AMERICAN EARTH

A Special Publication of THE LIBRARY OF AMERICA

EDITED BY
Bill McKibben

FOREWORD BY
Al Gore

AMERICAN EARTH

*Environmental Writing
Since Thoreau*

Visit our website at www.loa.org

Some of the material in this volume is reprinted with the permission of holders
of copyright and publishing rights. Acknowledgments are on pages 1005–22.

Distributed to the trade by Penguin Random House and in Canada by Penguin
Random House Canada, Ltd.

Design by Fearn Cutler de Vicq

Library of Congress Control Number: 2007940683

ISBN: 978–1–59853–020–9 (trade edition)
ISBN: 978–1–59853–024–7 (slipcase edition)

The Library of America—182
Fourth Printing

Printed in the United States of America

American Earth:
Environmental Writing Since Thoreau
has been made possible with publication support from

THE GOULD FAMILY FOUNDATION

and will be kept in print by its gift to
the Guardians of American Letters Fund,
established by The Library of America
to ensure that every volume
will be permanently available.

CONTENTS

FOREWORD

by *Al Gore*

It was a writer who first drew my attention to the environment, years before the word entered the public lexicon. My mother often read to my sister, Nancy, and me at the dinner table, and in 1962, she read to us from a new book, *Silent Spring*. It made an unmistakable impression. For the first time, I saw the connection between the twin poles of my childhood: the family farm in the lush Cumberland riverbed and the marble halls of Washington, D.C., where my father cast votes on behalf of his rural neighbors. "No witchcraft, no enemy action had silenced the rebirth of new life in this stricken world," Rachel Carson wrote of a model American town devastated by chemical pesticides. "The people had done it themselves." Carson opened my mind to the notion that human actions could affect the ecosystems we depend on, and she proclaimed a lofty new mission for self-government: to energize and empower the "millions to whom the beauty and the ordered world of nature still have meaning that is deep and imperative."

It is humbling for a politician—even a recovering one—to reflect on the role writers have played, and continue to play, in developing and shaping the environmental movement. A truth eloquently expressed has an influence greater than any elected official. This collection includes powerful writing by Rachel Carson as well as many other authors known for their attentiveness to the natural world: John Muir, Edward Abbey, John McPhee, Wendell Berry, Annie Dillard, Michael

Pollan, Bill McKibben. (When I was serving in the Senate, McKibben's description of the planetary impact of chlorofluorocarbons made such an impression on me that it led, among other things, to my receiving the honorific title "Ozone Man" from the first President Bush.) Of the political leaders included here, President Theodore Roosevelt's voice resonates most, and reminds us of the vision possible within government. As avid a writer and conservationist as he was a hunter, Roosevelt boomed in 1903 a truth that seems just as fresh today: "We have gotten past the stage, my fellow-citizens, when we are to be pardoned if we treat any part of our country as something to be skinned for two or three years for the use of the present generation, whether it is the forest, the water, the scenery."

Taken together, these essays, poems, cartoons, and speeches show how our country's attitude toward nature has developed and changed from Thoreau's time to our own. Above all, they show us that environmentalism, while inevitably a source of conflict, is inherent in our national character, a fundamental part of our heritage as Americans. Thomas Jefferson believed that closeness to the land was essential to a virtuous citizenry, and the great writers in this collection carry this vision forward in profound and divergent ways. Thoreau defiantly wrote: "The earth I tread on is not a dead, inert mass. It is a body—has a spirit—is organic—and fluid to the influence of its spirit—and to whatever particle of that spirit is in me." Others, like Walt Whitman, celebrated the vitality of American growth and progress, the "the unseen moral essence of all the vast materials of America" transforming into a "new society proportionate to Nature."

Throughout, as the best of our country's environmental writing beautifully reflects, Americans have intensely debated the rights and the responsibilities of each individual and of society as a whole. The current threat of global warming has spurred many writers to emulate the idealism and solitary self-reliance of Thoreau at Walden Pond. But just as he could not completely shut out his neighbors, Americans cannot shut out one another—or the rest of the world—if we are to restore the balance between the natural and the man-made.

We are entering a new era in which American environmentalism will help shape our standing in the world. As Abraham Lincoln told Congress in 1862, "as our case is new, so we must think anew, and act anew. We must disenthrall ourselves, and then we shall save our country." Within our rich history, we can find the wisdom and the spirit we need to disenthrall ourselves and fulfill what is perhaps our ultimate manifest destiny: to save our earth.

INTRODUCTION

I'm writing these words at 10,000 feet in the Yosemite backcountry, eight or nine hiking miles from Tuolumne Meadows where in 1889 Robert Underwood Johnson asked John Muir to write two pieces for his magazine describing the beauty of the Sierra and the need to protect it. The granite is as pure white, the lake in front me as deep blue as it was when Muir first took up his pen. Indeed it's arguably a better place now—no sheep graze here now, the "hoofed locusts" that ate the wildflower meadows in Muir's time. Instead, thousands of people arrive each day and disperse out into the wild, to walk, to look—to gaze with the precise awe that Muir was among the first to find the words for.

I'm writing these words at 10,000 feet in the Yosemite backcountry. A haze muddies the southwestern sky—it's from forest fires burning out of control not far away after the hottest July on record in the American West. There are only pitiful, shrinking fields of snow left even on the high peaks—the snowpack was 28 percent of normal this spring. A new study released last week showed that trees in Yosemite are dying at twice the rate of 20 years ago, apparently stressed by the change in climate.

This is a significant moment to be surveying the literature of American environmentalism. The movement—so often driven by a piece of writing—has won many great battles. There are hundreds of millions of acres of land conserved and laws passed to protect the most insignificant of flora and fauna; regulations have cleaned the air and water. And yet the war goes badly. So far the images and metaphors that these and other writers have produced—the rich heritage of American environmental writing, on which the movement continues to draw—have proved insufficient against the forces of expanding commerce and daily habit that drive global warming. The fight continues; the words in this anthology are still in play.

From the beginning American writing has concerned itself with the story of people and the natural world. Though the continent they landed on was in fact more densely populated and more substantially altered by Native Americans than the European settlers realized, it really was a "howling wilderness" compared with the Europe they'd left behind, long since cut over, divided, subdued. The "environment"— harsh winters, huge forests, broad deserts—was a character in our letters from the start, and early American accounts of the natural world— Bartram's journals of his Southeast trips, Lewis and Clark's chronicle of their journey of western discovery—are classics of the first rank.

But "environmental writing" is something different from these. As defined broadly by the pieces in this book, it takes as its subject the collision between people and the rest of the world, and asks searching questions about that collision: Is it necessary? What are its effects? Might there be a better way? To a considerable degree, environmental writing can be said to overlap with what is often called "nature writing" (a category ably surveyed by Robert Finch and John Elder's 1990 anthology *The Norton Book of Nature Writing*); but it subsumes and moves beyond it, seeking answers as well as consolation, embracing controversy, sometimes sounding an alarm. While it often celebrates nature, it also recognizes, implicitly or explicitly, that nature is no longer innocent or invulnerable. A diverse and multifarious concept, environmentalism at times seems to go almost underground for long stretches, not unlike some ephemeral stream in a hardwood forest. But when it resurfaces again it is usually stronger. And this stream, thankfully, has grown steadily broader in recent years, as more writers of different backgrounds and tastes have joined it as tributaries.

An argument can be made that environmental writing is America's single most distinctive contribution to the world's literature, and in this anthology I have sought to give a feel for how that writing—out of which emerged the first modern environmentalism—evolved intellectually and artistically. Other cultures are older and perhaps therefore more subtle in their observation of the endlessly fascinating dance of human beings. But only on this continent was Culture fully conscious while Economy went about the business of knocking down Nature. The ancient world, Europe, Asia—these underwent huge ecological changes before anyone was writing books. But the kind of disastrous deforestation that the ancient *Epic of Gilgamesh* only hints at, Aldo Leopold watched happen. And only here did that witness take place in a context of general affluence that made vigorous questioning possible—more and more of us were freed from the need to directly subdue the natural world in order to secure our dinner. We had more room for thinking. As a result, this is a literature with measurable effects. The body of writing anthologized here drove the political side of the movement more often than the other way round. Marsh and Muir gave us national parks, and Marshall and Zahniser the Wilderness Act.

One obvious difference between this and an anthology of nature writing is where it begins—not until the mid-19th century and the career of Henry David Thoreau. Thoreau, who spent many hours every day outdoors and was a fine botanizer and natural historian, meets anyone's definition of a naturalist. But he was much more: argumentative, eccentric, perhaps most of all deeply sensitive to the human culture around him. He was struck by the idea that the lives Americans had begun to lead were desperately divorced from reality, a reality that could be found in nature. "In wildness is the preservation of the world," he wrote famously—one of the great koans of American literature. Indeed, Thoreau had more than a little of both the eastern monk and the Old Testament prophet in him. *Walden* is almost scriptural in its pithy discursions. There are five ideas a page; it's no wonder that the book has never faded, that it lives at the very center of American writing.

But Thoreau was a Buddha with a receipt from the hardware store—his two-year experiment in living at Walden Pond is as practical as it is philosophical. He asks the twin questions that have become far more acute in the 150 years since his passing: "How much is enough?" and "How do I know what I really want?" Nothing about the age of Mc-Mansions, SUVs, or 500-channel cable systems would have surprised him. His lack of interest in the brand-new transatlantic telegraph ("but perchance the first news that will leak through the broad, flapping American ear will be that the Princess Adelaide has the whooping cough") defined the limits of the Information Age a century before anyone else even realized it was upon us.

In fact, there is something almost disconcerting about beginning this volume with Thoreau—he saw so far into the distance that it took decades for other writers to catch up with him and the questions he raised. It's as if Picasso had suddenly appeared in the mid-19th century—the history of art would not have been ready to make full sense of him. In many ways Thoreau seems to be speaking directly to our moment, far more directly than most of his immediate successors. So it's fitting that he ends this collection too, in Rebecca Solnit's graceful small essay that reminds us of the joy that balanced his sternness and made it bearable. (She reminds us as well that Thoreau was a tactical innovator, the proponent of an ethic of civil disobedience that would come to the fore of the environmental movement a century later.)

After the prophetic explosion that was Thoreau, American environmental writing and thought continued, even if at a more deliberate pace and sometimes at extended intervals, to drive the movement forward. From the ideas developed in writings like those collected here sprang the complex of laws and regulations, lobbying groups, wildernesses, and national parks that constitute one of this nation's great gifts to the world (and that make Washington's current environmental backsliding so particularly shameful). It's worth noting how each advance in environmental practice was preceded by a great book, a procession perhaps unique in American letters. There would have been a Civil War without *Uncle Tom's Cabin*, which is not to downplay its importance but merely to say that larger forces of economics and power were moving more or less inexorably; but by contrast most of what we call environmental progress has been voluntary, and often counter to the stronger tides of history.

Without George Perkins Marsh and his observations on the dangers of deforestation, it's not at all sure that the New York State legislature would have embarked on the quite extraordinary task of protecting the Adirondacks. Surely the grandeur of Yosemite Valley would have called forth a champion eventually, but without the ecstatic prose of John Muir, who invented a new grammar and vocabulary of wild delight from his afternoons in "the Range of Light," it's hard to imagine that the Sierra Club would have emerged to lead a century's worth of battles. Without Rachel Carson sounding the alarm when she did, it seems entirely likely that many more species of North American birds might have been doomed. There is much to be proud of in this literature; the movement it inspired has won a great many of the fights it picked. You can tick them off by noting the topics of the early essays in this book: national parks, the plumage trade, control of soil erosion, pesticides, smog. Each of the battles was against tall odds, and most absolutely required a witness or two to point the way—David Brower in the battle to save the Grand Canyon, for instance.

But there is no closure in this struggle. To look down that list is to realize that most of these battles were fought around the margins. The places we've managed to preserve, with few exceptions, were high, rocky, cold, or otherwise remote, and hence of limited economic value. The fights we've won have so far been mostly about smoothing the rough edges of progress—catalytic converters for cars and highway beautification, but not mass transit, much less bicycle cities.

Of all the images and the metaphors that have fueled environmentalism in the past, and that have been strong enough to accomplish these good and necessary works, the most important has been that of the wild. The wild, the pure, the clean: from Thoreau to Abbey, from Muir to Austin to Brower, that's been the key idea, the emotional trigger. It's been fuel enough to take us to the orbit that we needed to reach in the past. But as we set about the work that faces us now—the work of reorienting our lives to ward off the apocalypse that science now predicts—we must continue to find further images, further metaphors.

Consider the difference between the carbon monoxide molecule and the carbon dioxide molecule. The first is pollution as we've always known it—something noxious, and something mistaken. It results from a flaw in the engine—fix that incomplete combustion and the air above Los Angeles gets clearer. A catalytic converter is a $500 repair, and that you can accomplish with the emotional power of the wild. The Sierra Club did more than anyone else to pass the laws that cleaned our air, and though they talked about emphysema deaths and showed pictures of smoggy cities, their calendars showed far more pictures of alpine meadows and aspen groves in fall yellow. The head of steam that started building with Muir and ran at least through the first Earth Day was enough to meet that kind of challenge. Dirty bad, clean good.

But carbon dioxide, by contrast, isn't a mistake. It's the inevitable byproduct of fossil fuel combustion, and hence can't be controlled with a filter (the less carbon monoxide and particulates your car pours out, the more CO_2). You could control it only by moving quickly and sharply away from fossil fuel and toward a different kind of world—technologically different, with new sources of energy, but also quite likely different in its social and political forms, less obsessed with economic growth. This is an altogether higher orbit, involving much heavier lifting. The idea of the wild alone will not get us there.

A new fuel source is required, in both practical and metaphorical terms—a new fuel source that has been in the works for many years and is now starting to come into its own. The reader will note that the selections in this volume are weighted toward more recent writing, from the period beginning with the first Earth Day in 1970. In part that's because I think the writing is so good; there seems to be an almost inverse relationship between ecological decline and the rise of powerful voices. (It has been the great privilege of my professional life to be a small part of this group of writers—people like Terry Tempest Williams, Rick Bass, Barry Lopez, Richard Nelson, David Abram, Scott Russell Sanders. It is an interesting literary group for many reasons, including the fact that it exists largely outside the academy, and that most of its members are activists as well as writers.) But even more, it's because of my sense that these contemporary writers are doing the necessary work of seeking out ideas and images that will help America, and then the world, to confront the very much deeper problem we now face.

Scholars have often referred to these writers as "place-based," or talked about them cultivating a "sense of place." This is true—they write from the red rock desert, or the valleys that hug Montana's northern border. But they are interested in far more than mere description. What's key to understand is that this new generation of environmental writers rose to prominence in the years since 1980—the years since Ronald Reagan took office and the long-standing bipartisan commitment to environmental reform collapsed, the years when the systemic nature of our trouble came more sharply into focus. And the years when a kind of hyperindividualism became not just one strand in the American psyche, but pretty much the sole ideology of a continent.

Fighting the ideology that was laying waste to so much of the planet demanded going beyond that individualism. Many found the means to do that in the notion of "community"—a word almost as fuzzy and hard to pin down as "wild," but one that has emerged as an even more compelling source of motive energy for the environmental movement. This conception of community has its roots in science—in ecology, which time will tally as the most important emergent science of the 20th century, more so even than nuclear physics.

The central insight of ecology—that everything is connected—is hardly new. It found its greatest voice well over half a century ago in Aldo Leopold, a figure very nearly as prescient and ahead of his time as Thoreau. Leopold's gentle insistence that we needed an ethic large enough to encompass everything, including the land, helps us understand the natural world as more than a set of charismatic set pieces and helps us to understand that we need to play a much more careful role in that drama. It's no accident that Leopold spent his professional life in wildlife management, or that he found much of the pleasure of his private life in rebuilding the eroded soils and depleted forests of his Wisconsin homestead. Nor is it any surprise that he died helping neighbors battle a wildfire on their land. "Neighbors"—of all types—mattered profoundly.

The next great figure in this communitarian lineage may well be the poet Gary Snyder. He's an unlikely candidate at first blush—he came of age as a writer with the Beats, the great celebrants of the cult of individualism and wild nonconformity. (He's the model for Japhy Ryder in Kerouac's *The Dharma Bums*, and Kerouac is perhaps best thought of as a minor key Thoreau on his own voyage of self-discovery.) But Snyder left the U.S. in the early 1960s, just as the rest of the Beats helped launch the great carnival of individual liberation that we know as hippiedom. He spent much of the decade studying as a Zen monk, which was a very different task. And when he returned—though he was an icon of the San Francisco scene, whose poems nestled next to the *I Ching* on 10,000 bookshelves—he seemed more interested in the history of the California Indians than in the next cool fad. "Becoming native to your place" was his mantra—a commitment that involved discipline, hard work, and a willingness to learn from elders, be they plant, animal, or human communities.

If there was one elder above all others that people in this literary world were listening to, it was Wendell Berry. It's hard to imagine a more countercultural figure for our time than Berry, the lanky Kentucky tobacco farmer who had turned his back on an international literary life to work with horses on a farm down the road from where he'd grown up. Berry's poems, novels, and essays are of a piece—from his perch in rural America he was able to see more quickly than most the ruination that postwar consumer capitalism, with its emphasis on cheap and fast, was bringing to the American landscape and the American character. He counseled, by contrast, *responsibility*, to the soil and its inherent limits, to the human community and its inherent joys, sadnesses, and cycles. It is testimony to the power of his writing, and of his life, that he managed to make "responsibility" attractive to a great pool of readers; because he, more than anyone else, was swimming against the tide. He came of age as a writer at the precise moment when big agriculture was finishing its industrialization of rural America, when Wal-Mart and McDonalds were spreading the gospel of convenience, and when the liberations of the 1960s, for all their enormous benefits in so many areas, were devolving into something less attractive. The general ethic of "do your own thing," of marching to a different drummer—all of which traces back in some way toward Thoreau—came at a cost.

We were liberated to be hyperindividualists, in a way few humans had ever before been. In the decades since, that liberation has been experienced mainly through consumption. I remember, early in the rise of the SUV (the ultimate vehicle of choice for the 60s generation), this ad for Land Rover: "Celebrate Thoreau's Birthday: Drive Through a Pond." We've built ever larger houses, consumed ever more exotic foods, traveled ever farther around the globe. And in the process, of course, we've burned ever more fossil fuel. Indeed, the substitution of cheap oil for human labor is the greatest liberation of all, except that

1) we've started to run out;

2) the resulting CO_2 is wrecking the earth; and

3) as Berry has long suggested, none of it is making us particularly happy or fulfilled. Indeed, the most recent data show Americans far less satisfied with their lives than people in many other places, most of them poorer than we are. The reason seems to be our sharply felt lack of community, of connection with others.

Much recent environmental writing is about rebuilding that community. A surprising amount follows Berry's lead and concentrates on food—just in the past year or so, Michael Pollan and Barbara Kingsolver have written best sellers about relocalizing our eating, about escaping the republic of irresponsibility presided over by Cargill, Archer Daniels Midland, and the Burger King.

Not every modern author, of course, is marching in the same direction. One of the most beloved writers of recent times was Edward Abbey, and responsibility was not his watchword; anarchy was. But he and Berry traded encomiums, each trying to tag the other with the title of America's best essayist—and in the process agreed that wildness, the stark western landscapes that Abbey loved, needed tameness to make them possible, that the traditional American distinction between raped land and virgin land was unhealthy, and that therefore good stewardship—husbandry, to use the old term—was required.

In this new world, the farmer's market is as potent an emblem as the wilderness area, the smell of fresh-baked local bread as tonic as the tang of mountain air. And just in time. Because in a globally warming world we now know that it does no ultimate good to set aside a wilderness area if you don't also preserve the climate that makes it what it is. Environmentalism can no longer merely fix the excesses of our consumer culture. It needs to change that culture. This may be a quixotic task, at least in the short time allotted us by the atmospheric chemists to rein in our consumption. Some of the signs are good—indeed Wendell Berry has lived long enough to see farmer's markets become the fastest growing part of the American food economy. Others are not so good—Arctic ice, we learned last year, is melting so fast that the North may be free of its white cover in summer as early as 2020, barely more than a decade.

It's a race between physics and metaphysics, and environmentalism can no longer confine itself to the narrow sphere it has long inhabited. If it isn't as much about economics, sociology, and pop culture as it is about trees, mountains, and animals, it won't in the end matter. That's why this will be hopefully be the last anthology possible of "environmental writing." If we are to weather the ecological upheavals now bearing down upon us, the insights expressed by the writers in this book will need to become mainstream, no longer a dissident creed but a dominant one reflected in all our literature.

Wildness will always be essential—I write these words, again, while camped alone high in the Sierra, in a kind of quiet ecstasy. Essential, but not sufficient.

I've arranged this work chronologically, and my hope has been to give some sense of how environmental concern built to a great crest at Earth Day in 1970 and since has begun to explore new directions. This is a literature that twines around a movement (a movement whose history is beautifully detailed in Tom Turner's meticulous chronology). I've included only a few poems, and just tiny chunks of fiction, the latter usually to make some documentary point; both genres deserve anthologies of their own. Edwin Matthews' selection from the many iconic images that have contributed to environmental awareness over the years, prepared with the assistance of photo researcher Joan Hamilton, adds another important element to this collection.

This kind of volume requires a great deal of teamwork. My original plan went like this: I emailed everyone I know and asked them what they'd put in such a book. Therefore I'd like to thank everyone I know, and ask their forgiveness for not getting in everything that they suggested—many of my favorites came out too. As the winnowing began, the staff of The Library of America provided expert guidance and assistance, along with dozens of outside consultants who made many valuable suggestions. Edwin Matthews, who conceived of this book and secured its funding, and Tom Turner, senior editor at Earthjustice, were part of this project from the beginning and played an important role in shaping this volume in all its aspects. The final choices—the final mistakes—are mine, and they reflect my particular take on this literature, this movement, and this moment in time. They are offered in the hope that they will spur not only reflection but action as well.

Bill McKibben
August 2007

HENRY DAVID THOREAU

Henry David Thoreau (1817–1862) was born, grew up, lived out his life, and died in Concord, Massachusetts. He studied at Harvard from 1833 to 1837, then signed on as a teacher at Concord Academy but was dismissed for refusing to whip students. He and his brother John opened an elementary school in 1838, where, according to some authorities, they invented the idea of the field trip. John became sick in 1841 and the brothers closed the school; Henry went to live with Ralph Waldo Emerson, beginning a long friendship with him and with the other members of the Transcendental Club, among them Bronson Alcott and Margaret Fuller. The other transcendentalists experimented with communes like Brook Farm, but Thoreau was more solitary, and the most important years in his life began in 1845 when he took up residence in a small cabin he'd built on the shore of Walden Pond a short walk from town. He spent two years, two months, and two days there, experimenting with simplifying his life. Thoreau's isolation at Walden wasn't absolute or deliberately ascetic—he often returned to town to see friends and eat meals, had a steady stream of visitors (often too steady for his taste), and at one point engaged in a political protest, spending a night in Concord jail for his refusal to pay his poll tax. But it was notably productive: he returned to town with the draft of one book (*A Week on the Concord and Merrimack Rivers*) and the notes that he would spend the next six years turning into *Walden* (1854), perhaps the most remarkable book in the American canon. As dense as scripture, crowded with aphorism, *Walden* is full of enough ideas for a score of ordinary books. But it has lived as long and as fully as any other writing of its vintage and inspired all the best kinds of people: both Mahatma Gandhi and Martin Luther King Jr. claimed him as a major influence. Thoreau suffered from tuberculosis contracted during his college years; his condition worsened beginning in 1859, and he spent his last years revising his accounts of the Maine woods and other works. As he neared death his aunt Louisa asked him if he had made his peace with God. "I did not know we had ever quarreled," he said. He died at the age of 44.

Picking a few fragments from his writings is an impossible task; an anthology of American environmental writing might well be one-third Thoreau. Here are a few entries from his copious journals, and then the description from *Walden* of the building of the famous cabin. "Huckleberries," a late essay or lecture-text, shows the modern nature essay being born, with a small root giving way to a luxuriant growth of thought and speculation.

from **Journals**

Oct. 24th 1837.

The Mould our Deeds Leave.

Every part of nature teaches that the passing away of one life is the making room for another. The oak dies down to the ground, leaving within its rind a rich virgin mould, which will impart a vigorous life to an infant forest — — The pine leaves a sandy and sterile soil—the harder woods a strong and fruitful mould. — —

So this constant abrasion and decay makes the soil of my future growth. As I live now so shall I reap. If I grow pines and birches, my virgin mould will not sustain the oak, but pines and birches, or, perchance, weeds and brambles, will constitute my second growth. — —

March 6th 1838

— — How can a man sit down and quietly pare his nails, while the earth goes gyrating ahead amid such a din of sphere music, whirling him along about her axis some twenty four thousand miles between sun and sun?   but mainly in a circle some two millions of miles actual progress. And then such a hurly-burly on the surface—wind always blowing—now a zephyr, now a hurricane—tides never idle, ever fluctuating, no rest for Niagara, but perpetual ran-tan on those limestone rocks—and then that summer simmering which our ears are used to—

which would otherwise be christened confusion worse confounded, but is now ironically called "silence audible"—and above all the incessant tinkering named hum of industry—the hurrying to and fro and confused jabbering of men— Can man do less than get up and shake himself?

April 24th 1838.

Steam ships

—Men have been contriving new means and modes of motion— Steam ships have been westering during these late days and nights on the Atlantic waves—the fuglers of a new evolution to this generation — — Meanwhile plants spring silently by the brook sides—and the grim woods wave indifferent—the earth emits no howl—pot on fire simmers and seethes—and men go about their business. — —

Saturday March 19th 1842

When I walk in the fields of Concord and meditate on the destiny of this prosperous slip of the Saxon *family*—the unexhausted energies of this new country—I forget that this which is now Concord was once Musketaquid and that the *American race* has had its destiny also. Everywhere in the fields—in the corn and grain land—the earth is strewn with the relics of a race which has vanished as completely as if trodden in with the earth.

I find it good to remember the eternity behind me as well as the eternity before. Where ever I go I tread in the tracks of the Indian— I pick up the bolt which he has but just dropped at my feet. And if I consider destiny I am on his trail. I scatter his hearth stones with my feet, and pick out of the embers of his fire the simple but enduring implements of the wigwam and the chace— In planting my corn in the same furrow which yielded its increase to his support so long—I displace some memorial of him.

I have been walking this afternoon over a pleasant field planted with winter rye—near the house. Where this strange people once had their dwelling place. Another species of mortal men but little less wild to me than the musquash they hunted— Strange spirits—daemons—

whose eyes could never meet mine. With another nature—and another fate than mine— The crows flew over the edge of the woods, and wheeling over my head seemed to rebuke—as dark winged spirits more akin to the Indian than I. Perhaps only the present disguise of the Indian— If the new has a meaning so has the old.

Nature has her russet hues as well as green— Indeed our eye splits on every object, and we can as well take one path as the other— If I consider its history it is old—if its destiny it is new— I may see a part of an object or the whole— I will not be imposed on and think nature is old, because the season is advanced   I will study the botany of the mosses and fungi on the decayed—and remember that decayed wood is not old, but has just begun to be what it is. I need not think of the pine almond or the acorn and sapling when I meet the fallen pine or oak— more than of the generations of pines and oaks which have fed the young tree.

The new blade of the corn—the third leaf of the melon—these are not green but gray with time, but sere in respect of time.

September 12, 1851

2 PM To the Three Friends' Hill beyond Flints Pond—via RR. RWEs Wood Path S side Walden—Geo Heywood's Cleared Lot & Smith's orchards—return via E of Flints' P via Goose P & my old home to RR—

I go to Flints P. for the sake of the *Mt* view from the hill beyond looking over Concord. I have thought it the best especially in the winter which I can get in this neighborhood. It is worth the while to see the *Mts* in the horizon once a day. I have thus seen some earth which corresponds to my least earthly & trivial—to my most heaven-ward looking thoughts— The earth seen through an azure an etherial veil. They are the natural *temples* elevated brows of the earth—looking at which the thoughts of the beholder are naturally elevated and etherialized. I wish to see the earth through the medium of much air or heaven—for there is no paint like the air. *Mts* thus seen are worthy of worship. I go to Flints' Pond also to see a rippling lake & a reedy-island in its midst— Reed Island.

A man should feed his senses with the best that the land affords

At the entrance to the Deep Cut I heard the telegraph wire vibrating like an Æolian Harp. It reminded me suddenly—reservedly with a beautiful paucity of communication—even silently, such was its effect on my thoughts— It reminded me, I say, with a certain pathetic moderation—of what finer & deeper stirrings I was susceptible—which grandly set all argument & dispute aside— —a triumphant though transient exhibition of the truth. It told me by the faintest imaginable strain—it told me by the finest strain that a human ear can hear—yet conclusively & past all refutation—that there were higher infinitely higher plains of life—which it behoved me never to forget. As I was entering the Deep Cut the wind which was conveying a message to me from heaven dropt it on the wire of the telegraph which it vibrated as it past. I instantly sat down on a stone at the foot of the telegraph pole—& attended to the communication. It merely said "Bear in mind, Child—& never for an instant forget—that there are higher plains infinitely higher plains of life than this thou art now travelling on. Know that the goal is distant & is upward and is worthy all your life's efforts to attain to." And then it ceased and though I sat some minutes longer I heard nothing more.

There is every variety & degree of inspiration from mere fullness of life to the most rapt mood. A human soul is played on even as this wire—which now vibrates slowly & gently so that the passer can hardly hear it & anon the sound swells & vibrates with such intensity as if it would rend the wire—as far as the elasticity & tension of the wire permits—and now it dies away and is silent—& though the breeze continues to sweep over it, no strain comes from it—& the traveller hearkens in vain. It is no small gain to have this wire stretched through Concord though there may be no Office here. Thus I make my own use of the telegraph—without consulting the Directors—like the sparrows which I perceive use it extensively for a perch.

Shall I not go to this office to hear if there is any communication for me—as steadily as to the Post office in the village?

Tuesday Dec 30th

Mem. Go to the Deep Cut. The flies now crawl forth from the crevices all covered with dust, dreaming of summer—without life or energy enough to clean their wings

This afternoon being on fair Haven Hill I heard the sound of a saw—and soon after from the cliff saw two men sawing down a noble pine beneath about 40 rods off. I resolved to watch it till it fell—the last of a dozen or more which were left when the forest was cut and for 15 years have waved in solitary majesty over the sproutland. I saw them like beavers or insects gnawing at the trunk of this noble tree, the diminutive mannikins with their crosscut saw which could scarcely span it. It towered up a hundred feet as I afterward found by measurement—one of the tallest probably now in the township & straight as an arrow, but slanting a little toward the hill side. —its top seen against the frozen river & the hills of Conantum. I watch closely to see when it begins to move. Now the sawers stop—and with an axe open it a little on the side toward which it leans that it may break the faster. And now their saw goes again— Now surely it is going—it is inclined one quarter of the quadrant, and breathless I expect its crashing fall— But no I was mistaken it has not moved an inch, it stands at the same angle as at first. It is 15 minutes yet to its fall. Still its branches wave in the wind as if it were destined to stand for a century, and the wind soughs through its needles as of yore; it is still a forest tree—the most majestic tree that waves over Musketaquid. — The silvery sheen of the sunlight is reflected from its needles—it still affords an inaccessible crotch for the squirrel's nest—not a lichen has forsaken its mastlike stem— —its raking mast—the hill is the hull. Now's the moment—the mannikins at its base are fleeing from their crime—they have dropped the guilty saw & axe. How slowly & majestically it starts—as if it were only swayed by a summer breeze and would return without a sigh to its location in the air—& now it fans the hill side with its fall and it lies down to its bed in the valley from which it is never to rise, as softly as a feather, folding its green mantle about it like a warrior—as if tired of standing it embraced the earth with silent joy. — returning its elements to the dust again—but hark! there you only saw—but did not hear—

There now comes up a deafening crash to these rocks—advertising you that even trees do not die without a groan. It rushes to embrace the earth, & mingle its elements with the dust. And now all is still once more & forever both to eye & ear.

I went down and measured it. It was about 4 feet in diameter where it was sawed—about 100 feet long. Before I had reached it—the axe-men had already half divested it of its branches. Its gracefully spreading top was a perfect wreck on the hill side as if it had been made of glass—& the tender cones of one years growth upon its summit appealed in vain & too late to the mercy of the chopper. Already he has measured it with his axe—and marked out the mill logs it will make. And the space it occupied in upper air is vacant for the next 2 centuries. It is lumber   He has laid waste the air. When the fish hawk in the spring revisits the banks of the Musketaquid, he will circle in vain to find his accustomed perch. — & the henhawk will mourn for the pines lofty enough to protect her brood. A plant which it has taken two centuries to perfect rising by slow stages into the heavens—has this afternoon ceased to exist. Its sapling top had expanded to this January thaw as the forerunner of summers to come. Why does not the village bell sound a knell. I hear no knell tolled—I see no procession of mourners in the streets—or the woodland aisles— The squirrel has leapt to another tree—the hawk has circled further off—& has now settled upon a new eyre but the woodman is preparing to lay his axe at the root of that also.

Dec 31st

The 3d warm day.   now overcast and beginning to drizzle. Still it is inspiriting as the brightest weather—though the sun surely is not agoing to shine. There is a latent light in the mist—as if there were more electricity than usual in the air. These are warm foggy days in winter which excite us.

It reminds me this thick spring like weather, that I have not enough valued and attended to the pure clarity & brilliancy of the winter skies— Consider in what respects the winter sunsets differ from the summer ones. Shall I ever in summer evenings see so celestial a reach of blue sky contrasting with amber as I have seen a few days since—

The day sky in winter corresponds for clarity to the night sky in which the stars shine & twinkle so brightly in this latitude.

I am too late perhaps, to see the sand foliage in the deep cut— should have been there day before yesterday—it is now too wet & soft.

Yet in some places it is perfect. I see some perfect leopard's paws

These things suggest—that there is motion in the earth as well as on the surface; it lives & grows. It is warmed & influenced by the sun—just as my blood by my thoughts. I seem to see some of the life that is in the spring bud & blossom more intimately nearer its fountain head—the fancy sketches & designs of the artist. It is more simple & primitive growth. As if for ages sand and clay might have thus flowed into the forms of foliage—before plants were produced to clothe the earth. The earth I tread on is not a dead inert mass. It is a body—has a spirit—is organic—and fluid to the influence of its spirit—and to whatever particle of that spirit is in me. She is not dead but sleepeth. It is more cheering than the fertility & luxuriance of vineyards—this fundamental fertility near to the principle of growth. To be sure it is somewhat foecal and stercoral—. So the poet's creative moment is when the frost is coming out in the spring—but as in the case of some too easy poets—if the weather is too warm & rainy or long continued it becomes mere diarrhea—mud & clay relaxed. The poet must not have something pass his bowels merely—that is women's poetry.— He must have something pass his brain & heart and bowels too, it may be, altogether. — so he gets delivered— There is no end to the fine bowels here exhibited—heaps of liver—lights & bowels. Have you no bowels? Nature has some bowels.   and there again she is mother of humanity. Concord is a worthier place to live in—the globe is a worthier place for these creations   This slumbering life—that may wake. Even the solid globe is permeated by the living law. It is the most living of creatures. No doubt all creatures that live on its surface are but parasites.

1837–51

from **Walden; or, Life in the Woods**

Near the end of March, 1845, I borrowed an axe and went down to the woods by Walden Pond, nearest to where I intended to build my house, and began to cut down some tall arrowy white pines, still in their youth, for timber. It is difficult to begin without borrowing, but perhaps it is the most generous course thus to permit your fellow-men to have an interest in your enterprise. The owner of the axe, as he released his hold on it, said that it was the apple of his eye; but I returned it sharper than I received it. It was a pleasant hillside where I worked, covered with pine woods, through which I looked out on the pond, and a small open field in the woods where pines and hickories were springing up. The ice in the pond was not yet dissolved, though there were some open spaces, and it was all dark colored and saturated with water. There were some slight flurries of snow during the days that I worked there; but for the most part when I came out on to the railroad, on my way home, its yellow sand heap stretched away gleaming in the hazy atmosphere, and the rails shone in the spring sun, and I heard the lark and pewee and other birds already come to commence another year with us. They were pleasant spring days, in which the winter of man's discontent was thawing as well as the earth, and the life that had lain torpid began to stretch itself. One day, when my axe had come off and I had cut a green hickory for a wedge, driving it with a stone, and had placed the whole to soak in a pond hole in order to swell the wood, I saw a striped snake run into the water, and he lay on the bottom, apparently without inconvenience, as long as I staid there, or more than a quarter of an hour; perhaps because he had not yet fairly come out of the torpid state. It appeared to me that for a like reason men remain in their present low and primitive condition; but if they should feel the influence of the spring of springs arousing them, they would of necessity rise to a higher and more ethereal life. I had previously seen the snakes in frosty mornings in my path with portions of their bodies still numb and inflexible, waiting for the sun to thaw them. On the 1st of April it rained and melted the ice, and in the early part of the day, which was very foggy, I heard a stray goose groping about over the pond and cackling as if lost, or like the spirit of the fog.

So I went on for some days cutting and hewing timber, and also studs and rafters, all with my narrow axe, not having many communicable or scholar-like thoughts, singing to myself,—

> Men say they know many things;
> But lo! they have taken wings,—
> The arts and sciences,
> And a thousand appliances;
> The wind that blows
> Is all that any body knows.

I hewed the main timbers six inches square, most of the studs on two sides only, and the rafters and floor timbers on one side, leaving the rest of the bark on, so that they were just as straight and much stronger than sawed ones. Each stick was carefully mortised or tenoned by its stump, for I had borrowed other tools by this time. My days in the woods were not very long ones; yet I usually carried my dinner of bread and butter, and read the newspaper in which it was wrapped, at noon, sitting amid the green pine boughs which I had cut off, and to my bread was imparted some of their fragrance, for my hands were covered with a thick coat of pitch. Before I had done I was more the friend than the foe of the pine tree, though I had cut down some of them, having become better acquainted with it. Sometimes a rambler in the wood was attracted by the sound of my axe, and we chatted pleasantly over the chips which I had made.

By the middle of April, for I made no haste in my work, but rather made the most of it, my house was framed and ready for the raising. I had already bought the shanty of James Collins, an Irishman who worked on the Fitchburg Railroad, for boards. James Collins' shanty was considered an uncommonly fine one. When I called to see it he was not at home. I walked about the outside, at first unobserved from within, the window was so deep and high. It was of small dimensions, with a peaked cottage roof, and not much else to be seen, the dirt being raised five feet all around as if it were a compost heap. The roof was the soundest part, though a good deal warped and made brittle by the sun. Door-sill there was none, but a perennial passage for the hens under the door board. Mrs. C. came to the door and asked me to view it from the inside. The hens were driven in by my approach. It was dark, and had a dirt floor for the most part, dank, clammy, and aguish, only here a board and there a board which would not bear removal. She lighted a lamp to show me the inside of the roof and the walls, and also that the board floor extended under the bed, warning me not to step into the cellar, a sort of dust hole two feet deep. In her own words, they were "good boards overhead, good boards all around, and a good window,"—of two whole squares originally, only the cat had passed out that way lately. There was a stove, a bed, and a place to sit, an infant in the house where it was born, a silk parasol, gilt-framed looking-glass, and a patent new coffee mill nailed to an oak sapling, all told. The bargain was soon concluded, for James had in the mean while returned. I to pay four dollars and twenty-five cents to-night, he to vacate at five to-morrow morning, selling to nobody else meanwhile: I to take possession at six. It were well, he said, to be there early, and anticipate certain indistinct but wholly unjust claims on the score of ground rent and fuel. This he assured me was the only encumbrance. At six I passed him and his family on the road. One large bundle held their all,—bed, coffee-mill, looking-glass, hens,—all but the cat, she took to the woods and became a wild cat, and, as I learned afterward, trod in a trap set for woodchucks, and so became a dead cat at last.

I took down this dwelling the same morning, drawing the nails, and removed it to the pond side by small cartloads, spreading the boards on the grass there to bleach and warp back again in the sun. One early thrush gave me a note or two as I drove along the woodland path. I was informed treacherously by a young Patrick that neighbor Seeley, an Irishman, in the intervals of the carting, transferred the still tolerable, straight, and drivable nails, staples, and spikes to his pocket, and then stood when I came back to pass the time of day, and look freshly up, unconcerned, with spring thoughts, at the devastation; there being a dearth of work, as he said. He was there to represent spectatordom, and help make this seemingly insignificant event one with the removal of the gods of Troy.

I dug my cellar in the side of a hill sloping to the south, where a woodchuck had formerly dug his burrow, down through sumach and blackberry roots, and the lowest stain of vegetation, six feet square by seven deep, to a fine sand where potatoes would not freeze in any winter. The sides were left shelving, and not stoned; but the sun having never shone on them, the sand still keeps its place. It was but two hours' work. I took particular pleasure in this breaking of ground, for in almost all latitudes men dig into the earth for an equable temperature. Under the most splendid house in the city is still to be found the cellar where they store their roots as of old, and long after the superstructure has disappeared posterity remark its dent in the earth. The house is still but a sort of porch at the entrance of a burrow.

At length, in the beginning of May, with the help of some of my acquaintances, rather to improve so good an occasion for neighborliness than from any necessity, I set up the frame of my house. No man was ever more honored in the character of his raisers than I. They are destined, I trust, to assist at the raising of loftier structures one day. I began to occupy my house on the 4th of July, as soon as it was boarded and roofed, for the boards were carefully feather-edged and lapped, so that it was perfectly impervious to rain; but before boarding I laid the foundation of a chimney at one end, bringing two cartloads of stones up the hill from the pond in my arms. I built the chimney after my hoeing in the fall, before a fire became necessary for warmth, doing my cooking in the mean while out of doors on the ground, early in the morning: which mode I still think is in some respects more convenient and agreeable than the usual one. When it stormed before my bread was baked, I fixed a few boards over the fire, and sat under them to watch my loaf, and passed some pleasant hours in that way. In those days, when my hands were much employed, I read but little, but the least scraps of paper which lay on the ground, my holder, or tablecloth, afforded me as much entertainment, in fact answered the same purpose as the Iliad.

—

It would be worth the while to build still more deliberately than I did, considering, for instance, what foundation a door, a window, a cellar, a garret, have in the nature of man, and perchance never raising any superstructure until we found a better reason for it than our temporal necessities even. There is some of the same fitness in a man's building his own house that there is in a bird's building its own nest. Who knows but if men constructed their dwellings with their own hands, and provided food for themselves and families simply and honestly enough, the poetic faculty would be universally developed, as birds universally sing when they are so engaged? But alas! we do like cowbirds and cuckoos, which lay their eggs in nests which other birds have built, and cheer no traveller with their chattering and unmusical notes. Shall we forever resign the pleasure of construction to the carpenter? What does architecture amount to in the experience of the mass of men? I never in all my walks came across a man engaged in so simple and natural an occupation as building his house. We belong to the community. It is not the tailor alone who is the ninth part of a man; it is as much the preacher, and the merchant, and the farmer. Where is this division of labor to end? and what object does it finally serve? No doubt another *may* also think for me; but it is not therefore desirable that he should do so to the exclusion of my thinking for myself.

True, there are architects so called in this country, and I have heard of one at least possessed with the idea of making architectural ornaments have a core of truth, a necessity, and hence a beauty, as if it were a revelation to him. All very well perhaps from his point of view, but only a little better than the common dilettantism. A sentimental reformer in architecture, he began at the cornice, not at the foundation. It was only how to put a core of truth within the ornaments, that every sugar plum in fact might have an almond or caraway seed in it,— though I hold that almonds are most wholesome without the sugar,— and not how the inhabitant, the indweller, might build truly within and without, and let the ornaments take care of themselves. What reasonable man ever supposed that ornaments were something outward and in the skin merely,—that the tortoise got his spotted shell, or the shellfish its mother-o'-pearl tints, by such a contract as the inhabitants of

Broadway their Trinity Church? But a man has no more to do with the style of architecture of his house than a tortoise with that of its shell: nor need the soldier be so idle as to try to paint the precise *color* of his virtue on his standard. The enemy will find it out. He may turn pale when the trial comes. This man seemed to me to lean over the cornice and timidly whisper his half truth to the rude occupants who really knew it better than he. What of architectural beauty I now see, I know has gradually grown from within outward, out of the necessities and character of the indweller, who is the only builder,—out of some unconscious truthfulness, and nobleness, without ever a thought for the appearance; and whatever additional beauty of this kind is destined to be produced will be preceded by a like unconscious beauty of life. The most interesting dwellings in this country, as the painter knows, are the most unpretending, humble log huts and cottages of the poor commonly; it is the life of the inhabitants whose shells they are, and not any peculiarity in their surfaces merely, which makes them *picturesque*; and equally interesting will be the citizen's suburban box, when his life shall be as simple and as agreeable to the imagination, and there is as little straining after effect in the style of his dwelling. A great proportion of architectural ornaments are literally hollow, and a September gale would strip them off, like borrowed plumes, without injury to the substantials. They can do without *architecture* who have no olives nor wines in the cellar. What if an equal ado were made about the ornaments of style in literature, and the architects of our bibles spent as much time about their cornices as the architects of our churches do? So are made the *belles-lettres* and the *beaux-arts* and their professors. Much it concerns a man, forsooth, how a few sticks are slanted over him or under him, and what colors are daubed upon his box. It would signify somewhat, if, in any earnest sense, *he* slanted them and daubed it; but the spirit having departed out of the tenant, it is of a piece with constructing his own coffin,—the architecture of the grave, and "carpenter," is but another name for "coffin-maker." One man says, in his despair or indifference to life, take up a handful of the earth at your feet, and paint your house that color. Is he thinking of his last and narrow house? Toss up a copper for it as well. What an abundance of leisure he must have! Why do you take up a handful of dirt? Better paint your house your own complexion; let it turn pale or blush for you. An enterprise to improve the style of cottage architecture! When you have got my ornaments ready I will wear them.

Before winter I built a chimney, and shingled the sides of my house, which were already impervious to rain, with imperfect and sappy shingles made of the first slice of the log, whose edges I was obliged to straighten with a plane.

I have thus a tight shingled and plastered house, ten feet wide by fifteen long, and eight-feet posts, with a garret and a closet, a large window on each side, two trap doors, one door at the end, and a brick fireplace opposite. The exact cost of my house, paying the usual price for such materials as I used, but not counting the work, all of which was done by myself, was as follows; and I give the details because very few are able to tell exactly what their houses cost, and fewer still, if any, the separate cost of the various materials which compose them:—

Boards,	$8	03½,	mostly shanty boards.
Refuse shingles for roof and sides,	4	00	
Laths,	1	25	
Two second-hand windows with glass,	2	43	
One thousand old brick,	4	00	
Two casks of lime,	2	40	That was high.
Hair,	0	31	More than I needed.
Mantle-tree iron,	0	15	
Nails,	3	90	
Hinges and screws,	0	14	
Latch,	0	10	
Chalk,	0	01	
Transportation,	1	40	I carried a good part on my back
In all,	$28	12½	

These are all the materials excepting the timber stones and sand, which I claimed by squatter's right. I have also a small wood-shed adjoining, made chiefly of the stuff which was left after building the house.

I intend to build me a house which will surpass any on the main street in Concord in grandeur and luxury, as soon as it pleases me as much and will cost me no more than my present one.

I thus found that the student who wishes for a shelter can obtain one for a lifetime at an expense not greater than the rent which he now pays annually. If I seem to boast more than is becoming, my excuse is that I brag for humanity rather than for myself; and my shortcomings and inconsistencies do not affect the truth of my statement. Notwithstanding much cant and hypocrisy,—chaff which I find it difficult to separate from my wheat, but for which I am as sorry as any man,—I will breathe freely and stretch myself in this respect, it is such a relief to both the moral and physical system; and I am resolved that I will not through humility become the devil's attorney. I will endeavor to speak a good word for the truth. At Cambridge College the mere rent of a student's room, which is only a little larger than my own, is thirty dollars each year, though the corporation had the advantage of building thirty-two side by side and under one roof, and the occupant suffers the inconvenience of many and noisy neighbors, and perhaps a residence in the fourth story. I cannot but think that if we had more true wisdom in these respects, not only less education would be needed, because, forsooth, more would already have been acquired, but the pecuniary expense of getting an education would in a great measure vanish. Those conveniences which the student requires at Cambridge or elsewhere cost him or somebody else ten times as great a sacrifice of life as they would with proper management on both sides. Those things for which the most money is demanded are never the things which the student most wants. Tuition, for instance, is an important item in the term bill, while for the far more valuable education which he gets by associating with the most cultivated of his contemporaries no charge is made. The mode of founding a college is, commonly, to get up a subscription of dollars and cents, and then following blindly the principles of a division of labor to its extreme, a principle which should never be followed but with circumspection,—to call in a contractor who makes this a subject of speculation, and he employs Irishmen or other operatives actually to lay the foundations, while the students that are to be are said to be fitting themselves for it; and for these oversights successive generations have to pay. I think that it would be *better than this*, for the students, or those who desire to be benefited by it, even to lay the foundation themselves. The student who secures his coveted leisure and retirement by systematically shirking any labor necessary to man obtains but an ignoble and unprofitable leisure, defrauding himself of the experience which alone can make leisure fruitful. "But," says one, "you do not mean that the students should go to work with their hands instead of their heads?" I do not mean that exactly, but I mean something which he might think a good deal like that; I mean that they should not *play* life, or *study* it merely, while the community supports them at this expensive game, but earnestly *live* it from beginning to end. How could youths better learn to live than by at once trying the experiment of living? Methinks this would exercise their minds as much as mathematics. If I wished a boy to know something about the arts and sciences, for instance, I would not pursue the common course, which is merely to send him into the neighborhood of some professor, where any thing is professed and practised but the art of life;—to survey the world through a telescope or a microscope, and never with his natural eye; to study chemistry, and not learn how his bread is made, or mechanics, and not learn how it is earned; to discover new satellites to Neptune, and not detect the motes in his eyes, or to what vagabond he is a satellite himself; or to be devoured by the monsters that swarm all around him, while contemplating the monsters in a drop of vinegar. Which would have advanced the most at the end of a month,—the boy who had made his own jackknife from the ore which he had dug and smelted, reading as much as would be necessary for this,—or the boy who had attended the lectures on metallurgy at the Institute in the mean while, and had received a Rogers' penknife from his father? Which would be most likely to cut his fingers?—To my astonishment I was informed on leaving college that I had studied navigation!—why, if I had taken one turn down the harbor I should have known more about it. Even the *poor* student studies and is taught only *political* economy, while that economy of living which is synonymous with philosophy is not even sincerely professed in our colleges. The consequence is, that while he is reading Adam Smith, Ricardo, and Say, he runs his father in debt irretrievably.

As with our colleges, so with a hundred "modern improvements;" there is an illusion about them; there is not always a positive advance.

The devil goes on exacting compound interest to the last for his early share and numerous succeeding investments in them. Our inventions are wont to be pretty toys, which distract our attention from serious things. They are but improved means to an unimproved end, an end which it was already but too easy to arrive at; as railroads lead to Boston or New York. We are in great haste to construct a magnetic telegraph from Maine to Texas; but Maine and Texas, it may be, have nothing important to communicate. Either is in such a predicament as the man who was earnest to be introduced to a distinguished deaf woman, but when he was presented, and one end of her ear trumpet was put into his hand, had nothing to say. As if the main object were to talk fast and not to talk sensibly. We are eager to tunnel under the Atlantic and bring the old world some weeks nearer to the new; but perchance the first news that will leak through into the broad, flapping American ear will be that the Princess Adelaide has the whooping cough. After all, the man whose horse trots a mile in a minute does not carry the most important messages; he is not an evangelist, nor does he come round eating locusts and wild honey. I doubt if Flying Childers ever carried a peck of corn to mill.

One says to me, "I wonder that you do not lay up money; you love to travel; you might take the cars and go to Fitchburg to-day and see the country." But I am wiser than that. I have learned that the swiftest traveller is he that goes afoot. I say to my friend, Suppose we try who will get there first. The distance is thirty miles; the fare ninety cents. That is almost a day's wages. I remember when wages were sixty cents a day for laborers on this very road. Well, I start now on foot, and get there before night; I have travelled at that rate by the week together. You will in the mean while have earned your fare, and arrive there some time to-morrow, or possibly this evening, if you are lucky enough to get a job in season. Instead of going to Fitchburg, you will be working here the greater part of the day. And so, if the railroad reached round the world, I think that I should keep ahead of you; and as for seeing the country and getting experience of that kind, I should have to cut your acquaintance altogether.

Such is the universal law, which no man can ever outwit, and with regard to the railroad even we may say it is as broad as it is long. To make a railroad round the world available to all mankind is equivalent to grading the whole surface of the planet. Men have an indistinct notion that if they keep up this activity of joint stocks and spades long enough all will at length ride somewhere, in next to no time, and for nothing; but though a crowd rushes to the depot, and the conductor shouts "All aboard!" when the smoke is blown away and the vapor condensed, it will be perceived that a few are riding, but the rest are run over,—and it will be called, and will be, "A melancholy accident." No doubt they can ride at last who shall have earned their fare, that is, if they survive so long, but they will probably have lost their elasticity and desire to travel by that time. This spending of the best part of one's life earning money in order to enjoy a questionable liberty during the least valuable part of it, reminds me of the Englishman who went to India to make a fortune first, in order that he might return to England and live the life of a poet. He should have gone up garret at once. "What!" exclaim a million Irishmen starting up from all the shanties in the land, "is not this railroad which we have built a good thing?" Yes, I answer, *comparatively* good, that is, you might have done worse; but I wish, as you are brothers of mine, that you could have spent your time better than digging in this dirt.

* * *

I went to the woods because I wished to live deliberately, to front only the essential facts of life, and see if I could not learn what it had to teach, and not, when I came to die, discover that I had not lived. I did not wish to live what was not life, living is so dear; nor did I wish to practise resignation, unless it was quite necessary. I wanted to live deep and suck out all the marrow of life, to live so sturdily and Spartan-like as to put to rout all that was not life, to cut a broad swath and shave close, to drive life into a corner, and reduce it to its lowest terms, and, if it proved to be mean, why then to get the whole and genuine meanness of it, and publish its meanness to the world; or if it were sublime, to know it by experience, and be able to give a true account of it in my next excursion. For most men, it appears to me, are in a strange uncertainty about it, whether it is of the devil or of God, and have *somewhat hastily* concluded that it is the chief end of man here to "glorify God and enjoy him forever."

Still we live meanly, like ants; though the fable tells us that we were long ago changed into men; like pygmies we fight with cranes; it is error upon error, and clout upon clout, and our best virtue has for its occasion a superfluous and evitable wretchedness. Our life is frittered away by detail. An honest man has hardly need to count more than his ten fingers, or in extreme cases he may add his ten toes, and lump the rest. Simplicity, simplicity, simplicity! I say, let your affairs be as two or three, and not a hundred or a thousand; instead of a million count half a dozen, and keep your accounts on your thumb nail. In the midst of this chopping sea of civilized life, such are the clouds and storms and quick-sands and thousand-and-one items to be allowed for, that a man has to live, if he would not founder and go to the bottom and not make his port at all, by dead reckoning, and he must be a great calculator indeed who succeeds. Simplify, simplify. Instead of three meals a day, if it be necessary eat but one; instead of a hundred dishes, five; and reduce other things in proportion. Our life is like a German Confederacy, made up of petty states, with its boundary forever fluctuating, so that even a German cannot tell you how it is bounded at any moment. The nation itself, with all its so called internal improvements, which, by the way, are all external and superficial, is just such an unwieldy and overgrown establishment, cluttered with furniture and tripped up by its own traps, ruined by luxury and heedless expense, by want of calculation and a worthy aim, as the million households in the land; and the only cure for it as for them is in a rigid economy, a stern and more than Spartan simplicity of life and elevation of purpose. It lives too fast. Men think that it is essential that the *Nation* have commerce, and export ice, and talk through a telegraph, and ride thirty miles an hour, without a doubt, whether *they* do or not; but whether we should live like baboons or like men, is a little uncertain. If we do not get out sleepers, and forge rails, and devote days and nights to the work, but go to tinkering upon our *lives* to improve *them*, who will build railroads? And if railroads are not built, how shall we get to heaven in season? But if we stay at home and mind our business, who will want railroads? We do not ride on the railroad; it rides upon us. Did you ever think what those sleepers are that underlie the railroad? Each one is a man, an Irishman, or a Yankee man. The rails are laid on them, and they are covered with sand, and the cars run smoothly over them. They are sound sleepers, I assure you. And every few years a new lot is laid down and run over; so that, if some have the pleasure of riding on a rail, others have the misfortune to be ridden upon. And when they run over a man that is walking in his sleep, a supernumerary sleeper in the wrong position, and wake him up, they suddenly stop the cars, and make a hue and cry about it, as if this were an exception. I am glad to know that it takes a gang of men for every five miles to keep the sleepers down and level in their beds as it is, for this is a sign that they may sometime get up again.

Why should we live with such hurry and waste of life? We are determined to be starved before we are hungry. Men say that a stitch in time saves nine, and so they take a thousand stitches to-day to save nine to-morrow. As for *work*, we haven't any of any consequence. We have the Saint Vitus' dance, and cannot possibly keep our heads still. If I should only give a few pulls at the parish bell-rope, as for a fire, that is, without setting the bell, there is hardly a man on his farm in the outskirts of Concord, notwithstanding that press of engagements which was his excuse so many times this morning, nor a boy, nor a woman, I might almost say, but would forsake all and follow that sound, not mainly to save property from the flames, but, if we will confess the truth, much more to see it burn, since burn it must, and we, be it known, did not set it on fire,—or to see it put out, and have a hand in it, if that is done as handsomely; yes, even if it were the parish church itself. Hardly a man takes a half hour's nap after dinner, but when he wakes he holds up his head and asks, "What's the news?" as if the rest of mankind had stood his sentinels. Some give directions to be waked every half hour, doubtless for no other purpose; and then, to pay for it, they tell what they have dreamed. After a night's sleep the news is as indispensable as the breakfast. "Pray tell me any thing new that has happened to a man any where on this globe,"—and he reads it over his coffee and rolls, that a man has had his eyes gouged out this morning on the Wachito River; never dreaming the while that he lives in the dark unfathomed mammoth cave of this world, and has but the rudiment of an eye himself.

For my part, I could easily do without the post-office. I think that there are very few important communications made through it. To speak critically, I never received more than one or two letters in my life—I wrote this some years ago—that were worth the postage. The penny-post is, commonly, an institution through which you seriously offer a man that penny for his thoughts which is so often safely offered in jest. And I am sure that I never read any memorable news in a newspaper. If we read of one man robbed, or murdered, or killed by accident, or one house burned, or one vessel wrecked, or one steamboat blown up, or one cow run over on the Western Railroad, or one mad dog killed, or one lot of grasshoppers in the winter,—we never need read of another. One is enough. If you are acquainted with the principle, what do you care for a myriad instances and applications? To a philosopher all *news*, as it is called, is gossip, and they who edit and read it are old women over their tea. Yet not a few are greedy after this gossip. There was such a rush, as I hear, the other day at one of the offices to learn the foreign news by the last arrival, that several large squares of plate glass belonging to the establishment were broken by the pressure,—news which I seriously think a ready wit might write a twelvemonth or twelve years beforehand with sufficient accuracy. As for Spain, for instance, if you know how to throw in Don Carlos and the Infanta, and Don Pedro and Seville and Granada, from time to time in the right proportions,—they may have changed the names a little since I saw the papers,—and serve up a bull-fight when other entertainments fail, it will be true to the letter, and give us as good an idea of the exact state or ruin of things in Spain as the most succinct and lucid reports under this head in the newspapers: and as for England, almost the last significant scrap of news from that quarter was the revolution of 1649; and if you have learned the history of her crops for an average year, you never need attend to that thing again, unless your speculations are of a merely pecuniary character. If one may judge who rarely looks into the newspapers, nothing new does ever happen in foreign parts, a French revolution not excepted.

What news! how much more important to know what that is which was never old! "Kieou-pe-yu (great dignitary of the state of Wei) sent a man to Khoung-tseu to know his news. Khoung-tseu caused the messenger to be seated near him, and questioned him in these terms: What is your master doing? The messenger answered with respect: My master desires to diminish the number of his faults, but he cannot come to the end of them. The messenger being gone, the philosopher remarked: What a worthy messenger! What a worthy messenger!" The preacher, instead of vexing the ears of drowsy farmers on their day of rest at the end of the week,—for Sunday is the fit conclusion of an ill-spent week, and not the fresh and brave beginning of a new one,—with this one other draggle-tail of a sermon, should shout with thundering voice,— "Pause! Avast! Why so seeming fast, but deadly slow?"

Shams and delusions are esteemed for soundest truths, while reality is fabulous. If men would steadily observe realities only, and not allow themselves to be deluded, life, to compare it with such things as we know, would be like a fairy tale and the Arabian Nights' Entertainments. If we respected only what is inevitable and has a right to be, music and poetry would resound along the streets. When we are unhurried and wise, we perceive that only great and worthy things have any permanent and absolute existence,—that petty fears and petty pleasures are but the shadow of the reality. This is always exhilarating and sublime. By closing the eyes and slumbering, and consenting to be deceived by shows, men establish and confirm their daily life of routine and habit every where, which still is built on purely illusory foundations. Children, who play life, discern its true law and relations more clearly than men, who fail to live it worthily, but who think that they are wiser by experience, that is, by failure. I have read in a Hindoo book, that "there was a king's son, who, being expelled in infancy from his native city, was brought up by a forester, and, growing up to maturity in that state, imagined himself to belong to the barbarous race with which he lived. One of his father's ministers having discovered him, revealed to him what he was, and the misconception of his character was removed, and he knew himself to be a prince. So soul," continues the Hindoo philosopher, "from the circumstances in which it is placed, mistakes its own character, until the truth is revealed to it by some holy teacher, and then it knows itself to be *Brahme*." I perceive that we inhabitants of New England live this mean life that we do because our vision does not penetrate the surface of things. We think that that *is* which *appears* to be. If a man should walk through this town and see only the reality, where, think you, would the "Mill-dam" go to? If he should give us an account of the realities he beheld there, we should not recognize the place in his description. Look at a meeting-house, or a court-house, or a jail, or a shop, or a dwelling-house, and say what that thing really is before a true gaze, and they would all go to pieces in your account of them. Men esteem truth remote, in the outskirts of the system, behind the farthest star, before Adam and after the last man. In eternity there is indeed something true and sublime. But all these times and places and occasions are now and here. God himself culminates in the present moment, and will never be more divine in the lapse of all the ages. And we are enabled to apprehend at all what is sublime and noble only by the perpetual instilling and drenching of the reality which surrounds us. The universe constantly and obediently answers to our conceptions; whether we travel fast or slow, the track is laid for us. Let us spend our lives in conceiving then. The poet or the artist never yet had so fair and noble a design but some of his posterity at least could accomplish it.

Let us spend one day as deliberately as Nature, and not be thrown off the track by every nutshell and mosquito's wing that falls on the rails. Let us rise early and fast, or break fast, gently and without perturbation; let company come and let company go, let the bells ring and the children cry,—determined to make a day of it. Why should we knock under and go with the stream? Let us not be upset and overwhelmed in that terrible rapid and whirlpool called a dinner, situated in the meridian shallows. Weather this danger and you are safe, for the rest of the way is down hill. With unrelaxed nerves, with morning vigor, sail by it, looking another way, tied to the mast like Ulysses. If the engine whistles, let it whistle till it is hoarse for its pains. If the bell rings, why should we run? We will consider what kind of music they are like. Let us settle ourselves, and work and wedge our feet downward through the mud and slush of opinion, and prejudice, and tradition, and delusion, and appearance, that alluvion which covers the globe, through Paris and London, through New York and Boston and Concord, through church and state, through poetry and philosophy and religion, till we come to a hard bottom and rocks in place, which we can call *reality*, and say, This is, and no mistake; and then begin, having a *point d'appui*, below freshet and frost and fire, a place where you might found a wall or a state, or set a lamp-post safely, or perhaps a gauge, not a Nilometer, but a Realometer, that future ages might know how deep a freshet of shams and appearances had gathered from time to time. If you stand right fronting and face to face to a fact, you will see the sun glimmer on both its surfaces, as if it were a cimeter, and feel its sweet edge dividing you through the heart and marrow, and so you will happily conclude your mortal career. Be it life or death, we crave only reality. If we are really dying, let us hear the rattle in our throats and feel cold in the extremities; if we are alive, let us go about our business.

Time is but the stream I go a-fishing in. I drink at it; but while I drink I see the sandy bottom and detect how shallow it is. Its thin current slides away, but eternity remains. I would drink deeper; fish in the sky, whose bottom is pebbly with stars. I cannot count one. I know not the first letter of the alphabet. I have always been regretting that I was not as wise as the day I was born. The intellect is a cleaver; it discerns and rifts its way into the secret of things. I do not wish to be any more busy with my hands than is necessary. My head is hands and feet. I feel all my best faculties concentrated in it. My instinct tells me that my head is an organ for burrowing, as some creatures use their snout and fore-paws, and with it I would mine and burrow my way through these hills. I think that the richest vein is somewhere hereabouts; so by the divining rod and thin rising vapors I judge; and here I will begin to mine.

Walden; or, Life in the Woods (1854)

from **Huckleberries**

served my apprenticeship and have since done considerable jour-
neywork in the huckleberry field. Though I never paid for my
schooling and clothing in that way, it was some of the best schooling
that I got and paid for itself. Theodore Parker is not the only New England boy who has got his education by picking huckleberries, though
he may not have gone to Harvard thereafter, nor to any school more distant than the huckleberry field. *There* was the university itself where
you could learn the everlasting Laws, and Medicine and Theology, not
under Story, and Warren, and Ware, but far wiser professors than they.
Why such haste to go from the huckleberry field to the College yard?

As in old times they who dwelt on the heath, remote from towns,
being backward to adopt the doctrines which prevailed in towns, were
called heathen in a bad sense, so I trust that we dwellers in the huckleberry pastures, which are our heathlands, shall be slow to adopt the notions of large towns and cities, though perchance we may be nicknamed
huckleberry people. But the worst of it is that the emissaries of the
towns come more for our berries than they do for our salvation.

Occasionally, in still summer forenoons, when perhaps a mantua-
maker was to be dined, and a huckleberry pudding had been decided
on (by the authorities), I a lad of ten was despatched to a neighboring
hill alone. My scholastic education could be thus far tampered with,
and an excuse might be found. No matter how scarce the berries on the
near hills, the exact number necessary for a pudding could surely be
collected by eleven o'clock—and all ripe ones too though I turned some
round three times to be sure they were not premature. My rule in such
cases was never to eat one till my dish was full; for going a-berrying
implies more things than eating the berries. They at home got nothing
but the pudding, a comparatively heavy affair—but I got the forenoon
out of doors—to say nothing about the appetite for the pudding. They
got only the plums that were in the pudding, but I got the far sweeter
plums that never go into it.

At other times, when I had companions, some of them used to bring such remarkably shaped dishes, that I was often curious to see how the berries disposed of themselves in them. Some brought a coffee-pot to the huckleberry field, and such a vessel possessed this advantage at least, that if a greedy boy had skimmed off a handful or two on his way home, he had only to close the lid and give his vessel a shake to have it full again. I have seen this done all round when the party got as far homeward as the Dutch House. It can probably be done with any vessel that has much side to it.

There was a Young America then, which has become Old America, but its principles and motives are still the same, only applied to other things. Sometimes, just before reaching the spot—every boy rushed to the hill side and hastily selecting a spot—shouted 'I speak for this place,' indicating its bounds, and another 'I speak for that,' and so on— and this was sometimes considered good law for the huckleberry field. At any rate it is a law similar to this by which we have taken possession of the territory of Indians and Mexicans.

I once met with a whole family, father, mother, and children, ravaging a huckleberry field in this wise. They cut up the bushes as they went and beat them over the edge of a bushel basket, till they had it full of berries, ripe and green, leaves, sticks etc., and so they passed along out of my sight like wild men.

I well remember with what a sense of freedom and spirit of adventure I used to take my way across the fields with my pail, some years later, toward some distant hill or swamp, when dismissed for all day, and I would not now exchange such an expansion of all my being for all the learning in the world. Liberation and enlargement—such is the fruit which all culture aims to secure. I suddenly knew more about my books than if I had never ceased studying them. I found myself in a schoolroom where I could not fail to see and hear things worth seeing and hearing—where I could not help getting my lesson—for my lesson came to me. Such experience often repeated, was the chief encouragement to go to the Academy and study a book at last.

But ah we have fallen on evil days! I hear of pickers ordered out of the huckleberry fields, and I see stakes set up with written notices forbidding any to pick them. Some let their fields or allow so much for the picking. *Sic transit gloria ruris*. I do not mean to blame any, but all—to bewail our fates generally. We are not grateful enough that we have lived a part of our lives before these things occurred. What becomes of the true value of country life—what, if you must go to market for it? It has come to this, that the butcher now brings round our huckleberries in his cart. Why, it is as if the hangman were to perform the marriage ceremony. Such is the inevitable tendency of our civilization, to reduce huckleberries to a level with beef-steaks—that is to blot out four fifths of it, or the going a-huckleberrying, and leave only a pudding, that part which is the fittest accompaniment to a beef-steak. You all know what it is to go a-beef-steaking. It is to knock your old fellow laborer Bright on the head to begin with—or possibly to cut a steak from him running in the Abyssinian fashion and wait for another to grow there. The butcher's item in chalk on the door is now 'Calf's head and huckleberries.'

I suspect that the inhabitants of England and the continent of Europe have thus lost in a measure their natural rights, with the increase of population and monopolies. The wild fruits of the earth disappear before civilization, or only the husks of them are to be found in large markets. The whole country becomes, as it were, a town or beaten common, and almost the only fruits left are a few hips and haws.

What sort of a country is that where the huckleberry fields are private property? When I pass such fields on the highway, my heart sinks within me. I see a blight on the land. Nature is under a veil there. I make haste away from the accursed spot. Nothing could deform her fair face more. I cannot think of it ever after but as the place where fair and palatable berries, are converted into money, where the huckleberry is desecrated.

It is true, we have as good a right to make berries private property, as to make wild grass and trees such—it is not worse than a thousand other practices which custom has sanctioned—but that is the worst of it, for it suggests how bad the rest are, and to what result our civilization and division of labor naturally tend, to make all things venal.

A., a professional huckleberry picker, has hired B.'s field, and, we will suppose, is now gathering the crop, with a patent huckleberry horse rake.

C., a professed cook, is superintending the boiling of a pudding made of some of the berries.

While Professor D.—for whom the pudding is intended, sits in his library writing a book—a work on the *Vaccinieae* of course.

And now the result of this downward course will be seen in that work—which should be the ultimate fruit of the huckleberry field. It will be worthless. It will have none of the spirit of the huckleberry in it, and the reading of it will be a weariness of the flesh.

I believe in a different kind of division of labor—that Professor D. should be encouraged to divide himself freely between his library and the huckleberry field.

What I chiefly regret in this case, is the in effect dog-in-the-manger result; for at the same time that we exclude mankind from gathering berries in our field, we exclude them from gathering health and happiness and inspiration, and a hundred other far finer and nobler fruits than berries, which are found there, but which we have no notion of gathering and shall not gather ourselves, nor ever carry to market, for there is no market for them, but let them rot on the bushes.

We thus strike only one more blow at a simple and wholesome relation to nature. I do not know but this is the excuse of those who have lately taken to swinging bags of beans and ringing dumb bells. As long as the berries are free to all comers they are beautiful, though they may be few and small, but tell me that this is a blueberry swamp which somebody has hired, and I shall not want even to look at it. We so commit the berries to the wrong hands, that is to the hands of those who cannot appreciate them. This is proved by the fact that if we do not pay them some money, these parties will at once cease to pick them. They have no other interest in berries but a pecuniary one. Such is the constitution of our society that we make a compromise and permit the berries to be degraded, to be enslaved, as it were.

Accordingly in laying claim for the first time to the spontaneous fruit of our pastures, we are inevitably aware of a little meanness, and the merry berry party which we turn away naturally looks down on and despises us. If it were left to the berries to say who should have them, is it not likely that they would prefer to be gathered by the party of children in the hay-rigging, who have come to have a good time merely?

This is one of the taxes which we pay for having a rail-road. All our improvements, so called, tend to convert the country into the town. But I do not see clearly that these successive losses are ever quite made up to us. This suggests, as I have said, what origin and foundation many of our institutions have. I do not say this by way of complaining of this custom in particular, which is beginning to prevail—not that I love Caesar less but Rome more. It is my own way of living that I complain of as well as yours—and therefore I trust that my remarks will come home to you. I hope that I am not so poor a shot, like most clergymen, as to fire into a crowd of a thousand men without hitting somebody—though I do not aim at any one.

Thus we behave like oxen in a flower garden. The true fruit of Nature can only be plucked with a fluttering heart and a delicate hand, not bribed by any earthly reward. No hired man can help us to gather that crop.

Among the Indians, the earth and its productions generally were common and free to all the tribe, like the air and water—but among us who have supplanted the Indians, the public retain only a small yard or common in the middle of the village, with perhaps a grave-yard beside it, and the right of way, by sufferance, by a particular narrow route, which is annually becoming narrower, from one such yard to another. I doubt if you can ride out five miles in any direction without coming to where some individual is tolling in the road—and he expects the time when it will all revert to him or his heirs. This is the way we civilized men have arranged it.

I am not overflowing with respect and gratitude to the fathers who thus laid out our New England villages, whatever precedent they were influenced by, for I think that a 'prentice hand liberated from Old English prejudices could have done much better in this new world. If they were in earnest seeking thus far away 'freedom to worship God,' as some assure us—why did they not secure a little more of it, when it was so cheap and they were about it? At the same time that they built meeting-houses why did they not preserve from desecration and destruction far grander temples not made with hands?

What are the natural features which make a township handsome—and worth going far to dwell in? A river with its waterfalls—meadows, lakes—hills, cliffs or individual rocks, a forest and single ancient trees—such things are beautiful. They have a high use which dollars and cents never represent. If the inhabitants of a town were wise they would seek to preserve these things though at a considerable expense. For such things educate far more than any hired teachers or preachers, or any at present recognized system of school education.

I do not think him fit to be the founder of a state or even of a town who does not foresee the use of these things, but legislates as it were, for oxen chiefly.

It would be worth the while if in each town there were a committee appointed, to see that the beauty of the town received no detriment. If here is the largest boulder in the country, then it should not belong to an individual nor be made into door-steps. In some countries precious metals belong to the crown—so here more precious objects of great natural beauty should belong to the public.

Let us try to keep the new world new, and while we make a wary use of the city, preserve as far as possible the advantages of living in the country.

I think of no natural feature which is a greater ornament and treasure to this town than the river. It is one of the things which determine whether a man will live here or in another place, and it is one of the first objects which we show to a stranger. In this respect we enjoy a great advantage over those neighboring towns which have no river. Yet the town, as a corporation, has never turned any but the most purely utilitarian eyes upon it—and has done nothing to preserve its natural beauty.

They who laid out the town should have made the river available as a common possession forever. The town collectively should at least have done as much as an individual of taste who owns an equal area commonly does in England. Indeed I think that not only the channel but one or both banks of every river should be a public highway—for a river is not useful merely to float on. In this case, one bank might have been reserved as a public walk and the trees that adorned it have been protected, and frequent avenues have been provided leading to it from the main street. This would have cost but few acres of land and but little wood, and we should all have been gainers by it. Now it is accessible only at the bridges at points comparatively distant from the town, and there there is not a foot of shore to stand on unless you trespass on somebody's lot—and if you attempt a quiet stroll down the bank—you soon meet with fences built at right angles with the stream and projecting far over the water—where individuals, naturally enough, under the present arrangement—seek to monopolize the shore. At last we shall get our only view of the stream from the meeting house belfry.

As for the trees which fringed the shore within my remembrance—where are they? and where will the remnant of them be after ten years more?

So if there is any central and commanding hill-top, it should be reserved for the public use. Think of a mountain top in the township—even to the Indians a sacred place—only accessible through private grounds. A temple as it were which you cannot enter without trespassing—nay the temple itself private property and standing in a man's cow yard—for such is commonly the case. New Hampshire courts have lately been deciding, as if it was for them to decide, whether the top of Mount Washington belonged to A or B—and it being decided in favor of B, I hear that he went up one winter with the proper officers and took formal possession. That area should be left unappropriated for modesty and reverence's sake—if only to suggest that the traveller who climbs thither in a degree rises above himself, as well as his native valley, and leaves some of his grovelling habits behind.

I know it is a mere figure of speech to talk about temples nowadays, when men recognize none, and associate the word with heathenism. Most men, it appears to me, do not care for Nature, and would sell their share in all her beauty, for as long as they may live, for a stated and not very large sum. Thank God they cannot yet fly and lay waste the sky as well as the earth. We are safe on that side for the present. It is for the very reason that some do not care for these things that we need to combine to protect all from the vandalism of a few.

It is true, we as yet take liberties and go across lots in most directions but we naturally take fewer and fewer liberties every year, as we meet with more resistance, and we shall soon be reduced to the same straights they are in England, where going across lots is out of the question— and we must ask leave to walk in some lady's park.

There are a few hopeful signs. There is the growing *library*—and then the town does set trees along the highways. But does not the broad landscape itself deserve attention?

We cut down the few old oaks which witnessed the transfer of the township from the Indian to the white man, and perchance commence our museum with a cartridge box taken from a British soldier in 1775. How little we insist on truly grand and beautiful natural features. There may be the most beautiful landscapes in the world within a dozen miles of us, for aught we know—for their inhabitants do not value nor perceive them—and so have not made them known to others—but if a grain of gold were picked up there, or a pearl found in a fresh-water clam, the whole state would resound with the news.

Thousands annually seek the White Mountains to be refreshed by their wild and primitive beauty—but when the country was discovered a similar kind of beauty prevailed all over it—and much of this might have been preserved for our present refreshment if a little foresight and taste had been used.

I do not believe that there is a town in this country which realizes in what its true wealth consists.

I visited the town of Boxboro only eight miles west of us last fall— and far the handsomest and most memorable thing which I saw there, was its noble oak wood. I doubt if there is a finer one in Massachusetts. Let it stand fifty years longer and men will make pilgrimages to it from all parts of the country, and for a worthier object than to shoot squirrels in it—and yet I said to myself, Boxboro would be very like the rest of New England, if she were ashamed of that wood-land. Probably, if the history of this town is written, the historian will have omitted to say a word about this forest—the most interesting thing in it—and lay all the stress on the history of the parish.

It turned out that I was not far from right—for not long after I came across a very brief historical notice of Stow—which then included Boxboro—written by the Reverend John Gardiner in the *Massachusetts Historical Collections*, nearly a hundred years ago. In which Mr. Gardiner, after telling us who was his predecessor in the ministry, and when he himself was settled, goes on to say, 'As for any remarkables, I am of mind there have been the fewest of any town of our standing in the Province. . . . I can't call to mind above one thing worthy of public notice, and that is the grave of Mr. John Green' who, it appears, when in England, 'was made clerk of the exchequer' by Cromwell. 'Whether he was excluded the act of oblivion or not I cannot tell,' says Mr. Gardiner. At any rate he returned to New England and as Gardiner tells us 'lived and died, and lies buried in this place.'

I can assure Mr. Gardiner that he was not excluded from the act of oblivion.

It is true Boxboro was less peculiar for its woods at that date—but they were not less interesting absolutely.

I remember talking a few years ago with a young man who had undertaken to write the history of his native town—a wild and mountainous town far up country, whose very name suggested a hundred things to me, and I almost wished I had the task to do myself—so few of the original settlers had been driven out—and not a single clerk of the exchequer buried in it. But to my chagrin I found that the author was complaining of want of materials, and that the crowning fact of his story was that the town had been the residence of General C— and the family mansion was still standing.

I have since heard, however, that Boxboro is content to have that forest stand, instead of the houses and farms that might supplant it—not because of its beauty—but because the land pays a much larger tax now than it would then.

Nevertheless it is likely to be cut off within a few years for ship-timber and the like. It is too precious to be thus disposed of. I think that it would be wise for the state to purchase and preserve a few such forests.

If the people of Massachusetts are ready to found a professorship of Natural History—so they must see the importance of preserving some portions of nature herself unimpaired.

I find that the rising generation in this town do not know what an oak or a pine is, having seen only inferior specimens. Shall we hire a man to lecture on botany, on oaks for instance, our noblest plants— while we permit others to cut down the few best specimens of these trees that are left? It is like teaching children Latin and Greek while we burn the books printed in those languages.

I think that each town should have a park, or rather a primitive forest, of five hundred or a thousand acres, either in one body or several— where a stick should never be cut for fuel—nor for the navy, nor to make wagons, but stand and decay for higher uses—a common possession forever, for instruction and recreation.

All Walden wood might have been reserved, with Walden in the midst of it, and the Easterbrooks country, an uncultivated area of some four square miles in the north of the town, might have been our huckleberry field. If any owners of these tracts are about to leave the world without natural heirs who need or deserve to be specially remembered, they will do wisely to abandon the possession to all mankind, and not will them to some individual who perhaps has enough already—and so correct the error that was made when the town was laid out. As some give to Harvard College or another Institution, so one might give a forest or a huckleberry field to Concord. This town surely is an institution which deserves to be remembered. Forget the heathen in foreign parts, and remember the pagans and savages here.

We hear of cow commons and ministerial lots, but we want *men* commons and *lay* lots as well. There is meadow and pasture and woodlot for the town's poor, why not a forest and huckleberry field for the town's rich?

We boast of our system of education, but why stop at schoolmasters and schoolhouses? We are all schoolmasters and our schoolhouse is the universe. To attend chiefly to the desk or schoolhouse, while we neglect the scenery in which it is placed, is absurd. If we do not look out we shall find our fine schoolhouse standing in a cow yard at last.

It frequently happens that what the city prides itself on most is its park—those acres which require to be the least altered from their original condition.

Live in each season as it passes; breathe the air, drink the drink, taste the fruit, and resign yourself to the influences of each. Let these be your only diet-drink and botanical medicines.

In August live on berries, not dried meats and pemmican as if you were on shipboard making your way through a waste ocean, or in the Darien Grounds, and so die of ship-fever and scurvy. Some will die of ship-fever and scurvy in an Illinois prairie, they lead such stifled and scurvy lives.

Be blown on by all the winds. Open all your pores and bathe in all the tides of nature, in all her streams and oceans, at all seasons. Miasma and infection are from within, not without. The invalid brought to the brink of the grave by an unnatural life, instead of imbibing the great influence that nature is—drinks only of the tea made of a particular herb—while he still continues his unnatural life—saves at the spile and wastes at the bung. He does not love nature or his life and so sickens and dies and no doctor can save him.

Grow green with spring—yellow and ripe with autumn. Drink of each season's influence as a vial, a true panacea of all remedies mixed for your especial use. The vials of summer never made a man sick, only those which he had stored in his cellar. Drink the wines not of your own but of nature's bottling—not kept in a goat- or pig-skin, but in the skins of a myriad fair berries.

Let Nature do your bottling, as also your pickling and preserving.

For all nature is doing her best each moment to make us well. She exists for no other end. Do not resist her. With the least inclination to be well we should not be sick. Men have discovered, or think that they have discovered the salutariness of a few wild things only, and not of all nature. Why nature is but another name for health. Some men think that they are not well in Spring or Summer or Autumn or Winter, (if you will excuse the pun) it is only because they are not indeed *well*, that is fairly *in* those seasons.

c. 1861

GEORGE CATLIN

Better known as a painter than a writer, George Catlin (1796–1872) was, in fact, more driven by subject than medium. Obsessed with the American Indian's dwindling numbers, he resolved in mid-career to "use my art and so much of the labors of my future life as might be required in rescuing from oblivion the looks and customs of the vanishing races of native man in America." Much of that work, which took him across the American frontier for a decade, hangs on the walls of the most important museums in the country. But Catlin also learned much that couldn't be painted—including the story of how white Americans were purposefully slaughtering the great herds of buffalo that were the aboriginal larder. The questions raised in this account—about luxury and necessity, for instance—still echo in our debates over globalization and trade and other environmental issues.

from Letters and Notes on the Manners, Customs, and Condition of the North American Indians

It is generally supposed, and familiarly said that a man "*falls*" into a rêverie; but I seated myself in the shade a few minutes since, resolved to *force* myself into one; and for this purpose I laid open a small pocket-map of North America, and excluding my thoughts from every other object in the world, I soon succeeded in producing the desired illusion. This little chart, over which I bent, was seen in all its parts, as nothing but the green and vivid reality. I was lifted up upon an imaginary pair of wings, which easily raised and held me floating in the open air, from whence I could behold beneath me the Pacific and the Atlantic Oceans—the great cities of the East, and the mighty rivers.

I could see the blue chain of the great lakes at the North—the Rocky Mountains, and beneath them and near their base, the vast, and almost boundless plains of grass, which were speckled with the bands of grazing buffaloes!

The world turned gently around, and I examined its surface; continent after continent passed under my eye, and yet amidst them all, I saw not the vast and vivid green, that is spread like a carpet over the Western wilds of my own country. I saw not elsewhere in the world, the myriad herds of buffaloes—my eyes scanned in vain for they were not. And when I turned again to the wilds of my native land, I beheld them all in motion! For the distance of several hundreds of miles from North to South, they were wheeling about in vast columns and herds—some were scattered, and ran with furious wildness—some lay dead, and others were pawing the earth for a hiding-place—some were sinking down and dying, gushing out their life's blood in deep-drawn sighs— and others were contending in furious battle for the life they possessed, and the ground that they stood upon. They had long since assembled from the thickets, and secret haunts of the deep forest, into the midst of the treeless and bushless plains, as the place for their safety. I could see in an hundred places, amid the wheeling bands, and on their skirts and flanks, the leaping wild horse darting among them. I saw not the arrows, nor heard the twang of the sinewy bows that sent them; but I saw their victims fall!—on other steeds that rushed along their sides, I saw the glistening lances, which seemed to lay across them; their blades were blazing in the sun, till dipped in blood, and then I lost them! In other parts (and there were many), the vivid flash of *fire-arms* was seen—*their* victims fell too, and over their dead bodies hung suspended in air, little clouds of whitened smoke, from under which the flying horsemen had darted forward to mingle again with, and deal death to, the trampling throng.

So strange were men mixed (both red and white) with the countless herds that wheeled and eddyed about, that all below seemed one vast extended field of battle—whole armies, in some places, seemed to blacken the earth's surface;—in other parts, regiments, battalions, wings, platoons, rank and file, and *"Indian-file"*—all were in motion;

and death and destruction seemed to be the watch-word amongst them. In their turmoil, they sent up great clouds of dust, and with them came the mingled din of groans and trampling hoofs, that seemed like the rumbling of a dreadful cataract, or the roaring of distant thunder. Alternate pity and admiration harrowed up in my bosom and my brain, many a hidden thought; and amongst them a few of the beautiful notes that were once sung, and exactly in point: "*Quadrupedante putrem sonitu quatit ungula campum.*" Even such was the din amidst the quadrupeds of these vast plains. And from the craggy cliffs of the Rocky Mountains also were seen descending into the valley, the myriad Tartars, who had not horses to ride, but before their well-drawn bows the fattest of the herds were falling. Hundreds and thousands were strewed upon the plains—they were flayed, and their reddened carcasses left; and about them bands of wolves, and dogs, and buzzards were seen devouring them. Contiguous, and in sight, were the distant and feeble smokes of wigwams and villages, where the skins were dragged, and dressed for white man's luxury! where they were all sold for *whiskey*, and the poor Indians laid drunk, and were crying. I cast my eyes into the towns and cities of the East, and there I beheld buffalo robes hanging at almost every door for traffic; and I saw also the curling smokes of a thousand *Stills*—and I said, "Oh insatiable man, is thy avarice such! wouldst thou tear the skin from the back of the last animal of this noble race, *and rob thy fellow-man of his meat, and for it give him poison!*"

* * *

Many are the rudenesses and wilds in Nature's works, which are destined to fall before the deadly axe and desolating hands of cultivating man; and so amongst her ranks of *living*, of beast and human, we often find noble stamps, or beautiful colours, to which our admiration clings; and even in the overwhelming march of civilized improvements and refinements do we love to cherish their existence, and lend our efforts to preserve them in their primitive rudeness. Such of Nature's works are always worthy of our preservation and protection; and the further we become separated (and the face of the country) from that pristine wildness and beauty, the more pleasure does the mind of enlightened man feel in recurring to those scenes, when he can have them preserved for his eyes and his mind to dwell upon.

Of such "rudenesses and wilds," Nature has nowhere presented more beautiful and lovely scenes, than those of the vast prairies of the West; and of *man* and *beast*, no nobler specimens than those who inhabit them—the *Indian* and the *buffalo*—joint and original tenants of the soil, and fugitives together from the approach of civilized man; they have fled to the great plains of the West, and there, under an equal doom, they have taken up their *last abode*, where their race will expire, and their bones will bleach together.

It may be that *power* is *right*, and *voracity* a *virtue*; and that these people, and these noble animals, are *righteously* doomed to an issue that *will* not be averted. It can be easily proved—we have a civilized science that can easily do it, or anything else that may be required to cover the iniquities of civilized man in catering for his unholy appetites. It can be proved that the weak and ignorant have no *rights*—that there can be no virtue in darkness—that God's gifts have no meaning or merit until they are appropriated by civilized man—by him brought into the light, and converted to his use and luxury. We have a mode of reasoning (I forget what it is called) by which all this can be proved, and even more. The *word* and the *system* are entirely of *civilized* origin; and latitude is admirably given to them in proportion to the increase of civilized wants, which often require a *judge* to overrule the laws of nature. I say that *we* can prove such things; but an *Indian* cannot. It is a mode of reasoning unknown to him in his nature's simplicity, but admirably adapted to subserve the interests of the enlightened world, who are always their own judges, when dealing with the savage; and who, in the present refined age, have many appetites that can only be lawfully indulged, by proving God's laws defective.

It is not enough in this polished and extravagant age, that we get from the Indian his lands, and the very clothes from his back, but the food from their mouths must be stopped, to add a new and useless article to the fashionable world's luxuries. The ranks must be thinned, and the race exterminated, of this noble animal, and the Indians of the great plains left without the means of supporting life, that white men may figure a few years longer, enveloped in buffalo robes—that they may spread them, for their pleasure and elegance, over the backs of their sleighs, and trail them ostentatiously amidst the busy throng, as a thing of beauty and elegance that had been made for them!

Reader! listen to the following calculations, and forget them not. The buffaloes (the quadrupeds from whose backs your beautiful robes were taken, and whose myriads were once spread over the whole country, from the Rocky Mountains to the Atlantic Ocean) have recently fled before the appalling appearance of civilized man, and taken up their abode and pasturage amid the almost boundless prairies of the West. An instinctive dread of their deadly foes, who made an easy prey of them whilst grazing in the forest, has led them to seek the midst of the vast and treeless plains of grass, as the spot where they would be least exposed to the assaults of their enemies; and it is exclusively in those desolate fields of silence (yet of beauty) that they are to be found—and over these vast steppes, or prairies, have they fled, like the Indian, towards the "setting sun;" until their bands have been crowded together, and their limits confined to a narrow strip of country on this side of the Rocky Mountains.

This strip of country, which extends from the province of Mexico to lake Winnepeg on the North, is almost one entire plain of grass, which is, and ever must be, useless to cultivating man. It is here, and here chiefly, that the buffaloes dwell; and with, and hovering about them, live and flourish the tribes of Indians, whom God made for the enjoyment of that fair land and its luxuries.

It is a melancholy contemplation for one who has travelled as I have, through these realms, and seen this noble animal in all its pride and glory, to contemplate it so rapidly wasting from the world, drawing the irresistible conclusion too, which one must do, that its species is soon to be extinguished, and with it the peace and happiness (if not the actual existence) of the tribes of Indians who are joint tenants with them, in the occupancy of these vast and idle plains.

And what a splendid contemplation too, when one (who has travelled these realms, and can duly appreciate them) imagines them as they *might* in future be seen, (by some great protecting policy of government) preserved in their pristine beauty and wildness, in a *magnificent park*, where the world could see for ages to come, the native Indian in his classic attire, galloping his wild horse, with sinewy bow, and shield and lance, amid the fleeting herds of elks and buffaloes. What a beautiful and thrilling specimen for America to preserve and hold up to the view of her refined citizens and the world, in future ages! A *nation's Park*, containing man and beast, in all the wild and freshness of their nature's beauty!

I would ask no other monument to my memory, nor any other enrolment of my name amongst the famous dead, than the reputation of having been the founder of such an institution.

Such scenes might easily have been preserved, and still could be cherished on the great plains of the West, without detriment to the country or its borders; for the tracts of country on which the buffaloes have assembled, are uniformly sterile, and of no available use to cultivating man.

It is on these plains, which are stocked with buffaloes, that the finest specimens of the Indian race are to be seen. It is here that the savage is decorated in the richest costume. It is here, and here only, that his wants are all satisfied, and even the *luxuries* of life are afforded him in abundance. And here also is he the proud and honourable man (before he has had teachers or laws), above the imported wants, which beget meanness and vice; stimulated by ideas of honour and virtue, in which the God of Nature has certainly not curtailed him.

There are, by a fair calculation, more than 300,000 Indians, who are now subsisted on the flesh of the buffaloes, and by those animals supplied with all the luxuries of life which they desire, as they know of none others. The great variety of uses to which they convert the body and other parts of that animal, are almost incredible to the person who has not actually dwelt amongst these people, and closely studied their modes and customs. Every part of their flesh is converted into food, in one shape or another, and on it they entirely subsist. The robes of the animals are worn by the Indians instead of blankets—their skins when tanned, are used as coverings for their lodges, and for their beds; undressed, they are used for constructing canoes—for saddles, for bridles—l'arrêts, lasos, and thongs. The horns are shaped into ladles and spoons—the brains are used for dressing the skins—their bones are used for saddle trees—for war clubs, and scrapers for graining the robes—and others are broken up for the marrow-fat which is contained in them. Their sinews are used for strings and backs to their bows—for thread to string their beads and sew their dresses. The feet of the animals are boiled, with their hoofs, for the glue they contain, for fastening their arrow points, and many other uses. The hair from the head and shoulders, which is long, is twisted and braided into halters, and the tail is used for a fly brush. In this wise do these people convert and use the various parts of this useful animal, and with all these luxuries of life about them, and their numerous games, they are happy (God bless them) in the ignorance of the disastrous fate that awaits them.

Yet this interesting community, with its sports, its wildnesses, its languages, and all its manners and customs, could be perpetuated, and also the buffaloes, whose numbers would increase and supply them with food for ages and centuries to come, if a system of non-intercourse could be established and preserved. But such is not to be the case—the buffalo's doom is sealed, and with their extinction must assuredly sink into real despair and starvation, the inhabitants of these vast plains, which afford for the Indians, no other possible means of subsistence; and they must at last fall a prey to wolves and buzzards, who will have no other bones to pick.

It seems hard and cruel, (does it not?) that we civilized people with all the luxuries and comforts of the world about us, should be drawing from the backs of these useful animals the skins for our luxury, leaving their carcasses to be devoured by the wolves—that we should draw from that country, some 150 or 200,000 of their robes annually, the greater part of which are taken from animals that are killed expressly for the robe, at a season when the meat is not cured and preserved, and for each of which skins the Indian has received but a pint of whiskey!

Such is the fact, and that number or near it, are annually destroyed, in addition to the number that is necessarily killed for the subsistence of 300,000 Indians, who live entirely upon them. It may be said, perhaps, that the Fur Trade of these great western realms, which is now limited chiefly to the purchase of buffalo robes, is of great and national importance, and should and must be encouraged. To such a suggestion I would reply, by merely enquiring, (independently of the poor Indians' disasters,) how much more advantageously would such a capital be employed, both for the weal of the country and for the owners, if it were invested in machines for the manufacture of *woollen robes*, of equal and superior value and beauty; thereby encouraging the growers of wool, and the industrious manufacturer, rather than cultivating a taste for the use of buffalo skins; which is just to be acquired, and then, from necessity, to be dispensed with, when a few years shall have destroyed the last of the animals producing them.

It may be answered, perhaps, that the necessaries of life are given in exchange for these robes; but what, I would ask, are the necessities in Indian life, where they have buffaloes in abundance to live on? The Indians' necessities are entirely artificial—are all created; and when the buffaloes shall have disappeared in his country, which will be within *eight* or *ten* years, I would ask, who is to supply him with the necessaries of life then? and I would ask, further, (and leave the question to be answered ten years hence), when the skin shall have been stripped from the back of the last animal, who is to resist the ravages of 300,000 starving savages; and in their trains, 1,500,000 wolves, whom direst necessity will have driven from their desolate and gameless plains, to seek for the means of subsistence along our exposed frontier? God has everywhere supplied man in a state of Nature, with the necessaries of life, and before we destroy the game of his country, or teach him new desires, he has no wants that are not satisfied.

Amongst the tribes who have been impoverished and repeatedly removed, the necessaries of life are extended with a better grace from the hands of civilized man; 90,000 of such have already been removed, and they draw from Government some 5 or 600,000 dollars annually in cash; *which money passes immediately into the hands of white men*, and for it the necessaries of life *may be* abundantly furnished. But who, I would ask, are to furnish the Indians who have been instructed in this unnatural mode—living upon *such* necessaries, and even luxuries of life, extended to them by the hands of white men, when those annuities are at an end, and the skin is stripped from the last of the animals which God gave them for their subsistence?

Reader, I will stop here, lest you might forget to answer these important queries—these are questions which I know will puzzle the world—and, perhaps, it is not right that I should ask them.

Letters and Notes on the Manners, Customs, and
Condition of the North American Indians (1841)

LYDIA HUNTLEY SIGOURNEY

Lydia Sigourney (1791–1865) was among the most popular poets of her day, her work a perfect distillation of Victorian convention and sentimentality. That's why she's included here—to give some picture of how fashionable readers were beginning to think about nature and its destruction by the middle of the 19th century.

Fallen Forests

Man's warfare on the trees is terrible.
He lifts his rude hut in the wilderness,
And lo! the loftiest trunks, that age on age
Were nurtured to nobility, and bore
Their summer coronets so gloriously,
Fall with a thunder-sound, to rise no more.
He toucheth flame unto them, and they lie
A blackened wreck, their tracery and wealth
Of sky-fed emerald, madly spent to feed
An arch of brilliance for a single night,
And scaring thence the wild deer and the fox,
And the lithe squirrel from the nut-strewn home,
So long enjoyed.
     He lifts his puny arm,
And every echo of the axe doth hew
The iron heart of centuries away.
He entereth boldly to the solemn groves
On whose green altar-tops, since time was young,
The winged birds have poured their incense strain
Of praise and love, within whose mighty nave
The wearied cattle from a thousand hills
Have found their shelter mid the heat of day;
Perchance, in their mute worship pleasing Him
Who careth for the meanest He hath made.
I said he entereth to the sacred groves

Where Nature in her beauty bends to God,
And lo! their temple-arch is desecrate;
Sinks the sweet hymn, the ancient ritual fades,
And uptorn roots, and prostrate columns mark
The invader's footsteps.
                Silent years roll on,
His babes are men. His ant-heap dwelling grows
Too narrow, for his hand hath gotten wealth.
He builds a stately mansion, but it stands
Unblessed by trees. He smote them recklessly,
When their green arms were round him, as a guard
Of tutelary deities, and feels
Their maledictions, now the burning noon
Maketh his spirit faint. With anxious care
He casteth acorns in the earth, and woos
Sunbeam and rain; he planteth the young shoot,
And props it from the storm, but neither he,
Nor yet his children's children, shall behold
What he hath swept away.
                Methinks 't were well,
Not as a spoiler or a thief, to roam
O'er Nature's bosom, that sweet, gentle nurse
Who loveth us, and spreads a sheltering couch
When our brief task is o'er. On that green mound
Affection's hand may set the willow-tree,
Or train the cypress, and let none profane
Her pious care.
              Oh Father! grant us grace
In all life's toils, so, with a steadfast hand
Evil and good to poise, as not to mark
Our way with wrecks, nor when the sands of time
Run low, with saddened eye the past survey,
And mourn the rashness time can ne'er restore.

Scenes in My Native Land (1845)

SUSAN FENIMORE COOPER

Susan Fenimore Cooper (1813–1894), daughter of the novelist, traveled with her father in his later years and acted as his secretary. But she also kept a journal of her own, which she worked into her book *Rural Hours*, first published in 1850. Her voice is clear and compelling, and her eye is sharp—she stands in the last generation of eastern Americans who could plausibly recall the era when the farm fields "belonged to a wilderness," home of "the bear, the wolf, and the panther." She describes with great accuracy the ecological transitions that followed the arrival of Europeans in North America, including what we would now call the rise of invasive species. And she provides an early and altogether pleasing version of what would eventually be called the "nature essay," that form that gathers in power even as the integrity that it describes deteriorates.

from *Rural Hours*

Wednesday, 6th.—Coolish this morning. Chilly people have lighted their parlor fires. Last year we had strawberries the 6th of June, but the present season is more backward. Good walking weather to-day.

It is a pleasing part of the elegance of May, in a temperate climate, that few of the coarser weeds show themselves during that month; or, rather, at that early day, they do not appear in their true character. They are, of course, very troublesome to gardeners from the first, but they do not then obtrude themselves upon general attention. The season advances with great rapidity, however, and already these rude plants are beginning to show themselves in the forms by which we know them. The burdock and nettle, and thistle, &c., &c., are growing too plentifully under fences, and in waste spots; chickweed and purslane, &c., &c., spring up in the paths and beds so freely and so boldly, that it is the chief labor of the month to wage war upon their tribe.

It is remarkable that these troublesome plants have come very generally from the Old World; they do not belong here, but following the steps of the white man, they have crossed the ocean with him. A very large proportion of the most common weeds in our fields and gardens, and about our buildings, are strangers to the soil. It will be easy to name a number of these:—such, for instance, as the dock and the burdock, found about every barn and outbuilding; the common plaintains and mallows—regular path-weeds; the groundsel, purslane, pigweed, goose-foot, shepherd's-purse, and lamb's-quarters, so troublesome in gardens; the chickweed growing everywhere; the prinpernel, celandine, and knawel; the lady's thumb and May-weed; the common nettles and teazel; wild flax, stickseed, burweed, doorweed; all the mulleins; the most pestilent thistles, both the common sort and that which is erroneously called the Canada thistle; the sow thistles; the chess, corncockle, tares, bugloss, or blue-weed, and the pigeon-weed of the grain-fields; the darnel, yarrow, wild parsnip, ox-eye daisy, the wild garlick, the acrid buttercup, and the acrid St. John's wort of the meadows; the nightshades, Jerusalem artichoke, wild radish, wild mustard, or charlock, the poison hemlock, the henbane,—ay, even the very dandelion,* a plant which we tread under foot at every turn. Others still might be added to the list, which were entirely unknown to the red man, having been introduced by the European race, and are now choking up all our way-sides, forming the vast throng of foreign weeds. Some of these have come from a great distance, travelling round the world. The shepherd's-purse, with others, is common in China, on the most eastern coast of Asia. One kind of mallows belongs to the East Indies; another to the coast of the Mediterranean. The gimson weed, or Datura, is an Abyssinian plant, and the Nicandra came from Peru. It is supposed that the amaranths or greenweeds, so very common here, have also

*Dr. Torrey.

been introduced, though possibly only from the more southern parts of our own country.

Some few American plants have been also carried to Europe, where they have become naturalized; but the number is very small. The evening primrose, and the silkweed, among others, have sowed themselves in some parts of the Old World, transported, no doubt, with the tobacco, and maize, and potato, which are now so widely diffused over the Eastern continent, to the very heart of Asia. But even at home, on our own soil, the amount of native weeds is small when compared with the throngs brought from the Old World. The wild cucumber, a very troublesome plant, the great white convolvolus, the dodder, the field sorrel, the pokeweed, the silkweed, with one or two plantains and thistles, of the rarer kinds, are among the most important of those whose origin is clearly settled as belonging to this continent. It is also singular that among those tribes which are of a divided nature, some being natives, others introduced, the last are generally the most numerous; for instance, the native chickweeds, and plantains, and thistles, are less common here than the European varieties.

There are other naturalized plants frequent in neglected spots, about farm-houses, and along road-sides, which have already become so common as to be weeds; the simples and medicinal herbs, used for ages by the goodwives of England and Holland, were early brought over, and have very generally become naturalized,—catnip, mint, horehound, tansy, balm, comfrey, elecampane, &c., &c.,—immediately take root, spreading far and wide wherever they are allowed to grow. It is surprising how soon they become firmly established in a new settlement; we often observe them in this new country apart from any dwelling. At times we have found them nearly a mile from either garden or house. The seeds of naturalized plants seem, in many cases, to have floated across our lake upon the water; for we have found the European mint and catnip growing with the blue gentian immediately on the banks where the woods spread around in every direction for some distance.

The word weed varies much with circumstances; at times, we even apply it to the beautiful flower or the useful herb. A plant may be a weed, because it is noxious, or fetid, or unsightly, or troublesome, but it is rare indeed that all these faults are united in one individual of the vegetable race. Often the unsightly, or fetid, or even the poisonous plant, is useful, or it may be interesting from some peculiarity; and on the other hand, many others, troublesome from their numbers, bear pleasing flowers, taken singly. Upon the whole, it is not so much a natural defect which marks the weed, as a certain impertinent, intrusive character in these plants; a want of modesty, a habit of shoving themselves forward upon ground where they are not needed, rooting themselves in soil intended for better things, for plants more useful, more fragrant, or more beautiful. Thus the corn-cockle bears a fine flower, not unlike the mullein-pink of the garden, but then it springs up among the precious wheat, taking the place of the grain, and it is a weed; the flower of the thistle is handsome in itself, but it is useless, and it pushes forward in throngs by the way-side until we are weary of seeing it, and everybody makes war upon it; the common St. John's wort, again, has a pretty yellow blossom, and it has its uses also as a simple, but it is injurious to the cattle, and yet it is so obstinately tenacious of a place among the grasses, that it is found in every meadow, and we quarrel with it as a weed.

These noxious plants have come unbidden to us, with the grains and grasses of the Old World, the evil with the good, as usual in this world of probation—the wheat and tares together. The useful plants produce a tenfold blessing upon the labor of man, but the weed is also there, ever accompanying his steps, to teach him a lesson of humility. Certain plants of this nature—the dock, thistle, nettle, &c., &c.,—are known to attach themselves especially to the path of man; in widely different soils and climates, they are still found at his door. Patient care and toil can alone keep the evil within bounds, and it seems doubtful whether it lies within the reach of human means entirely to remove from the face of the earth one single plant of this peculiar nature, much less all their varieties. Has any one, even of the more noxious sorts, ever been utterly destroyed? Agriculture, with all the pride and power of science now at her command, has apparently accomplished but little in this way. Egypt and China are said to be countries in which weeds are comparatively rare; both regions have long been in a high state of cultivation, filled to overflowing with a hungry population, which neglects scarce a rood of the soil, and yet even in those lands, even upon the banks of the Nile, where the crops succeed each other without any interval throughout the whole year, leaving no time for weeds to extend themselves; even there, these noxious plants are not unknown, and the moment the soil is abandoned, only for a season, they return with renewed vigor.

In this new country, with a fresh soil, and a thinner population, we have not only weeds innumerable, but we observe, also, that briers and brambles seem to acquire double strength in the neighborhood of man; we meet them in the primitive forest, here and there, but they line our roads and fences, and the woods are no sooner felled to make ready for cultivation, than they spring up in profusion, the first natural produce of the soil. But in this world of mercy, the just curse is ever graciously tempered with a blessing; many a grateful fruit, and some of our most delightful flowers, grow among the thorns and briers, their fragrance and excellence reminding man of the sweets as well as the toils of his task. The sweet-briar, more especially, with its simple flower and delightful fragrance, unknown in the wilderness, but moving onward by the side of the ploughman, would seem, of all others, the husbandman's blossom.

* * *

Monday, 23d.—Just at the point where the village street becomes a road and turns to climb the hill-side, there stands a group of pines, a remnant of the old forest. There are many trees like these among the woods; far and near such may be seen rising from the hills, now tossing their arms in the stormy winds, now drawn in still and dark relief against the glowing evening sky. Their gaunt, upright forms standing about the hill-tops, and the ragged gray stumps of those which have fallen, dotting the smooth fields, make up the sterner touches in a scene whose general aspect is smiling. But although these old trees are common upon the wooded heights, yet the group on the skirts of the village stands alone among the fields of the valley; their nearer brethren have all been swept away, and these are left in isolated company, differing in character from all about them, a monument of the past.

It is upon a narrow belt of land, a highway and a corn-field on one side, a brook and an orchard on the other, that these trees are rooted; a strip of woodland connected with the forest on the hills above, and suddenly cut off where it approaches the first buildings of the village. There they stand, silent spectators of the wonderful changes that have come over the valley. Hundreds of winters have passed since the cones which contained the seed of that grove fell from the parent tree; centuries have elapsed since their heads emerged from the topmost wave of the sea of verdure to meet the sunshine, and yet it is but yesterday that their shadows first fell, in full length, upon the sod at their feet.

Sixty years since, those trees belonged to a wilderness; the bear, the wolf, and the panther brushed their trunks, the ungainly moose and the agile deer browsed at their feet; the savage hunter crept stealthily about their roots, and painted braves passed noiselessly on the war-path beneath their shade. How many successive generations of the red man have trod the soil they over-shadowed, and then sat down in their narrow graves—how many herds of wild creatures have chased each other through that wood, and left their bones to bleach among the fern and moss, there is no human voice can tell. We only know that the summer winds, when they filled the canvas of Columbus and Cabot, three hundred years ago, came sweeping over these forest pines, murmuring then as we hear them murmur to-day.

There is no record to teach us even the name of the first white man who saw this sequestered valley, with its limpid lake; it was probably some bold hunter from the Mohawk, chasing the deer, or in quest of the beaver. But while towns were rising on the St. Lawrence and upon the seaboard, this inland region lay still unexplored; long after trading-houses had been opened, and fields had been tilled, and battles had been fought to the north, south, east, ay, and even at many points westward, those pines stood in the heart of a silent wilderness. This little lake lay embedded in a forest until after the great struggle of the Revolution was over. A few months after the war was brought to an honorable close, Washington made a journey of observation among the inland waters of this part of the country; writing to a friend in France, he names this little lake, the source of a river, which, four degrees farther south, flows into the Chesapeake in near neighborhood with his own Potomac. As he passed along through a half-wild region, where the few marks of civilization then existing bore the blight of war, he conceived the outline of many of those improvements which have since been carried out by others, and have yielded so rich a revenue of prosperity. It is a pleasing reflection to those who live here, that while many important places in the country were never honored by his presence, Washington has trod the soil about our lake. But even at that late day, when the great and good man came, the mountains were still clothed in wood to the water's edge, and mingled with giant oaks and ashes, those tall pines waved above the valley.

At length, nearly three long centuries after the Genoese had crossed the ocean, the white man came to plant a home on this spot, and it was then the great change began; the axe and the saw, the forge and the wheel, were busy from dawn to dusk, cows and swine fed in thickets whence the wild beasts had fled, while the ox and the horse drew away in chains the fallen trunks of the forest. The tenants of the wilderness shrunk deeper within its bounds with every changing moon; the wild creatures fled away within the receding shades of the forest, and the red man followed on their track; his day of power was gone, his hour of pitiless revenge had passed, and the last echoes of the war-whoop were dying away forever among these hills, when the pale-faces laid their hearth-stones by the lake shore. The red man, who for thousands of years had been lord of the land, no longer treads the soil; he exists here only in uncertain memories, and in forgotten graves.

Such has been the change of the last half century. Those who from childhood have known the cheerful dwellings of the village, the broad and fertile farms, the well-beaten roads, such as they are to-day, can hardly credit that this has all been done so recently by a band of men, some of whom, white-headed and leaning on their staves, are still among us. Yet such is the simple truth. This village lies just on the borders of the tract of country which was opened and peopled immediately after the Revolution; it was among the earliest of those little colonies from the sea-board which struck into the wilderness at that favorable moment, and whose rapid growth and progress in civilization have become a by-word. Other places, indeed, have far surpassed this quiet borough; Rochester, Buffalo, and others of a later date, have become great cities, while this remains a rural village; still, whenever we pause to recall what has been done in this secluded valley during the lifetime of one generation, we must needs be struck with new astonishment. And throughout every act of work, those old pines were there. Unchanged themselves, they stand surrounded by objects over all of which a great change has passed. The open valley, the half-shorn hills, the paths, the flocks, the buildings, the woods in their second growth, even the waters in the different images they reflect on their bosom, the very race of men who come and go, all are different from what they were; and those calm old trees seem to heave the sigh of companionless age, as their coned heads rock slowly in the winds.

The aspect of the wood tells its own history, so widely does it differ in character from the younger groves waving in gay luxuriance over the valley. In the midst of smooth fields it speaks so clearly of the wilderness, that it is not the young orchard of yesterday's planting, but the aged native pines which seem the strangers on the ground. The pine of forest growth never fails to have a very marked character of its own; the gray shaft rises clear and unbroken by bend or bough, to more than half its great elevation, thence short horizontal limbs in successive fan-like growth surround the trunk to its summit, which is often crowned with a low crest of upright branches. The shaft is very fine from its great height and the noble simplicity of its lines; in coloring, it is a pure clear gray, having the lightest and the smoothest bark of all its tribe, and only occasionally mottled with patches of lichens. The white pine of this climate gathers but few mosses, unless in very moist situations; the very oldest trees are often quite free from them. Indeed, this is a tree seldom seen with the symptoms of a half-dead and decaying condition about it, like so many others; the gray line of a naked branch may be observed here and there, perhaps, a sign of age, but it generally preserves to the very last an appearance of vigor, as though keeping death at bay until struck to the heart, or laid low from the roots. It is true, this appearance may often prove deceptive; still, it is a peculiarity of our pine, that it preserves its verdure until the very last, unlike many other trees which are seen in the forest, half green, half gray, and lifeless.

The pine of the lawns or open groves and the pine of the forest differ very strikingly in outline; the usual pyramidal or conical form of the evergreen is very faintly traced on the short, irregular limbs of the forest tree; but what is lost in luxuriance and elegance is more than replaced by a peculiar character of wild dignity, as it raises its stern head high above the lesser wood, far overtopping the proudest rank of oaks. And yet, in their rudest shapes, they are never harsh; as we approach them, we shall always find something of the calm of age and the sweetness of nature to soften their aspect; there is a grace in the slow waving of their limbs in the higher air, which never fails; there is a mysterious melody in their breezy murmurs; there is an emerald light in their beautiful verdure, which lies in unfading wreaths, fresh and clear, about the heads of those old trees. The effect of light and shade on the foliage of those older forest pines is indeed much finer than what we see among their younger neighbors; the tufted branches, in their horizontal growth, are beautifully touched with circlets of a clear light, which is broken up and lost amid the confused medley of branches in trees of more upright growth. The long brown cones are chiefly pendulous, in clusters, from the upper branches; some seasons they are so numerous on the younger trees as to give their heads a decided brown coloring.

The grove upon the skirts of the village numbers, perhaps, some forty trees, varying in their girth from five or six to twelve feet; and in height, from a hundred and twenty to a hundred and sixty feet. Owing to their unscreened position and their height, these trees may be clearly distinguished for miles, whether from the lake, the hills, or the roads about the country—a land-mark overtopping the humble church-spires, and every object raised by man within the bounds of the valley. Their rude simplicity of outline, the erect, unbending trunks, their stern, changeless character, and their scanty drapery of foliage, unconsciously lead one to fancy them an image of some band of savage chiefs, emerging in a long, dark line from the glen in their rear, and gazing in wonder upon their former hunting-grounds in its altered aspect.

The preservation of those old pines must depend entirely upon the will of their owner; they are private property; we have no right to ask that they may be spared, but it is impossible to behold their hoary trunks and crested heads without feeling a hope that they may long continue unscathed, to look down upon the village which has sprung up at their feet. They are certainly one of the most striking objects in the county, and we owe a debt of gratitude to the hand which has so long preserved them, one of the honors of our neighborhood. It needs but a few short minutes to bring one of these trees to the ground; the rudest boor passing along the highway may easily do the deed; but how many years must pass ere its equal stand on the same spot! Let us pause to count the days, the months, the years; let us number the generations that must come and go, the centuries that must roll onward, ere the seed sown from this year's cones shall produce a wood like that before us. The stout arm so ready to raise the axe to-day, must grow weak with age, it must drop into the grave; its bone and sinew must crumble into dust long before another tree, tall and great as those, shall have grown from the cone in our hand. Nay, more, all the united strength of sinew, added to all the powers of mind, and all the force of will, of millions of men, can do no more toward the work than the poor ability of a single arm; these are of the deeds which time alone can perform. But allowing even that hundreds of years hence other trees were at length to succeed these with the same dignity of height and age, no other younger wood can ever claim the same connection as this, with a state of things now passed away forever; they cannot have that wild, stern character of the aged forest pines. This little town itself must fall to decay and ruin; its streets must become choked with bushes and brambles; the farms of the valley must be anew buried within the shades of a wilderness; the wild deer and the wolf, and the bear, must return from beyond the great lakes; the bones of the savage men buried under our feet must arise and move again in the chase, ere trees like those, with the spirit of the forest in every line, can stand on the same ground in wild dignity of form like those old pines now looking down upon our homes.

Rural Hours (1850)

TABLE ROCK ALBUM

Table Rock was a large shelf of rock that jutted out from the Canadian side of Niagara Falls, and during the early years of tourism in the area it offered the main vantage point for viewing the cataract. An album was left for visitors to record their thoughts. In this random sampling from a few weeks in 1847, it is worth noting both the care that these impromptu authors often took (hundreds of poems were written on the spot) and the deep connection in Americans' minds between natural spectacle and divine power. Much of Table Rock collapsed in 1850, and the rest was blown up in 1935 on the claim that it represented a safety hazard. By then, hydropower development was underway at the Falls; half the average flow of the river is now diverted through upstream turbines during daylight hours of prime tourist season, and much more the rest of the year.

from **Table Rock Album**

O thou, Niagara! no Eloquence can set forth thy own native, untiring, ceaseless Eloquence—roll on!—And you, ye Poets, stand abashed, nor dare attempt impossibilities.

D.

—

BY REQUEST.

Niagara! Monarch of earth's wonders,—reflection of Almightiness,—in thy celestial beauty, and thy dread magnificence, and ceaseless thunder song—roll on thy course—echoing ever the nothingness of man—the boundless majesty of God!

T. T. WATERMAN.

August 31, 1847.

—

A VOLUNTARY.

One would think that emotions of sublimity, knocked common sense into "pi" and stirred up foaming fancies in the intellect, something like the boiling waters in this double and twisted caldron down here; after looking over the Albums around here. Why the—Mammoth Cave—don't men know what they are going to write before they begin, and say it so, they and some others know, after it is written.

A KENTUCKIAN.

—

FAREWELL!

Thou Lord of water power—in thy Majestic Glory—thou art all and *more* than all my soul conceived thee,—I never dreamed thy wonders to be so numberless and vast! beauty in union with grandeur—here fill and elevate, and satisfy my soul.

Sept. 1, 1847.

—

While standing under the horse-shoe Fall,
Didn't *it* look grand—and *you* feel small?

THOMAS A. DWYN, *Dublin, Ireland.*

—

Majestic greatness sits, Niagara, upon thy brow,
And o'er thy rocks in thundering grandeur roll;—
We gaze, in silent wonder wrapped and humbly bow,
To thee, O God, who *thus* doth thrill our inmost soul.

B. T. ROMAINE AND LADY.

Albany, N. Y., Sept. 20th, 1847.

—

This is but the breathings of the great "I Am!" What must his anger be?

Mingled with mercy.

—

Roll on thou dark green flood, roll on, time measurest not thine age—eternity can but express thy end,—Creation's dawn witnessed thy earliest gush,—Creation's doom can but extinguish—thy perpetual rush.

—

Oh! God!! Great are thy works! Oh! Man!! How small are thine, when placed in the same view.

A COMSTOCK.

July 30th, 1847.   *Sandwich Islands.*

—

The Falls of "Niagara" far surpass any natural curiosity in the known world. No human eye that has not beheld this cataract can form any idea of its greatness. Like all the works of God's creation, it shows forth to his glory.

WARD CARPENTER,

August 3rd, 1847.   *Westchester Co., N. Y.*

—

Niagara—Here Nature holds its sway,
While man, with both delight and awe, doth
Gaze and wonder at its magnificence.

BOZ.

Table Rock Album (1850)

WALT WHITMAN

Walt Whitman (1819–1892), recognized by Ralph Waldo Emerson as America's first original poet, reminds us that most citizens of the 19th century (and for that matter the 20th) were not what we would now call environmentalists—even those with a great affection for the natural world or who are usually thought of as progressive. On the one hand, "This Compost," Whitman's haunting depiction of death turned to new life in the soil, is an ecological masterpiece; on the other hand, in "The Song of the Redwood-Tree," when describing California's noble redwoods he concedes their nobleness and then looks forward to seeing them cut down in order to build bold, brash, new California. It's important never to forget the titanic energy behind the idea of growth, especially in this period when America's ascent really began. Our sense of surging human destiny as an almost natural force is powerfully expressed by Whitman here. That sense may explain why environmentalism, with all its cautions and caveats, remains a dissident and not a dominant voice, right up to the present.

from **Leaves of Grass**

This Compost

1

Something startles me where I thought I was safest,
I withdraw from the still woods I loved,
I will not go now on the pastures to walk,
I will not strip the clothes from my body to meet my lover
    the sea,
I will not touch my flesh to the earth as to other flesh to
    renew me.

O how can it be that the ground itself does not sicken?
How can you be alive you growths of spring?
How can you furnish health you blood of herbs, roots,
  orchards, grain?
Are they not continually putting distemper'd corpses
  within you?
Is not every continent work'd over and over with sour
  dead?

Where have you disposed of their carcasses?
Those drunkards and gluttons of so many generations?
Where have you drawn off all the foul liquid and meat?
I do not see any of it upon you to-day, or perhaps I am
  deceiv'd,
I will run a furrow with my plough, I will press my spade
  through the sod and turn it up underneath,
I am sure I shall expose some of the foul meat.

2

Behold this compost! behold it well!
Perhaps every mite has once form'd part of a sick
  person—yet behold!
The grass of spring covers the prairies,
The bean bursts noiselessly through the mould in the
  garden,
The delicate spear of the onion pierces upward,
The apple-buds cluster together on the apple-branches,
The resurrection of the wheat appears with pale visage
  out of its graves,
The tinge awakes over the willow-tree and the mulberry-tree,
The he-birds carol mornings and evenings while the she-
  birds sit on their nests,
The young of poultry break through the hatch'd eggs,
The new-born of animals appear, the calf is dropt from the
  cow, the colt from the mare,

Out of its little hill faithfully rise the potato's dark green
      leaves,
Out of its hill rises the yellow maize-stalk, the lilacs bloom
      in the dooryards,
The summer growth is innocent and disdainful above all
      those strata of sour dead.

What chemistry!
That the winds are really not infectious,
That this is no cheat, this transparent green-wash of the
      sea which is so amorous after me,
That it is safe to allow it to lick my naked body all over
      with its tongues,
That it will not endanger me with the fevers that have
      deposited themselves in it,
That all is clean forever and forever,
That the cool drink from the well tastes so good,
That blackberries are so flavorous and juicy,
That the fruits of the apple-orchard and the orange-
      orchard, that melons, grapes, peaches, plums, will
      none of them poison me,
That when I recline on the grass I do not catch any disease,
Though probably every spear of grass rises out of what
      was once a catching disease.

Now I am terrified at the Earth, it is that calm and patient,
It grows such sweet things out of such corruptions,
It turns harmless and stainless on its axis, with such
      endless successions of diseas'd corpses,
It distills such exquisite winds out of such infused fetor,
It renews with such unwitting looks its prodigal, annual,
      sumptuous crops,
It gives such divine materials to men, and accepts such
      leavings from them at last.

1856

Song of the Redwood-Tree

1

A California song,

A prophecy and indirection, a thought impalpable to
      breathe as air,

A chorus of dryads, fading, departing, or hamadryads
      departing,

A murmuring, fateful, giant voice, out of the earth and sky,

Voice of a mighty dying tree in the redwood forest dense.

Farewell my brethren,

Farewell O earth and sky, farewell ye neighboring waters,

My time has ended, my term has come.

Along the northern coast,

Just back from the rock-bound shore and the caves,

In the saline air from the sea in the Mendocino country,

With the surge for base and accompaniment low and
      hoarse,

With crackling blows of axes sounding musically driven
      by strong arms,

Riven deep by the sharp tongues of the axes, there in the
      redwood forest dense,

I heard the mighty tree its death-chant chanting.

The choppers heard not, the camp shanties echoed not,

The quick-ear'd teamsters and chain and jack-screw men
      heard not,

As the wood-spirits came from their haunts of a thousand
      years to join the refrain,

But in my soul I plainly heard.

Murmuring out of its myriad leaves,

Down from its lofty top rising two hundred feet high,

Out of its stalwart trunk and limbs, out of its foot-thick
bark,

That chant of the seasons and time, chant not of the past
only but the future.

You untold life of me,

And all you venerable and innocent joys,

*Perennial hardy life of me with joys 'mid rain and many a
summer sun,*

And the white snows and night and the wild winds;

*0 the great patient rugged joys, my soul's strong joys
unreck'd by man,*

*(For know I bear the soul befitting me, I too have
consciousness, identity,*

And all the rocks and mountains have, and all the earth,)

Joys of the life befitting me and brothers mine,

Our time, our term has come.

Nor yield we mournfully majestic brothers,

We who have grandly fill'd our time;

With Nature's calm content, with tacit huge delight,

We welcome what we wrought for through the past,

And leave the field for them.

For them predicted long,

For a superber race, they too to grandly fill their time,

For them we abdicate, in them ourselves ye forest kings!

*In them these skies and airs, these mountain peaks, Shasta,
Nevadas,*

*These huge precipitous cliffs, this amplitude, these valleys,
far Yosemite,*

To be in them absorb'd, assimilated.

Then to a loftier strain,
Still prouder, more ecstatic rose the chant,
As if the heirs, the deities of the West,
Joining with master-tongue bore part.

Not wan from Asia's fetiches,
Nor red from Europe's old dynastic slaughter-house,
(Area of murder-plots of thrones, with scent left yet of
      wars and scaffolds everywhere,)
But come from Nature's long and harmless throes,
      peacefully builded thence,
These virgin lands, lands of the Western shore,
To the new culminating man, to you, the empire new,
You promis'd long, we pledge, we dedicate.

You occult deep volitions,
You average spiritual manhood, purpose of all, pois'd on
      yourself, giving not taking law,
You womanhood divine, mistress and source of all, whence
      life and love and aught that comes from life and love,
You unseen moral essence of all the vast materials of
      America, (age upon age working in death the same as
      life,)
You that, sometimes known, oftener unknown, really shape
      and mould the New World, adjusting it to Time and
      Space,
You hidden national will lying in your abysms, conceal'd but
      ever alert,
You past and present purposes tenaciously pursued, may-be
      unconscious of yourselves,
Unswerv'd by all the passing errors, perturbations of the
      surface;

*You vital, universal, deathless germs, beneath all creeds,
    arts, statutes, literatures,*
*Here build your homes for good, establish here, these areas
    entire, lands of the Western shore,*
We pledge, we dedicate to you.

For man of you, your characteristic race,
*Here may he hardy, sweet, gigantic grow, here tower
    proportionate to Nature,*
*Here climb the vast pure spaces unconfined, uncheck'd by
    wall or roof,*
*Here laugh with storm or sun, here joy, here patiently
    inure,*
*Here heed himself, unfold himself, (not others' formulas
    heed,) here fill his time,*
To duly fall, to aid, unreck'd at last,
To disappear, to serve.

Thus on the northern coast,
In the echo of teamsters' calls and the clinking chains, and
    the music of choppers' axes,
The falling trunk and limbs, the crash, the muffled shriek,
    the groan,
Such words combined from the redwood-tree, as of voices
    ecstatic, ancient and rustling,
The century-lasting, unseen dryads, singing, withdrawing,
All their recesses of forests and mountains leaving,
From the Cascade range to the Wahsatch, or Idaho far, or
    Utah,
To the deities of the modern henceforth yielding,
The chorus and indications, the vistas of coming
    humanity, the settlements, features all,
In the Mendocino woods I caught.

2

The flashing and golden pageant of California,
The sudden and gorgeous drama, the sunny and ample
    lands,
The long and varied stretch from Puget sound to Colorado
    south,
Lands bathed in sweeter, rarer, healthier air, valleys and
    mountain cliffs,
The fields of Nature long prepared and fallow, the silent,
    cyclic chemistry,
The slow and steady ages plodding, the unoccupied
    surface ripening, the rich ores forming beneath;
At last the New arriving, assuming, taking possession,
A swarming and busy race settling and organizing
    everywhere,
Ships coming in from the whole round world, and going
    out to the whole world,
To India and China and Australia and the thousand island
    paradises of the Pacific,
Populous cities, the latest inventions, the steamers on the
    rivers, the railroads, with many a thrifty farm, with
    machinery,
And wool and wheat and the grape, and diggings of
    yellow gold.

3

But more in you than these, lands of the Western shore,
(These but the means, the implements, the standing-
    ground,)
I see in you, certain to come, the promise of thousands of
    years, till now deferr'd,
Promis'd to be fulfill'd, our common kind, the race.

The new society at last, proportionate to Nature,
In man of you, more than your mountain peaks or stalwart
      trees imperial,
In woman more, far more, than all your gold or vines, or
      even vital air.

Fresh come, to a new world indeed, yet long prepared,
I see the genius of the modern, child of the real and ideal,
Clearing the ground for broad humanity, the true America,
      heir of the past so grand,
To build a grander future.

1874

GEORGE PERKINS MARSH

By the time he graduated at the top of his Dartmouth class in 1820, George Perkins Marsh (1801–1882) spoke French, Spanish, Portuguese, Italian, and German. A true polymath, he became a prominent lawyer in his native Vermont, served in Congress and as the American minister to Turkey and Greece, and lectured at Columbia on English philology and etymology, before President Lincoln sent him as the first U.S. ambassador to the new kingdom of Italy in 1861, a post he retained until the end of his life. His endless travels and his relentlessly discerning eye made it possible for him to write what can be regarded as the first major work of scientific environmentalism in American history, *Man and Nature* (1864), which argued from copious Mediterranean and New England examples that by cutting down our forests we risked turning our land dry and barren. The insight that humans could do profound damage to the natural world was novel and startling; if any 19th-century American could have understood what science now tells us about global warming, it would have been Marsh, who noted the changes in local climate that came from wanton cutting. In his own day, as the writer John Elder has pointed out in his recent and lovely *Pilgrimage to Vallombrosa* (2006), Marsh's insights led directly to the protection of New York's vast Adirondack Park and indirectly to the creation of a system of national parks and reserves. Marsh's writing can be fairly technical, and for many decades it lapsed into obscurity, but recent years have seen a steady revival in his reputation as what Lewis Mumford called "the fountainhead of the conservation movement." His family farm in Woodstock, Vermont, is now preserved as a national historical park.

from Man and Nature

Destructiveness of Man

Man has too long forgotten that the earth was given to him for usufruct alone, not for consumption, still less for profligate waste. Nature has provided against the absolute destruction of any of her elementary matter, the raw material of her works; the thunderbolt and the tornado, the most convulsive throes of even the volcano and the earthquake, being only phenomena of decomposition and recomposition. But she has left it within the power of man irreparably to derange the combinations of inorganic matter and of organic life, which through the night of æons she had been proportioning and balancing, to prepare the earth for his habitation, when, in the fulness of time, his Creator should call him forth to enter into its possession.

Apart from the hostile influence of man, the organic and the inorganic world are, as I have remarked, bound together by such mutual relations and adaptations as secure, if not the absolute permanence and equilibrium of both, a long continuance of the established conditions of each at any given time and place, or at least, a very slow and gradual succession of changes in those conditions. But man is everywhere a disturbing agent. Wherever he plants his foot, the harmonies of nature are turned to discords. The proportions and accommodations which insured the stability of existing arrangements are overthrown. Indigenous vegetable and animal species are extirpated, and supplanted by others of foreign origin, spontaneous production is forbidden or restricted, and the face of the earth is either laid bare or covered with a new and reluctant growth of vegetable forms, and with alien tribes of animal life. These intentional changes and substitutions constitute, indeed, great revolutions; but vast as is their magnitude and importance, they are, as we shall see, insignificant in comparison with the contingent and unsought results which have flowed from them.

The fact that, of all organic beings, man alone is to be regarded as essentially a destructive power, and that he wields energies to resist which, nature—that nature whom all material life and all inorganic substance obey—is wholly impotent, tends to prove that, though living in physical nature, he is not of her, that he is of more exalted parentage, and belongs to a higher order of existences than those born of her womb and submissive to her dictates.

There are, indeed, brute destroyers, beasts and birds and insects of prey—all animal life feeds upon, and, of course, destroys other life,—

but this destruction is balanced by compensations. It is, in fact, the very means by which the existence of one tribe of animals or of vegetables is secured against being smothered by the encroachments of another; and the reproductive powers of species, which serve as the food of others, are always proportioned to the demand they are destined to supply. Man pursues his victims with reckless destructiveness; and, while the sacrifice of life by the lower animals is limited by the cravings of appetite, he unsparingly persecutes, even to extirpation, thousands of organic forms which he cannot consume.*

The earth was not, in its natural condition, completely adapted to

---

*The terrible destructiveness of man is remarkably exemplified in the chase of large mammalia and birds for single products, attended with the entire waste of enormous quantities of flesh, and of other parts of the animal, which are capable of valuable uses. The wild cattle of South America are slaughtered by millions for their hides and horns; the buffalo of North America for his skin or his tongue; the elephant, the walrus, and the narwhal for their tusks; the cetacea, and some other marine animals, for their oil and whalebone; the ostrich and other large birds, for their plumage. Within a few years, sheep have been killed in New England by whole flocks, for their pelts and suet alone, the flesh being thrown away; and it is even said that the bodies of the same quadrupeds have been used in Australia as fuel for limekilns. What a vast amount of human nutriment, of bone, and of other animal products valuable in the arts, is thus recklessly squandered! In nearly all these cases, the part which constitutes the motive for this wholesale destruction, and is alone saved, is essentially of insignificant value as compared with what is thrown away. The horns and hide of an ox are not economically worth a tenth part as much as the entire carcass.

One of the greatest benefits to be expected from the improvements of civilization is, that increased facilities of communication will render it possible to transport to places of consumption much valuable material that is now wasted because the price at the nearest market will not pay freight. The cattle slaughtered in South America for their hides would feed millions of the starving population of the Old World, if their flesh could be economically preserved and transported across the ocean.

We are beginning to learn a better economy in dealing with the inorganic world. The utilization—or, as the Germans more happily call it, the Verwerthung, the *beworthing*—of waste from metallurgical, chemical, and manufacturing establishments, is among the most important results of the application of science to industrial purposes. The incidental products from the laboratories of manufacturing chemists often become more valuable than those for the preparation of which they were erected. The slags from silver refineries, and even from smelting houses of the coarser metals, have not unfrequently yielded to a second operator a better return than the first had derived from dealing with the natural ore; and the saving of lead carried off in the smoke of furnaces has, of itself, given a large profit on the capital invested in the works. A few years ago, an officer of an American mint was charged with embezzling gold committed to him for coinage. He insisted, in his defence, that much of the metal was volatilized and lost in refining and melting, and upon scraping the chimneys of the melting furnaces and the roofs of the adjacent houses, gold enough was found in the soot to account for no small part of the deficiency.

the use of man, but only to the sustenance of wild animals and wild vegetation. These live, multiply their kind in just proportion, and attain their perfect measure of strength and beauty, without producing or requiring any change in the natural arrangements of surface, or in each other's spontaneous tendencies, except such mutual repression of excessive increase as may prevent the extirpation of one species by the encroachments of another. In short, without man, lower animal and spontaneous vegetable life would have been constant in type, distribution, and proportion, and the physical geography of the earth would have remained undisturbed for indefinite periods, and been subject to revolution only from possible, unknown cosmical causes, or from geological action.

But man, the domestic animals that serve him, the field and garden plants the products of which supply him with food and clothing, cannot subsist and rise to the full development of their higher properties, unless brute and unconscious nature be effectually combated, and, in a great degree, vanquished by human art. Hence, a certain measure of transformation of terrestrial surface, of suppression of natural, and stimulation of artificially modified productivity becomes necessary. This measure man has unfortunately exceeded. He has felled the forests whose network of fibrous roots bound the mould to the rocky skeleton of the earth; but had he allowed here and there a belt of woodland to reproduce itself by spontaneous propagation, most of the mischiefs which his reckless destruction of the natural protection of the soil has occasioned would have been averted. He has broken up the mountain reservoirs, the percolation of whose waters through unseen channels supplied the fountains that refreshed his cattle and fertilized his fields; but he has neglected to maintain the cisterns and the canals of irrigation which a wise antiquity had constructed to neutralize the consequences of its own imprudence. While he has torn the thin glebe which confined the light earth of extensive plains, and has destroyed the fringe of semi-aquatic plants which skirted the coast and checked the drifting of the sea sand, he has failed to prevent the spreading of the dunes by clothing them with artificially propagated vegetation. He has ruthlessly warred on all the tribes of animated nature whose spoil he could convert to his own uses, and he has not protected the birds which prey on the insects most destructive to his own harvests.

Purely untutored humanity, it is true, interferes comparatively little with the arrangements of nature,* and the destructive agency of man becomes more and more energetic and unsparing as he advances in civ-

---

*It is an interesting and not hitherto sufficiently noticed fact, that the domestication of the organic world, so far as it has yet been achieved, belongs, not indeed to the savage state, but to the earliest dawn of civilization, the conquest of inorganic nature almost as exclusively to the most advanced stages of artificial culture. It is familiarly known to all who have occupied themselves with the psychology and habits of the ruder races, and of persons with imperfectly developed intellects in civilized life, that although these humble tribes and individuals sacrifice, without scruple, the lives of the lower animals to the gratification of their appetites and the supply of their other physical wants, yet they nevertheless seem to cherish with brutes, and even with vegetable life, sympathies which are much more feebly felt by civilized men. The popular traditions of the simpler peoples recognize a certain community of nature between man, brute animals, and even plants; and this serves to explain why the apologue or fable, which ascribes the power of speech and the faculty of reason to birds, quadrupeds, insects, flowers, and trees, is one of the earliest forms of literary composition.

In almost every wild tribe, some particular quadruped or bird, though persecuted as a destroyer of more domestic beasts, or hunted for food, is regarded with peculiar respect, one might almost say, affection. Some of the North American aboriginal nations celebrate a propitiatory feast to the manes of the intended victim before they commence a bear hunt; and the Norwegian peasantry have not only retained an old proverb which ascribes to the same animal "*ti Mænds Styrke og tolv Mænds Vid*," ten men's strength and twelve men's cunning; but they still pay to him something of the reverence with which ancient superstition invested him. The student of Icelandic literature will find in the saga of *Finnbogi hinn rami* a curious illustration of this feeling, in an account of a dialogue between a Norwegian bear and an Icelandic champion—dumb show on the part of Bruin, and chivalric words on that of Finnbogi—followed by a duel, in which the latter, who had thrown away his arms and armor in order that the combatants might meet on equal terms, was victorious. Drummond Hay's very interesting work on Morocco contains many amusing notices of a similar feeling entertained by the Moors toward the redoubtable enemy of their flocks—the lion.

This sympathy helps us to understand how it is that most if not all the domestic animals—if indeed they ever existed in a wild state—were appropriated, reclaimed and trained before men had been gathered into organized and fixed communities, that almost every known esculent plant had acquired substantially its present artificial character, and that the properties of nearly all vegetable drugs and poisons were known at the remotest period to which historical records reach. Did nature bestow upon primitive man some instinct akin to that by which she teaches the brute to select the nutritious and to reject the noxious vegetables indiscriminately mixed in forest and pasture?

This instinct, it must be admitted, is far from infallible, and, as has been hundreds of times remarked by naturalists, it is in many cases not an original faculty but an acquired and transmitted habit. It is a fact familiar to persons engaged in sheep husbandry in New England—and I have seen it confirmed by personal observation—that sheep bred where the common laurel, as it is called, *Kalmia angustifolia*, abounds, almost always avoid browsing upon the leaves of that plant, while those brought from districts where laurel is

ilization, until the impoverishment, with which his exhaustion of the natural resources of the soil is threatening him, at last awakens him to the necessity of preserving what is left, if not of restoring what has been wantonly wasted. The wandering savage grows no cultivated vegetable, fells no forest, and extirpates no useful plant, no noxious weed. If his skill in the chase enables him to entrap numbers of the animals on which he feeds, he compensates this loss by destroying also the lion, the tiger, the wolf, the otter, the seal, and the eagle, thus indirectly protecting the feebler quadrupeds and fish and fowls, which would otherwise become the booty of beasts and birds of prey. But with stationary life, or rather with the pastoral state, man at once commences an almost indiscriminate warfare upon all the forms of animal and vegetable existence around him, and as he advances in civilization, he gradually eradicates or transforms every spontaneous product of the soil he occupies.*

---

unknown, and turned into pastures where it grows, very often feed upon it and are poisoned by it. A curious acquired and hereditary instinct, of a different character, may not improperly be noticed here. I refer to that by which horses bred in provinces where quicksands are common avoid their dangers or extricate themselves from them. See BRÉMONTIER, *Mémoire sur les Dunes, Annales des Ponts et Chaussées,* 1833: *premier sémestre*, pp. 155–157.

It is commonly said in New England, and I believe with reason, that the crows of this generation are wiser than their ancestors. Scarecrows which were effectual fifty years ago are no longer respected by the plunderers of the cornfield, and new terrors must from time to time be invented for its protection.

Civilization has added little to the number of vegetable or animal species grown in our fields or bred in our folds, while, on the contrary, the subjugation of the inorganic forces, and the consequent extension of man's sway over, not the annual products of the earth only, but her substance and her springs of action, is almost entirely the work of highly refined and cultivated ages. The employment of the elasticity of wood and of horn, as a projectile power in the bow, is nearly universal among the rudest savages. The application of compressed air to the same purpose, in the blowpipe, is more restricted, and the use of the mechanical powers, the inclined plane, the wheel and axle, and even the wedge and lever, seems almost unknown except to civilized man. I have myself seen European peasants to whom one of the simplest applications of this latter power was a revelation.

*The difference between the relations of savage life, and of incipient civilization, to nature, is well seen in that part of the valley of the Mississippi which was once occupied by the mound builders and afterward by the far less developed Indian tribes. When the tillers of the fields which must have been cultivated to sustain the large population that once inhabited those regions perished or were driven out, the soil fell back to the normal forest state, and the savages who succeeded the more advanced race interfered very little, if at all, with the ordinary course of spontaneous nature.

Human and Brute Action Compared

It has been maintained by authorities as high as any known to modern science, that the action of man upon nature, though greater in *degree*, does not differ in *kind*, from that of wild animals. It appears to me to differ in essential character, because, though it is often followed by unforeseen and undesired results, yet it is nevertheless guided by a self-conscious and intelligent will aiming as often at secondary and remote as at immediate objects. The wild animal, on the other hand, acts instinctively, and, so far as we are able to perceive, always with a view to single and direct purposes. The backwoodsman and the beaver alike fell trees; the man that he may convert the forest into an olive grove that will mature its fruit only for a succeeding generation, the beaver that he may feed upon their bark or use them in the construction of his habitation. Human differs from brute action, too, in its influence upon the material world, because it is not controlled by natural compensations and balances. Natural arrangements, once disturbed by man, are not restored until he retires from the field, and leaves free scope to spontaneous recuperative energies; the wounds he inflicts upon the material creation are not healed until he withdraws the arm that gave the blow. On the other hand, I am not aware of any evidence that wild animals have ever destroyed the smallest forest, extirpated any organic species, or modified its natural character, occasioned any permanent change of terrestrial surface, or produced any disturbance of physical conditions which nature has not, of herself, repaired without the expulsion of the animal that had caused it.*

The form of geographical surface, and very probably the climate of a given country, depend much on the character of the vegetable life belonging to it. Man has, by domestication, greatly changed the habits and properties of the plants he rears; he has, by voluntary selection, immensely modified the forms and qualities of the animated creatures that serve him; and he has, at the same time, completely rooted out

---

*There is a possible—but only a possible—exception in the case of the American bison.

many forms of both vegetable and animal being.* What is there, in the influence of brute life, that corresponds to this? We have no reason to believe that in that portion of the American continent which, though peopled by many tribes of quadruped and fowl, remained uninhabited by man, or only thinly occupied by purely savage tribes, any sensible geographical change had occurred within twenty centuries before the epoch of discovery and colonization, while, during the same period, man had changed million of square miles, in the fairest and most fertile regions of the Old World, into the barrenest deserts.

The ravages committed by man subvert the relations and destroy the balance which nature had established between her organized and her inorganic creations; and she avenges herself upon the intruder, by letting loose upon her defaced provinces destructive energies hitherto kept in check by organic forces destined to be his best auxiliaries, but which he has unwisely dispersed and driven from the field of action. When the forest is gone, the great reservoir of moisture stored up in its vegetable mould is evaporated, and returns only in deluges of rain to wash away the parched dust into which that mould has been converted. The well-wooded and humid hills are turned to ridges of dry rock, which encumbers the low grounds and chokes the watercourses with its debris, and—except in countries favored with an equable distribution of rain through the seasons, and a moderate and regular inclination of surface—the whole earth, unless rescued by human art from the physical degradation to which it tends, becomes an assemblage of bald mountains, of barren, turfless hills, and of swampy and malarious plains. There are parts of Asia Minor, of Northern Africa, of Greece, and even of Alpine Europe, where the operation of causes set in action by man has brought the face of the earth to a desolation almost as complete as that of the moon; and though, within that brief space of time which we call "the historical period," they are known to have been cov-

---

*Whatever may be thought of the modification of organic species by natural selection, there is certainly no evidence that animals have exerted upon any form of life an influence analogous to that of domestication upon plants, quadrupeds, and birds reared artificially by man; and this is as true of unforeseen as of purposely effected improvements accomplished by voluntary selection of breeding animals.

ered with luxuriant woods, verdant pastures, and fertile meadows, they are now too far deteriorated to be reclaimable by man, nor can they become again fitted for human use, except through great geological changes, or other mysterious influences or agencies of which we have no present knowledge, and over which we have no prospective control. The earth is fast becoming an unfit home for its noblest inhabitant, and another era of equal human crime and human improvidence, and of like duration with that through which traces of that crime and that improvidence extend, would reduce it to such a condition of impoverished productiveness, of shattered surface, of climatic excess, as to threaten the depravation, barbarism, and perhaps even extinction of the species.*

* * *

Instability of American Life

All human institutions, associate arrangements, modes of life, have their characteristic imperfections. The natural, perhaps the necessary defect of ours, is their instability, their want of fixedness, not in form only, but even in spirit. The face of physical nature in the United States shares this incessant fluctuation, and the landscape is as variable as the habits of the population. It is time for some abatement in the restless love of change which characterizes us, and makes us almost a nomade rather than a sedentary people.† We have now felled forest enough

---

*——"And it may be remarked that, as the world has passed through these several stages of strife to produce a Christendom, so by relaxing in the enterprises it has learnt, does it tend downwards, through inverted steps, to wildness and the waste again. Let a people give up their contest with moral evil; disregard the injustice, the ignorance, the greediness, that may prevail among them, and part more and more with the Christian element of their civilization; and in declining this battle with sin, they will inevitably get embroiled with men. Threats of war and revolution punish their unfaithfulness; and if then, instead of retracing their steps, they yield again, and are driven before the storm, the very arts they had created, the structures they had raised, the usages they had established, are swept away; 'in that very day their thoughts perish.' The portion they had reclaimed from the young earth's ruggedness is lost; and failing to stand fast against man, they finally get embroiled with nature, and are thrust down beneath her ever-living hand."—MARTINEAU'S *Sermon, "The Good Soldier of Jesus Christ."*

†It is rare that a middle-aged American dies in the house where he was born, or an old man even in that which he has built; and this is scarely true of the rural districts, where every man owns his habitation, than of the city, where the majority live in hired

everywhere, in many districts far too much. Let us restore this one element of material life to its normal proportions, and devise means for maintaining the permanence of its relations to the fields, the meadows, and the pastures, to the rain and the dews of heaven, to the springs and rivulets with which it waters the earth. The establishment of an approximately fixed ratio between the two most broadly characterized distinctions of rural surface—woodland and plough land—would involve a certain persistence of character in all the branches of industry, all the occupations and habits of life, which depend upon or are immediately connected with either, without implying a rigidity that should exclude flexibility of accommodation to the many changes of external circumstance which human wisdom can neither prevent nor foresee, and would thus help us to become, more emphatically, a well-ordered and stable commonwealth, and, not less conspicuously, a people of progress.

---

houses. This life of incessant flitting is unfavorable for the execution of permanent improvements of every sort, and especially of those which, like the forest, are slow in repaying any part of the capital expended in them. It requires a very generous spirit in a landholder to plant a wood on a farm he expects to sell, or which he knows will pass out of the hands of his descendants at his death. But the very fact of having begun a plantation would attach the proprietor more strongly to the soil for which he had made such a sacrifice; and the paternal acres would have a greater value in the eyes of a succeeding generation, if thus improved and beautified by the labors of those from whom they were inherited. Landed property, therefore, the transfer of which is happily free from every legal impediment or restriction in the United States, would find, in the feelings thus prompted, a moral check against a too frequent change of owners, and would tend to remain long enough in one proprietor or one family to admit of gradual improvements which would increase its value both to the possessor and to the state.

Man and Nature (1864)

This short diatribe against billboards from Phineas T. Barnum's book *The Humbugs of the World* (1866) is a curiosity almost as great as the midget General Tom Thumb, the original Siamese twins, the "Feejee Mermaid," or the other amazements on which Barnum (1810–1891) built his fortune. The greatest of showmen, the "Shakespeare of advertising," Barnum is credited with the first billboards in New York City— poster-sized ads for his sideshows were first pasted up in the 1830s. But Barnum had his limits. Happy as he was to show unsuspecting rubes the 161-year-old former nurse of General George Washington, he was appalled by the "spiritual mediums" and other fakers of his day; in *Humbugs* he offered a $500 prize for anyone who could prove they actually communicated with the dead. And as this essay makes clear, he thought there was a time and a place for advertising too, a point that some have tried to make ever since. (See the somewhat less memorable remarks of Lyndon Johnson a century later at the signing of the Highway Beautification Act, on pages 395–98 in this anthology.)

from **The Humbugs of the World**

I cannot however permit this chapter to close without recording a protest in principle against that method of advertising of which Warren's on the Pyramid is an instance. Not that it is a crime or even an immorality in the usual sense of the words; but it is a violent offence against good taste, and a selfish and inexcusable destruction of other people's enjoyments. No man ought to advertise in the midst of landscapes or scenery, in such a way as to destroy or injure their beauty by introducing totally incongruous and relatively vulgar associations. Too many transactions of the sort have been perpetrated in our own country.

The principle on which the thing is done is, to seek out the most attractive spot possible—the wildest, the most lovely, and there, in the most staring and brazen manner to paint up advertisements of quack medicines, rum, or as the case may be, in letters of monstrous size, in the most obtrusive colors, in such a prominent place, and in such a lasting way as to destroy the beauty of the scene both thoroughly and permanently.

Any man with a beautiful wife or daughter would probably feel disagreeably, if he should find branded indelibly across her smooth white forehead, or on her snowy shoulder in blue and red letters such a phrase as this: "Try the Jigamaree Bitters!" Very much like this is the sort of advertising I am speaking of. It is not likely that I shall be charged with squeamishness on this question. I can readily enough see the selfishness and vulgarity of this particular sort of advertising, however.

It is outrageously selfish to destroy the pleasure of thousands, for the sake of a chance of additional gain. And it is an atrocious piece of vulgarity to flaunt the names of quack nostrums, and of the coarse stimulants of sots, among the beautiful scenes of nature. The pleasure of such places depends upon their freedom from the associations of every day concerns and troubles and weaknesses. A lovely nook of forest scenery, or a grand rock, like a beautiful woman, depends for much of its attractiveness upon the attendant sense of freedom from whatever is low; upon a sense of purity and of romance. And it is about as nauseous to find "Bitters" or "Worm Syrup" daubed upon the landscape, as it would be upon the lady's brow.

Since writing this I observe that two legislatures—those of New Hampshire and New York—have passed laws to prevent this dirty misdemeanor. It is greatly to their credit, and it is in good season. For it is matter of wonder that some more colossal vulgarian has not stuck up a sign a mile long on the Palisades. But it is matter of thankfulness too. At the White Mountains, many grand and beautiful views have been spoiled by these nostrum and bedbug souled fellows.

It is worth noticing that the chief haunts of the city of New York, the Central Park, has thus far remained unviolated by the dirty hands of these vulgar advertisers. Without knowing anything about it, I have no doubt whatever that the commissioners have been approached often by parties desiring the privilege of advertising within its limits. Among the advertising fraternity it would be thought a gigantic opportunity to be able to flaunt the name of some bug-poison, fly-killer, bowel-rectifier, or disguised rum, along the walls of the Reservoir; upon the delicate stone-work of the Terrace, or the graceful lines of the Bow Bridge; to nail up a tin sign on every other tree, to stick one up right in front of every seat; to keep a gang of young wretches thrusting pamphlet or handbill into every person's palm that enters the gate, to paint a vulgar sign across every gray rock; to cut quack words in ditch-work in the smooth green turf of the mall or ball-ground. I have no doubt that it is the peremptory decision and clear good taste of the Commissioners alone, which have kept this last retreat of nature within our crowded city from being long ago plastered and daubed with placards, hand-bills, sign-boards and paint, from side to side and from end to end, over turf, tree, rock, wall, bridge, archway, building and all.

The Humbugs of the World (1866)

JOHN MUIR

John Muir (1838–1914) was the next great figure after Thoreau in the parade of American environmentalists. He is most celebrated for his practical achievements: founding the Sierra Club (he served as its president for 22 years until his death) and preserving Yosemite. But he is a literary hero as well. Beyond its pragmatic force, Muir's prose introduced an ecstatic new grammar and vocabulary of wildness into the American imagination: in some sense, every national park on the planet owes its existence to the spell he cast. Muir was born in Scotland, but moved to a Wisconsin homestead at the age of 11. His father was abusive, working his son long hours and beating him until he had memorized most of the Bible. He rebelled by becoming a vagabond, and by asking powerful questions about the orthodoxies of his day and ours, especially the notion that people stood at the center of the universe. His *A Thousand-Mile Walk to the Gulf*, written in 1867, is especially trenchant in its sympathetic portrait of the alligator: "Honorable representatives of the great saurians of an older creation, may you long enjoy your lilies and rushes, and be blessed now and then with a mouthful of terror-stricken man by way of dainty!" Muir's evident pleasure in the prospect of an occasional successful alligator attack foreshadows current ideas about "anthropocentrism" among deep ecologists. His writings also anticipate the ecologist's sense of interconnectedness: "When we try to pick out anything by itself," he wrote in *My First Summer in the Sierra* (1911), "we find it hitched to everything else in the universe."

Muir's wanderings eventually led him to California, and then Yosemite, where he helped Louis Agassiz prove his controversial theories about glaciation. But he was more and more disgusted by the way that flocks of sheep were trashing the backcountry, and so he began writing a series of articles that led to the creation of the Sierra Club and the further protection of Yosemite. He was a friend of Theodore Roosevelt, but a sworn enemy of Roosevelt's chief forester, Gifford Pinchot, who had no use for pristine wilderness. His later years were saddened by the losing fight to save Yosemite's Hetch Hetchy Valley, which San Francisco dammed as a water source. But his long treks across the granite fastness of the Sierra had doubtless left him with joy enough for one lifetime: "This grand show is eternal. It is always sunrise somewhere; the dew is never all dried at once; a shower is forever falling; vapor is ever rising. Eternal sunrise, eternal sunset, eternal dawn and gloaming, on seas and continents and islands, each in its turn, as the round earth rolls."

from **A Thousand-Mile Walk to the Gulf**

A few hours later I dined with three men and three dogs. I was viciously attacked by the latter, who undertook to undress me with their teeth. I was nearly dragged down backward, but escaped unbitten. Liver pie, mixed with sweet potatoes and fat duff, was set before me, and after I had finished a moderate portion, one of the men, turning to his companion, remarked: "Wall, I guess that man quit eatin' 'cause he had nothin' more to eat. I'll get him more potato."

Arrived at a place on the margin of a stagnant pool where an alligator had been rolling and sunning himself. "See," said a man who lived here, "see, what a track that is! He must have been a mighty big fellow. Alligators wallow like hogs and like to lie in the sun. I'd like a shot at that fellow." Here followed a long recital of bloody combats with the scaly enemy, in many of which he had, of course, taken an important part. Alligators are said to be extremely fond of negroes and dogs, and naturally the dogs and negroes are afraid of them.

Another man that I met to-day pointed to a shallow, grassy pond before his door. "There," said he, "I once had a tough fight with an alligator. He caught my dog. I heard him howling, and as he was one of my best hunters I tried hard to save him. The water was only about knee-deep and I ran up to the alligator. It was only a small one about four feet long, and was having trouble in its efforts to drown the dog in the shallow water. I scared him and made him let go his hold, but before the poor crippled dog could reach the shore, he was caught again, and when I went at the alligator with a knife, it seized my arm. If it had been a little stronger it might have eaten me instead of my dog."

I never in all my travels saw more than one, though they are said to be abundant in most of the swamps, and frequently attain a length of nine or ten feet. It is reported, also, that they are very savage, oftentimes attacking men in boats. These independent inhabitants of the sluggish waters of this low coast cannot be called the friends of man, though I heard of one big fellow that was caught young and was partially civilized and made to work in harness.

Many good people believe that alligators were created by the Devil, thus accounting for their all-consuming appetite and ugliness. But doubtless these creatures are happy and fill the place assigned them by the great Creator of us all. Fierce and cruel they appear to us, but beautiful in the eyes of God. They, also, are his children, for He hears their cries, cares for them tenderly, and provides their daily bread.

The antipathies existing in the Lord's great animal family must be wisely planned, like balanced repulsion and attraction in the mineral kingdom. How narrow we selfish, conceited creatures are in our sympathies! how blind to the rights of all the rest of creation! With what dismal irreverence we speak of our fellow mortals! Though alligators, snakes, etc., naturally repel us, they are not mysterious evils. They dwell happily in these flowery wilds, are part of God's family, unfallen, undepraved, and cared for with the same species of tenderness and love as is bestowed on angels in heaven or saints on earth.

I think that most of the antipathies which haunt and terrify us are morbid productions of ignorance and weakness. I have better thoughts of those alligators now that I have seen them at home. Honorable representatives of the great saurians of an older creation, may you long enjoy your lilies and rushes, and be blessed now and then with a mouthful of terror-stricken man by way of dainty!

* * *

The world, we are told, was made especially for man—a presumption not supported by all the facts. A numerous class of men are painfully astonished whenever they find anything, living or dead, in all

God's universe, which they cannot eat or render in some way what they call useful to themselves. They have precise dogmatic insight of the intentions of the Creator, and it is hardly possible to be guilty of irreverence in speaking of *their* God any more than of heathen idols. He is regarded as a civilized, law-abiding gentleman in favor either of a republican form of government or of a limited monarchy; believes in the literature and language of England; is a warm supporter of the English constitution and Sunday schools and missionary societies; and is as purely a manufactured article as any puppet of a half-penny theater.

With such views of the Creator it is, of course, not surprising that erroneous views should be entertained of the creation. To such properly trimmed people, the sheep, for example, is an easy problem—food and clothing "for us," eating grass and daisies white by divine appointment for this predestined purpose, on perceiving the demand for wool that would be occasioned by the eating of the apple in the Garden of Eden.

In the same pleasant plan, whales are storehouses of oil for us, to help out the stars in lighting our dark ways until the discovery of the Pennsylvania oil wells. Among plants, hemp, to say nothing of the cereals, is a case of evident destination for ships' rigging, wrapping packages, and hanging the wicked. Cotton is another plain case of clothing. Iron was made for hammers and ploughs, and lead for bullets; all intended for us. And so of other small handfuls of insignificant things.

But if we should ask these profound expositors of God's intentions, How about those man-eating animals—lions, tigers, alligators—which smack their lips over raw man? Or about those myriads of noxious insects that destroy labor and drink his blood? Doubtless man was intended for food and drink for all these? Oh, no! Not at all! These are unresolvable difficulties connected with Eden's apple and the Devil. Why does water drown its lord? Why do so many minerals poison him? Why are so many plants and fishes deadly enemies? Why is the lord of creation subjected to the same laws of life as his subjects? Oh, all these things are satanic, or in some way connected with the first garden.

Now, it never seems to occur to these far-seeing teachers that Nature's object in making animals and plants might possibly be first of all the happiness of each one of them, not the creation of all for the happiness of one. Why should man value himself as more than a small part of the one great unit of creation? And what creature of all that the Lord has taken the pains to make is not essential to the completeness of that unit—the cosmos? The universe would be incomplete without man; but it would also be incomplete without the smallest transmicroscopic creature that dwells beyond our conceitful eyes and knowledge.

From the dust of the earth, from the common elementary fund, the Creator has made *Homo sapiens*. From the same material he has made every other creature, however noxious and insignificant to us. They are earthborn companions and our fellow mortals. The fearfully good, the orthodox, of this laborious patchwork of modern civilization cry "Heresy" on every one whose sympathies reach a single hair's breadth beyond the boundary epidermis of our own species. Not content with taking all of earth, they also claim the celestial country as the only ones who possess the kind of souls for which that imponderable empire was planned.

This star, our own good earth, made many a successful journey around the heavens ere man was made, and whole kingdoms of creatures enjoyed existence and returned to dust ere man appeared to claim them. After human beings have also played their part in Creation's plan, they too may disappear without any general burning or extraordinary commotion whatever.

Plants are credited with but dim and uncertain sensation, and minerals with positively none at all. But why may not even a mineral arrangement of matter be endowed with sensation of a kind that we in our blind exclusive perfection can have no manner of communication with?

But I have wandered from my object. I stated a page or two back that man claimed the earth was made for him, and I was going to say that venomous beasts, thorny plants, and deadly diseases of certain parts of the earth prove that the whole world was not made for him. When an animal from a tropical climate is taken to high latitudes, it may perish of cold, and we say that such an animal was never intended for so severe a climate. But when man betakes himself to sickly parts of the tropics and perishes, he cannot see that he was never intended for such deadly climates. No, he will rather accuse the first mother of the cause of the difficulty, though she may never have seen a fever district; or will consider it a providential chastisement for some self-invented form of sin.

Furthermore, all uneatable and uncivilizable animals, and all plants which carry prickles, are deplorable evils which, according to closet researches of clergy, require the cleansing chemistry of universal planetary combustion. But more than aught else mankind requires burning, as being in great part wicked, and if that transmundane furnace can be so applied and regulated as to smelt and purify us into conformity with the rest of the terrestrial creation, then the tophetization of the erratic genus Homo were a consummation devoutly to be prayed for. But, glad to leave these ecclesiastical fires and blunders, I joyfully return to the immortal truth and immortal beauty of Nature.

1867

A Wind-Storm in the Forests

The mountain winds, like the dew and rain, sunshine and snow, are measured and bestowed with love on the forests to develop their strength and beauty. However restricted the scope of other forest influences, that of the winds is universal. The snow bends and trims the upper forests every winter, the lightning strikes a single tree here and there, while avalanches mow down thousands at a swoop as a gardener trims out a bed of flowers. But the winds go to every tree, fingering every leaf and branch and furrowed bole; not one is forgotten; the Mountain Pine towering with outstretched arms on the rugged buttresses of the icy peaks, the lowliest and most retiring tenant of the dells; they seek and find them all, caressing them tenderly, bending them in lusty exercise, stimulating their growth, plucking off a leaf or limb as required, or removing an entire tree or grove, now whispering and cooing through the branches like a sleepy child, now roaring like the ocean; the winds blessing the forests, the forests the winds, with ineffable beauty and harmony as the sure result.

After one has seen pines six feet in diameter bending like grasses before a mountain gale, and ever and anon some giant falling with a crash that shakes the hills, it seems astonishing that any, save the lowest thickset trees, could ever have found a period sufficiently stormless to establish themselves; or, once established, that they should not, sooner or later, have been blown down. But when the storm is over, and we behold the same forests tranquil again, towering fresh and unscathed in erect majesty, and consider what centuries of storms have fallen upon them since they were first planted,—hail, to break the tender seedlings; lightning, to scorch and shatter; snow, winds, and avalanches, to crush and overwhelm,—while the manifest result of all this wild storm-culture is the glorious perfection we behold; then faith in Nature's forestry is established, and we cease to deplore the violence of her most destructive gales, or of any other storm-implement whatsoever.

There are two trees in the Sierra forests that are never blown down, so long as they continue in sound health. These are the Juniper and the Dwarf Pine of the summit peaks. Their stiff, crooked roots grip the storm-beaten ledges like eagles' claws, while their lithe, cord-like branches bend round compliantly, offering but slight holds for winds, however violent. The other alpine conifers—the Needle Pine, Mountain Pine, Two-leaved Pine, and Hemlock Spruce—are never thinned out by this agent to any destructive extent, on account of their admirable toughness and the closeness of their growth. In general the same is true of the giants of the lower zones. The kingly Sugar Pine, towering aloft to a height of more than 200 feet, offers a fine mark to storm-winds; but it is not densely foliaged, and its long, horizontal arms swing round compliantly in the blast, like tresses of green, fluent algæ in a brook; while the Silver Firs in most places keep their ranks well together in united strength. The Yellow or Silver Pine is more frequently overturned than any other tree on the Sierra, because its leaves and branches form a larger mass in proportion to its height, while in many places it is planted sparsely, leaving open lanes through which storms may enter with full force. Furthermore, because it is distributed along the lower portion of the range, which was the first to be left bare on the breaking up of the ice-sheet at the close of the glacial winter, the soil it is growing upon has been longer exposed to post-glacial weathering, and consequently is in a more crumbling, decayed condition than the fresher soils farther up the range, and therefore offers a less secure anchorage for the roots.

While exploring the forest zones of Mount Shasta, I discovered the path of a hurricane strewn with thousands of pines of this species. Great and small had been uprooted or wrenched off by sheer force, making a clean gap, like that made by a snow avalanche. But hurricanes capable of doing this class of work are rare in the Sierra, and when we have explored the forests from one extremity of the range to the other, we are compelled to believe that they are the most beautiful on the face of the earth, however we may regard the agents that have made them so.

There is always something deeply exciting, not only in the sounds of winds in the woods, which exert more or less influence over every mind, but in their varied waterlike flow as manifested by the movements of the trees, especially those of the conifers. By no other trees are they rendered so extensively and impressively visible, not even by the lordly tropic palms or tree-ferns responsive to the gentlest breeze. The waving of a forest of the giant Sequoias is indescribably impressive and sublime, but the pines seem to me the best interpreters of winds. They are mighty waving goldenrods, ever in tune, singing and writing wind-music all their long century lives. Little, however, of this noble tree-waving and tree-music will you see or hear in the strictly alpine portion of the forests. The burly Juniper, whose girth sometimes more than equals its height, is about as rigid as the rocks on which it grows. The slender lash-like sprays of the Dwarf Pine stream out in wavering ripples, but the tallest and slenderest are far too unyielding to wave even in the heaviest gales. They only shake in quick, short vibrations. The Hemlock Spruce, however, and the Mountain Pine, and some of the tallest thickets of the Two-leaved species bow in storms with considerable scope and gracefulness. But it is only in the lower and middle zones that the meeting of winds and woods is to be seen in all its grandeur.

One of the most beautiful and exhilarating storms I ever enjoyed in the Sierra occurred in December, 1874, when I happened to be exploring one of the tributary valleys of the Yuba River. The sky and the ground and the trees had been thoroughly rain-washed and were dry again. The day was intensely pure, one of those incomparable bits of California winter, warm and balmy and full of white sparkling sunshine, redolent of all the purest influences of the spring, and at the same time enlivened with one of the most bracing wind-storms conceivable. Instead of camping out, as I usually do, I then chanced to be stopping at the house of a friend. But when the storm began to sound, I lost no time in pushing out into the woods to enjoy it. For on such occasions Nature has always something rare to show us, and the danger to life and limb is hardly greater than one would experience crouching deprecatingly beneath a roof.

It was still early morning when I found myself fairly adrift. Delicious sunshine came pouring over the hills, lighting the tops of the pines, and setting free a steam of summery fragrance that contrasted strangely with the wild tones of the storm. The air was mottled with pine-tassels and bright green plumes, that went flashing past in the sunlight like birds pursued. But there was not the slightest dustiness, nothing less pure than leaves, and ripe pollen, and flecks of withered bracken and moss. I heard trees falling for hours at the rate of one every two or three minutes; some uprooted, partly on account of the loose, water-soaked condition of the ground; others broken straight across, where some weakness caused by fire had determined the spot. The gestures of the various trees made a delightful study. Young Sugar Pines, light and feathery as squirrel-tails, were bowing almost to the ground; while the grand old patriarchs, whose massive boles had been tried in a hundred storms, waved solemnly above them, their long, arching branches streaming fluently on the gale, and every needle thrilling and ringing and shedding off keen lances of light like a diamond. The Douglas

Spruces, with long sprays drawn out in level tresses, and needles massed in a gray, shimmering glow, presented a most striking appearance as they stood in bold relief along the hilltops. The madroños in the dells, with their red bark and large glossy leaves tilted every way, reflected the sunshine in throbbing spangles like those one so often sees on the rippled surface of a glacier lake. But the Silver Pines were now the most impressively beautiful of all. Colossal spires 200 feet in height waved like supple goldenrods chanting and bowing low as if in worship, while the whole mass of their long, tremulous foliage was kindled into one continuous blaze of white sun-fire. The force of the gale was such that the most steadfast monarch of them all rocked down to its roots with a motion plainly perceptible when one leaned against it. Nature was holding high festival, and every fiber of the most rigid giants thrilled with glad excitement.

I drifted on through the midst of this passionate music and motion, across many a glen, from ridge to ridge; often halting in the lee of a rock for shelter, or to gaze and listen. Even when the grand anthem had swelled to its highest pitch, I could distinctly hear the varying tones of individual trees,—Spruce, and Fir, and Pine, and leafless Oak,—and even the infinitely gentle rustle of the withered grasses at my feet. Each was expressing itself in its own way,—singing its own song, and making its own peculiar gestures,—manifesting a richness of variety to be found in no other forest I have yet seen. The coniferous woods of Canada, and the Carolinas, and Florida, are made up of trees that resemble one another about as nearly as blades of grass, and grow close together in much the same way. Coniferous trees, in general, seldom possess individual character, such as is manifest among Oaks and Elms. But the California forests are made up of a greater number of distinct species than any other in the world. And in them we find, not only a marked differentiation into special groups, but also a marked individuality in almost every tree, giving rise to storm effects indescribably glorious.

Toward midday, after a long, tingling scramble through copses of hazel and ceanothus, I gained the summit of the highest ridge in the neighborhood; and then it occurred to me that it would be a fine thing to climb one of the trees to obtain a wider outlook and get my ear close to the Æolian music of its topmost needles. But under the circumstances the choice of a tree was a serious matter. One whose instep was not very strong seemed in danger of being blown down, or of being struck by others in case they should fall; another was branchless to a considerable height above the ground, and at the same time too large to be grasped with arms and legs in climbing; while others were not favorably situated for clear views. After cautiously casting about, I made choice of the tallest of a group of Douglas Spruces that were growing close together like a tuft of grass, no one of which seemed likely to fall unless all the rest fell with it. Though comparatively young, they were about 100 feet high, and their lithe, brushy tops were rocking and swirling in wild ecstasy. Being accustomed to climb trees in making botanical studies, I experienced no difficulty in reaching the top of this one, and never before did I enjoy so noble an exhilaration of motion. The slender tops fairly flapped and swished in the passionate torrent, bending and swirling backward and forward, round and round, tracing indescribable combinations of vertical and horizontal curves, while I clung with muscles firm braced, like a bobolink on a reed.

In its widest sweeps my tree-top described an arc of from twenty to thirty degrees, but I felt sure of its elastic temper, having seen others of the same species still more severely tried—bent almost to the ground indeed, in heavy snows—without breaking a fiber. I was therefore safe, and free to take the wind into my pulses and enjoy the excited forest from my superb outlook. The view from here must be extremely beautiful in any weather. Now my eye roved over the piny hills and dales as over fields of waving grain, and felt the light running in ripples and broad swelling undulations across the valleys from ridge to ridge, as the shining foliage was stirred by corresponding waves of air. Oftentimes these waves of reflected light would break up suddenly into a kind of beaten foam, and again, after chasing one another in regular order, they would seem to bend forward in concentric curves, and disappear on some hillside, like sea-waves on a shelving shore. The quantity of light reflected from the bent needles was so great as to make whole groves appear as if covered with snow, while the black shadows beneath the trees greatly enhanced the effect of the silvery splendor.

Excepting only the shadows there was nothing somber in all this wild sea of pines. On the contrary, notwithstanding this was the winter season, the colors were remarkably beautiful. The shafts of the pine and libocedrus were brown and purple, and most of the foliage was well tinged with yellow; the laurel groves, with the pale undersides of their leaves turned upward, made masses of gray; and then there was many a dash of chocolate color from clumps of manzanita, and jet of vivid crimson from the bark of the madroños, while the ground on the hillsides, appearing here and there through openings between the groves, displayed masses of pale purple and brown.

The sounds of the storm corresponded gloriously with this wild exuberance of light and motion. The profound bass of the naked branches and boles booming like waterfalls; the quick, tense vibrations of the pine-needles, now rising to a shrill, whistling hiss, now falling to a silky murmur; the rustling of laurel groves in the dells, and the keen metallic click of leaf on leaf—all this was heard in easy analysis when the attention was calmly bent.

The varied gestures of the multitude were seen to fine advantage, so that one could recognize the different species at a distance of several miles by this means alone, as well as by their forms and colors, and the way they reflected the light. All seemed strong and comfortable, as if really enjoying the storm, while responding to its most enthusiastic greetings. We hear much nowadays concerning the universal struggle for existence, but no struggle in the common meaning of the word was manifest here; no recognition of danger by any tree; no deprecation; but rather an invincible gladness as remote from exultation as from fear.

I kept my lofty perch for hours, frequently closing my eyes to enjoy the music by itself, or to feast quietly on the delicious fragrance that was streaming past. The fragrance of the woods was less marked than that produced during warm rain, when so many balsamic buds and leaves are steeped like tea; but, from the chafing of resiny branches against each other, and the incessant attrition of myriads of needles, the gale was spiced to a very tonic degree. And besides the fragrance from these local sources there were traces of scents brought from afar. For this wind came first from the sea, rubbing against its fresh, briny waves, then distilled through the redwoods, threading rich ferny gulches, and spreading itself in broad undulating currents over many a flower-enameled ridge of the coast mountains, then across the golden plains, up the purple foot-hills, and into these piny woods with the varied incense gathered by the way.

Winds are advertisements of all they touch, however much or little we may be able to read them; telling their wanderings even by their scents alone. Mariners detect the flowery perfume of land-winds far at sea, and sea-winds carry the fragrance of dulse and tangle far inland, where it is quickly recognized, though mingled with the scents of a thousand land-flowers. As an illustration of this, I may tell here that I breathed sea-air on the Firth of Forth, in Scotland, while a boy; then was taken to Wisconsin, where I remained nineteen years; then, without in all this time having breathed one breath of the sea, I walked quietly, alone, from the middle of the Mississippi Valley to the Gulf of Mexico, on a botanical excursion, and while in Florida, far from the coast, my attention wholly bent on the splendid tropical vegetation about me, I suddenly recognized a sea-breeze, as it came sifting through the palmettos and blooming vine-tangles, which at once awakened and set free a thousand dormant associations, and made me a boy again in Scotland, as if all the intervening years had been annihilated.

Most people like to look at mountain rivers, and bear them in mind; but few care to look at the winds, though far more beautiful and sublime, and though they become at times about as visible as flowing water. When the north winds in winter are making upward sweeps over the curving summits of the High Sierra, the fact is sometimes published with flying snow-banners a mile long. Those portions of the winds thus embodied can scarce be wholly invisible, even to the darkest imagination. And when we look around over an agitated forest, we may see something of the wind that stirs it, by its effects upon the trees. Yonder it descends in a rush of waterlike ripples, and sweeps over the bending pines from hill to hill. Nearer, we see detached plumes and leaves, now speeding by on level currents, now whirling in eddies, or, escaping over the edges of the whirls, soaring aloft on grand, up-swelling domes of air, or tossing on flame-like crests. Smooth, deep currents, cascades, falls, and swirling eddies, sing around every tree and leaf, and over all the varied topography of the region with telling changes of form, like mountain rivers conforming to the features of their channels.

After tracing the Sierra streams from their fountains to the plains, marking where they bloom white in falls, glide in crystal plumes, surge gray and foam-filled in boulder-choked gorges, and slip through the woods in long, tranquil reaches—after thus learning their language and forms in detail, we may at length hear them chanting all together in one grand anthem, and comprehend them all in clear inner vision, covering the range like lace. But even this spectacle is far less sublime and not a whit more substantial than what we may behold of these storm-streams of air in the mountain woods.

We all travel the milky way together, trees and men; but it never occurred to me until this storm-day, while swinging in the wind, that trees are travelers, in the ordinary sense. They make many journeys, not extensive ones, it is true; but our own little journeys, away and back again, are only little more than tree-wavings—many of them not so much.

When the storm began to abate, I dismounted and sauntered down through the calming woods. The storm-tones died away, and, turning toward the east, I beheld the countless hosts of the forests hushed and tranquil, towering above one another on the slopes of the hills like a devout audience. The setting sun filled them with amber light, and seemed to say, while they listened, "My peace I give unto you."

As I gazed on the impressive scene, all the so-called ruin of the storm was forgotten, and never before did these noble woods appear so fresh, so joyous, so immortal.

c. 1878

from **My First Summer in the Sierra**

Sketching on the North Dome. It commands views of nearly all the valley besides a few of the high mountains. I would fain draw everything in sight—rock, tree, and leaf. But little can I do beyond mere outlines,—marks with meanings like words, readable only to myself,—yet I sharpen my pencils and work on as if others might possibly be benefited. Whether these picture-sheets are to vanish like fallen leaves or go to friends like letters, matters not much; for little can they tell to those who have not themselves seen similar wildness, and like a language have learned it. No pain here, no dull empty hours, no fear of the past, no fear of the future. These blessed mountains are so compactly filled with God's beauty, no petty personal hope or experience has room to be. Drinking this champagne water is pure pleasure, so is breathing the living air, and every movement of limbs is pleasure, while the whole body seems to feel beauty when exposed to it as it feels the camp-fire or sunshine, entering not by the eyes alone, but equally through all one's flesh like radiant heat, making a passionate ecstatic pleasure-glow not explainable. One's body then seems homogeneous throughout, sound as a crystal.

Perched like a fly on this Yosemite dome, I gaze and sketch and bask, oftentimes settling down into dumb admiration without definite hope of ever learning much, yet with the longing, unresting effort that lies at the door of hope, humbly prostrate before the vast display of God's power, and eager to offer self-denial and renunciation with eternal toil to learn any lesson in the divine manuscript.

It is easier to feel than to realize, or in any way explain, Yosemite grandeur. The magnitudes of the rocks and trees and streams are so delicately harmonized they are mostly hidden. Sheer precipices three thousand feet high are fringed with tall trees growing close like grass on the brow of a lowland hill, and extending along the feet of these precipices a ribbon of meadow a mile wide and seven or eight long, that seems like a strip a farmer might mow in less than a day. Waterfalls, five hundred to one or two thousand feet high, are so subordinated to the mighty cliffs over which they pour that they seem like wisps of smoke, gentle as floating clouds, though their voices fill the valley and make the rocks tremble. The mountains, too, along the eastern sky, and the domes in front of them, and the succession of smooth rounded waves between, swelling higher, higher, with dark woods in their hollows, serene in massive exuberant bulk and beauty, tend yet more to hide the grandeur of the Yosemite temple and make it appear as a subdued subordinate feature of the vast harmonious landscape. Thus every attempt to appreciate any one feature is beaten down by the overwhelming influence of all the others. And, as if this were not enough, lo! in the sky arises another mountain range with topography as rugged and substantial-looking as the one beneath it—snowy peaks and domes and shadowy Yosemite valleys—another version of the snowy Sierra, a new creation heralded by a thunder-storm. How fiercely, devoutly wild is Nature in the midst of her beauty-loving tenderness!—painting lilies, watering them, caressing them with gentle hand, going from flower to flower like a gardener while building rock mountains and cloud mountains full of lightning and rain. Gladly we run for shelter beneath an overhanging cliff and examine the reassuring ferns and mosses, gentle love tokens growing in cracks and chinks. Daisies, too, and ivesias, confiding wild children of light, too small to fear. To these one's heart goes home, and the voices of the storm become gentle. Now the sun breaks forth and fragrant steam arises. The birds are out singing on the edges of the groves. The west is flaming in gold and purple, ready for the ceremony of the sunset, and back I go to camp with my notes and pictures, the best of them printed in my mind as dreams. A fruitful day, without measured beginning or ending. A terrestrial eternity. A gift of good God.

Wrote to my mother and a few friends, mountain hints to each. They seem as near as if within voice-reach or touch. The deeper the solitude the less the sense of loneliness, and the nearer our friends. Now bread and tea, fir bed and good-night to Carlo, a look at the sky lilies, and death sleep until the dawn of another Sierra to-morrow.

July 21. Sketching on the Dome—no rain; clouds at noon about quarter filled the sky, casting shadows with fine effect on the white mountains at the heads of the streams, and a soothing cover over the gardens during the warm hours.

Saw a common house-fly and a grasshopper and a brown bear. The fly and grasshopper paid me a merry visit on the top of the Dome, and I paid a visit to the bear in the middle of a small garden meadow between the Dome and the camp where he was standing alert among the flowers as if willing to be seen to advantage. I had not gone more than half a mile from camp this morning, when Carlo, who was trotting on a few yards ahead of me, came to a sudden, cautious standstill. Down went tail and ears, and forward went his knowing nose, while he seemed to be saying, "Ha, what's this? A bear, I guess." Then a cautious advance of a few steps, setting his feet down softly like a hunting cat, and questioning the air as to the scent he had caught until all doubt vanished. Then he came back to me, looked me in the face, and with his speaking eyes reported a bear near by; then led on softly, careful, like an experienced hunter, not to make the slightest noise, and frequently looking back as if whispering, "Yes, it's a bear; come and I'll show you." Presently we came to where the sunbeams were streaming through between the purple shafts of the firs, which showed that we were nearing an open spot, and here Carlo came behind me, evidently sure that the bear was very near. So I crept to a low ridge of moraine boulders on the edge of a narrow garden meadow, and in this meadow I felt pretty sure the bear must be. I was anxious to get a good look at the sturdy mountaineer without alarming him; so drawing myself up noiselessly back of one of the largest of the trees I peered past its bulging buttresses, exposing only a part of my head, and there stood neighbor Bruin within a stone's throw, his hips covered by tall grass and flowers, and his front feet on the trunk of a fir that had fallen out into the meadow, which raised his head so high that he seemed to be standing erect. He had not yet seen me, but was looking and listening attentively, showing that in some way he was aware of our approach. I watched his gestures and tried to make the most of my opportunity to learn what I could about him, fearing he would catch sight of me and run away. For I had been told that this sort of bear, the cinnamon, always ran from his bad brother man, never showing fight unless wounded or in defense of young. He made a telling picture standing alert in the sunny forest garden. How well he played his part, harmonizing in bulk and color and shaggy hair with the trunks of the trees and lush vegetation, as natural a feature as any other in the landscape. After examining at leisure, noting the sharp muzzle thrust inquiringly forward, the long shaggy hair on his broad chest, the stiff, erect ears nearly buried in hair, and the slow, heavy way he moved his head, I thought I should like to see his gait in running, so I made a sudden rush at him, shouting and swinging my hat to frighten him, expecting to see him make haste to get away. But to my dismay he did not run or show any sign of running. On the contrary, he stood his ground ready to fight and defend himself, lowered his head, thrust it forward, and looked sharply and fiercely at me. Then I suddenly began to fear that upon me would fall the work of running; but I was afraid to run, and therefore, like the bear, held my ground. We stood staring at each other in solemn silence within a dozen yards or thereabouts, while I fervently hoped that the power of the human eye over wild beasts would prove as great as it is said to be. How long our awfully strenuous interview lasted, I don't know; but at length in the slow full-ness of time he pulled his huge paws down off the log, and with mag-nificent deliberation turned and walked leisurely up the meadow, stopping frequently to look back over his shoulder to see whether I was pursuing him, then moving on again, evidently neither fearing me very much nor trusting me. He was probably about five hundred pounds in weight, a broad, rusty bundle of ungovernable wildness, a happy fellow whose lines have fallen in pleasant places. The flowery glade in which I saw him so well, framed like a picture, is one of the best of all I have yet discovered, a conservatory of Nature's precious plant people. Tall lilies were swinging their bells over that bear's back, with geraniums, larkspurs, columbines, and daisies brushing against his sides. A place for angels, one would say, instead of bears.

In the great cañons Bruin reigns supreme. Happy fellow, whom no famine can reach while one of his thousand kinds of food is spared him. His bread is sure at all seasons, ranged on the mountain shelves like stores in a pantry. From one to the other, up or down he climbs, tasting and enjoying each in turn in different climates, as if he had journeyed thousands of miles to other countries north or south to enjoy their varied productions. I should like to know my hairy brothers better—though after this particular Yosemite bear, my very neighbor, had sauntered out of sight this morning, I reluctantly went back to camp for the Don's rifle to shoot him, if necessary, in defense of the flock. Fortunately I couldn't find him, and after tracking him a mile or two towards Mount Hoffman I bade him Godspeed and gladly returned to my work on the Yosemite Dome.

The house-fly also seemed at home and buzzed about me as I sat sketching, and enjoying my bear interview now it was over. I wonder what draws house-flies so far up the mountains, heavy gross feeders as they are, sensitive to cold, and fond of domestic ease. How have they been distributed from continent to continent, across seas and deserts and mountain chains, usually so influential in determining boundaries of species both of plants and animals. Beetles and butterflies are sometimes restricted to small areas. Each mountain in a range, and even the different zones of a mountain, may have its own peculiar species. But the house-fly seems to be everywhere. I wonder if any island in mid-ocean is flyless. The bluebottle is abundant in these Yosemite woods, ever ready with his marvelous store of eggs to make all dead flesh fly. Bumblebees are here, and are well fed on boundless stores of nectar and pollen. The honeybee, though abundant in the foothills, has not yet got so high. It is only a few years since the first swarm was brought to California.

A queer fellow and a jolly fellow is the grasshopper. Up the mountains he comes on excursions, how high I don't know, but at least as far and high as Yosemite tourists. I was much interested with the hearty enjoyment of the one that danced and sang for me on the Dome this afternoon. He seemed brimful of glad, hilarious energy, manifested by springing into the air to a height of twenty or thirty feet, then diving and springing up again and making a sharp musical rattle just as the lowest point in the descent was reached. Up and down a dozen times or

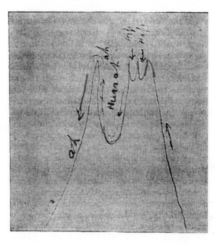

Track of singing dancing grasshopper in the air over North Dome

so he danced and sang, then alighted to rest, then up and at it again. The
curves he described in the air in diving and rattling resembled those
made by cords hanging loosely and attached at the same height at the
ends, the loops nearly covering each other. Braver, heartier, keener, care-
free enjoyment of life I have never seen or heard in any creature, great or
small. The life of this comic red-legs, the mountain's merriest child,
seems to be made up of pure, condensed gayety. The Douglas squirrel
is the only living creature that I can compare him with in exuberant,
rollicking, irrepressible jollity. Wonderful that these sublime mountains
are so loudly cheered and brightened by a creature so queer. Nature in
him seems to be snapping her fingers in the face of all earthly dejection
and melancholy with a boyish hip-hip-hurrah. How the sound is made
I do not understand. When he was on the ground he made not the
slightest noise, nor when he was simply flying from place to place, but
only when diving in curves, the motion seeming to be required for the
sound; for the more vigorous the diving the more energetic the corresponding outbursts of jolly rattling. I tried to observe him closely while
he was resting in the intervals of his performances; but he would not allow a near approach, always getting his jumping legs ready to spring

for immediate flight, and keeping his eyes on me. A fine sermon the little fellow danced for me on the Dome, a likely place to look for sermons in stones, but not for grasshopper sermons. A large and imposing pulpit for so small a preacher. No danger of weakness in the knees of the world while Nature can spring such a rattle as this. Even the bear did not express for me the mountain's wild health and strength and happiness so tellingly as did this comical little hopper. No cloud of care in his day, no winter of discontent in sight. To him every day is a holiday; and when at length his sun sets, I fancy he will cuddle down on the forest floor and die like the leaves and flowers, and like them leave no unsightly remains calling for burial.

Sundown, and I must to camp. Good-night, friends three,—brown bear, rugged boulder of energy in groves and gardens fair as Eden; restless, fussy fly with gauzy wings stirring the air around all the world; and grasshopper, crisp, electric spark of joy enlivening the massy sublimity of the mountains like the laugh of a child. Thank you, thank you all three for your quickening company. Heaven guide every wing and leg. Good-night friends three, good-night.

My First Summer in the Sierra (1911)

Hetch Hetchy Valley

Yosemite is so wonderful that we are apt to regard it as an exceptional creation, the only valley of its kind in the world; but Nature is not so poor as to have only one of anything. Several other yosemites have been discovered in the Sierra that occupy the same relative positions on the Range and were formed by the same forces in the same kind of granite. One of these, the Hetch Hetchy Valley, is in the Yosemite National Park about twenty miles from Yosemite and is easily accessible to all sorts of travelers by a road and trail that leaves the Big Oak Flat road at Bronson Meadows a few miles below Crane Flat, and to mountaineers by way of Yosemite Creek basin and the head of the middle fork of the Tuolumne.

It is said to have been discovered by Joseph Screech, a hunter, in 1850, a year before the discovery of the great Yosemite. After my first visit to it in the autumn of 1871, I have always called it the "Tuolumne Yosemite," for it is a wonderfully exact counterpart of the Merced Yosemite, not only in its sublime rocks and waterfalls but in the gardens, groves and meadows of its flowery park-like floor. The floor of Yosemite is about 4000 feet above the sea; the Hetch Hetchy floor about 3700 feet. And as the Merced River flows through Yosemite, so does the Tuolumne through Hetch Hetchy. The walls of both are of gray granite, rise abruptly from the floor, are sculptured in the same style and in both every rock is a glacier monument.

Standing boldly out from the south wall is a strikingly picturesque rock called by the Indians, Kolana, the outermost of a group 2300 feet high, corresponding with the Cathedral Rocks of Yosemite both in relative position and form. On the opposite side of the Valley, facing Kolana, there is a counterpart of the El Capitan that rises sheer and plain to a height of 1800 feet, and over its massive brow flows a stream which makes the most graceful fall I have ever seen. From the edge of the cliff to the top of an earthquake talus it is perfectly free in the air for a thousand feet before it is broken into cascades among talus boulders. It is in all its glory in June, when the snow is melting fast, but fades and vanishes toward the end of summer. The only fall I know with which it may fairly be compared is the Yosemite Bridal Veil; but it excels even that favorite fall both in height and airy-fairy beauty and behavior. Lowlanders are apt to suppose that mountain streams in their wild career over cliffs lose control of themselves and tumble in a noisy chaos of mist and spray. On the contrary, on no part of their travels are they more harmonious and self-controlled. Imagine yourself in Hetch Hetchy on a sunny day in June, standing waist-deep in grass and flowers (as I have often stood), while the great pines sway dreamily with scarcely perceptible motion. Looking northward across the Valley you see a plain, gray granite cliff rising abruptly out of the gardens and groves to a height of 1800 feet, and in front of it Tueeulala's silvery scarf burning with irised sun-fire. In the first white outburst at the head there is abundance of visible energy, but it is speedily hushed and concealed in divine repose, and its tranquil progress to the base of the cliff is like that of a downy feather in a still room. Now observe the fineness and marvelous distinctness of the various sun-illumined fabrics into which the water is woven; they sift and float from form to form down the face of that grand gray rock in so leisurely and unconfused a manner that you can examine their texture, and patterns and tones of color as you would a piece of embroidery held in the hand. Toward the top of the fall you see groups of booming, comet-like masses, their solid, white heads separate, their tails like combed silk interlacing among delicate gray and purple shadows, ever forming and dissolving, worn out by friction in their rush through the air. Most of these vanish a few hundred feet below the summit, changing to varied forms of cloud-like drapery. Near the bottom the width of the fall has increased from about twenty-five feet to a hundred feet. Here it is composed of yet finer tissues, and is still without a trace of disorder—air, water and sunlight woven into stuff that spirits might wear.

So fine a fall might well seem sufficient to glorify any valley; but here, as in Yosemite, Nature seems in nowise moderate, for a short distance to the eastward of Tueeulala booms and thunders the great Hetch Hetchy Fall, Wapama, so near that you have both of them in full view from the same standpoint. It is the counterpart of the Yosemite Fall, but has a much greater volume of water, is about 1700 feet in height, and appears to be nearly vertical, though considerably inclined, and is dashed into huge outbounding bosses of foam on projecting shelves and knobs. No two falls could be more unlike—Tueeulala out in the open sunshine descending like thistledown; Wapama in a jagged, shadowy gorge roaring and thundering, pounding its way like an earthquake avalanche.

Besides this glorious pair there is a broad, massive fall on the main river a short distance above the head of the Valley. Its position is something like that of the Vernal in Yosemite, and its roar as it plunges into a surging trout-pool may be heard a long way, though it is only about twenty feet high. On Rancheria Creek, a large stream, corresponding in position with the Yosemite Tenaya Creek, there is a chain of cascades joined here and there with swift flashing plumes like the one between the Vernal and Nevada Falls, making magnificent shows as they go their glacier-sculptured way, sliding, leaping, hurrahing, covered with crisp clashing spray made glorious with sifting sunshine. And besides all these a few small streams come over the walls at wide intervals, leaping from ledge to ledge with birdlike song and watering many a hidden cliff-garden and fernery, but they are too unshowy to be noticed in so grand a place.

The correspondence between the Hetch Hetchy walls in their trends, sculpture, physical structure, and general arrangement of the main rock-masses and those of the Yosemite Valley has excited the wondering admiration of every observer. We have seen that the El Capitan and Cathedral rocks occupy the same relative positions in both valleys; so also do their Yosemite points and North Domes. Again, that part of the Yosemite north wall immediately to the east of the Yosemite Fall has two horizontal benches, about 500 and 1500 feet above the floor, timbered with golden-cup oak. Two benches similarly situated and timbered occur on the same relative portion of the Hetch Hetchy north wall, to the east of Wapama Fall, and on no other. The Yosemite is bounded at the head by the great Half Dome. Hetch Hetchy is bounded in the same way, though its head rock is incomparably less wonderful and sublime in form.

The floor of the Valley is about three and a half miles long, and from a fourth to half a mile wide. The lower portion is mostly a level meadow about a mile long, with the trees restricted to the sides and the river banks, and partially separated from the main, upper, forested portion by a low bar of glacier-polished granite across which the river breaks in rapids.

The principal trees are the yellow and sugar pines, digger pine, incense cedar, Douglas spruce, silver fir, the California and golden-cup oaks, balsam cottonwood, Nuttall's flowering dogwood, alder, maple, laurel, tumion, etc. The most abundant and influential are the great yellow or silver pines like those of Yosemite, the tallest over two hundred feet in height, and the oaks assembled in magnificent groves with massive rugged trunks four to six feet in diameter, and broad, shady, widespreading heads. The shrubs forming conspicuous flowery clumps and tangles are manzanita, azalea, spiræa, brier-rose, several species of ceanothus, calycanthus, philadelphus, wild cherry, etc.; with abundance of showy and fragrant herbaceous plants growing about them or out in the open in beds by themselves—lilies, Mariposa tulips, brodiaeas, orchids, iris, spraguea, draperia, collomia, collinsia, castilleja, nemophila, larkspur, columbine, goldenrods, sunflowers, mints of many species, honeysuckle, etc. Many fine ferns dwell here also, especially the beautiful and interesting rock-ferns—pellaea, and cheilanthes of several species—fringing and rosetting dry rockpiles and ledges; woodwardia and asplenium on damp spots with fronds six or seven feet high; the delicate maiden-hair in mossy nooks by the falls, and the sturdy, broadshouldered pteris covering nearly all the dry ground beneath the oaks and pines.

It appears, therefore, that Hetch Hetchy Valley, far from being a plain, common, rock-bound meadow, as many who have not seen it seem to suppose, is a grand landscape garden, one of Nature's rarest and most precious mountain temples. As in Yosemite, the sublime rocks of its walls seem to glow with life, whether leaning back in repose or standing erect in thoughtful attitudes, giving welcome to storms and calms alike, their brows in the sky, their feet set in the groves and gay flowery meadows, while birds, bees, and butterflies help the river and waterfalls to stir all the air into music—things frail and fleeting and types of permanence meeting here and blending, just as they do in Yosemite, to draw her lovers into close and confiding communion with her.

Sad to say, this most precious and sublime feature of the Yosemite National Park, one of the greatest of all our natural resources for the uplifting joy and peace and health of the people, is in danger of being dammed and made into a reservoir to help supply San Francisco with water and light, thus flooding it from wall to wall and burying its gardens and groves one or two hundred feet deep. This grossly destructive commercial scheme has long been planned and urged (though water as pure and abundant can be got from sources outside of the people's park, in a dozen different places), because of the comparative cheapness of the dam and of the territory which it is sought to divert from the great uses to which it was dedicated in the Act of 1890 establishing the Yosemite National Park.

The making of gardens and parks goes on with civilization all over the world, and they increase both in size and number as their value is recognized. Everybody needs beauty as well as bread, places to play in and pray in, where Nature may heal and cheer and give strength to body and soul alike. This natural beauty-hunger is made manifest in the little window-sill gardens of the poor, though perhaps only a geranium slip in a broken cup, as well as in the carefully tended rose and lily gardens of the rich, the thousands of spacious city parks and botanical gardens, and in our magnificent National parks—the Yellowstone, Yosemite, Sequoia, etc.—Nature's sublime wonderlands, the admiration and joy of the world. Nevertheless, like anything else worth while, from the very beginning, however well guarded, they have always been subject to attack by despoiling gain-seekers and mischief-makers of every degree from Satan to Senators, eagerly trying to make everything immediately and selfishly commercial, with schemes disguised in smug-smiling philanthropy, industriously, shampiously crying, "Conservation, conservation, panutilization," that man and beast may be fed and the dear Nation made great. Thus long ago a few enterprising merchants utilized the Jerusalem temple as a place of business instead of a place of prayer, changing money, buying and selling cattle and sheep and doves; and earlier still, the first forest reservation, including only one tree, was likewise despoiled. Ever since the establishment of the Yosemite National Park, strife has been going on around its borders and I suppose this will go on as part of the universal battle between right and wrong, however much its boundaries may be shorn, or its wild beauty destroyed.

The first application to the Government by the San Francisco Supervisors for the commercial use of Lake Eleanor and the Hetch Hetchy Valley was made in 1903, and on December 22nd of that year it was denied by the Secretary of the Interior, Mr. Hitchcock, who truthfully said:

> Presumably the Yosemite National Park was created such by law because of the natural objects of varying degrees of scenic importance located within its boundaries, inclusive alike of its beautiful small lakes, like Eleanor, and its majestic wonders, like Hetch Hetchy and Yosemite Valley. It is the aggregation of such natural scenic features that makes the Yosemite Park a wonderland which the Congress of the United States sought by law to reserve for all coming time as nearly as practicable in the condition fashioned by the hand of the Creator—a worthy object of National pride and a source of healthful pleasure and rest for the thousands of people who may annually sojourn there during the heated months.

In 1907 when Mr. Garfield became Secretary of the Interior the application was renewed and granted; but under his successor, Mr. Fisher, the matter has been referred to a Commission, which as this volume goes to press still has it under consideration.

The most delightful and wonderful camp grounds in the Park are its three great valleys—Yosemite, Hetch Hetchy, and Upper Tuolumne; and they are also the most important places with reference to their positions relative to the other great features—the Merced and Tuolumne Cañons, and the High Sierra peaks and glaciers, etc., at the head of the rivers. The main part of the Tuolumne Valley is a spacious flowery lawn four or five miles long, surrounded by magnificent snowy mountains, slightly separated from other beautiful meadows, which together make a series about twelve miles in length, the highest reaching to the feet of Mount Dana, Mount Gibbs, Mount Lyell and Mount McClure. It is about 8500 feet above the sea, and forms the grand central High Sierra camp ground from which excursions are made to the noble mountains, domes, glaciers, etc.; across the Range to the Mono Lake and volcanoes and down the Tuolumne Cañon to Hetch Hetchy. Should Hetch Hetchy be submerged for a reservoir, as proposed, not only would it be utterly destroyed, but the sublime cañon way to the heart of the High Sierra would be hopelessly blocked and the great camping ground, as the watershed of a city drinking system, virtually would be closed to the public. So far as I have learned, few of all the thousands who have seen the park and seek rest and peace in it are in favor of this outrageous scheme.

One of my later visits to the Valley was made in the autumn of 1907 with the late William Keith, the artist. The leaf-colors were then ripe, and the great godlike rocks in repose seemed to glow with life. The artist, under their spell, wandered day after day along the river and through the groves and gardens, studying the wonderful scenery; and, after making about forty sketches, declared with enthusiasm that although its walls were less sublime in height, in picturesque beauty and charm Hetch Hetchy surpassed even Yosemite.

That any one would try to destroy such a place seems incredible; but sad experience shows that there are people good enough and bad enough for anything. The proponents of the dam scheme bring forward a lot of bad arguments to prove that the only righteous thing to do with the people's parks is to destroy them bit by bit as they are able. Their arguments are curiously like those of the devil, devised for the destruction of the first garden—so much of the very best Eden fruit going to waste; so much of the best Tuolumne water and Tuolumne scenery going to waste. Few of their statements are even partly true, and all are misleading.

Thus, Hetch Hetchy, they say, is a "low-lying meadow." On the contrary, it is a high-lying natural landscape garden, as the photographic illustrations show.

"It is a common minor feature, like thousands of others." On the contrary it is a very uncommon feature; after Yosemite, the rarest and in many ways the most important in the National Park.

"Damming and submerging it 175 feet deep would enhance its beauty by forming a crystal-clear lake." Landscape gardens, places of recreation and worship, are never made beautiful by destroying and burying them. The beautiful sham lake, forsooth, would be only an eyesore, a dismal blot on the landscape, like many others to be seen in the Sierra. For, instead of keeping it at the same level all the year, allowing

Nature centuries of time to make new shores, it would, of course, be full only a month or two in the spring, when the snow is melting fast; then it would be gradually drained, exposing the slimy sides of the basin and shallower parts of the bottom, with the gathered drift and waste, death and decay of the upper basins, caught here instead of being swept on to decent natural burial along the banks of the river or in the sea. Thus the Hetch Hetchy dam-lake would be only a rough imitation of a natural lake for a few of the spring months, an open sepulcher for the others.

"Hetch Hetchy water is the purest of all to be found in the Sierra, unpolluted, and forever unpollutable." On the contrary, excepting that of the Merced below Yosemite, it is less pure than that of most of the other Sierra streams, because of the sewerage of camp grounds draining into it, especially of the Big Tuolumne Meadows camp ground, occupied by hundreds of tourists and mountaineers, with their animals, for months every summer, soon to be followed by thousands from all the world.

These temple destroyers, devotees of ravaging commercialism, seem to have a perfect contempt for Nature, and, instead of lifting their eyes to the God of the mountains, lift them to the Almighty Dollar.

Dam Hetch Hetchy! As well dam for water-tanks the people's cathedrals and churches, for no holier temple has ever been consecrated by the heart of man.

The Yosemite (1912)

W.H.H. "Adirondack" Murray (1840–1904) was a Connecticut clergy-
man who also specialized in Sunday-night lectures on secular themes.
His favorite subject was the Great North Woods of the Adirondacks,
which survived intact well into the 19th century, long after almost all
of New England had been logged to stubble. He turned his lectures into
a book, of which this excerpt is the beginning; understandably, it
sparked a rush of tourists into the mountains, whom the locals called
"Murray's Fools." Some were dismayed to find Adirondack wildlife he
hadn't described (notably blackflies), but many more were as enchanted as the good reverend. Soon the Adirondacks were home to at
least 200 "great camps," well-appointed rustic retreats for the richest
Americans. All the potential and all the pitfalls of what we might now
call ecotourism were represented in the years that followed. On the one
hand, the area was soon overrun, and the attitudes that Murray took
toward his guides have helped define the relationship between vaca-
tioner and local ever since; on the other, the visitors provided a political
constituency that helped the New York State legislature decide to make
it the country's first really big protected landscape and a model for all
the parks, reserves, wildernesses, and refuges that would follow.

from **Adventures in the Wilderness**

The Wilderness

The Adirondack Wilderness, or the "North Woods," as it is sometimes called, lies between the Lakes George and Champlain on
the east, and the river St. Lawrence on the north and west. It reaches
northward as far as the Canada line, and southward to Booneville. Its
area is about that of the State of Connecticut. The southern part is known
as the Brown Tract Region, with which the whole wilderness by some

is confused, but with no more accuracy than any one county might be said to comprise an entire State. Indeed, "Brown's Tract" is the least interesting portion of the Adirondack region. It lacks the lofty mountain scenery, the intricate mesh-work of lakes, and the wild grandeur of the country to the north. It is the lowland district, comparatively tame and uninviting. Not until you reach the Racquette do you get a glimpse of the magnificent scenery which makes this wilderness to rival Switzerland. There, on the very ridge-board of the vast water-shed which slopes northward to the St. Lawrence, eastward to the Hudson, and southward to the Mohawk, you can enter upon a voyage the like of which, it is safe to say, the world does not anywhere else furnish. For hundreds of miles I have boated up and down that wilderness, going ashore only to "carry" around a fall, or across some narrow ridge dividing the otherwise connected lakes. For weeks I have paddled my cedar shell in all directions, swinging northerly into the St. Regis chain, westward nearly to Potsdam, southerly to the Black River country, and from thence penetrated to that almost unvisited region, the "South Branch," without seeing a face but my guide's, and the entire circuit, it must be remembered, was through a wilderness yet to echo to the lumberman's axe. It is estimated that a thousand lakes, many yet unvisited, lie embedded in this vast forest of pine and hemlock. From the summit of a mountain, two years ago, I counted, as seen by my naked eye, forty-four lakes gleaming amid the depths of the wilderness like gems of purest ray amid the folds of emerald-colored velvet. Last summer I met a gentleman on the Racquette who had just received a letter from a brother in Switzerland, an artist by profession, in which he said, that, "having travelled over all Switzerland, and the Rhine and Rhone region, he had not met with scenery which, judged from a purely artistic point of view, combined so many beauties in connection with such grandeur as the lakes, mountains, and forest of the Adirondack region presented to the gazer's eye." And yet thousands are in Europe to-day as tourists who never gave a passing thought to this marvellous country lying as it were at their very doors.

Another reason why I visit the Adirondacks, and urge others to do so, is because I deem the excursion eminently adapted to restore impaired health. Indeed, it is marvellous what benefit physically is often derived from a trip of a few weeks to these woods. To such as are afflicted with that dire parent of ills, dyspepsia, or have lurking in their system consumptive tendencies, I most earnestly recommend a month's experience among the pines. The air which you there inhale is such as can be found only in high mountainous regions, pure, rarefied, and bracing. The amount of venison steak a consumptive will consume after a week's residence in that appetizing atmosphere is a subject of daily and increasing wonder. I have known delicate ladies and fragile school-girls, to whom all food at home was distasteful and eating a pure matter of duty, average a gain of a pound per day for the round trip. This is no exaggeration, as some who will read these lines know. The spruce, hemlock, balsam, and pine, which largely compose this wilderness, yield upon the air, and especially at night, all their curative qualities. Many a night have I laid down upon my bed of balsam-boughs and been lulled to sleep by the murmur of waters and the low sighing melody of the pines, while the air was laden with the mingled perfume of cedar, of balsam and the water-lily. Not a few, far advanced in that dread disease, consumption, have found in this wilderness renewal of life and health. I recall a young man, the son of wealthy parents in New York, who lay dying in that great city, attended as he was by the best skill that money could secure. A friend calling upon him one day chanced to speak of the Adirondacks, and that many had found help from a trip to their region. From that moment he pined for the woods. He insisted on what his family called "his insane idea," that the mountain air and the aroma of the forest would cure him. It was his daily request and entreaty that he might go. At last his parents consented, the more readily because the physicians assured them that their son's recovery was impossible, and his death a mere matter of time. They started with him for the north in search of life. When he arrived at the point where he was to meet his guide he was too reduced to walk. The guide seeing his condition refused to take him into the woods, fearing, as he plainly expressed it, that he would "die on his hands." At last another guide was prevailed upon to serve him, not so much for the money, as he afterwards told me, but because he pitied the young man, and felt that "one so near death as he was should be gratified even in his whims."

The boat was half filled with cedar, pine, and balsam boughs, and the young man, carried in the arms of his guide from the house, was laid at full length upon them. The camp utensils were put at one end, the guide seated himself at the other, and the little boat passed with the living and the dying down the lake, and was lost to the group watching them amid the islands to the south. This was in early June. The first week the guide carried the young man on his back over all the portages, lifting him in and out of the boat as he might a child. But the healing properties of the balsam and pine, which were his bed by day and night, began to exert their power. Awake or asleep, he inhaled their fragrance. Their pungent and healing odors penetrated his diseased and irritated lungs. The second day out his cough was less sharp and painful. At the end of the first week he could walk by leaning on the paddle. The second week he needed no support. The third week the cough ceased entirely. From that time he improved with wonderful rapidity.

* * *

Guides

This is the most important of all considerations to one about to visit the wilderness. An ignorant, lazy, low-bred guide is a nuisance in camp and useless everywhere else. A skilful, active, well-mannered guide, on the other hand, is a joy and consolation, a source of constant pleasure to the whole party. With an ignorant guide you will starve; with a lazy one you will lose your temper; with a low-bred fellow you can have no comfort. Fortunate in the selection of your guide, you will be fortunate in everything you undertake clean through the trip. A good guide, like a good wife, is indispensable to one's success, pleasure, and peace. If I were to classify such guides as are nuisances, I should place at the head of the list the "witty guide." He is forever *talking*. He inundates the camp with gab. If you chance to have company, he is continually thrusting himself impertinently forward. He is possessed from head to foot with the idea that he is *smart*. He can never open his mouth unless it is to air his opinions or perpetrate some stale joke. He is always vulgar, not seldom profane. Avoid him as you would the plague.

Next in order comes the "talkative guide." The old Indian maxim, "Much talk, no hunt," I have found literally verified. A true hunter talks little. The habit of his skill is silence. In camp or afloat he is low-voiced and reticent. I have met but one exception to this rule. I will not name him, lest it give pain. He is a good hunter and a capital guide, in spite of his evil tendency to gab. This tendency is vicious in many ways. It is closely allied with that other vice,—*bragging*. Such a guide in a large party is apt to breed dispute and difference. He is very liable to give the gentleman who employs him the impression that others in the party are striving to "get ahead of him." Moreover, he is always interrupting you when you do not want to be interrupted. Silence, which is a luxury found only in the wilderness, flees at his approach. Beware of the talkative guide.

The next in order, and the last I shall mention, is the "lazy guide." Such a guide is the most vexatious creature you can have around. Nothing short of actual experience with one can give you an adequate impression. Now, a guide's duties, while not absolutely laborious, are nevertheless multiform. To discharge them well, a man should have a brisk, cheerful temperament and a certain pride in his calling. He should be quick, inventive, and energetic. With these qualities even ordinarily developed, a man makes a good guide; without them he is intolerable. A lazy guide is usually in appearance fleshy, lymphatic, dirty, and often well advanced in years. As a rule, avoid an old guide as you would an old horse. His few years' extra experience, compared to a younger man, cannot make good the decline of his powers and the loss of his ambition. A young, active fellow of thirty, with his reputation to make, is worth two who are fifty and egotistical. The worst sight I ever saw in the woods, the exhibition which stirred me most, was the spectacle of a fat, lazy lout of a guide lying on his stomach, reading a dime novel, while the gentleman who hired him was building "smudges." If he had been my guide, I would have smudged him! The "witty," "talkative," and "lazy guide" are the three hindrances to a party's happiness. If you find yourself or party burdened with either species, admonish kindly but firmly; and if this mild application will not suffice, turn him mercilessly adrift, and post him *by name* on your way out, at every camp and hotel, as an imposition and a pest. Make an example of one or two, and the rest would take the hint. Every respectable and worthy guide will thank you for it, and your conscience will have peace as over a duty fulfilled.

For the most part the "independent guides" are models of skill, energy, and faithfulness. I say "independent," to distinguish the class so called from another class yclept "hotel guides." The difference between the two classes is this: the "hotel guides" are paid so much per month by the hotel-keepers, and by them furnished to their boarders and such as come unprovided. This system is faulty in many respects. The "hotel guide" is not responsible to the party for its success, and therefore is not quickened to make his best endeavor. He has no reputation to make, as has the independent guide, for his service is secured to him for the season, by virtue of his connection with the hotel. Furthermore, the "hotel guide" is often unemployed for weeks if the season is dull; and, hanging around a frontier hotel in daily proximity to the bar, is very liable to beget that greatest of all vices in a guide,—*drunkenness*. If, on the other hand, the season is a crowded one, the proprietor finds it difficult to secure guides enough for his guests, and so must needs content himself with men totally unfit for the service. Thus it often happens that a party taking their guides at the hands of the landlord finds, when too late, that out of half a dozen guides, only one is capable, while the others are mere makeshifts, the good guide being sent along as a teacher and "boss" of the raw hands. I do not say that there are no good guides among those known as hotel guides, for there are; but as a *class* they are far inferior in character, skill, and habits to the others.

The independent guides, so called, are, as a whole, a capable and noble class of men. They know their calling thoroughly, and can be relied on. They have no other indorsement than such as the parties to which they act as guides give them; and as their chances of subsequent service depend upon their present success, they are stimulated to the utmost to excel. Between these and the hotel guides there exists a rivalry, and I might employ a stronger term. The independent guide feels, and is not slow to assert, his superiority. He is justified in doing it. The system of hotel guiding is wrong in theory and pernicious in practice. Every guide should be immediately responsible to the party hiring him. His chances of future employment should depend upon his present success. This is the only natural, simple, and equitable method. It is beneficial to both parties. The sportsman is well served; and the guide, if he is faithful, secures constant employment from season to season. Many of the best guides are engaged a year in advance.

I cannot let this opportunity pass unimproved of testifying to the capacity, skill, and faithfulness of a great majority of the guides through the Adirondack region. With many I am personally acquainted, and rejoice to number them among my friends. I have seen them under every circumstance of exposure and trial, of feasting and hunger, of health and sickness, and a more honest, cheerful, and patient class of men cannot be found the world over. Born and bred, as many of them were, in this wilderness, skilled in all the lore of woodcraft, handy with the rod, superb at the paddle, modest in demeanor and speech, honest to a proverb, they deserve and receive the admiration of all who make their acquaintance. Bronzed and hardy, fearless of danger, eager to please, uncontaminated with the vicious habits of civilized life, they are not unworthy of the magnificent surroundings amid which they dwell. Among them an oath is never heard, unless in moments of intense excitement. Vulgarity of speech is absolutely unknown, and theft a matter of horror and surprise. Measured by our social and intellectual facilities, their lot is lowly and uninviting, and yet to them there is a charm and fascination in it. Under the base of these overhanging mountains they were born. Upon the waters of these secluded lakes they have sported from earliest boyhood. The wilderness has unfolded to them its mysteries, and made them wise with a wisdom nowhere written in books. This wilderness is their home. Here they were born, here have they lived, and here it is that they expect to die. Their graves will be made under the pines where in childhood they played, and the sounds of wind and wave which lulled them to sleep when boys will swell the selfsame cadences in requiem over their graves. When they have passed away, tradition will prolong their virtues and their fame.

Adventures in the Wilderness (1869)

FREDERICK LAW OLMSTED

Central Park is America's most visited park—partly because it is in the middle of our biggest city, and partly because it is so wonderfully designed to welcome diverse uses. Frederick Law Olmsted (1822–1903), working with the architect Calvert Vaux, won the competition in the 1850s to design the park, and for the next decades defended his vision, then fairly unique, of a park designed for the common man. He and his associates went on to design such a huge number and variety of other parks and greenswards—from the U.S. Capitol Grounds to the Stanford campus, from Boston's Emerald Necklace to the grounds of Chicago's titanic Columbian Exposition—that he can fairly be said to have had as much impact on how we experience the natural world as the creators of the great national parks. He is also among the first exponents of what becomes a persistent theme: that "the environment" isn't confined to rural America, but needs to be a part of city life as well.

from *A Review of Recent Changes, and Changes Which Have Been Projected, in the Plans of the Central Park*

As the city grows larger, projects for the public benefit multiply, land becomes more valuable, and the Park more and more really central, applications for the use of ground upon it for various more or less plausible purposes, are likely to become increasingly frequent and increasingly urgent, and there will thus be a strong tendency to its conversion into a great, perpetual metropolitan Fair Ground, in the plan and administration of which no general purpose need be recognized, other than to offer, for the recreation of those who may visit it, a desultory collocation of miscellaneous entertainments, tangled together by a series of crooked roads and walks, and richly decorated with flowers and trees, fountains and statuary.

THE ONLY SOLID GROUND OF RESISTANCE TO DANGERS OF THIS CLASS WILL BE FOUND TO REST IN THE CONVICTION THAT THE PARK THROUGHOUT IS A SINGLE WORK OF ART, AND AS SUCH, SUBJECT TO THE PRIMARY LAW OF EVERY WORK OF ART, NAMELY, THAT IT SHALL BE FRAMED UPON A SINGLE, NOBLE MOTIVE, TO WHICH THE DESIGN OF ALL ITS PARTS, IN SOME MORE OR LESS SUBTLE WAY, SHALL BE CONFLUENT AND HELPFUL.

To find such a general motive of design for the Central Park it will be necessary to go back to the beginning and ask, for what worthy purpose could the city be required to take out and keep excluded from the field of ordinary urban improvements, a body of land in what was looked forward to as its very centre, so large as that assigned for the Park? For what such object of great prospective importance would a smaller body of land not have been adequate?

To these questions a sufficient answer can, we believe, be found in the expectation that the whole of the island of New York, would, but for such a reservation, before many years be occupied by buildings and paved streets; that millions upon millions of men were to live their lives upon this island, millions more to go out from it, or its immediate densely populated suburbs, only occasionally and at long intervals, and that all its inhabitants would assuredly suffer, in greater or less degree, according to their occupations and the degree of their confinement to it, from influences engendered by these conditions.

The narrow reservations previously made offered no relief from them, because they would soon be dominated by surrounding buildings, and because the noise, bustle, confinement and noxious qualities of the air of the streets would extend over them without important mitigation.

Provisions for the improvement of the ground, however, pointed to something more than mere exemption from urban conditions, namely, to the formation of an opposite class of conditions; conditions remedial of the influences of urban conditions.

Two classes of improvements were to be planned for this purpose: one directed to secure pure and wholesome air, to act through the lungs; the other to secure an antithesis of objects of vision to those of the streets and houses which should act remedially, by impressions on the mind and suggestions to the imagination.

The latter only require our present attention, and the first question with reference to them is: What class of objects are best adapted to the purpose?

Experience would lead most men to answer that they are chiefly such as give the characteristic charm to gardens, pleasure grounds, and rural landscapes. But some consideration may be required to determine by what mode of selection from among these, and by what general principle of arrangement, the highest practicable degree of the desired effect is to be attained.

It sometimes occurs that certain species of trees grow naturally, under conditions favoring such a result, in forms of extraordinary symmetry, their heads each having the outline of a haycock set upon a straight, perpendicular post. Occasionally several such trees may be found in nature growing together. Any number of objects of that character would have but limited value, if any, for the purpose of the Park, because it is a character more nearly compatible in a tree than any other with the convenience of men when living compactly in streets and houses. Trees of that form might be, and, in fact, sometimes are, grown along the streets of the city between rows of houses.

A series of rose bushes, grown in pots, trained to single stems, sustained by stakes, would have even less value. Trim beds of flowers, such as might be set on a drawing-room table, or in the fore-court of a city dwelling, still less.

A cluster of hornbeams and hemlocks, the trunks of some twisting over a crannied rock, the face of the rock brightened by lichens, and half veiled by tresses of vines growing over it from the rear, and its base lost in a tangle of ground pine, mosses and ferns, would be of considerable value, partly because of the greater difficulty of reconciling the presence of such an assemblage of natural objects with the requirements of convenience in the streets, but mainly because the intricate disposition of lights and shadows seen in the back parts of it would create a degree of obscurity not absolutely impenetrable, but sufficient to affect the imagination with a sense of mystery.

A broad stretch of slightly undulating meadow without defined edge, its turf lost in a haze of the shadows of scattered trees under the branches of which the eye would range, would be of even higher value, and if beyond this meadow occurred a depression of the surface, and the heads of other trees were seen again at an uncertain distance, the conditions would be most of all valuable for the purpose in view, first, because there would be positive assurance of a certain considerable extent of space free of all ordinary urban conditions, and, in the soft, smooth, tranquil surface of turf, of immunity from the bustling, violent and wearing influences which act upon the surface of the streets, and secondly, because the imagination, looking into the soft commingling lights and shadows and fading tints of color of the back ground would have encouragement to extend these purely rural conditions indefinitely.

Considering that large classes of rural objects and many types of natural scenery are not practicable to be introduced on the site of the Park—mountain, ocean, desert and prairie scenery for example—it will be found that the most valuable form that could have been prescribed is that which we have last indicated, and which may be distinguished from all others as pastoral. But the site of the Park having had a very heterogeneous surface, which was largely formed of solid rock, it was not desirable that the attempt should be made to reduce it all to the simplicity of pastoral scenery. What would the central motive of design require of the rest? Clearly that it should be given such a character as, while affording contrast and variety of scene, would, as much as possible, be confluent to the same end, namely, the constant suggestion to the imagination of an unlimited range of rural conditions.

The pleasing uncertainty and delicate, mysterious tone which *chiaro-oscuro* lends to the distance of an open pastoral landscape certainly cannot be paralleled in rugged ground, where the scope of vision is limited; but a similar influence on the mind, less only in degree, is experienced as we pass near the edge of a long stretch of natural woods, the outer trees disposed in irregular clusters, the lower branches sweeping the turf or bending over rocks, and underwood mingling at intervals with their foliage. Under such circumstances, although the eye nowhere penetrates far, an agreeable suggestion is conveyed to the imagination of freedom, and of interest beyond the objects which at any moment meet the eye. While, therefore, elements of scenery of this class (which may, for the present purpose, be distinguished as picturesque sylvan scenery) would both acquire and impart value from their contrast with the simpler elements of open pastoral landscapes, their effect, by tending to withdraw the mind to an indefinite distance from all objects associated with the streets and walls of the city, would be of the same character.

The question of localizing or adjusting these two classes of landscape elements to the various elements of the natural topography of the Park next occurs, the study of which must begin with the consideration that the Park is to be surrounded by an artificial wall, twice as high as the Great Wall of China, composed of urban buildings. Wherever this should appear across a meadow-view, the imagination would be checked abruptly at short range. Natural objects were thus required to be interposed, which, while excluding the buildings as much as possible from view, would leave an uncertainty as to the occupation of the space beyond, and establish a horizon line, composed, as much as possible, of verdure.

No one, looking into a closely-grown wood, can be certain that at a short distance back there are not glades or streams, or that a more open disposition of trees does not prevail.

A range of high woods, then, or of trees so disposed as to produce an effect, when seen from a short distance looking outwardly from the central parts of the Park, of a natural wood-side, must be regarded as more nearly indispensable to the purpose in view—that of relieving the visitor from the city—than any other available feature.

The site of the Park being naturally very broken and largely composed of masses of rock, the extent to which the meadow-like surfaces of pastoral scenery could be introduced in the plan was limited.

It was, then, first of all, required that such parts of the site as were available and necessary to the purpose should be assigned to the occupation of elements which would compose a wood-side, screening incongruous objects without the Park as much as possible from the view of observers within it.

Secondly, of the remaining ground, it was required to assign as much as was available to the occupation of elements which would compose tranquil, open, pastoral scenes.

Thirdly, it was required to assign all of the yet remaining ground to elements which would tend to form passages of scenery contrasting in depth of obscurity and picturesque character of detail with the softness and simplicity of the open landscapes.

There are other elements yet to be considered; but those thus classified and assigned to various quarters of the site alone contribute directly to the general characteristic purpose of the Park, and are, therefore, to be distinguished as its essential elements.

This should be clearly recognized. As neither glass, nor china, nor knives and forks, nor even table and chairs are the essential elements of a dinner, so neither bridges, towers, shelters, seats, refectories, statues, cages for birds and animals, nor even drives and walks are the essential elements of the Park. But as what is well designed to nourish the body and enliven the spirits through the stomach makes a dinner a dinner, so what is well designed to recreate the mind from urban oppressions through the eye, makes the Park the Park. All other elements of it are simply accessories of these essentials.

1872

J. STERLING MORTON

Before there was Earth Day, there was Arbor Day. J. Sterling Morton (1832–1902) was a prominent Nebraska pioneer who arrived there in 1854 and was appointed by President Buchanan to serve as secretary of the territory in 1858. He was interested in farming and forestry; with some combination of Muir's romanticism and Marsh's pragmatism, he felt that Nebraska needed more trees for many reasons, from natural beauty to natural windbreaks. His advocacy of a tree-planting day in the spring spread through American schools, and it soon became an official holiday in many states, celebrated on the last Friday in April: "the only anniversary in which humanity looks futureward instead of pastward."

About Trees

A tree is the perfection in strength, beauty, and usefulness of vegetable life. It stands majestic through the sun and storm of centuries. Resting in summer beneath its cooling shade, or sheltering besides its massive trunk from the chilling blast of winter, we are prone to forget the little seed whence it came. Trees are no respecters of persons. They grow as luxuriantly beside the cabin of the pioneer as against the palace of the millionaire. Trees are not proud. What is this tree? This great trunk, these stalwart limbs, these beautiful branches, these gracefully bending boughs, these gorgeous flowers, this flashing foliage and ripening fruit, purpling in the autumnal haze are only living materials organized in the laboratory of Nature's mysteries out of rain, sunlight, dews, and earth. On this spot, in this tree, a metamorphosis has so deftly taken place that it has failed to excite even the wonder of the majority of men.

Here, sixty years ago, a school boy planted an acorn. Spring came, then the germ of this oak began to attract the moisture of the soil. The shell of the acorn was then broken open by the internal growth of the embryo oak. It sent downward a rootlet to get soil and water, and upward it shot a stem to which the first pair of leaves was attached. These leaves are thick and fleshy. They constitute the greater bulk of the acorn. They are the first care-takers of the young oak. Once out of the earth and in the sunlight they expand, assume a finer texture, and begin their usefulness as nursing leaves, "folia nutrientia." They contain a store of starch elaborated in the parent oak which bore the acorn.

In tree infancy the nursing leaves take oxygen from the air, and through its influence the starch in the nursing leaves is transmuted into a tree baby-food, called dextrine, which is conveyed by the water absorbed during germination to the young rootlet and to the gemmule and also to the first aerial leaf. So fed, this leaf expands, and remains on the stem all summer. The nursing leaves die when the aerial leaves have taken their food away, and then the first stage of oakhood has begun. It has subterranean and superterranean organs, the former finding plant-food in the earth, and the latter gathering it in the air, the sunlight, and the storm. The rootlets in the dark depths of soil, the foliage in the sunlit air, begin now their common joint labor of constructing a majestic oak. Phosphates and all the delicacies of plant-food are brought in from the secret stores of the earth by the former, while foliage and twig and trunk are busy in catching sunbeams, air, and thunderstorms, to imprison in the annual increment of solid wood. There is no light coming from your wood, corncob, or coal fire which some vegetable Prometheus did not, in its days of growth, steal from the sun and secrete in the mysteries of a vegetable organism.

Combustion lets loose the captive rays and beams which growing plants imprisoned years, centuries, even eons ago, long before human life began its earthly career. The interdependence of animal and tree life is perennial. The intermission of a single season of a vegetable life and growth on the earth would exterminate our own and all the animal races. The trees, the forests are essential to man's health and life. When the last tree shall have been destroyed there will be no man left to mourn the improvidence and thoughtlessness of the forest-destroying race to which he belonged.

In all civilizations man has cut down and consumed, but seldom restored or replanted, the forests. In biblical times Palestine was lovely in the foliage of the palm, and the purpling grapes hung upon her hillsides and gleamed in her fertile valleys like gems in the diadems of her princes. But man, thoughtless of the future, careless of posterity, destroyed and replaced not; so, where the olive and the pomegranate and the vine once held up their luscious fruit for the sun to kiss, all is now infertility, desolation, desert, and solitude. The orient is dead to civilization, dead to commerce, dead to intellectual development. The orient died of treelessness.

From the grave of the eastern nations comes the tree monition to the western. The occident like the orient would expire with the destruction of all its forests and woodlands.

Twenty-five thousand acres of woodland are consumed by the railroads, the manufactories, and the homes of the United States every twenty-four hours. How many are planted? To avert treelessness, to improve the climatic conditions, for the sanitation and embellishment of home environments, for the love of the beautiful and useful combined in the music and majesty of a tree, as fancy and truth unite in an epic poem, Arbor Day was created. It has grown with the vigor and beneficence of a grand truth or a great tree. It faces the future. It is the only anniversary in which humanity looks futureward instead of pastward, in which there is a consensus of thought for those who are to come after us, instead of reflections concerning those who have gone before us. It is a practical anniversary. It is a beautiful anniversary. To the common schools of the country I confide its perpetuation and usefulness with the same abiding faith that I would commit the acorn to the earth, the tree to the soil, or transmit the light on the shore to far off ships on the waves beyond, knowing certainly that loveliness, comfort, and great contentment shall come to humanity everywhere because of its thoughtful and practical observance by all the civilized peoples of the earth.

Arbor Day Leaves (1893)

THEODORE ROOSEVELT

Theodore Roosevelt (1858–1919) is almost certainly the most *vigorous* president America has ever elected, and much of that energy was spent enjoying and protecting the nation's physical beauty. Born into a wealthy family, Roosevelt suffered from asthma. To build up his constitution he became a devoted fitness buff and outdoorsman, and the first of his many publications was a list of Adirondack birds. He spent time on a North Dakota ranch where he learned to ride, rope, and hunt (and where, as a deputy sheriff, he helped capture three outlaws who had stolen his riverboat). He served in posts as diverse as New York City police commissioner and Assistant Secretary of the Navy before organizing a volunteer cavalry regiment to fight in the Spanish-American War. His exploits at the head of these "Rough Riders" propelled him to the governorship of New York and then the vice-presidency, and he was climbing on New York's highest peak, Mt. Marcy, when a guide rushed up the trail with the word that McKinley, shot by an assassin, was dying. As president, he devoted much of his time to conservation, creating the beginning of the wildlife refuge system, establishing the Forest Service, and setting aside more land for national parks and preserves than all of his predecessors combined. Indeed, many spectacular spots across the West owe their protection to executive action from Roosevelt, who sometimes acted simply because someone wrote to him to describe a particularly striking place. Out of office in 1909, he undertook an African safari, collecting so many specimens that the Smithsonian was able to share his largesse with museums across the country; another expedition, this one to the Amazon, followed his unsuccessful bid for the presidency on the Progressive ticket in 1912. Like many of his other trips, it produced a book (one of 18 he would write), but it also left him weakened after a bout with malaria. He died in 1919 at the age of 60.

There's plenty to dislike about Roosevelt—he was bellicose and jingoistic. But he was also the most significant environmental president in American history, and the most engaging writer ever to sit in the Oval Office, as these two short letters (one to Frank Chapman, the great ornithologist who originated the tradition of Christmas Bird Counts, the other to the beloved writer John Burroughs) make clear. His Arizona speech splits the difference between the pragmatism of Pinchot, with its nod to irrigation, and the passion of Muir, with its hymn to the Grand Canyon.

To Frank Michler Chapman

Albany, February 16, 1899

My dear Mr. Chapman:

I need hardly say how heartily I sympathize with the purposes of the Audubon Society. I would like to see all harmless wild things, but especially all birds protected in every way. I do not understand how any man or woman who really loves nature can fail to try to exert all influence in support of such objects as those of the Audubon Society. Spring would not be spring without bird songs, any more than it would be spring without buds and flowers, and I only wish that besides protecting the songsters, the birds of the grove, the orchard, the garden and the meadow, we could also protect the birds of the sea shore and of the wilderness. The loon ought to be, and, under wise legislation, could be a feature of every Adirondack lake; ospreys, as everyone knows, can be made the tamest of the tame; and terns should be as plentiful along our shores as swallows around our barns. A tanager or a cardinal makes a point of glowing beauty in the green woods, and the cardinal among the white snows. When the bluebirds were so nearly destroyed by the severe winter a few seasons ago, the loss was like the loss of an old friend, or at least like the burning down of a familiar and dearly loved house. How immensely it would add to our forests if only the great logcock were still found among them! The destruction of the wild pigeon and the Carolina paraquet has meant a loss as severe as if the Catskills or the Palisades were taken away. When I hear of the destruction of a species I feel just as if all the works of some great writer had perished; as if we had lost all instead of only part of Polybius or Livy. *Very truly yours*

To John Burroughs

Washington, August 12, 1904

Dear Oom John:

I think that nothing is more amusing and interesting than the development of the changes made in wild beast character by the wholly unprecedented course of things in the Yellowstone Park. I have just had a letter from Buffalo Jones, describing his experiences in trying to get tin cans off the feet of the bears in the Yellowstone Park. There are lots of tin cans in the garbage heaps which the bears muss over, and it has now become fairly common for a bear to get his paw so caught in a tin can that he cannot get it off, and of course great pain and injury follow. Buffalo Jones was sent with another scout to capture, tie up and cure these bears. He roped two and got the can off of one, but the other tore himself loose, can and all, and escaped, owing, as Jones bitterly insists, to the failure of duty on the part of one of his brother scouts, whom he sneers at as "a foreigner." Think of the grizzly bear of the early Rocky Mountain hunters and explorers, and then think of the fact that part of the recognized duties of the scouts in the Yellowstone Park at this moment is to catch this same grizzly bear and remove tin cans from the bear's paws in the bear's interest!

The grounds of the White House are lovely now, and the most decorative birds in them are some redheaded woodpeckers.

Give my regards to Mrs. Burroughs. How I wish I could see you at Slabsides! But of course this summer there is no chance of that. *Always yours*

Speech at Grand Canyon, Arizona, May 6, 1903

Mr. Governor, and you, my Fellow-Citizens:

I am glad to be in Arizona to-day. From Arizona many gallant men came into the regiment which I had the honor to command. Arizona sent men who won glory on fought fields, and men to whom came a glorious and an honorable death fighting for the flag of their country. As long as I live it will be to me an inspiration to have served with Bucky O'Neill. I have met so many comrades whom I prize, for whom I feel respect and admiration and affection, that I shall not particularize among them except to say that there is none for whom I feel all of respect and admiration and affection more than for your Governor.

I have never been in Arizona before. It is one of the regions from which I expect most development through the wise action of the National Congress in passing the irrigation act. The first and biggest experiment now in view under that act is the one that we are trying in Arizona. I look forward to the effects of irrigation partly as applied by and through the government, still more as applied by individuals, and especially by associations of individuals, profiting by the example of the government, and possibly by help from it—I look forward to the effects of irrigation as being of greater consequence to all this region of country in the next fifty years than any other material movement whatsoever.

In the Grand Canyon, Arizona has a natural wonder which, so far as I know, is in kind absolutely unparalleled throughout the rest of the world. I want to ask you to do one thing in connection with it in your own interest and in the interest of the country—to keep this great wonder of nature as it now is. I was delighted to learn of the wisdom of the Santa Fe railroad people in deciding not to build their hotel on the brink of the canyon. I hope you will not have a building of any kind, not a summer cottage, a hotel, or anything else, to mar the wonderful grandeur, the sublimity, the great loneliness and beauty of the canyon.

Leave it as it is. You can not improve on it. The ages have been at work on it, and man can only mar it. What you can do is to keep it for your children, your children's children, and for all who come after you, as one of the great sights which every American if he can travel at all should see. We have gotten past the stage, my fellow-citizens, when we are to be pardoned if we treat any part of our country as something to be skinned for two or three years for the use of the present generation, whether it is the forest, the water, the scenery. Whatever it is, handle it so that your children's children will get the benefit of it. If you deal with irrigation, apply it under circumstances that will make it of benefit, not to the speculator who hopes to get profit out of it for two or three years, but handle it so that it will be of use to the home-maker, to the man who comes to live here, and to have his children stay after him. Keep the forests in the same way. Preserve the forests by use; preserve them for the ranchman and the stockman, for the people of the Territory, for the people of the region round about. Preserve them for that use, but use them so that they will not be squandered, that they will not be wasted, so that they will be of benefit to the Arizona of 1953 as well as the Arizona of 1903.

To the Indians here I want to say a word of welcome. In my regiment I had a good many Indians. They were good enough to fight and to die, and they are good enough to have me treat them exactly as squarely as any white man. There are many problems in connection with them. We must save them from corruption and from brutality; and I regret to say that at times we must save them from unregulated Eastern philanthropy. All I ask is a square deal for every man. Give him a fair chance. Do not let him wrong any one, and do not let him be wronged.

I believe in you. I am glad to see you. I wish you well with all my heart, and I know that your future will justify all the hopes we have.

MARY AUSTIN

The places where America first fell in love with "nature"—the Hudson River Valley, Niagara Falls—were in the moist East. Even when the West came into view, our first affections were for relatively lush locales, like Yellowstone and the Yosemite Valley. Mary Austin (1868–1934) was among the first to write with careful attention about the desert, and to do so in a way that managed to capture its beauty without indulging in undue sentimentality (in a sense, she's the ancestor of Ed Abbey, another unblinking desert rat). In the 1880s, after graduating from college, Austin homesteaded a piece of California land with her mother and her brother. Her life was not easy—a luckless marriage, a mentally retarded daughter, a brush with breast cancer—but the reception of *The Land of Little Rain* (1903) was strong enough to let her write steadily for the rest of her life, usually on Southwestern themes. She was an unflinching observer, as in her description of a pair of meadowlarks caught by a early heat wave and trying to keep their egg shaded: "at midday they stood, or drooped above it, half fainting with pitifully parted bills, between their treasure and the sun." Austin was tough, but also deeply human, and eventually she rigged a canvas screen to cast a shadow on the nest.

The Scavengers

Fifty-seven buzzards, one on each of fifty-seven fence posts at the rancho El Tejon, on a mirage-breeding September morning, sat solemnly while the white tilted travelers' vans lumbered down the Canada de los Uvas. After three hours they had only clapped their wings, or exchanged posts. The season's end in the vast dim valley of the San Joaquin is palpitatingly hot, and the air breathes like cotton wool. Through it all the buzzards sit on the fences and low hummocks, with wings spread fanwise for air. There is no end to them, and they smell to heaven. Their heads droop, and all their communication is a rare, horrid croak.

The increase of wild creatures is in proportion to the things they feed upon: the more carrion the more buzzards. The end of the third successive dry year bred them beyond belief. The first year quail mated sparingly; the second year the wild oats matured no seed; the third, cattle died in their tracks with their heads towards the stopped watercourses. And that year the scavengers were as black as the plague all across the mesa and up the treeless, tumbled hills. On clear days they betook themselves to the upper air, where they hung motionless for hours. That year there were vultures among them, distinguished by the white patches under the wings. All their offensiveness notwithstanding, they have a stately flight. They must also have what pass for good qualities among themselves, for they are social, not to say clannish.

It is a very squalid tragedy,—that of the dying brutes and the scavenger birds. Death by starvation is slow. The heavy-headed, rack-boned cattle totter in the fruitless trails; they stand for long, patient intervals; they lie down and do not rise. There is fear in their eyes when they are first stricken, but afterward only intolerable weariness. I suppose the dumb creatures know nearly as much of death as do their betters, who have only the more imagination. Their even-breathing submission after the first agony is their tribute to its inevitableness. It needs a nice discrimination to say which of the basket-ribbed cattle is likest to afford the next meal, but the scavengers make few mistakes. One stoops to the quarry and the flock follows.

Cattle once down may be days in dying. They stretch out their necks along the ground, and roll up their slow eyes at longer intervals. The buzzards have all the time, and no beak is dropped or talon struck until the breath is wholly passed. It is doubtless the economy of nature to have the scavengers by to clean up the carrion, but a wolf at the throat would be a shorter agony than the long stalking and sometime perchings of these loathsome watchers. Suppose now it were a man in this long-drawn, hungrily spied upon distress! When Timmie O'Shea was lost on Armogossa Flats for three days without water, Long Tom

Basset found him, not by any trail, but by making straight away for the points where he saw buzzards stooping. He could hear the beat of their wings, Tom said, and trod on their shadows, but O'Shea was past recalling what he thought about things after the second day. My friend Ewan told me, among other things, when he came back from San Juan Hill, that not all the carnage of battle turned his bowels as the sight of slant black wings rising flockwise before the burial squad.

There are three kinds of noises buzzards make,—it is impossible to call them notes,—raucous and elemental. There is a short croak of alarm, and the same syllable in a modified tone to serve all the purposes of ordinary conversation. The old birds make a kind of throaty chuckling to their young, but if they have any love song I have not heard it. The young yawp in the nest a little, with more breath than noise. It is seldom one finds a buzzard's nest, seldom that grown-ups find a nest of any sort; it is only children to whom these things happen by right. But by making a business of it one may come upon them in wide, quiet cañons, or on the lookouts of lonely, table-topped mountains, three or four together, in the tops of stubby trees or on rotten cliffs well open to the sky.

It is probable that the buzzard is gregarious, but it seems unlikely from the small number of young noted at any time that every female incubates each year. The young birds are easily distinguished by their size when feeding, and high up in air by the worn primaries of the older birds. It is when the young go out of the nest on their first foraging that the parents, full of a crass and simple pride, make their indescribable chucklings of gobbling, gluttonous delight. The little ones would be amusing as they tug and tussle, if one could forget what it is they feed upon.

One never comes any nearer to the vulture's nest or nestlings than hearsay. They keep to the southerly Sierras, and are bold enough, it seems, to do killing on their own account when no carrion is at hand. They dog the shepherd from camp to camp, the hunter home from the hill, and will even carry away offal from under his hand.

The vulture merits respect for his bigness and for his bandit airs, but he is a sombre bird, with none of the buzzard's frank satisfaction in his offensiveness.

The least objectionable of the inland scavengers is the raven, frequenter of the desert ranges, the same called locally "carrion crow." He is handsomer and has such an air. He is nice in his habits and is said to have likable traits. A tame one in a Shoshone camp was the butt of much sport and enjoyed it. He could all but talk and was another with the children, but an arrant thief. The raven will eat most things that come his way,—eggs and young of ground-nesting birds, seeds even, lizards and grasshoppers, which he catches cleverly; and whatever he is about, let a coyote trot never so softly by, the raven flaps up and after; for whatever the coyote can pull down or nose out is meat also for the carrion crow.

And never a coyote comes out of his lair for killing, in the country of the carrion crows, but looks up first to see where they may be gathering. It is a sufficient occupation for a windy morning, on the lineless, level mesa, to watch the pair of them eying each other furtively, with a tolerable assumption of unconcern, but no doubt with a certain amount of good understanding about it. Once at Red Rock, in a year of green pasture, which is a bad time for the scavengers, we saw two buzzards, five ravens, and a coyote feeding on the same carrion, and only the coyote seemed ashamed of the company.

Probably we never fully credit the interdependence of wild creatures, and their cognizance of the affairs of their own kind. When the five coyotes that range the Tejon from Pasteria to Tunawai planned a relay race to bring down an antelope strayed from the band, beside myself to watch, an eagle swung down from Mt. Pinos, buzzards materialized out of invisible ether, and hawks came trooping like small boys to a street fight. Rabbits sat up in the chaparral and cocked their ears, feeling themselves quite safe for the once as the hunt swung near them. Nothing happens in the deep wood that the blue jays are not all agog to tell. The hawk follows the badger, the coyote the carrion crow, and from their aerial stations the buzzards watch each other. What would be worth knowing is how much of their neighbor's affairs the new generations learn for themselves, and how much they are taught of their elders.

So wide is the range of the scavengers that it is never safe to say, eyewitness to the contrary, that there are few or many in such a place.

Where the carrion is, there will the buzzards be gathered together, and in three days' journey you will not sight another one. The way up from Mojave to Red Butte is all desertness, affording no pasture and scarcely a rill of water. In a year of little rain in the south, flocks and herds were driven to the number of thousands along this road to the perennial pastures of the high ranges. It is a long, slow trail, ankle deep in bitter dust that gets up in the slow wind and moves along the backs of the crawling cattle. In the worst of times one in three will pine and fall out by the way. In the defiles of Red Rock, the sheep piled up a stinking lane; it was the sun smiting by day. To these shambles came buzzards, vultures, and coyotes from all the country round, so that on the Tejon, the Ceriso, and the Little Antelope there were not scavengers enough to keep the country clean. All that summer the dead mummified in the open or dropped slowly back to earth in the quagmires of the bitter springs. Meanwhile from Red Rock to Coyote Holes, and from Coyote Holes to Haiwai the scavengers gorged and gorged.

The coyote is not a scavenger by choice, preferring his own kill, but being on the whole a lazy dog, is apt to fall into carrion eating because it is easier. The red fox and bobcat, a little pressed by hunger, will eat of any other animal's kill, but will not ordinarily touch what dies of itself, and are exceedingly shy of food that has been manhandled.

Very clean and handsome, quite belying his relationship in appearance, is Clark's crow, that scavenger and plunderer of mountain camps. It is permissible to call him by his common name, "Camp Robber:" he has earned it. Not content with refuse, he pecks open meal sacks, filches whole potatoes, is a gormand for bacon, drills holes in packing cases, and is daunted by nothing short of tin. All the while he does not neglect to vituperate the chipmunks and sparrows that whisk off crumbs of comfort from under the camper's feet. The Camp Robber's gray coat, black and white barred wings, and slender bill, with certain tricks of perching, accuse him of attempts to pass himself off among woodpeckers; but his behavior is all crow. He frequents the higher pine belts, and has a noisy strident call like a jay's, and how clean he and the frisk-tailed chipmunks keep the camp! No crumb or paring or bit of eggshell goes amiss.

High as the camp may be, so it is not above timber-line, it is not too high for the coyote, the bobcat, or the wolf. It is the complaint of the ordinary camper that the woods are too still, depleted of wild life. But what dead body of wild thing, or neglected game untouched by its kind, do you find? And put out offal away from camp over night, and look next day at the foot tracks where it lay.

Man is a great blunderer going about in the woods, and there is no other except the bear makes so much noise. Being so well warned beforehand, it is a very stupid animal, or a very bold one, that cannot keep safely hid. The cunningest hunter is hunted in turn, and what he leaves of his kill is meat for some other. That is the economy of nature, but with it all there is not sufficient account taken of the works of man. There is no scavenger that eats tin cans, and no wild thing leaves a like disfigurement on the forest floor.

The Land of Little Rain (1903)

NATHANIEL SOUTHGATE SHALER

Perhaps the most prominent American geologist of the late 19th century, Harvard professor and sometime poet Nathaniel Southgate Shaler (1841–1906) shows himself in this book from late in his career to be an able disciple of George Perkins Marsh and one of the early voices raised against the depletion of natural resources. It's important to understand that we could, in fact, have seen some of our troubles coming. (A few years before, for instance, the Nobel-winning Swedish chemist Svante Arrhenius had predicted and accurately calculated the scale of global warming from fossil fuel combustion.) But such voices were little heeded at the time—the surge of American growth and expansion was too intoxicating.

from **Man and the Earth**

The situation of man with reference to the material resources of the earth deserves more attention than has been given to it. Here and there students of the mineral deposits of certain countries, especially those of Great Britain, have computed the amounts of coal and iron within limited fields and estimated the probable time when those stores would be exhausted; but a general account of the tax that civilization makes on the fields it occupies and a forecast as to their endurance of the present and prospective demand on them is lacking. It is evident that such a fore-looking should be one of the first results of high culture. We may be sure that those who look back upon us and our deeds from the centuries to come will remark upon the manner in which we use our heritage, and theirs, as we are now doing, in the spendthrift's way, with no care for those to come. They will date the end of barbarism from the time when the generations began to feel that they rightfully had no more than a life estate in this sphere, with no right to squander the inheritance of their kind.

To see our position with reference to the resources of the earth it is well to begin by noting the fact that the lower animals, and primitive men as well, make no drain on its stores. They do not lessen the amount of soil or take from the minerals of the under-earth: in a small way they enrich it by their simple lives, for their forms are contributed to that store of chemically organized matter which serves the needs of those that come after them. With the first step upward, however, and ever in increasing measure as he mounts toward civilization, man becomes a spoiler. As soon as he attains the grade of a hunter he begins to disturb the balance of the life about him and in time he attains such success in the art that he exterminates the larger, and therefore the rarer, beasts. Thus when our *genus homo* comes into view, elephants of various species existed in considerable numbers in all the continents except Australia. Its first large accomplishment appears to have consisted in the extermination of these noble beasts in the Americas, in Europe, and in northern Asia. There is no historic record of this work, but the disappearance of the elephants can be well explained only by the supposition that they went down before the assault of vigorous men, as has been the case with many other species of large land animals.

So long as men remained in the estate of the hunter the damage they could do was limited to the destruction of the larger beasts and the birds, such as the moa, that could not fly. Prolific species, even of considerable size, such as the bisons, if they were nimble and combative, seem to have been able to hold the field against the attacks of primitive hunters. While in this station the tribes of men are never very numerous, for their wars, famines, and sorceries prevent their increase, which, under the most favorable conditions, is never rapid among savages. As soon, however, as stone implements begin to be replaced by those of metal, man begins to draw upon the limited stores of the under-earth, and with each advance in his arts the demand becomes the greater. In the first centuries of the iron age the requisition was much less than a pound each year for each person. Four centuries ago it probably did not exceed, even in the most civilized countries, ten pounds per capita each year. It appears to have been at something like that rate when the English colonies were founded in North America. At the present time, in the United States, it is at the average rate of about five hundred pounds per annum for every man, woman, and child in the land, and the demand is increasing with startling rapidity. It seems eminently probable that before the end of the present century, unless checked by a great advancement of cost, it will require a ton of iron each year to meet the progressive desires of this insatiable man.

Of the other long-used metals and other earth resources the increase in consumption is, with slight exceptions, as notable as in the case of iron; within a generation, mainly because of the use of the metal in electrical work, the need of copper has augmented even more rapidly than that of iron and the gain in the requirements is going on with exceeding speed. So, too, the demand for the other base metals long in use, zinc and tin, has been in nowise lessened by the more extended use of iron and copper; they are ever finding new places in the arts and a larger demand in the markets. As regards the so-called noble metals, silver and gold, the demand from the beginning has not been distinctly related to use, but to unlimited desire. Men have always wrested all they could of them from the earth or from each other, with little reference to the profit they won in the process. There has been of late something like a halt in the production of silver, except when it comes as a by-product, because it has generally been abandoned as a standard of value; but taken together the production of these precious metals has in modern times increased about as rapidly as that of iron. It is likely, however, that they will in time become of no economic importance.

As regards the earth's resources in the way of fuel—coal, oil, wood, petroleum, and peat—the history of the modern increase in demand is as evident and menacing as in the case of the metals. When the American English colonies were founded, coal had hardly begun to come into use in any country. It is doubtful if the output of the world amounted at that time to one hundred thousand tons, possibly to not more per capita of the folk in Europe than a pound, or about the same as iron at that late period in the so-called "iron age." At the present time the total production of Europe and North America amounts to an average of at least two tons per each unit of the population, and the increase goes on at a high ratio. Petroleum, practically unknown to the Occidental peoples until about half a century ago, has, with wonderful rapidity, become a necessity to all civilized and many barbaric peoples; the increase in the rate of consumption is swifter than that of any other earth product. Timber and peat, the primitive resources for light and heat, are the only earth products for which the demand has not greatly extended in modern times; it appears, indeed, to have shrunk in most civilized countries with the cheapening and diffusion of coal, due to the lessened cost of mining and of transportation.

The increase in the tax of the earth's resources is seen also in the very great number of substances which were unknown to the ancients, or disregarded by them, but which now find a large place in our arts. A comparison of the demands of three centuries ago with those of our day is interesting. In, say, 1600, when men were very much alive to the question of what they could gain, there were only about twenty substances, other than precious stones, for which they looked to the underground realm. Clays for the potter and bricklayer, whetstones and millstones, iron, copper, tin, gold, silver, lead, sand for glass, mica, coal, peat, salt, and mercury make up all the important elements of this list. At the present time, we more or less seriously depend on what is below the ground for several hundred substances or their immediate derivatives which find a place in our arts. Petroleum alone has afforded the basis of far more earth products than were in use at the time of the discovery of America. It gives us a large number of dyes and a host of medicines. It is indeed likely that the products immediately derived from the mineral oils exceed all those obtained from the earth at the time of Columbus—and each year brings additions to the demand.

The advance in needs of dynamic power, in modern times, has been even greater than in ponderable things. Even two centuries ago, the energy available for man's work was mainly limited to that obtained from domesticated animals. The wind served in a small measure through the sails of ships and of windmills, and there were water-wheels, but the average amount of energy at his service was certainly less than one horse-power per capita. At the present time it may safely be reckoned that in the United States and in European countries on a similar economic basis, the average amount is at least ten times as great, and the

present rate of increase quite as high as in the case of mineral resources. It is true, that, so far as water is concerned, this increase in the
demand for energy in the arts does not come as a tax on the store of the
under-earth, as it is obtained through solar energy which would otherwise be dissipated in space. But the use of falling water as a source of
power, though rapidly increasing, does not keep pace with that of coal,
which is obtained from a store which is in process of rapid exhaustion,
one that cannot be relied on for more than a few hundred years to
come:—if the world keeps the rate of consumption with which it enters
the twentieth century it will be exhausted before the twenty-third.

Man and the Earth (1905)

JOHN BURROUGHS

Of all the writers gathered in this book, none came close to being as popular in their day as John Burroughs (1837–1921), the man who reintroduced reading America to the natural world at the turn of the century. For several decades he may have been the most popular writer of any kind in the country—when he and President Theodore Roosevelt traveled across the U.S. by train in 1903, observers said the writer often drew more admirers at their whistle stops than the politician, soon to be returned to the White House. Burroughs was born in the sidehill farm country of the picturesque Catskills, where most of his best essays would be set. In 1863 he went to work in Washington as a clerk at the Currency Bureau, and during his decade in the capital he formed a close friendship with Walt Whitman, whose work he would herald throughout his life. He published his first collection of nature essays, *Wake-Robin*, in 1871; its success eventually let him move home to the Catskills, where he wrote many more of the charming pastoral pieces that earned him his following. They fit the tenor of their place—if John Muir was the craggy champion of the rugged West, John Burroughs is the lower-key bard of the lower-key, lower-elevation eastern mountains, the patron saint of the weekend cottage in the Berkshires. His gift for close observation and large meaning launched the nature essay as we know it, and his example launched a million people with knapsacks out into meadow and forest. Burroughs is not a sentimentalist, however— he was an indefatigable champion of both Whitman and Darwin, and his writing has slipped into undeserved obscurity in recent decades. Its quietness works quite powerfully in our over-amplified moment, his natural and fluent grace an implicit rebuke to an awful lot of more overheated prose.

The Art of Seeing Things

I

I do not purpose to attempt to tell my reader how to see things, but only to talk about the art of seeing things, as one might talk of any other art. One might discourse about the art of poetry, or of painting, or of oratory, without any hope of making one's readers or hearers poets or painters or orators.

The science of anything may be taught or acquired by study; the art of it comes by practice or inspiration. The art of seeing things is not something that may be conveyed in rules and precepts; it is a matter vital in the eye and ear, yea, in the mind and soul, of which these are the organs. I have as little hope of being able to tell the reader how to see things as I would have in trying to tell him how to fall in love or to enjoy his dinner. Either he does or he does not, and that is about all there is of it. Some people seem born with eyes in their heads, and others with buttons or painted marbles, and no amount of science can make the one equal to the other in the art of seeing things. The great mass of mankind are, in this respect, like the rank and file of an army: they fire vaguely in the direction of the enemy, and if they hit, it is more a matter of chance than of accurate aim. But here and there is the keen-eyed observer; he is the sharpshooter; his eye selects and discriminates, his purpose goes to the mark.

Even the successful angler seems born, and not made; he appears to know instinctively the ways of trout. The secret is, no doubt, love of the sport. Love sharpens the eye, the ear, the touch; it quickens the feet, it steadies the hand, it arms against the wet and the cold. What we love to do, that we do well. To know is not all; it is only half. To love is the other half. Wordsworth's poet was contented if he might enjoy the things which others understood. This is generally the attitude of the young and of the poetic nature. The man of science, on the other hand, is contented if he may understand the things that others enjoy: that is his enjoyment. Contemplation and absorption for the one; investigation and classification for the other. We probably all have, in varying degrees, one or the other of these ways of enjoying Nature: either the sympathetic and emotional enjoyment of her which the young and the artistic and the poetic temperament have, or the enjoyment through our knowing faculties afforded by natural science, or, it may be, the two combined, as they certainly were in such a man as Tyndall.

But nothing can take the place of love. Love is the measure of life: only so far as we love do we really live. The variety of our interests, the width of our sympathies, the susceptibilities of our hearts—if these do not measure our lives, what does? As the years go by, we are all of us more or less subject to two dangers, the danger of petrifaction and the danger of putrefaction; either that we shall become hard and callous, crusted over with customs and conventions till no new ray of light or of joy can reach us, or that we shall become lax and disorganized, losing our grip upon the real and vital sources of happiness and power. Now, there is no preservative and antiseptic, nothing that keeps one's heart young, like love, like sympathy, like giving one's self with enthusiasm to some worthy thing or cause.

If I were to name the three most precious resources of life, I should say books, friends, and nature; and the greatest of these, at least the most constant and always at hand, is nature. Nature we have always with us, an inexhaustible storehouse of that which moves the heart, appeals to the mind, and fires the imagination,—health to the body, a stimulus to the intellect, and joy to the soul. To the scientist Nature is a storehouse of facts, laws, processes; to the artist she is a storehouse of pictures; to the poet she is a storehouse of images, fancies, a source of inspiration; to the moralist she is a storehouse of precepts and parables; to all she may be a source of knowledge and joy.

II

There is nothing in which people differ more than in their powers of observation. Some are only half alive to what is going on around them. Others, again, are keenly alive: their intelligence, their powers of recognition, are in full force in eye and ear at all times. They see and hear everything, whether it directly concerns them or not. They never pass unseen a familiar face on the street; they are never oblivious of any interesting feature or sound or object in the earth or sky about them. Their power of attention is always on the alert, not by conscious effort, but by natural habit and disposition. Their perceptive faculties may be said to be always on duty. They turn to the outward world a more highly sensitized mind than other people. The things that pass before them are caught and individualized instantly. If they visit new countries, they see the characteristic features of the people and scenery at once. The impression is never blurred or confused. Their powers of observation suggest the sight and scent of wild animals; only, whereas it is fear that sharpens the one, it is love and curiosity that sharpens the other. The mother turkey with her brood sees the hawk when it is a mere speck against the sky; she is, in her solicitude for her young, thinking of hawks, and is on her guard against them. Fear makes keen her eye. The hunter does not see the hawk till his attention is thus called to it by the turkey, because his interests are not endangered; but he outsees the wild creatures of the plain and mountain,—the elk, the antelope, and the mountain-sheep,—he makes it his business to look for them, and his eyes carry farther than do theirs.

We may see coarsely and vaguely, as most people do, noting only masses and unusual appearances, or we may see finely and discriminatingly, taking in the minute and the specific. In a collection of stuffed birds, the other day, I observed that a wood thrush was mounted as in the act of song, its open beak pointing straight to the zenith. The taxidermist had not seen truly. The thrush sings with its beak but slightly elevated. Who has not seen a red squirrel or a gray squirrel running up and down the trunk of a tree? But probably very few have noticed that the position of the hind feet is the reverse in the one case from what it is in the other. In descending they are extended to the rear, the toe-nails hooking to the bark, checking and controlling the fall. In most pictures the feet are shown well drawn up under the body in both cases.

People who discourse pleasantly and accurately about the birds and flowers and external nature generally are not invariably good observers. In their walks do they see anything they did not come out to see? Is there any spontaneous or unpremeditated seeing? Do they make discoveries? Any bird or creature may be hunted down, any nest discovered, if you lay siege to it; but to find what you are not looking for, to catch the shy winks and gestures on every side, to see all the by-play going on around you, missing no significant note or movement, penetrating every screen with your eye-beams—that is to be an observer; that is to have "an eye practiced like a blind man's touch,"—a touch that can distinguish a white horse from a black,—a detective eye that reads the faintest signs. When Thoreau was at Cape Cod, he noticed that the horses there had a certain muscle in their hips inordinately developed by reason of the insecure footing in the ever-yielding sand. Thoreau's vision at times fitted things closely. During some great fête in Paris, the Empress Eugénie and Queen Victoria were both present. A reporter noticed that when the royal personages came to sit down, Eugénie looked behind her before doing so, to see that the chair was really there, but Victoria seated herself without the backward glance, knowing there must be a seat ready: there always had been, and there always would be, for her. The correspondent inferred that the incident showed the difference between born royalty and hastily made royalty. I wonder how many persons in that vast assembly made this observation; probably very few. It denoted a gift for seeing things.

If our powers of observation were quick and sure enough, no doubt we should see through most of the tricks of the sleight-of-hand man. He fools us because his hand is more dexterous than our eye. He captures our attention, and then commands us to see only what he wishes us to see.

In the field of natural history, things escape us because the actors are small, and the stage is very large and more or less veiled and obstructed. The movement is quick across a background that tends to conceal rather than expose it. In the printed page the white paper plays quite as important a part as the type and the ink; but the book of nature is on a different plan: the page rarely presents a contrast of black and white, or even black and brown, but only of similar tints, gray upon gray, green upon green, or drab upon brown.

By a close observer I do not mean a minute, cold-blooded specialist,—

> "a fingering slave,
> One who would peep and botanize
> Upon his mother's grave,"—

but a man who looks closely and steadily at nature, and notes the individual features of tree and rock and field, and allows no subtile flavor of the night or day, of the place and the season, to escape him. His senses are so delicate that in his evening walk he feels the warm and the cool streaks in the air, his nose detects the most fugitive odors, his ears the most furtive sounds. As he stands musing in the April twilight, he hears that fine, elusive stir and rustle made by the angleworms reaching out from their holes for leaves and grasses; he hears the whistling wings of the woodcock as it goes swiftly by him in the dusk; he hears the call of the kill-dee come down out of the March sky; he hears far above him in the early morning the squeaking cackle of the arriving blackbirds pushing north; he hears the soft, prolonged, lulling call of the little owl in the cedars in the early spring twilight; he hears at night the roar of the distant waterfall, and the rumble of the train miles across the country when the air is "hollow;" before a storm he notes how distant objects stand out and are brought near on those brilliant days that we call "weather-breeders." When the mercury is at zero or lower, he notes how the passing trains hiss and simmer as if the rails or wheels were red-hot. He reads the subtile signs of the weather. The stars at night forecast the coming day to him; the clouds at evening and at morning are a sign. He knows there is the wet-weather diathesis and the dry-weather diathesis, or, as Goethe said, water affirmative and water negative, and he interprets the symptoms accordingly. He is keenly alive to all outward impressions. When he descends from the hill in the autumn twilight, he notes the cooler air of the valley like a lake about him; he notes how, at other seasons, the cooler air at times settles down between the mountains like a vast body of water, as shown by the level line of the fog or the frost upon the trees.

The modern man looks at nature with an eye of sympathy and love where the earlier man looked with an eye of fear and superstition.

Hence he sees more closely and accurately; science has made his eye steady and clear. To a hasty traveler through the land, the farms and country homes all seem much alike, but to the people born and reared there, what a difference! They have read the fine print that escapes the hurried eye and that is so full of meaning. Every horizon line, every curve in hill or valley, every tree and rock and spring run, every turn in the road and vista in the landscape, has its special features and makes its own impression.

Scott wrote in his journal: "Nothing is so tiresome as walking through some beautiful scene with a minute philosopher, a botanist, or a pebble-gatherer, who is eternally calling your attention from the grand features of the natural picture to look at grasses and chuckie-stanes." No doubt Scott's large, generous way of looking at things kindles the imagination and touches the sentiments more than does this minute way of the specialist. The nature that Scott gives us is like the air and the water that all may absorb, while what the specialist gives us is more like some particular element or substance that only the few can appropriate. But Scott had his specialties, too, the specialties of the sportsman: he was the first to see the hare's eyes as she sat in her form, and he knew the ways of grouse and pheasants and trout. The ideal observer turns the enthusiasm of the sportsman into the channels of natural history, and brings home a finer game than ever fell to shot or bullet. He too has an eye for the fox and the rabbit and the migrating water-fowl, but he sees them with loving and not with murderous eyes.

III

So far as seeing things is an art, it is the art of keeping your eyes and ears open. The art of nature is all in the direction of concealment. The birds, the animals, all the wild creatures, for the most part try to elude your observation. The art of the bird is to hide her nest; the art of the game you are in quest of is to make itself invisible. The flower seeks to attract the bee and the moth by its color and perfume, because they are of service to it; but I presume it would hide from the excursionists and the picnickers if it could, because they extirpate it. Power of attention and a mind sensitive to outward objects, in these lies the secret of seeing things. Can you bring all your faculties to the front, like a house with many faces at the doors and windows; or do you live retired within yourself, shut up in your own meditations? The thinker puts all the powers of his mind in reflection: the observer puts all the powers of his mind in perception; every faculty is directed outward; the whole mind sees through the eye and hears through the ear. He has an objective turn of mind as opposed to a subjective. A person with the latter turn of mind sees little. If you are occupied with your own thoughts, you may go through a museum of curiosities and observe nothing.

Of course one's powers of observation may be cultivated as well as anything else. The senses of seeing and hearing may be quickened and trained as well as the sense of touch. Blind persons come to be marvelously acute in their powers of touch. Their feet find the path and keep it. They come to know the lay of the land through this sense, and recognize the roads and surfaces they have once traveled over. Helen Keller reads your speech by putting her hand upon your lips, and is thrilled by the music of an instrument through the same sense of touch. The perceptions of school-children should be trained as well as their powers of reflection and memory. A teacher in Connecticut, Miss Aiken,—whose work on mind-training I commend to all teachers,—has hit upon a simple and ingenious method of doing this. She has a revolving blackboard upon which she writes various figures, numbers, words, sentences, which she exposes to the view of the class for one or two or three seconds, as the case may be, and then asks them to copy or repeat what was written. In time they become astonishingly quick, especially the girls, and can take in a multitude of things at a glance. Detectives, I am told, are trained after a similar method; a man is led quickly by a show-window, for instance, and asked to name and describe the objects he saw there. Life itself is of course more or less a school of this kind, but the power of concentrated attention in most persons needs stimulating. Here comes in the benefit of manual-training schools. To *do* a thing, to make something, the powers of the mind must be focused. A boy in building a boat will get something that all the books in the world cannot give him. The concrete, the definite, the discipline of real things, the educational values that lie here, are not enough appreciated.

IV

The book of nature is like a page written over or printed upon with different-sized characters and in many different languages, interlined and cross-lined, and with a great variety of marginal notes and references. There is coarse print and fine print; there are obscure signs and hieroglyphics. We all read the large type more or less appreciatively, but only the students and lovers of nature read the fine lines and the footnotes. It is a book which he reads best who goes most slowly or even tarries long by the way. He who runs may read some things. We may take in the general features of sky, plain, and river from the express train, but only the pedestrian, the saunterer, with eyes in his head and love in his heart, turns every leaf and peruses every line. One man sees only the migrating water-fowls and the larger birds of the air; another sees the passing kinglets and hurrying warblers as well. For my part, my delight is to linger long over each page of this marvelous record, and to dwell fondly upon its most obscure text.

I take pleasure in noting the minute things about me. I am interested even in the ways of the wild bees, and in all the little dramas and tragedies that occur in field and wood. One June day, in my walk, as I crossed a rather dry, high-lying field, my attention was attracted by small mounds of fresh earth all over the ground, scarcely more than a handful in each. On looking closely, I saw that in the middle of each mound there was a hole not quite so large as a lead-pencil. Now, I had never observed these mounds before, and my curiosity was aroused. "Here is some fine print," I said, "that I have overlooked." So I set to work to try to read it; I waited for a sign of life. Presently I saw here and there a bee hovering about over the mounds. It looked like the honey-bee, only less pronounced in color and manner. One of them alighted on one of the mounds near me, and was about to disappear in the hole in the centre when I caught it in my hand. Though it stung me, I retained it and looked it over, and in the process was stung several times; but the pain was slight. I saw it was one of our native wild bees,

cousin to the leaf-rollers, that build their nests under stones and in decayed fence-rails. (In Packard I found it described under the name of
Andrena.) Then I inserted a small weed-stalk into one of the holes, and,
with a little trowel I carried, proceeded to dig out the nest. The hole was
about a foot deep; at the bottom of it I found a little semi-transparent,
membranous sac or cell, a little larger than that of the honey-bee; in this
sac was a little pellet of yellow pollen—a loaf of bread for the young
grub when the egg should have hatched. I explored other nests and
found them all the same. This discovery was not a great addition to my
sum of natural knowledge, but it was something. Now when I see the
signs in a field, I know what they mean: they indicate the tiny earthen
cradles of *Andrena*.

Near by I chanced to spy a large hole in the turf, with no mound of
soil about it. I could put the end of my little finger into it. I peered
down, and saw the gleam of two small, bead-like eyes. I knew it to be
the den of the wolf-spider. Was she waiting for some blundering insect
to tumble in? I say she, because the real ogre among the spiders is the
female. The male is small and of little consequence. A few days later I
paused by this den again and saw the members of the ogress scattered
about her own door. Had some insect Jack the Giant-Killer been there,
or had a still more formidable ogress, the sand-hornet, dragged her
forth and carried away her limbless body to her den in the bank?

What the wolf-spider does with the earth it excavates in making its
den is a mystery. There is no sign of it anywhere about. Does it force its
way down by pushing the soil to one side and packing it there firmly?
The entrance to the hole usually has a slight rim or hem to keep the
edge from crumbling in.

As it happened, I chanced upon another interesting footnote that very
day. I was on my way to a muck swamp in the woods, to see if the showy
lady's-slipper was in bloom. Just on the margin of the swamp, in the deep
shade of the hemlocks, my eye took note of some small, unshapely creature crawling hurriedly over the ground. I stooped down, and saw it
was some large species of moth just out of its case, and in a great hurry
to find a suitable place in which to hang itself up and give its wings a
chance to unfold before the air dried them. I thrust a small twig in its

way, which it instantly seized upon. I lifted it gently, carried it to drier ground, and fixed the stick in the fork of a tree, so that the moth hung free a few feet from the ground. Its body was distended nearly to the size of one's little finger, and surmounted by wings that were so crumpled and stubby that they seemed quite rudimentary. The creature evidently knew what it wanted, and knew the importance of haste. Instantly these rude, stubby wings began to grow. It was a slow process, but one could see the change from minute to minute. As the wings expanded, the body contracted. By some kind of pumping arrangement air was being forced from a reservoir in the one into the tubes of the other. The wings were not really growing, as they at first seemed to be, but they were unfolding and expanding under this pneumatic pressure from the body. In the course of about half an hour the process was completed, and the winged creature hung there in all its full-fledged beauty. Its color was checked black and white like a loon's back, but its name I know not. My chief interest in it, aside from the interest we feel in any new form of life, arose from the creature's extreme anxiety to reach a perch where it could unfold its wings. A little delay would doubtless have been fatal to it. I wonder how many human geniuses are hatched whose wings are blighted by some accident or untoward circumstance. Or do the wings of genius always unfold, no matter what the environment may be?

One seldom takes a walk without encountering some of this fine print on nature's page. Now it is a little yellowish-white moth that spreads itself upon the middle of a leaf as if to imitate the droppings of birds; or it is the young cicadas working up out of the ground, and in the damp, cool places building little chimneys or tubes above the surface to get more warmth and hasten their development; or it is a wood-newt gorging a tree-cricket, or a small snake gorging the newt, or a bird song with some striking peculiarity—a strange defect, or a rare excellence. Now it is a shrike impaling his victim, or blue jays mocking and teasing a hawk and dropping quickly into the branches to avoid his angry blows, or a robin hustling a cuckoo out of the tree where her nest is, or a vireo driving away a cowbird, or the partridge blustering about your feet till her young are hidden. One October morning I was walking along the road on the edge of the woods, when I came into a gentle shower of butternuts; one of them struck my hat-brim. I paused and looked about me; here one fell, there another, yonder a third. There was no wind blowing, and I wondered what was loosening the butternuts. Turning my attention to the top of the tree, I soon saw the explanation: a red squirrel was at work gathering his harvest. He would seize a nut, give it a twist, when down it would come; then he would dart to another and another. Farther along I found where he had covered the ground with chestnut burs; he could not wait for the frost and the winds; did he know that the burs would dry and open upon the ground, and that the bitter covering of the butternuts would soon fall away from the nut?

There are three things that perhaps happen near me each season that I have never yet seen—the toad casting its skin, the snake swallowing its young, and the larvæ of the moth and butterfly constructing their shrouds. It is a mooted question whether or not the snake does swallow its young, but if there is no other good reason for it, may they not retreat into their mother's stomach to feed? How else are they to be nourished? That the moth larva can weave its own cocoon and attach it to a twig seems more incredible. Yesterday, in my walk, I found a firm, silver-gray cocoon, about two inches long and shaped like an Egyptian mummy (probably *Promethea*), suspended from a branch of a bush by a narrow, stout ribbon twice as long as itself. The fastening was woven around the limb, upon which it turned as if it grew there. I would have given something to have seen the creature perform this feat, and then incase itself so snugly in the silken shroud at the end of this tether. By swinging free, its firm, compact case was in no danger from woodpeckers, as it might have been if resting directly upon a branch or tree-trunk. Near by was the cocoon of another species (*Cecropia*) that was fastened directly to the limb; but this was vague, loose, and much more involved and net-like. I have seen the downy woodpecker assaulting one of these cocoons, but its yielding surface and webby interior seemed to puzzle and baffle him.

I am interested even in the way each climbing plant or vine goes up the pole, whether from right to left, or from left to right,—that is, with the hands of a clock or against them,—whether it is under the law of the great cyclonic storms of the northern hemisphere, which all move against the hands of a clock, or in the contrary direction, like the cyclones in the southern hemisphere. I take pleasure in noting every little dancing whirlwind of a summer day that catches up the dust or the leaves before me, and every little funnel-shaped whirlpool in the swollen stream or river, whether or not they spin from right to left or the reverse. If I were in the southern hemisphere, I am sure I should note whether these things were under the law of its cyclones in this respect or under the law of ours. As a rule, our twining plants and toy whirlwinds copy our revolving storms and go against the hands of the clock. But there are exceptions. While the bean, the bittersweet, the morning-glory, and others go up from left to right, the hop, the wild buckwheat, and some others go up from right to left. Most of our forest trees show a tendency to wind one way or the other, the hard woods going in one direction, and the hemlocks and pines and cedars and butternuts and chestnuts in another. In different localities, or on different geological formations, I find these directions reversed. I recall one instance in the case of a hemlock six or seven inches in diameter, where this tendency to twist had come out of the grain, as it were, and shaped the outward form of the tree, causing it to make, in an ascent of about thirty feet, one complete revolution about a larger tree close to which it grew. On a smaller scale I have seen the same thing in a pine.

Persons lost in the woods or on the plains, or traveling at night, tend, I believe, toward the left. The movements of men and women, it is said, differ in this respect, one sex turning to the right and the other to the left.

I had lived in the world more than fifty years before I noticed a peculiarity about the rays of light one often sees diverging from an opening, or a series of openings, in the clouds, namely, that they are like spokes in a wheel, the hub, or centre, of which appears to be just there in the vapory masses, instead of being, as is really the case, nearly ninety-three millions of miles beyond. The beams of light that come through cracks or chinks in a wall do not converge in this way, but to the eye run parallel to one another. There is another fact: this fan-shaped display of converging rays is always immediately in front of the observer; that is, exactly between him and the sun, so that the central spoke or shaft in his front is always perpendicular. You cannot see this fan to the right or left of the sun, but only between you and it. Hence, as in the case of the rainbow, no two persons see exactly the same rays.

The eye sees what it has the means of seeing, and its means of seeing are in proportion to the love and desire behind it. The eye is informed and sharpened by the thought. My boy sees ducks on the river where and when I cannot, because at certain seasons he thinks ducks and dreams ducks. One season my neighbor asked me if the bees had injured my grapes. I said, "No; the bees never injure my grapes."

"They do mine," he replied; "they puncture the skin for the juice, and at times the clusters are covered with them."

"No," I said, "it is not the bees that puncture the skin; it is the birds."

"What birds?"

"The orioles."

"But I haven't seen any orioles," he rejoined.

"We have," I continued, "because at this season we think orioles; we have learned by experience how destructive these birds are in the vineyard, and we are on the lookout for them; our eyes and ears are ready for them."

If we think birds, we shall see birds wherever we go; if we think arrowheads, as Thoreau did, we shall pick up arrowheads in every field. Some people have an eye for four-leaved clovers; they see them as they walk hastily over the turf, for they already have them in their eyes. I once took a walk with the late Professor Eaton of Yale. He was just then specially interested in the mosses, and he found them, all kinds, everywhere. I can see him yet, every few minutes upon his knees, adjusting his eye-glasses before some rare specimen. The beauty he found in them, and pointed out to me, kindled my enthusiasm also. I once spent a summer day at the mountain home of a well-known literary woman and editor. She lamented the absence of birds about her house. I named a half-dozen or more I had heard or seen in her trees within an hour—

the indigo-bird, the purple finch, the yellowbird, the veery thrush, the red-eyed vireo, the song sparrow.

"Do you mean to say you have seen or heard all these birds while sitting here on my porch?" she inquired.

"I really have," I said.

"I do not see them or hear them," she replied, "and yet I want to very much."

"No," said I; "you only *want to want* to see and hear them."

You must have the bird in your heart before you can find it in the bush.

I was sitting in front of a farmhouse one day in company with the local Nimrod. In a maple tree in front of us I saw the great crested fly-catcher. I called the hunter's attention to it, and asked him if he had ever seen that bird before. No, he had not; it was a new bird to him. But he probably had seen it scores of times,—seen it without regarding it. It was not the game he was in quest of, and his eye heeded it not.

Human and artificial sounds and objects thrust themselves upon us; they are within our sphere, so to speak: but the life of nature we must meet halfway; it is shy, withdrawn, and blends itself with a vast neutral background. We must be initiated; it is an order the secrets of which are well guarded.

Leaf and Tendril (1908)

The Grist of the Gods

About all we have in mind when we think of the earth is this thin pellicle of soil with which the granite framework of the globe is clothed—a red and brown film of pulverized and oxidized rock, scarcely thicker, relatively, than the paint or enamel which some women put on their cheeks, and which the rains often wash away as a tear washes off the paint and powder. But it is the main thing to us. Out of it we came and unto it we return. "Earth to earth, and dust to dust." The dust becomes warm and animated for a little while, takes on form and color, stalks about recuperating itself from its parent dust underfoot, and then fades and is resolved into the original earth elements. We are built up out of the ground quite as literally as the trees are, but not quite so immediately. The vegetable is between us and the soil, but our dependence is none the less real. "As common as dust" is one of our sayings, but the common, the universal, is always our mainstay in this world. When we see the dust turned into fruit and flowers and grain by that intangible thing called vegetable life, or into the bodies of men and women by the equally mysterious agency of animal life, we think better of it. The trembling gold of the pond-lily's heart, and its petals like carved snow, are no more a transformation of a little black muck and ooze by the chemistry of the sunbeam than our bodies and minds, too, are a transformation of the soil underfoot.

We are rooted to the air through our lungs and to the soil through our stomachs. We are walking trees and floating plants. The soil which in one form we spurn with our feet, and in another take into our mouths and into our blood—what a composite product it is! It is the grist out of which our bread of life is made, the grist which the mills of the gods, the slow patient gods of Erosion, have been so long grinding—grinding probably more millions of years than we have any idea of. The original stuff, the pulverized granite, was probably not very nourishing, but the fruitful hand of time has made it so. It is the kind of grist that improves with the keeping, and the more the meal-worms have worked in it, the better the bread. Indeed, until it has been eaten and digested by our faithful servitors the vegetables, it does not make the loaf that is our staff of life. The more death has gone into it, the more life comes out of it; the more it is a cemetery, the more it becomes a nursery; the more the rocks perish, the more the fields flourish.

This story of the soil appeals to the imagination. To have a bit of earth to plant, to hoe, to delve in, is a rare privilege. If one stops to consider, one cannot turn it with his spade without emotion. We look back with the mind's eye through the vista of geologic time and we see islands and continents of barren, jagged rocks, not a grain of soil anywhere. We look again and behold a world of rounded hills and fertile valleys and plains, depth of soil where before were frowning rocks. The hand of time with its potent fingers of heat, frost, cloud, and air has passed slowly over the scene, and the miracle is done. The rocks turn to herbage, the fetid gases to the breath of flowers. The mountain melts down into a harvest field; volcanic scoria changes into garden mould; where towered a cliff now basks a green slope; where the strata yawned now bubbles a fountain; where the earth trembled, verdure now undulates. Your lawn and your meadow are built up of the ruins of the foreworld. The leanness of granite and gneiss has become the fat of the land. What transformation and promotion!—the decrepitude of the hills becoming the strength of the plains, the decay of the heights resulting in the renewal of the valleys!

Many of our hills are but the stumps of mountains which the hand of time has cut down. Hence we may say that if God made the mountains, time made the hills.

What adds to the wonder of the earth's grist is that the millstones that did the work and are still doing it are the gentle forces that career above our heads—the sunbeam, the cloud, the air, the frost. The rain's gentle fall, the air's velvet touch, the sun's noiseless rays, the frost's exquisite crystals, these combined are the agents that crush the rocks and pulverize the mountains, and transform continents of sterile granite into a world of fertile soils. It is as if baby fingers did the work of giant powder and dynamite. Give the clouds and the sunbeams time enough, and the Alps and the Andes disappear before them, or are transformed into plains where corn may grow and cattle graze. The snow falls as softly as down and lies almost as lightly, yet the crags crumble beneath it; compacted by gravity, out of it grew the tremendous ice sheet that ground off the mountain summits, that scooped out lakes and valleys, and modeled our northern landscapes as the sculptor his clay image.

Not only are the mills of the gods grinding here, but the great cosmic mill in the sidereal heavens is grinding also, and some of its dust reaches our planet. Cosmic dust is apparently falling on the earth at all times. It is found in the heart of hailstones and in Alpine snows, and helps make up the mud of the ocean floors.

During the unthinkable time of the revolution of the earth around the sun, the amount of cosmic matter that has fallen upon its surface from out the depths of space must be enormous. It certainly must enter largely into the composition of the soil and of the sedimentary rocks. Celestial dirt we may truly call it, star dust, in which we plant our potatoes and grain and out of which Adam was made, and every son of man since Adam—the divine soil in very fact, the garden of the Eternal, contributed to by the heavens above and all the vital forces below, incorruptible, forever purifying itself, clothing the rocky framework of the globe as with flesh and blood, making the earth truly a mother with a teeming fruitful womb, and her hills veritable mammary glands. The iron in the fruit and vegetables we eat, which thence goes into our blood, may, not very long ago, have formed a part of the cosmic dust that drifted for untold ages along the highways of planets and suns.

The soil underfoot, or that we turn with our plow, how it thrills with life or the potencies of life! What a fresh, good odor it exhales when we turn it with our spade or plow in spring! It is good. No wonder children and horses like to eat it!

How inert and dead it looks, yet what silent, potent fermentations are going on there—millions and trillions of minute organisms ready to further your scheme of agriculture or horticulture. Plant your wheat or your corn in it, and behold the miracle of a birth of a plant or a tree. How it pushes up, fed and stimulated by the soil, through the agency of heat and moisture! It makes visible to the eye the life that is latent or held in suspense there in the cool, impassive ground. The acorn, the chestnut, the maple keys, have but to lie on the surface of the moist earth to feel its power and send down rootlets to meet it.

From one point of view, what a ruin the globe is!—worn and crumbled and effaced beyond recognition, had we known it in its youth. Where once towered mountains are now only their stumps—low, fertile hills or plains. Shake down your great city with its skyscrapers till most of its buildings are heaps of ruins with grass and herbage growing upon them, and you have a hint of what has happened to the earth.

Again, one cannot but reflect what a sucked orange the earth will be in the course of a few more centuries. Our civilization is terribly expensive to all its natural resources; one hundred years of modern life doubtless exhausts its stores more than a millennium of the life of antiquity. Its coal and oil will be about used up, all its mineral wealth greatly depleted, the fertility of its soil will have been washed into the sea through the drainage of its cities, its wild game will be nearly extinct, its primitive forests gone, and soon how nearly bankrupt the planet will be!

There is no better illustration of the way decay and death play into the hands of life than the soil underfoot. The earth dies daily and has done so through countless ages. But life and youth spring forever from its decay; indeed, could not spring at all till the decay began. All the soil was once rock, perhaps many times rock, as the water that flows by may have been many times ice.

The soft, slow, aerial forces, how long and patiently they have worked! Oxygen has played its part in the way of oxidation and dioxidation of minerals. Carbon or carbonic acid has played its part, hydrogen has played its. Even granite yields slowly but surely to the action of rain-water. The sun is of course the great dynamo that runs the earth machinery and, through moisture and the air currents, reduces the rocks to soil. Without solar heat we should have no rain, and without rain we should have no soil. The decay of a mountain makes a hill of fertile fields. The soil, as we know it, is the product of three great processes—mechanical, chemical, and vital—which have been going on for untold ages. The mechanical we see in the friction of winds and waves and the grinding of glaciers, and in the destructive effects of heat and cold upon the rocks; the chemical in the solvent power of rain-water and of water charged with various acids and gases. The soil is rarely the color of the underlying rock from which it came, by reason of the action of the various gases of the atmosphere. Iron is black, but when turned into rust by the oxygen of the air, it is red.

The vital processes that have contributed to the soil we see going on about us in the decay of animal and vegetable matter. It is this process that gives the humus to the soil, in fact, almost humanizes it, making it tender and full of sentiment and memories, as it were, so that it responds more quickly to our needs and to our culture. The elements of the soil remember all those forms of animal and vegetable life of which they once made a part, and they take them on again the more readily. Hence the quick action of wood ashes upon vegetable life. Iron and lime and phosphorus that have once been taken up by growing plants and trees seem to have acquired new properties, and are the more readily taken up again.

The soil, like mankind, profits by experience, and grows deep and mellow with age. Turn up the cruder subsoil to the sun and air and to vegetable life, and after a time its character is changed; it becomes more gentle and kindly and more fertile.

All things are alike or under the same laws—the rocks, the soil, the soul of man, the trees in the forest, the stars in the sky. We have fertility, depth, geniality, in the ground underfoot, on the same terms upon which we have these things in human life and character.

We hardly realize how life itself has stored up life in the soil, how the organic has wedded and blended with the inorganic in the ground we walk upon. Many if not all of the sedimentary rocks that were laid down in the abysms of the old ocean, out of which our soil has been produced, and that are being laid down now, out of which future soils will be produced, were and are largely of organic origin, the leavings of untold myriads of minute marine animals that lived millions of years ago. Our limestone rocks, thousands of feet thick in places, the decomposition of which furnishes some of our most fertile soils, are mainly of plant and animal origin. The chalk hills of England, so smooth and plump, so domestic and mutton-suggesting, as Huxley says, are the leavings of minute creatures called *Globigerinæ*, that lived and died in the ancient seas in the remote past. Other similar creatures, *Radiolaria* and diatoms, have played an equally important part in contributing the foundation of our soils. Diatom earth is found in places in Virginia forty feet thick. The coral insects have also contributed their share to the soil-making rocks. Our marl-beds, our phosphatic and carbonaceous rocks, are all largely of animal origin. So that much of our soil has lived and died many times, and has been charged more and more during the geologic ages or eternities with the potencies of life.

Indeed, Huxley, after examining the discoveries of the *Challenger* expedition, says there are good grounds for the belief "that all the chief known constituents of the crust of the earth may have formed part of living bodies; that they may be the 'ash' of protoplasm."

This implies that life first appeared in the sea, and gave rise to untold myriads of minute organisms, that built themselves shells out of the mineral matter held in solution by the water. As these organisms perished, their shells fell to the bottom and formed the sedimentary rocks. In the course of ages these rocks were lifted up above the sea, and their decay and disintegration under the action of the elements formed our soil—our clays, our marls, our green sand—and out of this soil man himself is built up.

I do not wonder that the Creator found the dust of the earth the right stuff to make Adam of. It was half man already. I can easily believe that his spirit was evoked from the same stuff, that it was latent there, and in due time, under the brooding warmth of the creative energy, awoke to life.

If matter is eternal, as science leads us to believe, and creation and recreation a never-ending process, then the present world, with all its myriad forms of the organic and the inorganic, is only one of the infinite number of forms that matter must have assumed in past æons. The whole substance of the globe must have gone to the making of other globes such a number of times as no array of figures could express. Every one of the sixty or more primary elements that make up our own bodies and the solid earth beneath us must have played the same part in the drama of life and death, growth and decay, organic and inorganic, that it is playing now, and will continue to play through an unending future.

This gross matter seems ever ready to vanish into the transcendental. When the new physics is done with it, what is there left but spirit, or something akin to it? When the physicist has followed matter through all its transformations, its final disguise seems to be electricity. The solid earth is resolvable into electricity, which comes as near to spirit as anything we can find in the universe.

Our senses are too dull and coarse to apprehend the subtle and incessant play of forces about us—the finer play and emanations of matter that go on all about us and through us. From a lighted candle, or gas-jet, or glowing metal shoot corpuscles or electrons, the basic constituents of matter, of inconceivable smallness—a thousand times smaller than an atom of hydrogen—and at the inconceivable speed of 10,000 to 90,000 miles a second. Think how we are bombarded by these bullets as we sit around the lamp or under the gas-jet at night, and are all unconscious of them! We are immersed in a sea of forces and potentialities of which we hardly dream. Of the scale of temperatures, from absolute zero to the heat of the sun, human life knows only a minute fraction. So of the elemental play of forces about us and over us, terrestrial and celestial—too fine for our apprehension on the one hand, and too large on the other—we know but a fraction.

The quivering and the throbbing of the earth under our feet in changes of temperature, the bendings and oscillations of the crust under the tread of the great atmospheric waves, the vital fermentations and oxidations in the soil—are all beyond the reach of our dull senses. We hear the wind in the treetops, but we do not hear the humming of the sap in the trees. We feel the pull of gravity, but we do not feel the medium through which it works. During the solar storms and disturbances all our magnetic and electrical instruments are agitated, but you and I are all unconscious of the agitation.

There are no doubt vibrations from out the depths of space that might reach our ears as sound were they attuned to the ether as the eye is when it receives a ray of light. We might hear the rush of the planets along their orbits, we might hear the explosions and uprushes in the sun; we might hear the wild whirl and dance of the nebulæ, where suns and systems are being formed; we might hear the "wreck of matter and the crush of worlds" that evidently takes place now and then in the abysms of space, because all these things must send through the ether impulses and tremblings that reach our planet. But if we felt or heard or saw or were conscious of all that was going on in the universe, what a state of agitation we should be in! Our scale of apprehension is wisely limited, mainly to things that concern our well-being.

But let not care and humdrum deaden us to the wonders and the mysteries amid which we live, nor to the splendors and the glories. We need not translate ourselves in imagination to some other sphere or state of being to find the marvelous, the divine, the transcendent; we need not postpone our day of wonder and appreciation to some future time and condition. The true inwardness of this gross visible world, hanging like an apple on the bough of the great cosmic tree, and swelling with all the juices and potencies of life, transcends anything we have dreamed of super-terrestrial abodes. It is because of these things, because of the vitality, spirituality, oneness, and immanence of the universe as revealed by science, its condition of transcending time and space, without youth and without age, neither beginning nor ending, neither material nor spiritual, but forever passing from one into the other, that I was early and deeply impressed by Walt Whitman's lines:—

"There was never any more inception than there is now,
 Nor any more youth or age than there is now;
 And will never be any more perfection than there is now,
 Nor any more heaven or hell than there is now."

And I may add, nor any more creation than there is now, nor any more miracles, or glories, or wonders, or immortality, or judgment days, than there are now. And we shall never be nearer God and spiritual and transcendent things than we are now. The babe in its mother's womb is not nearer its mother than we are to the invisible sustaining and mothering powers of the universe, and to its spiritual entities, every moment of our lives.

The doors and windows of the universe are all open; the screens are all transparent. We are not barred or shut off; there is nothing foreign or unlike; we find our own in the stars as in the ground underfoot; this clod may become a man; yon shooting star may help redden his blood.

Whatever is upon the earth is of the earth; it came out of the divine soil, beamed upon by the fructifying heavens, the soul of man not less than his body.

I never see the spring flowers rising from the mould, or the pond-lilies born of the black ooze, that matter does not become transparent and reveal to me the working of the same celestial powers that fashioned the first man from the common dust.

Man's mind is no more a stranger to the earth than is his body. Is not the clod wise? Is not the chemistry underfoot intelligent? Do not the roots of the trees find their way? Do not the birds know their times and seasons? Are not all things about us filled to overflowing with mind-stuff? The cosmic mind is the earth mind, and the earth mind is man's mind, freed but narrowed, with vision but with erring reason, conscious but troubled, and—shall we say?—human but immortal.

Leaf and Tendril (1908)

Nature Near Home

After long experience I am convinced that the best place to study nature is at one's own home,—on the farm, in the mountains, on the plains, by the sea,—no matter where that may be. One has it all about him then. The seasons bring to his door the great revolving cycle of wild life, floral and faunal, and he need miss no part of the show.

At home one should see and hear with more fondness and sympathy. Nature should touch him a little more closely there than anywhere else. He is better attuned to it than to strange scenes. The birds about his own door are his birds, the flowers in his own fields and wood are his, the rainbow springs its magic arch across his valley, even the everlasting stars to which one lifts his eye, night after night, and year after year, from his own doorstep, have something private and personal about them. The clouds and the sunsets one sees in strange lands move one the more they are like the clouds and sunsets one has become familiar with at home. The wild creatures about you become known to you as they cannot be known to a passer-by. The traveler sees little of

Nature that is revealed to the home-stayer. You will find she has made her home where you have made yours, and intimacy with her there becomes easy. Familiarity with things about one should not dull the edge of curiosity or interest. The walk you take to-day through the fields and woods, or along the river-bank, is the walk you should take to-morrow, and next day, and next. What you miss once, you will hit upon next time. The happenings are at intervals and are irregular. The play of Nature has no fixed programme. If she is not at home to-day, or is in a non-committal mood, call to-morrow, or next week. It is only when the wild creatures are at home, where their nests or dens are made, that their characteristics come out.

If you would study the winter birds, for instance, you need not go to the winter woods to do so; you can bring them to your own door. A piece of suet on a tree in front of your window will bring chickadees, nuthatches, downy woodpeckers, brown creepers, and often juncos. And what interest you will take in these little waifs from the winter woods that daily or hourly seek the bounty you prepare for them! It is not till they have visited you for weeks that you begin to appreciate the bit of warmth and life they have added to your winter outlook. The old tree-trunk then wears a more friendly aspect. The great inhospitable out-of-doors is relenting a little; the cold and the snow have found their match, and it warms your heart to think that you can help these brave little feathered people to win the fight. Not a bit daunted are they at the fearful odds against them; the woods and groves seem as barren as deserts, the earth is piled with snow, the trees snap with the cold—no stores, no warmth anywhere, yet here are

> "these atoms in full breath
> Hurling defiance at vast death."

They are as cheery and active as if on a summer holiday.

The birds are sure to find the tidbit you put out for them on the tree in front of your window, because, sooner or later, at this season, they visit every tree. The picking is very poor and they work their territory over and over thoroughly. No tree in field or grove or orchard escapes them. The wonder is that in such a desert as the trees appear to be in winter, in both wood and field, these little adventurers can subsist at all. They reap a, to us, invisible harvest, but the rough dry bark of the trees is not such a barren waste as it seems. The amount of animal food in the shape of minute insects, eggs, and larvæ tucked away in cracks and crevices must be considerable, and, by dint of incessant peeping and prying into every seam and break in the bark, they get fuel enough to keep their delicate machinery going.

The brown creeper, with his long, slender, decurved bill, secures what the chickadee, with his short, straight bill, fails to get. The creeper works the trunk of the tree from the ground up in straight or in spiral lines, disappearing quickly round the trunk if he scents danger. He is more assimilatively colored than any of his winter congeners, being like a bit of animated bark itself in form and color, hence his range and movements are more limited and rigid than those of the woodpeckers and chickadees. The creeper is emphatically a tree-trunk bird. His enemies are shrikes and hawks, and the quickness with which he will dart around the trunk or flash away to another trunk shows what the struggle for life has taught his race.

The range of the nuthatch is greater than that of the creeper, in that he takes in more of the branches of the tree. He is quite conspicuously colored in his suit of black, light gray, blue, and white, and his power of movement is correspondingly varied. His bill is straight and heavier, and has an upward slant with the angle of the face that must serve him some useful purpose. He navigates the tree-trunks up and down and around, always keeping an eye on every source of danger in the air about him. I have never seen a nuthatch molested or threatened by any bird of prey, but his habitual attitude of watchfulness while exploring the tree-trunks, with head bent back and beak pointing out at right angles, shows clearly what the experience of his race has taught him. Danger evidently lurks in that direction, and black and white and blue are revealing colors in the neutral woods. But, however much the nuthatch may be handicapped by its coloration, it far outstrips the creeper in range and numbers. Its varied diet of nuts and insects no doubt gives it a more vigorous constitution, and makes it more adaptive. It is the vehicle of more natural life and energy.

How winter emphasizes the movements of wild life! The snow and the cold are the white paper upon which the print is revealed. A track of a mouse, a bird, a squirrel, or a fox shows us at a glance how the warm pulse of life defies the embargo of winter. From cracks and rents in the frigid zone which creep down upon us at this season there issue tiny jets of warm life which play about here and there as if in the heyday of summer. The woods snap and explode with the frost, the ground is choked with snow, no sign of food is there for bird or beast, and yet here are these tiny bundles of cheer and contentment in feathers—the chickadees, the nuthatches, and their fellows.

Field and Study (1919)

GIFFORD PINCHOT

If Thoreau and Muir are the great heroes of early conservationist thought, Gifford Pinchot (1865–1946) is often cast as the villain, a utilitarian immune to the beauty and spiritual meaning of the American landscape, whose only design for the vast forests under his control was that they "produce the largest possible amount of whatever crop or service will be most useful, and keep on producing it for generation after generation of men and trees." But in many ways Pinchot's formula represented an improvement over the prevailing standard—his father had made a fortune lumbering but felt he'd done permanent damage to the land. There was no scientific forestry in America, so Gifford went to France to study forest management and returned to take control of the forest tracts at Biltmore, the Vanderbilt estate in North Carolina. The experience he gained, and his aristocratic self-confidence, landed him the top job at what would become the U.S. Forest Service, and just as importantly the confidence of Theodore Roosevelt. Together they built the national forest system, an achievement that Congress would almost certainly have blocked had they argued for it on grounds of natural beauty rather than commercial potential. His other great legacy is the professional civil service that ran those forests, the embodiment of the era's belief in progressive and efficient government management. Pinchot had a talent for political infighting and intrigue, and he brushed aside anything that seemed romantic—he helped defeat Muir, for instance, in the battle over the dam at Hetch Hetchy. But he exemplified what was probably the prevailing American attitude toward our natural endowment—the forests were there for us to use, and we should use them carefully.

Prosperity

The most prosperous nation of to-day is the United States. Our unexampled wealth and well-being are directly due to the superb natural resources of our country, and to the use which has been made of them by our citizens, both in the present and in the past. We are prosperous because our forefathers bequeathed to us a land of marvellous resources still unexhausted. Shall we conserve those resources, and in our turn transmit them, still unexhausted, to our descendants?

Unless we do, those who come after us will have to pay the price of misery, degradation, and failure for the progress and prosperity of our day. When the natural resources of any nation become exhausted, disaster and decay in every department of national life follow as a matter of course. Therefore the conservation of natural resources is the basis, and the only permanent basis, of national success. There are other conditions, but this one lies at the foundation.

Perhaps the most striking characteristic of the American people is their superb practical optimism; that marvellous hopefulness which keeps the individual efficiently at work. This hopefulness of the American is, however, as short-sighted as it is intense. As a rule, it does not look ahead beyond the next decade or score of years, and fails wholly to reckon with the real future of the Nation. I do not think I have often heard a forecast of the growth of our population that extended beyond a total of two hundred millions, and that only as a distant and shadowy goal. The point of view which this fact illustrates is neither true nor far-sighted. We shall reach a population of two hundred millions in the very near future, as time is counted in the lives of nations, and there is nothing more certain than that this country of ours will some day support double or triple or five times that number of prosperous people if only we can bring ourselves so to handle our natural resources in the present as not to lay an embargo on the prosperous growth of the future.

We, the American people, have come into the possession of nearly four million square miles of the richest portion of the earth. It is ours to use and conserve for ourselves and our descendants, or to destroy. The fundamental question which confronts us is, What shall we do with it?

That question cannot be answered without first considering the condition of our natural resources and what is being done with them to-day. As a people, we have been in the habit of declaring certain of our resources to be inexhaustible. To no other resource more frequently than coal has this stupidly false adjective been applied. Yet our coal supplies are so far from being inexhaustible that if the increasing rate of consumption shown by the figures of the last seventy-five years continues to prevail, our supplies of anthracite coal will last but fifty years and of bituminous coal less than two hundred years. From the point of view of national life, this means the exhaustion of one of the most important factors in our civilization within the immediate future. Not a few coal fields have already been exhausted, as in portions of Iowa and Missouri. Yet, in the face of these known facts, we continue to treat our coal as though there could never be an end of it. The established coal-mining practice at the present date does not take out more than one-half the coal, leaving the less easily mined or lower grade material to be made permanently inaccessible by the caving in of the abandoned workings. The loss to the Nation from this form of waste is prodigious and inexcusable.

The waste in use is not less appalling. But five per cent. of the potential power residing in the coal actually mined is saved and used. For example, only about five per cent. of the power of the one hundred and fifty million tons annually burned on the railways of the United States is actually used in traction; ninety-five per cent. is expended unproductively or is lost. In the best incandescent electric lighting plants but one-fifth of one per cent. of the potential value of the coal is converted into light.

Many oil and gas fields, as in Pennsylvania, West Virginia, and the Mississippi Valley, have already failed, yet vast amounts of gas continue to be poured into the air and great quantities of oil into the streams. Cases are known in which great volumes of oil were systematically burned in order to get rid of it.

The prodigal squandering of our mineral fuels proceeds unchecked in the face of the fact that such resources as these, once used or wasted, can never be replaced. If waste like this were not chiefly thoughtless, it might well be characterized as the deliberate destruction of the Nation's future.

Many fields of iron ore have already been exhausted, and in still more, as in the coal mines, only the higher grades have been taken from the mines, leaving the least valuable beds to be exploited at increased cost or not at all. Similar waste in the case of other minerals is less serious only because they are less indispensable to our civilization than coal and iron. Mention should be made of the annual loss of millions of dollars worth of by-products from coke, blast, and other furnaces now thrown into the air, often not merely without benefit but to the serious injury of the community. In other countries these by-products are saved and used.

We are in the habit of speaking of the solid earth and the eternal hills as though they, at least, were free from the vicissitudes of time and certain to furnish perpetual support for prosperous human life. This conclusion is as false as the term "inexhaustible" applied to other natural resources. The waste of soil is among the most dangerous of all wastes now in progress in the United States. In 1896, Professor Shaler, than whom no one has spoken with greater authority on this subject, estimated that in the upland regions of the states south of Pennsylvania three thousand square miles of soil had been destroyed as the result of forest denudation, and that destruction was then proceeding at the rate of one hundred square miles of fertile soil per year. No seeing man can travel through the United States without being struck with the enormous and unnecessary loss of fertility by easily preventable soil wash. The soil so lost, as in the case of many other wastes, becomes itself a source of damage and expense, and must be removed from the channels of our navigable streams at an enormous annual cost. The Mississippi River alone is estimated to transport yearly four hundred million tons of sediment, or about twice the amount of material to be excavated from the Panama Canal. This material is the most fertile portion of our richest fields, transformed from a blessing to a curse by unrestricted erosion.

The destruction of forage plants by overgrazing has resulted, in the opinion of men most capable of judging, in reducing the grazing value of the public lands by one-half. This enormous loss of forage, serious though it be in itself, is not the only result of wrong methods of pasturage. The destruction of forage plants is accompanied by loss of surface soil through erosion; by forest destruction; by corresponding deterioration in the water supply; and by a serious decrease in the quality and weight of animals grown on overgrazed lands. These sources of loss from failure to conserve the range are felt to-day. They are accompanied by the certainty of a future loss not less important, for range lands once badly overgrazed can be restored to their former value but slowly or not at all. The obvious and certain remedy is for the Government to hold and control the public range until it can pass into the hands of settlers who will make their homes upon it. As methods of agriculture improve and new dry-land crops are introduced, vast areas once considered unavailable for cultivation are being made into prosperous homes; and this movement has only begun.

The single object of the public land system of the United States, as President Roosevelt repeatedly declared, is the making and maintenance of prosperous homes. That object cannot be achieved unless such of the public lands as are suitable for settlement are conserved for the actual home-maker. Such lands should pass from the possession of the Government directly and only into the hands of the settler who lives on the land. Of all forms of conservation there is none more important than that of holding the public lands for the actual home-maker.

It is a notorious fact that the public land laws have been deflected from their beneficent original purpose of home-making by lax administration, short-sighted departmental decisions, and the growth of an unhealthy public sentiment in portions of the West. Great areas of the public domain have passed into the hands, not of the home-maker, but of large individual or corporate owners whose object is always the making of profit and seldom the making of homes. It is sometimes urged that enlightened self-interest will lead the men who have acquired large holdings of public lands to put them to their most productive use, and it is said with truth that this best use is the tillage of small areas by small owners. Unfortunately, the facts and this theory disagree. Even the most cursory examination of large holdings throughout the West will refute the contention that the intelligent self-interest of large owners results promptly and directly in the making of homes. Few passions of the human mind are stronger than land hunger, and the large holder clings to his land until circumstances make it actually impossible for him to hold it any longer. Large holdings result in sheep or cattle ranges, in huge ranches, in great areas held for speculative rise in price, and not in homes. Unless the American homestead system of small free-holders is to be so replaced by a foreign system of tenantry, there are few things of more importance to the West than to see to it that the public lands pass directly into the hands of the actual settler instead of into the hands of the man who, if he can, will force the settler to pay him the unearned profit of the land speculator, or will hold him in economic and political dependence as a tenant. If we are to have homes on the public lands, they must be conserved for the men who make homes.

The lowest estimate reached by the Forest Service of the timber now standing in the United States is 1,400 billion feet, board measure; the highest, 2,500 billion. The present annual consumption is approximately 100 billion feet, while the annual growth is but a third of the consumption, or from 30 to 40 billion feet. If we accept the larger estimate of the standing timber, 2,500 billion feet, and the larger estimate of the annual growth, 40 billion feet, and apply the present rate of consumption, the result shows a probable duration of our supplies of timber of little more than a single generation.

Estimates of this kind are almost inevitably misleading. For example, it is certain that the rate of consumption of timber will increase enormously in the future, as it has in the past, so long as supplies remain to draw upon. Exact knowledge of many other factors is needed before closely accurate results can be obtained. The figures cited are, however, sufficiently reliable to make it certain that the United States has already crossed the verge of a timber famine so severe that its blighting effects will be felt in every household in the land. The rise in the price of lumber which marked the opening of the present century is the beginning of a vastly greater and more rapid rise which is to come. We must necessarily begin to suffer from the scarcity of timber long before our supplies are completely exhausted.

It is well to remember that there is no foreign source from which we can draw cheap and abundant supplies of timber to meet a demand per capita so large as to be without parallel in the world, and that the suffering which will result from the progressive failure of our timber has been but faintly foreshadowed by temporary scarcities of coal.

What will happen when the forests fail? In the first place, the business of lumbering will disappear. It is now the fourth greatest industry in the United States. All forms of building industries will suffer with it, and the occupants of houses, offices, and stores must pay the added cost. Mining will become vastly more expensive; and with the rise in the cost of mining there must follow a corresponding rise in the price of coal, iron, and other minerals. The railways, which have as yet failed entirely to develop a satisfactory substitute for the wooden tie (and must, in the opinion of their best engineers, continue to fail), will be profoundly affected, and the cost of transportation will suffer a corresponding increase. Water power for lighting, manufacturing, and transportation, and the movement of freight and passengers by inland waterways, will be affected still more directly than the steam railways. The cultivation of the soil, with or without irrigation, will be hampered by the increased cost of agricultural tools, fencing, and the wood needed for other purposes about the farm. Irrigated agriculture will suffer most of all, for the destruction of the forests means the loss of the waters as surely as night follows day. With the rise in the cost of producing food, the cost of food itself will rise. Commerce in general will necessarily be affected by the difficulties of the primary industries upon which it depends. In a word, when the forests fail, the daily life of the average citizen will inevitably feel the pinch on every side. And the forests have already begun to fail, as the direct result of the suicidal policy of forest destruction which the people of the United States have allowed themselves to pursue.

It is true that about twenty per cent. of the less valuable timber land in the United States remains in the possession of the people in the National Forests, and that it is being cared for and conserved to supply the needs of the present and to mitigate the suffering of the near future. But it needs no argument to prove that this comparatively small area will be insufficient to meet the demand which is now exhausting an area four times as great, or to prevent the suffering I have described. Measures of greater vigor are imperatively required.

The conception that water is, on the whole, the most important natural resource has gained firm hold in the irrigated West, and is making rapid progress in the humid East. Water, not land, is the primary value in the Western country, and its conservation and use to irrigate land is the first condition of prosperity. The use of our streams for irrigation and for domestic and manufacturing uses is comparatively well developed. Their use for power is less developed, while their use for transportation has only begun. The conservation of the inland waterways of the United States for these great purposes constitutes, perhaps, the largest single task which now confronts the Nation. The maintenance and increase of agriculture, the supply of clear water for domestic and manufacturing uses, the development of electrical power, transportation, and lighting, and the creation of a system of inland transportation by water whereby to regulate freight-rates by rail and to move the bulkier commodities cheaply from place to place, is a task upon the successful accomplishment of which the future of the Nation depends in a peculiar degree.

We are accustomed, and rightly accustomed, to take pride in the vigorous and healthful growth of the United States, and in its vast promise for the future. Yet we are making no preparation to realize what we so easily foresee and glibly predict. The vast possibilities of our great future will become realities only if we make ourselves, in a sense, responsible for that future. The planned and orderly development and conservation of our natural resources is the first duty of the United States. It is the only form of insurance that will certainly protect us against the disasters that lack of foresight has in the past repeatedly brought down on nations since passed away.

The Fight for Conservation (1910)

WILLIAM T. HORNADAY

William T. Hornaday (1854–1937) here chronicles a pioneering moment in conservation history, when Theodore Roosevelt helped win the fight against the "plumage trade" that was devastating bird populations around the world. Hornaday was an eminent American zoologist who served as head of the New York Zoological Park for many years; a rough sense of the reasons why the social justice and environmental movements have often parted ways may be garnered from the fact that he saw nothing wrong with exhibiting a live African pygmy, named Ota Benga, in the zoo's monkey house, later remarking that it was the "most amusing passage" in the institution's history. His 1913 book *Our Vanishing Wild Life*, from which this account is taken, has a strongly nativist edge: immigrants and negroes are singled out as villains for their hunting of indigenous fauna.

The Bird Tragedy on Laysan Island

In the far-away North Pacific Ocean, about seven hundred miles from Honolulu west-b'-north, lies the small island of Laysan. It is level, sandy, poorly planted by nature, and barren of all things likely to enlist the attention of predatory man. To the harassed birds of mid-ocean, it seemed like a secure haven, and for ages past it has been inhabited only by them. There several species of sea birds, large and small, have found homes and breeding places. Until 1909, the inhabitants consisted of the Laysan albatross, black-footed albatross, sooty tern, gray-backed tern, noddy tern, Hawaiian tern, white tern, Bonin petrel, two shearwaters, the red-tailed tropic bird, two boobies and the man-of-war bird.

Laysan Island is two miles long by one and one-half miles broad, and at times it has been literally covered with birds. Its bird life was first brought prominently to notice in 1891, by Henry Palmer, the agent of Hon. Walter Rothschild, and in 1902 and 1903 Walter K. Fisher and W. A. Bryan made further observations.

Ever since 1891 the bird life on Laysan has been regarded as one of the wonders of the bird world. One of the photographs taken prior to 1909 shows a vast plain, apparently a square mile in area, covered and crowded with Laysan albatrosses. They stand there on the level sand, serene, bulky and immaculate. Thousands of birds appear in one view—a very remarkable sight.

Naturally man, the ever-greedy, began to cast about for ways by which to convert some product of that feathered host into money. At first guano and eggs were collected. A tramway was laid down and small box-cars were introduced, in which the collected material was piled and pushed down to the packing place.

For several years this went on, and the birds themselves were not molested. At last, however, a tentacle of the feather-trade octopus reached out to Laysan. In an evil moment in the spring of 1909, a predatory individual of Honolulu and elsewhere, named Max Schlemmer, decided that the wings of those albatross, gulls and terns should be torn off and sent to Japan, whence they would undoubtedly be shipped to Paris, the special market for the wings of sea-birds slaughtered in the North Pacific.

Schlemmer the Slaughterer bought a cheap vessel, hired twenty-three phlegmatic and cold-blooded Japanese laborers, and organized a raid on Laysan. With the utmost secrecy he sailed from Honolulu, landed his bird-killers upon the sea-bird wonderland, and turned them loose upon the birds.

For several months they slaughtered diligently and without mercy. Apparently it was the ambition of Schlemmer to kill every bird on the island.

By the time the bird-butchers had accumulated between three and four car-loads of wings, and the carnage was half finished, William A. Bryan, Professor of Zoology in the College of Honolulu, heard of it and promptly wired the United States Government.

Without the loss of a moment the Secretary of the Navy despatched the revenue cutter *Thetis* to the shambles of Laysan. When Captain Jacobs arrived he found that in round numbers about *three hundred thousand* birds had been destroyed, and all that remained of them were several acres of bones and dead bodies, and about three carloads of wings, feathers and skins. It was evident that Schlemmer's intention was to kill all the birds on the island, and only the timely arrival of the *Thetis* frustrated that bloody plan.

The twenty-three Japanese poachers were arrested and taken to Honolulu for trial, and the *Thetis* also brought away all the stolen wings and plumage with the exception of one shedful of wings that had to be left behind on account of lack of carrying space. That old shed, with one end torn out, and supposed to contain nearly fifty thousand pairs of wings, was photographed by Prof. Dill in 1911, as shown herewith.

Three hundred thousand albatrosses, gulls, terns and other birds were butchered to make a Schlemmer holiday! Had the arrival of the *Thetis* been delayed, it is reasonably certain that every bird on Laysan would have been killed to satisfy the wolfish rapacity of one money-grubbing white man.

In 1911, the Iowa State University despatched to Laysan a scientific expedition in charge of Prof. Homer R. Dill. The party landed on the island on April 24 and remained until June 5, and the report of Professor Dill (U.S. Department of Agriculture) is consumedly interesting to the friends of birds. Here is what he has said regarding the evidences of bird-slaughter:

"Our first impression of Laysan was that the poachers had stripped the place of bird life. An area of over 300 acres on each side of the buildings was apparently abandoned. Only the shearwaters moaning in their burrows, the little wingless rail skulking from one grass tussock to another, and the saucy finch remained. It is an excellent example of what Prof. Nutting calls the survival of the inconspicuous.

"Here on every side are bones bleaching in the sun, showing where the poachers had piled the bodies of the birds as they stripped them of wings and feathers. In the old open guano shed were seen the remains of hundreds and possibly thousands of wings which were placed there but never cured for shipping, as the marauders were interrupted in their work.

"An old cistern back of one of the buildings tells a story of cruelty that surpasses anything else done by these heartless, sanguinary pirates, not excepting the practice of cutting wings from living birds and leaving them to die of hemorrhage. In this dry cistern the living birds were kept by hundreds to slowly starve to death. In this way the fatty tissue lying next to the skin was used up, and the skin was left quite free from grease, so that it required little or no cleaning during preparation.

"Many other revolting sights, such as the remains of young birds that had been left to starve, and birds with broken legs and deformed beaks were to be seen. Killing clubs, nets and other implements used by these marauders were lying all about. Hundreds of boxes to be used in shipping the bird skins were packed in an old building. It was very evident they intended to carry on their slaughter as long as the birds lasted.

"Not only did they kill and skin the larger species but they caught and caged the finch, honey eater, and miller bird. Cages and material for making them were found."—(Report of an Expedition to Laysan Island in 1911. By Homer R. Dill, page 12.)

The report of Professor Bryan contains the following pertinent paragraphs:

"This wholesale killing has had an appalling effect on the colony. * * It is conservative to say that fully one-half the number of birds of both species of albatross that were so abundant everywhere in 1903 have been killed. The colonies that remain are in a sadly decimated condition. * * Over a large part of the island, in some sections a hundred acres in a place, that ten years ago were thickly inhabited by albatrosses not a single bird remains, while heaps of the slain lie as mute testimony of the awful slaughter of these beautiful, harmless, and without doubt beneficial inhabitants of the high seas.

"While the main activity of the plume-hunters was directed against the albatrosses, they were by no means averse to killing anything in the bird line that came in their way. * * Fortunately, serious as were the depredations of the poachers, their operations were interrupted before any of the species had been completely exterminated."

But the work of the Evil Genius of Laysan did not stop with the slaughter of three hundred thousand birds. Mr. Schlemmer introduced rabbits and guinea-pigs; and these rapidly multiplying rodents now are threatening to consume every plant on the island. If the plants disappear, many of the insects will go with them; and this will mean the disappearance of the small insectivorous birds.

In February, 1909, President Roosevelt issued an executive order creating the Hawaiian Islands Reservation for Birds. In this are included Laysan and twelve other islands and reefs, some of which are inhabited by birds that are well worth preserving. By this act, we may feel that for the future the birds of Laysan and neighboring islets are secure from further attacks by the bloody-handed agents of the vain women who still insist upon wearing the wings and feathers of wild birds.

Our Vanishing Wild Life (1913)

THEODORE DREISER

One of America's great literary naturalists, Theodore Dreiser (1871–1945) turns his lens here, in a 1919 newspaper article, on the Standard Oil works in Bayonne, New Jersey. The result is a classic description of American industrial squalor and an early, albeit pessimistic, sounding of themes later addressed by the environmental justice movement. It is easy to fault Dreiser for his sense that these workers were of a less feeling, "not very attractive" order; we could also fault ourselves and face up to our current willingness to move dirty and dangerous occupations like these out of sight, to the sweatshops of Bangladesh or the coastal plain of China, for instance.

A Certain Oil Refinery

There is a section of land very near New York, lying at the extreme southern point of the peninsula known as Bayonne, which is given up to a peculiar business. The peninsula is a long neck of land lying between those two large bays which extend a goodly distance on either hand, one toward the city of Newark, the other toward the vast and restless ocean beyond Brooklyn. Stormy winds sweep over it at many periods of the year. The seagull and the tern fly high over its darksome roof-tops. Tall stacks and bare, red buildings and scores of rounded tanks spread helter-skelter over its surface, give it a dreary, unkempt and yet not wholly inartistic appearance which appeals, much as a grotesque deformity appeals or a masque intended to represent pain.

This section is the seat of a most prosperous manufacturing establishment, a single limb of a many-branched tree, and its business is the manufacturing, or rather refining, of oil. Of an ordinary business day you would not want a more inspiring picture of that which is known as manufacture. Great ships, inbound and outbound, from all ports of the world, lie anchored at its docks. Long trains of oil cars are backed in on many spurs of tracks, which branch from main-line arteries and stand like caravans of steel, waiting to carry new burdens of oil to the uttermost parts of the land. There are many buildings and outhouses of all shapes and dimensions which are continually belching forth smoke in a solid mass, and if you stand and look in any direction on a gloomy day you may see red fires which burn and gleam in a steady way, giving a touch of somber richness to a scene which is otherwise only a mass of black and gray.

This region is remarkable for the art, as for the toil of it, if nothing more. A painter could here find a thousand contrasts in black and gray and red and blue, which would give him ample labor for his pen or brush. These stacks are so tall, the building from which they spring so low. Spread out over a marshy ground which was once all seaweed and which now shows patches of water stained with iridescent oil, broken here and there with other patches of black earth to match the blacker buildings which abound upon it, you have a combination in shades and tones of one color which no artist could resist. A Whistler could make wonderful blacks and whites of this. A Vierge or a Shinn could show us what it means to catch the exact image of darkness at its best. A casual visitor, if he is of a sensitive turn, shudders or turns away with a sense of depression haunting him. It is a great world of gloom, done in lines of splendid activity, but full of the pathos of faint contrasts in gray and black.

At that, it is not so much the art of it that is impressive as the solemn life situation which it represents. These people who work in it—and there are thousands of them—are of an order which you would call commonplace. They are not very bright intellectually, of course, or they would not work here. They are not very attractive physically, for nature suits body to mind in most instances, and these bodies as a rule reflect the heaviness of the intelligence which guides them. They are poor Swedes and Poles, Hungarians and Lithuanians, people who in many instances do not speak our tongue as yet, and who are used to conditions so rough and bare that those who are used to conditions of even moderate comfort shudder at the thought of them. They live in tumble-down shacks next to "the works" and they arrange their domestic economies heaven only knows how. Wages are not high (a dollar or a dollar and a half a day is good pay in most instances), and many of them have families to support, large families, for children in all the poorer sections are always numerous. There are dark, minute stores, and as dark and meaner saloons, where many of them (the men) drink. Looking at the homes and the saloons hereabout, it would seem to you as though any grade of intelligence ought to do better than this, as if an all-wise, directing intelligence, which we once assumed nature to pos-sess, could not allow such homely, claptrap things to come into being. And yet here they are.

Taken as a mass, however, and in extreme heat or cold, under rain or snow, when the elements are beating about them, they achieve a swart solemnity, rise or fall to a somber dignity or misery for which na-ture might well be praised. They look so grim, so bare, so hopeless. Artists ought to make pictures of them. Writers ought to write of them. Musicians should get their inspiration for what is antiphonal and con-tra-puntal from such things. They are of the darker moods of nature, its meanest inspiration.

However, it is not of these houses alone that this picture is to be made, but of the work within the plant, its nature, its grayness, its in-tricacy, its rancidity, its commonplaceness, its mental insufficiency; for it is a routine, a process, lacking from one year's end to another any trace of anything creative—the filling of one vat and another, for in-stance, and letting the same settle; introducing into one vat and another a given measure of chemicals which are known to bring about separa-tion and purifications or, in other words, the process called refining; opening gates in tubes and funnels which drain the partially refined oils into other vats and finally into barrels and tanks, which are placed on cars or ships. You may find the how of it in any encyclopedia. But the interesting thing to me is that men work and toil here in a sickening atmosphere of blackness and shadow, of vile odors, of vile substances, of vile surroundings. You could not enter this yard, nor glance into one of these buildings, nor look at these men tramping by, without feeling that they were working in shadow and amid foul odors and gases, which decidedly are not conducive to either health or the highest order of intelligence.

Refuse tar, oil and acids greet the nostrils and sight everywhere. The great chimneys on either hand are either belching huge columns of black or blue smoke, or vapory blue gases, which come in at the windows. The ground under your feet is discolored by oil, and all the wagons, cars, implements, machinery, buildings, and the men, of course, are splotched and spotted with it. There seems to be no escape. The very air is full of smoke and oil.

It is in this atmosphere that thousands of men are working. You may see them trudging in in the morning, their buckets or baskets over their arms, a consistent pallor overspreading their faces, an irritating cough in some instances indicating their contact with the smoke and fumes; and you may see them trudging out again at night, marked with the same pallor, coughing with the same cough; a day of peculiar duties followed by a night in the somber, gray places which they call home. Another line of men is always coming in as they go out. It is a line of men which straggles over all of two miles and is coming or going during an hour, either of the morning or the night. There is no gayety in it, no enthusiasm. You may see depicted on these faces only the mental attitude which ensues where one is compelled to work at some thing in which there is nothing creative. It is really, when all is said and done, not a pleasant picture.

I will not say, however, that it is an unrelieved hardship for men to work so. "The Lord tempereth the wind to the shorn lamb" is an old proverb and unquestionably a true one. Indubitably these men do not feel as keenly about these things as some of the more exalted intellectual types in life, and it is entirely possible that a conception of what we know as "atmosphere" may never have found lodgment in their brains. Nevertheless, it is true that their physical health is affected to a certain extent, and it is also true that the home life to which they return is what it is, whether this be due to low intelligence or low wages, or both. The one complements the other, of course. If any attempt were made to better their condition physically or mentally, it might well be looked upon by them as meddling. At the same time it is true that up to this time nothing has been done to improve their condition. Doing anything more for them than paying them wages is not thought of.

A long trough, for instance, a single low wooden tub, in a small boarded-off space, in the boss teamsters' shanty, with neither soap nor towels and only the light that comes from a low door, is all the provision made for the host of "still-cleaners," the men who are engaged in the removal of the filthy refuse—tar, acids, and vile residuums from the stills and agitators. In connection with the boiler-room, where over three hundred men congregate at noontime and at night, there is to be found nothing better. You may see rows of grimy men congregate at noontime and at night, to eat their lunch or dinner, there is to be found nothing better. You may see rows of grimy men in various departments attempting to clean themselves under such circumstances, and still others walking away without any attempt at cleaning themselves before leaving. It takes too long. The idea of furnishing a clean dining-room in which to eat or a place to hang coats has never occurred to any one. They bring their food in buckets.

However, that vast problem, the ethics of employment, is not up for discussion in this instance: only the picture which this industry presents. On a gray day or a stormy one, if you have a taste for the somber, you have here all the elements of a gloomy labor picture which may not long endure, so steadily is the world changing. On the one hand, masters of great force and wealth, penurious to a degree, on the other the victims of this same penuriousness and indifference, dumbly accepting it, and over all this smoke and gas and these foul odors about all these miserable chambers. Truly, I doubt if one could wish a better hell for one's enemies than some of the wretched chambers here, where men rove about like troubled spirits in a purgatory of man's devising; nor any mental state worse than that in which most of these victims of Mother Nature find themselves. At the bottom nothing but darkness and thickness of wit, and dullness of feeling, let us say, and at the top the great brilliant blooms known to the world as the palaces and the office buildings and the private cars and the art collections of the principal owners of the stock of this concern. For those at the top, the brilliancy of the mansions of Fifth Avenue, the gorgeousness of the resorts of Newport and Palm Beach, the delights of intelligence and freedom; for those beneath, the dark chamber, the hanging smoke, pallor, foul odors, wretched homes. Yet who shall say that this is not the foreordained order of life? Can it be changed? Will it ever be, permanently? Who is to say?

The Color of a Great City (1923)

GENE STRATTON-PORTER

A daughter of the American Midwest in a time of rapid transition, Gene Stratton-Porter (1863–1924) wrote sugary (and extremely popular) fiction to underwrite her work in natural history. She spent much of her time wandering the Limberlost Swamp south of Geneva, Indiana, where she learned to photograph birds and flowers. Her novels, especially *Freckles* (1904) and *A Girl of the Limberlost* (1909), sold hundreds of thousands of copies, and her publisher allowed her to intersperse these tales with somewhat less saleable nature books—such as *Moths of the Limberlost* (1912). She was a great curiosity: one journalist wrote that she "lives in a swamp, arrays herself in man's clothes, and sallies forth in all weathers to study the secrets of nature. I believe she knows every bug, bird, and beast in the woods." She was also a fighter for the world she watched disappearing around her, as Standard Oil of Indiana drilled new wells and farmers drained more land. Her last book, published posthumously in 1927, was a collection of essays on environmental themes entitled *Let Us Highly Resolve*. "The resources of the country were so vast that it never occurred to any one to select the most valuable . . . and store them for the use of future generations," she wrote—and she was one of the early popular writers to try to set that failing right.

The Last Passenger Pigeon

The farm on which I lived as a child was one of the most beautiful at that time that I ever have seen. Three brooks of running water crossed its meadow and valley places. There were thickets and woods pastures between the open, plowed fields, and on the west there was one heavy piece of virgin timber where every bird of deep forest loved to home, and every bird of any kind could find the location it loved under the eaves of the barn, under the clapboards of the pig pens, in the corn bins, in the chimneys of the house, in the apple trees, in the thickets, beside the brooks, in the forest, and on the earth.

One of the birds with which I was daily familiar was the Passenger Pigeon. We had pigeons as well as doves, and all of us knew the difference between the soft grays, the smaller size and the note of the dove, and the larger frame of the pigeon with its more vivid plumage and red feet, with its whistling whirr of wing and its different call note. It is a fact that in the days of my childhood Nature was still so rampant that men waged destruction in every direction without thought. Nature seemed endlessly lavish; the springs were bubbling everywhere, half a dozen on our land; the water of the wide brooks was singing noisily on its way to the rivers and down to the sea; the grass was long and lush and shining; the forests walled us in everywhere. The cleared soil had been cleared at the expense of inroads into these same forests and this thing had been going on for more than a hundred years before my time. In the days of my childhood I can remember sitting on the gate post and watching the curling violet smoke spirals ascending heavenward in half a dozen different directions, and each of them meant that during the winter farmers had been cutting indiscriminately the finest hardwood timber that God ever made, as well as the softer woods. When a man started to clear a piece of land he chopped down *every tree on it*, cut the trunks into sections, rolled them into log heaps, and burned them to get them out of his way, in order that he might use the land for the growing of wheat, corn, and potatoes. In this way uncounted millions of dollars in bird's eye maple, cherry, in burled oak, golden oak, black walnut, hickory, and the red elm so sought after now for knife handles and gun butts went up in flames and smoke. Nowhere was there even one man who had the vision to see that the forests would eventually come to an end. In our own neighbourhood, lying in the heart of the greatest hardwood belt in the world, log heaps were burned that would to-day, at current prices, make many millionaires. And as the forests fell, the creeks and springs dried up, devastating winds swept from western prairies, and so the work of changing the climatic conditions of a world was well under way.

While the forests were being felled, the fur-bearing animals and all kinds of game birds were being driven farther and farther from the haunts of civilization. I can remember in childhood the haze of smoke that always drifted from the west when the Indians and white settlers rounded up the game and burned over large stretches of prairie to secure meat to cure for their winter food store. In our immediate neighbourhood there were nearly half of the neighbours who did not believe in cutting down the forest, in tilling land, in building big, fine homes and churches and schoolhouses, and paving roads. These men believed in living in log cabins in small clearings devoted to a potato patch and a few acres of corn. Water was drawn from springs. Of milk and butter there was none. The corn was ground for bread; the potatoes were buried for winter; the rivers and the forests furnished the fish and game. There was never a day in my childhood in which from every direction around us there could not be heard the crack of the rifle and diffusion of the shotgun in the hands of men hunting game for food, and the river banks were lined by persistent fishermen seining as they pleased. To an extent there was hunting and fishing in our own family. Three or four times a year Father and the boys took a day off, drove to the river, and came home with fish by the washtubful—huge big fish flushed with red around the gills and under parts that they called "red horses"; pucker-mouthed suckers nearly as big as I was; and big, bull-headed catfish, and the solid sweet meat of the black bass. My own fishing was confined to the chubs and shiners of the small creeks crossing our land until I reached an age when I was large enough to be taken along on some of the real fishing expeditions to the Wabash River or lakes near us.

Between Thanksgiving and Christmas, when the corn was husked and in the cribs, and the fall work all done, the boys were allowed to spend some time outside of their school work in hunting with guns and trapping game, and they frequently brought in unbelievable numbers of squirrels and rabbits. In our family we never hunted for nor ate the opossums and 'coons as did many of our neighbours. Father said he never opened his mouth to take a bite of 'possum that he did not think of its long, slick tail. It looked too much like a rat to suit him. He was perfectly satisfied with rations from our poultry yard and lambs and shoats. But Mother liked to have game to offer guests from the city who were tired of the meat that could be purchased at markets, and so the boys hunted until long strings of quail, rabbits, and squirrels, skinned, dressed, and frozen to bone hardness, hung in the store house ready for use on the arrival of unexpected guests. In those days it was no unusual thing for hunters to bring in wild turkeys and in the spring and fall wild ducks and geese that paused at our creeks during migration, while from the time I can remember until I was perhaps eight years of age, we always trapped quail.

There seemed to be an inexhaustible supply of them and very few of the neighbours paid any attention to anything so small as quail. They were out for big game that would supply a large, hungry family of growing children with meat, while many of them did not have bounteous supplies of the richest milk, cream, butter, lard, and tallow as we did. The quail traps that we made I very frequently helped in constructing. Long strips of light pine wood were cut perhaps three quarters of an inch square. These were built into small square pens beginning with the full length of the strips at the bottom, and each round, as they were laid up four-square, the strips were cut shorter until at a foot or so of height they drew into perhaps a nine-inch opening which was covered with a light board. On each of the four sides as these walls were built a heavy cord was crossed over each stick. These were drawn taut and tied at the top, resulting in a slatted structure that could be picked up in the hand and carried anywhere.

The method of setting one of these traps was interesting. A hair trigger in the shape of a figure four was deftly constructed from pine. The trap was taken to a place where quail were numerous, one edge of it raised and set on this trigger. Then in several directions leading from it wheat was dropped, a few grains at a time. The birds, striking these trails of wheat, would follow them up until they reached the trap beneath which was a generous supply. Usually as many birds as could crowd in would follow the lure and when they were busy picking the grains, some bird would espy the wheat on the trigger and the slightest touch would spring it. The trap would drop down covering anywhere from ten to twelve or fifteen birds. These were drawn and frozen as a delicacy to offer guests or in case of sickness.

Quail were so numerous that we were allowed as children to take the eggs. When we found a nest we might take a long stick and roll out and open one egg as a test. If the mother bird had been brooding until the egg was beginning to germinate, the nest was left and given every protection. If the eggs were fresh, we were permitted to bring them home and boil them hard for a treat. I am sure that no other egg was quite so delicious. But by the time I was ten years of age, we began to notice that quail were growing scarcer, so the edict went forth that no more eggs must be eaten and no more traps must be set. Father had discovered by bitter experience that when the quail were not ranging freely through his grain fields bugs and insect pests were damaging his grain until his crops were not so large as when the birds had been more numerous.

These things he studied out and began to pass along to his neighbours, even to put in his sermons that he preached in the pulpit. He began to see even that long ago that the springs were drying up, that the creeks were nearly dry in summer, that the rivers and lakes were lowering in volume, and from that time on our whole family began to practise and to preach conservation along every line.

One of the things that Father never would allow our boys to do was to shoot or to trap the Passenger Pigeons. I think very likely, from his training in Biblical lore, he had in the back of his head a sort of religious reverence for a pigeon or a dove that made him shield them when he did not the quail. He used to tell me that they were among the very oldest birds in the history of the world, that one of the bases of reckoning a man's wealth in Biblical times was to count his dovecotes, and he showed me how these were made and explained how the doves and the wild pigeons were used as a sacrifice to the Almighty, while every line of the Bible concerning these birds, many of them exquisitely poetical, was on his tongue's tip. Father and Mother never would permit the destruction of the wild pigeons which were even more numerous than were the quail. In fact, the pigeons came in such flocks that we frequently found places where they had settled so thickly on the branches of trees having brittle wood, such as maple and beech, that quite good-sized limbs had been broken down from the weight of the pigeons that swarmed over them to brood by night. In my childhood it was customary for men to take long poles and big bags and lanterns and go searching through the woods until they found one of these perching places of the pigeons. Then half-a-dozen men would flash the lanterns in such a manner that the lights would blind the birds, and with the clubs others would beat the birds from the limbs, strike them down and gather them up by the bagfull.

I remember being at the home of one of our neighbours on an errand for Mother one morning when the birds from a pigeon hunt were being dressed. I was shocked and horrified to see dozens of these beautiful birds, perhaps half of them still alive, struggling about with broken wings, backs, and legs, waiting to be skinned, split down the back, and dropped into the pot-pie kettle. I went home with a story that sickened me, and Father again cautioned our boys not to shoot even one wild pigeon. He said that so many were being taken that presently none would be left. That such a thing could happen in our own day as that the last of these beautiful birds might be exterminated, no one seriously dreamed. We merely used precaution as an eventuality that might remotely occur.

More mercy seemed to be exercised in the case of the doves. For one thing, they did not flock in numbers and could not be attacked in masses as were the pigeons. For another, they were smaller and it was difficult to secure enough of them to make a meal for even a small family, and it may have been, too, that their plaintive, cooing notes made an appeal to the heart that the pigeon did not possess. The pigeons were bigger birds; they had more meat on their bones; they persisted in their flocking tendencies throughout nesting and moulting seasons, so that a hunter, coming into pigeon territory, could be sure with a shotgun by day or a club by night of taking all the birds he could carry. Father said he had eaten a few of them, and that they were very delicious either in pot-pie or when the young were fried, but from my time on, in our family, and as far as our influence extended, the pigeons were protected. I never even tasted one, for which I am thankful. People everywhere spoke of these pigeon raids at night as a shame when any one mentioned them, especially raids where bags full of birds were maimed and living when carried away to suffer for hours before they were prepared for food by thoughtless and brutal hunters. Soon it became noticeable that the pigeons were not so numerous. We missed their alert call notes, their musical wings, their small clouds in flight. The work that they had done in gathering up untold quantities of weed seeds and chinquapins was missed and the seeds were left to germinate and become a pest, instead of pigeon food. By and by, people began to say that the pigeons were provoked and had gone on farther north to brood. Their powers of flight were well understood and it was known that they flew long distances when they chose. By the time our family moved from the country to the town of Wabash in order to give the three younger children the advantages of higher schooling, such a thing as a wild pigeon was not seen in our woods, and their notes were not heard either in spring or fall migration. Then items began to appear in the papers saying that the pigeons were very rapidly being exterminated, that people who were settling and residing in Michigan and farther north did not see any. Hunters missed them in territory they long had haunted. And in an amazingly short time people were beginning to watch and to listen for the pigeons, and to report that no one had either seen or heard of any.

About the year 1910, on a business trip to Cincinnati, following natural inclinations, I took a day off to visit the Zoölogical Gardens, and while I was going about among the different cages containing what was at that time the largest and finest and the most complete collection of wild birds and animals anywhere in the United States, from the babel of barking hyenas and restless wolves and groaning camels and grunting elephants and chattering monkeys trying to express their longing for home and freedom, all of them nearly breaking my heart in sympathy that creatures embodying the very essence of wild life should be so degraded and frightened and humiliated as were these things in captivity, while I was trying to steel my heart to go on through the collection to get an idea of what really might be there, I heard a faint little "See? See?" that I instantly recognized, and throwing up my head I saw, high among the confining wires of a cage, a male wild pigeon, and as I stood looking at the noble bird there presently flew across the cage to him from the ground below where she had been picking seed, a female. Before the birds had really become extinct someone had secured a pair and confined them in this cage, but they did not seem to have bred and reproduced themselves in captivity. A few years after this the papers recorded the fact that the male had died, and a few years later I read of the female having been sent, on her death, to the Smithsonian Institution in order that a dead bird might be preserved for future generations; while in one of our magazines at that time (I think the *National Geographic*) there was printed a photograph of this bird after she had been mounted.

Then I followed the history of the vanishing of the pigeons through the sporting and outing and ornithological magazines of the country up to the place where an award of one hundred dollars was offered to any one who would make known to the Audubon Societies of our country the homing place of even one wild pigeon. This award was gradually increased until it reached one thousand dollars. By that time I was beginning to publish records of my findings afield. From the first dove and martin of late February and early March, dependent on the season, to the last migrant wing of November, I was afield with a wagonload of cameras and paraphernalia doing what I could to wrest the secrets of the wild from Nature around me and in an effort to secure illustrations for the works on natural history that I was so intensely interested in writing, and to secure material that I incorporated very largely in books containing a slight amount of fiction as a bait for those who would not take their natural history unless it were sugar-coated.

It was in the busiest part of nesting time, late May and early June, and each day on which light was right for field photography, with the Limberlost as a centre, I was travelling to as distant a circumference as I could attain in any direction with my little black horse and my load of field paraphernalia. Usually my journeyings were to the south, the east, and the north of the Limberlost because to the south lay swampy outskirts, to the east and north wound the lure of the river. I knew more people in those directions and there were oil men who would help me with my work. But there were times when I went also to the west. There was one memorable day in 1912 on which one of the oil men had sent me word as to where I might find the nest of a bird that he thought very interesting, in a thicket of bushes in a fence corner on the land bordering a highway running north and south. I had travelled west on the broad highway leading from the village to the crossroad, found the location to which I had been directed, and tied my horse in a sheltered place. Then I had carried my cameras, set up and screened the one I wished to use, and focussed my lenses on the nest of a brooding hen goldfinch.

It was no wonder that my informant had thought this nest interesting. It began in the sharp angle of small twigs leaving the trunk of a scrub elm, and in order to reach the proper circumference for the nest at the top, the little hen had built in an unusual amount of foundation. The nest was all of nine or ten inches in depth from foundation to top. It was built with a base of tiny twigs and little bits of moss and dried seed pods with a conglomeration of little dried stuff that the mother bird could gather to raise up her foundations to the place where she began forming the hair cup that held her eggs for brooding. Over the outside of the nest, with her careful building and the dainty material she had used, there was almost the same effect of decoration that is sometimes found on the nest of a red-eyed vireo or a wood pewee, or some of the smaller birds that really do trim the outsides of their nests with bits of moss and decorate them with queer, tiny seed pods. The nest was very beautiful and the little greenish gold hen that brooded on it had reached maturity and years of such discretion and wisdom that she recognized my presence and my touch as that of a friend. Without very much to teach her, merely by a slow and careful approach, I had been able to set my camera and cover it near enough her nest to secure pictures that would not need enlargement.

The nest was sheltered from sun and rain by a branch above it that I could easily bend back for photographic purposes and release when I took the camera away. Running parallel with the fence and high enough above it to allow loads of hay to pass under through the gates or where the snake fences were laid down for the purpose, ran the lines of telephone wires crossing the country, but the wires were high enough to be out of my way and no post was set near where I wanted to work.

The brooding bird had left the nest at a period when I covered the camera with branches, but I had hardly settled myself among the screening bushes of an adjoining fence corner where I had a good view of the work I wished to do when she came back, perched on the edge of the nest and leaning over, with her bill turned her eggs and arranged them in a different position before she again resumed brooding. That picture I secured. By moving softly and waiting until she had brooded perhaps half an hour, I was able to reach the camera, change the plate holder, and reset the shutter. Having nothing else of importance on hand at the minute, I decided that I would remain in the fence corner an hour or two on the chance that she might again leave the nest and I might secure another pose of her on her return, or that the male bird near the noon hour might come with food for his brooding mate as had happened in a few rare instances before my lenses. At any rate, the chance seemed worth waiting for, and it was while I was waiting that far in the distance to the east a pair of ears that were as alert, I will venture to say, as any that ever went forth to field work, picked up a sound, and I raised my head and began watching, and presently I recognized that what I was hearing was the wing music of a bird that should reasonably have been a dove, but was not. The air waves that whistle from a dove's wings in flight make a beautiful sound to hear, but what I heard that morning I recognized as a different thing that was a familiar part of my childhood. I heard the whistling wings of a bird, but the tones were louder, differently vibrating from those of a dove, and the bird was coming straight toward me. Unconsciously I knelt up, holding to the bushes and staring into the sky, so presently I could see the bird approaching, headed straight toward the fence corner in which my camera was set, while it was not flying at much greater height than the wires above me.

This all happened so quickly that I was left in nearly a dazed condition when the bird curved down a bit in flight and alighted on the telephone wires so near to me. So quietly that I was almost breathless, I stared up at that bird and slowly my mouth fell open. I knew every dove that ever had been native to Indiana, and I had experienced an intimate acquaintance with one dove having a black band around its neck that had been carried in a cage from Egypt to our country, and had escaped its mistress to be captured at my hands. That bird I adored. I had worshipped it for the three days that it remained in my possession; then its owner, hearing that I had a wonderful dove with foreign history, came and proved her rights and carried away a bird that I would have given any reasonable sum to have owned.

This bird that I was kneeling there in the fence corner staring up at, this bird that had come to me with whistling wings and questing eyes, was as large as the largest domestic pigeon I ever had seen, but there was nothing domestic about it. It had the sleek feathering and the trim, alert carriage of the wild bird. But it had not the surety of a bird at home; it seemed restless and alarmed. Its beak and its feet and its nose were bright red. As it plumed its feathers and dressed its wings while it rested on the wire, I could see that over the top of its head and its shoulders there was the most exquisite metallic lustre of bronze and this bronze tempered out to shifting shades of lighter colour having the same evanescent tints across the breast. The back was a reddish slate-gray over which the bronze lights played, and here and there over its wings there seemed to be a tiny dark feather. The tail was long and had not many feathers in it, and the shape of the bird when it drew itself up and turned its head from side to side to study the landscape was beautiful. It remained intensely alert. It seemed to be searching for something. Its eyes were big and liquid and it constantly turned its head in all directions. As it struck the wire it uttered a queer cry. It was not in the least like the notes of doves or pigeons. It was in a high key and it was a questioning note. As nearly as I could translate it into words it cried: "See? See? See?" in hurried utterance.

When it had rested a few seconds, searching the landscape all around, it suddenly tilted forward, spread its wings, and called again loudly, listened intently, and then took up its flight straight west. There was not a bird in the ornithology of our country that this could have been except one of the very last of our wild pigeons. There was no possibility that I could have been mistaken. I had known the bird intimately in my youth. I had seen it not so long before in captivity in the Cincinnati gardens. In order to make sure that I was right, for even in tales you won't believe I can at times adduce evidence, I wrote to S. A. Stephan, for years General Manager of the Cincinnati Zoölogical Gardens, the finest gardens in the world at the time I last visited them, and asked him for the history of the Passenger Pigeons I had seen in captivity there and told him of how people here in California had sent me word of locations in which I could find a few remaining specimens of this noble bird, but search only resulted in Band Tailed or some other pigeon, never a true Passenger. Mr. Stephan wrote this letter in exact confirmation of my memory:

Dear Madam:

I received your letter and note that you are anxious to receive some information in regard to the wild Passenger Pigeons that we formerly had in the Cincinnati Zoo.

In 1878 we bought six pair of Passenger Pigeons. They hatched several young here, but after several years the old ones finally weakened and died off, as did also some of the young. In 1910 we just had two left. These were two that were hatched out here in the Garden—a male and a female. The male died when it was twenty-six years old, and the female died a few years afterward, and was twenty-eight years old. When the female died I presented it to the Smithsonian Institution at Washington, and they mounted it and have it on exhibition there at the present time.

I have been misinformed a number of times the same as you have from people in California who claimed they could get the wild Passenger Pigeons for us. One party went so far as to shoot one of the birds and send it to us in order for me to see whether or not it really was the Passenger Pigeon, but on investigation I found it was the Band Tailed Pigeon. I really believe that the wild Passenger Pigeons are extinct. I am offering $1,000.00 for a pair of them, not injured, but am most positive I will never succeed in getting them.

Yours very truly,
S. A. STEPHAN,
General Manager.

So here I was looking with all my soul at one specimen of a bird bearing on its head a price ranging from one hundred up, with no way and no desire to capture it. Since it was there, sound and alert, possibly in some far corner of the earth it might find a mate and perpetuate its species. At my hands, at least, it had its chance, while I never have seen another or heard of any one else who has. That one male specimen, flying alone, searching for a mate and its species, at a time when for many years a high price had been set on its head was a pathetic figure. It was a blasting accusation. It was no wonder that strained "See? See?" came to me as the best interpretation of its call note. The bird might very well have been crying "See? See? See what you have done to me! See what you have done to your beautiful land! Where are your great stretches of forest? Where are the fish-thronged rivers your fathers enjoyed? Where are the bubbling springs and the sparkling brooks? Why is this land parching with thirst even in the springtime? Why have you not saved the woods and the water and the wildflowers and the rustle of bird wings and the notes of their song? See what you have done to me! Where a few years ago I homed over your land in uncounted thousands, to-day I am alone. See me searching for a mate! See me hunting for a flock of my kind! See what you have done to me! See! See! See!"

Tales You Won't Believe (1925)

"Creation is still going on, the creative forces are as great and as active to-day as they have ever been, and to-morrow's morning will be as heroic as any of the world." That's the hopeful phrase on Henry Beston's gravestone, found next to the ocean on the coastal Maine farm where he spent most of his adult life. Beston's legacy is tied to the sea—particularly to the beaches of Cape Cod, where he came of age as a writer. After an early career as a teacher, journalist, and editor, a 38-year-old Beston (1888–1968) went for a two-week vacation to the small cottage he had built facing the Atlantic on Cape Cod's Nauset Beach. There he lingered for "a year in outer nature," producing a singularly spare and beautiful account of a place with few people and much sky, much sea, much life. (A slow writer, he sat down to turn his journals into something publishable only when the woman he loved, the writer Elizabeth Coatsworth, told him "No book, no marriage.") The small cabin became a National Literary Landmark, and then, somehow fittingly, it was swept out to sea in 1978 by a winter storm like the ones he described so well.

Orion Rises on the Dunes

So came August to its close, ending its last day with a night so luminous and still that a mood came over me to sleep out on the open beach under the stars. There are nights in summer when darkness and ebbing tide quiet the universal wind, and this August night was full of that quiet of absence, and the sky was clear. South of my house, between the bold fan of a dune and the wall of a plateau, a sheltered hollow opens seaward, and to this nook I went, shouldering my blankets sailorwise. In the star-shine the hollow was darker than the immense and solitary beach, and its floor was still pleasantly warm with the overflow of day.

I fell asleep uneasily, and woke again as one wakes out-of-doors. The vague walls about me breathed a pleasant smell of sand, there was no sound, and the broken circle of grass above was as motionless as something in a house. Waking again, hours afterward, I felt the air grown colder and heard a little advancing noise of waves. It was still night. Sleep gone and past recapture, I drew on my clothes and went to the beach. In the luminous east, two great stars aslant were rising clear of the exhalations of darkness gathered at the rim of night and ocean— Betelgeuse and Bellatrix, the shoulders of Orion. Autumn had come, and the Giant stood again at the horizon of day and the ebbing year, his belt still hidden in the bank of cloud, his feet in the deeps of space and the far surges of the sea.

My year upon the beach had come full circle; it was time to close my door. Seeing the great suns, I thought of the last time I marked them in the spring, in the April west above the moors, dying into the light and sinking. I saw them of old above the iron waves of black December, sparkling afar. Now, once again, the Hunter rose to drive summer south before him, once again autumn followed on his steps. I had seen the ritual of the sun; I had shared the elemental world. Wraiths of memories began to take shape. I saw the sleet of the great storm slanting down again into the grass under the thin seepage of moon, the blue-white spill of an immense billow on the outer bar, the swans in the high October sky, the sunset madness and splendour of the year's terns over the dunes, the clouds of beach birds arriving, the eagle solitary in the blue. And because I had known this outer and secret world, and been able to live as I had lived, reverence and gratitude greater and deeper than ever possessed me, sweeping every emotion else aside, and space and silence an instant closed together over life. Then time gathered again like a cloud, and presently the stars began to pale over an ocean still dark with remembered night.

During the months that have passed since that September morning some have asked me what understanding of Nature one shapes from so strange a year? I would answer that one's first appreciation is a sense that the creation is still going on, that the creative forces are as great and as active to-day as they have ever been, and that to-morrow's morning will be as heroic as any of the world. *Creation is here and now.* So near is man to the creative pageant, so much a part is he of the endless and incredible experiment, that any glimpse he may have will be but the revelation of a moment, a solitary note heard in a symphony thundering through debatable existences of time. Poetry is as necessary to comprehension as science. It is as impossible to live without reverence as it is without joy.

And what of Nature itself, you say—that callous and cruel engine, red in tooth and fang? Well, it is not so much of an engine as you think. As for "red in tooth and fang," whenever I hear the phrase or its intellectual echoes I know that some passer-by has been getting life from books. It is true that there are grim arrangements. Beware of judging them by whatever human values are in style. As well expect Nature to answer to your human values as to come into your house and sit in a chair. The economy of nature, its checks and balances, its measurements of competing life—all this is its great marvel and has an ethic of its own. Live in Nature, and you will soon see that for all its non-human rhythm, it is no cave of pain. As I write I think of my beloved birds of the great beach, and of their beauty and their zest of living. And if there are fears, know also that Nature has its unexpected and unappreciated mercies.

Whatever attitude to human existence you fashion for yourself, know that it is valid only if it be the shadow of an attitude to Nature. A human life, so often likened to a spectacle upon a stage, is more justly a ritual. The ancient values of dignity, beauty, and poetry which sustain it are of Nature's inspiration; they are born of the mystery and beauty of the world. Do no dishonour to the earth lest you dishonour the spirit of man. Hold your hands out over the earth as over a flame. To all who love her, who open to her the doors of their veins, she gives of her strength, sustaining them with her own measureless tremor of dark life. Touch the earth, love the earth, honour the earth, her plains, her valleys, her hills, and her seas; rest your spirit in her solitary places. For the gifts of life are the earth's and they are given to all, and they are the songs of birds at daybreak, Orion and the Bear, and dawn seen over ocean from the beach.

The Outermost House (1928)

Benton MacKaye (1879–1975) has brought enormous pleasure to untold numbers of Americans—less from his prose, which is occasionally cumbersome, than from his great footpath, the Appalachian Trail. A forester and planner, he was a cofounder of The Wilderness Society. But instead of being obsessed with the gorgeous West, he trained his eye on the populous eastern seaboard, and in *The New Exploration* became one of the first to diagnose urban and suburban sprawl. The A.T. was conceived only in part as the recreational trail it has become; it was also supposed to be a spine for connecting communities, allowing their individuality to flourish instead of being submerged in homogenizing, cookie-cutter growth. MacKaye's ideas remain provocative and beckon toward the emerging localist movements of the early 21st century.

The Indigenous and the Metropolitan

We have had a view from the top of New England. We have sighted our main theme—the contact of the indigenous and the metropolitan: two "worlds," two ideas of life, as distinct perhaps as the Greek and the Roman, and yet interwoven in utmost intimacy. The first job of our exploration will be to visualize their separate strands. Each is a separate environment: the indigenous appears to be a compound of the primeval and the colonial; the metropolitan appears to be a compound of the urban and the world-wide industrial. But let us watch appearances. In order to understand these compound environments better, and to separate their strands more readily, we shall analyze them into their various elements. There seem to be three basic "elemental environments," as we might call them. They are the following:

The Primeval—the environment of life's sources, of the common living-ground of all mankind.

The Rural—the environment of agriculture, of local common interests and all-round human living.

The Urban—the environment of manufacturing and trade, of the community of group interests and specialized living.

Let us look into each one of these:

The Primeval Environment. Abraham Lincoln once had this to say about Niagara Falls:

> The mere physical of Niagara Falls is a very small part of that world's wonder. Its power to excite reflection and emotion is its great charm. . . . It calls up the indefinite past. When Columbus first sought this continent—when Christ suffered on the cross—when Moses led Israel through the Red Sea—nay, even when Adam first came from the hand of his Maker: then, as now, Niagara was roaring here.

Thus spoke "the first American" about primeval America. This picture of the "mere physical" of America, and of "its power to excite reflection," makes a rough and ready visualization of the particular type of primeval environment on which the American nation was founded. Here is America of the "indefinite past," the America which "was roaring here" when "Columbus first sought this continent." Of course every other nation also has been founded ultimately upon some primeval base. But we are close to ours. Primeval America is well within the memory of men now living, and in spots it still hangs on. Such names as Daniel Boone and Lewis and Clark set forth a clean-cut background of mountain, forest, plain, and Indian life, whose yet unfaded color lingers on a people's retina and holds alive such other names as Niagara and Monadnock and Appalachian.

We spell these names and place them on our maps. We cleave to them as symbols anyhow of the happy hunting-ground for which they stood. We visualize the *name*. Our job now, in the new exploration, is to visualize the *thing*—the hunting-ground itself as a land in which to live, the actual restoration of the primeval American environment. In this we must take one region at a time. We are taking New England. Here indeed the true primeval has been largely swept away, though the spruce and fir of the Northwoods preserve much of their wild flavor (in Aroostook, in Coos, in the White and Green Mountains, and elsewhere). But the remote lands of New England, if not wholly primeval, are in large part *pastoral*. The semi-wooded upland pastures on the slopes and rugged summits of "up country" form an approach at least to the primeval, and give us definite sense of our "indefinite past."

Other types of the primeval American environment occur in other parts of America: the luxuriant hardwood forests of the Carolina Highland; the semi-tropical swamps of the Gulf Coast; the Arizona desert; the fir-flanked Cascades. Here in this "happy hunting-ground" we find the sources of life itself—in the forests, the waters, and the rest of nature's gifts. Here is our common *living-ground*.

The Rural Environment. As with the primeval environment, so with the rural—various American types have existed. These have been developed under various racial and climatic combinations: the Puritans in New England; the Cavaliers in Virginia; the French in Quebec and in Louisiana; the Spanish in California; the Scandinavian in Minnesota. The primeval environment is one bequeathed to us by God. All others are bequeathed by God with man's assistance. Hence enters, with man, the element of fallacy. But some environments approach more closely the primal needs than do some others: they reflect the wants of man *as* man (as genus Homo) rather than man as any particular race. One of these seems to be the environment brought over and developed by the Puritans in New England during our pre-Revolutionary period (1620 to 1776). To this we have already referred as the "colonial environment."

This is a type of rural environment; it is illustrated in the New England hill village. Though developed in its present form within recent centuries, it has come down to us from early Anglo-Saxon days; and its essential roots extend, probably, back into unrecorded times. The hill village is a pronounced example of a unit of humanity—a community—a definite "living together." The essence of its being is reflected in its physical layout. The Common is the nucleus of the village life—physically, legally, socially, for in and around this are fitted the various elements of human activity in all the structural symmetry of a starfish.

There are about five points to this starfish: religion, politics, education, commerce, home. There is the church (with its steeple); there is the town hall (with its stately Doric columns); and the little red brick school house; and the general store; and the thirty or so dwelling-houses, these last being placed around the Common and along the radiating roads. Tributary to this nucleus lies the territory within, say, a three-mile radius, which, with its fields of corn and hay, its sheep and cattle pastures, and its woodlots of white pine and hardwoods, forms (or once did form) the "physical resource" whose workings provide (or did once provide) the employment and support of the men and families constituting the little unit. And then, as part of the workings, there stood, along the stream at the bottom of the hill (in the real old colonial days), the three infant manufactures of food, clothing, and shelter, represented in the grist mill, shoddy mill, and sawmill.

The structural symmetry of the colonial environment was equaled by its cultural symmetry. The rural colonial village embodied a rounded, if elementary, development of genuine culture—physical, intellectual, artistic. Each season, being a reality and not a weather report, had its suitable activity. The "all-roundness" of colonial community living may be illustrated by noting some of its old-time play activities, showing as they do a primal, natural balance between outdoors and indoors, daytime and night, summer and winter.

There was the swimming-hole in the mill stream—and the flooding of the meadow for skating around the evening bonfire. There was the "after haying" picnic on the river intervale—and the "double-runner" coasting parties by February moonlight. There was baseball—and there was shinny: rainy-day pout fishing—and tracking rabbits. There was the mud scow on the spring meadow—and there was fishing through the ice. There was the illustrated lecture—on the planetary bodies or the Norman Conquest. There was *Evangeline* read aloud on a long solstice evening. There were May baskets on twilight doorsteps, with loud knockings and merry routs for conquest; there was "drop the handkerchief" on the Common. There was the midsummer authors' carnival. There was the strawberry festival on the green and the corn-husking on the barn floor. There was the farmers' supper and the ladies' autumn fair. (There were quadrilles and reels and slides.) There was the Grand Masquerade in the January thaw. The church bell rang out on the night before the Fourth, as the sleigh bells did on the night before Christmas.

This array of colonial cultural activity is not given in order to picture an ideal. Nor is it a dream of village life in eighteenth-century New England. In every one—and more—of the customs cited, I have myself taken part personally since the 1880's. Colonial village culture, therefore, is still near at hand. Of English origin, it is indigenous specially to New England, for here it developed its American form. Here still lie its deeply imbedded roots. The atmosphere of the colonial village and the mists arising from the primeval Niagara, both are imbedded in the indigenous America, both come to us out of "the indefinite past."

The Urban Environment. Frederic C. Howe has written an illuminating book called *The City: The Hope of Democracy.* Personally I am in thorough agreement with this hope—that is, for the *real city.* And if the real city is the hope of democracy, and self-government, then it seems to be the hope of something far deeper; namely, the ability of human kind happily to live together. As the ant hill or the beehive is a highly organized and concentrated community of the insect world, so the city is with respect to the human world. The city is a community *par excellence.* It is the village grown up—with the several points of the starfish symmetry developed to their fullest measure. But, understand—there is the same difference between the grown-up village and the overgrown village as between the grown-up youth and the overgrown boob. Village and city—each is *a community*—each is (or should be) for a population what the home should be for a family.

Let us look into our complete, symmetrical city, as a ready method of getting at the essence of the real urban environment. Our city is not only urban, but urbane; not merely the material fact, but also the spiritual form; not industrial alone, but cultural as well. Each point in our starfish is developed to a measure limited only by the confines of our civilization. The meeting-house becomes a cathedral; the town hall becomes the City Hall or the dome-topped legislative Capitol; the little red school becomes a humming university, and the store, a whirling terminal. The home remains a home. But inter-home relations must seek a different basis, since you have too many neighbors now to have *all* of them as intimates. A vital common interest in the Common will remain (provided the city is a real community), but the intimacy of friendship must be limited to numbers it can comprehend. Groups, therefore, are inevitable and new bonds of comradeship; and these are based less on geographic interest in any particular city section than on zeal for some section of the world or civilization. There is the "section" of sport, of art, of music, of drama, of literature, of science, of religion, of statesmanship, of technology, of economics, of what not. Thus are the points on the starfish subdivided and developed, each one, toward the nth power of our dreamed-for realization.

Each one of these groups is a little sphere unto itself. The city is not only a community, it is a conflux. We have already emphasized the point that the metropolis is a conflux of streams of traffic. So is the city. The real city, as a center of industry, is a conflux of streams of traffic; as a center of culture it is a conflux of streams of thought. Indeed each group is such a conflux. The single group within a city is like the post office in that city. The posted letter is a drop of water in a stream of ideas. Each such drop of water, starting in some home or business office or other source, flows first to the central postal station, thence to the station of some remote or near-by center, and thence again to some other home or business office, or some other destination. In each city post office certain streams converge, while others radiate outward. So with each group of people within that city who are occupied in the development of a single body of ideas—whether of business, or politics, or religion, or science, or art. Each group is a "station," having definite connections with many other stations; and around each, wherever it may be, there converge and radiate a myriad streams of thought. In this way each group within a city may form part of a world-wide whole, and to the extent to which this is so, we call such city in the true sense *cosmopolitan.*

Cosmopolitan does not mean standardized. Quite the reverse. It means adding to the world's variety rather than detracting therefrom. To borrow foreign ideas which can be adapted to our local or regional environment is one thing; to inflict our own patterns on foreign lands, regardless of their environments, is quite another thing. For us to borrow china tableware from the Chinese or skis from the Norwegians, or for the Indian to borrow the riding-horse from the European, who had got it from the Asiatic—these are cosmopolitan adaptations to home environment which enrich the color of the world by translating beauty from one country's medium into another's. For us to perpetrate upon the various peoples of the earth, regardless of race, land, or climate, a standard pattern of American pantaloons, or American cigars, or American movies—these are metropolitan intrusions on home environment which pauperize the color of the world by transporting ugliness from the factories of one country to the living-quarters of all others. Cosmopolitanism adds to the world's variety: metropolitanism adds to the world's monotony.

The city which is truly cosmopolitan is also individual, while the standardized city may be crudely provincial. An instance of the first is the City of Quebec: she is (or was when I first saw her) a capital instance of a city with a personality. She is French, and she is English; her reposeful heights reflect the Arctic wilderness and the early Canadian frontier, while her Lower Town suggests the Middle Ages: because she has variety, she is individual. On the other hand, take any of a dozen American so-called cities: if you have seen one, you have seen all; they have geometry, not personality.

A city, to be an individual, must first of all have unity: to be an interesting individual, it must to some extent be cosmopolitan. These seem to be the two bedrock essentials of the true urban environment. The unity must be of body and of soul. There must be definite geographic boundaries as with the early New England village, and no petering out in fattening, gelatinous suburban fringes: the true city is all heart with no fatty degeneration. There must be a common interest and soul—something equivalent to the village Common. Such combined unity, of form and substance, makes the complete community. The real city is the complement of the real village. One is a community of groups and specialized interests; the other is a community of human folks and all-round interests. In the one are focused world-wide forces through the medium of specialized cosmopolitan contacts; in the other, nearer alike to earth and to sky, are focused world-deep and cosmic forces through the more intimate medium of human and primal contacts.

We have now looked into each of the three basic elemental environments, the primeval, the rural, and the urban. We have viewed each as a normal entity. Let us next look into them as they actually occur as a part of present American life: view them, that is, as actual and somewhat abnormal entities. We shall take them up in reverse order, beginning with the urban environment. This environment in America has been so transformed that it may be considered as practically extinct, and the process itself of transformation may best be described by using an analogy and comparing the city to a pond.

As a city is defined as a "large town," so a lake may be defined as a "large pond." Suppose we have a little mill-pond, made by damming up a creek where it flows through a canyon. Say we want to enlarge our pond; that is, turn it into *a lake*. We build a higher dam, closing the canyon to a higher level. The waters of the creek and mill-pond rise to this higher level throughout the upper valley, deepening the mill-pond and widening its surface both upstream and on the sides. The pond becomes a lake.

Suppose this lake to be as large as can be held within the confines of the valley. It is bounded securely by crestlines on each side. But in one of these crestlines there is a gap, the bottom of which comes down within a few feet of the lake's surface.

Well, it is suggested that we have a larger lake: that we have a *super-lake*. So we raise the dam still higher. The waters begin to rise and extend their boundaries. They reach the level of the bottom of the gap. Still they go on rising. They begin to spill over the gap into the adjoining valley. Still the waters rise. They begin to flood the adjoining valley. Pretty soon they form a deluge.

Our lake, which was intact within its natural proper sphere (the valley), has now become a ruptured thing and uncontrolled. It spreads itself in headless devastating flight, knowing no confines. A "super-lake" indeed!

Of course no civil engineer would be idiot enough ever to let this happen; ever to allow the flow of the waters to get outside their safe and proper sphere. But we the people of this country, and of the world in general, allow this very thing to happen. Not with the flow of waters—no, but with the flow of population.

Not content in making a small town into a large town; in developing merely a larger community—a unit of humanity within its natural borders and confines: not content in making a *city*, we make a *super-city*. We handle the advancing flow of population toward the urban centers just as a mentally deficient engineer would handle the advancing flow of water down the valley. First we build a "dam." This consists of office buildings where jobs are to be had. The population must reach these office buildings in order to make a living. Then we allow the flood of folks to back up against this "dam" of office buildings until it backs far outside the confines of an integrated city and spills over on adjoining areas. This it does in a shapeless widening deluge of headless suburban massings which know no bounds or social structure.

What we call "suburban" (the under-city) is really "super-urban" (the over-city—the outer layers of the tide which overwhelms the city). Since there is usually no sharp line between suburbs and city proper, we have, in such centers as New York, Chicago, Detroit, and the other "Greater" cities, in truth no *city* at all. Instead we have what Mr. W. J. Wilgus of the New York Central Lines has graphically called a "massing of humanity."

These massings and floods of humanity follow closely the law which governs the massings and floods of waters—the law of gravitation. In level country, like the prairie around Chicago, they just spread out in an ever-widening disk. In hill country they creep through the valleys or along the shore lines, coalescing in linear bands, as up the Hudson valley or along the shore between Bridgeport and New Haven. They submerge whatever stands in their advancing path, whether village or open country. Thus the "hill village" retains its integrity as a community only so long as the tide remains below, but too often it has, like its sister village in the valley, been overpowered by the creeping mass and drowned beneath its waters. And so Arlington Heights and

Lexington within the Boston Basin, as Harlem and Chelsea long since upon Manhattan Island, have taken their places among the submerged villages of America.

But the first thing to become submerged is not the country village but the city itself as a true community. Since, as already noted, there is no clear-cut line between the city and the suburban (or super-urban) fringes, the city precincts become swallowed in the "lake" as much as the surrounding areas, and whatever color there may be in the original *urban environment* "runs" in the watery colorless fringes and becomes diluted into the all-pervading and standardized drabness of the *metropolitan environment*. That is what has happened to "Boston Town" and to "Little Old New York." It has happened to Washington, D.C., within my own memory, and it has happened to a dozen other American centers. These now have become "Great Cities" and hope to become "Titan Cities." Mr. Clarence S. Stein has a better name for them: he calls them "Dinosaur Cities." In each case the adjective is correct, but the substantive is nil; for, having ceased to be communities, they are no longer *cities*. Indeed *the city is the first victim of the metropolitan flood.*

And this situation is not to be dodged merely by having middle-sized towns. We have them now in plenty: so many in fact that we have a name for them—we call them "Main Streets." The average "Main Street" is neither village nor city. If it is yet a community it hopes soon not to be: it dreams to become, not a social structure like ancient Athens, but a social gelatin like modern New York. It is not a unit of humanity, it is an incipient "massing of humanity." It is, if anything, worse than the "Great City" itself. Cosmopolitan interests and contacts tend to mellow the metropolitanism of the one, while crass provincialism rowdyizes the metropolitanism of the other.

The true urban environment, therefore, seems to be submerged in America, for the time being, at all events, by what we have called the metropolitan environment. The city is being supplanted by the super-city. The community of definite social structure, developing within certain geographic confines around a common civic purpose, is being replaced by a standardized massing of humanity void of social structure, unbound by geographic confines, and uninspired by any common interest. Intimate self-government is being ironed out by generalized overhead administration. Mechanical standardization replaces human integration. Such seems to be the present actual situation respecting the urban environment. How about the rural environment?

The rural environment in America has also undergone a transformation, especially in the older portions of the country. The colonial village which we have pictured has, as an actuality, very largely disappeared. It has gone in two ways. First it has been submerged, in the manner already described, by the metropolitan "waters" of the supercity. This has been the fate of the villages lying within the great metropolitan districts—Boston, New York, and the other districts in eastern or Appalachian America. Next it has been "drained" to augment the "waters." This has been the fate largely of the villages lying within the back hill country of the Appalachian barrier itself. The disappearance in these two ways of the country village is reflected in the statistics of rural population of Appalachian America (the Atlantic and east central States). This in 1800 formed 96 per cent. of the total population; that is, almost everybody in America was then living in settlements containing less than 2,500 persons each. In 1920 only 43 per cent. of the people in this portion of America were living in rural settlements or areas. In New England the proportion has shrunk to 21 per cent.

The typical colonial village which we have described has become, in the up country of New England, for the most part a deserted village. The church and steeple remain, and the bell also, but it rings, if it rings at all, for a season only, and then for a waning congregation. The town hall is there, but the town meeting has been moved to a more populous precinct. The school house stands, but the pupils who are left in town are "merged" by motor bus in some other center. The independent store has become a chain store. The thirty dwelling-houses have become thirteen—or three. The outlying fields and pastures have largely become brushland (having shrunk since 1890 by 43 per cent.), and the woodlots are cut off a little faster than they grow. Below in the valley the grist mill has gone; the shoddy mill went long ago; the sawmill run by water power has been replaced by the steam portable.

The primeval environment, like the rural, has been affected in two ways. It has not been submerged, but vital particles of it have been captured by the influence of metropolitanism and made to some extent a portion of the metropolitan environment itself. This happens when a lofty summit like Mt. Washington, the acme of a little primeval world, is profaned and half obliterated by the erection of a modern hotel connected by cog-rail and motor road with the tourist world below. The complete primeval environment on a site of this kind consists of two halves: first, the summit itself as the superlative sample of the realm; and second, the vision in perspective of the realm in its entirety. The hotel leaves us the second half, impaired somewhat by the cacophony of the immediate environs; it practically obliterates the first half.

The other outstanding way in which the primeval environment has been affected is by depletion of the forests. This point has long been emphasized, and by many able writers and exponents. The development of the forest as a psychologic resource must go hand in hand with the development of timber as a physical resource, and this will come to pass when, gradually, timber mining is replaced by timber culture.

We have now examined, both as normal potentialities and as present actualities, the three "elemental environments." Together they seem to form, when normally developed, a complete and rounded external world adapted to man's psychologic needs. The primeval is the environment of man's contact with nature; the rural (or communal) is the environment of fundamental human relations; the urban (or cosmopolitan) is the communal environment compounded. Each one of these spheres is a basic natural resource in man's development, and depletion in any one of them means a corresponding depletion in man's life.

Each of these environments is rooted squarely in the earth, not only the primeval and the communal but the cosmopolitan as well, for this is merely a collection of indigenous experiences from other lands. They form the indigenous world, the fundamental world of man's needs as a cultured being. In a sense they form the substance of the ideal world of normal contacts and reactions wherein the course of man's evolution might run smoothly were it not for the injection therein from time to time of some exotic substance. Something of this sort seemingly has come to pass, in America and elsewhere, within the past century. A rootless, aimless, profoundly disharmonized environment has replaced the indigenous one.

This new world is the metropolitan world. It is "a world without a country." Its reactions are born not of nature's soil, but of artificiality; they are reverse to the reactions of the natural normal sphere. Instead of means being adapted to achieve ends, the ends are distorted to fit established means; in lieu of industry being made to achieve culture, culture is made to echo the intonations of industry; oil paints are manufactured not to promote art, art is manufactured to advertise oil paints. Yet this unnatural tendency of the metropolitan process has come about in a seemingly natural way. The machine spells freedom from primitive industry and raw-boned nature, and if one machine makes one unit of freedom, then, we argue, ten machines must make ten units. But, of course, they do no such thing. We wake up to find ourselves no longer serfs to nature's soil but to find ourselves instead the slaves to man's machine. We have within our exogenous world swapped the old boss for a new one. The mastership belongs no longer to nature in the raw, but to "nature dressed up in modern clothes."

The great struggle of the immediate future will be between man himself and man's machine. One form of this struggle promises to be a contest between two realms. One of these is that potential realm of permanent human innate desire, whose power awaits its development to actuality even as the potential sphere of water power within the mountain stream. This human realm (or sphere) has in America a twofold residence: first in the gradually awakening common mind of a large portion of the country's people; and second in the actual territory and landscape of a large portion of the country itself. This potential awakening common mind, groping unconsciously for a complete environment, would base itself on psychologic resource as well as physical, and, to secure man's innate natural ends, would harness *the machine* as the machine has harnessed natural means and power. This we may call the innate or indigenous portion of civilization. The other realm consists of the exogenous or metropolitan portion. Here is the real war of civilization.

This struggle will be taking place not alone in America, but on every other continent. It will be a contest between the aggressive mechanized portion of Western European society (so-called Western civilization) and the indigenous portion of every society invaded, including the indigenous portion of American society. The contest in this country will be between Metropolitan America and Indigenous America. These now stand vis-à-vis, not only psychologically but physically and geographically. The metropolitan world we have compared to a mechanized framework; also we have compared it to an invading army and to an invading flood of water. It is all of these: it is a mechanized molten framework of industry which flows, as we have said, in accordance with the law of gravitation. First it occupies the lower valley, such as the locality of the Boston Basin, obliterating the original urban environment of "Boston Town." Next in finger-like projections it flows, glacier-wise, toward the outskirts, obliterating such rural village and environment as comes within its wake. Then, its projections narrowing, it flows along the railways and motor roads back through the hinterland, starting little centers of provincial metropolitanism in the Main Street towns and around the numerous gasoline stations. Finally here and there it crawls up some mountain summit and obliterates a strategic particle of the primeval environment. It is mightiest in the valleys and weakest on the mountain ridges. The strategy of the indigenous world is just the other way. It is still mighty within the primeval environment, as along the ridgeways of the Appalachian barrier, including such ranges as the Green Mountains in New England. It is strong also in such regions as up country, where, although the farms and villages are depleted, the resources both physical and psychologic are still there, and are yet open to restoration and renewed development. But down in the lower valleys and around the big centers the metropolitan world, as we have shown, is in virtual possession, and any improvement in environment awaits the complex process of reformation from within.

The metropolitan world, then, may be considered as an exotic intrusion or "flow" into certain portions of the innate or indigenous world. Considered thus, and not merely as a static framework, it becomes the dominant part of the flow of population and of the industrial migration to which we have referred in a previous chapter. The control and guidance of this flow and migration we have stated to be the fundamental problem of regional engineering toward the goal set up by Governor Smith of New York, which was "the making of the mold in which future generations shall live." The particular aspect of this problem treated of in this Philosophy of Regional Planning is the strategy of the indigenous world with respect to its contact with this metropolitan flow. This strategy consists, roughly speaking, in developing the indigenous environments (primeval, rural, and communal) and in confining the encroachments of the metropolitan environment. As applied to this country, therefore, it consists in developing the Indigenous America and in confining the Metropolitan America. This procedure requires the consideration of a number of important questions with respect both to ends and to means, as well as to further background on the subject of the American setting. We shall, therefore, look next into something of the history and causes which have shaped the particular contact in this country of indigenous and metropolitan environments as these have been disclosed in the present chapter.

The New Exploration: A Philosophy of Regional Planning (1928)

J. N. "DING" DARLING

"Ding" Darling (1876–1962), two-time winner of the Pulitzer Prize for his editorial cartoons, was an ardent conservationist throughout his life. In 1934, F.D.R. appointed him to head the Bureau of Biological Survey (now the U.S. Fish and Wildlife Service). A national wildlife refuge on Florida's Sanibel Island is named in his memory.

What a few more seasons will do to the ducks

New York *Herald*, September 17, 1930

1. Thomas Cole and William Cullen Bryant in the wilderness of the Catskill Mountains (Asher B. Durand, *Kindred Spirits*, 1849).

2. George Catlin, *Buffalo Hunt, Approaching in a Ravine* (from *Catlin's North American Indian Portfolio*, 1845).

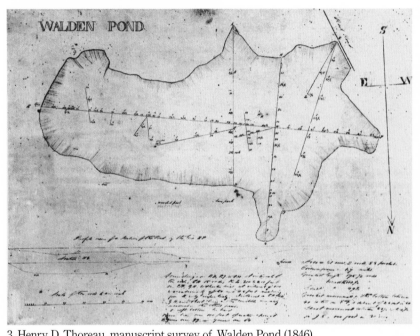

3. Henry D. Thoreau, manuscript survey of Walden Pond (1846).

RURAL HOURS,

BY a Lady

Red-Throated Humming Bird.

NEW YORK

G. P. PUTNAM

1851.

4. Hand-colored title page of Susan Fenimore Cooper's *Rural Hours* (1851).

WALDEN;

OR,

LIFE IN THE WOODS.

By HENRY D. THOREAU,

AUTHOR OF "A WEEK ON THE CONCORD AND MERRIMACK RIVERS."

I do not propose to write an ode to dejection, but to brag as lustily as chanticleer in the morning, standing on his roost, if only to wake my neighbors up. — Page 92.

BOSTON:

TICKNOR AND FIELDS.

M DCCC LIV.

5. Title page of Henry D. Thoreau's *Walden* (1854), with an engraving of Thoreau's cabin based on a sketch by Sophia Thoreau.

6–7. Lydia Huntley Sigourney (1859) and George Perkins Marsh (c. 1861) photographed at Mathew Brady's New York studio.

8. James Wallace Black, *Artists' Falls, North Conway* (1854).

9. Carleton Watkins, *Trees and Cabin with Yosemite Falls in Background* (1861). Watkins' photographs helped persuade Congress to pass legislation in 1864 protecting Yosemite Valley.

10. Carleton Watkins, *The Three Graces, 272 Feet* (c. 1865–66).

11. William Henry Jackson, *Elk with Velvet on its Antlers, Yellowstone National Park* (1871).

12. Charles Leander Weed, *Yosemite Valley from Mariposa Trail* (1864).
In June 1859 Weed became the first photographer to venture into Yosemite.

13. B. F. Upton, *On the Drive, Pineries of Minnesota* (c. 1867–75).

14. Buffalo skulls at Michigan Carbon Works, a Detroit charcoal and fertilizer factory (c. 1880).

15. Currier & Ives' *The Falls of Niagara (From the Canada Side)*, engraved by Parsons & Atwater after a painting by B. Hess (c. 1868).

16. William Henry Jackson, *Old Faithful* (1870); in March 1872, influenced by Jackson's photographs, Congress made Yellowstone the first national park in the U.S.

17. Albert Bierstadt, *Hetch Hetchy Canyon* (1875); Hetch Hetchy was flooded in 1923 to provide water and electricity for San Francisco.

The Catskills.

SUNRISE FROM SOUTH MOUNTAIN

18. Harry Fenn (S. V. Hunt, engraver), *The Catskills: Sunrise from South Mountain* (from *Picturesque America*, 1873).

19. Timothy H. O'Sullivan, *Ancient Ruins in the Cañon de Chelle, N.M.* (1873).

20. *St. Peter's Dome on the C.S. & C.C. Short Line, Colo.* (1901); the scenery on the Cripple Creek rail route "bankrupts the English language," Theodore Roosevelt is reported to have said.

21. *"A Bare Faced Steal"* (1905); feeding the bears, once a popular attraction at Yellowstone, was banned in 1970.

22. Darius Kinsey, *On the Spring Boards and in the Undercut, Washington Bolt Cutter and His Daughters* (1905).

23. Darius Kinsey, *Logging in the Cascade Mountains, near Seattle* (c. 1906).

24. Theodore Roosevelt and John Muir at Glacier Point, Yosemite, during a private trip to the backcountry (1903).

25. John Burroughs and John Muir at the Grand Canyon (1909).

26. John Muir with a Sierra Club group on the trail to Hetch Hetchy, California (1909).

27. Herbert W. Gleason, *Northwest Cove of Walden, Ice Breaking Up (Train in Distance)* (1920).

28. *Walden in Winter (Arching Limb)*, a lantern slide used in Herbert W. Gleason's popular conservation lectures, hand-colored by his wife, Lulu Rounds Gleason (1917).

29. Alma Lavenson, *Zion Canyon (The Light Beyond)* (1927). In 1909, President Taft protected Zion as a national monument.

30. Gifford Pinchot at Partlow Lake in New York's Adirondack Park (c. 1892, the year the Park was created).

31. Mary Austin (c. 1920).

32. Gene Stratton-Porter
in California (c. 1920).

33. Arthur Rothstein, *Dust Clouds over Texas Panhandle* (1936).

34. Aldo Leopold examining red pines near his shack in Sauk County, Wisconsin (1946), where he wrote much of *A Sand County Almanac*.

35. Leopold's shack (c. 1936).

36. Sigurd Olson stocking Minnesota's Crooked Lake—now protected as part of the Boundary Waters Canoe Area—with smallmouth bass fingerlings (1940).

37. Ansel Adams, *Mount McKinley and Wonder Lake, Denali National Park, Alaska* (1947).

Bob Marshall (1901–1939) was born in New York City to a prominent family, and reborn each summer in the Adirondack Mountains of New York. There, with his brother George, he became the first to list and climb the 46 High Peaks, and legend has it that on one of those mountaintops he conceived of the need for a league of people to protect what wilderness remained intact in the United States. The Wilderness Society was formally founded in 1935 with Marshall as its main pillar and Benton MacKaye and Aldo Leopold, among others, on its board. The group laid the foundation for the Wilderness Act passed by Congress in 1964, and the second-largest wilderness in the lower 48, a massive Montana complex of pristine forest and peak, bears his name. Marshall also explored in Alaska in the 1930s. This piece, published posthumously, describes some of his early explorations in the Brooks Range. Marshall was among the first Europeans, and perhaps the first humans, to wander this country; he named the Gates of the Arctic mountains, which serve as the core of what is now America's largest national park.

from **Wintertrip into New Country**

The whole trip, you might say, started over an argument. The issue was whether Clear River, one of the three main tributaries of the North Fork of the Koyukuk, headed against the Arctic Divide. Since nobody was ever known to have been even close to its source, the discussions were entirely conjectural based on knowledge of adjacent drainage. The vote of those who hazarded an opinion was four to four, with Ernie Johnson the leader of the believers in the Arctic Divide origin, and I the chief opponent of this viewpoint. When Ernie had been in Wiseman over New Year's, 1931, he had suggested we should resolve the doubt by following the river to its source when the days grew longer in March. This would also give him an opportunity to seek new hunting grounds. I had more work planned already than I could possibly ever accomplish, but the chance of following an unknown river to its source in mid-winter seemed more important than anything else. Besides, the trip would give me an opportunity to study timber line on another major drainage, and thus make my investigation more complete. I thought we could well tie in a visit to the gold-mining settlements at Wild Lake where Ernie had friends; we could mush to the lake after our exploration of Clear River and return to Wiseman via Bettles. It sounded splendid and I agreed to accompany Ernie.

The community gave us a great farewell dance the night before we were to leave Wiseman. Then, when Ernie's dogs were sick the next day from the medicine he had given them to eradicate worms, there was a second farewell the next night. But even worms have their ends, so on March 6, well danced, we hit the trail and mushed fourteen miles to the old Charlie Yale cabin on Glacier River, which Al Retzlaf and I had visited in 1929.

The second day we mushed twenty hard miles to an old prospector's cabin on Bonanza Creek, which had such a low roof I must have put a permanent dent in my head from constant violent contact. The third day we covered twelve easy miles to a cabin which Ernie had built at the junction of the Tinayguk River and North Fork. There were no remarkable events or scenery on either of these days, yet they left a vivid memory of that world of three pure, unblended colors through which we traveled for sixteen consecutive days of perfect weather—the base of fresh, white snow, the dark, green spruce trees set upon it, and the clear, blue sky as a covering. Everywhere we looked we saw the sparkle of snow crystals where the bright sun reflected from the surface.

Perhaps a word is in order here about our equipment and method of travel.

To begin with, what does a person wear for a mid-winter journey in the Arctic? First, there must be something which will insulate the body and keep the heat in. Second, something, either leather or closely woven cloth, which will keep the wind out. Third, everything must be fitting loosely, especially footwear, so as not to impede the circulation of the blood. Most important, a person must be sure not to wear so much that he perspires, because it is disastrous to get wet. Most people who froze to death in this north country first got wet, either by breaking through overflows or by sweating. Wetness means ice in short order, and no matter how much clothing one has on, it is impossible to warm up with a coat of ice against the body. The only thing one can do is build a fire and dry out before it is too late. Of course, when the temperature is only 10 or 20 below, and no wind is blowing, a little perspiration is no cause for worry.

I wore a suit of medium-heavy wool underwear, an ordinary flannel shirt, a pair of light wool pants, a pair of cotton overalls (to break the wind and keep the snow from sticking to the wool), a sleeveless sweater, one of those closely woven, green Filson cruising jackets, and a light cloth parka over everything. The parka had no buttons, could be slipped over the head, came down a little below the knees, and had no vent to let the wind get through. On one or two fairly cold days—it was never more than 31 below—I wore a caribou-fur parka while riding the back end of my sled. For my head I used a muskrat cap with pieces covering my ears and the sides of my face. There was a hood on the parka which came way over in front, and was a great protection from the wind. On my feet I wore three pairs of wool socks, inner soles, and moose-skin moccasins with eight-inch tops. My hands were protected by anything from wool mittens inside and wool-lined leather mittens outside, to just canvas gloves, depending on how cold it was.

Our method of travel was by dogs. Ernie had one sled with four dogs, I had another with three. Between us we carried about 450 pounds of equipment. Half of this consisted of dog feed, in the form of dried salmon, tallow, cornmeal, rice, and oatmeal.

We used three principal ways of traveling by sled. If there was a well-broken trail, or if we happened to be following a recently overflowed river with fresh ice, we just stood on the rear end of the runners, steering by pressure one way or the other on the handle bars, and let the dogs pull us, except on up-grades where we ran along behind.

If the trail was at all drifted, especially on side hills, it became very difficult to hold the sled on the trail merely by steering from the rear, so we geepoled ahead. The geepole is a stick which protrudes in front of the sled on the gee, or right side, and by pushing on it one way or the other the sled can easily be kept where you want it. While geepoling, depending on how fast the dogs could travel, we walked or ran on snowshoes just in front of the sled and astraddle of the towline by which the dogs were hitched.

If the snow was very deep and soft, the dogs could not get footing and sank to the bottom at every step. Then we had to snowshoe ahead on our smallest pair of snowshoes, working hard at every step packing the snow down so that the dogs could have it a little easier. When the going was particularly bad, we both snowshoed ahead and let the dogs follow. At other times one of us geepoled the two sleds which we coupled together, one behind the other.

At the Tinayguk River cabin, to which Ernie referred as "home" although it was forty miles from the nearest neighbor, we broke up our load. We left about half our food and dog feed for the Wild River part of our journey, storing it in Ernie's cache, a little log cabin built on poles about eight feet high. The poles were girdled part way up by tin to prevent clawed animals from climbing them. In this country with its camp robbers, weasels, grizzly bears, and, worst of all, wolverines, storing food is a problem.

Not so bright and early the next morning we set out for Clear River. It was only four miles to the mouth. Nine miles beyond it Ernie had left a tent when he had gone up about two weeks earlier in a futile effort to find some signs of fur. His old trail had not drifted badly, so we had a relatively easy time. This was fortunate because it gave us leisure to enjoy the Clear River canyon, where, first on one side of the river and then on the other, rock walls rose straight up for one or two hundred feet, bright yellow surfaces mixed with white snow, and capped with spruce trees which grew to the very edge of the cliffs. Al Retzlaf and I had looked down into this canyon in the summer of 1929, when we and our horses climbed the Moving Mountain.

Next morning we broke camp early, taking the tent and stove with us, and continuing up the canyon.

The sky was cloudless and blue, snow sparkled over everything. After ten miles of winding among precipices, the country opened out, and we found ourselves among well-rounded, rolling hills, which did not seem at all like the customary topography of the Brooks Range. Miles to the north, however, some jagged peaks loomed, making the landscape less unfamiliar.

Most of this day we geepoled, but there were some overflowed places where we had the finest riding on the runners. There were also a couple of stretches which had overflowed so recently that they had not frozen yet so that there was a shallow layer of icy water over the solid ice beneath. Here we changed our moccasins for mukluks— waterproof sealskin boots with the fur turned in.

As we progressed upstream the timber became more and more scarce, until we came to a patch which we thought might be the last. Just above it Clear River entered another canyon which blocked the view farther upstream. As we did not wish to make camp among the dwarf willows after dark, we stopped here for the night. The timber was on a bench, 40 feet above the river. It took us half an hour to break an uphill trail a couple of hundred yards to the timber, but the view it gave us, even more than the shelter, made this effort a cheap price to pay.

Making camp in loose snow, several feet deep, in which one sinks practically to the bottom the instant snowshoes are removed, is an interesting experience, at least for one brought up in a civilization where shelter comes ready made.

Our routine in camp was the result of many a night out in the deep snow. We would start with nothing but two bundled sleds, a wilderness in which a shelter had never yet been erected, and more (Ernie) or less (I) personal competence to combine the two into something safe and comfortable. Our procedure generally began by Ernie tramping down with his snowshoes a space big enough to pitch the 9 by 9 tent, with a little extra room to prevent our sinking clear to our waists the moment we stepped outside our tent. Then we usually hitched the tent to trees by ropes at either end of the ridge, and stretched out the wall ropes to trees, shrubs, or specially cut poles, whichever happened to be most handy. Meanwhile I would hack down a green spruce for blocks on which to set the stove, saving the boughs to spread on top of the snow inside the tent. Ernie would cut more boughs, and soon we would forget we were roosting on snow, unless we happened to look under the stove.

Before we started out in the morning, Ernie always filled the stove with shavings, kindling, and dry sticks of wood, so that once it was set up and the stovepipe attached at night, we would have a roaring fire in a few moments. Getting a fire started quickly was most important in really cold weather. Even in relatively mild weather the sooner the fire got going the better, because all cooking had to wait until we had melted enough snow to get the water we required. For melting the snow we used five-gallon gasoline cans, with one side cut out. Each night we used three of them, half full of water, two for cooking dog feed and one for ourselves.

But with melting the snow our nightly task was far from finished. Wood had to be cut. The dogs had to be unhitched and tied to trees. Spruce-bough bedding had to be prepared for them. Then we had to take in our own bedding and spread it out on our boughs. We had to scrape the snow from our socks, overalls, and moccasins, and hang them up to dry. When a little of the snow was melted we started the tea water, and after that the rest of the supper. While we were eating and afterward, the dog feed would be cooking. After supper there would be dishwashing, sewing, repairing snowshoes, and—most tedious of all—crawling, head first, into a sleeping bag to change films in total darkness. When the dog feed was done we would take it outside, pour it into separate pans for each dog, and let it cool. Just before going to bed we would serve it.

This may sound like a lot of work, and actually we were kept busy until ten or eleven o'clock. Nevertheless these evenings were very pleasant. Ernie was a simple but excellent cook, and the meals he prepared added real joy to our life after a day of mushing. The *pièce de résistance* of our suppers was always a pot of boiled meat. Ernie believed it essential for healthy camp life to avoid too much frying, and above all to avoid burned grease. The meat was tender sheep, which Ernie had shot late in the fall. With the natural cold-storage facilities of the Arctic there was no trouble in keeping meat all winter. We varied our suppers by boiling lima beans, peas, dried vegetables, rice, or macaroni with the meat. One potful lasted us for two nights. On the second night it was only necessary to thaw out and heat what was left from the first. The same was true of fruit. We always had a pot of dried apples and cranberries cooked and ready for immediate use. The only fresh cooking necessary for supper on the second night was tea, biscuits, and sometimes rice or macaroni.

At supper and after came the period of leisurely conversation. Ernie had taken along *Kristin Lavransdatter* and Whitehead's *Science and the Modern World*, while I had 1,217 pages of Tolstoi's *War and Peace* (which Ernie had read along with *Anna Karenina* during his last two-month trip in the wilderness). But we were both so busy talking that neither of us read a single page. Ernie had remarkably broad interests, bred from vast reading during thousands of solitary evenings in camp. Our conversations varied in subject matter from midwestern Methodist moral notions of the school teacher and Tolstoi's overworking of the phenomenon of love at first sight to the work of the physicists Albert A. Michelson and Robert A. Millikan and how it tied up with the cosmic-ray theory. The most recurring theme, however, was Ernie's love for the wilderness.

"If I had a hundred thousand dollars today," he said with his slight Swedish accent, "I wouldn't quit this life in the hills. I'd get a little better equipment, and I'd go Outside and get married, but I'd come right back in here again. I know what the life Outside is like and it don't appeal to me. I've lived this free life in here too long."

Referring to a notoriously parsimonious local citizen, he said, "The man was indignant because we opened a can of corn. 'It costs too much,' he'd say. Now there's no sense to that. We're here such a short time and a person can get so much pleasure out of good eating, he's a fool if he don't take that pleasure while he can."

Like the majority of Koyukukers, Ernie was very contemptuous of the modern, high-power publicity explorers like Wilkins, Byrd, and the

Roosevelts. Concerning the Byrd Expedition he said: "Jesus Christ, do they call that exploring? Why, they had everything they could ask for except women. That foodstuff they had they could live on in luxury all the time. They don't know anything about hardships. They ought to get out in the hills here where they have to live on themselves, and can't radio for help every time they get in trouble."

Bed for both of us consisted of a heavy, winter sheepskin, as soft as a coiled spring mattress, laid on the boughs. Over this we spread our sleeping bags and crawled in. The stove would burn for two or three hours after we retired, keeping the tent as warm as a house. Then it would gradually chill off to outside temperature, until about five or five-thirty. At that time Ernie, who always slept nearest the door of the stove, would start the fire, while I would crack the ice on the top of the water can and fill the coffee pot. Then we would drop back into our bags for a delicious half hour of dozing while the tent was warming and the water heating.

Our regular breakfast was sheep steaks fried in olive oil (another of Ernie's dietetic hobbies; he is death on lard or bacon grease), hot cakes, coffee, and fruit. After breakfast we would dress for the trail, and if we were moving camp tear down the tent, pack up the sleds, and hitch up the dogs.

On the morning after reaching the timber patch above Clear River canyon, however, we didn't break camp. Not knowing what lay ahead, we determined on a day of reconnaissance. So we hitched up the sleds, empty except for our heavy parkas, a change of footwear for emergency, extra gloves, mukluks, a lunch including a large thermos bottle filled with hot coffee, and my photographic outfit.

As soon as we started, the dogs tore down the 40-foot slope to the river so fast that we had to ride the brakes hard to keep from dashing the sleds to pieces among the trees. We swung out on the clear ice of the river, and started up the dark canyon at a pace of nine or ten miles an hour. The canyon was not very deep, but the walls were so steep that three hours after sunrise it seemed like late evening.

Then all at once we were out of the canyon, at the foot of a great sunny amphitheater, perhaps six miles long and three or four miles wide. The floor was as gently tilted as any agricultural valley might have been. There were scattered stands of spruce timber as far as we could see. On either side mountains rose for about 2,000 feet steeply, but not precipitously, except at the very summits. Only at the upper end of the valley, from which we could see three deep gorges emerging, was there any sign of those incredibly jagged summits which typify the upper North Fork country. It was a peaceful, cheerful valley, all sunlight and flawlessly blue sky and snow.

After a couple of miles we came to the end of the river's overflow. We left the river, and from now on the snow was so deep that we had to plod along on snowshoes, breaking trail for the dogs. It was work, but work filled with delight in the beauty of that bright valley, the increasing wildness of the country ahead, and the mystery of which gorge before us carried the main tributary of this never-followed river. Halfway up the valley, I looked back beyond where our camp lay and was startled by the sight of a rock chimney, about 300 or 400 feet on the sides we could see, rising from the drainage to the east. All the way up the valley we kept looking back at this gigantic rock which bore a striking resemblance to Chimney Rock in the Kaniksu National Forest in Idaho. We called it Chimney Mountain.

If this sight was startling, it was nothing compared with the revelation of fresh grandeur which was awaiting us when we reached the head of the amphitheater. We discovered that Clear River emerged from none of the three gorges we had imagined, but from a hidden valley which turned almost at right angles to the east. I cannot convey in words my feeling in finding this broad valley lying there, just as fresh and untrammeled as at the dawn of geological eras hundreds of millions of years ago. Nor is there any adequate way of describing the scenery, beyond giving the measurements and outlines: Eight miles long, one and a half wide, U-shaped, flanked by mountains rising 2,000–3,000 feet almost straight out of it. I could mention dozens of thousand-foot sheer precipices; I could liken the valley to a Yosemite without waterfalls, but with rock domes beside which the world-renowned Half Dome would be trivial—yet with all that, I would not have conveyed the sense of the continuous, exulting feeling of immensity; of the thrill of seeing gigantic

pinnacles on every side overhanging gorges; of the great, white, serrated skyline at the head of the valley, built of towering summits nearly
a mile higher than where we were; and of the freshness of the all-
covering snow, the blue sky, the clarity and sparkle of the mid-winter
atmosphere.

Perfect as this valley seemed from its foot, its ascent unfolded new
scenery so magnificent that the first view seemed like only a tourist's
glimpse of the real beauty. For into this wide major valley, ten unique
gorges debouched. I say unique because every one had a character and
individuality which made it stand out unforgettably. In the continental
United States every one would be considered worthy of preservation as
a national monument.

c. 1931

Archy the cockroach was Don Marquis' (1878–1937) great creation. The conceit went like this: at night the bug would emerge from his nest and jump on the keys of Marquis' typewriter, producing his column for him. (Archy couldn't jump on the "shift" key simultaneously, so his writings are mostly in the lower-case.) The works of Archy and his cat friend Mehitabel have been steadily in print since the 1920s; here you get a sense of the mood of the eastern cities in the era of Depression and Dust Bowl.

what the ants are saying

dear boss i was talking with an ant
the other day
and he handed me a lot of
gossip which ants the world around
are chewing over among themselves

i pass it on to you
in the hope that you may relay it to other
human beings and hurt their feelings with it
no insect likes human beings
and if you think you can see why
the only reason i tolerate you is because
you seem less human to me than most of them
here is what the ants are saying

it wont be long now it wont be long
man is making deserts of the earth
it wont be long now
before man will have used it up

so that nothing but ants
and centipedes and scorpions
can find a living on it
man has oppressed us for a million years
but he goes on steadily
cutting the ground from under
his own feet making deserts deserts deserts

we ants remember
and have it all recorded
in our tribal lore
when gobi was a paradise
swarming with men and rich
in human prosperity
it is a desert now and the home
of scorpions ants and centipedes

what man calls civilization
always results in deserts
man is never on the square
he uses up the fat and greenery of the earth
each generation wastes a little more
of the future with greed and lust for riches

north africa was once a garden spot
and then came carthage and rome
and despoiled the storehouse
and now you have sahara
sahara ants and centipedes

toltecs and aztecs had a mighty
civilization on this continent
but they robbed the soil and wasted nature

and now you have deserts scorpions ants and centipedes
and the deserts of the near east
followed egypt and babylon and assyria
and persia and rome and the turk
the ant is the inheritor of tamerlane
and the scorpion succeeds the caesars

america was once a paradise
of timberland and stream
but it is dying because of the greed
and money lust of a thousand little kings
who slashed the timber all to hell
and would not be controlled
and changed the climate
and stole the rainfall from posterity
and it wont be long now
it wont be long
till everything is desert
from the alleghenies to the rockies
the deserts are coming
the deserts are spreading
the springs and streams are drying up
one day the mississippi itself
will be a bed of sand
ants and scorpions and centipedes
shall inherit the earth

men talk of money and industry
of hard times and recoveries
of finance and economics
but the ants wait and the scorpions wait
for while men talk they are making deserts all the time
getting the world ready for the conquering ant

drought and erosion and desert
because men cannot learn

rainfall passing off in flood and freshet
and carrying good soil with it
because there are no longer forests
to withhold the water in the
billion meticulations of the roots

it wont be long now it won't be long
till earth is barren as the moon
and sapless as a mumbled bone

dear boss i relay this information
without any fear that humanity
will take warning and reform
                                        archy

The Lives and Times of Archy and Mehitabel (1935)

Born into relative prosperity on an Iowa farm, Caroline Henderson (1877–1966) graduated from Mt. Holyoke College in 1901. She seemed set for some kind of conventionally secure life, until she nearly died of diphtheria in 1907. When she recovered, she was determined to pursue her girlhood dream of farming on the frontier, and so she established a quarter-section on the High Plains near Eva, Oklahoma. She met her husband, an itinerant named Will, when he came as part of a crew to dig her well. They settled down to grow wheat on land that was arid even before the Dust Bowl, and where the forces of modernizing agriculture were already starting to drive crop prices down and drive many of their neighbors off the land. To supplement their income in the years before World War I, Henderson wrote a popular series of columns as the "Homestead Lady" for *Ladies World*, and then in the 1930s a series of letters for the *Atlantic* that, though stoic, described the essential horror of that most epic of American environmental crises, the Dust Bowl—not just outside, where crops were buried beneath the sand, but even inside, at the center of the home, where the grit of the dust sapped the grit of the homesteaders. The Hendersons managed to keep their farm until their retirement, but it was always a bitter struggle, and Henderson wrote very little except letters to friends in the decades after these pieces.

Letter from the Dust Bowl

EVA, OKLAHOMA
June 30, 1935

MY DEAR EVELYN:—

Your continued interest in our effort to 'tie a knot in the end of the rope and hang on' is most stimulating. Our recent transition from rain-soaked eastern Kansas with its green pasture, luxuriant foliage, abundance of flowers, and promise of a generous harvest, to the dust-covered desolation of No Man's Land was a difficult change to crowd into one short day's travel. Eleanor has laid aside the medical books for a time. Wearing our shade hats, with handkerchiefs tied over our faces and vaseline in our nostrils, we have been trying to rescue our home from the accumulations of wind-blown dust which penetrates wherever air can go. It is an almost hopeless task, for there is rarely a day when at some time the dust clouds do not roll over. 'Visibility' approaches zero and everything is covered again with a silt-like deposit which may vary in depth from a film to actual ripples on the kitchen floor. I keep oiled cloths on the window sills and between the upper and lower sashes. They help just a little to retard or collect the dust. Some seal the windows with the gummed-paper strips used in wrapping parcels, but no method is fully effective. We buy what appears to be red cedar sawdust with oil added to use in sweeping our floors, and do our best to avoid inhaling the irritating dust.

In telling you of these conditions I realize that I expose myself to charges of disloyalty to this western region. A good Kansas friend suggests that we should imitate the Californian attitude toward earthquakes and keep to ourselves what we know about dust storms. Since the very limited rains of May in this section gave some slight ground for renewed hope, optimism has been the approved policy. Printed articles or statements by journalists, railroad officials, and secretaries of small-town Chambers of Commerce have heralded too enthusiastically the return of prosperity to the drouth region. And in our part of the country that is the one durable basis for any prosperity whatever. There is nothing else to build upon. But you wished to know the truth, so I am telling you the actual situation, though I freely admit that the facts are themselves often contradictory and confusing.

Early in May, with no more grass or even weeds on our 640 acres than on your kitchen floor, and even the scanty remnants of dried grasses from last year cut off and blown away, we decided, like most of our neighbors, to ship our cattle to grass in the central part of the state. We sent 27 head, retaining here the heifers coming fresh this spring. The shipping charge on our part of the carload was $46. Pasture costs us $7.00 for a cow and calf for the season and $5.00 for a yearling. Whether this venture brings profit or loss depends on whether the cattle make satisfactory gains during the summer and whether prices remain reasonable or fall back to the level that most people would desire. We farmers here in the United States might as well recognize that we are a minority group, and that the prevailing interest of the nation as a whole is no longer agricultural. Hay for the horses and the heifers remaining here cost us $23 per ton, brought by truck from eastern Oklahoma.

The day after we shipped the cattle, the long drouth was temporarily broken by the first effective moisture in many months—about one and one-quarter inches in two or three gentle rains. All hope of a wheat crop had been abandoned by March or April.

Contrary to many published reports, a good many people had left this country either temporarily or permanently before any rains came. And they were not merely 'drifters,' as is frequently alleged. In May a friend in the southwestern county of Kansas voluntarily sent me a list of the people who had already left their immediate neighborhood or were packed up and ready to go. The list included 109 persons in 26 families, substantial people, most of whom had been in that locality over ten years, and some as long as forty years. In these families there had been two deaths from dust pneumonia. Others in the neighborhood were ill at that time. Fewer actual residents have left our neighborhood, but on a sixty-mile trip yesterday to procure tractor repairs we saw many pitiful reminders of broken hopes and apparently wasted effort. Little abandoned homes where people had drilled deep wells for the precious water, had set trees and vines, built reservoirs, and fenced in gardens,—with everything now walled in or half buried by banks of drifted soil,—told a painful story of loss and disappointment. I grieved especially over one lonely plum thicket buried to the tips of the twigs, and a garden with a fence closely built of boards for wind protection, now enclosing only a hillock of dust covered with the blue-flowered bull nettles which no winds or sands discourage.

It might give you some notion of our great 'open spaces' if I tell you that on the sixty-mile trip, going by a state road over which our mail comes from the railroad, and coming back by a Federal highway, we encountered only one car, and no other vehicles of any sort. And this was on Saturday, the farmers' marketing day!

The coming of the long-desired rain gave impetus to the Federal projects for erosion control. Plans were quickly made, submitted to groups of farmers in district gatherings, and put into operation without delay.

The proposition was that, in order to encourage the immediate listing of abandoned wheat ground and other acreage so as to cut down wind erosion, the Federal Government would contribute ten cents per acre toward the expense of fuel and oil for tractors or feed for horses, if the farmers would agree to list not less than one fourth of the acreage on contour lines. Surveys were made promptly for all farmers signing contracts for either contour listing or terracing. The latest report states that within the few weeks since the programme was begun in our county 299,986 acres have been ploughed or listed on these contour lines—that is, according to the lay of the land instead of on straight lines with right-angled turns as has been the usual custom.

The plan has been proposed and carried through here as a matter of public policy for the welfare of all without reproach or humiliation to anyone. It should be remembered that 1935 is the fourth successive year of drouth and crop failure through a great part of the high plains region, and the hopelessly low prices for the crop of 1931 gave no chance to build up reserves for future needs. If the severe critics of all who in any way join in government plans for the saving of homes and the restoration of farms to a productive basis could only understand how vital a human problem is here considered, possibly their censures might be less bitter and scornful.

At any rate the contour listing has been done over extensive areas. If rains come to carry forward the feed crops now just struggling up in the furrows, the value of the work can be appraised. The primary intention of the plan for contour listing is to distribute rainfall evenly over the fields and prevent its running off to one end of the field or down the road to some creek or drainage basin. It is hoped that the plan will indirectly tend to lessen wind erosion by promoting the growth of feed crops, restoration of humus to denuded surfaces, and some protection through standing stubbles and the natural coverage of weeds and unavoidable wastes. One great contributing cause of the terrible dust storms of the last two years has been the pitiful bareness of the fields resulting from the long drouth.

I am not wise enough to forecast the result. We have had two most welcome rains in June—three quarters of an inch and one-half inch. Normally these should have been of the utmost benefit, though they by no means guarantee an abundant feed crop from our now sprouting seeds as many editorial writers have decreed, and they do nothing toward restoring subsoil moisture. Actually the helpful effects of the rains have been for us and for other people largely destroyed by the drifting soil from abandoned, unworked lands around us. It fills the air and our eyes and noses and throats, and, worst of all, our furrows, where tender shoots are coming to the surface only to be buried by the smothering silt from the fields of rugged individualists who persist in their right to do nothing.

A fairly promising piece of barley has been destroyed for us by the merciless drift from the same field whose sands have practically buried the little mulberry hedge which has long sheltered our buildings from the northwest winds. Large spaces in our pastures are entirely bare in spite of the rains. Most of the green color, where there is any grazing, is due to the pestilent Russian thistles rather than to grass. Our little locust grove which we cherished for so many years has become a small pile of fence posts. With trees and vines and flowers all around you, you can't imagine how I miss that little green shaded spot in the midst of the desert glare.

Naturally you will wonder why we stay where conditions are so extremely disheartening. Why not pick up and leave as so many others have done? It is a fair question, but a hard one to answer.

Recently I talked with a young university graduate of very superior attainments. He took the ground that in such a case sentiment could and should be disregarded. He may be right. Yet I cannot act or feel or think as if the experiences of our twenty-seven years of life together had never been. And they are all bound up with the little corner to which we have given our continued and united efforts. To leave voluntarily—to break all these closely knit ties for the sake of a possibly greater comfort elsewhere—seems like defaulting on our task. We may *have* to leave. We can't hold out indefinitely without some return from the land, some source of income, however small. But I think I can never go willingly or without pain that as yet seems unendurable.

There are also practical considerations that serve to hold us here, for the present. Our soil is excellent. We need only a little rain—less than in most places—to make it productive. No one who remembers the wheat crops of 1926, 1929, 1931, can possibly regard this as permanently submarginal land. The newer methods of farming suggest possibilities of better control of moisture in the future. Our entire equipment is adapted to the type of farming suitable for this country and would have to be replaced at great expense with the tools needed in some other locality. We have spent so much in trying to keep our land from blowing away that it looks foolish to walk off and leave it, when somewhat more favorable conditions seem now to 'cast their shadows before.' I scarcely need to tell you that there is no use in thinking of either renting or selling farm property here at present. It is just a place to stand on—if we can keep the taxes paid—and work and hope for a better day. We could realize nothing whatever from all our years of struggle with which to make a fresh start.

We long for the garden and little chickens, the trees and birds and wild flowers of the years gone by. Perhaps if we do our part these good things may return some day, for others if not for ourselves.

Will joins me in earnest hopes for your recovery. The dust has been particularly aggravating to his bronchial trouble, but he keeps working on. A great reddish-brown dust cloud is rising now from the southeast, so we must get out and do our night work before it arrives. Our thoughts go with you.

The Atlantic, May 1936

DONALD CULROSS PEATTIE

Soon after its publication, the Limited Editions Club chose Donald Culross Peattie's *An Almanac for Moderns* (1935) as the book of its moment "most likely to become a classic." Instead it has dropped into obscurity, partly because his style is a little stilted and purple, but also because times changed. Peattie (1898–1964) was a deep believer in the Order of the Universe as Understood by Science—biologists, physicists, and astronomers, "those who have looked most deeply," were the "surest, serenest" men he knew, because they understood that "the immutable order of nature is on our side. It is on the side of life." This would become a harder confidence to share just a few years later, once the physicists had exploded the first big bombs. This small piece captures his sense that everything is going to be okay—even the obnoxious starling, that interloper, is actually mostly to the good.

Birds That Are New Yorkers

February is a good month in which to make friends with the birds of a great city. It is often deemed the dullest page in the bright almanac of birds. For all of nature February is the last, not the second, month of the year. It is the hour before the dawn when, it is customary to say, nothing of interest happens. Practically no birds arrive in February on their Spring migrations, and almost none of the Winter visitants depart.

Yet where others have long despised to look, be sure that there is at least a grain of gold undiscovered, and sometimes a whole lode. The spirit of discovery, true scientific discovery, is, after all, not concerned with the rare, but with the tremendous importance of the usual. A skylark on your penthouse potted pine would be a sensational accident, but it would be nothing else. A city pigeon's strutting on your office window sill is, for all that is already known about pigeons, still the more significant event.

The biology of the pigeon, his marvelous adaptability, his intelligence, the fascination of his Mendelian strains, bred, interbred, and bred out again to the normal—these in the end surpass any meaning that a skylark would have if he chanted some morning at your window. For, after all, skylarks have been tried—they were introduced around Flatbush, only to perish after a few years—and are found wanting. Wanting, that is, in nature's prime demand, ability to survive.

The ability to survive constant association with human beings is the first prerequisite of those birds that do not merely pass through the city in Winter but make of it a more or less permanent home. Since you yourself, and all of us, largely make these conditions, it is interesting to see how they look to the birds. And this is the picture:

A jumble of peaks and canyons having nothing about them that, to bird intelligence, means a memorable landmark; a glare of lights by night, many of them swaying, all of them blinding; a powerful upward draft from all high buildings, so strong as to toss airplanes about like corks at sea; insect fare very nearly nil, and grain supply scarcely better; nesting sites rare or totally lacking for all birds that demand a tree, a shrub, or a tuft of grass; constant danger from traffic, from dislodgement of the nest, from hungry, prowling cats and rats; absence in the modern city of telegraph lines for perches; and, frequently, the definite hostility of the city authorities, who are prepared, if a bird enjoys any success at all, to blast him out of town with a fire hose, or to shoot him or poison his food or trap him.

The advantages are few, but real. They include warmth and shelter in Winter, great opportunities for scavenging around refuse piles, and an absence of competition from other species.

And now begins the biological fascination of the study of city birds, a pursuit that needs no instruments nor field trips to further it, for the phenomenon of their adaptation lies all about us ready for our understanding. We grasp it so readily because it is, in many respects, identical with our experiences as social denizens of the vast human rookery we call a city.

Obviously, to begin with, those birds would succeed within these strict limits of life which were inherently adaptable and educable. They must possess some previous experience of humanity, and food habits which are close to ours, or at least not confined in a finikin way to a few forest insects or the nectar of flowers. There will have also to be a high prolificity, to cover the accident rate incident upon living where humans order all things only for their own convenience.

And, finally, these metropolitan singers will have to be possessed of many human qualities. They must be social, able to endure and enjoy crowding, able to act as a flock, to pool common interests and make concerted attacks upon local problems. They certainly need intelligence, and it is probable that they need more of a vocabulary, more power to communicate, than we find in the solitary singer in the woods.

Now when all these conditions are imposed, how many native American birds would measure up to them? Considering only the birds of the Northeastern States, there come to my mind few besides grackles, some of the swallows, crows, jays and, in their restricted element, harbor gulls. Out of these, only our common harbor or herring gull—a cosmopolite of ports the world around—is actually a common city bird, and that of course not outside the fringe of docks and watersides.

As a scavenger of city and ocean refuse the gull is invaluable. And, it seems, to be useful to man is the best chance of survival which any animal can have. Not only is the gull protected by law in civilized communities; he has one other great survival value—his flesh is nauseous and inedible. He is not worth killing.

It is not surprising that all the rest of our regular resident city birds should be European species. For the conditions of life in Europe have been at work for centuries in selecting out for survival only the creatures that get along with the human species. They must be clever, and adaptable, and able sturdily to hold their own; but they must, however thieving, predatory or mischievous, not carry their aggressive characteristics so far that man will make a concerted effort to destroy them. If they cannot be good like the pigeons, they must be able to gauge the limits of man's patience to a nicety, like the English sparrows, and just escape his most awful wrath.

The white man introduced many changes when he came to America. He brought with him new weapons—plow and axe, dog and horse, drainage and guns. He broke open the museum of ancient American life, a crowded exhibit of delicate antiquities to which nothing new could be added without first clearing something away. And European man instinctively cleared away everything unfamiliar to him. The buffalo was monarch here, but wild, untamed, unpedigreed, and the white man preferred domesticated, servile cattle. He exterminated the passenger pigeon and put the barnyard pigeon in its place. He upset the balance of nature, and never since has he been able to restore it.

The least unfortunate of his efforts has been the introduction of the common pigeon, more correctly the rock dove of Europe. This creature was established in early times by the first colonists, and as a pet his right to be here has never been denied. But it is only recently that ornithologists have actually begun to measure his intelligence.

We all see the pigeons in the streets, but few of us stop to wonder where they nest, or in what season. We never see their squabs, yet we know that, uncared for, these gentle denizens of the skyscrapers are not diminishing in numbers. In short, quite characteristically, we take for granted the most mysterious and astonishing facts about us; we exclaim only over exceptions and coincidences without meaning, such as the fortuitous landing of a dazed woodcock on the windowsill of the headquarters of the Audubon Society, high above New York.

A less endearing immigrant, but one just as thoroughly Americanized, is the sparrow that we rather unjustly call English. It was deliberately introduced at Brooklyn in 1851 and 1852, and in a short time it had spread as widely as in Australia. Intended to eat up a harmful insect pest, it soon had earned for itself the reputation of the prime and classic example of a pest.

War has been waged on the domestic sparrow, with guns and poisoned grain and traps. But it was two unforeseen influences that checked the triumphs of *Passer domesticus*. First, the coming of the automobile and the consequent disappearance of the horse from our streets changed the course of sparrow history, for this guttersnipe thrives best around horses. Next, the advent of the starlings introduced a challenger. In a few fast rounds the starling has pretty well won the title.

The domestic sparrow will never pass completely from our city scene, for his very prolificity will sustain him. Or rather, his wife's industrious matronhood, for the female sparrow is often seen carrying straw for a nest in February, and as many as four broods are crowded into the year's cycle.

Eugene Schieffelin, one of the first to import house sparrows, not content with his misguided good works, continued in the same vein in 1890 and 1891 by releasing one hundred starlings in Central Park. They were also deliberately introduced in Baltimore and Washington, and at the present writing are becoming common as far west as Illinois. The general verdict is that we have got rid of a cat by importing a tiger.

The indictment against the starling is a long one. He gangs up on other birds, invading the home sites of such valuable native species as nest in hollows and under eaves, like the robin, flicker, woodpeckers, swallows and bluebirds. And by the use of concerted numbers, starlings defeat rival species individually. The endless gabbling of these birds in their dingy, spotted, untidy Winter plumage, makes the streets and squares where they congregate look and sound very like a hobo college.

But there are things to be said in the starling's favor. He was long ago voted by the farmers of England the most useful bird, from his habit of destroying insect pests. In the great drought of 1934 starlings in Illinois helped put an end to the frightful chinch bug menace. The crow-like intelligence of starlings makes them interesting neighbors, and to see them go wheeling out, several hundred in a flock, in perfect formation, gives a lift to the heart that loves gallantry.

Finding the faults in city birds, we are shown a mirror of our own kind. They are quarrelsome, tolerant of dirt, greedy, and distinctly promiscuous, having those polygamous and polyandrous tendencies one must regretfully call all too human. This cliff-dwelling life of ours, so ancient and so modern, seems to call forth our own failings in our animal neighbors. But when we complain of them we should remember that we cannot expect hermit thrushes to live on Broadway. It is starlings and pigeons and sparrows or nothing—and when one must rub elbows with neighbors, it is wisest to find in them all the good there is.

The New York Times Magazine, February 16, 1936

In 1988, the eminent Harvard critic Helen Vendler published an essay in *The New Yorker* that attempted to read Robinson Jeffers (1887–1962) out of the American canon. He had not, she insisted, done the hard psychological work of coming to terms with his childhood, resisting the "introspection" required of a major poet. It was a revealing comment, less perhaps about Jeffers than about prevailing literary standards. Jeffers' precise point was that living in one's head, out of contact with the physical world that surrounds us, defined the modern disease. That was what he fought against, and his work found allies among those who loved the rugged California coast and those who understood wild places everywhere. The recipient of a first-rate education (by 12 he had mastered Greek and Latin and could speak French and German fluently), he studied medicine at USC and forestry at the University of Washington before settling in Carmel and building, stone by stone, a kind of small castle he called Tor House. He began producing epic poems, all of which took up the theme that man did not stand alone at the center of the universe. He was a Nietzschean and in certain ways a crank, but to argue à la Vendler that he was badly adjusted is perhaps to presume that the world as we know it is well-adjusted. Environmentalists, especially those of a radical philosophical bent, have often found him sympathetic: for many years the journal of Friends of the Earth was called *Not Man Apart*.

The Answer

Then what is the answer?—Not to be deluded by dreams.
To know that great civilizations have broken down into
     violence, and their tyrants come, many times before.
When open violence appears, to avoid it with honor or
     choose the least ugly faction; these evils are essential.

To keep one's own integrity, be merciful and uncorrupted
        and not wish for evil; and not be duped
By dreams of universal justice or happiness. These dreams
        will not be fulfilled.
To know this, and know that however ugly the parts
        appear the whole remains beautiful. A severed hand
Is an ugly thing, and man dissevered from the earth and
        stars and his history . . . for contemplation or in
        fact . . .
Often appears atrociously ugly. Integrity is wholeness, the
        greatest beauty is
Organic wholeness, the wholeness of life and things, the
        divine beauty of the universe. Love that, not man
Apart from that, or else you will share man's pitiful
        confusions, or drown in despair when his days
        darken.

1935

Carmel Point

The extraordinary patience of things!
This beautiful place defaced with a crop of suburban
        houses—
How beautiful when we first beheld it,
Unbroken field of poppy and lupin walled with clean cliffs;
No intrusion but two or three horses pasturing,
Or a few milch cows rubbing their flanks on the outcrop
        rock-heads—
Now the spoiler has come: does it care?
Not faintly. It has all time. It knows the people are a tide
That swells and in time will ebb, and all

Their works dissolve. Meanwhile the image of the pristine
      beauty
Lives in the very grain of the granite,
Safe as the endless ocean that climbs our cliff.—As for us:
We must uncenter our minds from ourselves;
We must unhumanize our views a little, and become
      confident
As the rock and ocean that we were made from.

1953

JOHN STEINBECK

John Steinbeck (1902–1968), who won the Nobel Prize, was one of the great observers among American writers—*The Grapes of Wrath* (1939) grew out of a seven-part series he wrote for his hometown *San Francisco News* about the Okies flooding into California's Central Valley to escape the Dust Bowl ravaging the Plains. He listened with heart as well as head—the degree to which he identified with these men and women can be measured by the number of people who called him a "communist" once it was published.

from **The Grapes of Wrath**

To the red country and part of the gray country of Oklahoma, the last rains came gently, and they did not cut the scarred earth. The plows crossed and recrossed the rivulet marks. The last rains lifted the corn quickly and scattered weed colonies and grass along the sides of the roads so that the gray country and the dark red country began to disappear under a green cover. In the last part of May the sky grew pale and the clouds that had hung in high puffs for so long in the spring were dissipated. The sun flared down on the growing corn day after day until a line of brown spread along the edge of each green bayonet. The clouds appeared, and went away, and in a while they did not try any more. The weeds grew darker green to protect themselves, and they did not spread any more. The surface of the earth crusted, a thin hard crust, and as the sky became pale, so the earth became pale, pink in the red country and white in the gray country.

In the water-cut gullies the earth dusted down in dry little streams. Gophers and ant lions started small avalanches. And as the sharp sun struck day after day, the leaves of the young corn became less stiff and erect; they bent in a curve at first, and then, as the central ribs of strength grew weak, each leaf tilted downward. Then it was June, and the sun shone more fiercely. The brown lines on the corn leaves widened and moved in on the central ribs. The weeds frayed and edged back toward their roots. The air was thin and the sky more pale; and every day the earth paled.

In the roads where the teams moved, where the wheels milled the ground and the hooves of the horses beat the ground, the dirt crust broke and the dust formed. Every moving thing lifted the dust into the air: a walking man lifted a thin layer as high as his waist, and a wagon lifted the dust as high as the fence tops, and an automobile boiled a cloud behind it. The dust was long in settling back again.

When June was half gone, the big clouds moved up out of Texas and the Gulf, high heavy clouds, rain-heads. The men in the fields looked up at the clouds and sniffed at them and held wet fingers up to sense the wind. And the horses were nervous while the clouds were up. The rain-heads dropped a little spattering and hurried on to some other country. Behind them the sky was pale again and the sun flared. In the dust there were drop craters where the rain had fallen, and there were clean splashes on the corn, and that was all.

A gentle wind followed the rain clouds, driving them on northward, a wind that softly clashed the drying corn. A day went by and the wind increased, steady, unbroken by gusts. The dust from the roads fluffed up and spread out and fell on the weeds beside the fields, and fell into the fields a little way. Now the wind grew strong and hard and it worked at the rain crust in the corn fields. Little by little the sky was darkened by the mixing dust, and the wind felt over the earth, loosened the dust, and carried it away. The wind grew stronger. The rain crust broke and the dust lifted up out of the fields and drove gray plumes into the air like sluggish smoke. The corn threshed the wind and made a dry, rushing sound. The finest dust did not settle back to earth now, but disappeared into the darkening sky.

The wind grew stronger, whisked under stones, carried up straws and old leaves, and even little clods, marking its course as it sailed across the fields. The air and the sky darkened and through them the sun shone redly, and there was a raw sting in the air. During a night the wind raced faster over the land, dug cunningly among the rootlets of the corn, and the corn fought the wind with its weakened leaves until the roots were freed by the prying wind and then each stalk settled wearily sideways toward the earth and pointed the direction of the wind.

The dawn came, but no day. In the gray sky a red sun appeared, a dim red circle that gave a little light, like dusk; and as that day advanced, the dusk slipped back toward darkness, and the wind cried and whimpered over the fallen corn.

Men and women huddled in their houses, and they tied handkerchiefs over their noses when they went out, and wore goggles to protect their eyes.

When the night came again it was black night, for the stars could not pierce the dust to get down, and the window lights could not even spread beyond their own yards. Now the dust was evenly mixed with the air, an emulsion of dust and air. Houses were shut tight, and cloth wedged around doors and windows, but the dust came in so thinly that it could not be seen in the air, and it settled like pollen on the chairs and tables, on the dishes. The people brushed it from their shoulders. Little lines of dust lay at the door sills.

In the middle of that night the wind passed on and left the land quiet. The dust-filled air muffled sound more completely than fog does. The people, lying in their beds, heard the wind stop. They awakened when the rushing wind was gone. They lay quietly and listened deep into the stillness. Then the roosters crowed, and their voices were muffled, and the people stirred restlessly in their beds and wanted the morning. They knew it would take a long time for the dust to settle out of the air. In the morning the dust hung like fog, and the sun was as red as ripe new blood. All day the dust sifted down from the sky, and the next day it sifted down. An even blanket covered the earth. It settled on the corn, piled up on the tops of the fence posts, piled up on the wires; it settled on roofs, blanketed the weeds and trees.

The people came out of their houses and smelled the hot stinging air and covered their noses from it. And the children came out of the houses, but they did not run or shout as they would have done after a rain. Men stood by their fences and looked at the ruined corn, drying fast now, only a little green showing through the film of dust. The men were silent and they did not move often. And the women came out of the houses to stand beside their men—to feel whether this time the men would break. The women studied the men's faces secretly, for the corn could go, as long as something else remained. The children stood near by, drawing figures in the dust with bare toes, and the children sent exploring senses out to see whether men and women would break. The children peeked at the faces of the men and women, and then drew careful lines in the dust with their toes. Horses came to the watering troughs and nuzzled the water to clear the surface dust. After a while the faces of the watching men lost their bemused perplexity and became hard and angry and resistant. Then the women knew that they were safe and that there was no break. Then they asked, What'll we do? And the men replied, I don't know. But it was all right. The women knew it was all right, and the watching children knew it was all right. Women and children knew deep in themselves that no misfortune was too great to bear if their men were whole. The women went into the houses to their work, and the children began to play, but cautiously at first. As the day went forward the sun became less red. It flared down on the dust-blanketed land. The men sat in the doorways of their houses; their hands were busy with sticks and little rocks. The men sat still—thinking—figuring.

The Grapes of Wrath (1939)

WOODY GUTHRIE

"This Land Is Your Land," written in 1940, has been sung around so many camp fires that people tend not to notice how radical it is—the idea that this land really is *ours*, and the very nature of the land (the fog, the wind, the sand) shouts out that point. Woody Guthrie (1912–1967) was the great folksinger of the 20th century, the voice of the Dust Bowl and of the union movement. "This Land" was written in response to Kate Smith's bombastic recording of Irving Berlin's "God Bless America," and it is set to the tune of a Baptist hymn (and Carter Family hit) called "When the World's on Fire." Guthrie revised the lyrics a number of times over the years; this version comes from a pamphlet he illustrated and published himself in 1945. Bob Dylan and Peter, Paul, and Mary recorded their own versions of the song in the 1960s, and Bruce Springsteen in the 1970s. Were I in charge of such matters, it would alternate weeks with "America the Beautiful" as our national anthem.

This Land Is Your Land

CHORUS:
This land is your land, this land is my land,
From the redwood forest to the New York island,
The Canadian mountain to the gulf stream waters,
This land is made for you and me.

As I go walking this ribbon of highway
I see above me this endless skyway
And all around me the wind keeps saying:
This land is made for you and me.

I roam and I ramble and I follow my footsteps
Till I come to the sands of her mineral desert
The mist is lifting and the voice is saying:
This land is made for you and me.

Where the wind is blowing I go a-strolling
The wheat field waving and the dust a-rolling
The fog is lifting and the wind is saying:
This land is made for you and me.

Nobody living can ever stop me
As I go walking my freedom highway
Nobody living can make me turn back
This land is made for you and me.

1945

MARJORY STONEMAN DOUGLAS

Marjory Stoneman Douglas (1890–1998) was born long enough ago that in college she joined a club promoting the right of women to vote; she lived long enough to receive the Presidential Medal of Freedom from Bill Clinton. And along the way, through a combination of writing and political activism, she did more than anyone else to try to preserve the Everglades, the great "river of grass" that gently drains Florida. After working for her father's paper, the *Miami Herald*, she became a freelance writer in the 1920s, producing stories for magazines like *The Saturday Evening Post*. In 1947 she published *The Everglades: River of Grass*, a book that changed what people thought of when they heard the word "swamp." Though the southern chunk of the Glades was protected as a national park that same year, the state's rampant development continued, and by the 1960s Douglas found herself becoming an environmental advocate for the preservation of the endangered ecosystem. She founded Friends of the Everglades, rallied to defeat plans for an airport on the park's northern edge, and helped raise the ruckus that eventually led to sweeping and extensive plans to restore the flow of the great sheet of water.

from **The Everglades: River of Grass**

The Everglades begin at Lake Okeechobee.

That is the name later Indians gave the lake, a name almost as recent as the word "Everglades." It means "Big Water." Everybody knows it.

Yet few have any idea of those pale, seemingly illimitable waters. Over the shallows, often less than a foot deep but seven hundred fifty or so square miles in actual area, the winds in one gray swift moment can shatter the reflections of sky and cloud whiteness standing still in that shining, polished, shimmering expanse. A boat can push for hours in a day of white sun through the short, crisp lake waves and there will be nothing to be seen anywhere but the brightness where the color of the water and the color of the sky become one. Men out of sight of land can stand in it up to their armpits and slowly "walk in" their long nets to the waiting boats. An everglade kite and his mate, questing in great solitary circles, rising and dipping and rising again on the wind currents, can look down all day long at the water faintly green with floating water lettuce or marked by thin standing lines of reeds, utter their sharp goat cries, and be seen and heard by no one at all.

There are great shallow islands, all brown reeds or shrubby trees thick in the water. There are masses of water weeds and hyacinths and flags rooted so long they seem solid earth, yet there is nothing but lake bottom to stand on. There the egret and the white ibis and the glossy ibis and the little blue herons in their thousands nested and circled and fed.

A long northeast wind, a "norther," can lash all that still surface to dirty vicious gray and white, over which the rain mists shut down like stained rolls of wool, so that from the eastern sand rim under dripping cypresses or the west ridge with its live oaks, no one would guess that all that waste of empty water stretched there but for the long monotonous wash of waves on unseen marshy shores.

Saw grass reaches up both sides of that lake in great enclosing arms, so that it is correct to say that the Everglades are there also. But south, southeast and southwest, where the lake water slopped and seeped and ran over and under the rock and soil, the greatest mass of the saw grass begins. It stretches as it always has stretched, in one thick enormous curving river of grass, to the very end. This is the Everglades.

It reaches one hundred miles from Lake Okeechobee to the Gulf of Mexico, fifty, sixty, even seventy miles wide. No one has ever fought his way along its full length. Few have ever crossed the northern wilderness of nothing but grass. Down that almost invisible slope the water moves. The grass stands. Where the grass and the water are there is the heart, the current, the meaning of the Everglades.

The grass and the water together make the river as simple as it is unique. There is no other river like it. Yet within that simplicity, enclosed within the river and bordering and intruding on it from each side, there is subtlety and diversity, a crowd of changing forms, of thrusting teeming life. And all that becomes the region of the Everglades.

The truth of the river is the grass. They call it saw grass. Yet in the botanical sense it is not grass at all so much as a fierce, ancient, cutting sedge. It is one of the oldest of the green growing forms in this world.

There are many places in the South where this saw grass, with its sharp central fold and edges set with fine saw teeth like points of glass, this sedge called *Cladium jamaicensis*, exists. But this is the greatest concentration of saw grass in the world. It grows fiercely in the fresh water creeping down below it. When the original saw grass thrust up its spears into the sun, the fierce sun, lord and power and first cause over the Everglades as of all the green world, then the Everglades began. They lie wherever the saw grass extends: 3,500 square miles, hundreds and thousands and millions, of acres, water and saw grass.

The first saw grass, exactly as it grows today, sprang up and lived in the sweet water and the pouring sunlight, and died in it, and from its own dried and decaying tissues and tough fibers bright with silica sprang up more fiercely again. Year after year it grew and was fed by its own brown rotting, taller and denser in the dark soil of its own death. Year after year, hundreds after hundreds of years, not so long as any geologic age but long in botanic time, far longer than anyone can be sure of, the saw grass grew. Four thousand years, they say, it must at least have grown like that, six feet, ten feet, twelve feet, even fifteen in places of deepest water. The edged and folded swords bristled around the delicate straight tube of pith that burst into brown flowering. The brown seed, tight enclosed after the manner of sedges, ripened in dense brownness. The seed was dropped and worked down in the water and its own ropelike mat of roots. All that decay of leaves and seed covers and roots was packed deeper year after year by the elbowing upthrust of its own life. Year after year it laid down new layers of virgin muck under the living water.

There are places now where the depth of the muck is equal to the height of the saw grass. When it is uncovered and brought into the sunlight, its stringy and grainy dullness glitters with the myriad unrotted silica points, like glass dust.

At the edges of the Glades, and toward those southern- and south-westernmost reaches where the great estuary or delta of the Glades river takes another form entirely, the saw grass is shorter and more sparse, and the springy, porous muck deposit under it is shallower and thinner. But where the saw grass grows tallest in the deepest muck, there goes the channel of the Glades.

The water winks and flashes here and there among the saw-grass roots, as the clouds are blown across the sun. To try to make one's way among these impenetrable tufts is to be cut off from all air, to be beaten down by the sun and ripped by the grassy saw-toothed edges as one sinks in mud and water over the roots. The dried yellow stuff holds no weight. There is no earthly way to get through the mud or the standing, keen-edged blades that crowd these interminable miles.

Or in the times of high water in the old days, the flood would rise until the highest tops of that sharp grass were like a thin lawn standing out of water as blue as the sky, rippling and wrinkling, linking the pools and spreading and flowing on its true course southward.

A man standing in the center of it, if he could get there, would be as lost in saw grass, as out of sight of anything but saw grass as a man drowning in the middle of Okeechobee—or the Atlantic Ocean, for that matter—would be out of sight of land.

The water moves. The saw grass, pale green to deep-brown ripeness, stands rigid. It is moved only in sluggish rollings by the vast push of the winds across it. Over its endless acres here and there the shadows of the dazzling clouds quicken and slide, purple-brown, plum-brown, mauve-brown, rust-brown, bronze. The bristling, blossoming tops do not bend easily like standing grain. They do not even in their own growth curve all one way but stand in edged clumps, curving against each other, all the massed curving blades making millions of fine arching lines that at a little distance merge to a huge expanse of brown wires or bristles or, farther beyond, to deep-piled plush. At the horizon they become velvet. The line they make is an edge of velvet against the infinite blue, the blue-and-white, the clear fine primrose yellow, the burning brass and crimson, the molten silver, the deepening hyacinth sky.

The clear burning light of the sun pours daylong into the saw grass and is lost there, soaked up, never given back. Only the water flashes and glints. The grass yields nothing.

Nothing less than the smashing power of some hurricane can beat it down. Then one can see, from high up in a plane, where the towering weight and velocity of the hurricane was the strongest and where along the edges of its whorl it turned less and less savagely and left the saw grass standing. Even so, the grass is not flattened in a continuous swath but only here and here and over there, as if the storm bounced or lifted and smashed down again in great hammering strokes or enormous cat-licks.

Only one force can conquer it completely and that is fire. Deep in the layers of muck there are layers of ashes, marks of old fires set by lightning or the early Indians. But in the early days the water always came back and there were long slow years in which the saw grass grew and died, laying down again its tough resilient decay.

This is the saw grass, then, which seems to move as the water moved, in a great thick arc south and southwestward from Okeechobee to the Gulf. There at the last imperceptible incline of the land the saw grass goes along the headwaters of many of those wide, slow, mangrove-bordered fresh-water rivers, like a delta or an estuary into which the salt tides flow and draw back and flow again.

The mangrove becomes a solid barrier there, which by its strong, arched and labyrinthine roots collects the sweepage of the fresh water and the salt and holds back the parent sea. The supple branches, the oily green leaves, set up a barrier against the winds, although the hurricanes prevail easily against them. There the fresh water meets the incoming salt, and is lost.

It may be that the mystery of the Everglades is the saw grass, so simple, so enduring, so hostile. It was the saw grass and the water which divided east coast from west coast and made the central solitudes that held in them the secrets of time, which has moved here so long unmarked.

The Everglades: River of Grass (1947)

Ecology was the great emergent science of the 20th century, and its central insight was that everything is connected. Aldo Leopold (1887–1948) is often described as the father of environmental ethics, and his "land ethic" is a landmark in American philosophical thought. But the idea that "a thing is right when it tends to preserve the integrity, stability, and beauty of the biotic community" is as much a pragmatic insight as an ethical one, and it grew from a lifetime out in the natural world. After a rural midwestern childhood he went to Yale's Forestry School and then entered the infant U.S. Forest Service, both institutions under the sway of Gifford Pinchot's forthright utilitarianism. Much of his early career was spent in the desert Southwest, and it was there that he began to develop the principles that made him the founder of wildlife management in the United States. His 1933 textbook *Game Management* is still in print—and so, of course, is his classic account, in "Thinking Like a Mountain," of the day he changed his mind about killing wolves, the key Damascus Road story of American environmental conversion. In 1924, he helped to preserve the Gila Wilderness, part of New Mexico's Gila National Forest; in 1935 he joined Bob Marshall, Benton MacKaye, and others in founding The Wilderness Society. He was moving beyond Pinchot—or perhaps synthesizing the warring impulses of Pinchot and his old adversary John Muir—when he decided that effective conservation required truly wild lands as a baseline. But his vision went well beyond wilderness. In many ways his "land ethic" offered an early attempt to ground environmentalism in every action and decision. It was his words in *A Sand County Almanac* (1949) that would provide his greatest legacy: the explicit recognition that the human community needed to extend its boundaries to include "soils, waters, plants, and animals, or collectively: the land." He died fighting a brush fire near his Sand County shack.

Marshland Elegy

A dawn wind stirs on the great marsh. With almost imperceptible slowness it rolls a bank of fog across the wide morass. Like the white ghost of a glacier the mists advance, riding over phalanxes of tamarack, sliding across bog-meadows heavy with dew. A single silence hangs from horizon to horizon.

Out of some far recess of the sky a tinkling of little bells falls soft upon the listening land. Then again silence. Now comes a baying of some sweet-throated hound, soon the clamor of a responding pack. Then a far clear blast of hunting horns, out of the sky into the fog.

High horns, low horns, silence, and finally a pandemonium of trumpets, rattles, croaks, and cries that almost shakes the bog with its nearness, but without yet disclosing whence it comes. At last a glint of sun reveals the approach of a great echelon of birds. On motionless wing they emerge from the lifting mists, sweep a final arc of sky, and settle in clangorous descending spirals to their feeding grounds. A new day has begun on the crane marsh.

—

A sense of time lies thick and heavy on such a place. Yearly since the ice age it has awakened each spring to the clangor of cranes. The peat layers that comprise the bog are laid down in the basin of an ancient lake. The cranes stand, as it were, upon the sodden pages of their own history. These peats are the compressed remains of the mosses that clogged the pools, of the tamaracks that spread over the moss, of the cranes that bugled over the tamaracks since the retreat of the ice sheet. An endless caravan of generations has built of its own bones this bridge into the future, this habitat where the oncoming host again may live and breed and die.

To what end? Out on the bog a crane, gulping some luckless frog, springs his ungainly hulk into the air and flails the morning sun with mighty wings. The tamaracks re-echo with his bugled certitude. He seems to know.

—

Our ability to perceive quality in nature begins, as in art, with the pretty. It expands through successive stages of the beautiful to values as yet uncaptured by language. The quality of cranes lies, I think, in this higher gamut, as yet beyond the reach of words.

This much, though, can be said: our appreciation of the crane grows with the slow unraveling of earthly history. His tribe, we now know, stems out of the remote Eocene. The other members of the fauna in which he originated are long since entombed within the hills. When we hear his call we hear no mere bird. We hear the trumpet in the orchestra of evolution. He is the symbol of our untamable past, of that incredible sweep of millennia which underlies and conditions the daily affairs of birds and men.

And so they live and have their being—these cranes—not in the constricted present, but in the wider reaches of evolutionary time. Their annual return is the ticking of the geologic clock. Upon the place of their return they confer a peculiar distinction. Amid the endless mediocrity of the commonplace, a crane marsh holds a paleontological patent of nobility, won in the march of aeons, and revocable only by shotgun. The sadness discernible in some marshes arises, perhaps, from their once having harbored cranes. Now they stand humbled, adrift in history.

Some sense of this quality in cranes seems to have been felt by sportsmen and ornithologists of all ages. Upon such quarry as this the Holy Roman Emperor Frederick loosed his gyrfalcons. Upon such quarry as this once swooped the hawks of Kublai Khan. Marco Polo tells us: 'He derives the highest amusement from sporting with gyrfalcons and hawks. At Changanor the Khan has a great Palace surrounded by a fine plain where are found cranes in great numbers. He causes millet and other grains to be sown in order that the birds may not want.'

The ornithologist Bengt Berg, seeing cranes as a boy upon the Swedish heaths, forthwith made them his life work. He followed them to Africa and discovered their winter retreat on the White Nile. He says of his first encounter: 'It was a spectacle which eclipsed the flight of the roc in the Thousand and One Nights.'

—

When the glacier came down out of the north, crunching hills and gouging valleys, some adventuring rampart of the ice climbed the Baraboo Hills and fell back into the outlet gorge of the Wisconsin River. The swollen waters backed up and formed a lake half as long as the state, bordered on the east by cliffs of ice, and fed by the torrents that fell from melting mountains. The shorelines of this old lake are still visible; its bottom is the bottom of the great marsh.

The lake rose through the centuries, finally spilling over east of the Baraboo range. There it cut a new channel for the river, and thus drained itself. To the residual lagoons came the cranes, bugling the defeat of the retreating winter, summoning the on-creeping host of living things to their collective task of marsh-building. Floating bogs of sphagnum moss clogged the lowered waters, filled them. Sedge and leatherleaf, tamarack and spruce successively advanced over the bog, anchoring it by their root fabric, sucking out its water, making peat. The lagoons disappeared, but not the cranes. To the moss-meadows that replaced the ancient waterways they returned each spring to dance and bugle and rear their gangling sorrel-colored young. These, albeit birds, are not properly called chicks, but *colts*. I cannot explain why. On some dewy June morning watch them gambol over their ancestral pastures at the heels of the roan mare, and you will see for yourself.

One year not long ago a French trapper in buckskins pushed his canoe up one of the moss-clogged creeks that thread the great marsh. At this attempt to invade their miry stronghold the cranes gave vent to loud and ribald laughter. A century or two later Englishmen came in covered wagons. They chopped clearings in the timbered moraines that border the marsh, and in them planted corn and buckwheat. They did not intend, like the Great Khan at Changanor, to feed the cranes. But the cranes do not question the intent of glaciers, emperors, or pioneers. They ate the grain, and when some irate farmer failed to concede their usufruct in his corn, they trumpeted a warning and sailed across the marsh to another farm.

There was no alfalfa in those days, and the hill-farms made poor hay land, especially in dry years. One dry year someone set a fire in the tamaracks. The burn grew up quickly to bluejoint grass, which, when cleared of dead trees, made a dependable hay meadow. After that, each August, men appeared to cut hay. In winter, after the cranes had gone South, they drove wagons over the frozen bogs and hauled the hay to their farms in the hills. Yearly they plied the marsh with fire and axe, and in two short decades hay meadows dotted the whole expanse.

Each August when the haymakers came to pitch their camps, singing and drinking and lashing their teams with whip and tongue, the cranes whinnied to their colts and retreated to the far fastnesses. 'Red shitepokes' the haymakers called them, from the rusty hue which at that season often stains the battleship-gray of crane plumage. After the hay was stacked and the marsh again their own, the cranes returned, to call down out of October skies the migrant flocks from Canada. Together they wheeled over the new-cut stubbles and raided the corn until frosts gave the signal for the winter exodus.

These haymeadow days were the Arcadian age for marsh dwellers. Man and beast, plant and soil lived on and with each other in mutual toleration, to the mutual benefit of all. The marsh might have kept on producing hay and prairie chickens, deer and muskrat, crane-music and cranberries forever.

The new overlords did not understand this. They did not include soil, plants, or birds in their ideas of mutuality. The dividends of such a balanced economy were too modest. They envisaged farms not only around, but *in* the marsh. An epidemic of ditch-digging and land-booming set in. The marsh was gridironed with drainage canals, speckled with new fields and farmsteads.

But crops were poor and beset by frosts, to which the expensive ditches added an aftermath of debt. Farmers moved out. Peat beds dried, shrank, caught fire. Sun-energy out of the Pleistocene shrouded the countryside in acrid smoke. No man raised his voice against the waste, only his nose against the smell. After a dry summer not even the winter snows could extinguish the smoldering marsh. Great pockmarks were burned into field and meadow, the scars reaching down to the sands of the old lake, peat-covered these hundred centuries. Rank weeds sprang out of the ashes, to be followed after a year or two by aspen scrub. The cranes were hard put, their numbers shrinking with the remnants of unburned meadow. For them, the song of the power shovel came near being an elegy. The high priests of progress knew nothing of cranes, and cared less. What is a species more or less among engineers? What good is an undrained marsh anyhow?

For a decade or two crops grew poorer, fires deeper, wood-fields larger, and cranes scarcer, year by year. Only reflooding, it appeared, could keep the peat from burning. Meanwhile cranberry growers had, by plugging drainage ditches, reflooded a few spots and obtained good yields. Distant politicians bugled about marginal land, over-production, unemployment relief, conservation. Economists and planners came to look at the marsh. Surveyors, technicians, CCC's, buzzed about. A counter-epidemic of reflooding set in. Government bought land, resettled farmers, plugged ditches wholesale. Slowly the bogs are re-wetting. The fire-pocks become ponds. Grass fires still burn, but they can no longer burn the wetted soil.

All this, once the CCC camps were gone, was good for cranes, but not so the thickets of scrub popple that spread inexorably over the old burns, and still less the maze of new roads that inevitably follow governmental conservation. To build a road is so much simpler than to think of what the country really needs. A roadless marsh is seemingly as worthless to the alphabetical conservationist as an undrained one was to the empire-builders. Solitude, the one natural resource still undowered of alphabets, is so far recognized as valuable only by ornithologists and cranes.

Thus always does history, whether of marsh or market place, end in paradox. The ultimate value in these marshes is wildness, and the crane is wildness incarnate. But all conservation of wildness is self-defeating, for to cherish we must see and fondle, and when enough have seen and fondled, there is no wilderness left to cherish.

—

Some day, perhaps in the very process of our benefactions, perhaps in the fullness of geologic time, the last crane will trumpet his farewell and spiral skyward from the great marsh. High out of the clouds will fall the sound of hunting horns, the baying of the phantom pack, the tinkle of little bells, and then a silence never to be broken, unless perchance in some far pasture of the Milky Way.

* * *

Odyssey

X had marked time in the limestone ledge since the Paleozoic seas covered the land. Time, to an atom locked in a rock, does not pass.

The break came when a bur-oak root nosed down a crack and began prying and sucking. In the flash of a century the rock decayed, and X was pulled out and up into the world of living things. He helped build a flower, which became an acorn, which fattened a deer, which fed an Indian, all in a single year.

From his berth in the Indian's bones, X joined again in chase and flight, feast and famine, hope and fear. He felt these things as changes in the little chemical pushes and pulls that tug timelessly at every atom. When the Indian took his leave of the prairie, X moldered briefly underground, only to embark on a second trip through the bloodstream of the land.

This time it was a rootlet of bluestem that sucked him up and lodged him in a leaf that rode the green billows of the prairie June, sharing the common task of hoarding sunlight. To this leaf also fell an uncommon task: flicking shadows across a plover's eggs. The ecstatic plover, hovering overhead, poured praises on something perfect: perhaps the eggs, perhaps the shadows, or perhaps the haze of pink phlox that lay on the prairie.

When the departing plovers set wing for the Argentine, all the bluestems waved farewell with tall new tassels. When the first geese came out of the north and all the bluestems glowed wine-red, a forehanded deermouse cut the leaf in which X lay, and buried it in an underground nest, as if to hide a bit of Indian summer from the thieving frosts. But a fox detained the mouse, molds and fungi took the nest apart, and X lay in the soil again, foot-loose and fancy-free.

Next he entered a tuft of side-oats grama, a buffalo, a buffalo chip, and again the soil. Next a spiderwort, a rabbit, and an owl. Thence a tuft of sporobolus.

All routines come to an end. This one ended with a prairie fire, which reduced the prairie plants to smoke, gas, and ashes. Phosphorus and potash atoms stayed in the ash, but the nitrogen atoms were gone with the wind. A spectator might, at this point, have predicted an early end of the biotic drama, for with fires exhausting the nitrogen, the soil might well have lost its plants and blown away.

But the prairie had two strings to its bow. Fires thinned its grasses, but they thickened its stand of leguminous herbs: prairie clover, bush clover, wild bean, vetch, lead-plant, trefoil, and Baptisia, each carrying its own bacteria housed in nodules on its rootlets. Each nodule pumped nitrogen out of the air into the plant, and then ultimately into the soil. Thus the prairie savings bank took in more nitrogen from its legumes than it paid out to its fires. That the prairie is rich is known to the humblest deermouse; why the prairie is rich is a question seldom asked in all the still lapse of ages.

Between each of his excursions through the biota, X lay in the soil and was carried by the rains, inch by inch, downhill. Living plants retarded the wash by impounding atoms; dead plants by locking them to their decayed tissues. Animals ate the plants and carried them briefly uphill or downhill, depending on whether they died or defecated higher or lower than they fed. No animal was aware that the altitude of his death was more important than his manner of dying. Thus a fox caught a gopher in a meadow, carrying X uphill to his bed on the brow of a ledge, where an eagle laid him low. The dying fox sensed the end of his chapter in foxdom, but not the new beginning in the odyssey of an atom.

An Indian eventually inherited the eagle's plumes, and with them propitiated the Fates, whom he assumed had a special interest in Indians. It did not occur to him that they might be busy casting dice against gravity; that mice and men, soils and songs, might be merely ways to retard the march of atoms to the sea.

One year, while X lay in a cottonwood by the river, he was eaten by a beaver, an animal that always feeds higher than he dies. The beaver starved when his pond dried up during a bitter frost. X rode the carcass down the spring freshet, losing more altitude each hour than heretofore in a century. He ended up in the silt of a backwater bayou, where he fed a crayfish, a coon, and then an Indian, who laid him down to his last sleep in a mound on the riverbank. One spring an oxbow caved the bank, and after one short week of freshet X lay again in his ancient prison, the sea.

An atom at large in the biota is too free to know freedom; an atom back in the sea has forgotten it. For every atom lost to the sea, the prairie pulls another out of the decaying rocks. The only certain truth is that its creatures must suck hard, live fast, and die often, lest its losses exceed its gains.

—

It is the nature of roots to nose into cracks. When Y was thus released from the parent ledge, a new animal had arrived and begun redding up the prairie to fit his own notions of law and order. An oxteam turned the prairie sod, and Y began a succession of dizzy annual trips through a new grass called wheat.

The old prairie lived by the diversity of its plants and animals, all of which were useful because the sum total of their co-operations and competitions achieved continuity. But the wheat farmer was a builder of categories; to him only wheat and oxen were useful. He saw the useless pigeons settle in clouds upon his wheat, and shortly cleared the skies of them. He saw the chinch bugs take over the stealing job, and fumed because here was a useless thing too small to kill. He failed to see the downward wash of over-wheated loam, laid bare in spring against the pelting rains. When soil-wash and chinch bugs finally put an end to wheat farming, Y and his like had already traveled far down the watershed.

When the empire of wheat collapsed, the settler took a leaf from the old prairie book: he impounded his fertility in livestock, he augmented it with nitrogen-pumping alfalfa, and he tapped the lower layers of the loam with deep-rooted corn.

But he used his alfalfa, and every other new weapon against wash, not only to hold his old plowings, but also to exploit new ones which, in turn, needed holding.

So, despite alfalfa, the black loam grew gradually thinner. Erosion engineers built dams and terraces to hold it. Army engineers built levees and wing-dams to flush it from the rivers. The rivers would not flush, but raised their beds instead, thus choking navigation. So the engineers built pools like gigantic beaver ponds, and Y landed in one of these, his trip from rock to river completed in one short century.

On first reaching the pool, Y made several trips through water plants, fish, and waterfowl. But engineers build sewers as well as dams, and down them comes the loot of all the far hills and the sea. The atoms that once grew pasque-flowers to greet the returning plovers now lie inert, confused, imprisoned in oily sludge.

Roots still nose among the rocks. Rains still pelt the fields. Deermice still hide their souvenirs of Indian summer. Old men who helped destroy the pigeons still recount the glory of the fluttering hosts. Black and white buffalo pass in and out of red barns, offering free rides to itinerant atoms.

* * *

Thinking Like a Mountain

A deep chesty bawl echoes from rimrock to rimrock, rolls down the mountain, and fades into the far blackness of the night. It is an outburst of wild defiant sorrow, and of contempt for all the adversities of the world.

Every living thing (and perhaps many a dead one as well) pays heed to that call. To the deer it is a reminder of the way of all flesh, to the pine a forecast of midnight scuffles and of blood upon the snow, to the coyote a promise of gleanings to come, to the cowman a threat of red ink at the bank, to the hunter a challenge of fang against bullet. Yet behind these obvious and immediate hopes and fears there lies a deeper meaning, known only to the mountain itself. Only the mountain has lived long enough to listen objectively to the howl of a wolf.

Those unable to decipher the hidden meaning know nevertheless that it is there, for it is felt in all wolf country, and distinguishes that country from all other land. It tingles in the spine of all who hear wolves by night, or who scan their tracks by day. Even without sight or sound of wolf, it is implicit in a hundred small events: the midnight whinny of a pack horse, the rattle of rolling rocks, the bound of a fleeing deer, the way shadows lie under the spruces. Only the ineducable tyro can fail to sense the presence or absence of wolves, or the fact that mountains have a secret opinion about them.

My own conviction on this score dates from the day I saw a wolf die. We were eating lunch on a high rimrock, at the foot of which a turbulent river elbowed its way. We saw what we thought was a doe fording the torrent, her breast awash in white water. When she climbed the bank toward us and shook out her tail, we realized our error: it was a wolf. A half-dozen others, evidently grown pups, sprang from the willows and all joined in a welcoming mêlée of wagging tails and playful maulings. What was literally a pile of wolves writhed and tumbled in the center of an open flat at the foot of our rimrock.

In those days we had never heard of passing up a chance to kill a wolf. In a second we were pumping lead into the pack, but with more excitement than accuracy: how to aim a steep downhill shot is always confusing. When our rifles were empty, the old wolf was down, and a pup was dragging a leg into impassable slide-rocks.

We reached the old wolf in time to watch a fierce green fire dying in her eyes. I realized then, and have known ever since, that there was something new to me in those eyes—something known only to her and to the mountain. I was young then, and full of trigger-itch; I thought that because fewer wolves meant more deer, that no wolves would mean hunters' paradise. But after seeing the green fire die, I sensed that neither the wolf nor the mountain agreed with such a view.

—

Since then I have lived to see state after state extirpate its wolves. I have watched the face of many a newly wolfless mountain, and seen the south-facing slopes wrinkle with a maze of new deer trails. I have seen every edible bush and seedling browsed, first to anaemic desuetude, and then to death. I have seen every edible tree defoliated to the height of a saddlehorn. Such a mountain looks as if someone had given God a new pruning shears, and forbidden Him all other exercise. In the end the starved bones of the hoped-for deer herd, dead of its own too-much, bleach with the bones of the dead sage, or molder under the high-lined junipers.

I now suspect that just as a deer herd lives in mortal fear of its wolves, so does a mountain live in mortal fear of its deer. And perhaps with better cause, for while a buck pulled down by wolves can be re-placed in two or three years, a range pulled down by too many deer may fail of replacement in as many decades.

So also with cows. The cowman who cleans his range of wolves does not realize that he is taking over the wolf's job of trimming the herd to fit the range. He has not learned to think like a mountain. Hence we have dustbowls, and rivers washing the future into the sea.

—

We all strive for safety, prosperity, comfort, long life, and dullness. The deer strives with his supple legs, the cowman with trap and poison, the statesman with pen, the most of us with machines, votes, and dollars, but it all comes to the same thing: peace in our time. A measure of suc-cess in this is all well enough, and perhaps is a requisite to objective thinking, but too much safety seems to yield only danger in the long run. Perhaps this is behind Thoreau's dictum: In wildness is the sal-vation of the world. Perhaps this is the hidden meaning in the howl of the wolf, long known among mountains, but seldom perceived among men.

* * *

The Land Ethic

When god-like Odysseus returned from the wars in Troy, he hanged all on one rope a dozen slave-girls of his household whom he suspected of misbehavior during his absence.

This hanging involved no question of propriety. The girls were property. The disposal of property was then, as now, a matter of expe-diency, not of right and wrong.

Concepts of right and wrong were not lacking from Odysseus'

Greece: witness the fidelity of his wife through the long years before at last his black-prowed galleys clove the wine-dark seas for home. The ethical structure of that day covered wives, but had not yet been extended to human chattels. During the three thousand years which have since elapsed, ethical criteria have been extended to many fields of conduct, with corresponding shrinkages in those judged by expediency only.

The Ethical Sequence

This extension of ethics, so far studied only by philosophers, is actually a process in ecological evolution. Its sequences may be described in ecological as well as in philosophical terms. An ethic, ecologically, is a limitation on freedom of action in the struggle for existence. An ethic, philosophically, is a differentiation of social from anti-social conduct. These are two definitions of one thing. The thing has its origin in the tendency of interdependent individuals or groups to evolve modes of co-operation. The ecologist calls these symbioses. Politics and economics are advanced symbioses in which the original free-for-all competition has been replaced, in part, by co-operative mechanisms with an ethical content.

The complexity of co-operative mechanisms has increased with population density, and with the efficiency of tools. It was simpler, for example, to define the anti-social uses of sticks and stones in the days of the mastodons than of bullets and billboards in the age of motors.

The first ethics dealt with the relation between individuals; the Mosaic Decalogue is an example. Later accretions dealt with the relation between the individual and society. The Golden Rule tries to integrate the individual to society; democracy to integrate social organization to the individual.

There is as yet no ethic dealing with man's relation to land and to the animals and plants which grow upon it. Land, like Odysseus' slave-girls, is still property. The land-relation is still strictly economic, entailing privileges but not obligations.

The extension of ethics to this third element in human environment is, if I read the evidence correctly, an evolutionary possibility and an ecological necessity. It is the third step in a sequence. The first two have already been taken. Individual thinkers since the days of Ezekiel and Isaiah have asserted that the despoliation of land is not only inexpedient but wrong. Society, however, has not yet affirmed their belief. I regard the present conservation movement as the embryo of such an affirmation.

An ethic may be regarded as a mode of guidance for meeting ecological situations so new or intricate, or involving such deferred reactions, that the path of social expediency is not discernible to the average individual. Animal instincts are modes of guidance for the individual in meeting such situations. Ethics are possibly a kind of community instinct in-the-making.

The Community Concept

All ethics so far evolved rest upon a single premise: that the individual is a member of a community of interdependent parts. His instincts prompt him to compete for his place in that community, but his ethics prompt him also to co-operate (perhaps in order that there may be a place to compete for).

The land ethic simply enlarges the boundaries of the community to include soils, waters, plants, and animals, or collectively: the land.

This sounds simple: do we not already sing our love for and obligation to the land of the free and the home of the brave? Yes, but just what and whom do we love? Certainly not the soil, which we are sending helter-skelter downriver. Certainly not the waters, which we assume have no function except to turn turbines, float barges, and carry off sewage. Certainly not the plants, of which we exterminate whole communities without batting an eye. Certainly not the animals, of which we have already extirpated many of the largest and most beautiful species. A land ethic of course cannot prevent the alteration, management, and use of these 'resources,' but it does affirm their right to continued existence, and, at least in spots, their continued existence in a natural state.

In short, a land ethic changes the role of *Homo sapiens* from conqueror of the land-community to plain member and citizen of it. It implies respect for his fellow-members, and also respect for the community as such.

In human history, we have learned (I hope) that the conqueror role is eventually self-defeating. Why? Because it is implicit in such a role that the conqueror knows, *ex cathedra*, just what makes the community clock tick, and just what and who is valuable, and what and who is worthless, in community life. It always turns out that he knows neither, and this is why his conquests eventually defeat themselves.

In the biotic community, a parallel situation exists. Abraham knew exactly what the land was for: it was to drip milk and honey into Abraham's mouth. At the present moment, the assurance with which we regard this assumption is inverse to the degree of our education.

The ordinary citizen today assumes that science knows what makes the community clock tick; the scientist is equally sure that he does not. He knows that the biotic mechanism is so complex that its workings may never be fully understood.

That man is, in fact, only a member of a biotic team is shown by an ecological interpretation of history. Many historical events, hitherto explained solely in terms of human enterprise, were actually biotic interactions between people and land. The characteristics of the land determined the facts quite as potently as the characteristics of the men who lived on it.

Consider, for example, the settlement of the Mississippi valley. In the years following the Revolution, three groups were contending for its control: the native Indian, the French and English traders, and the American settlers. Historians wonder what would have happened if the English at Detroit had thrown a little more weight into the Indian side of those tipsy scales which decided the outcome of the colonial migration into the cane-lands of Kentucky. It is time now to ponder the fact that the cane-lands, when subjected to the particular mixture of forces represented by the cow, plow, fire, and axe of the pioneer, became bluegrass. What if the plant succession inherent in this dark and bloody ground had, under the impact of these forces, given us some worthless sedge, shrub, or weed? Would Boone and Kenton have held out? Would there have been any overflow into Ohio, Indiana, Illinois, and Missouri? Any Louisiana Purchase? Any transcontinental union of new states? Any Civil War?

Kentucky was one sentence in the drama of history. We are commonly told what the human actors in this drama tried to do, but we are seldom told that their success, or the lack of it, hung in large degree on the reaction of particular soils to the impact of the particular forces exerted by their occupancy. In the case of Kentucky, we do not even know where the bluegrass came from—whether it is a native species, or a stowaway from Europe.

Contrast the cane-lands with what hindsight tells us about the Southwest, where the pioneers were equally brave, resourceful, and persevering. The impact of occupancy here brought no bluegrass, or other plant fitted to withstand the bumps and buffetings of hard use. This region, when grazed by livestock, reverted through a series of more and more worthless grasses, shrubs, and weeds to a condition of unstable equilibrium. Each recession of plant types bred erosion; each increment to erosion bred a further recession of plants. The result today is a progressive and mutual deterioration, not only of plants and soils, but of the animal community subsisting thereon. The early settlers did not expect this: on the ciénegas of New Mexico some even cut ditches to hasten it. So subtle has been its progress that few residents of the region are aware of it. It is quite invisible to the tourist who finds this wrecked landscape colorful and charming (as indeed it is, but it bears scant resemblance to what it was in 1848).

This same landscape was 'developed' once before, but with quite different results. The Pueblo Indians settled the Southwest in pre-Columbian times, but they happened *not* to be equipped with range livestock. Their civilization expired, but not because their land expired.

In India, regions devoid of any sod-forming grass have been settled, apparently without wrecking the land, by the simple expedient of carrying the grass to the cow, rather than vice versa. (Was this the result of some deep wisdom, or was it just good luck? I do not know.)

In short, the plant succession steered the course of history; the pioneer simply demonstrated, for good or ill, what successions inhered in the land. Is history taught in this spirit? It will be, once the concept of land as a community really penetrates our intellectual life.

The Ecological Conscience

Conservation is a state of harmony between men and land. Despite nearly a century of propaganda, conservation still proceeds at a snail's pace; progress still consists largely of letterhead pieties and convention oratory. On the back forty we still slip two steps backward for each forward stride.

The usual answer to this dilemma is 'more conservation education.' No one will debate this, but is it certain that only the *volume* of education needs stepping up? Is something lacking in the *content* as well?

It is difficult to give a fair summary of its content in brief form, but, as I understand it, the content is substantially this: obey the law, vote right, join some organizations, and practice what conservation is profitable on your own land; the government will do the rest.

Is not this formula too easy to accomplish anything worth-while? It defines no right or wrong, assigns no obligation, calls for no sacrifice, implies no change in the current philosophy of values. In respect of land-use, it urges only enlightened self-interest. Just how far will such education take us? An example will perhaps yield a partial answer.

By 1930 it had become clear to all except the ecologically blind that southwestern Wisconsin's topsoil was slipping seaward. In 1933 the farmers were told that if they would adopt certain remedial practices for five years, the public would donate CCC labor to install them, plus the necessary machinery and materials. The offer was widely accepted, but the practices were widely forgotten when the five-year contract period was up. The farmers continued only those practices that yielded an immediate and visible economic gain for themselves.

This led to the idea that maybe farmers would learn more quickly if they themselves wrote the rules. Accordingly the Wisconsin Legislature in 1937 passed the Soil Conservation District Law. This said to farmers, in effect: *We, the public, will furnish you free technical service and loan you specialized machinery, if you will write your own rules for land-use. Each county may write its own rules, and these will have the force of law.* Nearly all the counties promptly organized to accept the proffered help, but after a decade of operation, *no county has yet written a single rule.* There has been visible progress in such practices as strip-cropping, pasture renovation, and soil liming, but none in fencing woodlots against grazing, and none in excluding plow and cow from steep slopes. The farmers, in short, have selected those remedial practices which were profitable anyhow, and ignored those which were profitable to the community, but not clearly profitable to themselves.

When one asks why no rules have been written, one is told that the community is not yet ready to support them; education must precede rules. But the education actually in progress makes no mention of obligations to land over and above those dictated by self-interest. The net result is that we have more education but less soil, fewer healthy woods, and as many floods as in 1937.

The puzzling aspect of such situations is that the existence of obligations over and above self-interest is taken for granted in such rural community enterprises as the betterment of roads, schools, churches, and baseball teams. Their existence is not taken for granted, nor as yet seriously discussed, in bettering the behavior of the water that falls on the land, or in the preserving of the beauty or diversity of the farm landscape. Land-use ethics are still governed wholly by economic self-interest, just as social ethics were a century ago.

To sum up: we asked the farmer to do what he conveniently could to save his soil, and he has done just that, and only that. The farmer who clears the woods off a 75 per cent slope, turns his cows into the clearing, and dumps its rainfall, rocks, and soil into the community creek, is still (if otherwise decent) a respected member of society. If he puts lime on his fields and plants his crops on contour, he is still entitled to all the privileges and emoluments of his Soil Conservation District. The District is a beautiful piece of social machinery, but it is coughing along on two cylinders because we have been too timid, and too anxious for quick success, to tell the farmer the true magnitude of his obligations. Obligations have no meaning without conscience, and the problem we face is the extension of the social conscience from people to land.

No important change in ethics was ever accomplished without an internal change in our intellectual emphasis, loyalties, affections, and convictions. The proof that conservation has not yet touched these foundations of conduct lies in the fact that philosophy and religion have not yet heard of it. In our attempt to make conservation easy, we have made it trivial.

Substitutes for a Land Ethic

When the logic of history hungers for bread and we hand out a stone, we are at pains to explain how much the stone resembles bread. I now describe some of the stones which serve in lieu of a land ethic.

One basic weakness in a conservation system based wholly on economic motives is that most members of the land community have no economic value. Wildflowers and songbirds are examples. Of the 22,000 higher plants and animals native to Wisconsin, it is doubtful whether more than 5 per cent can be sold, fed, eaten, or otherwise put to economic use. Yet these creatures are members of the biotic community, and if (as I believe) its stability depends on its integrity, they are entitled to continuance.

When one of these non-economic categories is threatened, and if we happen to love it, we invent subterfuges to give it economic importance. At the beginning of the century songbirds were supposed to be disappearing. Ornithologists jumped to the rescue with some distinctly shaky evidence to the effect that insects would eat us up if birds failed to control them. The evidence had to be economic in order to be valid.

It is painful to read these circumlocutions today. We have no land ethic yet, but we have at least drawn nearer the point of admitting that birds should continue as a matter of biotic right, regardless of the presence or absence of economic advantage to us.

A parallel situation exists in respect of predatory mammals, raptorial birds, and fish-eating birds. Time was when biologists somewhat overworked the evidence that these creatures preserve the health of game by killing weaklings, or that they control rodents for the farmer, or that they prey only on 'worthless' species. Here again, the evidence had to be economic in order to be valid. It is only in recent years that we hear the more honest argument that predators are members of the community, and that no special interest has the right to exterminate them for the sake of a benefit, real or fancied, to itself. Unfortunately this enlightened view is still in the talk stage. In the field the extermination of predators goes merrily on: witness the impending erasure of the timber wolf by fiat of Congress, the Conservation Bureaus, and many state legislatures.

Some species of trees have been 'read out of the party' by economics-minded foresters because they grow too slowly, or have too low a sale value to pay as timber crops: white cedar, tamarack, cypress, beech, and hemlock are examples. In Europe, where forestry is ecologically more advanced, the non-commercial tree species are recognized as members of the native forest community, to be preserved as such, within reason. Moreover some (like beech) have been found to have a valuable function in building up soil fertility. The interdependence of the forest and its constituent tree species, ground flora, and fauna is taken for granted.

Lack of economic value is sometimes a character not only of species or groups, but of entire biotic communities: marshes, bogs, dunes, and 'deserts' are examples. Our formula in such cases is to relegate their conservation to government as refuges, monuments, or parks. The difficulty is that these communities are usually interspersed with more valuable private lands; the government cannot possibly own or control such scattered parcels. The net effect is that we have relegated some of them to ultimate extinction over large areas. If the private owner were ecologically minded, he would be proud to be the custodian of a reasonable proportion of such areas, which add diversity and beauty to his farm and to his community.

In some instances, the assumed lack of profit in these 'waste' areas has proved to be wrong, but only after most of them had been done away with. The present scramble to reflood muskrat marshes is a case in point.

There is a clear tendency in American conservation to relegate to government all necessary jobs that private landowners fail to perform. Government ownership, operation, subsidy, or regulation is now widely prevalent in forestry, range management, soil and watershed management, park and wilderness conservation, fisheries management, and migratory bird management, with more to come. Most of this growth in governmental conservation is proper and logical, some of it is inevitable. That I imply no disapproval of it is implicit in the fact that I have spent most of my life working for it. Nevertheless the question arises: What is the ultimate magnitude of the enterprise? Will the tax base carry its eventual ramifications? At what point will governmental conservation, like the mastodon, become handicapped by its own dimensions? The answer, if there is any, seems to be in a land ethic, or some other force which assigns more obligation to the private landowner.

Industrial landowners and users, especially lumbermen and stockmen, are inclined to wail long and loudly about the extension of government ownership and regulation to land, but (with notable exceptions) they show little disposition to develop the only visible alternative: the voluntary practice of conservation on their own lands.

When the private landowner is asked to perform some unprofitable act for the good of the community, he today assents only with outstretched palm. If the act costs him cash this is fair and proper, but when it costs only forethought, open-mindedness, or time, the issue is at least debatable. The overwhelming growth of land-use subsidies in recent years must be ascribed, in large part, to the government's own agencies for conservation education: the land bureaus, the agricultural colleges, and the extension services. As far as I can detect, no ethical obligation toward land is taught in these institutions.

To sum up: a system of conservation based solely on economic self-interest is hopelessly lopsided. It tends to ignore, and thus eventually to eliminate, many elements in the land community that lack commercial value, but that are (as far as we know) essential to its healthy functioning. It assumes, falsely, I think, that the economic parts of the biotic clock will function without the uneconomic parts. It tends to relegate to government many functions eventually too large, too complex, or too widely dispersed to be performed by government.

An ethical obligation on the part of the private owner is the only visible remedy for these situations.

The Land Pyramid

An ethic to supplement and guide the economic relation to land pre-supposes the existence of some mental image of land as a biotic mech-anism. We can be ethical only in relation to something we can see, feel, understand, love, or otherwise have faith in.

The image commonly employed in conservation education is 'the balance of nature.' For reasons too lengthy to detail here, this figure of speech fails to describe accurately what little we know about the land mechanism. A much truer image is the one employed in ecology: the biotic pyramid. I shall first sketch the pyramid as a symbol of land, and later develop some of its implications in terms of land-use.

Plants absorb energy from the sun. This energy flows through a circuit called the biota, which may be represented by a pyramid con-sisting of layers. The bottom layer is the soil. A plant layer rests on the soil, an insect layer on the plants, a bird and rodent layer on the insects, and so on up through various animal groups to the apex layer, which consists of the larger carnivores.

The species of a layer are alike not in where they came from, or in what they look like, but rather in what they eat. Each successive layer depends on those below it for food and often for other services, and each in turn furnishes food and services to those above. Proceeding up-ward, each successive layer decreases in numerical abundance. Thus, for every carnivore there are hundreds of his prey, thousands of their prey, millions of insects, uncountable plants. The pyramidal form of the system reflects this numerical progression from apex to base. Man shares an intermediate layer with the bears, raccoons, and squirrels which eat both meat and vegetables.

The lines of dependency for food and other services are called food chains. Thus soil-oak-deer-Indian is a chain that has now been largely converted to soil-corn-cow-farmer. Each species, including ourselves, is a link in many chains. The deer eats a hundred plants other than oak, and the cow a hundred plants other than corn. Both, then, are links in a hundred chains. The pyramid is a tangle of chains so complex as to seem disorderly, yet the stability of the system proves it to be a highly organized structure. Its functioning depends on the co-operation and competition of its diverse parts.

In the beginning, the pyramid of life was low and squat; the food chains short and simple. Evolution has added layer after layer, link after link. Man is one of thousands of accretions to the height and complexity of the pyramid. Science has given us many doubts, but it has given us at least one certainty: the trend of evolution is to elaborate and diversify the biota.

Land, then, is not merely soil; it is a fountain of energy flowing through a circuit of soils, plants, and animals. Food chains are the living channels which conduct energy upward; death and decay return it to the soil. The circuit is not closed; some energy is dissipated in decay, some is added by absorption from the air, some is stored in soils, peats, and long-lived forests; but it is a sustained circuit, like a slowly augmented revolving fund of life. There is always a net loss by downhill wash, but this is normally small and offset by the decay of rocks. It is deposited in the ocean and, in the course of geological time, raised to form new lands and new pyramids.

The velocity and character of the upward flow of energy depend on the complex structure of the plant and animal community, much as the upward flow of sap in a tree depends on its complex cellular organization. Without this complexity, normal circulation would presumably not occur. Structure means the characteristic numbers, as well as the characteristic kinds and functions, of the component species. This interdependence between the complex structure of the land and its smooth functioning as an energy unit is one of its basic attributes.

When a change occurs in one part of the circuit, many other parts must adjust themselves to it. Change does not necessarily obstruct or divert the flow of energy; evolution is a long series of self-induced changes, the net result of which has been to elaborate the flow mechanism and to lengthen the circuit. Evolutionary changes, however, are usually slow and local. Man's invention of tools has enabled him to make changes of unprecedented violence, rapidity, and scope.

One change is in the composition of floras and faunas. The larger predators are lopped off the apex of the pyramid; food chains, for the first time in history, become shorter rather than longer. Domesticated species from other lands are substituted for wild ones, and wild ones are moved to new habitats. In this world-wide pooling of faunas and floras, some species get out of bounds as pests and diseases, others are extinguished. Such effects are seldom intended or foreseen; they represent unpredicted and often untraceable readjustments in the structure. Agricultural science is largely a race between the emergence of new pests and the emergence of new techniques for their control.

Another change touches the flow of energy through plants and animals and its return to the soil. Fertility is the ability of soil to receive, store, and release energy. Agriculture, by overdrafts on the soil, or by too radical a substitution of domestic for native species in the superstructure, may derange the channels of flow or deplete storage. Soils depleted of their storage, or of the organic matter which anchors it, wash away faster than they form. This is erosion.

Waters, like soil, are part of the energy circuit. Industry, by polluting waters or obstructing them with dams, may exclude the plants and animals necessary to keep energy in circulation.

Transportation brings about another basic change: the plants or animals grown in one region are now consumed and returned to the soil in another. Transportation taps the energy stored in rocks, and in the air, and uses it elsewhere; thus we fertilize the garden with nitrogen gleaned by the guano birds from the fishes of seas on the other side of the Equator. Thus the formerly localized and self-contained circuits are pooled on a world-wide scale.

The process of altering the pyramid for human occupation releases stored energy, and this often gives rise, during the pioneering period, to a deceptive exuberance of plant and animal life, both wild and tame. These releases of biotic capital tend to becloud or postpone the penalties of violence.

—

This thumbnail sketch of land as an energy circuit conveys three basic ideas:

(1) That land is not merely soil.

(2) That the native plants and animals kept the energy circuit open; others may or may not.

(3) That man-made changes are of a different order than evolution-ary changes, and have effects more comprehensive than is intended or foreseen.

These ideas, collectively, raise two basic issues: Can the land adjust itself to the new order? Can the desired alterations be accomplished with less violence?

Biotas seem to differ in their capacity to sustain violent conversion. Western Europe, for example, carries a far different pyramid than Cae-sar found there. Some large animals are lost; swampy forests have become meadows or plow-land; many new plants and animals are in-troduced, some of which escape as pests; the remaining natives are greatly changed in distribution and abundance. Yet the soil is still there and, with the help of imported nutrients, still fertile; the waters flow normally; the new structure seems to function and to persist. There is no visible stoppage or derangement of the circuit.

Western Europe, then, has a resistant biota. Its inner processes are tough, elastic, resistant to strain. No matter how violent the alterations, the pyramid, so far, has developed some new *modus vivendi* which pre-serves its habitability for man, and for most of the other natives.

Japan seems to present another instance of radical conversion with-out disorganization.

Most other civilized regions, and some as yet barely touched by civi-lization, display various stages of disorganization, varying from initial symptoms to advanced wastage. In Asia Minor and North Africa diag-nosis is confused by climatic changes, which may have been either the cause or the effect of advanced wastage. In the United States the degree of disorganization varies locally; it is worst in the Southwest, the Ozarks, and parts of the South, and least in New England and the Northwest. Better land-uses may still arrest it in the less advanced regions. In parts of Mexico, South America, South Africa, and Australia a violent and ac-celerating wastage is in progress, but I cannot assess the prospects.

This almost world-wide display of disorganization in the land seems to be similar to disease in an animal, except that it never culmi-nates in complete disorganization or death. The land recovers, but at some reduced level of complexity, and with a reduced carrying capacity for people, plants, and animals. Many biotas currently regarded as 'lands of opportunity' are in fact already subsisting on exploitative agriculture, i.e. they have already exceeded their sustained carrying capacity. Most of South America is overpopulated in this sense.

In arid regions we attempt to offset the process of wastage by reclamation, but it is only too evident that the prospective longevity of reclamation projects is often short. In our own West, the best of them may not last a century.

The combined evidence of history and ecology seems to support one general deduction: the less violent the manmade changes, the greater the probability of successful readjustment in the pyramid. Violence, in turn, varies with human population density; a dense population requires a more violent conversion. In this respect, North America has a better chance for permanence than Europe, if she can contrive to limit her density.

This deduction runs counter to our current philosophy, which assumes that because a small increase in density enriched human life, that an indefinite increase will enrich it indefinitely. Ecology knows of no density relationship that holds for indefinitely wide limits. All gains from density are subject to a law of diminishing returns.

Whatever may be the equation for men and land, it is improbable that we as yet know all its terms. Recent discoveries in mineral and vitamin nutrition reveal unsuspected dependencies in the up-circuit: incredibly minute quantities of certain substances determine the value of soils to plants, of plants to animals. What of the down-circuit? What of the vanishing species, the preservation of which we now regard as an esthetic luxury? They helped build the soil; in what unsuspected ways may they be essential to its maintenance? Professor Weaver proposes that we use prairie flowers to reflocculate the wasting soils of the dust bowl; who knows for what purpose cranes and condors, otters and grizzlies may some day be used?

Land Health and the A-B Cleavage
A land ethic, then, reflects the existence of an ecological conscience, and this in turn reflects a conviction of individual responsibility for the

health of the land. Health is the capacity of the land for self-renewal. Conservation is our effort to understand and preserve this capacity.

Conservationists are notorious for their dissensions. Superficially these seem to add up to mere confusion, but a more careful scrutiny reveals a single plane of cleavage common to many specialized fields. In each field one group (A) regards the land as soil, and its function as commodity-production; another group (B) regards the land as a biota, and its function as something broader. How much broader is admittedly in a state of doubt and confusion.

In my own field, forestry, group A is quite content to grow trees like cabbages, with cellulose as the basic forest commodity. It feels no inhibition against violence; its ideology is agronomic. Group B, on the other hand, sees forestry as fundamentally different from agronomy because it employs natural species, and manages a natural environment rather than creating an artificial one. Group B prefers natural reproduction on principle. It worries on biotic as well as economic grounds about the loss of species like chestnut, and the threatened loss of the white pines. It worries about a whole series of secondary forest functions: wildlife, recreation, watersheds, wilderness areas. To my mind, Group B feels the stirrings of an ecological conscience.

In the wildlife field, a parallel cleavage exists. For Group A the basic commodities are sport and meat; the yardsticks of production are ciphers of take in pheasants and trout. Artificial propagation is acceptable as a permanent as well as a temporary recourse—if its unit costs permit. Group B, on the other hand, worries about a whole series of biotic side-issues. What is the cost in predators of producing a game crop? Should we have further recourse to exotics? How can management restore the shrinking species, like prairie grouse, already hopeless as shootable game? How can management restore the threatened rarities, like trumpeter swan and whooping crane? Can management principles be extended to wildflowers? Here again it is clear to me that we have the same A-B cleavage as in forestry.

In the larger field of agriculture I am less competent to speak, but there seem to be somewhat parallel cleavages. Scientific agriculture was actively developing before ecology was born, hence a slower penetration of ecological concepts might be expected. Moreover the farmer, by the very nature of his techniques, must modify the biota more radically than the forester or the wildlife manager. Nevertheless, there are many discontents in agriculture which seem to add up to a new vision of 'biotic farming.'

Perhaps the most important of these is the new evidence that poundage or tonnage is no measure of the food-value of farm crops; the products of fertile soil may be qualitatively as well as quantitatively superior. We can bolster poundage from depleted soils by pouring on imported fertility, but we are not necessarily bolstering food-value. The possible ultimate ramifications of this idea are so immense that I must leave their exposition to abler pens.

The discontent that labels itself 'organic farming,' while bearing some of the earmarks of a cult, is nevertheless biotic in its direction, particularly in its insistence on the importance of soil flora and fauna.

The ecological fundamentals of agriculture are just as poorly known to the public as in other fields of land-use. For example, few educated people realize that the marvelous advances in technique made during recent decades are improvements in the pump, rather than the well. Acre for acre, they have barely sufficed to offset the sinking level of fertility.

In all of these cleavages, we see repeated the same basic paradoxes: man the conqueror *versus* man the biotic citizen; science the sharpener of his sword *versus* science the searchlight on his universe; land the slave and servant *versus* land the collective organism. Robinson's injunction to Tristram may well be applied, at this juncture, to *Homo sapiens* as a species in geological time:

> Whether you will or not
> You are a King, Tristram, for you are one
> Of the time-tested few that leave the world,
> When they are gone, not the same place it was.
> Mark what you leave.

The Outlook

It is inconceivable to me that an ethical relation to land can exist without love, respect, and admiration for land, and a high regard for its value. By value, I of course mean something far broader than mere economic value; I mean value in the philosophical sense.

Perhaps the most serious obstacle impeding the evolution of a land ethic is the fact that our educational and economic system is headed away from, rather than toward, an intense consciousness of land. Your true modern is separated from the land by many middlemen, and by innumerable physical gadgets. He has no vital relation to it; to him it is the space between cities on which crops grow. Turn him loose for a day on the land, and if the spot does not happen to be a golf links or a 'scenic' area, he is bored stiff. If crops could be raised by hydroponics instead of farming, it would suit him very well. Synthetic substitutes for wood, leather, wool, and other natural land products suit him better than the originals. In short, land is something he has 'outgrown.'

Almost equally serious as an obstacle to a land ethic is the attitude of the farmer for whom the land is still an adversary, or a taskmaster that keeps him in slavery. Theoretically, the mechanization of farming ought to cut the farmer's chains, but whether it really does is debatable.

One of the requisites for an ecological comprehension of land is an understanding of ecology, and this is by no means co-extensive with 'education'; in fact, much higher education seems deliberately to avoid ecological concepts. An understanding of ecology does not necessarily originate in courses bearing ecological labels; it is quite as likely to be labeled geography, botany, agronomy, history, or economics. This is as it should be, but whatever the label, ecological training is scarce.

The case for a land ethic would appear hopeless but for the minority which is in obvious revolt against these 'modern' trends.

The 'key-log' which must be moved to release the evolutionary process for an ethic is simply this: quit thinking about decent land-use as solely an economic problem. Examine each question in terms of what is ethically and esthetically right, as well as what is economically expedient. A thing is right when it tends to preserve the integrity, stability, and beauty of the biotic community. It is wrong when it tends otherwise.

It of course goes without saying that economic feasibility limits the tether of what can or cannot be done for land. It always has and it always will. The fallacy the economic determinists have tied around our collective neck, and which we now need to cast off, is the belief that economics determines *all* land-use. This is simply not true. An innumerable host of actions and attitudes, comprising perhaps the bulk of all land relations, is determined by the land-users' tastes and predilections, rather than by his purse. The bulk of all land relations hinges on investments of time, forethought, skill, and faith rather than on investments of cash. As a land-user thinketh, so is he.

I have purposely presented the land ethic as a product of social evolution because nothing so important as an ethic is ever 'written.' Only the most superficial student of history supposes that Moses 'wrote' the Decalogue; it evolved in the minds of a thinking community, and Moses wrote a tentative summary of it for a 'seminar.' I say tentative because evolution never stops.

The evolution of a land ethic is an intellectual as well as emotional process. Conservation is paved with good intentions which prove to be futile, or even dangerous, because they are devoid of critical understanding either of the land, or of economic land-use. I think it is a truism that as the ethical frontier advances from the individual to the community, its intellectual content increases.

The mechanism of operation is the same for any ethic: social approbation for right actions: social disapproval for wrong actions.

By and large, our present problem is one of attitudes and implements. We are remodeling the Alhambra with a steam-shovel, and we are proud of our yardage. We shall hardly relinquish the shovel, which after all has many good points, but we are in need of gentler and more objective criteria for its successful use.

A Sand County Almanac (1949)

Like many pieces in this anthology—*Silent Spring, The Fate of the Earth, The End of Nature*—"The Fog" first appeared in *The New Yorker,* which under longtime editor William Shawn took emerging environmental issues seriously before most other publications. Berton Rouché (1911–1994), a *New Yorker* regular best known for his articles about medical detection, here takes up one of the first dramatic American cases of acute toxic pollution. The Donora smog did its killing in an era when people tended to blithely dismiss pollution as "the smell of money." It's worth recalling how recently in American history the air in our industrial cities was as lethal as the witches' brew that now lingers above the factories of China, and how much we owe the generation of environmentalists who helped clean up these most obvious forms of pollution.

The Fog

The Monongahela River rises in the middle Alleghenies and seeps for a hundred and twenty-eight miles through the iron and bituminous-coal fields of northeastern West Virginia and southwestern Pennsylvania to Pittsburgh. There, joining the Allegheny River, it becomes the wild Ohio. It is the only river of any consequence in the United States that flows due north, and it is also the shortest. Its course is cramped and crooked, and flanked by bluffs and precipitous hills. Within living memory, its waters were quick and green, but they are murky now with pollution, and a series of locks and dams steady its once tumultuous descent, rendering it navigable from source to mouth. Traffic on the Monongahela is heavy. Its shipping, which consists almost wholly of coal barges pushed by wheezy, coal-burning stern-wheelers, exceeds in tonnage that of the Panama Canal. The river is densely industrialized. There are trucking highways along its narrow banks and interurban lines and branches of the Pennsylvania Railroad and the New York Central and smelters and steel plants and chemical works and glass factories and foundries and coke plants and machine shops and zinc mills, and its hills and bluffs are scaled by numerous blackened mill towns. The blackest of them is the borough of Donora, in Washington County, Pennsylvania.

Donora is twenty-eight miles south of Pittsburgh and covers the tip of a lumpy point formed by the most convulsive of the Monongahela's many horseshoe bends. Though accessible by road, rail, and river, it is an extraordinarily secluded place. The river and the bluffs that lift abruptly from the water's edge to a height of four hundred and fifty feet enclose it on the north and east and south, and just above it to the west is a range of rolling but even higher hills. On its outskirts are acres of sidings and rusting gondolas, abandoned mines, smoldering slag piles, and gulches filled with rubbish. Its limits are marked by sooty signs that read, "Donora. Next to Yours the Best Town in the U.S.A." It is a harsh, gritty town, founded in 1901 and old for its age, with a gaudy main street and a thousand identical gaunt gray houses. Some of its streets are paved with concrete and some are cobbled, but many are of dirt and crushed coal. At least half of them are as steep as roofs, and several have steps instead of sidewalks. It is treeless and all but grass-less, and much of it is slowly sliding downhill. After a rain, it is a smear of mud. Its vacant lots and many of its yards are mortally gullied, and one of its three cemeteries is an eroded ruin of gravelly clay and top-pled tombstones. Its population is 12,300. Two-thirds of its men, and a substantial number of its women, work in its mills. There are three of them—a steel plant, a wire plant, and a zinc-and-sulphuric-acid plant—all of which are operated by the American Steel & Wire Co., a subsidiary of the United States Steel Corporation, and they line its river front for three miles. They are huge mills. Some of the buildings are two blocks long, many are five or six stories high, and all of them bristle with hundred-foot stacks perpetually plumed with black or red or sulphurous yellow smoke.

Donora is abnormally smoky. Its mills are no bigger or smokier than many, but their smoke, and the smoke from the passing boats and trains, tends to linger there. Because of the crowding bluffs and sheltering hills, there is seldom a wind, and only occasionally a breeze, to dispel it. On still days, unless the skies are high and buoyantly clear, the lower streets are always dim and there is frequently a haze on the heights. Autumn is the smokiest season. The weather is close and dull then, and there are persistent fogs as well. The densest ones generally come in October. They are greasy, gagging fogs, often intact even at high noon, and they sometimes last for two or three days. A few have lasted as long as four. One, toward the end of October, 1948, hung on for six. Unlike its predecessors, it turned out to be of considerably more than local interest. It was the second smoke-contaminated fog in history ever to reach a toxic density. The first such fog occurred in Belgium, in an industrialized stretch of the Meuse Valley, in 1930. During it several hundred people were prostrated, sixty of them fatally. The Donora fog struck down nearly six thousand. Twenty of them—five women and fifteen men—died. Nobody knows exactly what killed them, or why the others survived. At the time, not many of the stricken expected to.

The fog closed over Donora on the morning of Tuesday, October 26th. The weather was raw, cloudy, and dead calm, and it stayed that way as the fog piled up all that day and the next. By Thursday, it had stiffened adhesively into a motionless clot of smoke. That afternoon, it was just possible to see across the street, and, except for the stacks, the mills had vanished. The air began to have a sickening smell, almost a taste. It was the bittersweet reek of sulphur dioxide. Everyone who was out that day remarked on it, but no one was much concerned. The smell of sulphur dioxide, a scratchy gas given off by burning coal and melting ore, is a normal concomitant of any durable fog in Donora. This time, it merely seemed more penetrating than usual.

At about eight-thirty on Friday morning, one of Donora's eight physicians, Dr. Ralph W. Koehler, a tense, stocky man of forty-eight, stepped to his bathroom window for a look at the weather. It was, at best, unchanged. He could see nothing but a watery waste of rooftops islanded in fog. As he was turning away, a shimmer of movement in the distance caught his eye. It was a freight train creeping along the river-bank just south of town, and the sight of it shook him. He had never seen anything quite like it before. "It was the smoke," he says. "They were firing up for the grade and the smoke was belching out, but it didn't rise. I mean it didn't go up at all. It just spilled out over the lip of the stack like a black liquid, like ink or oil, and rolled down to the ground and lay there. My God, it just lay there! I thought, Well, God damn—and they talk about needing smoke control up in Pittsburgh! I've got a heart condition, and I was so disgusted my heart began to act up a little. I had to sit down on the edge of the tub and rest a minute."

Dr. Koehler and an associate, Dr. Edward Roth, who is big, heavy-set, and in his middle forties, share an office on the second floor of a brownstone building one block up from the mills, on McKean Avenue, the town's main street. They have one employee, a young woman named Helen Stack, in whom are combined an attractive receptionist, an efficient secretary, and a capable nurse. Miss Stack was the first to reach the office that morning. Like Dr. Koehler and many other Dono-rans, she was in uncertain spirits. The fog was beginning to get on her nerves, and she had awakened with a sore throat and a cough and sup-posed that she was coming down with a cold. The appearance of the office deepened her depression. Everything in it was smeared with a kind of dust. "It wasn't just ordinary soot and grit," she says. "There was something white and scummy mixed up in it. It was just wet ash from the mills, but I didn't know that then. I almost hated to touch it, it was so nasty-looking. But it had to be cleaned up, so I got out a cloth and went to work." When Miss Stack had finished, she lighted a ciga-rette and sat down at her desk to go through the mail. It struck her that the cigarette had a very peculiar taste. She held it up and sniffed at the smoke. Then she raised it to her lips, took another puff, and doubled up in a paroxysm of coughing. For an instant, she thought she was going to be sick. "I'll never forget that taste," she says. "Oh, it was awful! It was sweet and horrible, like something rotten. It tasted the way the fog smelled, only ten times worse. I got rid of the cigarette as fast as I could and drank a glass of water, and then I felt better. What puzzled me was I'd smoked a cigarette at home after breakfast and it had tasted all right. I didn't know what to think, except that maybe it was because the fog wasn't quite as bad up the hill as here downstreet. I guess I thought my cold was probably partly to blame. I wasn't really uneasy. The big Halloween parade the Chamber of Commerce puts on every year was to be held that night, and I could hear the workmen down in the street putting up the decorations. I knew the committee wouldn't be going ahead with the parade if they thought anything was wrong. So I went on with my work, and pretty soon the Doctors came in from their early calls and it was just like any other morning."

The office hours of Dr. Koehler and Dr. Roth are the same, from one to three in the afternoon and from seven to nine at night. Whenever possible in the afternoon, Dr. Koehler leaves promptly at three. Because of his unsteady heart, he finds it desirable to rest for a time before dinner. That Friday afternoon, he was just getting into his coat when Miss Stack announced a patient. "He was wheezing and gasping for air," Dr. Koehler says, "but there wasn't anything very surprising about that. He was one of our regular asthmatics, and the fog gets them every time. The only surprising thing was that he hadn't come in sooner. The fact is, none of our asthmatics had been in all week. Well, I did what I could for him. I gave him a shot of adrenalin or aminophyllin—some antispasmodic—to dilate the bronchia, so he could breathe more easily, and sent him home. I followed him out. I didn't feel so good myself."

Half an hour after Dr. Koehler left, another gasping asthmatic, an elderly steelworker, tottered into the office. "He was pretty wobbly," Miss Stack says. "Dr. Roth was still in his office, and saw him right away. I guess he wasn't much better when he came out, because I remember thinking, Poor fellow. There's nothing sadder than an asthmatic when the fog is bad. Well, he had hardly gone out the door when I heard a terrible commotion. I thought, Oh, my gosh, he's fallen down the stairs! Then there was an awful yell. I jumped up and dashed out into the hall. There was a man I'd never seen before sort of draped over the banister. He was kicking at the wall and pulling at the banister and moaning and choking and yelling at the top of his voice, 'Help! Help me! I'm dying!' I just stood there. I was petrified. Then Dr. Brown, across the hall, came running out, and he and somebody else helped the man on up the stairs and into his office. Just then, my phone began to ring. I almost bumped into Dr. Roth. He was coming out to see what was going on. When I picked up the phone, it was just like hearing that man in the hall again. It was somebody saying somebody was dying. I said Dr. Roth would be right over, but before I could even tell him, the phone started ringing again. And the minute I hung up the receiver, it rang again. That was the beginning of a terrible night. From that minute on, the phone never stopped ringing. That's the honest truth. And they were all alike. Everybody who called up said the same thing. Pain in the abdomen. Splitting headache. Nausea and vomiting. Choking and couldn't get their breath. Coughing up blood. But as soon as I got over my surprise, I calmed down. Hysterical people always end up by making me feel calm. Anyway, I managed to make a list of the first few calls and gave it to Dr. Roth. He was standing there with his hat and coat on and his bag in his hand and chewing on his cigar, and he took the list and shook his head and went out. Then I called Dr. Koehler, but his line was busy. I don't remember much about the next hour. All I know is I kept trying to reach Dr. Koehler and my phone kept ringing and my list of calls kept getting longer and longer."

One of the calls that lengthened Miss Stack's list was a summons to the home of August Z. Chambon, the burgess, or mayor, of Donora. The patient was the Burgess's mother, a widow of seventy-four, who lives with her son and his wife. "Mother Chambon was home alone that afternoon," her daughter-in-law says. "August was in Pittsburgh on business and I'd gone downstreet to do some shopping. It took me forever, the fog was so bad. Even the inside of the stores was smoky. So I didn't get home until around five-thirty. Well, I opened the door and stepped into the hall, and there was Mother Chambon. She was lying on the floor, with her coat on and a bag of cookies spilled all over beside her. Her face was blue, and she was just gasping for breath and in terrible pain. She told me she'd gone around the corner to the bakery a few minutes before, and on the way back the fog had got her. She said she barely made it to the house. Mother Chambon has bronchial trouble, but I'd never seen her so bad before. Oh, I was frightened! I helped her up—I don't know how I ever did it—and got her into bed. Then I called the doctor. It took me a long time to reach his office, and then he wasn't in. He was out making calls. I was afraid to wait until he could get here—Mother Chambon was so bad, and at her age and all—so I called another doctor. He was out, too. Finally, I got hold of Dr. Levin and he said he'd come right over, and he finally did. He gave her an injection that made her breathe easier and something to put her to sleep. She slept for sixteen solid hours. But before Dr. Levin left, I told him that there seemed to be an awful lot of sickness going on all of a sudden. I was coughing a little myself. I asked him what was happening. 'I don't know,' he said. 'Something's coming off, but I don't know what.'"

Dr. Roth returned to his office at a little past six to replenish his supply of drugs. By then, he, like Dr. Levin, was aware that something was coming off. "I knew that whatever it was we were up against was serious," he says. "I'd seen some very pitiful cases, and they weren't all asthmatics or chronics of any kind. Some were people who had never been bothered by fog before. I was worried, but I wasn't bewildered. It was no mystery. It was obvious—all the symptoms pointed to it—that the fog and smoke were to blame. I didn't think any further than that. As a matter of fact, I didn't have time to think or wonder. I was too damn busy. My biggest problem was just getting around. It was almost impossible to drive. I even had trouble finding the office. McKean Avenue was solid coal smoke. I could taste the soot when I got out of the car, and my chest felt tight. On the way up the stairs, I started coughing and I couldn't stop. I kept coughing and choking until my stomach turned over. Fortunately, Helen was out getting something to eat—I just made it to the office and into the lavatory in time. My God, I was sick! After a while, I dragged myself into my office and gave myself an injection of adrenalin and lay back in a chair. I began to feel better. I felt so much better I got out a cigar and lighted up. That practically finished me. I took one pull, and went into another paroxysm of coughing. I probably should have known better—cigars had tasted terrible all day—but I hadn't had that reaction before. Then I heard the phone ringing. I guess it must have been ringing off and on all along. I thought about answering it, but I didn't have the strength to move. I just lay there in my chair and let it ring."

When Miss Stack came into the office a few minutes later, the telephone was still ringing. She had answered it and added the call to her list before she realized that she was not alone. "I heard someone groaning," she says. "Dr. Roth's door was open and I looked in. I almost jumped, I was so startled. He was slumped down in his chair, and his face was brick red and dripping with perspiration. I wanted to help him, but he said there wasn't anything to do. He told me what had happened. 'I'm all right now,' he said. 'I'll get going again in a minute. You go ahead and answer the phone.' It was ringing again. The next thing I knew, the office was full of patients, all of them coughing and groaning. I was about ready to break down and cry. I had talked to Dr. Koehler by that time and he knew what was happening. He had been out on calls from home. 'I'm coughing and sick myself,' he said, 'but I'll go out again as soon as I can.' I tried to keep calm, but with both Doctors sick and the office full of patients and the phone ringing, I just didn't know which way to turn. Dr. Roth saw two or three of the worst patients. Oh, he looked ghastly! He really looked worse than some of the patients. Finally, he said he couldn't see any more, that the emergency house calls had to come first, and grabbed up his stuff and went out. The office was still full of patients, and I went around explaining things to them. It was awful. There wasn't anything to do but close up, but I've never felt so heartless. Some of them were so sick and miserable. And right in the middle of everything the parade came marching down the street. People were cheering and yelling, and the bands were playing. I could hardly believe my ears. It just didn't seem possible."

The sounds of revelry that reached Miss Stack were deceptive. The parade, though well attended, was not an unqualified success. "I went out for a few minutes and watched it," the younger Mrs. Chambon says. "It went right by our house. August wasn't home yet, and after what had happened to Mother Chambon, I thought it might cheer me up a little. It did and it didn't. Everybody was talking about the fog and wondering when it would end, and some of them had heard there was sickness, but nobody seemed at all worried. As far as I could tell, all the sick people were old. That made things look not too bad. The fog always affects the old people. But as far as the parade was concerned, it was a waste of time. You really couldn't see a thing. They were just like shadows marching by. It was kind of uncanny. Especially since most of the people in the crowd had handkerchiefs tied over their nose and mouth to keep out the smoke. All the children did. But, even so, everybody was coughing. I was glad to get back in the house. I guess everybody was. The minute it was over, everybody scattered. They just vanished. In two minutes there wasn't a soul left on the street. It was as quiet as midnight."

Among the several organizations that participated in the parade was the Donora Fire Department. The force consists of about thirty volunteers and two full-time men. The latter, who live at the firehouse, are the chief, John Volk, a wiry man in his fifties, and his assistant and driver, a hard, round-faced young man named Russell Davis. Immediately after the parade, they returned to the firehouse. "As a rule," Chief Volk says, "I like a parade. We've got some nice equipment here, and I don't mind showing it off. But I didn't get much pleasure out of that one. Nobody could see us, hardly, and we couldn't see them. That fog was black as a derby hat. It had us all coughing. It was a relief to head for home. We hadn't much more than got back to the station, though, and got the trucks put away and said good night to the fellows than the phone rang. Russ and I were just sitting down to drink some coffee. I dreaded to answer it. On a night like that, a fire could have been real mean. But it wasn't any fire. It was a fellow up the street, and the fog had got him. He said he was choking to death and couldn't get a doctor, and what he wanted was our inhalator. He needed air. Russ says I just stood there with my mouth hanging open. I don't remember what I thought. I guess I was trying to think what to do as much as anything else. I didn't disbelieve him—he sounded half dead already—but, naturally, we're not supposed to go running around treating the sick. But what the hell, you can't let a man die! So I told him O.K. I told Russ to take the car and go. The way it turned out, I figure we did the right thing. I've never heard anybody say different."

"That guy was only the first," Davis says. "From then on, it was one emergency call after another. I didn't get to bed until Sunday. Neither did John. I don't know how many calls we had, but I do know this: We had around eight hundred cubic feet of oxygen on hand when I started out Friday night, and we ended up by borrowing from McKeesport and Monessen and Monongahela and Charleroi and everywhere around here. I never want to go through a thing like that again. I was laid up for a week after. There never was such a fog. You couldn't see your hand in front of your face, day or night. Hell, even inside the station the air was blue. I drove on the left side of the street with my head out the window, steering by scraping the curb. We've had bad fogs here before. A guy lost his car in one. He'd come to a fork in the road and didn't know where he was, and got out to try and tell which way to go. When he turned back to his car, he couldn't find it. He had no idea where it was until, finally, he stopped and listened and heard the engine. That guided him back. Well, by God, this fog was so bad you couldn't even get a car to idle. I'd take my foot off the accelerator and—bango!—the engine would stall. There just wasn't any oxygen in the air. I don't know how I kept breathing. I don't know how anybody did. I found people laying in bed and laying on the floor. Some of them were laying there and they didn't give a damn whether they died or not. I found some down in the basement with the furnace draft open and their head stuck inside, trying to get air that way. What I did when I got to a place was throw a sheet or a blanket over the patient and stick a cylinder of oxygen underneath and crack the valves for fifteen minutes or so. By God, that rallied them! I didn't take any myself. What I did every time I came back to the station was have a little shot of whiskey. That seemed to help. It eased my throat. There was one funny thing about the whole thing. Nobody seemed to realize what was going on. Everybody seemed to think he was the only sick man in town. I don't know what they figured was keeping the doctors so busy. I guess everybody was so miserable they just didn't think."

Toward midnight, Dr. Roth abandoned his car and continued his rounds on foot. He found not only that walking was less of a strain but that he made better time. He walked the streets all night, but he was seldom lonely. Often, as he entered or left a house, he encountered a colleague. "We all had practically the same calls," Dr. M. J. Hannigan, the president of the Donora Medical Association, says. "Some people called every doctor in town. It was pretty discouraging to finally get someplace and drag yourself up the steps and then be told that Dr. So-and-So had just been there. Not that I blame them, though. Far from it. There were a couple of times when I was about ready to call for help myself. Frankly, I don't know how any of us doctors managed to hold out and keep going that night."

Not all of them did. Dr. Koehler made his last call that night at one o'clock. "I had to go home," he says. "God knows I didn't want to. I'd hardly made a dent in my list. Every time I called home or the Physicians' Exchange, it doubled. But my heart gave out. I couldn't go on any longer without some rest. The last thing I heard as I got into bed was my wife answering the phone. And the phone was the first thing I heard in the morning. It was as though I hadn't been to sleep at all." While Dr. Koehler was bolting a cup of coffee, the telephone rang again. This time, it was Miss Stack. They conferred briefly about the patients he had seen during the night and those he planned to see that morning. Among the latter was a sixty-four-year-old steelworker named Ignatz Hollowitti. "One of the Hollowitti girls, Dorothy, is a good friend of mine," Miss Stack says. "So as soon as I finished talking to Dr. Koehler, I called her to tell her that Doctor would be right over. I wanted to relieve her mind. Dorothy was crying when she answered the phone. I'll never forget what she said. She said, 'Oh, Helen—my dad just died! He's dead!' I don't remember what I said. I was simply stunned. I suppose I said what people say. I must have. But all I could think was, My gosh, if people are dying—why, this is tragic! Nothing like this has ever happened before!'"

Mr. Hollowitti was not the first victim of the fog. He was the sixth. The first was a retired steelworker of seventy named Ivan Ceh. According to the records of the undertaker who was called in—Rudolph Schwerha, whose establishment is the largest in Donora—Mr. Ceh died at one-thirty Saturday morning. "I was notified at two," Mr. Schwerha says. "There is a note to such effect in my book. I thought nothing, of course. The call awakened me from sleep, but in my profession anything is to be expected. I reassured the bereaved and called my driver and sent him for the body. He was gone forever. The fog that night was impossible. It was a neighborhood case—only two blocks to go, and my driver works quick—but it was thirty minutes by the clock before I heard the service car in the drive. At that moment, again the phone rang. Another case. Now I was surprised. Two different cases so soon together in this size town doesn't happen every day. But there was no time then for thinking. There was work to do. I must go with my driver for the second body. It was in the Sunnyside section, north of town, too far in such weather for one man alone. The fog, when we got down by the mills, was unbelievable. Nothing could be seen. It was like a blanket. Our fog lights were useless, and even with the fog spotlight on, the white line in the street was invisible. I began to worry. What if we should bump a parked car? What if we should fall off the road? Finally, I told my driver, 'Stop! I'll take the wheel. You walk in front and show the way.' So we did that for two miles. Then we were in the country. I know that section like my hand, but we had missed the house. So we had to turn around and go back. That was an awful time. We were on the side of a hill, with a terrible drop on one side and no fence. I was afraid every minute. But we made it, moving by inches, and pretty soon I found the house. The case was an old man and he had died all of a sudden. Acute cardiac dilation. When we were ready, we started back. Then I began to feel sick. The fog was getting me. There was an awful tickle in my throat. I was coughing and ready to vomit. I called to my driver that I had to stop and get out. He was ready to stop, I guess. Already he had walked four or five miles. But I envied him. He was well and I was awful sick. I leaned against the car, coughing and gagging, and at last I riffled a few times. Then I was much better. I could drive.

So we went on, and finally we were home. My wife was standing at the door. Before she spoke, I knew what she would say. I thought, Oh, my God—another! I knew it by her face. And after that came another. Then another. There seemed to be no end. By ten o'clock in the morning, I had nine bodies waiting here. Then I heard that DeRienzo and Lawson, the other morticians, each had one. Eleven people dead! My driver and I kept looking at each other. What was happening? We didn't know. I thought probably the fog was the reason. It had the smell of poison. But we didn't know."

Mr. Schwerha's bewilderment was not widely shared. Most Donorans were still unaware Saturday morning that anything was happening. They had no way of knowing. Donora has no radio station, and its one newspaper, the *Herald-American*, is published only five days a week, Monday through Friday. It was past noon before a rumor of widespread illness began to drift through town. The news reached August Chambon at about two o'clock. In addition to being burgess, an office that is more an honor than a livelihood, Mr. Chambon operates a moving-and-storage business, and he had been out of town on a job all morning. "There was a message waiting for me when I got home," he says. "John Elco, of the Legion, had called and wanted me at the Borough Building right away. I wondered what the hell, but I went right over. It isn't like John to get excited over nothing. The fog didn't even enter my mind. Of course, I'd heard there were some people sick from it. My wife had told me that. But I hadn't paid it any special significance. I just thought they were like Mother—old people that were always bothered by fog. Jesus, in a town like this you've got to expect fog. It's natural. At least, that's what I thought then. So I was astonished when John told me that the fog was causing sickness all over town. I was just about floored. That's a fact. Because I felt fine myself. I was hardly even coughing much. Well, as soon as I'd talked to John and the other fellows he had rounded up, I started in to do what I could. Something had already been done. John and Cora Vernon, the Red Cross director, were setting up an emergency-aid station in the Community Center. We don't have a hospital here. The nearest one is at

Charleroi. Mrs. Vernon was getting a doctor she knew there to come over and take charge of the station, and the Legion was arranging for cars and volunteer nurses. The idea was to get a little organization in things—everything was confused as hell—and also to give our doctors a rest. They'd been working steady for thirty-six hours or more. Mrs. Vernon was fixing it so when somebody called a doctor's number, they would be switched to the Center and everything would be handled from there. I've worked in the mills and I've dug coal, but I never worked any harder than I worked that day. Or was so worried. Mostly I was on the phone. I called every town around here to send supplies for the station and oxygen for the firemen. I even called Pittsburgh. Maybe I overdid it. There was stuff pouring in here for a week. But what I wanted to be was prepared for anything. The way that fog looked that day, it wasn't ever going to lift. And then the rumors started going around that now people were dying. Oh, Jesus! Then I was scared. I heard all kinds of reports. Four dead. Ten dead. Thirteen dead. I did the only thing I could think of. I notified the State Health Department, and I called a special meeting of the Council and our Board of Health and the mill officials for the first thing Sunday morning. I wanted to have it right then, but I couldn't get hold of everybody—it was Saturday night. Every time I looked up from the phone, I'd hear a new rumor. Usually a bigger one. I guess I heard everything but the truth. What I was really afraid of was that they might set off a panic. That's what I kept dreading. I needn't have worried, though. The way it turned out, half the town had hardly heard that there was anybody even sick until Sunday night, when Walter Winchell opened his big mouth on the radio. By then, thank God, it was all over."

The emergency-aid station, generously staffed and abundantly supplied with drugs and oxygen inhalators, opened at eight o'clock Saturday night. "We were ready for anything and prepared for the worst," Mrs. Vernon says. "We even had an ambulance at our disposal. Phillip DeRienzo, the undertaker, loaned it to us. But almost nothing happened. Altogether, we brought in just eight patients. Seven, to be exact. One was dead when the car arrived. Three were very bad and we sent them to the hospital in Charleroi. The others we just treated and sent home.

It was really very queer. The fog was as black and nasty as ever that night, or worse, but all of a sudden the calls for a doctor just seemed to trickle out and stop. It was as though everybody was sick who was going to be sick. I don't believe we had a call after midnight. I knew then that we'd seen the worst of it."

Dr. Roth had reached that conclusion, though on more slender evidence, several hours before. "I'd had a call about noon from a woman who said two men roomers in her house were in bad shape," he says. "It was nine or nine-thirty by the time I finally got around to seeing them. Only, I never saw them. The landlady yelled up to them that I was there, and they yelled right back, 'Tell him never mind. We're O.K. now.' Well, that was good enough for me. I decided things must be letting up. I picked up my grip and walked home and fell into bed. I was dead-beat."

There was no visible indication that the fog was beginning to relax its smothering grip when the group summoned by Burgess Chambon assembled at the Borough Building the next morning to discuss the calamity. It was another soggy, silent, midnight day. "That morning was the worst," the Burgess says. "It wasn't just that the fog was still hanging on. We'd begun to get some true facts. We didn't have any real idea how many people were sick. That didn't come out for months. We thought a few hundred. But we did have the number of deaths. It took the heart out of you. The rumors hadn't come close to it. It was eighteen. I guess we talked about that first. Then the question of the mills came up. The smoke. L. J. Westhaver, who was general superintendent of the steel and wire works then, was there, and so was the head of the zinc plant, M. M. Neale. I asked them to shut down for the duration. They said they already had. They had started banking the fires at six that morning. They went on to say, though, that they were sure the mills had nothing to do with the trouble. We didn't know what to think. Everybody was at a loss to point the finger at anything in particular. There just didn't seem to be any explanation. We had another meeting that afternoon. It was the same thing all over again. We talked and we wondered and we worried. We couldn't think of anything to do that hadn't already been done. I think we heard about the nineteenth death before we broke up. We thought for a week that was the last. Then one more finally died. I don't remember exactly what all we did or said that afternoon. What I remember is after we broke up. When we came out of the building, it was raining. Maybe it was only drizzling then—I guess the real rain didn't set in until evening—but, even so, there was a hell of a difference. The air was different. It didn't get you any more. You could breathe."

The investigation of the disaster lasted almost a year. It was not only the world's first full-blooded examination of the general problem of air pollution but one of the most exhaustive inquiries of any kind ever made in the field of public health. Its course was directed jointly by Dr. Joseph Shilen, director of the Bureau of Industrial Hygiene of the Pennsylvania Department of Health, and Dr. J. G. Townsend, chief of the Division of Industrial Hygiene of the United States Public Health Service, and at times it involved the entire technical personnel of both agencies. The Public Health Service assigned to the case nine engineers, seven physicians, six nurses, five chemists, three statisticians, two meteorologists, two dentists, and a veterinarian. The force under the immediate direction of Dr. Shilen, though necessarily somewhat smaller, was similarly composed.

The investigation followed three main lines, embracing the clinical, the environmental, and the meteorological aspects of the occurrence. Of these, the meteorological inquiry was the most nearly conclusive. It was also the most reassuring. It indicated that while the situation of Donora is unwholesomely conducive to the accumulation of smoke and fog, the immediate cause of the October, 1948, visitation was a freak of nature known to meteorologists as a temperature inversion. This phenomenon is, as its name suggests, characterized by a temporary, and usually brief, reversal of the normal atmospheric conditions, in which the air near the earth is warmer than the air higher up. Its result is a more or less complete immobilization of the convection currents in the lower air by which gases and fumes are ordinarily carried upward, away from the earth.

The clinical findings, with one or two exceptions, were more confirmatory than illuminating. One of the revelations, which was gleaned from several months of tireless interviewing, was that thousands, rather than just hundreds, had been ill during the fog. For the most part, the findings demonstrated, to the surprise of neither the investigators nor the Donora physicians, that the affection was essentially an irritation of the respiratory tract, that its severity increased in proportion to the age of the victim and his predisposition to cardio-respiratory ailments, and that the ultimate cause of death was suffocation.

The environmental study, the major phase of which was an analysis of the multiplicity of gases emitted by the mills, boats, and trains, was, in a positive sense, almost wholly unrewarding. It failed to determine the direct causative agent. Still, its results, though negative, were not without value. They showed, contrary to expectation, that no one of the several stack gases known to be irritant—among them fluoride, chloride, hydrogen sulphide, cadmium oxide, and sulphur dioxide—could have been present in the air in sufficient concentration to produce serious illness. "It seems reasonable to state," Dr. Helmuth H. Schrenk, chief of the Environmental Investigations Branch of the Public Health Service's Division of Industrial Hygiene, has written of this phase of the inquiry, "that while no single substance was responsible for the . . . episode, the syndrome could have been produced by a combination, or summation of the action, of two or more of the contaminants. Sulphur dioxide and its oxidation products, together with particulate matter [soot and fly ash], are considered significant contaminants. However, the significance of the other irritants as important adjuvants to the biological effects cannot be finally estimated on the basis of present knowledge. It is important to emphasize that information available on the toxicological effects of mixed irritant gases is meagre and data on possible enhanced action due to adsorption of gases on particulate matter is limited." To this, Dr. Leonard A. Scheele, Surgeon General of the Service, has added, "One of the most important results of the study is to show us what we do not know."

Funeral services for most of the victims of the fog were held on Tuesday, November 2nd. Monday had been a day of battering rain, but the weather cleared in the night, and Tuesday was fine. "It was like a day in spring," Mr. Schwerha says. "I think I have never seen such a beautiful blue sky or such a shining sun or such pretty white clouds. Even the trees in the cemetery seemed to have color. I kept looking up all day."

The New Yorker, September 30, 1950

EDWIN WAY TEALE

Though he won the Pulitzer for *Wandering Through Winter* in 1966, Edwin Way Teale's work really belongs here, a little further back in the history of American nature writing—in that period after World War II and before Rachel Carson when it was easier and perhaps expected to be genial about the natural world and its prospects. In *North with the Spring* (1951), he began his great lifetime project of following the seasons across the American landscape, recounting his 17,000-mile journey in a black Buick, from the Everglades to the melting snows of New Hampshire. If he tended to shy away from controversy, Teale (1899–1980) was nevertheless prescient about the future ("Time and space—time to be alone, space to move about—these may well become the great scarcities of tomorrow") and always clear on what counted: "The difference between utility and utility plus beauty is the difference between telephone wires and the spider's web."

The Longest Day

During all the days of our travels—in the Everglades, along the delta marshes, on a barrier island, in the Great Smokies, among the pine barrens and the Lilliput forests of Cape Cod and the green hills of the border—we had wondered vaguely about this final twenty-four hours of spring. What would the day be like? Where would we be? What would we be doing? In what surroundings, bright or gloomy, would we come to the end of our travels with a season?

Now we knew the answers. This was the final day, the summit of the spring.

We awoke before four o'clock. Already a clear sky was brightening above the birchtops outside our cabin window in Crawford Notch. By four, robins were singing and the wooded steeps above us echoed with the calling of an ovenbird. Then came the pure sweet strain of the whitethroat, most moving of all the voices of this north-country choir. Long before five even the bottom of the deep ravine, where dusk comes swiftly and dawn is retarded, was filled with daylight. With this sunrise the tide of light reached its annual flood to begin the long slow rollback to the low ebb of December.

During that day—between the earliest sunrise and the latest sunset of the spring—we roamed amid the beauty and grandeur of the mountains. They formed a fitting climax for our travels with the spring. Where else except in America would that journey have carried us through such variedly impressive scenery, such altering forms of plant and animal life, such diverse events of natural history interest?

I remember we stopped for a long time that afternoon to watch the dance of the Mayflies above Echo Lake and Profile Lake below the Great Stone Face. All through Franconia Notch, over the two lakes and the Pemigewasset River, these pale-yellow ephemera drifted through the air, luminous in every open space lighted by the lengthening rays of late afternoon. Half a hundred hung in a small cloud above one spot on the shore of Echo Lake. Spotlighted by long fingers of sunshine coming through the treetops, they bobbed and turned and fluttered in a shining throng that extended from about two to six feet above the ground. Here hour after hour they engaged in a curious mating performance such as we had never witnessed before.

Every few minutes one of the dancers would leave the throng and climb steeply into the air. At a height of eight or ten feet it would turn downward and plunge in an almost vertical descent through the May fly cloud. A foot or so from the ground it would level off and curve upward again. During each swift descent, as the diving insect passed through the bobbing dancers, three or four would dart in pursuit. Apparently the plunging May fly was the female, those that joined in the pursuit the males. All through the sunset and on into the twilight this love dance of the ephemera continued.

A mile to the north, where Lafayette Brook tumbles down a rocky ravine on a plunging descent toward Gale River, we heard the last bird chorus of the spring. All up the mountain steeps hermit thrushes and whitethroats and wood thrushes and veeries and olive-backed thrushes sang in the sunset. From time to time a small dark form fluttered into the air above the trees of the ravine. Clear and sweet, a warbling, twittering jumble of notes came down to us. We were hearing the flight song of the ovenbird—the mysterious, never-identified "night warbler" of Thoreau's *Journal.*

In this choir whitethroats predominated. We grew to recognize different singers by variations in pitch and quality. One would begin with a long, exquisite violin note and others up the ravine, some higher pitched, others lower pitched, would repeat the sad sweet overtones of their melody. It is a song of the New World, a song of hope and confidence; it is a song of the Old World, a song of wisdom and sadness. It seems to put to music the bravery of the spirit, the courage of the frail.

In an often-quoted admonition, Mark Twain advised famous men to think up their last words beforehand rather than to depend on the inspiration of the moment. If we had planned beforehand the ending of spring's longest day, nothing we could have imagined would have excelled the glory of that final sunset. From the high aerie of the bridge spanning Lafayette Brook we watched it spread across the sky over the darkening mountains that, range on range, rolled away into the west. As the warmth of the sunlight ebbed and the air grew chill in the valleys below us, rivers of mist rose above rivers of water. The winding course of every stream was marked by vapor in the air above it. Gazing down, we could trace the progress of invisible watercourses meandering through the forest below. Contour lines had been traced on the air by mist.

During one time of strange and eerie beauty, all the curls and billows of the mist glowed red, rising like slow tongues and sheets of fire above the treetops tinged by the flames of the western sky. Nowhere else on our trip except over the lonely barrier beach at Bull's Island had we encountered so memorable a sunset as this final fading of the daylight in these final hours of spring. It was the sunset of the day, the sunset of the season, the sunset of our trip with the spring.

Unseen in the brilliance of midday, a new moon—a faint greenish-silver parenthesis mark in the sky—had moved across the zenith. Now, as the colors faded in the west and the long slow twilight of the summer solstice began, it increased in brightness. Below it in the deep dusk of the valley toward Franconia, pinpoints of electric lights at farms and villages glittered in the gathering night. Here in this wild and beautiful spot amid the mountains, the dark woods, the rising mist, the new moon hanging above the silhouettes of the peaks, we waited, in spite of the night chill, until the last sunlight of the spring had ebbed from the sky.

Miles to the south, in a cabin by the Pemigewasset, later that night we built a blazing fire of birch logs in the fireplace. We sat for a long time in the warmth of this flickering hearth-fire talking of our journey with a season, of our incomparable good fortune, of the adventures we had shared together. Never in our lives would there be another spring like this. It was late when we stepped out to look at the sky. From horizon to horizon the heavens were clear, filled with the glinting of the stars. And almost as we looked, in the night, under the stars, spring was gone. It was summer when we awoke.

Everywhere in the Northern Hemisphere spring had come and gone. The season had swept far to the north; it had climbed mountains; it had passed into the sky. Like a sound, spring spreads and spreads until it is swallowed up in space. Like the wind, it moves across the map invisible; we see it only in its effects. It appears like the tracks of the breeze on a field of wheat, like shadows of wind-blown clouds, like tossing branches that reveal the presence of the invisible, the passing of the unseen. So spring had spread from Georgia to North Carolina, from Virginia to Canada, leaving consequences beyond number in its wake. We longed for a thousand springs on the road instead of this one. For spring is like life. You never grasp it entire; you touch it here, there; you know it only in parts and fragments. Reflecting thus as we started south on that first morning of summer—on the day of the summer solstice, the longest day of the year—we were well aware that it is only on the calendar that spring comes to so sudden a termination. In reality its end is a gradual change. Season merges with season in a slow transition into another life.

Driving home to a house where all the calendars marked February and where piles of mail recorded four months on their postmarks, we crossed the Whitestone Bridge onto Long Island. And then—so near the irrevocable end of our journey—we turned aside, we wandered about, we made delays. We followed the Jones Beach parkway to its end, we visited the Massapequa cedars, we stopped at a pond where wild ducks sunned themselves on a grassy bank, we drove nearly a hundred miles before we swung into our driveway. Even then I let the engine idle, loath to cut the switch. Reluctantly I turned the key. The sudden stopping of the motor put a period to our long adventure with the spring.

North with the Spring (1951)

HELEN AND SCOTT NEARING

Helen (1904–1995) and Scott (1883–1983) Nearing were the somewhat stern parents of the back-to-the-land movement that blossomed in the 1960s. In 1932, after Scott lost his college teaching post for his political radicalism, the couple moved to rural Vermont, where they began a lifelong experiment in self-sufficient living, one that continued 20 years later after a move to coastal Maine. The lessons and prescriptions they offered in *Living the Good Life* (1954) and subsequent books inspired many to visit them and many more to emulate their example; their Maine home is now preserved as The Good Life Center.

from **Living the Good Life**

Things were moving fast—perhaps too fast. We were getting in deep. Was it too deep? We had acquired three neglected farms and were starting off at sugaring, of which we knew nothing. Where were these events leading us? Did the sweeping changes in our way of life mean commitments and entanglements which we would regret later on? We had to be wary as well as watchful. Our situation could be summed up in three paragraphs.

We were in the country. We had land. We had all the wood we could use, for the cutting. We had an adequate supply of food from the gardens. We had time, a purpose, energy, enough ingenuity and imagination, a tiny cash income from maple and a little cash money on hand.

We were on a run-down, run-out farm. We were living in a poorly built wooden house through which the winter winds swept like water through a sieve. We owned a timber tract that would come into its own only in twenty to thirty years. We owned the place next door, another run-down farm, equipped with wretched buildings. Our soil was swampy, rough and rocky, mostly covered with second growth, but there was a small amount of good timber left on it. Our gardens were promising, but the main garden was too low and wet to be really productive.

We were in good health. We were solvent in that we had no debts. We were fairly hopeful of the future, but inexperienced in the ways of subsistence living and somewhat uncertain as to how we should proceed. After due consideration and in the spirit of the times, we drew up a ten year plan.

This plan was not made out of whole cloth, all at once. It was modified by experience, as we went along. It was flexible, but in principle and usually in practice we stuck to it. Suppose we set down the main points which the plan covered when we outlined it in the middle 1930's.

1. *We wish to set up a semi-self-contained household unit, based largely on a use economy, and, as far as possible, independent of the price-profit economy which surrounds us.*

The Great Depression had brought millions of bread-winners face to face with the perils which lurked for those who, in a commodity economy based on wage-paid labor, purchase their livelihood in the open market. The wage and salary workers did not own their own jobs, nor did they have any part in deciding economic policy nor in selecting those who carried policy into effect. The many unemployed in 1932 did not lose their jobs through any fault of their own, yet they found themselves workless, in an economy based on cash payment for the necessaries and decencies. Though their incomes had ceased, their outgo for food, shelter and clothing ate up their accumulated savings and threw them into debt. Since we were proposing to go on living in this profit-price economy, we had to accept its dread implications or find a workable alternative. We saw that alternative in a semi-subsistence livelihood.

We would attempt to carry on this self-subsistent economy by the following steps: (1) Raising as much of our own food as local soil and climatic conditions would permit. (2) Bartering our products for those which we could not or did not produce. (3) Using wood for fuel and cutting it ourselves. (4) Putting up our own buildings with stone and wood from the place, doing the work ourselves. (5) Making such implements as sleds, drays, stone-boats, gravel screens, ladders. (6) Holding down to the barest minimum the number of implements, tools, gadgets and machines which we might buy from the assembly lines of big business.* (7) If we had to have such machines for a few hours or days in a year (plough, tractor, rototiller, bull-dozer, chain-saw), we would rent or trade them from local people instead of buying and owning them.

2. *We have no intention of making money, nor do we seek wages or profits. Rather we aim to earn a livelihood, as far as possible on a use economy basis. When enough bread labor has been performed to secure the year's living, we will stop earning until the next crop season.*

Ideas of "making money" or "getting rich" have given people a perverted view of economic principles. The object of economic effort is not money, but livelihood. Money cannot feed, clothe or shelter. Money is a medium of exchange,—a means of securing the items that make up livelihood. It is the necessaries and decencies which are important, not the money which may be exchanged for them. And money must be paid for, like anything else. Robert Louis Stevenson wrote in *Men and Books*, "Money is a commodity to be bought or not to be bought, a luxury in which we may either indulge or stint ourselves, like any other. And there are many luxuries that we may legitimately prefer to it, such as a grateful conscience, a country life, or the woman of our inclination."[†]

People brought up in a money economy are taught to believe in the importance of getting and keeping money. Time and again folk told us, "You can't afford to make syrup. You won't make any money that way." One year a neighbor, Harold Field, kept a careful record of the labor he

---

*All through the years in Vermont we had one expensive, indispensable machine, a half-ton pick-up truck. The first one was a Dodge; later came Fords and Chevrolets, until we got a Jeep, which proved incomparably superior to the others because of its four-wheel drive. If we had done our driving on concrete highways, the four-wheel mechanism would have been superfluous, but on back roads, across fields and through the woods, up and down hills, in mud, snow, slush and on ice, the four-wheel drive paid for its extra cost in one season. Occasionally there might be something, logs, for example, which we could not handle in a pick-up with a body 48 inches wide by 78 inches long, though we did rig up a device that enabled us to carry easily and in quantity, standard iron pipe lengths 21 feet long and even longer poles. The pick-up handled lumber, gravel, stone, lime, cement, top-soil, cord wood and sugar wood, freight and express. It also delivered our sugar products, and carried us many thousand miles each year.

[†]Lon.: Chatto & Windus   1888   p. 143

put in during the syrup season and of the sale price of his product, and figured that he got only 67 cents an hour for his time. In view of these figures, the next year he did not tap out because sugaring paid less than wage labor. But, during that syrup season he found no chance to work for wages, so he didn't even make the 67 cents an hour.

Our attitude was quite different. We kept careful cost figures, but we never used them to determine whether we should or should not make syrup. We tapped our trees as each sap season came along. Our figures showed us what the syrup had cost. When the season was over and the syrup on hand, we wrote to various correspondents in California or Florida, told them what our syrup had cost, and exchanged our product for equal value of their citrus, walnuts, olive oil or raisins. As a result of these transactions, we laid in a supply of items at no cash outlay, which we could not ourselves produce. Our livelihood base was broadened as the result of our efforts in the sugar bush and the sap house.

We also sold our syrup and sugar on the open market. In selling anything, we tried to determine exact costs and set our prices not in terms of what the traffic would bear but in terms of the costs,—figuring in our own time at going day wages.

Just as each year we estimated the amount of garden produce needed for our food, so we tried to foresee the money required to meet our cash obligations. When we had the estimated needs, we raised no more crops and made no more money for that period. In a word, we were trying to make a livelihood, and once our needs in this direction were covered, we turned our efforts in other directions,—toward social activities, toward avocations such as reading, writing, music making, toward repairs or replacements of our equipment.

3. *All of our operations will be kept on a cash and carry basis. No bank loans. No slavery to interest on mortgages, notes and I.O.U's.*

Under any economy, people who rent out money live on easy street. Whether as individuals or banking establishments, they lend money, take security and live on a rich harvest of interest and the proceeds of forced sales. The money lenders are able to enjoy comfort and luxury, without doing any productive labor. It is the borrowing producers who pay the interest or lose their property. Farmers and home owners by the thousands lost everything they had during the Great Depression because they could not meet interest payments. We decided to buy for cash or not at all.

4. *We will make our cash crop from maple syrup and will work out a cooperative arrangement wherever possible.* We made a cooperative agreement with Floyd Hurd and his family under which we would work together and divide the syrup crop in proportion to land and tools owned and the work done by each party. We began this arrangement in 1935 and continued it for six years with the Hurds, later carrying it on with other people.

5. *We will put syrup production on an efficient basis, replace the old Hoard sugarhouse with a modern building and equip it with new tools.* We did this in 1935, we building the new sugarhouse and the Hurds buying a large new evaporator. We also decided to convert part of our syrup crop into maple sugar, for which there was a ready sale. The complete story of this effort has been told in detail in *The Maple Sugar Book.*

6. *So long as the income from the sale of maple syrup and sugar covers our needs we will not sell anything else from the place. Any garden or other surpluses will be shared with neighbors and friends in terms of their needs.*

This latter practice was carried out generally in the valley. Rix Knight had extra pear trees. In a good season he distributed bushels to any of us who had no pears. Jack Lightfoot let us pick his spare apples and let others cut Christmas greens, free of charge. We brought firewood to those who needed it, and many garden products. Our chief delight was growing, picking and giving away sweet peas. We grew these in profusion,—double rows 60 to 100 feet long, each year. Whenever taking a trip to town in blooming season (July to frost of late September) we filled baskets and basins with dozens of bunches and gave them out during the day to friends and strangers alike. Grocers, dentist friends, gas station attendants, utter strangers on the street,—all were the delighted recipients of the fragrant blossoms. One woman, after endeavoring to pay for a large bunch, was heard to go off muttering, "I've lived too near New York too long to understand such practices."

Living the Good Life (1954)

What John Muir was to the Sierra Nevada and Marjory Stoneman Douglas to the Everglades, Sigurd Olson (1899–1982) was to the vast lake country on America's northern border—both chief chronicler and chief defender. Born in Chicago, he made his home for most of his life in Ely, Minnesota, where until 1947 he was dean of the local junior college. He traveled the Quetico-Superior country, often by canoe (and sometimes, as in this piece, on ice skates), and came to believe that the wild offered something spiritual and essential to modern man. His conservation work was untiring (and often angered his neighbors): he served as president of both The Wilderness Society and the National Parks Association, helped draft the federal Wilderness Act, and was instrumental in establishing Point Reyes National Seashore in California, the Arctic National Wildlife Range (now Refuge) in Alaska, and Voyageurs National Park in Minnesota. But his conservation work drew on the power of his words, which inspired many to the cause and many more to visit the lands he described. "The way of a canoe is the way of the wilderness and of a freedom almost forgotten," he wrote; "it is an antidote to insecurity, the open door to waterways of ages past and a way of life with profound and abiding satisfactions."

Northern Lights

The lights of the aurora moved and shifted over the horizon. Sometimes there were shafts of yellow tinged with green, then masses of evanescence which moved from east to west and back again. Great streamers of bluish white zigzagged like a tremendous trembling curtain from one end of the sky to the other. Streaks of yellow and orange and red shimmered along the flowing borders. Never for a moment were they still, fading until they were almost completely gone, only to dance forth again in renewed splendor with infinite combinations and startling patterns of design.

The lake lay like a silver mirror before me, and from its frozen surface came subterranean rumblings, pressure groans, sharp reports from the newly forming ice. As far as I could see, the surface was clear and shining. That ice was something to remember here in the north, for most years the snows come quickly and cover the first smooth glaze of freezing almost as soon as it is formed, or else the winds ruffle the surface of the crystallizing water and fill it with ridges and unevenness. But this time there had been no wind or snow to interfere, and the ice everywhere was clear—seven miles of perfect skating, something to dream about in years to come.

Hurriedly I strapped on my skates, tightened the laces, and in a moment was soaring down the path of shifting light which stretched endlessly before me. Out in the open away from shore there were few cracks—stroke—stroke—stroke—long and free, and I knew the joy that skating and skiing can give, freedom of movement beyond myself. But to get the feel of soaring, there must be miles of distance and conditions must be right. As I sped down the lake, I was conscious of no effort, only of the dancing lights in the sky and a sense of lightness and exaltation.

Shafts of light shot up into the heavens above me and concentrated there in a final climactic effort in which the shifting colors seemed drained from the horizons to form one gigantic rosette of flame and yellow and greenish purple. Suddenly I grew conscious of the reflections from the ice itself and that I was skating through a sea of changing color caught between the streamers above and below. At that moment I was part of the aurora, part of its light and of the great curtain that trembled above me.

Those moments of experience are rare. Sometimes I have known them while swimming in the moonlight, again while paddling a canoe when there was no wind and the islands seemed inverted and floating on the surface. I caught it once when the surf was rolling on an ocean coast and I was carried on the crest of a wave that had begun a thousand miles away. Here it was once more—freedom of movement and detachment from the earth.

Down the lake I went straight into the glistening path, speeding through a maze of changing color—stroke—stroke—stroke—the ringing of steel on ice, the sharp, reverberating rumbles of expansion below. Clear ice for the first time in years, and the aurora blazing away above it.

At the end of the lake I turned and saw the glittering lights of Winton far behind me. I lay down on the ice to rest. The sky was still bright and I watched the shifting lights come and go. I knew what the astronomers and the physicists said, that they were caused by sunspots and areas of gaseous disturbance on the face of the sun that bombarded the earth's stratosphere with hydrogen protons and electrons which in turn exploded atoms of oxygen, nitrogen, helium, and the other elements surrounding us. Here were produced in infinite combinations all the colors of the spectrum. It was all very plausible and scientific, but tonight that explanation left me cold. I was in no mood for practicality, for I had just come skating down the skyways themselves and had seen the aurora from the inside. What did the scientists know about what I had done? How could they explain what had happened to me and the strange sensations I had known?

Much better the poem of Robert Service telling of the great beds of radium emanating shafts of light into the northern darkness of the Yukon and how men went mad trying to find them. How infinitely more satisfying to understand and feel the great painting by Franz Johnson of a lone figure crossing a muskeg at night with the northern lights blazing above it. I stood before that painting in the Toronto Art Gallery one day and caught all the stark loneliness, all the beauty and the cold of that scene, and for a moment forgot the busy city outside.

I like to think of them as the ghost dance of the Chippewas. An Indian once told me that when a warrior died, he gathered with his fellows along the northern horizon and danced the war dances they had known on earth. The shifting streamers and the edgings of color came from the giant headdresses they wore. I was very young when I first saw them that way, and there were times during those enchanted years when I thought I could distinguish the movements of individual bodies as they rushed from one part of the sky to another. I knew nothing then of protons or atoms and saw the northern lights as they should be seen. I knew, too, the wonderment that only a child can know and a beauty that is enhanced by mystery.

As I lay there on the ice and thought of these things I wondered if legendry could survive scientific truth, if the dance of the protons would replace the ghost dance of the Chippewas. I wondered as I began to skate toward home if anything—even knowing the physical truth— could ever change the beauty of what I had seen, the sense of unreality. Indian warriors, exploding atoms, beds of radium—what difference did it make? What counted was the sense of the north they gave me, the fact that they typified the loneliness, the stark beauty of frozen muskegs, lakes, and forests. Those northern lights were part of me and I of them.

On the way back I noticed that there was a half-moon over the cluster of lights in the west. I skirted the power dam at the mouth of the Kawishiwi River, avoiding the blaze of its light on the black water below the spillway. Then suddenly the aurora was gone and the moon as well.

Stroke—stroke—stroke—the shores were black now, pinnacled spruce and shadowed birch against the sky. At the landing I looked back. The ice was still grumbling and groaning, still shaping up to the mold of its winter bed.

The Singing Wilderness (1956)

It's possible that E. B. White's biggest contribution to an environmental worldview was his trilogy of essentially perfect children's books— *Stuart Little* (1945), *Charlotte's Web* (1952), and *The Trumpet of the Swan* (1970)—each of which extended the moral imagination deep into the animal kingdom. But for all the pleasure of those works and for all the funny "Talk of the Town" pieces and cartoon captions and light verse that White (1899–1985) wrote for *The New Yorker*, the classic essays he wrote from the mid-1930s to the early 1960s may be the real heart of his work. These years—which spanned the Depression, World War II, the growth of the United Nations down the street from his home in Manhattan's Turtle Bay neighborhood, and the spread of atomic weapons—were as confused and chaotic as any in American history. Against the serene backdrop of his summer house on the coast of Maine, and against the gentle play of his prose, the specter of a world darkened by the new danger of radioactive fallout seemed especially eerie and sad.

Sootfall and Fallout

TURTLE BAY,
OCTOBER 18

This is a dark morning in the apartment, but the block is gay with yellow moving vans disgorging Mary Martin's belongings in front of a house a couple of doors east of here, into which (I should say from the looks of things) she is moving. People's lives are so exposed at moments like this, their possessions lying naked in the street, the light of day searching out every bruise and mark of indoor living. It is an unfair exposé—end tables with nothing to be at the end of, standing lamps with their cords tied up in curlers, bottles of vermouth craning their long necks from cartons of personal papers, and every wastebasket carrying its small cargo of miscellany. The vans cause a stir in the block. Heads appear in the windows of No. 230, across the way. Passersby stop on the sidewalk and stare brazenly into the new home through the open door. I have a mezzanine seat for the performance; like a Peeping Tom, I lounge here in my bathrobe and look down, held in the embrace of a common cold, before which scientists stand in awe although they have managed to split the atom, infect the topsoil with strontium 90, break the barrier of sound, and build the Lincoln Tunnel.

What a tremendous lot of stuff makes up the cumulus called "the home"! The trivet, the tiny washboard, the fire tools, the big copper caldron large enough to scale a hog in, the metal filing cabinets, the cardboard filing cabinets, the record-player, the glass and the china invisible in their barrels, the carpet sweeper. (I wonder whether Miss Martin knows that she owns an old-fashioned carpet sweeper in a modern shade of green.) And here comes a bright little hacksaw, probably the apple of Mr. Halliday's eye. When a writing desk appears, the movers take the drawers out, to lighten the load, and I am free to observe what a tangle Mary Martin's stationery and supplies are in—like my wife's, everything at sixes and sevens. And now the bed, under the open sky above Forty-eighth Street. And now the mattress. A wave of decency overtakes me. I avert my gaze.

The movers experience the worst trouble with two large house plants, six-footers, in their great jars. The jars, on being sounded, prove to be a third full of water and have to be emptied into the gutter. Living things are always harder to lift, somehow, than inanimate objects, and I think any mover would rather walk up three flights with a heavy bureau than go into a waltz with a rubber plant. There is really no way for a man to put his arms around a big house plant and still remain a gentleman.

Out in back, away from the street, the prospect is more pleasing. The yellow cat mounts the wisteria vine and tries to enter my bedroom, stirred by dreams of a bullfinch in a cage. The air is hazy, smoke and fumes being pressed downward in what the smog reporter of the *Times* calls "a wigwam effect." I don't know what new gadget the factories of Long Island are making today to produce such a foul vapor—probably a new jet applicator for the relief of nasal congestion. But whatever it is, I would swap it for a breath of fresh air. On every slight stirring of the breeze, the willow behind Mary Martin's wigwam lets drop two or three stylish yellow leaves, and they swim lazily down like golden fish to where Paul, the handyman, waits with his broom. In the ivy border along the wall, watchful of the cat, three thrushes hunt about among the dry leaves. I can't pronounce "three thrushes," but I can see three thrushes from this window, and this is the first autumn I have ever seen three at once. An October miracle. I think they are hermits, but the visibility is so poor I can't be sure.

This section of Manhattan boasts the heaviest sootfall in town, and the United States of America boasts the heaviest fallout in the world, and when you take the sootfall and the fallout and bring smog in on top of them, I feel I am in a perfect position to discuss the problem of universal pollution. The papers, of course, are full of the subject these days, as they follow the Presidential campaigners around the nation from one contaminated area to another.

I have no recent figures on sootfall in the vicinity of Third Avenue, but the *Times* last Saturday published some figures on fallout from Dr. Willard F. Libby, who said the reservoir of radioactive materials now floating in the stratosphere from the tests of all nations was roughly twenty-four billion tons. That was Saturday. Sunday's *Times* quoted Dr. Laurence H. Snyder as saying, "In assessing the potential harm [of weapons-testing], statements are always qualified by a phrase such as 'if the testing of weapons continues at the present rate . . .' This qualification is usually obsolete by the time the statement is printed." I have an idea the figure twenty-four billion tons may have been obsolete when it appeared in the paper. It may not have included, for instance, the radioactive stuff from the bomb the British set off in Australia a week or two ago. Maybe it did, maybe it didn't. The point of Dr. Snyder's remark is clear; a thermonuclear-arms race is, as he puts it, self-accelerating. Bomb begets bomb. A begets H. Anything you can build, I can build bigger.

"Unhappily," said Governor Harriman the other night, "we are still thinking in small, conventional terms, and with unwarranted complacency."

The habit of thinking in small, conventional terms is, of course, not limited to us Americans. You could drop a leaflet or a Hubbard squash on the head of any person in any land and you would almost certainly hit a brain that was whirling in small, conventional circles. There is something about the human mind that keeps it well within the confines of the parish, and only one outlook in a million is non-parochial. The impression one gets from campaign oratory is that the sun revolves around the earth, the earth revolves around the United States, and the United States revolves around whichever city the speaker happens to be in at the moment. This is what a friend of mine used to call the Un-Copernican system. During a Presidential race, candidates sometimes manage to create the impression that their thoughts are ranging widely and that they have abandoned conventional thinking. I love to listen to them when they are in the throes of these quadrennial seizures. But I haven't heard much from either candidate that sounded unconventional— although I have heard some things that sounded sensible and sincere. A candidate could easily commit political suicide if he were to come up with an unconventional thought during a Presidential tour.

I think Man's gradual, creeping contamination of the planet, his sending up of dust into the air, his strontium additive in our bones, his discharge of industrial poisons into rivers that once flowed clear, his mixing of chemicals with fog on the east wind add up to a fantasy of such grotesque proportions as to make everything said on the subject seem pale and anemic by contrast. I hold one share in the corporate earth and am uneasy about the management. Dr. Libby said there is new evidence that the amount of strontium reaching the body from topsoil impregnated by fallout is "considerably less than the seventy per cent of the topsoil concentration originally estimated." Perhaps we should all feel elated at this, but I don't. The correct amount of strontium with which to impregnate the topsoil is *no* strontium. To rely on "tolerances" when you get into the matter of strontium 90, with three sovereign bomb testers already testing, independently of one another, and about fifty potential bomb testers ready to enter the stratosphere with their contraptions, is to talk with unwarranted complacency. I belong to a small, unconventional school that believes that *no* rat poison is the correct amount to spread in the kitchen where children and puppies can get at it. I believe that *no* chemical waste is the correct amount to discharge into the fresh rivers of the world, and I believe that if there is a way to trap the fumes from factory chimneys, it should be against the law to set these deadly fumes adrift where they can mingle with fog and, given the right conditions, suddenly turn an area into another Donora, Pa.

"I have seen the smoky fury of our factories—rising to the skies," said President Eisenhower cheerfully as he addressed the people of Seattle last night. Well, I can see the smoky fury of our factories drifting right into this room this very minute; the fury sits in my throat like a bundle of needles, it explores my nose, chokes off my breath, and makes my eyes burn. The room smells like a slaughterhouse. And the phenomenon gets a brief mention in the morning press.

One simple, unrefuted fact about radioactive substances is that scientists do not agree about the "safe" amount. All radiation is harmful, all of it shortens life, all is cumulative, nobody keeps track of how much he gets in the form of X-rays and radiotherapy, and all of it affects not only the recipient but his heirs. Both President Eisenhower and Governor Stevenson have discussed H-bomb testing and the thermonuclear scene, and their views differ. Neither of them, it seems to me, has quite told the changing facts of life on earth. Both tend to speak of national security as though it were still capable of being dissociated from universal well-being; in fact, sometimes in these political addresses it sounds as though this nation, or any nation, through force of character or force of arms, could damn well rise *above* planetary considerations, as though we were greater than our environment, as though the national verve somehow transcended the natural world.

"Strong we shall stay free," said President Eisenhower in Pittsburgh. And Governor Stevenson echoed the statement in Chicago: ". . . only the strong can be free."

This doctrine of freedom through strength deserves a second look. It would have served nicely in 1936, but nobody thought of it then.

Today, with the H-bomb deterring war, we are free and we are militarily strong, but the doctrine is subject to a queer, embarrassing amendment. Today it reads, "Strong we shall stay free, *provided we do not have to use our strength.*" That's not quite the same thing. What was true in 1936, if not actually false today, is at best a mere partial, or half, truth. A nation wearing atomic armor is like a knight whose armor has grown so heavy he is immobilized; he can hardly walk, hardly sit his horse, hardly think, hardly breathe. The H-bomb is an extremely effective deterrent to war, but it has little virtue as a *weapon* of war, because it would leave the world uninhabitable.

For a short while following the release of atomic energy, a strong nation was a secure nation. Today no nation, whatever its thermonuclear power, is a strong nation in the sense that it is a fully independent nation. All are weak, and all are weak from the same cause: each depends on the others for salvation, yet none admits this dependence, and there is absolutely no machinery for interdependence. The big nations are weak because the strength has gone out of their arms—which are too terrifying to use, too poisonous to explode. The little nations are weak because they have always been relatively weak and now they have to breathe the same bad air as the big ones. Ours is a balance, as Mr. Stevenson put it, not of power but of terror. If anything, the H-bomb rather favors small nations that don't as yet possess it; they feel slightly more free to jostle other nations, having discovered that a country can stick its tongue out quite far these days without provoking war, so horrible are war's consequences.

The atom, then, is a proper oddity. It has qualified the meaning of national security, it has very likely saved us from a third world war, it has given a new twist to the meaning of power, and it has already entered our bones with a cancer-producing isotope. Furthermore, it has altered the concept of personal sacrifice for moral principle. Human beings have always been willing to shed their blood for what they believed in. Yesterday this was clear and simple; we would pay in blood because, after the price was exacted, there was still a chance to make good the gain. But the modern price tag is not blood. Today our leaders and the leaders of other nations are, in effect, saying, "We will defend our beliefs not alone with our blood—by God, we'll defend them, if we have to, with our genes." This is bold, resolute talk, and one can't help admiring the spirit of it. I admire the spirit of it, but the logic of it eludes me. I doubt whether any noble principle—or any ignoble principle, either, for that matter—can be preserved at the price of genetic disintegration.

The thing I watch for in the speeches of the candidates is some hint that the thermonuclear-arms race may be bringing people nearer together, rather than forcing them farther apart. I suspect that because of fallout we may achieve a sort of universality sooner than we bargained for. Fallout may compel us to fall in. The magic-carpet ride on the mushroom cloud has left us dazed—we have come so far so fast. There is a passage in Anne Lindbergh's book "North to the Orient" that captures the curious lag between the mind and the body during a plane journey, between the slow unfolding of remembered images and the swift blur of modern flight. Mrs. Lindbergh started her flight to the Orient by way of North Haven, her childhood summer home. "The trip to Maine," she wrote, "used to be a long and slow one. There was plenty of time in the night, spattered away in the sleeper, in the morning spent ferrying across the river at Bath, in the afternoon syncopated into a series of calls on one coast town after another—there was plenty of time to make the mental change coinciding with our physical change. . . . But on this swift flight to North Haven in the *Sirius* my mind was so far behind my body that when we flew over Rockland Harbor the familiar landmarks below me had no reality."

Like the girl in the plane, we have arrived, but the familiar scene lacks reality. We cling to old remembered forms, old definitions, old comfortable conceptions of national coziness, national self-sufficiency. The Security Council meets solemnly and takes up Suez, eleven sovereign fellows kicking a sovereign ditch around while England threatens war to defend her "lifelines," when modern war itself means universal contamination, universal deathlines, and the end of ditches. I would feel more hopeful, more *secure*, if the Councilmen suddenly changed their tune and began arguing the case for mud turtles and other ancient denizens of ponds and ditches. That is the thing at stake now, and it is what will finally open the Canal to the world's ships in perfect concord.

Candidates for political office steer clear of what Mrs. Luce used to call "globaloney," for fear they may lose the entire American Legion vote and pick up only Norman Cousins. Yet there are indications that supranational ideas are alive in the back of a few men's minds. Through the tangle of verbiage, the idea of "common cause" skitters like a shy bird. Mr. Dulles uses the word "interdependent" in one sentence, then returns promptly to the more customary, safer word "independent." We give aid to Yugoslavia to assure her "independence," and the very fact of the gift is proof that neither donor nor recipient enjoys absolute independence any more; the two are locked in mortal *inter*dependence. Mr. Tito says he is for "new forms and new laws." I haven't the vaguest notion of what he means by that, and I doubt whether he has, either. Certainly there are no *old* laws, if by "laws" he means enforceable rules of conduct by which the world community is governed. But I'm for new forms, all right. Governor Stevenson, in one of his talks, said, "Nations have become so accustomed to living in the dark that they find it hard to learn to live in the light." What light? The light of government? If so, why not say so? President Eisenhower ended a speech the other day with the phrase "a peace of justice in a world of law." Everything else in his speech dealt with a peace of justice in a world of anarchy.

The riddle of disarmament, the riddle of peace, seems to me to hang on the interpretation of these conflicting and contradictory phrases—and on whether or not the men who use them really mean business. Are we independent or interdependent? We can't possibly be both. Do we indeed seek a peace of justice in a world of law, as the President intimates? If so, when do we start, and how? Are we for "new forms," or will the old ones do? In 1945, after the worst blood bath in history, the nations settled immediately back into old forms. In its structure, the United Nations reaffirms everything that caused World War II. At the end of a war fought to defeat dictators, the U.N. welcomed Stalin and Perón to full membership, and the Iron Curtain quickly descended to put the seal of authority on this inconsistent act. The drafters of the Charter assembled in San Francisco and defended their mild, inadequate format with the catchy phrase "Diplomacy is the art of the possible." Meanwhile, a little band of physicists met in a squash court and said, "The hell with the art of the possible. Watch this!"

The world organization debates disarmament in one room and, in the next room, moves the knights and pawns that make national arms imperative. This is not justice and law, and this is not light. It is not new forms. The U.N. is modern in intent, antique in shape. In San Francisco in 1945, the victor nations failed to create a constitution that placed a higher value on principle than on sovereignty, on common cause than on special cause. The world of 1945 was still a hundred per cent parochial. The world of 1956 is still almost a hundred per cent parochial. But at last we have a problem that is clearly a community problem, devoid of nationality—the problem of the total pollution of the planet.

We have, in fact, a situation in which the deadliest of all weapons, the H-bomb, together with its little brother, the A-bomb, is the latent source of great agreement among peoples. The bomb is universally hated, and it is universally feared. We cannot escape it with collective security; we shall have to face it with united action. It has given us a few years of grace without war, and now it offers us a few millenniums of oblivion. In a paradox of unbelievable jocundity, the shield of national sovereignty suddenly becomes the challenge of national sovereignty. And, largely because of events beyond our control, we are able to sniff the faint stirring of a community ferment—something every man can enjoy.

The President speaks often of "the peaceful uses of atomic energy," and they are greatly on his mind. I believe the peaceful use of atomic energy that should take precedence over all other uses is this: stop it from contaminating the soil and the sea, the rain and the sky, and the bones of man. That is elementary. It comes ahead of "good-will" ships and it comes ahead of cheap power. What good is cheap power if your child already has an incurable cancer?

The hydrogen-garbage-disposal program unites the people of the earth in a common anti-litterbug drive for salvation. Radioactive dust has no nationality, is not deflected by boundaries; it falls on Turk and

Texan impartially. The radio-strontium isotope finds its way into the milk of Soviet cow and English cow with equal ease. This simple fact profoundly alters the political scene and calls for political leaders to echo the physicists and say, "Never mind the art of the possible. Watch this!"

To me, living in the light means an honest attempt to discover the germ of common cause in a world of special cause, even against the almost insuperable odds of parochialism and national fervor, even in the face of the dangers that always attend political growth. Actually, nations are already enjoying little pockets of unity. The European coal-steel authority is apparently a success. The U.N., which is usually impotent in political disputes, has nevertheless managed to elevate the world's children and the world's health to a community level. The trick is to encourage and hasten this magical growth, this benign condition—encourage it and get it on paper, while children still have healthy bones and before we have all reached the point of no return. It will not mean the end of nations; it will mean the true beginning of nations.

Paul-Henri Spaak, addressing himself to the Egyptian government the other day, said, "We are no longer at the time of the absolute sovereignty of states." We are not, and we ought by this time to know we are not. I just hope we learn it in time. In the beautiful phrase of Mrs. Lindbergh's, there used to be "plenty of time in the night." Now there is hardly any time at all.

Well, this started out as a letter and has turned into a discourse. But I don't mind. If a candidate were to appear on the scene and come out for the dignity of mud turtles, I suppose people would hesitate to support him, for fear he had lost his reason. But he would have my vote, on the theory that in losing his reason he had kept his head. It is time men allowed their imagination to infect their intellect, time we all rushed headlong into the wilder regions of thought where the earth again revolves around the sun instead of around the Suez, regions where no individual and no group can blithely assume the right to sow the sky with seeds of mischief, and where the sovereign nation at last begins to function as the true friend and guardian of sovereign man.

The New Yorker, November 3, 1956

A lifelong academic who specialized in paleontology, Loren Eiseley (1907–1977) was best known for what he called his "concealed essays" that use personal anecdote to get at some scientific truth. Among other things, he was able to probe and to convey to readers the almost impossible scales of time and distance that geologists and physicists and evolutionary biologists were coming to understand by mid-century. *The Immense Journey* (1957), concerned mostly with the evolution of the universe, was his first book and his most popular, but he produced widely read essays for the rest of his life, presaging other top-notch popularizers like Carl Sagan or Stephen Jay Gould.

How Flowers Changed the World

If it had been possible to observe the Earth from the far side of the solar system over the long course of geological epochs, the watchers might have been able to discern a subtle change in the light emanating from our planet. That world of long ago would, like the red deserts of Mars, have reflected light from vast drifts of stone and gravel, the sands of wandering wastes, the blackness of naked basalt, the yellow dust of endlessly moving storms. Only the ceaseless marching of the clouds and the intermittent flashes from the restless surface of the sea would have told a different story, but still essentially a barren one. Then, as the millennia rolled away and age followed age, a new and greener light would, by degrees, have come to twinkle across those endless miles.

This is the only difference those far watchers, by the use of subtle instruments, might have perceived in the whole history of the planet Earth. Yet that slowly growing green twinkle would have contained the epic march of life from the tidal oozes upward across the raw and unclothed continents. Out of the vast chemical bath of the sea—not from the deeps, but from the element-rich, light-exposed platforms of the continental shelves—wandering fingers of green had crept upward along the meanderings of river systems and fringed the gravels of forgotten lakes.

In those first ages plants clung of necessity to swamps and watercourses. Their reproductive processes demanded direct access to water. Beyond the primitive ferns and mosses that enclosed the borders of swamps and streams the rocks still lay vast and bare, the winds still swirled the dust of a naked planet. The grass cover that holds our world secure in place was still millions of years in the future. The green marchers had gained a soggy foothold upon the land, but that was all. They did not reproduce by seeds but by microscopic swimming sperm that had to wriggle their way through water to fertilize the female cell. Such plants in their higher forms had clever adaptations for the use of rain water in their sexual phases, and survived with increasing success in a wet land environment. They now seem part of man's normal environment. The truth is, however, that there is nothing very "normal" about nature. Once upon a time there were no flowers at all.

A little while ago—about one hundred million years, as the geologist estimates time in the history of our four-billion-year-old planet—flowers were not to be found anywhere on the five continents. Wherever one might have looked, from the poles to the equator, one would have seen only the cold dark monotonous green of a world whose plant life possessed no other color.

Somewhere, just a short time before the close of the Age of Reptiles, there occurred a soundless, violent explosion. It lasted millions of years, but it was an explosion, nevertheless. It marked the emergence of the angiosperms—the flowering plants. Even the great evolutionist, Charles Darwin, called them "an abominable mystery," because they appeared so suddenly and spread so fast.

Flowers changed the face of the planet. Without them, the world we know—even man himself—would never have existed. Francis Thompson, the English poet, once wrote that one could not pluck a flower without troubling a star. Intuitively he had sensed like a naturalist the enormous interlinked complexity of life. Today we know that the appearance of the flowers contained also the equally mystifying emergence of man.

If we were to go back into the Age of Reptiles, its drowned swamps and birdless forests would reveal to us a warmer but, on the whole, a sleepier world than that of today. Here and there, it is true, the serpent heads of bottom-feeding dinosaurs might be upreared in suspicion of their huge flesh-eating compatriots. Tyrannosaurs, enormous bipedal caricatures of men, would stalk mindlessly across the sites of future cities and go their slow way down into the dark of geologic time.

In all that world of living things nothing saw save with the intense concentration of the hunt, nothing moved except with the grave sleep-walking intentness of the instinct-driven brain. Judged by modern standards, it was a world in slow motion, a cold-blooded world whose occupants were most active at noonday but torpid on chill nights, their brains damped by a slower metabolism than any known to even the most primitive of warm-blooded animals today.

A high metabolic rate and the maintenance of a constant body temperature are supreme achievements in the evolution of life. They enable an animal to escape, within broad limits, from the overheating or the chilling of its immediate surroundings, and at the same time to maintain a peak mental efficiency. Creatures without a high metabolic rate are slaves to weather. Insects in the first frosts of autumn all run down like little clocks. Yet if you pick one up and breathe warmly upon it, it will begin to move about once more.

In a sheltered spot such creatures may sleep away the winter, but they are hopelessly immobilized. Though a few warm-blooded mammals, such as the woodchuck of our day, have evolved a way of reducing their metabolic rate in order to undergo winter hibernation, it is a survival mechanism with drawbacks, for it leaves the animal helplessly exposed if enemies discover him during his period of suspended animation. Thus bear or woodchuck, big animal or small, must seek, in this time of descending sleep, a safe refuge in some hidden den or burrow. Hibernation is, therefore, primarily a winter refuge of small, easily concealed animals rather than of large ones.

A high metabolic rate, however, means a heavy intake of energy in order to sustain body warmth and efficiency. It is for this reason that even some of these later warm-blooded mammals existing in our day have learned to descend into a slower, unconscious rate of living during the winter months when food may be difficult to obtain. On a slightly higher plane they are following the procedure of the cold-blooded frog sleeping in the mud at the bottom of a frozen pond.

The agile brain of the warm-blooded birds and mammals demands a high oxygen consumption and food in concentrated forms, or the creatures cannot long sustain themselves. It was the rise of the flowering plants that provided that energy and changed the nature of the living world. Their appearance parallels in a quite surprising manner the rise of the birds and mammals.

Slowly, toward the dawn of the Age of Reptiles, something over two hundred and fifty million years ago, the little naked sperm cells wriggling their way through dew and raindrops had given way to a kind of pollen carried by the wind. Our present-day pine forests represent plants of a pollen-disseminating variety. Once fertilization was no longer dependent on exterior water, the march over drier regions could be extended. Instead of spores simple primitive seeds carrying some nourishment for the young plant had developed, but true flowers were still scores of millions of years away. After a long period of hesitant evolutionary groping, they exploded upon the world with truly revolutionary violence.

The event occurred in Cretaceous times in the close of the Age of Reptiles. Before the coming of the flowering plants our own ancestral stock, the warm-blooded mammals, consisted of a few mousy little creatures hidden in trees and underbrush. A few lizard-like birds with carnivorous teeth flapped awkwardly on ill-aimed flights among archaic shrubbery. None of these insignificant creatures gave evidence of any remarkable talents. The mammals in particular had been around for some millions of years, but had remained well lost in the shadow of the mighty reptiles. Truth to tell, man was still, like the genie in the bottle, encased in the body of a creature about the size of a rat.

As for the birds, their reptilian cousins the Pterodactyls flew farther and better. There was just one thing about the birds that paralleled the physiology of the mammals. They, too, had evolved warm blood and its accompanying temperature control. Nevertheless, if one had been seen stripped of his feathers, he would still have seemed a slightly uncanny and unsightly lizard.

Neither the birds nor the mammals, however, were quite what they seemed. They were waiting for the Age of Flowers. They were waiting for what flowers, and with them the true encased seed, would bring. Fish-eating, gigantic leather-winged reptiles, twenty-eight feet from wing tip to wing tip, hovered over the coasts that one day would be swarming with gulls.

Inland the monotonous green of the pine and spruce forests with their primitive wooden cone flowers stretched everywhere. No grass hindered the fall of the naked seeds to earth. Great sequoias towered to the skies. The world of that time has a certain appeal but it is a giant's world, a world moving slowly like the reptiles who stalked magnificently among the boles of its trees.

The trees themselves are ancient, slow-growing and immense, like the redwood groves that have survived to our day on the California coast. All is stiff, formal, upright and green, monotonously green. There is no grass as yet; there are no wide plains rolling in the sun, no tiny daisies dotting the meadows underfoot. There is little versatility about this scene; it is, in truth, a giant's world.

A few nights ago it was brought home vividly to me that the world has changed since that far epoch. I was awakened out of sleep by an unknown sound in my living room. Not a small sound—not a creaking timber or a mouse's scurry—but a sharp, rending explosion as though an unwary foot had been put down upon a wine glass. I had come instantly out of sleep and lay tense, unbreathing. I listened for another step. There was none.

Unable to stand the suspense any longer, I turned on the light and passed from room to room glancing uneasily behind chairs and into closets. Nothing seemed disturbed, and I stood puzzled in the center of the living room floor. Then a small button-shaped object upon the rug caught my eye. It was hard and polished and glistening. Scattered over the length of the room were several more shining up at me like wary little eyes. A pine cone that had been lying in a dish had been blown the length of the coffee table. The dish itself could hardly have been the source of the explosion. Beside it I found two ribbon-like strips of a velvety-green. I tried to place the two strips together to make a pod. They twisted resolutely away from each other and would no longer fit.

I relaxed in a chair, then, for I had reached a solution of the midnight disturbance. The twisted strips were wistaria pods that I had brought in a day or two previously and placed in the dish. They had chosen midnight to explode and distribute their multiplying fund of life down the length of the room. A plant, a fixed, rooted thing, immobilized in a single spot, had devised a way of propelling its offspring across open space. Immediately there passed before my eyes the million airy troopers of the milkweed pod and the clutching hooks of the sandburs. Seeds on the coyote's tail, seeds on the hunter's coat, thistledown mounting on the winds—all were somehow triumphing over life's limitations. Yet the ability to do this had not been with them at the beginning. It was the product of endless effort and experiment.

The seeds on my carpet were not going to lie stiffly where they had dropped like their antiquated cousins, the naked seeds on the pine-cone scales. They were travelers. Struck by the thought, I went out next day and collected several other varieties. I line them up now in a row on my desk— so many little capsules of life, winged, hooked or spiked. Every one is an angiosperm, a product of the true flowering plants. Contained in these little boxes is the secret of that far-off Cretaceous explosion of a hundred million years ago that changed the face of the planet. And somewhere in here, I think, as I poke seriously at one particularly resistant seedcase of a wild grass, was once man himself.

When the first simple flower bloomed on some raw upland late in the Dinosaur Age, it was wind pollinated, just like its early pine-cone relatives. It was a very inconspicuous flower because it had not yet evolved the idea of using the surer attraction of birds and insects to achieve the transportation of pollen. It sowed its own pollen and received the pollen of other flowers by the simple vagaries of the wind. Many plants in regions where insect life is scant still follow this principle today. Nevertheless, the true flower—and the seed that it produced—was a profound innovation in the world of life.

In a way, this event parallels, in the plant world, what happened among animals. Consider the relative chance for survival of the exteriorly deposited egg of a fish in contrast with the fertilized egg of a mammal, carefully retained for months in the mother's body until the young animal (or human being) is developed to a point where it may survive. The biological wastage is less—and so it is with the flowering plants. The primitive spore, a single cell fertilized in the beginning by a swimming sperm, did not promote rapid distribution, and the young plant, moreover, had to struggle up from nothing. No one had left it any food except what it could get by its own unaided efforts.

By contrast, the true flowering plants (angiosperm itself means "encased seed") grew a seed in the heart of a flower, a seed whose development was initiated by a fertilizing pollen grain independent of outside moisture. But the seed, unlike the developing spore, is already a fully equipped *embryonic plant* packed in a little enclosed box stuffed full of nutritious food. Moreover, by featherdown attachments, as in dandelion or milkweed seed, it can be wafted upward on gusts and ride the wind for miles; or with hooks it can cling to a bear's or a rabbit's hide; or like some of the berries, it can be covered with a juicy, attractive fruit to lure birds, pass undigested through their intestinal tracts and be voided miles away.

The ramifications of this biological invention were endless. Plants traveled as they had never traveled before. They got into strange environments heretofore never entered by the old spore plants or stiff pinecone-seed plants. The well-fed, carefully cherished little embryos raised their heads everywhere. Many of the older plants with more primitive reproductive mechanisms began to fade away under this unequal contest. They contracted their range into secluded environments. Some, like the giant redwoods, lingered on as relics; many vanished entirely.

The world of the giants was a dying world. These fantastic little seeds skipping and hopping and flying about the woods and valleys brought with them an amazing adaptability. If our whole lives had not been spent in the midst of it, it would astound us. The old, stiff, sky-reaching wooden world had changed into something that glowed here and there with strange colors, put out queer, unheard-of fruits and little intricately carved seed cases, and, most important of all, produced concentrated foods in a way that the land had never seen before, or dreamed of back in the fish-eating, leaf-crunching days of the dinosaurs.

That food came from three sources, all produced by the reproductive system of the flowering plants. There were the tantalizing nectars and pollens intended to draw insects for pollenizing purposes, and which are responsible also for that wonderful jeweled creation, the hummingbird. There were the juicy and enticing fruits to attract larger animals, and in which tough-coated seeds were concealed, as in the tomato, for example. Then, as if this were not enough, there was the food in the actual seed itself, the food intended to nourish the embryo. All over the world, like hot corn in a popper, these incredible elaborations of the flowering plants kept exploding. In a movement that was almost instantaneous, geologically speaking, the angiosperms had taken over the world. Grass was beginning to cover the bare earth until, today, there are over six thousand species. All kinds of vines and bushes squirmed and writhed under new trees with flying seeds.

The explosion was having its effect on animal life also. Specialized groups of insects were arising to feed on the new sources of food and, incidentally and unknowingly, to pollinate the plant. The flowers bloomed and bloomed in ever larger and more spectacular varieties. Some were pale unearthly night flowers intended to lure moths in the evening twilight, some among the orchids even took the shape of female spiders in order to attract wandering males, some flamed redly in the light of noon or twinkled modestly in the meadow grasses. Intricate mechanisms splashed pollen on the breasts of hummingbirds, or stamped it on the bellies of black, grumbling bees droning assiduously from blossom to blossom. Honey ran, insects multiplied, and even the descendants of that toothed and ancient lizard-bird had become strangely altered.

Equipped with prodding beaks instead of biting teeth they pecked the seeds and gobbled the insects that were really converted nectar.

Across the planet grasslands were now spreading. A slow continental upthrust which had been a part of the early Age of Flowers had cooled the world's climates. The stalking reptiles and the leather-winged black imps of the seashore cliffs had vanished. Only birds roamed the air now, hot-blooded and high-speed metabolic machines.

The mammals, too, had survived and were venturing into new domains, staring about perhaps a bit bewildered at their sudden eminence now that the thunder lizards were gone. Many of them, beginning as small browsers upon leaves in the forest, began to venture out upon this new sunlit world of the grass. Grass has a high silica content and demands a new type of very tough and resistant tooth enamel, but the seeds taken incidentally in the cropping of the grass are highly nutritious. A new world had opened out for the warm-blooded mammals. Great herbivores like the mammoths, horses and bisons appeared. Skulking about them had arisen savage flesh-feeding carnivores like the now extinct dire wolves and the saber-toothed tiger.

Flesh eaters though these creatures were, they were being sustained on nutritious grasses one step removed. Their fierce energy was being maintained on a high, effective level, through hot days and frosty nights, by the concentrated energy of the angiosperms. That energy, thirty per cent or more of the weight of the entire plant among some of the cereal grasses, was being accumulated and concentrated in the rich proteins and fats of the enormous game herds of the grasslands.

On the edge of the forest, a strange, old-fashioned animal still hesitated. His body was the body of a tree dweller, and though tough and knotty by human standards, he was, in terms of that world into which he gazed, a weakling. His teeth, though strong for chewing on the tough fruits of the forest, or for crunching an occasional unwary bird caught with his prehensile hands, were not the tearing sabers of the great cats. He had a passion for lifting himself up to see about, in his restless, roving curiosity. He would run a little stiffly and uncertainly, perhaps, on his hind legs, but only in those rare moments when he ventured out upon the ground. All this was the legacy of his climbing days; he had a hand with flexible fingers and no fine specialized hoofs upon which to gallop like the wind.

If he had any idea of competing in that new world, he had better forget it; teeth or hooves, he was much too late for either. He was a ne'er-do-well, an in-betweener. Nature had not done well by him. It was as if she had hesitated and never quite made up her mind. Perhaps as a consequence he had a malicious gleam in his eye, the gleam of an outcast who has been left nothing and knows he is going to have to take what he gets. One day a little band of these odd apes—for apes they were—shambled out upon the grass; the human story had begun.

Apes were to become men, in the inscrutable wisdom of nature, because flowers had produced seeds and fruits in such tremendous quantities that a new and totally different store of energy had become available in concentrated form. Impressive as the slow-moving, dim-brained dinosaurs had been, it is doubtful if their age had supported anything like the diversity of life that now rioted across the planet or flashed in and out among the trees. Down on the grass by a streamside, one of those apes with inquisitive fingers turned over a stone and hefted it vaguely. The group clucked together in a throaty tongue and moved off through the tall grass foraging for seeds and insects. The one still held, sniffed, and hefted the stone he had found. He liked the feel of it in his fingers. The attack on the animal world was about to begin.

If one could run the story of that first human group like a speeded-up motion picture through a million years of time, one might see the stone in the hand change to the flint ax and the torch. All that swarming grassland world with its giant bison and trumpeting mammoths would go down in ruin to feed the insatiable and growing numbers of a carnivore who, like the great cats before him, was taking his energy indirectly from the grass. Later he found fire and it altered the tough meats and drained their energy even faster into a stomach ill adapted for the ferocious turn man's habits had taken.

His limbs grew longer, he strode more purposefully over the grass. The stolen energy that would take man across the continents would fail him at last. The great Ice Age herds were destined to vanish. When they did so, another hand like the hand that grasped the stone by the river long ago would pluck a handful of grass seed and hold it contemplatively.

In that moment, the golden towers of man, his swarming millions, his turning wheels, the vast learning of his packed libraries, would glimmer dimly there in the ancestor of wheat, a few seeds held in a muddy hand. Without the gift of flowers and the infinite diversity of their fruits, man and bird, if they had continued to exist at all, would be today unrecognizable. Archaeopteryx, the lizard-bird, might still be snapping at beetles on a sequoia limb; man might still be a nocturnal insectivore gnawing a roach in the dark. The weight of a petal has changed the face of the world and made it ours.

The Immense Journey (1957)

WILLIAM O. DOUGLAS

The environmental fight has often been waged by lawyers, not a species known for eloquent prose. But on the occasion of *Sierra Club* v. *Morton*, Supreme Court justice William O. Douglas delivered a dissent that, though it lacked the force of law, nonetheless stands out. Douglas (1898–1980) was the longest-serving Supreme Court justice in U.S. history; appointed by F.D.R. in 1939, the young New Dealer served until 1975. A westerner, he spent his life hiking and wrote often of his adventures in the Cascades; his description here of Glacier Peak, from *My Wilderness: The Pacific West* (1960), is a good example. In 1969, the Sierra Club sued to stop a ski resort planned in Mineral King valley in the southern Sierra Nevada, which was surrounded on three sides by Sequoia National Park. The Supreme Court eventually ruled that the club had failed to allege that the development would harm the club, its programs, or its members and therefore the organization lacked "standing to sue." Douglas, in his celebrated dissent (reprinted here without its extensive footnotes and § *et seq*s), argued that *someone* should be able to speak for nature itself. The Sierra Club revised its pleadings to allege harm, returned to the district court, and got the resort blocked. This opened the courthouse door for hundreds of lawsuits to follow.

from **My Wilderness: The Pacific West**

Glacier Peak

I sat on a knife-edged ridge in the northern Cascades, lost in thought. At my back the canyon dropped sheer for two thousand feet. The south slope at my feet made up into a deep, grassy bowl. Coming up, I had discovered that this bowl was dotted with painted cups—some yellow, some red. I had also found on these south slopes an amazing variety of lousewort. The one that caught my fancy was the elephants' heads. It has a purplish stem with a crowded spike of many flowers, shaped like little elephant heads, slightly fragrant, and deep pink in color. There were tiger lilies in abundance. Heather—some white, some lavender—made gay streaks. And the bees were busy in it. The pasqueflower—now in seed—showed its dainty plumes. A wide variety of sedges covered this bowl, and oval-leafed bilberry bushes—some in fruit that would soon be ripe—made up a large portion of the ground cover. In some hollows currant bushes grew luxuriantly; and this August their branches were heavy with deep-red fruit. Mountain ash was brilliant with its red berries.

There was, to my surprise, very little bunch grass here. The sides of this bowl had innumerable trails made by the deer and mountain goats. Sheep had once been in here, and they did their usual damage. This bowl at my feet already showed signs of washing. This is indeed fragile land, whose thin topsoil clings precariously to the sharp pitches of the canyons.

A bright buttercup, hardly an inch high, greeted me as I reached the tip. And a patch of grayish-green lupine, whose flowers were so tiny they almost went unnoticed, offered me a resting place.

This ridge was no more than 7000 feet high. Yet it was above tree line. The pines, the hemlock, the cedars were far below me. Only a few alpine fir with small purple cones that brightened their crowns were in this life zone; and I had left the last clump of them a few hundred feet down.

Glacier Peak (10,436 feet), higher than all Washington mountains except for Rainier, Adams, and Baker, dominated the southern skyline. It was draped with glaciers. Everywhere I looked there were peaks showing glaciers. These mountains lie so close to the Pacific that they are beneficiaries of most of its moisture. Each year's snowfall is deep, and packs down into permanent snow fields and gradually builds into the blue ice of living glaciers that hang permanently on the precipitous shoulders of these peaks.

The glacier that dug out the chasm where Lake Chelan lies was seventy-five miles long. One who travels to the head of Stehekin Valley can see several living fragments of it. Most of the glaciers in the northern

Cascades are now small; and some send tons of debris into their canyons on warm days. Some are fast receding. Others are great tumbles of *séracs* and crevasses. Some ice fields make up into a radial glacier system that was characteristic of the ice age. And some of these living glaciers are extensive, Honeycomb on Glacier Peak extending more than three miles.

Some of the northern Cascades are lava. Glacier Peak is indeed a volcanic cone. Pumice—so light it will float in water—is found here. Near Red Pass at the headwaters of the Whitechuck River, southwest of Glacier Peak, is the site of an old blowhole where a hill of pumice was ejected and piled in the fashion of a mound of tailings at the entrance of a drift. Pumice also lies at great depth in the river valleys of the Chiwawa and Entiat. Granite joined basalt when the earth's surface folded and buckled. These up-turned slabs formed great massifs, commanding steep canyons. Some walls are as highly polished as those in Yosemite. There are shales, limestone, and sandstone here too. And the grays of granite often shade into pinks and reds.

These peaks—which someday will be ranked with our greatest ones—are as yet little known. Glacier Peak is not visible from any major highway. Foothills hide the alpine area. The peaks are locked into a remote area that is a true recluse. This inner realm is remote and exquisite. Man did not plan it that way. The Glacier Peak area is a wilderness by sheer accident. Civilization so far has passed it by. A miner's helicopter is sometimes seen. High overhead a passenger plane makes a fleeting passage. But there are not many noises apart from those made by wind and water.

The view from any ridge in this range shows more snow and ice than any of our mountains south of Alaska. This is also a land that bursts with cascades of cold, clear water. Every ravine, every canyon has crystal-clear streams. High meadows spout ice-cold creeks. All of the water is safe to drink. It is pure distillation from a true wilderness.

On this lonely ridge I was not more than two days' hike from road's end. Yet it seemed I had left civilization far, far behind. I was so remote from cities and factories and farms that it seemed I was on another planet. Will the next generation ever have the chance to experience the same feeling of serenity and composure that comes when man faces the wilderness alone? This was my soliloquy as Cragg Gilbert, following a different route, joined me. I put the question to him and we talked a half hour or more about it.

If the population of this nation doubles by the end of this century (as it will if present trends continue), all the country along the coast from the Canadian border to Eugene, Oregon, will be one continuous urban and suburban area. The Pacific Northwest will be as saturated with population as Los Angeles is today. The sea will be one escape from civilization; the mountains another. The Glacier Peak area, if left roadless and intact, will offer perpetual physical and spiritual therapy. For its rugged nature—its steep canyons, forbidding glaciers, and knife-edged ridges—will be a magnet to those who have daring and fortitude.

"There should be some training grounds for them," Cragg added.

I mentioned John Muir's comparison of wild mountain sheep and domestic sheep. He found the latter quite dull, the former exciting. Nature builds strength and character competitively. Domesticated animals, like men and women of cities, get lazy habits. They become dependent on others, losing the drive and initiative that marked the species in the beginning. This loss of character can be disastrous to a race of men who, apartment-born, never experience the challenge that nature demands of all her children. This race of apartment-born people is of the earth, yet not a vital part of it. It is coddled and protected, utterly dependent on machines for its existence. It does not know how to pit human ingenuity against the universe; it therefore has no key to survival against disaster.

Men need testing grounds to develop these capacities. They cannot flower at Coney Island or at the ball park. Men need to know the elemental challenges that sea and mountains present. They need to know what it is to be alive and to survive when great storms come. They need to unlock the secrets of streams, lakes, and canyons and to find how these treasures are veritable storehouses of inspiration. They must experience the sense of mastery of adversity. They must find a peak or a ridge that they reach under their own power alone.

—

Cragg and I were disturbed. Before striking into the heart of the northern Cascades we had scouted its fringes. Roads were threatening at most points of the compass. On the west a road has already crept within a mile or so of Cascade Pass. Another presses into Bridge Creek from the east. Some, coming in from the south, are pointed like daggers at the heart of this remote area.

This is not the only threat. Forest Service plans call for the logging of some of the deep, narrow valleys that lie at the foot of Glacier Peak. Suiattle is one; Agnes is another. These are low valleys as far western country goes. We had come in by Lake Chelan (1100 feet), meeting Ray Courtney at Stehekin and packing in from there. We traveled the South Fork of Agnes Creek, reaching Suiattle Pass (5983 feet) in two days. At the start there were song sparrows and rattlesnakes, and with them poplar, alder, willow, and ponderosa pine. Raspberries and blackberries were thick. There was the fragrant snowbrush in these lower reaches, and much ocean spray. These—including the song sparrows and snakes—were soon left behind. White firs and red firs appeared, and in their shade I saw the bright-leaved Oregon grape, a host of the delicate twinflower, and masses of meadow foam. The forest floor is thick with kinnikinnick. Vine maple flourishes here. The snowberry—the bush that Lewis and Clark brought back from their expedition and that Jefferson sent to Paris as a decorative plant—is abundant. Its red flowers had gone when we traveled Agnes Creek and its white pulpy fruit was well formed. This fruit has two seeds greatly loved by chipmunks. They remove the seeds quite deftly, leaving only the pulp. They were beginning their snowberry harvest as we passed.

Higher up the canyon came the western hemlock, the Alaska cedar, and the red cedar. They flourish at a three-thousand-foot altitude, growing to immense size. They are the plums in the Agnes Creek pudding that the lumbermen want. And the Forest Service seems bent on letting them have what they want.

This hemlock-cedar forest is an inspiring sight. The shade is so thick that no grass grows. The tall, delicious blueberry grows lush. Somewhat below it stands the slim Solomon plume with strikingly translucent leaves. Lower still is the baldhip rose. There's a fourth bush that is more associated with the Pacific coast line than the Cascades. It is the devil's club, whose stalks bristle with spines but whose young leaves deer and horses adore. These four, in the main, make up the understory of the hemlock-cedar forest.

Agnes Creek Canyon is for the most part a narrow, V-shaped valley. The waters of the creek are clear and cold. They form one cascade after another, and below each is a deep pool where rainbow trout, pointed upstream, watch for morsels that are washed down.

The canyon is so narrow for much of the way that there is hardly room for more than the trail and the creek. There are not many places that offer the room necessary for tents and campfires. We stopped at one, and my small Himalayan tent had to crowd close to the trail. The truth is that a road up Agnes Creek—which would be built if this canyon were lumbered—would occupy most of the space. A road would not serve the purposes of recreation for those who come by car. The valley has few broad reaches where camp sites could be erected for the motorist. Agnes Creek, with its sharp canyon walls and its skimpy ground cover, would wash terribly. Agnes Creek—now as clear and pure as wildness can make any water—would run mud and silt. Lumber interests would be served; the man who built the road would make a fortune—but the harsh gully that would be left would stand for decades as a monument to the folly of an age that has tried to convert man into a statistic. That act of desecration would prove that the powers that be downgrade values that cannot be converted into dollar signs. What is true of Agnes Creek is in large measure true of Suiattle Creek, also doomed to being raped by saw and ax.

The Glacier Peak area is so little known it has few friends. Those bent on exploiting it, therefore, have a great advantage. They hope to perfect their plans before the public is aware of the great treasure that is here. The Forest Service is under the pressure of these powerful interests to do their bidding. The men in government who will decide the fate of this invaluable bit of wilderness have themselves not seen it. Even the local Forest Service men have probed very, very few canyons and high meadows. Who then will defend the Glacier Peak area?

These were the things Cragg and I discussed on a high ridge before we climbed Plummer Peak (7870 feet). Back in camp at Image Lake, we took up where we had left off. Bill Obertauffer, who had brought a group of Mazamas into Image Lake, joined us as the sun was setting. We stood on a knoll fringed by alpine fir, watching the sun turn the ice of Glacier Peak purple and then red. Suiattle River lay below us. The dark green of conifers filled this rich valley. Instead of deep forests where boys and girls would walk quietly and reverently as they approached the sanctuaries of Glacier Peak, there might soon be ugly stumps. Image Lake—whose value in terms of sheer beauty and inspiration is incalculable—was also threatened. For Miner's Ridge, where it lies, is to be left out of the proposed wilderness area. The reason? Mining interests want to chew it up in search of copper.

I mentioned that scientists had discovered that one ton of granite contains about four grams of uranium and twelve grams of thorium. Nuclear management could get out of these properties energy equivalent to that released on the burning of fifty tons of coal. "Now we can find new uses for our granite mountains," I sarcastically added.

"Think of putting any of these peaks or ridges through a rock crusher," Bill said. "How sacrilegious can we get?"

The exposure of Miner's Ridge to spoliation by mining interests seemed unthinkable to those of us who knew it and had come to love it. The gutting of Suiattle Valley, which lies at the feet of Glacier Peak, seemed equally profane. Harsh gullies and ugly wasteland would take the place of deep, dark forests that now are the haunts of deer, cougar, bobcat, wolverine, and bear. Glacier Peak would tower over a wasteland where gullies had been washed clear of topsoil.

This is not a speculative matter. Clear-cutting in the Far West produces deep scars on slopes. A canyon of trees restful to the eyes is invariably supplanted by a canyon of rocks and debris. A harvest of pine in Florida or Georgia means a new crop a few decades hence. But the harvest of the timber in the canyons of our western mountains often produces torrential runoffs of water that turn a fertile place into a sterile wasteland. The Cascades are cruelly scarred by these operations.

Thousands of years will pass before vegetation can produce the humus necessary for a new forest.

Cragg, Bill, and I talked of these things. The emphasis which these two sturdy mountaineers gave to the spiritual values of the wilderness reminded me of a meeting I had attended where federal fieldmen had discussed protests by citizens of plans for spraying sagebrush land. They roared with laughter when it was reported that a little old lady opposed the plan because the wild flowers would be destroyed.

Yet was not her right to search out a painted cup or a tiger lily as inalienable as the right of stockmen to search out grass or of a lumberman to claim a tree? The aesthetic values of the wilderness are as much our inheritance as the veins of copper and coal in our hills and the forests in our mountains.

My Wilderness: The Pacific West (1960)

Dissent in Sierra Club *v.* Morton

April 19, 1972

MR. JUSTICE DOUGLAS, dissenting.

I share the views of my Brother BLACKMUN and would reverse the judgment below.

The critical question of "standing" would be simplified and also put neatly in focus if we fashioned a federal rule that allowed environmental issues to be litigated before federal agencies or federal courts in the name of the inanimate object about to be dispoiled, defaced, or invaded by roads and bulldozers and where injury is the subject of public outrage. Contemporary public concern for protecting nature's ecological equilibrium should lead to the conferral of standing upon environmental objects to sue for their own preservation. This suit would therefore be more properly labeled as *Mineral King* v. *Morton*.

Inanimate objects are sometimes parties in litigation. A ship has a legal personality, a fiction found useful for maritime purposes. The corporation sole—a creature of ecclesiastical law—is an acceptable adversary and large fortunes ride on its cases. The ordinary corporation is a "person" for purposes of the adjudicatory processes, whether it represents proprietary, spiritual, aesthetic, or charitable causes.

So it should be as respects valleys, alpine meadows, rivers, lakes, estuaries, beaches, ridges, groves of trees, swampland, or even air that feels the destructive pressures of modern technology and modern life. The river, for example, is the living symbol of all the life it sustains or nourishes—fish, aquatic insects, water ouzels, otter, fisher, deer, elk, bear, and all other animals, including man, who are dependent on it or who enjoy it for its sight, its sound, or its life. The river as plaintiff speaks for the ecological unit of life that is part of it. Those people who have a meaningful relation to that body of water—whether it be a fisherman, a canoeist, a zoologist, or a logger—must be able to speak for the values which the river represents and which are threatened with destruction.

I do not know Mineral King. I have never seen it nor travelled it, though I have seen articles describing its proposed "development." The Sierra Club in its complaint alleges that "One of the principal purposes of the Sierra Club is to protect and conserve the national resources of the Sierra Nevada Mountains." The District Court held that this uncontested allegation made the Sierra Club "sufficiently aggrieved" to have "standing" to sue on behalf of Mineral King.

Mineral King is doubtless like other wonders of the Sierra Nevada such as Tuolumne Meadows and the John Muir Trail. Those who hike it, fish it, hunt it, camp in it, or frequent it, or visit it merely to sit in solitude and wonderment are legitimate spokesmen for it, whether they may be a few or many. Those who have that intimate relation with the inanimate object about to be injured, polluted, or otherwise despoiled are its legitimate spokesmen.

The Solicitor General, whose views on this subject are in the Appendix to this opinion, takes a wholly different approach. He considers the problem in terms of "government by the Judiciary." With all respect, the problem is to make certain that the inanimate objects, which are the very core of America's beauty, have spokesmen before they are destroyed. It is, of course, true that most of them are under the control of a federal or state agency. The standards given those agencies are usually expressed in terms of the "public interest." Yet "public interest" has so many differing shades of meaning as to be quite meaningless on the environmental front. Congress accordingly has adopted ecological standards in the National Environmental Policy Act of 1969, and guidelines for agency action have been provided by the Council on Environmental Quality of which Russell E. Train is Chairman.

Yet the pressures on agencies for favorable action one way or the other are enormous. The suggestion that Congress can stop action which is undesirable is true in theory; yet even Congress is too remote to give meaningful direction and its machinery is too ponderous to use very often. The federal agencies of which I speak are not venal or corrupt. But they are notoriously under the control of powerful interests who manipulate them through advisory committees, or friendly working relations, or who have that natural affinity with the agency which in time develops between the regulator and the regulated. As early as 1894, Attorney General Olney predicted that regulatory agencies might become "industry-minded," as illustrated by his forecast concerning the Interstate Commerce Commission:

> "The Commission is or can be made of great use to the railroads. It satisfies the public clamor for supervision of the railroads, at the same time that supervision is almost entirely nominal. Moreover, the older the Commission gets to be, the more likely it is to take a business and railroad view of things." M. Josephson, *The Politicos* (1938).

Years later a court of appeals observed, "the recurring question which has plagued public regulation of industry [is] whether the regulatory agency is unduly oriented toward the interests of the industry it is designed to regulate, rather than the public interest it is supposed to protect."

The Forest Service—one of the federal agencies behind the scheme to despoil Mineral King—has been notorious for its alignment with lumber companies, although its mandate from Congress directs it to consider the various aspects of multiple use in its supervision of the national forests.

The voice of the inanimate object, therefore, should not be stilled. That does not mean that the judiciary takes over the managerial functions from the federal agency. It merely means that before these priceless bits of Americana (such as a valley, an alpine meadow, a river, or a lake) are forever lost or are so transformed as to be reduced to the eventual rubble of our urban environment, the voice of the existing beneficiaries of these environmental wonders should be heard.

Perhaps they will not win. Perhaps the bulldozers of "progress" will plow under all the aesthetic wonders of this beautiful land. That is not the present question. The sole question is, who has standing to be heard?

Those who hike the Appalachian Trail into Sunfish Pond, New Jersey, and camp or sleep there, or run the Allagash in Maine, or climb the Guadalupes in West Texas, or who canoe and portage the Quetico Superior in Minnesota, certainly should have standing to defend those natural wonders before courts or agencies, though they live 3,000 miles away. Those who merely are caught up in environmental news or propaganda and flock to defend these waters or areas may be treated differently. That is why these environmental issues should be tendered by the inanimate object itself. Then there will be assurances that all of the forms of life which it represents will stand before the court—the pileated woodpecker as well as the coyote and bear, the lemmings as well as the trout in the streams. Those inarticulate members of the ecological group cannot speak. But those people who have so frequented the place as to know its values and wonders will be able to speak for the entire ecological community.

Ecology reflects the land ethic; and Aldo Leopold wrote in *A Sand County Almanac* (1949), "The land ethic simply enlarges the boundaries of the community to include soils, waters, plants, and animals, or collectively, the land."

That, as I see it, is the issue of "standing" in the present case and controversy.

Sierra Club v. *Morton,* 405 U.S. 727 (1972)

Environmentalists are sometimes accused of spending too little time thinking about cities, or of considering them inferior to unspoiled countryside or untouched wilderness. But of course city living is much more efficient in many ways than any of the alternatives. (In terms of energy use, New York City, with its excellent mass transit and tiny apartments, is the greenest city in America.) In her influential book *The Death and Life of Great American Cities* (1961), Jane Jacobs (1916–2006) battled what she felt were destructive ideas in modern urban planning, and the revitalization of many downtown cores owes a great deal to her sense of what people wanted from the places where they lived. In the section that follows, she argues that an overly sentimental view of nature was responsible for the rampant suburbanization of North America.

from **The Death and Life of Great American Cities**

Now we must dig a little deeper into the bog of intellectual misconceptions about cities in which orthodox reformers and planners have mired themselves (and the rest of us). Underlying the city planners' deep disrespect for their subject matter, underlying the jejune belief in the "dark and foreboding" irrationality or chaos of cities, lies a long-established misconception about the relationship of cities—and indeed of men—with the rest of nature.

Human beings are, of course, a part of nature, as much so as grizzly bears or bees or whales or sorghum cane. The cities of human beings are as natural, being a product of one form of nature, as are the colonies of prairie dogs or the beds of oysters. The botanist Edgar Anderson has written wittily and sensitively in *Landscape* magazine from time to time about cities as a form of nature. "Over much of the world," he comments, "man has been accepted as a city-loving creature." Nature watching, he points out, "is quite as easy in the city as in the country; all one has to do is accept Man as a part of Nature. Remember that as a specimen of *Homo sapiens* you are far and away most likely to find that species an effective guide to deeper understanding of natural history."

A curious but understandable thing happened in the eighteenth century. By then, the cities of Europeans had done well enough by them, mediating between them and many harsh aspects of nature, so that something became popularly possible which previously had been a rarity—sentimentalization of nature, or at any rate, sentimentalization of a rustic or a barbarian relationship with nature. Marie Antoinette playing milkmaid was an expression of this sentimentality on one plane. The romantic idea of the "noble savage" was an even sillier one, on another plane. So, in this country, was Jefferson's intellectual rejection of cities of free artisans and mechanics, and his dream of an ideal republic of self-reliant rural yeomen—a pathetic dream for a good and great man whose land was tilled by slaves.

In real life, barbarians (and peasants) are the least free of men—bound by tradition, ridden by caste, fettered by superstitions, riddled by suspicion and foreboding of whatever is strange. "City air makes free," was the medieval saying, when city air literally did make free the runaway serf. City air still makes free the runaways from company towns, from plantations, from factory-farms, from subsistence farms, from migrant picker routes, from mining villages, from one-class suburbs.

Owing to the mediation of cities, it became popularly possible to regard "nature" as benign, ennobling and pure, and by extension to regard "natural man" (take your pick of how "natural") as so too. Opposed to all this fictionalized purity, nobility and beneficence, cities, not being fictions, could be considered as seats of malignancy and—obviously—the enemies of nature. And once people begin looking at nature as if it were a nice big St. Bernard dog for the children, what could be more natural than the desire to bring this sentimental pet into the city too, so the city might get some nobility, purity and beneficence by association?

There are dangers in sentimentalizing nature. Most sentimental ideas imply, at bottom, a deep if unacknowledged disrespect. It is no accident that we Americans, probably the world's champion sentimentalizers about nature, are at one and the same time probably the world's most voracious and disrespectful destroyers of wild and rural countryside.

It is neither love for nature nor respect for nature that leads to this schizophrenic attitude. Instead, it is a sentimental desire to toy, rather patronizingly, with some insipid, standardized, suburbanized shadow of nature—apparently in sheer disbelief that we and our cities, just by virtue of being, are a legitimate part of nature too, and involved with it in much deeper and more inescapable ways than grass trimming, sunbathing, and contemplative uplift. And so, each day, several thousand more acres of our countryside are eaten by the bulldozers, covered by pavement, dotted with suburbanites who have killed the thing they thought they came to find. Our irreplaceable heritage of Grade I agricultural land (a rare treasure of nature on this earth) is sacrificed for highways or supermarket parking lots as ruthlessly and unthinkingly as the trees in the woodlands are uprooted, the streams and rivers polluted and the air itself filled with the gasoline exhausts (products of eons of nature's manufacturing) required in this great national effort to cozy up with a fictionalized nature and flee the "unnaturalness" of the city.

The semisuburbanized and suburbanized messes we create in this way become despised by their own inhabitants tomorrow. These thin dispersions lack any reasonable degree of innate vitality, staying power, or inherent usefulness as settlements. Few of them, and these only the most expensive as a rule, hold their attraction much longer than a generation; then they begin to decay in the pattern of city gray areas. Indeed, an immense amount of today's city gray belts was yesterday's dispersion closer to "nature." Of the buildings on the thirty thousand acres of already blighted or already fast-blighting residential areas in northern New Jersey, for example, half are less than forty years old. Thirty years from now, we shall have accumulated new problems of blight and decay over acreages so immense that in comparison the present problems of the great cities' gray belts will look piddling. Nor, however destructive, is this something which happens accidentally or without the use of will. This is exactly what we, as a society, have willed to happen.

Nature, sentimentalized and considered as the antithesis of cities, is apparently assumed to consist of grass, fresh air and little else, and this ludicrous disrespect results in the devastation of nature even formally and publicly preserved in the form of a pet.

For example, up the Hudson River, north of New York City, is a state park at Croton Point, a place for picnicking, ballplaying and looking at the lordly (polluted) Hudson. At the Point itself is—or was— a geological curiosity: a stretch of beach about fifteen yards long where the blue-gray clay, glacially deposited there, and the action of the river currents and the sun combined to manufacture clay dogs. These are natural sculptures, compacted almost to the density of stone, and baked, and they are of a most curious variety, from breathtakingly subtle and simple curving forms to fantastic concoctions of more than Oriental splendor. There are only a few places in the entire world where clay dogs may be found.

Generations of New York City geology students, along with picnickers, tired ballplayers and delighted children, treasure hunted among the clay dogs and carried their favorites home. And always, the clay, the river and the sun made more, and more, and more, inexhaustibly, no two alike.

Occasionally through the years, having been introduced to the clay dogs long ago by a geology teacher, I would go back to treasure hunt among them. A few summers ago, my husband and I took our children to the Point so they might find some and also so they might see how they are made.

But we were a season behind improvers on nature. The slope of muddy clay that formed the little stretch of unique beach had been demolished. In its place was a rustic retaining wall and an extension of the park's lawns. (The park had been augmented—statistically.) Digging beneath the new lawn here and there—for we can desecrate the next man's desecrations as well as anyone—we found broken bits of clay dogs, mashed by the bulldozers, the last evidence of a natural process that may well have been halted here forever.

Who would prefer this vapid suburbanization to timeless wonders?

What kind of park supervisor would permit such vandalism of nature? An all too familiar kind of mind is obviously at work here: a mind seeing only disorder where a most intricate and unique order exists; the same kind of mind that sees only disorder in the life of city streets, and itches to erase it, standardize it, suburbanize it.

The two responses are connected: Cities, as created or used by city-loving creatures are unrespected by such simple minds because they are not bland shadows of cities suburbanized. Other aspects of nature are equally unrespected because they are not bland shadows of nature suburbanized. Sentimentality about nature denatures everything it touches.

Big cities and countrysides can get along well together. Big cities need real countryside close by. And countryside—from man's point of view—needs big cities, with all their diverse opportunities and productivity, so human beings can be in a position to appreciate the rest of the natural world instead of to curse it.

Being human is itself difficult, and therefore all kinds of settlements (except dream cities) have problems. Big cities have difficulties in abundance, because they have people in abundance. But vital cities are not helpless to combat even the most difficult of problems. They are not passive victims of chains of circumstances, any more than they are the malignant opposite of nature.

Vital cities have marvelous innate abilities for understanding, communicating, contriving and inventing what is required to combat their difficulties. Perhaps the most striking example of this ability is the effect that big cities have had on disease. Cities were once the most helpless and devastated victims of disease, but they became great disease conquerors. All the apparatus of surgery, hygiene, microbiology, chemistry, telecommunications, public health measures, teaching and research hospitals, ambulances and the like, which people not only in cities but also outside them depend upon for the unending war against premature mortality, are fundamentally products of big cities and would be inconceivable without big cities. The surplus wealth, the productivity, the close-grained juxtaposition of talents that permit society to support advances such as these are themselves products of our organization into cities, and especially into big and dense cities.

It may be romantic to search for the salves of society's ills in slow-moving rustic surroundings, or among innocent, unspoiled provincials, if such exist, but it is a waste of time. Does anyone suppose that, in real life, answers to any of the great questions that worry us today are going to come out of homogeneous settlements?

Dull, inert cities, it is true, do contain the seeds of their own destruction and little else. But lively, diverse, intense cities contain the seeds of their own regeneration, with energy enough to carry over for problems and needs outside themselves.

The Death and Life of Great American Cities (1961)

RACHEL CARSON

Rachel Carson (1907–1964) is so closely identified with *Silent Spring* (1962) that it surprises many readers to learn of her earlier literary successes. As one of the first female professionals at the U.S. Fish and Wildlife Service, she published a trilogy of books about the oceans in the 1940s and 1950s. All were successful, and one—*The Sea Around Us* (1951)—won the National Book Award and remained on the *New York Times* best-seller list for a then-record 86 weeks. Think Jacques Cousteau, but in print—it would have been more than a good life's work to introduce so many Americans to the glories of marine ecology. But history had larger plans for Carson. She had been following reports of problems with the wonder-pesticide DDT almost since its introduction in the wake of World War II. Had the chemical been used in small doses for localized control of pestilent mosquitoes (as it currently is across much of the developing world), it might never have become a problem. Instead, American farmers were using as much as two pounds of the poison per acre on crops like cotton, and its effects were showing up throughout the food chain, especially in birds. Carson collected the data, and in a great imaginative feat put it together in her stunning metaphor of a spring gone silent. The book was serialized in *The New Yorker* prior to its publication, and despite a huge assault from the chemical industry, much of it predicated on the idea that a lady writer was likely to be hysterical in her reactions, she carried the day. Not only did the U.S. move to restrict the chemical, thus saving our national symbol, the bald eagle, but more importantly, the idea had been firmly planted that perhaps modernity was not as problem-free as we might have imagined. From that notion sprang most of what has followed for environmentalism.

from **Silent Spring**

A Fable for Tomorrow

There was once a town in the heart of America where all life seemed to live in harmony with its surroundings. The town lay in the midst of a checkerboard of prosperous farms, with fields of grain and hillsides of orchards where, in spring, white clouds of bloom drifted above the green fields. In autumn, oak and maple and birch set up a blaze of color that flamed and flickered across a backdrop of pines. Then foxes barked in the hills and deer silently crossed the fields, half hidden in the mists of the fall mornings.

Along the roads, laurel, viburnum and alder, great ferns and wild-flowers delighted the traveler's eye through much of the year. Even in winter the roadsides were places of beauty, where countless birds came to feed on the berries and on the seed heads of the dried weeds rising above the snow. The countryside was, in fact, famous for the abundance and variety of its bird life, and when the flood of migrants was pouring through in spring and fall people traveled from great distances to observe them. Others came to fish the streams, which flowed clear and cold out of the hills and contained shady pools where trout lay. So it had been from the days many years ago when the first settlers raised their houses, sank their wells, and built their barns.

Then a strange blight crept over the area and everything began to change. Some evil spell had settled on the community: mysterious maladies swept the flocks of chickens; the cattle and sheep sickened and died. Everywhere was a shadow of death. The farmers spoke of much illness among their families. In the town the doctors had become more and more puzzled by new kinds of sickness appearing among their patients. There had been several sudden and unexplained deaths, not only among adults but even among children, who would be stricken suddenly while at play and die within a few hours.

There was a strange stillness. The birds, for example—where had they gone? Many people spoke of them, puzzled and disturbed. The feeding stations in the backyards were deserted. The few birds seen anywhere were moribund; they trembled violently and could not fly. It was a spring without voices. On the mornings that had once throbbed with the dawn chorus of robins, catbirds, doves, jays, wrens, and scores of other bird voices there was now no sound; only silence lay over the fields and woods and marsh.

On the farms the hens brooded, but no chicks hatched. The farmers complained that they were unable to raise any pigs—the litters were small and the young survived only a few days. The apple trees were coming into bloom but no bees droned among the blossoms, so there was no pollination and there would be no fruit.

The roadsides, once so attractive, were now lined with browned and withered vegetation as though swept by fire. These, too, were silent, deserted by all living things. Even the streams were now lifeless. Anglers no longer visited them, for all the fish had died.

In the gutters under the eaves and between the shingles of the roofs, a white granular powder still showed a few patches; some weeks before it had fallen like snow upon the roofs and the lawns, the fields and streams.

No witchcraft, no enemy action had silenced the rebirth of new life in this stricken world. The people had done it themselves.

This town does not actually exist, but it might easily have a thousand counterparts in America or elsewhere in the world. I know of no community that has experienced all the misfortunes I describe. Yet every one of these disasters has actually happened somewhere, and many real communities have already suffered a substantial number of them. A grim specter has crept upon us almost unnoticed, and this imagined tragedy may easily become a stark reality we all shall know.

What has already silenced the voices of spring in countless towns in America? This book is an attempt to explain.

And No Birds Sing

Like the robin, another American bird seems to be on the verge of extinction. This is the national symbol, the eagle. Its populations have dwindled alarmingly within the past decade. The facts suggest that something is at work in the eagle's environment which has virtually destroyed its ability to reproduce. What this may be is not yet definitely known, but there is some evidence that insecticides are responsible.

The most intensively studied eagles in North America have been those nesting along a stretch of coast from Tampa to Fort Myers on the western coast of Florida. There a retired banker from Winnipeg, Charles Broley, achieved ornithological fame by banding more than 1000 young bald eagles during the years 1939–49. (Only 166 eagles had been banded in all the earlier history of birdbanding.) Mr. Broley banded eagles as young birds during the winter months before they had left their nests. Later recoveries of banded birds showed that these Florida-born eagles range northward along the coast into Canada as far as Prince Edward Island, although they had previously been considered nonmigratory. In the fall they return to the South, their migration being observed at such famous vantage points as Hawk Mountain in eastern Pennsylvania.

During the early years of his banding, Mr. Broley used to find 125 active nests a year on the stretch of coast he had chosen for his work. The number of young banded each year was about 150. In 1947 the production of young birds began to decline. Some nests contained no eggs; others contained eggs that failed to hatch. Between 1952 and 1957, about 80 per cent of the nests failed to produce young. In the last year of this period only 43 nests were occupied. Seven of them produced young (8 eaglets); 23 contained eggs that failed to hatch; 13 were used merely as feeding stations by adult eagles and contained no eggs. In 1958 Mr. Broley ranged over 100 miles of coast before finding and banding one eaglet. Adult eagles, which had been seen at 43 nests in 1957, were so scarce that he observed them at only 10 nests.

Although Mr. Broley's death in 1959 terminated this valuable series of uninterrupted observations, reports by the Florida Audubon Society, as well as from New Jersey and Pennsylvania, confirm the trend that may well make it necessary for us to find a new national emblem. The reports of Maurice Broun, curator of the Hawk Mountain Sanctuary, are especially significant. Hawk Mountain is a picturesque mountaintop in southeastern Pennsylvania, where the easternmost ridges of the Appalachians form a last barrier to the westerly winds before dropping away toward the coastal plain. Winds striking the mountains are deflected upward so that on many autumn days there is a continuous updraft on which the broad-winged hawks and eagles ride without effort, covering many miles of their southward migration in a day. At Hawk Mountain the ridges converge and so do the aerial highways. The result is that from a widespread territory to the north birds pass through this traffic bottleneck.

In his more than a score of years as custodian of the sanctuary there, Maurice Broun has observed and actually tabulated more hawks and eagles than any other American. The peak of the bald eagle migration comes in late August and early September. These are assumed to be Florida birds, returning to home territory after a summer in the North. (Later in the fall and early winter a few larger eagles drift through. These are thought to belong to a northern race, bound for an unknown wintering ground.) During the first years after the sanctuary was established, from 1935 to 1939, 40 per cent of the eagles observed were yearlings, easily identified by their uniformly dark plumage. But in recent years these immature birds have become a rarity. Between 1955 and 1959, they made up only 20 per cent of the total count, and in one year (1957) there was only one young eagle for every 32 adults.

Observations at Hawk Mountain are in line with findings elsewhere. One such report comes from Elton Fawks, an official of the Natural Resources Council of Illinois. Eagles—probably northern nesters—winter along the Mississippi and Illinois Rivers. In 1958 Mr. Fawks reported that a recent count of 59 eagles had included only one immature bird. Similar indications of the dying out of the race come from the world's only sanctuary for eagles alone, Mount Johnson Island in the Susquehanna River. The island, although only 8 miles above Conowingo Dam and about half a mile out from the Lancaster County shore, retains its primitive wildness. Since 1934 its single eagle nest has been under observation by Professor Herbert H. Beck, an ornithologist of Lancaster and custodian of the sanctuary. Between 1935 and 1947 use of the nest was regular and uniformly successful. Since 1947, although the adults have occupied the nest and there is evidence of egg laying, no young eagles have been produced.

On Mount Johnson Island as well as in Florida, then, the same situation prevails—there is some occupancy of nests by adults, some production of eggs, but few or no young birds. In seeking an explanation, only one appears to fit all the facts. This is that the reproductive capacity of the birds has been so lowered by some environmental agent that there are now almost no annual additions of young to maintain the race.

Exactly this sort of situation has been produced artificially in other birds by various experimenters, notably Dr. James DeWitt of the United States Fish and Wildlife Service. Dr. DeWitt's now classic experiments on the effect of a series of insecticides on quail and pheasants have established the fact that exposure to DDT or related chemicals, even when doing no observable harm to the parent birds, may seriously affect reproduction. The way the effect is exerted may vary, but the end result is always the same. For example, quail into whose diet DDT was introduced throughout the breeding season survived and even produced normal numbers of fertile eggs. But few of the eggs hatched. "Many embryos appeared to develop normally during the early stages of incubation, but died during the hatching period," Dr. DeWitt said. Of those that did hatch, more than half died within 5 days. In other tests in which both pheasants and quail were the subjects, the adults produced no eggs whatever if they had been fed insecticide-contaminated diets throughout the year. And at the University of California, Dr. Robert Rudd and Dr. Richard Genelly reported similar findings. When pheasants received dieldrin in their diets, "egg production was markedly lowered and chick survival was poor." According to these authors, the delayed but lethal effect on the young birds follows from storage of dieldrin in the yolk of the egg, from which it is gradually assimilated during incubation and after hatching.

This suggestion is strongly supported by recent studies by Dr. Wallace and a graduate student, Richard F. Bernard, who found high concentrations of DDT in robins on the Michigan State University campus. They found the poison in all of the testes of male robins examined, in developing egg follicles, in the ovaries of females, in completed but un-laid eggs, in the oviducts, in unhatched eggs from deserted nests, in embryos within the eggs, and in a newly hatched, dead nestling.

These important studies establish the fact that the insecticidal poison affects a generation once removed from initial contact with it. Storage of poison in the egg, in the yolk material that nourishes the developing embryo, is a virtual death warrant and explains why so many of De-Witt's birds died in the egg or a few days after hatching.

Laboratory application of these studies to eagles presents difficulties that are nearly insuperable, but field studies are now under way in Florida, New Jersey, and elsewhere in the hope of acquiring definite evidence as to what has caused the apparent sterility of much of the eagle population. Meanwhile, the available circumstantial evidence points to insecticides. In localities where fish are abundant they make up a large part of the eagle's diet (about 65 per cent in Alaska; about 52 per cent in the Chesapeake Bay area). Almost unquestionably the eagles so long studied by Mr. Broley were predominantly fish eaters. Since 1945 this particular coastal area has been subjected to repeated sprayings with DDT dissolved in fuel oil. The principal target of the aerial spraying was the salt-marsh mosquito, which inhabits the marshes and coastal areas that are typical foraging areas for the eagles. Fishes and crabs were killed in enormous numbers. Laboratory analyses of their tissues revealed high concentrations of DDT—as much as 46 parts per million. Like the grebes of Clear Lake, which accumulated heavy concentrations of insecticide residues from eating the fish of the lake, the eagles have almost certainly been storing up the DDT in the tissues of their bodies. And like the grebes, the pheasants, the quail, and the robins, they are less and less able to produce young and to preserve the continuity of their race.

From all over the world come echoes of the peril that faces birds in our modern world. The reports differ in detail, but always repeat the theme of death to wildlife in the wake of pesticides. Such are the stories of hundreds of small birds and partridges dying in France after vine stumps were treated with an arsenic-containing herbicide, or of partridge shoots in Belgium, once famous for the numbers of their birds, denuded of partridges after the spraying of nearby farmlands.

In England the major problem seems to be a specialized one, linked with the growing practice of treating seed with insecticides before sowing. Seed treatment is not a wholly new thing, but in earlier years the chemicals principally used were fungicides. No effects on birds seem to have been noticed. Then about 1956 there was a change to dual-purpose treatment; in addition to a fungicide, dieldrin, aldrin, or heptachlor was added to combat soil insects. Thereupon the situation changed for the worse.

In the spring of 1960 a deluge of reports of dead birds reached British wildlife authorities, including the British Trust for Ornithology, the Royal Society for the Protection of Birds, and the Game Birds Association. "The place is like a battlefield," a landowner in Norfolk wrote. "My keeper has found innumerable corpses, including masses of small birds—Chaffinches, Greenfinches, Linnets, Hedge Sparrows, also House Sparrows . . . the destruction of wild life is quite pitiful." A gamekeeper wrote: "My Partridges have been wiped out with the dressed corn, also some Pheasants and all other birds, hundreds of birds have been killed . . . As a lifelong gamekeeper it has been a distressing experience for me. It is bad to see pairs of Partridges that have died together."

In a joint report, the British Trust for Ornithology and the Royal Society for the Protection of Birds described some 67 kills of birds—a far from complete listing of the destruction that took place in the spring of 1960. Of these 67, 59 were caused by seed dressings, 8 by toxic sprays.

A new wave of poisoning set in the following year. The death of 600 birds on a single estate in Norfolk was reported to the House of Lords, and 100 pheasants died on a farm in North Essex. It soon became evident that more counties were involved than in 1960 (34 compared with 23). Lincolnshire, heavily agricultural, seemed to have suffered most, with reports of 10,000 birds dead. But destruction involved all of agricultural England, from Angus in the north to Cornwall in the south, from Anglesey in the west to Norfolk in the east.

In the spring of 1961 concern reached such a peak that a special committee of the House of Commons made an investigation of the matter, taking testimony from farmers, landowners, and representatives of the Ministry of Agriculture and of various governmental and nongovernmental agencies concerned with wildlife.

"Pigeons are suddenly dropping out of the sky dead," said one witness. "You can drive a hundred or two hundred miles outside London and not see a single kestrel," reported another. "There has been no parallel in the present century, or at any time so far as I am aware, [this is] the biggest risk to wildlife and game that ever occurred in the country," officials of the Nature Conservancy testified.

Facilities for chemical analysis of the victims were most inadequate to the task, with only two chemists in the country able to make the tests (one the government chemist, the other in the employ of the Royal Society for the Protection of Birds). Witnesses described huge bonfires on which the bodies of the birds were burned. But efforts were made to have carcasses collected for examination, and of the birds analyzed, all but one contained pesticide residues. The single exception was a snipe, which is not a seed-eating bird.

Along with the birds, foxes also may have been affected, probably indirectly by eating poisoned mice or birds. England, plagued by rabbits, sorely needs the fox as a predator. But between November 1959 and April 1960 at least 1300 foxes died. Deaths were heaviest in the same counties from which sparrow hawks, kestrels, and other birds of prey virtually disappeared, suggesting that the poison was spreading through the food chain, reaching out from the seed eaters to the furred and feathered carnivores. The actions of the moribund foxes were those of animals poisoned by chlorinated hydrocarbon insecticides. They were seen wandering in circles, dazed and half blind, before dying in convulsions.

The hearings convinced the committee that the threat to wildlife was "most alarming"; it accordingly recommended to the House of Commons that "the Minister of Agriculture and the Secretary of State for Scotland should secure the immediate prohibition for the use as seed dressings of compounds containing dieldrin, aldrin, or heptachlor, or chemicals of comparable toxicity." The committee also recommended more adequate controls to ensure that chemicals were adequately tested under field as well as laboratory conditions before being put on the market. This, it is worth emphasizing, is one of the great blank spots in pesticide research everywhere. Manufacturers' tests on the common laboratory animals—rats, dogs, guinea pigs—include no wild species, no birds as a rule, no fishes, and are conducted under controlled and artificial conditions. Their application to wildlife in the field is anything but precise.

England is by no means alone in its problem of protecting birds from treated seeds. Here in the United States the problem has been most troublesome in the rice-growing areas of California and the South. For a number of years California rice growers have been treating seed with DDT as protection against tadpole shrimp and scavenger beetles which sometimes damage seedling rice. California sportsmen have enjoyed excellent hunting because of the concentrations of waterfowl and pheasants in the rice fields. But for the past decade persistent reports of bird losses, especially among pheasants, ducks, and blackbirds, have come from the rice-growing counties. "Pheasant sickness" became a well-known phenomenon: birds "seek water, become paralyzed, and are found on the ditch banks and rice checks quivering," according to one observer. The "sickness" comes in the spring, at the time the rice fields are seeded. The concentration of DDT used is many times the amount that will kill an adult pheasant.

The passage of a few years and the development of even more poisonous insecticides served to increase the hazard from treated seed. Aldrin, which is 100 times as toxic as DDT to pheasants, is now widely used as a seed coating. In the rice fields of eastern Texas, this practice has seriously reduced the populations of the fulvous tree duck, a tawny-colored, gooselike duck of the Gulf Coast. Indeed, there is some reason to think that the rice growers, having found a way to reduce the populations of blackbirds, are using the insecticide for a dual purpose, with disastrous effects on several bird species of the rice fields.

As the habit of killing grows—the resort to "eradicating" any creature that may annoy or inconvenience us—birds are more and more finding themselves a direct target of poisons rather than an incidental one. There is a growing trend toward aerial applications of such deadly poisons as parathion to "control" concentrations of birds distasteful to farmers. The Fish and Wildlife Service has found it necessary to express serious concern over this trend, pointing out that "parathion treated areas constitute a potential hazard to humans, domestic animals, and wildlife." In southern Indiana, for example, a group of farmers went together in the summer of 1959 to engage a spray plane to treat an area of river bottomland with parathion. The area was a favored roosting site for thousands of blackbirds that were feeding in nearby cornfields. The problem could have been solved easily by a slight change in agricultural practice—a shift to a variety of corn with deep-set ears not accessible to the birds—but the farmers had been persuaded of the merits of killing by poison, and so they sent in the planes on their mission of death.

The results probably gratified the farmers, for the casualty list included some 65,000 red-winged blackbirds and starlings. What other wildlife deaths may have gone unnoticed and unrecorded is not known. Parathion is not a specific for blackbirds: it is a universal killer. But such rabbits or raccoons or opossums as may have roamed those bottomlands and perhaps never visited the farmers' cornfields were doomed by a judge and jury who neither knew of their existence nor cared.

And what of human beings? In California orchards sprayed with this same parathion, workers handling foliage that had been treated *a month* earlier collapsed and went into shock, and escaped death only through skilled medical attention. Does Indiana still raise any boys who roam through woods or fields and might even explore the margins of a river? If so, who guarded the poisoned area to keep out any who might wander in, in misguided search for unspoiled nature? Who kept vigilant watch to tell the innocent stroller that the fields he was about to enter were deadly—all their vegetation coated with a lethal film? Yet at so fearful a risk the farmers, with none to hinder them, waged their needless war on blackbirds.

In each of these situations, one turns away to ponder the question: Who has made the decision that sets in motion these chains of poisonings, this ever-widening wave of death that spreads out, like ripples when a pebble is dropped into a still pond? Who has placed in one pan of the scales the leaves that might have been eaten by the beetles and in the other the pitiful heaps of many-hued feathers, the lifeless remains of the birds that fell before the unselective bludgeon of insecticidal poisons? Who has decided—who has the *right* to decide—for the countless legions of people who were not consulted that the supreme value is a world without insects, even though it be also a sterile world ungraced by the curving wing of a bird in flight? The decision is that of the authoritarian temporarily entrusted with power; he has made it during a moment of inattention by millions to whom beauty and the ordered world of nature still have a meaning that is deep and imperative.

Silent Spring (1962)

In the postwar years, as the population of the suburbs ringing the eastern cities swelled, people talked frequently of the "eastern megalopolis"—in the typically overheated prose of *Time* magazine from 1966, a "coruscating corridor of light, an unbroken, 450-mile-long conglomeration" of humanity stretching from Boston to Washington. Russell Baker (b. 1925), though he grew up in small-town Virginia, was a star citizen of that megalopolis—a reporter in the Washington bureau of *The New York Times*. Beginning in 1962 he wrote the Observer column for the *Times* op-ed page, two or three columns a week that established him as a wry and savvy onlooker during one of America's most tumultuous periods. Environmental concern was always a hallmark of the *Times* (editorial page editor John B. Oakes was a tireless and effective advocate of anything ecological), and in this small essay Baker captures the wary eye with which the establishment was starting to view unchecked "progress."

The Great Paver

WASHINGTON, Feb. 6—One of the happier events of the winter has been the preliminary success in Boston of an experiment in getting commuters off the highways and onto the railroads.

With a cut in commuter fares and improved service, Boston has found that enough people have switched from car to rail to afford noticeable relief from the traffic glut that was strangling the city. Some people suspect that the revival of rail travel is only temporary, that it has something to do with the bad winter weather and the novelty of the experiment, and that it will prove, with the first warm day in April, to have been only a nice dream.

There is a small clique little known outside insiders' circles that will be extremely pained if the Boston experiment should work. The director of this tiny but immensely powerful group, whose tentacles reach even into the Mafia, is known only as The Great Paver.

His dream, which he would dismiss as implausible if concocted by one of Ian Fleming's villains, is to pave the entire United States with concrete and asphalt. He envisions a nation buried under six-lane, limited-access turnpikes. When the last blade of American grass is buried, he plans to go on to pave Europe. Then Asia. And on and on until the whole planet is coated in cement. Today American—tomorrow the world.

Accusations that The Great Paver is power mad are unfair. True, he has henchmen whose motives are not unselfish. We all know the motives of the oil cartel and the notorious auto repair syndicate whose goals correspond with The Great Paver's. The Great Paver, however, is utterly principled.

His philosophy is summed up in the sentence with which he refutes every attempt to stop him: "The world must move cars."

Seeing thousands of cars jammed up in the city's narrow arteries, he has thrown concrete over houses and shops and covered the parks with asphalt to let the traffic move. When human beings have protested, he has told them simply: "The world must move cars."

Now, of course, he has learned that new superexpressways pour more cars into more narrow arteries. He realizes, not entirely without sorrow, that there can be no end until the entire continent is utterly and completely paved.

The Great Paver has been especially active in Washington lately. He has laid concrete all over the beautiful Virginia hills across the Potomac and is busy pouring it through the lush Maryland valleys. With splendid highways now surrounding the capital, there is nothing to do but buy a car or two and get out and drive on them.

And so, with the lovelier and lovelier highways luring more and more motorists, it has become increasingly difficult to move. The Great Paver has the answer on blueprints showing immense concrete loops constricting the capital's center, new Potomac bridges feeding Virginia's backed-up thousands into Washington's parklands and magnificent new interchanges of unspeakable complexity.

There is even, rumor has it, a secret sketch of the finished Washington which shows an endless vista of concrete broken only by a round protuberance identifiable as the upper part of the Capitol dome and by the very tip of the Washington Monument.

Like most cities, Washington has been dangerously slow in awakening to the presence of The Great Paver. In desperately belated haste, it has thrown together a plan for mass transit system as an alternative to burial by highway. And in the Senate, Mike Mansfield, the Democratic leader, has introduced a bill to prevent the paving of one of the city's finer parks. (The Senator lives in the doomed area.)

These measures, however, look to be too little and too late. The Great Paver rarely loses a battle. "The world must move cars" has proven a powerful argument everywhere else and few cities are as powerless to defend themselves as poor, spiritless, ungoverned old Washington.

Its best hope may be that Boston's experiment in rails might work. In view of past experience with The Paver, however, there is not much reason to hope.

The New York Times, February 7, 1963

ELIOT PORTER

Eliot Porter (1901–1990), a Harvard-educated doctor turned photographer, helped train the American eye to see the natural world in new ways. Birds were his principal subject for much of his career; a Guggenheim fellowship helped him experiment with a process that let him make richly saturated color prints. Increasingly his photographs captured the minutiae of the natural world, almost the opposite of Ansel Adams' sublime landscapes. In 1960 he organized an exhibition that paired many of his pictures with quotations from Thoreau's essays and journals. David Brower (see pages 554–58 in this volume) turned the exhibit into a book, *In Wildness Is the Preservation of the World* (1962), and that book took off, launching the Sierra Club on a publishing mission that would produce dozens of influential volumes. Porter's pictures of the soon-to-be-dammed Glen Canyon in *The Place No One Knew* (1963) helped enormously in the fight to keep the Colorado running free through the Grand Canyon; later books by other contributors showed the Adirondacks, Baja, the Galapagos, and the Smokies. As essayist and critic Rebecca Solnit has written, "His photographs have come to embody what we look for and value in the natural world, what the public often tries to photograph, and what a whole genre of photography imitates. The work is so compelling that it eventually becomes how we see and imagine, rather than what we look at . . . We live in a world Porter helped invent." His images and words, alas, are at best merely the best record we have of Glen Canyon, which was lost to Glen Canyon Dam and is now submerged under Lake Powell.

The Living Canyon

The architect, the life-giver, and the moderator of Glen Canyon is the Colorado River. It slips along serenely, riffled only in the few places where boulder-filled narrows confine it, for nearly two hundred miles. For all the serenity, the first canyon experience is too over-whelming to let you take in more than the broadest features and bold-est strokes. The eye is numbed by vastness and magnificence, and passes over the fine details, ignoring them in a defense against surfeit. The big features, the massive walls and towers, the shimmering vistas, the enveloping light, are all hypnotizing, shutting out awareness of the particular.

Later you begin to focus on the smaller, more familiar, more com-prehensible objects which, when finally seen in the context of the whole, are endowed with a wonder no less than the total. It is from them that the greatest rewards come. Then you see for the first time the velvety lawns of young tamarisks sprouting on the wet sandbars just vacated by the retreating flood, or notice how the swirling surface of the green, opaque river converts light reflected from rocks and trees and sky into a moire of interlacing lines and coils of color, or observe the festooned, evocative designs etched into the walls by water and lichens.

It is an intimate canyon. The feeling of intimacy comes partly from your being able to travel through it by boat—from a close association unknown in a canyon seen only from above or dipped into at only a few places. The intimacy also comes from the calmness and congeniality of the river and the closeness of the walls. Life along the banks and bars is unhurried. Every bend offers a good campsite. Clear springs are not far apart, providing in a shaded setting of mossy, dripping rocks and wildflowers welcome respite from the heat of noon. At evening, in the glow of burnished cliffs, a quiet peace settles on the boatmen gathered close to their campfire, their subdued voices accentuating the faint gur-gling of the big river slipping past its banks. With night spreading fast and stars appearing in the diminished sky, the canyon's dimly silhouet-ted walls give comfort and security.

The rocks through which the canyon was carved are old monolithic sandstones rising hundreds of feet, in places straight from the water. The Wingate formation at the upper end weathers through vertical cracks extending down from the surface into massive, burnt-red, columnar blocks and slabs. When these break off and fall, shattering on the steep, narrow talus bordering the river, they strew the slope with upended, jagged fragments; their faces, like the cliff above, oxidize to a polished purple-black. This dark varnish, reflecting the sky, turns in the shade to deep metallic blue but in the sun shines a dazzling white. Downstream the Wingate formation drops out of sight below the surface. Its place is taken by Navajo sandstone, and the character of the cliffs changes strikingly. Here the plateau weathers into round domes and the rim is less sharp. Water streaks the walls with ribbons of color that cling like folds of wet curtains to the rock. The dark stains are caused by the algae and lichens that manage to grow in the occasional films of moisture; the bluish-white bands mark where chemicals have been leached.

The Navajo sandstone cleaves to produce immense arches and bays and all manner of rippled and shell-like structures. Imposed on these shapes, giving emphasis by contrast, oxidation has added to the yellow and orange stone a blue and purple cast; and lichens following the same pattern superimpose on north-facing walls a texture of tapestry. Slabs spall off the cliffs from time to time, one layer after another. The fresh scars and those of great antiquity add their own infinite variety to that of the tapestries. High on the face of the canyon walls in many places, like the pupilless eyes of marble statues, huge lenticular depressions have flaked out—the beginnings of caves, in which water oozes out along the fracture lines. If the caves are shaded, they contain a heavy growth of maidenhair fern and mimulus.

The tributaries of Glen Canyon are a unique natural museum exhibiting examples of erosion found nowhere else in the world. The walls of the canyon as a whole are like worm-eaten wood, riddled with tunnels on an enormous scale. The smooth bores of their unroofed, twisting holes converge on the common river channel. Most of them are quite short, no more than a mile in length, the shortest snaking back only two or three turns before ending abruptly in a circular chamber surrounding a pool into which a trickle may descend through a sculptured channel.

The similarity of the tributary ground plans shows that the same forces were at work molding them. Their courses are S-curves twisting back into the sandstone of the Colorado Plateau. Some straighten out as they advance headward, but others twist for miles back from the river—like Twilight Canyon, which my youngest son followed for fifty-seven turns without coming to an end or detecting a lessening of the height of its walls. It and several other canyons are dry and dead; nothing grows among heaped-up boulders. No flowers spring from the barren walls, and no water stays, unless it is deeply shaded under a massively undercut wall. Such a canyon is no place to be caught in a flash flood.

But most side canyons, even those carrying no permanent stream, are rich with plant life. For all the havoc the floods work against lifeless structures, they are ineffective against the frailest living things which, like the sea algae of a surf-bound coast, bend to their irresistible force and spring back after the torrent has passed, and the power of fertility soon reseeds the plants that are uprooted. Grasses, flowers, canes, and vines cover the sand banks at the bends. Oaks grow almost impenetrably in the sunniest spots and redbud fills the shady corners. Cottonwoods remember where the water was.

Down all the tributaries pour intermittent floods burdened with sand, each grain a chisel able to liberate imprisoned grains from the ancient walls. The streams batter the canyonsides, tearing away all loose material, and gouging out deep troughs. The narrowness of some canyons—their sides may be hundreds of feet high and less than six feet apart at the bottom—is dramatic evidence of the rapidity of erosion. A few evidently started as tight meanders in the surface rock, in which fast corrasion deepened the channels into wide passages beneath interlocking walls. At the sharpest bends the pounding waters have scooped out deep caves, the girdling walls of which envelop an opposite rounded peninsula of rock. These gigantic structures are like loosely articulated elements of an immobile ball and socket joint. If you stand facing outward in the stream bed in one of these caves and look up at the top of the dome-shaped inner wall, you see the sky as a crescent of blue, bounded above by the overhanging dark surface of the cave rising behind you. The magnitude of these awesome shapes expanding over your head out of the confines of the canyon floor is a test of credulity.

Of all the phenomena of the side canyons, it is the light, even in the farthest depths of the narrowest canyon, that evokes the ultimate in awe. In somber, rocky caverns of purple and ocher stone into which the sun rarely strikes, shallow pools glitter brassily from sunlit cliffs high overhead. Wherever there is a damp cleft, maidenhair fern and scarlet lobelia and white columbine grow. Their drooping leaves turn a dusky cyan-green in the blue shadows, creating a subdued, almost funereal atmosphere.

It is reflection that imparts magic to the waters of the Glen Canyon and its tributaries. Every pool and rill, every sheet of flowing water, every wet rock and seep—these mirror with enameled luster the world about. In narrow chasms streams of melted gems flow over purple sand past banks of verdant willow. Small puddles, like shining eyes, fuse the colors of pink rocks and cerulean sky, and wet ripples of mud may do the same thing. In the changing light nothing remains the same from year to year or hour to hour. Flood and drouth, heat and cold, life and death alter the finer details incessantly, but they leave unchanged the grand plan and the enchanting quality of the Colorado's masterwork.

The first explorers of Glen Canyon, the Powell party, well appreciated its beauty and remarked on it often enough in their accounts to have established its reputation as a wonderland of the Colorado. Later visitors probably did not especially notice its finer aspects for they were lured there by the hope of sudden riches. They came in barges with tools and dredges and machinery to extract gold from the river's sands and gravel benches, but they were frustrated by the difficulties of their operations and returned with empty hands, losing even the wealth they had invested. They left a more permanent mark than their scratchings or the disintegrating machinery they abandoned—the names they gave to the places where they strived, lost heart, and died. Their memorials are places like Smith Bar, California Bar, Klondike and Dead Man bars, and Stanton's Dredge—crazily tilted and rusting in mid river.

But now another kind of invasion is taking place—one that will obliterate all the places that bear the nostalgic names, wipe them out for all foreseeable time. Thus, with nothing tangible to evoke the past, even the memory of the river's history will be destroyed. This final act of destruction is, as it was with Colorado River goldseekers fifty years ago, materially motivated. The wealth of the Colorado this time is its power, ostensibly at least, although there are those who see a less forthright purpose—the ambition of a federal bureau to build an empire out of river development, with sincere regard, no doubt, for one kind of public welfare, but with disregard of many less tangible aspects of human well-being. Glen Canyon dam may appear to exemplify this ambition. But neither does its imposing magnitude alone justify it, nor can the dam serve all the beneficial functions attributed to it in the process of obtaining legislative support or as a subsequent apology.

The waters impounded by this plug of artificial stone spread back through Glen Canyon and for one hundred eighty-six miles in all, inundating the sparkling river, swallowing its luminous cliffs and tapestried walls, and extinguishing far into the long, dim, distant future everything that gave it life. As the waters creep into the side canyons, enveloping one by one their mirroring pools, drowning their bright flowers, backing up their clear, sweet springs with stale flood water, a fine opaque silt settles over all, covering rocks and trees alike with a gray slimy ooze. Darkness pervades the canyons. Death and the thickening, umbrageous gloom take over where life and shimmering light were the glory of the river.

Glen Canyon's forms of life have been separated from the world by the canyon's depth as well as by its desert borders. Its vegetation has been reproducing for centuries, most of the species probably arriving from the outside world by way of the river. Its animals, too, are isolated, a few having developed their own races in the flow of evolutionary processes within the restricted canyon environment. The birds are the most conspicuous. It is their nature to live conspicuous lives—they fly. They advertise their presence by song, even when they seem to be skulking in the thickets. In the spring the willow and tamarisk jungles of the river's edge ring with the cheerful sibilance of yellow warblers. From among the broken rocks of dry talus comes the bright chant of the rock wren, and higher up from the cliff side, the canyon wren's deliberate down-scale notes echo melodiously. Added to these sweet songs, there are some unmelodious, comic sounds issuing frequently from the thickets—the harsh clucking, cawing, and whistling of the yellow-breasted chat that lurks mostly unseen in the densest underbrush but occasionally bursts from the top of a bush in awkward, wing-clapping, nuptial flight.

Great blue herons, with their four-toe prints, mark the muddy border of every lagoon and shallow backwash, where they have stood motionless watching for small fish or frogs. Approached too closely, they rise smoothly, legs dangling, their powerful wings beating slowly in unhurried flight down the river.

In the side canyons, along the narrow water courses where deep pools are carved in rock and the flow is clear and constant, lives a small, plump, gray bird with stumpy tail, the water ouzel. A favorite haunt is the narrows in Bridge Canyon, on the trail to Rainbow Bridge. He is truly aquatic, and although not web-footed, he is as much at home in the water as a duck. He makes his living in the flowing streams and cascades of high country and canyons of the west; he cannot live without them and he never departs far from them. He builds his roofed nest and rears his young in the spray of waterfalls. When first encountered he will probably be bobbing on a stone in midstream, and to your astonishment he may suddenly plunge into the foaming water. Over his somber dark gray suit he instantly slips a resplendent jacket of shiny silver bubbles and walks about on the bottom picking up aquatic larvae here and there showing as little concern as he would on dry land. In a moment he pops out again, leaving his bright diving suit behind and, as dry as before he dove in, continues about his business. He is apparently pleased with his mode of life, bursting into song most unexpectedly after emerging from one of his underwater foraging expeditions. He sings his ebullient, varied song throughout the year for no other assignable reason than the sheer joy of doing so, for he is the only audience when he sings unheard in the mist of a thundering cascade.

To the murmuring and chattering by the river, the raven's harsh caw is added now and then from a high ledge or from a point in the air where he has found a balance between the law of gravity and the law of convection. He hangs there, rocking slightly as he drifts and soars, seeking out the current, his black profile punctuating his words. He is a bird of parts, but he is no show-off nor does he hide his talents. He saves a particular quality in his voice for special occasions, and though he cannot sing, he is able to introduce a bell-like quality into his croak which adds a musical touch without melody. He does not live just to exist, but appears to delight in his greatest accomplishment—flight. A small group may spend hours playing in the air currents, soaring effortlessly, chasing one another in an endless game—diving, swooping wing to wing, turning upside down in a wild exuberant melee, racing past the face of a cliff, feeling desperately for the upsurge that will give an advantage, uttering guttural cries that release all their pent-up excitement just as children cry out in their play. Who can say this is not an expression of joy?

But it is dark now, quiet above the bank except for the river's soft voice. I turn in my sleeping bag toward the east, where a faint light is just perceptible. Soon it will give way to the waxing twilight of morning and the world will fill with color. This is a positive time, a time of expansion and increase and expectation. In the waning twilight of evening everything is closing down and in retreat, but at dawn each moment is brighter; the path into light, into activity, is full of hope and renewed energy and the promise of clarity. The sun, still a long way beneath the rim, routs the last stars down the brightening sky. They make a pale stand in the thinning shadow of the earth, until Venus alone holds out, resisting the stampede. Directly overhead fleecy clouds sail from the northwest across the narrow, rock-enclosed sky, preserving the order of their ranks while their shapes shift and flow. A tinge of pink is spreading over them, changing gradually to salmon and then to yellow, when suddenly from some notch in the horizon the sun bursts into this hemisphere. It lights the top of a butte, transforming it into a metallic crown. Slowly the color slips down its sides, copperplating them and enveloping the canyon in warmth. The river, still in shadow, picks up color and multiplies it, converting gray stones along its muddy bank into uncut lapis lazuli embedded in molten bronze. Blue highlights thread the dry sand ripples. Day is near and will soon blaze into the canyon depths.

All the bizarre morning colors fade with the day's advance. Purple banks and blue dunes become common mud and sand. The river becomes muddy green. The rocks turn to brick and clay as the sun climbs above the canyon rim.

We have our breakfast, pack our few possessions, and are ready to shove off into the current lapping at the loaded boats. We check the sands again for forgotten objects, postponing the final moment, loath to depart the little world which for a night's stop was the focus of our lives in an eternity of timeless existence. We push the boats out, wading knee deep in mud to gain the deeper water before climbing on board. The day is bright and still. No wind ruffles the glassy surface of the river, lined with swirling striae by the upwelling current. The mirrored sandstone cliffs are distorted near the boat, but down the river's reach they are nearly perfectly reflected. In the winding canyon dark and light reflections replace one another in slow succession. The gentle wake of the boat breaks these images into undulating spots and patches, each wave for a moment holding a fragment of sky mixed with golden globules of sunlit rock.

The striped walls of Glen Canyon pass slowly by, progressively revealing and concealing the breaks in their defenses. Often the walls are so sharply undercut by the river that there is no talus, not even a sand bank or bar, to separate them from the water. Some of them are sliced unexpectedly by narrow perpendicular slots. At high water the river deposits its load in them—sand dropping in the eddies at the entrances and finer sediments precipitating in the quietest waters. Back in the slots these fingers of the river blend into a bank of gray ooze which thickens into a slippery bed of clay of uncertain depth extending from wall to wall. After the spring run-off has subsided and the river withdrawn, these slots are left plugged to their mouths with mud and silt that dries slowly to a cracked, crusted surface you can walk on. But the first local freshet will wash it all out.

Like the half-concealed passages into long forgotten tombs, these narrow slots give no hint of the strange sights inside their portals. We plunge apprehensively into the mud and water. Sometimes it is waist-deep; sometimes we have to swim. We struggle through the sucking clay, one laborious step at a time, to harder ground where we make our unimpeded way within.

In Anasazi Canyon, after traversing a winding corridor of tangled woodbine gardens, we find ourselves at last in a circular arena, confronted by overhanging, inaccessible walls. Dark viridescent lumps of moss dot the surface and, trembling in a perpetual current of air, green fern tenacles grow around them from the slippery rock. From a groove at a higher level a thin stream slides into a black and fathomless pond. The whole interior of this tenebrous chamber, with wavy greenery lining its sides, is like the ciliated cavity of a huge sea anemone.

In Cathedral Canyon, beyond a series of immense, vaulted bends, we come to a sudden closing in of the walls where the floor disappears into a water-filled trough no wider than a man's body. Swimming through it is a dreamlike adventure. Shivering, we glide along like seals, chin deep in the water, through still depths into an inscrutable solitude. Only the hollow sound of our splashing reverberates along the contorted channel back into the stony labyrinth. Now and then the mysterious bottom, a stone or a graveled ledge, rises to surprise us. We climb over wedged boulders from one ribbon pool to another in a journey reminiscent of Xanadu, "through caverns measureless to man." A sudden shaft of sun, giving a dimension of reality, penetrates the upper stories through an unseen window. It lights a strip of wall a dazzling yellow and is reflected to our eyes at water level from the thin curved edge where the pool laps the rock in gentle undulations, like golden threads reaching ahead to delineate for a moment the wavering separation of water from stone. At the end a wisp of a waterfall drops from unseen heights overhead, slipping over a smooth and algaed chute into a slatey pool. Shivering, we retrace our way, glad to emerge at last into the August sun.

Little Arch, we discover, is a short canyon, ending in a waterfall up which an earlier explorer cut shallow steps in the wet sandstone. We follow these and are led through pools in a tortured narrow trough to a roofed room in the ocherous rock. It is dry on one side where a sand bank is heaped up; the other side extends a few feet into a moist alcove giving egress—through a chimney leading straight up to the sky—to the free air of the plateau high overhead. The sides of the chimney have been ground into concave plaques lying one above the other like immense elongated scales. An infernal light spreads down this tube and suffuses the chamber, dyeing our faces and half-naked bodies a dull furnace red. Our imaginations, turning to the violent events that must periodically take place in this cavern, picture the enveloping spray and hear the roar of water as it pours down the chimney in a tumultuous, thundering rush.

Weather in the canyon country is not always good. Storms sweep over it from the northwest, the outriggers of disturbances down from the Aleutians, and may last for a week, enveloping the canyon in mist and rain. More usually, summer's bad weather is local and short-lived. Storms develop over the bordering plateaus, spreading out over the encircling land until darkening thunderheads rumble their warning. Down in the canyon, where the cliff-edged sky is narrow, they can surprise you. A white-edged, black cloud rises above the canyon rim, lightning flickers, a crash ricochets down the canyon, and the first drops spatter dark wet circles on the red sandstone. They evaporate quickly from the hot surface but their replacements come fast. A dusty smell pervades the hot air. The rain curves into the canyon in gusts, bright points and streaks against dark cliffs. The drops seem to float down but they strike the face hard. The black cloud now possesses the entire opening of sky and a cold wind sweeps through the canyon. Another flash of lightning brightens the obscurity and thunder crashes again, much louder, reverberating from higher terraces, rolling and rumbling up and down the gorge, dying in the cul de sacs. The rain comes down hard now. The wet cliffs have lost all color, but glisten like mercury from the sheets of water pouring over them. Through the notches and dips in the rim, wherever the walls were streaked, streams pour down. Through larger notches torrents spume over, free-falling hundreds of feet with a roar, some white and clean, others brown and murky. The noise of falling water and the rush of the rising creek drown out all but the thunder.

The downpour retreats as quickly as it came, and the waterfalls diminish, then cease. The sun comes out again, the rocks dry off, a few puddles lingering in their hollows, and the trees glitter and drip briefly. The creek runs brown and full and is the last to return to its peaceful pace.

In the canyon itself the days flow through your consciousness as the river flows along its course, without a break and with hardly a ripple to disturb their smoothness. Problems fade from the forefront of your mind. Duration becomes a serene timeless flow without landmarks, without interruptions, without the insistent beckoning of obligations. The river supplies and in a sense supplants the need for a measure of time. The current becomes the time on which you move. Things happen and days pass. They exist simply in a heap of impressions and memories, all different and yet all of one kind. There is no more liberating or healing experience. It penetrates to the very core of being, scattering anxieties, untangling knots, re-creating the spirit.

To put the world, and yourself at the same time, in a valid perspective you must remove yourself from the demands of both. The world's demands fade the faster, but nonetheless surely your own will shrink to acceptable proportions and cannot sally forth to attack you. In the wilderness of Glen Canyon you do not assail yourself. You glide on into the day unpursued, living, as all good river travelers should, in the present.

The Place No One Knew (1963)

HOWARD ZAHNISER

Howard Zahniser (1906–1964) wrote the fewest sentences in this book, but they are the ones that protected the most American soil. In 1945 Zahniser became executive secretary of The Wilderness Society, which had been formed ten years earlier by Robert Marshall. A few years later he initiated a discussion in the conservation movement about the need for a formal wilderness system, and he spent the rest of his life pursuing that dream. He lobbied tirelessly, and, at his vacation cabin in the central Adirondacks, drafted the language that would create new federal wilderness modeled on that New York State preserve. He died four months before the final passage of the wilderness bill, but his key sentence—"an area where the earth and its community of life are untrammeled by man, where man is a visitor who does not remain"—was the anchor of the final text. Congress has never before or since been as poetic, as philosophical, or as selfless and farseeing.

from **The Wilderness Act of 1964**

AN ACT
To establish a National Wilderness Preservation System for the permanent good of the whole people, and for other purposes.

Be it enacted by the Senate and House of Representatives of the United States of America in Congress assembled.

SHORT TITLE

SECTION 1. This Act may be cited as the "Wilderness Act".

WILDERNESS SYSTEM ESTABLISHED STATEMENT OF POLICY

SEC. 2. (a) In order to assure that an increasing population, accompanied by expanding settlement and growing mechanization, does not

occupy and modify all areas within the United States and its possessions, leaving no lands designated for preservation and protection in
their natural condition, it is hereby declared to be the policy of the Congress to secure for the American people of present and future generations the benefits of an enduring resource of wilderness. For this
purpose there is hereby established a National Wilderness Preservation
System to be composed of federally owned areas designated by Congress as "wilderness areas", and these shall be administered for the use
and enjoyment of the American people in such manner as will leave
them unimpaired for future use and enjoyment as wilderness, and so as
to provide for the protection of these areas, the preservation of their
wilderness character, and for the gathering and dissemination of information regarding their use and enjoyment as wilderness; and no Federal lands shall be designated as "wilderness areas" except as provided
for in this Act or by a subsequent Act.

(b) The inclusion of an area in the National Wilderness Preservation System notwithstanding, the area shall continue to be managed by
the Department and agency having jurisdiction thereover immediately
before its inclusion in the National Wilderness Preservation System unless otherwise provided by Act of Congress. No appropriation shall be
available for the payment of expenses or salaries for the administration
of the National Wilderness Preservation System as a separate unit nor
shall any appropriations be available for additional personnel stated as
being required solely for the purpose of managing or administering areas solely because they are included within the National Wilderness
Preservation System.

DEFINITION OF WILDERNESS

(c) A wilderness, in contrast with those areas where man and his
own works dominate the landscape, is hereby recognized as an area
where the earth and its community of life are untrammeled by man,
where man himself is a visitor who does not remain. An area of wilderness is further defined to mean in this Act an area of undeveloped Federal land retaining its primeval character and influence, without
permanent improvements or human habitation, which is protected and

managed so as to preserve its natural conditions and which (1) generally appears to have been affected primarily by the forces of nature, with the imprint of man's work substantially unnoticeable; (2) has outstanding opportunities for solitude or a primitive and unconfined type of recreation; (3) has at least five thousand acres of land or is of sufficient size as to make practicable its preservation and use in an unimpaired condition; and (4) may also contain ecological, geological, or other features of scientific, educational, scenic, or historical value.

1964

Lyndon Baines Johnson (1908–1973) signed the Highway Beautification Act and gave this short and sentimental speech, but it was really the work of his wife, Lady Bird Johnson, who died in 2007. Her campaign to plant flowers in cities and remove billboards and junkyards from American highways prompted her to move beyond the ancillary role expected of a First Lady: she started sitting in on legislative strategy sessions and lobbying members of Congress for their votes. In the gathering tumult of the 1960s it may have seemed like a small project, but in fact it meant a big fight with the powerful outdoor advertising lobby. And for a woman who had been born in 1912 and grown up rich in rural Texas, it was a way to enter that confusing political maelstrom. "Getting on the subject of beautification is like picking up a tangled skein of wool," she wrote in her diary on January 27, 1965; "all the threads are interwoven—recreation and pollution and mental health, and the crime rate, and rapid transit, and highway beautification, and the war on poverty, and parks—national, state, and local. It is hard to hitch the conversation into one straight line, because everything leads to something else."

Remarks at the Signing of the Highway Beautification Act of 1965

Secretary Gardner, distinguished Members of the leadership of the Congress and Members of the Congress, and all other lovers of beauty:

America likes to think of itself as a strong and stalwart and expanding Nation. It identifies itself gladly with the products of its own hands. We frequently point with pride and with confidence to the products of our great free enterprise system—management and labor.

These are and these should be a source of pride to every American. They are certainly the source of American strength. They are truly the fountainhead of American wealth. They are actually a part of America's soul.

But there is more to America than raw industrial might. And when you go through what I have gone through the last 2 weeks you constantly think of things like that. You no longer get your computers in and try to count your riches.

There is a part of America which was here long before we arrived, and will be here, if we preserve it, long after we depart: the forests and the flowers, the open prairies and the slope of the hills, the tall mountains, the granite, the limestone, the caliche, the unmarked trails, the winding little streams—well, this is the America that no amount of science or skill can ever recreate or actually ever duplicate.

This America is the source of America's greatness. It is another part of America's soul as well.

When I was growing up, the land itself was life. And when the day seemed particularly harsh and bitter, the land was always there just as nature had left it—wild, rugged, beautiful, and changing, always changing.

And really, how do you measure the excitement and the happiness that comes to a boy from the old swimming hole in the happy days of yore, when I used to lean above it; the old sycamore, the baiting of a hook that is tossed into the stream to catch a wily fish, or looking at a graceful deer that leaps with hardly a quiver over a rock fence that was put down by some settler a hundred years or more ago?

How do you really put a value on the view of the night that is caught in a boy's eyes while he is stretched out in the thick grass watching the million stars that we never see in these crowded cities, breathing the sounds of the night and the birds and the pure, fresh air while in his ears are the crickets and the wind?

Well, in recent years I think America has sadly neglected this part of America's national heritage. We have placed a wall of civilization between us and between the beauty of our land and of our countryside. In our eagerness to expand and to improve, we have relegated nature to a weekend role, and we have banished it from our daily lives.

Well, I think that we are a poorer Nation because of it, and it is something I am not proud of. And it is something I am going to do something about. Because as long as I am your President, by choice of your people, I do not choose to preside over the destiny of this country and to hide from view what God has gladly given it.

And that is why today there is a great deal of real joy within me, and within my family, as we meet here in this historic East Room to sign the Highway Beautification Act of 1965.

Now, this bill does more than control advertising and junkyards along the billions of dollars of highways that the people have built with their money—public money, not private money. It does more than give us the tools just to landscape some of those highways.

This bill will bring the wonders of nature back into our daily lives.

This bill will enrich our spirits and restore a small measure of our national greatness.

As I rode the George Washington Memorial Parkway back to the White House only yesterday afternoon, I saw nature at its purest. And I thought of the honor roll of names—a good many of you are sitting here in the front row today—that made this possible. And as I thought of you who had helped and stood up against private greed for public good, I looked at those dogwoods that had turned red, and the maple trees that were scarlet and gold. In a pattern of brown and yellow, God's finery was at its finest. And not one single foot of it was marred by a single, unsightly, man-made construction or obstruction—no advertising signs, no old, dilapidated trucks, no junkyards. Well, doctors could prescribe no better medicine for me, and that is what I said to my surgeon as we drove along.

This bill does not represent everything that we wanted. It does not represent what we need. It does not represent what the national interest requires. But it is a first step, and there will be other steps. For though we must crawl before we walk, we are going to walk.

I remember the fierce resolve of a man that I admired greatly, a great leader of a great people, Franklin D. Roosevelt. He fought a pitched battle in 1936 with private interests whose target was private gain. And I shall long remember the words that I believe he echoed at

Madison Square Garden, when he declared to the Nation that the forces of selfishness had not only met their match, but these forces had met their master.

Well, I have not asked you to come here today to tell you that I have a desire to master anyone. But until the clock strikes the last hour of the time allotted to me as President by vote of all the people of this country, I will never turn away from the duty that my office demands or the vigilance that my oath of office requires.

And this administration has no desire to punish or to penalize any private industry, or any private company, or any group, or any organization of complex associations in this Nation. But we are not going to allow them to intrude their own specialized private objective on the larger public trust.

Beauty belongs to all the people. And so long as I am President, what has been divinely given to nature will not be taken recklessly away by man.

This Congress is to be thanked for the bill that you have given us. I wish it could have been more, but I realize, too, that there are other views to be considered in our system of checks and balances.

The grandchildren of those of you in this country that may have mocked and ridiculed us today, someday will point with pride to the public servants who are here in this room, who cast their lot with the people.

And unless I miss my guess, history will remember on its honor roll those of you whom the camera brings into focus in this room today, who stood up and were counted when that roll was called that said we are going to preserve at least a part of what God gave us.

Thank you very much.

October 22, 1965

KENNETH E. BOULDING

The economist Kenneth Boulding (1910–1993) once essayed this bit of doggerel, in his 1969 "Ballad of Ecological Awareness":

> One principle that is an ecological upsetter
> Is that if anything is good, then more of it is better,
> And this misunderstanding sets us very, very wrong,
> For no relation in the world is linear for long.

It encompasses his fundamental argument, one that in the end may be a far more radical challenge to the orthodoxies of neoclassical economic theory than the failed Marxist experiments of the 20th century. Economists were used to treating environmental damage as an "externality" and assuming that growth would forever create more solutions than problems. Boulding's work—followed by a number of other brave dissenters like Herman Daly and Robert Costanza—seems more prophetic with each passing year, as accelerating growth seems to be leading us straight into an ever warmer world.

from **The Economics of the Coming Spaceship Earth**

The closed earth of the future requires economic principles which are somewhat different from those of the open earth of the past. For the sake of picturesqueness, I am tempted to call the open economy the "cowboy economy," the cowboy being symbolic of the illimitable plains and also associated with reckless, exploitative, romantic, and violent behavior, which is characteristic of open societies. The closed economy of the future might similarly be called the "spaceman" economy, in which the earth has become a single spaceship, without unlimited reservoirs of anything, either for extraction or for pollution, and in which, therefore, man must find his place in a cyclical ecological system which is capable of continuous reproduction of material form even though it cannot escape having inputs of energy. The difference between the two types of economy becomes most apparent in the attitude towards consumption. In the cowboy economy, consumption is regarded as a good thing and production likewise; and the success of the economy is measured by the amount of the throughput from the "factors of production," a part of which, at any rate, is extracted from the reservoirs of raw materials and noneconomic objects, and another part of which is output into the reservoirs of pollution. If there are infinite reservoirs from which material can be obtained and into which effluvia can be deposited, then the throughput is at least a plausible measure of the success of the economy. The gross national product is a rough measure of this total throughput. It should be possible, however, to distinguish that part of the GNP which is derived from exhaustible and that which is derived from reproducible resources, as well as that part of consumption which represents effluvia and that which represents input into the productive system again. Nobody, as far as I know, has ever attempted to break down the GNP in this way, although it would be an interesting and extremely important exercise, which is unfortunately beyond the scope of this paper.

By contrast, in the spaceman economy, throughput is by no means a desideratum, and is indeed to be regarded as something to be minimized rather than maximized. The essential measure of the success of the economy is not production and consumption at all, but the nature, extent, quality, and complexity of the total capital stock, including in this the state of the human bodies and minds included in the system. In the spaceman economy, what we are primarily concerned with is stock maintenance, and any technological change which results in the maintenance of a given total stock with a lessened throughput (that is, less production and consumption) is clearly a gain. This idea that both production and consumption are bad things rather than good things is very strange to economists, who have been obsessed with the income-flow concepts to the exclusion, almost, of capital-stock concepts.

There are actually some very tricky and unsolved problems involved in the questions as to whether human welfare or well-being is to be regarded as a stock or a flow. Something of both these elements seems actually to be involved in it, and as far as I know there have been practically no studies directed towards identifying these two dimensions of human satisfaction. Is it, for instance, eating that is a good thing, or is it being well fed? Does economic welfare involve having nice clothes, fine houses, good equipment, and so on, or is it to be measured by the depreciation and the wearing out of these things? I am inclined myself to regard the stock concept as most fundamental, that is, to think of being well fed as more important than eating, and to think even of so-called services as essentially involving the restoration of a depleting psychic capital. Thus I have argued that we go to a concert in order to restore a psychic condition which might be called "just having gone to a concert," which, once established, tends to depreciate. When it depreciates beyond a certain point, we go to another concert in order to restore it. If it depreciates rapidly, we go to a lot of concerts; if it depreciates slowly, we go to few. On this view, similarly, we eat primarily to restore bodily homeostasis, that is, to maintain a condition of being well fed, and so on. On this view, there is nothing desirable in consumption at all. The less consumption we can maintain a given state with, the better off we are. If we had clothes that did not wear out, houses that did not depreciate, and even if we could maintain our bodily condition without eating, we would clearly be much better off.

It is this last consideration, perhaps, which makes one pause. Would we, for instance, really want an operation that would enable us to restore all our bodily tissues by intravenous feeding while we slept? Is there not, that is to say, a certain virtue in throughput itself, in activity itself, in production and consumption itself, in raising food and in eating it? It would certainly be rash to exclude this possibility. Further interesting problems are raised by the demand for variety. We certainly do not want a constant state to be maintained; we want fluctuations in the state. Otherwise there would be no demand for variety in food, for variety in scene, as in travel, for variety in social contact, and so on.

The demand for variety can, of course, be costly, and sometimes it seems to be too costly to be tolerated or at least legitimated, as in the case of marital partners, where the maintenance of a homeostatic state in the family is usually regarded as much more desirable than the variety and excessive throughput of the libertine. There are problems here which the economics profession has neglected with astonishing single-mindedness. My own attempts to call attention to some of them, for instance, in two articles,* as far as I can judge, produced no response whatever; and economists continue to think and act as if production, consumption, throughput, and the GNP were the sufficient and adequate measure of economic success.

It may be said, of course, why worry about all this when the space-man economy is still a good way off (at least beyond the lifetimes of any now living), so let us eat, drink, spend, extract and pollute, and be as merry as we can, and let posterity worry about the spaceship earth. It is always a little hard to find a convincing answer to the man who says, "What has posterity ever done for me?" and the conservationist has always had to fall back on rather vague ethical principles postulating identity of the individual with some human community or society which extends not only back into the past but forward into the future. Unless the individual identifies with some community of this kind, conservation is obviously "irrational." Why should we not maximize the welfare of this generation at the cost of posterity? "*Après nous, le déluge*" has been the motto of not insignificant numbers of human societies. The only answer to this, as far as I can see, is to point out that the welfare of the individual depends on the extent to which he can identify himself with others, and that the most satisfactory individual identity is that which identifies not only with a community in space but also with a community extending over time from the past into the future. If this kind of identity is recognized as desirable, then posterity has a voice, even if it does not have a vote; and in a sense, if its voice can influence

---

*K. E. Boulding, "The Consumption Concept in Economic Theory," *American Economic Review*, 35:2 (May 1945), pp. 1–14; and "Income or Welfare?," *Review of Economic Studies*, 17 (1949–50), pp. 77–86.

votes, it has votes too. This whole problem is linked up with the much larger one of the determinants of the morale, legitimacy, and "nerve" of a society, and there is a great deal of historical evidence to suggest that a society which loses its identity with posterity and which loses its positive image of the future loses also its capacity to deal with present problems, and soon falls apart.[*]

Even if we concede that posterity is relevant to our present problems, we still face the question of time-discounting and the closely related question of uncertainty-discounting. It is a well-known phenomenon that individuals discount the future, even in their own lives. The very existence of a positive rate of interest may be taken as at least strong supporting evidence of this hypothesis. If we discount our own future, it is certainly not unreasonable to discount posterity's future even more, even if we do give posterity a vote. If we discount this at 5 per cent per annum, posterity's vote or dollar halves every fourteen years as we look into the future, and after even a mere hundred years it is pretty small—only about $1\frac{1}{2}$ cents on the dollar. If we add another 5 per cent for uncertainty, even the vote of our grandchildren reduces almost to insignificance. We can argue, of course, that the ethical thing to do is not to discount the future at all, that time-discounting is mainly the result of myopia and perspective, and hence is an illusion which the moral man should not tolerate. It is a very popular illusion, however, and one that must certainly be taken into consideration in the formulation of policies. It explains, perhaps, why conservationist policies almost have to be sold under some other excuse which seems more urgent, and why, indeed, necessities which are visualized as urgent, such as defense, always seem to hold priority over those which involve the future.

All these considerations add some credence to the point of view which says that we should not worry about the spaceman economy at all, and that we should just go on increasing the GNP and indeed the gross world product, or GWP, in the expectation that the problems of the future can be left to the future, that when scarcities arise, whether

[*]Fred L. Polak, *The Image of the Future*, Vols. I and II, translated by Elise Boulding (New York: Sythoff, Leyden and Oceana, 1961).

this is of raw materials or of pollutable reservoirs, the needs of the then present will determine the solutions of the then present, and there is no use giving ourselves ulcers by worrying about problems that we really do not have to solve. There is even high ethical authority for this point of view in the New Testament, which advocates that we should take no thought for tomorrow and let the dead bury their dead. There has always been something rather refreshing in the view that we should live like the birds, and perhaps posterity is for the birds in more senses than one; so perhaps we should all call it a day and go out and pollute something cheerfully. As an old taker of thought for the morrow, however, I cannot quite accept this solution; and I would argue, furthermore, that tomorrow is not only very close, but in many respects it is already here. The shadow of the future spaceship, indeed, is already falling over our spendthrift merriment. Oddly enough, it seems to be in pollution rather than in exhaustion that the problem is first becoming salient. Los Angeles has run out of air, Lake Erie has become a cesspool, the oceans are getting full of lead and DDT, and the atmosphere may become man's major problem in another generation, at the rate at which we are filling it up with gunk. It is, of course, true that at least on a microscale, things have been worse at times in the past. The cities of today, with all their foul air and polluted waterways, are probably not as bad as the filthy cities of the pretechnical age. Nevertheless, that fouling of the nest which has been typical of man's activity in the past on a local scale now seems to be extending to the whole world society; and one certainly cannot view with equanimity the present rate of pollution of any of the natural reservoirs, whether the atmosphere, the lakes, or even the oceans.

Environmental Quality in a Growing Economy (1966)

Lynn White Jr. (1907–1987) had a long career as a professor of medieval history at Princeton, Stanford, and UCLA, but he is remembered for this one article, published in 1967 as debates about ecology were reaching full volume. In it he posits that the seeds of environmental destruction lie in the Christian worldview: that man should hold dominion over nature, and that man, formed in God's image, is different from and superior to all else. His essay provoked storms of controversy, but it also prompted many Christians over the next few decades to develop an increasingly resonant environmental theology. White's call at the end of the essay for a more "Franciscan" ethic among Christians is beginning to be answered: in 2006, many of the nation's leading evangelicals broke with the Bush administration over global warming and urged swift action, on the grounds that God calls us to be good stewards of the creation.

from *The Historical Roots of Our Ecologic Crisis*

Until recently, agriculture has been the chief occupation even in "advanced" societies; hence, any change in methods of tillage has much importance. Early plows, drawn by two oxen, did not normally turn the sod but merely scratched it. Thus, cross-plowing was needed and fields tended to be squarish. In the fairly light soils and semiarid climates of the Near East and Mediterranean, this worked well. But such a plow was inappropriate to the wet climate and often sticky soils of northern Europe. By the latter part of the 7th century after Christ, however, following obscure beginnings, certain northern peasants were using an entirely new kind of plow, equipped with a vertical knife to cut the line of the furrow, a horizontal share to slice under the sod, and a moldboard to turn it over. The friction of this plow with the soil was so great that it normally required not two but eight oxen. It attacked the land with such violence that cross-plowing was not needed, and fields tended to be shaped in long strips.

In the days of the scratch-plow, fields were distributed generally in units capable of supporting a single family. Subsistence farming was the presupposition. But no peasant owned eight oxen: to use the new and more efficient plow, peasants pooled their oxen to form large plow-teams, originally receiving (it would appear) plowed strips in proportion to their contribution. Thus, distribution of land was based no longer on the needs of a family but, rather, on the capacity of a power machine to till the earth. Man's relation to the soil was profoundly changed. Formerly man had been part of nature; now he was the exploiter of nature. Nowhere else in the world did farmers develop any analogous agricultural implement. Is it coincidence that modern technology, with its ruthlessness toward nature, has so largely been produced by descendants of these peasants of northern Europe?

This same exploitive attitude appears slightly before A.D. 830 in Western illustrated calendars. In older calendars the months were shown as passive personifications. The new Frankish calendars, which set the style for the Middle Ages, are very different: they show men coercing the world around them—plowing, harvesting, chopping trees, butchering pigs. Man and nature are two things, and man is master.

These novelties seem to be in harmony with larger intellectual patterns. What people do about their ecology depends on what they think about themselves in relation to things around them. Human ecology is deeply conditioned by beliefs about our nature and destiny—that is, by religion. To Western eyes this is very evident in, say, India or Ceylon. It is equally true of ourselves and of our medieval ancestors.

The victory of Christianity over paganism was the greatest psychic revolution in the history of our culture. It has become fashionable today to say that, for better or worse, we live in "the post-Christian age." Certainly the forms of our thinking and language have largely ceased to be Christian, but to my eye the substance often remains amazingly akin to that of the past. Our daily habits of action, for example, are dominated by an implicit faith in perpetual progress which was unknown either to Greco-Roman antiquity or to the Orient. It is rooted in, and is indefensible apart from, Judeo-Christian teleology. The fact that Communists share it merely helps to show what can be demonstrated on many other grounds: that Marxism, like Islam, is a Judeo-Christian heresy. We continue today to live, as we have lived for about 1700 years, very largely in a context of Christian axioms.

What did Christianity tell people about their relations with the environment?

While many of the world's mythologies provide stories of creation, Greco-Roman mythology was singularly incoherent in this respect. Like Aristotle, the intellectuals of the ancient West denied that the visible world had had a beginning. Indeed, the idea of a beginning was impossible in the framework of their cyclical notion of time. In sharp contrast, Christianity inherited from Judaism not only a concept of time as nonrepetitive and linear but also a striking story of creation. By gradual stages a loving and all-powerful God had created light and darkness, the heavenly bodies, the earth and all its plants, animals, birds, and fishes. Finally, God had created Adam and, as an afterthought, Eve to keep man from being lonely. Man named all the animals, thus establishing his dominance over them. God planned all of this explicitly for man's benefit and rule: no item in the physical creation had any purpose save to serve man's purposes. And, although man's body is made of clay, he is not simply part of nature: he is made in God's image.

Especially in its Western form, Christianity is the most anthropocentric religion the world has seen. As early as the 2nd century both Tertullian and Saint Irenaeus of Lyons were insisting that when God shaped Adam he was foreshadowing the image of the incarnate Christ, the Second Adam. Man shares, in great measure, God's transcendence of nature. Christianity, in absolute contrast to ancient paganism and Asia's religions (except, perhaps, Zoroastrianism), not only established a dualism of man and nature but also insisted that it is God's will that man exploit nature for his proper ends.

At the level of the common people this worked out in an interesting way. In Antiquity every tree, every spring, every stream, every hill had its own *genius loci*, its guardian spirit. These spirits were accessible to men, but were very unlike men; centaurs, fauns, and mermaids show their ambivalence. Before one cut a tree, mined a mountain, or dammed a brook, it was important to placate the spirit in charge of that particular situation, and to keep it placated. By destroying pagan animism, Christianity made it possible to exploit nature in a mood of indifference to the feelings of natural objects.

It is often said that for animism the Church substituted the cult of saints. True; but the cult of saints is functionally quite different from animism. The saint is not *in* natural objects; he may have special shrines, but his citizenship is in heaven. Moreover, a saint is entirely a man; he can be approached in human terms. In addition to saints, Christianity of course also had angels and demons inherited from Judaism and perhaps, at one remove, from Zoroastrianism. But these were all as mobile as the saints themselves. The spirits *in* natural objects, which formerly had protected nature from man, evaporated. Man's effective monopoly on spirit in this world was confirmed, and the old inhibitions to the exploitation of nature crumbled.

When one speaks in such sweeping terms, a note of caution is in order. Christianity is a complex faith, and its consequences differ in differing contexts. What I have said may well apply to the medieval West, where in fact technology made spectacular advances. But the Greek East, a highly civilized realm of equal Christian devotion, seems to have produced no marked technological innovation after the late 7th century, when Greek fire was invented. The key to the contrast may perhaps be found in a difference in the tonality of piety and thought which students of comparative theology find between the Greek and the Latin Churches. The Greeks believed that sin was intellectual blindness, and that salvation was found in illumination, orthodoxy—that is, clear thinking. The Latins, on the other hand, felt that sin was moral evil, and that salvation was to be found in right conduct. Eastern theology has been intellectualist. Western theology has been voluntarist. The Greek saint contemplates; the Western saint acts. The implications of Christianity for the conquest of nature would emerge more easily in the Western atmosphere.

The Christian dogma of creation, which is found in the first clause of all the Creeds, has another meaning for our comprehension of today's ecologic crisis. By revelation, God had given man the Bible, the Book of Scripture. But since God had made nature, nature also must reveal the divine mentality. The religious study of nature for the better understanding of God was known as natural theology. In the early Church, and always in the Greek East, nature was conceived primarily as a symbolic system through which God speaks to men: the ant is a sermon to sluggards; rising flames are the symbol of the soul's aspiration. This view of nature was essentially artistic rather than scientific. While Byzantium preserved and copied great numbers of ancient Greek scientific texts, science as we conceive it could scarcely flourish in such an ambience.

However, in the Latin West by the early 13th century natural theology was following a very different bent. It was ceasing to be the decoding of the physical symbols of God's communication with man and was becoming the effort to understand God's mind by discovering how his creation operates. The rainbow was no longer simply a symbol of hope first sent to Noah after the Deluge: Robert Grosseteste, Friar Roger Bacon, and Theodoric of Freiberg produced startlingly sophisticated work on the optics of the rainbow, but they did it as a venture in religious understanding. From the 13th century onward, up to and including Leibnitz and Newton, every major scientist, in effect, explained his motivations in religious terms. Indeed, if Galileo had not been so expert an amateur theologian he would have got into far less trouble: the professionals resented his intrusion. And Newton seems to have regarded himself more as a theologian than as a scientist. It was not until the late 18th century that the hypothesis of God became unnecessary to many scientists.

It is often hard for the historian to judge, when men explain why they are doing what they want to do, whether they are offering real reasons or merely culturally acceptable reasons. The consistency with which scientists during the long formative centuries of Western science said that the task and the reward of the scientist was "to think God's thoughts after him" leads one to believe that this was their real motivation. If so, then modern Western science was cast in a matrix of Christian theology. The dynamism of religious devotion, shaped by the Judeo-Christian dogma of creation, gave it impetus.

We would seem to be headed toward conclusions unpalatable to many Christians. Since both *science* and *technology* are blessed words in our contemporary vocabulary, some may be happy at the notions, first, that, viewed historically, modern science is an extrapolation of natural theology and, second, that modern technology is at least partly to be explained as an Occidental, voluntarist realization of the Christian dogma of man's transcendence of, and rightful mastery over, nature. But, as we now recognize, somewhat over a century ago science and technology—hitherto quite separate activities—joined to give mankind powers which, to judge by many of the ecologic effects, are out of control. If so, Christianity bears a huge burden of guilt.

I personally doubt that disastrous ecologic backlash can be avoided simply by applying to our problems more science and more technology. Our science and technology have grown out of Christian attitudes toward man's relation to nature which are almost universally held not only by Christians and neo-Christians but also by those who fondly regard themselves as post-Christians. Despite Copernicus, all the cosmos rotates around our little globe. Despite Darwin, we are *not*, in our hearts, part of the natural process. We are superior to nature, contemptuous of it, willing to use it for our slightest whim. The newly elected Governor of California, like myself a churchman but less troubled than I, spoke for the Christian tradition when he said (as is alleged), "when you've seen one redwood tree, you've seen them all." To a Christian a tree can be no more than a physical fact. The whole concept of the sacred grove is alien to Christianity and to the ethos of the West. For nearly 2 millennia Christian missionaries have been chopping down sacred groves, which are idolatrous because they assume spirit in nature.

What we do about ecology depends on our ideas of the man-nature relationship. More science and more technology are not going to get us out of the present ecologic crisis until we find a new religion, or rethink our old one. The beatniks, who are the basic revolutionaries of our time, show a sound instinct in their affinity for Zen Buddhism, which conceives of the man-nature relationship as very nearly the mirror image of the Christian view. Zen, however, is as deeply conditioned by Asian history as Christianity is by the experience of the West, and I am dubious of its viability among us.

Possibly we should ponder the greatest radical in Christian history since Christ: Saint Francis of Assisi. The prime miracle of Saint Francis is the fact that he did not end at the stake, as many of his left-wing followers did. He was so clearly heretical that a General of the Franciscan Order, Saint Bonaventura, a great and perceptive Christian, tried to suppress the early accounts of Franciscanism. The key to an understanding of Francis is his belief in the virtue of humility—not merely for the individual but for man as a species. Francis tried to depose man from his monarchy over creation and set up a democracy of all God's creatures. With him the ant is no longer simply a homily for the lazy, flames a sign of the thrust of the soul toward union with God; now they are Brother Ant and Sister Fire, praising the Creator in their own ways as Brother Man does in his.

Later commentators have said that Francis preached to the birds as a rebuke to men who would not listen. The records do not read so: he urged the little birds to praise God, and in spiritual ecstasy they flapped their wings and chirped rejoicing. Legends of saints, especially the Irish saints, had long told of their dealings with animals but always, I believe, to show their human dominance over creatures. With Francis it is different. The land around Gubbio in the Apennines was being ravaged by a fierce wolf. Saint Francis, says the legend, talked to the wolf and persuaded him of the error of his ways. The wolf repented, died in the odor of sanctity, and was buried in consecrated ground.

What Sir Steven Runciman calls "the Franciscan doctrine of the animal soul" was quickly stamped out. Quite possibly it was in part inspired, consciously or unconsciously, by the belief in reincarnation held by the Cathar heretics who at that time teemed in Italy and southern France, and who presumably had got it originally from India. It is significant that at just the same moment, about 1200, traces of metempsychosis are found also in western Judaism, in the Provençal *Cabbala*. But

Francis held neither to transmigration of souls nor to pantheism. His view of nature and of man rested on a unique sort of pan-psychism of all things animate and inanimate, designed for the glorification of their transcendent Creator, who, in the ultimate gesture of cosmic humility, assumed flesh, lay helpless in a manger, and hung dying on a scaffold.

I am not suggesting that many contemporary Americans who are concerned about our ecologic crisis will be either able or willing to counsel with wolves or exhort birds. However, the present increasing disruption of the global environment is the product of a dynamic technology and science which were originating in the Western medieval world against which Saint Francis was rebelling in so original a way. Their growth cannot be understood historically apart from distinctive attitudes toward nature which are deeply grounded in Christian dogma. The fact that most people do not think of these attitudes as Christian is irrelevant. No new set of basic values has been accepted in our society to displace those of Christianity. Hence we shall continue to have a worsening ecologic crisis until we reject the Christian axiom that nature has no reason for existence save to serve man.

The greatest spiritual revolutionary in Western history, Saint Francis, proposed what he thought was an alternative Christian view of nature and man's relation to it: he tried to substitute the idea of the equality of all creatures, including man, for the idea of man's limitless rule of creation. He failed. Both our present science and our present technology are so tinctured with orthodox Christian arrogance toward nature that no solution for our ecologic crisis can be expected from them alone. Since the roots of our trouble are so largely religious, the remedy must also be essentially religious, whether we call it that or not. We must rethink and refeel our nature and destiny. The profoundly religious, but heretical, sense of the primitive Franciscans for the spiritual autonomy of all parts of nature may point a direction. I propose Francis as a patron saint for ecologists.

Science, March 10, 1967

The observant reader may have noticed a lack of poke-in-the-ribs humor in this collection. Environmentalists tend toward the somber, mostly for the same reason as morticians. But Ed Abbey (1927–1989) was the marvelous exception, a master of anarchy and irreverence and one of the funniest writers America has produced since Mark Twain. I remember a day spent touring his beloved Arches National Monument in the backcountry near Moab, Utah. Because he refused to let me pay tribute in the form of a $5 admission fee to the park rangers at the gate, we instead drove for miles, took down a fence, and forced my rental car through a series of improbable rutted washes to reach our goal, cackling the whole way. Exploits like this, but involving dynamite, make his *The Monkey Wrench Gang* (1975) surely the greatest environmental action novel—and helped give birth to the radical green group Earth First! But his good cheer, calculated crudity, and pointed political incorrectness may mask for some readers the seriousness of his project: in *Desert Solitaire* (1968), a book which may last a very long time, he describes a summer in the ranger cabin in that red rock desert country. His hope, he says at the start, is to "confront, immediately and directly if it's possible, the bare bones of existence, the elemental and fundamental, the bedrock which sustains us. I want to be able to look at and into a juniper tree, a piece of quartz, a vulture, a spider, and see it as it is in itself, devoid of all humanly ascribed qualities." If you're venturing into the uncharted territory beyond anthropocentrism, it's good to have someone as human as Abbey for a guide.

Polemic: Industrial Tourism and the National Parks

I like my job. The pay is generous; I might even say munificent: $1.95 per hour, earned or not, backed solidly by the world's most powerful

Air Force, biggest national debt, and grossest national product. The fringe benefits are priceless: clean air to breathe (after the spring sandstorms); stillness, solitude and space; an unobstructed view every day and every night of sun, sky, stars, clouds, mountains, moon, cliffrock and canyons; a sense of time enough to let thought and feeling range from here to the end of the world and back; the discovery of something intimate—though impossible to name—in the remote.

The work is simple and requires almost no mental effort, a good thing in more ways than one. What little thinking I do is my own and I do it on government time. Insofar as I follow a schedule it goes about like this:

For me the work week begins on Thursday, which I usually spend in patrolling the roads and walking out the trails. On Friday I inspect the campgrounds, haul firewood, and distribute the toilet paper. Saturday and Sunday are my busy days as I deal with the influx of weekend visitors and campers, answering questions, pulling cars out of the sand, lowering children down off the rocks, tracking lost grandfathers and investigating picnics. My Saturday night campfire talks are brief and to the point. "Everything all right?" I say, badge and all, ambling up to what looks like a cheerful group. "Fine," they'll say; "how about a drink?" "Why not?" I say.

By Sunday evening most everyone has gone home and the heavy duty is over. Thank God it's Monday, I say to myself the next morning. Mondays are very nice. I empty the garbage cans, read the discarded newspapers, sweep out the outhouses and disengage the Kleenex from the clutches of cliffrose and cactus. In the afternoon I watch the clouds drift past the bald peak of Mount Tukuhnikivats. (*Someone* has to do it.)

Tuesday and Wednesday I rest. Those are my days off and I usually set aside Wednesday evening for a trip to Moab, replenishing my supplies and establishing a little human contact more vital than that possible with the tourists I meet on the job. After a week in the desert, Moab (pop. 5500, during the great uranium boom), seems like a dazzling metropolis, a throbbing dynamo of commerce and pleasure. I walk the single main street as dazed by the noise and neon as a country boy on his first visit to Times Square. (Wow, I'm thinking, this is great.)

After a visit to Miller's Supermarket, where I stock up on pinto beans and other necessities, I am free to visit the beer joints. All of them are busy, crowded with prospectors, miners, geologists, cowboys, truckdrivers and sheepherders, and the talk is loud, vigorous, blue with blasphemy. Although differences of opinion have been known to occur, open violence is rare, for these men treat one another with courtesy and respect. The general atmosphere is free and friendly, quite unlike the sad, sour gloom of most bars I have known, where nervous men in tight collars brood over their drinks between out-of-tune TV screens and a remorseless clock. Why the difference?

I have considered the question and come up with the following solution:

1. These prospectors, miners, etc. have most of them been physically active all day out-of-doors at a mile or more above sea level; they are comfortably tired and relaxed.

2. Most of them have been working alone; the presence of a jostling crowd is therefore not a familiar irritation to be borne with resignation but rather an unaccustomed pleasure to be enjoyed.

3. Most of them are making good wages and/or doing work they like to do; they are, you might say, happy. (The boom will not last, of course, but this is forgotten. And the ethical and political implications of uranium exploitation are simply unknown in these parts.)

4. The nature of their work requires a combination of skills and knowledge, good health and self-reliance, which tends to inspire self-confidence; they need not doubt their manhood. (Again, everything is subject to change.)

5. Finally, Moab is a Mormon town with funny ways. Hard booze is not sold across the bar except in the semiprivate "clubs." Nor even standard beer. These hard-drinking fellows whom I wish to praise are trying to get drunk on three-point-two! They rise somewhat heavily from their chairs and barstools and tramp, with frequency and a squelchy, sodden noise, toward the pissoirs at the back of the room, more waterlogged than intoxicated.

In the end the beer halls of Moab, like all others, become to me depressing places. After a few games of rotation pool with my friend

Viviano Jacquez, a reformed sheepherder turned dude wrangler (a dubious reform), I am glad to leave the last of those smoky dens around midnight and to climb into my pickup and take the long drive north and east back to the silent rock, the unbounded space and the sweet clean air of my outpost in the Arches.

Yes, it's a good job. On the rare occasions when I peer into the future for more than a few days I can foresee myself returning here for season after season, year after year, indefinitely. And why not? What better sinecure could a man with small needs, infinite desires, and philosophic pretensions ask for? The better part of each year in the wilderness and the winters in some complementary, equally agreeable environment—Hoboken perhaps, or Tiajuana, Nogales, Juarez . . . one of the border towns. Maybe Tonopah, a good tough Nevada mining town with legal prostitution, or possibly Oakland or even New Orleans—some place grimy, cheap (since I'd be living on unemployment insurance), decayed, hopelessly corrupt. I idle away hours dreaming of the wonderful winter to come, of the chocolate-colored mistress I'll have to rub my back, the journal spread open between two tall candles in massive silver candlesticks, the scrambled eggs with green chile, the crock of homebrew fermenting quietly in the corner, etc., the nights of desperate laughter with brave young comrades, burning billboards, and defacing public institutions. . . . Romantic dreams, romantic dreams.

For there is a cloud on my horizon. A small dark cloud no bigger than my hand. Its name is Progress.

The ease and relative freedom of this lovely job at Arches follow from the comparative absence of the motorized tourists, who stay away by the millions. And they stay away because of the unpaved entrance road, the unflushable toilets in the campgrounds, and the fact that most of them have never even heard of Arches National Monument. (Could there be a more genuine testimonial to its beauty and integrity?) All this must change.

I'd been warned. On the very first day Merle and Floyd had mentioned something about developments, improvements, a sinister Master Plan. Thinking that *they* were the dreamers, I paid little heed and had soon forgotten the whole ridiculous business. But only a few days ago something happened which shook me out of my pleasant apathy.

I was sitting out back on my 33,000-acre terrace, shoeless and shirtless, scratching my toes in the sand and sipping on a tall iced drink, watching the flow of evening over the desert. Prime time: the sun very low in the west, the birds coming back to life, the shadows rolling for miles over rock and sand to the very base of the brilliant mountains. I had a small fire going near the table—not for heat or light but for the fragrance of the juniper and the ritual appeal of the clear flames. For symbolic reasons. For ceremony. When I heard a faint sound over my shoulder I looked and saw a file of deer watching from fifty yards away, three does and a velvet-horned buck, all dark against the sundown sky. They began to move. I whistled and they stopped again, staring at me. "Come on over," I said, "have a drink." They declined, moving off with casual, unhurried grace, quiet as phantoms, and disappeared beyond the rise. Smiling, thoroughly at peace, I turned back to my drink, the little fire, the subtle transformations of the immense landscape before me. On the program: rise of the full moon.

It was then I heard the discordant note, the snarling whine of a jeep in low range and four-wheel-drive, coming from an unexpected direction, from the vicinity of the old foot and horse trail that leads from Balanced Rock down toward Courthouse Wash and on to park headquarters near Moab. The jeep came in sight from beyond some bluffs, turned onto the dirt road, and came up the hill toward the entrance station. Now operating a motor vehicle of any kind on the trails of a national park is strictly forbidden, a nasty bureaucratic regulation which I heartily support. My bosom swelled with the righteous indignation of a cop: by God, I thought, I'm going to write these sons of bitches a ticket. I put down the drink and strode to the housetrailer to get my badge.

Long before I could find the shirt with the badge on it, however, or the ticket book, or my shoes or my park ranger hat, the jeep turned in at my driveway and came right up to the door of the trailer. It was a gray jeep with a U.S. Government decal on the side—Bureau of Public Roads—and covered with dust. Two empty water bags flapped at the bumper. Inside were three sunburned men in twill britches and engineering boots, and a pile of equipment: transit case, tripod, survey rod, bundles of wooden stakes. (*Oh no!*) The men got out, dripping with dust, and the driver grinned at me, pointing to his parched open mouth and making horrible gasping noises deep in his throat.

"Okay," I said, "come on in."

It was even hotter inside the trailer than outside but I opened the refrigerator and left it open and took out a pitcher filled with ice cubes and water. As they passed the pitcher back and forth I got the full and terrible story, confirming the worst of my fears. They were a survey crew, laying out a new road into the Arches.

And when would the road be built? Nobody knew for sure; perhaps in a couple of years, depending on when the Park Service would be able to get the money. The new road—to be paved, of course—would cost somewhere between half a million and one million dollars, depending on the bids, or more than fifty thousand dollars per linear mile. At least enough to pay the salaries of ten park rangers for ten years. Too much money, I suggested—they'll never go for it back in Washington.

The three men thought that was pretty funny. Don't worry, they said, this road will be built. I'm worried, I said. Look, the party chief explained, you *need* this road. He was a pleasant-mannered, soft-spoken civil engineer with an unquestioning dedication to his work. A very dangerous man. Who *needs* it? I said; we get very few tourists in this park. That's why you need it, the engineer explained patiently; look, he said, when this road is built you'll get ten, twenty, thirty times as many tourists in here as you get now. His men nodded in solemn agreement, and he stared at me intently, waiting to see what possible answer I could have to that.

"Have some more water," I said. I had an answer all right but I was saving it for later. I knew that I was dealing with a madman.

As I type these words, several years after the little episode of the gray jeep and the thirsty engineers, all that was foretold has come to pass. Arches National Monument has been developed. The Master Plan has been fulfilled. Where once a few adventurous people came on weekends to camp for a night or two and enjoy a taste of the primitive and remote, you will now find serpentine streams of baroque automobiles pouring in and out, all through the spring and summer, in numbers that would have seemed fantastic when I worked there: from 3,000 to 30,000 to 300,000 per year, the "visitation," as they call it, mounts ever upward. The little campgrounds where I used to putter around reading three-day-old newspapers full of lies and watermelon seeds have now been consolidated into one master campground that looks, during the busy season, like a suburban village: elaborate housetrailers of quilted aluminum crowd upon gigantic camper-trucks of Fiberglas and molded plastic; through their windows you will see the blue glow of television and hear the studio laughter of Los Angeles; knobby-kneed oldsters in plaid Bermudas buzz up and down the quaintly curving asphalt road on motorbikes; quarrels break out between campsite neighbors while others gather around their burning charcoal briquettes (ground campfires no longer permitted—not enough wood) to compare electric toothbrushes. The Comfort Stations are there, too, all lit up with electricity, fully equipped inside, though the generator breaks down now and then and the lights go out, or the sewage backs up in the plumbing system (drain fields were laid out in sand over a solid bed of sandstone), and the water supply sometimes fails, since the 3000-foot well can only produce about 5gpm—not always enough to meet the demand. Down at the beginning of the new road, at park headquarters, is the new entrance station and visitor center, where admission fees are collected and where the rangers are going quietly nuts answering the same three basic questions five hundred times a day: (1) Where's the john? (2) How long's it take to see this place? (3) Where's the Coke machine?

Progress has come at last to the Arches, after a million years of neglect. Industrial Tourism has arrived.

What happened to Arches Natural Money-mint is, of course, an old story in the Park Service. All the famous national parks have the same problems on a far grander scale, as everyone knows, and many other problems as yet unknown to a little subordinate unit of the system in a backward part of southeastern Utah. And the same kind of development that has so transformed Arches is under way, planned or completed in many more national parks and national monuments. I will mention only a few examples with which I am personally familiar:

The newly established Canyonlands National Park. Most of the major points of interest in this park are presently accessible, over passable dirt roads, by car—Grandview Point, Upheaval Dome, part of the White Rim, Cave Spring, Squaw Spring campground and Elephant Hill. The more difficult places, such as Angel Arch or Druid Arch, can be reached by jeep, on horseback or in a one- or two-day hike. Nevertheless the Park Service had drawn up the usual Master Plan calling for modern paved highways to most of the places named and some not named.

Grand Canyon National Park. Most of the south rim of this park is now closely followed by a conventional high-speed highway and interrupted at numerous places by large asphalt parking lots. It is no longer easy, on the South Rim, to get away from the roar of motor traffic, except by descending into the canyon.

Navajo National Monument. A small, fragile, hidden place containing two of the most beautiful cliff dwellings in the Southwest—Keet Seel and Betatakin. This park will be difficult to protect under heavy visitation, and for years it was understood that it would be preserved in a primitive way so as to screen out those tourists unwilling to drive their cars over some twenty miles of dirt road. No longer so: the road has been paved, the campground enlarged and "modernized," and the old magic destroyed.

Natural Bridges National Monument. Another small gem in the park system, a group of three adjacent natural bridges tucked away in the canyon country of southern Utah. Formerly you could drive your car (over dirt roads, of course) to within sight of and easy walking distance—a hundred yards?—of the most spectacular of the three bridges. From there it was only a few hours walking time to the other two. All three could easily be seen in a single day. But this was not good enough for the developers. They have now constructed a paved road into the heart of the area, *between* the two biggest bridges.

Zion National Park. The northwestern part of this park, known as the Kolob area, has until recently been saved as almost virgin wilderness. But a broad highway, with banked curves, deep cuts and heavy fills, that will invade this splendid region, is already under construction.

Capitol Reef National Monument. Grand and colorful scenery in a rugged land—south-central Utah. The most beautiful portion of the park was the canyon of the Fremont River, a great place for hiking, camping, exploring. And what did the authorities do? They built a state highway through it.

Lee's Ferry. Until a few years ago a simple, quiet, primitive place on the shores of the Colorado, Lee's Ferry has now fallen under the protection of the Park Service. And who can protect it against the Park Service? Powerlines now bisect the scene; a 100-foot pink water tower looms against the red cliffs; tract-style houses are built to house the "protectors"; natural campsites along the river are closed off while all campers are now herded into an artificial steel-and-asphalt "campground" in the hottest, windiest spot in the area; historic buildings are razed by bulldozers to save the expense of maintaining them while at the same time hundreds of thousands of dollars are spent on an unneeded paved entrance road. And the administrators complain of *vandalism*.

I could easily cite ten more examples of unnecessary or destructive development for every one I've named so far. What has happened in these particular areas, which I chance to know a little and love too much, has happened, is happening, or will soon happen to the majority of our national parks and national forests, despite the illusory protection of the Wilderness Preservation Act, unless a great many citizens rear up on their hind legs and make vigorous political gestures demanding implementation of the Act.

There may be some among the readers of this book, like the earnest engineer, who believe without question that any and all forms of construction and development are intrinsic goods, in the national parks as well as anywhere else, who virtually identify quantity with quality and therefore assume that the greater the quantity of traffic, the higher the value received. There are some who frankly and boldly advocate the eradication of the last remnants of wilderness and the complete subjugation of nature to the requirements of—not man—but industry. This is a courageous view, admirable in its simplicity and power, and with the weight of all modern history behind it. It is also quite insane. I cannot attempt to deal with it here.

There will be other readers, I hope, who share my basic assumption that wilderness is a necessary part of civilization and that it is the primary responsibility of the national park system to preserve *intact and undiminished* what little still remains.

Most readers, while generally sympathetic to this latter point of view, will feel, as do the administrators of the National Park Service, that although wilderness is a fine thing, certain compromises and adjustments are necessary in order to meet the ever-expanding demand for outdoor recreation. It is precisely this question which I would like to examine now.

The Park Service, established by Congress in 1916, was directed not only to administer the parks but also to "provide for the enjoyment of same in such manner and by such means as will leave them unimpaired for the enjoyment of future generations." This appropriately ambiguous language, employed long before the onslaught of the automobile, has been understood in various and often opposing ways ever since. The Park Service, like any other big organization, includes factions and factions. The Developers, the dominant faction, place their emphasis on the words *"provide for the enjoyment."* The Preservers, a minority but also strong, emphasize the words *"leave them unimpaired."* It is apparent, then, that we cannot decide the question of development versus preservation by a simple referral to holy writ or an attempt to guess the intention of the founding fathers; we must make up our own minds and decide for ourselves what the national parks should be and what purpose they should serve.

The first issue that appears when we get into this matter, the most important issue and perhaps the only issue, is the one called *accessibility*. The Developers insist that the parks must be made fully accessible not only to people but also to their machines, that is, to automobiles, motorboats, etc. The Preservers argue, in principle at least, that wilderness and motors are incompatible and that the former can best be experienced, understood, and enjoyed when the machines are left behind where they belong—on the superhighways and in the parking lots, on the reservoirs and in the marinas.

What does accessibility mean? Is there any spot on earth that men have not proved accessible by the simplest means—feet and legs and heart? Even Mt. McKinley, even Everest, have been surmounted by men on foot. (Some of them, incidentally, rank amateurs, to the horror and indignation of the professional mountaineers.) The interior of the Grand Canyon, a fiercely hot and hostile abyss, is visited each summer by thousands and thousands of tourists of the most banal and unadventurous type, many of them on foot—self-propelled, so to speak—and the others on the backs of mules. Thousands climb each summer to the summit of Mt. Whitney, highest point in the forty-eight United States, while multitudes of others wander on foot or on horseback through the ranges of the Sierras, the Rockies, the Big Smokies, the Cascades and the mountains of New England. Still more hundreds and thousands float or paddle each year down the currents of the Salmon, the Snake, the Allagash, the Yampa, the Green, the Rio Grande, the Ozark, the St. Croix and those portions of the Colorado which have not yet been destroyed by the dam builders. And most significant, these hordes of nonmotorized tourists, hungry for a taste of the difficult, the original, the real, do not consist solely of people young and athletic but also of old folks, fat folks, pale-faced office clerks who don't know a rucksack from a haversack, and even children. The one thing they all have in common is the refusal to live always like sardines in a can—they are determined to get outside of their motorcars for at least a few weeks each year.

This being the case, why is the Park Service generally so anxious to accommodate that other crowd, the indolent millions born on wheels and suckled on gasoline, who expect and demand paved highways to lead them in comfort, ease and safety into every nook and corner of the national parks? For the answer to that we must consider the character of what I call Industrial Tourism and the quality of the mechanized tourists—the Wheelchair Explorers—who are at once the consumers, the raw material and the victims of Industrial Tourism.

Industrial Tourism is a big business. It means money. It includes the motel and restaurant owners, the gasoline retailers, the oil corporations, the road-building contractors, the heavy equipment manufacturers, the state and federal engineering agencies and the sovereign, all-powerful automotive industry. These various interests are well organized, command more wealth than most modern nations, and are represented in Congress with a strength far greater than is justified in any constitutional or democratic sense. (Modern politics is expensive— power follows money.) Through Congress the tourism industry can bring enormous pressure to bear upon such a slender reed in the executive branch as the poor old Park Service, a pressure which is also exerted on every other possible level—local, state, regional—and through advertising and the well-established habits of a wasteful nation.

When a new national park, national monument, national seashore, or whatever it may be called is set up, the various forces of Industrial Tourism, on all levels, immediately expect action—meaning specifically a road-building program. Where trails or primitive dirt roads already exist, the Industry expects—it hardly needs to ask—that these be developed into modern paved highways. On the local level, for example, the first thing that the superintendent of a new park can anticipate being asked, when he attends his first meeting of the area's Chamber of Commerce, is not "Will roads be built?" but rather "When does construction begin?" and "Why the delay?"

(The Natural Money-Mint. With supersensitive antennae these operatives from the C. of C. look into red canyons and see only green, stand among flowers snorting out the smell of money, and hear, while thunderstorms rumble over mountains, the fall of a dollar bill on motel carpeting.)

Accustomed to this sort of relentless pressure since its founding, it is little wonder that the Park Service, through a process of natural selection, has tended to evolve a type of administration which, far from resisting such pressure, has usually been more than willing to accommodate it, even to encourage it. Not from any peculiar moral weakness but simply because such well-adapted administrators are themselves believers in a policy of economic development. "Resource management" is the current term. Old foot trails may be neglected, back-country ranger stations left unmanned, and interpretive and protective services inadequately staffed, but the administrators know from long experience that millions for asphalt can always be found; Congress is always willing to appropriate money for more and bigger paved roads, anywhere—particularly if they form loops. Loop drives are extremely popular with the petroleum industry—they bring the motorist right back to the same gas station from which he started.

Great though it is, however, the power of the tourist business would not in itself be sufficient to shape Park Service policy. To all accusations of excessive development the administrators can reply, as they will if pressed hard enough, that they are giving the public what it wants, that their primary duty is to serve the public not preserve the wilds. "Parks are for people" is the public-relations slogan, which decoded means that the parks are for people-in-automobiles. Behind the slogan is the assumption that the majority of Americans, exactly like the managers of the tourist industry, expect and demand to see their national parks from the comfort, security, and convenience of their automobiles.

Is this assumption correct? Perhaps. Does that justify the continued and increasing erosion of the parks? It does not. Which brings me to the final aspect of the problem of Industrial Tourism: the Industrial Tourists themselves.

They work hard, these people. They roll up incredible mileages on their odometers, rack up state after state in two-week transcontinental motor marathons, knock off one national park after another, take millions of square yards of photographs, and endure patiently the most prolonged discomforts: the tedious traffic jams, the awful food of park cafeterias and roadside eateries, the nocturnal search for a place to sleep or camp, the dreary routine of One-Stop Service, the endless lines of creeping traffic, the smell of exhaust fumes, the ever-proliferating Rules & Regulations, the fees and the bills and the service charges, the boiling radiator and the flat tire and the vapor lock, the surly retorts of room clerks and traffic cops, the incessant jostling of the anxious crowds, the irritation and restlessness of their children, the worry of their wives, and the long drive home at night in a stream of racing cars against the lights of another stream racing in the opposite direction, passing now and then the obscure tangle, the shattered glass, the patrolman's lurid blinker light, of one more wreck.

Hard work. And risky. Too much for some, who have given up the struggle on the highways in exchange for an entirely different kind of vacation—out in the open, on their own feet, following the quiet trail through forest and mountains, bedding down at evening under the stars, when and where they feel like it, at a time when the Industrial Tourists are still hunting for a place to park their automobiles.

Industrial Tourism is a threat to the national parks. But the chief victims of the system are the motorized tourists. They are being robbed and robbing themselves. So long as they are unwilling to crawl out of their cars they will not discover the treasures of the national parks and will never escape the stress and turmoil of those urban-suburban complexes which they had hoped, presumably, to leave behind for a while.

How to pry the tourists out of their automobiles, out of their back-breaking upholstered mechanized wheelchairs and onto their feet, onto the strange warmth and solidity of Mother Earth again? This is the problem which the Park Service should confront directly, not evasively, and which it cannot resolve by simply submitting and conforming to the automobile habit. The automobile, which began as a transportation convenience, has become a bloody tyrant (50,000 lives a year), and it is the responsibility of the Park Service, as well as that of everyone else concerned with preserving both wilderness and civilization, to begin a campaign of resistance. The automotive combine has almost succeeded in strangling our cities; we need not let it also destroy our national parks.

It will be objected that a constantly increasing population makes resistance and conservation a hopeless battle. This is true. Unless a way is found to stabilize the nation's population, the parks cannot be saved. Or anything else worth a damn. Wilderness preservation, like a hundred other good causes, will be forgotten under the overwhelming pressure of a struggle for mere survival and sanity in a completely urbanized, completely industrialized, ever more crowded environment. For my own part I would rather take my chances in a thermonuclear war than live in such a world.

Assuming, however, that population growth will be halted at a tolerable level before catastrophe does it for us, it remains permissible to talk about such things as the national parks. Having indulged myself in a number of harsh judgments upon the Park Service, the tourist industry, and the motoring public, I now feel entitled to make some constructive, practical, sensible proposals for the salvation of both parks and people.

(1) No more cars in national parks. Let the people walk. Or ride horses, bicycles, mules, wild pigs—anything—but keep the automobiles and the motorcycles and all their motorized relatives out. We have agreed not to drive our automobiles into cathedrals, concert halls, art museums, legislative assemblies, private bedrooms and the other sanctums of our culture; we should treat our national parks with the same deference, for they, too, are holy places. An increasingly pagan and hedonistic people (thank God!), we are learning finally that the forests and mountains and desert canyons are holier than our churches. Therefore let us behave accordingly.

Consider a concrete example and what could be done with it: Yosemite Valley in Yosemite National Park. At present a dusty milling confusion of motor vehicles and ponderous camping machinery, it could be returned to relative beauty and order by the simple expedient of requiring all visitors, at the park entrance, to lock up their automobiles and continue their tour on the seats of good workable bicycles supplied free of charge by the United States Government.

Let our people travel light and free on their bicycles—nothing on the back but a shirt, nothing tied to the bike but a slicker, in case of rain. Their bedrolls, their backpacks, their tents, their food and cooking kits will be trucked in for them, free of charge, to the campground of their choice in the Valley, by the Park Service. (Why not? The roads will still be there.) Once in the Valley they will find the concessioners waiting, ready to supply whatever needs might have been overlooked, or to furnish rooms and meals for those who don't want to camp out.

The same thing could be done at Grand Canyon or at Yellowstone or at any of our other shrines to the out-of-doors. There is no compelling reason, for example, why tourists need to drive their automobiles to the very brink of the Grand Canyon's south rim. They could *walk* that last mile. Better yet, the Park Service should build an enormous parking lot about ten miles south of Grand Canyon Village and another east of Desert View. At those points, as at Yosemite, our people could emerge from their steaming shells of steel and glass and climb upon horses or bicycles for the final leg of the journey. On the rim, as at present, the hotels and restaurants will remain to serve the physical needs of the park visitors. Trips along the rim would also be made on foot, on horseback, or—utilizing the paved road which already exists— on bicycles. For those willing to go all the way from one parking lot to the other, a distance of some sixty or seventy miles, we might provide bus service back to their cars, a service which would at the same time effect a convenient exchange of bicycles and/or horses between the two terminals.

What about children? What about the aged and infirm? Frankly, we need waste little sympathy on these two pressure groups. Children too small to ride bicycles and too heavy to be borne on their parents' backs need only wait a few years—if they are not run over by automobiles they will grow into a lifetime of joyous adventure, if we save the parks and *leave them unimpaired for the enjoyment of future generations.* The aged merit even less sympathy: after all they had the opportunity to see the country when it was still relatively unspoiled. However, we'll stretch a point for those too old or too sickly to mount a bicycle and let them ride the shuttle buses.

I can foresee complaints. The motorized tourists, reluctant to give up the old ways, will complain that they can't see enough without their automobiles to bear them swiftly (traffic permitting) through the parks. But this is nonsense. A man on foot, on horseback or on a bicycle will see more, feel more, enjoy more in one mile than the motorized tourists can in a hundred miles. Better to idle through one park in two weeks than try to race through a dozen in the same amount of time. Those who are familiar with both modes of travel know from experience that this is true; the rest have only to make the experiment to discover the same truth for themselves.

They will complain of physical hardship, these sons of the pioneers. Not for long; once they rediscover the pleasures of actually operating their own limbs and senses in a varied, spontaneous, voluntary style, they will complain instead of crawling back into a car; they may even object to returning to desk and office and that dry-wall box on Mossy Brook Circle. The fires of revolt may be kindled—which means hope for us all.

(2) No more new roads in national parks. After banning private automobiles the second step should be easy. Where paved roads are already in existence they will be reserved for the bicycles and essential in-park services, such as shuttle buses, the trucking of camping gear and concessioners' supplies. Where dirt roads already exist they too will be reserved for nonmotorized traffic. Plans for new roads can be discarded and in their place a program of trail-building begun, badly needed in some of the parks and in many of the national monuments. In mountainous areas it may be desirable to build emergency shelters along the trails and bike roads; in desert regions a water supply might have to be provided at certain points—wells drilled and handpumps installed if feasible.

Once people are liberated from the confines of automobiles there will be a greatly increased interest in hiking, exploring, and back-country packtrips. Fortunately the parks, by the mere elimination of motor traffic, will come to seem far bigger than they are now—there will be more room for more persons, an astonishing expansion of space. This follows from the interesting fact that a motorized vehicle, when not at rest, requires a volume of space far out of proportion to its size. To illustrate: imagine a lake approximately ten miles long and on the average one mile wide. A single motorboat could easily circumnavigate the lake in an hour; ten motorboats would begin to crowd it; twenty or thirty, all in operation, would dominate the lake to the exclusion of any other form of activity; and fifty would create the hazards, confusion, and turmoil that make pleasure impossible. Suppose we banned motorboats and allowed only canoes and rowboats; we would see at once that the lake seemed ten or perhaps a hundred times bigger. The same thing holds true, to an even greater degree, for the automobile. Distance and space are functions of speed and time. Without expending a single dollar from the United States Treasury we could, if we wanted to, multiply the area of our national parks tenfold or a hundredfold—simply by banning the private automobile. The next generation, all 250 million of them, would be grateful to us.

(3) Put the park rangers to work. Lazy scheming loafers, they've wasted too many years selling tickets at toll booths and sitting behind desks filling out charts and tables in the vain effort to appease the mania for statistics which torments the Washington office. Put them to work. They're supposed to be rangers—make the bums range; kick them out of those overheated air-conditioned offices, yank them out of those overstuffed patrol cars, and drive them out on the trails where they should be, leading the dudes over hill and dale, safely into and back out of the wilderness. It won't hurt them to work off a little office fat; it'll do them good, help take their minds off each other's wives, and give them a chance to get out of reach of the boss—a blessing for all concerned.

They will be needed on the trail. Once we outlaw the motors and stop the road-building and force the multitudes back on their feet, the people will need leaders. A venturesome minority will always be eager to set off on their own, and no obstacles should be placed in their path; let them take risks, for Godsake, let them get lost, sunburnt, stranded, drowned, eaten by bears, buried alive under avalanches—that is the right and privilege of any free American. But the rest, the majority, most of them new to the out-of-doors, will need and welcome assistance, instruction and guidance. Many will not know how to saddle a horse, read a topographical map, follow a trail over slickrock, memorize landmarks, build a fire in rain, treat snakebite, rappel down a cliff, glissade down a glacier, read a compass, find water under sand, load a burro, splint a broken bone, bury a body, patch a rubber boat, portage a waterfall, survive a blizzard, avoid lightning, cook a porcupine, comfort a girl during a thunderstorm, predict the weather, dodge falling rock, climb out of a box canyon, or pour piss out of a boot. Park rangers know these things, or should know them, or used to know them and can relearn; they will be needed. In addition to this sort of practical guide service the ranger will also be a bit of a naturalist, able to edify the party in his charge with the natural and human history of the area, in detail and in broad outline.

Critics of my program will argue that it is too late for such a radical reformation of a people's approach to the out-of-doors, that the pattern is too deeply set, and that the majority of Americans would not be willing to emerge from the familiar luxury of their automobiles, even briefly, to try the little-known and problematic advantages of the bicycle, the saddle horse, and the footpath. This might be so; but how can we be sure unless we dare the experiment? I, for one, suspect that millions of our citizens, especially the young, are yearning for adventure, difficulty, challenge—they will respond with enthusiasm. What we must do, prodding the Park Service into the forefront of the demonstration, is provide these young people with the opportunity, the assistance, and the necessary encouragement.

How could this most easily be done? By following the steps I have proposed, plus reducing the expenses of wilderness recreation to the minimal level. Guide service by rangers should, of course, be free to the public. Money saved by *not* constructing more paved highways into the parks should be sufficient to finance the cost of bicycles and horses for the entire park system. Elimination of automobile traffic would allow the Park Service to save more millions now spent on road maintenance, police work and paper work. Whatever the cost, however financed, the benefits for park visitors in health and happiness—virtues unknown to the statisticians—would be immeasurable.

Excluding the automobile from the heart of the great cities has been seriously advocated by thoughtful observers of our urban problems. It seems to me an equally proper solution to the problems besetting our national parks. Of course it would be a serious blow to Industrial Tourism and would be bitterly resisted by those who profit from that industry. Exclusion of automobiles would also require a revolution in the thinking of Park Service officialdom and in the assumptions of most American tourists. But such a revolution, like it or not, is precisely what is needed. The only foreseeable alternative, given the current trend of things, is the gradual destruction of our national park system.

Let us therefore steal a slogan from the Development Fever Faction in the Park Service. The parks, they say, are for people. Very well. At the main entrance to each national park and national monument we shall erect a billboard one hundred feet high, two hundred feet wide, gorgeously filigreed in brilliant neon and outlined with blinker lights, exploding stars, flashing prayer wheels and great Byzantine phallic symbols that gush like geysers every thirty seconds. (You could set your watch by them.) Behind the fireworks will loom the figure of Smokey the Bear, taller than a pine tree, with eyes in his head that swivel back and forth, watching YOU, and ears that actually twitch. Push a button and Smokey will recite, for the benefit of children and government officials who might otherwise have trouble with some of the big words, in a voice ursine, loud and clear, the message spelled out on the face of the billboard. To wit:

HOWDY FOLKS. WELCOME. THIS IS YOUR NATIONAL PARK, ESTAB-
LISHED FOR THE PLEASURE OF YOU AND ALL PEOPLE EVERYWHERE.
PARK YOUR CAR, JEEP, TRUCK, TANK, MOTORBIKE, MOTORBOAT, JET-
BOAT, AIRBOAT, SUBMARINE, AIRPLANE, JETPLANE, HELICOPTER, HOV-
ERCRAFT, WINGED MOTORCYCLE, SNOWMOBILE, ROCKETSHIP, OR ANY
OTHER CONCEIVABLE TYPE OF MOTORIZED VEHICLE IN THE WORLD'S
BIGGEST PARKINGLOT BEHIND THE COMFORT STATION IMMEDIATELY
TO YOUR REAR. GET OUT OF YOUR MOTORIZED VEHICLE, GET ON
YOUR HORSE, MULE, BICYCLE OR FEET, AND COME ON IN.
ENJOY YOURSELVES. THIS HERE PARK IS FOR *people*.

The survey chief and his two assistants did not stay very long. Letting them go in peace, without debate, I fixed myself another drink, returned to the table in the backyard and sat down to await the rising of the moon.

My thoughts were on the road and the crowds that would pour upon it as inevitably as water under pressure follows every channel which is opened to it. Man is a gregarious creature, we are told, a social being. Does that mean he is also a herd animal? I don't believe it, despite the character of modern life. The herd is for ungulates, not for men and women and their children. Are men no better than sheep or cattle, that they must live always in view of one another in order to feel a sense of safety? I can't believe it.

We are preoccupied with time. If we could learn to love space as deeply as we are now obsessed with time, we might discover a new meaning in the phrase *to live like men.*

At what distance should good neighbors build their houses? Let it be determined by the community's mode of travel: if by foot, four miles; if by horseback, eight miles; if by motorcar, twenty-four miles; if by airplane, ninety-six miles.

Recall the Proverb: "Set not thy foot too often in thy neighbor's house, lest he grow weary of thee and hate thee."

The sun went down and the light mellowed over the sand and distance and hoodoo rocks "pinnacled dim in the intense inane." A few stars appeared, scattered liberally through space. The solitary owl called.

Finally the moon came up, a golden globe behind the rocky fretwork of the horizon, a full and delicate moon that floated lightly as a leaf upon the dark slow current of the night. A face that watched me from the other side.

The air grew cool. I put on boots and shirt, stuffed some cheese and raisins in my pocket, and went for a walk. The moon was high enough to cast a good light when I reached the place where the gray jeep had first come into view. I could see the tracks of its wheels quite plainly in the sand and the route was well marked, not only by the tracks but by the survey stakes planted in the ground at regular fifty-foot intervals and by streamers of plastic ribbon tied to the brush and trees.

Teamwork, that's what made America what it is today. Teamwork and initiative. The survey crew had done their job; I would do mine. For about five miles I followed the course of their survey back toward headquarters, and as I went I pulled up each little wooden stake and threw it away, and cut all the bright ribbons from the bushes and hid them under a rock. A futile effort, in the long run, but it made me feel good. Then I went home to the trailer, taking a shortcut over the bluffs.

Desert Solitaire (1968)

PAUL R. EHRLICH

Paul Ehrlich (b. 1932) appeared more than 20 times on *The Tonight Show* with Johnny Carson, which gives you some idea of just how scared about the future people suddenly became in the late 1960s. Though his original scientific work, which won him many prizes and a faculty slot at Stanford while still in his twenties, was in lepidoptery, Ehrlich's particular passion was human population. He believed, as these passages from *The Population Bomb* (1968) make clear, that there was no emergency greater than the exponential increase in human numbers. Though some of his predictions have been proven inaccurate, and some have found his descriptions of the developing world to be tainted by a colonialist mentality, it's worth noting that his loud alarm helped spur the spread of family planning worldwide. In the subsequent four decades, the average woman on this planet went from having six children to fewer than three, and the demographers now predict that human numbers, currently above six billion, may not soon double again—one of the few global environmental statistics heading in the right direction.

from **The Population Bomb**

The Problem

I have understood the population explosion intellectually for a long time. I came to understand it emotionally one stinking hot night in Delhi a couple of years ago. My wife and daughter and I were returning to our hotel in an ancient taxi. The seats were hopping with fleas. The only functional gear was third. As we crawled through the city, we entered a crowded slum area. The temperature was well over 100, and the air was a haze of dust and smoke. The streets seemed alive with people. People eating, people washing, people sleeping. People visiting, arguing, and screaming. People thrusting their hands through the taxi window, begging. People defecating and urinating. People clinging to buses. People herding animals. People, people, people, people. As we moved slowly through the mob, hand horn squawking, the dust, noise, heat, and cooking fires gave the scene a hellish aspect. Would we ever get to our hotel? All three of us were, frankly, frightened. It seemed that anything could happen—but, of course, nothing did. Old India hands will laugh at our reaction. We were just some overprivileged tourists, unaccustomed to the sights and sounds of India. Perhaps, but since that night I've known the *feel* of overpopulation.

Too Many People

Americans are beginning to realize that the undeveloped countries of the world face an inevitable population-food crisis. Each year food production in undeveloped countries falls a bit further behind burgeoning population growth, and people go to bed a little bit hungrier. While there are temporary or local reversals of this trend, it now seems inevitable that it will continue to its logical conclusion: mass starvation. The rich are going to get richer, but the more numerous poor are going to get poorer. Of these poor, a minimum of three and one-half million will starve to death this year, mostly children. But this is a mere handful compared to the numbers that will be starving in a decade or so. And it is now too late to take action to save many of those people.

In a book about population there is a temptation to stun the reader with an avalanche of statistics. I'll spare you most, but not all, of that. After all, no matter how you slice it, population is a numbers game. Perhaps the best way to impress you with numbers is to tell you about the "doubling time"—the time necessary for the population to double in size.

It has been estimated that the human population of 6000 B.C. was about five million people, taking perhaps one million years to get there from two and a half million. The population did not reach 500 million until almost 8,000 years later—about 1650 A.D. This means it doubled roughly once every thousand years or so. It reached a billion people around 1850, doubling in some 200 years. It took only 80 years or so for the next doubling, as the population reached two billion around 1930. We have not completed the next doubling to four billion yet, but we now have well over three billion people. The doubling time at present seems to be about 37 years.[1] Quite a reduction in doubling times: 1,000,000 years, 1,000 years, 200 years, 80 years, 37 years. Perhaps the meaning of a doubling time of around 37 years is best brought home by a theoretical exercise. Let's examine what might happen on the absurd assumption that the population continued to double every 37 years into the indefinite future.

If growth continued at that rate for about 900 years, there would be some 60,000,000,000,000,000 people on the face of the earth. Sixty million billion people. This is about 100 persons for each square yard of the Earth's surface, land and sea. A British physicist, J. H. Fremlin,[2] guessed that such a multitude might be housed in a continuous 2,000-story building covering our entire planet. The upper 1,000 stories would contain only the apparatus for running this gigantic warren. Ducts, pipes, wires, elevator shafts, etc., would occupy about half of the space in the bottom 1,000 stories. This would leave three or four yards of floor space for each person. I will leave to your imagination the physical details of existence in this ant heap, except to point out that all would not be black. Probably each person would be limited in his travel. Perhaps he could take elevators through all 1,000 residential stories but could travel only within a circle of a few hundred yards' radius on any floor. This would permit, however, each person to choose his friends from among some ten million people! And, as Fremlin points out, entertainment on the worldwide TV should be excellent, for at any time "one could expect some ten million Shakespeares and rather more Beatles to be alive."

Could growth of the human population of the Earth continue beyond that point? Not according to Fremlin. We would have reached a "heat limit." People themselves, as well as their activities, convert other

1. Since this was written, 1968 figures have appeared, showing that the doubling time is now 35 years.
2. J. H. Fremlin, "How Many People Can the World Support?" *New Scientist,* October 29, 1964.

forms of energy into heat which must be dissipated. In order to permit this excess heat to radiate directly from the top of the "world building" directly into space, the atmosphere would have been pumped into flasks under the sea well before the limiting population size was reached. The precise limit would depend on the technology of the day. At a population size of one billion billion people, the temperature of the "world roof" would be kept around the melting point of iron to radiate away the human heat generated.

The Population Bomb (1968)

GARRETT HARDIN

Garrett Hardin (1915–2003), like Lynn White Jr., had a long academic career and is remembered for a single paper—really, almost a single phrase: "the tragedy of the commons." This essay has been enormously influential, mostly for its hard-nosed "realism" about the need for control. Although global population pressures have begun to abate, mostly through education and voluntary choice, in recent years activists have rehabilitated the idea of the commons in many spheres, arguing that the privatization of life pushed hard by American conservatives has undermined human communities.

from **The Tragedy of the Commons**

The tragedy of the commons develops in this way. Picture a pasture open to all. It is to be expected that each herdsman will try to keep as many cattle as possible on the commons. Such an arrangement may work reasonably satisfactorily for centuries because tribal wars, poaching, and disease keep the numbers of both man and beast well below the carrying capacity of the land. Finally, however, comes the day of reckoning, that is, the day when the long-desired goal of social stability becomes a reality. At this point, the inherent logic of the commons remorselessly generates tragedy.

As a rational being, each herdsman seeks to maximize his gain. Explicitly or implicitly, more or less consciously, he asks, "What is the utility *to me* of adding one more animal to my herd?" This utility has one negative and one positive component.

1) The positive component is a function of the increment of one animal. Since the herdsman receives all the proceeds from the sale of the additional animal, the positive utility is nearly +1.

2) The negative component is a function of the additional overgrazing created by one more animal. Since, however, the effects of overgrazing are shared by all the herdsmen, the negative utility for any particular decision-making herdsman is only a fraction of -1.

Adding together the component partial utilities, the rational herdsman concludes that the only sensible course for him to pursue is to add another animal to his herd. And another; and another. . . . But this is the conclusion reached by each and every rational herdsman sharing a commons. Therein is the tragedy. Each man is locked into a system that compels him to increase his herd without limit—in a world that is limited. Ruin is the destination toward which all men rush, each pursuing his own best interest in a society that believes in the freedom of the commons. Freedom in a commons brings ruin to all.

Some would say that this is a platitude. Would that it were! In a sense, it was learned thousands of years ago, but natural selection favors the forces of psychological denial.[1] The individual benefits as an individual from his ability to deny the truth even though society as a whole, of which he is a part, suffers. Education can counteract the natural tendency to do the wrong thing, but the inexorable succession of generations requires that the basis for this knowledge be constantly refreshed.

A simple incident that occurred a few years ago in Leominster, Massachusetts, shows how perishable the knowledge is. During the Christmas shopping season the parking meters downtown were covered with plastic bags that bore tags reading: "Do not open until after Christmas. Free parking courtesy of the mayor and city council." In other words, facing the prospect of an increased demand for already scarce space, the city fathers reinstituted the system of the commons. (Cynically, we suspect that they gained more votes than they lost by this retrogressive act.)

In an approximate way, the logic of the commons has been understood for a long time, perhaps since the discovery of agriculture or the invention of private property in real estate. But it is understood

1. G. Hardin, Ed. *Population, Evolution, and Birth Control* (Freeman, San Francisco, 1964), p. 56.

mostly only in special cases which are not sufficiently generalized. Even at this late date, cattlemen leasing national land on the western ranges demonstrate no more than an ambivalent understanding, in constantly pressuring federal authorities to increase the head count to the point where over-grazing produces erosion and weed-dominance. Likewise, the oceans of the world continue to suffer from the survival of the philosophy of the commons. Maritime nations still respond automatically to the shibboleth of the "freedom of the seas." Professing to believe in the "inexhaustible resources of the oceans," they bring species after species of fish and whales closer to extinction.[2]

The National Parks present another instance of the working out of the tragedy of the commons. At present, they are open to all, without limit. The parks themselves are limited in extent—there is only one Yosemite Valley—whereas population seems to grow without limit. The values that visitors seek in the parks are steadily eroded. Plainly, we must soon cease to treat the parks as commons or they will be of no value to anyone.

What shall we do? We have several options. We might sell them off as private property. We might keep them as public property, but allocate the right to enter them. The allocation might be on the basis of wealth, by the use of an auction system. It might be on the basis of merit, as defined by some agreed-upon standards. It might be by lottery. Or it might be on a first-come, first-served basis, administered to long queues. These, I think, are all the reasonable possibilities. They are all objectionable. But we must choose—or acquiesce in the destruction of the commons that we call our National Parks.

Pollution

In a reverse way, the tragedy of the commons reappears in problems of pollution. Here it is not a question of taking something out of the commons, but of putting something in—sewage, or chemical, radioactive, and heat wastes into water; noxious and dangerous fumes into the air; and distracting and unpleasant advertising signs into the

2. S. McVay, *Sci. Amer.* **216** (No. 8), 13 (1966).

line of sight. The calculations of utility are much the same as before. The rational man finds that his share of the cost of the wastes he discharges into the commons is less than the cost of purifying his wastes before releasing them. Since this is true for everyone, we are locked into a system of "fouling our own nest," so long as we behave only as independent, rational, free-enterprisers.

The tragedy of the commons as a food basket is averted by private property, or something formally like it. But the air and waters surrounding us cannot readily be fenced, and so the tragedy of the commons as a cesspool must be prevented by different means, by coercive laws or taxing devices that make it cheaper for the polluter to treat his pollutants than to discharge them untreated. We have not progressed as far with the solution of this problem as we have with the first. Indeed, our particular concept of private property, which deters us from exhausting the positive resources of the earth, favors pollution. The owner of a factory on the bank of a stream—whose property extends to the middle of the stream—often has difficulty seeing why it is not his natural right to muddy the waters flowing past his door. The law, always behind the times, requires elaborate stitching and fitting to adapt it to this newly perceived aspect of the commons.

The pollution problem is a consequence of population. It did not much matter how a lonely American frontiersman disposed of his waste. "Flowing water purifies itself every 10 miles," my grandfather used to say, and the myth was near enough to the truth when he was a boy, for there were not too many people. But as population became denser, the natural chemical and biological recycling processes became overloaded, calling for a redefinition of property rights.

How To Legislate Temperance?

Analysis of the pollution problem as a function of population density uncovers a not generally recognized principle of morality, namely: *the morality of an act is a function of the state of the system at the time it is performed.*[3] Using the commons as a cesspool does not harm the

3. J. Fletcher, *Situation Ethics* (Westminster, Philadelphia, 1966).

general public under frontier conditions, because there is no public; the same behavior in a metropolis is unbearable. A hundred and fifty years ago a plainsman could kill an American bison, cut out only the tongue for his dinner, and discard the rest of the animal. He was not in any important sense being wasteful. Today, with only a few thousand bison left, we would be appalled at such behavior.

In passing, it is worth noting that the morality of an act cannot be determined from a photograph. One does not know whether a man killing an elephant or setting fire to the grassland is harming others until one knows the total system in which his act appears. "One picture is worth a thousand words," said an ancient Chinese; but it may take 10,000 words to validate it. It is as tempting to ecologists as it is to reformers in general to try to persuade others by way of the photographic shortcut. But the essense of an argument cannot be photographed: it must be presented rationally—in words.

That morality is system-sensitive escaped the attention of most codifiers of ethics in the past. "Thou shalt not . . ." is the form of traditional ethical directives which make no allowance for particular circumstances. The laws of our society follow the pattern of ancient ethics, and therefore are poorly suited to governing a complex, crowded, changeable world. Our epicyclic solution is to augment statutory law with administrative law. Since it is practically impossible to spell out all the conditions under which it is safe to burn trash in the back yard or to run an automobile without smog-control, by law we delegate the details to bureaus. The result is administrative law, which is rightly feared for an ancient reason—*Quis custodiet ipsos custodes?*—"Who shall watch the watchers themselves?" John Adams said that we must have "a government of laws and not men." Bureau administrators, trying to evaluate the morality of acts in the total system, are singularly liable to corruption, producing a government by men, not laws.

Prohibition is easy to legislate (though not necessarily to enforce); but how do we legislate temperance? Experience indicates that it can be accomplished best through the mediation of administrative law. We limit possibilities unnecessarily if we suppose that the sentiment of

Quis custodiet denies us the use of administrative law. We should rather retain the phrase as a perpetual reminder of fearful dangers we cannot avoid. The great challenge facing us now is to invent the corrective feedbacks that are needed to keep custodians honest. We must find ways to legitimate the needed authority of both the custodians and the corrective feedbacks.

Freedom To Breed Is Intolerable

The tragedy of the commons is involved in population problems in another way. In a world governed solely by the principle of "dog eat dog"—if indeed there ever was such a world—how many children a family had would not be a matter of public concern. Parents who bred too exuberantly would leave fewer descendants, not more, because they would be unable to care adequately for their children. David Lack and others have found that such a negative feedback demonstrably controls the fecundity of birds.[4] But men are not birds, and have not acted like them for millenniums, at least.

If each human family were dependent only on its own resources; *if* the children of improvident parents starved to death; *if*, thus, over-breeding brought its own "punishment" to the germ line—*then* there would be no public interest in controlling the breeding of families. But our society is deeply committed to the welfare state,[5] and hence is confronted with another aspect of the tragedy of the commons.

In a welfare state, how shall we deal with the family, the religion, the race, or the class (or indeed any distinguishable and cohesive group) that adopts overbreeding as a policy to secure its own aggrandizement?[6] To couple the concept of freedom to breed with the belief that everyone born has an equal right to the commons is to lock the world into a tragic course of action.

Unfortunately this is just the course of action that is being pursued

---

4. D. Lack, *The Natural Regulation of Animal Numbers* (Clarendon Press, Oxford, 1954).

5. H. Girvetz, *From Wealth to Welfare* (Stanford Univ. Press, Stanford, Calif., 1950).

6. G. Hardin, *Perspec. Biol. Med.* **6,** 366 (1963).

by the United Nations. In late 1967, some 30 nations agreed to the following:[7]

> The Universal Declaration of Human Rights describes the family as the natural and fundamental unit of society. It follows that any choice and decision with regard to the size of the family must irrevocably rest with the family itself, and cannot be made by anyone else.

It is painful to have to deny categorically the validity of this right; denying it, one feels as uncomfortable as a resident of Salem, Massachusetts, who denied the reality of witches in the 17th century. At the present time, in liberal quarters, something like a taboo acts to inhibit criticism of the United Nations. There is a feeling that the United Nations is "our last and best hope," that we shouldn't find fault with it; we shouldn't play into the hands of the archconservatives. However, let us not forget what Robert Louis Stevenson said: "The truth that is suppressed by friends is the readiest weapon of the enemy." If we love the truth we must openly deny the validity of the Universal Declaration of Human Rights, even though it is promoted by the United Nations. We should also join with Kingsley Davis[8] in attempting to get Planned Parenthood–World Population to see the error of its ways in embracing the same tragic ideal.

Conscience Is Self-Eliminating

It is a mistake to think that we can control the breeding of mankind in the long run by an appeal to conscience. Charles Galton Darwin made this point when he spoke on the centennial of the publication of his grandfather's great book. The argument is straightforward and Darwinian.

People vary. Confronted with appeals to limit breeding, some people will undoubtedly respond to the plea more than others. Those who have more children will produce a larger fraction of the next generation than those with more susceptible consciences. The difference will be accentuated, generation by generation.

7. U. Thant, *Int. Planned Parenthood News*, No. 168 (February 1968), p. 3.
8. K. Davis, *Science* **158,** 730 (1967).

In C. G. Darwin's words: "It may well be that it would take hundreds of generations for the progenitive instinct to develop in this way, but if it should do so, nature would have taken her revenge, and the variety *Homo contracipiens* would become extinct and would be replaced by the variety *Homo progenitivus.*"[9]

The argument assumes that conscience or the desire for children (no matter which) is hereditary—but hereditary only in the most general formal sense. The result will be the same whether the attitude is transmitted through germ cells, or exosomatically, to use A. J. Lotka's term. (If one denies the latter possibility as well as the former, then what's the point of education?) The argument has here been stated in the context of the population problem, but it applies equally well to any instance in which society appeals to an individual exploiting a commons to restrain himself for the general good—by means of his conscience. To make such an appeal is to set up a selective system that works toward the elimination of conscience from the race.

Pathogenic Effects of Conscience

The long-term disadvantage of an appeal to conscience should be enough to condemn it; but has serious short-term disadvantages as well. If we ask a man who is exploiting a commons to desist "in the name of conscience," what are we saying to him? What does he hear?—not only at the moment but also in the wee small hours of the night when, half asleep, he remembers not merely the words we used but also the nonverbal communication cues we gave him unawares? Sooner or later, consciously or subconsciously, he senses that he has received two communications, and that they are contradictory: (i) (intended communication) "If you don't do as we ask, we will openly condemn you for not acting like a responsible citizen"; (ii) (the unintended communication) "If you *do* behave as we ask, we will secretly condemn you for a simpleton who can be shamed into standing aside while the rest of us exploit the commons."

Everyman then is caught in what Bateson has called a "double

9. S. Tax, Ed., *Evolution after Darwin* (Univ. of Chicago Press, Chicago, 1960), vol. 2, p. 469.

bind." Bateson and his co-workers have made a plausible case for viewing the double bind as an important causative factor in the genesis of schizophrenia.[10] The double bind may not always be so damaging, but it always endangers the mental health of anyone to whom it is applied. "A bad conscience," said Nietzsche, "is a kind of illness."

To conjure up a conscience in others is tempting to anyone who wishes to extend his control beyond the legal limits. Leaders at the highest level succumb to this temptation. Has any President during the past generation failed to call on labor unions to moderate voluntarily their demands for higher wages, or to steel companies to honor voluntary guidelines on prices? I can recall none. The rhetoric used on such occasions is designed to produce feelings of guilt in noncooperators.

For centuries it was assumed without proof that guilt was a valuable, perhaps even an indispensable, ingredient of the civilized life. Now, in this post-Freudian world, we doubt it.

Paul Goodman speaks from the modern point of view when he says: "No good has ever come from feeling guilty, neither intelligence, policy, nor compassion. The guilty do not pay attention to the object but only to themselves, and not even to their own interests, which might make sense, but to their anxieties."[11]

One does not have to be a professional psychiatrist to see the consequences of anxiety. We in the Western world are just emerging from a dreadful two-centuries-long Dark Ages of Eros that was sustained partly by prohibition laws, but perhaps more effectively by the anxiety-generating mechanisms of education. Alex Comfort has told the story well in *The Anxiety Makers*;[12] it is not a pretty one.

Since proof is difficult, we may even concede that the results of anxiety may sometimes, from certain points of view, be desirable. The larger question we should ask is whether, as a matter of policy, we should ever encourage the use of a technique the tendency (if not the intention) of which is psychologically pathogenic. We hear much talk these days of responsible parenthood; the coupled words are incorpo-

10. G. Bateson, D. D. Jackson, J. Haley, J. Weakland, *Behav. Sci.* **1,** 251 (1956).

11. P. Goodman, *New York Rev. Books* **10**(8), 22 (23 May 1968).

12. A. Comfort, *The Anxiety Makers* (Nelson, London, 1967).

rated into the titles of some organizations devoted to birth control. Some people have proposed massive propaganda campaigns to instill responsibility into the nation's (or the world's) breeders. But what is the meaning of the word responsibility in this context? Is it not merely a synonym for the word conscience? When we use the word responsibility in the absence of substantial sanctions are we not trying to browbeat a free man in a commons into acting against his own interest? Responsibility is a verbal counterfeit for a substantial *quid pro quo*. It is an attempt to get something for nothing.

If the word responsibility is to be used at all, I suggest that it be in the sense Charles Frankel uses it.[13] "Responsibility," says this philosopher, "is the product of definite social arrangements." Notice that Frankel calls for social arrangements—not propaganda.

Mutual Coercion Mutually Agreed Upon

The social arrangements that produce responsibility are arrangements that create coercion, of some sort. Consider bank-robbing. The man who takes money from a bank acts as if the bank were a commons. How do we prevent such action? Certainly not by trying to control his behavior solely by a verbal appeal to his sense of responsibility. Rather than rely on propaganda we follow Frankel's lead and insist that a bank is not a commons; we seek the definite social arrangements that will keep it from becoming a commons. That we thereby infringe on the freedom of would-be robbers we neither deny nor regret.

The morality of bank-robbing is particularly easy to understand because we accept complete prohibition of this activity. We are willing to say "Thou shalt not rob banks," without providing for exceptions. But temperance also can be created by coercion. Taxing is a good coercive device. To keep downtown shoppers temperate in their use of parking space we introduce parking meters for short periods, and traffic fines for longer ones. We need not actually forbid a citizen to park as long as he wants to; we need merely make it increasingly expensive for him to do so. Not prohibition, but carefully biased options are what

13. C. Frankel, *The Case for Modern Man* (Harper, New York, 1955), p. 203.

we offer him. A Madison Avenue man might call this persuasion; I prefer the greater candor of the word coercion.

Coercion is a dirty word to most liberals now, but it need not forever be so. As with the four-letter words, its dirtiness can be cleansed away by exposure to the light, by saying it over and over without apology or embarrassment. To many, the word coercion implies arbitrary decisions of distant and irresponsible bureaucrats; but this is not a necessary part of its meaning. The only kind of coercion I recommend is mutual coercion, mutually agreed upon by the majority of the people affected.

To say that we mutually agree to coercion is not to say that we are required to enjoy it, or even to pretend we enjoy it. Who enjoys taxes? We all grumble about them. But we accept compulsory taxes because we recognize that voluntary taxes would favor the conscienceless. We institute and (grumblingly) support taxes and other coercive devices to escape the horror of the commons.

An alternative to the commons need not be perfectly just to be preferable. With real estate and other material goods, the alternative we have chosen is the institution of private property coupled with legal inheritance. Is this system perfectly just? As a genetically trained biologist I deny that it is. It seems to me that, if there are to be differences in individual inheritance, legal possession should be perfectly correlated with biological inheritance—that those who are biologically more fit to be the custodians of property and power should legally inherit more. But genetic recombination continually makes a mockery of the doctrine of "like father, like son" implicit in our laws of legal inheritance. An idiot can inherit millions, and a trust fund can keep his estate intact. We must admit that our legal system of private property plus inheritance is unjust—but we put up with it because we are not convinced, at the moment, that anyone has invented a better system. The alternative of the commons is too horrifying to contemplate. Injustice is preferable to total ruin.

It is one of the peculiarities of the warfare between reform and the status quo that it is thoughtlessly governed by a double standard. Whenever a reform measure is proposed it is often defeated when its opponents triumphantly discover a flaw in it. As Kingsley Davis has pointed out,[14] worshippers of the status quo sometimes imply that no reform is possible without unanimous agreement, an implication contrary to historical fact. As nearly as I can make out, automatic rejection of proposed reforms is based on one of two unconscious assumptions: (i) that the status quo is perfect; or (ii) that the choice we face is between reform and no action; if the proposed reform is imperfect, we presumably should take no action at all, while we wait for a perfect proposal.

But we can never do nothing. That which we have done for thousands of years is also action. It also produces evils. Once we are aware that the status quo is action, we can then compare its discoverable advantages and disadvantages with the predicted advantages and disadvantages of the proposed reform, discounting as best we can for our lack of experience. On the basis of such a comparison, we can make a rational decision which will not involve the unworkable assumption that only perfect systems are tolerable.

Recognition of Necessity

Perhaps the simplest summary of this analysis of man's population problems is this: the commons, if justifiable at all, is justifiable only under conditions of low-population density. As the human population has increased, the commons has had to be abandoned in one aspect after another.

First we abandoned the commons in food gathering, enclosing farm land and restricting pastures and hunting and fishing areas. These restrictions are still not complete throughout the world.

Somewhat later we saw that the commons as a place for waste disposal would also have to be abandoned. Restrictions on the disposal of domestic sewage are widely accepted in the Western world; we are still struggling to close the commons to pollution by automobiles, factories, insecticide sprayers, fertilizing operations, and atomic energy installations.

In a still more embryonic state is our recognition of the evils of the

14. J. D. Roslansky, *Genetics and the Future of Man* (Appleton-Century-Crofts, New York, 1966), p. 177.

commons in matters of pleasure. There is almost no restriction on the propagation of sound waves in the public medium. The shopping public is assaulted with mindless music, without its consent. Our government is paying out billions of dollars to create supersonic transport which will disturb 50,000 people for every one person who is whisked from coast to coast 3 hours faster. Advertisers muddy the airwaves of radio and television and pollute the view of travelers. We are a long way from outlawing the commons in matters of pleasure. Is this because our Puritan inheritance makes us view pleasure as something of a sin, and pain (that is, the pollution of advertising) as the sign of virtue?

Every new enclosure of the commons involves the infringement of somebody's personal liberty. Infringements made in the distant past are accepted because no contemporary complains of a loss. It is the newly proposed infringements that we vigorously oppose; cries of "rights" and "freedom" fill the air. But what does "freedom" mean? When men mutually agreed to pass laws against robbing, mankind became more free, not less so. Individuals locked into the logic of the commons are free only to bring on universal ruin; once they see the necessity of mutual coercion, they become free to pursue other goals. I believe it was Hegel who said, "Freedom is the recognition of necessity."

The most important aspect of necessity that we must now recognize, is the necessity of abandoning the commons in breeding. No technical solution can rescue us from the misery of overpopulation. Freedom to breed will bring ruin to all. At the moment, to avoid hard decisions many of us are tempted to propagandize for conscience and responsible parenthood. The temptation must be resisted, because an appeal to independently acting consciences selects for the disappearance of all conscience in the long run, and an increase in anxiety in the short.

The only way we can preserve and nurture other and more precious freedoms is by relinquishing the freedom to breed, and that very soon. "Freedom is the recognition of necessity"—and it is the role of education to reveal to all the necessity of abandoning the freedom to breed. Only so, can we put an end to this aspect of the tragedy of the commons.

Science, December 13, 1968

Philip K. Dick (1928–1982) was one of the foremost science-fiction writers in the transitional era between space opera and the modern genre. His novels, of which *Do Androids Dream of Electric Sheep?* (1968) is perhaps the most famous, foreshadow the surprising bleakness that would come to dominate the SF aisle in the age of William Gibson and futuristic cinema, from *Blade Runner* (1982, based on *Androids*) to *The Matrix* (1999). This dystopian bent comes, I think, from the prediction that human scale and human values may not survive their inevitable collision with new technologies—technologies whose demands and dimensions may come to overwhelm our own.

from Do Androids Dream of Electric Sheep?

He broke off. Because, all at once, he had seen their animals.

A powerful corporation, he realized, would of course be able to afford this. In the back of his mind, evidently, he had anticipated such a collection; it was not surprise that he felt but more a sort of yearning. He quietly walked away from the girl, toward the closest pen. Already he could smell them, the several scents of the creatures standing or sitting, or, in the case of what appeared to be a raccoon, asleep.

Never in his life had he personally seen a raccoon. He knew the animal only from 3-D films shown on television. For some reason the dust had struck that species almost as hard as it had the birds—of which almost none survived, now. In an automatic response he brought out his much-thumbed Sidney's and looked up raccoon with all the sublistings. The list prices, naturally, appeared in italics; like Percheron horses, none existed on the market for sale at any figure. Sidney's catalogue simply listed the price at which the last transaction involving a raccoon had taken place. It was astronomical.

"His name is Bill," the girl said from behind him. "Bill the raccoon. We acquired him just last year from a subsidiary corporation." She pointed past him and he then perceived the armed company guards, standing with their machine guns, the rapid-fire little light Skoda issue; the eyes of the guards had been fastened on him since his car landed. And, he thought, my car is clearly marked as a police vehicle.

"A major manufacturer of androids," he said thoughtfully, "invests its surplus capital on living animals."

"Look at the owl," Rachael Rosen said. "Here, I'll wake it up for you." She started toward a small, distant cage, in the center of which jutted up a branching dead tree.

There are no owls, he started to say. Or so we've been told. Sidney's, he thought; they list it in their catalogue as extinct: the tiny, precise type, the *E*, again and again throughout the catalogue. As the girl walked ahead of him he checked to see, and he was right. Sidney's never makes a mistake, he said to himself. We know that, too. What else can we depend on?

"It's artificial," he said, with sudden realization; his disappointment welled up keen and intense.

"No." She smiled and he saw that she had small even teeth, as white as her eyes and hair were black.

"But Sidney's listing," he said, trying to show her the catalogue. To prove it to her.

The girl said, "We don't buy from Sidney's or from any animal dealer. All our purchases are from private parties and the prices we pay aren't reported." She added, "Also we have our own naturalists; they're now working up in Canada. There's still a good deal of forest left, comparatively speaking, anyhow. Enough for small animals and once in a while a bird."

For a long time he stood gazing at the owl, who dozed on its perch. A thousand thoughts came into his mind, thoughts about the war, about the days when owls had fallen from the sky; he remembered how in his childhood it had been discovered that species upon species had become extinct and how the 'papes had reported it each day—foxes one morning, badgers the next, until people had stopped reading the perpetual animal obits.

He thought, too, about his need for a real animal; within him an actual hatred once more manifested itself toward his electric sheep, which he had to tend, had to care about, as if it lived. The tyranny of an object, he thought. It doesn't know I exist. Like the androids, it had no ability to appreciate the existence of another. He had never thought of this before, the similarity between an electric animal and an andy. The electric animal, he pondered, could be considered a subform of the other, a kind of vastly inferior robot. Or, conversely, the android could be regarded as a highly developed, evolved version of the ersatz animal. Both viewpoints repelled him.

"If you sold your owl," he said to the girl Rachael Rosen, "how much would you want for it, and how much of that down?"

"We would never sell our owl." She scrutinized him with a mixture of pleasure and pity; or so he read her expression. "And even if we sold it, you couldn't possibly pay the price. What kind of animal do you have at home?"

"A sheep," he said. "A black-faced Suffolk ewe."

"Well, then you should be happy."

"I'm happy," he answered. "It's just that I always wanted an owl, even back before they all dropped dead." He corrected himself. "All but yours."

Rachael said, "Our present crash program and overall planning call for us to obtain an additional owl which can mate with Scrappy." She indicated the owl dozing on its perch; it had briefly opened both eyes, yellow slits which healed over as the owl settled back down to resume its slumber. Its chest rose conspicuously and fell, as if the owl, in its hypnagogic state, had sighed.

Do Androids Dream of Electric Sheep? (1968)

COLIN FLETCHER

Many of the writers in this book inspired Americans to go outdoors and take a hike; Colin Fletcher (1922–2007) told them how to do it. Fletcher was Welsh by birth, but his life was as American as you can get. In 1958 he hiked from Mexico to Oregon, and in 1963 he became the first person to walk the entire Grand Canyon within the rim, a trip described in his fine book *The Man Who Walked Through Time* (1968). The techniques he developed on those trips became the backbone of *The Complete Walker* (1969), which in its four editions has now sold more than half a million copies. The book, which grew fatter with each subsequent edition, took backpacking from the age of canvas rucksacks to the Gore-Tex era, from pemmican bars to collapsible espresso pots. But some of Fletcher's advice—particularly about packing light— never changed. And his exuberant enthusiasm for actually getting out on the trail created countless new apostles of wilderness who became the core of the post-Earth Day environmental movement.

A Sample Day in the Kitchen

Not to mention the bedroom, and most other departments too.) (Meticulously applicable only to those who operate on the Fletcher in-sleeping-bag culinary system.)

Something stirs inside you, and you half-open one eye. Stars and blackness, nothing more. You close the eye. But the something keeps on stirring, and after a moment you slide another inch toward consciousness and turn your head to the east and reopen the eye. It is there all right, a pale blue backing to the distant peaks. You sigh, pull up one arm inside the mummy bag, and check that the luminous hands of your watch say five o'clock.

After a decent interval you loosen the drawstrings of the mummy bag so that there is just enough room for you to slip on the shirt (which has been keeping the draft off your shoulders all night) and the down jacket (which you have been lying on). Then, still half-cocooned in the mummy bag, you sit up, reach back into the pack (which is propped up against the staff, just behind your head), and take out your shorts (which are waiting on top of everything else) and the pillow-size bag containing the day's rations (which is just underneath the shorts). From the ticket pocket of the shorts you fumble out book matches and an empty Lipton tea-bag wrapper. You stuff the shorts down into the mummy bag to warm. Next you take the flashlight out of one of your boots (which are standing just off to the left of the air mattress). Then you put the tea-bag wrapper down in the little patch you cleared for the stove last night (on the right side of bed, because the wind was blowing from the left last night; and very close to the groundsheet so that you don't have to stretch). You set the tea-bag wrapper alight and hold the stove (which is waiting close by) by its handle, just above the burning paper. Soon, you see in the beam of the flashlight that gasoline is welling up from the nozzle. You put the stove down on the tea bag, snuffing out the flame. Gasoline seeps down the generator of the stove and into the little depression in the bowl, encircling the generator. When the depression is full, you close the stove valve and ignite the gasoline. When it has almost burned away, you reopen the valve. If you time it dead right, the last guttering flame ignites the jet. Otherwise, you light it with another match. The stove roars healthily, almost waking you up.

You check that the roaring stove is standing quite firm, reach out for the larger of the cooking pots (which you half-filled with water after dinner last night—because you know what you are like in the morning—and which spent the night back near the pack, off to one side, where no restless movement of your body could possibly knock it over). You put the pot on the stove. Next you put on your hat (which was hanging by its chin band from the top of the pack-frame) because you are now conscious enough to feel chilly on the back of your head where there used to be plenty of hair when you were younger. Then you reach out for the smaller cooking pot (which is also back in safety beside the pack, and in which you last night put two ounces of dehydrated fruit cocktail and a shade more water than was necessary to reconstitute it). You remove the cup from inside this pot (it stayed clean there overnight) and put it ready on the stove-cover platform (which is still beside the stove, where you used it for dinner last night). You leave the spoon in the pot (it too stayed clean and safe there overnight). You pour a little more water into the pot from a canteen, squirt in some milk powder (the squirter stood all night beside the pot), stir, and add about two ounces of cereal mix. Then you lean back against the pack, still warm and comfortable in the mummy bag, and begin to eat the fruit and cereal mixture. The pale blue band along the eastern horizon broadens.

Soon—without needing to use the flashlight now—you see steam jetting out from the pot on the stove. You remove the pot, lift its cover and drop in one tea bag (which you put ready on top of the pot at the same time as you took the cereal out of the day's-ration bag). You leave the label hanging outside so that later, when the tea is strong enough, you can lift the bag out. Then you turn off the stove. And suddenly the world is very quiet and very beautiful, and for the first time that morning you really look at the silhouetted peaks and at the shadows that are the valleys. You swirl the teapot a couple of times to suffuse the tea, take a few more mouthfuls of fruit-and-cereal, then pour a cupful of tea, squirt-add milk, spoon in copious sugar (the sugar container also spent the night beside the pots), and take the first luxurious sip. Warmth flows down your throat, spreads outward. Your brain responds. Still sluggishly, it takes another step toward full focus.

And so, sitting there at ease, leaning back against the pack, you eat breakfast. You eat it fairly fast today, because you have twenty miles to go, and by eleven o'clock it will be hot. You keep pouring fresh cups of hot tea, and each one tells. Spoonful by spoonful, you eat the fruit-and-cereal. It is very sweet, and it tastes good. When it is finished you chew a stick of beef jerky. And all the time the world and the day are unfolding above and below and around you. The light eases from gray toward blue. The valleys begin to emerge from their shadow, the peaks to gain a third dimension. The night, you realize, has already slipped away.

Do not let the menu deceive you: there is no better kind of breakfast.

When the meal is over you wash up rather sketchily (there is plenty of water, but time presses). You re-bag the food and utensils and stove and stow them away in the pack. The light moves on from blue toward pink. Still inside the mummy bag, you put on your shorts. And (because this is a day in a book) you time it just right. The sun moves majestically up from behind those distant peaks, exploding the blue and the pink into gold, at the very moment you need its warmth—at the very moment that the time arrives for you to pluck up your courage and forsake the mummy bag and put on socks and boots. Ten minutes later you are walking. Another half hour and you are wide awake.

(This is only a sample morning, of course—a not-too-cold morning on which you know there is a hot and fairly long day ahead. If the night had been really cold, or the dew so heavy that it soaked the mummy bag and everything else, you would probably have waited for the sun to make the world bearable or to dry out all that extra and unnecessary load of water. If, on the other hand, the day promised to be horribly long, or its noonday heat burningly hot, you would have set the something to stir inside you even earlier—probably suffering a restless night thereby, unless you are a more efficient alarm clock than I am—and would have finished breakfast in time to start walking as soon as it was light enough to do so safely. By contrast, this might have been a rest day. Then, you would simply have dozed until you got tired of dozing, and afterward made breakfast—or have woken yourself up first by diving into lake or river. But whatever the variations—unless you decided to catch fish for breakfast and succeeded—the basic food theme would have remained very much the same.)

You walk all morning, following a trail that twists along beside a pure, rushing mountain creek. Every hour, you halt for ten minutes. At every halt you take the cup from the belt clip at your waist and dip it into the creek and drink as much of the sensuously cool water as you want. And at every halt—except perhaps the first, when breakfast is still adequately with you—you take the bag of raisins-and-mintcake out of the nibble pocket and munch a few raisins and fragments of mintcake. At each succeeding halt you tend to eat rather more; but, without giving the matter much direct thought, you ration against the hours ahead. In mid-morning, a stick of beef jerky helps replenish the protein supply. Later, you boost the quickly available energy, and the fats too, with a piece of chocolate.

Just after noon, you stop for lunch. You choose the place carefully—almost more carefully than the site for a night camp, because you will spend more waking hours there. You most often organize the day with a long midday halt, not only because it means that you avoid walking through the worst of the heat but also because you have found noon a more comfortable and rewarding time than late evening to swim and wash and launder and doze and read and write notes and dream and mosey around looking at rocks and stones and fish and lizards and sandflies and trees and panoramas and cloud shadows and all the other important things. A long lunch halt also means that you split the day's effort into two slabs, with a good long rest in between. Come to think of it, perhaps this after all is the really critical factor.

Anyway, you choose your lunch site carefully. You find a perfect place, in a shady hollow beside the creek, to prop up the pack and roll out the groundsheet and then the air mattress and mummy bag (yes, mummy bag, for cushioning effect), and within three minutes of halting you have a set-up virtually identical to the one you woke up in that morning.

The soup of the day is mushroom. The directions could hardly be simpler: "Empty the contents into 1 liter (4 measuring cups) of hot water and bring to the boil. Cover and simmer for 5–10 minutes." So you light the stove and boil as much water as you know from experience you need for soup (what *you* need, not necessarily four measuring cups). You stir in the soup powder, add a smidgen of thyme (after rubbing it lightly in the palm of your hand), replace the cover at a very slight tilt so that the simmering soup will not boil over, reduce the heat as far as it will go (a mildly delicate business), and meditate for five minutes, stretched out tiredly but luxuriously on the mummy bag. After five minutes you add a dollop of margarine to the soup, stir, and pour out the first cupful. You leave the rest simmering. When you pour the second cup you turn off the stove and put the pot in the warmest place around—a patch of dry, sandy soil that happens to lie in a shaft of sunlight. Within half an hour of halting you have finished the soup and dropped off into a catnap.

When you wake up you wash all pots and utensils—thoroughly now, because there is time as well as water. You use sand as a scourer, grass as a cleaning cloth, detergent powder as detergent powder, and the creek for rinsing. (If the pots had looked very dirty and you had been "out" for a long time, or if an upset stomach had made you suspicious about cleanliness, you might—if there was fuel to spare—have put spoon and cup into the small pot and the small pot and some water into the big pot and boil-sterilized the whole caboosh.)

Next you do a couple of chores that you have made more or less automatic action after lunch, so that you will not overlook them. You decide on the menu for the next twenty-four hours and make the necessary transfers from bulk-ration bag to current-day's bag—including the refilling from the bagged reserve of the containers of milk (an everyday chore) and sugar and salt (once a week). You also replenish the nibble pocket: raisins, mintcake, energy bar. If necessary, you put a new book of matches in the ticket pocket of your shorts or long pants or both. (You carry a book in each.)

Then you refill the stove. You use the funnel and take great care not to spill precious fuel, but the aluminum bottle is brimful and some gasoline dribbles down its side. Still, you expected this slight wastage; and you know that it won't happen in a day or two, once the level in the bottle drops.

(Naturally, it does not matter much what time of day you choose to do these chores. In winter, for example, when the days are short, you'll probably just snatch a quick lunch and will do the reapportionment and refilling during the early hours of the long, long darkness. But on each trip you try to get into the habit of doing the chores at about the same time each day, because you know that otherwise you may find yourself fumbling down into the pack for the bulk-food bag in the middle of a meal, and at the same moment hear the dying bleat of an almost empty stove.)

For the next two or three or four or even five hours you either do some of the many make-and-mend chores that always keep piling up (washing, laundering, writing notes, and so on), or you mosey around and do the important matters that you came for (rocks, lizards, cloud shadows), or you simply sit and contemplate. Or you devote the time to a combination of all these things. But at the end of that time, when you know you ought to be walking again within half an hour, you brew up a sizable pot of tea (this particular day, you too are walking on a British passport). And because there are still four hours to darkness and night camp and dinner, you eat half an energy bar. Then you pack everything away, hoist up the pack, and start walking—leaving behind as the only signs of occupation a rectangle of crushed grass that will recover within hours, and, where the stove stood, a tiny circle that you manage to conceal anyway by pulling the grass stems together.

You find yourself walking in desert now (a shade miraculously, it's true, but it suits our book purposes better to have it happen that way) and it is very hot. Because you expect to find no more water until you come to a spring about noon the following day, you have filled all three half-gallon canteens you brought with you. Now, you go easy on the water. You still drink as well as munch at every hourly halt. And you drink enough. But only just enough. Enough, that is, to take the edge off any emerging hint of thirst. At the first couple of halts this blunting process calls for only a very small sip or two. Later you need a little more. But always, before you swallow the precious liquid, you swirl it around your mouth to wash away the dryness and the scum.

One canteen has to be non-fumble available at halts, but direct sunlight would quickly turn its water tepid. So you put it inside the pack—on top, but insulated by a down jacket.

With an hour to go to darkness, and a promise already there of the coolness that will come when the sun drops behind the parched, encircling hills, you begin to feel tired—not so much muscle-weary as plain running out of energy. So at the hourly halt you pour some water into the lid of one cooking pot, squirt-add milk, and pour in some cereal mixture. (Looked at objectively, this cereal snack always seems a highly inefficient business. It ought to be enough to take from the nibble pocket a booster bonus of raisins or chocolate or the remaining half energy bar. But the cereal snack seems to work better, so you go on doing it.)

At this final pre-camp halt you empty into the inner cooking pot the dehydrated beans and mixed vegetables that are on the day's dinner menu, and add salt and just enough water to reconstitute them. (Presoaked like this, they cook in ten minutes rather than half an hour.) You know from experience how much water to add. It is surprisingly little: barely enough to cover them. You add as little as possible, to reduce the danger of spillage, and from now on, when you take the pack off, you are careful to keep it upright.

You walk until it is too dark to go on (keeping a canny rattlesnake-watch during the last hour, because this is their time of day). You camp in any convenient place that is level enough, though it is a kitchen advantage, stovewise, to have adequate shelter from desert winds (usually *down* canyons at night).

Dinner is the main meal of the day, but it is very simple to prepare. It has to be. You are tired now. And because the rising sun will be coercing you on your way again in less than eight hours, you don't want to waste time. So as soon as you halt you roll out the groundsheet and air mattress and sleeping bag and sit thankfully down and set up the kitchen just as you did last night and at lunch-time, except that because of a hump in the ground and a gentle but growing crosswind you find it expedient to put everything on the other side of the bed. Even before you take off your boots, you empty the already soft vegetables out of the small pot into the big one, scraping the stickily reluctant scraps out with the spoon and swirling the small pot clean with the water you're going to need to cook the meal anyway. You add a little or a lot of water according to whether you fancy tonight's stew in the form of a near-soup or an off-putty goo. (Only experience will teach you how much water achieves what consistency. For painless experience, start with near-soups that won't burn, and then work down toward goo. Your methods are rough and ready, so you will from time to time add the pleasures of surprise to those of variety.) You light the stove (using the flashlight to check when the gasoline wells up) and put the big pot on it, uncovered. Then you crumble one meat bar onto the vegetables and sprinkle in about one fifth of a package of oxtail soup and a couple of shakes of pepper and a healthy dose of hand-rubbed oregano. You stir and cover. Next you take off your boots and put them within easy reach, on the opposite side of the bed from the kitchen, and put your socks in the boots. Then you anoint your feet with rubbing alcohol, taking care to keep it well away from the stove, and blow up the air mattress (whatever you do, don't leave this breath-demanding chore until after dinner).

At this point, steam issues from the stew pot. You reduce the heat to dead-low or thereabouts (taking care not to turn the stove off in the process), stir the compound a couple of times, inhale appreciatively and replace the cover. While dinner simmers toward fruition you empty two ounces of dehydrated peaches and a little water into the small cooking pot and put it ready for breakfast, up alongside the pack. Then you jot down a few thoughts in your notebook, stir the stew and sample it, find the beans are not quite soft yet. So you study the map and worry a bit about the morning's route, put map and pen and pencil and eyeglasses and thermometer into the bedside boots, take off your shorts and slide halfway down into the mummy bag out of the wind, and stir the stew again and find all ready. You pour-and-spoon out a cupful, leaving the balance on the stove because the wind is blowing distinctly cool now. And then, leaning comfortably back against the pack and watching the sky and the black peaks meld, you eat, cupful by cupful, your dinner. You finish it—just. Then you spoon-scrape out every last possible fragment and polish-clean the pot and cup and spoon with a piece of toilet paper. You put the paper under the stove so that you can burn it in the morning. Then you put cup and spoon into the breakfast-readied small pot, pour the morning tea water into the big pot, set the big pot alongside the small one and the sugar and milk containers alongside them both, put the current day's ration bag into the pack (where it is moderately safe from mice and their night allies) and your shorts on top of it, lean one canteen against the boots so that you can reach out and grasp it during the night without doing more than loosen the mummy-bag drawstrings, zipper and drawstring yourself into the bag, wind your watch, belch once, remind yourself what time you want the something to stir in the morning, and go to sleep.*

---

*The elapsed time between halting and going to sleep will obviously vary with many factors, including how eager you are to get to sleep. It is difficult to give meaningful average times. You just don't measure such things very often. The only time I remember doing so was under conditions markedly similar to those of our sample evening. I was in no particular hurry, but I did not dally. And I happened to notice as I wound my watch that it was exactly forty minutes since I had halted.

The Complete Walker (1968)

R. BUCKMINSTER FULLER

I once interviewed R. Buckminster Fuller (1895–1983). That is to say, I once held a microphone in front of his mouth while he embarked on a stunning, elliptical, and semi-connected 20-minute ramble that touched on everything from rocket travel to architecture to why he wore three watches (so that he could know the time where he was, where he was going, and at his home base). Fuller considered himself a citizen of the Earth, and he considered the Earth in need of considerable improvement, which he was willing to arrange. Some of his inventions— notably the geodesic dome, which could sustain its own weight even when blown up to enormous size as in the American pavilion at Montreal's Expo '67—were great successes. Others, like the three-wheeled Dymaxion Car, were not. But Fuller at heart was an environmentalist, deeply concerned with the question he poses in this essay: "Does humanity have a chance to survive lastingly and successfully on planet Earth, and if so, how?" He thought that the growth of knowledge, combined with the ability to recycle the Earth's materials, offered a way out for a planet in peril, and his exuberance was persuasive for many. Marshall McLuhan, who shared the same essential optimism about the emerging infosphere, coined the term "global village." Fuller's "Spaceship Earth" is the other great description of our planet from the moment of new insight that coincided with the first views back from outer space.

Spaceship Earth

Our little Spaceship Earth is only eight thousand miles in diameter, which is almost a negligible dimension in the great vastness of space. Our nearest star—our energy-supplying mother-ship, the Sun—is ninety-two million miles away, and the next nearest star is one hundred thousand times further away. It takes two and one-half years for light to get to us from the next nearest energy supply ship star. That is the kind of space-distanced pattern we are flying. Our little Spaceship Earth is right now travelling at sixty thousand miles an hour around the sun and is also spinning axially, which, at the latitude of Washington, D.C., adds approximately one thousand miles per hour to our motion. Each minute we both spin at one hundred miles and zip in orbit at one thousand miles. That is a whole lot of spin and zip. When we launch our rocketed space capsules at fifteen thousand miles an hour, that additional acceleration speed we give the rocket to attain its own orbit around our speeding Spaceship Earth is only one-fourth greater than the speed of our big planetary spaceship.

Spaceship Earth was so extraordinarily well invented and designed that to our knowledge humans have been on board it for two million years not even knowing that they were on board a ship. And our spaceship is so superbly designed as to be able to keep life regenerating on board despite the phenomenon, entropy, by which all local physical systems lose energy. So we have to obtain our biological life-regenerating energy from another spaceship—the sun.

Our sun is flying in company with us, within the vast reaches of the Galactic system, at just the right distance to give us enough radiation to keep us alive, yet not close enough to burn us up. And the whole scheme of Spaceship Earth and its live passengers is so superbly designed that the Van Allen belts, which we didn't even know we had until yesterday, filter the sun and other star radiation which as it impinges upon our spherical ramparts is so concentrated that if we went nakedly outside the Van Allen belts it would kill us. Our Spaceship Earth's designed infusion of that radiant energy of the stars is processed in such a way that you and I can carry on safely. You and I can go out and take a sunbath, but are unable to take in enough energy through our skins to keep alive. So part of the invention of the Spaceship Earth and its biological life-sustaining is that the vegetation on the land and the algae in the sea, employing photosynthesis, are designed to impound the life-regenerating energy for us to adequate amount.

But we can't eat all the vegetation. As a matter of fact, we can eat very little of it. We can't eat the bark nor wood of the trees nor the grasses. But insects can eat these, and there are many other animals and creatures that can. We get the energy relayed to us by taking the milk and meat from the animals. The animals can eat the vegetation, and there are a few of the fruits and tender vegetation petals and seeds that we can eat. We have learned to cultivate more of those botanical edibles by genetical inbreeding.

That we are endowed with such intuitive and intellectual capabilities as that of discovering the genes and the R.N.A. and D.N.A. and other fundamental principles governing the fundamental design controls of life systems as well as of nuclear energy and chemical structuring is part of the extraordinary design of the Spaceship Earth, its equipment, passengers, and internal support systems. It is therefore paradoxical but strategically explicable, as we shall see, that up to now we have been mis-using, abusing, and polluting this extraordinary chemical energy-interchanging system for successfully regenerating all life aboard our planetary spaceship.

One of the interesting things to me about our spaceship is that it is a mechanical vehicle, just as is an automobile. If you own an automobile, you realize that you must put oil and gas into it, and you must put water in the radiator and take care of the car as a whole. You begin to develop quite a little thermodynamic sense. You know that you're either going to have to keep the machine in good order or it's going to be in trouble and fail to function. We have not been seeing our Spaceship Earth as an integrally-designed machine which to be persistently successful must be comprehended and serviced in total.

Now there is one outstandingly important fact regarding Spaceship Earth, and that is that no instruction book came with it. I think it's very significant that there is no instruction book for successfully operating our ship. In view of the infinite attention to all other details displayed by our ship, it must be taken as deliberate and purposeful that an instruction book was omitted. Lack of instruction has forced us to find that there are two kinds of berries—red berries that will kill us and red berries that will nourish us. And we had to find out ways of telling which-was-which red berry before we ate it or otherwise we would die. So we were forced, because of a lack of an instruction book, to use our intellect, which is our supreme faculty, to devise scientific experimental procedures and to interpret effectively the significance of the experimental findings. Thus, because the instruction manual was missing we are learning how we safely can anticipate the consequences of an increasing number of alternative ways of extending our satisfactory survival and growth—both physical and metaphysical.

Quite clearly, all of life as designed and born is utterly helpless at the moment of birth. The human child stays helpless longer than does the young of any other species. Apparently it is part of the invention "man" that he is meant to be utterly helpless through certain anthropological phases and that, when he begins to be able to get on a little better, he is meant to discover some of the physical leverage-multiplying principles inherent in universe as well as the many nonobvious resources around him which will further compoundingly multiply his knowledge-regenerating and life-fostering advantages.

I would say that designed into this Spaceship Earth's total wealth was a big safety factor which allowed man to be very ignorant for a long time until he had amassed enough experiences from which to extract progressively the system of generalized principles governing the increases of energy managing advantages over environment. The designed omission of the instruction book on how to operate and maintain Spaceship Earth and its complex life-supporting and regenerating systems has forced man to discover retrospectively just what his most important forward capabilities are. His intellect had to discover itself. Intellect in turn had to compound the facts of his experience. Comprehensive reviews of the compounded facts of experiences by intellect brought forth awareness of the generalized principles underlying all special and only superficially-sensed experiences. Objective employment of those generalized principles in rearranging the physical resources of environment seems to be leading to humanity's eventually total success and readiness to cope with far vaster problems of universe.

To comprehend this total scheme we note that long ago a man went through the woods, as you may have done, and I certainly have, trying to find the shortest way through the woods in a given direction. He found trees fallen across his path. He climbed over those crisscrossed trees and suddenly found himself poised on a tree that was slowly teetering. It happened to be lying across another great tree, and the other end of the tree on which he found himself teetering lay under a third great fallen tree. As he teetered he saw the third big tree lifting. It seemed impossible to him. He went over and tried using his own muscles to lift that great tree. He couldn't budge it. Then he climbed back atop the first smaller tree, purposefully teetering it, and surely enough it again elevated the larger tree. I'm certain that the first man who found such a tree thought that it was a magic tree, and may have dragged it home and erected it as man's first totem. It was probably a long time before he learned that any stout tree would do, and thus extracted the concept of the generalized principle of leverage out of all his earlier successive special-case experiences with such accidental discoveries. Only as he learned to generalize fundamental principles of physical universe did man learn to use his intellect effectively.

Once man comprehended that any tree would serve as a lever his intellectual advantages accelerated. Man freed of special-case superstition by intellect has had his survival potentials multiplied millions fold. By virtue of the leverage principles in gears, pulleys, transistors, and so forth, it is literally possible to do more with less in a multitude of physio-chemical ways. Possibly it was this intellectual augmentation of humanity's survival and success through the metaphysical perception of generalized principles which may be objectively employed that Christ was trying to teach in the obscurely told story of the loaves and the fishes.

Operating Manual for Spaceship Earth (1969)

STEPHANIE MILLS

If you want to know what it felt like to be young and idealistic in the late 1960s, you could do worse than read Stephanie Mills' commencement address to her classmates at Mills College in California. Her vow not to have children made headlines across the country; it was, after all, the era of Paul Ehrlich and the population bomb. Mills (b. 1948) has gone on to a distinguished career as a writer and social critic—she has called herself a Luddite and eschews the computer and the Internet. "I'm content with the pace, volume, and style of communication I do enjoy," she says, and indeed in her 2002 book *Epicurean Simplicity* she focuses on the finer points of some basic pleasures: gardening, bicycling, friendship.

Mills College Valedictory Address

Traditionally, commencement exercises are the occasion for fatuous comments on the future of the graduates present. This future is generally painted in glowing terms, characterized as long and happy. My depressing comment on that rosy future, that infinite future, is that it is a hoax. Our days as a race on this planet are, at this moment, numbered, and the reason for our finite, unrosy future is that we are breeding ourselves out of existence. Within the next ten years, we will witness widespread famines and possible global plagues raging through famine-weakened populations. Soon we may have to ask ourselves grisly questions like, "Will I be willing to shoot my neighbor if he tries to steal my last loaf of bread? Will I be forced to become a cannibal?"

The hideous fact that we are reproducing so rapidly that it is conceivable that our means of sustenance will be grossly inadequate within ten years was foreseen nearly two centuries ago. In 1798, Thomas Robert Malthus, in his "Essay on the Principle of Population," said, "Population, when unchecked, increases in a geometrical ratio. Subsistence increases only in an arithmetical ratio." We have had nearly two hundred years to think over the consequences of that projection, yet at the turn of the century, people were arrested in New York for distributing birth control information, and only last year, Pope Paul the Sixth issued an encyclical which forbade the members of his flock to use contraceptives. At this point in our history as a race, Dr. Paul Ehrlich of Stanford has observed, "Anyone . . . who stands in the way of measures to bring down the birth rate is automatically working for a rise in the death rate."

So—we have had at least a two hundred years' warning, yet in nineteen sixty-nine, still, virtually nothing is being done by anyone with enough power to substantially affect the situation. Mind you, I said affect, not eliminate. One of the more depressing aspects of the problem is that we cannot escape unscathed. Dr. Ehrlich and others say that immediate action must be taken simply to minimize the consequences. And *if* this action is taken, which it probably won't be, the psychological damage that we will all suffer is great. One of the suggestions for reducing the range of the disaster is the involuntary sterilization of any person who has produced more than two children. This may sound grossly inhumane, and perhaps it is to an extent, since our identities as men and women are so conditioned by our reproductive functions. I am terribly saddened by the fact that the most humane thing for me to do is to have no children at all. But the piper is finally demanding payment.

As an ex-potential parent, I have asked myself what kind of world my children would grow up in. And the answer was, "Not very pretty, not very clean. Sad, in fact." Because, you see, if the population continues to grow, the facilities to accommodate that population must grow, too. Thus we have more highways and fewer trees, more electricity and fewer undammed rivers, more cities and less clean air. Mankind has spread across the face of the earth like a great unthinking, unfeeling cancer. We have horribly disfigured this planet, ungrateful and shortsighted animals that we are. Our frontier spirit involves no reverence for any forms of life other than our own, and now we are even threatening ourselves with the ultimate disrespect of suicide. Perhaps we are unconsciously expiating our guilt, but it is just this quality—unconsciousness—that we must fight in ourselves. Rather than blindly walking into the abyss, we must take warning and try to extricate ourselves from it before it is really too late.

Too often, members of the so-called real world, that is the non-academic world, by some people's definition, are willing to dismiss the warnings and insights of the unreal, academic world. This often-made distinction and subsequent dismissal is a result of practicing a peculiar brand of pragmatism. It is the kind of pragmatism which says, "Let's be realistic—it just isn't profitable to develop an electric automobile." This kind of pragmatism is false, nearsighted, and a very shallow form of self-delusion. One of the advantages of a college education is escaping this kind of pragmatism for four years, being free of the small reality of earning a living. From this freedom comes a long-range perspective, which is a desperate necessity—not a luxury. Colleges are hot-beds of this kind of necessity. For four years I have been spared the reality of car payments and refrigerators, and in these four years, I have had more and more to come to grips with the awesome reality of human survival on this planet. Coping with this reality has not been a privilege, and certainly not a luxury. It is a very disheartening responsibility.

One of the reasons that it is so disheartening is the knowledge that it would be easier for me to leave this ivory tower to earn a living as a cocktail waitress than to earn a living as a crusader, of sorts, for human survival. If I had enough time, I'd try to get rich, become a philanthropist, and endow a foundation. But I have less than ten years, and so, for that matter, do you. This business of impending extinction is something that the so-called real and unreal worlds share. I can't eat a dollar bill, and Howard Hughes can't eat my diploma. The real and unreal worlds both have to become pragmatic on a grand scale, or there won't be any worlds left. We must come together to face this overwhelming human reality, and to do so, we probably must circumvent the so-called political realities which limit our ability to move quickly to lessen the gravity of this disaster. Political realities are, after all, only constructs for dealing with situations, and as mental constructs, they assume a note of unreality—especially when they obscure reality. Political realities are clouding this issue of human survival every day. On the primary level, there is the political reality that we simply can't go into a country and force it at gunpoint to adopt population-control measures. Still, we go into countries and increase their death rates at gunpoint. On a secondary level, there is the political reality that this situation is far less interesting to our government than the space program, anti-ballistic missiles, or even the size of print on cigarette packages. This conspicuous lack of interest may be due to the fact that there is hardly anybody, save a few desperate individuals, lobbying to save the human race. And the absence of a lobby may be due to the fact that pushing to save the human race will turn no one an instant profit. There is no material or political gain in the issue as of this moment.

And, as of this moment, the problem seems vaguely unreal. Some of us have never gone hungry a day in our lives. Starvation is a remote concept. The shelves of grocery stores are still crammed with things to eat. Why should I believe that anything will happen to change that? You and I should believe that the famine can and will happen if for no other reason than that we still may be able to do something. And doing something to save the human race has always been a fond dream of idealists both over and under thirty.

June 1, 1969

In October 1955, the Beat school of American writers went public with a reading at the Six Gallery in San Francisco. Allen Ginsberg's *Howl* was the highlight of the evening, but Gary Snyder (b. 1930) was there as well, reading one of his now-classic early poems, "A Berry Feast." In the years since, while the Beat flame blazed very high and then guttered, Snyder has built one of the more important careers in American letters, a career that has gone beyond movements and fads and that has been sustained by his concern for the natural world. Snyder, unlike most of the Beats, was intimately connected with that world from the beginning—a child of the Pacific Northwest who spent his early years climbing high mountains and working in fire towers and on logging crews (Japhy Ryder, the hero of Kerouac's 1958 *The Dharma Bums*, is based on Snyder). While many of the 1950s avant-garde grew interested in Eastern thought, Snyder took the project more seriously than most—he lived from 1956 to 1968 in Japan, often in a Zen monastery. He returned to the U.S. at the height of the counterculture years, and again found himself at the forefront. His darkly comic poem about that eco-icon Smokey the Bear dates from that period, and was soon followed by *Turtle Island* (1974), which won the Pulitzer Prize and was on the bookshelf of every commune and back-to-the-land homestead. Turtle Island was an aboriginal name for the North American continent, and much of his work in recent decades has explored the ecological power of indigenous understanding, always with the hope that all Americans might decide to settle in and become "native to their place."

Smokey the Bear Sutra

Once in the Jurassic, about 150 million years ago,
the Great Sun Buddha in this corner of the Infinite
Void gave a great Discourse to all the assembled elements

and energies: to the standing beings, the walking beings,
the flying beings, and the sitting beings—even grasses,
to the number of thirteen billion, each one born from a
seed, were assembled there: a Discourse concerning
Enlightenment on the planet Earth.

"In some future time, there will be a continent called
America. It will have great centers of power called
such as Pyramid Lake, Walden Pond, Mt. Rainier, Big Sur,
Everglades, and so forth; and powerful nerves and
        channels
such as Columbia River, Mississippi River, and Grand
        Canyon.
The human race in that era will get into troubles all over
its head, and practically wreck everything in spite of
its own strong intelligent Buddha-nature."

"The twisting strata of the great mountains and the
        pulsings
of great volcanoes are my love burning deep in the earth.
My obstinate compassion is schist and basalt and
granite, to be mountains, to bring down the rain. In that
future American Era I shall enter a new form: to cure
the world of loveless knowledge that seeks with blind
        hunger;
and mindless rage eating food that will not fill it."

And he showed himself in his true form of
        SMOKEY THE BEAR.

A handsome smokey-colored brown bear standing on his hind
legs, showing that he is aroused and watchful.

Bearing in his right paw the Shovel that digs to the truth beneath appearances; cuts the roots of useless attachments, and flings damp sand on the fires of greed and war;

His left paw in the Mudra of Comradely Display—indicating that all creatures have the full right to live to their limits and that deer, rabbits, chipmunks, snakes, dandelions, and lizards all grow in the realm of the Dharma;

Wearing the blue work overalls symbolic of slaves and laborers, the countless men oppressed by a civilization that claims to save but only destroys;

Wearing the broad-brimmed hat of the West, symbolic of the forces that guard the Wilderness, which is the Natural State of the Dharma and the True Path of man on earth; all true paths lead through mountains—

With a halo of smoke and flame behind, the forest fires of the kali-yuga, fires caused by the stupidity of those who think things can be gained and lost whereas in truth all is contained vast and free in the Blue Sky and Green Earth of One Mind;

Round-bellied to show his kind nature and that the great earth has food enough for everyone who loves her and trusts her;

Trampling underfoot wasteful freeways and needless suburbs; smashing the worms of capitalism and totalitarianism;

Indicating the Task: his followers, becoming free of cars, houses, canned food, universities, and shoes, master the Three Mysteries of their own Body, Speech, and Mind; and fearlessly chop down the rotten trees and prune out the sick limbs of this country America and then burn the leftover trash.

Wrathful but Calm, Austere but Comic, Smokey the Bear will
Illuminate those who would help him; but for those who would
hinder or slander him,

HE WILL PUT THEM OUT.

Thus his great Mantra:

Namah samanta vajranam chanda maharoshana
Sphataya hum traka ham mam

"I DEDICATE MYSELF TO THE UNIVERSAL DIAMOND
BE THIS RAGING FURY DESTROYED"

And he will protect those who love woods and rivers,
Gods and animals, hobos and madmen, prisoners and sick
people, musicians, playful women, and hopeful children;

And if anyone is threatened by advertising, air pollution,
or the police, they should chant SMOKEY THE BEAR'S
WAR SPELL:

DROWN THEIR BUTTS
CRUSH THEIR BUTTS
DROWN THEIR BUTTS
CRUSH THEIR BUTTS

And SMOKEY THE BEAR will surely appear to put the enemy
out with his vajra-shovel.

Now those who recite this Sutra and then try to put it in
practice will accumulate merit as countless as the sands
of Arizona and Nevada,
Will help save the planet Earth from total oil slick,
Will enter the age of harmony of man and nature,
Will win the tender love and caresses of men, women, and
beasts

Will always have ripe blackberries to eat and a sunny spot
     under a pine tree to sit at,
AND IN THE END WILL WIN HIGHEST PERFECT
ENLIGHTENMENT.

       thus have we heard.

          (may be reproduced free forever)

           1969

Covers the Ground

"When California was wild, it was one sweet bee-garden . . ."
John Muir

Down the Great Central Valley's
blossoming almond orchard acres
lines of tree trunks shoot a glance through
     as the rows flash by—

And the ground is covered with
cement culverts standing on end,
house-high & six feet wide
culvert after culvert far as you can see
     covered with
mobile homes, pint-size portable housing, johnny-on-the-spots,
concrete freeway, overpass, underpass,
     exit floreals, entrance curtsies, railroad bridge,
long straight miles of divider oleanders;
scrappy ratty grass and thistle, tumbled barn, another age,

yards of tractors, combines lined up—
new bright-painted units down at one end,
old stuff broke and smashed down at the other,
cypress tree spires, frizzy lonely palm tree,
steep and gleaming
fertilizer tank towers fine-line catwalk in the sky—

    covered with walnut orchard acreage
irrigated, pruned and trimmed;
with palleted stacks of cement bricks
    waiting for yellow fork trucks;
quarter-acre stacks of wornout car tires,
dust clouds blowing off the new plowed fields,
taut-strung vineyards trimmed out even on the top,

cubic blocks of fresh fruit loading boxes,
long aluminum automated chicken-feeder houses,
    spring fur of green weed
    comes on last fall's hard-baked ground,
        beyond "Blue Diamond Almonds"
come the rows of red-roofed houses
& the tower that holds catfood
with a red / white checkered sign

crows whuff over almond blossoms
beehives sit tight between fruit tree ranks
eucalyptus boughs shimmer in the wind—a pale blue hip-roof
house   behind a weathered fence—
crows in the almonds
    trucks on the freeways,
        Kenworth, Peterbilt, Mack,
        rumble diesel depths,
like boulders bumping in an outwash glacial river

drumming to a not-so-ancient text

> *"The Great Central Plain of California*
> *was one smooth bed of honey-bloom*
> > *400 miles, your foot would press*
> *a hundred flowers at every step*
> *it seemed one sheet of plant gold;*
>
> *all the ground was covered*
> *with radiant corollas ankle-deep:*
> *bahia, madia, madaria, burielia,*
> *chrysopsis, grindelia,*
> > *wherever a bee might fly—"*

us and our stuff just covering the ground.

Mountains and Rivers Without End (1996)

DENIS HAYES

Denis Hayes (b. 1944) grew up in the paper-mill town of Camas, Washington, but it wasn't the sulfur fumes or the clearcuts that turned him into an environmental activist. That came later, when as a student at Harvard's Kennedy School of Government he was required to intern in a government office. He was hired by Sen. Gaylord Nelson, a Democrat from Wisconsin, and was asked to organize teach-ins across the country about the environmental movement. These gathered momentum and turned into the first Earth Day in 1970. Hayes has spent the rest of his life in the movement, running everything from the Solar Energy Research Institute to the Green Seal consumer-certification effort to the Bullitt Foundation, which funds environmental efforts from its base in Seattle. But he has also reappeared on schedule to lead the major Earth Day anniversaries in 1990 and 2000. Some have criticized those later efforts as too corporate or celebrity-driven, but no one ever denies the power of Earth Day 1970. In Hayes' words, "it forged traditional conservationists into a union with newer constituencies worried about urban and industrial issues, thus giving birth to the modern environmental movement."

The Beginning

Sylvan Theater, Washington, D.C., April 22

I suspect that the politicians and businessmen who are jumping on the environmental bandwagon don't have the slightest idea what they are getting into. They are talking about filters on smokestacks while we are challenging corporate irresponsibility. They are bursting with pride about plans for totally inadequate municipal sewage treatment plants; we are challenging the ethics of a society that, with only 6 percent of the world's population, accounts for more than half of the world's annual consumption of raw materials.

Our country is stealing from poorer nations and from generations yet unborn. We seem to have a reverse King Midas touch. Everything we touch turns to garbage—142 million tons of smoke, 7 million junked cars, 30 million tons of paper, 28 billion bottles, 48 billion cans each year. We waste riches in planned obsolescence and invest the overwhelming bulk of our national budget in ABMs and MIRVs and other means of death. Russia can destroy every American twelve times; America can destroy every Russian forty times. I guess that is supposed to mean that we are ahead.

We're spending insanely large sums on military hardware instead of eliminating hunger and poverty. We squander our resources on moon dust while people live in wretched housing. We still waste lives and money on a war that we should never have entered and should get out of immediately.

We have made Vietnam an ecological catastrophe. Vietnam was once capable of producing a marketable surplus of grain. Now America must feed her. American bombs have pockmarked Vietnam with more than 2.6 million craters a year, some of them thirty feet deep. We spent $73 million on defoliation in Vietnam last year alone, much of it on 2,4,5-T, a herbicide we've now found causes birth defects. We dumped defoliants on Vietnam at the rate of 10,000 pounds a month, and in the last fiscal year alone we blackened 6,600 square miles. We cannot pretend to be concerned with the environment of this or any other country as long as we continue the war in Vietnam or wage war in Cambodia, Laos, or anywhere else.

But even if that war were over tomorrow, we would still be killing this planet. We are systematically destroying our land, our streams, and our seas. We foul our air, deaden our senses, and pollute our bodies. And it's getting worse.

America's political and business institutions don't seem yet to have realized that some of us want to live in this country thirty years from now. They had better come to recognize it soon. We don't have very much time. We cannot afford to give them very much time.

When it comes to salvaging the environment, the individual is almost powerless. You can pick up litter, and if you're diligent, you may be able to find some returnable bottles. But you are forced to breathe the lung-corroding poison which companies spew into the air. You cannot buy electricity from a power company which does not pollute. You cannot find products in biodegradable packages. You cannot even look to the manufacturer for reliable information on the ecological effects of a product.

You simply can't live an ecologically sound life in America. That is not one of the options open to you. Go shopping and you find dozens of laundry products; it seems like a tremendous array unless you know that most are made by three companies, and the differences in cleaning power are almost negligible. If you really want to be ecologically sound, you won't buy any detergents—just some old-fashioned laundry soap and a bit of soda. But there's nothing on those packages to tell you the phosphate content, and there's nothing in the supermarket to tell you, only meaningless advertising that keeps dunning you.

We are learning. In response, industry has turned the environmental problem over to its public relations men. We've been deluged with full-page ads about pollution problems and what's being done about them. It would appear from most of them that things are fine and will soon be perfect. But the people of America are still coughing. And our eyes are running, and our lungs are blackening, and our property is corroding, and we're getting angry. We're getting angry at half-truths, angry at semitruths, and angry at outright lies.

We are tired of being told that we are to blame for corporate depredations. Political and business leaders once hoped that they could turn the environmental movement into a massive antilitter campaign. They have failed. We have learned not to place our faith in regulatory agencies that are supposed to act in the public interest. We have learned not to believe the advertising that sells us presidents the way it sells us useless products.

We will not appeal any more to the conscience of institutions because institutions have no conscience. If we want them to do what is right, we must make them do what is right. We will use proxy fights, lawsuits, demonstrations, research, boycotts, ballots—whatever it takes. This may be our last chance. If environment is a fad, it's going to be our last fad.

Things as we know them are falling apart. There is an unease across this country today. People know that something is wrong. The war is part of it, but most critics of the war have, from the beginning, known that the war is only a symptom of something much deeper. Poor people have long known what is wrong. Now the alley garbage, the crowding and the unhappiness and the crime have spread beyond the ghetto and a whole society is coming to realize that it must drastically change course.

We are building a movement, a movement with a broad base, a movement which transcends traditional political boundaries. It is a movement that values people more than technology, people more than political boundaries and political ideologies, people more than profit. It will be a difficult fight. Earth Day is the beginning.

Earth Day—The Beginning (1970)

JOSEPH LELYVELD

Joe Lelyveld (b. 1937), executive editor of *The New York Times* from 1994 to 2001, manages in this straightforward piece of reporting to capture the flavor of the first Earth Day. It wasn't like the other protests of the era—the civil rights and antiwar gatherings that by then had begun to turn sour. There was an air of joy and hope and sheer pleasure at being outside—it was so much fun, in fact, that almost 40 years later many communities continue to celebrate April 22 as a kind of unofficial holiday. But the passion unleashed that day also had direct political consequences—organizers targeted unsympathetic members of Congress in that year's mid-term elections, and their successful efforts (seven incumbents were defeated) scared Washington into passing the landmark environmental laws that began the clean-up of urban air and rural rivers alike.

Millions Join Earth Day Observances Across the Nation

Huge, light-hearted throngs ambled down autoless streets here yesterday as the city heeded Earth Day's call for a regeneration of a polluted environment by celebrating an exuberant rite of spring.

If the environment had any enemies they did not make themselves known. Political leaders, governmental departments and corporations hastened to line up in the ranks of those yearning for a clean, quiet, fume-free city.

For two hours, except for crosstown traffic, the internal-combustion engine was barred from Fifth Avenue between 59th and 14th Streets: the only wheeled vehicle to go down the avenue during this period was a horse-drawn buggy carrying members of a Harlem block association.

Fourteenth Street between Third and Seventh Avenues, left free for pedestrians between noon and midnight, became an ecological carnival.

The Consolidated Edison Company, identified by many environmentalists as a prime enemy, draped orange and blue bunting from the lampposts. And balloons stamped with the slogans of the peace and population-control movements—"War is the worst pollution" and "Stop at two"—drifted over the crowds.

Union Square, the focus for scores of Earth Day observances and teach-ins throughout the metropolitan area, saw the kind of crowds it had rarely seen since the turbulent days of the thirties, when it was a favorite arena for leftists.

At any given time there were probably 20,000 people in the square, but the crowds were constantly on the move, so it was likely that many more than 100,000 passed through the square in the course of the day.

One section of the crowd was content to stand on 14th Street in front of a huge, brightly painted rostrum and listen to talks on the urgent crises of the day.

It was here that the festivities were officially ended at 10:40 P.M., with a brief announcement to that effect by an unidentified speaker, followed by the dousing of the floodlights.

The crowds continued to stroll along the traffic-free streets of the area until midnight, when the police barriers began coming down, and cars and trucks once more swept along 14th Street and the surrounding streets.

Earlier, other visitors had rambled through the booths around the square where particular causes were stressed—clean air and peace, urban planning and voluntary sterilization, conservation and wildlife preservation.

Each visitor to the square had to improvise his own Earth Day, by deciding where to spend his time. Some resolved the range of choices by taking part in a nonstop Frisbee game on Union Square Park's piebald lawns. Thousands crowded into a block-long polyethylene "bubble" on 17th Street to breathe pure, filtered air; before the enclosure had been open to the public for a half an hour the pure air carried unmistakable whiffs of marijuana.

Mayor Lindsay, in a brief speech, helped set the general theme of the day. "Behind the complex predictions and obscure language," he said, "beyond words like ecology, environment and pollution there is a simple question: Do we want to live or die?"

The Mayor was among those who brought up the war in Vietnam as an environmental concern. "Pure water will not wash away the stain of an immoral war," he declared.

Indeed, there was hardly a subject that has aroused demonstrators in the last five years that was not recapitulated in the course of the day.

At midafternoon, the full range in mood of protests was reflected in a musical counterpoint: On 14th Street the folk singer Odetta was singing "We Shall Overcome" while at the other end of the square a rock group was chanting, "Power to the people!"

But for its sponsors and its youthful participants, Earth Day was less a demonstration than a secular revival meeting. The hope was that citizens would pause and consider what they could do as individuals to fight pollution. To this end, the Environmental Action Coalition sold a "New York Pollution Survival Kit" with a list of 40 actions that individuals could take to fight noise, waste and dirt.

A quotation from Pogo on one of the booths caught this side of Earth Day: "We have met the enemy and they is us."

Senator Charles E. Goodell was greeted at a rally at New York University with a leaflet calling his speech "the biggest cause of air pollution." The speech called for harsher enforcement procedures by Federal agencies concerned with the environment.

Governor Rockefeller was greeted in Union Square with scattered cries of "Fascist pig!" Earlier he spoke in Prospect Park and rode a bicycle there.

Before he left Albany he signed a bill organizing anti-pollution activities under a Department of Environmental Conservation; a similar bill was signed by Gov. William T. Cahill in New Jersey.

But mostly the politicians were greeted by inattention. Organizers in the Environmental Action Coalition said they had been under pressure from candidates for Governor here—Mr. Rockefeller, Arthur J. Goldberg, Howard J. Samuels and Robert M. Morgenthau—to make room for them on their platform, but refused because they did not want the day to take a political cast.

An exception was made for Representative Richard L. Ottinger, who is seeking the Democratic nomination for the Senate, on account of his support of conservation groups seeking to clean up the Hudson River.

Mr. Ottinger denounced Governor Rockefeller and his new department, saying the Governor was merely "putting a new name on the same old door," behind which "you will find the same tired bureaucracy that protects the exploiters and polluters."

Con Edison braced itself for demonstrations outside its headquarters at Irving Place and 14th Street, imposing elaborate security precautions at the one entrance it left open. But the biggest crowd near there was the line forming across the street at Lüchow's restaurant for the bratwurst on sale at a sidewalk cafe.

The first schoolchildren arriving in Union Square early this morning for a special Earth Day cleanup were fourth-graders from the Sacred Heart School at Fifth Avenue and 91st Street. They were handed brooms, shovels and rakes, all with the compliments of Con Edison.

Mayor Lindsay stopped by the square to chat with the schoolgirls, then left in an electric-powered bus, also compliments of Con Edison.

"The coalition people are delighted with us," a Con Edison spokesman said. Actually, the coalition organizers were complaining that the utility company and others were spending more on advertising their support of Earth Day than they were on Earth Day itself.

On 14th Street a "guerrilla" theater group acted out a skit portraying the plight of a hibernating bear who awakes to find a Con Edison nuclear reactor had been built above his cave.

On Fifth Avenue, a youthful group of demonstrators called attention to the utility company's connection with fishkills in the Hudson River by displaying several dead fish. "You're next, people! You're next!" they cried.

The holiday mood on Fifth Avenue was exemplified by members of the architectural firm of Warner, Burns, Toan & Lunde, who spread a yellow-and-white quilt on the asphalt near 57th Street, put a tulip in a wine bottle for a centerpiece and enjoyed a picnic in the sun. A laughing crowd gathered around them and sang, "Happy Earth Day to You."

But a handful seemed to be irritated; among these was Katherine Duffy, a secretary for the American Standard Plumbing Company, who surveyed the crowds and said: "This is terrible, especially if you have only one hour for lunch."

Mayor Lindsay liked the transformation. "This is the first time I've walked down Fifth Avenue without getting booed half the distance," he said, pausing in front of St. Patrick's Cathedral.

Some of the most fervent Earth Day activities took place in areas remote from crowds. To name only a few of many, there were the students of John Dewey High School in Brooklyn who borrowed Park Department tools to clear off Plumb Beach near Flatbush Avenue; the community group that planted shrubs in Carl Schurz Park on East End Avenue and the group of Finch College students who washed the windows of a Lexington Avenue local subway train on their way to Union Square.

Similar activities attracted enthusiastic cleanup squads in the suburbs. Students from the Highlands Junior High School in White Plains painted the city's ramshackle railroad station and landscaped its grounds. In Rockland County, Pearl River students cleaned a public park and a stream that runs through the village.

Mayor Lindsay, who put in a full Earth Day moving tirelessly from one event to the next in his electric bus, returned to Union Square in the evening for a second speech. After that the speeches stopped and the platform was taken over by amateur rock groups. The side-streets and park emptied, but a large crowd remained on hand on 14th Street.

The New York Times, April 23, 1970

JONI MITCHELL & MARVIN GAYE

If you want to understand how Americans felt about the environment in the years around the first Earth Day—if you want to understand the waves of passion that produced the Clean Air Act and the Clean Water Act and the other laws that a reluctant President Nixon felt compelled to sign—you could do worse than listen to these enormous hits by Joni Mitchell and Marvin Gaye, which share a mood of head-shaking sadness even though they come from artists who were poles apart.

Joni Mitchell (b. 1943) grew up in western Canada and began her singing career in the coffeehouses of Toronto and then New York. Her work tended toward the personal and confessional, but her biggest hit, "Big Yellow Taxi," was much more political. She told a journalist not long after its release that the idea had come to her in a Honolulu hotel room: "Living in Los Angeles, smog-choked L.A., is bad enough but the last straw came when I visited Hawaii for the first time. It was night time when we got there, so I didn't get my first view of the scenery until I got up the next morning. The hotel room was quite high up so in the distance I could see the blue Pacific Ocean. I walked over to the balcony and there was the picture-book scenery, palm tree swaying in the breeze and all. Then I looked down and there was this ugly concrete car park in the hotel grounds. I thought 'They paved paradise and put up a parking lot.'"

Marvin Gaye (1939–1984) grew up in Washington, D.C., and began singing in his father's church. Early in the 1960s he met Berry Gordy, who signed him for his new Motown Records label. Gaye recorded hit after hit ("I Heard It Through the Grapevine") and sang classic duets with Tammi Terrell ("Ain't No Mountain High Enough"). But when Terrell died of a brain tumor in 1970, Gaye went into seclusion. He returned after a year with an album, *What's Going On* (which included "Mercy Mercy Me"), so different from his Motown hits that Gordy at first refused to release it. When he relented, it went to the top of the charts and has since been ranked as one of the top ten record albums of all time. Told from the point of view of a returning Vietnam veteran, it is a chronicle of profound despair at the dysfunction of American society—not least its disintegrating environment.

Big Yellow Taxi

They paved paradise,
Put up a parking lot
With a pink hotel, a boutique,
And a swinging hot spot

Don't it always seem to go
That you don't know what you've got
'til it's gone
They paved paradise
Put up a parking lot

They took all the trees
Put 'em in a tree museum
And they charged the people
A dollar and a half just to see 'em

(*Chorus*)

Hey farmer farmer
Put away that DDT now
Give me spots on my apples
But leave me the birds and the bees—
Please!

(*Chorus*)

Late last night,
I heard the screen door slam
And a big yellow taxi
Took away my old man

   (*Chorus*)

I said:

   (*Chorus*)

Ladies of the Canyon (1970)

Mercy Mercy Me (The Ecology)

Oh, mercy mercy me
Oh things ain't what they used to be
(No no)

Where did all the blue skies go?
Poison is the wind that blows
From the north and south and east

   (*Chorus*)

Ah things ain't what they used to be, no no
Oil wasted on the ocean and upon our seas
Fish full of mercury

   (*Chorus*)

Radiation underground and in the sky
Animals and birds who live nearby are dying

(*Chorus*)

What about this overcrowded land?
How much more abuse from man can she stand?

My sweet Lord
My sweet Lord
My sweet Lord

What's Going On (1971)

John McPhee (b. 1931) is renowned not only for his quiet and impeccable prose, but also for his range—he has written about everything from basketball to oranges. Arguably his most important book was *Encounters with the Archdruid* (1971), whose portrait of David Brower helped cement Brower's position at the forefront of the burgeoning environmental movement. McPhee uses an interesting device: he sets Brower in three different environments with three different antagonists. In the following excerpt, on the Colorado River, Brower engages the greatest dam-builder of the era. He doesn't win every argument, but his infectious love for the natural world always seems to carry the day.

from Encounters with the Archdruid

Seven years earlier, we could have flown north through Glen Canyon at an altitude of four hundred feet over the riverbed, and that, in a way, is what we did now. We got into a nineteen-foot gray boat—its hull molded for speed, a Buick V-6 engine packed away somewhere, a two-way radio, and the black-lettered words *United States Government* across the stern—and up the lake we went at twenty knots, for three days spraying arches of clear water toward red-and-black-streaked tapestry walls, pinnacle spires, and monument buttes. The Utah canyonland had been severed halfway up by a blue geometric plane, creating a waterscape of interrupted shapes, spectacularly unnatural, spectacularly beautiful. If we stopped for lunch, nudging up to a cool shadowing wall, we were in fact four hundred feet up the sheer side of what had been an immense cliff above the river, and was still an immense cliff—Wingate, Kayenta, Navajo Sandstones—above the lake. The boat sped on among hemispherical islands that had once been mountainous domes. It wheeled into Caprian bays. Arched overhangs formed grottoes in what had once been the lofty ceilings of natural amphitheatres.

Above the sound of the engine, Dominy shouted, "Who but Dominy would build a lake in the desert? Look at the country around here! No vegetation. No precipitation. It's just not the setting for a lake under any natural circumstances. Yet it is the most beautiful lake in the world."

"A thousand people a year times ten thousand years times ten thousand years will never see what was there," Brower said. He pointed straight down into the water. Then he opened a can of beer. The beer was in a big container full of ice. The ice had been made from water of the reservoir—reclaimed pellets of the Colorado. The container held dozens of cans of beer and soft drinks, enough for ten men anywhere else, but even on the lake the air was as dry as paper and the sun was a desert sun, and we held those cans in the air like plasma, one after another, all day long. Brower, the aesthetician, likes beer cans. Not for him are the simple biases of his throng. He really appreciates the cans themselves—their cylindrical simplicity, their beautifully crafted lithography. Brower's love of beauty is so powerful it leaps. It sometimes lands in unexpected places. Looking out over the lake at canyon walls flashing in reflected light, he slowly turned his Budweiser in his hand, sipped a little, and then said, "Lake Powell does not exist. I have never seen anything like it before. It's an incredibly beautiful reservoir. It must be the most beautiful reservoir in the world. I just wish you could hold the water level where it is now, Floyd."

Dominy smiled. The lake would become more and more beautiful as it continued to fill, he said. It would go up another hundred and twenty feet, revising vistas as it rose, and the last thirty-five feet would be the most dramatic, because the water at that elevation would reach far into the canyon-land.

"You can't duplicate this experience—this lake—anywhere else," Brower said. "But neither can you enjoy the original experience. That's the trouble. I camped under here once. It was a beautiful campsite. The river was one unending campsite. The ibis, the egrets, the wild blue herons are gone. Their habitat is gone—the mudbanks along the river."

"We've covered up a lot of nice stuff, there's no question about that, but you've got to admit that as far as views are concerned we've opened up a lot. Look. You can see mountains."

"The Henry Mountains," Brower said. "They were the last mountain range discovered in the lower forty-eight."

For my part, I kept waiting to see the lake. "Lake," as I sensed the word, called to mind a fairly compact water-filled depression in high terrain, with bends and bays perhaps obscuring some parts from others, but with a discernible center, a middle, a place that was farther from shore than any other, and from which a sweeping view of shore-line could be had in all directions. This was a provincialism, based on a Saranac, a Sunapee, a Mooselookmeguntic, and it had left me unprepared for Lake Powell, a map of which looks like a diagram of the human nervous system. The deep spinal channel of Glen Canyon, which was once the path of the Colorado, is now the least interesting part of Lake Powell. The long, narrow bays that reach far into hundreds of tributary canyons are the absorbing places to enter—the boat rounding bends between ever-narrowing walls among reflections of extraordinary beauty on wind-slickened rock. These were the places—these unimaginably deep clefts in the sandstone—that most stirred and most saddened Brower, who remembered wading through clear pools under cottonwood trees four hundred feet below the arbitrary level on which we floated.

In Face Canyon, the boat idled slowly and moved almost silently through still water along bending corridors of rock. "There used to be pools and trees in this little canyon," Brower said. "Cottonwoods, willows."

"Poison ivy, jimsonweed," Dominy said.

"Little parks with grasses. Water always running," Brower went on.

The rock, dark with the oxidation known as desert varnish, appeared to be a rich blue. Desert varnish somehow picks up color from the sky. The notes of a canyon wren descended the pentatonic scale. "That's the music here—the best there is," Brower said. "There used to be paper shells of surface mud on the floor of this canyon, cracking, peeling. Damn it, that was handsome."

"On balance, I can't lament what's been covered up," Dominy said.

In Cascade Canyon, on a ledge that had once been hundreds of feet high, grew a colony of mosses and ferns. "Now there's a hanging garden that's going to get water beyond its wildest dreams," Dominy said. "But unfortunately, like welfare, the water is going to drown it."

In Brower's memory, the most beautiful place in all the region of Glen Canyon was a cavernous space, under vaulting rock walls, that had been named the Cathedral in the Desert. The great walls arched toward one another, forming high and almost symmetrical overlapping parabolas. They enclosed about an acre of ground, in which had grown willows, grasses, columbine, and maidenhair fern. The center of this scene was a slim waterfall, no more than a foot in diameter, that fell sixty feet into a deep and foaming pool. From it a clear stream had flowed through the nave and out to the Colorado. The government boat now entered the Cathedral. Dominy switched off the engine. Water was halfway to the ceiling, and the waterfall was about ten feet high. It was cool in there, and truly beautiful—the vaulted ceiling, the sound of the falling water, the dancing and prismatic reflections, the echo of whispers. It had been beautiful in there before the reservoir came, and it would continue to be so, in successive stages, until water closed the room altogether.

A cabin cruiser came into the Cathedral. In it were a middle-aged couple and an older man. They asked what branch of the government we represented.

"I'm the Commissioner of Reclamation," Dominy said.

"Holy mackerel!" said the younger man.

"This lake is beautiful," the woman said.

"Thank you," Dominy said.

Back in the sunlight, Dominy worried about Brower's lobstering skin. "It would be a terrible thing to get this wildlife enthusiast out here and burn him up," he said.

"I'm red-faced not from the sun but from anger," Brower said.

"Red-faced with anger at my destructive tactics," said Dominy. "See that buoy? That's the Colorado River under water. The buoy is exactly over the original riverbed. Fabulous. Fabulous." The buoy floated on fifty or sixty fathoms of water.

The boat's radio crackled with heavy static as Park Service rangers made contact with one another. One ranger commented on "the unusual companionship" that was loose on the lake.

Dominy gave his cowboy yell, and said, "Hell, if those rangers could see us now! Dave, in spite of your bad judgment, you're a hell of a nice guy."

"I have nothing but bias," Brower said.

Skiers whipped by, going south. "Some of these bastards come up here and ski for fifty miles," Dominy said.

We cruised into the vicinity of a large natural rock span called Gregory Arch, which was now thirty-five feet beneath us. "If I could swim, I would want to go down and lay a wreath on Gregory Arch, because we've covered it up," Dominy said. "Dave, now that we've cemented our friendship, let me ask you: Why didn't you make a fuss about Gregory Arch?"

"We didn't know about it."

"No one else did, either. No one could have helped you."

"The public's evaluation of a place they may not have ever seen is what will save a place—it is what saved Grand Canyon. It's what might have saved Glen Canyon."

"Saved? For every person who could ever have gotten in here when this place was in its natural state, God damn it, there will be hundreds of thousands who will get in here, into all these side canyons—on the water highways. It's your few against the hundreds. Kids can see this place. Eighty-year-olds. People who can't walk."

"Ninety-nine per cent of the population can walk."

"Before I built this lake, not six hundred people had been in here in recorded history."

"By building this lake," Brower said, "mankind has preëmpted a hundred and eighty-six thousand acres of habitat for its own exclusive use."

"I'm a fair man," said Dominy. "Just to show you how fair I am, I'll say this: When we destroyed Glen Canyon, we destroyed something really beautiful. But we brought in something else."

"Water."

"You can lament all you want what we covered up. What we got is beautiful, and it's accessible."

The boat, in Labyrinth Canyon, drifted in a film of tamarisk needles, driftwood, bits of Styrofoam, bobbing beer cans, plastic lids. "We conservationists call this Dominy soup," Brower said.

On ledges above the soup were dozens of potholes, some of them very large, and Brower silently drew circles in the air to indicate how, over centuries, these enormous holes in the sandstone had been made by small rocks in swirling water. He and Dominy climbed out of the boat onto a ledge and lowered themselves into a pothole that was eleven feet in diameter and fifteen feet deep. There they began to argue about evaporation—through which, inevitably, a percentage of water in storage will be lost. Six hundred thousand acre-feet of water would annually evaporate from the surface of Lake Powell when full, Brower asserted, and Dominy did not like being baited on his own ground. Something spiralled in his mind like the stones that had cut the hole he was standing in, and eventually he burst out, "Don't give me that evaporation crap! If we didn't store the water, it wouldn't be here."

Brower danced away, came back, and jabbed lightly. "The water is stored only to produce kilowatts anyway," he said.

"We don't release one God-damned acre-foot of water from Lake Powell just to produce kilowatts," Dominy said.

Brower nodded solemnly in disbelief. He moved in again, shifting his grounds of complaint, and mentioned the huge aeolian sand deposits—millions of tons of fine sand clinging to hollows in the cliffsides—that regularly plop into Lake Powell as the rising water gets to them. Conservationists had suggested that Lake Powell was all but filling with these sands and that the very shores of the lake were crumbling into the water.

"The stuff melts on contact!" Dominy shouted. "You know you're exaggerating! Stretch the truth, that's all you conservationists do. When water hits it, that stuff melts like powder. The unstable material goes, but the walls of Jericho won't come down. The cliffs aren't coming down." He climbed out of the pothole.

Brower pointed to strange striations in jagged shapes on the opposite canyon wall. "That is hieroglyphic, written centuries ago by God Himself," he said.

"Yeah? What does it say?" said Dominy.

"It says, 'Don't flood it.'"

Encounters with the Archdruid (1971)

FRIENDS OF THE EARTH

Before Kyoto and Rio there was Stockholm. In June 1972, the U.N. Conference on the Human Environment—a huge international event, with a cast of thousands—attempted to come to some global consensus about the earth's ecological crises. Richard Nixon hailed the results of the conclave, which endorsed U.S. proposals to halt commercial whaling, regulate ocean dumping, and set up a World Heritage Trust to preserve wilderness areas. It was a moment of both enormous concern and enormous optimism, and this short excerpt from *The Stockholm Conference: Only One Earth* (1972)—a report prepared for the historic meeting by Amory Lovins and Friends of the Earth—captures some of the mood.

from Only One Earth

The earth is very old: more than 4,000,000,000 years old, an age we can write but not imagine. We do not know just how the earth was made. Somehow it gathered into a spinning ball. Its quivering crust slowly began to cool and take shape, a bleak and violent place. Winds of poison blew across its empty seas. But when more than 1,000,000,000 years had passed and the searing fire-tides had ebbed, the mixing of dead atoms in some strange swamp or ocean made by chance a new kind of matter: groups of atoms that could help others like themselves to form, that could break apart other groups and take their energy, that could absorb sunlight and store its energy. When the workings of time and chance brought these new kinds of matter together and linked them to each other in a great cycle driven by the sun, a new kind of chemistry was born, with such power that it swept the whole world, and gentled it, and changed it from brown to green.

For the past 3,000,000,000 years, sunlight has fed the growth of this new chemistry. Very slowly, larger and more complex groups of atoms have built themselves by trial and error; different patterns of atoms have come together to make cells, and cells to make tissues, and tissues to make organs, and organs to make redwoods and bees and sharks and hawks and men: things so wonderful that we know almost nothing of how they are put together.

Of course, most of the ways in which atoms have happened to arrange themselves have not been good for much. The plants and animals that live today are made of the select few patterns of atoms that did work well enough to survive; and for each living thing that has survived, there have been thousands of 'mistakes' that are no longer here. By now there has been so much chance mixing of atoms that most of the ways in which groups of (say) a few hundred of them can be put together have already been tried somewhere; and most of the patterns that are not here probably are not here for a good reason—they did not work well enough for plants and animals to make more like them. Yet at the same time, this chance trying of many ways of putting atoms together is still going on: life is never still, always trying to become something else, something more efficient and stable and strong. Life changes to meet its needs: as Robinson Jeffers wrote,

> What but the wolf's tooth whittled so fine
>   The fleet limbs of the antelope?
> What but fear winged the birds, and hunger
>   Jewelled with such eyes the great goshawk's head?

In the midst of this ceaseless change, life holds to one central truth: that all the matter and energy needed for life moves in great closed circles from which nothing escapes and to which only the driving fire of the sun is added. Life devours itself: everything that eats is itself eaten; everything that can be eaten is eaten; every chemical that is made by life can be broken down by life; all the sunlight that can be used is used. Of all that there is on earth, nothing is taken away by life and nothing is added by life—but nearly everything is used by life, used and reused in thousands of complex ways, moved through vast chains of plants and animals and back again to the beginning. Any break in these chains can spoil the whole. The web of life has so many threads that a few can be broken without making it all unravel (and if this were not so, life could not have survived the normal accidents of weather and time), but still the snapping of each thread makes the whole web shudder, and weakens it. Thus in the complex world of living things everything depends on everything else, all life is the same life, every effect is a cause, nothing can happen by itself. You can never do just one thing: the effects of what you do in the world will always spread out like ripples in a pond, and will make faraway and long-delayed changes you have never thought about. Yet you can never do nothing either, for you too are part of the web. Doing just as you have always done is itself doing something, and this too has effects.

The earth is round. We have known this for hundreds of years, but few people even today see what it means: that everywhere on earth, linked by cause and effect, is in a sense the same place, and that there is only so much earth and sky and water: so much and no more. We do not have unlimited amounts of anything—of land, of wind, of rain, of food, of sunlight, of a way to throw things; for the earth is round, and roundness means limits. Nor do we have immeasurable amounts of anything—for the amounts have been measured and, lately, found wanting. For the first time in his short history, man is now facing the limits of the earth that he likes to call his.

Getting It In Proportion

Man does not like to think his history is short, but so it is—so short that it is the merest instant in the earth's history. To see this, to put man's life in context with the earth's, imagine the whole history of the earth compressed into the six-day week of the Biblical Creation—a scale that makes eight thousand years pass in a single second. The first day and a half of this week are too early for life, which does not appear until about Tuesday noon. During the rest of Tuesday, and also Wednesday, Thursday, Friday, and well into Saturday, life expands and transforms the planet: life becomes more diverse, more stable, more beautiful; life makes a home for itself and adapts itself to live there. At four in the afternoon on Saturday, the age of reptiles comes onstage; at nine in the evening it goes offstage, but pelicans and redwoods are already here, lifeforms now threatened by man's wish to have the whole world to himself.

Man does not appear on the earth until three minutes before Saturday midnight. A second before midnight, man the hunter becomes man the farmer, and wandering tribesmen becomes villagers. Two-fifths of a second before midnight, Tutenkhamon rules Egypt. A third of a second before midnight, K'ung fu-tzŭ and Gautama Buddha walk the earth. A fortieth of a second before midnight, the Industrial Revolution begins. It is midnight now, and some people are saying we can go on at the rate that has worked for this fortieth of a second, because we know all the answers. Do we really know that much?

The Stockholm Conference: Only One Earth (1972)

WENDELL BERRY

The steadiest, most grounded and distinctive voice in contemporary writing about the environment doubtless belongs to Wendell Berry. Born in the summer of 1934 on a farm in Henry County, Kentucky, that his family had worked for four generations, he seemed likely to be the one who "escaped." After earning his masters at the University of Kentucky, he won a Wallace Stegner writing fellowship at Stanford, where he spent 1958 and 1959 studying with the noted writer in a seminar that also included Ed Abbey, Larry McMurtry, and Ken Kesey—as much literary firepower as may ever have slouched in the same classroom. A Guggenheim fellowship took him to France and Italy, after which he taught English at NYU until 1964. And then—in contravention of most of the laws of American success—he returned to Kentucky, bought a 125-acre farm on the banks of the Kentucky River near its confluence with the Ohio, and commenced growing tobacco and other crops much in the manner of his forebears. He also began writing the essays, poems, stories, and novels that have earned him his unrivaled place as the voice of a new agrarianism, with an old fidelity to place and neighbor, and a prophetic sense of the world as a runaway train nearing some kind of sad crash. It is almost impossible to select a few small fragments from his vast body of work, and especially difficult to neglect the stories and novels that in the most profound and lovely way make his case for community—community that embraces not only one's neighbors but also the land. Berry has occasionally been dismissed as nostalgic or sentimental, but in fact he is one of our most realistic writers, the least prone to the delusion that a way of life dependent on short-term exploitation of the soil and one's fellow man can be durable or satisfying. You cannot read his words without wishing in some corner of your heart to be a small farmer in a working community—I've often found framed copies of the Mad Farmer poems on the walls of people who have returned to the land, taken up the challenge of fitting into place. Berry has lived long enough to see his ideas take root: he is the father of the farmers' market, now the fastest-growing part of our food economy. If Wal-Mart has an antonym, it's Wendell Berry.

Manifesto: The Mad Farmer Liberation Front

Love the quick profit, the annual raise,
vacation with pay. Want more
of everything ready made. Be afraid
to know your neighbors and to die.
And you will have a window in your head.
Not even your future will be a mystery
any more. Your mind will be punched in a card
and shut away in a little drawer.
When they want you to buy something
they will call you. When they want you
to die for profit they will let you know.
So, friends, every day do something
that won't compute. Love the Lord.
Love the world. Work for nothing.
Take all that you have and be poor.
Love someone who does not deserve it.
Denounce the government and embrace
the flag. Hope to live in that free
republic for which it stands.
Give your approval to all you cannot
understand. Praise ignorance, for what man
has not encountered he has not destroyed.
Ask the questions that have no answers.
Invest in the millennium. Plant sequoias.
Say that your main crop is the forest
that you did not plant,
that you will not live to harvest.
Say that the leaves are harvested
when they have rotted into the mold.

Call that profit. Prophesy such returns.
Put your faith in the two inches of humus
that will build under the trees
every thousand years.
Listen to carrion—put your ear
close, and hear the faint chattering
of the songs that are to come.
Expect the end of the world. Laugh.
Laughter is immeasurable. Be joyful
though you have considered all the facts.
So long as women do not go cheap
for power, please women more than men.
Ask yourself: Will this satisfy
a woman satisfied to bear a child?
Will this disturb the sleep
of a woman near to giving birth?
Go with your love to the fields.
Lie easy in the shade. Rest your head
in her lap. Swear allegiance
to what is nighest your thoughts.
As soon as the generals and the politicos
can predict the motions of your mind,
lose it. Leave it as a sign
to mark the false trail, the way
you didn't go. Be like the fox
who makes more tracks than necessary,
some in the wrong direction.
Practice resurrection.

The Country of Marriage (1973)

The Making of a Marginal Farm

One day in the summer of 1956, leaving home for school, I stopped on the side of the road directly above the house where I now live. From there you could see a mile or so across the Kentucky River Valley, and perhaps six miles along the length of it. The valley was a green trough full of sunlight, blue in its distances. I often stopped here in my comings and goings, just to look, for it was all familiar to me from before the time my memory began: woodlands and pastures on the hillsides; fields and croplands, wooded slew-edges and hollows in the bottoms; and through the midst of it the tree-lined river passing down from its headwaters near the Virginia line toward its mouth at Carrollton on the Ohio.

Standing there, I was looking at land where one of my great-great-great-grandfathers settled in 1803, and at the scene of some of the happiest times of my own life, where in my growing-up years I camped, hunted, fished, boated, swam, and wandered—where, in short, I did whatever escaping I felt called upon to do. It was a place where I had happily been, and where I always wanted to be. And I remember gesturing toward the valley that day and saying to the friend who was with me: "That's all I need."

I meant it. It was an honest enough response to my recognition of its beauty, the abundance of its lives and possibilities, and of my own love for it and interest in it. And in the sense that I continue to recognize all that, and feel that what I most need is here, I can still say the same thing.

And yet I am aware that I must necessarily mean differently—or at least a great deal more—when I say it now. Then I was speaking mostly from affection, and did not know, by half, what I was talking about. I was speaking of a place that in some ways I knew and in some ways cared for, but did not live in. The differences between knowing a place and living in it, between cherishing a place and living responsibly in it, had not begun to occur to me. But they are critical differences, and understanding them has been perhaps the chief necessity of my experience since then.

I married in the following summer, and in the next seven years lived in a number of distant places. But, largely because I continued to feel that what I needed was here, I could never bring myself to want to live in any other place. And so we returned to live in Kentucky in the summer of 1964, and that autumn bought the house whose roof my friend and I had looked down on eight years before, and with it "twelve acres more or less." Thus I began a profound change in my life. Before, I had lived according to expectation rooted in ambition. Now I began to live according to a kind of destiny rooted in my origins and in my life. One should not speak too confidently of one's "destiny;" I use the word to refer to causes that lie deeper in history and character than mere intention or desire. In buying the little place known as Lanes Landing, it seems to me, I began to obey the deeper causes.

We had returned so that I could take a job at the University of Kentucky in Lexington. And we expected to live pretty much the usual academic life: I would teach and write; my "subject matter" would be, as it had been, the few square miles in Henry County where I grew up. We bought the tiny farm at Lanes Landing, thinking that we would use it as a "summer place," and on that understanding I began, with the help of two carpenter friends, to make some necessary repairs on the house. I no longer remember exactly how it was decided, but that work had hardly begun when it became a full-scale overhaul.

By so little our minds had been changed: this was not going to be a house to visit, but a house to live in. It was as though, having put our hand to the plow, we not only did not look back, but could not. We renewed the old house, equipped it with plumbing, bathroom, and oil furnace, and moved in on July 4, 1965.

Once the house was whole again, we came under the influence of the "twelve acres more or less." This acreage included a steep hillside pasture, two small pastures by the river, and a "garden spot" of less than half an acre. We had, besides the house, a small barn in bad shape, a good large building that once had been a general store, and a small garage also in usable condition. This was hardly a farm by modern standards, but it was land that could be used, and it was unthinkable that we would not use it. The land was not good enough to afford the possibility of a cash income, but it would allow us to grow our food— or most of it. And that is what we set out to do.

In the early spring of 1965 I had planted a small orchard; the next spring we planted our first garden. Within the following six or seven years we reclaimed the pastures, converted the garage into a henhouse, rebuilt the barn, greatly improved the garden soil, planted berry bushes, acquired a milk cow—and were producing, except for hay and grain for our animals, nearly everything that we ate: fruit, vegetables, eggs, meat, milk, cream, and butter. We built an outbuilding with a meat room and a food-storage cellar. Because we did not want to pollute our land and water with sewage, and in the process waste nutrients that should be returned to the soil, we built a composting privy. And so we began to attempt a life that, in addition to whatever else it was, would be responsibly agricultural. We used no chemical fertilizers. Except for a little rotenone, we used no insecticides. As our land and our food became healthier, so did we. And our food was of better quality than any that we could have bought.

We were not, of course, living an idyll. What we had done could not have been accomplished without difficulty and a great deal of work. And we had made some mistakes and false starts. But there was great satisfaction, too, in restoring the neglected land, and in feeding ourselves from it.

Meanwhile, the forty-acre place adjoining ours on the downriver side had been sold to a "developer," who planned to divide it into lots for "second homes." This project was probably doomed by the steepness of the ground and the difficulty of access, but a lot of bulldozing—and a lot of damage—was done before it was given up. In the fall of 1972, the place was offered for sale and we were able to buy it.

We now began to deal with larger agricultural problems. Some of this new land was usable; some would have to be left in trees. There were perhaps fifteen acres of hillside that could be reclaimed for pasture, and about two and a half acres of excellent bottomland on which we would grow alfalfa for hay. But it was a mess, all of it badly neglected, and a considerable portion of it badly abused by the developer's bulldozers. The hillsides were covered with thicket growth; the bottom was shoulder high in weeds; the diversion ditches had to be restored; a bulldozed gash meant for "building sites" had to be mended; the barn needed a new foundation, and the cistern a new top; there were no fences. What we had bought was less a farm than a reclamation project—which has now, with a later purchase, grown to seventy-five acres.

While we had only the small place, I had got along very well with a Gravely "walking tractor" that I owned, and an old Farmall A that I occasionally borrowed from my Uncle Jimmy. But now that we had increased our acreage, it was clear that I could not continue to depend on a borrowed tractor. For a while I assumed that I would buy a tractor of my own. But because our land was steep, and there was already talk of a fuel shortage—and because I liked the idea—I finally decided to buy a team of horses instead. By the spring of 1973, after a lot of inquiring and looking, I had found and bought a team of five-year-old sorrel mares. And—again by the generosity of my Uncle Jimmy, who has never thrown any good thing away—I had enough equipment to make a start.

Though I had worked horses and mules during the time I was growing up, I had never worked over ground so steep and problematical as this, and it had been twenty years since I had worked a team over ground of any kind. Getting started again, I anticipated every new task with uneasiness, and sometimes with dread. But to my relief and delight, the team and I did all that needed to be done that year, getting better as we went along. And over the years since then, with that team and others, my son and I have carried on our farming the way it was carried on in my boyhood, doing everything with our horses except baling the hay. And we have done work in places and in weather in which a tractor would have been useless. Experience has shown us—or re-shown us—that horses are not only a satisfactory and economical means of power, especially on such small places as ours, but are probably *necessary* to the most conservative use of steep land. Our farm, in fact, is surrounded by potentially excellent hillsides that were maintained in pasture until tractors replaced the teams.

Another change in our economy (and our lives) was accomplished in the fall of 1973 with the purchase of our first wood-burning stove. Again the petroleum shortage was on our minds, but we also knew that from the pasture-clearing we had ahead of us we would have an abundance of wood that otherwise would go to waste—and when that was gone we would still have our permanent wood lots. We thus expanded our subsistence income to include heating fuel, and since then have used our furnace only as a "backup system" in the coldest weather and in our absences from home. The horses also contribute significantly to the work of fuel-gathering; they will go easily into difficult places and over soft ground or snow where a truck or a tractor could not move.

As we have continued to live on and from our place, we have slowly begun its restoration and healing. Most of the scars have now been mended and grassed over, most of the washes stopped, most of the buildings made sound; many loads of rocks have been hauled out of the fields and used to pave entrances or fill hollows; we have done perhaps half of the necessary fencing. A great deal of work is still left to do, and some of it— the rebuilding of fertility in the depleted hillsides—will take longer than we will live. But in doing these things we have begun a restoration and a healing in ourselves.

I should say plainly that this has not been a "paying proposition." As a reclamation project, it has been costly both in money and in effort. It seems at least possible that, in any other place, I might have had little interest in doing any such thing. The reason I have been interested in doing it here, I think, is that I have felt implicated in the history, the uses, and the attitudes that have depleted such places as ours and made them "marginal."

I had not worked long on our "twelve acres more or less" before I saw that such places were explained almost as much by their human history as by their nature. I saw that they were not "marginal" because they ever were unfit for human use, but because in both culture and character *we* had been unfit to use them. Originally, even such steep slopes as these along the lower Kentucky River Valley were deep-soiled and abundantly fertile; "jumper" plows and generations of carelessness impoverished them. Where yellow clay is at the surface now, five feet of good soil may be gone. I once wrote that on some of the nearby uplands one walks as if "knee-deep" in the absence of the original soil. On these steeper slopes, I now know, that absence is shoulder-deep.

That is a loss that is horrifying as soon as it is imagined. It happened easily, by ignorance, indifference, "a little folding of the hands to sleep." It cannot be remedied in human time; to build five feet of soil takes perhaps fifty or sixty thousand years. This loss, once imagined, is potent with despair. If a people in adding a hundred and fifty years to itself subtracts fifty thousand from its land, what is there to hope?

And so our reclamation project has been, for me, less a matter of idealism or morality than a kind of self-preservation. A destructive history, once it is understood as such, is a nearly insupportable burden. Understanding it is a disease of understanding, depleting the sense of efficacy and paralyzing effort, unless it finds healing work. For me that work has been partly of the mind, in what I have written, but that seems to have depended inescapably on work of the body and of the ground. In order to affirm the values most native and necessary to me—indeed, to affirm my own life as a thing decent in possibility—I needed to know in my own experience that this place did not have to be abused in the past, and that it can be kindly and conservingly used now.

With certain reservations that must be strictly borne in mind, our work here has begun to offer some of the needed proofs.

Bountiful as the vanished original soil of the hillsides may have been, what remains is good. It responds well—sometimes astonishingly well—to good treatment. It never should have been plowed (some of it never should have been cleared), and it never should be plowed again. But it can be put in pasture without plowing, and it will support an excellent grass sod that will in turn protect it from erosion, if properly managed and not overgrazed.

Land so steep as this cannot be preserved in row crop cultivation.

To subject it to such an expectation is simply to ruin it, as its history shows. Our rule, generally, has been to plow no steep ground, to maintain in pasture only such slopes as can be safely mowed with a horse-drawn mower, and to leave the rest in trees. We have increased the numbers of livestock on our pastures gradually, and have carefully rotated the animals from field to field, in order to avoid overgrazing. Under this use and care, our hillsides have mended and they produce more and better pasturage every year.

As a child I always intended to be a farmer. As a young man, I gave up that intention, assuming that I could not farm and do the other things I wanted to do. And then I became a farmer almost unintentionally and by a kind of necessity. That wayward and necessary becoming—along with my marriage, which has been intimately a part of it—is the major event of my life. It has changed me profoundly from the man and the writer I would otherwise have been.

There was a time, after I had left home and before I came back, when this place was my "subject matter." I meant that too, I think, on the day in 1956 when I told my friend, "That's all I need." I was regarding it, in a way too easy for a writer, as a mirror in which I saw myself. There was obviously a sort of narcissism in that—and an inevitable superficiality, for only the surface can reflect.

In coming home and settling on this place, I began to *live* in my subject, and to learn that living in one's subject is not at all the same as "having" a subject. To live in the place that is one's subject is to pass through the surface. The simplifications of distance and mere observation are thus destroyed. The obsessively regarded reflection is broken and dissolved. One sees that the mirror was a blinder; one can now begin to see where one is. One's relation to one's subject ceases to be merely emotional or esthetical, or even merely critical, and becomes problematical, practical, and responsible as well. Because it must. It is like marrying your sweetheart.

Though our farm has not been an economic success, as such success is usually reckoned, it is nevertheless beginning to make a kind of economic sense that is consoling and hopeful. Now that the largest expenses of purchase and repair are behind us, our income from the place is beginning to run ahead of expenses. As income I am counting the value of shelter, subsistence, heating fuel, and money earned by the sale of livestock. As expenses I am counting maintenance, newly purchased equipment, extra livestock feed, newly purchased animals, reclamation work, fencing materials, taxes, and insurance.

If our land had been in better shape when we bought it, our expenses would obviously be much smaller. As it is, once we have completed its restoration, our farm will provide us a home, produce our subsistence, keep us warm in winter, and earn a modest cash income. The significance of this becomes apparent when one considers that most of this land is "unfarmable" by the standards of conventional agriculture, and that most of it was producing nothing at the time we bought it.

And so, contrary to some people's opinion, it *is* possible for a family to live on such "marginal" land, to take a bountiful subsistence and some cash income from it, and, in doing so, to improve both the land and themselves. (I believe, however, that, at least in the present economy, this should not be attempted without a source of income other than the farm. It is now extremely difficult to pay for the best of farmland by farming it, and even "marginal" land has become unreasonably expensive. To attempt to make a living from such land is to impose a severe strain on land and people alike.)

I said earlier that the success of our work here is subject to reservations. There are only two of these, but both are serious.

The first is that land like ours—and there are many acres of such land in this country—can be conserved in use only by competent knowledge, by a great deal more work than is required by leveler land, by a devotion more particular and disciplined than patriotism, and by ceaseless watchfulness and care. All these are cultural values and resources, never sufficiently abundant in this country, and now almost obliterated by the contrary values of the so-called "affluent society."

One of my own mistakes will suggest the difficulty. In 1974 I dug a small pond on a wooded hillside that I wanted to pasture occasionally. The excavation for that pond—as I should have anticipated, for I had better reason than I used—caused the hillside to slump both above and below. After six years the slope has not stabilized, and more expense and trouble will be required to stabilize it. A small hillside farm will not survive many mistakes of that order. Nor will a modest income.

The true remedy for mistakes is to keep from making them. It is not in the piecemeal technological solutions that our society now offers, but in a change of cultural (and economic) values that will encourage in the whole population the necessary respect, restraint, and care. Even more important, it is in the possibility of settled families and local communities, in which the knowledge of proper means and methods, proper moderations and restraints, can be handed down, and so accumulate in place and stay alive; the experience of one generation is not adequate to inform and control its actions. Such possibilities are not now in sight in this country.

The second reservation is that we live at the lower end of the Kentucky River watershed, which has long been intensively used, and is increasingly abused. Strip mining, logging, extractive farming, and the digging, draining, roofing, and paving that go with industrial and urban "development," all have seriously depleted the capacity of the watershed to retain water. This means not only that floods are higher and more frequent than they would be if the watershed were healthy, but that the floods subside too quickly, the watershed being far less a sponge, now, than it is a roof. The floodwater drops suddenly out of the river, leaving the steep banks soggy, heavy, and soft. As a result, great strips and blocks of land crack loose and slump, or they give way entirely and disappear into the river in what people here call "slips."

The flood of December 1978, which was unusually high, also went down extremely fast, falling from banktop almost to pool stage within a couple of days. In the aftermath of this rapid "drawdown," we lost a block of bottom-land an acre square. This slip, which is still crumbling, severely damaged our place, and may eventually undermine two buildings. The same flood started a slip in another place, which threatens a third building. We have yet another building situated on a huge (but, so far, very gradual) slide that starts at the river and, aggravated by two state highway cuts, goes almost to the hilltop. And we have serious river bank erosion the whole length of our place.

What this means is that, no matter how successfully we may control erosion on our hillsides, our land remains susceptible to a more serious cause of erosion that we cannot control. Our river bank stands literally at the cutting edge of our nation's consumptive economy. This, I think, is true of many "marginal" places—it is true, in fact, of many places that are not marginal. In its consciousness, ours is an upland society; the ruin of watersheds, and what that involves and means, is little considered. And so the land is heavily taxed to subsidize an "affluence" that consists, in reality, of health and goods stolen from the unborn.

Living at the lower end of the Kentucky River watershed is what is now known as "an educational experience"—and not an easy one. A lot of information comes with it that is severely damaging to the reputation of our people and our time. From where I live and work, I never have to look far to see that the earth does indeed pass away. But however that is taught, and however bitterly learned, it is something that should be known, and there is a certain good strength in knowing it. To spend one's life farming a piece of the earth so passing is, as many would say, a hard lot. But it is, in an ancient sense, the human lot. What saves it is to love the farming.

Recollected Essays (1981)

Preserving Wildness

The argument over the proper relation of humanity to nature is becoming, as the sixties used to say, polarized. And the result, as before, is bad talk on both sides. At one extreme are those who sound as if they are entirely in favor of nature; they assume that there is no necessary disjuncture or difference between the human estate and the estate of nature, that human good is in some simple way the same as natural good. They believe, at least in principle, that the biosphere is an egalitarian system, in which all creatures, including humans, are equal in value and have an equal right to live and flourish. These people tend to stand aloof from the issue of the proper human use of nature. Indeed, they have begun to use "stewardship" (meaning the responsible use of nature) as a term of denigration.

At the other extreme are the nature conquerors, who have no patience with an old-fashioned outdoor farm, let alone a wilderness. These people divide all reality into two parts: human good, which they define as profit, comfort, and security; and everything else, which they understand as a stockpile of "natural resources" or "raw materials," which will sooner or later be transformed into human good. The aims of these militant tinkerers invariably manage to be at once unimpeachable and suspect. They wish earnestly, for example, to solve what they call "the problem of hunger"—if it can be done glamorously, comfortably, and profitably. They believe that the ability to do something is the reason to do it. According to a recent press release from the University of Illinois College of Agriculture, researchers there are looking forward to "food production without either farmers or farms." (This is perhaps the first explicit acknowledgment of the program that has been implicit in the work of the land-grant universities for forty or fifty years.)

If I had to choose, I would join the nature extremists against the technology extremists, but this choice seems poor, even assuming that it is possible. I would prefer to stay in the middle, not to avoid taking sides, but because I think the middle *is* a side, as well as the real location of the problem.

The middle, of course, is always rather roomy and bewildering territory, and so I should state plainly the assumptions that define the ground on which I intend to stand:

1. We live in a wilderness, in which we and our works occupy a tiny space and play a tiny part. We exist under its dispensation and by its tolerance.

2. This wilderness, the universe, is *somewhat* hospitable to us, but it is also absolutely dangerous to us (it is going to kill us, sooner or later), and we are absolutely dependent upon it.

3. That we depend upon what we are endangered by is a problem not solvable by "problem solving." It does not have what the nature romantic or the technocrat would regard as a solution. We are not going back to the Garden of Eden, nor are we going to manufacture an Industrial Paradise.

4. There does exist a possibility that we can live more or less in harmony with our native wilderness; I am betting my life that such a harmony is possible. But I do not believe that it can be achieved simply or easily or that it can ever be perfect, and I am certain that it can never be made, once and for all, but is the forever unfinished lifework of our species.

5. It is not possible (at least, not for very long) for humans to intend their own good specifically or exclusively. We cannot intend our good, in the long run, without intending the good of our place—which means, ultimately, the good of the world.

6. To use or not to use nature is not a choice that is available to us; we can live only at the expense of other lives. Our choice has rather to do with how and how much to use. This is not a choice that can be decided satisfactorily in principle or in theory; it is a choice intransigently impractical. That is, it must be worked out in local practice because, by necessity, the practice will vary somewhat from one locality to another. There is, thus, no *practical* way that we can intend the good of the world; practice can only be local.

7. If there is no escape from the human use of nature, then human good cannot be simply synonymous with natural good.

What these assumptions describe, of course, is the human predicament. It is a spiritual predicament, for it requires us to be properly humble and grateful; time and again, it asks us to be still and wait. But it is also a practical problem, for it requires us to *do* things.

In going to work on this problem it is a mistake to proceed on the basis of an assumed division or divisibility between nature and humanity, or wildness and domesticity. But it is also a mistake to assume that there is no difference between the natural and the human. If these things could be divided, our life would be far simpler and easier than it is, just as it would be if they were not different. Our problem, exactly, is that the human and the natural are indivisible, and yet are different.

The indivisibility of wildness and domesticity, even within the fabric of human life itself, is easy enough to demonstrate. Our bodily life, to begin at the nearest place, is half wild. Perhaps it is more than half wild, for it is dependent upon reflexes, instincts, and appetites that we do not cause or intend and that we cannot, or had better not, stop. We live, partly, because we are domestic creatures—that is, we participate in our human economy to the extent that we "make a living"; we are able, with variable success, to discipline our appetites and instincts in order to produce this artifact, this human living. And yet it is equally true that we breathe and our hearts beat and we survive as a species because we are wild.

The same is true of a healthy human economy as it branches upward out of the soil. The topsoil, to the extent that it is fertile, is wild; it is a dark wilderness, ultimately unknowable, teeming with wildlife. A forest or a crop, no matter how intentionally husbanded by human foresters or farmers, will be found to be healthy precisely to the extent that it is wild—able to collaborate with earth, air, light, and water in the way common to plants before humans walked the earth. We know from experience that we can increase our domestic demands upon plants so far that we force them into kinds of failure that wild plants do not experience.

Breeders of domestic animals, likewise, know that, when a breeding program is too much governed by human intention, by economic considerations, or by fashion, uselessness is the result. Size or productivity, for instance, will be gained at the cost of health, vigor, or reproductive ability. In other words, so-called domestic animals must remain half wild, or more than half, because they are creatures of nature. Humans are intelligent enough to select for a type of creature; they are not intelligent enough to *make* a creature. Their efforts to make an entirely domestic animal, like their efforts to make an entirely domestic human, are doomed to failure because they do not have and undoubtedly are never going to have the full set of production standards for the making of creatures. From a human point of view, then, creature making is wild. The effort to make plants, animals, and humans ever more governable by human intentions is continuing with more determination and more violence than ever, but that does not mean that it is nearer to success. It means only that we are increasing the violence and the magnitude of the expectable reactions.

To be divided against nature, against wildness, then, is a human disaster because it is to be divided against ourselves. It confines our identity as creatures entirely within the bounds of our own understanding, which is invariably a mistake because it is invariably reductive. It reduces our largeness, our mystery, to a petty and sickly comprehensibility.

But to say that we are not divided and not dividable from nature is not to say that there is no difference between us and the other creatures. Human nature partakes of nature, participates in it, is dependent on it, and yet is different from it. We feel the difference as discomfort or difficulty or danger. Nature is not easy to live with. It is hard to have rain on your cut hay, or floodwater over your cropland, or coyotes in your sheep; it is hard when nature does not respect your intentions, and she never does exactly respect them. Moreover, such problems belong to all of us, to the human lot. Humans who do not experience them are exempt only because they are paying (or underpaying) other humans such as farmers to deal with nature on their behalf. Further, it is not just agriculture-dependent humanity that has had to put up with natural dangers and frustrations; these have been the lot of hunting and gathering societies also, and the wild creatures do not always live comfortably or easily with nature either.

But humans differ most from other creatures in the extent to which they must be *made* what they are—that is, in the extent to which they are artifacts of their culture. It is true that what we might as well call culture does go into the making of some birds and animals, but this teaching is so much less than the teaching that makes a human as to be almost a different thing. To take a creature who is biologically a human and to make him or her fully human is a task that requires many years (some of us sometimes fear that it requires more than a lifetime), and this long effort of human making is necessary, I think, because of our power. In the hierarchy of power among the earth's creatures, we are at the top, and we have been growing stronger for a long time. We are now, to ourselves, incomprehensibly powerful, capable of doing more damage than floods, storms, volcanoes, and earthquakes. And so it is more important than ever that we should have cultures capable of making us into humans—creatures capable of prudence, justice, fortitude, temperance, and the other virtues. For our history reveals that, stripped of the restraints, disciplines, and ameliorations of culture, humans are not "natural," not "thinking animals" or "naked apes," but monsters—indiscriminate and insatiable killers and destroyers. We differ from other creatures, partly, in our susceptibility to monstrosity. It is perhaps for this reason that, in the wake of the great wars of our century, we have seen poets such as T. S. Eliot, Ezra Pound, and David Jones making an effort to reweave the tattered garment of culture and to reestablish the cultural tasks, which are, as Pound put it, "To know the histories / to know good from evil / And know whom to trust." And we see, if we follow Pound a little further, that the recovery of culture involves, leads to, or is the recovery of nature:

> the trees rise
> and there is a wide sward between them
> . . . myrrh and olibanum on the altar stone
> giving perfume,
>   and where was nothing
> now is furry assemblage
>   and in the boughs now are voices . . .

In the recovery of culture *and* nature is the knowledge of how to farm well, how to preserve, harvest, and replenish the forests, how to make, build, and use, return and restore. In this *double* recovery, which is the recovery of our humanity, is the hope that the domestic and the wild can exist together in lasting harmony.

—

This doubleness of allegiance and responsibility, difficult as it always is, confusing as it sometimes is, apparently is inescapable. A culture that does not measure itself by nature, by an understanding of its debts to nature, becomes destructive of nature and thus of itself. A culture that does not measure itself by its own best work and the best work of other cultures (the determination of which is its unending task) becomes destructive of itself and thus of nature.

Harmony is one phase, the good phase, of the inescapable dialogue between culture and nature. In this phase, humans consciously and conscientiously ask of their work: Is this good for us? Is this good for our place? And the questioning and answering in this phase is minutely particular: It can occur only with reference to particular artifacts, events, places, ecosystems, and neighborhoods. When the cultural side of the dialogue becomes too theoretical or abstract, the other phase, the bad one, begins. Then the conscious, responsible questions are not asked; acts begin to be committed and things to be made on their own terms for their own sakes, culture deteriorates, and nature retaliates.

The awareness that we are slowly growing into now is that the earthly wildness that we are so complexly dependent upon is at our mercy. It has become, in a sense, our artifact because it can only survive by a human understanding and forbearance that we now must make. The only thing we have to preserve nature with is culture; the only thing we have to preserve wildness with is domesticity.

To me, this means simply that we are not safe in assuming that we can preserve wildness by making wilderness preserves. Those of us who see that wildness and wilderness need to be preserved are going to have to understand the dependence of these things upon our domestic economy and our domestic behavior. If we do not have an economy capable of valuing in particular terms the durable good of localities and communities, then we are not going to be able to preserve anything. We are going to have to see that, if we want our forests to last, then we must make wood products that last, for our forests are more threatened by shoddy workmanship than by clear-cutting or by fire. Good workmanship—that is, careful, considerate, and loving work—requires us to think considerately of the whole process, natural and cultural, involved in the making of wooden artifacts, because the good worker does not share the industrial contempt for "raw material." The good worker loves the board before it becomes a table, loves the tree before it yields the board, loves the forest before it gives up the tree. The good worker understands that a badly made artifact is both an insult to its user and a danger to its source. We could say, then, that good forestry begins with the respectful husbanding of the forest that we call stewardship and ends with well-made tables and chairs and houses, just as good agriculture begins with stewardship of the fields and ends with good meals.

In other words, conservation is going to prove increasingly futile and increasingly meaningless if its proscriptions are not answered positively by an economy that rewards and enforces good use. I would call this a loving economy, for it would strive to place a proper value on all the materials of the world, in all their metamorphoses from soil and water, air and light to the finished goods of our towns and households, and I think that the only effective motive for this would be a particularizing love for local things, rising out of local knowledge and local allegiance.

Our present economy, by contrast, does not account for affection at all, which is to say that it does not account for value. It is simply a description of the career of money as it preys upon both nature and human society. Apparently because our age is so manifestly unconcerned for the life of the spirit, many people conclude that it places an undue value on material things. But that cannot be so, for people who valued material things would take care of them and would care for the sources of them. We could argue that an age that *properly* valued and cared for material things would be an age properly spiritual. In my part of the country, the Shakers, "unworldly" as they were, were the true materialists, for they truly valued materials. And they valued them in the only way that such things *can* be valued in practice: by good workmanship, both elegant and sound. The so-called materialism of our own time is, by contrast, at once indifferent to spiritual concerns and insatiably destructive of the material world. And I would call our economy, not materialistic, but abstract, intent upon the subversion of both spirit and matter by abstractions of value and of power. In such an economy, it is impossible to value anything that one *has*. What one has (house or job, spouse or car) is only valuable insofar as it can be exchanged for what one believes that one wants—a limitless economic process based upon boundless dissatisfaction.

Now that the practical processes of industrial civilization have become so threatening to humanity and to nature, it is easy for us, or for some of us, to see that practicality needs to be made subject to spiritual values and spiritual measures. But we must not forget that it is also necessary for spirituality to be responsive to practical questions. For human beings the spiritual and the practical are, and should be, inseparable. Alone, practicality becomes dangerous; spirituality, alone, becomes feeble and pointless. Alone, either becomes dull. Each is the other's discipline, in a sense, and in good work the two are joined.

"The dignity of toil is undermined when its necessity is gone," Kathleen Raine says, and she is right. It is an insight that we dare not ignore, and I would emphasize that it applies to *all* toil. What is not needed is frivolous. Everything depends on our right relation to necessity—and therefore on our right definition of necessity. In defining our necessity, we must be careful to discount the subsidies, the unrepaid borrowings, from nature that have so far sustained industrial civilization: the "cheap" fossil fuels and ores; the forests that have been cut down and not replanted; the virgin soils of much of the world, whose fertility has not been replenished.

And so, though I am trying to unspecialize the idea and the job of preserving wildness, I am not against wilderness preservation. I am only pointing out, as the Reagan administration has done, that the wildernesses we are trying to preserve are standing squarely in the way of our present economy, and that the wildernesses cannot survive if our economy does not change.

The reason to preserve wilderness is that we need it. We need wilderness of all kinds, large and small, public and private. We need to go now and again into places where our work is disallowed, where our hopes and plans have no standing. We need to come into the presence of the unqualified and mysterious formality of Creation. And I would agree with Edward Abbey that we need as well some tracts of what he calls "absolute wilderness," which "through general agreement none of us enters at all."

We need wilderness also because wildness—nature—is one of our indispensable studies. We need to understand it as our source and preserver, as an essential measure of our history and behavior, and as the ultimate definer of our possibilities. There are, I think, three questions that must be asked with respect to a human economy in any given place:

1. What is here?
2. What will nature permit us to do here?
3. What will nature help us to do here?

The second and third questions are obviously the ones that would define agendas of practical research and of work. If we do not work with and within natural tolerances, then we will not be permitted to work for long. It is plain enough, for example, that if we use soil fertility faster than nature can replenish it, we are proposing an end that we do not desire. And to ignore the possibility of help from nature makes farming, for example, too expensive for farmers—as we are seeing. It may make life too expensive for humans.

But the second and third questions are ruled by the first. They cannot be answered—they cannot intelligently be asked—until the first has been answered. And yet the first question has not been answered, or asked, so far as I know, in the whole history of the American economy. All the great changes, from the Indian wars and the opening of agricultural frontiers to the inauguration of genetic engineering, have been made without a backward look and in ignorance of whereabouts. Our response to the forest and the prairie that covered our present fields was to get them out of the way as soon as possible. And the obstructive human populations of Indians and "inefficient" or small farmers have been dealt with in the same spirit. We have never known what we were doing because we have never known what we were *un*doing. We cannot know what we are doing until we know what nature would be doing if we were doing nothing. And that is why we need small native wildernesses widely dispersed over the countryside as well as large ones in spectacular places.

However, to say that wilderness and wildness are indispensable to us, indivisible from us, is not to say that we can find sufficient standards for our life and work in nature. To suggest that, for humans, there is a simple equation between "natural" and "good" is to fall prey immediately to the cynics who love to point out that, after all, "everything is natural." They are, of course, correct. Nature provides bountifully for her children, but, as we would now say, she is also extremely permissive. If her children want to destroy one another entirely or to commit suicide, that is all right with her. There is nothing, after all, more natural than the extinction of species; the extinction of *all* species, we must assume, would also be perfectly natural.

Clearly, if we want to argue for the existence of the world as we know it, we will have to find some way of qualifying and supplementing this relentless criterion of "natural." Perhaps we can do so only by a reaffirmation of a lesser kind of naturalness—that of self-interest. Certainly human self-interest has much wickedness to answer for, and we are living in just fear of it; nevertheless, we must take care not to condemn it absolutely. After all, we value this passing work of nature that we call "the natural world," with its graceful plenty of animals and plants, precisely because *we* need it and love it and want it for a home.

We are creatures obviously subordinate to nature, dependent upon a wild world that we did not make. And yet we are joined to that larger nature by our own nature, a part of which is our self-interest. A common complaint nowadays is that humans think the world is "anthropocentric," or human-centered. I understand the complaint; the assumptions of so-called anthropocentrism often result in gross and dangerous insubordination. And yet I don't know how the human species can avoid some version of self-centeredness; I don't know how any species can. An earthworm, I think, is living in an earthworm-centered world; the thrush who eats the earthworm is living in a thrush-centered world; the hawk who eats the thrush is living in a hawk-centered world. Each creature, that is, does what is necessary in its own behalf, and is domestic in its own *domus* or home.

Humans differ from earthworms, thrushes, and hawks in their capacity to do more—in modern times, a great deal more—in their own behalf than is necessary. Moreover, the vast majority of humans in the industrial nations are guilty of this extravagance. One of the oldest human arguments is over the question of how much is necessary. How much must humans do in their own behalf in order to be fully human? The number and variety of the answers ought to notify us that we never have known for sure, and yet we have the disquieting suspicion that, almost always, the honest answer has been "less."

We have no way to work at this question, it seems to me, except by perceiving that, in order to have the world, we must share it, both with each other and with other creatures, which is immediately complicated by the further perception that, in order to live in the world, we must use it somewhat at the expense of other creatures. We must acknowledge both the centrality and the limits of our self-interest. One can hardly imagine a tougher situation.

But in the recognition of the difficulty of our situation is a kind of relief, for it makes us give up the hope that a solution can be found in a simple preference for humanity over nature or nature over humanity. The only solutions we have ahead of us will need to be worked for and worked out. They will have to be practical solutions, resulting in good local practice. There is work to do that can be done.

As we undertake this work, perhaps the greatest immediate danger lies in our dislike of ourselves as a species. This is an understandable dislike—we are justly afraid of ourselves—but we are nevertheless obliged to think and act out of a proper self-interest and a genuine self-respect as human beings. Otherwise, we will allow our dislike and fear of ourselves to justify further abuses of one another and the world. We must come to terms with the fact that it is not natural to be disloyal to one's own kind.

For these reasons, there is great danger in the perception that "there are too many people," whatever truth may be in it, for this is a premise from which it is too likely that somebody, sooner or later, will proceed to a determination of *who* are the surplus. If we conclude that there are too many, it is hard to avoid the further conclusion that there are some we do not need. But how many do we need, and which ones? Which ones, now apparently unnecessary, may turn out later to be indispensable? We do not know; it is a part of our mystery, our wildness, that we do not know.

I would argue that, at least for us in the United States, the conclusion that "there are too many people" is premature, not because I know that there are *not* too many people, but because I do not think we are prepared to come to such a conclusion. I grant that questions about population size need to be asked, but they are not the *first* questions that need to be asked.

The "population problem," initially, should be examined as a problem, not of quantity, but of pattern. Before we conclude that we have too many people, we must ask if we have people who are misused, people who are misplaced, or people who are abusing the places they have. The facts of most immediate importance may be, not how many we are, but where we are and what we are doing. At any rate, the attempt to solve our problems by reducing our numbers may be a distraction from the overriding population statistic of our time: that *one* human with a nuclear bomb and the will to use it is 100 percent too many. I would argue that it is not human fecundity that is overcrowding the world so much as technological multipliers of the power of individual humans. The worst disease of the world now is probably the ideology of technological heroism, according to which more and more people willingly cause large-scale effects that they do not foresee and that they cannot control. This is the ideology of the professional class of the industrial nations—a class whose allegiance to communities and places has been dissolved by their economic motives and by their educations. These are people who will go anywhere and jeopardize anything in order to assure the success of their careers.

We may or may not have room for more people, but it is certain that we do not have more room for technological heroics. We do not need any more thousand-dollar solutions to ten-dollar problems or million-dollar solutions to thousand-dollar problems—or multibillion-dollar solutions where there was never a problem at all. We have no way to compute the inhabitability of our places; we cannot weigh or measure the pleasures we take in them; we cannot say how many dollars domestic tranquillity is worth. And yet we must now learn to bear in mind the memory of communities destroyed, disfigured, or made desolate by technological events, as well as the memory of families dispossessed, displaced, and impoverished by "labor-saving" machines. The issue of human obsolescence may be more urgent for us now than the issue of human population.

The population issue thus leads directly to the issue of proportion and scale. What is the proper amount of power for a human to use? What are the proper limits of human enterprise? How may these proprieties be determined? Such questions may seem inordinately difficult, but that is because we have gone too long without asking them. One of the fundamental assumptions of industrial economics has been that such questions are outmoded and that we need never ask them again. The failure of that assumption now requires us to reconsider the claims of wildness and to renew our understanding of the old ideas of propriety and harmony.

When we propose that humans should learn to behave properly with respect to nature so as to place their domestic economy harmoniously upon and within the sustaining and surrounding wilderness, then we make possible a sort of landscape criticism. Then we can see that it is not primarily the number of people inhabiting a landscape that determines the propriety of the ratio and the relation between human domesticity and wildness, but it is the way the people divide the landscape and use it. We can see that it is the landscape of monoculture in which both nature and humanity are most at risk. We feel the human fragility of the huge one-class housing development, just as we feel the natural fragility of the huge one-crop field.

Looking at the monocultures of industrial civilization, we yearn with a kind of homesickness for the humanness and the naturalness of a highly diversified, multipurpose landscape, democratically divided, with many margins. The margins are of the utmost importance. They are the divisions between holdings, as well as between kinds of work and kinds of land. These margins—lanes, streamsides, wooded fencerows, and the like—are always freeholds of wildness, where limits are set on human intention. Such places are hospitable to the wild lives of plants and animals and to the wild play of human children. They enact, within the bounds of human domesticity itself, a human courtesy toward the wild that is one of the best safeguards of designated tracts of true wilderness. This is the landscape of harmony, safer far for life of all kinds than the landscape of monoculture. And we should not neglect to notice that, whereas the monocultural landscape is totalitarian in tendency, the landscape of harmony is democratic and free.

Home Economics (1987)

Annie Dillard (b. 1945) received her M.A. in English for a thesis on Thoreau and *Walden*. A few years later she took up a similar project, hers centered on Tinker Creek, in the Blue Ridge Mountains near Roanoke. She walked the woods endlessly and turned over in her mind the beauty, the cruelty, the meaning and the lack of meaning in what she witnessed. By most accounts she wrote up her notes into a book in a kind of fever, producing *Pilgrim at Tinker Creek* (1974), which not only won the Pulitzer Prize but also the bigger award: a raft of readers who felt as if their perceptions had been powerfully shifted.

Fecundity

I

I wakened myself last night with my own shouting. It must have been that terrible yellow plant I saw pushing through the flood-damp soil near the log by Tinker Creek, the plant as fleshy and featureless as a slug, that erupted through the floor of my brain as I slept, and burgeoned into the dream of fecundity that woke me up.

I was watching two huge luna moths mate. Luna moths are those fragile ghost moths, fairy moths, whose five-inch wings are swallow-tailed, a pastel green bordered in silken lavender. From the hairy head of the male sprouted two enormous, furry antennae that trailed down past his ethereal wings. He was on top of the female, hunching repeatedly with a horrible animal vigor.

It was the perfect picture of utter spirituality and utter degradation. I was fascinated and could not turn away my eyes. By watching them I in effect permitted their mating to take place and so committed myself to accepting the consequences—all because I wanted to see what would happen. I wanted in on a secret.

And then the eggs hatched and the bed was full of fish. I was standing across the room in the doorway, staring at the bed. The eggs hatched before my eyes, on my bed, and a thousand chunky fish swarmed there in a viscid slime. The fish were firm and fat, black and white, with triangular bodies and bulging eyes. I watched in horror as they squirmed three feet deep, swimming and oozing about in the glistening, transparent slime. Fish in the bed!—and I awoke. My ears still rang with the foreign cry that had been my own voice.

For nightmare you eat wild carrot, which is Queen Anne's lace, or you chew the black seeds of the male peony. But it was too late for prevention, and there is no cure. What root or seed will erase that scene from my mind? Fool, I thought: child, you child, you ignorant, innocent fool. What did you expect to see—angels? For it was understood in the dream that the bed full of fish was my own fault, that if I had turned away from the mating moths the hatching of their eggs wouldn't have happened, or at least would have happened in secret, elsewhere. I brought it upon myself, this slither, this swarm.

I don't know what it is about fecundity that so appalls. I suppose it is the teeming evidence that birth and growth, which we value, are ubiquitous and blind, that life itself is so astonishingly cheap, that nature is as careless as it is bountiful, and that with extravagance goes a crushing waste that will one day include our own cheap lives, Henle's loops and all. Every glistening egg is a memento mori.

After a natural disaster such as a flood, nature "stages a comeback." People use the optimistic expression without any real idea of the pressures and waste the comeback involves. Now, in late June, things are popping outside. Creatures extrude or vent eggs; larvae fatten, split their shells, and eat them; spores dissolve or explode; root hairs multiply, corn puffs on the stalk, grass yields seed, shoots erupt from the earth turgid and sheathed; wet muskrats, rabbits, and squirrels slide into the sunlight, mewling and blind; and everywhere watery cells divide and swell, swell and divide. I can like it and call it birth and regeneration, or I can play the devil's advocate and call it rank fecundity—and say that it's hell that's a-poppin'.

This is what I plan to do. Partly as a result of my terrible dream, I have been thinking that the landscape of the intricate world that I have painted is inaccurate and lopsided. It is too optimistic. For the notion of the infinite variety of detail and the multiplicity of forms is a pleasing one; in complexity are the fringes of beauty, and in variety are generosity and exuberance. But all this leaves something vital out of the picture. It is not one pine I see, but a thousand. I myself am not one, but legion. And we are all going to die.

In this repetition of individuals is a mindless stutter, an imbecilic fixedness that must be taken into account. The driving force behind all this fecundity is a terrible pressure I also must consider, the pressure of birth and growth, the pressure that splits the bark of trees and shoots out seeds, that squeezes out the egg and bursts the pupa, that hungers and lusts and drives the creature relentlessly toward its own death. Fecundity, then, is what I have been thinking about, fecundity and the pressure of growth. Fecundity is an ugly word for an ugly subject. It is ugly, at least, in the eggy animal world. I don't think it is for plants.

I never met a man who was shaken by a field of identical blades of grass. An acre of poppies and a forest of spruce boggle no one's mind. Even ten square miles of wheat gladdens the hearts of most people, although it is really as unnatural and freakish as the Frankenstein monster; if man were to die, I read, wheat wouldn't survive him more than three years. No, in the plant world, and especially among the flowering plants, fecundity is not an assault on human values. Plants are not our competitors; they are our prey and our nesting materials. We are no more distressed at their proliferation than an owl is at a population explosion among field mice.

After the flood last year I found a big tulip-tree limb that had been wind-thrown into Tinker Creek. The current dragged it up on some rocks on the bank, where receding waters stranded it. A month after the flood I discovered that it was growing new leaves. Both ends of the branch were completely exposed and dried. I was amazed. It was like the old fable about the corpse's growing a beard; it was as if the woodpile in my garage were suddenly to burst greenly into leaf. The way plants persevere in the bitterest of circumstances is utterly heartening.

I can barely keep from unconsciously ascribing a will to these plants, a do-or-die courage, and I have to remind myself that coded cells and mute water pressure have no idea how grandly they are flying in the teeth of it all.

In the lower Bronx, for example, enthusiasts found an ailanthus tree that was fifteen feet long growing from the corner of a garage roof. It was rooted in and living on "dust and roofing cinders." Even more spectacular is a desert plant, *Ibervillea sonorae*—a member of the gourd family—that Joseph Wood Krutch describes. If you see this plant in the desert, you see only a dried chunk of loose wood. It has neither roots nor stems; it's like an old gray knot-hole. But it is alive. Each year before the rainy season comes, it sends out a few roots and shoots. If the rain arrives, it grows flowers and fruits; these soon wither away, and it reverts to a state as quiet as driftwood.

Well, the New York Botanical Garden put a dried *Ibervillea sonorae* on display in a glass case. "For seven years," says Joseph Wood Krutch, "without soil or water, simply lying in the case, it put forth a few anticipatory shoots and then, when no rainy season arrived, dried up again, hoping for better luck next year." That's what I call flying in the teeth of it all.

(It's hard to understand why no one at the New York Botanical Garden had the grace to splash a glass of water on the thing. Then they could say on their display case label, "This is a live plant." But by the eighth year what they had was a dead plant, which is precisely what it had looked like all along. The sight of it, reinforced by the label "Dead *Ibervillea sonorae*," would have been most melancholy to visitors to the botanical garden. I suppose they just threw it away.)

The growth pressure of plants can do an impressive variety of tricks. Bamboo can grow three feet in twenty-four hours, an accomplishment that is capitalized upon, *legendarily*, in that exquisite Asian torture in which a victim is strapped to a mesh bunk a mere foot above a bed of healthy bamboo plants whose wood-like tips have been sharpened. For the first eight hours he is fine, if jittery; then he starts turning into a collander, by degrees.

Down at the root end of things, blind growth reaches astonishing proportions. So far as I know, only one real experiment has ever been performed to determine the extent and rate of root growth, and when you read the figures, you see why. I have run into various accounts of this experiment, and the only thing they don't tell you is how many lab assistants were blinded for life.

The experimenters studied a single grass plant, winter rye. They let it grow in a greenhouse for four months; then they gingerly spirited away the soil—under microscopes, I imagine—and counted and measured all the roots and root hairs. In four months the plant had set forth 378 miles of roots—that's about three miles a day—in 14 million distinct roots. This is mighty impressive, but when they get down to the root hairs, I boggle completely. In those same four months the rye plant created 14 *billion* root hairs, and those little strands placed end-to-end just about wouldn't quit. In a single *cubic inch* of soil, the length of the root hairs totaled 6000 miles.

Other plants use the same water power to heave the rock earth around as though they were merely shrugging off a silken cape. Rutherford Platt tells about a larch tree whose root had cleft a one-and-one-half ton boulder and hoisted it a foot into the air. Everyone knows how a sycamore root will buckle a sidewalk, a mushroom will shatter a cement basement floor. But when the first real measurements of this awesome pressure were taken, nobody could believe the figures.

Rutherford Platt tells the story in *The Great American Forest*, one of the most interesting books ever written: "In 1875, a Massachusetts farmer, curious about the growing power of expanding apples, melons and squashes, harnessed a squash to a weight-lifting device which had a dial like a grocer's scale to indicate the pressure exerted by the expanding fruit. As the days passed, he kept piling on counterbalancing weight; he could hardly believe his eyes when he saw his vegetables quietly exerting a lifting force of 5 thousand pounds per square inch. When nobody believed him, he set up exhibits of harnessed squashes and invited the public to come and see. The *Annual Report of the Massachusetts Board of Agriculture*, 1875, reported: 'Many thousands of men, women, and children of all classes of society visited it. *Mr. Penlow* watched it day and night, making hourly observations; *Professor*

Parker was moved to write a poem about it; *Professor Seelye* declared that he positively stood in awe of it.'"

All this is very jolly. Unless perhaps I were strapped down above a stand of growing, sharpened bamboo, I am unlikely to feel the faintest queasiness either about the growth pressure of plants, or their fecundity. Even when the plants get in the way of human "culture," I don't mind. When I read how many thousands of dollars a city like New York has to spend to keep underground water pipes free of ailanthus, ginkgo, and sycamore roots, I cannot help but give a little cheer. After all, water pipes are almost always an excellent source of water. In a town where resourcefulness and beating the system are highly prized, these primitive trees can fight city hall and win.

But in the animal world things are different, and human feelings are different. While we're in New York, consider the cockroaches under the bed and the rats in the early morning clustered on the porch stoop. Apartment houses are hives of swarming roaches. Or again: in one sense you could think of Manhattan's land as high-rent, high-rise real estate; in another sense you could see it as an enormous breeding ground for rats, acres and acres of rats. I suppose that the rats and the cockroaches don't do so much actual damage as the roots do; nevertheless, the prospect does not please. Fecundity is anathema only in the animal. "Acres and acres of rats" has a suitably chilling ring to it that is decidedly lacking if I say, instead, "acres and acres of tulips."

The landscape of earth is dotted and smeared with masses of apparently identical individual animals, from the great Pleistocene herds that blanketed grasslands to the gluey gobs of bacteria that clog the lobes of lungs. The oceanic breeding grounds of pelagic birds are as teeming and cluttered as any human Calcutta. Lemmings blacken the earth and locusts the air. Grunion run thick in the ocean, corals pile on pile, and protozoans explode in a red tide stain. Ants take to the skies in swarms, mayflies hatch by the millions, and molting cicadas coat the trunks of trees. Have you seen the rivers run red and lumpy with salmon?

Consider the ordinary barnacle, the rock barnacle. Inside every one of those millions of hard white cones on the rocks—the kind that bruises your heel as you bruise its head—is of course a creature as alive as you or I. Its business in life is this: when a wave washes over it, it sticks out twelve feathery feeding appendages and filters the plankton for food. As it grows, it sheds its skin like a lobster, enlarges its shell, and reproduces itself without end. The larvae "hatch into the sea in milky clouds." The barnacles encrusting a single half mile of shore can leak into the water a million million larvae. How many is that to a human mouthful? In sea water they grow, molt, change shape wildly, and eventually, after several months, settle on the rocks, turn into adults, and build shells. Inside the shells they have to shed their skins. Rachel Carson was always finding the old skins; she reported: "Almost every container of sea water that I bring up from the shore is flecked with white, semitransparent objects. . . . Seen under the microscope, every detail of structure is perfectly represented. . . . In the little cellophane-like replicas I can count the joints of the appendages; even the bristles, growing at the bases of the joints, seem to have been slipped intact out of their casings." All in all, rock barnacles may live four years.

My point about rock barnacles is those million million larvae "in milky clouds" and those shed flecks of skin. Sea water seems suddenly to be but a broth of barnacle bits. Can I fancy that a million million human infants are more real?

What if God has the same affectionate disregard for us that we have for barnacles? I don't know if each barnacle larva is of itself unique and special, or if we the people are essentially as interchangeable as bricks. My brain is full of numbers; they swell and would split my skull like a shell. I examine the trapezoids of skin covering the back of my hands like blown dust motes moistened to clay. I have hatched, too, with millions of my kind, into a milky way that spreads from an unknown shore.

I have seen the mantis's abdomen dribbling out eggs in wet bubbles like tapioca pudding glued to a thorn. I have seen a film of a termite queen as big as my face, dead white and featureless, glistening with slime, throbbing and pulsing out rivers of globular eggs. Termite workers, who looked like tiny longshoremen unloading the *Queen Mary*, licked each egg as fast as it was extruded to prevent mold. The whole world is an incubator for incalculable numbers of eggs, each one coded minutely and ready to burst.

The egg of a parasite chalcid wasp, a common small wasp, multiplies unassisted, making ever more identical eggs. The female lays a single fertilized egg in the flaccid tissues of its live prey, and that one egg divides and divides. As many as two thousand new parasitic wasps will hatch to feed on the host's body with identical hunger. Similarly—only more so—Edwin Way Teale reports that a lone aphid, without a partner, breeding "unmolested" for one year, would produce so many living aphids that, although they are only a tenth of an inch long, together they would extend into space twenty-five hundred *light-years*. Even the average goldfish lays five thousand eggs, which she will eat as fast as she lays, if permitted. The sales manager of Ozark Fisheries in Missouri, which raises commercial goldfish for the likes of me, said, "We produce, measure, and sell our product by the ton." The intricacy of Ellery and aphids multiplied mindlessly into tons and light-years is more than extravagance; it is holocaust, parody, glut.

The pressure of growth among animals is a kind of terrible hunger. These billions must eat in order to fuel their surge to sexual maturity so that they may pump out more billions of eggs. And what are the fish on the bed going to eat, or the hatched mantises in the Mason jar going to eat, but each other? There is a terrible innocence in the benumbed world of the lower animals, reducing life there to a universal chomp. Edwin Way Teale, in *The Strange Lives of Familiar Insects*—a book I couldn't live without—describes several occasions of meals mouthed under the pressure of a hunger that knew no bounds.

You remember the dragonfly nymph, for instance, which stalks the bottom of the creek and the pond in search of live prey to snare with its hooked, unfolding lip. Dragonfly nymphs are insatiable and mighty. They clasp and devour whole minnows and fat tadpoles. Well, a dragonfly nymph, says Teale, "has even been seen climbing up out of the water on a plant to attack a helpless dragonfly emerging, soft and rumpled, from its nymphal skin." Is this where I draw the line?

It is between mothers and their offspring that these feedings have truly macabre overtones. Look at lacewings. Lacewings are those fragile green insects with large, rounded transparent wings. The larvae eat enormous numbers of aphids, the adults mate in a fluttering rush of instinct, lay eggs, and die by the millions in the first cold snap of fall. Sometimes, when a female lays her fertile eggs on a green leaf atop a slender stalked thread, she is hungry. She pauses in her laying, turns around, and eats her eggs one by one, then lays some more, and eats them, too.

Anything can happen, and anything does; what's it all about? Valerie Eliot, T. S. Eliot's widow, wrote in a letter to the London *Times*: "My husband, T. S. Eliot, loved to recount how late one evening he stopped a taxi. As he got in the driver said: 'You're T. S. Eliot.' When asked how he knew, he replied: 'Ah, I've got an eye for a celebrity. Only the other evening I picked up Bertrand Russell, and I said to him, "Well, Lord Russell, what's it all about," and, do you know, he couldn't tell me.'" Well, Lord God, asks the delicate, dying lacewing whose mandibles are wet with the juice secreted by her own ovipositor, what's it all about? ("And do you know . . .")

Planarians, which live in the duck pond, behave similarly. They are those dark laboratory flatworms that can regenerate themselves from almost any severed part. Arthur Koestler writes, "during the mating season the worms become cannibals, devouring everything alive that comes their way, including their own previously discarded tails which were in the process of growing a new head." Even such sophisticated mammals as the great predator cats occasionally eat their cubs. A mother cat will be observed licking the area around the umbilical cord of the helpless newborn. She licks, she licks, she licks until something snaps in her brain, and she begins eating, starting there, at the vulnerable belly.

Although mothers devouring their own offspring is patently the more senseless, somehow the reverse behavior is the more appalling. In the death of the parent in the jaws of its offspring I recognize a universal drama that chance occurrence has merely telescoped, so that I can see all the players at once. Gall gnats, for instance, are common small flies. Sometimes, according to Teale, a gall gnat larva, which does not resemble the adult in the least, and which has certainly not mated, nevertheless produces within its body eggs, live eggs, which then hatch within its soft tissues. Sometimes the eggs hatch alive even within the quiescent body of the pupa. The same incredible thing occasionally occurs within the fly genus *Miastor*, again to both larvae and pupae. "These eggs hatch within their bodies and the ravenous larvae which emerge immediately begin devouring their parents." In this case, I know what it's all about, and I wish I didn't. The parents die, the next generation lives, *ad majorem gloriam*, and so it goes. If the new generation hastens the death of the old, it scarcely matters; the old has served its one purpose, and the direct processing of proteins is tidily all in the family. But think of the invisible swelling of ripe eggs inside the pupa as wrapped and rigid as a mummified Egyptian queen! The eggs burst, shatter her belly, and emerge alive, awake, and hungry from a mummy case which they crawl over like worms and feed on till it's gone. And then they turn to the world.

"To prevent a like fate," Teale continues, "some of the ichneumon flies, those wasplike parasites which deposit their eggs in the body tissues of caterpillars, have to scatter their eggs while in flight at times when they are unable to find their prey and the eggs are ready to hatch within their bodies."

You are an ichneumon. You mated and your eggs are fertile. If you can't find a caterpillar on which to lay your eggs, your young will starve. When the eggs hatch, the young will eat any body in which they find themselves, so if you don't kill them by emitting them broadcast over the landscape, they'll eat you alive. But if you let them drop over the fields you will probably be dead yourself, of old age, before they even hatch to starve, and the whole show will be over and done, and a wretched one it was. You feel them coming, and coming, and you struggle to rise. . . .

Not that the ichneumon is making any conscious choice. If she were, her dilemma would be truly the stuff of tragedy; Aeschylus need have looked no further than the ichneumon. That is, it would be the stuff of real tragedy if only Aeschylus and I could convince you that the ichneumon is really and truly as alive as we are, and that what happens to it matters. Will you take it on faith?

Here is one last story. It shows that the pressures of growth gang aft agley. The clothes moth, whose caterpillar eats wool, sometimes goes into a molting frenzy which Teale blandly describes as "curious": "A curious paradox in molting is the action of a clothes-moth larva with insufficient food. It sometimes goes into a 'molting frenzy,' changing its skin repeatedly and getting smaller and smaller with each change." Smaller and smaller . . . can you imagine the frenzy? Where shall we send our sweaters? The diminution process could, in imagination, extend to infinity, as the creature frantically shrinks and shrinks and shrinks to the size of a molecule, then an electron, but never can shrink to absolute nothing and end its terrible hunger. I feel like Ezra: "And when I heard this thing, I rent my garment and my mantle, and plucked off the hair of my head and of my beard, and sat down astonied."

II

I am not kidding anyone if I pretend that these awesome pressures to eat and breed are wholly mystifying. The million million barnacle larvae in a half mile of shore water, the rivers of termite eggs, and the light-years of aphids ensure the living presence, in a scarcely concerned world, of ever more rock barnacles, termites, and aphids.

It's chancy out there. Dog whelks eat rock barnacles, worms invade their shells, shore ice razes them from the rocks and grinds them to a powder. Can you lay aphid eggs faster than chickadees can eat them? Can you find a caterpillar, can you beat the killing frost?

As far as lower animals go, if you lead a simple life you probably face a boring death. Some animals, however, lead such complicated lives that not only do the chances for any one animal's death at any minute multiply greatly, but so also do the *varieties* of the deaths it might die. The ordained paths of some animals are so rocky they are preposterous. The horsehair worm in the duck pond, for instance, wriggling so serenely near the surface, is the survivor of an impossible series of squeaky escapes. I did a bit of research into the life cycles of these worms, which are shaped exactly like hairs from a horse's tail, and learned that although scientists are not exactly sure what happens to any one species of them, they think it might go something like this:

You start with long strands of eggs wrapped around vegetation in the duck pond. The eggs hatch, the larvae emerge, and each seeks an aquatic host, say a dragonfly nymph. The larva bores into the nymph's body, where it feeds and grows and somehow escapes. Then if it doesn't get eaten it swims over to the shore where it encysts on submersed plants. This is all fairly improbable, but not impossibly so.

Now the coincidences begin. First, presumably, the water level of the duck pond has to drop. This exposes the vegetation so that the land host organism can get at it without drowning. Horsehair worms have various land hosts, such as crickets, beetles, and grasshoppers. Let's say ours can only make it if a grasshopper comes along. Fine. But the grasshopper had best hurry, for there is only so much fat stored in the encysted worm, and it might starve. Well, here comes just the right species of grasshopper, and it is obligingly feeding on shore vegetation. Now I have not observed any extensive grazing of grasshoppers on any grassy shores, but obviously it must occur. Bingo, then, the grasshopper just happens to eat the encysted worm.

The cyst bursts. The worm emerges in all its hideous length, up to thirty-six inches, inside the body of the grasshopper, on which it feeds. I presume that the worm must eat enough of its host to stay alive, but not so much that the grasshopper will keel over dead far from water. Entomologists have found tiger beetles dead and dying on the water whose insides were almost perfectly empty except for the white coiled bodies of horsehair worms. At any rate, now the worm is almost an adult, ready to reproduce. But first it's got to get out of this grasshopper.

Biologists don't know what happens next. If at the critical stage the grasshopper is hopping in a sunny meadow away from a duck pond or ditch, which is entirely likely, then the story is over. But say it happens to be feeding near the duck pond. The worm perhaps bores its way out of the grasshopper's body, or perhaps is excreted. At any rate, there it is on the grass, drying out. Now the biologists have to go so far as to invoke a "heavy rain," falling from heaven at this fortuitous moment, in order to get the horsehair worm back into the water where it can mate and lay more seemingly doomed eggs. You'd be thin, too.

Other creatures have it just about as easy. A blood fluke starts out as an egg in human feces. If it happens to fall into fresh water it will live only if it happens to encounter a certain species of snail. It changes in the snail, swims out, and now needs to find a human being in the water in order to bore through his skin. It travels around in the man's blood, settles down in the blood vessels of his intestine, and turns into a sexually mature blood fluke, either male or female. Now it has to find another fluke, of the opposite sex, who also just happens to have traveled the same circuitous route and landed in the same unfortunate man's intestinal blood vessels. Other flukes lead similarly improbable lives, some passing through as many as four hosts.

But it is for gooseneck barnacles that I reserve the largest measure of awe. Recently I saw photographs taken by members of the *Ra* expedition. One showed a glob of tar as big as a softball, jetsam from a larger craft, which Heyerdahl and his crew spotted in the middle of the Atlantic Ocean. The tar had been in the sea for a long time; it was overgrown with gooseneck barnacles. The gooseneck barnacles were entirely incidental, but for me they were the most interesting thing about the whole expedition. How many gooseneck barnacle larvae must be dying out there in the middle of vast oceans for every one that finds a glob of tar to fasten to? You've seen gooseneck barnacles washed up on the beach; they grow on old ship's timber, driftwood, strips of rubber—anything that's been afloat in the sea long enough. They do not resemble rock barnacles in the least, although the two are closely related. They have pinkish shells extending in a flattened oval from a flexible bit of "gooseneck" tissue that secures them to the substratum.

I have always had a fancy for these creatures, but I'd always assumed that they lived near shores, where chance floating holdfasts are more likely to occur. What are they doing—what are the larvae doing—out there in the middle of the ocean? They drift and perish, or, by some freak accident in a world where anything can happen, they latch and flourish. If I dangled my hand from the deck of the *Ra* into the sea, could a gooseneck barnacle fasten there? If I gathered a cup of ocean water, would I be holding a score of dying and dead barnacle larvae? Should I throw them a chip? What kind of a world is this, anyway? Why not make fewer barnacle larvae and give them a decent chance? Are we dealing in life, or in death?

I have to look at the landscape of the blue-green world again. Just think: in all the clean beautiful reaches of the solar system, our planet alone is a blot; our planet alone has death. I have to acknowledge that the sea is a cup of death and the land is a stained altar stone. We the living are survivors huddled on flotsam, living on jetsam. We are escapees. We wake in terror, eat in hunger, sleep with a mouthful of blood.

Death: W. C. Fields called death "the Fellow in the Bright Nightgown." He shuffles around the house in all the corners I've forgotten, all the halls I dare not call to mind or visit for fear I'll glimpse the hem of his shabby, dazzling gown disappearing around a turn. This is the monster evolution loves. How could it be?

The faster death goes, the faster evolution goes. If an aphid lays a million eggs, several might survive. Now, my right hand, in all its human cunning, could not make one aphid in a thousand years. But these aphid eggs—which run less than a dime a dozen, which run absolutely free—can make aphids as effortlessly as the sea makes waves. Wonderful things, wasted. It's a wretched system. Arthur Stanley Eddington, the British physicist and astronomer who died in 1944, suggested that all of "Nature" could conceivably run on the same deranged scheme. "If indeed she has no greater aim than to provide a home for her greatest experiment, Man, it would be just like her methods to scatter a million stars whereof one might haply achieve her purpose." I doubt very much that this is the aim, but it seems clear on all fronts that this is the method.

Say you are the manager of the Southern Railroad. You figure that you need three engines for a stretch of track between Lynchburg and Danville. It's a mighty steep grade. So at fantastic effort and expense you have your shops make nine thousand engines. Each engine must be fashioned just so, every rivet and bolt secure, every wire twisted and wrapped, every needle on every indicator sensitive and accurate.

You send all nine thousand of them out on the runs. Although there are engineers at the throttles, no one is manning the switches. The engines crash, collide, derail, jump, jam, burn. . . . At the end of the massacre you have three engines, which is what the run could support in the first place. There are few enough of them that they can stay out of each others' paths.

You go to your board of directors and show them what you've done. And what are they going to say? You know what they're going to say. They're going to say: It's a hell of a way to run a railroad.

Is it a better way to run a universe?

Evolution loves death more than it loves you or me. This is easy to write, easy to read, and hard to believe. The words are simple, the concept clear—but you don't believe it, do you? Nor do I. How could I, when we're both so lovable? Are my values then so diametrically opposed to those that nature preserves? This is the key point.

Must I then part ways with the only world I know? I had thought to live by the side of the creek in order to shape my life to its free flow. But I seem to have reached a point where I must draw the line. It looks as though the creek is not buoying me up but dragging me down. Look: Cock Robin may die the most gruesome of slow deaths, and nature is no less pleased; the sun comes up, the creek rolls on, the survivors still sing. I cannot feel that way about your death, nor you about mine, nor either of us about the robin's—or even the barnacles'. We value the individual supremely, and nature values him not a whit. It looks for the moment as though I might have to reject this creek life unless I want to be utterly brutalized. Is human culture with its values my only real home after all? Can it possibly be that I should move my anchor-hold to the side of a library? This direction of thought brings me abruptly to a fork in the road where I stand paralyzed, unwilling to go on, for both ways lead to madness.

Either this world, my mother, is a monster, or I myself am a freak.

Consider the former: the world is a monster. Any three-year-old can see how unsatisfactory and clumsy is this whole business of reproducing and dying by the billions. We have not yet encountered any god who is as merciful as a man who flicks a beetle over on its feet. There is not a people in the world who behaves as badly as praying mantises. But wait, you say, there is no right and wrong in nature; right and wrong is a human concept. Precisely: we are moral creatures, then, in an amoral world. The universe that suckled us is a monster that does not care if we live or die—does not care if it itself grinds to a halt. It is fixed and blind, a robot programmed to kill. We are free and seeing; we can only try to outwit it at every turn to save our skins.

This view requires that a monstrous world running on chance and death, careening blindly from nowhere to nowhere, somehow produced wonderful us. I came from the world, I crawled out of a sea of amino acids, and now I must whirl around and shake my fist at that sea and cry Shame! If I value anything at all, then I must blindfold my eyes when I near the Swiss Alps. We must as a culture disassemble our telescopes and settle down to backslapping. We little blobs of soft tissue crawling around on this one planet's skin are right, and the whole universe is wrong.

Or consider the alternative.

Julian of Norwich, the great English anchorite and theologian, cited, in the manner of the prophets, these words from God: "See, I am God: see, I am in all things: see, I never lift my hands off my works, nor ever shall, without end. . . . How should anything be amiss?" But now not even the simplest and best of us sees things the way Julian did. It seems to us that plenty is amiss. So much is amiss that I must consider the second fork in the road, that creation itself is blamelessly, benevolently askew by its very free nature, and that it is only human feeling that is freakishly amiss. The frog that the giant water bug sucked had, presumably, a rush of pure feeling for about a second, before its brain turned to broth. I, however, have been sapped by various strong feelings about the incident almost daily for several years.

Do the barnacle larvae care? Does the lacewing who eats her eggs care? If they do not care, then why am I making all this fuss? If I am a freak, then why don't I hush?

Our excessive emotions are so patently painful and harmful to us as a species that I can hardly believe that they evolved. Other creatures manage to have effective matings and even stable societies without great emotions, and they have a bonus in that they need not ever mourn. (But some higher animals have emotions that we think are similar to ours: dogs, elephants, otters, and the sea mammals mourn their dead. Why do that to an otter? What creator could be so cruel, not to kill otters, but to let them care?) It would seem that emotions are the curse, not death—emotions that appear to have devolved upon a few freaks as a special curse from Malevolence.

All right then. It is our emotions that are amiss. We are freaks, the world is fine, and let us all go have lobotomies to restore us to a natural state. We can leave the library then, go back to the creek lobotomized, and live on its banks as untroubled as any muskrat or reed. You first.

Of the two ridiculous alternatives, I rather favor the second. Although it is true that we are moral creatures in an amoral world, the world's amorality does not make it a monster. Rather, I am the freak. Perhaps I don't need a lobotomy, but I could use some calming down, and the creek is just the place for it. I must go down to the creek again. It is where I belong, although as I become closer to it, my fellows appear more and more freakish, and my home in the library more and more limited. Imperceptibly at first, and now consciously, I shy away from the arts, from the human emotional stew. I read what the men with telescopes and microscopes have to say about the landscape. I read about the polar ice, and I drive myself deeper and deeper into exile from my own kind. But, since I cannot avoid the library altogether—the human culture that taught me to speak in its tongue—I bring human values to the creek, and so save myself from being brutalized.

What I have been after all along is not an explanation but a picture. This is the way the world is, altar and cup, lit by the fire from a star that has only begun to die. My rage and shock at the pain and death of individuals of my kind is the old, old mystery, as old as man, but forever fresh, and completely unanswerable. My reservations about the fecundity and waste of life among other creatures is, however, mere squeamishness. After all, I'm the one having the nightmares. It is true that many of the creatures live and die abominably, but I am not called upon to pass judgment. Nor am I called upon to live in that same way, and those creatures who are are mercifully unconscious.

I don't want to cut this too short. Let me pull the camera back and look at that fork in the road from a distance, in the larger context of the speckled and twining world. It could be that the fork will disappear, or that I will see it to be but one of many interstices in a network, so that it is impossible to say which line is the main part and which is the fork.

The picture of fecundity and its excesses and of the pressures of growth and its accidents is of course no different from the picture I painted before of the world as an intricate texture of a bizarre variety of forms. Only now the shadows are deeper. Extravagance takes on a sinister, wastrel air, and exuberance blithers. When I added the dimension of time to the landscape of the world, I saw how freedom grew the beauties and horrors from the same live branch. This landscape is the same as that one, with a few more details added, and a different emphasis. I see squashes expanding with pressure and a hunk of wood rapt on the desert floor. The rye plant and the Bronx ailanthus are literally killing themselves to make seeds, and the animals to lay eggs. Instead of one goldfish swimming in its intricate bowl, I see tons and tons of goldfish laying and eating billions and billions of eggs. The point of all the eggs is of course to make goldfish one by one—nature loves the *idea* of the individual, if not the individual himself—and the point of a goldfish is pizzazz. This is familiar ground. I merely failed to mention that it is death that is spinning the globe.

It is harder to take, but surely it's been thought about. I cannot really get very exercised over the hideous appearance and habits of some deep-sea jellies and fishes, and I exercise easy. But about the topic of my own death I am decidedly touchy. Nevertheless, the two phenomena are two branches of the same creek, the creek that waters the world. Its source is freedom, and its network of branches is infinite. The graceful mockingbird that falls drinks there and sips in the same drop a beauty that waters its eyes and a death that fledges and flies.

The petals of tulips are flaps of the same doomed water that swells and hatches in the ichneumon's gut.

That something is everywhere and always amiss is part of the very stuff of creation. It is as though each clay form had baked into it, fired into it, a blue streak of nonbeing, a shaded emptiness like a bubble that not only shapes its very structure but that also causes it to list and ultimately explode. We could have planned things more mercifully, perhaps, but our plan would never get off the drawing board until we agreed to the very compromising terms that are the only ones that being offers.

The world has signed a pact with the devil; it had to. It is a covenant to which every thing, even every hydrogen atom, is bound. The terms are clear: if you want to live, you have to die; you cannot have mountains and creeks without space, and space is a beauty married to a blind man. The blind man is Freedom, or Time, and he does not go anywhere without his great dog Death. The world came into being with the signing of the contract. A scientist calls it the Second Law of Thermodynamics. A poet says, "The force that through the green fuse drives the flower/Drives my green age." This is what we know. The rest is gravy.

Pilgrim at Tinker Creek (1974)

LEWIS THOMAS

"I am a member of a fragile species, still new to the earth, the youngest creatures of any scale, here only a few moments as evolutionary time is measured, a juvenile species, a child of a species," Lewis Thomas (1913–1993) wrote in his last book, *The Fragile Species* (1992); "we are only tentatively set in place, error-prone, at risk of fumbling, in real danger at the moment of leaving behind only a thin layer of our fossils." Thomas was a doctor for 50 years, dean of two medical schools, and president of the Memorial Sloan-Kettering Cancer Center, but he is best known for the column he began writing in 1971 for the *New England Journal of Medicine*, "Notes of a Biology Watcher." Those columns were first collected in *The Lives of a Cell* in 1974, which managed to win two National Book Awards, one for Arts and Letters and the other for Science. They centered on his fascination with symbiosis—the mutually beneficial relationship between organisms. That obsession allowed him to see the world in some sense as a single cell, an insight that he thought offered real hope for avoiding a quick evolutionary end for our kind. He once told an interviewer that although he was very worried about ecological trouble, "I think we're undoubtedly here to stay, provided we are able to continue our social development and become more accomplished in the skills of thinking together as members of a social species."

The World's Biggest Membrane

Viewed from the distance of the moon, the astonishing thing about the earth, catching the breath, is that it is alive. The photographs show the dry, pounded surface of the moon in the foreground, dead as an old bone. Aloft, floating free beneath the moist, gleaming membrane of bright blue sky, is the rising earth, the only exuberant thing in this part of the cosmos. If you could look long enough, you would see the swirling of the great drifts of white cloud, covering and uncovering the half-hidden masses of land. If you had been looking for a very long, geologic time, you could have seen the continents themselves in motion, drifting apart on their crustal plates, held afloat by the fire beneath. It has the organized, self-contained look of a live creature, full of information, marvelously skilled in handling the sun.

It takes a membrane to make sense out of disorder in biology. You have to be able to catch energy and hold it, storing precisely the needed amount and releasing it in measured shares. A cell does this, and so do the organelles inside. Each assemblage is poised in the flow of solar energy, tapping off energy from metabolic surrogates of the sun. To stay alive, you have to be able to hold out against equilibrium, maintain imbalance, bank against entropy, and you can only transact this business with membranes in our kind of world.

When the earth came alive it began constructing its own membrane, for the general purpose of editing the sun. Originally, in the time of prebiotic elaboration of peptides and nucleotides from inorganic ingredients in the water on the earth, there was nothing to shield out ultraviolet radiation except the water itself. The first thin atmosphere came entirely from the degassing of the earth as it cooled, and there was only a vanishingly small trace of oxygen in it. Theoretically, there could have been some production of oxygen by photodissociation of water vapor in ultraviolet light, but not much. This process would have been self-limiting, as Urey showed, since the wave lengths needed for photolysis are the very ones screened out selectively by oxygen; the production of oxygen would have been cut off almost as soon as it occurred.

The formation of oxygen had to await the emergence of photosynthetic cells, and these were required to live in an environment with sufficient visible light for photosynthesis but shielded at the same time against lethal ultraviolet. Berkner and Marshall calculate that the green cells must therefore have been about ten meters below the surface of water, probably in pools and ponds shallow enough to lack strong convection currents (the ocean could not have been the starting place).

You could say that the breathing of oxygen into the atmosphere was the result of evolution, or you could turn it around and say that evolution was the result of oxygen. You can have it either way. Once the photosynthetic cells had appeared, very probably counterparts of today's blue-green algae, the future respiratory mechanism of the earth was set in place. Early on, when the level of oxygen had built up to around 1 per cent of today's atmospheric concentration, the anaerobic life of the earth was placed in jeopardy, and the inevitable next stage was the emergence of mutants with oxidative systems and ATP. With this, we were off to an explosive developmental stage in which great varieties of respiring life, including the multicellular forms, became feasible.

Berkner has suggested that there were two such explosions of new life, like vast embryological transformations, both dependent on threshold levels of oxygen. The first, at 1 per cent of the present level, shielded out enough ultraviolet radiation to permit cells to move into the surface layers of lakes, rivers, and oceans. This happened around 600 million years ago, at the beginning of the Paleozoic era, and accounts for the sudden abundance of marine fossils of all kinds in the record of this period. The second burst occurred when oxygen rose to 10 per cent of the present level. At this time, around 400 million years ago, there was a sufficient canopy to allow life out of the water and onto the land. From here on it was clear going, with nothing to restrain the variety of life except the limits of biologic inventiveness.

It is another illustration of our fantastic luck that oxygen filters out the very bands of ultraviolet light that are most devastating for nucleic acids and proteins, while allowing full penetration of the visible light needed for photosynthesis. If it had not been for this semipermeability, we could never have come along.

The earth breathes, in a certain sense. Berkner suggests that there may have been cycles of oxygen production and carbon dioxide consumption, depending on relative abundances of plant and animal life, with the ice ages representing periods of apnea. An overwhelming richness of vegetation may have caused the level of oxygen to rise above today's concentration, with a corresponding depletion of carbon dioxide. Such a drop in carbon dioxide may have impaired the "greenhouse" property of the atmosphere, which holds in the solar heat otherwise lost by radiation from the earth's surface. The fall in temperature would in turn have shut off much of living, and, in a long sigh, the level of oxygen may have dropped by 90 per cent. Berkner speculates that this is what happened to the great reptiles; their size may have been all right for a richly oxygenated atmosphere, but they had the bad luck to run out of air.

Now we are protected against lethal ultraviolet rays by a narrow rim of ozone, thirty miles out. We are safe, well ventilated, and incubated, provided we can avoid technologies that might fiddle with that ozone, or shift the levels of carbon dioxide. Oxygen is not a major worry for us, unless we let fly with enough nuclear explosives to kill off the green cells in the sea; if we do that, of course, we are in for strangling.

It is hard to feel affection for something as totally impersonal as the atmosphere, and yet there it is, as much a part and product of life as wine or bread. Taken all in all, the sky is a miraculous achievement. It works, and for what it is designed to accomplish it is as infallible as anything in nature. I doubt whether any of us could think of a way to improve on it, beyond maybe shifting a local cloud from here to there on occasion. The word "chance" does not serve to account well for structures of such magnificence. There may have been elements of luck in the emergence of chloroplasts, but once these things were on the scene, the evolution of the sky became absolutely ordained. Chance suggests alternatives, other possibilities, different solutions. This may be true for gills and swim-bladders and forebrains, matters of detail, but not for the sky. There was simply no other way to go.

We should credit it for what it is: for sheer size and perfection of function, it is far and away the grandest product of collaboration in all of nature.

It breathes for us, and it does another thing for our pleasure. Each day, millions of meteorites fall against the outer limits of the membrane and are burned to nothing by the friction. Without this shelter, our surface would long since have become the pounded powder of the moon. Even though our receptors are not sensitive enough to hear it, there is comfort in knowing that the sound is there overhead, like the random noise of rain on the roof at night.

The Lives of a Cell (1974)

DAVID R. BROWER

The most important environmental leader of the second half of the 20th century, David Brower (1912–2000) makes many appearances in the pages of this volume. He is the hero of John McPhee's *Encounters with the Archdruid* (see pages 493–99) and he published books of photographs by artists like Eliot Porter (pages 380–91). Born in Berkeley, Brower was the preeminent rock climber of the early years of American alpinism. He led the first ascent of New Mexico's Shiprock in 1939, and it was sheer pleasure to sit with him in Yosemite Valley, one of his trademark martinis in hand, and watch him point out the dozens of routes he'd pioneered up out of that granite paradise. But if he joined the Sierra Club as a climber, he would transform it—and environmentalism—as its executive director in the 1950s and 1960s. He took what was largely a hiking club and turned it into the most potent political force in American environmentalism (and a prototype for crusading NGOs around the world). Much of his genius was channeled into publishing—in the 1960s he created the series of Sierra Club books that allowed many Americans their first real glimpses of the emotionally charged landscape of the American West, in the process helping build support for national parks in the North Cascades and elsewhere and creating a mass constituency for wilderness, at that time a pretty rarefied taste. Brower was not an organization man—the Sierra Club's board eventually tired of his independence and forced him to resign, whereupon he founded Friends of the Earth, which became an international version of the Sierra Club and which allowed him to expand his work beyond wilderness to all the other environmental issues that the 1970s brought to the fore. Eventually he proved too ungovernable for that group as well, so he quit in 1986 and devoted the rest of his years to the Earth Island Institute. Though his resumé may sound as if he specialized in conflict (and though he always advised environmentalists to leave compromises to the politicians), he was in fact beloved throughout the activist community, always willing to lend a hand to other people's causes and always willing to talk deep into the night at the local bar with whatever young environmentalists he could find.

The Third Planet: Operating Instructions

This planet has been delivered wholly assembled and in perfect working condition, and is intended for fully automatic and trouble-free operation in orbit around its star, the sun. However, to insure proper functioning, all passengers are requested to familiarize themselves fully with the following instructions.

Warning:

Loss or even temporary misplacement of these instructions may result in calamity. Passengers who must proceed without the benefit of these rules are likely to cause considerable damage before they can learn the proper operating procedures for themselves.

A. COMPONENTS:

It is recommended that passengers become completely familiar with the following planetary components:

1. Air:

The air accompanying this planet is not replaceable. Enough has been supplied to cover the land and the water, but not very deeply. In fact, if the atmosphere were reduced to the density of water, then it would be a mere 33 feet deep. In normal use, the air is self-cleaning. It may be cleaned in part if excessively soiled. The passengers' lungs will be of help—up to a point. However, they will discover that anything they throw, spew, or dump into the air will return to them in due course. Since passengers will need to use the air, on the average, every five seconds, they should treat it accordingly.

2. Water:

The water supplied with this planet isn't replaceable either. The operating water supply is very limited: If the earth were the size of an egg, all the water on it would fit in a single drop. The water contains many creatures, almost all of which eat and may be eaten; these creatures may be eaten by human passengers. If disagreeable things are dispersed in the planet's water, however, caution should be observed, since the water creatures concentrate the disagreeable things in their tissues. If human passengers then eat the water creatures, they will add disagreeable things to their diet. In general, passengers are advised not to disdain water, because that is what they mostly are.

3. Land:

Although the surface of this planet is varied and seems abundant, only a small amount of land is suited to growing things, and that essential part should not be misused. It is also recommended that no attempt be made to disassemble the surface too deeply inasmuch as the land is supported by a molten and very hot underlayer that will grow little but volcanoes.

4. Life:

The above components help make life possible. There is only one life per passenger and it should be treated with dignity. Instructions covering the birth, operation and maintenance, and disposal for each living entity have been thoughtfully provided. These instructions are contained in a complex language, called the DNA code, that is not easily understood. However, this does not matter, as the instructions are fully automatic. Passengers are cautioned, however, that radiation and many dangerous chemicals can damage the instructions severely. If in this way living species are destroyed, or rendered unable to reproduce, the filling of reorders is subject to long delays.

5. Fire:

This planet has been designed and fully tested at the factory for totally safe operation with fuel constantly transmitted from a remote source, the sun, provided at absolutely no charge. *The following must be observed with greatest care*: The planet comes with a limited reserve fuel supply, contained in fossil deposits, which should be used only in emergencies. Use of this reserve fuel supply entails hazards, including the release of certain toxic metals, which must be kept out of the air and the food supply of living things. The risk will not be appreciable if the use of the emergency fuel is extended over the operating life of the planet. Rapid use, if sustained only for a brief period, may produce unfortunate results.

B. MAINTENANCE:

The kinds of maintenance will depend upon the number and constituency of the passengers. If only a few million human passengers wish to travel at a given time, no maintenance will be required and no reservations will be necessary. The planet is self-maintaining and the external fuel source will provide exactly as much energy as is needed or can be safely used. However, if a very large number of people insist on boarding at one time, serious problems will result, requiring costly solutions.

C. OPERATION:

Barring extraordinary circumstances, it is necessary only to observe the mechanism periodically and to report any irregularities to the Smithsonian Institution. However, if, owing to misuse of the planet's mechanism, observations show a substantial change in the predictable patterns of sunrise and sunset, passengers should prepare to leave the vehicle.

D. EMERGENCY REPAIRS:

If through no responsibility of the current passengers, damage to the planet's operating mechanism has been caused by ignorant or careless action of the previous travelers, it is best to request the Manufacturer's assistance (best obtained through prayer).

Final note:

Upon close examination, this planet will be found to consist of complex and fascinating detail in design and structure. Some passengers, upon discovering these details in the past, have attempted to replicate or improve the design and structure, or have even claimed to have invented them. The Manufacturer, having among other things invented the opposable thumb, may be amused by this. It is reliably reported that at this point, however, it appears to the Manufacturer that the full panoply of consequences of this thumb idea of His will not be without an element of unwelcome surprise.

The New York Times Magazine, March 16, 1975

Many of the writers in this book are mystics of one kind or another, dissidents, romantics, philosophers. Amory Lovins (b. 1947), on the contrary, is the polymathic policy wonk of contemporary environmentalism. "I don't do problems, I do solutions," he once told the *New Yorker* writer Elizabeth Kolbert. David Brower first discovered him working as a research fellow at Oxford, and trying to block an open-pit copper mine that had been planned for the mountains of Wales. But Lovins' real talent was for thinking about resource systems, especially energy, and after the oil crunch in 1973 his ideas began to gain wide attention. This piece was published in 1976 in *Foreign Affairs*, and has provided much of the template for thinking about energy policy in the years since. Should we pursue more of what we have—coal mines, oil wells, nuclear reactors—or should we seek the "soft path" of conservation, renewable energy, and distributed generation? Lovins was asking these questions before anyone was worried about global warming, but they have become ever more pressing—and his vision has found receptive audiences in recent years not only in many Fortune 500 companies but also in some corners of the Defense Department. His Rocky Mountain Institute continues to publish important studies—most recently *Winning the Oil Endgame* (2004)—and to pioneer by example as well as exhortation: their headquarters, high in the mountains near Aspen, is so well-insulated that even in midwinter sunlight and body heat manage to keep it warm enough to grow bananas in the atrium.

from Energy Strategy: The Road Not Taken?

V

There exists today a body of energy technologies that have certain specific features in common and that offer great technical, economic

FIGURE 1

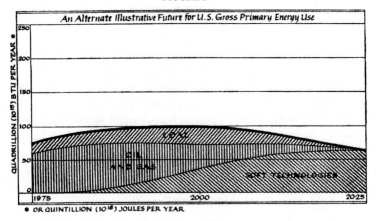

An Alternate Illustrative Future for U.S. Gross Primary Energy Use

* OR QUINTILLION (10¹⁸) JOULES PER YEAR

and political attractions, yet for which there is no generic term. For lack of a more satisfactory term, I shall call them "soft" technologies: a textural description, intended to mean not vague, mushy, speculative or ephemeral, but rather flexible, resilient, sustainable and benign. Energy paths dependent on soft technologies, illustrated in Figure 1, will be called "soft" energy paths, as the "hard" technologies sketched in Section II constitute a "hard" path (in both senses). The distinction between hard and soft energy paths rests not on how much energy is used, but on the technical and sociopolitical *structure* of the energy system, thus focusing our attention on consequent and crucial political differences.

In Figure 1, then, the social structure is significantly shaped by the rapid deployment of soft technologies. These are defined by five characteristics:

— They rely on renewable energy flows that are always there whether we use them or not, such as sun and wind and vegetation: on energy income, not on depletable energy capital.

— They are diverse, so that energy supply is an aggregate of very many individually modest contributions, each designed for maximum effectiveness in particular circumstances.

— They are flexible and relatively low-technology—which does not mean unsophisticated, but rather, easy to understand and use without esoteric skills, accessible rather than arcane.

— They are matched in *scale* and in geographic distribution to end-use needs, taking advantage of the free distribution of most natural energy flows.

— They are matched in *energy quality* to end-use needs: a key feature that deserves immediate explanation.

People do not want electricity or oil, nor such economic abstractions as "residential services," but rather comfortable rooms, light, vehicular motion, food, tables, and other real things. Such end-use needs can be classified by the physical nature of the task to be done. In the United States today, about 58 percent of all energy at the point of end use is required as heat, split roughly equally between temperatures above and below the boiling point of water. (In Western Europe the low-temperature heat alone is often a half of all end-use energy.) Another 38 percent of all U.S. end-use energy provides mechanical motion: 31 percent in vehicles, 3 percent in pipelines, 4 percent in industrial electric motors. The rest, a mere 4 percent of delivered energy, represents *all* lighting, electronics, telecommunications, electrometallurgy, electrochemistry, arc-welding, electric motors in home appliances and in railways, and similar end uses which now *require* electricity.

Some 8 percent of all our energy end use, then, requires electricity for purposes other than low-temperature heating and cooling. Yet, since we actually use electricity for many such low-grade purposes, it now meets 13 percent of our end-use needs—and its generation consumes 29 percent of our fossil fuels. A hard energy path would increase this 13 percent figure to 20–40 percent (depending on assumptions) by the year 2000, and far more thereafter. But this is wasteful because the laws of physics require, broadly speaking, that a power station change three units of fuel into two units of almost useless waste heat plus one unit of electricity. This electricity can do more difficult kinds of work than can the original fuel, but unless this extra quality and versatility are used to advantage, the costly process of upgrading the fuel—and losing two-thirds of it—is all for naught.

Plainly we are using premium fuels and electricity for many tasks for which their high energy quality is superfluous, wasteful and expensive, and a hard path would make this inelegant practice even more common. Where we want only to create temperature differences of tens of degrees, we should meet the need with sources whose potential is tens or hundreds of degrees, not with a flame temperature of thousands or a nuclear temperature of millions—like cutting butter with a chainsaw.

For some applications, electricity is appropriate and indispensable: electronics, smelting, subways, most lighting, some kinds of mechanical work, and a few more. But these uses are already oversupplied, and for the other, dominant uses remaining in our energy economy this special form of energy cannot give us our money's worth (in many parts of the United States today it already costs $50–120 per barrel-equivalent). Indeed, in probably no industrial country today can additional supplies of electricity be used to thermodynamic advantage which would justify their high cost in money and fuels.

So limited are the U.S. end uses that really require electricity that by applying careful technical fixes to them we could reduce their 8 percent total to about 5 percent (mainly by reducing commercial overlighting), whereupon we could probably cover all those needs with present U.S. hydroelectric capacity plus the cogeneration capacity available in the mid-to-late 1980s.* Thus an affluent industrial economy could advantageously operate with no central power stations at all! In practice we would not necessarily want to go that far, at least not for a long time; but the possibility illustrates how far we are from supplying energy only in the quality needed for the task at hand.

A feature of soft technologies as essential as their fitting end-use needs (for a different reason) is their appropriate scale, which can achieve important types of economies not available to larger, more centralized systems. This is done in five ways, of which the first is reducing

*The scale of potential conservation in this area is given in M. Ross and R. H. Williams, "Assessing the Potential for Fuel Conservation," forthcoming in *Technology Review*; the scale of potential cogeneration capacity is from P. W. McCracken *et al.*, *Industrial Energy Center Study*, Dow Chemical Co. *et al.*, report to NSF, PB-243 824, National Technical Information Service (Springfield, Va.), June 1975.

and sharing overheads. Roughly half your electricity bill is fixed distribution costs to pay the overheads of a sprawling energy system: transmission lines, transformers, cables, meters and people to read them, planners, headquarters, billing computers, interoffice memos, advertising agencies. For electrical and some fossil-fuel systems, distribution accounts for more than half of total capital cost, and administration for a significant fraction of total operating cost. Local or domestic energy systems can reduce or even eliminate these infrastructure costs. The resulting savings can far outweigh the extra costs of the dispersed maintenance infrastructure that the small systems require, particularly where that infrastructure already exists or can be shared (e.g., plumbers fixing solar heaters as well as sinks).

Small scale brings further savings by virtually eliminating distribution losses, which are cumulative and pervasive in centralized energy systems (particularly those using high-quality energy). Small systems also avoid direct diseconomies of scale, such as the frequent unreliability of large units and the related need to provide instant "spinning reserve" capacity on electrical grids to replace large stations that suddenly fail. Small systems with short lead times greatly reduce exposure to interest, escalation and mistimed demand forecasts—major indirect diseconomies of large scale.

The fifth type of economy available to small systems arises from mass production. Consider, as Henrik Harboe suggests, the 100-odd million cars in this country. In round numbers, each car probably has an average cost of less than $4,000 and a shaft power over 100 kilowatts (134 horsepower). Presumably a good engineer could build a generator and upgrade an automobile engine to a reliable, 35-percent-efficient diesel at no greater total cost, yielding a mass-produced diesel generator unit costing less than $40 per kw. In contrast, the motive capacity in our central power stations—currently totaling about 1/40 as much as in our cars—costs perhaps ten times more per kw, partly because it is not mass-produced. It is not surprising that at least one foreign car maker hopes to go into the wind-machine and heat-pump business. Such a market can be entered incrementally, without the billions of dollars' investment required for, say, liquefying natural gas or gasifying coal. It may require a production philosophy oriented toward technical simplicity, low replacement cost, slow obsolescence, high reliability, high volume and low markup; but these are familiar concepts in mass production. Industrial resistance would presumably melt when—as with pollution-abatement equipment—the scope for profit was perceived.

* * *

IX

Perhaps the most profound difference between the soft and hard paths is their domestic sociopolitical impact. Both paths, like any 50-year energy path, entail significant social change. But the kinds of social change needed for a hard path are apt to be much less pleasant, less plausible, less compatible with social diversity and personal freedom of choice, and less consistent with traditional values than are the social changes that could make a soft path work.

It is often said that, on the contrary, a soft path must be repressive; and coercive paths to energy conservation and soft technologies can indeed be imagined. But coercion is not necessary and its use would signal a major failure of imagination, given the many policy instruments available to achieve a given technical end. Why use penal legislation to encourage roof insulation when tax incentives and education (leading to the sophisticated public understanding now being achieved in Canada and parts of Europe) will do? Policy tools need not harm lifestyles or liberties if chosen with reasonable sensitivity.

In contrast to the soft path's dependence on pluralistic consumer choice in deploying a myriad of small devices and refinements, the hard path depends on difficult, large-scale projects requiring a major social commitment under centralized management. We have noted in Section II the extraordinary capital intensity of centralized, electrified high technologies. Their similarly heavy demands on other scarce resources—skills, labor, materials, special sites—likewise cannot be met by market allocation, but require compulsory diversion from whatever priorities are backed by the weakest constituencies. Quasi-warpowers legislation to this end has already been seriously proposed. The hard path, sometimes portrayed as the bastion of free enterprise and free markets, would instead be a world of subsidies, $100-billion bailouts, oligopolies, regulations, nationalization, eminent domain, corporate statism.

Such dirigiste autarchy is the first of many distortions of the political fabric. While soft technologies can match any settlement pattern, their diversity reflecting our own pluralism, centralized energy sources encourage industrial clustering and urbanization. While soft technologies give everyone the costs and benefits of the energy system he chooses, centralized systems allocate benefits to suburbanites and social costs to politically weaker rural agrarians. Siting big energy systems pits central authority against local autonomy in an increasingly divisive and wasteful form of centrifugal politics that is already proving one of the most potent constraints on expansion.

In an electrical world, your lifeline comes not from an understandable neighborhood technology run by people you know who are at your own social level, but rather from an alien, remote, and perhaps humiliatingly uncontrollable technology run by a faraway, bureaucratized, technical elite who have probably never heard of you. Decisions about who shall have how much energy at what price also become centralized—a politically dangerous trend because it divides those who use energy from those who supply and regulate it.

The scale and complexity of centralized grids not only make them politically inaccessible to the poor and weak, but also increase the likelihood and size of malfunctions, mistakes and deliberate disruptions. A small fault or a few discontented people become able to turn off a country. Even a single rifleman can probably black out a typical city instantaneously. Societies may therefore be tempted to discourage disruption through stringent controls akin to a garrison state. In times of social stress, when grids become a likely target for dissidents, the sector may be paramilitarized and further isolated from grass-roots politics.

If the technology used, like nuclear power, is subject to technical surprises and unique psychological handicaps, prudence or public clamor may require generic shutdowns in case of an unexpected type of malfunction: one may have to choose between turning off a country and persisting in potentially unsafe operation. Indeed, though many in the

$100-billion quasi-civilian nuclear industry agree that it could be politically destroyed if a major accident occurred soon, few have considered the economic or political implications of putting at risk such a large fraction of societal capital. How far would governments go to protect against a threat—even a purely political threat—a basket full of such delicate, costly and essential eggs? Already in individual nuclear plants, the cost of a shutdown—often many dollars a second—weighs heavily, perhaps too heavily, in operating and safety decisions.

Any demanding high technology tends to develop influential and dedicated constituencies of those who link its commercial success with both the public welfare and their own. Such sincerely held beliefs, peer pressures, and the harsh demands that the work itself places on time and energy all tend to discourage such people from acquiring a similarly thorough knowledge of alternative policies and the need to discuss them. Moreover, the money and talent invested in an electrical program tend to give it disproportionate influence in the counsels of government, often directly through staff-swapping between policy- and mission-oriented agencies. This incestuous position, now well developed in most industrial countries, distorts both social and energy priorities in a lasting way that resists political remedy.

For all these reasons, if nuclear power were clean, safe, economic, assured of ample fuel, and socially benign per se, it would still be unattractive because of the political implications of the kind of energy economy it would lock us into. But fission technology also has unique sociopolitical side-effects arising from the impact of human fallibility and malice on the persistently toxic and explosive materials in the fuel cycle. For example, discouraging nuclear violence and coercion requires some abrogation of civil liberties*; guarding long-lived wastes against geological or social contingencies implies some form of hierarchical social rigidity or homogeneity to insulate the technological priesthood from social turbulence; and making political decisions about nuclear

---

*R. Ayres, *10 Harvard Civil Rights-Civil Liberties Law Review*, Spring 1975, pp. 369–443; J. H. Barton, "Intensified Nuclear Safeguards and Civil Liberties," report to USNRC, Stanford Law School, October 21, 1975.

hazards which are compulsory, remote from social experience, disputed, unknown, or unknowable, may tempt governments to bypass democratic decision in favor of elitist technocracy.*

Even now, the inability of our political institutions to cope with nuclear hazard is straining both their competence and their perceived legitimacy. There is no scientific basis for calculating the likelihood or the maximum long-term effects of nuclear mishaps, or for guaranteeing that those effects will not exceed a particular level; we know only that all precautions are, for fundamental reasons, inherently imperfect in essentially unknown degree. Reducing that imperfection would require much social engineering whose success would be speculative. Technical success in reducing the hazards would not reduce, and might enhance, the need for such social engineering. The most attractive political feature of soft technologies and conservation—the alternatives that will let us avoid these decisions and their high political costs—may be that, like motherhood, everyone is in favor of them.

X

Civilization in this country, according to some, would be inconceivable if we used only, say, half as much electricity as now. But that is what we did use in 1963, when we were at least half as civilized as now. What would life be like at the per capita levels of primary energy that we had in 1910 (about the present British level) but with doubled efficiency of energy use and with the important but not very energy-intensive amenities we lacked in 1910, such as telecommunications and modern medicine? Could it not be at least as agreeable as life today? Since the energy needed today to produce a unit of GNP varies more than 100-fold depending on what good or service is being produced, and since GNP in turn hardly measures social welfare, why must energy and welfare march forever in lockstep? Such questions today can be neither answered nor ignored.

Underlying energy choices are real but tacit choices of personal values. Those that make a high-energy society work are all too apparent.

*H. P. Green, *43 George Washington Law Review*, March 1975, pp. 791–807.

Those that could sustain life-styles of elegant frugality are not new; they are in the attic and could be dusted off and recycled. Such values as thrift, simplicity, diversity, neighborliness, humility and craftsmanship—perhaps most closely preserved in politically conservative communities—are already, as we see from the ballot box and the census, embodied in a substantial social movement, camouflaged by its very pervasiveness. Offered the choice freely and equitably, many people would choose, as Herman Daly puts it, "growth in things that really count rather than in things that are merely countable": choose not to transform, in Duane Elgin's phrase, "a rational concern for material well-being into an obsessive concern for unconscionable levels of material consumption."

Indeed, we are learning that many of the things we had taken to be the benefits of affluence are really remedial costs, incurred in the pursuit of benefits that might be obtainable in other ways without those costs. Thus much of our prized personal mobility is really involuntary traffic made necessary by the settlement patterns which cars create. Is that traffic a cost or a benefit?

Pricked by such doubts, our inflated craving for consumer ephemerals is giving way to a search for both personal and public purpose, to reexamination of the legitimacy of the industrial ethic. In the new age of scarcity, our ingenious strivings to substitute abstract (therefore limitless) wants for concrete (therefore reasonably bounded) needs no longer seem so virtuous. But where we used to accept unquestioningly the facile (and often self-serving) argument that traditional economic growth and distributional equity are inseparable, new moral and humane stirrings now are nudging us. We can now ask whether we are not already so wealthy that further growth, far from being essential to addressing our equity problems, is instead an excuse not to mobilize the compassion and commitment that could solve the same problems with or without the growth.

Finally, as national purpose and trust in institutions diminish, governments, striving to halt the drift, seek ever more outward control. We are becoming more uneasily aware of the nascent risk of what a Stanford Research Institute group has called ". . . 'friendly fascism'—a managed society which rules by a faceless and widely dispersed complex of warfare-welfare-industrial-communications-police bureaucracies with a technocratic ideology." In the sphere of politics as of personal values, could many strands of observable social change be converging on a profound cultural transformation whose implications we can only vaguely sense: one in which energy policy, as an integrating principle, could be catalytic?*

It is not my purpose here to resolve such questions—only to stress their relevance. Though fuzzy and unscientific, they are the beginning and end of any energy policy. Making values explicit is essential to preserving a society in which diversity of values can flourish.

Some people suppose that a soft energy path entails mainly social problems, a hard path mainly technical problems, so that since in the past we have been better at solving the technical problems, that is the kind we should prefer to incur now. But the hard path, too, involves difficult social problems. We can no longer escape them; we must choose which kinds of social problems we want. The most important, difficult, and neglected questions of energy strategy are not mainly technical or economic but rather social and ethical. They will pose a supreme challenge to the adaptability of democratic institutions and to the vitality of our spiritual life.

*W. W. Harman, *An Incomplete Guide to the Future*, Stanford Alumni Association, 1976.

Foreign Affairs, October 1976

N. SCOTT MOMADAY

N. Scott Momaday (b. 1934) has a rare and interesting vantage point for thinking about the relationship between Americans and the natural world. His mother was the daughter of pioneers, though with some Indian blood. She adopted the name Little Moon, attended an Indian school in Kansas, and eventually married Momaday's father, a Kiowa. A novelist whose first book, *House Made of Dawn*, won the Pulitzer in 1969, he has thought more straightforwardly than most of us about the continent's long aboriginal heritage, and the radically different ways in which his Native American and European ancestors related to the land. This essay was published as part of *National Geographic*'s celebration of the Bicentennial in 1976; the poem interspersed throughout is also Momaday's, from his collection *The Gourd Dancer* (1976).

A First American Views His Land

First Man
behold:
the earth
glitters
with leaves;
the sky
glistens
with rain.
Pollen
is borne
on winds
that low
and lean
upon
mountains.

Cedars
blacken
the slopes—
and pines.

One hundred centuries ago. There is a wide, irregular landscape in what is now northern New Mexico. The sun is a dull white disk, low in the south; it is a perfect mystery, a deity whose coming and going are inexorable. The gray sky is curdled, and it bears very close upon the earth. A cold wind runs along the ground, dips and spins, flaking drift from a pond in the bottom of a ravine. Beyond the wind the silence is acute. A man crouches in the ravine, in the darkness there, scarcely visible. He moves not a muscle; only the wind lifts a lock of his hair and lays it back along his neck. He wears skins and carries a spear. These things in particular mark his human intelligence and distinguish him as the lord of the universe. And for him the universe is especially *this* landscape; for him the landscape is an element like the air. The vast, virgin wilderness is by and large his whole context. For him there is no possibility of existence elsewhere.

Directly there is a blowing, a rumble of breath deeper than the wind, above him, where some of the hard clay of the bank is broken off and the clods roll down into the water. At the same time there appears on the skyline the massive head of a long-horned bison, then the hump, then the whole beast, huge and black on the sky, standing to a height of seven feet at the hump, with horns that extend six feet across the shaggy crown. For a moment it is poised there; then it lumbers obliquely down the bank to the pond. Still the man does not move, though the beast is now only a few steps upwind. There is no sign of what is about to happen; the beast meanders; the man is frozen in repose.

Then the scene explodes. In one and the same instant the man springs to his feet and bolts forward, his arm cocked and the spear held high, and the huge animal lunges in panic, bellowing, its whole weight thrown violently into the bank, its hooves churning and chipping earth into the air, its eyes gone wide and wild and white. There is a moment in which its awful, frenzied motion is wasted, and it is mired and helpless in its fear, and the man hurls the spear with his whole strength, and the point is driven into the deep, vital flesh, and the bison in its agony staggers and crashes down and dies.

This ancient drama of the hunt is enacted again and again in the landscape. The man is preeminently a predator, the most dangerous of all. He hunts in order to survive; his very existence is simply, squarely established upon that basis. But he hunts also because he can, because he has the means; he has the ultimate weapon of his age, and his prey is plentiful. His relationship to the land has not yet become a moral equation.

But in time he will come to understand that there is an intimate, vital link between the earth and himself, a link that implies an intricate network of rights and responsibilities. In some unimagined future he will understand that he has the ability to devastate and perhaps destroy his environment. That moment will be one of extreme crisis in his evolution.

The weapon is deadly and efficient. The hunter has taken great care in its manufacture, especially in the shaping of the flint point, which is an extraordinary thing. A larger flake has been removed from each face, a groove that extends from the base nearly to the tip. Several hundred pounds of pressure, expertly applied, were required to make these grooves. The hunter then is an artisan, and he must know how to use rudimentary tools. His skill, manifest in the manufacture of this artifact, is unsurpassed for its time and purpose. By means of this weapon is the Paleo-Indian hunter eminently able to exploit his environment.

Thousands of years later, about the time that Columbus begins his first voyage to the New World, another man, in the region of the Great Lakes, stands in the forest shade on the edge of a sunlit brake. In a while a deer enters into the pool of light. Silently the man fits an arrow to a bow, draws aim, and shoots. The arrow zips across the distance and strikes home. The deer leaps and falls dead.

But this latter-day man, unlike his ancient predecessor, is only incidentally a hunter; he is also a fisherman, a husbandman, even a physician. He fells trees and builds canoes; he grows corn, squash, and beans, and he gathers fruits and nuts; he uses hundreds of species of wild plants for food, medicine, teas, and dyes. Instead of one animal, or two or three, he hunts many, none to extinction as the Paleo-Indian may have done. He has fitted himself far more precisely into the patterns of the wilderness than did his ancient predecessor. He lives on the land; he takes his living from it; but he does not destroy it. This distinction supports the fundamental ethic that we call conservation today. In principle, if not yet in name, this man is a conservationist.

These two hunting sketches are far less important in themselves than is that long distance between them, that whole possibility within the dimension of time. I believe that in that interim there grew up in the mind of man an idea of the land as sacred.

> *At dawn*
> *eagles*
> *lie and*
> *hover*
> *above*
> *the plain*
> *where light*
> *gathers*
> *in pools.*
> *Grasses*
> *shimmer*
> *and shine.*
> *Shadows*
> *withdraw*
> *and lie*
> *away*
> *like smoke.*

"The earth is our mother. The sky is our father." This concept of nature, which is at the center of the Native American world view, is familiar to us all. But it may well be that we do not understand entirely what that concept is in its ethical and philosophical implications.

I tell my students that the American Indian has a unique investment in the American landscape. It is an investment that represents perhaps thirty thousand years of habitation. That tenure has to be worth something in itself—a great deal, in fact. The Indian has been here a long time; he is at home here. That simple and obvious truth is one of the most important realities of the Indian world, and it is integral in the Indian mind and spirit.

How does such a concept evolve? Where does it begin? Perhaps it begins with the recognition of beauty, the realization that the physical world *is* beautiful. We don't know much about the ancient hunter's sensibilities. It isn't likely that he had leisure in his life for the elaboration of an aesthetic ideal. And yet the weapon he made was beautiful as well as functional. It has been suggested that much of the minute chipping along the edges of his weapon served no purpose but that of aesthetic satisfaction.

A good deal more is known concerning that man of the central forests. He made beautiful boxes and dishes out of elm and birch bark, for example. His canoes were marvelous, delicate works of art. And this aesthetic perception was a principle of the whole Indian world of his time, as indeed it is of our time. The contemporary Native American is a man whose strong aesthetic perceptions are clearly evident in his arts and crafts, in his religious ceremonies, and in the stories and songs of his rich oral tradition. This, in view of the pressures that have been brought to bear upon the Indian world and the drastic changes that have been effected in its landscape, is a blessing and an irony.

Consider for example the Navajos of the Four Corners area. In recent years an extensive coal-mining operation has mutilated some of their most sacred land. A large power plant in that same region spews a contamination into the sky that is visible for many miles. And yet, as much as any people of whom I have heard, the Navajos perceive and celebrate the beauty of the physical world.

There is a Navajo ceremonial song that celebrates the sounds that are made in the natural world, the particular voices that beautify the earth:

> *Voice above,*
> *Voice of thunder,*
> *Speak from the*
> *dark of clouds;*
> *Voice below,*
> *Grasshopper voice,*
> *Speak from the*
> *green of plants;*
> *So may the earth*
> *be beautiful.*

There is in the motion and meaning of this song a comprehension of the world that is peculiarly native, I believe, that is integral in the Native American mentality. Consider: The singer stands at the center of the natural world, at the source of its sound, of its motion, of its life. Nothing of that world is inaccessible to him or lost upon him. His song is filled with reverence, with wonder and delight, and with confidence as well. He knows something about himself and about the things around him— and he knows that he knows. I am interested in what he sees and hears; I am interested in the range and force of his perception. Our immediate impression may be that his perception is narrow and deep—vertical. After all, "voice above . . . voice below," he sings. But is it vertical only? At each level of his expression there is an extension of his aware- ness across the whole landscape. The voice above is the voice of thunder, and thunder rolls. Moreover, it issues from the impalpable dark clouds and runs upon their horizontal range. It is a sound that in- tegrates the whole of the atmosphere. And even so, the voice below, that of the grasshopper, issues from the broad plain and multiplicity of plants. And of course the singer is mindful of much more than thunder and insects; we are given in his song the wide angle of his vision and his hearing—and we are given the testimony of his dignity, his trust, and his deep belief.

This comprehension of the earth and air is surely a matter of morality, for it brings into account not only man's instinctive reaction to his environment but the full realization of his humanity as well, the achievement of his intellectual and spiritual development as an individual and as a race.

In my own experience I have seen numerous examples of this regard for nature. My grandfather Mammedaty was a farmer in his mature years; his grandfather was a buffalo hunter. It was not easy for Mammedaty to be a farmer; he was a Kiowa, and the Kiowas never had an agrarian tradition. Yet he had to make his living, and the old, beloved life of roaming the plains and hunting the buffalo was gone forever. Even so, as much as any man before him, he fitted his mind and will and spirit to the land; there was nothing else. He could not have conceived of living apart from the land.

In *The Way to Rainy Mountain* I set down a small narrative that belongs in the oral tradition of my family. It indicates something essential about the Native American attitude toward the land:

"East of my grandmother's house, south of the pecan grove, there is buried a woman in a beautiful dress. Mammedaty used to know where she is buried, but now no one knows. If you stand on the front porch of the house and look eastward towards Carnegie, you know that the woman is buried somewhere within the range of your vision. But her grave is unmarked. She was buried in a cabinet, and she wore a beautiful dress. How beautiful it was! It was one of those fine buckskin dresses, and it was decorated with elk's teeth and beadwork. That dress is still there, under the ground."

It seems to me that this statement is primarily a declaration of love for the land, in which the several elements—the woman, the dress, and this plain—are at last become one reality, one expression of the beautiful in nature. Moreover, it seems to me a peculiarly Native American expression in this sense: that the concentration of things that are explicitly remembered—the general landscape, the simple, almost abstract nature of the burial, above all the beautiful dress, which is wholly singular in kind (as well as in its function within the narrative)—is especially Indian in character. The things that are *not* explicitly remembered—the woman's name, the exact location of her grave—are the things that matter least in the special view of the storyteller. What matters here is the translation of the woman into the landscape, a translation particularly signified by means of the beautiful and distinctive dress, an *Indian* dress.

When I was a boy, I lived for several years at Jemez Pueblo, New Mexico. The Pueblo Indians are perhaps more obviously invested in the land than are other people. Their whole life is predicated upon a thorough perception of the physical world and its myriad aspects. When I first went there to live, the cacique, or chief, of the Pueblos was a venerable old man with long, gray hair and bright, deep-set eyes. He was entirely dignified and imposing—and rather formidable in the eyes of a boy. He excited my imagination a good deal. I was told that this old man kept the calendar of the tribe, that each morning he stood on a certain spot of ground near the center of the town and watched to see where the sun appeared on the skyline. By means of this solar calendar did he know and announce to his people when it was time to plant, to harvest, to perform this or that ceremony. This image of him in my mind's eye—the old man gazing each morning after the ranging sun— came to represent for me the epitome of that real harmony between man and the land that signifies the Indian world.

One day when I was riding my horse along the Jemez River, I looked up to see a long caravan of wagons and people on horseback and on foot. Men, women, and children were crossing the river ahead of me, moving out to the west, where most of the cultivated fields were, the farmland of the town. It was a wonderful sight to see, this long procession, and I was immediately deeply curious. I wanted to investigate, but it was not in me to do so at once, for that racial reserve, that sense of propriety that is deep-seated in Native American culture, stayed me, held me up. Then I saw someone coming toward me on horseback, galloping. It was a friend of mine, a boy of my own age. "Come on," he said. "Come with us." "Where are you going?" I asked casually. But he would not tell me. He simply laughed and urged me to come along, and of course I was very glad to do so. It was a bright spring morning, and

I had a good horse under me, and the prospect of adventure was delicious. We moved far out across the eroded plain to the farthest fields at the foot of a great red mesa, and there we planted two large fields of corn. And afterward, on the edge of the fields, we sat on blankets and ate a feast in the shade of a cottonwood grove. Later I learned it was the cacique's fields we planted. And this is an ancient tradition at Jemez. The people of the town plant and tend and harvest the cacique's fields, and in the winter the hunters give to him a portion of the meat that they bring home from the mountains. It is as if the cacique is himself the translation of man, every man, into the landscape.

I have not forgotten that day, nor shall I forget it. I remember the warm earth of the fields, the smooth texture of seeds in my hands, and the brown water moving slowly and irresistibly among the rows. Above all I remember the spirit in which the procession was made, the work was done, and the feasting was enjoyed. It was a spirit of communion, of the life of each man in relation to the life of the planet and of the infinite distance and silence in which it moves. We made, in concert, an appropriate expression of that spirit.

One afternoon an old Kiowa woman talked to me, telling me of the place in Oklahoma in which she had lived for a hundred years. It was the place in which my grandparents, too, lived; and it is the place where I was born. And she told me of a time even further back, when the Kiowas came down from the north and centered their culture in the red earth of the southern plains. She told wonderful stories, and as I listened, I began to feel more and more sure that her voice proceeded from the land itself. I asked her many things concerning the Kiowas, for I wanted to understand all that I could of my heritage. I told the old woman that I had come there to learn from her and from people like her, those in whom the old ways were preserved. And she said simply: "It is good that you have come here." I believe that her word "good" meant many things; for one thing it meant *right*, or *appropriate*. And indeed it was appropriate that she should speak of the land. She was eminently qualified to do so. She had a great reverence for the land, and an ancient perception of it, a perception that is acquired only in the course of many generations.

It is this notion of the appropriate, along with that of the beautiful, that forms the Native American perspective on the land. In a sense these considerations are indivisible; Native American oral tradition is rich with songs and tales that celebrate natural beauty, the beauty of the natural world. What is more appropriate to our world than that which is beautiful?

> *At noon*
> *turtles*
> *enter*
> *slowly*
> *into*
> *the warm*
> *dark loam.*
> *Bees hold*
> *the swarm.*
> *Meadows*
> *recede*
> *through planes*
> *of heat*
> *and pure*
> *distance.*

Very old in the Native American world view is the conviction that the earth is vital, that there is a spiritual dimension to it, a dimension in which man rightly exists. It follows logically that there are ethical imperatives in this matter. I think: Inasmuch as I am in the land, it is appropriate that I should affirm myself in the spirit of the land. I shall celebrate my life in the world and the world in my life. In the natural order man invests himself in the landscape and at the same time incorporates the landscape into his own most fundamental experience. This trust is sacred.

The process of investment and appropriation is, I believe, preeminently a function of the imagination. It is accomplished by means of an act of the imagination that is especially ethical in kind. We are what we imagine ourselves to be. The Native American is someone who thinks of himself, imagines himself in a particular way. By virtue of his experience his idea of himself comprehends his relationship to the land.

And the quality of this imagining is determined as well by racial and cultural experience. The Native American's attitudes toward this landscape have been formulated over a long period of time, a span that reaches back to the end of the Ice Age. The land, *this* land, is secure in his racial memory.

In our society as a whole we conceive of the land in terms of ownership and use. It is a lifeless medium of exchange; it has for most of us, I suspect, no more spirituality than has an automobile, say, or a refrigerator. And our laws confirm us in this view, for we can buy and sell the land, we can exclude each other from it, and in the context of ownership we can use it as we will. Ownership implies use, and use implies consumption.

But this way of thinking of the land is alien to the Indian. His cultural intelligence is opposed to these concepts; indeed, for him they are all but inconceivable quantities. This fundamental distinction is easier to understand with respect to ownership than to use, perhaps. For obviously the Indian does use, and has always used, the land and the available resources in it. The point is that *use* does not indicate in any real way his idea of the land. "Use" is neither his word nor his idea. As an Indian I think: "You say that I *use* the land, and I reply, yes, it is true; but it is not the first truth. The first truth is that I *love* the land; I see that it is beautiful; I delight in it; I am alive in it."

In the long course of his journey from Asia and in the realization of himself in the New World, the Indian has assumed a deep ethical regard for the earth and sky, a reverence for the natural world that is antipodal to that strange tenet of modern civilization that seemingly has it that man must destroy his environment. It is this ancient ethic of the Native American that must shape our efforts to preserve the earth and the life upon and within it.

*At dusk
the gray
foxes
stiffen
in cold;
blackbirds
are fixed
in white
branches.
Rivers
follow
the moon,
the long
white track
of the
full moon.*

National Geographic, July 1976

LESLIE MARMON SILKO

Although she has told interviewers that she sees herself as "a citizen of the world" and not of the United States alone, Leslie Marmon Silko (b. 1948) is in certain ways as American a writer as it's possible to be. She grew up on the edge of the Laguna Pueblo in New Mexico, of mixed Native American, European, and Mexican ancestry. In her first great book, *Ceremony* (1977), she tackled the question of how Tayo, a shell-shocked World War II veteran, might regain his sanity upon his return to the Southwest. The answer involves understanding, with the help of Native American tradition, that cosmos and humanity are parts of a whole, and that harmony between them is an achievable goal—the grail that animates most great environmental writing. In subsequent works—especially the sprawling and mesmerizing *Almanac of the Dead* (1991)—she links her region with much of the rest of the indigenous world, helping draw the atlas of place-based resistance to the encroachments of global consumerism.

from **Ceremony**

The trail was parallel to the top of the orange sandrock mesa. It was almost too narrow for a horse, and the mare sent a stream of pebbles and small rocks rolling down the steep slopes. He leaned forward over her shoulders to make the climb easier. The sun was moving higher into the sky, and the cliffs of the mesa radiated the sun's warmth. He stopped her near the top and tied his jacket behind the saddle, over the bedroll and sack of food. He looked at the sky: it had a bright blue intensity that only autumn and the movement of the sun from its summer place in the sky could give it. He studied the sky all the rest of the way up; the mare had only one direction to go because the trail had become too narrow even for her to turn around. At the top, the wind was cold. He stopped to put on his jacket and rest the mare. Below, the house was hidden by the foothills, but the country beyond it spread out before him in all directions. To the east was the Rio Puerco Valley, where the river had cut a deep narrow arroyo that now carried the water too low to benefit the valley land. Years of wind and no rain had finally stripped the valley down to dark gray clay, where only the bluish salt bush could grow. Beyond the Rio Puerco, to the southeast, he could see the blue mountains east of the Rio Grande, where the rich valley was full of their cities. But from this place there was no sign the white people had ever come to this land; they had no existence then, except as he remembered them. So for a while he forgot, and sought out the southern peaks that were thin blue and skeletal in the great distance.

The mountain had been named for the swirling veils of clouds, the membranes of foggy mist clinging to the peaks, then leaving them covered with snow. This morning the mountain was dusted with snow, and the blue-gray clouds were unwinding from the peaks. He pulled the mare away from her grazing and remounted. He trotted her west, across the grassy flat toward the *cerros*, gently rounded hills of dark lava rock which were covered with a thin crust of topsoil and grass, edged with thickets of scrub oak. The pine trees grew in groves along the ridges above the dry lake-bed flats; but as he rode closer to the mountain, the land ascended into a solid pine forest, and the scrub oak and grass grew only in small clearings.

The white ranchers called this place North Top, but he remembered it by the story Josiah had told him about a hunter who walked into a grassy meadow up here and found a mountain-lion cub chasing butterflies; as long as the hunter sang a song to the cub, it continued to play. But when the hunter thought of the cub's mother and was afraid, the mountain-lion cub was startled, and ran away. The Laguna people had always hunted up there. They went up the slopes of the cone-shaped peaks in the summer, when the deer were reddish brown, the hair short and shining while they browsed in meadows above the treeline to avoid the heat. In late fall, as the deer moved down with each snowstorm, the people hunted the foothills and *cerros* and the grassy dry lake flats of the big plateau. And finally, in the winter, when the deer had heavy dark gray coats and the bitter snow winds drove them down twisting narrow trails, the Laguna hunters found them, fat from acorns and piñons growing in the narrow steep canyons below the rim.

All but a small part of the mountain had been taken. The reservation boundary included only a canyon above Encinal and a few miles of timber on the plateau. The rest of the land was taken by the National Forest and by the state which later sold it to white ranchers who came from Texas in the early 1900s. In the twenties and thirties the loggers had come, and they stripped the canyons below the rim and cut great clearings on the plateau slopes. The logging companies hired full-time hunters who fed entire logging camps, taking ten or fifteen deer each week and fifty wild turkeys in one month. The loggers shot the bears and mountain lions for sport. And it was then the Laguna people understood that the land had been taken, because they couldn't stop these white people from coming to destroy the animals and the land. It was then too that the holy men at Laguna and Acoma warned the people that the balance of the world had been disturbed and the people could expect droughts and harder days to come.

White ranchers pastured cattle there, especially during the dry years when no grass grew below the mountain. They fattened them on the plateau during the summer, and brought them down to the buyers in late fall. Tayo rode past white-faced Herefords standing around a windmill; they stared at him and the horse stupidly. He did not expect to find Josiah's cattle near Herefords, because the spotted cattle were so rangy and wild; but without Betonie he wouldn't have hoped to find the cattle at all. Until the previous night, old Betonie's vision of stars, cattle, a woman, and a mountain had seemed remote; he had been wary, especially after he found the stars, and they were in the north. It seemed more likely to find the spotted cattle in the south, far far in the south—the direction they had always gone. The last time Josiah had seen them, the cattle had been wandering southwest along the boundary between the reservation and state land. When Tayo told Robert he was going north, up into the mountains to look for the cattle, Robert shrugged his shoulders and shook his head. "Maybe," he said, "maybe.

I guess once somebody got them, they could have taken them just about anywhere." So he had gone, not expecting to find anything more than the winter constellation in the north sky overhead; but suddenly Betonie's vision was a story he could feel happening—from the stars and the woman, the mountain and the cattle would come.

Tayo stopped the mare by a pine tree on a ridge near a scrub-oak thicket. He tied the lariat rope around her neck and slipped off the bridle to let her graze. He untied the food sack from behind the saddle and walked over to the tree. Layers of reddish brown pine needles sank softly under his feet, and he brushed aside the pine cones before he sat down. From where he sat, the world looked as if it were more than half blue sky closing around like a dome. The sun was leaning into the southwest sky. He chewed the jerky as carefully as the mare chewed the grass, pushing against cords of gristle with his tongue, feeling the slippery fibers give way between his teeth. He swallowed the last piece of jerky and felt it roll with the urgency and excitement in his belly.

The Texans who bought the land fenced it and posted signs in English and Spanish warning trespassers to keep out. But the people from the land grants and the people from Laguna and Acoma ignored the signs and hunted deer; occasionally, the Mexicans took a cow. So later on, the ranchers hired men to patrol on horseback, carrying .30-30s in saddle scabbards. But the armed riders made little difference because there were miles and miles of fence and two or three hunters could easily slip between them. Still, he would have to be careful. When he located the cattle, he would drive them back. He had the bill of sale from Ulibarri buttoned in his shirt pocket just in case.

He got up feeling happy and excited. He would take the cattle home again, and they would follow the plans Josiah had made and raise a new breed of cattle that could live in spite of drought and hard weather. He tied the lunch sack under the bedroll and pulled the bridle back over the mare's ears. He rode west along the south rim of the plateau, watching for sudden movements that were speckled white. The barbed wire fence paralleled the rim, and he could see bits of belly hair the deer left on the barbed wire where their trails crossed the fence. Fences had never stopped the speckled cattle either, but there was no sign they had been there. So he rode north, looking for another fence that might be holding them.

He rode miles across dry lake flats and over rocky *cerros* until he came to a high fence of heavy-gauge steel mesh with three strands of barbed wire across the top. It was a fence that could hold the spotted cattle. The white man, Floyd Lee, called it a wolf-proof fence; but he had poisoned and shot all the wolves in the hills, and the people knew what the fence was for: a thousand dollars a mile to keep Indians and Mexicans out; a thousand dollars a mile to lock the mountain in steel wire, to make the land his.

He was examining the fence and the way the wire was buried underground so animals could not crawl or dig under it, when from the corner of his eye he saw something move. They were too far away for him to see the brands, and the light brown spots were difficult to make out on their light hides, but they moved like deer, on long thin legs. It was them.

They were strung out on the south slope of a round lava rock hill, moving west along the fence line. He watched them disappear over a ridge, and in a few minutes he saw the lead cow reappear on the far slope, still following the fence line. They had worn a path into the ground along the south boundary fence, walking relentlessly back and forth from east to west, as if waiting for some chance to escape, for some big pine to blow down in the wind and tear open a gate to the south. South: the direction was lodged deep in their bones.

He moved quickly; his hands were shaking. The mare snorted and shied away from the sudden motions. He held the reins tight and moved closer to her, slowly, speaking softly. He patted her neck until she was calm again. He looked at the hill where the cattle had disappeared, and fumbled untying the saddle strings; he pulled the bedroll loose and reached into the folds of the blankets. Next to a rope the most important tool a rider carried was a pair of fencing pliers. Hundreds of miles of barbed-wire fence marked boundaries and kept the cattle and horses from wandering. Josiah taught him to watch for loose strands of wire and breaks in the fence; he taught Tayo how to mend them before any livestock strayed off reservation land. He helped Tayo stitch a leather holster for the pliers one evening after supper, and he reminded him that you never knew when you might be traveling some place and a fence might get in your way. Josiah had nodded toward Mount Taylor when he said it.

He pulled on his work gloves, and he cut through four strands of heavy steel wire before he realized he was standing where anyone might see him. He looked around quickly for a fence rider on horseback or a patrol in a pickup truck. His heart was pounding, and he remembered the hide-and-go-seek games of a long time ago, when he had lain flat on the ground, trying hard not to pee in his pants. He threw down the pliers and pulled off the gloves. He could think more clearly after he pissed. There was no reason to hurry. The cattle would be easy to find because they stayed close to the south boundary fence. In a few hours it would be dark, and he could go after them. It would be simple. There was no reason to hurry or make foolish mistakes.

He tied the mare in a clearing surrounded by a thicket of scrub oak. He sat under a scrub oak and picked up acorns from the ground around him. The oak leaves were already fading from dark green to light yellow, and within the week they would turn gold and bright red. The acorns were losing their green color too, and the hulls were beginning to dry out. By the time the leaves fell and the acorns dropped, he would be home with the cattle.

The sun was hanging low in the branches of the pines at the top of the ridge; the thicket and clearing were in deep shadow. The wind rustled the oak leaves, and the mare's shit sent steam into the cold air. He crouched down with his hands in his pockets and the collar of his jacket pulled up to his ears. Up here, winter was already close. He ate another piece of jerky and a handful of parched corn, waiting for the dark. He swallowed water from the canteen and watched the sky for the autumn evening stars to appear.

He fed the mare a handful of parched corn and lifted her unshod hooves to check for damage from the sharp lava rock. He didn't know how well she could run at night over this rocky, unfamiliar country. The dry lake flats and scrub-oak ridges could be confusing. The rolling hills scattered with lava rock and the pine ridges between clearings were almost indistinguishable from one another. He had been fooled by them before when he had gone hunting with Rocky and Robert and Josiah. They had left the truck parked in plain view, at the edge of a pine ridge. But at the end of the day, when he and Rocky had started walking back, they expected to see the old green truck parked on every ridge that came into sight. They weren't lost, because they knew where they were, but the green truck was lost. They kept hiking across dry lake flats and over oak- and pine-covered ridges, saying to each other, "This time, this will be the place," until finally Josiah and Robert came bouncing over the rocky flats in the green truck and picked them up.

Tayo rode the mare slowly along the fence, looking for a place that could be easily located, even at night. He would have only one chance to drive the cattle through the hole in the fence, and while he searched desperately for the opening, they could scatter in every direction. He stopped by a dead pine. Lightning had split it down the middle, and around the charred core, where the bark had peeled away, the tree had weathered silver. Behind it there was an outcrop of lava that made a knob on top of the ridge. He dismounted and went to work on the wire.

The strands of wire were four inches apart and a quarter of an inch thick. He had to stop to shake the muscle cramps from his hands. The moon was rising early. He worked on his knees, cutting away the wire at ground level, where it continued under the surface six inches deep to discourage coyotes and wolves from digging under it. He tried to clear a place to kneel, but the ground was almost solid with pebbles and rocks. After the first ten feet of cutting and bending back the wire, his knees went numb; he felt cold air on his skin and knew that his Levis were worn through at both knees. He was thinking about the cattle and how they had ended up on Floyd Lee's land. If he had seen the cattle on land-grant land or in some Acoma's corral, he wouldn't have hesitated to say "stolen." But something inside him made him hesitate to say it now that the cattle were on a white man's ranch. He had a crazy desire to believe that there had been some mistake, that Floyd Lee had gotten them innocently, maybe buying them from the real thieves. Why did he hesitate to accuse a white man of stealing but not a Mexican or an Indian? He took off his gloves and stuck his hands inside his jacket to wipe the broken blisters on his shirt. Sweat made the raw skin sting all the way up both arms, leaving his shoulders with a dull ache. He knew then he had learned the lie by heart—the lie which they had wanted him to learn: only brown-skinned people were thieves; white people didn't steal, because they always had the money to buy whatever they wanted.

The lie. He cut into the wire as if cutting away at the lie inside himself. The liars had fooled everyone, white people and Indians alike; as long as people believed the lies, they would never be able to see what had been done to them or what they were doing to each other. He wiped the sweat off his face onto the sleeve of his jacket. He stood back and looked at the gaping cut in the wire. If the white people never looked beyond the lie, to see that theirs was a nation built on stolen land, then they would never be able to understand how they had been used by the witchery; they would never know that they were still being manipulated by those who knew how to stir the ingredients together: white thievery and injustice boiling up the anger and hatred that would finally destroy the world: the starving against the fat, the colored against the white. The destroyers had only to set it into motion, and sit back to count the casualties. But it was more than a body count; the lies devoured white hearts, and for more than two hundred years white people had worked to fill their emptiness; they tried to glut the hollowness with patriotic wars and with great technology and the wealth it brought. And always they had been fooling themselves, and they knew it.

The cut in the fence was a good twenty feet wide, large enough for the cattle to find. He walked back to the horse and put away the pliers. He poured water over the raw skin on his hands and drank what was left in the canteen; he pissed one more time.

The moon was bright, and the rolling hills and dry lake flats reflected a silvery light illusion that everything was as visible as if seen in broad daylight. But the mare stumbled and threw him hard against the saddle horn, and he realized how deceptive the moonlight was; exposed root tips and dark rocks waited in deep shadows cast by the moon. Their lies would destroy this world.

Ceremony (1977)

R. CRUMB

R. Crumb (b. 1943) is usually described as "the founding father of underground comics." His menagerie of characters includes Fritz the Cat and Mr. Natural, and his chief obsessions, explored from his base in the Haight-Ashbury, include sex, repression, and early-American folk and blues records. But in the years around the first Earth Day, every radical paid at least some attention to the ecological consequences of "normal" life in America, and Crumb (who would also go on to illustrate an edition of Edward Abbey's *The Monkey Wrench Gang* in 1985) was no exception. Here is his "A Short History of America."

To visit Wes Jackson's Land Institute in Salina, Kansas, is to see a vision of a nearly forgotten past and a hopeful, future rural America. (He's down a dirt road from the present—the giant grain elevators and the big-box stores.) Jackson (b. 1936), a plant geneticist by training, has long argued that our current farming practices are eroding topsoil, draining aquifers and petroleum resources, and destroying small farm communities. His plan: an agriculture that works *with* nature for long-term durability. He's assembled a team of PhDs who are patiently trying to figure out how to grow wheat and other crops perennially instead of annually—that is, to create a prairie that produces food, one that doesn't need to be plowed each year and doused with herbicides. The early results are promising, not only with wheat but also with sorghum and sunflower, and with the solar-powered farm his team has built. An old friend of Wendell Berry, Jackson also hosts an annual Prairie Festival each fall that has become one of the gathering points for farm-minded environmentalists. A MacArthur Fellow, his books include *New Roots for Agriculture* (1980), *Altars of Unhewn Stone* (1987), and *Consulting the Genius of the Place* (2010).

Outside the Solar Village: One Utopian Farm

Many of the most lively, intimate expressions of spirit spring from the joyous, continuous contact of human beings with a particular locality. They feel the age-long spirit of this valley or that hill each with its trees and rocks and special tricks of weather, as the seasons unfold in their endless charm. If life can be made secure in each community and if the rewards of the different communities are distributed justly, there will flower in every community not only those who attain joy in daily, productive work well done; but also those who paint and sing and tell stories with the flavor peculiar to their own valley, well-loved hill, or broad prairie . . . Every community can become something distinctly precious in its own right. Children will not try to escape as they grow up. They will look ahead to the possibility of enriching the traditions of their ancestors.

—Henry Wallace

The year is 2030 in a world with increased consciousness. People everywhere—on farms, in villages, and in cities—have sustainability as their central paradigm. They think globally and act locally. Regional semi-self-sufficiency is emphasized but the principles of the New Age Farmers are the same from New England to Southern California.

Our utopian farm is in Kansas, below the 39th parallel and east of the 98th meridian. The area averages about 28 inches of rainfall each year but the evaporation is in excess of rainfall. This is farming country which, before being plowed more than a century ago, was a biotically rich landscape. Stories handed down through the grandparents tell school-age children how the breaking of this virgin sod sounded like the opening of a zipper. A few miles east is the western edge of the vast Tallgrass Prairie, dominated by such species as Big Bluestem, Indiangrass and Switchgrass. Scarcely thirty miles to the west are the mixed prairies dominated by Bluestem and Sideoats Grama.

Because of the minimal landscape relief, the Great Plains is one of the few regions where it makes sense to divide the land into one mile square parcels. A road surrounds almost every square mile. This is a land which, after the "Great Plowing" in the early 1900's, supported such high-producing annual crops as wheat, sorghum, milo and soybeans. Before 1990 only native pastureland and roadsides carried the grasses that were characteristic of the region before the European arrived. This prairie land, mostly because of forced grazing, has long since lost 20 or 25 native prairie species. What was left was not prairie but grassland. During most of the last century, wheat was an important export crop for the region; we are fortunate that even more grassland wasn't plowed. Church leaders, farmers and grain men had said that we must sell grain to feed a hungry world. This was a moral veneer over a basically economic consideration, but it was enough to discourage the initial development of mixed perennials. Traditional crops were proven producers regardless of their tremendous toll on finite energy resources, finite soil and, for western corn growers, finite fossil ground water.

But now in 2030 the settlement pattern differs drastically from what it was in 1980. In this immediate area, each family lives on 160 acres, or four families per square mile (640 acres). The dwellings of most families are near the middle of the square mile section but on their own property. Therefore, within 300 yards of each other are usually 16—20 people. Their small village and main trading center, which includes both school and churches, is two and a half miles away from our farm. No one in the rural service area of the village is ever any farther away. The village's service area covers 16 square miles (four miles on each side) and includes 64 farm families totaling about 250 people.

Westward, in the mixed prairie, one half section (320 acres) is needed to support a single family, and nearly 200 miles west of the mixed grass country, in the short grass prairie, two square miles is usually necessary to support a family. Eastward and in some of the West, it is another story. Along the Missouri in Nebraska, the southwestern half of Minnesota, most of Iowa, in southeastern Wisconsin, northern Indiana, northwestern Ohio, east central Michigan; along the Mississippi in western Tennessee and northwestern Mississippi; in much of the Sacramento Valley, as well as in numerous other localized areas throughout the country, fewer than ten acres—but never more than twenty—are enough to support a family. It is not that production is always higher than in our area, it is just that a combination of factors, including rainfall, makes a sustainable yield more assured. The carrying capacity of the land is so varied that when we say the average farm, nationwide, is forty acres, we must immediately realize the limited meaning of that statistic.

Regardless of farm size, the village population seldom exceeds the farm population by more than a factor of two. An entire community in our region comprises around 750 people, including the 260 people on farms. Let us compare this to the distribution pattern nationwide. The population of the United States is around 300 million and is scheduled to stabilize completely in the next seven years, in spite of the fact that zero population growth procedures have been in effect since the early 1980's. The momentum of that past is still with us, though insignificantly so. But it is the distribution of the population which has been radically altered over the last 50 years.

Most of the major cities have experienced drastic declines and the number of cities of 40,000 or less has greatly increased. Optimum city size was widely discussed in the last century. Many of the New Age pioneers concluded, though there was nothing like unanimous agreement, that much of the social pathology of our former urban areas could be attributed to the spiritual dangers which arise when people no longer know or feel their rootedness in the land. When heat comes from a stove, food from a grocery store, building materials from the lumber yard and the automobile from the showroom floor, the spiritual loss is devastating to the society. It doesn't necessarily take a city of a million, many concluded, to provide the "critical mass" necessary to help a large number of humans live up to a broad spectrum of their innate potentialities. A population of 40,000 seems to have a special energy. When Notre Dame was begun, the Paris population was 35,000. Renaissance Florence was also around 35–40,000. Regional cities now seldom exceed 40,000 and there are somewhat fewer than 4,000 such cities totaling less than 160 million people. Of course, some of the major cities still contain a few million people, but they are mostly empty, and much of their area now produces food, clothing and shelter where concrete and stone formerly dominated the environment. The civilization was a long time in learning that, by and large, the only people who really liked the big city life were merchants and intellectuals.

Of the 300 million people in the United States, some 20 million, or about one fifteenth of the population, work in the rural areas associated with rangeland and forestry. Nearly 10 million families totaling about 40 million people are living on 400 million acres of cropland. This amounts to a little over 13 percent of the total population, well over twice the percentage of 50 years ago and nearly three times the total rural population of that time. The rural villages, however, have twice as many people as the countryside they support. I mentioned earlier that the land holdings vary drastically in size. For example, in much of northeastern Illinois, a family of four can live on five acres. This puts 128 small farms or 512 people on each square mile. This is a very high density, but the productivity of the land is the determining factor. Over 8,000 people live within the 16-square-mile rural service area. Its supporting village has over 16,000 people.

Our solar village of 500 or so is necessarily different from the northeastern Illinois village of 16,000. Aside from the differing political dynamics associated with different sizes and densities, there is a commonness of purpose best reflected in the numerous bioshelters which grow what might be described as a healthful diet, though not an abundance of calories. (The fields provide most of the protein and carbohydrates for this society and it is up to the people in the villages and cities to provide vegetables and fruits and a certain amount of animal protein, mostly from fish, in the passive bioshelters, which were pioneered by the New Alchemists in the last century.) The major differences among these villages lie in how different regions' village people work with farmers to meet the expectations of the land. A pluralistic society does not preclude the possibility of holding a common allegiance.

Neither does pluralism mean that certain patterns of young and old cannot be similar everywhere. Throughout the country, older people have the option of living in the village but their presence is cherished on the farm. Nearly all have chosen to live in the village but most return to the farm daily to assist their family and neighbors in various chores. These are the people who play the most important part in the children's education.

Most communities now emphasize the value of history, and history becomes more real when adults tell personal stories which link the past to the present. The stories are about heroes, the prophets of the solar age and the pioneers in the era of decentralization and land resettlement, and villainous corporations more concerned about avoiding liability payments legally, than protecting the environment. The older people tell of a past in which nuclear power was tried, discovered to be filled with unresolvable uncertainties, and abandoned. Many of these older people lived during what is now called the "Age of the Recognition of Limits." These former doom-watching pioneers were like the children of Israel who had escaped the grasp of the Egyptians and then wandered in the wilderness for 40 years, saddled with their own slave mentality, waiting for a new generation of free minds to develop and be fit for life in the promised land. Many of the pioneers have readily admitted their earlier addiction to all the consumer products of affluence and work hard at teaching their young the true source of sustenance and health—the land. They are living reminders that this sunpowered civilization has arrived as the result of nothing less than a religious reformation.

The strong new land ethic has resulted in a different concept of land ownership. Under the Land Trust System, land is not owned by individuals in the same sense that it was 50 years ago. Nevertheless, it can be passed on from one generation to the next, and people have a strong sense of ownership. They cannot do exactly as they please with the property. They cannot willfully pollute it with toxic chemicals, sell it off for housing developments, or in any way speculate with it. Such wasteful exploitation discounts too much of the future. Activity which is potentially destructive is prohibited by a board of non-farming elders from the village; at least half of them have been farmers for 20 years or more. The board includes two members from the regional city, and both sexes are equally represented.

On our farm, the well-insulated house is partially underground and equipped with both passive and active solar installations for hot water and space heating. Though it is 100% solar, a wood stove is in place as a back up. A water-pumping windmill and two wind-electric systems provide power for the farmstead. A combination of technologies from the past are appropriate for the farm's water system. A water-pumping windmill brings water to tanks for the livestock and household use. Trenching machines and plastic pipe are used to deliver the water wherever needed for human convenience. One wind generator takes care of all refrigeration needs and simply cools the deepfreeze and refrigerator when the wind is blowing. Since the refrigerator itself is the "accumulator," no batteries are needed. The other wind-electric system consists of an induction motor which kicks in when the output of the wind-powered generator is greater than the load on the service line. The induction motor, which is similar to that found on washing machines in the 1930's, is plugged into the wall receptacle and runs the kilowatt-hour meter backward, giving the farmstead an electrical energy credit. A special meter records the number of hours generated. If this household wishes to break even on the utility bill, its unit must provide four kilowatts of electricity to a privately-owned utility for each one it receives. There is just enough electricity generated in the area from both wind and low-head hydroelectric turbines to supply the needs of the countryside, village, and regional city. This is because in the last 50 years, solar for space and hot water heating has become so widespread. In combination with the appropriate design and construction of new shelters, heating needs have been met with a modest amount of wood, grown for the specific purpose of backing up the solar systems.

In the 20 acres of creek bottom land, people grow such annual monocultures as wheat, corn, rye, barley and oats. Orchards and vegetable gardens are near the houses. Canning of garden products takes place outside, using energy derived from concentrating collectors. Dried foods take precedence over canned foods and root crops are very important.

A single solar hog house on wheels is large enough to accommodate no more than two sows and twenty feeder pigs. A similar solar chicken house, surrounded by a twenty-five-foot square fence, accommodates from twenty-five to fifty chickens. About half are frying chickens, which are eaten during the summer months. Unlike the chickens grown in closed confinement fifty years ago, these animals experience few tumors, and the yolk of their eggs is a brilliant gold.

Pigs and chickens "graze" on fresh pasture during the growing season. Their mobile pens are easily advanced a few feet each day with hand levers operated by school children or grandparents from the village. The mobile pens allow for an economy of fencing materials. This managed migration simulates the migration of large animals in pre-settlement times. Only the breeding stock for pigs, plus the laying hens and two roosters are maintained throughout the winter.

The one large outbuilding is devoted to covering the small amount of machinery. The expensive equipment consists of a small, multiple harvesting combine, a forty-five horsepower tractor and a hay baler. The combine has a seven-foot cutter bar and runs off the tractor's power take-off.

The traction and transportation fuel needs are met with alcohol, derived from crops grown on the farm. The "fuel forty" is the principle energy producer. It grows a six-species polyculture consisting of five grasses and one legume. These species are selected for their high carbohydrate content and relatively low protein yield. This forty-acre field averages about twenty barrels of crude oil equivalent per year. Livestock are cycled onto this acreage for a few weeks each year to enhance the crumb structure of the soil.

Nationwide, roughly 25%, or approximately 100 million acres of cropland, is devoted to growing alcohol fuels. The yield amounts to about 50 million barrels of oil equivalent. An additional 7 million barrels equivalent is gained in the form of methanol from the farm. In 1979, this would have amounted to only a three-day supply of oil, or less than 1% of the annual consumption.

One hundred years ago approximately twenty-five percent of the total acreage was devoted to horses and mules for traction purposes. Now, about eight barrels of crude equivalent, or only ten percent of the total acreage on the farm, is devoted to farm traction. This is because horses and mules would burn energy just standing around being horses and mules, but the tractor can be turned off. However, the tractor cannot become pregnant and build a replacement on solar energy. A pregnant mare at rest is not really resting. Furthermore, parts wear out on the tractor and cannot be replaced by ordinary cell division as with the traction animal. Nevertheless, from the point of view of total energy expenditure, the tractor is used rather than the beast of burden, so long as other livestock are around to enhance the crumb structure of the soil. The other twelve barrels equivalent from the fuel forty, representing about fifteen percent of the total acreage, is sent to the village and city for their liquid fuel needs.

The alcohol fuel "refinery" requires some elaboration. Organic material produced at the farm is delivered to a privately-owned or co-op still in the village. The production of portable liquid fuels is part of a fine-grained approach to our over-all energy needs. It has become economically feasible as farming methods have become less energy-intensive and less capital-intensive. It wasn't economically feasible in the 1980's and produced very little net energy, but the agricultural sector was enthusiastic about producing alcohol fuel from farm crops. Hundreds of on-farm stills were built and closed down in 18 months after federal and state subsidies were withdrawn. Major stills costing $20 million and more were built, and many closed within three years after losing the subsidies. In those years, each automobile would consume in calories what nearly two dozen people would consume in the same period. American farmers learned a valuable and painful lesson about the potential of alcohol fuel production to meet the enormous energy demands of that time. Soil loss accelerated during this period, and farmers gradually learned to curtail their alcohol production programs to a very moderate level.

Another source of energy comes from the "multiple purpose forty." Leaf and stem material are harvested from an herbaceous polyculture after the early summer seed harvest, and converted into methanol equivalent to two to five barrels of crude oil a year. In the fall, some of the net wood production of the woodlot and orchard is also converted. Upon arrival at the still, all organic matter is weighed, moisture is determined, and nutrients are calculated. The farmer may sell some or all of his alcohol into the public sector, but the nutrients left over after distillation are returned to the farm and usually spread on the field or woodlot from which they were taken. Of course human waste is returned to the fields from all over. This is to prevent soil mining and reduce the amount of chemical fertilizer applied.

One concern which is constantly being discussed and fine-tuned in discussions has to do with what tools and equipment should be owned and operated by the farm and which ones made available through the rental place in the village. At this time the rental place provides an Easy Flo fertilizer distributor (for Phosphorus and nitrogen), a chisel which is attached to the tractor to break sod-bound soils, seed bed preparation equipment for the annual crops, plus numerous other pieces of equipment which are not frequently used.

People on this land have a deep distrust of commercially-produced chemicals. It is amazing that this distrust began to develop some forty years ago in the churches. In many seminaries during the 1980's, many students began to discuss the Genesis version of the Creation as possibly contributing to much of the environmental problem. During the 1970's, the dominion question had been much discussed. Since most defenders of the Genesis story had insisted that dominion was not the current word, but that stewardship was implied, church people began to relax. That turned out to be a rather unimportant consideration. During the 1980's another discussion began, much more quietly. The emphasis this time was on the cultural impact of a subtlety in our religious heritage. The culture fostered, however unwittingly, the belief that we are a separate creation. After all, the creation story held that the earth and the living world were created and then there was a pause. Following the pause, in a special effort, came human beings. But our biologists in the last century demonstrated that the same 20 amino acids are in the redwood, the snail, the human and the elm tree, as well as in the lowly microbe. Furthermore, the nucleotides, which make up the code, are mostly the same throughout. Native Americans had talked about brother wolf and sister tree long before these discoveries. Now in our churches it is frequently mentioned that our cells have had no evolutionary experience with such and such a pesticide, or that the concentration of a "natural" chemical much greater than our tissues have ever experienced is to be avoided. A toxic level is defined as a quantity beyond our cells' evolutionary standards.

Because a sustainable agriculture is more important than a highly productive one, upland crops consist of recently developed herbaceous perennial polycultures. The polycultures are ensembles of species developed by the land grant universities through the experiment stations. Perennials were selected because of their soil-holding capability.

High-yielding, nutritious seed-producing perennials were first inventoried in numerous experimental gardens. Next, an intense selection program was initiated to increase the yield of the individual species. Later, thousands of species combinations were tried. From then on, plant breeders sought to improve performance of individual species within the polyculture environment. These perennial polycultures have several distinct advantages over the former annual monocultures.

First, soil loss has been reduced to replacement levels. We had expected this, for the reduction of soil loss was a major motivation behind the extensive research. Secondly, spring water has returned to the area. Many springs are now trickling all year around, and the total microhydroelectric capacity has increased, along with a rise in the water table. The land with the perennial vegetation has become a huge battery for stored "electricity." A third advantage is that the energy required for maintenance and harvest after the initial planting is just five percent of that required by the former high-yielding annual monocultures. And finally, although the usual pathogens and insects are still around, they do not reach epidemic proportions.

Our particular farm has fields consisting mostly of grasses, a few legumes, and even members of the sunflower family. Some of the fields are harvested in early summer; some, in the fall. The early summer or July harvest in one field includes descendants of Intermediate wheatgrass, Canada wild rye, Sideoats Grama, Tall wheatgrass and Stueve's Lespedeza. The fall harvest consists of four grasses, a legume and a member of the sunflower family. The grasses include descendants of switchgrass, sand lovegrass, Indian Grass, and weeping lovegrass. The legume, Wild Senna, and a perennial soybean provide nitrogen and some seed, and a high-yielding descendant of the Gray-headed Coneflower produces seeds with two important oils.

Some of the early objections to the difficulty of harvest and separation of seeds from the polycultures were quickly overcome when agricultural engineers began to invent new machinery. In fact—and this is ironic—the return to polycultures only became possible in our age of mechanization. Some have since made the argument that monoculture arose because of the need to harvest small seeds efficiently when all we had was hand labor. The age of mechanization, then, has allowed us to develop an agriculture that closely mimics the vegetative structure in pre-agricultural times. Much of the machinery has allowed us to return to the psyche of hunters and gatherers again, but of course in a modern context.

The fossil fuels used during the transition era, 1985–2025, as we moved from mining and destruction of land as a way of life to the solar age, afforded us opportunities not only in plant breeding, but in animal improvement as well. This period gave us the chance to develop crops that were less dependent on humans. The same was true with the livestock. For example, American Bison were crossed with domestic cattle and the thicker hides made the critters more resistant to severe winters. In a way, we are now using solar energy (stored in grass) to maintain barns—the hides of animals. Protective shelter made of lumber for large animals is not necessary.

Grandparents amuse children with stories about square tomatoes and featherless chickens. The featherless chicken was developed in the 1970's by reductionistic technologists who thought they would help corporate chicken growers and processors to cut costs in cleaning chickens. The consequence was a funny-looking chicken that required such a warm environment that the energy costs were in excess of the cleaning costs. The moral of the story is that big money is a sure license for big foolishness.

Livestock are moved from one polyculture to another in a rhythm that does not jeopardize flowering and seed set. Most grazing does occur in areas that produce seed for human consumption, but certain polycultures are grown for the livestock exclusively. A few weeks before slaughter, buffalo/beef graze on mixed perennials that are setting seed. This is a weak simulation of the feedlot of former times. No hay is hauled to the barn for winter feeding, for there is no barn. Some of the hay is windrowed with a side-delivery rake and left, but most raked hay is rolled into 1000–1200 pound bales and left in the field. This system reduces the need to spend time and energy moving hay and manure, and the nutrients are left where they are most useful.

The movement of livestock on the farm turns out to be critical. In natural ecosystems there were no fences. Even though we are forced to use fences for all our livestock, our management program recognizes that animal wastes on the farm contribute to the crumb structure of the soil, which allows the soil to release nutrients slowly while holding moisture.

Many of the problems caused by farming techniques of the 1960's and 1970's have been solved in this new era. Seed bed preparation occurs mostly where the few acres of annuals are grown, and since tillage has been dramatically reduced, soil loss is almost non-existent. Silting of streams is minimal, and more species and larger populations of fish thrive in the waterways. Energy-expensive terracing is no longer as necessary, and where check dams and small farm ponds exist, they serve the farmer mostly as pools for growing catfish. Irrigation is reduced, because hundreds of springs have been reborn. Fertilizer application is minimal because the diversity of crops has maintained a better nutrient balance with less nutrient run-off. The record-breaking fish kills because of fertilizer and feedlot run-off during the last century are now only part of the legends about our unenlightened grandparents. Weeding is essentially a thing of the past, except in gardens and where annual monocultures are grown. Pesticide application is almost non-existent because of both polyculture and a broader genetic base in our crops. A broader genetic base in livestock and the demise of high-density feedlots have made the use of antibiotics for livestock seldom necessary. The life of farm machinery has increased by a factor of sixteen in the last fifty years. All of these changes have resulted in a drastic cut in energy consumption for farm production.

The major changes began to surface during the 1980's, when a few young agricultural professionals, having adopted a sustainable agriculture as their goal, looked for the sustainable alternatives rather than placing their bets on corporately-controlled agriculture. In many respects, they were the true heroes of the era. Some took the theory of the quantitative gene developed during the 1960's and, along with the known virtues of hybrid vigor, made repeated breakthroughs in new crop development.

There was a unifying theme from Massachusetts to Kansas to California. People recognized that in the long run and often in the short run, land determines. Citizens sought to meet the expectations of the land and to look at the natural ecosystems of different regions as the standards against which to judge their agricultural practices.

Suddenly, as is so often the case with profound statements, there was a new meaning to the words Thoreau uttered from the Concord Lyceum in the mid 1800's: "In wildness is the preservation of the world."

The policy-makers began to take seriously the prediction of Charles Lindbergh: "The human future depends on our ability to combine the knowledge of science with the wisdom of wildness."

When this concept was applied to our farms, they became waterproof, diversified family hearths. Our fields are no longer vulnerable, oil-hungry monocultures, although they are not wilderness either.

But without wilderness, we would not have developed a sustainable agriculture and culture. The practice of stewardship is now both easy and effective; for plowshares have been beaten into appropriate tools and war against our Earth Mother is practiced no more.

New Roots for Agriculture (1980)

LOIS MARIE GIBBS

Lois Gibbs (b. 1951) was a young wife and mother when she and her husband, a chemical worker, bought a house in the Love Canal section of Niagara Falls, New York. In 1978, she discovered that her seven-year-old son, who had had persistent health problems, was going to school on the site of a toxic waste dump. Local authorities brushed aside her questions, so she took on the role of environmental activist, helping track the illnesses of other neighborhood children, circulating petitions, and trying to get something done about the contamination. When it became clear that almost no one in the community could afford to move—they couldn't sell their homes—she and her neighbors tried to force federal action, at one point going so far as to take two EPA officials hostage. She later walked onstage at the Democratic National Convention and talked a cornered Jimmy Carter into promising mortgage assistance for the relocated residents. The Love Canal fight gave birth to the Superfund program for cleaning up heavily contaminated sites; Gibbs went on to form the Citizens Clearinghouse for Hazardous Waste (now the Center for Health, Environment and Justice), which has helped organize communities like hers against polluters. America's sense of sublime nature had first been formed at the great cataract a few miles from Love Canal; it was sadly apt that centuries later Niagara Falls became a byword for contamination, but Gibbs' bold actions helped spur a much-needed new working-class environmental activism.

from **Love Canal: My Story**

If you drove down my street *before Love Canal* (that's what I call what happened to us), you might have thought it looked like a typical American small town that you would see in a TV movie—neat bungalows, many painted white, with neatly clipped hedges or freshly painted fences. The houses are generally small but comfortable; at that time ("before Love Canal" in 1978) they sold for about $30,000. If you came in the summertime, you would have seen men painting their houses or adding an extra room, women taking care of gardens, and children riding bicycles and tricycles on the sidewalks or playing in the backyards.

You would see something quite different today. Since Love Canal, the houses nearest the canal area have been boarded up and abandoned. Many have homemade signs and graffiti, vividly telling what happened to make this a ghost town. The once-neat gardens are overgrown, the lawns uncut. A high chain-link fence surrounds the houses nearest the canal. The area is deserted. The fence is a reminder of the 22,000 tons of poisons buried there, poisons that can cause cancer, that can cause mothers to miscarry or give birth to deformed children, poisons that can make children and adults sick, many of them in ways doctors only dimly understand.

When we moved into our house on 101st Street in 1972, I didn't even know Love Canal was there. It was a lovely neighborhood in a quiet residential area, with lots of trees and lots of children outside playing. It seemed just the place for our family. We have two children—Michael, who was born just before we moved in, and Melissa (Missy), born June 12, 1975. I was twenty-six. I liked the neighborhood because it was in the city but out of it. It was convenient. There was a school within walking distance. I liked the idea of my children being able to walk to the 99th Street School. The school's playground was part of a big, open field with houses all around. Our new neighbors told us that the developers who sold them their houses said the city was going to put a park on the field.

It is really something, if you stop and think of it, that underneath that field were poisons, and on top of it was a grade school and a playground. We later found out that the Niagara Falls School Board knew the filled-in canal was a toxic dump site. We also know that they knew it was dangerous because, when the Hooker Chemical Corporation sold it to them for one dollar, Hooker put a clause in the deed declaring that the corporation would not be responsible for any harm that came to anyone from *chemicals* buried there. That one-dollar school site turned out to be some bargain!

Love Canal actually began for me in June 1978 with Mike Brown's articles in the Niagara Falls *Gazette*. At first, I didn't realize where the canal was. Niagara Falls has two sets of streets numbered the same. Brown's articles said Love Canal was between 99th and 97th streets, but I didn't think he meant the place where my children went to school or where I took them to play on the jungle gyms and swings. Although I read the articles, I didn't pay much attention to them. One article did stand out, though. In it, Mike Brown wrote about monkeys subjected to PCB's having miscarriages and deformed offspring.

One of his later articles pointed out that the school had been built over the canal. Still, I paid little attention. It didn't affect me, Lois Gibbs. I thought it was terrible; but I lived on the other side of Pine Avenue. Those poor people over there on the other side were the ones who had to worry. The problem didn't affect me, so I wasn't going to bother doing anything about it, and I certainly wasn't going to speak out about it. Then when I found out the 99th Street School was indeed on top of it, I was alarmed. My son attended that school. He was in kindergarten that year. I decided I needed to do some investigating.

I went to my brother-in-law, Wayne Hadley, a biologist and, at the time, a professor at the State University of New York at Buffalo. He had worked on environmental problems and knew a lot about chemicals. I asked him to translate some of that jibber-jabber in the articles into English. I showed Wayne Mike Brown's articles listing the chemicals in the canal and asked what they were. I was really alarmed by his answer. Some of the chemicals, he said, can affect the nervous system. Just a little bit, even the amount that's in paint or gasoline, can kill brain cells. I still couldn't believe it; but if it *were* true, I wanted to get Michael out of that 99th Street School.

I went down to the offices of the *Gazette* and was surprised to learn how many articles there were on Love Canal. It not only surprised me, it panicked me! The articles listed the chemicals and described some reactions to them. One is damage to the central nervous system.

(Michael had begun having seizures after he started school.) Another is leukemia and other blood diseases. (Michael's white blood cell count had gone down.) The doctor said that might have been caused by the medication he took for his epilepsy, but now I wasn't so sure. Michael had started school in September and had developed epilepsy in December; in February his white blood count dropped.

All of a sudden, everything seemed to fall into place. There's no history of epilepsy in either my family or my husband's. So why should Michael develop it? He had always been sensitive to medication. I could never give him an aspirin like a normal baby because he would get sick to his stomach or break out in a rash. I couldn't give him *anything* because of that sensitivity. If it were true that Michael was more sensitive than most other children, then whatever chemicals were buried under the school would affect him more than they did other children in the school, or even more than my daughter Missy, who has always been a strong, lively child. The chemicals probably would not affect Missy, at least not right away. I wasn't thinking then about long-term effects. (A year and a half later, Missy was hospitalized for a blood-platelet disorder, but later she was fine.)

I went over all the articles with Wayne, and decided Michael definitely should not attend that school—nor, for that matter, should any child. They shouldn't even play on that playground. Wayne was worried about his son Eric. He and my sister Kathy used to leave Eric for me to baby-sit while they were at work.

I was stunned that the school board had allowed a school to be built on such a location. Even today, it doesn't seem possible that, knowing there were dangerous chemicals buried there, someone could put up a *school* on the site. The 99th Street School had over 400 children that year, one of its lowest annual enrollments.

I was about to get my first lesson in dealing with officials. When I started, I was interested only in myself and my child. I didn't stop to think about the other children in the neighborhood. I considered sending Michael to a Catholic School, and I even looked into the possibility; but I'm not Catholic, and my husband Harry didn't approve of a strict religious education. Besides, there were plenty of other schools in Niagara

Falls. We had a choice. My choice was to send Michael to another public school.

I called the superintendent of schools, and told him I wanted my son removed from that school. I explained what I believed was Michael's problem, his susceptibility to chemicals and drugs of all kinds. I also told him what I was sure he already knew, that the school was sitting on a toxic waste dump site. I repeated that I wanted Michael transferred. He could finish the school year; but he wasn't going to attend that school the next year.

The superintendent told me I couldn't do that. He couldn't transfer a child merely because the child's mother didn't want him to go to a particular school. I would need statements from two doctors, anyway. I thought that was ridiculous, that there was already reason enough for my child to be moved: the school was over a chemical dump site, and Michael had been sick *after* he started attending the school. But I went to my pediatrician and asked him for a statement. He agreed to send one to the superintendent. I also went to my family doctor and explained about the canal. I told her about my fears and about the change in Michael's health since he started attending the school. She also agreed to write a statement for the school.

After awhile, I called the superintendent back. He wasn't in; he was at a meeting. It was the first of many calls. Finally, after I had called once or twice a day for two weeks, he returned my phone calls. It was a strange conversation. At first, he said he hadn't gotten the doctors' statements. Then he contradicted himself by referring to them. He said Michael could not be removed from the school, based on those statements, because the statements alleged that the area was contaminated. If the area were contaminated, then it wasn't only Michael who should be removed; all the children should be removed. The superintendent said that he did not believe the area was contaminated, and, finally, that they weren't about to close the 99th Street School.

I was furious. I wasn't going to send my child to a place that was poisoned. The thoughts that can go through a person's head. I thought that I, as a person, had rights, that I ought to have a choice, and that one of those choices was not to send my child to school in a contaminated place. Like many people, I can be stubborn when I get angry. I decided to go door-to-door and see if the other parents in the neighborhood felt the same way. That way, maybe something could be done. At the time, though, I didn't really think of it as "organizing."

It wasn't just the phone call with the superintendent that convinced me I had to do something. I called the president of the 99th Street School PTA and asked her if she could help me, or if she could at least tell me whom to go to or what to do. She said she was about to go on vacation. I got the feeling she wasn't interested. She seemed to be pushing me away, as if she didn't want to have anything to do with me.

I was disappointed and angry. School would open again in two months, and I wasn't going to let my child go back to that school. I didn't care what I had to do to prevent it. I wasn't going to send him to a private school, either. First of all, we couldn't afford it; and second, I thought parents had the right to send their children to schools that were safe.

As I said, I decided to go door-to-door with a petition. It seemed like a good idea to start near the school, to talk to the mothers nearest it. I had already heard that a lot of the residents near the school had been upset about the chemicals for the past couple of years. I thought they might help me. I had never done anything like this, however, and I was frightened. I was afraid a lot of doors would be slammed in my face, that people would think I was some crazy fanatic. But I decided to do it anyway. I went to 99th and Wheatfield and knocked on my first door. There was no answer. I just stood there, not knowing what to do. It was an unusually warm June day and I was perspiring. I thought: *What am I doing here? I must be crazy. People are going to think I am. Go home, you fool!* And that's just what I did.

It was one of those times when I had to sit down and face myself. I was afraid of making a fool of myself, I had scared myself, and I had gone home. When I got there, I sat at the kitchen table with my petition in my hand, thinking. *Wait. What if people do slam doors in your face? People may think you're crazy. But what's more important—what people think or your child's health? Either you're going to do something or you're going to have to admit you're a coward and not do it.* I decided to wait until the next day—partly to figure out exactly how I was going to do this but more, I think, to build my self-confidence.

The next day, I went out on my own street to talk to people I knew. It was a little easier to be brave with them. If I could convince people I knew—friends—maybe it would be less difficult to convince others. I started with the home of Michael's best friend, Curtis. His mother Kathy had gone over to her mother's with the children, but his father was at home. We talked and talked about the chemicals and the harm they could do. I think I talked more because of nerves and less because I had a lot to say. Finally, I asked him if he would sign my petition. I held my breath, waiting for him to say, "I won't, you're crazy!" But he signed. He agreed with me. He said: "I'm not going to send Curtis there, either. Curtis is hyperactive. If the canal does cause all the problems you say it does, because of the chemicals, well, maybe that's Curtis's problem. Maybe it isn't a psychological problem. Maybe it has something to do with the chemicals."* I was relieved—and pleased. I thought to myself, *Gee, this is going to be easy. I guess it isn't so bad after all.* I had a lot to learn.

At first, I went to my friends' houses. I went to the back door, as I always did when I visited a neighbor. Each house took about twenty or twenty-five minutes. They wanted to know about Love Canal. Many of the people who lived farther from the canal than 97th or 99th streets didn't even know the canal existed; they thought the area was a field. Some had heard about Love Canal, but they didn't realize where it was, and they didn't pay much attention to the issue—just as I hadn't. So I spent a lot of time giving them the background, explaining what Love Canal was. Something began to happen to me as I went around talking to these people. It was hot and humid that summer. My mother kept saying I was crazy to do it. I was losing weight, mainly because I didn't

---

*In this book I am going to write as though people were actually saying certain things, because that's the way I remember what was said. I can't guarantee that they used exactly those words, but what they did say was similar to the way I have written it, and the meaning is the same.

have much time to eat. My house was a mess because I wasn't home. Dinner was late, and Harry sometimes was upset. Between the kids and the heat, I was getting very tired. But something drove me on. I kept going door-to-door, still on my own street. When I finished 101st, I did 102d; when I finished those two streets, I felt ready to go back to 99th Street, where I had begun by running home afraid of looking foolish.

Just before going back to 99th Street, I called a woman who lived on 97th Street. Her backyard abutted the canal. I had read about her in the newspaper. She was one of the people who had been organizing others. She said she would be willing to help, but nothing ever happened. Somehow something about her voice didn't sound right. Although I didn't realize it at the time, I was getting another lesson: even though we all have common problems, we don't always work together.

I shouldn't have been too surprised when I discovered later that emergencies like this bring out the best and the worst in people. Sometimes people have honest differences about the best way to solve a problem. Sometimes, however, people have big egos; it's more important for them to be up front and draw attention to themselves than cooperate with others in working for a cause. I really did have a lot to learn. At the time, there were a lot of small groups organizing. Tom Heisner and Karen Schroeder, who lived right on the canal, had started getting people together, and they were doing a good job, though we later had our differences.

I started at the south end of 99th Street. It turned out that that was the end of the canal most severely affected. The first person I spoke to was Mr. Frain. I knocked on his door, introduced myself, and told him I had a petition demanding that the school be closed down. Our children's lives were being threatened. He understood right away and signed my petition. Then he showed me the steps to his front porch. The steps had separated from the house. They were about two inches lower than where they should have been and about an inch and a half away from the foundation. It looked as if the soil were sinking, but Mr. Frain didn't know why or what it meant. He asked me if I could talk to anyone, or if I could see if someone would come out and look at it. I didn't know what to do. Because he was so concerned, I told him I would try, and left.

It was terribly warm and humid that day. The closer I got to the canal, the more I could smell it. I could *feel* it, too, it was so humid. The odor seemed to hang in the thick air. My nose began to run, and my eyes were watering. I thought it was psychosomatic. I hadn't been eating properly and I was tired. Maybe, I thought, I'm just oversensitive. But my consciousness of the danger of the chemicals was not yet roused. Now I won't even drink the city water. I buy bottled water.

As I proceeded down 99th Street, I developed a set speech. I would tell people what I wanted. But the speech wasn't all that necessary. It seemed as though every home on 99th Street had someone with an illness. One family had a young daughter with arthritis. They couldn't understand why she had it at her age. Another daughter had had a miscarriage. The father, still a fairly young man, had had a heart attack. I went to the next house, and there, people would tell me *their* troubles. People were reaching out; they were telling me their troubles in hopes I would do something. But I didn't know anything to do. I was also confused. I just wanted to stop children from going to that school. Now look at all those other health problems! Maybe they were related to the canal. But even if they were, what could I do?

As I continued going door-to-door, I heard more. The more I heard, the more frightened I became. This problem involved much more than the 99th Street School. The entire community seemed to be sick! Then I remembered my own neighbors. One who lived on the left of my husband and me was suffering from severe migraines and had been hospitalized three or four times that year. Her daughter had kidney problems and bleeding. A woman on the other side of us had gastrointestinal problems. A man in the next house down was dying of lung cancer and he didn't even work in industry. The man across the street had just had lung surgery. I thought about Michael; maybe there *was* more to it than just the school. I didn't understand how chemicals could get all the way over to 101st Street from 99th; but the more I thought about it, the more frightened I became—for my family and for the whole neighborhood.

Everything was unbelievable. I worried that I was exaggerating, or that people were exaggerating their complaints. I talked it over with

Wayne. Luckily, he knew someone who might be able to help us—a Dr. Beverly Paigen, who is a biologist, geneticist, and cancer research scientist at the Roswell Park Memorial Institute, a world-famous research hospital in Buffalo. We went to see Dr. Paigen. She is a wonderful, brave person who, like Wayne, had been involved in environmental-pollution fights. She asked us to bring some soil samples so she could do an Ames test. The Ames test is a quick way of determining potentially dangerous effects of chemicals. When bacteria are exposed to mutagenic chemicals, Dr. Paigen told us, they reproduce abnormally.

I continued to go door-to-door. I was becoming more worried because of the many families with children who had birth defects. Then I learned something even more frightening: there had been five crib deaths within a few short blocks.

I was still getting people's cooperation and interest, but I was soon to learn that not everyone felt the same way I did. The woman on 97th Street who had done some organizing never provided any help. We never argued; in fact, she never said anything. One day, while I was knocking on doors, I noticed her riding on her bicycle. She seemed to be watching me. I was both puzzled and intimidated mainly because my self-confidence wasn't yet all that high. I thought we had a common problem, that we should be working together. But she had tried to organize the neighborhood; therefore, it was her neighborhood, her territory. Maybe she felt I was stepping on her toes.

I finally got up my courage and walked over. "Hi," I said. She was in front of her house. A tree in the front yard was wilted. It looked sick, as though it were dying. We stood in the yard and talked. She told me she couldn't use her backyard, that everything there was dead. She asked what I was doing, and I told her. Her voice suddenly turned cold. She warned me about rocking the boat, telling me not to make waves. She had already taken care of the problem. She had been working hard, talking to a number of politicians, and she didn't want me to undo what she had done.

I was taken aback. I explained that I didn't want to "undo" anything, that I wanted to work *with* her. It was a very hot day. I was dying of the heat. I wanted a cigarette or a cold drink—I didn't know which.

There we were, standing in the hot sun, with the only shade coming from a dying tree, and she was telling me how everything was all right. I didn't know what to think. I had to go home and figure this out. I went home, but not because I was frightened. I just needed time to think, to figure out what was happening.

The New York State Health Department held a public meeting in June 1978. It was the first one I attended. Dr. Nicholas Vianna and some of his staff explained that they were going to do environmental and health studies. They wanted to take samples—of blood, air, and soil, as well as from sump pumps. They wanted to find out if there really was a problem. They would study only the first ring of houses, though, the ones with backyards abutting Love Canal. Bob Matthews, Niagara Falls city engineer, was there to explain the city's plan for remedial construction. They all sat in front of a big, green chalkboard on the stage in the auditorium of the 99th Street School.

I didn't understand everything that was said, especially about determining whether there was a problem. A pretty young woman carefully dressed, with a lovely scarf, spoke articulately. Her dog's nose had been burned when it sniffed the ground in her yard. She kept asking Dr. Vianna: "What does this mean? How did he burn his nose?" She said the dog was suffering, that her children loved the dog and loved playing with him; but she was willing to have the dog put away if Dr. Vianna would first test the dog.

That was a new reaction to me, one I hadn't come across in my canvassing. How *did* the dog burn his nose? Did that mean chemicals were on the surface? I knew there were health problems, and I felt the school should be closed; but I hadn't actually *seen* any chemicals. I felt a chill. This was a new danger, and a more ominous one. A man got up and said he couldn't put his daughter out in his own backyard because if he did, the soles of her feet would burn. The man thought chemicals were causing it. His daughter was with him. She was a cute little thing, only eighteen months old, with curly dark hair. Imagine he couldn't let her play in his own backyard, and he didn't know why!

Dr. Vianna had no answer. "We are investigating. We will see what we can do." That was all he would, or could, say. When the audience realized that he didn't have any answers, the meeting became emotional. There were about seventy-five people in that warm, humid auditorium. Everyone was hot, and we could smell the canal. The heat must have had something to do with the short tempers. Next, Dr. Vianna advised people who lived near the canal not to eat any vegetables from their gardens. With that, the little girl's father became very upset. "Look—my kid can't play in the yard because her feet get burned. My neighbor's dog burns his nose in the yard. We can't eat out of the garden. What's going on here? What is this *all about?*"

Dr. Vianna just kept saying, "I don't know. We are investigating. It's too early to tell."

Then Bob Matthews discussed the remedial construction plan. He used the chalkboard to show us how a system of tile pipes would run the length of the canal on both sides. He said the canal was like a bathtub that was overflowing. He was talking to us as though we were children! He said it was like putting a fat woman in a bathtub causing the water to overflow onto the floor. The tile system would collect the overflow. Then it would be pumped out and treated by filtering it through charcoal. After it had been cleaned by the charcoal, it would be pumped down to the sewers and everything would be all right. The overflow-filtering system would also draw the chemicals away from the backyards, which would be clean again.

I asked him about the underground springs that feed into the canal. What would happen to them? He ignored the question, repeating, "It's like putting a fat lady in a bathtub." "That's not what I mean," I said, "I'm talking about *underground* streams. What happens to them? We are so close to the Niagara River. How will your overflow system shut those springs off?" Someone else observed that the tile drains would be only twelve feet deep. "What if the chemicals are forty feet down? The canal is probably forty feet deep." Another person said there were many types of chemicals in there. How was the city engineer going to get them out? No one would, or could, give us straight answers. The audience was getting frustrated and angry. They wanted answers.

I asked Dr. Vianna if the 99th Street School was safe. He answered that the air readings on the school had come back clean. But there we were, sitting in the school auditorium, smelling chemicals! I said: "You are telling me there are chemicals there. You are going to build this big, elaborate system to take the fat lady out of the bathtub and collect all this overflow. You tell us the air tests clean. But you also tell us we can't eat the vegetables. How can these kids be safe walking on the playground? How can it be safe?" "Have the children walk on the sidewalk," Dr. Vianna said. "Make sure they don't cut across the canal or walk on the canal itself."

I couldn't believe what I was hearing. I asked again: "How can you say all that when the playground is on the canal?" He didn't have an answer. He just said: "You are their mother. You can limit the time they play on the canal." I wondered if he had any children.

By now the audience was really frustrated, and so was I. People began walking out, muttering, furious. There were no answers. They didn't understand, and they were becoming frightened.

Love Canal: My Story (1982)

JONATHAN SCHELL

I can remember the havoc in the quiet offices of *The New Yorker* in the weeks after Jonathan Schell's *The Fate of the Earth* (1982) was serialized in the magazine. It was like a scene from a movie—messengers would arrive daily with canvas bags literally bursting with mail. The essay hit people so hard, I think, because it moved discussion of nuclear war beyond the merely geopolitical and raised the specter of global environmental catastrophe. While John Hersey's *Hiroshima* (1946) had helped Americans imagine the human horror of a single explosion, Schell (1943–2014) helped us imagine the existential awfulness of the world after a nuclear exchange. That vision spurred the nuclear freeze movement, and by the end of the decade even Ronald Reagan was musing about doing away with nuclear weapons. It wasn't the first time Schell had influenced our political life. As a very young reporter, he'd gone to Vietnam for *The New Yorker*, producing *The Village of Ben Suc* (1967), which made perfectly clear how little the American military really understood the war they were fighting. His "Notes and Comment" in *The New Yorker* throughout the Watergate years pounded away at Richard Nixon's constitutional crimes. In this century, writing for *The Nation*, Schell mounted one of the first persistent critiques of the Bush administration's war in Iraq. But it is *The Fate of the Earth* for which he will be remembered—as the first writer fully to come to terms with the meaning of the awesome new power latent in our military technology.

from **The Fate of the Earth**

Regarded objectively, as an episode in the development of life on earth, a nuclear holocaust that brought about the extinction of mankind and other species by mutilating the ecosphere would constitute an evolutionary setback of possibly limited extent—the first to result from a deliberate action taken by the creature extinguished but perhaps no greater than any of several evolutionary setbacks, such as the extinction of the dinosaurs, of which the geological record offers evidence. (It is, of course, impossible to judge what course evolution would take after human extinction, but the past record strongly suggests that the reappearance of man is not one of the possibilities. Evolution has brought forth an amazing variety of creatures, but there is no evidence that any species, once extinguished, has ever evolved again. Whether or not nature, obeying some law of evolutionary progress, would bring forth another creature equipped with reason and will, and capable of building, and perhaps then destroying, a world, is one more unanswerable question, but it is barely conceivable that some gifted new animal will pore over the traces of our self-destruction, trying to figure out what went wrong and to learn from our mistakes. If this should be possible, then it might justify the remark once made by Kafka: "There is infinite hope, but not for us." If, on the other hand, as the record of life so far suggests, terrestrial evolution is able to produce only once the miracle of the qualities that we now associate with human beings, then all hope rides with human beings.) However, regarded subjectively, from within human life, where we are all actually situated, and as something that would happen to us, human extinction assumes awesome, inapprehensible proportions. It is of the essence of the human condition that we are born, live for a while, and then die. Through mishaps of all kinds, we may also suffer untimely death, and in extinction by nuclear arms the number of untimely deaths would reach the limit for any one catastrophe: everyone in the world would die. But although the untimely death of everyone in the world would in itself constitute an unimaginably huge loss, it would bring with it a separate, distinct loss that would be in a sense even huger—the cancellation of all future generations of human beings. According to the Bible, when Adam and Eve ate the fruit of the tree of knowledge God punished them by withdrawing from them the privilege of immortality and dooming them and their kind to die. Now our species has eaten more deeply of the fruit of the tree of knowledge, and has brought itself face to face with a second death—the death of mankind. In doing so, we have caused a basic change in the circumstances in which life was given to us, which is to say that we have altered the human condition. The distinctness of this second death from the deaths of all the people on earth can be illustrated by picturing two different global catastrophes. In the first, let us suppose that most of the people on earth were killed in a nuclear holocaust but that a few million survived and the earth happened to remain habitable by human beings. In this catastrophe, billions of people would perish, but the species would survive, and perhaps one day would even repopulate the earth in its former numbers. But now let us suppose that a substance was released into the environment which had the effect of sterilizing all the people in the world but otherwise leaving them unharmed. Then, as the existing population died off, the world would empty of people, until no one was left. Not one life would have been shortened by a single day, but the species would die. In extinction by nuclear arms, the death of the species and the death of all the people in the world would happen together, but it is important to make a clear distinction between the two losses; otherwise, the mind, overwhelmed by the thought of the deaths of the billions of living people, might stagger back without realizing that behind this already ungraspable loss there lies the separate loss of the future generations.

The possibility that the living can stop the future generations from entering into life compels us to ask basic new questions about our existence, the most sweeping of which is what these unborn ones, most of whom we will never meet even if they are born, mean to us. No one has ever thought to ask this question before our time, because no generation before ours has ever held the life and death of the species in its hands. But if we hardly know how to comprehend the possible deaths in a holocaust of the billions of people who are already in life how are we to comprehend the life or death of the infinite number of possible people who do not yet exist at all? How are we, who are a part of human life, to step back from life and see it whole, in order to assess the meaning of its disappearance? To kill a human being is murder, and there are those who believe that to abort a fetus is also murder, but what crime is it to cancel the numberless multitude of unconceived people? In what court is such a crime to be judged? Against whom is it committed? And what law does it violate? If we find the nuclear peril to be somehow abstract, and tend to consign this whole elemental issue to "defense experts" and other dubiously qualified people, part of the reason, certainly, is that the future generations really are abstract—that is to say, without the tangible existence and the unique particularities that help to make the living real to us. And if we find the subject strangely "impersonal" it may be in part because the unborn, who are the ones directly imperilled by extinction, are not yet persons. What are they, then? They lack the individuality that we often associate with the sacredness of life, and may at first thought seem to have only a shadowy, mass existence. *Where* are they? Are they to be pictured lined up in a sort of fore-life, waiting to get into life? Or should we regard them as nothing more than a pinch of chemicals in our reproductive organs, toward which we need feel no special obligations? What standing should they have among us? How much should their needs count in competition with ours? How far should the living go in trying to secure their advantage, their happiness, their existence?

The individual person, faced with the metaphysical-seeming perplexities involved in pondering the possible cancellation of people who do not yet exist—an apparently extreme effort of the imagination, which seems to require one first to summon before the mind's eye the countless possible people of the future generations and then to consign these incorporeal multitudes to a more profound nothingness—might well wonder why, when he already has his own death to worry about, he should occupy himself with this other death. Since our own individual death promises to inflict a loss that is total and final, we may find the idea of a second death merely redundant. After all, can everything be taken away from us twice? Moreover, a person might reason that even if mankind did perish he wouldn't have to know anything about it, since in that event he himself would perish. There might actually be something consoling in the idea of having so much company in death. In the midst of universal death, it somehow seems out of order to want to go on living oneself. As Randall Jarrell wrote in his poem "Losses," thinking back to his experience in the Second World War, "it was not dying: everybody died."

However, the individual would misconceive the nuclear peril if he tried to understand it primarily in terms of personal danger, or even in terms of danger to the people immediately known to him, for the nuclear peril threatens life, above all, not at the level of individuals, who already live under the sway of death, but at the level of everything that individuals hold in common. Death cuts off life; extinction cuts off birth. Death dispatches into the nothingness after life each person who has been born; extinction in one stroke locks up in the nothingness before life all the people who have not yet been born. For we are finite beings at both ends of our existence—natal as well as mortal—and it is the natality of our kind that extinction threatens. We have always been able to send people to their death, but only now has it become possible to prevent all birth and so doom all future human beings to uncreation. The threat of the loss of birth—a beginning that is over and done with for every living person—cannot be a source of immediate, selfish concern; rather, this threat assails everything that people hold in common, for it is the ability of our species to produce new generations which assures the continuation of the world in which all our common enterprises occur and have their meaning. Each death belongs inalienably to the individual who must suffer it, but birth is our common possession. And the meaning of extinction is therefore to be sought first not in what each person's own life means to him but in what the world and the people in it mean to him.

In its nature, the human world is, in Hannah Arendt's words, a "common world," which she distinguishes from the "private realm" that belongs to each person individually. (Somewhat surprisingly, Arendt, who devoted so much of her attention to the unprecedented evils that have appeared in our century, never addressed the issue of nuclear arms; yet I have discovered her thinking to be an indispensable foundation for reflection on this question.) The private realm, she writes in "The Human Condition," a book published in 1958, is made up of "the passions of the heart, the thoughts of the mind, the delights of the senses," and terminates with each person's death, which is the most solitary of all human experiences. The common world, on the other hand, is made up of all institutions, all cities, nations, and other communities, and all works of fabrication, art, thought, and science, and it survives the death of every individual. It is basic to the common world that it encompasses not only the present but all past and future generations. "The common world is what we enter when we are born and what we leave behind when we die," Arendt writes. "It transcends our life-span into past and future alike; it was there before we came and will outlast our brief sojourn in it. It is what we have in common not only with those who live with us, but also with those who were here before and with those who will come after us." And she adds, "Without this transcendence into a potential earthly immortality, no politics, strictly speaking, no common world, and no public realm is possible." The creation of a common world is the use that we human beings, and we alone among the earth's creatures, have made of the biological circumstance that while each of us is mortal, our species is biologically immortal. If mankind had not established a common world, the species would still outlast its individual members and be immortal, but this immortality would be unknown to us and would go for nothing, as it does in the animal kingdom, and the generations, unaware of one another's existence, would come and go like waves on the beach, leaving everything just as it was before. In fact, it is only because humanity has built up a common world that we can fear our destruction as a species. It may even be that man, who has been described as the sole creature that knows that it must die, can know this only because he lives in a common world, which permits him to imagine a future beyond his own life. This common world, which is unharmed by individual death but depends on the survival of the species, has now been placed in jeopardy by nuclear arms. Death and extinction are thus complementary, dividing between them the work of undoing, or threatening to undo, everything that human beings are or can ever become, with death terminating the life of each individual and extinction imperilling the common world shared by all. In one sense, extinction is less terrible than death, since extinction can be avoided, while death is inevitable; but in another sense extinction is more terrible—is the more radical nothingness—because extinction ends death just as surely as it ends birth and life. Death is only death; extinction is the death of death.

The world is made a common one by what Arendt calls "publicity," which insures that "everything that appears in public can be seen and heard by everybody." She writes, "A common world can survive the coming and going of the generations only to the extent that it appears in public. It is the publicity of the public realm which can absorb and make shine through the centuries whatever men may want to save from the natural ruin of time." But this publicity does not only shine on human works; it also brings to light the natural foundations of life, enabling us to perceive what our origins are. It thereby permits us not only to endow things of our own making with a degree of immortality but to see and appreciate the preëxisting, biological immortality of our species and of life on the planet, which forms the basis for any earthly immortality whatever. The chief medium of the publicity of the common world is, of course, language, whose possession by man is believed by many to be what separates him from the other animals; but there are also the other "languages" of the arts and sciences. And standing behind language is that of which language is expressive—our reason, our psyche, our will, and our spirit. Through these, we are capable of entering into the lives of others, and of becoming aware that we belong to a community of others that is as wide as our species. The foundation of a common world is an exclusively human achievement, and to live in a common world—to speak and listen to one another, to read, to write, to know about the past and look ahead to the future, to receive the achievements of past generations, and to pass them on, together with achievements of our own, to future generations, and otherwise to participate in human enterprises that outlast any individual life—is part of what it means to be human, and by threatening all this nuclear weapons threaten a part of our humanity. The common world is not something that can be separated from the life we now live; it is intrinsic to our existence—something as close to us as the words we speak and the thoughts we think using those words. Descartes's famous axiom "I think, therefore I am" has perhaps been more extensively rebutted than any other single philosophical proposition. The rebuttal by Lewis Mumford happens to amount to a description of each person's indebtedness to the common world and to the common biological inheritance that the common world has brought to light. "Descartes forgot that before he uttered these words 'I think' . . . he needed the coöperation of countless fellow-beings, extending back to his own knowledge as far as the thousands of years that Biblical history recorded," Mumford writes in "The Pentagon of Power," a book published in 1970. "Beyond that, we know now he needed the aid of an even remoter past that mankind too long remained ignorant of: the millions of years required to transform his dumb animal ancestors into conscious human beings." In our long and arduous ascent out of biological darkness, it seems, we forgot our indebtedness to the natural world of our origins, and now, in consequence, threaten to plunge ourselves into an even deeper darkness. The nuclear predicament is thus in every sense a crisis of life in the common world. Only because there is a common world, in which knowledge of the physical world accumulates over the generations, can there be a threat to the common world and to its natural foundations. Only because there is a common world, which permits us knowledge of other generations and of the terrestrial nature of which human life is a part, can we worry about, or even know of, that threat. And only because there is a common world can we hope, by concerting our actions, to save ourselves and the earth.

The common world has been the work of every generation that has lived in it, back to the remotest ages. Much as poets begin by using language as they find it but, usually as an unself-conscious consequence of their work, leave usage slightly altered behind them, people in general pursue their various ends in the yielding medium of the world and shape its character by their actions. But although the world receives the imprint of the lives of those who pass through it, it has never been given to any single generation to dictate the character of the world. Not even the most thoroughgoing totalitarian regimes have succeeded in wholly shaping the lives of their peoples. One has only to think of Alexander Solzhenitsyn growing up in the Soviet Union but drawing so much of his spiritual sustenance from earlier centuries of Russian life, or to think of China, where so many of the customs and qualities of the people have outlasted what was probably the longest and most concentrated assault in history by a government on the national tradition of its own country, to realize how deeply a people's past is woven into its present.

The links binding the living, the dead, and the unborn were described by Edmund Burke, the great eighteenth-century English conservative, as a "partnership" of the generations. He wrote, "Society is indeed a contract. . . . It is a partnership in all science; a partnership in all art; a partnership in every virtue, and in all perfection. As the ends of such a partnership cannot be obtained except in many generations, it becomes a partnership not only between those who are living, but between those who are living, those who are dead, and those who are to be born." Pericles offered a similar, though not identical, vision of the common life of the generations in his funeral oration, in which he said that all Athens was a "sepulchre" for the remembrance of the soldiers who had died fighting for their city. Thus, whereas Burke spoke of common tasks that needed many generations for their achievement, Pericles spoke of the immortality that the living confer on the dead by remembering their sacrifices. In the United States, Abraham Lincoln seemed to combine these two thoughts when he said in his Gettysburg address that the sacrifices of the soldiers who had died at Gettysburg laid an obligation on the living to devote themselves to the cause for which the battle had been fought. And, indeed, every political observer or political actor of vision has recognized that if life is to be fully human it must take cognizance of the dead and the unborn.

But now our responsibilities as citizens in the common world have been immeasurably enlarged. In the pre-nuclear common world, we were partners in the protection of the arts, the institutions, the customs, and all "perfection" of life; now we are also partners in the protection of life itself. Burke described as a common inheritance the achievements that one generation passed along to the next. "By a constitutional policy, working after the pattern of nature, we receive, we hold, we transmit our government and our privileges, in the same manner in which we enjoy and transmit our property and our lives," he wrote. "The institutions of policy, the goods of fortune, the gifts of Providence, are handed down, to us and from us, in the same course and order." These words appear in Burke's "Reflections on the Revolution in France"—the revolution being an event that filled him with horror, for in it he believed he saw a single generation violently destroying in a few years the national legacy of hundreds of years. But, whether or not he was right in thinking that the inheritance of France was being squandered by its recipients, the inheriting generations and their successors were at least biologically intact. In our time, however, among the items in the endangered inheritance the inheritors find themselves. Each generation of mankind still receives, holds, and transmits the inheritance from the past, but, being now a part of that inheritance, each generation *is received, is held, and is transmitted*, so that receiver and received, holder and held, transmitter and transmitted are one. Yet our jeopardy is only a part of the jeopardy of all life, and the largest item in the inheritance that we receive, hold, and must transmit is the entire ecosphere. So deep is the change in the structure of human life brought about by this new peril that in retrospect the Burkean concern about the "perfection" of life, indispensable as this concern is to the quality of our existence, seems like only the barest hint or suggestion of the incomparably more commanding obligation that is laid on us by the nuclear predicament. It strikes modern ears as prophetic that when Burke sought to describe the permanence in human affairs which he so valued he often resorted to metaphors drawn from the natural world—speaking, for example, of a "pattern of nature" that human society should imitate—as though he had had a premonition that an almost habitually revolutionary mankind would one day proceed from tearing society apart to tearing the natural world apart. Speaking of the society into which each of us is born, Burke angrily asked whether it could be right to "hack that aged parent in pieces." His words have acquired a deeper meaning than he could ever have foretold for them now that the parent in question is not merely human society but the earth itself.

The Fate of the Earth (1982)

WILLIAM CRONON

William Cronon (b. 1954) is one of the deans of environmental history, a recent and growing part of the discipline that asks how landscape has affected people and vice-versa. This selection, from his first book, *Changes in the Land* (1983), helped New Englanders understand the legacy with which they lived—a legacy of ignorance in many ways. But it also helped people reconfigure the New World in their minds as a place that had been rearranged by aboriginal cultures long before the arrival of Europeans. Cronon went on to write important essays on the American West and a magnificent history of Chicago's emergence from the land that surrounds it (*Nature's Metropolis*, 1991); he also stirred much ire in environmental circles by questioning the historical reality of "wilderness" in a 1995 essay. One of his largest legacies is the great number of young environmental historians he has helped to train, who are now reshaping our sense of the past of every corner of the continent.

Seasons of Want and Plenty

In describing New England's natural abundance so enthusiastically, the colonists were misleading in two ways; in the process, they revealed the assumptions by which they misconstrued the supposed "poverty" of the Indians. Those who sought to promote colonial enterprises tended to put the best possible face on everything they encountered in the New World. Selective reporting, exaggeration, and outright lies could all be useful tools in accomplishing this task. Captain Christopher Levett felt it necessary to inform readers of his 1628 account of New England that he would not "as some have done to my knowledge, speak more than is true." English readers must not be taken in by descriptions which made New England out to be a veritable paradise of milk and honey. "I will not tell you," Levett wrote,

> that you may smell the corn fields before you see the land; neither must men think that corn doth grow naturally, (or on trees,) nor will the deer come when they are called, or stand still and look on a man until he shoot him, not knowing a man from a beast; nor the fish leap into the kettle, nor on the dry land, neither are they so plentiful, that you may dip them up in baskets, nor take cod in nets to make a voyage, which is no truer than that the fowls will present themselves to you with spits through them.

If the myths which Levett criticized had anything in common, it was their vision of a landscape in which wealth and sustenance could be achieved with little labor. Hopes for great windfall profits had fueled New World enterprises ever since the triumphs of Cortes, and were reinforced by traditions as old as the Garden of Eden. When English immigrants exaggerated the wealth of New England, they dreamed of a world in which returns to human labor were far greater than in England.[1]

Because their hopes led them to expect a land of plenty, early visitors introduced a second distortion into their accounts. Even when what they wrote was literally true, they often failed to note that it was not *always* true. Just as the habitats of New England formed a patchwork quilt on the landscape, the plenty of one being matched by the poverty of another, so too did those habitats change from month to month, the abundance of one season giving few clues to what a place might be like at other times of the year. Most early descriptions were written by spring and summer visitors, who naturally saw only the times when fish, fruit, and fowl were all too numerous to count. Would-be English settlers thus formed their vision of New England from accounts

1. Christopher Levett, "Voyage into New England" (1628), *Massachusetts Historical Society Collections*, 3rd ser., 3 (1843), p. 179. Virginia probably suffered most from this kind of exaggeration, but see Thomas Morton, *New English Canaan* (1632), Charles F. Adams, ed., *Pubs. of the Prince Society*, XIV (Boston, 1883), pp. 231–3, for tendencies in the same direction. William Morrell's "Poem on New-England" (ca. 1623), *Massachusetts Historical Society Collections*, 1st ser., 1 (1792), pp. 125–39, is also a good example.

that concentrated the summer's seasonal wealth into an image of perpetual abundance. If the result was not disaster, it was at least disappointment. "When I remember the high commendations some have given of the place," wrote one chastened colonist, "I have thought the reason thereof to be this, that they wrote surely in strawberry time."[2]

New England's seasonal cycles were little different from those of Europe. If anything, its summers were hotter and its winters colder. Colonists were prevented from realizing this only by their own high expectations of laborless wealth: many initially seemed to believe that strawberry time would last all year. Captain Levett wrote of one early attempt at settlement in which the colonists "neither applied themselves to planting of corn nor taking of fish, more than for their present use, but went about to build castles in the air, and making of forts, neglecting the plentiful time of fishing." They did so because their myths told them that the plentiful times would never end, but their refusal to lay up stores for the winter meant that many starved to death. The pattern occurred repeatedly, whether at Sagadahoc, Plymouth, or Massachusetts Bay: colonists came without adequate food supplies and died. At Plymouth alone, half the Pilgrims were dead before the first winter was over. Those who had experienced the New England cold knew better, and warned that new arrivals who hoped to survive must bring provisions to last the year and a half before settlements could become self-sustaining. "Trust not too much on us for Corne at this time," wrote a spokesman for the Pilgrims, "for by reason of this last company that came, depending wholy upon us, we shall have little enough till harvest." This was hardly the advice one would send from a land of infinite plenty. The problem was perhaps stated most plaintively by the Massachusetts colonist John Pond, who in 1631 wrote his parents, "I pray you remember me as your child . . . we do not know how long we may subsist, for we cannot live here without provisions from ould eingland."[3]

2. Quoted by Thomas Hutchinson, *The History of the Colony and Province of Massachusetts-Bay* (1765), Lawrence Shaw Mayo, ed. (Cambridge, MA, 1936), I, p. 405.

3. Levett, "Voyage," p. 182; *A Relation of the English Plantation at Plimoth* (1622), facsimile edition, Readex Microprint (1966) (henceforth cited as *Mourt's Relation*), p. 63; John [?] Pond to William Pond, March 15, 1630/1, in Everett Emerson, ed., *Letters from*

In New England, most colonists anticipated that they would be able to live much as they had done in England, in an artisanal and farming community with work rhythms, class relations, and a social order similar to the one they had left behind—the only difference being their own improved stature in society. There were many misconceptions involved in this vision, but the one most threatening to survival was the simple fact that establishing European relations of production in the New World was a far more complicated task than most colonists realized. Even to set up farms was a struggle. Once colonists had done this, adjusting to the New England ecosystem by re-creating the annual agricultural cycles which had sustained them in England, starving times became relatively rare. But for the first year or two, before European subsistence patterns had been reproduced, colonists found themselves forced to rely either on what little they had brought with them or on what New England's inhabitants—whether English or Indian—were willing to provide. Few colonists expected that they would have to go abegging like this. At most, they contemplated supplementing their food stores by trading with the Indians; and as one promoter argued, should the Indians be reluctant to trade, it would be easy enough "to bring them all in subjection, and make this provision." Many colonists arrived believing that they could survive until their first harvest simply by living as the Indians supposedly did, off the unplanted bounties of nature. Colonists were assured by some that Indian men got their livelihood with "small labour but great pleasure." Thomas Morton spoke of Indians for whom "the beasts of the forrest there doe serve to furnish them at any time when they please." If this were true, then surely Englishmen could do no worse. John Smith told his readers that, in New England, "nature and liberty affoords us that freely which in *England* we want, or it costeth us deerly." The willingness of colonists to believe such arguments, and hazard their lives upon them, was testimony to

New England (Amherst, MA, 1976), p. 65. See Neil Salisbury, *Manitou and Providence* (New York, 1982), pp. 81–2, 111–18, for evidence that Indian refusal to trade also lay at the root of the Sagadahoc and Wessagusset failures. On differences between American and European climates, see Karen Ordahl Kupperman, "The Puzzle of American Climate in the Early Colonial Period," *American Historical Review*, 87 (1982), pp. 1262–89.

how little they understood both the New England environment and the ways Indians actually lived in it.[4]

A central fact of temperate ecosystems like those of New England is their periodicity: they are tied to overlapping cycles of light and dark, high and low tides, waxing and waning moons, and especially the long and short days which mean hot and cold seasons. Each plant and animal species makes its adjustments to these various cycles, so that the flowing of sap in trees, the migration of birds, the spawning of fish, the rutting of deer, and the fruiting of plants all have their special times of the year. A plant that stores most of its food energy in its roots during the winter will transfer much of that energy first to its leaves and then to its seeds as the warmer months progress. Such patterns of energy concentration are cru- cial to any creature which seeks to eat that plant. Because animals, in- cluding people, feed on plants and other animals, the ways they obtain their food are largely determined by the cycles in which other species lead their lives. Just as a fox's summer diet of fruit and insects shifts to rodents and birds during the winter, so too did the New England Indians seek to obtain their food wherever it was seasonally most concentrated in the New England ecosystem. Doing so required an intimate understanding of the habits and ecology of other species, and it was this knowledge that the English discovered they lacked.[5]

4. John Smith, *The Generall Historie of Virginia* (1624), facsimile edition, Readex Microprint (1966), pp. 211, 219; Morrell, "New England," p. 131; Morton, *Canaan*, p. 177; James A. Henretta, *The Evolution of American Society, 1700–1815* (Lexington, MA, 1973), pp. 31–9. Exaggerated expectations were not limited to the English. Pierre Biard's *Relation* (in Reuben Gold Thwaites, ed., *Jesuit Relations, III, Acadia, 1611–1616* [Cleve- land, 1897], pp. 65–7) supplies a wonderful French example: ". . . we Frenchmen are so willing to go there with our eyes shut and our heads down; believing, for example, that in Canada, when we are hungry, all we will have to do is go to an Island, and there by the skillful use of a club, right and left, we can bring down birds each as big as a duck, with every blow. This is well said, as our people have done this more than once and in more than one place. It is all very well, if you are never hungry except when these birds are on the Islands, and if even then you happen to be near them. But if you are fifty or sixty leagues away, what are you going to do?" Good discussions of these colonial assumptions about the New World can be found in Karen O. Kupperman, *Settling with the Indians* (Totowa, NJ, 1980); in Edmund S. Morgan's classic, "The Labor Problem at Jamestown, 1607–18," *American Historical Review*, 76 (1971), pp. 595–611; and his *American Slavery, American Freedom* (New York, 1975).

5. For general introductions to photoperiodism, see Robert L. Smith, *Ecology and Field Biology* (New York, 1966), pp. 98–126; Robert E. Ricklefs, *Ecology*, 2nd ed. (New York, 1979),

Indian communities had learned to exploit the seasonal diversity of their environment by practicing mobility: their communities characteristically refused to stay put. The principal social and economic grouping for precolonial New England Indians was the village, a small settlement with perhaps a few hundred inhabitants organized into extended kin networks. Villages, rather than the larger and better-known units called tribes or confederacies, were the centers around which Indian interactions with the environment revolved. But villages were not fixed geographical entities: their size and location changed on a seasonal basis, communities breaking up and reassembling as social and ecological needs required. Wherever villagers expected to find the greatest natural food supplies, there they went. When fish were spawning, many Indian families might gather at a single waterfall to create a dense temporary settlement in which feasting and celebration were the order of the day; when it was time to hunt in the fall, the same families might be found scattered over many square miles of land. All aspects of Indian life hinged on this mobility. Houses, consisting of wooden frames covered by grass mats or bark, were designed to be taken apart and moved in a few hours. For some groups, the shape of houses changed from season to season to accommodate different densities of population: small wigwams housing one or two families in the summer became in the winter extended longhouses holding many families. When food had to be stored while a village moved elsewhere, it was left in carefully constructed underground pit-barns, where it could be retrieved when needed. Tools and other property were either light and easily carried or just as readily abandoned and remade when needed in a new location. As Thomas Morton observed, "They love not to bee cumbered with many utensilles."[6]

pp. 280–306; and Edward J. Kormondy, *Concepts of Ecology* (Englewood Cliffs, NJ, 1969), pp. 140–54.

6. Roger Williams, *A Key into the Language of America* (1643), John J. Teunissen and Evelyn J. Hinz, eds. (Detroit, 1973), pp. 127–8; Morton, *Canaan*, p. 177. On the changing shape of wigwams, see William Wood, *New England's Prospect* (1634), Alden T. Vaughan, ed. (Amherst, MA, 1977), p. 113; H. P. Biggar, ed., *The Works of Samuel de Champlain*, 6 vols. (Toronto, 1922–36), maps; Daniel Gookin, "Historical Collections of the Indians in New England," *Massachusetts Historical Society Collections*, 1st ser., (1792), p. 150; William C. Sturtevant, "Two 1761 Wigwams at Niantic, Connecticut," *American Antiquity*, 40 (1975), pp. 437–44; and Bernard G. Hoffman, *The Historical Ethnography of the Micmac in the Sixteenth and Seventeenth Centuries*, Ph.D. Thesis, UCLA, 1955, p. 135.

The seasonal cycles within which a village moved depended on the habitats available to it: Indians who had access to the seashore, for instance, could lead rather different lives than their inland counterparts. Important as habitat differences were, however, the crucial distinction between Indian communities was whether or not they had adopted agriculture. In general, Indians south of the Kennebec River in Maine raised crops as part of their annual subsistence cycles; more northern Indians, on the other hand, as Verrazzano noted in 1524, showed "no sign of cultivation." Verrazzano quite reasonably attributed the absence of agriculture in the north to soil which would produce neither fruit nor grain "on account of its sterility": climatic conditions in fact made grain raising an increasingly risky business the farther north an Indian people lived. Because the ability to grow crops had drastic implications for the way a village conducted the rest of its food-gathering activities, it is best to begin our description of Indian subsistence strategies in the north, where Indians were entirely dependent on the natural abundance of the ecosystem. Only in the north did Indians live entirely as hunter-gatherers, people who bore at least superficial resemblance to the creatures of English fantasy who captured nature's bounties with "small labor but great pleasure."[7]

In the north, spring commenced "when the leaves begin to sprout, when the wild geese appear, when the fawns of moose attain to a certain size in the bellies of their mothers, and when the seals bear their young." Most especially, the northern spring began when the ice broke up; then inland populations moved to coastal sites where they repaired fishing gear—nets, tackle, weirs, birchbark canoes—in anticipation of the spawning runs. For Maine Indians who had access to the coast, probably well over half the yearly food supply came from the rivers and seashore. In late March, the smelt arrived in streams and rivers in such quantities that one could not put a "hand into the water, without encountering them." They were followed in April by the alewives, sturgeon, and salmon, so that spawning runs furnished a major share of

7. Lawrence C. Wroth, ed., *The Voyages of Giovanni de Verrazzano, 1524–1528* (New Haven, 1970), p. 140.

the food supply from March through May. By early May, nonspawning fish were also providing food. Offshore were cod which had to be caught with hook and line. Closer to land were tidewater and ground fish, such as brook trout, smelt, striped bass, and flounder, all of which could be caught with weirs and nets, and the larger sturgeon and salmon, which were usually harpooned. In the tidal zone were the scallops, clams, mussels, and crabs which women and children gathered as a steady base for the village diet. As described by the Jesuit Pierre Biard, this phase of the northern Indians' subsistence cycle was especially flush: "From the month of May up to the middle of September, they are free from all anxiety about their food; for the cod are upon the coast, and all kinds of fish and shellfish."[8]

The arrival of the alewives also heralded the coming of the migratory birds, including the large ducks which Biard called bustards, whose eggs were over twice as large as ordinary European hens' eggs. Not only could women and children gather birds' eggs while men fished; they could capture the birds themselves with snares or clubs. Bird migrations made their biggest contribution to Indian food supplies in April, May, September, and October, when Canada geese, brants, mourning doves, and miscellaneous ducks passed through; other birds, albeit in fewer numbers, could be caught during the summer as well. By July and August, strawberries, raspberries, and blueberries were ripening, providing food not only for Indians but for flocks of passenger pigeons and other

8. Hoffman, *Micmac Ethnography*, is superb on northern subsistence cycles; his diagram of these has been published in "Ancient Tribes Revisited," *Ethnohistory*, 14 (1967), p. 21. The northern documents of the French Jesuits are exceptionally fine: these include Biard, *Relation*, pp. 79–85; Nicolas Denys, *The Description and Natural History of the Coasts of North America (Acadia)* (1672), William F. Ganong, ed. (Toronto, Champlain Society Publications, II, 1908); and Chrestien Le Clercq, *New Relations of Gaspesia* (1691), William F. Ganong, ed., (Toronto, Champlain Society Publications, V, 1910). I have used them extensively in the discussion which follows, even though they fall outside the regional boundaries of New England, because documentary coverage of the Maine Indians is poor and northern New England Indians were much more like their Canadian neighbors than the Indians to the south. The best modern account of the Maine Indians is Frank G. Speck, *Penobscot Man* (Philadelphia, 1940). Quotations in this paragraph are from LeClercq, *Gaspesia*, p. 137; and Biard, *Relation*, p. 81. Hoffman, *Micmac Ethnography*, p. 160, argues that cod was not a major component of the northern coastal diet, despite Biard's claims to the contrary.

birds which nested in the area. In addition to birds, various coastal mammals—whales, porpoises, walruses, and seals—were hunted and eaten. Nuts, berries, and other wild plants were gathered as they became available. In all ways, the summer was a time of plenty.

Things changed in September. Toward the middle of the month, Indian populations moved inland to the smaller creeks, where eels could be caught as they returned from their spawning in the sea. From October through March, villages broke into small family bands that subsisted on beaver, caribou, moose, deer, and bear. Men were responsible for killing these animals, while women maintained the campsite and did all hauling and processing of the slaughtered meat. If snows were heavy and animals could be easily tracked, hunting provided an adequate food supply; if the snow failed to stay on the ground, on the other hand, it was easy to starve. Northern Indians accepted as a matter of course that the months of February and March, when the animals they hunted were lean and relatively scarce, would be times of little food.[9]

European visitors had trouble comprehending this Indian willingness to go hungry in the late winter months. They were struck by the northern Indians' apparent refusal to store more than a small amount of the summer's plenty for winter use. As the Jesuit Chrétien Le Clercq remarked:

> They are convinced that fifteen to twenty lumps of meat, or of fish dried or cured in the smoke, are more than enough to support them for the space of five to six months. Since, however, they are a people of good appetite, they consume their provisions very much sooner than they expect. This exposes them often to the danger of dying from hunger, through lack of the provision which they could easily possess in abundance if they would only take the trouble to gather it.

9. Biard, *Relation*, pp. 83, 101–3; Denys, *Acadia*, pp. 405, 422–3; Bruce J. Bourque, "Aboriginal Settlement and Subsistence on the Maine Coast," *Man in the Northeast*, 6 (Fall 1973), pp. 3–20; John Gyles, "Memoirs of Odd Adventures, Strange Deliverances, etc." (1736), in Alden T. Vaughan and Edward W. Clark, eds., *Puritans among the Indians* (Cambridge, MA, 1981), p. 103. Note again the nomenclature problem here: there are no bustards (Biard's *outardes*) in North America. We cannot be sure to which species he was referring.

Here again was the paradox of want in a land of plenty. To a European sensibility, it made no sense to go hungry if one knew in advance that there would be little food in winter. Colonists who starved did so because they learned too late how ill informed they had been about the New World's perpetual abundance. Although the myth died hard, those who survived it were reasonably quick to revise their expectations. When Europeans inquired why nonagricultural Indians did not do the same, the Indians replied, "It is all the same to us, we shall stand it well enough; we spend seven and eight days, even ten sometimes, without eating anything, yet we do not die." What they said was true: Indians died from starvation much less frequently than did early colonists, so there was a certain irony in European criticisms of Indians on this score. Whatever the contradictions of their own position, however, the colonists could not understand Indian attitudes toward winter food shortages. Consciously choosing hunger, rather than working harder in the leisurely times of summer, seemed a fool's decision.[10]

One effect of that choice, however, was to hold northern Indians to low population densities. The ecological principle known as Liebig's Law states that biological populations are limited not by the total annual resources available to them but by the minimum amount that can be found at the scarcest time of the year. Different species meet this restriction in different ways, and the mechanism—conscious or unconscious— whereby northern Indians restrained their fertility is not clear. However they accomplished this feat, its effects were self-evident: the low Indian populations of the precolonial northern forests had relatively little impact on the ecosystems they inhabited. The very abundance which so impressed the Europeans was testimony to this fact. By keeping population densities low, the food scarcities of winter guaranteed the abundance of spring, and contributed to the overall stability of human relationships to the ecosystem. In this, northern New England

10. Le Clercq, *Gaspesia*, p. 110; James Sullivan, "The History of the Penobscot Indians," *Massachusetts Historical Society Collections*, 1st ser., 9 (1804), p. 228; Biard, *Relation*, p. 107.

Indians were typical of hunting and gathering peoples around the world.[11]

The farming Indians of southern New England, among whom the earliest English colonists made their settlements, also engaged in hunting and gathering, but their ability to raise crops put them in a fundamentally different relationship with their environment. The very decision to engage in agriculture requires the creation of at least enough seed surplus to assure that planting can be done the following year, and opens the possibility of growing and storing enough food to carry a population through the winter with much less dependence on the vagaries of the hunt. Grain made up perhaps one-half to two-thirds of the southern New England diet, thereby reducing southern reliance on other foodstuffs; in comparison, northern Indians who raised no grain at all had to obtain two to three times more food energy from hunting and fishing. More importantly, nothing in the northern diet could be stored through the scarce times of winter as effectively as grain, making starvation a much less serious threat in the south than in the north.[12]

The ability of agriculture to smooth out the seasonal scarcities of wild foodstuffs had major consequences for the sizes of Indian populations in New England. The nonagricultural Indians of Maine sustained population densities, on average, of perhaps 41 persons per hundred square miles. The crop-raising Indians of southern New England, on

11. Eugene P. Odum, *Fundamentals of Ecology*, 3rd ed. (Philadelphia, 1971), pp. 106–39, explicates Liebig's Law and other environmental constraints on populations. It is unclear whether the starvation periods which French Jesuits observed among northern Indian populations at the beginning of the seventeenth century were typical of precolonial times. There is at least some reason to believe that the famines may have been the result of Indians having shifted their subsistence patterns to include trade with Europeans along the coast of Maine and Nova Scotia. Hoffman, *Micmac Ethnography*, pp. 229–33, gives the arguments against viewing the seventeenth-century starvations as normal; see also Bourque, "Aboriginal Settlement." On general hunter-gatherer behavior, see Richard B. Lee and Irven DeVore, eds., *Man the Hunter* (New York, 1968); and Marshall Sahlins, *Stone Age Economics* (Chicago, 1972).

12. M. K. Bennett, "The Food Economy of the New England Indians, 1605–75," *Journal of Political Economy*, 63 (1955), pp. 391–3. (Historians generally use Bennett's figures fairly uncritically, but there are many problems with them. See notes 16 and 20 below.)

the other hand, probably maintained 287 persons on an identical amount of land, a sevenfold difference. When these two broad groups were combined, the total Indian population of New England probably numbered somewhere between 70,000 and 100,000 people in 1600. (Lest this seem unimpressive, one should remember that the *English* population of New England was smaller than this even at the beginning of the eighteenth century, having reached only 93,000 people by 1700.) The crucial role of agriculture in maintaining so large an Indian population in precolonial New England is clear: although agricultural and non-agricultural peoples inhabited roughly equal areas of southern and northern New England respectively, those who raised crops contributed over 80 percent of the total population.[13]

Although southern Indians engaged in many of the same annual hunting and fishing activities as northern ones, their concentration on the raising of crops can be seen even in the names they gave their months. Northern Indians named their lunar months in terms of seasonal changes in animal populations, referring to the egg laying of birds, the running of salmon, the molting of geese, the hibernation of bears, and so on. By contrast, southern Indians chose the names of their months with an entirely different emphasis. The fur trader John Pynchon recorded that the Agawam Indian village near Springfield, Massachusetts, began its year with the month of Squannikesos, which included part of April and part of May, and whose name meant "when they set Indian corn." This was followed by various months whose names indicated the weeding of corn, the hilling of corn, the ripening of corn, the coming of the frost, the middle of winter, the thawing of ice, and the catching of fish. The southern cycle of months was thus remarkable

13. The debate over pre-Columbian Indian population figures has generated an extensive literature, and my text conveys only the roughest outlines of its conclusions. See the bibliographical essay for a survey of this material. My own argument follows the discussions in Francis Jennings, *The Invasion of America* (Chapel Hill, 1975), pp. 15–31; S. F. Cook, *The Indian Populations of New England in the Seventeenth Century* (Berkeley, 1976); and especially Dean R. Snow, *The Archaeology of New England* (New York, 1980), pp. 31–42, whose density figures I have converted from square kilometers to square miles. Colonial population figures are from U. S. Bureau of the Census, *Historical Statistics of the United States* (Washington, 1975), Table Z 1–19, p. 1168.

in having only a single reference to the animals which so dominated the northern calendar, an indication of how much agriculture had transformed Indian lives there.[14]

As the Agawam calendar shows, southern Indians began their annual subsistence cycles by moving to their summer fields and preparing the ground by working it with clamshell hoes. According to the Dutch traveler Isaack de Rasieres, the Indians "make heaps like molehills, each about two and a half feet from the others, which they sow or plant in April with maize, in each heap five or six grains." Because the earth was not stirred deeply by this method, much of the soil was left intact and erosion was thereby held to a minimum. As the young plants grew, soil was raised around them to create low mounds which strengthened their roots against the attacks of birds. Maize was not an easy crop to raise: as de Rasieres noted, it was "a grain to which much labor must be given, with weeding and earthing-up, or it does not thrive." Perhaps partly for this reason, Indian farmers, unlike European ones, used their cornfields to raise more than just corn. When Champlain observed Indian fields near the mouth of the Saco River, he noted that

> with the corn they put in each hill three or four Brazilian beans [kidney beans], which are of different colors. When they grow up, they interlace with the corn, which reaches to the height of from five to six feet; and they keep the ground very free from weeds. We saw there many squashes, and pumpkins, and tobacco, which they likewise cultivate.

14. Northern month names can be found in Le Clercq, *Gaspesia*, pp. 137–9; Hoffman, *Micmac Ethnography*, p. 246; Biard, *Relation*, pp. 79–83; and Philip K. Bock, "Micmac," in Trigger, *Northeast*, p. 111. Southern calendars are in Eva L. Butler, "Algonkian Culture and Use of Maize in Southern New England," *Bulletin of the Archaeological Society of Connecticut*, 22 (December 1948), pp. 10–11; "Indian Names of the Months," *New England Historical and Genealogical Register*, 10 (1856), p. 166; and Gordon M. Day, "An Agawam Fragment," *International Journal of American Linguistics*, 33 (1967), pp. 244–7. See also the discussion in Peter A. Thomas, "Contrastive Subsistence Strategies and Land Use as Factors for Understanding Indian-White Relations in New England," *Ethnohistory*, 23 (1976), pp. 1–18. The Abenaki calendar given by Sebastian Rasles in *Dictionary of the Abnaki Language in North America* (Cambridge, MA, 1833), p. 478, includes two or three months referring to maize cultivation.

It was not an agriculture that looked very orderly to a European eye accustomed to monocultural fields. Cornstalks served as beanpoles, squashes sent their tendrils everywhere, and the entire surface of the field became a dense tangle of food plants. But, orderly or not, such gardens had the effect, as John Winthrop, Jr., said, of "loading the Ground with as much as it will beare," creating very high yields per acre, discouraging weed growth, and preserving soil moisture. Moreover, although Indians may or may not have realized it, the resulting harvest of beans and corn provided the amino acids necessary for a balanced diet of vegetable protein.[15]

Except for tobacco, crops were primarily the responsibility of women. Roger Williams wrote that Indian women "constantly beat all their corne with hand: they plant it, dresse it, gather it, barne it, beat it, and take as much paines as any people in the world" with it. As with the hunting Indians of northern New England, the sexual division of labor for the agricultural peoples of southern New England was very well defined, women performing those jobs which were most compatible with simultaneous child-care. This meant tasks which were generally repetitive, which could be easily interrupted, which did not require travel too far from home, and which did not suffer if one performed them while giving most of one's attention to the children. In the non-agricultural north, women's work involved gathering shellfish and birds on the shore, collecting wild plants, trapping small rodents, making garments, keeping camp, and the whole range of food-processing activities; but meat gathered by men probably supplied half or more of a village's food. In the south, on the other hand, agriculture changed this

15. Isaack de Rasieres to Samuel Blommaert, ca. 1628, in Sydney V. James, Jr., ed., *Three Visitors to Early Plymouth* (Plimoth Plantation, 1963), p. 71; Samuel de Champlain, *Voyages of Samuel de Champlain*, W. L. Grant, ed. (New York, 1907), p. 62. On multiple crop farming, see Fulmer Mood, "John Winthrop, Jr., on Indian Corn," *New England Quarterly*, 10 (1937), pp. 128–9; Williams, *Key*, pp. 170–1; Carl Sauer, "The Agency of Man on the Earth," in William L. Thomas, ed., *Man's Role in Changing the Face of the Earth* (Chicago, 1956), pp. 56–7; Harold C. Conklin, "An Ethnoecological Approach to Shifting Agriculture," *Transactions of the New York Academy of Science*, 2nd ser., 17 (1954), pp. 133–42; Conklin, "The Study of Shifting Cultivation," *Current Anthropology*, 2 (1961), pp. 27–61; and Howard S. Russell, "New England Indian Agriculture," *Bulletin of the Massachusetts Archaeological Society*, 22 (1961), pp. 58–61.

sexual division and made women much more important than men in providing food. A single Indian woman could raise anywhere from twenty-five to sixty bushels of corn by working an acre or two, enough to provide half or more of the annual caloric requirements for a family of five. When corn was combined with the other foods for which they were responsible, women may have contributed as much as three-fourths of a family's total subsistence needs.[16]

Crops were planted between March and late June, the event often being timed by the leafing of certain trees or the arrival of the alewives. While women worked the fields, men erected weirs on the rivers and fished the spring spawning runs. By March, most beans and corn remaining from the previous harvest were probably needed as seed for planting, so that fish and migratory birds became the chief sources of food from late winter through midsummer. Contrary to what American myth has long held, it is quite unlikely that alewives or other fish were used as fertilizer in Indian fields, notwithstanding the legendary role of the Pilgrims' friend Squanto in teaching colonists this practice. Squanto probably learned the technique while being held captive in Europe, and if any Indians used it in New England, they did so in an extremely limited area. Having no easy way to transport large quantities of fish from river to field, and preferring quite sensibly to avoid such back-breaking work, Indians simply abandoned their fields when the soil lost its fertility. As William Wood wrote, "The Indians who are too lazy to catch fish plant corn eight or ten years in one place without it,

16. Williams, *Key*, p. 121; Judith K. Brown, "A Note on the Division of Labor by Sex," *American Anthropologist*, 72 (1970), pp. 1073–8. Note that I refer here only to the sexual division of food-producing activities; I make no effort to consider the total allocation of physical or nonphysical work. On the productivity of maize agriculture, see Peter A. Thomas, *In the Maelstrom of Change: The Indian Trade and Cultural Process in the Middle Connecticut River Valley, 1635–1665*, Ph.D. Thesis, University of Massachusetts, 1979, p. 109; Williams, *Key*, p. 171; Bennett, "Food Economy," pp. 391–3. Bennett's figures for corn's contribution to the Indian diet are probably exaggerated: he derived them by estimating total caloric requirements for an average person, subtracting Williams's corn yield estimates as distributed on a per capita basis, and allocating the remainder to noncorn foods. Such an algorithm obviously privileges corn at the expense of other foods, fails to consider waste, and assumes that corn was consumed at a constant level all year long. My discussion in the text shows why I think this unlikely; see also note 20 below.

having very good crops." Fertilizing fields with fish, as the English eventually did, seemed to Indians a wholly unnecessary labor.[17]

Once crops were planted and weeded, they needed less attention for two or three months, until the ripening corn had to be guarded against marauding birds before being harvested. (De Rasieres explained how some birds, probably passenger pigeons, were known as "maize thieves" because "they flatten the corn in any place where they alight, just as if cattle had lain there.") During these months, villages tended to disperse and families moved their individual wigwams to other planting and gathering sites. Women, who owned the wigwams and most household goods, moved their camps from field to field as necessary, and then to points along the coast where they gathered seafood and the cattails used in making mats for wigwams. Camps occasionally had to be moved in the summer simply to escape the fleas which tended to breed around human habitations. Wigwams were also moved if a death occurred in one, or if a settlement was threatened by war.[18]

Men fanned out from these bases for extended fishing and hunting trips. They might disappear into the woods for ten days at a time to build a dugout canoe that would allow them to fish deep water with harpoon or hook and line. Southern New England boats were made from decay-resistant chestnut and were heavy enough to require several hands to launch; in the north, paper birch, which did not grow in southeastern New England, was used to create the much lighter and

17. Mood, "Winthrop on Corn," p. 126; Wood, *Prospect*, p. 35; James, *Plymouth Visitors*, pp. 7–9. The case against Indian fish fertilizer was first made by Erhard Rostlund, "The Evidence for the Use of Fish as Fertilizer in Aboriginal North America," *Journal of Geography*, 56 (1957), pp. 222–8; and Lynn Ceci has put forward the strongest collection of arguments in "Fish Fertilizer: A Native North American Practice?" *Science*, 188 (1975), pp. 26–30. She replies to critics in *Science*, 189 (1975), pp. 946–50. On the exhaustion of grain stores by late winter, see Lorraine E. Williams, *Ft. Shantok and Ft. Corchaug: A Comparative Study of Seventeenth Century Culture Contact in the Long Island Sound Area*, Ph.D. Thesis, New York University, 1972, p. 232, which confirms my critique of Bennett with the help of archaeological evidence.

18. James, *Plymouth Visitors*, p. 79; Williams, *Key*, pp. 128, 163; Wood, *Prospect*, p. 114; Butler, "Maize," pp. 18–19; Mood, "Winthrop on Corn," p. 126; John Josselyn, "An Account of Two Voyages to New-England" (1675), *Massachusetts Historical Society Collections*, 3rd ser., 3 (1833), p. 296.

more familiar birchbark canoes. Whether birch or chestnut, these tippy boats might be taken a mile or more offshore at night to hunt sturgeon by torchlight, or be run down the rapids of rivers in search of salmon or eels. Used for these purposes, canoes could be very dangerous indeed. Roger Williams spoke from personal experience when he said, "It is wonderfull to see how they will venture in those Canoes, and how (being oft overset as I have myself been with them) they will swim a mile, yea two or more safe to Land." Such danger was typical of male work. Whereas the relatively steady labor of agriculture and gathering allowed women to provide the largest share of a village's food without moving far from home, the hunting and fishing of animal protein had much different requirements. These activities took men far from the main camp for many days at a time, and exposed them to much greater risk of injury or death. Hunting and fishing both had irregular work rhythms which sometimes required many intense hours of labor under hard conditions, and sometimes long hours of idleness. Times in camp were often periods of relative leisure and recuperation for men.[19]

As summer drew to a close, female food production reached a climax and male hunting activities began to contribute a greater share of the village's food. Autumn saw the harvesting of corn in addition to the gathering of acorns, chestnuts, groundnuts, and other wild plants. It was a time of extensive festivals when many hundreds of people gathered in dense settlements and consumed much of this surplus food. Gambling, dancing, and eating were combined with rituals—similar to the potlatch ceremonies of the Pacific Northwest—in which wealthy individuals gave away much of what they owned to establish reciprocal relations of obligation with potential followers or allies. The harvest saw greater surplus than any other time of year, and so was often the preferred season for going to war, when food stores both at home and in enemy territory would be at their peak. But once the harvest celebrations were over, Indian households struck their wigwams, stored the

19. Williams, *Key*, pp. 176, 178; Denys, *Acadia*, pp. 407, 420–2; Biard, *Relation*, p. 83; Josselyn, *Two Voyages*, pp. 305–6.

bulk of their corn and beans, and moved to campsites to conduct the fall hunt.[20]

From October to December, when animals like bear and deer were at their fattest, southern villages, much like their counterparts in the north, broke into small bands to assure maximum coverage of the hunting territory. Again the sexual division of labor came into play. Men hunted steadily, using a variety of techniques. Game might be stalked with bow and arrow by a lone hunter or by groups of two or three hundred men working together. It might be snared with traps specially designed to capture a single species; William Bradford, for instance, accidentally walked into a trap strong enough to hold a full-grown deer. Or game might be run between specially planted hedges more than a mile in length until it was finally driven onto the weapons of waiting hunters. Nothing required a greater knowledge of animal behavior than the winter hunt. While men remained in the field, women hauled dead game back to camp. There they butchered and processed it, preparing the hides for clothing, cooking the meat, and smoking some of it for use later in the winter.[21]

By late December, when the snows finally came, the village had probably reassembled in heavily wooded valleys well protected from the weather, where fuel for campfires was easy to obtain. For the rest of the winter, men continued to hunt and fish the surrounding area on snowshoes, while women remained in camp making garments and living on

20. Butler, "Maize," pp. 24–6; Williams, *Key*, p. 231; Wood, *Prospect*, pp. 103–5; Gookin, "Historical Collections," p. 153. Thomas, *Maelstrom of Change*, p. 348, gives archaeological evidence that there was a greater fall consumption of berries than historical sources note. On the range of foods gathered, see Lucia S. Chamberlain, "Plants Used by the Indians of Eastern North America," *American Naturalist*, 35 (1901), pp. 1–10; Gretchen Beardsley, "The Groundnut as Used by the Indians of Eastern North America," *Papers of the Michigan Academy of Sciences, Arts, and Letters*, 25 (1940), pp. 507–15; and Frederic W. Warner, "The Foods of the Connecticut Indians," *Bulletin of the Archaeological Society of Connecticut*, 37 (1972), pp. 27–47. The massive fall consumption of corn in these festivals argues against the assumption in Bennett's overly aggregated statistics that corn was eaten at a constant level year round.

21. Williams, *Key*, pp. 128, 224; Wood, *Prospect*, p. 106; *Mourt's Relation*, p. 8; Thomas, *Maelstrom of Change*, pp. 106–8.

meat and stored grain. Especially for men away from camp, winter was a time of occasional hunger between kills; most carried only a small store of parched corn flour called *nocake* as traveling fare. Like their hunting kindred to the north, they accepted such hunger as inevitable and bore it with stoicism. As Samuel Lee reported, the Indians were "very patient in fasting, & will gird in their bellies till they meet with food; but then none more gluttons or drunk on occasion. Theyle eat 10 times in 24 houres, when they have a beare or a deere."[22]

The hunt provided a crucial source of protein and vitamins during the winter. A single season's catch for a southern New England village of about 400 inhabitants might bring in over 8,500 pounds of edible deer meat and over 7,000 pounds of bear, the two animals which together contributed more than three-fourths of an inland village's winter meat supply. (Coastal Indians who relied more heavily on seafood killed smaller amounts of large game.) Whether or not this meat was essential to a community's survival—given the availability of stored beans and grain—the skins of these and other furbearing animals would furnish the village's clothing for the following year. Simple measurements of caloric content thus tend to undervalue the importance of the fall and winter hunt to an agricultural village's subsistence cycle. Hundreds of square miles had to be stalked to obtain skins for the skirts, leggings, shirts, moccasins, and other articles of clothing Indians would need in the months ahead.[23]

The relationship of the southern New England Indians to their environment was thus, if anything, even more complicated than that of

22. Josselyn, *Two Voyages,* pp. 302–4; Morton, *Canaan,* p. 138; Butler, "Maize," pp. 28–30; Gookin, "Historical Collections," p. 150; George Lyman Kittredge, ed., "Letters of Samuel Lee and Samuel Sewall Relating to New England and the Indians," *Publications of the Colonial Society of Massachusetts,* 14 (1912), p. 148.

23. Thomas, *Maelstrom of Change,* pp. 355–7; Josselyn, *Two Voyages,* p. 297. My arguments about the relationship between hunting, meat, and clothing are derived from Harold Hickerson, "The Virginia Deer and Intertribal Buffer Zones in the Upper Mississippi Valley," in Anthony Leeds and Andrew P. Vayda, eds., *Men, Culture and Animals,* AAAS, Publication No. 78 (1965), pp. 43–65; and Richard Michael Gramly, "Deerskins and Hunting Territories: Competition for a Scarce Resource of the Northeastern Woodlands," *American Antiquity,* 42 (1977), pp. 601–5. Gramly overstates the importance of deer, but his arguments are otherwise sound.

the northern Indians. To the seasons of hunting and fishing shared by both groups were added the agricultural cycles which increased the available food surplus and so enabled denser populations to sustain themselves. In both areas, the mobility of village sites and the shift between various subsistence bases reduced potential strains on any particular segment of the ecosystem, keeping the overall human burden low. But in clearing land for planting and thus concentrating the food base, southern Indians were taking a most important step in reshaping and manipulating the ecosystem.

Clearing fields was relatively easy. By setting fire to wood piled around the base of standing trees, Indian women destroyed the bark and so killed the trees; the women could then plant corn amid the leafless skeletons that were left. During the next several years, many of the trees would topple and could be entirely removed by burning. As one Indian remembered, "An industrious woman, when great many dry logs are fallen, could burn off as many logs in one day as a smart man can chop in two or three days time with an axe." However efficient they were at such clearing, Indian women were frugal with their own labor, and sought to avoid even this much work for as long as they could. That meant returning to the same field site for as long as possible, usually eight to ten years. In time, the soil gradually lost its fertility and eventually necessitated movement to a new field. (Soil exhaustion was to some extent delayed by the action of the nitrogen-fixing beans which Indian women planted with the corn; whether they were aware of it or not, this was one of the side benefits of planting multicrop fields.)[24]

The annual reoccupation of fixed village and planting sites meant that the area around field and camp experienced heavy human use: intensive food gathering, the accumulation of garbage, and, most importantly, the consumption of firewood. One of the main reasons Indians moved to winter camps was that their summer sites had been stripped of the fuel essential for winter fires. Indians believed in big fires—one

24. "Extract from an Indian History," *Massachusetts Historical Society Collections*, 1st ser., 9 (1804), p. 101; a paraphrased version of this can be found in Hedrick Aupaumut, *First Annual Report of the American Society for Promoting the Civilization and General Improvement of the Indian Tribes of the United States* (New Haven, 1824), pp. 41–2.

colonist said that "their Fire is instead of our bed cloaths"—and burned wood heavily all night long, both summer and winter. Such practices could not long be maintained on a single site. As Morton said, "They use not to winter and summer in one place, for that would be a reason to make fuell scarse." The Indians were thus no strangers to the fuel shortages so familiar to the English, even if Indian scarcities were more local. When Verrazzano found twenty-five to thirty leagues of treeless land in Narragansett Bay, or Higginson spoke of thousands of acres in a similar state near Boston, they were observing the effects of agricultural Indians returning to fixed village sites and so consuming their forest energy supply. Indeed, when the Indians wondered why English colonists were coming to their land, the first explanation that occurred to them was a fuel shortage. Roger Williams recounted:

> This question they oft put to me: Why come the *Englishmen* hither? and measuring others by themselves; they say, It is because you want *firing*: for they, having burnt up the *wood* in one place, (wanting draughts [animals] to bring *wood* to them) they are faine to follow the *wood*; and so to remove to a fresh new place for the *woods* sake.

Williams regarded this merely as a quaint instance of Indian provincialism, but in one ironic sense, given what we know of the English forests of the seventeenth century, the Indians were perhaps shrewder than he knew.[25]

The effect of southern New England Indian villages on their environment was not limited to clearing fields or stripping forests for firewood. What most impressed English visitors was the Indians' burning of extensive sections of the surrounding forest once or twice a year. "The Salvages," wrote Thomas Morton, "are accustomed to set fire of

---

25. Morton, *Canaan*, p. 138; Williams, *Key*, pp. 107, 138; see also William Christie MacLeod, "Fuel and Early Civilization," *American Anthropologist*, N.S., 27 (1925), pp. 344–6; Wroth, *Verrazzano*, p. 139; Higginson, *Plantation*, p. 308. Le Clerq gives us a nice portrait of the garbage problems which also led Indians to move their campsites: "They are filthy and vile in their wigwams, of which the approaches are filled with excrements, feathers, chips, shreds of skins, and very often with entrails of the animals or the fishes which they take in hunting or fishing" (*Gaspesia*, p. 253).

the Country in all places where they come, and to burne it twize a yeare, viz: at the Spring, and the fall of the leafe." Here was the reason that the southern forests were so open and parklike; not because the trees naturally grew thus, but because the Indians preferred them so. As William Wood observed, the fire "consumes all the underwood and rubbish which otherwise would overgrow the country, making it un-passable, and spoil their much affected hunting." The result was a for-est of large, widely spaced trees, few shrubs, and much grass and herbage. "In those places where the Indians inhabit," said Wood, "there is scarce a bush or bramble or any cumbersome underwood to be seen in the more champion ground." By removing underwood and fallen trees, the Indians reduced the total accumulated fuel at ground level. With only small nonwoody plants to consume, the annual fires moved quickly, burned with relatively low temperatures, and soon extin-guished themselves. They were more ground fires than forest fires, not usually involving larger trees, and so they rarely grew out of control. Fires of this kind could be used to drive game for hunting, to clear fields for planting, and, on at least one occasion, to fend off European invaders.[26]

26. Quotations are from Morton, *Canaan*, p. 172; Wood, *Prospect*, p. 38; and, on fending off invaders, Martin Pring, "A Voyage Set Out from the Citie of Bristoll, 1603," in Henry S. Burrage, ed., *Early English and French Voyages* (New York, 1906), p. 351. Other primary documents on burning are Higginson, p. 308; Edward Johnson, *Johnson's Wonder-Working Providence*, J. Franklin Jameson, ed. (New York, 1910), p. 85; Benjamin Trumbull, *A Complete History of Connecticut* (Hartford, 1797), p. 23. The classic essay on Indian burning is Gordon M. Day, "The Indian as an Ecological Factor in the Northeastern Forest," *Ecology*, 34 (1953), pp. 329–46; see also the various articles cited in the biblio-graphical essay. The chief critique of this interpretation of Indian burning is Hugh M. Raup, "Recent Changes of Climate and Vegetation in Southern New England and Adjacent New York," *Journal of the Arnold Arboretum*, 18 (1937), pp. 79–117. Raup believed that "to picture a wholesale conflagration in Massachusetts, Rhode Island, Connecticut, and south-ern New York State as would involve most of the inflammable woods every year, or even every 10 to 20 years, is inconceivable" (p. 84). In this, he failed to take account of the reduced fuel burden at ground level in forests which are repeatedly burned; the very fact of regular burning kept ground fires from reaching the canopy. But Raup was no doubt right that the *entirety* of southern New England was never regularly burned; I have limited the claims of my argument to the local vicinity of village sites. A recent article defends Raup but basically confirms my emphasis on local burning: Emily W. B. Russell, "Indian-Set Fires in the Forests of the Northeastern United States," *Ecology*, 64 (1983), pp. 78–88.

Northern Indians do not appear to have engaged in such burning. Because they did not practice agriculture and so were less tied to particular sites, they had less incentive to alter the environment of a given spot. Their chief mode of transportation was the canoe, so that they had less need of an open forest for traveling. Moreover, many of the northern tree species were not well adapted to repeated burning, and northern forests tended to accumulate enough fuel at ground level that, once a fire got started, it usually reached the canopy and burned out of control. Conditions in southern New England were quite different. Denser, fixed settlements encouraged heavy use of more limited forest areas, and most inland travel was by land. The trees of the southern forest, once fully grown, suffered little more than charred bark if subjected to ground fires of short duration. If destroyed, they regenerated themselves by sprouting from their roots: chestnuts, oaks, and hickories, the chief constituents of the southern upland forests, are in fact sometimes known as "sprout hardwoods." Repeated fires tended to destroy trees and shrubs which lacked this ability, including hemlock, beech, and juniper. Even the white pine, which often sprang up after large forest fires, tended to be killed off if subjected to regular burning because of its inability to sprout, and so was uncommon in the vicinity of active Indian settlements.[27]

Colonial observers understood burning as being part of Indian efforts to simplify hunting and facilitate travel; most failed to see its subtler ecological effects. In the first place, it increased the rate at which forest nutrients were recycled into the soil, so that grasses, shrubs, and nonwoody plants tended to grow more luxuriantly following a fire than

27. Regina Flannery, "An Analysis of Coastal Algonquian Culture," *Catholic University Anthropological Series*, 7 (1939), pp. 14, 167; Day, "Indian as Ecological Factor," pp. 338–9. Northern hardwood forests in the Midwest were probably burned completely by lightning and man-made fires on a hundred-year cycle, but the same was apparently not true of the northern New England forest. See Orrie L. Loucks, "Evolution of Diversity, Efficiency and Community Stability," *American Zoologist*, 10 (1970), pp. 17–25; Sidney S. Frissell, Jr., "The Importance of Fire as a Natural Ecological Factor in Itasca State Park, Minnesota," *Quaternary Research*, 3 (1973), pp. 397–407; Craig C. Lorimer, "The Presettlement Forest and Natural Disturbance Cycle of Northeastern Maine," *Ecology*, 58 (1977), pp. 139–48; and F. Herbert Bormann and Gene E. Likens, "Catastrophic Disturbance and the Steady State in Northern Hardwood Forests," *American Scientist*, 67 (1979), pp. 660–9.

they had before. Especially on old Indian fields, fire created conditions favorable to strawberries, blackberries, raspberries, and other gatherable foods. Grasses like the little bluestem were rare in a mature forest, but in a forest burned by Indians they became abundant. The thinning of the forest canopy, which resulted from the elimination of smaller trees, allowed more light to reach the forest floor and further aided such growth. The soil became warmer and drier, discouraging tree species which preferred moister conditions—beech, sugar maple, red maple, black birch—and favoring drier species like oaks when regular burning was allowed to lapse. Burning also tended to destroy plant diseases and pests, not to mention the fleas which inevitably became abundant around Indian settlements. Roger Williams summed up these effects by commenting that "this burning of the Wood to them they count a Benefit, both for destroying of vermin, and keeping downe the Weeds and thickets."[28]

Selective Indian burning thus promoted the mosaic quality of New England ecosystems, creating forests in many different states of ecological succession. In particular, regular fires promoted what ecologists call the "edge effect." By encouraging the growth of extensive regions which resembled the boundary areas between forests and grasslands, Indians created ideal habitats for a host of wildlife species. Of all early American observers, only the astute Timothy Dwight seems to have commented on this phenomenon. "The object of these conflagrations," he wrote, "was to produce fresh and sweet pasture for the purpose of alluring the deer to the spots on which they had been kindled." The effect was even subtler than Dwight realized: because the enlarged edge areas actually raised the total herbivorous food supply, they not merely attracted game but helped create much larger populations of it. Indian

28. Williams, *Key*, pp. 165, 168, 191. On fire effects discussed in this and the subsequent paragraph, see William A. Niering, *et al.*, "Prescribed Burning in Southern New England: Introduction to Long-Range Studies," *Proceedings of the Annual Tall Timbers Fire Ecology Conference*, 10 (1970), pp. 267–86; Silas Little, "Effects of Fire on Temperate Forests: Northeastern United States," in T. T. Kozlowski and C. E. Ahlgren, eds., *Fire and Ecosystems* (New York, 1974), pp. 225–50; and the articles in the special October 1973 issue of *Quaternary Research*, especially the superb summary in the Introduction by H. E. Wright, Jr., and M. L. Heinselman, pp. 319–28.

burning promoted the increase of exactly those species whose abundance so impressed English colonists: elk, deer, beaver, hare, porcupine, turkey, quail, ruffed grouse, and so on. When these populations increased, so did the carnivorous eagles, hawks, lynxes, foxes, and wolves. In short, Indians who hunted game animals were not just taking the "unplanted bounties of nature"; in an important sense, they were harvesting a foodstuff which they had consciously been instrumental in creating.[29]

Few English observers could have realized this. People accustomed to keeping domesticated animals lacked the conceptual tools to realize that Indians were practicing a more distant kind of husbandry of their own. To the colonists, only Indian women appeared to do legitimate work; the men idled away their time in hunting, fishing, and wantonly burning the woods, none of which seemed like genuinely productive activities to Europeans. English observers often commented about how hard Indian women worked. "It is almost incredible," Williams wrote, "what burthens the poore women carry of *Corne*, of *Fish*, of *Beanes*, of *Mats*, and a childe besides." The criticism of Indian males in such remarks was usually explicit. "Their wives are their slaves," wrote Christopher Levett, "and do all the work; the men will do nothing but kill beasts, fish, etc." For their part, Indian men seemed to acknowledge that their wives were a principal source of wealth and mocked Englishmen for not working their wives harder. According to the lawyer Thomas Lechford, "They say, *Englishman* much foole, for spoiling good working creatures, meaning women: And when they see any of our *English* women sewing with their needles, or working coifes, or such things, they will cry out, Lazie squaes."[30]

Part of the problem with these cross-cultural criticisms was the inability or refusal by either side to observe fully how much each sex was con-

29. Odum, *Fundamentals of Ecology*, pp. 157–9; Timothy Dwight, *Travels in New England and New York* (1821), Barbara Miller Solomon, ed. (Cambridge, MA, 1969), IV, pp. 38–9; Williams, *Key*, p. 165. E. L. Jones discusses these edge effects in his "Creative Disruptions in American Agriculture, 1620–1820," *Agricultural History*, 48 (1974), pp. 514–15, although I think he becomes confused when he describes burned forests as dense, dark, and deep, with few birds. Exactly the opposite was the case.

30. Quotations on women's work are from Williams, *Key*, p. 122 (in which he refers specifically to the loads women bear in moving camp); Levett, "Voyage," p. 178; and Thomas Lechford, *Plain Dealing* (1642), *Massachusetts Historical Society Collections*, 3rd

tributing to the total food supply. Indian men, seeing Englishmen working in the fields, could not understand why English *women* were not doing such work. At the same time, they failed to see the contributions colonial women were actually making: gardening, cooking, spinning and weaving textiles, sewing clothing, tending milch cows, making butter and cheese, caring for children, and so on. The English, for their part, had trouble seeing hunting and fishing—which most regarded as leisure activities— as involving real labor, and so tended to brand Indian men as lazy. "The Men," wrote Francis Higginson, "for the most part live idely, they doe nothing but hunt and fish: their wives set their Corne and doe all their other worke." It is quite possible that Indian women—like women in many cultures—did indeed bear a disproportionate share of the work burden. But even if the advent of agriculture in southern New England had shifted the balance between meat and vegetables in the Indian diet—lowering the importance of meat and incidentally changing the significance of each sex's role in acquiring food—the annual subsistence cycle still saw Indian communities giving considerable attention to hunting meat, the tradition- ally more masculine activity. As we shall see, the English used this Indian reliance on hunting not only to condemn Indian men as lazy savages but to deny that Indians had a rightful claim to the land they hunted. European perceptions of what constituted a proper use of the environment thus rein- forced what became a European ideology of conquest.[31]

The relationships of the New England Indians to their environment, whether in the north or the south, revolved around the wheel of the sea- sons: throughout New England, Indians held their demands on the

ser., 3 (1833), p. 103. See also Morrell, "New England," p. 136; and Wood, *Prospect*, pp. 92, 115–16. Two recent articles assert a much more egalitarian relationship between Indian men and women: Robert Steven Grumet, "Sunksquaws, Shamans, and Tradeswomen: Middle Atlantic Coastal Algonkian Women During the 17th and 18th Centuries," in Mona Etienne and Eleanor Leacock, eds., *Women and Colonization* (New York, 1980), pp. 43–62; and Trudie Lamb, "Squaw Sachems: Women Who Rule," *Artifacts*, 9:2 (Winter/Spring 1981), pp. 1–3. These both argue from the experience of elite women in leadership roles, and Grumet seems to me unsuccessful in proving his claim that the sexual division of la- bor was not fairly strict.

31. Francis Higginson, *New-Englands Plantation* (1630), *Massachusetts Historical So- ciety Proceedings*, 62 (1929), p. 316. For further materials on sexual work roles, see James Axtell, ed., *The Indian Peoples of Eastern America: A Documentary History of the Sexes* (New York, 1981), pp. 103–39.

ecosystem to a minimum by moving their settlements from habitat to habitat. As one of the earliest European visitors noted, "They move . . . from one place to another according to the richness of the site and the season." By using other species when they were most plentiful, Indians made sure that no single species became overused. It was a way of life to match the patchwork of the landscape. On the coast were fish and shell-fish, and in the salt marshes were migratory birds. In the forests and low-land thickets were deer and beaver; in cleared upland fields were corn and beans; and everywhere were the wild plants whose uses were too numerous to catalog. For New England Indians, ecological diversity, whether natural or artificial, meant abundance, stability, and a regular supply of the things that kept them alive.[32]

The ecological relationships which the English sought to reproduce in New England were no less cyclical than those of the Indians; they were only simpler and more concentrated. The English too had their seasons of want and plenty, and rapidly adjusted their false expectations of perpetual natural wealth to match New World realities. But whereas Indian villages moved from habitat to habitat to find maximum abundance through minimal work, and so reduce their impact on the land, the English believed in and required permanent settlements. Once a village was established, its improvements—cleared fields, pastures, buildings, fences, and so on—were regarded as more or less fixed features of the landscape. English fixity sought to replace Indian mobility; here was the central conflict in the ways Indians and colonists interacted with their environments. The struggle was over two ways of living and using the seasons of the year, and it expressed itself in how two peoples conceived of property, wealth, and boundaries on the landscape.

32. Wroth, *Verrazzano*, p. 139. In areas where a diversity of habitats was lacking, like central Vermont, Indian populations were very low or absent. See William A. Bayreuther, "Environmental Diversity as a Factor in Modeling Prehistoric Settlement Patterns: Southeastern Vermont's Black River Valley," *Man in the Northeast*, 19 (1980), pp. 83–93. But see also Gordon M. Day, "The Indian Occupation of Vermont," *Vermont History*, 33 (1965), pp. 365–74.

Changes in the Land (1983)

Alice Walker wrote this piece to celebrate the birth of Martin Luther King Jr., and it helps mark the increasing confluence of social justice and environmental ideas. Walker (b. 1944) grew up in Georgia, the eighth child of sharecroppers. She made it out: first to Spelman College and then to Sarah Lawrence, where she became active in the civil rights movement of the early 1960s. In 1982, just before this talk, she published *The Color Purple*, a spectacularly successful novel about the struggle against racism and patriarchy that was made into a well-received movie and a Broadway musical. She writes with lovely muscularity, no more so than in this short essay about power in the world and how it has affected the earth.

Everything Is a Human Being

> . . There are people who think that only people have emotions like *pride, fear, and joy, but those who know will tell you all things are alive, perhaps not in the same way we are alive, but each in its own way, as should be, for we are not all the same. And though different from us in shape and life span, different in Time and Knowing, yet are trees alive. And rocks. And water. And all know emotion.*
>
> —*Anne Cameron*, DAUGHTERS OF COPPER WOMAN*

Some years ago a friend and I walked out into the countryside to listen to what the Earth was saying, and to better hear our own thoughts. We had prepared ourselves to experience what in the old days would have been called a vision, and what today probably has no name that is not found somewhat amusing by many. Because there is

*Vancouver: Press Gang, 1981.

no longer countryside that is not owned by someone, we stopped at the entrance to a large park, many miles distant from the city. By the time we had walked a hundred yards, I felt I could go no farther and lay myself down where I was, across the path in a grove of trees. For several hours I lay there, and other people entering the park had to walk around me. But I was hardly aware of them. I was in intense dialogue with the trees.

As I was lying there, really across their feet, I felt or "heard" with my feelings the distinct request from them that I remove myself. But these are not feet, I thought, peering at them closely, but roots. Roots do not tell you to go away. It was then that I looked up and around me into the "faces." These "faces" were all middle-aged to old conifers, and they were all suffering from some kind of disease, the most obvious sign of which was a light green fungus, resembling moss and lichen, that nearly covered them, giving them—in spite of the bright spring sunlight—an eerie, fantastical aspect. Beneath this greenish envelopment, the limbs of the trees, the "arms," were bent in hundreds of shapes in a profusion of deformity. Indeed, the trees reminded me of nothing so much as badly rheumatoid elderly people, as I began to realize how difficult, given their bent shapes, it would be for their limbs to move freely in the breeze. Clearly these were sick people, or trees; irritable, angry, and growing old in pain. And they did not want me lying on their gnarled and no doubt aching feet.

Looking again at their feet, or roots—which stuck up all over the ground and directly beneath my cheek—I saw that the ground from which they emerged was gray and dead-looking, as if it had been poisoned. Aha, I thought, this is obviously a place where chemicals were dumped. The soil has been poisoned, the trees afflicted, slowly dying, and they do not like it. I hastily communicated this deduction to the trees and asked that they understand it was not I who had done this. I just moved to this part of the country, I said. But they were not appeased. Get up. Go away, they replied. But I refused to move. Nor could I. I needed to make them agree to my innocence.

The summer before this encounter I lived in the northern hills of California, where much logging is done. Each day on the highway, as I went to buy groceries or to the river to swim, I saw the loggers' trucks, like enormous hearses, carrying the battered bodies of the old sisters and brothers, as I thought of them, down to the lumberyards in the valley. In fact, this sight, in an otherwise peaceful setting, distressed me— as if I lived in a beautiful neighborhood that daily lost hundreds of its finest members, while I sat mournful but impotent beside the avenue that carried them away.

It was of this endless funeral procession that I thought as I lay across the feet of the sick old relatives whose "safe" existence in a public park (away from the logging trucks) had not kept them safe at all.

I *love* trees, I said.

Human, *please*, they replied.

But I do not cut you down in the prime of life. I do not haul your mutilated and stripped bodies shamelessly down the highway. It is the lumber companies, I said.

Just go away, said the trees.

All my life you have meant a lot to me, I said. I love your grace, your dignity, your serenity, your generosity . . .

Well, said the trees, before I actually finished this list, we find you without grace, without dignity, without serenity, and there is no generosity in you either—just ask any tree. You butcher us, you burn us, you grow us only to destroy us. Even when we grow ourselves, you kill us, or cut off our limbs. That we are alive and have feelings means nothing to you.

But *I*, as an individual, am innocent, I said. Though it did occur to me that I live in a wood house, I eat on a wood table, I sleep on a wood bed.

My uses of wood are modest, I said, and always tailored to my needs. I do not slash through whole forests, destroying hundreds of trees in the process of "harvesting" a few.

But finally, after much discourse, I understood what the trees were telling me: Being an individual doesn't matter. Just as human beings perceive all trees as one (didn't a U.S. official say recently that "when you've seen one tree, you've seen 'em all"?), all human beings, to the trees, are one. We are judged by our worst collective behavior, since it is so vast; not by our singular best. The Earth holds us responsible for our crimes against it, not as individuals, but as a species—this was the message of the trees. I found it to be a terrifying thought. For I had assumed that the Earth, the spirit of the Earth, noticed exceptions—those who wantonly damage it and those who do not. But the Earth is wise. It has given itself into the keeping of all, and all are therefore accountable.

And how hard it will be to change our worst behavior!

Last spring I moved even deeper into the country, and went eagerly up the hill from my cabin to start a new garden. As I was patting the soil around the root of a new tomato plant, I awakened a small garden snake who lived in the tomato bed. Though panicked and not knowing at the time what kind of snake it was, I tried calmly to direct it out of the garden, now that I, a human being, had arrived to take possession of it. It went. The next day, however, because the tomato bed *was* its home, the snake came back. Once more I directed it away. The third time it came back, I called a friend—who thought I was badly frightened, from my nervous behavior—and he killed it. It looked very small and harmless, hanging from the end of his hoe.

Everything I was ever taught about snakes—that they are dangerous, frightful, repulsive, sinister—went into the murder of this snake person, who was only, after all, trying to remain in his or her home, perhaps the only home he or she had ever known. Even my ladylike "nervousness" in its presence was learned behavior. I knew at once that killing the snake was not the first act that should have occurred in my new garden, and I grieved that I had apparently learned nothing, as a human being, since the days of Adam and Eve.

Even on a practical level, killing this small, no doubt bewildered and disoriented creature made poor sense, because throughout the summer snakes just like it regularly visited the garden (and deer, by the way, ate all the tomatoes), so that it appeared to me that the little snake I killed was always with me. Occasionally a very large mama or papa snake wandered into the cabin yard, as if to let me know its child had been murdered, and it knew who was responsible for it.

These garden snakes, said my neighbors, are harmless; they eat mice and other pests that invade the garden. In this respect, they are even helpful to humans. And yet, I am still afraid of them, because that is how I was taught to be. Deep in the psyche of most of us there is this fear—and long ago, I do not doubt, in the psyche of ancient peoples, there was a similar fear of trees. And of course a fear of other human beings, for that is where all fear of natural things leads us: to fear of ourselves, fear of each other, and fear even of the spirit of the Universe, because out of fear we often greet its outrageousness with murder.

> That fall, they say, the last of the bison herds was slaughtered by the Wasichus.* I can remember when the bison were so many that they could not be counted, but more and more Wasichus came to kill them until there were only heaps of bones scattered where they used to be. The Wasichus did not kill them to eat; they killed them for the metal that makes them crazy, and they took only the hides to sell. Sometimes they did not even take the hides, only the tongues; and I have heard that fire-boats came down the Missouri River loaded with dried bison tongues. You can see that the men who did this were crazy. Sometimes they did not even take the tongues; they just killed and killed because they liked to do that. When we hunted bison, we killed only what we needed. And when there was nothing left but heaps of bones, the Wasichus came and gathered up even the bones and sold them.
>
> —BLACK ELK SPEAKS[†]

In this way, the Wasichus starved the Indians into submission, and forced them to live on impoverished "reservations" in their own land. Like the little snake in my garden, many of the Indians returned again and again to their ancient homes and hunting grounds, only to be driven off with greater and greater brutality until they were broken or killed.

---

[*]Wasichu was a term used by the Oglala Sioux to designate the white man, but it had no reference to the color of his skin. It means: He who takes the fat. It is possible to be white and not a Wasichu or to be a Wasichu and not white. In the United States, historically speaking, Wasichu of color have usually been in the employ of the military, which is the essence of Wasichu.

[†]By John G. Neihardt (New York: William Morrow, 1932).

The Wasichus in Washington who ordered the slaughter of bison and Indian and those on the prairies who did the deed are frequently thought of, by some of us, as "fathers of our country," along with the Indian killers and slave owners Washington and Jefferson and the like.

Yet what "father" would needlessly exterminate any of his children?

Are not the "fathers," rather, those Native Americans, those "wild Indians" like Black Elk, who said, "It is the story of all life that is holy and is good to tell, and of us two-leggeds sharing in it with the four-leggeds and the wings of the air and all green things; for these are children of one mother and their father is one Spirit"?

Indeed, America, the country, acts so badly, so much like a spoiled adolescent boy, because it has never acknowledged the "fathers" that existed before the "fathers" of its own creation. It has been led instead—in every period of its brief and troubled history—by someone who might be called Younger Brother (after the character in E. L. Doctorow's novel *Ragtime*, set in turn-of-the-century America), who occasionally blunders into good and useful deeds, but on the whole never escapes from the white Victorian house of racist and sexist repression, puritanism, and greed.

The Wasichu speaks, in all his U.S. history books, of "opening up virgin lands." Yet there were people living here, on "Turtle Island," as the Indians called it, for thousands of years; but living so gently on the land that to Wasichu eyes it looked untouched. Yes, it was "still," as they wrote over and over again, with lust, "virginal." If it were a bride, the Wasichus would have permitted it to wear a white dress. For centuries on end Native Americans lived on the land, making love to it through worship and praise, without once raping or defiling it. The Wasichus— who might have chosen to imitate the Indians, but didn't because to them the *Indians* were savages—have been raping and defiling it since the day they came. It is ironic to think that if the Indians who were here then "discovered" America as it is now, they would find little reason to want to stay. This is a fabulous *land*, not because it is a country, but because it is soaked in so many years of love. And though the Native Americans fought as much as any other people among themselves (much to their loss!), never did they fight against the earth, which they correctly perceived as their mother, or against their father, the sky, now thought of mainly as "outer space," where primarily bigger and "better" wars have a projected future.

The Wasichus may be fathers of the country, but the Native Americans, the Indians, are the parents ("guardians," as they've always said they are) of the land.* And, in my opinion, as Earthling above all, we must get to know these parents "from our mother's side" before it is too late. It has been proved that the land can exist without the country—and be better for it; it has not been proved (though some space enthusiasts appear to think so) that the country can exist without the land. And the land is being killed.

Sometimes when I teach, I try to help my students understand what it must feel like to be a slave. Not many of them can go to South Africa and ask the black people enslaved by the Wasichus there, or visit the migrant-labor camps kept hidden from their neighborhoods, so we talk about slavery as it existed in America, a little over a hundred years ago. One day I asked if any of them felt they had been treated "like dirt." No; many of them felt they had been treated badly at some time in their lives (they were largely middle class and white) but no one felt he or she had been treated like dirt. Yet what pollution you breathe, I pointed out, which the atmosphere also breathes; what a vast number of poisons you eat with your food, which the Earth has eaten just before you. How unexpectedly many of you will fall ill and die from cancer because the very ground on which you build your homes will be carcinogenic. As the Earth is treated "like dirt"—its dignity demeaned by wanton dumpings of lethal materials all across its proud face and in its crystal seas—so are we all treated.

Some of us have become used to thinking that woman is the nigger of the world, that a person of color is the nigger of the world, that a

*Though much of what we know of our Indian ancestors concerns the male, it is good to remember who produced him; that women in some tribes were shamans, could vote, and among the Onondaga still elect the men who lead the tribe. And, inasmuch as "women's work" has always involved cleaning up after the young, as well as teaching them principles by which to live, we have our Indian female parent to thank for her care of Turtle Island, as well as the better documented male who took her instructions so utterly to heart.

poor person is the nigger of the world. But, in truth, Earth itself has become the nigger of the world. It is perceived, ironically, as other, alien, evil, and threatening by those who are finding they cannot draw a healthful breath without its cooperation. While the Earth is poisoned, everything it supports is poisoned. While the Earth is enslaved, none of us is free. While the Earth is "a nigger," it has no choice but to think of us all as Wasichus. While it is "treated like dirt," so are we.

In this time, when human life—because of human greed, avarice, ignorance, and fear—hangs by a thread, it is of disarmament that every thoughtful person thinks; for regardless of whether we all agree that we deserve to live, or not, as a species, most of us have the desire. But disarmament must also occur in the heart and in the spirit. We must absolutely reject the way of the Wasichu that we are so disastrously traveling, the way that respects most (above nature, obviously above life itself, above even the spirit of the Universe) the "metal that makes men crazy." The United States, the country, has no doubt damned its soul because of how it has treated others, and if it is true that we reap what we sow, as a country we have only to recognize the poison inside us as the poison we forced others to drink. But the land is innocent. It is still Turtle Island, and more connected to the rest of the Universe than to the United States government. It is beginning to throw up the poisons it has been forced to drink, and we must help it by letting go of our own; for until it is healthy and well, we cannot be.

Our primary connection is to the Earth, our mother and father; regardless of who "owns" pieces and parts, we, as sister and brother beings to the "four-leggeds (and the fishes) and the wings of the air," share the whole. No one should be permitted to buy a part of our Earth to dump poisons in, just as we would not sell one of our legs to be used as a trash can.

Many of us are afraid to abandon the way of the Wasichu because we have become addicted to his way of death. The Wasichu has promised us so many good things, and has actually delivered several. But "progress," once claimed by the present chief of the Wasichus to be their "most important product," has meant hunger, misery, enslavement, unemployment, and worse to millions of people on the globe. The many time-saving devices we have become addicted to, because of our "progress," have freed us to watch endless reruns of commercials, sitcoms, and murders.

Our thoughts must be on how to restore to the Earth its dignity as a living being; how to stop raping and plundering it as a matter of course. We must begin to develop the consciousness that everything has equal rights because existence itself is equal. In other words, we are all here: trees, people, snakes, alike. We must realize that even tiny insects in the South American jungle know how to make plastic, for instance; they have simply chosen not to cover the Earth with it. The Wasichu's uniqueness is not his ability to "think" and "invent"—from the evidence, almost everything does this in some fashion or other—it is his profound unnaturalness. His lack of harmony with other peoples and places, and with the very environment to which he owes his life.

In James Mooney's *Myths of the Cherokee and Sacred Formulas of the Cherokees*, collected between 1887 and 1890, he relates many interesting practices of the original inhabitants of this land, among them the custom of asking pardon of slain or offended animals. And in writing about the needless murder of the snake who inhabited our garden—the snake's and mine—I ask its pardon and, in the telling of its death, hope to save the lives of many of its kin.

> The missionary Washburn [says Mooney] tells how among the Cherokees of Arkansas, he was once riding along, accompanied by an Indian on foot, when they discovered a poisonous snake coiled beside the path. "I observed Blanket turned aside to avoid the serpent, but made no sign of attack, and I requested the interpreter to get down and kill it. He did so, and I then inquired of Blanket why he did not kill the serpent. He answered, 'I never kill snakes and so snakes never kill me.'"
>
> The trader Henry [Mooney observes elsewhere] tells of similar behavior among the Objibwa of Lake Superior in 1764. While gathering wood he was startled by a sudden rattle. . . . "I no sooner saw the snake, than I hastened to the canoe, in order to procure my gun; but, the Indians observing what I was doing, inquired the occasion, and being informed, begged me to

desist. At the same time, they followed me to the spot, with their pipes and tobacco pouches in their hands. On returning, I found the snake still coiled.

"The Indians, on their part, surrounded it, all addressing it by turns, and calling it their *grandfather*, but yet keeping at some distance. During this part of the ceremony, they filled their pipes; and now each blew the smoke toward the snake, who, as it appeared to me, really received it with pleasure. In a word, after remaining coiled, and receiving incense, for the space of half an hour, it stretched itself along the ground, in visible good humor. Its length was between four and five feet. Having remained outstretched for some time, at last it moved slowly away, the Indians following it, and still addressing it by the title of grandfather, beseeching it to take care of their families during their absence, and to be pleased to open the heart of Sir William Johnson (the British Indian Agent, whom they were about to visit) so that he might *show them charity*, and fill their canoe with rum. One of the chiefs added a petition, that the snake would take no notice of the insult which had been offered by the Englishman, who would even have put him to death, but for the interference of the Indians, to whom it was hoped he would impute no part of the offense. They further requested, that he would remain, and inhabit their country, and not return among the English. . . ."

What makes this remarkable tale more so is that the "bite" of the Englishman's rum was to afflict the Indians far more severely than the bite of any tremendous number of poisonous snakes.

That the Indians were often sexist, prone to war, humanly flawed, I do not dispute. It is their light step upon the Earth that I admire and would have us emulate. The new way to exist on the Earth may well be the ancient way of the steadfast lovers of this particular land. No one has better appreciated Earth than the Native American. Whereas to the Wasichus only the white male attains full human status, everything to the Indian was a relative. Everything was a human being.

As I finish writing this, I notice a large spider sleeping underneath my desk. It does not look like me. It is a different size. But that it loves life as I do, I have no doubt. It is something to think about as I study its many strange but oddly beautiful dozen or so legs, its glowing coral-and-amber coloring, its thick web, whose intricate pattern I would never be able to duplicate. Imagine building your house from your own spit!

In its modesty, its fine artistry and self-respecting competency, is it not like some gay, independent person many of us have known? Perhaps a rule for permissible murder should be that beyond feeding and clothing and sheltering ourselves, even abundantly, we should be allowed to destroy only what we ourselves can re-create. We cannot re-create this world. We cannot re-create "wilderness." We cannot even, truly, re-create ourselves. Only our behavior can we re-create, or create anew.

> Hear me, four quarters of the world—a relative I am! Give me the strength to walk the soft earth, a relative to all that is! Give me the eyes to see and the strength to understand, that I may be like you. . . .
>
> Great Spirit, Great Spirit, my Grandfather, all over the earth the faces of living things are all alike. With tenderness have these come up out of the ground. Look upon these faces of children without number and with children in their arms, that they may face the winds and walk the good road to the day of quiet.
> —BLACK ELK SPEAKS

Note

The Onondagas are the "Keepers of the Fire" of the Six Nation Confederacy in New York state. The Confederacy (originally composed of five nations) is perhaps the oldest democratic union of nations in the Western world, dating back roughly to the time of the Magna Carta. It is governed under an ancient set of principles known as the "Gayaneshakgowa," or Great Law of Peace, which in written form is the constitution of the Six Nation Confederacy.

This remarkable document contains what well may have been the first detailed pronouncements on democratic popular elections, the consent of the governed, the need to monitor and approve the behavior of governmental leaders, the importance of public opinion, the rights of women, guarantees of free speech and religion, and the equitable distribution of wealth.

Benjamin Franklin and Thomas Jefferson acknowledged in the mid-18th century that their own ideas for a democratic confederacy were based largely on what they had learned from the Six Nations. A century later Friedrich Engels paid a similar tribute to the Great Law of Peace while making his contribution to the theory of Marxism.

—Jon Stewart, Pacific News Service

Living by the Word (1989)

E. O. Wilson (b. 1929) has delivered staggering insights on the average of one a decade. In the 1960s, he and Robert MacArthur coined the phrase "island biogeography" to explain the effects of habitat size and isolation on extinction rates, work that is now a key tool in conservation planning. In the 1970s, he coined the term "sociobiology" to argue for a strong genetic role in human behavior, an idea that offended left-wing orthodoxies of the time (his classes at Harvard were routinely interrupted by protesters), but that won him the Pulitzer Prize for *On Human Nature* (1979). In 1984 his book *Biophilia* proposed that humans had an innate affection for other living systems, deeply rooted in our biology. His life would certainly seem to prove the case: he took up the lifelong study of ants as a child, in part because an eye injury made it easier for him to study small species he could observe up close. As his academic fame grew, he used it tirelessly to advocate for conservation, especially a strategy for protecting "hotspots" around the tropics that were particularly rich in diverse species. And in recent years he has worked hard to bridge the divide between science and religion, arguing for a common interest in the protection of creation.

Bernhardsdorp

At Bernhardsdorp on an otherwise ordinary tropical morning, the sunlight bore down harshly, the air was still and humid, and life appeared withdrawn and waiting. A single thunderhead lay on the horizon, its immense anvil shape diminished by distance, an intimation of the rainy season still two or three weeks away. A footpath tunneled through the trees and lianas, pointing toward the Saramacca River and far beyond, to the Orinoco and Amazon basins. The woodland around the village struggled up from the crystalline sands of the Zanderij formation.

It was a miniature archipelago of glades and creekside forest enclosed by savanna—grassland with scattered trees and high bushes. To the south it expanded to become a continuous lacework fragmenting the savanna and transforming it in turn into an archipelago. Then, as if conjured upward by some unseen force, the woodland rose by stages into the triple-canopied rain forest, the principal habitat of South America's awesome ecological heartland.

In the village a woman walked slowly around an iron cooking pot, stirring the fire beneath with a soot-blackened machete. Plump and barefoot, about thirty years old, she wore two long pigtails and a new cotton dress in a rose floral print. From politeness, or perhaps just shyness, she gave no outward sign of recognition. I was an apparition, out of place and irrelevant, about to pass on down the footpath and out of her circle of required attention. At her feet a small child traced meanders in the dirt with a stick. The village around them was a cluster of no more than ten one-room dwellings. The walls were made of palm leaves woven into a herringbone pattern in which dark bolts zigzagged upward and to the onlooker's right across flesh-colored squares. The design was the sole indigenous artifact on display. Bernhardsdorp was too close to Paramaribo, Surinam's capital, with its flood of cheap manufactured products to keep the look of a real Arawak village. In culture as in name, it had yielded to the colonial Dutch.

A tame peccary watched me with beady concentration from beneath the shadowed eaves of a house. With my own taxonomist's eye I registered the defining traits of the collared species, *Dicotyles tajacu*: head too large for the piglike body, fur coarse and brindled, neck circled by a pale thin stripe, snout tapered, ears erect, tail reduced to a nub. Poised on stiff little dancer's legs, the young male seemed perpetually fierce and ready to charge yet frozen in place, like the metal boar on an ancient Gallic standard.

A note: Pigs, and presumably their close relatives the peccaries, are among the most intelligent of animals. Some biologists believe them to be brighter than dogs, roughly the rivals of elephants and porpoises. They form herds of ten to twenty members, restlessly patrolling territories of about a square mile. In certain ways they behave more like wolves and dogs than social ungulates. They recognize one another as individuals, sleep with their fur touching, and bark back and forth when on the move. The adults are organized into dominance orders in which the females are ascendant over males, the reverse of the usual mammalian arrangement. They attack in groups if cornered, their scapular fur bristling outward like porcupine quills, and can slash to the bone with sharp canine teeth. Yet individuals are easily tamed if captured as infants and their repertory stunted by the impoverishing constraints of human care.

So I felt uneasy—perhaps the word is embarrassed—in the presence of a captive individual. This young adult was a perfect anatomical specimen with only the rudiments of social behavior. But he was much more: a powerful presence, programed at birth to respond through learning steps in exactly the collared-peccary way and no other to the immemorial environment from which he had been stolen, now a mute speaker trapped inside the unnatural clearing, like a messenger to me from an unexplored world.

I stayed in the village only a few minutes. I had come to study ants and other social insects living in Surinam. No trivial task: over a hundred species of ants and termites are found within a square mile of average South American tropical forest. When all the animals in a randomly selected patch of woodland are collected together and weighed, from tapirs and parrots down to the smallest insects and roundworms, one third of the weight is found to consist of ants and termites. If you close your eyes and lay your hand on a tree trunk almost anywhere in the tropics until you feel something touch it, more times than not the crawler will be an ant. Kick open a rotting log and termites pour out. Drop a crumb of bread on the ground and within minutes ants of one kind or another drag it down a nest hole. Foraging ants are the chief predators of insects and other small animals in the tropical forest, and termites are the key animal decomposers of wood. Between them they form the conduit for a large part of the energy flowing through the forest. Sunlight to leaf to caterpillar to ant to anteater to jaguar to maggot to humus to termite to dissipated heat: such are the links that compose the great energy network around Surinam's villages.

I carried the standard equipment of a field biologist: camera; canvas satchel containing forceps, trowel, ax, mosquito repellent, jars, vials of alcohol, and notebook; a twenty-power hand lens swinging with a reassuring tug around the neck; partly fogged eyeglasses sliding down the nose and khaki shirt plastered to the back with sweat. My attention was on the forest; it has been there all my life. I can work up some appreciation for the travel stories of Paul Theroux and other urbanophile authors who treat human settlements as virtually the whole world and the intervening natural habitats as troublesome barriers. But everywhere I have gone—South America, Australia, New Guinea, Asia—I have thought exactly the opposite. Jungles and grasslands are the logical destinations, and towns and farmland the labyrinths that people have imposed between them sometime in the past. I cherish the green enclaves accidentally left behind.

Once on a tour of Old Jerusalem, standing near the elevated site of Solomon's Throne, I looked down across the Jericho Road to the dark olive trees of Gethsemane and wondered which native Palestinian plants and animals might still be found in the shade underneath. Thinking of "Go to the ant, thou sluggard; consider her ways," I knelt on the cobblestones to watch harvester ants carry seeds down holes to their subterranean granaries, the same food-gathering activity that had impressed the Old Testament writer, and possibly the same species at the very same place. As I walked with my host back past the Temple Mount toward the Muslim Quarter, I made inner calculations of the number of ant species found within the city walls. There was a perfect logic to such eccentricity: the million-year history of Jerusalem is at least as compelling as its past three thousand years.

At Bernhardsdorp I imagined richness and order as an intensity of light. The woman, child, and peccary turned into incandescent points. Around them the village became a black disk, relatively devoid of life, its artifacts adding next to nothing. The woodland beyond was a luminous bank, sparked here and there by the moving lights of birds, mammals, and larger insects.

I walked into the forest, struck as always by the coolness of the shade beneath tropical vegetation, and continued until I came to a small glade that opened onto the sandy path. I narrowed the world down to the span of a few meters. Again I tried to compose the mental set—call it the naturalist's trance, the hunter's trance—by which biologists locate more elusive organisms. I imagined that this place and all its treasures were mine alone and might be so forever in memory—if the bulldozer came.

In a twist my mind came free and I was aware of the hard workings of the natural world beyond the periphery of ordinary attention, where passions lose their meaning and history is in another dimension, without people, and great events pass without record or judgment. I was a transient of no consequence in this familiar yet deeply alien world that I had come to love. The uncounted products of evolution were gathered there for purposes having nothing to do with me; their long Cenozoic history was enciphered into a genetic code I could not understand. The effect was strangely calming. Breathing and heartbeat diminished, concentration intensified. It seemed to me that something extraordinary in the forest was very close to where I stood, moving to the surface and discovery.

I focused on a few centimeters of ground and vegetation. I willed animals to materialize, and they came erratically into view. Metallic-blue mosquitoes floated down from the canopy in search of a bare patch of skin, cockroaches with variegated wings perched butterfly-like on sunlit leaves, black carpenter ants sheathed in recumbent golden hairs filed in haste through moss on a rotting log. I turned my head slightly and all of them vanished. Together they composed only an infinitesimal fraction of the life actually present. The woods were a biological maelstrom of which only the surface could be scanned by the naked eye. Within my circle of vision, millions of unseen organisms died each second. Their destruction was swift and silent; no bodies thrashed about, no blood leaked into the ground. The microscopic bodies were broken apart in clean biochemical chops by predators and scavengers, then assimilated to create millions of new organisms, each second.

Ecologists speak of "chaotic regimes" that rise from orderly processes and give rise to others in turn during the passage of life from lower to higher levels of organization. The forest was a tangled bank tumbling down to the grassland's border. Inside it was a living sea through which I moved like a diver groping across a littered floor. But I knew that all around me bits and pieces, the individual organisms and their populations, were working with extreme precision. A few of the species were locked together in forms of symbiosis so intricate that to pull out one would bring others spiraling to extinction. Such is the consequence of adaptation by coevolution, the reciprocal genetic change of species that interact with each other through many life cycles. Eliminate just one kind of tree out of hundreds in such a forest, and some of its pollinators, leafeaters, and woodborers will disappear with it, then various of their parasites and key predators, and perhaps a species of bat or bird that depends on its fruit—and when will the reverberations end? Perhaps not until a large part of the diversity of the forest collapses like an arch crumbling as the keystone is pulled away. More likely the effects will remain local, ending with a minor shift in the overall pattern of abundance among the numerous surviving species. In either case the effects are beyond the power of present-day ecologists to predict. It is enough to work on the assumption that all of the details matter in the end, in some unknown but vital way.

After the sun's energy is captured by the green plants, it flows through chains of organisms dendritically, like blood spreading from the arteries into networks of microscopic capillaries. It is in such capillaries, in the life cycles of thousands of individual species, that life's important work is done. Thus nothing in the whole system makes sense until the natural history of the constituent species becomes known. The study of every kind of organism matters, everywhere in the world. That conviction leads the field biologist to places like Surinam and the outer limits of evolution, of which this case is exemplary:

> The three-toed sloth feeds on leaves high in the canopy of the lowland forests through large portions of South and Central America. Within its fur live tiny moths, the species *Cryptoses choloepi*, found nowhere else on Earth. When a sloth descends

to the forest floor to defecate (once a week), female moths leave the fur briefly to deposit their eggs on the fresh dung. The emerging caterpillars build nests of silk and start to feed. Three weeks later they complete their development by turning into adult moths, and then fly up into the canopy in search of sloths. By living directly on the bodies of the sloths, the adult *Cryptoses* assure their offspring first crack at the nutrient-rich excrement and a competitive advantage over the myriad of other coprophages.

At Bernhardsdorp the sun passed behind a small cloud and the woodland darkened. For a moment all that marvelous environment was leveled and subdued. The sun came out again and shattered the vegetative surfaces into light-based niches. They included intensely lighted leaf tops and the tops of miniature canyons cutting vertically through tree bark to create shadowed depths two or three centimeters below. The light filtered down from above as it does in the sea, giving out permanently in the lowermost recesses of buttressed tree trunks and penetralia of the soil and rotting leaves. As the light's intensity rose and fell with the transit of the sun, silverfish, beetles, spiders, bark lice, and other creatures were summoned from their sanctuaries and retreated back in alternation. They responded according to receptor thresholds built into their eyes and brains, filtering devices that differ from one kind of animal to another. By such inborn controls the species imposed a kind of prudent self-discipline. They unconsciously halted their population growth before squeezing out competitors, and others did the same. No altruism was needed to achieve this balance, only specialization. Coexistence was an incidental by-product of the Darwinian advantage that accrued from the avoidance of competition. During the long span of evolution the species divided the environment among themselves, so that now each tenuously preempted certain of the capillaries of energy flow. Through repeated genetic changes they sidestepped competitors and built elaborate defenses against the host of predator species that relentlessly tracked them through matching genetic countermoves. The result was a splendid array of specialists, including moths that live in the fur of three-toed sloths.

Now to the very heart of wonder. Because species diversity was created prior to humanity, and because we evolved within it, we have never fathomed its limits. As a consequence, the living world is the natural domain of the most restless and paradoxical part of the human spirit. Our sense of wonder grows exponentially: the greater the knowledge, the deeper the mystery and the more we seek knowledge to create new mystery. This catalytic reaction, seemingly an inborn human trait, draws us perpetually forward in a search for new places and new life. Nature is to be mastered, but (we hope) never completely. A quiet passion burns, not for total control but for the sensation of constant advance.

At Bernhardsdorp I tried to convert this notion into a form that would satisfy a private need. My mind maneuvered through an unending world suited to the naturalist. I looked in reverie down the path through the savanna woodland and imagined walking to the Saramacca River and beyond, over the horizon, into a timeless reconnaissance through virgin forests to the land of magical names, Yékwana, Jívaro, Sirionó, Tapirapé, Siona-Secoya, Yumana, back and forth, never to run out of fresh jungle paths and glades.

The same archetypal image has been shared in variations by others, and most vividly during the colonization of the New World. It comes through clearly as the receding valleys and frontier trails of nineteenth-century landscape art in the paintings of Albert Bierstadt, Frederick Edwin Church, Thomas Cole, and their contemporaries during the crossing of the American West and the innermost reaches of South America.

In Bierstadt's *Sunset in Yosemite Valley* (1868), you look down a slope that eases onto the level valley floor, where a river flows quietly away through waist-high grass, thickets, and scattered trees. The sun is near the horizon. Its dying light, washing the surface in reddish gold, has begun to yield to blackish green shadows along the near side of the valley. A cloud bank has lowered to just beneath the tops of the sheer rock walls. More protective than threatening, it has transformed the valley into a tunnel opening out through the far end into a sweep of land. The world beyond is obscured by the blaze of the setting sun into which we are forced to gaze in order to see that far. The valley, empty of people, is safe: no fences, no paths, no owners. In a few minutes we could walk to the river, make camp, and afterward explore away from the banks at leisure. The ground in sight is human-sized, measured literally by foot strides and strange new plants and animals large enough to be studied at twenty paces. The dreamlike quality of the painting rolls time forward: what might the morning bring? History is still young, and human imagination has not yet been chained by precise geographic knowledge. Whenever we wish, we can strike out through the valley to the unknown terrain beyond, to a borderland of still conceivable prodigies—bottomless vales and boundless floods, in Edgar Allan Poe's excited imagery, "and chasms, and caves and Titan woods with forms that no man can discover." The American frontier called up the old emotions that had pulled human populations like a living sheet over the world during the ice ages. The still unfallen western world, as Melville wrote of the symbolizing White Steed in *Moby Dick*, "revived the glories of those primeval times when Adam walked majestic as a god."

Then a tragedy: this image is almost gone. Although perhaps as old as man, it has faded during our own lifetime. The wildernesses of the world have shriveled into timber leases and threatened nature reserves. Their parlous state presents us with a dilemma, which the historian Leo Marx has called the machine in the garden. The natural world is the refuge of the spirit, remote, static, richer even than human imagination. But we cannot exist in this paradise without the machine that tears it apart. We are killing the thing we love, our Eden, progenitrix, and sibyl. Human beings are not captive peccaries, natural creatures torn from a sylvan niche and imprisoned within a world of artifacts. The noble savage, a biological impossibility, never existed. The human relation to nature is vastly more subtle and ambivalent, probably for this reason. Over thousands of generations the mind evolved within a ripening culture, creating itself out of symbols and tools, and genetic advantage accrued from planned modifications of the environment. The unique operations of the brain are the result of natural selection operating through the filter of culture. They have suspended us between the two antipodal ideals of nature and machine, forest and city, the natural and the artifactual, relentlessly seeking, in the words of the geographer Yi-Fu Tuan, an equilibrium not of this world.

So at Bernhardsdorp my own thoughts were inconstant. They skipped south to the Saramacca and on deep into the Amazon basin, the least spoiled garden on Earth, and then swiftly back north to Paramaribo and New York, greatest of machines. The machine had taken me there, and if I ever seriously thought of confronting nature without the conveniences of civilization, reality soon regained my whole attention. The living sea is full of miniature horrors designed to reduce visiting biologists to their constituent amino acids in quick time. Arboviruses visit the careless intruder with a dismaying variety of chills and diarrhea. Breakbone fever swells the joints to agonizing tightness. Skin ulcers spread remorselessly outward from thorn scratches on the ankle. Triatoma assassin bugs suck blood from the sleeper's face during the night and leave behind the fatal microorganisms of Chagas' disease—surely history's most unfair exchange. Leishmaniasis, schistosomiasis, malignant tertian malaria, filariasis, echinococcosis, onchocerciasis, yellow fever, amoebic dysentery, bleeding bot-fly cysts . . . evolution has devised a hundred ways to macerate livers and turn blood into a parasite's broth. So the romantic voyager swallows chloraquin, gratefully accepts gamma globulin shots, sleeps under mosquito netting, and remembers to pull on rubber boots before wading in freshwater streams. He hopes that enough fuel was put into the Land Rover that morning, and he hurries back to camp in time for a hot meal at dusk.

The impossible dilemma caused no problem for ancestral men. For millions of years human beings simply went at nature with everything they had, scrounging food and fighting off predators across a known world of a few square miles. Life was short, fate terrifying, and reproduction an urgent priority: children, if freely conceived, just about replaced the family members who seemed to be dying all the time. The population flickered around equilibrium, and sometimes whole bands became extinct. Nature was something out there—nameless and limitless, a force to beat against, cajole, and exploit.

If the machine gave no quarter, it was also too weak to break the wilderness. But no matter: the ambiguity of the opposing ideals was a superb strategy for survival, just so long as the people who used it stayed sufficiently ignorant. It enhanced the genetic evolution of the brain and generated more and better culture. The world began to yield, first to the agriculturists and then to technicians, merchants, and circumnavigators. Humanity accelerated toward the machine antipode, heedless of the natural desire of the mind to keep the opposite as well. Now we are near the end. The inner voice murmurs *You went too far*, and disturbed the world, and gave away too much for your control of Nature. Perhaps Hobbes's definition is correct, and this will be the hell we earned for realizing truth too late. But I demur in all this. I suggest otherwise: the same knowledge that brought the dilemma to its climax contains the solution. Think of scooping up a handful of soil and leaf litter and spreading it out on a white ground cloth, in the manner of the field biologist, for close examination. This unprepossessing lump contains more order and richness of structure, and particularity of history, than the entire surfaces of all the other (lifeless) planets. It is a miniature wilderness that can take almost forever to explore.

Tease apart the adhesive grains with the aid of forceps, and you will expose the tangled rootlets of a flowering plant, curling around the rotting veins of humus, and perhaps some larger object such as the boat-shaped husk of a seed. Almost certainly among them will be a scattering of creatures that measure the world in millimeters and treat this soil sample as traversable: ants, spiders, springtails, armored oribatid mites, enchytraeid worms, millipedes. With the aid of a dissecting microscope, proceed on down the size scale to the roundworms, a world of scavengers and fanged predators feeding on them. In the hand-held microcosm all these creatures are still giants in a relative sense. The organisms of greatest diversity and numbers are invisible or nearly so. When the soil-and-litter clump is progressively magnified, first with a compound light microscope and then with scanning electron micrographs, specks of dead leaf expand into mountain ranges and canyons, soil particles become heaps of boulders. A droplet of moisture trapped between root hairs grows into an underground lake, surrounded by a three-dimensional swamp of moistened humus. The niches are defined by both topography and nuances in chemistry, light, and temperature shifting across fractions of a millimeter. Organisms now come into view for which the soil sample is a complete world. In certain places are found the fungi: cellular slime molds, the one-celled chitin-producing chytrids, minute gonapodyaceous and oomycete soil specialists, Kickxellales, Eccrinales, Endomycetales, and Zoopagales. Contrary to their popular reputation, the fungi are not formless blobs, but exquisitely structured organisms with elaborate life cycles. The following is a recently discovered extreme specialization, the example of the sloth moth repeated on a microscopic scale:

> In water films and droplets, attack cells of an oomycete, *Haptoglossa mirabilis*, await the approach of small, fat wormlike animals the biologists call rotifers. Each cell is shaped like a gun; its anterior end is elongated to form a barrel, which is hollowed out to form a bore. At the base of the bore is a complicated explosive device. When a rotifer swims close, the attack cell detects its characteristic odor and fires a projectile of infective tissue through the barrel and into its body. The fungal cells proliferate through the victim's tissues and then metamorphose into a cylindrical fruiting body, from which exit tubes sprout. Next tiny spores separate themselves inside the fruiting body, swim out the exit tubes with the aid of whip-shaped hairs, and settle down to form new attack cells. They await more rotifers, prepared to trigger the soundless explosion that will commence a new life cycle.

Still smaller than the parasitic fungi are the bacteria, including colony-forming polyangiaceous species, specialized predators that consume other bacteria. All around them live rich mixtures of rods, cocci, coryneforms, and slime azotobacteria. Together these microorganisms metabolize the entire spectrum of live and dead tissue. At the moment of discovery some are actively growing and fissioning, while others lie dormant in wait for the right combination of nutrient chemicals. Each species is kept at equilibrium by the harshness of the environment. Any one, if allowed to expand without restriction for a few weeks, would multiply exponentially, faster and faster, until it weighed more than the entire Earth. But in reality the individual organism simply dissolves and assimilates whatever appropriate fragments of plants and animals come to rest near it. If the newfound meal is large enough, it may succeed in growing and reproducing briefly before receding back into the more normal state of physiological quiescence.

Biologists, to put the matter as directly as possible, have begun a second reconnaissance into the land of magical names. In exploring life they have commenced a pioneering adventure with no imaginable end. The abundance of organisms increases downward by level, like layers in a pyramid. The handful of soil and litter is home for hundreds of insects, nematode worms, and other larger creatures, about a million fungi, and ten billion bacteria. Each of the species of these organisms has a distinct life cycle fitted, as in the case of the predatory fungus, to the portion of the microenvironment in which it thrives and reproduces. The particularity is due to the fact that it is programed by an exact sequence of nucleotides, the ultimate molecular units of the genes.

The amount of information in the sequence can be measured in bits. One bit is the information required to determine which of two equally likely alternatives is chosen, such as heads or tails in a coin toss. English words average two bits per letter. A single bacterium possesses about ten million bits of genetic information, a fungus one billion, and an insect from one to ten billion bits according to species. If the information in just one insect—say an ant or beetle—were to be translated into a code of English words and printed in letters of standard size, the string would stretch over a thousand miles. Our lump of earth contains information that would just about fill all fifteen editions of the *Encyclopaedia Britannica*.

To see what such molecular information can do, consider a column of ants running across the floor of a South American forest. Riding on the backs of some of the foragers are minute workers of the kind usually confined to duties within the underground nursery chambers. The full significance of hitchhiking is problematic, but at the very least the act helps to protect the colony against parasites. Tiny flies, members of the family Phoridae, hover above the running foragers. From time to time a fly dives down to thrust an egg into the neck of one of them. Later the egg hatches into a maggot that burrows deeper into the ant's body. The maggot grows rapidly, transforms into a pupa, and eventually erupts through the cuticle as an adult fly to restart the life cycle. The divebombers find the runners easy targets when they are burdened with a fragment of food. But when one also carries a hitchhiker, the smaller ant is able to chase the intruder away with its jaws and legs. It serves as a living fly whisk.

The brain of the fly or of the fly-whisk ant, when dissected out and placed in a drop of saline solution on a glass slide, resembles a grain of sugar. Although barely visible to the naked eye, it is a complete command center that choreographs the insect's movements through its entire adult cycle. It signals the precise hour for the adult to emerge from the pupal case; it processes the flood of signals transduced to it by the outer sensors; and it directs the performance of about twenty behavioral acts through nerves in the legs, antennae, and mandibles. The fly and the ant are hardwired in a manner unique to their respective species and hence radically different from each other, so that predator is implacably directed against prey, flier against runner, solitaire against colony member.

With advanced techniques it has been possible to begin mapping insect nervous systems in sufficient detail to draw the equivalent of wiring diagrams. Each brain consists of somewhere between a hundred thousand and a million nerve cells, most of which send branches to a thousand or more of their neighbors. Depending on their location, individual cells appear to be programed to assume a particular shape and to transmit messages only when stimulated by coded discharges from neighbor units that feed into them. In the course of evolution, the entire system has been miniaturized to an extreme. The fatty sheaths surrounding the axon shafts of the kind found in larger animals have been largely stripped away, while the cell bodies are squeezed off to one side of the multitudinous nerve connections. Biologists understand in very general terms how the insect brain might work as a complete on-board computer, but they are a long way from explaining or duplicating such a device in any detail.

The great German zoologist Karl von Frisch once said of his favorite organism that the honeybee is like a magic well: the more you draw from it, the more there is to draw. But science is in no other way mystical. Its social structure is such that anyone can follow most enterprises composing it, as observer if not as participant, and soon you find yourself on the boundaries of knowledge.

You start with the known: in the case of the honeybee, where it nests, its foraging expeditions, and its life cycle. Most remarkable at this level is the waggle dance discovered by von Frisch, the tail-wagging movement performed inside the hive to inform nestmates of the location of newly discovered flower patches and nest sites. The dance is the closest approach known in the animal kingdom to a true symbolic language. Over and over again the bee traces a short line on the vertical surface of the comb, while sister workers crowd in close behind. To return to the start of the line, the bee loops back first to the left and then to the right and so produces a figure-eight. The center line contains the message. Its length symbolically represents the distance from the hive to the goal, and its angle away from a line drawn straight up on the comb, in other words away from twelve o'clock, represents the angle to follow right or left of the sun when leaving the hive. If the bee dances straight up the surface of the comb, she is telling the others to fly toward the sun. If she dances ten degrees to the right, she causes them to go ten degrees right of the sun. Using such directions alone, the members of the hive are able to harvest nectar and pollen from flowers three miles or more from the hive.

The revelation of the waggle-dance code has pointed the way to deeper levels of biological investigation, and a hundred new questions. How does the bee judge gravity while on the darkened comb? What does it use for a guide when the sun goes behind a cloud? Is the waggle dance inherited or must it be learned? The answers create new concepts that generate still more mysteries. To pursue them (and we are now certainly at the frontier) investigators must literally enter the bee itself, exploring its nervous system, the interplay of its hormones and behavior, the processing of chemical cues by its nervous system. At the level of cell and tissue, the interior of the body will prove more technically challenging than the external workings of the colony first glimpsed. We are in the presence of a biological machine so complicated that to understand just one part of it—wings, heart, ovary, brain—can consume many lifetimes of original investigation.

And if that venture were somehow to be finished, it will merely lead on down into the essence of the machine, to the interior of cells and the giant molecules that compose their distinctive parts. Questions about process and meaning then take center stage. What commits an embryonic cell to become part of the brain instead of a respiratory unit? Why does the mother's blood invest yolk in the growing egg? Where are the genes that control behavior? Even in the unlikely event that all this microscopic domain is successfully mapped, the quest still lies mostly ahead. The honeybee, *Apis mellifera*, is the product of a particular history. Through fossil remains in rock and amber, we know that its lineage goes back at least 50 million years. Its contemporary genes were assembled by an astronomical number of events that sorted and recombined the constituent nucleotides. The species evolved as the outcome of hourly contacts with thousands of other kinds of plants and animals along the way. Its range expanded and contracted across Africa and Eurasia in a manner reminiscent of the fortunes of a human tribe. Virtually all this history remains unknown. It can be pursued to any length by those who take a special interest in *Apis mellifera* and seek what Charles Butler called its "most sweet and sov'raigne fruits" when he launched the modern scientific study of the honeybee in 1609.

Every species is a magic well. Biologists have until recently been satisfied with the estimate that there are between three and ten million of them on Earth. Now many believe that ten million is too low. The upward revision has been encouraged by the increasingly successful penetration of the last great unexplored environment of the planet, the canopy of the tropical rain forest, and the discovery of an unexpected number of new species living there. This layer is a sea of branches, leaves, and flowers crisscrossed by lianas and suspended about one hundred feet above the ground. It is one of the easiest habitats to locate—from a distance at least—but next to the deep sea the most difficult to reach. The tree trunks are thick, arrow-straight, and either slippery smooth or covered with sharp tubercles. Anyone negotiating them safely to the top must then contend with swarms of stinging ants and wasps. A few athletic and adventurous younger biologists have begun to overcome the difficulties by constructing special pulleys, rope catwalks, and observation platforms from which they can watch high arboreal animals in an undisturbed state. Others have found a way to sample the insects, spiders, and other arthropods with insecticides and quick-acting knockdown agents. They first shoot lines up into the canopy, then hoist the chemicals up in canisters and spray them out into the surrounding vegetation by remote control devices. The falling insects and other organisms are caught in sheets spread over the ground. The creatures discovered by these two methods have proved to be highly specialized in their food habits, the part of the tree in which they live, and the time of the year when they are active. So an unexpectedly large number of different kinds are able to coexist. Hundreds can fit comfortably together in a single tree top. On the basis of a preliminary statistical projection from these data, Terry L. Erwin, an entomologist at the National Museum of Natural History, has estimated that there may be thirty million species of insects in the world, most limited to the upper vegetation of the tropical forests.

Although such rough approximations of the diversity of life are not too difficult to make, the exact number of species is beyond reach because—incredibly—the majority have yet to be discovered and specimens placed in museums. Furthermore, among those already classified no more than a dozen have been studied as well as the honeybee. Even *Homo sapiens*, the focus of billions of dollars of research annually, remains a seemingly intractable mystery. All of man's troubles may well arise, as Vercors suggested in *You Shall Know Them*, from the fact that we do not know what we are and do not agree on what we want to become. This crucial inadequacy is not likely to be remedied until we have a better grasp of the diversity of the life that created and sustains us. So why hold back? It is a frontier literally at our fingertips, and the one for which our spirit appears to have been explicitly designed.

I walked on through the woodland at Bernhardsdorp to see what the day had to offer. In a decaying log I found a species of ant previously known only from the midnight zone of a cave in Trinidad. With the aid of my hand lens I identified it from its unique combination of teeth, spines, and body sculpture. A month before I had hiked across five miles of foothills in central Trinidad to find it in the original underground habitat. Now suddenly here it was again, nesting and foraging in the open. Scratch from the list what had been considered the only "true" cave ant in the world—possessed of workers pale yellow, nearly eyeless, and sluggish in movement. Scratch the scientific name *Spelaeomyrmex*, meaning literally cave ant, as a separate taxonomic entity. I knew that it would have to be classified elsewhere, into a larger and more conventional genus called *Erebomyrma*, ant of Hades. A small quick victory, to be reported later in a technical journal that specializes on such topics and is read by perhaps a dozen fellow myrmecologists. I turned to watch some huge-eyed ants with the formidable name *Gigantiops destructor*. When I gave one of the foraging workers a freshly killed termite, it ran off in a straight line across the forest floor. Thirty feet away it vanished into a small hollow tree branch that was partly covered by decaying leaves. Inside the central cavity I found a dozen workers and their mother queen—one of the first colonies of this unusual insect ever recorded. All in all, the excursion had been more productive than average. Like a prospector obsessed with ore samples, hoping for gold, I gathered a few more promising specimens in vials of ethyl alcohol and headed home, through the village and out onto the paved road leading north to Paramaribo.

Later I set the day in my memory with its parts preserved for retrieval and closer inspection. Mundane events acquired the raiment of symbolism, and this is what I concluded from them: That the naturalist's journey has only begun and for all intents and purposes will go on forever. That it is possible to spend a lifetime in a magellanic voyage around the trunk of a single tree. That as the exploration is pressed, it will engage more of the things close to the human heart and spirit. And if this much is true, it seems possible that the naturalist's vision is only a specialized product of a biophilic instinct shared by all, that it can be elaborated to benefit more and more people. Humanity is exalted not because we are so far above other living creatures, but because knowing them well elevates the very concept of life.

Biophilia (1984)

CÉSAR CHÁVEZ

César Chávez (1927–1993) was perhaps the greatest Latino social activist in American history. Born in Arizona to Mexican parents, he grew up a migrant laborer harvesting the crops of the Imperial, Sacramento, and San Joaquin valleys—Oxnard for beans, San Jose for apricots, on and on. Chávez completed school through the eighth grade, and after a stint in the Navy married and returned to the migrant life. He became a community organizer in the 1950s and started labor-organizing among grape pickers in the 1960s. His United Farm Workers movement used every kind of tactic from protest marches to nationwide boycotts to win historic contract victories with wine makers and table-grape growers between 1965 and 1970. His speech urging one such boycott, in 1986, is a reminder that low wages are not the only form of exploitation.

Wrath of Grapes Boycott Speech

I am speaking to you about our Wrath of Grapes Boycott because I believe our greatest court, the court of last resort, is the American people. And I believe that once you have taken a few moments to hear this message you will concur in this verdict along with a million other North Americans who are already committed to the largest grape boycott in history. The worth of humans is involved here.

I see us as one family. We cannot turn our backs on each other and our future. We farm workers are closest to food production. We were the first to recognize the serious health hazards of agriculture pesticides to both consumers and ourselves.

Twenty years ago over 17 million Americans united in a grape boycott campaign that transformed the simple act of refusing to buy grapes into a powerful and effective force against poverty and injustice.

Through the combined strengths of a national boycott, California farm workers won many of the same rights as other workers—the right to organize and negotiate with growers.

But we also won a critical battle for all Americans. Our first contracts banned the use of DDT, DDE, Dieldrin on crops, years before the federal government acted.

Twenty years later our contracts still seek to limit the spread of poison in our food and fields, but we need your help once again if we are to succeed.

A powerful self-serving alliance between the California governor and the $4 billion agricultural industry has resulted in a systematic and reckless poisoning of not only California farm workers but of grape consumers throughout our nation and Canada.

The hard won law enacted in 1975 has been trampled beneath the feet of self-interest. Blatant violations of California labor laws are constantly ignored. And worst of all, the indiscriminate and even illegal use of dangerous pesticides has radically increased in the last decade causing illness, permanent disability, and even death.

We must not allow the governor of California and the selfish interests of California grape growers to threaten lives throughout North America.

We have known for many years that pesticides used in agriculture pollute the air, earth, and water, contaminate animals and humans, and are found in the tissue of newborn infants and mothers' milk. This March, the *New York Times* reported that the Environmental Protection Agency finally considers pesticide pollution its most urgent problem, noting virtually everyone is exposed to pesticides.

The Environmental Protection Agency experts have warned that

#1—Pesticide residue is being found in a growing number of food products.

#2—Some poisons registered for use in the last thirty years cause cancer, mutations, and birth defects.

#3—Most chemicals on the market have insufficient and sometimes fraudulent test results.

#4—Underground water supplies of twenty-three states are already tainted, and farm workers suffer some pesticide-induced illness in alarming numbers.

Consumers must be alerted now that no one can actually define or measure so called safe exposure to residual poison that accumulates in the human body, as environments differ and each person's tolerance is unique. What might be safe statistically for the average healthy forty year old male might irreparably harm an elderly consumer, a child, or the baby of a pregnant mother.

What we do know absolutely is that human lives are worth more than grapes and that innocent looking grapes on the table may disguise poisonous residues hidden deep inside where washing cannot reach.

Let me share the frightening facts with you. Last July the *New York Times* and national television reported that nearly one thousand California, Pacific Northwest, Alaskan, and Canadian consumers became ill as the result of eating watermelons tainted with the powerful insecticide Aldicarb, labeled the most acutely toxic pesticide registered in the United States. Yet Aldicarb cannot be legally used on watermelons.

In June local agriculture officials quarantined fields in Delano, California, grape ranches because residues of the pesticide Orthene were found in the vineyards; yet Orthene cannot be legally used on table grapes.

And a new study shows pesticides used in growing may be responsible for the illness of over three hundred thousand of the nation's 4 million farm workers.

But of the twenty-seven legally restricted toxic poisons currently used on grapes, at least five are potentially as dangerous or more hazardous to consumers and grape workers than deadly Aldicarb and Orthene.

Here are five major threats to your health that cling to California table grapes:

—Parathion and Phosdrin—are highly poisonous insecticides, similar to nerve gas, and are responsible for the majority of deaths and serious poisoning of farm workers. They cause birth defects and are carcinogens.

—Captan—a proven cancer-causing and birth-defect producing agent (fungicide).

—Dinoseb—a highly toxic herbicide that has caused worker deaths.

—methyl bromide—a more potent mutagen (an agent affecting genetic material) than mustard gas and is a highly poisonous and proven carcinogen.

Statistics and news articles do not relate the real cost, the human anguish that originates from poisons on our food. They do not tell the tragedies I personally learn of daily.

How can I explain these chemicals to three-year-old Amalia Larios, who will never walk, born with a spinal defect due to pesticide exposure of her mother.

What statistics are important to Adrian Espinoza, seven years old and dying of cancer with eight other children, whose only source of water was polluted with pesticides.

What headlines can justify the loss of irrigator Manuel Anaya's right hand, amputated due to recurrent infection from powerful herbicides added to the water he worked with in the fields.

How do we comfort the mother of maimed and stillborn infants, the parents who watch their teenage children sicken or die.

What report can be cited at the hospital beds I visit, at growing numbers of wakes I attend.

What court will hear the case of thirty-two-year-old Juan Chaboya, murdered by deadly chemicals in the freshly sprayed fields outside San Diego, his dead body dumped by the growers forty-five miles away at a Tijuana clinic. What excuse for justice will we offer his four children and his widow if we do nothing.

Now is the time for all of us to stand as a family and demand a response in the name of decency. Too much is at stake. This is a battle that none of us can afford to lose because it is a fight for the future of America. It is a fight we can win, and it is a fight that everyone can join.

Add your voice to our demands of decency as we call for

#1—A ban on the five most dangerous pesticides used in grape production—Parathion, Phosdrin, Dinoseb, methyl bromide, and Captan.

#2—A joint UFW/grower testing program for poisonous residues on grapes sold in stores with the results made public.

#3—Free and fair elections for farm workers to decide whether to organize and negotiate contracts limiting the use of dangerous poisons in the fields.

#4—Good faith bargaining.

Until these demands of decency are met, we will carry the message of the Wrath of Grapes Boycott from state to state. Ten years ago, 12 percent of the country boycotted grapes and the growers were forced to accountability. California Governor Deukmejian and agribusiness cannot withstand the judgment of outraged consumers who refused to purchase their tainted products. Every month over 1 million grape consumers like yourselves receive our message across North America. State and federal law makers, mayors and city councils, religious and labor leaders, students and senior citizens, mothers and fathers, rich and poor, concerned individuals in every walk of life have endorsed the Wrath of Grapes Boycott. With their commitment and their donations, they in turn have reached out to their friends and relatives to help bind the foundation of a growing coalition of decency.

Now I am reaching out to you for help because consumers and farm workers must stand together as one family if we are to be heard. I am not asking you to give up wine or raisins. I am asking you to give us your commitment and valuable support.

I am asking you to join us now and be counted to join the growing family of individuals who will boycott grapes until the demands of decency have been met.

And hard as it is for me to ask for money, I am asking you to contribute to the cause—$100, $50, $15, whatever you can afford, whatever you would have spent on grapes this year. Insure that every week 1 million more consumers will know the truth.

You have my personal pledge that every cent of your contributions will be spent on the Wrath of Grapes Campaign bringing this message into every home in America because this message is the source of our combined strength.

My friends, the wrath of grapes is a plague born of selfish men that is indiscriminately and undeniably poisoning us all. Our only protection is to boycott the grapes, and our only weapon is the truth. If we unite we can only triumph for ourselves, for our children, and for their children. We look forward to hearing from you soon.

1986

BARRY LOPEZ

Barry Lopez (b. 1945) has won most of the honors an American writer can claim, notably the National Book Award for his classic *Arctic Dreams: Imagination and Desire in a Northern Landscape* (1986). Born in New York and schooled at Notre Dame, he has spent most of his life in the West, often looking northward. He has also become in certain ways the elder of the disparate tribe of nature writers across the continent, helping new voices emerge and coordinating projects like the recent and critically acclaimed *Home Ground* (2006), which gathered together 40 authors and set them the task of defining terms from landscape geography. This finely observed essay about a band of stranded sperm whales on the coast of his adopted home state makes clear how much American attitudes toward nature have changed over the last century—the sheer despair at seeing these animals die, who not long ago were hunted mercilessly, says much about the influence of nature writing, and not least of Lopez' own rigorous and gentle work.

A Presentation of Whales

On that section of the central Oregon coast on the evening of June 16, 1979, gentle winds were blowing onshore from the southwest. It was fifty-eight degrees. Under partly cloudy skies the sea was running with four-foot swells at eight-second intervals. Moderately rough. State police cadets Jim Clark and Steve Bennett stood at the precipitous edge of a foredune a few miles south of the town of Florence, peering skeptically into the dimness over a flat, gently sloping beach. Near the water's edge they could make out a line of dark shapes, and what they had taken for a practical joke, the exaggeration a few moments before of a man and a woman in a brown Dodge van with a broken headlight, now sank in for the truth.

Clark made a hasty, inaccurate count and plunged with Bennett down the back of the dune to their four-wheel-drive. Minutes before, they had heard the voice of Corporal Terry Crawford over the radio; they knew he was patrolling in Florence. Rather than call him, they drove the six miles into town and parked across the street from where he was issuing a citation to someone for excessive noise. When Crawford had finished, Clark went over and told him what they had seen. Crawford drove straight to the Florence State Police office and phoned his superiors in Newport, forty-eight miles up the coast. At that point the news went out over police radios: thirty-six large whales, stranded and apparently still alive, were on the beach a mile south of the mouth of the Siuslaw River.

There were, in fact, forty-one whales—twenty-eight females and thirteen males, at least one of them dying or already dead. There had never been a stranding quite like it. It was first assumed that they were gray whales, common along the coast, but they were sperm whales: *Physeter catodon.* Deep-ocean dwellers. They ranged in age from ten to fifty-six and in length from thirty to thirty-eight feet. They were apparently headed north when they beached around 7:30 P.M. on an ebbing high tide.

The information shot inland by phone, crossing the Coast Range to radio and television stations in the more-populous interior of Oregon, in a highly charged form: giant whales stranded on a public beach accessible by paved road on a Saturday night, still alive. Radio announcers urged listeners to head for the coast to "save the whales." In Eugene and Portland, Greenpeace volunteers, already alerted by the police, were busy throwing sheets and blankets into their cars. They would soak them in the ocean, to cool the whales.

The news moved as quickly through private homes and taverns on the central Oregon coast, passed by people monitoring the police bands. In addition to phoning Greenpeace—an international organization with a special interest in protecting marine mammals—the police contacted the Oregon State University Marine Science Center in South Beach near Newport, and the Oregon Institute of Marine Biology in Charleston, fifty-eight miles south of Florence. Bruce Mate, a marine mammalogist at the OSU Center, phoned members of the Northwest Regional [Stranding] Alert Network and people in Washington, D.C.

By midnight, the curious and the awed were crowded on the beach, cutting the night with flashlights. Drunks, ignoring the whales' sudden thrashing, were trying to walk up and down on their backs. A collie barked incessantly; flash cubes burst at the huge, dark forms. Two men inquired about reserving some of the teeth, for scrimshaw. A federal agent asked police to move people back, and the first mention of disease was in the air. Scientists arrived with specimen bags and rubber gloves and fishing knives. Greenpeace members, one dressed in a bright orange flight suit, came with a large banner. A man burdened with a television camera labored over the foredune after them. They wished to tie a rope to one whale's flukes, to drag it back into the ocean. The police began to congregate with the scientists, looking for a rationale to control the incident.

In the intensifying confusion, as troopers motioned onlookers back (to "restrain the common herd of unqualified mankind," wrote one man later in an angry letter-to-the-editor), the thinking was that, somehow, the whales might be saved. Neal Langbehn, a federal protection officer with the National Marine Fisheries Service, denied permission to one scientist to begin removing teeth and taking blood samples. In his report later he would write: "It was my feeling that the whales should be given their best chance to survive."

This hope was soon deemed futile, as it had appeared to most of the scientists from the beginning—the animals were hemorrhaging under the crushing weight of their own flesh and were beginning to suffer irreversible damage from heat exhaustion. The scientific task became one of securing as much data as possible.

As dawn bloomed along the eastern sky, people who had driven recreational vehicles illegally over the dunes and onto the beach were issued citations and turned back. Troopers continued to warn people over bullhorns to please stand away from the whales. The Oregon Parks Department, whose responsibility the beach was, wanted no part of the growing confusion. The U.S. Forest Service, with jurisdiction over land in the Oregon Dunes National Recreation Area down to the foredune, was willing to help, but among all the agencies there was concern over limited budgets; there were questions, gently essayed, about the conflict of state and federal enforcement powers over the body parts of an endangered species. A belligerent few in the crowd shouted objections as the first syringes appeared, and yelled to scientists to produce permits that allowed them to interfere in the death of an endangered species.

Amid this chaos, the whales, sealed in their slick black neoprene skins, mewed and clicked. They slammed glistening flukes on the beach, jarring the muscles of human thighs like Jell-O at a distance of a hundred yards. They rolled their dark, purple-brown eyes at the scene and blinked.

They lay on the western shore of North America like forty-one derailed boxcars at dawn on a Sunday morning, and in the days that followed, the worst and the best of human behavior was shown among them.

The sperm whale, for many, is the most awesome creature of the open seas. Imagine a forty-five-year-old male fifty feet long, a slim, shiny black animal with a white jaw and marbled belly cutting the surface of green ocean water at twenty knots. Its flat forehead protects a sealed chamber of exceedingly fine oil; sunlight sparkles in rivulets running off folds in its corrugated back. At fifty tons it is the largest carnivore on earth. Its massive head, a third of its body length, is scarred with the beak, sucker, and claw marks of giant squid, snatched out of subterranean canyons a mile below, in a region without light, and brought writhing to the surface. Imagine a four-hundred-pound heart the size of a chest of drawers driving five gallons of blood at a stroke through its aorta: a meal of forty salmon moving slowly down twelve-hundred feet of intestine; the blinding, acrid fragrance of a two-hundred-pound wad of gray ambergris lodged somewhere along the way; producing sounds more shrill than we can hear—like children shouting on a distant playground—and able to sort a cacophony of noise: electric crackling of shrimp, groaning of undersea quakes, roar of upwellings, whining of porpoise, hum of oceanic cables. With skin as sensitive as the inside of your wrist.

What makes them awesome is not so much these things, which are discoverable, but the mysteries that shroud them. They live at a remarkable distance from us and we have no *Pioneer II* to penetrate their world. Virtually all we know of sperm whales we have learned on the slaughter decks of oceangoing whalers and on the ways at shore stations. We do not even know how many there are; in December 1978, the Scientific Committee of the International Whaling Commission said it could not set a quota for a worldwide sperm whale kill—so little was known that any number written down would be ridiculous.*

The sperm whale, in all its range of behaviors—from the enraged white bull called Mocha Dick that stove whaling ships off the coast of Peru in 1810, to a nameless female giving birth to a fourteen-foot, one-ton calf in equatorial waters in the Pacific—remains distant. The general mystery is enhanced by specific mysteries: the sperm whale's brain is larger than the brain of any other creature that ever lived. Beyond the storage of incomprehensible amounts of information, we do not know what purpose such size serves. And we do not know what to make of its most distinctive anatomical feature, the spermaceti organ. An article in *Scientific American*, published several months before the stranding, suggests that the whale can control the density of its spermaceti oil, thereby altering its specific gravity to assist it in diving. It is argued also that the huge organ, located in the head, serves as a means of generating and focusing sound, but there is not yet any agreement on these speculations.

Of the many sperm whale strandings in recorded history, only three have been larger than the one in Oregon. The most recent was of fifty-six on the eastern Baja coast near Playa San Rafael on January 6, 1979. But the Florence stranding is perhaps the most remarkable. Trained scientists arrived almost immediately; the site was easily accessible, with even an airstrip close by. It was within an hour's drive of

---

*A quota of 5000 was nevertheless set. In June 1979, within days of the Florence stranding but apparently unrelated to it, the IWC dropped the 1980 world sperm whale quota to 2203 and set aside the Indian Ocean as a sanctuary. (By 1987 the quota was 0, though special exemptions permit some 200 sperm whales still to be taken worldwide.)

two major West Coast marine-science centers. And the stranding seemed to be of a whole social unit. That the animals were still alive meant live blood specimens could be taken. And by an uncanny coincidence, a convention of the American Society of Mammalogists was scheduled to convene June 18 at Oregon State University in Corvallis, less than a two-hour drive away. Marine experts from all over the country would be there. (As it turned out, some of them would not bother to come over; others would secure access to the beach only to take photographs; still others would show up in sports clothes—all they had—and plunge into the gore that by the afternoon of June 18 littered the beach.)

The state police calls to Greenpeace on the night of June 16 were attempts to reach informed people to direct a rescue. Michael Piper of Greenpeace, in Eugene, was the first to arrive with a small group at about 1:30 A.M., just after a low tide at 12:59 A.M.

"I ran right out of my shoes," Piper says. The thought that they would still be alive—clicking and murmuring, their eyes tracking human movement, lifting their flukes, whooshing warm air from their blowholes—had not penetrated. But as he ran into the surf to fill a bucket to splash water over their heads, the proportions of the stranding and the impending tragedy overwhelmed him.

"I knew, almost from the beginning, that we were not going to get them out of there, and that even if we did, their chances of survival were a million to one," Piper said.

Just before dawn, a second contingent of Greenpeace volunteers arrived from Portland. A Canadian, Michael Bailey, took charge and announced there was a chance with the incoming tide that one of the smaller animals could be floated off the beach and towed to sea (weights ranged from an estimated three and a half to twenty-five tons). Bruce Mate, who would become both scientific and press coordinator on the beach (the latter to his regret), phoned the Port of Coos Bay to see if an ocean-going tug or fishing vessel would be available to anchor offshore and help—Bailey's crew would ferry lines through the surf with a Zodiac boat. No one in Coos Bay was interested. A commercial helicopter service with a Skycrane capable of lifting nine tons also begged off. A call to the Coast Guard produced a helicopter, but people there pronounced any attempt to sky-tow a whale too dangerous.

The refusal of help combined with the apparent futility of the effort precipitated a genuinely compassionate gesture: Bailey strode resolutely into the freezing water and, with twenty-five or thirty others, amid flailing flukes, got a rope around the tail of an animal that weighed perhaps three or four tons. The waves knocked them down and the whale yanked them over, but they came up sputtering, to pull again. With the buoyancy provided by the incoming tide they moved the animal about thirty feet. The effort was heroic and ludicrous. As the rope began to cut into the whale's flesh, as television cameramen and press photographers crowded in, Michael Piper gave up his place on the rope in frustration and waded ashore. Later he would remark that, for some, the whale was only the means to a political end—a dramatization of the plight of whales as a species. The distinction between the suffering individual, its internal organs hemorrhaging, its flukes sliced by the rope, and the larger issue, to save the species, confounded Piper.

A photograph of the Greenpeace volunteers pulling the whale showed up nationally in newspapers the next day. A week later, a marine mammalogist wondered if any more damaging picture could have been circulated. It would convince people something could have been done, when in fact, he said, the whales were doomed as soon as they came ashore.

For many, transfixed on the beach by their own helplessness, the value of the gesture transcended the fact.

By midmorning Piper was so disturbed, so embarrassed by the drunks and by people wrangling to get up on the whales or in front of photographers, that he left. As he drove off through the crowds (arriving now by the hundreds, many in campers and motor homes), gray whales were seen offshore, with several circling sperm whales. "The best thing we could have done," Piper said, alluding to this, "was offer our presence, to be with them while they were alive, to show some compassion."

Irritated by a callous (to him) press that seemed to have only one question—Why did they come ashore?—Piper had blurted out that the whales may have come ashore "because they were tired of running" from commercial whalers. Scientists scoffed at the remark, but Piper, recalling it a week later, would not take it back. He said it was as logical as any other explanation offered in those first few hours.

Uneasy philosophical disagreement divided people on the beach from the beginning. Those for whom the stranding was a numinous event were estranged by the clowning of those who regarded it as principally entertainment. A few scientists irritated everyone with their preemptive, self-important air. When they put chain saws to the lower jaws of dead sperm whales lying only a few feet from whales not yet dead, there were angry shouts of condemnation. When townspeople kept at bay—"This is history, dammit," one man screamed at a state trooper, "and I want my kids to see it!"—saw twenty reporters, each claiming an affiliation with the same weekly newspaper, gain the closeness to the whales denied them, there were shouts of cynical derision.

"The effect of all this," said Michael Gannon, director of a national group called Oregonians Cooperating to Protect Whales, of the undercurrent of elitism and outrage, "was that it interfered with the spiritual and emotional ability of people to deal with the phenomenon. It was like being at a funeral where you were not allowed to mourn."

Bob Warren, a patrolman with the U.S. Forest Service, said he was nearly brought to tears by what faced him Sunday morning. "I had no conception of what a whale beaching would be like. I was apprehensive about it, about all the tourists and the law-enforcement atmosphere. When I drove up, the whole thing hit me in the stomach: I saw these *numbers*, these damn orange numbers—41, 40, 39—spray-painted on these dying animals. The media were coming on like the marines, in taxicabs, helicopters, low-flying aircraft. Biologists were saying, 'We've got to *euthanize* them.' It made me sick."

By this time Sunday morning, perhaps five hundred people had gathered; the crowd would swell to more than two thousand before evening, in spite of a drizzling rain. The state trooper who briefed Warren outlined the major problems: traffic was backing up on the South Jetty Road almost five miles to U.S. 101; the whales' teeth were "as valuable as gold" and individuals with hammers and saws had been warned away already; people were sticking their hands in the whales' mouths and were in danger of being killed by the pounding flukes; and there was a public-health problem—the whales might have come ashore with a communicable disease. (According to several experts, the danger to public health was minor, but in the early confusion it served as an excuse to keep the crowd back so scientists could work. Ironically, the threat would assume a life of its own two days later and scientists would find themselves working frantically ahead of single-minded state burial crews.)

One of the first things Warren and others did was to rope off the whales with orange ribbon and lath stakes, establishing a line beyond which the public was no longer permitted. Someone thoughtful among them ran the ribbon close enough to one whale to allow people to peer into the dark eyes, to see scars left by struggling squid, lamprey eels, and sharp boulders on the ocean floor, the patches of diatoms growing on the skin, the marbling streaking back symmetrically from the genital slit, the startlingly gentle white mouth ("What a really beautiful and chaste-looking mouth!" Melville wrote. "From floor to ceiling lined, or rather papered with a glistening white membrane, glossy as bridal satins"), to see the teeth, gleaming in the long, almost absurdly narrow jaw. In *The Year of the Whale*, Victor Scheffer describes the tooth as "creamy white, a cylinder lightly curved, a thing of art which fits delightfully in the palm of my hand."

The temptation to possess—a Polaroid of oneself standing over a whale, a plug of flesh removed with a penknife, a souvenir squid beak plucked deftly from an exposed intestine by a scientist—was almost palpable in the air.

"From the beginning," Warren continued, "I was operating on two levels: as a law-enforcement officer with a job, and as a person." He escorted people away from the whales, explaining as well as he could the threat of disease, wishing himself to reach out with them, to touch the animals. He recalls his rage watching people poke at a sensitive area under the whales' eyes to make them react, and calmly directing people to step back, to let the animals die in peace. Nothing could be done, he would say. How do you know? they would ask. He didn't.

Warren was awed by the sudden, whooshing breath that broke the silence around an animal perhaps once every fifteen minutes, and saddened by the pitiable way some of them were mired with their asymmetrical blowhole sanded in, dead. Near those still breathing he drove in lath stakes with the word LIVE written on them. The hopelessness of it, he said, and the rarity of the event were rendered absurd by his having to yell into a bullhorn, by the blood on the beach, the whales' blinking, the taunters hoisting beer cans to the police.

One of the things about being human, Warren reflected, is learning to see beyond the vulgar. Along with the jocose in the crowd, he said, there were hundreds who whispered to each other, as if in a grove of enormous trees. And faces that looked as though they were awaiting word of relatives presumed dead in an air crash. He remembers in particular a man in his forties, "dressed in polyesters," who stood with his daughter in a tidal pool inside the barrier, splashing cool water on a whale. Warren asked them to please step back. "Why?" the man asked. Someone in the crowd yelled an obscenity at Warren. Warren thought to himself: Why is there no room for the decency of this gesture?

The least understood and perhaps most disruptive incident on the beach on that first day was the attempt of veterinarians to kill the whales, first by injecting M–99, a morphine-base drug, then by ramming pipes into their pleural cavities to collapse their lungs, and finally by severing major arteries and letting them bleed to death. The techniques were crude, but no one knew enough sperm whale anatomy or physiology to make a clean job of it, and no one wanted to try some of the alternatives—from curare to dynamite—that would have made the job quicker. The ineptitude of the veterinarians caused them a private embarrassment to which they gave little public expression. Their frustration at their own inability to do anything to "help" the whales was exacerbated by nonscientists demanding from the sidelines that the animals be "put out of their misery." (The reasons for attempting euthanasia were poorly understood, philosophically and medically, and the issue nagged people long after the beach bore not a trace of the incident itself.)

As events unfolded on the beach, the first whale died shortly after the stranding, the last almost thirty-six hours later; suffocation and overheating were the primary causes. By waiting as long as they did to try to kill some of the animals and by allowing others to die in their own time, pathologists, toxicologists, parasitologists, geneticists, and others got tissues of poor quality to work with.* The disappointment was all the deeper because never had so many scientists been in a position to gather so much information. (Even with this loss and an initial lack of suitable equipment—chemicals to preserve tissues, blood-analysis kits, bone saws, flensing knives—the small core of twenty or so scientists "increased human knowledge about sperm whales several hundred percent," according to Mate.)

The fact that almost anything learned was likely to be valuable was meager consolation to scientists hurt by charges that they were cold and brutal people, irreverently jerking fetuses from the dead. Among these scientists were people who sat alone in silence, who departed in anger, and who broke down and cried.

No one knows why whales strand. It is almost always toothed whales that do, rather than baleen whales, most commonly pilot whales, Atlantic white-sided dolphins, false killer whales, and sperm whales—none of which are ordinarily found close to shore. Frequently they strand on gently sloping beaches. Among the more tenable explanations: 1) extreme social cohesion, where one sick animal is relentlessly followed ashore by many healthy animals; 2) disease or parasitic infec-

*A subsequent report, presented at a marine-mammals conference in Seattle in October 1979, made it clear that the whales began to suffer the effects of heat stress almost immediately. The breakdown of protein structures in their tissues made discovery of a cause of death difficult; from the beginning, edema, capillary dilation, and hemorrhaging made their recovery unlikely. Ice, seawater pumps, and tents for shade rather than Zodiac boats and towlines were suggested if useful tissue was to be salvaged in the future from large whales.

tion that affects the animals' ability to navigate: 3) harassment, by predators and, deliberate or inadvertent, by humans; 4) a reversion to phylogenetically primitive escape behavior—get out of the water—precipitated by stress.

At a public meeting in Florence—arranged by the local librarian to explain to a public kept off the beach what had happened, and to which invited scientists did not come—other explanations were offered. Someone had noticed whales splashing in apparent confusion near a river dredge and thought the sound of its engines might have driven the whales crazy. Local fishermen said there had been an unusual, near-shore warm current on June 16, with a concentration of plankton so thick they had trouble penetrating it with their depth finders. Another suggestion was that the whales might have been temporarily deranged by poisons in diatoms concentrated in fish they were eating.

The seventy-five or so people at the meeting seemed irritated that there was no answer, as did local reporters looking for an end to the story. Had scientists been there it is unlikely they could have suggested one. The beach was a gently sloping one, but the Florence whales showed no evidence of parasitism or disease, and modern research makes it clear that no single explanation will suffice. For those who would blame the machinations of modern man, scientists would have pointed out that strandings have been recorded since the time of Aristotle's *Historia animalium*.

The first marine biologist to arrive on the beach, at 3:30 A.M. Sunday, was Michael Graybill, a young instructor from the Oregon Institute of Marine Biology. He was not as perplexed as other scientists would be; a few months before he had dismantled the rotting carcass of a fifty-six-foot sperm whale that had washed ashore thirty miles south of Florence.

Graybill counted the animals, identified them as sperm whales, noted that, oddly, there were no nursing calves or obviously young animals, and that they all seemed "undersized." He examined their skin and eyes, smelled their breath, looked for signs of oral and anal discharge, and began the task of sexing and measuring the animals.

Driving to the site, Graybill worried most about someone "bashing their teeth out" before he got there. He wasn't worried about communicable disease; he was "willing to gamble" on that. He regarded efforts to save the whales, however, as unnatural interference in their death. Later, he cynically observed "how much 'science' took place at the heads of sperm whales" where people were removing teeth; and he complained that if they really cared about the worldwide fate of whales, Greenpeace volunteers would have stayed to help scientists with postmortems. (Some did. Others left because they could not stand to watch the animals die.)

Beginning Sunday morning, scientists had their first chance to draw blood from live, unwounded sperm whales (they used comparatively tiny one-and-a-half-inch, 18-gauge hypodermic needles stuck in vessels near the surface of the skin on the flukes). With the help of a blue, organic tracer they estimated blood volume at five hundred gallons. In subsequent stages, blubber, eyes, teeth, testicles, ovaries, stomach contents, and specific tissues were removed—the teeth for aging, the eyes for corneal cells to discover genetic relationships within the group. Postmortems were performed on ten females; three near-term fetuses were removed. An attempt was made to photograph the animals systematically.

The atmosphere on the beach shifted perceptibly over the next six days. On Sunday, a cool, cloudy day during which it rained, as many as three thousand people may have been on the beach. Police finally closed the access road to the area to discourage more from coming. Attempts to euthanize the animals continued, the jaws of the dead were being sawed off, and, in the words of one observer, "there was a television crew with a backdrop of stranded whales every twenty feet on the foredune."

By Monday the crowds were larger, but, in the estimation of a Forest Service employee, "of a higher quality. The type of people who show up at an automobile accident were gone; these were people who really wanted to see the whales. It was a four-and-a-half-mile walk in from the highway, and I talked with a woman who was seven months pregnant who made it and a man in a business suit and dress shoes who drove all the way down from Seattle."

Monday afternoon the crowds thinned. The beach had become a scene of postmortem gore sufficient to turn most people away. The outgoing tide had carried off gallons of blood and offal, drawing spiny dogfish sharks and smoothhound sharks into the breakers. As the animals died, scientists cut into them to relieve gaseous pressure—the resultant explosions could be heard half a mile away. A forty-pound chunk of liver whizzed by someone's back-turned shoulders; sixty feet of pearly-gray intestine unfurled with a snap against the sky. By evening the beach was covered with more than a hundred tons of intestines. Having to open the abdominal cavities so precipitately precluded, to the scientists' dismay, any chance of an uncontaminated examination.

By Tuesday the beach was closed to the public. The whale carcasses were being prepared for burning and burial, a task that would take four days, and reporters had given up asking why the stranding had happened, to comment on the stench.

The man responsible for coordinating scientific work at the stranding, thirty-three-year-old Bruce Mate, is well regarded by his colleagues. Deborah Duffield, a geneticist from Portland State University, reiterated the feelings of several when she said of him: "The most unusual thing was that he got all of us with our different, sometimes competing, interests to work together. You can't comprehend what an extraordinary achievement that is in a situation like this."

On the beach Mate was also the principal source of information for the press. Though he was courteous to interviewers and careful not to criticize a sometimes impatient approach, one suspected he was disturbed by the role and uncertain what, if anything, he owed the nonscientific community.

In his small, cramped office at the Marine Science Center in South Beach, Mate agreed that everyone involved—scientists, environmentalists, the police, the state agencies, the public—took views that were occasionally in opposition and that these views were often proprietary. He thought it was the business of science to obtain data and physical spec-imens on the beach, thereby acquiring rights of "ownership," and yet he acknowledged misgivings about this because he and others involved are to some extent publicly funded scientists.

The task that faced him was deceptively simple: get as much infor-mation as possible off the beach before the burning crews, nervous about a public-health hazard and eager to end the incident, destroyed the animals. But what about the way science dominated the scene, get-ting the police, for example, to keep the crowd away so science could exercise its proprietary interest? "I don't know how to cope with the public's desire to come and see. Letting those few people onto the beach would have precluded our getting that much more information to give to a much larger, national audience."

What about charges that science operated in a cold-blooded and, in the case of trying to collapse the whales' lungs, ignorant way? "Coming among these whales, watching them die and in some cases helping them to die—needless suffering is almost incomprehensible to me . . ." Mate paused, studied the papers on his desk, unsatisfied, it seemed, with his tack; ". . . there are moral and ethical questions here. It's like dealing with terminal cancer."

No one, he seemed to suggest, liked how fast it had all happened.

Had he been worried about anything on the beach? "Yes! I was ap-palled at the way professional people were going about [postmortems] without gloves. I was afraid for the Greenpeace people in a potentially life-threatening situation in the surf." He was also afraid that it would all get away from him because of the unknowns. What, in fact, *did* one save when faced with such an enormous amount of bone and tissue? But he came away happy. "This was the greatest scientific shot anyone ever had with large whales." After a moment he added, "If it happened tomorrow, we would be four times better."

Sitting at his desk, nursing a pinched nerve in his back, surrounded by phone messages from the press, he seemed seasoned.

Mate's twenty-seven-year-old graduate assistant, Jim Harvey, arrived on the beach at dawn on Sunday. At the first sight of the whales from the top of the dunes, strung out nose to flukes in a line five or six hundred yards long, the waves of a high tide breaking over them, Harvey simply sat down, awestruck at their size and number. He felt deeply sad, too, but as he drew near he felt "a rush of exhilaration, because there was so much information to be gathered." He could not get over the feeling, as he worked, of the size of them. (One afternoon a scientist stood confounded in a whale's abdomen, asking a colleague next to him, "Where's the liver?")

Deborah Duffield said of her experience on the beach: "It hurt me more than watching human beings die. I couldn't cope with the pain, the futility. . . . I just turned into myself. It brought out the scientist in me." Another scientist spoke of his hostility toward the sullen crowd, of directing that anger at himself, of becoming cold and going to work.

For Harvey and others, there was one incident that broke scientific concentration and brought with it a feeling of impropriety. Several scientists had started to strip blubber from a dead whale. Suddenly the whale next to it began pounding the beach with its flukes. The pounding continued for fifteen minutes—lifting and slamming the flukes to the left, lifting and slamming the flukes to the right.

When the animal quieted, they resumed work.

"Scientists rarely get a chance to express their feelings," Harvey said. "I was interested in other people's views, and I wanted to share mine, which are biological. I noticed some people who sat quietly for a long time behind the barriers in religious stances. I very much wanted to know their views. So many of the people who came down here were so sympathetic and full of concern—I wished I had the time to talk to them all." Harvey remembered something vividly. On the first day he put his face near the blowhole of one of the whales: a cylinder of clean, warm, humid air almost a foot in diameter blew back his hair.

"My view on it," said Joe Davis of the Oregon Parks Department, "wasn't the scientific part. My thought on it now is how nice it would have been to have been somewhere else." His smile falls between wryness and regret.

When something remarkable happens and bureaucrats take it for only a nuisance, it is often stripped of whatever mystery it may hold.

The awesome becomes common. Joe Davis, park manager at Honeyman Dunes State Park, adjacent to the stranding, was charged by the state with getting rid of the whales. He said he didn't take a moment to wonder at the mystery of it.

If ethical problems beset scientists, and mystical considerations occupied other onlookers, a set of concerns more prosaic confronted the police and the Oregon Parks Department. On Sunday night, June 17, police arrested a man in a camouflage suit caught breaking teeth out of a whale's jaw with a hammer and chisel. That night (and the next, and the next) people continued to play games with the police. The Parks Department, for its part, was faced with the disposal of five hundred tons of whale flesh that county environmental and health authorities said they couldn't burn—the solution to the problem at Playa San Rafael—and scientists said couldn't be buried. If buried, the carcasses would become hard envelopes of rotting flesh, the internal organs would liquefy and leach out onto the beach, and winter storms would uncover the whole mess.

This controversy, the public-health question, what to do about excessive numbers of press people, and concern over who was going to pay the bill (the Forest Service had donated tools, vehicles, and labor, but two bulldozers had had to be hired, at a hundred dollars and sixty dollars an hour) precipitated a meeting in Florence on Tuesday morning, June 19. A Forest Service employee, who asked not to be identified, thought the pressures that led to the meeting marked a difference between those who came to the beach out of compassion and genuine interest and those for whom it was "only a headache."

The principal issue, after an agreement was reached to burn the whales, then bury them, was who was going to pay. The state was reluctant; the scientists were impoverished. (It would be months before Mate would begin to recover $5,000 of his own money advanced to pay for equipment, transportation, and bulldozer time. "No one wants to fund work that's finished," Mate observed sardonically.) Commercial firms were averse to donating burning materials, or even transportation for them; G.P. Excavating of Florence did reduce rental fees on its bulldozers by about one-third and "broke even" after paying its operators.

The state finally took responsibility for the disposal and assumed the $25,000 cleanup bill, but it wanted to hear nothing about science's wish to salvage skeletons—it wanted the job finished.* Arrangements were made to bring in a crew of boys from the Young Adult Conservation Corps, and the Forest Service, always, it seemed, amenable, agreed to donate several barrels of Alumagel, a napalmlike substance.

It was further decided to ban the public from the beach during the burning, for health and safety reasons. Only the disposal crews, scientists, police, and selected press would be admitted. The criterion for press admittance was possession of "a legitimate press card."

The role of the press at such events is somewhat predictable. They will repeatedly ask the same, obvious questions; they will often know little of the science involved; occasionally they will intimidate and harass in order to ascertain (or assign) blame. An upper-level Forest Service employee accused the press of asking "the most uninteresting and intimidating kinds of questions." A State Parks employee felt the press fostered dissension over who was going to pay for the disposal. He was also angry with newspaper people for ignoring "the human side," the fact that many state police troopers worked long hours of overtime, and that Forest Service employees performed a number of menial tasks in an emotionally charged environment of rotting flesh. "After a week of sixteen-hour days, your nerves are raw, you stink, you just want to get away from these continual questions."

In the press's defense, the people who objected most were those worried about criticism of their own performance and those deeply frustrated by the trivialization of the event. The press—probing, perhaps inexpertly—made people feel no more than their own misgivings.

The publisher of the local *Siuslaw News*, Paul Holman, said before it was over that the whale stranding had become a nuisance. When police closed the road to the beach a man in a stateside truck began ferrying

---

*Three months later on September 6, 1979, an eighty-five-foot female blue whale washed ashore in Northern California. Ensuing argument over responsibility for disposal prevented scientists from going near the whale until September 13, by which time it had been severely battered on the rocks and vandalized.

people the four and a half miles to the whales for a dollar each. And a dollar back. The local airport, as well as tourist centers offering seaplane rides, were doing a "land-office business" in flyovers. Gas station operators got tired of telling tourists how to get to the beach. The Florence City Hall was swamped with calls about the burning, one from a man who was afraid his horses would be killed by the fallout on his pasture. Dune-buggy enthusiasts were angry at whale people who for two days blocked access to their hill-climbing area.

Whatever its interest, the press was largely gone by Monday afternoon. As the burning and burying commenced, the number of interested scientists also thinned. By Wednesday there were only about thirty people left on the beach. Bob Adams, acting director of the Lane Regional Air Pollution Authority, was monitoring the smoke. Neal Langbehn of the National Marine Fisheries Service stood guard over a pile of plastic-wrapped sperm whale jaws. Michael Graybill led a team flensing out skulls. The state fretted over a way to keep the carcasses burning. (It would finally be done with thousands of automobile and truck tires, cordwood, diesel fuel, and Alumagel.) As Mate watched he considered the threshold of boredom in people, and mourned the loss, among other things, of forty-one sperm whale skeletons.

A journalist, one of the last two or three, asked somebody to take her picture while she stood with a small poodle in her arms in front of the burning pits.

As is often the case with such events, what is salvaged is as much due to goodwill as it is to expertise. The Forest Service was widely complimented for helping, and Stafford Owen, the acting area ranger at the agency's Oregon Dunes National Recreation Area during the incident, tried to say why: "Most of us aren't highly educated people. We have had to work at a variety of things all our lives—operating a chain saw, repairing a truck engine, running a farm. We had the skills these doctors and scientists needed."

A soft-spoken colleague, Gene Large, trying to elaborate but not to make too much of himself, said, "I don't think the scientists had as much knowledge [of large mammalian anatomy] as I did. When it came to it, I had to show some of them where the ribs were." After a moment, Large said, "Trying to cut those whales open with a chain saw was like trying to slaughter a beef with a pen knife." "I didn't enjoy any part of it," Large said of the dismembering with chain saws and winches. "I think the older you get, the more sensitive you get." He mentioned an older friend who walked away from a dead, fifteen-foot, near-term fetus being lifted out of a gutted whale, and for a time wouldn't speak.

On Wednesday afternoon the whales were ignited in pits at the foot of the foredune. As they burned they were rendered, and when their oil caught fire they began to boil in it. The seething roar was muffled by a steady onshore breeze; the oily black smoke drifted southeast over the dunes, over English beach grass and pearly everlasting, sand verbena, and the purple flowers of beach pea, green leaves of sweet clover, and the bright yellow blooms of the monkey flower. It thinned until it disappeared against a weak-blue sky.

While fire cracked the blubber of one-eyed, jawless carcasses, a bulldozer the size of a two-car garage grunted in a trench being dug to the north for the last of them. These were still sprawled at the water's edge. Up close, the black, blistered skin, bearing scars of knives and gouging fingernails, looked like the shriveled surface of a pond evaporated beneath a summer sun. Their gray-blue innards lay about on the sand like bags of discarded laundry. Their purple tongues were wedged in retreat in their throats. Spermaceti oil dripped from holes in their heads, solidifying in the wind to stand in translucent stalagmites twenty inches high. Around them were tidal pools opaque with coagulated blood and, beyond, a pink surf.

As far as I know, no novelist, no historian, no moral philosopher, no scholar of Melville, no rabbi, no painter, no theologian had been on the beach. No one had thought to call them or to fly them in. At the end they would not have been allowed past the barricades.

The whales made a sound, someone had said, like the sound a big fir makes breaking off the stump just as the saw is pulled away. A thin screech.

Crossing Open Ground (1988)

W. S. MERWIN

W. S. Merwin's home in the perfectly named Maui town of Haiku is one of my favorite places in the world to visit. When Merwin (b. 1927) moved there decades ago, it was as barren as any of the other cut-over plantation lands on the Hawaiian Islands. But for many years he has divided his days between writing and planting, and in that time his acreage has become not a formal garden but a palm jungle, with species from around the world that he has grown from seed and then transplanted along the small hollow that drops to a stream. It is a luxuriant and soft place, a kind of antidote to the coruscating despair that marks much of Merwin's poetry. His work—which has won him both the Pulitzer and the National Book Award—returns again and again to his anger at the way our culture has separated people and nature. "The Pennsylvania I grew up in and loved as a child isn't there . . . it's been strip-mined: it really is literally not there," he once told an interviewer. If his palm forest is one answer, another is his work on behalf of Hawaiian culture and the environment to which it's so closely linked. He and his wife, Paula, were instrumental in helping to rally support for saving the largest tropical rain forest left in the U.S., a low-elevation tract on the Big Island threatened by a careless geothermal development.

Place

On the last day of the world
I would want to plant a tree

what for
not for the fruit

the tree that bears the fruit
is not the one that was planted

I want the tree that stands
in the earth for the first time

with the sun already
going down

and the water
touching its roots

in the earth full of the dead
and the clouds passing

one by one
over its leaves

The Rain in the Trees (1988)

BILL McKIBBEN

I was born in 1960, grew up in the suburbs, and wrote for *The New Yorker*'s quintessentially urban "Talk of the Town" column for five years after graduating from college. But I moved to the Adirondack Mountains, the East's largest wilderness, in 1987, and there began work on *The End of Nature* (1989). The first book for a general audience about global warming, it combines reporting on the emerging science with a sometimes despairing meditation on the idea that now no place on earth is beyond the altering touch of humans. In years since, I've written many other books and helped organize large-scale demonstrations against global warming.

from **The End of Nature**

Almost every day, I hike up the hill out my back door. Within a hundred yards the woods swallows me up, and there is nothing to remind me of human society—no trash, no stumps, no fence, not even a real path. Looking out from the high places, you can't see road or house; it is a world apart from man. But once in a while someone will be cutting wood farther down the valley, and the snarl of a chain saw will fill the woods. It is harder on those days to get caught up in the timeless meaning of the forest, for man is nearby. The sound of the chain saw doesn't blot out all the noises of the forest or drive the animals away, but it does drive away the feeling that you are in another, separate, timeless, wild sphere.

Now that we have changed the most basic forces around us, the noise of that chain saw will always be in the woods. We have changed the atmosphere, and that will change the weather. The temperature and rainfall are no longer to be entirely the work of some separate, uncivilizable force, but instead in part a product of our habits, our economies, our ways of life. Even in the most remote wilderness, where the strictest laws forbid the felling of a single tree, the sound of that saw will be clear, and a walk in the woods will be changed—tainted—by its whine. The world outdoors will mean much the same thing as the world indoors, the hill the same thing as the house.

An idea, a relationship, can go extinct, just like an animal or a plant. The idea in this case is "nature," the separate and wild province, the world apart from man to which he adapted, under whose rules he was born and died. In the past, we spoiled and polluted parts of that nature, inflicted environmental "damage." But that was like stabbing a man with toothpicks: though it hurt, annoyed, degraded, it did not touch vital organs, block the path of the lymph or blood. We never thought that we had wrecked nature. Deep down, we never really thought we could: it was too big and too old; its forces—the wind, the rain, the sun—were too strong, too elemental.

But, quite by accident, it turned out that the carbon dioxide and other gases we were producing in our pursuit of a better life—in pursuit of warm houses and eternal economic growth and of agriculture so productive it would free most of us from farming—*could* alter the power of the sun, could increase its heat. And that increase *could* change the patterns of moisture and dryness, breed storms in new places, breed deserts. Those things may or may not have yet begun to happen, but it is too late to altogether prevent them from happening. We have produced the carbon dioxide—we are ending nature.

We have not ended rainfall or sunlight; in fact, rainfall and sunlight may become more important forces in our lives. It is too early to tell exactly how much harder the wind will blow, how much hotter the sun will shine. That is for the future. But the *meaning* of the wind, the sun, the rain—of nature—has already changed. Yes, the wind still blows—but no longer from some other sphere, some inhuman place.

In the summer, my wife and I bike down to the lake nearly every afternoon for a swim. It is a dogleg Adirondack lake, with three beaver lodges, a blue heron, some otter, a family of mergansers, the occasional loon. A few summer houses cluster at one end, but mostly it is surrounded by wild state land. During the week we swim across and back, a trip of maybe forty minutes—plenty of time to forget everything but the feel of the water around your body and the rippling, muscular joy of a hard kick and the pull of your arms.

But on the weekends, more and more often, someone will bring a boat out for waterskiing, and make pass after pass up and down the lake. And then the whole experience changes, changes entirely. Instead of being able to forget everything but yourself, and even yourself except for the muscles and the skin, you must be alert, looking up every dozen strokes to see where the boat is, thinking about what you will do if it comes near. It is not so much the danger—few swimmers, I imagine, ever die by Evinrude. It's not even so much the blue smoke that hangs low over the water. It's that the motorboat gets in your mind. You're forced to think, not feel—to think of human society and of people. The lake is utterly different on these days, just as the planet is utterly different now.

* * *

There is also another emotional response—one that corresponds to the cry "What will I do without him?" when someone vital dies.

I took a day's hike last fall, walking Mill Creek from the spot where it runs by my door to the place where it crosses the main county road near Wevertown. It's a distance of maybe nine miles as the car flies, but rivers are far less efficient, and endlessly follow pointless, time-wasting, uneconomical meanders and curves. Mill Creek cuts some fancy figures, and so I was able to feel a bit exploratory—a budget Bob Marshall. In a strict sense, it wasn't much of an adventure. I stopped at the store for a liverwurst sandwich at lunchtime, the path was generally downhill, the temperature stuck at an equable 55 degrees, and since it was the week before the hunting season opened I didn't have to sing as I walked to keep from getting shot. On the other hand, I had made an arbitrary plan—to follow the creek—and, as a consequence, I spent hours stumbling through overgrown marsh, batting at ten-foot saplings and vines, emerging only every now and then, scratched and weary, into the steeper wooded sections. When Thoreau was on Katahdin, nature said to him, "I have never made this soil for thy feet, this air for thy breathing, these rocks for thy neighbors. I cannot pity nor fondle thee there, but forever relentlessly drive thee hence to where I *am* kind. Why seek me where I have not called thee, and then complain because you find me but a stepmother?" Nature said this to me on Mill Creek, or at least it said, "Go home and tell your wife you walked to Wevertown." I felt I should have carried a machete, or employed a macheteist. (The worst thing about battling through brake and bramble of this sort is that it's so anonymous—gray sticks, green stalks with reddish thorns, none of them to be found in any of the many guides and almanacs on my shelf.) And though I started the day with eight dry socks, none saw noon in that pleasant state.

If it was all a little damp and in a minor key, the sky was nonetheless bright blue, and rabbits kept popping out from my path, and pheasants fired up between my legs, and at each turning some new gift appeared: a vein of quartz, or a ridge where the maples still held their leaves, or a pine more than three feet in diameter that beavers had gnawed all the way around and halfway through and then left standing—a forty-foot sculpture. It was October, so there weren't even any bugs. And always the plash of the stream in my ear. It isn't Yosemite, the Mill Creek Valley, but its small beauties are absorbing, and one can say with Muir on his mountaintop, "Up here all the world's prizes seem as nothing."

And so what if it isn't nature primeval? One of our neighbors has left several kitchen chairs along his stretch of the bank, spaced at fifty-yard intervals for comfort in fishing. At one old homestead, a stone chimney stands at either end of a foundation now filled by a graceful birch. Near the one real waterfall, a lot of rusty pipe and collapsed concrete testifies to the old mill that once stood there. But these aren't disturbing sights—they're almost comforting, reminders of the way that nature has endured and outlived and with dignity reclaimed so many schemes and disruptions of man. (A mile or so off the creek, there's a mine where a hundred and fifty years ago a visionary tried to extract pigment for paint and pack it out on mule and sledge. He rebuilt after a fire; finally an avalanche convinced him. The path in is faint now, but his chimney, too, still stands, a small Angkor Wat of free enterprise.)

Large sections of the area were once farmed; but the growing season is not much more than a hundred days, and the limits established by that higher authority were stronger than the (powerful) attempts of individual men to circumvent them, and so the farms returned to forest, with only a dump of ancient bottles or a section of stone wall as a memorial. (Last fall, though, my wife and I found, in one abandoned meadow, a hop vine planted at least a century before. It was still flowering, and with its blossoms we brewed beer.) These ruins are humbling sights, reminders of the negotiations with nature that have established the world as we know it.

Changing socks (soaking for merely clammy) in front of the waterfall, I thought back to the spring before last, when a record snowfall melted in only a dozen or so warm April days. A little to the south, an inflamed stream washed out a highway bridge, closing the New York Thruway for months. Mill Creek filled till it was a river, and this waterfall, normally one of those diaphanous-veil affairs, turned into a cataract. It filled me with awe to stand there then, on the shaking ground and think, This is what nature is capable of.

But as I sat there this time, and thought about the dry summer we'd just come through, there was nothing awe-inspiring or instructive, or even lulling, in the fall of the water. It suddenly seemed less like a waterfall than like a spillway to accommodate the overflow of a reservoir. That didn't decrease its beauty, but it changed its meaning. It has begun or will soon begin to rain and snow when the particular mix of chemicals we've injected into the atmosphere adds up to rain or snow—when they make it hot enough over some tropical sea to form a cloud and send it this way. I had no more control, in one sense, over this process than I ever did. But it felt different, and lonelier. Instead of a world where rain had an independent and mysterious existence, the rain had become a subset of human activity: a phenomenon like smog or commerce or the noise from the skidder towing logs on Cleveland Road—all things over which I had no control, either. The rain bore a brand; it was a steer, not a deer. And that was where the loneliness came from. There's nothing there except us. There's no such thing as nature anymore—that other world that isn't business and art and breakfast is now not another world, and there is nothing except us alone.

At the same time that I felt lonely, though, I also felt crowded, without privacy. We go to the woods in part to escape. But now there is nothing except us and so there is no escaping other people. As I walked in the autumn woods I saw a lot of sick trees. With the conifers, I suspected acid rain. (At least I have the luxury of only suspecting; in too many places, they *know*). And so who walked with me in the woods? Well, there were the presidents of the Midwest utilities who kept explaining why they had to burn coal to make electricity (cheaper, fiduciary responsibility, no *proof* it kills trees) and then there were the congressmen who couldn't bring themselves to do anything about it (personally favor but politics the art of compromise, very busy with the war on drugs) and before long the whole human race had arrived to explain its aspirations. We like to drive, they said, air conditioning is a necessity nowadays, let's go to the mall. By this point, the woods were pretty densely populated. As I attempted to escape, I slipped on another rock, and in I went again. Of course, the person I was fleeing most fearfully was myself, for I drive (I drove forty thousand miles one year), and I'm burning a collapsed barn behind the house next week because it is much the cheapest way to deal with it, and I live on about four hundred times what Thoreau conclusively proved was enough, so I've done my share to take this independent, eternal world and turn it into a science-fair project (and not even a good science-fair project but a cloddish one, like pumping poison into an ant farm and "observing the effects").

The walk along Mill Creek, or any stream, or up any hill, or through any woods, is changed forever—changed as profoundly as when it shifted from pristine and untracked wilderness to mapped and deeded and cultivated land. Our local shopping mall now has a club of people who go "mall walking" every day. They circle the shopping center en masse—Caldor to Sears to J. C. Penney, circuit after circuit with an occasional break to shop. This seems less absurd to me now than it did at first. I like to walk in the outdoors not solely because the air is cleaner but because outdoors we venture into a sphere larger than ourselves. Mall walking involves too many other people, and too many purely human sights, ever to be more than good-natured exercise. But now, out in the wild, the sunshine on one's shoulders is a reminder that man has cracked the ozone, that, thanks to us, the atmosphere absorbs where once it released.

The greenhouse effect is a more apt name than those who coined it imagined. The carbon dioxide and trace gases act like the panes of glass on a greenhouse—the analogy is accurate. But it's more than that. We have built a greenhouse, *a human creation*, where once there bloomed a sweet and wild garden.

The End of Nature (1989)

ROBERT D. BULLARD

When Robert Bullard (b. 1946) was a newly minted sociology professor, his lawyer wife asked him to collect data for a lawsuit she had filed against a company trying to site a landfill in the middle of a black middle-class Houston neighborhood. When he started looking at the evidence, Bullard told *Grist* magazine, "I saw that one hundred percent of all the city-owned landfills in Houston were in black neighborhoods, though blacks made up only twenty-five percent of the population. . . . That's how I got dragged into this"—"this" being a career devoted to chronicling the degree to which people of color were the victims of a disproportionate share of the nation's pollution. Bullard's work, and especially his landmark book *Dumping in Dixie* (1990), helped give birth to the environmental justice movement, which has challenged predominantly white mainstream environmental organizations to devote more of their time and resources to people paying the biggest price for "progress." This challenge at first rankled some white environmentalists, who felt they were under attack, but it has slowly yielded a more diverse movement and new ways of thinking about environmental equity. The stakes involved are revealed more clearly with increased awareness about climate change: the industrialized North continues to dump damaging emissions in the backyards of the Third World.

from Dumping in Dixie

The environmental movement in the United States emerged with agendas that focused on such areas as wilderness and wildlife preservation, resource conservation, pollution abatement, and population control. It was supported primarily by middle- and upper-middle-class whites. Although concern about the environment cut across racial and class lines, environmental activism has been most pronounced among individuals who have above-average education, greater access to economic resources, and a greater sense of personal efficacy.[1]

Mainstream environmental organizations were late in broadening their base of support to include blacks and other minorities, the poor, and working-class persons. The "energy crisis" in the 1970s provided a major impetus for the many environmentalists to embrace equity issues confronting the poor in this country and in the countries of the Third World.[2] Over the years, environmentalism has shifted from a "participatory" to a "power" strategy, where the "core of active environmental movement is focused on litigation, political lobbying, and technical evaluation rather than on mass mobilization for protest marches."[3]

An abundance of documentation shows blacks, lower-income groups, and working-class persons are subjected to a disproportionately large amount of pollution and other environmental stressors in their neighborhoods as well as in their workplaces.[4] However, these groups have only been marginally involved in the nation's environmental movement. Problems facing the black community have been topics of much discussion in recent years. (Here, we use sociologist James

1. See Frederick R. Buttel and William L. Flinn, "Social Class and Mass Environmental Beliefs: A Reconsideration," *Environment and Behavior* 10 (September 1978): 433–450; Kenneth M. Bachrach and Alex J. Zautra, "Coping with Community Stress: The Threat of a Hazardous Waste Landfill," *Journal of Health and Social Behavior* 26 (June 1985): 127–141; Paul Mohai, "Public Concern and Elite Involvement in Environmental-Conservation Issues," *Social Science Quarterly* 66 (December 1985): 820–838.

2. Denton E. Morrison, "The Soft Cutting Edge of Environmentalism: Why and How the Appropriate Technology Notion Is Changing the Movement," *Natural Resources Journal* 20 (April 1980): 275–298.

3. Allan Schnaiberg, *The Environment: From Surplus to Scarcity* (New York: Oxford University Press, 1980), pp. 366–377.

4. See Morris E. Davis, "The Impact of Workplace Health and Safety on Black Workers: Assessment and Prognosis," *Labor Studies Journal* 4 (Spring 1981): 29–40; Richard Kazis and Richard Grossman, *Fear at Work: Job Blackmail, Labor, and the Environment* (New York: Pilgrim Press, 1983), Chapter 1; W. J. Kruvant, "People, Energy, and Pollution," in Dorothy K. Newman and Dawn Day, eds., *The American Energy Consumer* (Cambridge, Mass.: Ballinger, 1975), pp. 125–167; Robert D. Bullard, "Solid Waste Sites and the Black Houston Community," *Sociological Inquiry* 53 (Spring 1983): 273–288; Robert D. Bullard, "Endangered Environs: The Price of Unplanned Growth in Boomtown Houston," *California Sociologist* 7 (Summer 1984): 85–101; Robert D. Bullard and Beverly H. Wright, "Dumping Grounds in a Sunbelt City," *Urban Resources* 2 (Winter 1985): 37–39.

Blackwell's definition of the black community, "a highly diversified set of interrelated structures and aggregates of people who are held together by forces of white oppression and racism."[5]) Race has not been eliminated as a factor in the allocation of community amenities.

Research on environmental quality in black communities has been minimal. Attention has been focused on such problems as crime, drugs, poverty, unemployment, and family crisis. Nevertheless, pollution is exacting a heavy toll (in health and environmental costs) on black communities across the nation. There are few studies that document, for example, the way blacks cope with environmental stressors such as municipal solid-waste facilities, hazardous-waste landfills, toxic-waste dumps, chemical emissions from industrial plants, and on-the-job hazards that pose extreme risks to their health. Coping in this case is seen as a response to stress and is defined as "efforts, both action-oriented and intrapsychic, to manage, i.e., master, tolerate, reduce, minimize, environmental and internal demands, conflicts among them, which tax or exceed a person's resources."[6] Coping strategies employed by individuals confronted with a stressor are of two general types: *problem-focused coping* (e.g., individual and/or group efforts to directly address the problem) and *emotion-focused coping* (e.g., efforts to control one's psychological response to the stressor). The decision to take direct action or to tolerate a stressor often depends on how individuals perceive their ability to do something about or have an impact on the stressful situation. Personal efficacy, therefore, is seen as a factor that affects environmental and political activism.[7]

5. James E. Blackwell, *The Black Community: Diversity and Unity* (New York: Harper and Row, 1985), p. xiii.

6. Richard E. Lazarus and Raymond Launier, "Stress-Related Transactions Between Persons and Environment," in Lawrence A. Pervin and Michael Lewis, eds., *Perspectives in International Psychology* (New York: Plenum, 1978), pp. 297–327; Bachrach and Zautra, "Coping with Community Stress," pp. 127–129.

7. See Anthony M. Orum, "On Participation in Political Movements," *Journal of Applied Behavioral Science* 10 (April/June 1974): 181–207; Daniel L. Collins, Andrew Baum, and Jerome E. Singer, "Coping with Chronic Stress at Three Mile Island: Psychological and Biological Evidence," *Health Psychology* 2 (1983): 149–166; Mohai, "Public Concern and Elite Involvement," p. 832.

Much research has been devoted to analyzing social movements in the United States. For example, hundreds of volumes have been written in the past several years on the environmental, labor, antiwar, and civil rights movements. Despite this wide coverage, there is a dearth of material on the convergence (and the divergence, for that matter) of environmentalism and social justice advocacy. This appears to be the case in and out of academia. Moreover, few social scientists have studied environmentalism among blacks and other ethnic minorities. This oversight is rooted in historical and ideological factors and in the composition of the core environmental movement and its largely white middle-class profile.

Many of the interactions that emerged among core environmentalists, the poor, and blacks can be traced to distributional equity questions. How are the benefits and burdens of environmental reform distributed? Who gets what, where, and why? Are environmental inequities a result of racism or class barriers or a combination of both? After more than two decades of modern environmentalism, the equity issues have not been resolved. There has been, however, some change in the way environmental problems are presented by mainstream environmental organizations. More important, environmental equity has now become a major item on the local (grassroots) as well as national civil rights agenda.[8]

Much of the leadership in the civil rights movement came from historically black colleges and universities (HBCUs). Black college students were on the "cutting edge" in leading sit-in demonstrations at lunch counters, libraries, parks, and public transit systems that operated under Jim Crow laws. In *The Origins of the Civil Rights Movement*, Aldon D. Morris wrote:

> The tradition of protest is transmitted across generations by older relatives, black institutions, churches, and protest organizations. Blacks interested in social change inevitably gravitate

8. Robert D. Bullard and Beverly H. Wright, "Environmentalism and the Politics of Equity: Emergent Trends in the Black Community," *Mid-American Review of Sociology* 12 (Winter 1987): 21–37.

to this "protest community," where they hope to find solutions to a complex problem.

The modern civil rights movement fits solidly into this rich tradition of protest. Like the slave revolts, the Garvey Movement, and the March on Washington, it was highly organized. Its significant use of the black religious community to accomplish political goals also linked the modern movement to the earlier mass movements which also relied heavily on the church.[9]

Social justice and the elimination of institutionalized discrimination were the major goals of the civil rights movement. Many of the HBCUs are located in some of the most environmentally polluted communities in the nation. These institutions and their students, thus, have a vested interest in seeing that improvements are made in local environmental quality. Unlike their move to challenge other forms of inequity, black student-activists have been conspicuously silent and relatively inactive on environmental problems. Moreover, the resources and talents of the faculties at these institutions have also been underutilized in assisting affected communities in their struggle against polluters, including government and private industries.

The problem of polluted black communities is not a new phenomenon. Historically, toxic dumping and the location of locally unwanted land uses (LULUs) have followed the "path of least resistance," meaning black and poor communities have been disproportionately burdened with these types of externalities. However, organized black resistance to toxic dumping, municipal waste facility siting, and discriminatory environmental and land-use decisions is a relatively recent phenomenon.[10] Black environmental concern has been present but too often has not been followed up with action.

Ecological concern has remained moderately high across nearly all segments of the population. Social equity and concern about distributive

9. Aldon D. Morris, *The Origins of the Civil Rights Movement: Black Communities Organizing for Change* (New York: Free Press, 1984), p. x.

10. See Robert D. Bullard and Beverly H. Wright, "Blacks and the Environment," *Humboldt Journal of Social Relations* 14 (Summer 1987): 165–184; Bullard, "Solid Waste Sites and the Black Houston Community," pp. 273–288; Bullard, "Endangered Environs," pp. 84–102.

impacts, however, have not fared so well over the years. Low-income and minority communities have had few advocates and lobbyists at the national level and within the mainstream environmental movement. Things are changing as environmental problems become more "potent political issues [and] become increasingly viewed as threatening public health."[11]

The environmental movement of the 1960s and 1970s, dominated by the middle class, built an impressive political base for environmental reform and regulatory relief. Many environmental problems of the 1980s and 1990s, however, have social impacts that differ somewhat from earlier ones. Specifically, environmental problems have had serious regressive impacts. These impacts have been widely publicized in the media, as in the case of the hazardous-waste problems at Love Canal and Times Beach. The plight of polluted minority communities is not as well known as the New York and Missouri tragedies. Nevertheless, a disproportionate burden of pollution is carried by the urban poor and minorities.[12]

Few environmentalists realized the sociological implications of the not-in-my-backyard (NIMBY) phenomenon.[13] Given the political climate of the times, the hazardous wastes, garbage dumps, and polluting industries were likely to end up in somebody's backyard. But whose backyard? More often than not, these LULUs ended up in poor, powerless, black communities rather than in affluent suburbs. This pattern has proven to be the rule, even though the benefits derived from industrial waste production are directly related to affluence.[14] Public officials and private industry have in many cases responded to the NIMBY phenomenon using the place-in-blacks'-backyard (PIBBY) principle.[15]

11. Riley E. Dunlap, "Public Opinion on the Environment in the Reagan Era: Polls, Pollution, and Politics Revisited," *Environment* 29 (July/August 1987): 6–11, 32–37.

12. Brian J. L. Berry, ed., *The Social Burden of Environmental Pollution: A Comparative Metropolitan Data Source* (Cambridge, Mass.: Ballinger, 1977); Sam Love, "Ecology and Social Justice: Is There a Conflict," *Environmental Action* 4 (1972): 3–6; Julian McCaull, "Discriminatory Air Pollution: If the Poor Don't Breathe," *Environment* 19 (March 1976): 26–32; Vernon Jordon, "Sins of Omission," *Environmental Action* 11 (April 1980): 26–30.

13. Denton E. Morrison, "How and Why Environmental Consciousness Has Trickled Down," in Allan Schnaiberg, Nicholas Watts, and Klaus Zimmermann, eds., *Distributional Conflict in Environmental-Resource Policy* (New York: St. Martin's Press, 1986), pp. 187–220.

14. Robert D. Bullard and Beverly H. Wright, "The Politics of Pollution: Implications for the Black Community," *Phylon* 47 (March 1986): 71–78.

15. Bullard and Wright, "Environmentalism and the Politics of Equity," p. 28.

Social activists have begun to move environmentalism to the left in an effort to address some of the distributional impact and equity issues.[16] Documentation of civil rights violations has strengthened the move to make environmental quality a basic right of all individuals. Rising energy costs and a continued erosion of the economy's ability to provide jobs (but not promises) are factors that favor blending the objectives of labor, minorities, and other "underdogs" with those of middle-class environmentalists.[17] Although ecological sustainability and socioeconomic equality have not been fully achieved, there is clear evidence that the 1980s ushered in a new era of cooperation between environmental and social justice groups. While there is by no means a consensus on complex environmental problems, the converging points of view represent the notion that "environmental problems and . . . material problems have common roots."[18]

When analyzing the convergence of these groups, it is important to note the relative emphasis that environmental and social justice organizations give to "instrumental" versus "expressive" activities.[19] Environmental organizations have relied heavily on environmentally oriented expressive activities (outdoor recreation, field trips, social functions, etc.), while the social justice movements have made greater use of goal-oriented instrumental activities (protest demonstrations, mass rallies, sit-ins, boycotts, etc.) in their effort to produce social change.[20]

The push for environmental equity in the black community has much in common with the development of the modern civil rights movement that began in the South. That is, protest against discrimination has evolved from "organizing efforts of activists functioning through a well-developed indigenous base."[21] Indigenous black institutions, organizations,

16. Richard P. Gale, "The Environmental Movement and the Left: Antagonists or Allies?" *Sociological Inquiry* 53 (Spring 1983): 179–199.

17. Craig R. Humphrey and Frederick R. Buttel, *Environment, Energy, and Society* (Belmont, Calif.: Wadsworth Publishing Co., 1982), p. 253.

18. Ibid.

19. Arthur P. Jacoby and Nicholas Babchuk, "Instrumental Versus Expressive Voluntary Associations," *Sociology and Social Research* 47 (1973): 461–471.

20. Gale, "The Environmental Movement and the Left," p. 191.

21. Morris, *The Origins of the Civil Rights Movement*, p. xii.

leaders, and networks are coming together against polluting industries and discriminatory environmental policies. This book addresses this new uniting of blacks against institutional barriers of racism and classism.

Alsen (Louisiana)

Alsen is an unincorporated community located on the Mississippi River several miles north of Baton Rouge, Louisiana's state capital. The community had a population of 1,104 individuals in 1980 of whom 98.9 percent were black. Alsen developed as a rural community of black landowners to its present status as a stable, working-class suburban enclave. The median income for families in 1980 was $17,188. A total of 19.4 percent of Alsen's residents are below the poverty level, a percentage well below that of blacks nationally and in Louisiana. Typical homes in the area are woodframe or brick-veneer style. More than three-fourths (77.4 percent) of the year-round occupied homes in the community are occupied by owners and 22.6 percent by renters.[22] The community still maintains much of its small-town flavor. Many of the local residents have roots in the community dating back several generations.

Alsen lies at the beginning of the 85-mile industrial corridor where one-quarter of America's petrochemicals are produced. The chemical corridor begins in Baton Rouge and follows the Mississippi River down to the southeastern rim of New Orleans. The tiny town of Alsen sits in the shadow of Huey Long's skyscraper-capitol building and the towering petrochemical plants that dot the Mississippi River. This area also has been dubbed the "cancer corridor" because the air, ground, and water are full of carcinogens, mutagens, and embryotoxins. The area has been described as a "massive human experiment" and a "national sacrifice zone."[23]

The petrochemical industry has played an important role in Louisiana's economy, especially south Louisiana. More than 165,000 persons were employed in the state's petrochemical industry at its peak

22. U.S. Bureau of the Census, *Neighborhood Statistics Program: Narrative Profile of Neighborhoods in Baton Rouge and East Baton Rouge, LA* (Washington, D.C.: U.S. Government Printing Office, 1982), pp. 2–4.

23. David Maraniss and Michael Weisskopf, "Jobs and Illness in Petrochemical Corridor," *Washington Post*, December 22, 1987, p. 1; Brown, *The Toxic Cloud,* pp. 152–161.

in 1982. This single industry accounted for one out of every three tax dollars collected by the state.[24] The Baton Rouge area has paid a high price—industrial pollution—for the concentration of so many chemical companies in its midst. These companies discharge more than 150,000 tons of pollutants into the city's air each year. The bulk of these air pollutants are in the form of sulfur dioxides, nitrogen oxides, carbon monoxides, and hydrocarbons.

Louisiana is not a large state. It ranks thirty-one in land area of all states. Despite its relatively compact size, it managed to import more than 305.6 million pounds of hazardous waste in 1983.[25] Much of this waste was shipped into south Louisiana. In 1986, the state had 33.2 percent of the nation's total permitted hazardous-waste landfill capacity among active sites. Much of Louisiana's hazardous waste generated by the petrochemical industries is dumped in the Baton Rouge area. The only commercial hazardous-waste site in the Baton Rouge area is the Rollins Environmental Services facility, located adjacent to the Alsen community.

The Rollins site was the fourth largest in the nation, representing 11.3 percent of remaining permitted capacity in 1986.[26] The Rollins hazardous-waste landfill and incinerator have been a constant sore point for the nearby Alsen residents. The waste site has been the source of numerous odor and health complaints from nearby community residents and workers at the plant. The plant was cited for more than 100 state and federal violations between 1980 and 1985 but did not pay any penalties. Mary McCastle, a 72-year-old grandmother and Alsen community leader, summed up her community's running battle with Rollins:

> We had no warning Rollins was coming in here. When they did come in we didn't know what they were dumping. We did know that it was making us sick. People used to have nice gardens

24. Bob Anderson, Mike Dunn, and Sonny Alabarado, "Prosperity in Paradise: Louisiana's Chemical Legacy," *Morning Advocate*, April 25, 1985, p. 3.

25. Brown, *The Toxic Cloud*, p. 157.

26. Commission for Racial Justice, *Toxic Wastes and Race in the United States*, p. 66.

and fruit trees. They lived off their gardens and only had to buy meat. Some of us raised hogs and chickens. But not after Rollins came in. Our gardens and animals were dying out. Some days the odors from the plant would be nearly unbearable. We didn't know what was causing it. We later found out that Rollins was burning hazardous waste.[27]

Air quality in the Alsen community became a cause for alarm. Local residents began to question the company's right to spew pollutants on their community. Complaints were filed with the Louisiana Department of Environmental Quality (LDEQ) with no immediate results. Although local citizens registered their displeasure with the waste facility's operation, they got little attention from state environmental officials. Annie Bowdry, the director of the Alsen Community Center—a nonprofit human services program—described the state's response (or lack of response) to Alsen's needs:

Alsen is black and a nowhere place stuck out in the parish. It's not incorporated. It didn't count. It was not until after state environmental officials visited the community that citizen complaints were taken seriously. State officials could not believe that people endured everyday the terrible odors from the Rollins plant.[28]

In late 1980, residents began organizing to stop the contamination of their community. Local leaders recognized the fact that they were going up against a giant corporation. The annual revenue in Rollins from hazardous waste alone was more than $69 million. Citizens were also aware that the company provided jobs—although few Alsen residents worked at the company. Alsen residents were determined to take a stand based on what was best for the health and welfare of their community. In early 1981, local citizens filed a multimillion dollar class-action lawsuit against Rollins. The lawsuit and subsequent state monitoring of the air quality problem in Alsen forced the company to reduce the pollutants from the waste site. Public opposition to the

27. Interview with Mary McCastle, June 23, 1988, Alsen, Louisiana.
28. Interview with Annie Bowdry, June 23, 1988, Alsen, Louisiana.

Rollins hazardous-waste facility intensified in the mid-1980s when citizen groups and environmentalists (Greenpeace, Sierra Club, and some local grassroots groups) turned out in force to oppose an application by the firm to burn PCBs at its incinerator. This protest was successful in blocking the PCBs burn.

Alsen residents were outraged that their lawsuit against Rollins dragged on for so long. Local citizens were angry that Louisiana DEQ officials took so long to believe the horror stories of Alsen's air pollution problem. They wondered why it was so difficult to resolve this problem. Admon McCastle, a native of Alsen, saw racism as the root of his community's dilemma:

> More than 15 years ago, a wealthy white property owner next to Rollins received a half million dollar settlement from the company for the death of his cattle after water spilled onto his pasture. Yet, Rollins has failed to recognize it is harming people, not cows, in the Alsen community. When I look at this, I have to say racism has played a big part in the company's actions and the state's inaction.[29]

After dragging on for more than six years, the lawsuit was finally settled out of court in November 1987. The settlement, however, splintered the community. Residents were polarized into "money versus health" factions. Each plaintiff in the lawsuit received "an average of $3,000 the day before Christmas."[30] There was a "take the money and run" atmosphere that prevailed in the battle-weary community. Opponents of the secret-settlement agreement point to the need for continual health monitoring in the community. This is not a small point since the plaintiffs were required to sign away their right to sue Rollins for any future health-related problems. Annie Bowdry lodged her opposition to the settlement:

> We wanted to establish a health clinic in Alsen that would be administered by the state [Louisiana] and paid for by Rollins.

---

29. Interview with Admon McCastle, June 23, 1988, Alsen Louisiana.
30. Ibid.

Since Rollins made the people sick, they should have to pay for the operation of the clinic. All at once, someone mentioned money and the health clinic proposal went out the window. My feelings about the whole thing is a dollar cannot buy my health. But if I knew I was contaminated in time, then maybe a cure for me could be found. If not for me, then maybe for my children.[31]

Overall, life in the Alsen community has improved since residents have become more informed on the hazardous-waste problem and convinced state officials to closely monitor air quality in their community. Although economic concessions were extracted from Rollins through an out-of-court settlement, the community was left without a health facility of its own. Moreover, the settlement agreement shielded the waste disposal company from any future health-related lawsuits by the Alsen plaintiffs. Alsen residents still must drive to Baton Rouge for health care services.

The community's pollution problem is far from over because numerous chemical plants are still clustered along the Mississippi River just a short distance from their homes. This problem will likely remain as long as the backbone of Louisiana's economy remains heavily dependent on its "chemical corridor." More important, increased public opposition and tougher environmental regulations have made it more difficult to site new hazardous-waste facilities. The Rollins hazardous-waste landfill and incinerator, thus, take on added state and regional importance.

Louisiana, dubbed the "sportsman's paradise," has become an environmental nightmare as a result of lax regulations, unbridled production of toxic chemicals, and heavy dependence on the petrochemical industry as the backbone of the state's economy.

31. Interview with Annie Bowdry.

Dumping in Dixie (1990)

38. Ansel Adams, *El Capitan, Yosemite National Park, California* (1952).

39. Donora, Pennsylvania, on November 3, 1948. A day earlier, funeral services were held for victims of the Donora smog—a cloud of toxic gases that also sickened thousands of residents.

40. An insecticidal fogging machine in its first public test sprays DDT at Jones Beach, New York, July 8, 1945.

41. Cleveland firemen battle a blaze—one of many over the years—on the polluted Cuyahoga River, November 3, 1952.

42. Eliot Porter, *Pool in a Brook, Brook Pond, New Hampshire, October 4, 1953.*

43. Eliot Porter, *Arch and Box Elder Tree, Davis Gulch, Escalante River, Lake Powell, Utah, May 12, 1965.*

44. Charles Pratt, *Woman and Flowering Tree, Hoboken, New Jersey* (c. 1963).

45. Philip Hyde, *South Rim in Winter, Grand Canyon, Arizona* (1964).

46. Rachel Carson, author of the newly published *Silent Spring* (1962).

47. Hugh Barnes, David Brower, and Eliot Porter (*l. to r.*) examining proofs for *"In Wildness Is the Preservation of the World"*—the first of the Sierra Club's "Exhibit Format" books—at Barnes Press in New York (c. 1962).

48. Stanley Mouse/Mouse Studios, poster for 10th Biennial Sierra Club Wilderness Conference (1967).

49. Robert Rauschenberg, Earth Day poster (1970).

50. Earth Day in New York City (1970).

51. Gary Snyder (1969).

52. Earth Day (1970).

53. N. Scott Momaday (c. 1969).

54. A dead bird, covered in oil, in the wake of an oil spill off the coast of Santa Barbara (1969).

55. The "Blue Marble" (1972); taken by an *Apollo 17* crewmember, this was the first clear photograph of an illuminated whole Earth.

56. Robert Adams, *Newly Occupied Tract Houses, Colorado Springs* (1968).

57. Stephen Shore, *Second Street East and South Main Street, Kalispell, Montana, August 22, 1974.*

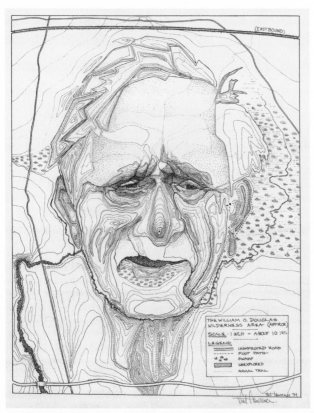

58. A portrait of the Supreme Court Justice and conservationist as a relief map: Vint Lawrence's *The William O. Douglas Wilderness Area* (1974).

59. Edward Abbey in the Aztec Peak lookout tower, where he worked as a fire spotter (Tonto National Forest, Arizona, c. 1979).

60. Scott and Helen Nearing at home in Harborside, Maine (1975).

61. Earth Day organizer Denis Hayes (1970).

62. Marjory Stoneman Douglas, canoeing with a Miccosukee Indian at the Miccosukee Cultural Center in the Everglades (1983).

63. Lois Gibbs at Love Canal (1978).

64. Timothy O'Sullivan, *Green River Buttes, Green River, Wyoming* (1872).

65. O'Sullivan revisited: Mark Klett & Gordon Bushaw for the Rephotographic Survey Project, *Castle Rock, Green River, Wyoming* (1979).

66. Emmet Gowin, *Aeration Pond, Toxic Water Treatment Facility, Pine Bluff, Arkansas* (1989).

67. John Pfahl, *Trojan Nuclear Plant, Columbia River, Oregon, October 1982*. The plant was shut down in 1992 after radioactive steam leaked from a cracked pipe; the cooling tower was demolished in 2006.

68. Julia Butterfly Hill in the branches of Luna, a redwood in the Headwaters Forest near Eureka, California. Hill lived in the tree for over two years to protect it from loggers (1998).

69. George Schaller, wildlife biologist, with a snow leopard kitten (c. 2000).

70. David Quammen in India's Gir Forest National Park, tracking endangered Asiatic lions (1997).

71. E. O. Wilson with a model ant (2002).

72. Robert Dawson, *Polluted New River, Calexico, California* (1989).

73. Kim Stringfellow, *Pumping Out Flood Water, Salton Sea Beach, California* (2004). The increasingly polluted Salton Sea—created by an engineering accident in 1905–06—has become an important habitat for migratory birds.

74. Richard Misrach, *Hazardous Waste Containment Site, Dow Chemical Corporation* (1998).

75. Robert Glenn Ketchum, *The Chainsaws of Summer* (Tongass Rainforest, Alaska, 1992).

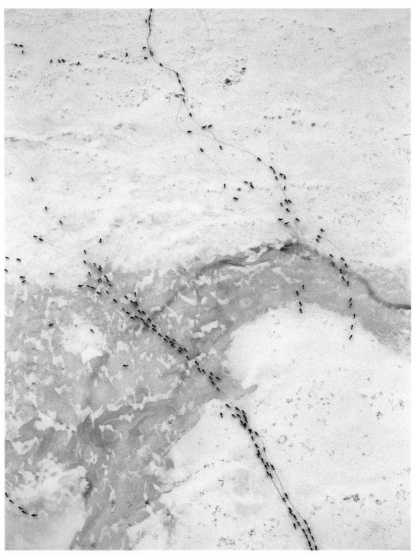

76. Subhankar Banerjee, *Caribou Migration I* (from the series *Oil and the Caribou*, 2002). Banerjee's photographs of the Arctic National Wildlife Refuge were introduced on the Senate floor during the 2003 debate over oil-drilling in the Refuge.

77. Subhankar Banerjee, *Polar Bear on Bernard Harbor* (from the series *Oil and the Caribou*, 2001).

78. A demonstration against salvage logging in the roadless areas of Oregon's Siskiyou National Forest (Christopher LaMarca, from the *Forest Defenders* series, 2005).

79. Anti-pollution protestors from Greenaction for Health & Environmental Justice and the local community block the entrance to a power plant in San Francisco's Hunters Point neighborhood (2004).

80. Chris Jordan, *Sawdust, Tacoma* (2004).

81. Edward Burtynsky, *Oxford Tire Pile #1, Westley, California* (1999).

82. Mitch Epstein, *Amos Coal Power Plant, Raymond, West Virginia* (2004).

MARY OLIVER

Mary Oliver (b. 1935) has won every award there is to win, including the Pulitzer and the National Book Award, but she is also one of those rare contemporary poets whose words are very much in the public realm: I've heard this poem, for instance, at more than one wedding, more than one graduation. She had a poet's upbringing—as a teenager she lived for a while in the home of Edna St. Vincent Millay, before heading off to Vassar—and she has published book after book without interruption. More than anything else, she's a joyous chronicler of the natural world, her verse filled with details from her daily walks near her Cape Cod home.

The Summer Day

Who made the world?
Who made the swan, and the black bear?
Who made the grasshopper?
This grasshopper, I mean—
the one who has flung herself out of the grass,
the one who is eating sugar out of my hand,
who is moving her jaws back and forth instead of up and down—
who is gazing around with her enormous and complicated eyes.
Now she lifts her pale forearms and thoroughly washes her face.
Now she snaps her wings open, and floats away.
I don't know exactly what a prayer is.
I do know how to pay attention, how to fall down
into the grass, how to kneel down in the grass,
how to be idle and blessed, how to stroll through the fields,
which is what I have been doing all day.
Tell me, what else should I have done?

Doesn't everything die at last, and too soon?
Tell me, what is it you plan to do
with your one wild and precious life?

House of Light (1990)

I once was hiking with Terry Tempest Williams (b. 1959) in my Adirondacks, and we came upon a newt in its red eft phase on the trail—a commonplace in the moist East, but a kind of bewildering and glistening orange jewel to someone used to the arid West. She sat there transfixed for a good half hour, caught in the wonder. That kind of close attention, applied to the workings of her family, her Mormon community, and the Utah desert where she's spent most of her life, has made her among the most beloved of contemporary writers about the natural world. Her now-classic *Refuge: An Unnatural History of Family and Place* (1991), from which these excerpts are drawn, tells two stories, one of the threat that the rising water of Great Salt Lake poses to a bird sanctuary on its edge and another of the death of her mother from the same cancer that had already claimed many other women in her family. She is convinced (and convincing) that living downwind from the Nevada nuclear test range in the 1950s has something to do with that run of sorrow, and she's been relentless as an opponent of that testing and as an advocate for protection of Utah's desert wilds, not always a popular stand in a conservative state. Her many other books include an essay collection *An Unspoken Hunger* (1994) and *Leap* (2000), a wildly imaginative meditation on a Hieronymus Bosch painting.

from Refuge: An Unnatural History of Family and Place

lake level: 4204.70'

Great Salt Lake is about twenty-five minutes from our home. From the mouth of Emigration Canyon where we live, I drive west past Brigham Young standing on top of "This Is the Place" monument. When I reach Foothill Drive, I turn right, pass the University of

Utah and make another right, heading east until I meet South Temple, which requires a left-hand turn. I arrive a few miles later at Eagle Gate, a bronze arch that spans State Street. I turn right once more. One block later, I turn left on North Temple and pass the Mormon Tabernacle on Temple Square. From here, I simply follow the gulls west, past the Salt Lake City International Airport.

Great Salt Lake: wilderness adjacent to a city; a shifting shoreline that plays havoc with highways; islands too stark, too remote to inhabit; water in the desert that no one can drink. It is the liquid lie of the West.

I recall an experiment from school: we filled a cup with water—the surface area of the contents was only a few square inches. Then we poured the same amount of water into a large, shallow dinner plate—it covered nearly a square foot. Most lakes in the world are like cups of water. Great Salt Lake, with its average depth measuring only thirteen feet, is like the dinner plate. We then added two or three tablespoons of salt to the cup of water for the right amount of salinity to complete the analogue.

The experiment continued: we let the plate and cup of water stand side by side on the window sill. As they evaporated, we watched the plate of water dry up becoming encrusted with salt long before the cup. The crystals were beautiful.

Because Great Salt Lake lies on the bottom of the Great Basin, the largest closed system in North America, it is a terminal lake with no outlet to the sea.

The water level of Great Salt Lake fluctuates wildly in response to climatic changes. The sun bears down on the lake an average of about 70 percent of the time. The water frequently reaches ninety degrees Fahrenheit, absorbing enough energy to evaporate almost four feet of water annually. If rainfall exceeds the evaporation rate, Great Salt Lake rises. If rainfall drops below the evaporation rate, the lake recedes. Add the enormous volume of stream inflow from the high Wasatch and Uinta Mountains in the east, and one begins to see a portrait of change.

Great Salt Lake is cyclic. At winter's end, the lake level rises with mountain runoff. By late spring, it begins to decline when the weather becomes hot enough that loss of water by evaporation from the surface is greater than the combined inflow from streams, ground water, and precipitation. The lake begins to rise again in the autumn, when the temperature decreases, and the loss of water by evaporation is exceeded by the inflow.

Since Captain Howard Stansbury's *Exploration and Survey of the Great Salt Lake, 1852,* the water level has varied by as much as twenty feet, altering the shoreline in some places by as much as fifteen miles. Great Salt Lake is surrounded by salt flats, sage plains, and farmland; a slight rise in the water level extends its area considerably. In the past twenty years, Great Salt Lake's surface area has fluctuated from fifteen hundred square miles to its present twenty-five hundred square miles. Great Salt Lake is now approximately the size of Delaware and Rhode Island. It has been estimated that a ten foot rise in Great Salt Lake would cover an additional two hundred forty square miles.

To understand the relationship that exists at Great Salt Lake between area and volume, imagine pouring one inch of water into the bottom of a paper cone. It doesn't take much water to raise an inch. However, if you wanted to raise the water level one inch at the top of the cone, the volume of water added would have to increase considerably. The lake bed of Great Salt Lake is cone-shaped. It takes more water to raise the lake an inch when it is at high-level, and less water to raise it in low-level years.

Natives of the Great Basin, of the Salt Lake Valley in particular, speak about Great Salt Lake in the shorthand of lake levels. For example, in 1963, Great Salt Lake retreated to its historic low of 4191'. Ten years later, Great Salt Lake reached its historic mean, 4200'— about the same level explorers John Fremont and Howard Stansbury encountered in the 1840s and 50s.

On September 18, 1982, Great Salt Lake began to rise because of a series of storms that occurred earlier in the month. The precipitation of 7.04 inches for the month (compared to an annual average of about fifteen inches from 1875 to 1982) made it the wettest September on record for Salt Lake City. The lake continued to rise for the next ten months as a result of greater-than-average snowfall during the winter and spring of 1982–83, and unseasonably cool weather (thus little evaporation) during the spring of 1983. The rise from September 18, 1982 to June 30, 1983, was 5.1′, the greatest seasonal rise ever recorded.

During these years, talk on the streets of Salt Lake City has centered around the lake: 4204′ and rising. It is no longer just a backdrop for spectacular sunsets. It is the play of urban drama. Everyone has their interests. 4211.6′ was the historic high recorded in the 1870's. City officials knew the Salt Lake City International Airport would be underwater if the Great Salt Lake rose to 4220′. Developments along the lakeshore were sunk at 4208′. Farmers whose land was being flooded in daily increments were trying desperately to dike or sell. And the Southern Pacific Railroad labors to maintain their tracks above water, twenty-four hours a day, three hundred sixty-five days a year, and has been doing so since 1959.

My interest lay at 4206′, the level which, according to my topographical map, meant the flooding of the Bear River Migratory Bird Refuge.

There are those birds you gauge your life by. The burrowing owls five miles from the entrance to the Bear River Migratory Bird Refuge are mine. Sentries. Each year, they alert me to the regularities of the land. In spring, I find them nesting, in summer they forage with their young, and by winter they abandon the Refuge for a place more comfortable.

What is distinctive about these owls is their home. It rises from the alkaline flats like a clay-covered fist. If you were to peek inside the tightly clenched fingers, you would find a dark-holed entrance.

"Tttss! Tttss! Tttss!"

That is no rattlesnake. Those are the distress cries of the burrowing owl's young.

Adult burrowing owls will stand on top of the mound with their prey before them, usually small rodents, birds, or insects. The entrance is littered with bones and feathers. I recall finding a swatch of yellow feathers like a doormat across the threshold—meadowlark, maybe. These small owls pursue their prey religiously at dusk.

Burrowing owls are part of the desert community, taking advantage of the abandoned burrows of prairie dogs. Historically, bison would move across the American Plains, followed by prairie dog towns which would aerate the soil after the weight of stampeding hooves. Black-footed ferrets, rattlesnakes, and burrowing owls inhabited the edges, finding an abundant food source in the communal rodents.

With the loss of desert lands, a decline in prairie dog populations is inevitable. And so go the ferret and burrowing owl. Rattlesnakes are more adaptable.

In Utah, prairie dogs and black-footed ferrets are endangered species, with ferrets almost extinct. The burrowing owl is defined as "threatened," a political step away from endangered status. Each year, the burrowing owls near the Refuge become more blessed.

The owls had staked their territory just beyond one of the bends in the Bear River. Whenever I drove to the Bird Refuge, I stopped at their place first and sat on the edge of the road and watched. They would fly around me, their wings sometimes spanning two feet. Undulating from post to post, they would distract me from their nest. Just under a foot long, they have a body of feathers the color of wheat, balanced on two long, spindly legs. They can burn grasses with their stare. Yellow eyes magnifying light.

The protective hissing of baby burrowing owls is an adaptive memory of their close association with prairie rattlers. Snake or owl? Who wants to risk finding out.

In the summer of 1983, I worried about the burrowing owls, wondering if the rising waters of Great Salt Lake had flooded their home, too. I was relieved to find not only their mound intact, but four owlets standing on its threshold. One of the Refuge managers stopped on the road and commented on what a good year it had been for them.

"Good news," I replied. "The lake didn't take everything."

That was late August when huge concentrations of shorebirds were still feeding between submerged shadescale.

A few months later, a friend of mine, Sandy Lopez, was visiting from Oregon. We had spoken of the Bird Refuge many times. The whistling swans had arrived, and it seemed like a perfect day for the marsh.

To drive to the Bear River Migratory Bird Refuge from Salt Lake City takes a little over one hour. I have discovered the conversation that finds its way into the car often manifests itself later on the land.

We spoke of rage. Of women and landscape. How our bodies and the body of the earth have been mined.

"It has everything to do with intimacy," I said. "Men define intimacy through their bodies. It is physical. They define intimacy with the land in the same way."

"Many men have forgotten what they are connected to," my friend added. "Subjugation of women and nature may be a loss of intimacy within themselves."

She paused, then looked at me.

"Do you feel rage?"

I didn't answer for some time.

"I feel sadness. I feel powerless at times. But I'm not certain what rage really means."

Several miles passed.

"Do you?" I asked.

She looked out the window. "Yes. Perhaps your generation, one behind mine, is a step removed from the pain."

We reached the access road to the Refuge and both took out our binoculars, ready for the birds. Most of the waterfowl had migrated, but a few ruddy ducks, redheads, and shovelers remained. The marsh glistened like cut topaz.

As we turned west about five miles from the Refuge, a mile or so from the burrowing owl's mound, I began to speak of them, *Athene cunicularia*. I told Sandy about the time when my grandmother and I first discovered them. It was in 1960, the same year she gave me my Peterson's *Field Guide to Western Birds*. I know because I dated their picture. We have come back every year since to pay our respects. Generations of burrowing owls have been raised here. I turned to my friend and explained how four owlets had survived the flood.

We anticipated them.

About a half mile away, I could not see the mound. I took my foot off the gas pedal and coasted. It was as though I was in unfamiliar country.

The mound was gone. Erased. In its place, fifty feet back, stood a cinderblock building with a sign, CANADIAN GOOSE GUN CLUB. A new fence crushed the grasses with a handwritten note posted: KEEP OUT.

We got out of the car and walked to where the mound had been for as long as I had a memory. Gone. Not a pellet to be found.

A blue pickup pulled alongside us.

"Howdy." They tipped their ball caps. "What y'all lookin' for?"

I said nothing. Sandy said nothing. My eyes narrowed.

"We didn't kill 'em. Those boys from the highway department came and graveled the place. Two bits, they did it. I mean, you gotta admit those ground owls are messy little bastards. They'll shit all over hell if ya let 'em. And try and sleep with 'em hollering at ya all night long. They had to go. Anyway, we got bets with the county they'll pop up someplace around here next year."

The three men in the front seat looked up at us, tipped their caps again. And drove off.

Restraint is the steel partition between a rational mind and a violent one. I knew rage. It was fire in my stomach with no place to go.

I drove out to the Refuge on another day. I suppose I wanted to see the mound back in place with the family of owls bobbing on top. Of course, they were not.

I sat on the gravel and threw stones.

By chance, the same blue pickup with the same three men pulled alongside: the self-appointed proprietors of the newly erected Canadian Goose Gun Club.

"Howdy, ma'am. Still lookin' for them owls, or was it sparrows?"

One winked.

Suddenly in perfect detail, I pictured the burrowing owls' mound— that clay-covered fist rising from the alkaline flats. The exact one these beergut-over-beltbuckled men had leveled.

I walked calmly over to their truck and leaned my stomach against their door. I held up my fist a few inches from the driver's face and slowly lifted my middle finger to the sky.

"This is for you—from the owls and me."

My mother was appalled—not so much over the loss of the burrowing owls, although it saddened her, but by my behavior. Women did not deliver obscene gestures to men, regardless. She shook her head, saying she had no idea where I came from.

In Mormon culture, that is one of the things you do know—history and geneology. I come from a family with deep roots in the American West. When the expense of outfitting several thousand immigrants to Utah was becoming too great for the newly established church, leaders decided to furnish the pioneers with small two-wheeled carts about the size of those used by apple peddlers, which could be pulled by hand from Missouri to the Salt Lake Valley. My ancestors were part of these original "handcart companies" in the 1850s. With faith, they would endure. They came with few provisions over the twelve-hundred-mile trail. It was a small sacrifice in the name of religious freedom. Almost one hundred and fifty years later, we are still here.

I am the oldest child in our family, a daughter with three younger brothers: Steve, Dan, and Hank.

My parents, John Henry Tempest, III, and Diane Dixon Tempest, were married in the Mormon Temple in Salt Lake City on September 18, 1953. My husband, Brooke Williams, and I followed the same tradition and were married on June 2, 1975. I was nineteen years old.

Our extended family includes both maternal and paternal grandparents: Lettie Romney Dixon and Donald "Sanky" Dixon, Kathryn Blackett Tempest and John Henry Tempest, Jr.

Aunts, uncles, and cousins are many, extending familial ties all across the state of Utah. If I ever wonder who I am, I simply attend a Romney family reunion and find myself in the eyes of everyone I meet. It is comforting and disturbing, at once.

I have known five of my great-grandparents intimately. They tutored me in stories with a belief that lineage mattered. Genealogy is in our blood. As a people and as a family, we have a sense of history. And our history is tied to land.

I was raised to believe in a spirit world, that life exists before the earth and will continue to exist afterward, that each human being, bird, and bulrush, along with all other life forms had a spirit life before it came to dwell physically on the earth. Each occupied an assigned sphere of influence, each has a place and a purpose.

It made sense to a child. And if the natural world was assigned spiritual values, then those days spent in wildness were sacred. We learned at an early age that God can be found wherever you are, especially outside. Family worship was not just relegated to Sunday in a chapel.

Our weekends were spent camped alongside a small stream in the Great Basin, in the Stansbury Mountains or Deep Creeks. My father would take the boys rabbit hunting while Mother and I would sit on a log in an aspen grove and talk. She would tell me stories of how when she was a girl she would paint red lips on the trunks of trees to practice kissing. Or how she would lie in her grandmother's lucerne patch and watch clouds.

"I have never known my full capacity for solitude," she would say.

"Solitude?" I asked.

"The gift of being alone. I can never get enough."

The men would return anxious for dinner. Mother would cook over a green Coleman stove as Dad told stories from his childhood—like the time his father took away his BB gun for a year because he shot off the heads of every red tulip in his mother's garden, row after row after row. He laughed. We laughed. And then it was time to bless the food.

After supper, we would spread out our sleeping bags in a circle, heads pointing to the center like a covey of quail, and watch the Great Basin sky fill with stars. Our attachment to the land was our attachment to each other.

The days I loved most were the days at Bear River. The Bird Refuge was a sanctuary for my grandmother and me. I call her "Mimi." We would walk along the road with binoculars around our necks and simply watch birds. Hundreds of birds. Birds so exotic to a desert child it forced the imagination to be still. The imagined was real at Bear River.

I recall one bird in particular. It wore a feathered robe of cinnamon, white, and black. Its body rested on long, thin legs. Blue legs. On the edge of the marsh, it gracefully lowered its head and began sweeping the water side to side with its delicate, upturned bill.

"Plee-ek! Plee-ek! Plee-ek!"

Three more landed. My grandmother placed her hand gently on my shoulder and whispered, "avocets." I was nine years old.

At ten, Mimi thought I was old enough to join the Audubon Society on a special outing to the wetlands surrounding Great Salt Lake. We boarded a greyhound bus in downtown Salt Lake and drove north on U.S. Highway 91, paralleling the Wasatch Mountains on our right and Great Salt Lake on our left. Once relaxed and out of the city, we were handed an official checklist of birds at the Bear River Migratory Bird Refuge.

"All members are encouraged to take copious notes and keep scrupulous records of birds seen," proclaimed the gray-haired, pony-tailed woman passing out cards.

"What do copious and scrupulous mean?" I asked my grandmother.

"It means pay attention," she said. I pulled out my notebook and drew pictures of the backs of birdwatchers' heads.

Off the highway, the bus drove through the small town of Brigham City with its sycamore-lined streets. It's like most Utah settlements with its Mormon layout: a chapel for weekly worship, a tabernacle for communal events, and a temple nearby (in this case Logan) where sacred rites are performed. Lawns are well groomed and neighborhoods are immaculate. But the banner arched over Main Street makes this town unique. In neon lights it reads, BRIGHAM CITY: GATEWAY TO THE WORLD'S GREATEST GAME BIRD REFUGE. So welded to the local color of this community, I daresay no one sees the sign anymore, except newcomers and perhaps the birds that fly under it.

A small, elderly man with wire-rimmed glasses and a worn golf cap, stood at the front of the bus and began speaking into the handheld microphone: "Ladies and gentlemen, in approximately ten miles we will be entering the Bear River Migratory Bird Refuge, America's first waterfowl sanctuary, established by a special act of Congress on April 23, 1928."

I was confused. I thought the marsh had been created in the spirit world first and on earth second. I never made the connection that God and Congress were in cahoots. Mimi said she would explain the situation later.

The man went on to say that the Bird Refuge was located at the delta of the Bear River, which poured into the Great Salt Lake. This I understood.

"People, this bus is a clock. Eyes forward, please. Straight ahead is twelve o'clock; to the rear is six. Three o'clock is on your right. Any bird identified from this point on will be noted accordingly."

The bus became a bird dog, a labrador on wheels, which decided where high noon would be simply by pointing in that direction. What time would it be if a bird decided to fly from nine o'clock to three o'clock? Did that make the bird half past nine or quarter to three? Even more worrisome to me was the possibility of a flock of birds flying between four and five o'clock. Would you say, "Twenty birds after four? Four-thirty?" Or simply move the hands of the clock forward to five? I decided not to bother my grandmother with these particulars and, instead, retreated to my unindexed field guide and turned to the color plates of ducks.

"Ibises at two o'clock!"

The brakes squeaked the bus to a halt. The doors opened like bellows and we all filed out. And there they were, dozens of white-faced glossy ibises grazing in the field. Their feathers on first glance were chestnut, but with the slightest turn they flashed iridescences of pink, purple, and green.

Another flock landed nearby. And another. And another. They coasted in diagonal lines with their heads and necks extended, their long legs trailing behind them, seeming to fall forward on hinges the second before they touched ground. By now, we must have been watching close to a hundred ibises probing the farmlands adjacent to the marsh.

Our leader told us they were eating earthworms and insects.

"Good eyes," I thought, as I could only see their decurved bills like scythes disappearing behind the grasses. I watched the wind turn each feather as the birds turned the soil.

Mimi whispered to me how ibises are the companions of gods. "Ibis escorts Thoth, the Egyptian god of wisdom and magic, who is the guardian of the Moon Gates in heaven. And there are two colors of ibis—one black and one white. The dark bird is believed to be associated with death, the white bird a celebration of birth."

I looked out over the fields of black ibis.

"When an ibis tucks its head underwing to sleep, it resembles a heart. The ibis knows empathy," my grandmother said. "Remember that, alongside the fact it eats worms."

She also told me that if I could learn a new way to tell time, I could also learn a new way to measure distance.

"The stride of an ibis was a measurement used in building the great temples of the Nile."

I sat down by the rear wheels of the bus and pondered the relationship between an ibis at Bear River and an ibis foraging on the banks of the Nile. In my young mind, it had something to do with the magic of birds, how they bridge cultures and continents with their wings, how they mediate between heaven and earth.

Back on the bus and moving, I wrote in my notebook "one hundred white-faced glossy ibises—companions of the gods."

Mimi was pleased. "We could go home now," she said. "The ibis makes the day."

But there were more birds. Many, many more. Within the next few miles, ducks, geese, and shorebirds were sighted around "the clock." The bus drove past all of them. With my arms out the window, I tried to touch the wings of avocets and stilts. I knew these birds from our private trips to the Refuge. They had become relatives.

As the black-necked stilts flew alongside the silver bus, their long legs trailed behind them like red streamers.

"*Ip-ip-ip! Ip-ip-ip!*"

Their bills were not flattened and upturned like avocets, but straight as darning needles.

The wind massaged my face. I closed my eyes and sat back in my seat.

Mimi and I got out of the bus and ate our lunch on the riverbank. Two western grebes, ruby-eyed and serpentine, fished, diving at good prospects. They surfaced with silver minnows struggling between sharp mandibles. Violet-green swallows skimmed the water for midges as a snowy egret stood on the edge of the spillway.

With a crab sandwich in one hand and binoculars in the other, Mimi explained why the Bird Refuge had in fact, been created.

"Maybe the best way to understand it," she said, "is to realize the original wetlands were recreated. It was the deterioration of the marshes at Bear River Bay that led to the establishment of a sanctuary."

"How?" I asked.

"The marshes were declining for several reasons: the diversion of water from the Bear River for irrigation, the backing-up of brine from Great Salt Lake during high-water periods, excessive hunting, and a dramatic rise in botulism, a disease known then as 'western duck disease.'

"The creation of the Bear River Migratory Bird Refuge helped to preserve the freshwater character of the marsh. Dikes were built to hold the water from the Bear River to stabilize, manage, and control water levels within the marsh. This helped to control botulism and at the same time keep out the brine. Meanwhile, the birds flourished."

After lunch, I climbed the observation tower at the Refuge headquarters. Any fear of heights I may have had moving up the endless flights of steel stairs was replaced by the bird's eye view before me. The marsh appeared as a green and blue mosaic where birds remained in a fluid landscape.

In the afternoon, we drove the twenty-two-mile loop around the Refuge. The roads capped the dikes which were bordered by deep channels of water with bulrush and teasel. We saw ruddy ducks (the man sitting behind us called them "blue bills"), shovelers, teals, and wigeons. We watched herons and egrets and rails. Red-wing blackbirds poised on cattails sang with long-billed marsh wrens as muskrats swam inside shadows created by clouds. Large families of Canada geese occupied the open water, while ravens flushed the edges for unprotected nests with eggs.

The marsh reflected health as concentric circles rippled outward from a mallard feeding "bottoms up."

By the end of the day, Mimi and I had marked sixty-seven species on our checklist, many of which I had never seen before. A short-eared owl hovered over the cattails. It was the last bird we saw as we left the Refuge.

I fell asleep on my grandmother's lap. Her strong, square hands resting on my forehead shielded the sun from my eyes. I dreamed of water and cattails and all that is hidden.

* * *

Epilogue

I belong to a Clan of One-Breasted Women. My mother, my grand-mothers, and six aunts have all had mastectomies. Seven are dead. The two who survive have just completed rounds of chemotherapy and radiation.

I've had my own problems: two biopsies for breast cancer and a small tumor between my ribs diagnosed as a "borderline malignancy."

This is my family history.

Most statistics tell us breast cancer is genetic, hereditary, with rising percentages attached to fatty diets, childlessness, or becoming pregnant after thirty. What they don't say is living in Utah may be the greatest hazard of all.

We are a Mormon family with roots in Utah since 1847. The "word of wisdom" in my family aligned us with good foods—no coffee, no tea, tobacco, or alcohol. For the most part, our women were finished having their babies by the time they were thirty. And only one faced breast cancer prior to 1960. Traditionally, as a group of people, Mormons have a low rate of cancer.

Is our family a cultural anomaly? The truth is, we didn't think about it. Those who did, usually the men, simply said, "bad genes." The women's attitude was stoic. Cancer was part of life. On February 16, 1971, the eve of my mother's surgery, I accidently picked up the telephone and overheard her ask my grandmother what she could expect.

"Diane, it is one of the most spiritual experiences you will ever encounter."

I quietly put down the receiver.

Two days later, my father took my brothers and me to the hospital to visit her. She met us in the lobby in a wheelchair. No bandages were visible. I'll never forget her radiance, the way she held herself in a purple velvet robe, and how she gathered us around her.

"Children, I am fine. I want you to know I felt the arms of God around me."

We believed her. My father cried. Our mother, his wife, was thirty-eight years old.

A little over a year after Mother's death, Dad and I were having dinner together. He had just returned from St. George, where the Tempest Company was completing the gas lines that would service southern Utah. He spoke of his love for the country, the sandstoned landscape, bare-boned and beautiful. He had just finished hiking the Kolob trail in Zion National Park. We got caught up in reminiscing, recalling with fondness our walk up Angel's Landing on his fiftieth birthday and the years our family had vacationed there.

Over dessert, I shared a recurring dream of mine. I told my father that for years, as long as I could remember, I saw this flash of light in the night in the desert—that this image had so permeated my being that I could not venture south without seeing it again, on the horizon, illuminating buttes and mesas.

"You did see it," he said.

"Saw what?"

"The bomb. The cloud. We were driving home from Riverside, California. You were sitting on Diane's lap. She was pregnant. In fact, I remember the day, September 7, 1957. We had just gotten out of the Service. We were driving north, past Las Vegas. It was an hour or so before dawn, when this explosion went off. We not only heard it, but felt it. I thought the oil tanker in front of us had blown up. We pulled over and suddenly, rising from the desert floor, we saw it, clearly, this golden-stemmed cloud, the mushroom. The sky seemed to vibrate with an eerie pink glow. Within a few minutes, a light ash was raining on the car."

I stared at my father.

"I thought you knew that," he said. "It was a common occurrence in the fifties."

It was at this moment that I realized the deceit I had been living under. Children growing up in the American Southwest, drinking contaminated milk from contaminated cows, even from the contaminated breasts of their mothers, my mother—members, years later, of the Clan of One-Breasted Women.

It is a well-known story in the Desert West, "The Day We Bombed Utah," or more accurately, the years we bombed Utah: above ground atomic testing in Nevada took place from January 27, 1951, through July 11, 1962. Not only were the winds blowing north covering "low-use segments of the population" with fallout and leaving sheep dead in their tracks, but the climate was right. The United States of the 1950s was red, white, and blue. The Korean War was raging. McCarthyism was rampant. Ike was it, and the cold war was hot. If you were against nuclear testing, you were for a communist regime.

Much has been written about this "American nuclear tragedy." Public health was secondary to national security. The Atomic Energy Commissioner, Thomas Murray, said, "Gentlemen, we must not let anything interfere with this series of tests, nothing."

Again and again, the American public was told by its government, in spite of burns, blisters, and nausea, "It has been found that the tests may be conducted with adequate assurance of safety under conditions prevailing at the bombing reservations." Assuaging public fears was simply a matter of public relations. "Your best action," an Atomic Energy Commission booklet read, "is not to be worried about fallout." A news release typical of the times stated, "We find no basis for concluding that harm to any individual has resulted from radioactive fallout."

On August 30, 1979, during Jimmy Carter's presidency, a suit was filed, *Irene Allen* v. *The United States of America*. Mrs. Allen's case was the first on an alphabetical list of twenty-four test cases, representative of nearly twelve hundred plaintiffs seeking compensation from the United States government for cancers caused by nuclear testing in Nevada.

Irene Allen lived in Hurricane, Utah. She was the mother of five children and had been widowed twice. Her first husband, with their two oldest boys, had watched the tests from the roof of the local high school. He died of leukemia in 1956. Her second husband died of pancreatic cancer in 1978.

In a town meeting conducted by Utah Senator Orrin Hatch, shortly before the suit was filed, Mrs. Allen said, "I am not blaming the government, I want you to know that, Senator Hatch. But I thought if my testimony could help in any way so this wouldn't happen again to any of the generations coming up after us . . . I am happy to be here this day to bear testimony of this."

God-fearing people. This is just one story in an anthology of thousands.

On May 10, 1984, Judge Bruce S. Jenkins handed down his opinion. Ten of the plaintiffs were awarded damages. It was the first time a federal court had determined that nuclear tests had been the cause of cancers. For the remaining fourteen test cases, the proof of causation was not sufficient. In spite of the split decision, it was considered a landmark ruling. It was not to remain so for long.

In April 1987, the Tenth Circuit Court of Appeals overturned Judge Jenkins's ruling on the ground that the United States was protected from suit by the legal doctrine of sovereign immunity, a centuries-old idea from England in the days of absolute monarchs.

In January 1988, the Supreme Court refused to review the Appeals Court decision. To our court system it does not matter whether the United States government was irresponsible, whether it lied to its citizens, or even that citizens died from the fallout of nuclear testing. What matters is that our government is immune: "The King can do no wrong."

In Mormon culture, authority is respected, obedience is revered, and independent thinking is not. I was taught as a young girl not to "make waves" or "rock the boat."

"Just let it go," Mother would say. "You know how you feel, that's what counts."

For many years, I have done just that—listened, observed, and quietly formed my own opinions, in a culture that rarely asks questions because it has all the answers. But one by one, I have watched the women in my family die common, heroic deaths. We sat in waiting rooms hoping for good news, but always receiving the bad. I cared for them, bathed their scarred bodies, and kept their secrets. I watched beautiful women become bald as Cytoxan, cisplatin, and Adriamycin were injected into their veins. I held their foreheads as they vomited green-black bile, and I shot them with morphine when the pain became inhuman. In the end, I witnessed their last peaceful breaths, becoming a midwife to the rebirth of their souls.

The price of obedience has become too high.

The fear and inability to question authority that ultimately killed rural communities in Utah during atmospheric testing of atomic weapons is the same fear I saw in my mother's body. Sheep. Dead sheep. The evidence is buried.

I cannot prove that my mother, Diane Dixon Tempest, or my grand-mothers, Lettie Romney Dixon and Kathryn Blackett Tempest, along with my aunts developed cancer from nuclear fallout in Utah. But I can't prove they didn't.

My father's memory was correct. The September blast we drove through in 1957 was part of Operation Plumbbob, one of the most inten-sive series of bomb tests to be initiated. The flash of light in the night in the desert, which I had always thought was a dream, developed into a family nightmare. It took fourteen years, from 1957 to 1971, for cancer to manifest in my mother—the same time, Howard L. Andrews, an author-ity in radioactive fallout at the National Institutes of Health, says radia-tion cancer requires to become evident. The more I learn about what it means to be a "downwinder," the more questions I drown in.

What I do know, however, is that as a Mormon woman of the fifth generation of Latter-day Saints, I must question everything, even if it means losing my faith, even if it means becoming a member of a border tribe among my own people. Tolerating blind obedience in the name of patriotism or religion ultimately takes our lives.

When the Atomic Energy Commission described the country north of the Nevada Test Site as "virtually uninhabited desert terrain," my family and the birds at Great Salt Lake were some of the "virtual unin-habitants."

One night, I dreamed women from all over the world circled a blazing fire in the desert. They spoke of change, how they hold the moon in their bellies and wax and wane with its phases. They mocked the presumption of even-tempered beings and made promises that they would never fear the witch inside themselves. The women danced wildly as sparks broke away from the flames and entered the night sky as stars.

And they sang a song given to them by Shoshone grandmothers:

Ah ne nah, nah	Consider the rabbits
nin nah nah—	How gently they walk on the earth—
ah ne nah, nah	Consider the rabbits
nin nah nah—	How gently they walk on the earth—
Nyaga mutzi	We remember them
oh ne nay—	We can walk gently also—
Nyaga mutzi	We remember them
oh ne nay—	We can walk gently also—

The women danced and drummed and sang for weeks, preparing themselves for what was to come. They would reclaim the desert for the sake of their children, for the sake of the land.

A few miles downwind from the fire circle, bombs were being tested. Rabbits felt the tremors. Their soft leather pads on paws and feet recognized the shaking sands, while the roots of mesquite and sage were smoldering. Rocks were hot from the inside out and dust devils hummed unnaturally. And each time there was another nuclear test, ravens watched the desert heave. Stretch marks appeared. The land was losing its muscle.

The women couldn't bear it any longer. They were mothers. They had suffered labor pains but always under the promise of birth. The red hot pains beneath the desert promised death only, as each bomb became a stillborn. A contract had been made and broken between human beings and the land. A new contract was being drawn by the women, who understood the fate of the earth as their own.

Under the cover of darkness, ten women slipped under a barbed-wire fence and entered the contaminated country. They were trespassing. They walked toward the town of Mercury, in moonlight, taking their cues from coyote, kit fox, antelope squirrel, and quail. They moved quietly and deliberately through the maze of Joshua trees. When a hint of daylight appeared they rested, drinking tea and sharing their rations of food. The women closed their eyes. The time had come to protest with the heart, that to deny one's genealogy with the earth was to commit treason against one's soul.

At dawn, the women draped themselves in mylar, wrapping long streamers of silver plastic around their arms to blow in the breeze. They wore clear masks, that became the faces of humanity. And when they arrived at the edge of Mercury, they carried all the butterflies of a summer day in their wombs. They paused to allow their courage to settle.

The town that forbids pregnant women and children to enter because of radiation risks was asleep. The women moved through the streets as winged messengers, twirling around each other in slow motion, peeking inside homes and watching the easy sleep of men and women. They were astonished by such stillness and periodically would utter a shrill note or low cry just to verify life.

The residents finally awoke to these strange apparitions. Some simply stared. Others called authorities, and in time, the women were apprehended by wary soldiers dressed in desert fatigues. They were taken to a white, square building on the other edge of Mercury. When asked who they were and why they were there, the women replied, "We are mothers and we have come to reclaim the desert for our children."

The soldiers arrested them. As the ten women were blindfolded and handcuffed, they began singing:

> *You can't forbid us everything*
> *You can't forbid us to think—*
> *You can't forbid our tears to flow*
> *And you can't stop the songs that we sing.*

The women continued to sing louder and louder, until they heard the voices of their sisters moving across the mesa:

> *Ah ne nah, nah*
> *nin nah nah—*
> *Ah ne nah, nah*
> *nin nah nah—*
> *Nyaga mutzi*

oh ne nay—
Nyaga mutzi
oh ne nay—

"Call for reinforcements," one soldier said.

"We have," interrupted one woman, "we have—and you have no idea of our numbers."

I crossed the line at the Nevada Test Site and was arrested with nine other Utahns for trespassing on military lands. They are still conducting nuclear tests in the desert. Ours was an act of civil disobedience. But as I walked toward the town of Mercury, it was more than a gesture of peace. It was a gesture on behalf of the Clan of One-Breasted Women.

As one officer cinched the handcuffs around my wrists, another frisked my body. She found a pen and a pad of paper tucked inside my left boot.

"And these?" she asked sternly.

"Weapons," I replied.

Our eyes met. I smiled. She pulled the leg of my trousers back over my boot.

"Step forward, please," she said as she took my arm.

We were booked under an afternoon sun and bused to Tonopah, Nevada. It was a two-hour ride. This was familiar country. The Joshua trees standing their ground had been named by my ancestors, who believed they looked like prophets pointing west to the Promised Land. These were the same trees that bloomed each spring, flowers appearing like white flames in the Mojave. And I recalled a full moon in May, when Mother and I had walked among them, flushing out mourning doves and owls.

The bus stopped short of town. We were released.

The officials thought it was a cruel joke to leave us stranded in the desert with no way to get home. What they didn't realize was that we were home, soul-centered and strong, women who recognized the sweet smell of sage as fuel for our spirits.

Refuge (1991)

RICK BASS

The wolf has long been a preeminent symbol of American wilderness—feared, reviled, systematically destroyed, and then slowly allowed a chance to come back. By the 1990s the wolf had been extirpated from most of its range in the lower 48, but healthy populations in Minnesota and Wisconsin set the stage for reintroduction efforts in, among other places, Yellowstone Park. Despite the bitter opposition of ranchers, the new packs proved both huge draws for tourists and a salutary part of western ecosystems. Few American writers have taken the measure of the animal as powerfully as Rick Bass (b. 1958), writing here not about reintroduced animals but about a pack that drifted on its own down from Canada. A native of Texas who first came to prominence with stories of his brief career as a petroleum geologist in *Oil Notes* (1989), Bass relocated to the remote and wild Yaak Valley of northern Montana, where he has waged a passionate fight to gain wilderness protection for a landscape besieged by large-scale logging. Known for books like *The Lost Grizzlies* (1995) and his massive, magical novel *Where the Sea Used to Be* (1998), Bass lives, literally and in his writing, on the border between the human and the wild. When the former overwhelms the latter, he warns, the damage goes both ways.

from The Ninemile Wolves

They say not to anthropomorphize—not to think of them as having feelings, not to think of them as being able to think—but late at night I like to imagine that they are killing: that another deer has gone down in a tangle of legs, tackled in deep snow; and that, once again, the wolves are feeding. That they have saved themselves, once again. That the deer or moose calf, or young dumb elk is still warm (steam rising from the belly as that part which contains the entrails is opened first), is now dead, or dying.

They eat everything, when they kill, even the snow that soaks up the blood.

This all goes on usually at night. They catch their prey from behind, often, but also by the nose, the face, the neck—whatever they can dart in and grab without being kicked. When the prey pauses, or buckles, it's over; the prey's hindquarters, or neck, might be torn out, and in that manner, the prey flounders. The wolves swarm it, then. They don't have thumbs. All they've got is teeth, long legs, and—I have to say this—great hearts.

I can say what I want to say. I gave up my science badge a long time ago. I've interviewed maybe a hundred people for or against wolves. The ones who are "for" wolves, they have an agenda: wilderness, and freedom for predators, for prey, for everything. The ones who are "against" wolves have an agenda: they've got vested financial interests. It's about money—more and more money—for them. They perceive the wolves to be an obstacle to frictionless cash flow.

The story's so rich. I can begin anywhere.

I can start with prey, which is what controls wolf numbers (not the other way around), or with history, which is rich in sin, cruelty, sensationalism (poisonings, maimings, torture). You can start with biology, or politics, or you can start with family, with loyalty, and even with the mystic-tinged edges of fate, which is where I choose to begin. It's all going to come together anyway. It has to. We're all following the wolf. To pretend anything else—to pretend that we are protecting the wolf, for instance, or *managing* him—is nonsense of the kind of immense proportions of which only our species is capable.

We're following the wolf. He's returning to Montana after sixty years.

The history of wolves in the West—of wolves in this country—is pretty well documented. Even by the turn of the century they were being diminished, and the wolves were all killed so quickly, and with such essentially religious zeal that we never had time to learn about them, and about their place on the land. And about our place on it. The wolves sure as hell didn't have time to learn about the government's wolf-, buffalo-, and Indian-killing program, and—well, I've got to say it—cows. Our culture has replaced buffalo with cattle, and wolves kill and eat cows, sometimes.

Peter Matthiessen writes in *Wildlife in America* that "with the slaughter of the bison and other hoofed animals in the late nineteenth century, the wolves . . . turned their attention to . . . livestock, which was already abundant on the grasslands." In the absence of bison, there was the bison's replacement: cattle. The wolves preyed upon these new intruders, without question, but ranchers and the government overreacted just a *tad*. Until very recently, the score stood at Cows, 99,200,000; Wolves, 0.

It took a lot of money to kill every last wolf out of the West. We behaved badly doing it: setting them on fire, feeding them ground-up glass, et cetera. Some people say it was the ranchers who kept the wolves out; others say the government. Other people say this country's lost its wildness, that it's no place for a wolf anymore, that already, wolves are like dinosaurs. There's room for sheep and cows, yes, and deer and elk and other plant eaters—but these woods are not the same woods they were sixty years ago. Even the shadows of trees in the forest are different, the wind's different.

There are a lot of people who believe that last part: that predators are out of date. And that Rocky Mountain gray wolves are the most old-fashioned, out-of-date predator of all. Sometimes I detect, even among wolves' most ardent well-wishers, a little chagrin that wolves succumbed so *easily*: that they wilted before the grazing juggernaut and federal predator-extinction programs of the 1920s. But with the government having been honed into fighting trim by practice on the "Indian problem," the wolves really had no chance. What's interesting (and wise) is that once the West's wolves were exterminated, they *stayed* exterminated. Canada's wolves did not repopulate the gaping wound of our wolf-free country.

Canada's always had the wolves, about 50,000 of them; so many wolves that there's even been a "hunting" (read: *killing*—people don't eat wolves) season on them. Which may not be so bad, in places, because it probably helps keep those wolves wild. With the mild winters of the greenhouse eighties, ungulate populations have increased dramatically. Using Canada as a base, wolves, or rumors of wolves, have historically trickled across the border, making shy, hidden, and often ill-fated sorties into the U.S., hanging out in the deep timber of northwestern Montana, eating deer and trying to stay away from people. The prey that wolves chase is most often found in valley bottoms—along rivers, where ranches and villages are located. I like to think of the wolves hanging back in the woods, up in the mountains, *longing* for the river bottoms, but too wild, too smart, to descend. The deer down along the rivers, among the people, among the barking dogs, among the intricate road systems, are in a way protected from everything but overpopulation, disease and starvation.

The wolves watching those tempting Montana river bottoms, and longing, but then—wild—drifting back into Canada.

But the thing that defines a wolf more than anything—better than DNA, better than fur, teeth, green eyes, better than even the low, mournful howl—is the way it *travels*. The home range of wolves in the northern Rockies averages 200 to 300 square miles, and ranges of 500 square miles are not uncommon. Montana could not be avoided by Canadian wolves. There are too many deer, too many elk: too many for the few predators that still exist.

Glacier National Park, right on the Montana–Canada line, has sometimes harbored a pack, sometimes two, but that's all. In Glacier, the Magic and Wigwam and Camas packs averaged between fifteen and thirty animals in the 1970s and 1980s. The Wigwam pack held the most mystery—eight of their nine members simply disappeared, over the course of a few days in 1989. Poaching is suspected, but they could also have been "assassinated"—wolves will often fight to the death if another pack crosses their boundary. (Deer have learned to seek out these boundaries, the line between two packs' territories acting as a sort of demilitarized zone—a ridge separating two valleys, perhaps, or an uplift between two river forks.)

The Glacier wolves served as a hope, a *longing*, for the rest of Montana, and gave lovely possibility to the occasional rumors that leapt up around the area, in nearby valleys—the Tobacco and Yaak valleys to the west and Swan Valley to the south. But the wolves that left Glacier, if they were indeed the ones being spotted, never (to any scientist's knowledge) mated—never formed what the biologists call the "pair bond" of an alpha male and alpha female—and it was thought that the sightings were unusually large coyotes. There's not as much similarity between the two as you'd think: coyotes often have a lot of red in their coats, and their muzzles are sharper, reminding me of screwdrivers, and their ears are larger and more pointy-looking. Coyotes are 25 percent to 50 percent smaller than long-legged wolves, and wolves have "fur around their face," and a ruffed coat, like a cape, up across their shoulders; coyotes' necks look bare by comparison.

Rumors of wolves outside of Glacier kept drifting in, increasing steadily through the 1980s, which fanned the hopes of those people desiring wolves. A poll taken in 1990 showed that two-thirds of Montanans believed wolves should be allowed to return to the state, while one-third thought wolves should be locked out. In the summer of 1988, in my valley, a mile south of Canada, I saw two big gray wolves—a mated pair, I hoped—lope through the woods, running north, headed to the border; later that winter, friends told me they'd seen a big black wolf and a gray wolf on the other side of their frozen lake, on several mornings, which indicated there might possibly, hopefully, be a pack. They're filtering south, even as you're reading this—moving through the trees, mostly, and eating a deer about every third day; they're coming down out of Canada, and the wild ones are trying to stay out of the populated river bottoms. The less wild ones—well, sometimes people see those.

It's been theorized that in addition to Montana's high deer population, hunting pressure in Canada may be helping send wolves back south, all along the U.S.–Canadian border—into the Cascades, the Olympics, northern Idaho and northwestern Montana, even along Montana's Front Range—but the main reason seems to be game overabundance, a dangerous excess, the simple response of predator-and-prey cycles. Like the tides and the pull of the moon, it's not a thing that we've been able to mess up, yet. It still works, or tries to. The recent warm winters in Montana have led deer and elk populations to all-time highs. There haven't been any dramatic disease die-offs in recent memory, no massive winter kills, no outbreaks of starvation and land-gone-ragged. The deer populations keep climbing as if *desiring* that outcome, though, and each summer you see more and more fawns; each fall you see more and more deer. The deer have the run of the woods, though mountain lion populations are increasing rapidly to join in on the feast. You've got to drive slowly at night. It's hard to find anyone living in the country who hasn't struck a deer at least once, late at night, no matter how carefully he drives. Usually if you hit a deer, you stop and put it in the back of your truck and drive on home and clean it and eat it (illegal, of course, but not immoral)—but sometimes the out-of-town people will keep going after striking a deer, leaving the deer dead on the side of the road or even *in* the road, and in the morning, if you live nearby, you'll hear the ravens, and then later in the afternoon, the little slinky-dog coyotes barking at one another, and by that night, everything's gone: meat, bones, hooves, even the hide.

I should point out that that's the scientists' belief—that Montana's huge deer populations are bringing the wolves back. There is another thought that occurs to me, though I'm sure the scientists would have nothing to do with this idea. I've been reading all the old case histories of wolves in this country and following the new histories, and the species doesn't seem to have changed in a hundred years, a hundred generations. The intricacy of their pack structure—the hierarchy of dominance and submission—is well documented, as is their territoriality, their fierce protection of borders, and their love of travel, of exploring those borders.

But these new wolves—I get the sense that they're a little different. Wiser, of course—even if only bearing wise blood but not knowing it. They seem to be a little *edgier*—pushing for those edges. All wolves travel like crazy, but these new wolves seem a little restless even for their species. They're trying to trickle down, like roots spreading fingers into weathered rock. And this time we'll be able to find out if human nature, and our politics, have changed—metamorphosed, perhaps, into something more advanced—or if at the base our politics are still those of Indian killers.

The wolves intend to find out, too.

Everything travels fast for a wolf. They went from huge buffalo-supported packs of twenty and thirty animals to near-extinction with great speed, and it is in their blood to recover with great speed, given the right conditions. Sixty years is only a blink, and it is a predator's genetic duty to endure hard times—very hard times—along with the sweet times.

The old wolves were natives, residents. These new wolves are foreigners, pioneers: explorers. It could be argued that wolves are never more wolflike than when they're exploring, trying to claim, or reclaim, new territory, rather than holding on and defending old borders. It could be argued that our perverse resistance to wolves helps them _remain_ wolves, that they need that great arm's distance to remain always outside of other communities, except perhaps for the community of ravens.

Is the base of our history unchanging, like some _batholith_ of sin—are we irretrievable killers?—or can we exist with wolves, this time? I believe we are being given another chance, an opportunity to demonstrate our ability to change. This time, we have a chance to let a swaying balance be struck: not just for wolves, but for humans, too. If I could say any one thing to politicians, and to people with guns and poison (and sheep and cows), it would be this: that to have the balance the majority of people claim to long for, it must be struck by the wolves as much as by the people. The wolves must have some say in defining it, or it will not be valid. And since they do not speak our language, it might be rough for a while: for three years, or five years, or maybe even ten.

I'd always thought of the "typical" wolf as being a smoke-gray color, but the wolves from Glacier are solid black half the time. It took me a while to get used to this—the black ones seemed, in my mind, more like dogs—but now I prefer seeing the black ones; the shining black coat sets off their green eyes in a way that seems to give the eyes more internal fire than they already have. Old-timers around the town of Libby tell how there used to be a lot of wolves in the Yaak Valley at the turn of the century, and how so many of them were black. I like a black wolf, though this is a long story, and there's not going to be time for what I do or don't like.

Wolf packs in northwestern Montana average between six and ten animals. These numbers are a function of both the social characteristics of the individuals within the pack and of game size and availability. It doesn't take many wolves to hunt the ubiquitous white-tailed deer. There's lots of game, and not many established wolf territories yet; a lot of free country just for the taking, room for "dispersers"—ambitious, aggressive, or outcast lone wolves—to expand into. It's an eerie form of recapitulation, not unlike, perhaps, our own species' westward expansion two hundred years ago. One healthy wolf can bring down one white-tail by itself. If a wolf in northwestern Montana isn't an alpha (breeding) wolf but desires to be, there's nothing to prevent him or her from taking off across the next ridge and over into the next valley, which, for now, is probably not wolf-occupied—containing instead only deer, elk and moose, and probably people, and maybe cattle.

In parts of Alaska and Minnesota, on the other hand, other packs' territories are already "taken," and the primary prey species is often moose. This creates more pressure to stay in a pack, even if it means being a beta or more subordinate pack member. It takes at least three or four wolves, absolute minimum, to bring down a moose, and the packs do better with around a dozen.

The one exception to this Montana average of six to ten animals per pack—and that's the lovely thing about wolves, you can never count on them to be counted on—was the giant pack that built up in Glacier, the Camas pack. It numbered, briefly, *twenty* members, and has since split into two packs, north and south, which range along the Flathead River. Because they're all family it's thought that—unlike other packs—the Camas wolves won't fight to the death if they stray into each other's territory. Mollie Matteson, a biologist in Montana, reports that members of the north and south packs even visited each other's dens in the summer of 1990, with "considerable going back and forth." (The alpha female of the north pack is the mother of the breeding female in the south pack.)

So Glacier's doing okay for wolves, for now. Soon enough—too soon—this story is going to have to lead away from wolf sociology and enter the dense woods of human sociology, and once that forest is entered, it may be a long time before the wolves in question emerge. I want to hold off from entering that place for as long as I can. Once the wolves in question get into that tangle of bureaucracy and human pinball, biological lies and manipulations, there's no telling where the wolves will emerge finally—or if they'll simply vanish—but already, in this story, they're moving inexorably toward that dark grove.

Usually the image one gets of wolves is of a deer running through the forest, with the wolves close behind. But in this forest, the image I get is of the wolf pack running through the trees, hurdling logs, with people chasing them, people running close behind. Not just ranchers and wolf-lovers are following them, but men and women in suits—politicians, and worse—and scientists, too, with all sorts of drugs and needles and electrical equipment. Some of the wolves will be captured and will succumb or be tamed, but others will break off from the pack that's being pursued, will escape, and continue weaving through the woods. As long as there are a lot of deer, these dispersers have a chance—a good chance.

Despite their deer-catching skills and wild, leave-away hearts, the odds for survival are stacked a little higher against disperser wolves. Wolf biologist Diane Boyd has documented wolves leaving the Glacier area and traveling as far as 500 miles. David Mech begins one of the chapters in his book, *The Wolf*, with an old Russian proverb that says, "The wolf is kept fed by his feet"—but traveling, and movement, seems to feed the wolf's soul, as well; it's nothing for them to cover twenty miles overnight on a hunt. The farthest recorded twenty-four-hour distance was traveled by a wolf in Scandinavia that went 125 miles in a day and a night, under pressure from dogs and hunters.

The farthest overall dispersal is 1500 kilometers (over 829 miles) by a wolf in Canada, an act which, if undertaken by any of the Glacier wolves, would put them clearly into the prey-infested woods of Yellowstone. Three more hops and a skip, as in the movement of a knight on a chess board, would take them back into southern Colorado, one of the country's areas richest in wolf lore. Yellowstone is supposedly another story from what this book's about—the biologists for the U.S. Fish & Wildlife Service (USF&WS) say, "Don't get this mixed up with Yellowstone"—but one thing I've learned in reading and asking about wolves in Montana over the last three years is that *nothing*'s a different story. It's all being woven together, more than a computer can hold, and certainly more than someone's mind—scientist or not—can assimilate.

What this story is about, this part of the weave, is the young Ninemile pack whose mother wandered all the way down into the country west of Missoula, into the mountains south and west of giant Flathead Lake, within easy striking distance of Idaho—within sight of Idaho, from the highest peaks. These pups raised themselves—were orphaned by fate while they still had their baby teeth—and in a brave move ripe with political festerings, were kept alive by USF&WS biologists whose job as mandated by federal law is "to preserve and protect endangered species," of which these six pups most certainly were: the Rocky Mountain gray wolf, *Canis lupus irremotus.* The Latin name, as *Missoulian* reporter Sherry Devlin has pointed out, translates roughly, wonderfully, into meaning "The Wolf Who Is Always Showing Up."

The Ninemile Wolves (1992)

ALAN DURNING

Alan Durning (b. 1964) worked as researcher at the Worldwatch Institute in Washington D.C., in the 1980s. The Institute, run by the eco-statistician Lester Brown, served as a kind of clearinghouse for environmental data, and as he labored on annual "State of the World" reports Durning became one of the first people to see that exponential increases in consumption were driving ecological destruction. He documented that trend in *How Much Is Enough?* (1992), a book that also pointed toward suggestive evidence that past a certain point consumption wasn't making people very happy. Following his own advice about community, he relocated to Seattle with his family, where he works with the Sightline Institute to build durable, delightful neighborhoods across the Pacific Northwest. In recent years, more and more environmentalists have focused on consumption as the driving force behind perils like global warming; in a sense, it is replacing population increase as the main factor driving ecological decline.

The Dubious Rewards of Consumption

The avarice of mankind is insatiable," wrote Aristotle 23 centuries ago, describing the way that as each desire is satisfied, a new one seems to appear in its place. That observation forms the first precept of economic theory, and is confirmed by much of human experience. A century before Christ, the Roman philosopher Lucretius wrote: "We have lost our taste for acorns. So [too] we have abandoned those couches littered with herbage and heaped with leaves. So the wearing of wild beasts' skins has gone out of fashion. . . . Skins yesterday, purple and gold today—such are the baubles that embitter human life with resentment."[1]

---

1. Aristotle, *Politics*, and Lucretius, *On the Nature of the Universe*, both quoted in Goldian VandenBroeck, ed., *Less Is More: The Art of Voluntary Poverty* (New York: Harper & Row, 1978).

Nearly 2,000 years later, Leo Tolstoy echoed Lucretius: "Seek among men, from beggar to millionaire, one who is contented with his lot, and you will not find one such in a thousand. . . . Today we must buy an overcoat and galoshes, tomorrow, a watch and a chain; the next day we must install ourselves in an apartment with a sofa and a bronze lamp; then we must have carpets and velvet gowns; then a house, horses and carriages, paintings and decorations."[2]

Contemporary chroniclers of wealth concur. For decades Lewis Lapham, born into an oil fortune, has been asking people how much money they would need to be happy. "No matter what their income," he reports, "a depressing number of Americans believe that if only they had twice as much, they would inherit the estate of happiness promised them in the Declaration of Independence. The man who receives $15,000 a year is sure that he could relieve his sorrow if he had only $30,000 a year; the man with $1 million a year knows that all would be well if he had $2 million a year. . . . Nobody," he concludes, "ever has enough."[3]

If human desires are in fact infinitely expandable, consumption is ultimately incapable of providing fulfillment—a logical consequence ignored by economic theory. Indeed, social scientists have found striking evidence that high-consumption societies, just as high-living individuals, consume ever more without achieving satisfaction. The allure of the consumer society is powerful, even irresistible, but it is shallow nonetheless.

Measured in constant dollars, the world's people have consumed as many goods and services since 1950 as all previous generations put together. Since 1940, Americans alone have used up as large a share of the earth's mineral resources as did everyone before them combined. Yet this historical epoch of titanic consumption appears to have failed to make the consumer class any happier. Regular surveys by the National Opinion Research Center of the University of Chicago reveal, for

2. Tolstoy, *My Religion*, quoted in VandenBroeck, *Less is More*.
3. Lewis H. Lapham, *Money and Class in America: Notes and Observations on Our Civil Religion* (New York: Weidenfeld & Nicolson, 1988).

example, that no more Americans report they are "very happy" now than in 1957. The "very happy" share of the population has fluctuated around one third since the mid-fifties, despite near-doublings in both gross national product and personal consumption expenditures per capita.[4]

A landmark study in 1974 revealed that Nigerians, Filipinos, Panamanians, Yugoslavians, Japanese, Israelis, and West Germans all ranked themselves near the middle on a happiness scale. Confounding any attempt to correlate material prosperity with happiness, low-income Cubans and affluent Americans both reported themselves considerably happier than the norm, and citizens of India and the Dominican Republic, less so. As psychologist Michael Argyle writes, "There is very little difference in the levels of reported happiness found in rich and very poor countries."[5]

Any relationship that does exist between income and happiness is relative rather than absolute. The happiness that people derive from consumption is based on whether they consume more than their neighbors and more than they did in the past. Thus, psychological data from diverse societies such as the United States, the United Kingdom, Israel, Brazil, and India show that the top income strata tend to be slightly happier than the middle strata, and the bottom group tends to be least happy. The upper classes in any society are more satisfied with their

4. Worldwatch Institute estimate of consumption since 1950 based on gross world product data from Angus Maddison, *The World Economy in the 20th Century* (Paris: Organisation for Economic Co-operation and Development, 1989); minerals from Ralph C. Kirby and Andrew S. Prokopovitsh, "Technological Insurance Against Shortages in Minerals and Metals," *Science*, February 20, 1976; opinion surveys from Michael Worley, National Opinion Research Center, University of Chicago, Chicago, Ill., private communication, September 19, 1990; gross national product per capita and personal consumption expenditures are adjusted for inflation from U.S. Bureau of the Census, *Statistical Abstract of the United States: 1991* (Washington, D.C.: U.S. Government Printing Office, 1991).

5. International comparison from R.A. Easterlin, "Does Economic Growth Improve the Human Lot? Some Empirical Evidence," cited in Michael Argyle, *The Psychology of Happiness* (New York: Methuen, 1987); quote from ibid. Similar arguments are found in Angus Campbell, *The Sense of Well-being in America: Recent Patterns and Trends* (New York: McGraw-Hill, 1981), in Paul Wachtel, *The Poverty of Affluence* (Philadelphia: New Society Publishers, 1989), and in F.E. Trainer, *Abandon Affluence* (Atlantic Highlands, N.J.: Zed Books, 1985).

lives than the lower classes are, but they are no more satisfied than the upper classes of much poorer countries—nor than the upper classes were in the less affluent past. Consumption is thus a treadmill, with everyone judging their status by who is ahead and who is behind.[6]

That treadmill yields some absurd results. During the casino years of the mid-eighties, for example, many New York investment bankers who earned "only" $600,000 a year felt poor, suffering anxiety and self-doubt. On less than $600,000, they simply were unable to keep up with the Joneses. One despondent dealmaker lamented, "I'm nothing. You understand that, nothing. I earn $250,000 a year, but it's nothing, and I'm nobody."[7]

From afar, such sentiments appear to reflect unadulterated greed. But on closer inspection they look more like evidence of humans' social nature. We are beings who need to belong. In the consumer society, that need to be valued and respected by others is acted out through consumption. As one Wall Street banker put it to the *New York Times*, "Net worth equals self-worth." Buying things becomes both a proof of self-esteem ("I'm worth it," chants one shampoo advertisement) and a means to social acceptance—a token of what turn-of-the-century economist Thorstein Veblen termed "pecuniary decency." Much consumption is motivated by this desire for approval: wearing the right clothes, driving the right car, and living in the right quarters are all simply ways of saying, "I'm OK. I'm in the group."[8]

In much the same way that the satisfaction of consumption derives from matching or outdoing others, it also comes from outdoing last year. Thus individual happiness is more a function of rising consumption than of high consumption as such. The reason, argues Stanford University economist Tibor Scitovsky, is that consumption is addictive: each luxury quickly becomes a necessity, and a new luxury must be found. This is as true for the young Chinese factory worker exchanging

6. Argyle, *The Psychology of Happiness.*

7. Brooke Kroeger, "Feeling Poor on $600,000 a Year," *New York Times*, April 26, 1987; dealmaker quoted in Lapham, *Money and Class in America.*

8. Banker quoted in Kroeger, "Feeling Poor on $600,000 a Year"; Veblen quoted in Lapham, *Money and Class in America.*

a radio for a black-and-white television as it is for the German junior executive trading in a BMW for a Mercedes.[9]

Luxuries become necessities between generations as well. People measure their current material comforts against the benchmark set in their own childhood. So each generation needs more than the previous did to be satisfied. Over a few generations, this process can redefine prosperity as poverty. The ghettos of the United States and Europe have things such as televisions that would have awed the richest neighborhoods of centuries past, but that does not diminish the scorn the consumer class heaps on slum dwellers, nor the bitterness felt by the modernized poor.[10]

With consumption standards perpetually rising, society is literally insatiable. The definition of a "decent" standard of living—the necessities of life for a member in good standing in the consumer society— endlessly shifts upward. The child whose parents have not purchased the latest video game feels ashamed to invite friends home. Teenagers without an automobile do not feel equal to their peers. In the clipped formulation of economists, "Needs are socially defined, and escalate with the rate of economic progress."[11]

The relationships between consumption and satisfaction are thus subtle, involving comparisons over time and with social norms. Yet studies on happiness indicate a far less subtle fact as well. The main determinants of happiness in life are not related to consumption at all—prominent among them are satisfaction with family life, especially marriage, followed by satisfaction with work, leisure to develop talents, and friendships.[12]

These factors are all an order of magnitude more significant than

9. Argyle, *The Psychology of Happiness*; Tibor Scitovsky, *The Joyless Economy* (New York: Oxford University Press, 1976).

10. Intergenerational rise of consumption standards from Eileen M. Crimmins et al., "Preference Changes Among American Youth: Family, Work, and Goods Aspirations, 1976–86," *Population and Development Review*, March 1991; redefining prosperity as poverty from Scitovsky, *The Joyless Economy*.

11. Endlessly shifting standard of decent living from Scitovsky, *The Joyless Economy*; quote from Crimmins et al., "Preference Changes Among American Youth."

12. Argyle, *Psychology of Happiness*.

income in determining happiness, with the ironic result that, for example, suddenly striking it rich can make people miserable. Million-dollar lottery winners commonly become isolated from their social networks, lose the structure and meaning that work formerly gave their lives, and find themselves estranged from even close friends and family. Similarly, analysts such as Scitovsky believe that reported happiness is higher at higher incomes largely because the skilled jobs of the well-off are more interesting than the routine labor of the working class. Managers, directors, engineers, consultants, and the rest of the professional elite enjoy more challenging and creative pursuits, and therefore receive more psychological rewards, than those lower on the business hierarchy.[13]

Oxford University psychologist Michael Argyle's comprehensive work *The Psychology of Happiness* concludes: "The conditions of life which really make a difference to happiness are those covered by three sources—social relations, work and leisure. And the establishment of a satisfying state of affairs in these spheres does not depend much on wealth, either absolute or relative." Indeed, some evidence suggests that social relations, especially in households and communities, are neglected in the consumer society; leisure likewise fares worse among the consumer class than many assume.[14]

The fraying social fabric of the consumer society, though it cannot be measured, reveals itself poignantly in discussions with the elderly. In 1978, researcher Jeremy Seabrook interviewed scores of older people in the English working class about their experience of rising prosperity. Despite dramatic gains in consumption and material comforts their parents and grandparents could never have hoped for, they were more disillusioned than content. One man told Seabrook, "People aren't satisfied, only they don't seem to know why they're not. The only chance of satisfaction we can imagine is getting more of what we've got now. But it's what we've got now that makes everybody dissatisfied. So what will more of it do, make us more satisfied, or more dissatisfied?"[15]

---

13. Scitovsky, *The Joyless Economy.*
14. Argyle, *Psychology of Happiness.*
15. Jeremy Seabrook, *What Went Wrong?* (New York: Pantheon Books, 1978).

The elders Seabrook interviewed were afraid for their children, who they saw as adrift in a profoundly materialistic world. They were afraid of vandals, muggers, and rapists, who seemed ruthless in a way they could not understand. They felt isolated from their neighbors, and unconnected to their communities. Affluence, as they saw it, had broken the bonds of mutual assistance that adversity once forged. In the end, they were waiting out their days in their sitting rooms, each with his or her own television.[16]

Mutual dependence for day-to-day sustenance—a basic characteristic of life for those who have not achieved the consumer class—bonds people as proximity never can. Yet those bonds have severed with the sweeping advance of the commercial mass market into realms once dominated by family members and local enterprise. Members of the consumer class enjoy a degree of personal independence unprecedented in human history, yet hand in hand comes a decline in our attachments to each other. Informal visits between neighbors and friends, family conversation, and time spent at family meals have all diminished in the United States since mid-century.[17]

Indeed, the present generation of young Americans believes that being good parents is equivalent to providing lots of goodies. Raising a family remains an important life goal for them, but spending time with their children does not. According to the survey research of Eileen Crimmins and her colleagues at the University of California, Los Angeles, American high school seniors express a strong desire "to give their children better opportunities than they have had," but not to "spend more time with their children." In high schoolers' minds, "better opportunities" apparently means "more goods." Writing in *Population and Development Review*, the researchers note, "Who would have foreseen a decade ago that clothes with designer labels and computer video games would be 'essential' inputs to a happy child?"[18]

16. Ibid.
17. Time spent visiting and conversing from John S. Robinson, "How Americans Use Time," *The Futurist*, September/October 1991; time at meals from Scitovsky, *The Joyless Economy*.
18. Crimmins et al., "Preference Changes Among American Youth."

Over the past century, the mass market has taken over an increasing number of the productive tasks once provided within the household, diminishing people's practical reliance on one another. More and more, flush with cash but pressed for time, we opt for the conveniences of prepared, packaged foods, miracle cleaning products, and disposable everythings—from napkins to cameras.

Part of the reason for this transformation of the household economy is that as consumer-class women emancipated themselves from the most tedious types of housework, men did not step in to fill the gap. Instead, housework shifted into the mass market, paid for out of the proceeds of women's new jobs. As both men and women left the home, gutting the household economy, housework was shunted to the money economy.

The sexual imbalance in housework persists, and, if anything, women's total workload has grown as the household changed from a unit of joint production and consumption into a passive, consuming entity. American women in the early sixties, for example, did as many hours of housework as their grandmothers had done in the twenties, despite dozens of "labor-saving" devices. And while American women, on average, have reduced their hours of housework somewhat since 1965, most of them have also taken jobs outside the home. American men's hours of housework, meanwhile, have barely increased at all since 1965. Data from the United Kingdom suggest a similar trend there.[19]

The commercialization of the household economy has cost the natural world dearly. Chores that shift out of the house take more resources to perform. Shirts pressed in commercial establishments require two trips, often by car, to the laundry. Meals from the take-out

19. U.S. women's housework before 1965 from David P. Ross and Peter J. Usher, *From the Roots Up: Economic Development as if Community Mattered* (Croton-on-Hudson, N.Y.: The Bootstrap Press, 1986), and from Herman E. Daly and John B. Cobb, Jr., *For the Common Good: Redirecting the Economy Toward Community, the Environment, and a Sustainable Future* (Boston: Beacon Press, 1989); women's housework since 1965 from Robinson, "How Americans Use Time"; U.K. housework from Ross and Usher, *From the Roots Up*.

restaurant or the frozen foods section multiply the packaging materials and transport energy used to nourish a family.

In the ideal household in the consumer society, people do little for themselves. We do not cook our food from scratch (55 percent of America's consumer food budget is spent on restaurant meals and ready-to-eat convenience foods). We neither mend nor press nor make our own clothes. We neither bake nor build nor do repairs for ourselves. We produce little besides children, and once we have done that, we have a diminishing role. Day-care franchises are more expedient for watching youngsters than the old-fashioned, now dispersed, extended family. Disposable diapers (typically 3,000 of them in the first year, at a cost of $570) have displaced cloth ones.[20]

The evolution of the household from producer to consumer is evident in housing designs in affluent nations. Older houses had pantries, workshops, sewing rooms, built-in clothes hampers, and laundry chutes. New homes have compact kitchens equipped for little more than heating prepared foods. Laundry rooms and root cellars gave way to hot tubs and home entertainment centers. Basement workshops were compressed into utility closets, to make room for pool tables and large-screen televisions. Even gardening, one of the vestigial forms of household production still popular among the consumer class, is gradually turning into a form of consumption, as purchased inputs replace backyard resources. Britons, for example, spent about $3 billion on their gardens and lawns in 1991, up from $1 billion a decade earlier.[21]

Like the household, the community economy has atrophied—or been dismembered—under the blind force of the money economy. Shopping malls, superhighways, and "strips" have replaced corner stores, local restaurants, and neighborhood theaters—the things that

20. U.S. food budget from Leonard L. Berry, "Market to the Perception," *American Demographics*, February 1990; diapers from Blayne Cutler, "Rock-A-Buy Baby," *American Demographics*, January 1990.

21. History from Susan Strasser, *Satisfaction Guaranteed: The Making of the American Mass Market* (New York: Pantheon Books, 1989), from Witold Rybczinski, "Living Smaller," *Atlantic Monthly*, February 1991, and from Nicholas Lemann, "Stressed Out in Suburbia," *Atlantic Monthly*, November 1989; British gardens from Jennifer Foote, "How Does the Garden Grow?" *Newsweek*, July 15, 1991.

help create a sense of common identity and community in an area. Traditional communities are all but extinct in some nations. In the United States, where the demise of local economies is furthest advanced, many neighborhoods are little more than a place to sleep, where neighbors share only a video rental franchise and a convenience store. Americans move, on average, every five years, and develop little attachment to those who live near them.[22]

The transformation of retailing is a leading cause of the decline of traditional community in the global consumer society. British researchers Carl Gardner and Julie Shepard describe the way civic and collective identity erode with the dwindling of local merchants. "The town center, once the natural focus for the people who live and work there, has . . . lost its individual characteristics and any reference to its unique past. Now it is merely a cloned version of dozens of others up and down the country. Outside shopping hours . . . many town and city centers have, as a result of the retail mono-culture, become shuttered, barren, lifeless spaces."[23]

Another human cost of the consumer society appears to be an acceleration of the pace of life. Psychologist Robert Levine of California State University, Fresno, measured everything from the average walking speed on city streets to the average talking speed of postal clerks in six countries to show that the pace of life accelerates as countries industrialize and commercialize. Japanese urbanites moved fastest, followed by Americans, English, Taiwanese, and Italians. Indonesians moved most slowly of all. As nations get richer, in other words, they hurry up.[24]

Renegade economist E. F. Schumacher proposed an economic law canonizing that observation in 1978: "The amount of genuine leisure available in a society is generally in inverse proportion to the amount of labor-saving machinery it employs." The more people value time—

22. History from Dolores Hayden, *Redesigning the American Dream: The Future of Housing, Work, and Family Life* (New York: W.W. Norton & Co., 1984); frequency of moving from Robert Reich, "A Question of Geography," *New Republic*, May 9, 1988.

23. Carl Gardner and Julie Shepard, *Consuming Passion: The Rise of Retail Culture* (London: Unwin Hyman, 1990).

24. Robert V. Levine, "The Pace of Life," *American Scientist*, September/October 1990.

and therefore take pains to save it—the less able they are to relax and enjoy it. Leisure time becomes too valuable to "waste" in idleness, and even physical exercise becomes a form of consumption. In 1989, Americans devoted the wages of 1 billion working hours to buying such sports clothing as Day-Glo Lycra body suits, wind-tunnel-tested bicycling shoes, rain jackets woven from space-age polymers, and designer hiking shorts. Leisure wear has replaced leisure as the reward for labor. In Japan, meanwhile, a *reja bumu* (leisure boom) has combined with rising concern for nature to pump up sales of fuel-guzzling four-wheel-drive Range Rovers from England and cabins made of imported American logs.[25]

Working hours in industrial countries, despite the reductions trade unionists have won in the past century, still exceed typical working hours before the Industrial Revolution. "In medieval Europe," observes Witold Rybczynski, a professor of architecture at McGill University in Montreal who studies leisure, "religious festivals reduced the work year to well below the modern level of 2,000 hours."[26]

The consumer society fails to deliver on its promise of fulfillment through material comforts because human wants are insatiable, human needs are socially defined, and the real sources of personal happiness are elsewhere. Indeed, the strength of social relations and the quality of leisure—both crucial psychological determinants of happiness in life—appear as much diminished as enhanced in the consumer class. The consumer society, it seems, has impoverished us by raising our income.

25. E. F. Schumacher, *Good Work* (New York: Harper & Row Publishers, 1979); George Watson, "The Decay of Idleness," *Wilson Quarterly*, Spring 1991; leisure wear from Witold Rybczynski, "Waiting for the Weekend," *Atlantic Monthly*, August 1991; Sepp Linhart, "From Industrial to Postindustrial Society: Changes in Japanese Leisure-Related Values and Behavior," *Journal of Japanese Studies*, Summer 1988; Range Rovers from T. R. Reid, "U.S. Automakers Grind Gears in Japan," *Washington Post*, September 23, 1990; "With Permit Rules Relaxed, Log Cabin Sales Are Soaring," *Japan Economic Journal*, August 4, 1990.
    26. Rybczynski, "Waiting for the Weekend."

How Much Is Enough? (1992)

SCOTT RUSSELL SANDERS

For a long time nature writing was mostly about going out to some lovely and unknown place and bringing back the tale. There's still some of that, but in recent decades more and more of those who do this kind of writing have concentrated on building a life in their own place and observing the close-at-hand. This phenomenon is especially notable in the case of Scott Russell Sanders (b. 1945), because he has spent his life in the kind of midwestern locale often considered nondescript and uninteresting, "flyover country." In his capable hands, however, the natural and human drama of Indiana and Ohio seem all the more remarkable for their quietness. The title of the 1993 book from which this essay comes is *Staying Put: Making a Home in a Restless World*. By sticking to the limestone country around Bloomington for most of his adult life, Sanders' sense of his local "place" has acquired a richness that most writers and academics, by habit or inclination often a transient tribe, can only envy.

After the Flood

A river poured through the landscape I knew as a child. It was the power of the place, gathering rain and snowmelt, surging through the valley under sun, under ice, under the bellies of fish and the curled brown boats of sycamore leaves. You will need a good map of Ohio to find the river I am talking about, the West Branch of the Mahoning. The stretch of it I knew best no longer shows on maps, a stretch that ran between wooded slopes and along the flanks of cornfields and pastures in the township of Charlestown, in Portage County, a rural enclave surrounded by the smokestacks and concrete of Akron, Youngstown, and Cleveland in the northeastern corner of the state.

Along that river bottom I gathered blackberries and hickory nuts, trapped muskrats, rode horses, followed baying hounds on the scent of raccoons. Spring and fall, I walked barefoot over the tilled fields, alert for arrowheads. Along those slopes I helped a family of Swedish farmers collect buckets of maple sap. On the river itself I skated in winter and paddled in summer, I pawed through gravel bars in search of fossils, I watched hawks preen and pounce, I courted and canoed and idled. This remains for me a primal landscape, imprinted on my senses, a place by which I measure every other place.

It is also, now, a drowned landscape. In the early 1960s, when I was in high school, politicians and bankers and realtors ordained that the Mahoning should be snared. A dam was built, the river died, and water backed up over most of the land I knew. No city needed the water for drinking. The reservoir, named after a man who had never lived in that valley, provided owners of loud boats with another playground for racing and waterskiing, and provided me with a lesson in loss. If the loss were mine alone, the story would not be worth telling. My grieving for a drowned landscape is private, a small ache in a bruised world. But the building of the dam, the obliteration of that valley, the displacement of people and beasts, these were public acts, the sort of acts we have been repeating from coast to coast as we devour the continent.

Like many townships in farm country, remote from the offices where the fate of land is decided, Charlestown has suffered more than one erasure. Long before the building of the reservoir, the government had already sliced away the northern third of the township for an arsenal, a wild, murderous place I have written about elsewhere as a paradise of bombs. On current maps of the township that upper third is blank white, and most of the remaining two-thirds, flooded by the reservoir, is vacant blue. Merely by looking at the map, one can tell that here is a sacrificial zone.

Returning to one's native ground, always tricky, becomes downright treacherous when the ground is at the bottom of a lake. Unwilling to dive through so much water, I can return to that drowned landscape, as I can return to childhood, only by diving through memory.

I had just become a teenager when the government began purchasing the farms and trailers and shacks that would be in the path of the reservoir. (If there had been mansions and factories in the way, the politicians would have doomed a different valley.) Among the first to be un-housed was the Swedish family, old Mr. Sivvy and his two unmarried children, who had farmed that bottom land with big-shouldered horses, whose silage I had pitchforked in the steaming silo, whose cows I had fed, whose maple syrup I had savored hot from the vat. Uprooted, the old man soon died. The children bought a new farm on high ground, trying to start over, but it was no good, the soil too thin, worn out, no black bottom land, no fat maples, no river pouring through it. All down the valley it was the same, people forced to move by a blizzard of gov-ernment paper, occasionally by the sheriff, in a few instances by the ar-rival of bulldozers at their front door.

While gangs of men with dynamite and dump trucks tore down the condemned buildings, other gangs with earthmovers and cement mixers slowly raised a wall across the river. For a year I watched it rise, while I wooed a girl who lived on a ridge overlooking the dam site. Crooners purred love songs from the stereo in her parlor, against an accompani-ment of chuffs and shouts and whistles from the valley below. I studied the contours of that girl's face while the river's contours were bullied into the shape of blueprints. The huge concrete forms, the tinkertoy scaf-folds, the blasting, the snort of compressors, the lurch of heavy ma-chines are confused in me now with the memory of damp hands and lingering kisses. The girl and I broke up, but the concrete held. There-after, I avoided that ridge, and did not see the laying of the dam's final tier, did not see the steel gates close. By the time I graduated from high school, water was beginning to lap over the banks of the Mahoning, but I could not bear to go down to the river and look.

When I left Ohio for college, my family left as well, trailing my father's work to Louisiana. My childhood friends dispersed—to war, to jail, to distant marriages and jobs, to cities where lights glittered and dollars sang. I had scant reason to visit that flooded township and good reason to keep my distance. Why rush to see a muddy expanse of anni-hilating water?

Some years later, however, duties carried me through the northeastern corner of Ohio, within an hour's drive of my old neighborhood. I had not planned to make a detour. Yet the names of towns emblazoned on huge green signs along the highway tugged at me. The shapes of chimneys and roofs, the colors of barns, the accents in fast-food booths and gas stations, all drew me off the interstate onto the roads of Portage County, up the stream of recollection toward that childhood place.

The season of my return was late winter, after the last snow and before the first plowing, before grass resumed its green sizzle, before trees blurred with leaves. The shape of the land lay exposed. It was a gray day, a day to immunize one against nostalgia, a day safe, I supposed, for facing up to what I had lost. Surely I was prepared by now to see the great erasure. I was a man, and had put behind me a boy's affection for a stretch of river and a patch of dirt. New places had claimed me, thereby loosening the grip of that old landscape. Still, to ease my way back, before going to the reservoir I drove through the county seat, Ravenna, which had scarcely changed, and then through Edinburgh, Atwater, Deerfield, Palmyra, Paris, Wayland—tiny crossroad settlements where I had played baseball and eaten pie and danced—and these, too, had scarcely changed. Circling, I drew closer and closer to the blue splotch on the map.

The best way to approach the water, I decided, was along the road where, for half our years in Charlestown, my family had lived on five acres with horses and rabbits and dogs. Surely our gray-shingled house would still be there, safe on its ridge above the lake, even if most of the land I had known was drowned. So I turned from the highway onto that curving, cracked, tar-slick road, looking for the familiar. But at the corner, where there should have been a farmhouse, a silo, a barn, there was only a billboard marking the entrance to the West Branch Reservation. The fields where I had baled hay now bristled with a young woods. There was no house in the hollow where the road dipped down, where the family of Seventh Day Adventists used to live with their stacks of apocalyptic pamphlets and their sad-eyed children. The spinster's white bungalow was gone, along with the battered bus in the side yard which had served her for a chicken coop. Yard after yard had grown up in brush, and the shade trees spread darkness over their own seedlings. No mail boxes leaned on posts beside the road, no driveways broke the fringe of weeds. The trailer park was gone, the haunted house was gone, the tar-paper shanty where the drunk mechanic beat his wife and the wife beat her kids and the kids wailed, that was gone, and so was every last trailer and cottage and privy and shack, all down the blacktopped mile to our place.

I recognized our place by the two weeping willows out front. My father and I had planted those willows from slips, had fenced them round to protect the tender bark from deer, had watered and weeded and nursed them along. By the day of my visit those twigs had burgeoned into yellow fountains some fifty feet high, brimming over the woods that used to be our cleared land, woods that flourished where our house and barn had stood. I did not get out of the car. I could see from the road all that I was ready to see. The dense thicket, bare of leaves, was the color of rusty iron. Aside from the willows, no hint of our work or ownership survived.

I felt a fool. During the years of my absence, while my mind had suffered the waters to rise through the forest and up the ravines onto the margins of our land, I had preserved the gray-shingled house, the low white barn, the lilacs and forsythia, the orchard and pasture, the garden, the lawn. And yet, all the while, cedar and sumac and brambles, like the earth's dark fur, had been pushing up through my past.

Sight of the reservoir, surely, could not be worse. I continued down the road through the vigorous woods. Not a house, not a barn, not a plowed field. The first clearing I came to was half a mile farther on, at the spot where a man named Ferry had lived. He used to let the neighborhood kids swim in his pond, even after a boastful boy dived into a rock and drowned. We knew that when we knocked at Mr. Ferry's door, raising money for school or scouts, he would buy whatever we had to sell. He was a tender man. He loved his wife so much that when she died he planted a thousand white pines in her memory. The pines, spindly in my recollection, had grown into a forest by the day of my return.

In place of Mr. Ferry's house and yard there was a state campground now, encircled by the spiky green palisade of pines. The entrance booth was boarded up. A placard outside instructed campers to deposit their fees—so much for trailers, so much for tents—in the box below. There was no box below, only a slab of plywood with ragged holes from which the screws had been ripped. Nor were there any campers on this wintry afternoon. As I drove through the vacant lot, the only sounds were the crunch of gravel beneath my tires and the yawp of blue jays overhead and the shoosh of wind through the pines.

I pulled away from the campground and drove on. My mind raced ahead along the road as I remembered it, steeply downhill between fat maples and patchy sycamores to the river and the steel-girdered bridge. I had rolled down that hill in a school bus, swayed down on horseback, hurtled down on bicycle and sled, run down on foot. The slope and feel of it, fixed inside me, became my standard for all hills. From the bridge I had watched the river's current raveling over sandbars, minnows flickering in the shallows, water-striders dimpling the surface. Now and again, when the sun was right, I had spied my own face peering up from the stream. In memory, the road stretched on beyond the bridge, passing the tin-roofed shed where the maple syrup boiled, passing the Sivvy farm, rising up the far slope to a T-junction with a ridgeline road. Turn left from there, and I would go to the high school. Turn right, and I would go to the barbershop and feed store. As my thoughts raced ahead of the car, inside me the valley opened and the river flexed its long sleek muscle.

Rounding the curve, however, I had to slam on the brakes to avoid running into a guardrail that blocked the road. Beyond the railing, where valley and bridge and river should have been, flat gray water spread away toward distant hills. You know this moment from dream: You are in a familiar room, but when you turn to leave, where a door should be there is a wall; or you come up behind someone you love, speak her name, yet when she turns around her face is blank; or you find the story of the universe written on a page, but when you draw close to read it, the letters dissolve. Waters of separation, waters of oblivion, waters of death.

I got out of the car and pressed my thighs against the cold steel barricade and stared. Gray, flat, empty lake. Not even a boat to redeem the emptiness. A lone crow slowly pumped toward the horizon on glossy black wings. Along the shore, a few sycamores still thrust up their mottled branches. Except for those trees, the pavement beneath my boots, and hills too high for water to claim, everything I knew had been swept away.

My worst imaginings had failed to prepare me for this. I stood there dazed. I could not take it in, so much had been taken away. For a long spell I leaned against the guardrail and dredged up everything I could remember of what lay beneath the reservoir. But memory was at last defeated by the blank gray water. No effort of mind could restore the river or drain the valley. I surrendered to what my eyes were telling me. Only then was I truly exiled.

Those who built the dam had their reasons. You have heard the litany: flood control, recreation, development. I very much doubt that more human good has come from that muddy, silting, rarely frequented lake than came from the cultivated valley and wild woods and free-flowing river. I am suspicious of the logic that would forestall occasional floods by creating a permanent one. But I do not wish to debate the merits of dams. I mean only to speak of how casually, how relentlessly we sever the bonds between person and place.

One's native ground is the place where, since before you had words for such knowledge, you have known the smells, the seasons, the birds and beasts, the human voices, the houses, the ways of working, the lay of the land, and the quality of light. It is the landscape you learn before you retreat inside the illusion of your skin. You may love the place if you flourished there, or hate the place if you suffered there. But love it or hate it, you cannot shake free. Even if you move to the antipodes, even if you become intimate with new landscapes, you still bear the impression of that first ground.

I am all the more committed to know and care for the place I have come to as an adult because I have lost irretrievably the childhood landscapes that gave shape to my love of the earth. The farm outside Memphis where I was born has vanished beneath parking lots and the poison-perfect lawns of suburbs. The arsenal, with its herds of deer grazing on the grassy roofs of ammunition bunkers, is locked away behind chain-link fences, barbed wire, and guns. And the Mahoning

Valley has been drowned. In our century, in our country, no fate could be more ordinary.

Of course, in mourning the drowned valley I also mourn my drowned childhood. The dry land preserved the traces of my comings and goings, the river carried the reflection of my beardless face. Yet even as a boy I knew that landscape was incomparably older than I, and richer, and finer. Some of the trees along the Mahoning had been rooted there when the first white settlers arrived from New England. Hawks had been hunting and deer had been drinking there since before our kind harnessed oxen. The gravels, laden with fossils, had been shoved there ten thousand years ago by glaciers. The river itself was the offspring of glaciers, a channel for meltwater to follow toward the Ohio, and thence to the Mississippi and the Gulf of Mexico. What I knew of the land's own history made me see that expanse of water as a wound.

Loyalty to place arises from sources deeper than narcissism. It arises from our need to be at home on the earth. We marry ourselves to the creation by knowing and cherishing a particular place, just as we join ourselves to the human family by marrying a particular man or woman. If the marriage is deep, divorce is painful. My drive down that unpeopled road and my desolate watch beside the reservoir gave me a hint of what others must feel when they are wrenched from their place. I say a *hint* because my loss is mild compared to what others have lost.

I think of the farmers who saw their wood lots and fields go under the flood. I think of the Miami and Shawnee who spoke of belonging to that land as a child belongs to a mother, and who were driven out by white soldiers. I think of the hundred other tribes that were herded onto reservations far from the graves of their ancestors. I think of the Africans who were yanked from their homes and bound in chains and shipped to this New World. I think about refugees, set in motion by hunger or tyranny or war. I think about children pushed onto the streets by cruelty or indifference. I think about migrant workers, dust bowl émigrés, all the homeless wanderers. I think about the poor everywhere—and it is overwhelmingly the poor—whose land is gobbled by strip mines, whose neighborhoods are wiped out by highways and shopping malls, whose villages are destroyed by bombs, whose forests are despoiled by chain saws and executive fountain pens.

The word *nostalgia* was coined in 1688 as a medical term, to provide an equivalent for the German word meaning homesickness. We commonly treat homesickness as an ailment of childhood, like mumps or chickenpox, and we treat nostalgia as an affliction of age. On our lips, nostalgia usually means a sentimental regard for the trinkets and fashions of an earlier time, for an idealized past, for a vanished youth. We speak of a nostalgia for the movies of the 1930s, say, or the hair-cuts of the 1950s. It is a shallow use of the word. The two Greek roots of *nostalgia* literally mean *return pain*. The pain comes not from returning home but from longing to return. Perhaps it is inevitable that a nation of immigrants—who shoved aside the native tribes of this continent, who enslaved and transported Africans, who still celebrate motion as if humans were dust motes—that such a nation should lose the deeper meaning of this word. A footloose people, we find it difficult to honor the lifelong, bone-deep attachment to place. We are slow to acknowledge the pain in yearning for one's native ground, the deep anguish in not being able, ever, to return.

On a warmer day I might have taken off my clothes and stepped over the guardrail and waded on down that road under the lake. Where the water was too deep, I could have continued in a boat, letting down a line to plumb the bottom. I would not be angling for death, which is far too easy to catch, but for life. To touch the ground even through a length of rope would be some consolation. The day was cold, however, and I was far from anyone who knew my face. So I climbed into the car and turned away and drove back through the resurgent woods.

Staying Put (1993)

GEORGE B. SCHALLER

The Tibetan red deer, the Vietnamese warty pig, the snow leopard—in a world that is often considered fully mapped and tracked, George Schaller (b. 1933) has managed to find animals others had thought extinct, to uncover populations so elusive that others had never studied them. And he has managed to make the results matter in more than scientific journals: his books have converted many to the conservation cause and helped create some of the largest wildlife refuges on earth. Born in Germany, Schaller moved as a boy to Missouri, then went to the University of Alaska intent on studying wildlife. After an early expedition with Olaus Murie to the Brooks Range in northeast Alaska, he headed to Africa where he was one of the first biologists to study gorillas in the wild. His talent for close observation in the field was matched by his gift for figuring out larger meanings: "No one who looks into a gorilla's eyes—intelligent, gentle, vulnerable—can remain unchanged, for the gap between ape and human vanishes; we know that the gorilla still lives within us," he said. In later years, working under difficult political circumstances, he studied pandas, tigers, the Himalayan blue sheep, the Serengeti lion. And he studied humans closely enough to realize that he could use the appeal of these "charismatic megafauna" to win the protection of the habitat on which they and many smaller species depend.

from *The Last Panda*

The ridge lunged upward like a dragon's spine bristling with fir and birch, and clouds were low and flying out from the mountains. Snow from a late-winter storm balanced on boughs and logs. When a riffle of wind stirred the branches, the snow drifted down in crystal veils that added a ghostlike radiance to the forest. Bamboo grew in the understory, the crowded ranks of stems claiming the hillside so completely that the light beneath the bamboo's canopy was a translucent undersea green. The sunless scent of moss and moldering wood choked the gloom. The bamboo was rigid with frost, and a dense silence hung over the ridge; there was no movement and seemingly no life.

In the stillness, leaves suddenly rustled and a stem cracked like breaking glass. Shrouded in bamboo was a giant panda, a female, slumped softly in the snow, her back propped against a shrub. Leaning to one side, she reached out and hooked a bamboo stem with the ivory claws of a forepaw, bent in the stem, and with a fluid movement bit it off near the base. Stem firmly grasped, she sniffed it to verify that it was indeed palatable, and then ate it end-first like a stalk of celery. While her powerful molars sectioned and crushed the stem, she glanced around for another, her movements placid and skillful, a perfect ecological integration between panda and bamboo. She ate within a circle of three feet, moved a few steps and ate some more, consuming only coarse stems and discarding the leafy tops; she then sat hunched, forepaws in her lap, drowsy and content. Within a circle of three thousand feet was her universe, all that she needed: bamboo, a mate, a snug tree-den in which to bear young.

Minutes later, she ambled in her rolling sailor's gait to a nearby spur where among gnarled rhododendrons she halted. No bamboo grew here. A shaft of sun escaped through a fissure of cloud and penetrated the twilight. Among bamboo the panda's form and color had seemed blurred and difficult to define; now in sun the panda shone with sparkling clarity. Near her was a massive fir. She knew that tree: it was a landmark, it defined the edge of her favored haunts, it served as a scentpost. The tree's many dimensions helped give her an identity. The snow around the tree was unmarked by tracks, but when she sniffed the bark, she learned that a male had marked the site with his anal glands a few days before. Though she fixed the scent in her mind, she did not cover his odors with hers.

She angled down to the nearest bamboo patch and there once again foraged, the recycling of bamboo being the essence of her existence.

She lived leisurely. Alone in these heights, the panda conveyed a sense of absolute solitude, an isolation that was almost mythic. A flock of tit-babblers skittered like airborne mice through the bamboo above her head, yet her small dark eyes showed no awareness. Having eaten, she rolled over to sleep, her body at rest in the snow against a log, her dense coat making her impervious to the elements.

From below, near where forest gave way to field, came the sound of an ax. The bamboo around her like armor against intruders, she listened and then moved away, shunning any possible confrontation. She traveled on a private path along the slope, insinuating herself from thicket to thicket, moving like a cloud shadow, navigating with precision through the sea of stems, with only her tracks a record of her silent passing.

The Last Panda (1993)

"A great deal of nature writing," Ellen Meloy once wrote, "sounds like a cross between a chloroform stupor and a high Mass." Her own prose is often wonderfully wry, and occasionally enraged. Meloy (1946–2004) was born in California and lived for a time in Montana, but then moved to the desert Southwest in the 1980s and found—not unlike Mary Austin almost a century before—the landscape she was made for. Her book *The Anthropology of Turquoise* (2002) was a finalist for the Pulitzer Prize, and her writings about the Colorado Plateau live on. Las Vegas, meanwhile, has only continued to grow, faster than any other American city in recent years, an ongoing reproof both to the desert landscape and to the ideas of restraint and humility that have marked much of American environmental writing.

The Flora and Fauna of Las Vegas

> *Human domination over nature is quite simply an illusion, a passing dream by a naïve species. It is an illusion that has cost us much, ensnared us in our own designs, given us a few boasts to make about our courage and genius, but all the same it is an illusion. Do what we will, the Colorado will one day find an unimpeded way to the sea.*
>
> DONALD WORSTER, *Under Western Skies*

Ascent. Summit. Descent. The interstate highway, the asphalt river, slips off the Colorado Plateau, rises and falls over the Great Basin's rhythmic contours of basin and range, and flows southwest toward the Mojave Desert. In basin the highway crosses the Sevier River, which the 1776 Domínguez-Escalante expedition, ever hoping to find a Pacific passage, erroneously linked with the Green River in the Uinta Basin. Through range the meticulously graveled and graded highway slopes bury Fremont village sites, their remains relocated to museums to make way for the four-lane. A few petroglyph panels are visible from the road. We cannot study them. We cannot get off the highway. No exit. The panels pass in a blur, ancient peeps drowned by billboard shouts: IT'S THE REAL THING.

The flanks of the Tushar and Pavant ranges tip us into the Parowan Valley, where we nose the truck south into the current of traffic through Mormon farm towns, each with identical, master-design brick churches surrounded by weekday-empty aprons of tarmac. Only Kmart has more parking lot. Solid and impervious, the churches may be rocket ships in disguise. When the Rapture comes, the Saints will simply hop in and blast off, smothering the apron in the dense vapor of afterburners without singeing a leaf on God's flora. Near Cedar City I glimpse a roadkill that may or may not be a poodle flung from a recreational vehicle. At a rest stop a teenager lifts his muscle shirt and stares at his navel. We're closer, I think. We have entered the gravitational field.

Most of the billboards in St. George advertise Nevada casinos, luring Utahns over the nearby state line to Mesquite or Las Vegas, the pull on their retirement dollar stronger than the pull of their faith. Flanked by the Beaver Dam Mountains and Hurricane Cliffs, St. George hemorrhages subdivisions and factory outlet malls and a lunatic compulsion to have the most golf courses in the universe, irrigated by the Virgin River, soon to be dammed, IMAXed, and deflowered of rare desert tortoises. Perhaps St. Georgians deserve all the golf they can muster. Many are Downwinders, human receptacles of nuclear fallout that scars their lives with seemingly endless tragedy.

During the atmospheric nuclear testing in the Nevada desert west of St. George from 1951 to 1962, it was the Atomic Energy Commission's practice to wait until the wind blew toward Utah before detonating its "shots" in order to avoid contaminating populous Las Vegas or Los Angeles. An AEC memo declassified two decades after the test era described the people living in the fallout's path as "a low-use segment of the population." Loyal to a government they believed to be divinely inspired, taught by their church never to challenge authority, assured by that authority that the radiation was harmless, Utah's patriotic Mormons endured the toxic showers with little objection.

When Utahns and Nevadans reported their symptoms and fears, public health officials told them that only their "neurosis" about the bombs would make them ill. When women reported burns, peeling skin, nausea, and diarrhea—all symptoms of radiation sickness—when they said their hair, fingernails, and toenails fell out after a cloud of fallout passed over them, their doctors wrote "change of life" or "housewife's syndrome" or "recent hysterectomy" on their charts. The dangers of radiation were known but suppressed, a "noble lie" deemed a necessary cost of national security and the fight against communism. Bomb after bomb exploded, some of them, like Shot Harry in 1953, extremely "dirty" and lethal, showering fallout throughout the West. Each nuclear test released radiation in amounts comparable to the radiation released at Chernobyl in 1986. In at least two ways the Nevada tests were nothing like Chernobyl: There were 126 detonations. None was an accident.

At the Nevada state line we cast aside Utah's wholesome aura for its nemesis. Behind: Leave it to Beaver. Ahead: Sodom and Gomorrah. In dusk that sizzles at 103 degrees, the land sprawls in bowls of creosote bush cupped by serrated ribs of rock. Over a long rise, past a convoy of trucks afloat in mirages of diesel and heat, we top the crest of the final ridge and behold the valley below, an island of neon capped in sludgy brown smog, ringed by a rabid housing boom. Las Vegas. The Meadows.

We grind down the freeway past warehouses and a cinder-block wall over which a life-size white plaster elephant, rogue prop from a theme park, curls its trunk, flares its ears, and rests ivory tusks on the barrier that separates its lunging charge from the highway's shoulder. Oleander bushes, carbon monoxide–tolerant but poisonous in their own right—they once offed a few Boy Scouts who peeled their thin branches, impaled hot dogs on their tips, and roasted a lethal meal—line the freeway then surrender to a chute of concrete, where we fry without air-conditioning in the gridlock of an exit bottleneck, surrounded by chilled limousines and Porsches. No one leaps out to save our lives. The ambient light is pale yellow, like the inside of a banana peel.

Why this pilgrimage from Desolation Canyon to Glitter Gulch, from cougar-blessed red-rock wilderness to the apex of engineered fantasy, from mesmerization to masochism? Why have we ventured so far from the river? Because our river is here beneath our smoldering, heat-frayed, about-to-explode radials. Only in Egypt are more people dependent on the flow of one river than the people of Clark County, Nevada. By controlling the Colorado River through the state's southern tip, Nevadans freed themselves from the constraints posed by puny, ill-timed rainfall that otherwise barely sustained darkling beetles, chuckwallas, and creosote bushes. In the Dam Century no place was too remote or too parched to reach with a lifeline, and the Colorado River, by this point carrying water from the Green, San Juan, Virgin, and other tributaries, is Las Vegas's intravenous feeding, its umbilical to prosperity, the force that pulsates the neon through the tubes. Here the River immolates its wild treasures on the altar of entrepreneurial spirit. We have chosen to devote much of the West's greatest waterway to this city. Las Vegas is the twentieth century's ultimate perversion of the River and the site of a twenty-first-century water war.

For every river rat this visit is mandatory. We cannot know the River until we know this place. Our pilgrimage also carries corollary missions. I hope to learn what Las Vegans know about their water. There is field research to be done. And I want everyone in the Excalibur Hotel and Casino, a massive, pseudomedieval, castellated grotesquerie with jousting matches, banquets, and 4,032 hotel rooms—4,032 *toilets*—to flush their toilets at precisely the same moment.

I wait in the truck while Mark registers at the hotel, the only vehicle-enclosed human in Nevada without a veneer of tinted safety glass between her and the rude assault of Real Air. I cannot go into the hotel because Real Air has fused my skin to the Naugahyde panel inside the truck door. My earrings, a Hopi man-in-the-maze design inlaid in silver, conduct so much heat, they sear man-in-the-maze–shaped burns on my neck.

The second thing Mark says to the waitress as we pump freon through our organs inside an air-conditioned restaurant: "Are you real?" She has a practiced tolerance for stupid questions and a tattoo on her left breast. The menu offers an entree called Heavy Trim Beef Primals. "I'd like a cheeseburger, please, hold the onions," Mark says, Green River sand spilling from his cuffs as he passes her the menu. "Are you real?"

The restaurant seethes with slick-haired bloodsuckers in sharkskin suits on cappuccino breaks from their drug harems and sieges of women wearing very short skirts who should not, Vegas being the one place where they can get away with this. The bun-grazing skirt on the cigarette girl remains immobile as she vigorously diversifies her cigarette-shy market by peddling illuminated Yo-Yos. The diners' sunburns, freshly acquired while powerboating on nearby Lake Mead, radiate sufficient heat to melt the ice in our water glasses. While we played Lost Tribe of the Oligocene on the river, male strippers became passé and musical revues with full-figured dancers became the rage: SENSATIONAL. TALENTED. PUDGY, proclaims one flashing Strip marquee.

"What are you in the mood for?" Mark asks about the evening's casino crawl. "Knights? Rome? The circus? The tropics? Urban South American festivities?" We settle on the Tropicana, an island-theme concoction whose grand entry sprouts the huge plaster heads of tiki gods from tidy plots of stale-smelling hothouse petunias, ferns, fountains, and sprinkler heads pumping liquid no faster than the desert air can evaporate it. The fountains, a bartender informs us, use wastewater recycled from guests' rooms. Despite his admonitions and fervent offers of bottled designer water, we down tap water by the gallons, never slaking our thirst. The bartender knows where his water comes from: Lake Mead, he says. We slug it down. Chlorine Lite with a bouquet of Evinrude.

In Las Vegas the best survival strategy is a wholesale reduction of Self to imbecilic dipstick, easily managed in these clockless, windowless mazes of flashing lights and blaring gaming devices with nary a molecule of The Environment allowed across the transom. The idea is complete disconnection from Earth, a realignment of the senses through a techno-collage of myths and fantasies conjured by corporate hacks. At the Tropicana I inspect each potted palm for signs of life. Then we transfer to the Rio, Where It Is Always Carnival and not much different from the other casinos save for the Brazilian motif and the tiny televisions mounted above each video poker machine. I peer into the foliage of potted banana trees, expecting at least a cricket. No palm, no leaf, no pot is real, only the cigarette butts.

Mark disappears, mumbling about the anthropology of dental-floss bikinis and a stripper named Bunny Fajitas. Before I'm trampled to death by a shriek of Rotarians from Pocatello, I duck away to rest on an outskirt, unused stair step. From there I watch a terrified woman in bright native African dress clutch the rail of a descending escalator in a death grip. At the escalator's foot, her family nurses her down in their melodic native tongue—from Senegal, perhaps, evidently an escalatorless nation. She survives. Everyone hugs. Hoover Dam's turbines juice the guitars and keyboards of a live band in the lobby. Smurf Intellect, Los Deli Meats, Heavy Trim Beef Primals, I didn't catch the name but the lyrics concern whips. A man in a crisp white shirt and dark slacks (waiter? missionary?) tells me I cannot sit on this step. I cannot sit anywhere, he asserts officiously, except on the stools at bars, poker and slot machines, and blackjack tables. He stares down his nose at me as if I had dripped cobra spit on his shoes and barks, "You must leave." Where's the river? Take me to the river. Take me to Senegal. At the Excalibur no one can be persuaded to induce hydro-gridlock by a simultaneous political flush of their toilets. Water simply seems too bounteous; it fills hoses, sprinklers, fountains, waterfalls, water slides, swimming pools, wishing wells, moats, fish tanks, and artificial lakes, it greens an epidemic of golf courses and chills a million cocktails.

A grown man in scarlet doublet and mustard yellow panty hose plops a tinsel wreath on my head and recites a sonnet in bad high-school Chaucer, prologue to a halfhearted sell on tickets to a jousting tournament. Somehow he knows I'm not the jousting type, but he lets me keep the wreath. A woman standing next to a video poker machine catches my eye: Liv Ullmann face, shorts, running shoes, a thick blond braid down her back, a dippy smile across a tanned face. She is singing from *The Sound of Music*. In strikingly muscular arms she clutches a grocery bag filled with folded newspapers. She rivets her gaze on the video machine as if it were Christopher Plummer or an Alp and belts out, "The hills are alive . . ."

Daft with the sheer profusion of man-made matter, Mark and I return to our hotel room and fling ourselves onto the bed, hot, weighty sheets draped over our fantasy-stuffed bodies, our feet protruding like Jesus' under the shroud in Mantegna's painting *The Lamentation Over the Dead Christ*. Sometime in the fitful night, a voice crackles over the intercom box above the bathroom doorway. "Please do not panic," the voice urges us. "The fire alarms mean nothing. Please stay in your rooms."

The river of traffic streaming down the Strip will kill me if I back up three feet off the boulevard curb, where I'm in the bushes risking my life to study nature in Vegas's endangered vacant lots, its postage-stamp plots of unpaved Mojave. The inventory so far: crickets, ants, pigeons, wind-strewn "escort girl" flyers as numerous as scutes on a pit viper, and a playing card (the king of spades). Cowbirds (those toxic parents!) chase kazooing cicadas through muffler-sizzled oleander bushes too spindly in foliage to hide the random upturned shopping cart or shade me from sunlight intensified by its infinite reflection off chrome and windshields. I observe one stunted specimen of Aleppo pine, *Pinus halepensis*, a drought-tolerant Mediterranean import largely relegated to freeways and residential areas. I find few bugs in the bush and plenty in the yellow pages under "Pests": termites, earwigs, roaches, pill bugs, silverfish, scorpions, plus rodents and a category called "olive control." Physiographically the Mojave Desert is a transitional province between the Great Basin to the north and the Sonoran Desert to the south. Biological boundaries of all three deserts mix here, so one would expect creosote bush, catclaw, mesquite, yucca, geckos, horned lizards, and the like. But hardly a particle of native flora or fauna lives in Strip habitat. I crawl out of the bushes and hike to safety. Off to find the meadows, *las vegas*.

Negligible rainfall, barely four inches annually, comes to the austere bowl of desert in which Las Vegas spreads. Over a century and a half ago, a carpet of spring-fed grasslands grew in this basin, an oasis in a sea of thorns, alkali, and dust. Except for an occasional flash flood through the washes, the nearby mountains flushed little moisture from their peaks. The basin's water came from an underground aquifer created during the Pleistocene, when rainfall was abundant. Big Springs surfaced in a mad gurgle to form the headwaters of Las Vegas Creek, which flowed easterly along the valley floor then disappeared into the sand. An exploration party in 1844 recorded the creek's temperature at 115 degrees. Eleven years later a Mormon mission watered travelers between Salt Lake City and California settlements. The missionaries also mined lead from an ore vein along the nearby Colorado River and shipped it north to be made into bullets by the church's public works unit. The missionaries took it upon themselves—these were busy people—to teach the Indians, mostly Paiute, "farming and hygiene," although no one bothered to ask the Indians if they cared to farm or needed help in attending to their bodies. Nineteenth-century zealotry seemed obsessed with putting natives behind plows, in pants. "Discontent with the teepee and the Indian camp," claimed Merrill Gates of the U.S. Board of Indian Commissioners in the 1880s, "is needed to get the Indian out of the blanket and into trousers—and trousers with a pocket in them, and with a pocket that aches to be filled with dollars!"

By 1907 wells tapped much of the groundwater. Their strength— good water at constant pressure—and cheap land lured more settlers, who drained the meadows for crops and pasture. For nearly fifty years water flowed into farm, pipe, and oblivion; no one capped the wells until 1955. Las Vegas Creek had dried up five years before. Big Springs, now under pavement and the lock and key of the municipal water district, surfaced no more, and parts of the Las Vegas Valley had subsided as much as five feet, so much water had been mined. The meadows disappeared but for a trace, I was told, at Lions Club and Fantasy Park near downtown Las Vegas.

I drive to Fantasy Park on a boulevard that parallels a brief stretch of creek straitjacketed by concrete riprap. The creek begins and ends in enormous culverts; it merely belches aboveground for a few blocks so people can throw their litter into it. Fantasy Park grows limp-leafed trees in even rows, and despite a posting that the park is for children twelve and under, a few prostrate bodies of napping transients drop bombs of drool into a rather seedy lawn. Casino blitz envelops the park, buffered by mortuaries. Downtown Las Vegas, once heartland of the economy of sin, is now an outlier to the upscale Strip. Unless razed, it has no space for the entertainment mall, the computer-programmed volcano, artificial rain forest, concourse of Roman statuary, circus, castle, or thirty-story pyramid.

However outstripped by the illusion vendors of the nineties, surely downtown Las Vegas scores highest for the Stupidity of Man exhibit's best archival photograph. The 1951 photograph shows Vegas Vic, a landmark, sixty-foot-high neon cowboy on the cornice of the Pioneer Club, beckoning the pilgrims to girls, gambling, and glitz. His thumb is up, his cigarette dangles from his lips. Behind Vegas Vic and the cityscape rises a white-hot cloud on a slender stem, one of the atom wranglers' earliest bombs, popped off on ground zero less than a hundred miles away.

In Fantasy Park the homeless nappers awaken and roll off what would be the meadows' last stand had a lawn not replaced them. One of the men zombie-walks across the turf to the Binary Plasma Center. Two others approach me for spare change, grass clippings stuck to their sweaty T-shirts. I donate my Fun Book, a collection of courtesy coupons for drinks, playing chips, and discounts at beauty parlors. Casually I ask them where Las Vegas water comes from. The answer is unanimous: the faucet.

Las Vegas's faucets feed one of the highest per-capita water consumption rates in the nation, serving over 800,000 residents, twenty million visitors a year, and a monthly influx of several thousand new residents, most of them quality-of-life refugees from California. To feed the housing boom and the gaming industry's insatiable quest for the next great attraction, Las Vegas will likely be using every last drop of its legal share of Colorado River by the year 2002. It has considered buying water from a desalination plant in Santa Barbara, California, to trade with Los Angeles for rights to more Colorado River water. Las Vegas secured the last of the unappropriated groundwater in its own valley and seeks unclaimed water from the nearby Virgin River. It has also applied to import water from aquifers beneath the "empty" basins in Nevada's outback—fossil water, the ancient rain stored since the Pleistocene and rationed to the surface in spring creeks and seeps that give life to bighorn sheep, fish, lizards, plants, birds, and ranchers. The controversy pits rural Nevada against Las Vegas, sparking memories of a water grab by another lifestyle-obsessed megalopolis: the plumbing of eastern Sierra Nevada runoff by the city of Los Angeles during the early century, an exportation that drained the Owens Valley nearly dry. Sierra water, stored in snowpack, renews itself. Nevada's aquifers would be mined.

While everyone tries to predict the nature of a twenty-first century water war, thousands more newcomers unpack and scream for faucets. Unless a tarantula leaps up and bites off their lips, few seem to notice they live in a desert. At the Las Vegas Natural History Museum, my next research stop, the feature exhibit is a three-hundred-gallon tank swarming with those fascinating Mojave Desert endemics: live sharks.

What does it take to make this emphatically arid place livable? Shade and water. The endless ripple of malls, warehouses, manufacturing plants, minicasinos, restaurants, car dealers, trailer parks, and spanking new residential estates beyond Strip and city speak of a desert culture carried leagues beyond those amenities by a titanic appetite. America's deserts became habitable by virtue of artifice, the replacement of natural flora, a rearrangement of contours, and most significant, the realignment of water: tap the springs and creeks, recontour the basin and flats, harness massive quantities of power and water from a river that flows through the chocolate brown andesite breccia walls of a primeval canyon that in the process is obliterated. We are on our way to Hoover Dam.

The basin cants away from the city toward the rough jumble of peaks above the Colorado River and Hoover's reservoir, Lake Mead. Someone has unpacked platter after platter of hundred-acre subdivisions, repeated motifs of flamingo pink and turquoise stucco with red, Spanish-style tile roofs. Concrete lining reroutes washes and arroyos to take the summer's flash floods somewhere, elsewhere. Hefty stucco walls enclose each community, deterring entry by thieves, perverts, Gila monsters, and lawn-spoiling Russian olive trees. The self-contained suburbs boast names like Legacy Legends and Verde Viejo. Who could lure real-estate dollars to places with names like Hell's Skillet, Arsenic Springs, Donkey Butt Wash, Limp Dick Crick?

The morning sizzles at ninety-six degrees before eight o'clock. Close to the dam, cars creep bumper to bumper beneath the giant towers and webs of transmission lines that carry rivers of energy to Nevada, California, and Arizona. We park short of the dam and join the queue under a skimpy aluminum ramada to await a shuttle bus that takes tourists the last few miles to the dam's crest. A sign reads WATCH FOR BIGHORN SHEEP, but everyone watches for the shuttle, deep-roasted outside their air-conditioned vehicles, red ants gnawing their ankles. Desolation Canyon has accustomed Mark and me to such discomfort, although we cannot assume a relaxed Fremont squat on the ground because it is covered in broken glass. For an hour we stand like stoic Kalahari hosts among rather testy Eskimo guests.

Several years ago I shed mud-caked river shoes and rude shorts, dressed respectably, and walked into the visitor center of another Colorado River megadam. Politely I asked the receptionist, "What would this river look like without the dam?" (Should I have flung my participles about so carelessly? Used *did* instead of *would*? Was Dr. Freud in the room?) The receptionist looked at me as if I had just stuffed angry sharks into his pants. "Excuse me for a moment," he rasped, and disappeared behind an office door. The floor vibrated quietly as turbines somewhere in the dam's bowels mangled their requisite five hundred cats a minute. These dams unnerve me, they push encephalitic fluids against my skull, they hair up my tongue as though I had been licking lightbulb filaments. I felt the River's pressure, the lurking power of the outlaw. Before the receptionist returned I had to leave.

Today, at Hoover Dam, I have promised Mark I shall be on my best behavior. Alas, as the humming voltaics lop three years off our life spans, the courage I conjured to haul myself into the innards of Hoover suddenly fails, research be damned. We flee back to the truck and drive across the dam.

The angular rock of Black Canyon tilts, coils, and juts in colors that range from dark brown to purplish black. A construction road cut exposes a bright pink interior, a rock version of a yawning hippopotamus. No one spoke up for a wild Black Canyon, no moss-backed biocentric heretics suggested that humanity view nature as a mother rather than a pet or slave. In the thirties everyone was speaking up for jobs and relief from the Depression.

Lieutenant Joseph Christmas Ives of the U.S. Topographical Engineers, who traveled up the Colorado River in a steamboat in 1857–58, had set the tone for Black Canyon as an aesthetic void. He dismissed the river as unnavigable, the Grand Canyon as "Hell," and the entire region as a "profitless locality." After entering Black Canyon, Ives wrote, "there is nothing to do but leave." The expedition's artist and topographer, Baron F. W. von Egloffstein, rendered an already dramatic landscape with ponderous mannerisms and romantic exaggerations. His engravings show Hadean walls of impenetrable rock enclosing a sunless, impossibly deep chasm, the landscape of nightmare.

Major John Wesley Powell's 1869 party emerged from the Grand Canyon at the Grand Wash Cliffs, ending their arduous journey from Wyoming not far from the Hoover Dam site. Flavell and Montéz floated through Black Canyon in 1896, the Kolb brothers in 1911, and barely a handful of river explorers saw it after them. When the Birdseye party, a U.S. Geological Survey crew, passed through in 1923, the canyon already hummed with activity. They met a number of surveyors and engineers who were seeking the exact spot for the first big nail in the snake's body.

Gridlock stalls us on the dam's crest, where shuttles disgorge tourists who line up to buy tickets to make the descent into the powerhouse. "People still come here, drawn by the spirit of the Colorado," a tour brochure proclaims. I desperately seek river spirit to the left of the dam crest—a hundred miles upcanyon across Lake Mead, amidst Jet Skis, Wave Runners, houseboats, fluorescent jet boats, and a fifty-foot bathtub ring—and to its right—the undrowned canyon squirting a limpid stream from the dam's foot. Nearly a quarter mile below the rims of Black Canyon, the Río Colorado runs cold and clear, bereft of its red-brown complexion, its silt and peculiar native fish. It is neither *río* nor *colorado* but a thin, blue-green lake slackened by Lake Mohave, the reservoir behind the next dam sixty-seven miles downstream, another stair step in the plumbing that extends the remainder of the Colorado's course to the dry sands of Mexico.

We U-turn on the Arizona flank of the dam and cross back over the crest, ensnared in a second gridlock, the extent of our tour of the monumental wedge that in Frank Waters's words "stands in its desert gorge like a fabulous, unearthly dream." My father, who watched Los Angeles boom and bloom on Colorado River water and hydropower as he grew up in the twenties and thirties, remembers that Boulder Dam, as Hoover Dam was first named, put men to work, four thousand Depression-starved men who desperately needed work, and food on the table of hungry families. Between 1931 and 1935 dam workers poured three and a quarter million cubic yards of concrete into this chasm with hardly a sandbar or ledge for footing and the indefatigable river roaring through the bypass tunnels, exposing the Mesozoic bedrock and ooze of a watercourse thirteen million years in the making. I peer over Hoover's lip and think of the workers who fell to their deaths during construction. Legend says they still lie buried in the dam they built, limbs outstretched in descent now ossified in concrete. The dam was not poured in a solid mass. Solid, it would have dried 125 years later. Workers constructed a 726.4-foot-high stack of house-sized forms, two hundred hollow wooden boxes filled with concrete cooled by refrigerant piped through copper tubing, forms now hidden under the smooth, arching sheath of concrete athwart the dark walls of Black Canyon. Under construction, Hoover Dam looked like Swiss cheese.

We drive by the transmission towers for a final dose of electromagnetic radiation and up the switchbacks behind a fuchsia and apple green pickup truck pulling a fuchsia and apple green trailer loaded with a pair of fuchsia and apple green Jet Skis. Lake Mead spreads to the northeast, saved from suffocation by Glen Canyon Dam upstream. Glen trapped the millions of tons of sediment that were filling Lake Mead at an alarming rate soon after Hoover Dam was built, threatening to render Hoover useless in about a hundred years. Lake Powell and its arms up Cataract Canyon and the Dirty Devil, San Juan, and other tributary rivers now hold the sediment behind Glen Canyon Dam. With Glen, the Colorado River's delta has moved from the Gulf of California to Nevada and Utah.

Hoover Dam rid the "natural menace," as the Bureau of Reclamation calls the virgin Colorado River, of its mud and its fury. During our tenure in the West, before the dam and since, we have loved neither mud nor fury. We have never loved this river. We have made war on it as if it were a pack of proud, unruly, elusive Apaches. Chase them down, catch them, tame them. Put pants on them. Hoover, Glen, and the others, triumphs in the reduction of wild river to tool, stand as secular cathedrals to environmental mastery, the monolithic beads in the necklace of river from Wyoming to Mexico, monuments to our species' uncanny ability to know how to do things and our failure to ask whether the environmental consequences might simply be too great.

Las Vegas makes no bones about its premier commodity—honest fraud—but I don't care much for the place. The exceptions, however, are the pink tongues on the pudgy white tigers in their all-white neo-Babylonian habitat box on the entry concourse of the Mirage Hotel and Casino. Each time I visit the tigers, they sleep behind their plate-glass shield, their languid, pot-bellied bodies sprawled across elevated benches, those sweet tongues drowsily lolling below exquisitely whiskered cheeks. The Mirage sucks a river of people off the Strip onto its moving sidewalks, channels them past the narcoleptic cats and a wall-sized aquarium of parrotfish, wrasses, angelfish, sharks, and other tropical prisoners, and spills them into the tributaries that flow to gaming rooms, bars, shops, and restaurants. Earlier I had seen the *Sound of Music* woman sleeping on a patch of Strip lawn, a bag lady with one grocery bag and the body of a marathon runner. Now she is here, singing to the poker machines, and I would gleefully join her had I not the singing voice of gargled bats. Like mobile tide pools, a shoal of Frenchmen in bright aloha shirts riffles noisily forward with the stream. Perched on bar stools like herons on a riverbank are Vegas's sunset women, hard-fleshed, sinewy women in crayon makeup, pink stilettos, and gazes to convince the most egocentric lout that they know far more than he does. These women should be allowed to run Las Vegas. They probably do.

In the bar beneath the Mirage's artificial rain forest, Mark sips a herbivore's daiquiri afloat with Chinese parasols, fruit, carrots, celery, and other verdure. He scouts for naysaying casino personnel while I dive under the table and crawl around the rain forest in search of wildlife. The thicket grows bromeliads, ferns, philodendrons, cricket noises, and roof-raking palm trees that thrust fat boles up through the epoxied floor. The philodendrons are real. I emerge, harvest the crop from my daiquiri, and study the couple across from us, whose furtive looks reveal that some outlaw love may soon be consummated.

Our cocktail server, who thinks her water comes from California but is not sure, enlightens us about the construction crews that were furiously ingesting the Strip's remnant open spaces. We had seen the activity earlier in the day, and we wondered about the new building in the parking lot behind the Circus Circus Casino.

"What are they building at Circus Circus?" Mark asks.

"That's the Grand Slam Canyon," she tells us, clearing the table of peach pits, orange rinds, celery leaves, kelp.

Grand Slam Canyon promises the Grand Canyon without the Grand Canyon's pesky discomforts—its infernal heat, wind, roadlessness, and size that defies the three-day vacation, its cacti, lizards, snakes, biting insects, burro poop, boulders, rapids, the possibility of death. Amidst hundred-foot peaks, swimming pools, water slides, pueblos, and a replica of the Grand Canyon's Havasu Falls, inside a climate-controlled, vented, pink womb of a dome, Grand Slam Canyon visitors will fly through rapids and waterfalls in a roller coaster. They will, as the woman on Desolation's boat ramp once wondered about the Green River, *take out at the same place they put in*. The River made better than itself.

By midnight my tongue is furry and dry, as if I had swallowed a mouthful of casino carpet. We walk outside the Mirage, where a hundred or more spectators watch a volcano erupt in the palm garden, upstaging a rising moon, spewing fire from propane burners and sloshing wastewater down its tiered slopes. Out from nowhere a single, frantic female mallard duck, her underside lit to molten gold by the tongues of flame, tries desperately to land in the volcano's moat. Mark and I stare incredulously at the duck, two faces pointed skyward among hundreds pointed volcano-ward. Unable to land in this perilous jungle of people, lights, and fire, the duck veers down the block toward Caesars Palace. With a sudden *ffzzt* and a shower of sparks barely distinguishable from the ambient neon, the duck incinerates in the web of transmission lines slicing through a seventy-foot gap in the Strip high-rises, a skein of wire and cable that surges with the power of the River.

Raven's Exile (1994)

"As a girl, even though I was shy, not given to argument, I was one day able to say to the Sunday school teacher, who believed we were in the house of the Lord, that I felt God when I sat under a tree," Linda Hogan (b. 1947) once told an interviewer. "It was there, with the tree, that I felt the love of the earth, smelling the soft soil, the blades of grass growing even as I sat." Hogan is of Chickasaw ancestry, and she has become a widely honored and well-loved novelist and essayist. With Brenda Peterson she co-edited the important anthology *Intimate Nature: The Bond Between Women and Animals* (1999).

Dwellings

Not far from where I live is a hill that was cut into by the moving water of a creek. Eroded this way, all that's left of it is a broken wall of earth that contains old roots and pebbles woven together and exposed. Seen from a distance, it is only a rise of raw earth. But up close it is something wonderful, a small cliff dwelling that looks almost as intricate and well made as those the Anasazi left behind when they vanished mysteriously centuries ago. This hill is a place that could be the starry skies of night turned inward into the thousand round holes where solitary bees have lived and died. It is a hill of tunneling rooms. At the mouths of some of the excavations, half-circles of clay beetle out like awnings shading a doorway. It is earth that was turned to clay in the mouths of the bees and spit out as they mined deeper into their dwelling places.

This place where the bees reside is at an angle safe from rain. It faces the southern sun. It is a warm and intelligent architecture of memory, learned by whatever memory lives in the blood. Many of the holes still contain the gold husks of dead bees, their faces dry and gone, their flat eyes gazing out from death's land toward the other uninhab-ited half of the hill that is across the creek from these catacombs.

The first time I found the residence of the bees, it was dusty summer. The sun was hot, and land was the dry color of rust. Now and then a car rumbled along the dirt road and dust rose up behind it before settling back down on older dust. In the silence, the bees made a soft droning hum. They were alive then, and working the hill, going out and returning with pollen, in and out through the holes, back and forth between day-light and the cooler, darker regions of inner earth. They were flying an invisible map through air, a map charted by landmarks, the slant of light, and a circling story they told one another about the direction of food held inside the center of yellow flowers.

Sitting in the hot sun, watching the small bees fly in and out around the hill, hearing the summer birds, the light breeze, I felt right in the world. I belonged there. I thought of my own dwelling places, those real and those imagined. Once I lived in a town called Manitou, which means "Great Spirit," and where hot mineral springwater gurgled beneath the streets and rose up into open wells. I felt safe there. With the underground movement of water and heat a constant reminder of other life, of what lives beneath us, it seemed to be the center of the world.

A few years after that, I wanted silence. My daydreams were full of places I longed to be, shelters and solitudes. I wanted a room apart from others, a hidden cabin to rest in. I wanted to be in a redwood for-est with trees so tall the owls called out in the daytime. I daydreamed of living in a vapor cave a few hours away from here. Underground, warm, and moist, I thought it would be the perfect world for staying out of cold winter, for escaping the noise of living.

And how often I've wanted to escape to a wilderness where a hu-man hand has not been in everything. But those were only dreams of peace, of comfort, of a nest inside stone or woods, a sanctuary where a dream or life wouldn't be invaded.

Years ago, in the next canyon west of here, there was a man who fol-lowed one of those dreams and moved into a cave that could only be reached by climbing down a rope. For years he lived there in comfort, like a troglodite. The inner weather was stable, never too hot, too cold, too wet, or too dry. But then he felt lonely. His utopia needed a woman. He went to town until he found a wife. For a while after the marriage, his wife climbed down the rope along with him, but before long she didn't want the mice scurrying about in the cave, or the untidy bats that wanted to hang from stones of the ceiling. So they built a door. Because of the closed entryway, the temperature changed. They had to put in heat. Then the inner moisture of earth warped the door, so they had to have air-conditioning, and after that the earth wanted to go about life in its own way and it didn't give in to the people.

In other days and places, people paid more attention to the strong-headed will of earth. Once homes were built of wood that had been felled from a single region in a forest. That way, it was thought, the house would hold together more harmoniously, and the family of walls would not fall or lend themselves to the unhappiness or arguments of the inhabitants.

An Italian immigrant to Chicago, Aldo Piacenzi, built birdhouses that were dwellings of harmony and peace. They were the incredible spired shapes of cathedrals in Italy. They housed not only the birds, but also his memories, his own past. He painted them the watery blue of his Mediterranean, the wild rose of flowers in a summer field. Inside them was straw and the droppings of lives that laid eggs, fledglings who grew there. What places to inhabit, the bright and sunny birdhouses in dreary alleyways of the city.

One beautiful afternoon, cool and moist, with the kind of yellow light that falls on earth in these arid regions, I waited for barn swallows to return from their daily work of food gathering. Inside the tunnel where they live, hundreds of swallows had mixed their saliva with mud and clay, much like the solitary bees, and formed nests that were perfect as a potter's bowl. At five in the evening, they returned all at once, a dark, flying shadow. Despite their enormous numbers and the crowding together of nests, they didn't pause for even a moment before entering the nests, nor did they crowd one another. Instantly they vanished into the nests. The tunnel went silent. It held no outward signs of life.

But I knew they were there, filled with the fire of living. And what a marriage of elements was in those nests. Not only mud's earth and water, the fire of sun and dry air, but even the elements contained one another. The bodies of prophets and crazy men were broken down in that soil.

I've noticed often how when a house is abandoned, it begins to sag. Without a tenant, it has no need to go on. If it were a person, we'd say it is depressed or lonely. The roof settles in, the paint cracks, the walls and floorboards warp and slope downward in their own natural ways, telling us that life must stay in everything as the world whirls and tilts and moves through boundless space.

One summer day, cleaning up after long-eared owls where I work at a rehabilitation facility for birds of prey, I was raking the gravel floor of a flight cage. Down on the ground, something looked like it was moving. I bent over to look into the pile of bones and pellets I'd just raked together. There, close to the ground, were two fetal mice. They were new to the planet, pink and hairless. They were so tenderly young. Their faces had swollen blue-veined eyes. They were nestled in a mound of feathers, soft as velvet, each one curled up smaller than an infant's ear, listening to the first sounds of earth. But the ants were biting them. They turned in agony, unable to pull away, not yet having the arms or legs to move, but feeling, twisting away from, the pain of the bites. I was horrified to see them bitten out of life that way. I dipped them in water, as if to take away the sting, and let the ants fall in the bucket. Then I held the tiny mice in the palm of my hand. Some of the ants were drowning in the water. I was trading one life for another, exchanging the lives of ants for those of mice, but I hated their suffering, and hated even more that they had not yet grown to a life, and already they inhabited the miserable world of pain. Death and life feed each other. I know that.

Inside these rooms where birds are healed, there are other lives besides those of mice. There are fine gray globes the wasps have woven together, the white cocoons of spiders in a corner, the downward tunneling anthills. All these dwellings are inside one small walled space, but I think most about the mice. Sometimes the downy nests fall out of the walls where their mothers have placed them out of the way of their enemies. When one of the nests falls, they are so well made and soft, woven mostly from the chest feathers of birds. Sometimes the leg of a small quail holds the nest together like a slender cornerstone with dry, bent claws. The mice have adapted to life in the presence of their enemies, adapted to living in the thin wall between beak and beak, claw and claw. They move their nests often, as if a new rafter or wall will protect them from the inevitable fate of all our returns home to the deeper, wider nest of earth that houses us all.

One August at Zia Pueblo during the corn dance I noticed tourists picking up shards of all the old pottery that had been made and broken there. The residents of Zia know not to take the bowls and pots left behind by the older ones. They know that the fragments of those earlier lives need to be smoothed back to earth, but younger nations, travelers from continents across the world who have come to inhabit this land, have little of their own to grow on. The pieces of earth that were formed into bowls, even on their way home to dust, provide the new people a lifeline to an unknown land, help them remember that they live in the old nest of earth.

It was in early February, during the mating season of the great horned owls. It was dusk, and I hiked up the back of a mountain to where I'd heard the owls a year before. I wanted to hear them again, the voices so tender, so deep, like a memory of comfort. I was halfway up the trail when I found a soft, round nest. It had fallen from one of the barebranched trees. It was a delicate nest, woven together of feathers, sage, and strands of wild grass. Holding it in my hand in the rosy twilight, I noticed that a blue thread was entwined with the other gatherings there. I pulled at the thread a little, and then I recognized it. It was a thread from one of my skirts. It was blue cotton. It was the unmistakable color and shape of a pattern I knew. I liked it, that a thread of my life was in an abandoned nest, one that had held eggs and new life. I took the nest home. At home, I held it to the light and looked more closely. There, to my surprise, nestled into the gray-green sage, was a gnarl of black hair. It was also unmistakable. It was my daughter's hair, cleaned from a brush and picked up out in the sun beneath the maple tree, or the pit cherry where birds eat from the overladen, fertile branches until only the seeds remain on the trees.

I didn't know what kind of nest it was, or who had lived there. It didn't matter. I thought of the remnants of our lives carried up the hill that way and turned into shelter. That night, resting inside the walls of our home, the world outside weighed so heavily against the thin wood of the house. The sloped roof was the only thing between us and the universe. Everything outside of our wooden boundaries seemed so large. Filled with night's citizens, it all came alive. The world opened in the thickets of the dark. The wild grapes would soon ripen on the vines. The burrowing ones were emerging. Horned owls sat in treetops. Mice scurried here and there. Skunks, fox, the slow and holy porcupine, all were passing by this way. The young of the solitary bees were feeding on pollen in the dark. The whole world was a nest on its humble tilt, in the maze of the universe, holding us.

Dwellings (1995)

David Abram (b. 1957) put himself through college performing sleight-of-hand magic at Alice's Restaurant, the Berkshires eatery made famous in Arlo Guthrie's song. He was good enough to have gone to Vegas, but instead he won a Watson fellowship and used it to wander Asia. He would perform a few tricks at the edge of some provincial bazaar and wait for the local shaman to get in touch; then he'd spend weeks or months sharing trade secrets and, more importantly, imbibing a new worldview, one in which the boundaries between people and the natural world were thinner and more porous. His landmark book *The Spell of the Sensuous* (1996), which begins with this selection from those Asian backwaters, covers a huge intellectual distance—before he's done Abram has revitalized the philosophical school of phenomenology and considered the birth of written alphabets. But always he's concerned with reintroducing Americans to the actual experience of the natural world, with "beginning to honor and value our direct sensory experience: the tastes and smells in the air, the feel of the wind as it caresses the skin, the feel of the ground under our feet as we walk upon it."

from *The Ecology of Magic*
A Personal Introduction to the Inquiry

Late one evening I stepped out of my little hut in the rice paddies of eastern Bali and found myself falling through space. Over my head the black sky was rippling with stars, densely clustered in some regions, almost blocking out the darkness between them, and more loosely scattered in other areas, pulsing and beckoning to each other. Behind them all streamed the great river of light with its several tributaries. Yet the Milky Way churned beneath me as well, for my hut was set in the middle of a large patchwork of rice paddies, separated from each other by narrow two-foot-high dikes, and these paddies were all filled with water. The surface of these pools, by day, reflected perfectly the blue sky, a reflection broken only by the thin, bright green tips of new rice. But by night the stars themselves glimmered from the surface of the paddies, and the river of light whirled through the darkness underfoot as well as above; there seemed no ground in front of my feet, only the abyss of star-studded space falling away forever.

I was no longer simply beneath the night sky, but also *above* it— the immediate impression was of weightlessness. I might have been able to reorient myself, to regain some sense of ground and gravity, were it not for a fact that confounded my senses entirely: between the constellations below and the constellations above drifted countless fireflies, their lights flickering like the stars, some drifting up to join the clusters of stars overhead, others, like graceful meteors, slipping down from above to join the constellations underfoot, and all these paths of light upward and downward were mirrored, as well, in the still surface of the paddies. I felt myself at times falling through space, at other moments floating and drifting. I simply could not dispel the profound vertigo and giddiness; the paths of the fireflies, and their reflections in the water's surface, held me in a sustained trance. Even after I crawled back to my hut and shut the door on this whirling world, I felt that now the little room in which I lay was itself floating free of the earth.

Fireflies! It was in Indonesia, you see, that I was first introduced to the world of insects, and there that I first learned of the great influence that insects—such diminutive entities—could have upon the human senses. I had traveled to Indonesia on a research grant to study magic—more precisely, to study the relation between magic and medicine, first among the traditional sorcerers, or *dukuns*, of the Indonesian archipelago, and later among the *dzankris*, the traditional shamans of Nepal. One aspect of the grant was somewhat unique: I was to journey into rural Asia not outwardly as an anthropologist or academic researcher, but as a magician in my own right, in hopes of gaining a more direct access to the local sorcerers. I had been a professional sleight-of-hand magician for five years back in the United States, helping to put myself through college by performing in clubs and restaurants throughout New England. I had, as well, taken a year off from my studies in the psychology of perception to travel as a street magician through Europe and, toward the end of that journey, had spent some months in London, England, exploring the use of sleight-of-hand magic in psychotherapy, as a means of engendering communication with distressed individuals largely unapproachable by clinical healers.[1] The success of this work suggested to me that sleight-of-hand might lend itself well to the curative arts, and I became, for the first time, interested in the relation, largely forgotten in the West, between folk medicine and magic.

It was this interest that led to the aforementioned grant, and to my sojourn as a magician in rural Asia. There, my sleight-of-hand skills proved invaluable as a means of stirring the curiosity of the local shamans. For magicians—whether modern entertainers or indigenous, tribal sorcerers—have in common the fact that they work with the malleable texture of perception. When the local sorcerers gleaned that I had at least some rudimentary skill in altering the common field of perception, I was invited into their homes, asked to share secrets with them, and eventually encouraged, even urged, to participate in various rituals and ceremonies.

But the focus of my research gradually shifted from questions regarding the application of magical techniques in medicine and ritual curing toward a deeper pondering of the relation between traditional magic and the animate natural world. This broader concern seemed to hold the keys to the earlier questions. For none of the several island sorcerers that I came to know in Indonesia, nor any of the *dzankris* with whom I lived in Nepal, considered their work as ritual healers to be their major role or function within their communities. Most of them, to be sure, *were* the primary healers or "doctors" for the villages in their vicinity, and they were often spoken of as such by the inhabitants of those villages. But the villagers also sometimes spoke of them, in low

1. This work was done at the Philadelphia Association, a therapeutic community directed by Dr. R. D. Laing and his associates.

voices and in very private conversations, as witches (or "lejaks" in Bali), as dark magicians who at night might well be practicing their healing spells backward (or while turning to the left instead of to the right) in order to afflict people with the very diseases that they would later work to cure by day. Such suspicions seemed fairly common in Indonesia, and often were harbored with regard to the most effective and powerful healers, those who were most renowned for their skill in driving out illness. For it was assumed that a magician, in order to expel malevolent influences, must have a strong understanding of those influences and demons—even, in some areas, a close rapport with such powers. I myself never consciously saw any of those magicians or shamans with whom I became acquainted engage in magic for harmful purposes, nor any convincing evidence that they had ever done so. (Few of the magicians that I came to know even accepted money in return for their services, although they did accept gifts in the way of food, blankets, and the like.) Yet I was struck by the fact that none of them ever did or said anything to counter such disturbing rumors and speculations, which circulated quietly through the regions where they lived. Slowly, I came to recognize that it was through the agency of such rumors, and the ambiguous fears that such rumors engendered in the village people, that the sorcerers were able to maintain a basic level of privacy. If the villagers did not entertain certain fears about the local sorcerer, then they would likely come to obtain his or her magical help for every little malady and disturbance; and since a more potent practitioner must provide services for several large villages, the sorcerer would be swamped from morning to night with requests for ritual aid. By allowing the inevitable suspicions and fears to circulate unhindered in the region (and sometimes even encouraging and contributing to such rumors), the sorcerer ensured that *only* those who were in real and profound need of his skills would dare to approach him for help.

This privacy, in turn, left the magician free to attend to what he acknowledged to be his primary craft and function. A clue to this function may be found in the circumstance that such magicians rarely dwell at the heart of their village; rather, their dwellings are commonly at the spatial periphery of the community or, more often, out beyond the edges of the village—amid the rice fields, or in a forest, or a wild cluster of boulders. I could easily attribute this to the just-mentioned need for privacy, yet for the magician in a traditional culture it seems to serve another purpose as well, providing a spatial expression of his or her symbolic position with regard to the community. For the magician's intelligence is not encompassed *within* the society; its place is at the edge of the community, mediating *between* the human community and the larger community of beings upon which the village depends for its nourishment and sustenance. This larger community includes, along with the humans, the multiple nonhuman entities that constitute the local landscape, from the diverse plants and the myriad animals—birds, mammals, fish, reptiles, insects—that inhabit or migrate through the region, to the particular winds and weather patterns that inform the local geography, as well as the various landforms—forests, rivers, caves, mountains—that lend their specific character to the surrounding earth.

The traditional or tribal shaman, I came to discern, acts as an intermediary between the human community and the larger ecological field, ensuring that there is an appropriate flow of nourishment, not just from the landscape to the human inhabitants, but from the human community back to the local earth. By his constant rituals, trances, ecstasies, and "journeys," he ensures that the relation between human society and the larger society of beings is balanced and reciprocal, and that the village never takes more from the living land than it returns to it—not just materially but with prayers, propitiations, and praise. The scale of a harvest or the size of a hunt are always negotiated between the tribal community and the natural world that it inhabits. To some extent every adult in the community is engaged in this process of listening and attuning to the other presences that surround and influence daily life. But the shaman or sorcerer is the exemplary voyager in the intermediate realm between the human and the more-than-human worlds, the primary strategist and negotiator in any dealings with the Others.

And it is only as a result of her continual engagement with the animate powers that dwell beyond the human community that the traditional magician is able to alleviate many individual illnesses that arise *within* that community. The sorcerer derives her ability to cure ailments from her more continuous practice of "healing" or balancing the community's relation to the surrounding land. Disease, in such cultures, is often conceptualized as a kind of systemic imbalance within the sick person, or more vividly as the intrusion of a demonic or malevolent presence into his body. There are, at times, malevolent influences within the village or tribe itself that disrupt the health and emotional well-being of susceptible individuals within the community. Yet such destructive influences within the human community are commonly traceable to a disequilibrium between that community and the larger field of forces in which it is embedded. Only those persons who, by their everyday practice, are involved in monitoring and maintaining the relations *between* the human village and the animate landscape are able to appropriately diagnose, treat, and ultimately relieve personal ailments and illnesses arising *within* the village. Any healer who was not simultaneously attending to the intertwined relation between the human community and the larger, more-than-human field, would likely dispel an illness from one person only to have the same problem arise (perhaps in a new guise) somewhere else in the community. Hence, the traditional magician or medicine person functions primarily as an intermediary between human and nonhuman worlds, and only secondarily as a healer.[2] Without a continually adjusted awareness of the relative balance or imbalance between the human group and its nonhuman environ, along with the skills necessary to modulate that primary relation, any "healer" is worthless—indeed, not a healer at all. The medicine person's primary allegiance, then, is not to the human community, but to the earthly web of relations in which that community is embedded—it is from this that his or her power to alleviate human illness derives—and this sets the local magician apart from other persons.

2. A simple illustration of this may be found among many of the indigenous peoples of North America, for whom the English term "medicine" commonly translates a word meaning "power"—specifically, the sacred power received by a human person from a particular animal or other nonhuman entity. Thus, a particular *medicine person* may be renowned for her "badger medicine" or "bear medicine," for his "eagle medicine," "elk medicine," or even "thunder medicine." It is from their direct engagement with these nonhuman powers that medicine persons derive their own abilities, including their ability to cure human ailments.

The primacy for the magician of nonhuman nature—the centrality of his relation to other species and to the earth—is not always evident to Western researchers. Countless anthropologists have managed to overlook the ecological dimension of the shaman's craft, while writing at great length of the shaman's rapport with "supernatural" entities. We can attribute much of this oversight to the modern, civilized assumption that the natural world is largely determinate and mechanical, and that that which is regarded as mysterious, powerful, and beyond human ken must therefore be of some other, nonphysical realm *above* nature, "supernatural."

The oversight becomes still more comprehensible when we realize that many of the earliest European interpreters of indigenous lifeways were Christian missionaries. For the Church had long assumed that only human beings have intelligent souls, and that the other animals, to say nothing of trees and rivers, were "created" for no other reason than to serve humankind. We can easily understand why European missionaries, steeped in the dogma of institutionalized Christianity, assumed a belief in supernatural, otherworldly powers among those tribal persons whom they saw awestruck and entranced by nonhuman (but nevertheless natural) forces. What is remarkable is the extent to which contemporary anthropology still preserves the ethnocentric bias of these early interpreters. We no longer describe the shamans' enigmatic spirit-helpers as the "superstitious claptrap of heathen primitives"—we have cleansed ourselves of at least *that* much ethnocentrism; yet we still refer to such enigmatic forces, respectfully now, as "supernaturals"—for we are unable to shed the sense, so endemic to scientific civilization, of nature as a rather prosaic and predictable realm, unsuited to such mysteries. Nevertheless, that which is regarded with the greatest awe and wonder by indigenous, oral cultures is, I suggest, none other than what we view as nature itself. The deeply mysterious powers and entities with whom the shaman enters into a rapport are ultimately the same forces—the same plants, animals, forests, and winds—that to literate, "civilized" Europeans are just so much scenery, the pleasant backdrop of our more pressing human concerns.

The most sophisticated definition of "magic" that now circulates through the American counterculture is "the ability or power to alter one's consciousness at will." No mention is made of any *reason* for altering one's consciousness. Yet in tribal cultures that which we call "magic" takes its meaning from the fact that humans, in an indigenous and oral context, experience their own consciousness as simply one form of awareness among many others. The traditional magician cultivates an ability to shift out of his or her common state of consciousness precisely in order to make contact with the other organic forms of sensitivity and awareness with which human existence is entwined. Only by temporarily shedding the accepted perceptual logic of his culture can the sorcerer hope to enter into relation with other species on their own terms; only by altering the common organization of his senses will he be able to enter into a rapport with the multiple nonhuman sensibilities that animate the local landscape. It is this, we might say, that defines a shaman: the ability to readily slip out of the perceptual boundaries that demarcate his or her particular culture—boundaries reinforced by social customs, taboos, and most importantly, the common speech or language—in order to make contact with, and learn from, the other powers in the land. His magic is precisely this heightened receptivity to the meaningful solicitations—songs, cries, gestures—of the larger, more-than-human field.

Magic, then, in its perhaps most primordial sense, is the experience of existing in a world made up of multiple intelligences, the intuition that every form one perceives—from the swallow swooping overhead to the fly on a blade of grass, and indeed the blade of grass itself—is an *experiencing* form, an entity with its own predilections and sensations, albeit sensations that are very different from our own.

To be sure, the shaman's ecological function, his or her role as intermediary between human society and the land, is not always obvious at first blush, even to a sensitive observer. We see the sorcerer being called upon to cure an ailing tribesman of his sleeplessness, or perhaps simply to locate some missing goods; we witness him entering into trance and sending his awareness into other dimensions in search of insight and aid. Yet we should not be so ready to interpret these dimensions as "supernatural," nor to view them as realms entirely "internal" to the personal psyche of the practitioner. For it is likely that the "inner world" of our Western psychological experience, like the supernatural heaven of Christian belief, originates in the loss of our ancestral reciprocity with the animate earth. When the animate powers that surround us are suddenly construed as having less significance than ourselves, when the generative earth is abruptly defined as a determinate object devoid of its own sensations and feelings, then the sense of a wild and multiplicitous otherness (in relation to which human existence has always oriented itself) must migrate, either into a supersensory heaven beyond the natural world, or else into the human skull itself—the only allowable refuge, in this world, for what is ineffable and unfathomable.

But in genuinely oral, indigenous cultures, the sensuous world itself remains the dwelling place of the gods, of the numinous powers that can either sustain or extinguish human life. It is not by sending his awareness out beyond the natural world that the shaman makes contact with the purveyors of life and health, nor by journeying into his personal psyche; rather, it is by propelling his awareness laterally, outward into the depths of a landscape at once both sensuous and psychological, the living dream that we share with the soaring hawk, the spider, and the stone silently sprouting lichens on its coarse surface.

The magician's intimate relationship with nonhuman nature becomes most evident when we attend to the easily overlooked background of his or her practice—not just to the more visible tasks of curing and ritual aid to which she is called by individual clients, or to the larger ceremonies at which she presides and dances, but to the content of the prayers by which she prepares for such ceremonies, and to the countless ritual gestures that she enacts when alone, the daily propitiations and praise that flow from her toward the land and *its* many voices.

All this attention to nonhuman nature was, as I have mentioned, very far from my intended focus when I embarked on my research into the uses of magic and medicine in Indonesia, and it was only gradually that I became aware of this more subtle dimension of the native magician's craft. The first shift in my preconceptions came rather quietly, when I was staying for some days in the home of a young "balian," or magic practitioner, in the interior of Bali. I had been provided with a simple bed in a separate, one-room building in the balian's family compound (most compound homes, in Bali, are comprised of several separate small buildings, for sleeping and for cooking, set on a single enclosed plot of land), and early each morning the balian's wife came to bring me a small but delicious bowl of fruit, which I ate by myself, sitting on the ground outside, leaning against the wall of my hut and watching the sun slowly climb through the rustling palm leaves. I noticed, when she delivered the fruit, that my hostess was also balancing a tray containing many little green plates: actually, they were little boat-shaped platters, each woven simply and neatly from a freshly cut section of palm frond. The platters were two or three inches long, and within each was a little mound of white rice. After handing me my breakfast, the woman and the tray disappeared from view behind the other buildings, and when she came by some minutes later to pick up my empty bowl, the tray in her hands was empty as well.

The second time that I saw the array of tiny rice platters, I asked my hostess what they were for. Patiently, she explained to me that they were offerings for the household spirits. When I inquired about the Balinese term that she used for "spirit," she repeated the same explanation, now in Indonesian, that these were gifts for the spirits of the family compound, and I saw that I had understood her correctly. She handed me a bowl of sliced papaya and mango, and disappeared around the corner. I pondered for a minute, then set down the bowl, stepped to the side of my hut, and peered through the trees. At first unable to see her, I soon caught sight of her crouched low beside the corner of one of the other buildings, carefully setting what I presumed was one of the offerings on the ground at that spot. Then she stood up with the tray, walked to the other visible corner of the same building, and there slowly and carefully set another offering on the ground. I returned to my bowl of fruit and finished my breakfast. That afternoon, when the rest of the household was busy, I walked back behind the building where I had seen her set down the two offerings. There were the little green platters, resting neatly at the two rear corners of the building. But the mounds of rice that had been within them were gone.

The next morning I finished the sliced fruit, waited for my hostess to come by for the empty bowl, then quietly headed back behind the buildings. Two fresh palm-leaf offerings sat at the same spots where the others had been the day before. These were filled with rice. Yet as I gazed at one of these offerings, I abruptly realized, with a start, that one of the rice kernels was actually moving.

Only when I knelt down to look more closely did I notice a line of tiny black ants winding through the dirt to the offering. Peering still closer, I saw that two ants had already climbed onto the offering and were struggling with the uppermost kernel of rice; as I watched, one of them dragged the kernel down and off the leaf, then set off with it back along the line of ants advancing on the offering. The second ant took another kernel and climbed down with it, dragging and pushing, and fell over the edge of the leaf, then a third climbed onto the offering. The line of ants seemed to emerge from a thick clump of grass around a nearby palm tree. I walked over to the other offering and discovered another line of ants dragging away the white kernels. This line emerged from the top of a little mound of dirt, about fifteen feet away from the buildings. There was an offering on the ground by a corner of my building as well, and a nearly identical line of ants. I walked into my room chuckling to myself: the balian and his wife had gone to so much trouble to placate the household spirits with gifts, only to have their offerings stolen by little six-legged thieves. What a waste! But then a strange thought dawned on me: what if the ants were the very "household spirits" to whom the offerings were being made?

I soon began to discern the logic of this. The family compound, like most on this tropical island, had been constructed in the vicinity of several ant colonies. Since a great deal of cooking took place in the compound (which housed, along with the balian and his wife and children, various members of their extended family), and also much preparation of elaborate offerings of foodstuffs for various rituals and festivals in the surrounding villages, the grounds and the buildings at the compound were vulnerable to infestations by the sizable ant population. Such invasions could range from rare nuisances to a periodic or even constant siege. It became apparent that the daily palm-frond offerings served to preclude such an attack by the natural forces that surrounded (and underlay) the family's land. The daily gifts of rice kept the ant colonies occupied—and, presumably, satisfied. Placed in regular, repeated locations at the corners of various structures around the compound, the offerings seemed to establish certain boundaries between the human and ant communities; by honoring this boundary with gifts, the humans apparently hoped to persuade the insects to respect the boundary and not enter the buildings.

Yet I remained puzzled by my hostess's assertion that these were gifts "for the spirits." To be sure, there has always been some confusion between our Western notion of "spirit" (which so often is defined in contrast to matter or "flesh"), and the mysterious presences to which tribal and indigenous cultures pay so much respect. I have already alluded to the gross misunderstandings arising from the circumstance that many of the earliest Western students of these other customs were Christian missionaries all too ready to see occult ghosts and immaterial phantoms where the tribespeople were simply offering their respect to the local winds. While the notion of "spirit" has come to have, for us in the West, a primarily anthropomorphic or human association, my encounter with the ants was the first of many experiences suggesting to me that the "spirits" of an indigenous culture are primarily those modes of intelligence or awareness that do *not* possess a human form.

As humans, we are well acquainted with the needs and capacities of the human body—we *live* our own bodies and so know, from within, the possibilities of our form. We cannot know, with the same familiarity and intimacy, the lived experience of a grass snake or a snapping turtle; we cannot readily experience the precise sensations of a hummingbird sipping nectar from a flower or a rubber tree soaking up sunlight. And yet we do know how it feels to sip from a fresh pool of water or to bask and stretch in the sun. Our experience may indeed be a variant of these other modes of sensitivity; nevertheless, we cannot, as humans, precisely experience the living sensations of another form. We do not know, with full clarity, their desires or motivations; we cannot know, or can never be sure that we know, what they know. That the deer does experience sensations, that it carries knowledge of how to orient in the land, of where to find food and how to protect its young, that it knows well how to survive in the forest without the tools upon which we depend, is readily evident to our human senses. That the mango tree has the ability to create fruit, or the yarrow plant the power to reduce a child's fever, is also evident. To humankind, these Others are purveyors of secrets, carriers of intelligence that we ourselves often need: it is these Others who can inform us of unseasonable changes in the weather, or warn us of imminent eruptions and earthquakes, who show us, when foraging, where we may find the ripest berries or the best route to follow back home. By watching them build their nests and shelters, we glean clues regarding how to strengthen our own dwellings, and their deaths teach us of our own. We receive from them countless gifts of food, fuel, shelter, and clothing. Yet still they remain Other to us, inhabiting their own cultures and displaying their own rituals, never wholly fathomable.

Moreover, it is not only those entities acknowledged by Western civilization as "alive," not only the other animals and the plants that speak, as spirits, to the senses of an oral culture, but also the meandering river from which those animals drink, and the torrential monsoon rains, and the stone that fits neatly into the palm of the hand. The mountain, too, has its thoughts. The forest birds whirring and chattering as the sun slips below the horizon are vocal organs of the rain forest itself.[3]

---

3. To the Western mind such views are likely to sound like reckless "projections" of human consciousness into inanimate and dumb materials, suitable for poetry perhaps, but having nothing, in fact, to do with those actual birds or that forest. Such is our common view. This text will examine the possibility that it is civilization that has been confused, and not indigenous peoples. It will suggest, and provide evidence, that one perceives a world at all only by projecting oneself into that world, that one makes contact with things and others only by actively participating in them, lending one's sensory imagination to things in order to discover how they alter and transform that imagination, how they reflect us back changed, how they are different from us. It will suggest that perception is *always* participatory, and hence that modern humanity's denial of awareness in nonhuman nature is borne not by any conceptual or scientific rigor, but rather by an inability, or a refusal, to fully perceive other organisms.

Bali, of course, is hardly an aboriginal culture; the complexity of its temple architecture, the intricacy of its irrigation systems, the resplendence of its colorful festivals and crafts all bespeak the influence of various civilizations, most notably the Hindu complex of India. In Bali, nevertheless, these influences are thoroughly intertwined with the indigenous animism of the Indonesian archipelago; the Hindu gods and goddesses have been appropriated, as it were, by the more volcanic, eruptive spirits of the local terrain.

Yet the underlying animistic cultures of Indonesia, like those of many islands in the Pacific, are steeped as well in beliefs often referred to by ethnologists as "ancestor worship," and some may argue that the ritual reverence paid to one's long-dead human ancestors (and the assumption of their influence in present life), easily invalidates my assertion that the various "powers" or "spirits" that move through the discourse of indigenous, oral peoples are ultimately tied to nonhuman (but nonetheless sentient) forces in the enveloping landscape.

This objection rests upon certain assumptions implicit in Christian civilization, such as the assumption that the "spirits" of dead persons necessarily retain their human form, and that they reside in a domain outside of the physical world to which our senses give us access. However, most indigenous tribal peoples have no such ready recourse to an immaterial realm outside earthly nature. Our strictly human heavens and hells have only recently been abstracted from the sensuous world that surrounds us, from this more-than-human realm that abounds in its own winged intelligences and cloven-hoofed powers. For almost all oral cultures, the enveloping and sensuous earth remains the dwelling place of both the living *and* the dead. The "body"—whether human or otherwise—is not yet a mechanical object in such cultures, but is a magical entity, the mind's own sensuous aspect, and at death the body's decomposition into soil, worms, and dust can only signify the gradual reintegration of one's ancestors and elders into the living landscape, from which all, too, are born.

Each indigenous culture elaborates this recognition of metamorphosis in its own fashion, taking its clues from the particular terrain in which it is situated. Often the invisible atmosphere that animates the visible world— the subtle presence that circulates both within us and between all things—

retains within itself the spirit or breath of the dead person until the time when that breath will enter and animate another visible body—a bird, or a deer, or a field of wild grain. Some cultures may burn, or "cremate," the body in order to more completely return the person, as smoke, to the swirling air, while that which departs as flame is offered to the sun and stars, and that which lingers as ash is fed to the dense earth. Still other cultures may dismember the body, leaving certain parts in precise locations where they will likely be found by condors, or where they will be consumed by mountain lions or by wolves, thus hastening the re-incarnation of that person into a particular animal realm within the landscape. Such examples illustrate simply that death, in tribal cultures, initiates a metamorphosis wherein the person's presence does not "vanish" from the sensible world (where would it go?) but rather remains as an animating force within the vastness of the landscape, whether subtly, in the wind, or more visibly, in animal form, or even as the eruptive, ever to be appeased, wrath of the volcano. "Ancestor worship," in its myriad forms, then, is ultimately another mode of attentiveness to nonhuman nature; it signifies not so much an awe or reverence of human powers, but rather a reverence for those forms that awareness takes when it is *not* in human form, when the familiar human embodiment dies and decays to become part of the encompassing cosmos.

This cycling of the human back into the larger world ensures that the other forms of experience that we encounter—whether ants, or willow trees, or clouds—are never absolutely alien to ourselves. Despite the obvious differences in shape, and ability, and style of being, they remain at least distantly familiar, even familial. It is, paradoxically, this perceived kinship or consanguinity that renders the difference, or otherness, so eerily potent.[4]

4. The similarity between such animistic worldviews and the emerging perspective of contemporary ecology is not trivial. Atmospheric geochemist James Lovelock, elucidating the well-known Gaia hypothesis—a theory stressing the major role played by organic life in the ceaseless modulation of the earth's atmospheric and climatic conditions—insists that the geological environment is itself constituted by organic life, and by the products of organic metabolism. In his words, we inhabit "a world that is the breath and bones of our ancestors." See, for instance, "Gaia: the World as Living Organism," in the *New Scientist*, December 18, 1986, as well as *Scientists on Gaia*, ed. Stephen Schneider and Penelope Boston (Cambridge: M.I.T. Press, 1991).

Several months after my arrival in Bali, I left the village in which I was staying to visit one of the pre-Hindu sites on the island. I arrived on my bicycle early in the afternoon, after the bus carrying tourists from the coast had departed. A flight of steps took me down into a lush, emerald valley, lined by cliffs on either side, awash with the speech of the river and the sighing of the wind through high, unharvested grasses. On a small bridge crossing the river I met an old woman carrying a wide basket on her head and holding the hand of a little, shy child; the woman grinned at me with the red, toothless smile of a beetle nut chewer. On the far side of the river I stood in front of a great moss-covered complex of passageways, rooms, and courtyards carved by hand out of the black volcanic rock.

I noticed, at a bend in the canyon downstream, a further series of caves carved into the cliffs. These appeared more isolated and remote, unattended by any footpath I could discern. I set out through the grasses to explore them. This proved much more difficult than I anticipated, but after getting lost in the tall grasses, and fording the river three times, I at last found myself beneath the caves. A short scramble up the rock wall brought me to the mouth of one of them, and I entered on my hands and knees. It was a wide but low opening, perhaps only four feet high, and the interior receded only about five or six feet into the cliff. The floor and walls were covered with mosses, painting the cave with green patterns and softening the harshness of the rock; the place, despite its small size—or perhaps because of it—had an air of great friendliness. I climbed to two other caves, each about the same size, but then felt drawn back to the first one, to sit cross-legged on the cushioning moss and gaze out across the emerald canyon. It was quiet inside, a kind of intimate sanctuary hewn into the stone. I began to explore the rich resonance of the enclosure, first just humming, then intoning a simple chant taught to me by a balian some days before. I was delighted by the overtones that the cave added to my voice, and sat there singing for a long while. I did not notice the change in the wind outside, or the cloud shadows darkening the valley, until the rains broke—suddenly and with great force. The first storm of the monsoon!

I had experienced only slight rains on the island before then, and was startled by the torrential downpour now sending stones tumbling along the cliffs, building puddles and then ponds in the green landscape below, swelling the river. There was no question of returning home—I would be unable to make my way back through the flood to the valley's entrance. And so, thankful for the shelter, I recrossed my legs to wait out the storm. Before long the rivulets falling along the cliff above gathered themselves into streams, and two small waterfalls cascaded across the cave's mouth. Soon I was looking into a solid curtain of water, thin in some places, where the canyon's image flickered unsteadily, and thickly rushing in others. My senses were all but overcome by the wild beauty of the cascade and by the roar of sound, my body trembling inwardly at the weird sense of being sealed into my hiding place.

And then, in the midst of all this tumult, I noticed a small, delicate activity. Just in front of me, and only an inch or two to my side of the torrent, a spider was climbing a thin thread stretched across the mouth of the cave. As I watched, it anchored another thread to the top of the opening, then slipped back along the first thread and joined the two at a point about midway between the roof and the floor. I lost sight of the spider then, and for a while it seemed that it had vanished, thread and all, until my focus rediscovered it. Two more threads now radiated from the center to the floor, and then another; soon the spider began to swing between these as on a circular trellis, trailing an ever-lengthening thread which it affixed to each radiating rung as it moved from one to the next, spiraling outward. The spider seemed wholly undaunted by the tumult of waters spilling past it, although every now and then it broke off its spiral dance and climbed to the roof or the floor to tug on the radii there, assuring the tautness of the threads, then crawled back to where it left off. Whenever I lost the correct focus, I waited to catch sight of the spinning arachnid, and then let its dancing form gradually draw the lineaments of the web back into visibility, tying my focus into each new knot of silk as it moved, weaving my gaze into the ever-deepening pattern.

And then, abruptly, my vision snagged on a strange incongruity: another thread slanted across the web, neither radiating nor spiraling from the central juncture, violating the symmetry. As I followed it with

my eyes, pondering its purpose in the overall pattern, I began to realize that it was on a different plane from the rest of the web, for the web
slipped out of focus whenever this new line became clearer. I soon saw
that it led to its own center, about twelve inches to the right of the first,
another nexus of forces from which several threads stretched to the
floor and the ceiling. And then I saw that there was a *different* spider
spinning this web, testing its tautness by dancing around it like the
first, now setting the silken cross weaves around the nodal point and
winding outward. The two spiders spun independently of each other,
but to my eyes they wove a single intersecting pattern. This widening
of my gaze soon disclosed yet another spider spiraling in the cave's
mouth, and suddenly I realized that there were *many* overlapping webs
coming into being, radiating out at different rhythms from myriad centers poised—some higher, some lower, some minutely closer to my eyes
and some farther—between the stone above and the stone below.

I sat stunned and mesmerized before this ever-complexifying expanse of living patterns upon patterns, my gaze drawn like a breath
into one converging group of lines, then breathed out into open space,
then drawn down into another convergence. The curtain of water had
become utterly silent—I tried at one point to hear it, but could not. My
senses were entranced.

I had the distinct impression that I was watching the universe
being born, galaxy upon galaxy. . . .

Night filled the cave with darkness. The rain had not stopped. Yet,
strangely, I felt neither cold nor hungry—only remarkably peaceful and
at home. Stretching out upon the moist, mossy floor near the back of
the cave, I slept.

When I awoke, the sun was staring into the canyon, the grasses below
rippling with bright blues and greens. I could see no trace of the webs, nor
their weavers. Thinking that they were invisible to my eyes without the
curtain of water behind them, I felt carefully with my hands around and
through the mouth of the cave. But the webs were gone. I climbed down to
the river and washed, then hiked across and out of the canyon to where my
cycle was drying in the sun, and headed back to my own valley.

I have never, since that time, been able to encounter a spider without feeling a great strangeness and awe. To be sure, insects and spiders are not the only powers, or even central presences, in the Indonesian universe. But they were *my* introduction to the spirits, to the magic afoot in the land. It was from them that I first learned of the intelligence that lurks in nonhuman nature, the ability that an alien form of sentience has to echo one's own, to instill a reverberation in oneself that temporarily shatters habitual ways of seeing and feeling, leaving one open to a world all alive, awake, and aware. It was from such small beings that my senses first learned of the countless worlds within worlds that spin in the depths of this world that we commonly inhabit, and from them that I learned that my body could, with practice, enter sensorially into these dimensions. The precise and minuscule craft of the spiders had so honed and focused my awareness that the very webwork of the universe, of which my own flesh was a part, seemed to be being spun by their arcane art. I have already spoken of the ants, and of the fireflies, whose sensory likeness to the lights in the night sky had taught me the fickleness of gravity. The long and cyclical trance that we call malaria was also brought to me by insects, in this case mosquitoes, and I lived for three weeks in a feverish state of shivers, sweat, and visions.

I had rarely before paid much attention to the natural world. But my exposure to traditional magicians and seers was shifting my senses; I became increasingly susceptible to the solicitations of nonhuman things. In the course of struggling to decipher the magicians' odd gestures or to fathom their constant spoken references to powers unseen and unheard, I began to *see* and to *hear* in a manner I never had before. When a magician spoke of a power or "presence" lingering in the corner of his house, I learned to notice the ray of sunlight that was then pouring through a chink in the roof, illuminating a column of drifting dust, and to realize that that column of light was indeed a power, influencing the air currents by its warmth, and indeed influencing the whole mood of the room; although I had not consciously seen it before, it had already been structuring my experience. My ears began to attend, in a new way, to the songs of birds—no longer just a melodic background to human speech, but meaningful speech in its own right, responding to and commenting on events in the surrounding earth. I became a student of subtle differences: the way a breeze may flutter a single leaf on a whole tree, leaving the other leaves silent and unmoved (had not that leaf, then, been brushed by a magic?); or the way the intensity of the sun's heat expresses itself in the precise rhythm of the crickets. Walking along the dirt paths, I learned to slow my pace in order to *feel* the difference between one nearby hill and the next, or to taste the presence of a particular field at a certain time of day when, as I had been told by a local *dukun*, the place had a special power and proffered unique gifts. It was a power communicated to my senses by the way the shadows of the trees fell at that hour, and by smells that only then lingered in the tops of the grasses without being wafted away by the wind, and other elements I could only isolate after many days of stopping and listening.

And gradually, then, other animals began to intercept me in my wanderings, as if some quality in my posture or the rhythm of my breathing had disarmed their wariness; I would find myself face-to-face with monkeys, and with large lizards that did not slither away when I spoke, but leaned forward in apparent curiosity. In rural Java, I often noticed monkeys accompanying me in the branches overhead, and ravens walked toward me on the road, croaking. While at Pangandaran, a nature preserve on a peninsula jutting out from the south coast of Java ("a place of many spirits," I was told by nearby fishermen), I stepped out from a clutch of trees and found myself looking into the face of one of the rare and beautiful bison that exist only on that island. Our eyes locked. When it snorted, I snorted back; when it shifted its shoulders, I shifted my stance; when I tossed my head, it tossed *its* head in reply. I found myself caught in a nonverbal conversation with this Other, a gestural duet with which my conscious awareness had very little to do. It was as if my body in its actions was suddenly being motivated by a wisdom older than my thinking mind, as though it was held and moved by a logos, deeper than words, spoken by the Other's body, the trees, and the stony ground on which we stood.

The Spell of the Sensuous (1996)

If you look up Jack Turner's bio on the website for Jackson Hole's famed Exum Guide Service, it says: "Guide for 38 years. Pioneer climbing in Colorado and extensive climbing in Yosemite and the Tetons. Veteran of 40 expeditions and treks in Pakistan, Peru, Nepal, China, Tibet, and India." In other words, Turner (b. 1942) has earned the right to say a few words about wild places, and he said them, with an edge, in *The Abstract Wild* (1996), the fierce and wonderful book from which this essay is drawn. He argues that much of what passes for "wilderness" on this continent has been so managed that it no longer means very much—Yosemite Valley has become Coney Island. But he also offers the possibility of real engagement, of encounters persistent and exposed enough to leave a mark.

The Song of the White Pelican

I am a pelican of the wilderness.—Psalms

I am lounging on the summit of the Grand Teton surrounded by blocks of quartz and a cobalt sky. It is mid-morning in July—warm, still, and so clear the distant ranges seem etched into the horizon. To the east, the Absaroka, Gros Ventre, and Wind River; to the south, the Salt, Snake, and Caribou; to the west the Big Hole and the Lost River; and to the north, the Centennial, Madison, Gallatin, and Beartooth. Directly north, and closer, is the still-snowy summit of the Pitchstone Plateau, and beyond it the fuzzy blur of a geyser somewhere near Old Faithful. To the northeast are slices of Yellowstone Lake.

Despite the breadth of view I always feel this summit is a place of great simplicity. I have just climbed the Exum, or south, ridge of the Grand Teton with clients. They are taking photographs. Since I have climbed the Grand for thirty years, I have my pictures, and since I am fifteen years older than my oldest client, I am tired. So I rest and enjoy the clarity and count shades of blue as the sky pales into the mountains. Then I hear a faint noise above me, and my heart says, "Pelicans."

The sounds are faint, so faint they are sometimes lost—a trace of clacking in the sky. It is even harder to see them. Tiny glints, like slivers of ice, are occasionally visible, then invisible, then visible again as the sheen of their feathers strikes just the right angle to the sun. With binoculars we see them clearly: seventeen white pelicans soaring in a tight circle. I have seen them here before, as well as from the summit of Symmetry Spire and from the long ridge of Rendezvous Peak. But it is rare—in part, I think, because the conditions for hearing and seeing them are so rare. Perhaps they are often above us, but with the wind and clouds and the ever-present anxiety of climbing, we fail to notice them.

The white pelican (*Pelecanus erythrorhynchos*), one of seven species in the world, is a large bird often weighing twenty pounds, with some individuals reaching thirty pounds. The only other pelican in North America, the brown pelican (*Pelecanus occidentalis*), is smaller and restricted to the coasts. The white pelican's wingspan reaches nine and a half feet, equal to the California condor's. Of North American birds, only the trumpeter swan is consistently larger.

Though huge, a pelican, like all birds, consists mostly of feathers, flesh, and air. The beak, skull, feet, and bones of a twenty-five-pound pelican weigh but twenty-three ounces. Its plumage is brilliant white except for the black primaries and outer secondaries, and pale yellow plumes on the crown of the head during breeding season. Occasionally there is pale yellow on the chest. Their eyes are the color of fine slate.

The summit of the Grand Teton is 13,770 feet high, and the pelicans above us are at the limit of unaided human vision. Since in good light a flock of white pelicans is easily visible at a mile, these pelicans are at least a mile above us, or higher than 19,000 feet. This seems high for any bird, but geese have been photographed at 29,000 feet, ravens are a nuisance on the South Col of Everest at 26,000 feet, and I have watched flocks of Brahminy ducks from Siberia cross the ridge between Everest and Cho Oyu, which is 19,500 feet at its low point. So although 19,000 feet is impressive, and no one knows how high pelicans can or do fly, the more interesting question is this: What are they *doing* up there? Soaring. Clacking. Yes, but why? I don't think anybody knows, and this mystery, along with the inevitable speculations, are a large part of why I find them so appealing.

For years I asked biologists and birders about pelican sounds, and they are unanimous: they have never heard a pelican make a sound. The popular bird books do not mention pelican sounds, and most of the technical literature reports that pelicans are mute except when breeding. Then the authors go on to admit they have spent little time around breeding pelicans. There are, of course, good reasons for this. The white pelican so dislikes human presence during breeding season that if approached, they will abandon their nests and raft on nearby water. The eggs, or chicks, are then exposed to the sun, to cold, and to the depredations of the ever-present gulls. An hour, or less, is sufficient to wipe out the breeding colony. If repeatedly harassed, white pelicans will abandon a rookery forever. For these reasons, monitoring the white pelican population is usually done from airplanes, increasingly with aerial photography. In one sense this is commendable, but in another it is sad, for fewer and fewer people know less and less about pelicans. The hard data are known—the average length of the bill, the average time of arrival and departure during migration, the average number of eggs—and no doubt will increase, but our understanding of pelicans, a way of knowing that requires intimacy, is nil.

We could, of course, let pelicans come to us. This is the difference between seeking and stalking and just sitting and waiting. It is an old difference, as old as hunting, but a difference that is hard for us to choose because we are, as a nation and as a civilization, a people of seeking and stalking, though exactly why this is so remains fugitive.

I used to visit an old Sherpa in Khumbu who had served on perhaps fifty Himalayan expeditions. His name was Dawa Tensing and he lived in a village just north of Thyangboche Monastery on the trail to

Everest. He was famous for saying, "So many people coming, coming, always looking, never finding, always coming back again. Why?" Once, in all sincerity, he asked me: "Is America beautiful? Why you always come back here?"

It took a long time for Dawa's "Why?" to sink into my thick skull, and it took even longer to prefer his question to the closure of an answer. I suspect now that if we wish to know pelicans intimately, we must begin with a preference for questions and a preference for sitting and waiting. Perhaps it would be better if ornithologists were to become glider pilots, mountaineers, and fishermen, flying in the thermals, lounging atop great peaks, fishing great rivers, and waiting for pelicans to come to them.

If we sit quietly in the places of pelicans, I believe they *will* come to us. I have been sitting in a cabin in a national park for portions of sixteen years now. Although I do not feed wild animals, the eagles come and watch me from a nearby snag, a red squirrel sits by my elbow while I shave, martens and weasels look in my window, and deer and elk nip the weeds by the porch. Moose sometimes sleep on the porch— and scare the wits out of me when I go out at night to pee.

Dōgen's famous lines in the *Genjo Koan* are always suggestive, even when removed from their spiritual context:

> That the self advances and confirms the ten thousand things is called delusion;
> That the ten thousand things advance and confirm the self is enlightenment.[1]

The Japanese word here translated as "enlightenment" can also be translated as "intimacy." Perhaps it is time to realize that the knowledge won from hard data is limited; perhaps it is time to allow wild animals to establish the degree of intimacy between us. No radio collars, no netting, no banding, no intrusion into their lives. We wait; they decide.

---

1. Quoted in Maezumi, *The Way of Everyday Life*, n.p.

A few people have spent time sitting with pelicans. In 1962 George Schaller spent 367 hours sitting in a canoe watching pelicans breed.[2] He heard lots of sounds. Other researchers have noted that pelicans hiss when angry, snap their mandibles together as a warning, and while mating make sounds that have been variously described as piglike or low-toned grunts, subdued croaking, a deep-voiced, murmuring groan, and grunting quacks. Audubon said they made a sound like blowing through the bunghole of a cask.

Although pelicans do make sounds, they are, relative to other birds, quite silent. There may be phylogenetic reasons for this. The newer species of birds are the most vocal and produce the greatest variety of sounds, while pelicans are very old—they've been around thirty-five to forty million years. We have one fossil record from the Pliocene, and we know they have been in the American West since the Pleistocene. Ornithologists have discovered prehistoric nesting sites on mountains that were once islands rising from the Pleistocene lakes that covered much of the Great Basin.

The silence of pelicans, along with their great age, contributes to their dignity. And this is no doubt augmented by the fact that the pelican is not a popular bird. The Hamilton stores in Yellowstone offer no pelican postcards or posters or stuffed pelicans or pelican candles or pelican-shaped coffee mugs—the kind of merchandise that nibbles at the dignity of other animals.

The white pelican, in short, is a quiet, dignified bird. The ones in Yellowstone are also friendly. Although biologists stress that pelicans are always in flocks (except for stragglers during migration), and that they are timid, anyone who fishes Yellowstone knows that they are often solitary, sort of like fly fishermen; and after fishing Yellowstone's waters for thirty-three years, I believe that white pelicans are fond of their fishing kin. Their reason is probably a good pelican reason, a sustained

2. Schaller, "Breeding Behavior of the White Pelican." Although it is somewhat dated, Schaller's article contains a bibliography of works on the white pelicans of Yellowstone Lake.

meditation on "anything that spends that much time trying to catch trout can't be all bad." For although other pelicans eat rough fish, especially carp, 98 to 100 percent of a Yellowstone pelican's diet is *Salmo clarki lewisi*, otherwise known as the black-spotted trout or, more formally, as the westslope cutthroat. On my off days I am consoled by the firm belief that the karma of those who subsist on trout is superior to those who subsist on carp.

Still, there must be a touch of condescension in the birds' view of fly fishermen. Pelicans have been observed struggling with twenty-four-inch trout, and they are sometimes so bloated by success they have to vomit so they can lose enough weight to fly. On an average day, a Yellowstone pelican will eat more than four pounds of cutthroats. If the average fly fisherman had to catch four pounds of trout a day to survive, there would be fewer *Homo sapiens* than pelicans—and lots of carcasses surrounded by three thousand dollars' worth of high-tech fishing gear.

Unlike the brown pelican, the white pelican does not dive for fish. It fishes with its bill and the flabby, stretchy gular pouch that hangs beneath it. The pelican is very clever with this pouch, using it as a dip net to catch fish, fluttering it to cool off (it is filled with blood vessels), and in one instance of a pelican in captivity, catching balls with it and throwing them back up into the air. Since its bill is about a foot long, the pelican must feed near the surface of the water, probably the top two or three feet. In deep water a group of pelicans will form a semicircle and by thrashing their wings and generally creating chaos drive fish into shallow water where they can reach them. But if fishing alone on a river, the pelican is attracted to fish feeding near the surface, and that means fish that are feeding on emerging aquatic insects and hatches.

The Yellowstone River is a great dry-fly river—what better place for a bird that must feed near the surface? If you go to the estuary below the lake during the gray drake mayfly hatch in late July, you will occasionally see pelicans floating amidst a blizzard of fly lines and mayflies, and performing upstream and downstream ferries like skilled kayakers to avoid all the people standing in the river. The novice fishermen are trying to match the huge duns, the pelicans and their followers are attending to the spinner fall.

Buffalo Ford, a picnic area with a small island offshore that divides the river and provides good holding water for trout, is another favorite place of pelicans and fishermen. I have seen pelicans work this water just like an angler works a dry fly or an emerger. They land above the good water and float into the deep pool at the head of the island, then alongside the deep trench of the main current that flows between the east side of the island and the far shore; after reaching the tailwater below the island, they lift off and fly back to the head of the good water. Then they do this again and again—just like the rest of the folks fishing the ford.

But every time they land on the river, it looks like a disaster. They drop the backs of their huge wings, throw out their feet like wheels, and land with a controlled crash—like a 747. Every time, they almost nose over; every time, they just make it. Then, to regain their composure, they tuck their bills into their chests with that snotty, satisfied-English-butler look and casually paddle off after more trout, buoyant as a well-greased fly. As the poet Onitsura says,

> The water-bird
> Looks heavy,—
> But it floats![3]

Because I guide in the Tetons all summer, I have little time for fishing, but when work slows, I fish the Yellowstone River and, afterward, on my way home, I stop at the Lake Hotel. I tell myself it is for dinner, but this is just an excuse to sit in the lounge, listen to the string quartet that plays during the summer months, and watch the light on Yellowstone Lake. The owners recently repainted the lounge in civilized pale green, rose, mauve, and cream. I like to sit in a wicker wing chair, drink margaritas, and listen to music that does not remind me of machines. Last year the first violinist was a young woman who played beautifully. Her skin was a color found only inside seashells. Bent to her violin, she swayed in oblivion, concealed in the solitude of her music, fully present, but lost, as luminous and self-contained and remote as a star.

3. In Blythe, *Haiku*, vol. 4, 1259.

Just visible above her shoulder, through the bay windows at the end of the lounge, was the lake, speckled with whitecaps. In the distance stretched its southeast arm. The slant of evening light and the ever-present storm clouds darkened its western shore, while sunlight revealed light rock or fresh snow on the peaks of the Absaroka. Farther, almost concealed by clouds, were Colter Peak, Turret Peak, the Trident, the Two-Ocean Plateau. Farther still was the Thorofare, the wildest, most remote place in the lower forty-eight states.

At the tip of this southeast arm, just west of where the Yellowstone River enters the lake, and roughly a half mile off the western and southern shores, are the Molly Islands. If you were to stand on the shore, you would see two spits of sand named Sandy Island and Rocky Island. They are small, low, and sparsely dappled with Scouler willow, nettles, sky pilot, and cinquefoil. Until recently these remote islands were the only white pelican rookery in Wyoming, the chosen home of strange white birds thirty-five million years old.

The sweep of all this pleases me—the wing chair, the cold tequila, the precision of the music, the woman's passion for her violin, the view into that wildest place. It reminds me why, unlike some of my more radical environmental friends, I do not wish to return to the Pleistocene.

The first sighting of a white pelican in Yellowstone was reported by the Stuart party in 1863. Like good Americans they promptly shot one near what is now Pelican Creek. This set the tone for our relations with white pelicans for the next century. The population was nearly wiped out in the late twenties when it was discovered that the pelican carried a parasite that infected cutthroat trout. This, in addition to their high consumption of trout, led to their slaughter. It was not an isolated act of stupidity. In 1918 the Utah Department of Fish and Game went to Hat Island, which was then a major breeding colony in the Great Salt Lake, and clubbed and shot hundreds of pelicans and herons.

The slaughter of pelicans fifty years ago is one reason we don't see more of them, and why the species is vulnerable. Another reason is the loss of habitat. Of the twenty-three breeding colonies in the American West, only five major sites remain. Many, like the Molly Islands, are small. In 1980 there were only 285 nests on the Molly Islands, and, unfortunately, the islands are so low they are vulnerable to flooding. According to the topographic map, Sandy Island is only 6 feet above the lake and Rocky Island is only 9. When Schaller studied the colony in 1962, the lake rose 2.3 feet in June from a heavy snow pack and wiped out at least 80 pelican nests. It is conceivable that a heavier runoff would flood the islands and cause the pelicans to abandon the colony. That there are more than 100,000 breeding White Pelicans in North America would not diminish our loss.

For years there has been an effort to have the white pelican listed as endangered. The U.S. population is vulnerable, especially in Wyoming, where the white pelican is listed as a "Priority 1 species," one needing "immediate attention and active management to ensure that extirpation or a significant decline in the breeding population" does not occur.

On the Molly Islands, pelican chicks hatch when the bison calves drop. (They are exceptionally ugly: nothing looks so like a dinosaur as a pelican chick.) Soon thereafter, in a striking example of natural timing, the shallow streams around Yellowstone Lake become choked with spawning cutthroats laying billions of eggs in pelican-heaven water. Trout eat the unprotected eggs of other trout, larger trout eat little trout, and all of them are gobbled up by grizzlies, California gulls, and pelicans in a wild frenzy of gluttony and sex. It's a good time to be a pelican chick.

After ten or eleven weeks the chicks begin to fly, and soon afterwards they must become aware of the Teton range fifty miles to the southwest and clearly visible from above the southeast arm of Yellowstone Lake. From this direction the so-called Cathedral Group of peaks—Teewinot, Mount Owen, and the Grand Teton—resembles a pyramid. If you were a soaring bird, you would want to go there, and the white pelican is a soaring bird par excellence. Like the great pelagic wanderers, pelicans have wings with a high ratio of length to width. They are built to soar and they soar well—thirty-five million years of constant feedback and fine-tuned design make a difference. Anyone writing on pelicans mentions their soaring, and most have watched them disappear into the blue—the phrase usually used is some variation of "at the limit of human vision."

Of all places available to pelicans, mountains provide the most opportunities for soaring. Where the prevailing wind meets a mountain, it flows over it like water over a boulder in a rapid. Just as beyond the boulder is a hole followed by smaller standing waves, so there are standing "wave trains" of air currents beyond the mountain, and pelicans can soar up each one. Since our prevailing summer wind is from the southwest, the wave trains behind the Grand Teton point straight toward the Molly Islands.

Pelicans can also soar in thermals. As the ground warms, patches of warmer air rise, puff out at the top, peel off, and are sucked back into the vortex that keeps rising again and again through the center of the thermal. The stronger the rise, the stronger the thermal, and the tighter the circle a soaring bird can cut. The Teton range has strong thermals, and the pelicans above the Grand Teton always soar in tight circles, carving into the wind for lift, then dropping around for the tailwind, then farther around and into the wind again for more lift. Thermals tend to stack up in a long "thermal street" and drift downwind, allowing a pelican to climb in one thermal, cut out and glide to the next, climb again, cut out again—all with virtually no expenditure of energy. In the summer, the Grand Teton's thermals stack up in a line heading toward the Molly Islands.

Pelicans also soar in thunderheads, which suck cold air down from the upper atmosphere. When it hits the ground, it spreads out, displacing warmer air which, in turn, goes upward, creating more good soaring places. The Grand Teton has some of the most dazzling thunderstorms of any place on the planet, with lightning to match. During the most intense period of one recent storm, lightning struck every two minutes, and the storm lasted sixteen hours. Pelicans often wander the edges of great storms and I envy them this freedom, even with its risks. In one account, thirty-three pelicans were knocked out of the air by lightning in Nebraska. In a storm in Utah, twenty-seven were killed. The same thing must happen over the Tetons.

Ten years ago my guided party was hit four times by ground currents while descending the Grand Teton. We watched green bolts of lightning ricochet through glaciers like bullets. Yet I still climb mountains, and pelicans still soar in thunderheads. After thirty-five million years, they must know about lightning and its risks, just as mountaineers do, but it no more changes their behavior than it changes ours.

So there are many good reasons for the pelicans to be above the Grand Teton, but exactly why remains a mystery. The pelicans we see there in July are not migrating. Yellowstone pelicans winter in Mexico and the Sea of Cortéz. Then in late March or early April they fly to the Great Salt Lake. In late April or early May they fly to the Molly Islands. Perhaps the pelicans over the Grand Teton in July are returning from a foraging mission. Perhaps they are nonbreeding adults on a lark. Perhaps someone will put a radio collar on one and find out, though I hope not. Whatever science would discover is not worth the intrusion into their wild lives. What interests me is not that pelicans can soar, that soaring is useful, or that they soar here. What interests me is the question of whether pelicans love to soar.

The pelican's love of soaring is only hinted at in ornithological literature, but it is there. In his *Handbook of North American Birds*, volume one, Ralf Palmer uses the word "indulge" in the cryptic grammar of scientific description. He says the pelicans "often indulge in high-soaring flights" and that "while soaring in stormy weather [they] may indulge in aerial acrobatics with much swooping and diving." This is not exactly the language of mechanistic science. Does this mean that pelicans are, sometimes at least, soaring for pleasure? Do they play in thunderheads for fun? Do they fly in thunderheads knowing full well the danger? Do they experience ecstasy while soaring so indulgently? What could it mean to attribute these emotions to a bird?

Consider Doug Peacock's film footage of the grizzly he named Happy Bear.[4] In the spring, when the streams are still frozen, Happy Bear likes to sit on his butt in small meadow streams and break off chunks of ice, bite them, push them underwater with his huge paws,

4. *Peacock's War,* Bullfrog Films, 1989.

then bite them again when they pop up. He does this a lot. I don't think we can say why Happy Bear is doing this without using analogies and metaphors from human emotional life.

Or consider the gulls in Guy Murchie's *Song of the Sky*:

> Many a time I have seen sea gulls at the big Travis Air Base near San Francisco flapping nonchalantly among the huge ten-engined B-36 bombers while their motors were being run up. The smoke whipping from the jets in four straight lines past the tail accompanied by that soul-shaking roar would have been enough to stampede a herd of elephants but the sea gulls often flew right into the tornado just for fun. When the full blast struck them they would simply disappear, only to turn up a few seconds later a quarter mile downwind, apparently having enjoyed the experience as much as a boy running through a hose—even coming around eager-eyed for more.[5]

Simply disappear. Like paddling a kayak into Lava Falls.

It is not popular now to attribute human characteristics and processes to wild animals, since it projects onto the Other our biases and perceptions and limits our view of their difference. But all description is merely analogy and metaphor, and as such is forever imperfect and respectful of mystery. We are more ignorant and limited than we can conceive. Even scientific descriptions and theories are contingent and subject to revision. We do not understand even our dog or cat, not to mention a vole. Even our knowledge of those we know best—our lovers and friends—is fragile and often mistaken. Our knowledge of strangers in our own culture is even more fragile, and it seems that despite our volumes of social science, we have no understanding of native peoples. Language may probe the mystery of the Other, but the Other remains a mystery.

We also fail to appreciate that many of our descriptions and explanations of human behavior are appropriations from wild animals: the lion-hearted hero, the wolfish cad, the foxy lady. And this suggests that life is a spectrum where unity is more pervasive than difference—a

5. Quoted in Krutch and Ericksson, *A Treasury of Birdlore*, 31.

rudimentary truth for the Apache and the Bushman, but a truth ignored by our epistemologies.

It is no more odd to say that pelicans love to soar and do so in *ecstasy* than it is to say what we so commonly say of human love and ecstasy: that our heart soars. Or, to take another example, to describe meditation as Dōgen does in the *Mountains and Rivers Sutra*: "Because mountains are high and broad, the way of riding the clouds is always reached in the mountains; the inconceivable power of soaring in the wind comes freely from the mountains."[6]

Some people fear that extending a human vocabulary to wild animals erodes their Otherness. But what is *not Other*? Are we not all, from one perspective, Other to each and every being in the universe? And at the same time, and from another perspective, do we not all share an elemental wildness that burns forth in each life?

When I see white pelicans riding mountain thermals, I feel their exaltation, their love of open sky and big clouds. Their fear of lightning is my fear, and I extend to them the sadness of descent. I believe the reasons they are soaring over the Grand Teton are not so different from the reasons we climb mountains, sail gliders into great storms, and stand in rivers with tiny pieces of feathers from a French duck's butt attached to a barbless hook at the end of sixty feet of a sixty-dollar string thrown by a thousand-dollar wand. Indeed, in love and ecstasy we are closest to the Other, for passion is at the root of all life and shared by all life. In passion, all beings are at their wildest; in passion, we—like pelicans—make strange noises that defy scientific explanation.

If pelicans are soaring above the Grand Teton in ecstasy, how should we describe their clacking? I can find only one reference in our immense literature on birds to the clacking that pelicans make at high altitude. In his *Life Histories of North American Petrels and Pelicans and Their Allies*, Arthur Cleveland Bent quotes Dr. P. L. Hatch as saying, "This immense bird usually signals his arrival in the early part of April by his characteristic notes from an elevation beyond the range of vision except under the most favorable circumstances. The sound of those notes

6. Dōgen Zenji, *Moon in a Dewdrop*, 97.

is difficult to describe, but unforgettable when once certainly heard from their aerial heights." Why do they utter that unforgettable sound only when they are so far up in the sky—at the limit of our vision? Olaus Murie once said of the coyote's howl that "if the coyote could reflect and speak he would say this is his song, simply that."[7] Simply that: the song of coyote. All things have their song, and few questions about songs have answers.

I believe the clacking in the sky over the Grand Teton is the song of the white pelican. I believe they sing their song in ecstasy, from joy in an experience unique to their perfections. I know climbers who whistle, sing, and yodel when they are up in the sky. William Blake died singing to the angels he knew were leading him to heaven. Some sing, some whistle, some yip, some clack in the sky, some make love to a violin. Why saw at strings of gut stretched over holes in burnished wood? Why sing cantatas and masses and chorales?

All life contains its anguish, even a trout-eating pelican's life—the Buddha's first noble truth. But all life must occasionally experience a release. In passion and ecstasy, all life lets go—of what?

7. Murie, *A Field Guide to Animal Tracks*, 96.

The Abstract Wild (1996)

CARL ANTHONY & RENÉE SOULE

Ecologists have often concluded that boundaries between different landscapes offer the richest niches. Carl Anthony (b. 1939) has inhabited similar borderlands since the start of his work. The publisher of *Race, Poverty and Environment Journal*, he was an early voice addressing issues of environmental justice. Although his work has focused on cities (particularly the Bay Area of northern California where he founded the Urban Habitat program), he also served as president of the Earth Island Institute, an organization whose intellectual lineage stretches straight back to John Muir and the birth of the wilderness movement. As demonstrated in this essay, co-written with Renée Soule—who has advocated an ecological approach to psychology for two decades and taught nonviolent communication skills at San Quentin prison—Anthony has always worked to bridge division instead of sharpen it. As he says, "In the inner cities, the problem is that people have tended to see jobs and economic development as a social, political, and economic issue, and not as an environmental issue. And environmentalists tend to see their issues as being separate from the social and racial justice issues. But actually, they are operating in the same universe; in fact, they are two sides of the same coin." In the wake of Hurricane Katrina, his words are especially prophetic.

A Multicultural Approach to Ecopsychology

Our commitment to a multicultural approach to ecopsychology arose out of a collaborative research project called "Race, Ecopsychology and the City." Over the course of six months, we discovered that the blending of these three seemingly disparate themes (race, ecopsychology, the city) gave them a coherency that doesn't exist if each stands alone. Racism is overwhelming, but viewing it from an ecopsychological perspective gives rise to new information and new possibilities of healing. We also found that the city, and not only the wilderness, is an appropriate place to apply ecopsychology. For where else in nature does the human psyche and the whole of nature come together to create a truly eco-psychological environment? In the bustle of a constructed urban setting, we see human psychology and values manifest in created physical forms. This is where deep ecopsychological work can be practically applied. Cities must be made whole and aesthetic if wild habitats are to survive with integrity.

Most importantly, if ecopsychology can't address real problems within human communities (like racism and urban desolation), then for those interested in deep social and ecological healing, the field wouldn't be big enough to warrant one's lifetime dedication. This project tested limits and promise of ecopsychology, and we're happy to say that we discovered both room to grow and a lot of promise.

During a recent celebration of Black history month, organized by a group of environmentalists anxious to get people of color more interested in the natural world, a young African American man told the following story. Many years ago as teenagers living in Stockton, California, he and his brother decided that, to make a little extra money, they would hire themselves out as farm workers for the day. They got up at 4:30 in the morning and dressed in time to be down at the local intersection where the truck comes by for day workers. They hopped on the truck, which made its way to the fields of Central Valley.

The journey took more than an hour. When they arrived, with the sun rising higher in the sky, they were put to work in the fields picking onions. The ground had been loosened by a tractor, and the smell of the onions, mixed with the odor of the thick rich soil, was pleasant. But it was a back breaking task to spend hours bent over, pulling up and loading the onions into sacks, to be picked up by the tractor which followed them. It was hot. They worked hard, taking an occasional break throughout the long day. With money borrowed from the owner of the farm they could buy soft drinks and food. At sun down, when they got paid, they realized they had spent as much on food and drink as they had made, and somehow, in the confusion, they had missed the truck going back to Stockton. They didn't have enough money to take the bus back. So they walked.

It took them from 8:30 at night, until 2:00 in the morning to get back, and they laughed all the way. Finally, at two in the morning, hot, sweaty and tired, they arrived at home, and made a vow to each other: they would never, ever set foot on a farm again.

This story can be seen as a metaphor for the historical experience of African Americans whose cultural experience of the land is quite different than many people of European heritage. African Americans worked the land in the South for many generations, first as slaves, then as sharecroppers without the opportunity to own the land, and without pay. Given the public invisibility and harshness of these rural experiences, it is not surprising that African Americans may have a different feeling about the land than privileged people of European heritage. The depth of humiliation, the feeling of outrage has totally colored the young men's perception of that experience of the land, leading to a feeling of detachment and avoidance of emotional engagement with rural life.

We offer this as one striking example of the psychological perspective that needs to be included in both an enduring conservation ethic and any form of ecological healing.

Ecopsychology is not only about our relationship to nature in wild places, for our response to urban realities is not divorced from our ancient fear of wild territories. In his remarkably candid book of stories *Race*, Studs Terkel (1992) recounts an episode of a young European American woman, a politically liberal college professor from a suburban community, who found herself driving through a desolate inner city neighborhood as the sun was going down. As her car approached a deserted intersection, she saw three young, African American men running toward her, frantically waving their hands in the air.

In a moment of panic she found the buttons on the panel beside her. She electronically rolled up the windows, locked all four doors of the car, and stepped on the gas so forcefully you could hear the tires screech. She drove four blocks, faster than it was safe before she realized she was going the wrong way on a one way street.

Although this young woman had in her life and work done everything she could to promote social justice, when confronted in an unfamiliar environment with the threat of survival, she faced a moment of truth. The men approaching the car were, apparently, signaling that she was going the wrong way. But in fright she had misread what they were trying to tell her. For her, the inner city was a wilderness, a place for shadowy fears to appear as terrifying reality. Down deep, she was afraid of black people, and her fear had caused her to recklessly endanger her life.

One could argue that this little anecdote about a frightened middle class woman at sundown in an inner city neighborhood has nothing to do with society's relationship to the natural world. But consider first that the episode is taking place as nightfall approaches. How much of her fear comes from the gut gripping combination of being caught in darkness in an unfamiliar world? We are taught that it is childish to be afraid of the dark. In darkness, however, we can no longer rely on our eyesight, and from a physiological point of view we must rely on other untrained and unreliable senses for information, including our imagination.

Consider too that the episode described above takes place in an abandoned and desolate part of the city, with burned-out buildings, vacant, garbage-filled lots now inhabited by only a third of the population for which it was designed, devoid of signs of life, paved over and forgotten. How much of her emotional reaction is an unconscious fear of retribution and guilt for being implicated in the prodigious waste of abandoned sections of the city? There is also the painful reminder that these are displaced people. They do not own their land, nor are they flourishing in this desolate urban habitat. In many ways, the young men remind us of the terrible fact that cities the world over are filled with refugees. Glitter, glitz and steel-enforced concrete structures cannot refute the fact that urban populations by definition are peoples who cannot feed themselves. In an urban environment, the prey-predator relationship exists between human beings.

The lessons of both social justice and ecopsychology are simple and the same. They involve living in connection, feeling the connection, honoring and then acting from that place of being connected. In many ways it is cities that clearly teach us about interdependence. Every person one sees is in some way part of one's own existence. What keeps one alive in the city are the people who drive the trucks, who work in offices, wheeling and dealing and making connections to the life-giving countryside whence come food, water, building materials. With every move, a city is stretching beyond its boundaries to sustain its heat, energy and life. Signs and lessons of interdependence are everywhere, providing we do not hide behind the glass and steel structures feeling separate, independent and perhaps smugly superior. We are all in this together, redwoods, mountain lions, the little kid down the street, the Mexican immigrant who picked radishes this morning.

Both social justice advocates and ecopsychologists look directly at how issues of racism and responsibility to the more-than-human world affect each of us on a very personal level. As the world grows smaller and human population increases, escaping these issues will be increasingly unavoidable.

Denial is a glaring challenge facing both advocates of social justice and ecopsychologists. Clear-cuts hide behind tree-lined highways. Economic and racial segregation still divide cities, creating taboo areas in urban habitats. Invisibility is one of the main symptoms of denial. Environmental and social justice issues are often "simply not on the agenda." Breaking through denial to a place of compassionate, creative responsibility is not easy. Ecopsychologists recognize the limited effectiveness of pounding people with horrific facts and statistics about poverty in America did not stop the welfare bill from passing.

Certainly we all need to "own our history" and acknowledge that much of our wealth rests upon exploitation of people and natural landscapes, but direct blame is not an effective way to motivate change. Both social justice advocates and environmentalists need to find ways of presenting facts that invite participation rather fear-based apathy. Both need to help people find the strength and courage it takes to face the truth, and look each other in the eye. This shared challenge is itself common ground.

Ecology can be seen as a way of life in the sense that its range of relationships and scope of healing includes everyone. In a sense, it is a "family psychology" where one's family includes all of life, including past and future generations. Monoculture is not only dull, but deadly to natural systems, including human society AND psychology. Complexity rests upon diversity, as does resourceful intelligence and love. Maintaining a stance of inclusivity is risky, but in an exciting way. Complexity and diversity constantly challenge cherished assumptions. But learning is inevitable if one is open to the risk of making mistakes. In fact, making mistakes is advisable. Fear is par for the course, and therefore so are confidence and courage.

One surprising benefit of diversity is that of feeling more firmly rooted in one's sense of self: a personal identity flexible enough to listen to, understand, and honor the experiences and values of another without erosion of one's own integrity. This core integrity comes from holding an ongoing intention to "stand corrected" without being subsumed by the perspectives of others. Everybody's story is vital to the integrity of the whole, including one's own.

Ecologists and social justice advocates both promote respect for diversity. That respect depends upon a mature capacity to embrace and even celebrate apparent contradictions. This internal stance of inclusivity is the key to ecopsychology, where a healthy multicultural, multibiotic, multiregional and multifaceted psyche merges and blends gracefully with Earth's ecology.

The Humanistic Psychologist, 1998

"We must make the rescue of the environment the central organizing principle for civilization." With that phrase in his 1992 book *Earth in the Balance* Al Gore (b. 1948) became America's most important environmental politician at the turn of the 21st century. Gore, the son of a senator from Tennessee, won the same seat in 1984. In the Senate he held hearings that helped bring global warming to public attention, and the publication of his powerful book helped convince environmentalists that his ascension to the vice-presidency under Bill Clinton in 1992 would herald dramatic change. Most were disappointed; the administration, faced with an unsympathetic Congress, didn't expend much political capital on green issues, and when Gore ran for president in 2000 many accused him of avoiding the issue. When the Supreme Court denied him the presidency after that bitter election he stayed out of the public eye for several years. He kept lecturing on climate change, however, and in 2006 producer Laurie David released a documentary based on his slideshow. *An Inconvenient Truth* won an Oscar, and, coupled with the destruction of Hurricane Katrina, brought global warming to the forefront of American politics. He was awarded, along with the Intergovernmental Panel on Climate Change, the 2007 Nobel Peace Prize. The committee praised "their efforts to build up and disseminate greater knowledge about man-made climate change, and to lay the foundations for the measures that are needed to counteract such change."

Speech at the Kyoto Climate Change Conference

Prime Minister Hashimoto and President Figueres, President Kinza Clodumar, other distinguished heads of state, distinguished delegates, ladies and gentlemen.

It is an honor to be here at this historic gathering, in this ancient capital of such beauty and grace. On behalf of President Clinton and the

American people, and our U.S. negotiator, Ambassador Stu Eizenstat, I salute our Japanese hosts for their gracious hospitality, and offer a special thank you to Prime Minister Hashimoto, and to our chairs, Minister Ohki, and Ambassador Estrada, for their hard work and leadership.

Since we gathered at the Rio Conference in 1992, both scientific consensus and political will have come a long way. If we pause for a moment and look around us, we can see how extraordinary this gathering really is.

We have reached a fundamentally new stage in the development of human civilization, in which it is necessary to take responsibility for a recent but profound alteration in the relationship between our species and our planet. Because of our new technological power and our growing numbers, we now must pay careful attention to the consequences of what we are doing to the Earth—especially to the atmosphere.

There are other parts of the Earth's ecological system that are also threatened by the increasingly harsh impact of thoughtless behavior: the poisoning of too many places where people—especially poor people—live, and the deaths of too many children—especially poor children—from polluted water and dirty air; the dangerous and unsustainable depletion of ocean fisheries; and the rapid destruction of critical habitats—rain forests, temperate forests, borial forests, wetlands, coral reefs, and other precious wellsprings of genetic variety upon which the future of humankind depends.

But the most vulnerable part of the Earth's environment is the very thin layer of air clinging near to the surface of the planet, that we are now so carelessly filling with gaseous wastes that we are actually altering the relationship between the Earth and the Sun—by trapping more solar radiation under this growing blanket of pollution that envelops the entire world.

The extra heat which cannot escape is beginning to change the global patterns of climate to which we are accustomed, and to which we have adapted over the last 10,000 years.

Last week we learned from scientists that this year, 1997, with only three weeks remaining, will be the hottest year since records have been kept. Indeed, nine of the 10 hottest years since the measurements began have come in the last 10 years. The trend is clear. The human consequences—and the economic costs—of failing to act are unthinkable. More record floods and droughts. Diseases and pests spreading to new areas. Crop failures and famines. Melting glaciers, stronger storms, and rising seas.

Our fundamental challenge now is to find out whether and how we can change the behaviors that are causing the problem.

To do so requires humility, because the spiritual roots of our crisis are pridefulness and a failure to understand and respect our connections to God's Earth and to each other.

Each of the 160 nations here has brought unique perspectives to the table, but we all understand that our work in Kyoto is only a beginning. None of the proposals being debated here will solve the problem completely by itself. But if we get off to the right start here, we can quickly build momentum as we learn together how to meet this challenge. Our first step should be to set realistic and achievable, binding emissions limits, which will create new markets for new technologies and new ideas that will, in turn, expand the boundaries of the possible and create new hope. Other steps will then follow. And then, ultimately, we will achieve a safe overall concentration level for greenhouse gases in the Earth's atmosphere.

This is the step-by-step approach we took in Montreal 10 years ago to address the problem of ozone depletion. And it is working.

This time, success will require first and foremost that we heal the divisions among us.

The first and most important task for developed countries is to hear the immediate needs of the developing world. And let me say, the United States has listened and we have learned.

We understand that your first priority is to lift your citizens from the poverty so many endure and build strong economies that will assure a better future. This is your right: it will not be denied.

And let me be clear in our answer to you: we do not want to founder on a false divide. Reducing poverty and protecting the Earth's environment are both critical components of truly sustainable development. We want to forge a lasting partnership to achieve a better future. One key is mobilizing new investment in your countries to ensure that you have higher standards of living, with modern, clean and efficient technologies.

That is what our proposals for emissions trading and joint implementation strive to do.

To our partners in the developed world, let me say we have listened and learned from you as well. We understand that while we share a common goal, each of us faces unique challenges.

You have shown leadership here, and for that we are grateful. We came to Kyoto to find new ways to bridge our differences. In doing so, however, we must not waiver in our resolve. For our part, the United States remains firmly committed to a strong, binding target that will reduce our own emissions by nearly 30 percent from what they would otherwise be—a commitment as strong, or stronger, than any we have heard here from any country. The imperative here is to do what we promise, rather than to promise what we cannot do.

All of us, of course, must reject the advice of those who ask us to believe there really is no problem at all. We know their arguments; we have heard others like them throughout history. For example, in my country, we remember the tobacco company spokesmen who insisted for so long that smoking did no harm. To those who seek to obfuscate and obstruct, we say: we will not allow you to put narrow special interests above the interests of all humankind.

So what does the United States propose that we do?

The first measure of any proposal must be its environmental merit, and ours is environmentally solid and sound.

It is strong and comprehensive, covering all six significant greenhouse gases. It recognizes the link between the air and the land, including both sources and sinks. It provides the tools to ensure that targets can be met—offering emissions trading, joint implementation and research as powerful engines of technology development and transfer. It further reduces emissions—below 1990 levels—in the years 2012 and beyond. It provides the means to ensure that all nations can join us on their own terms in meeting this common challenge.

It is also economically sound. And, with strict monitoring and accountability, it ensures that we will keep our bond with one another.

Whether or not agreement is reached here, we will take concrete steps to help meet this challenge. President Clinton and I understand that our first obligation is to address this issue at home. I commit to you today that the United States is prepared to act—and will act.

For my part, I have come here to Kyoto because I am both determined and optimistic that we can succeed. I believe that by our coming together in Kyoto we have already achieved a major victory, one both of substance and of spirit. I have no doubt that the process we have started here inevitably will lead to a solution in the days or years ahead.

Some of you here have, perhaps, heard from your home capitals that President Clinton and I have been burning up the phone lines, consulting and sharing new ideas. Today let me add this. After talking with our negotiators this morning and after speaking on the telephone from here a short time ago with President Clinton, I am instructing our delegation right now to show increased negotiating flexibility if a comprehensive plan can be put in place, one with realistic targets and timetables, market mechanisms, and the meaningful participation of key developing countries.

Earlier this century, the Scottish mountain climber, W. H. Murray, wrote: "Until one is committed there is hesitancy, the chance to draw back, always ineffectiveness. Concerning all acts of initiative . . . there is one elementary truth, the ignorance of which kills countless ideas and splendid plans: that the moment one definitely commits oneself, providence moves, too."

So let us press forward. Let us resolve to conduct ourselves in such a way that our children's children will read about the "Spirit of Kyoto," and remember well the place and the time where humankind first chose to embark together on a long-term sustainable relationship between our civilization and the Earth's environment.

In that spirit, let us transcend our differences and commit to secure our common destiny: a planet whole and healthy, whose nations are at peace, prosperous and free; and whose people everywhere are able to reach for their God-given potential.

December 8, 1997

RICHARD NELSON

Richard Nelson (b. 1941) is best known for his anthropological writings on the native peoples of the Far North. The year he spent with Eskimos on the Alaskan North Slope, in 1964–65, studying how they hunted and traveled on the sea ice, "made a different person of me and shaped the entire course of my life." Returning to his native Wisconsin, he shaped the material into an academic thesis, but luckily a publisher intervened and issued it as *Hunters of the Northern Ice* (1969). The book was followed by other anthropological excursions (and by Nelson's move to southeastern Alaska); these grew steadily more personal, culminating with *The Island Within* (1989), his classic account of self-discovery on an island near his Sitka home that draws on both Koyukon Indian teachings and ecological science. Like most of the great contemporary nature writers, Nelson is a devoted environmental activist—in his case he's been crucial in the fight to save the Tongass National Forest from clearcutting. But it is his sheer power of observation—natural observation and self-observation—that may be his greatest gift, well-displayed in this passage from the beginning of *Heart and Blood* (1997), his book about America's most ubiquitous large mammal, the deer. Annie Dillard once compared him to Cormac McCarthy, another writer's writer: "His rhetorical pitch was as wild as Thoreau's on Katahdin, transporting as Shakespeare pushing art into the realms that ennoble the reader." Yep.

from **Heart and Blood: Living with Deer in America**

June 12. A chill northwesterly breeze winnows down over the muskeg, shaking through pearly blossomed Labrador tea and purple-berried juniper. Brown, brittle grass and newly sprouted sedges shiver at the margins of rippling ponds. Above the muskeg and beyond a high, wooded ridge stands the brooding, conical wall of Kluksa Mountain, overcast shrouding its rim. Snow-filled ravines cleave upward through the talus like ivory spokes, giving the mountain a cold, forbidding look. I shrug against gusts that seep through my blue jeans and wool jacket. Yet there's a promise of summer in the wheezy, ethereal notes of a varied thrush chiming first on one pitch and then another, like a rainbow spilling from an indigo cloud.

In spite of rough water that made boating a misery, and regardless of the unseasonably cold weather with passing fits of rain, something impelled me to head out across Haida Strait with Keta this morning. It was partly the simple wish to abandon town and spend a quiet day here on the island. And it was partly a notion about deer; not just that I wanted to see them, but a desire of mine whose fulfillment fell somewhere between extreme unlikelihood and rock-solid impossibility. Along the North Pacific coast—as in most northern regions of the continent— the first half of June is fawning time. And despite the tremendous odds against wandering into the right place at precisely the right moment, I have allowed myself to dream of seeing a wild deer give birth.

To measure the improbability of witnessing this event, consider the experience of Leonard Lee Rue III, writer, naturalist, and preeminent wildlife photographer. Rue spent decades working closely with his favorite subject in both wild and confined situations, and by the mid-1980s, he estimated that he'd taken more than 100,000 photographs of deer. And yet, he writes in his 1978 classic, *The Deer of North America*: "I have been most fortunate in being able to witness the birth of fawns on two different occasions. Both does were semi-tame, living on a deer preserve." In other words, although millions of fawns are born each year in every imaginable cranny of our continent, there's very little chance that anyone is going to see it happen except within a fenced enclosure or perhaps a suburban backyard. On this wild, remote island, I could just as well spend my time searching the woods for stray albatrosses or watching the sky for unknown comets.

However, it's vaguely realistic to imagine stumbling across a sequestered fawn, perhaps seeing an infant blacktail with its mother, even watching it nurse—if not this year, then maybe sometime in the future. Over the past few weeks I've visited the island often, motivated by these peculiar and farfetched ambitions. But in fact, I'd be satisfied to encounter any deer at all, especially to stalk near enough for a glimpse into its daily life.

Trekking slowly toward the center of the muskeg, Keta and I follow an elongated rise that overlooks a grassy, undulating terrain with scattered copses of shore pine, scrubby juniper thickets, and twisting streamlets connecting hundreds of tiny ponds. Somewhere inland from us, a greater yellowlegs pours ceaseless, warbling whistles, growing louder as we hike along the ridge. Eventually I spot the mottled, stilt-legged shorebird fluttering from one dead tree to another, still ranting. Many times I've been scolded by a yellowlegs after inadvertently walking too close to its nest, and I've seen these birds get just as agitated over a deer or bear. The first possibility tempts me to head that way for a closer look, but the second encourages me to mind my own business.

While I ponder this dilemma, Keta picks up a hard scent, not on the ground but drifting in the northwest wind, meaning there's almost certainly a deer close by in a direction opposite from that of the yellowlegs. The aroma must be pretty thick, judging by Keta's fidgety behavior; just when I want her to keep still, she's prancing from side to side, raising and lowering her snout, gazing up into the wind. After she settles down we make our way across lower ground and through patches of deer cabbage—small plants with a single leaf like an umbrella perched on a fingerlength stalk. Some are freshly clipped, leaving empty stems with no crowning leaf, and hoofprints sunk deep into the moss identify the nibbler. Keta sniffs eagerly, sampling a mix of smells like a kid eating a dozen kinds of candy at once. From her excited behavior I'd guess a deer browsed here within the hour.

Angling west, still on the scent, we trek along another low rise affording good views on either side, so I stop to peruse the terrain. This muskeg is one of my favorites; I've walked every part of it innumerable times while hunting or bird-watching or exploring, often with friends, and I've had many encounters with the wild animals who live here—especially black-tailed deer. These experiences run through my mind whenever I come here, filling the land with memories, strengthening my attachment to it, rooting it more deeply inside me.

Near this spot, I once found the skeletons of two small bucks, a fork-horn and a spike, lying a few yards apart, and both of them had drastically asymmetrical antlers—long on one side, very short on the other. Another time I found several patches of thick, chalky material mixed with beach gravel lying around like cow pies, unlike anything I'd ever seen before. I finally realized they were droppings of a bear who had eaten blubber from a dead whale on the nearby shore.

From Keta's excitement I know we're still immersed in thick scent, so I stalk meticulously ahead—lifting each foot clear of the crunchy grass, worming through snarled juniper branches, bending and bracing and standing off balance and peering all around—on the assumption that we could come across something at any moment. Again and again Keta reaches for the breeze, delving farther into the trail of scent and urging me closer to whatever made it. I know she wants to turn directly upwind, but that would take us down off the ridge, into a broad meadow that seems too open for deer at midday, especially given my preoccupation with does and fawns. So I keep on as before, figuring our best chance is the ridge with its intermingled grassy swatches, thickets, and pines.

But while I focus on what I presume and infer, Keta focuses on what she *knows*, on the truth of this moment as revealed by her impeccable senses. She probes the air more intently as the scent grows richer and thicker. She swings up into the wind as if she has no choice, as if the pleasure or promise of the smell is more than she can resist. She comes back when I point insistently at the ground beside me but soon veers off again, balancing her own determination against mine.

Eventually I yield, figuring there's no harm in taking a look that way before we get back on course. Respecting the strength of Keta's interest, I give her the lead and pick every step deliberately, trying to make no sound at all, waiting for each little gust and then moving while the wind's bluster conceals the noise of my clumsy feet. I hesitate, study the terrain ahead, and move again. The muskeg looks abandoned and austere in the jostling wind and gray light, beneath the pallid, scudding clouds. In the distance I hear a robin's song, lilting and fading on the breeze. I stop to listen, but keep scanning up into the wind that Keta finds so promising and fertile.

When I'm about to take a step, I notice almost by chance a small tan-colored blotch, bright and sharp edged, incongruous amid the sere grass and ashy trunks and deep-green boughs. I catch myself and ease my foot back to the ground, Keta halting close at my side. Is it a deer, I wonder, as I lift the binoculars, or a patch of dry, faded moss?

Blacktail . . . doe . . . lying in a small oval of bare ground, legs folded tight against her flanks, head raised to keep watch. Because she's curled like a dog, I can see both her front and hind quarters, showing the breadth of her chest, the muscular bulge of her thighs, the broad ridge of her back, the shaggy fur of her tail. She seems very round, partly because she's resting on her side, partly because her belly seems unusually full.

Perhaps it's that look of fullness. Perhaps it's the way this deer has chosen to rest, lying on one side rather than belly down with forelegs tucked under her chest. Perhaps it's just because the season is right and because for so long I've carried this fervent wish. Whatever the reason, a thought flutters through my mind: she's going to have a fawn. Then it vanishes in the flood of reason and sensibility: never in such an open place as this, never just as Keta and I happen along, never would I have such blind, blundering luck.

I lower the binoculars, pleased that we've come across a bedded deer in plain sight and seemingly unaware of us. Instead of trying to stalk closer I sink down onto a dry tussock covered with reindeer lichen and crowberry—an ideal perch. Beside it, within easy reach, is a small muskeg pond a few inches deep, dimpled with water striders. I slip off my little backpack and glance at my watch—2:20 P.M.

Keta sits beside me, pressing heavily against my leg, raising her muzzle urgently to the wind, quivering with excitement. She knows as well as I do there's a deer close by, but luckily she can't see it from her low vantage. I rub her silky black fur, hoping she'll calm down, fearing she might whine or jitter noisily in the dry grass. She resists when I gently force her to lie down, then stands immediately, nose high, leaning toward the deer.

This is a fair-sized doe, as indicated by the brightness of the white patches on her neck and the long, narrow shape of her head. Her lusterless winter coat has just begun to shed, revealing patches of sleek, rust-colored summer fur. She's looking directly toward us, ears in a wide V and funneled to pick up the slightest sound, as if she might have glimpsed us or heard our rustlings. As fate would have it, Keta and I are surrounded by grass and tussocks with no shrubs to screen us from the deer's view or protect us from the wind. If she stays bedded for long, this is going to be an extremely cold watch. The deer's place is better than ours, in the lee of a small mound with a windscreen of waist-high junipers and sapling pines. Between us is a gentle swale fretted with bushes, sapling trees, and mossy patches. Luckily we're straight downwind and the northwester flows unwaveringly—so there's no chance the deer could catch our scent.

After 10 uneventful minutes the doe abruptly stands. Good news, I think, hoping she'll start to browse so we can sneak closer while she's distracted. On the other hand, she may slip off into the concealment of brushier terrain or she might see us from her higher vantage. But the deer just stands there, facing away from us with her back arched and her body strangely hunched. Then she flips up her tail and holds it for a moment curved stiffly over her back, the muscles unnaturally tensed, hairs standing on end as if they'd been stimulated by an electric shock—something altogether different from the waving vertical flag of an alarmed deer. Afterward she relaxes, walks a few steps, and to my great surprise lies down again, facing us with her head high.

This seems unusual—a bedded deer standing up and then lying back down in the same place. For a while she gazes our way, the great orbs of her eyes opened wide and black as midnight sky. Then she shifts her ears back and forth, visibly slackens, and looks off toward the runneled face of Kluksa Mountain, as if she were wholly at peace.

A bunch of chickadees flits in among the nearby pines, clinging to the boughs, probing their beaks under the loose bark and into the cleavages between needles, hunting for insects. Then, darting from tree to tree, they work their way toward the doe, who twitches her ears but otherwise ignores them. How I envy those little birds, perched within a few feet of her, their chittery notes falling around her like a shower of sequins.

Ten minutes later the doe stands, hunches her body again, turns around a few times with her tail rigidly erect, and then lies back down. Suddenly, my earlier fancy becomes a clear and plausible thought: she must be coming into labor! And yet I'm still convinced fawning is one event in a wild deer's life that I'll never see. Squinting through the binoculars until my arms throb, I now realize there's a conspicuous bulge in her belly, shaped like a basketball and far back near the hips. Is it the cold wind or the hard surge of excitement that sets me shivering?

The deer stands, immediately lies down, then rests for another 10 minutes before getting up and turning aimlessly, still oddly hunched, tail arched over her back like a drawn bow. And what I see now takes away all remaining doubt: beneath her erect tail is a conspicuous, dark, dilated opening.

Whenever the doe stands Keta picks up a flush of scent, so I press her to the ground and scratch her belly to keep her soothed and distracted. Deer can interrupt labor if they sense danger, so our doe might startle away, and even if she moved a few steps I'd no longer see her. After being totally immobile for almost an hour, lightly dressed and exposed to the wind, I've started shaking uncontrollably, and I'm afflicted with a nearly overpowering urge to move, warm up, sneak closer to her. She's only a few street-widths away, but the scrabble of brush, dry grass, and saturated, squishy moss would be impossible to traverse quietly. Above all, I'd be crazy to risk losing what is being given here.

For a while the doe lies quite still, intermittently flipping her tail; then every few minutes she rolls sharply on her side, straightens and stiffens her neck, and reaches out with her chin, ears laid back, eyes half closed. Although I hear no sound, her movements and expressions telegraph pain. Then she stands and turns several times, once again showing the dilated place beneath her tail.

Slowly, carefully, I pull a short rope from my pack and fasten one end to a shrub, the other to Keta's collar, with very little slack so she can't move around. I'm quaking so hard I can barely tie the knots, and when I tense my muscles to stir up a little warmth, my back and arms threaten to cramp. I've never realized how much a person's nose drips on a cold day until now, when I can't make the tiniest sniffle and don't dare raise a sleeve for the traditional swipe.

The doe paces awkwardly back and forth on her patch of bare ground, then lies down again, keeping very still. Head raised, she glances around constantly as if she's tense and disquieted. From a human standpoint she seems profoundly alone, terribly vulnerable—which of course she is—and this fills me with compassion. A woman in her situation would be surrounded by midwives and companions, or nurses and doctors; she'd be supported, encouraged, touched, consoled, attended, assisted. I would sit with the deer and protect her from harm, if only I could displace her fear. But she can know only the predator inside me, not the watcher.

A light drizzle falls, just enough to set the grass and leaves glistening. In the quiet moments that follow, the deer rolls on her side and sprawls to her fullest length with her neck stretched out, head wavering up and down, tail flashing and tensing. What happens next is so sudden and so unexpected—despite all that's come before—that I am wholly unprepared to see it.

Still lying on one side, she raises her uppermost hind leg off the ground, arches her neck, and reaches her head back. Then, out from beneath the flared white tail slips something long and wet and shining and very dark.

I want to jump and shout aloud for the joy of it, but instead I hold the binoculars to my eyes, arms aching and muscles shivering.

Half visible beside the mother's loins, a dusky-brown mass gathers itself together, moves in confused, spasmodic jerks, and becomes a fawn—a tiny, throbbing, trembling, living fleck of earth.

Reaching back along her flank, the doe begins vigorously licking her child, and as she pulls away the clinging membranes, the fawn thrusts her muzzle into the cold breeze, opens her mouth, and draws her first breath—taking in the same air that sustains every creature on earth, the air that surrounds this unlikely congeries of doe, fawn, dog, and human.

Through newly opened eyes, this tiny deer sees the island where she will live through her seasons of sunshine and rain, blizzard and frost, abundance and hardship; where she will learn the mosaic of landscape and trail, find membership in a society of deer, grow sleek and graceful and quick, present herself to courting bucks, and bring on fawns of her own. During these beginning moments of her life, she sees the prodigious wall of Kluksa Mountain that will loom above her from now until the moment of her death. The deer is born into a home more purely and absolutely than I could ever imagine.

I hear a series of short, high-pitched bleats drifting on the wind, almost surely from the fawn. The doe stands and licks her offspring, then raises her head, flicking her tongue in and out. Her lifted tail reveals the distended pinkish opening from which the fawn was born. A few minutes later she moves back to her original bed and lies down facing our way. The tiny deer—still very dark, wet, and slick—crawls over against her mother's belly and nuzzles up between her legs, as if to begin nursing.

Over the next 15 minutes the doe alternates between licking her child and licking herself, while the little one keeps trying to stand: front end up and back end down, back end up and front end down, wobbling precariously the whole time. At last, she turns so I can see her tiny face and her enormous, blinking eyes. Then she braces up onto her hind legs, straightens her spindly forelegs . . . and stands. But she flops down almost immediately and crawls close to her mother, who licks her once again.

The doe seems almost completely focused on her fawn, and I can't endure the cold any longer, so after whispering stern orders in Keta's ear I begin an excruciatingly careful stalk, keeping myself screened behind bushy pines, holding for long intervals between each step, moving stiffly and awkwardly after the protracted wait, still shaking like grass in the wind.

The fawn's coat is much darker than the doe's and it's aswarm with miniature white spots. She moves around constantly on quaking, rubbery legs, often arching her tail toward her back—much as her mother did in labor—showing a miniature white flash.

I have never approached a deer so fastidiously, twisting between close-grown shrubs, worming under low boughs, parting grass with my hands before bringing down each foot, struggling across murky seeps, creeping in slow motion like a slug on a cold morning. It's taken half an hour to cover 25 yards, but at least the shivering has stopped and I feel gloriously warm inside.

An hour after giving birth the doe still licks her fawn's shoulders, neck, face, and flanks—her raspy tongue tugging at the fur. When the fawn half squats, apparently to urinate or defecate, the mother licks beneath her infant's tail. Again and again the tiny deer stands and flops down . . . this animal destined someday to unleash herself in tremendous, vaulting leaps.

I somehow avoid any serious missteps until I've come within 10 yards of the deer and then a tuft of grass crackles under my boot. The doe stands abruptly and stares, but I'm hidden behind a patch of junipers, bending out just enough to see her. Her eyes blink slowly, her nostrils pinch and flare, her pinkish tongue swipes across her nose. I stay absolutely motionless for 20 minutes, letting her settle down while I figure out a way around the snarled junipers. For much of this time the doe licks her fawn while the little one bumps against her udder, searching for the tiny nipples.

When the deer child is an hour and a half old she clambers atop a small mound beside her mother's head, up into the full clear light and the wind, and there she stands, her forelegs braced like tripod stilts, hind legs bent so her hocks nearly touch the ground, her fur now dry and frizzy and light tawny brown.

I've started to cross a narrow stream—two inches of water flowing over a bed of organic ooze that bubbles noisily as my boots sink into it. This isn't lost on the doe, who watches and listens, trapping me in the little swamp. Future paleontologists might find my bones here, but despite their limber imaginations I doubt they'll ever surmise how it happened.

After browsing halfheartedly the doe reclines beside her fawn, staring at me but showing no trace of fear, while the wobbly infant sniffs her mother's huge gray ear. A burnished-brown streak runs between the fawn's eyes, and another from its forehead to the shiny black of its muzzle, making a distinct cross on its face. Nearby, juncos flit from pine to pine, tittering softly.

I keep looking back, trying to see Keta, hoping she's curled up on the grass, not chewing the rope to free herself and bring all this to an end. But she's completely hidden from view. Of course, I owe this experience to Keta, whose persistence brought me here, so when it's over she'll have the cookie in my pack.

Two hours after the fawn's birth and three hours since we first arrived, I'm still trying to close the distance between myself and the doe. The doe stares and listens intently to the rustling of my jacket sleeves, the grumbling of my empty stomach, the sponging of moss beneath my feet. Under ordinary circumstances she'd have fled long ago. Although I'm mostly hidden, and she probably doesn't know what I am, she knows an intruder is precisely here. Perhaps because of this she walks over to the resting fawn, who stretches up to nurse.

Squirming through the juniper thicket, I can't help making noises that must sound to the doe like crumpling paper. Suddenly, as if I had leapt out in front of her, she jars to full alarm, flags her tail, and struts a short distance, which puts me in plain sight with nothing taller than a blade of grass between us. She gazes first at me, then at her child, who makes a faint sound more like a high-pitched bird's whistle than a deer's bleat. The doe funnels her ears, raises and lowers her head, then returns to gently nuzzle her fawn as if its voice made everything else irrelevant. Now I believe I can come as close as common sense and etiquette allow.

She moves about 20 feet from the fawn and 20 feet from me, then starts nibbling the grass, displacing her nervous energy the way an anxious cat licks herself. Meanwhile, the tiny deer weaves around unsteadily, poking her nose into the scrubby pines, the grass tussocks, the crowberries, the Labrador tea, the sphagnum moss, the marsh marigolds, the arctic starflowers, the pink-blossomed laurel, and crispy-leaved deer cabbage—plants that will soon feed and fatten her, transforming the island's soil and waters into a lovely, bounding creature.

While the fawn keeps busy exploring, the doe's phantom grazing leads to something remarkable. She pulls from the grass a long, flaccid, shiny, crimson ribbon of afterbirth and in less than a minute she's eaten it. Then she moves around the place licking the earth and eating plants soiled with birth fluids, eliminating all signs and odors that could lead a predator to her fawn. For a while, the little deer will have no scent, so even a bear, despite its incomparable sense of smell, might pass within a few yards, yet never realize there's an easy kill nearby.

Finally, I step into the opening where the birth took place and we stand 10 feet apart. The doe walks off, stares for a long minute, then comes determinedly back, her head lowered and ears up, muscles tense and enervated as if she might charge straight into me. For the first time, the fawn turns away from her mother and sees me. Perhaps it's emblematic of the latter twentieth century that a deer born at the wild edge looks into the eyes of a man within two hours of her birth. Showing no trace of fear, she wobbles in my direction, making high-pitched bleats.

The doe comes to intervene, but the fawn keeps on moving toward me, her legs straddled, body wavering awkwardly from side to side, until I have to ease away. The doe watches for a moment, wags her ears, and then steps directly between us to prevent the fawn from advancing closer. I could easily have touched the little deer, but didn't want to afflict her with my scent, and now I could easily touch the mother deer, but it seems inconsiderate and excessive.

The fawn, who surely regards me as an ordinary fixture of the landscape, pushes eagerly for her mother's milk and I hear the soft rhythms of her suckling. Afterward she stands under the doe's belly, peering up at me with great, glinting eyes. I can scarcely believe how endearingly and impossibly tiny she is. The fawn's body is smaller than a cat's, probably weighing around five pounds, perched atop long, gangly legs about the diameter of my thumb. I suppose her back isn't more than 12 inches above the moss. She has a short, snubby face, shining black nose, and great, floppy rabbit ears. Along her backbone is a two-inch-wide strip of plain mahogany brown, with a row of about 20 white spots on either side, and her flanks are densely, randomly speckled. She pokes her snout into a juniper bush, touches brittle twigs and boughs, pulls back and vigorously shakes her head. Then she pinches her ears and slips in among the bushes.

Putting some distance between us, the doe walks easily away, but she pauses to nibble at the grass so her little one stays close. Because the wind holds perfectly, without ebbing or eddying, she's had no chance to catch my scent; otherwise she'd be gone by now. When I try to follow, she faces me and stamps all four feet as if she's running in place, as if she's trying to bluff me away, as if she'd like to drive me off but can't bring herself to do it. Embarrassed by her uneasiness and by the directness of my own intrusion, I slowly back away.

At this point the doe makes a decisive move. Turning abruptly, she circles downwind from me, and there—four hours after I first saw her—she blunders into my dense, flooding scent. She lifts her snout in little twitches, eyes wide and muscles hard, taking in a rank human pungence that tears every trace of ambivalence out of her. She stamps her front hooves, takes a few powerful bounds, stops to look back, then springs away, all four feet aloft, snorting and zigzagging, drumming the earth like a heartbeat. She halts behind a thicket and snorts repeatedly, as if she hopes to lure me away like a bird feigning a broken wing.

I have no choice but to leave quickly, after pausing for one last look at the fawn. Apparently her mother's snorts triggered an instinct to hide and freeze, because the little one is curled up beneath a juniper bush, perfectly still for the first time since she was born. Her tiny brown sides rise and fall, her great eyes stare unblinking, and she waits.

I turn away, look back once more, and hurry off so the mother can return.

The doe is still snorting when I reach the place where I left Keta, still snorting when I untie the dog and give her a grateful hug, still snorting as we hurry off down the muskeg, making plenty of noise so the mother will know we've gone.

My legs seem to fly over the moss as if I've become weightless, and my body is filled with the energy of euphoria. Keta revels back and forth in front of me, happy to be together again and jubilant in her freedom.

How to explain that the impossible has happened? This is what I've most desired for years, although I felt sure it was utterly beyond reach. Even if I'd gone to an enclosure or a zoo the timing was just too implausible. And yet I've now seen a wild deer born, and on this wild island where my love for deer was born. I remember what the Koyukon elders teach: that everything we receive from nature comes to us as a gift.

The fawn and I live from these same earthly gifts—the air we breathe, the water we drink, the food we eat. Looking at the fawn, I see myself, being born and flinging out into the world, to live and grow and die, and someday to feed other life, nurturing further generations in turn. Because I hunt in these muskegs every fall, our fates might someday conjoin. For this I feel neither guilt nor sadness, only gratitude and joyful affinity.

Lovely deer, you are always in my heart, dancing down the dawn into the light. Lovely deer, you are always in my blood, dancing down the dusk into the night.

Heart and Blood (1997)

DAVID QUAMMEN

"At 4:15 that morning I'm awake in my tent, preparing for the day's walk by duct-taping over the sores and raw spots on my toes, ankles, and heels," David Quammen (b. 1948) wrote in the fall of 1999 as he set off behind biologist Michael Fay and nine pygmies on perhaps the wildest adventure of recent decades—a straight-line "transect" that began in the Congo and would continue to the coast of Gabon. Duct tape, he continued, "holds amazingly well through a day of swamp slogging, and although peeling off the first batch isn't fun, removal becomes easier on later evenings when there's no more hair on your feet." Quammen is as tough as any writer in this book—physically, obviously, but also mentally. The former Rhodes Scholar has avoided sentimentality (shunning the term "nature writer" as if allergic) and taken as his main subject the most complex of all ecological questions: evolution. For 15 years he entertained readers of *Outside* magazine with his column "Natural Acts," but he was storing up anecdotes and understanding for the magisterial books—particularly *Song of the Dodo* (1996) and *Monster of God* (2003)—that have marked the mature height of his career. Environmentalists routinely argue that we stand on the edge of a "sixth great extinction," but Quammen is one of the very few who has done the intellectual and journalistic heavy lifting to make it clear why that's true, and to show what we need to do if we are to head off a catastrophic blow to biodiversity.

Planet of Weeds

Tallying the losses of Earth's animals and plants

Hope is a duty from which paleontologists are exempt. Their job is to take the long view, the cold and stony view, of triumphs and catastrophes in the history of life. They study the fossil record, that erratic selection of petrified shells, carapaces, bones, teeth, tree trunks, leaves, pollen, and other biological relics, and from it they attempt to discern the lost secrets of time, the big patterns of stasis and change, the trends of innovation and adaptation and refinement and decline that have blown like sea winds among ancient creatures in ancient ecosystems. Although life is their subject, death and burial supply all their data. They're the coroners of biology. This gives to paleontologists a certain distance, a hyperopic perspective beyond the reach of anxiety over outcomes of the struggles they chronicle. If hope is the thing with feathers, as Emily Dickinson said, then it's good to remember that feathers don't generally fossilize well. In lieu of hope and despair, paleontologists have a highly developed sense of cyclicity. That's why I recently went to Chicago, with a handful of urgently grim questions, and called on a paleontologist named David Jablonski. I wanted answers unvarnished with obligatory hope.

Jablonski is a big-pattern man, a macroevolutionist, who works fastidiously from the particular to the very broad. He's an expert on the morphology and distribution of marine bivalves and gastropods—or clams and snails, as he calls them when speaking casually. He sifts through the record of those mollusk lineages, preserved in rock and later harvested into museum drawers, to extract ideas about the origin of novelty. His attention roams back through 600 million years of time. His special skill involves framing large, resonant questions that can be answered with small, lithified clamshells. For instance: By what combinations of causal factor and sheer chance have the great evolutionary innovations arisen? How quickly have those innovations taken hold? How long have they abided? He's also interested in extinction, the converse of abidance, the yang to evolution's yin. Why do some species survive for a long time, he wonders, whereas others die out much sooner? And why has the rate of extinction—low throughout most of Earth's history—spiked upward cataclysmically on just a few occasions? How do those cataclysmic episodes, known in the trade as mass extinctions, differ in kind as well as degree from the gradual process of species extinction during the millions of years between? Can what struck in the past strike again?

The concept of mass extinction implies a biological crisis that spanned large parts of the planet and, in a relatively short time, eradicated a sizable number of species from a variety of groups. There's no absolute threshold of magnitude, and dozens of different episodes in geologic history might qualify, but five big ones stand out: Ordovician, Devonian, Permian, Triassic, Cretaceous. The Ordovician extinction, 439 million years ago, entailed the disappearance of roughly 85 percent of marine animal species—and that was before there were any animals *on land.* The Devonian extinction, 367 million years ago, seems to have been almost as severe. About 245 million years ago came the Permian extinction, the worst ever, claiming 95 percent of all known animal species and therefore almost wiping out the animal kingdom altogether. The Triassic, 208 million years ago, was bad again, though not nearly so bad as the Permian. The most recent was the Cretaceous extinction (sometimes called the K-T event because it defines the boundary between two geologic periods, with K for Cretaceous, never mind why, and T for Tertiary), familiar even to schoolchildren because it ended the age of dinosaurs. Less familiarly, the K-T event also brought extinction of the marine reptiles and the ammonites, as well as major losses of species among fish, mammals, amphibians, sea urchins, and other groups, totaling 76 percent of all species. In between these five episodes occurred some lesser mass extinctions, and throughout the intervening lulls extinction continued, too—but at a much slower pace, known as the background rate, claiming only about one species in any major group every million years. At the background rate, extinction is infrequent enough to be counterbalanced by the evolution of new species. Each of the five major episodes, in contrast, represents a drastic net loss of species diversity, a deep trough of biological impoverishment from which Earth only slowly recovered. How slowly? How long is the lag between a nadir of impoverishment and a recovery to ecological fullness? That's another of Jablonski's research interests. His rough estimates run to 5 or 10 million years. What drew me to this man's work, and then to his doorstep, were his special competence on mass extinctions and his willingness to discuss the notion that a sixth one is in progress now.

Some people will tell you that we as a species, *Homo sapiens*, the savvy ape, all 5.9 billion of us in our collective impact, are destroying the world. Me, I won't tell you that, because "the world" is so vague, whereas what we are or aren't destroying is quite specific. Some people will tell you that we are rampaging suicidally toward a degree of global wreckage that will result in our own extinction. I won't tell you that either. Some people say that the environment will be the paramount political and social concern of the twenty-first century, but what they mean by "the environment" is anyone's guess. Polluted air? Polluted water? Acid rain? A frayed skein of ozone over Antarctica? Greenhouse gases emitted by smokestacks and cars? Toxic wastes? None of these concerns is the big one, paleontological in scope, though some are more closely entangled with it than others. If the world's air is clean for humans to breathe but supports no birds or butterflies, if the world's waters are pure for humans to drink but contain no fish or crustaceans or diatoms, have we solved our environmental problems? Well, I suppose so, at least as environmentalism is commonly construed. That clumsy, confused, and presumptuous formulation "the environment" implies viewing air, water, soil, forests, rivers, swamps, deserts, and oceans as merely a milieu within which something important is set: human life, human history. But what's at issue in fact is not an environment; it's a living world.

Here instead is what I'd like to tell you: The consensus among conscientious biologists is that we're headed into another mass extinction, a vale of biological impoverishment commensurate with the big five. Many experts remain hopeful that we can brake that descent, but my own view is that we're likely to go all the way down. I visited David Jablonski to ask what we might see at the bottom.

On a hot summer morning, Jablonski is busy in his office on the second floor of the Hinds Geophysical Laboratory at the University of Chicago. It's a large open room furnished in tall bookshelves, tables piled high with books, stacks of paper standing knee-high off the floor. The walls are mostly bare, aside from a chart of the geologic time scale, a clipped cartoon of dancing tyrannosaurs in red sneakers, and a poster from a Rodin exhibition quietly appropriate to the overall theme of eloquent stone. Jablonski is a lean forty-five-year-old man with a dark full beard. Educated at Columbia and Yale, be came to Chicago in 1985 and has helped make its paleontology program perhaps the country's best. Although in not many hours he'll be leaving on a trip to Alaska, he has been cordial about agreeing to this chat. Stepping carefully, we move among the piled journals, reprints, and photocopies. Every pile represents a different research question, he tells me. "I juggle a lot of these things all at once because they feed into one another." That's exactly why I've come: for a little rigorous intellectual synergy.

Let's talk about mass extinctions, I say. When did someone first realize that the concept might apply to current events, not just to the Permian or the Cretaceous?

He begins sorting through memory, back to the early 1970s, when the full scope of the current extinction problem was barely recognized. Before then, some writers warned about "vanishing wildlife" and "endangered species," but generally the warnings were framed around individual species with popular appeal, such as the whooping crane, the tiger, the blue whale, the peregrine falcon. During the 1970s a new form of concern broke forth—call it wholesale concern—from the awareness that unnumbered millions of narrowly endemic (that is, unique and localized) species inhabit the tropical forests and that those forests were quickly being cut. In 1976, a Nairobi-based biologist named Norman Myers published a paper in *Science* on that subject; in passing, he also compared current extinctions with the rate during what he loosely called "the 'great dying' of the dinosaurs." David Jablonski, then a graduate student, read Myers's paper and tucked a copy into his files. This was the first time, as Jablonski recalls, that anyone tried to quantify the rate of present-day extinctions. "Norman was a pretty lonely guy, for a long time, on that," he says. In 1979, Myers published *The Sinking Ark*, explaining the problem and offering some rough projections. Between the years 1600 and 1900, by his tally, humanity had caused the extinction of about 75 known species, almost all of them mammals and birds. Between 1900 and 1979, humans had extinguished about another 75 known species, representing a rate well above the rate of known losses during the Cretaceous extinction. But even more worrisome was the inferable rate of unrecorded extinctions, recent and now impending, among plants and animals still unidentified by science. Myers guessed that 25,000 plant species presently stood jeopardized, and maybe hundreds of thousands of insects. "By the time human communities establish ecologically sound life-styles, the fallout of species could total several million." Rereading that sentence now, I'm struck by the reckless optimism of his assumption that human communities eventually will establish "ecologically sound life-styles."

Although this early stab at quantification helped to galvanize public concern, it also became a target for a handful of critics, who used the inexactitude of the numbers to cast doubt on the reality of the problem. Most conspicuous of the naysayers was Julian Simon, an economist at the University of Maryland, who argued bullishly that human resourcefulness would solve all problems worth solving, of which a decline in diversity of tropical insects wasn't one.

In a 1986 issue of *New Scientist*, Simon rebutted Norman Myers, arguing from his own construal of select data that there was "no obvious recent downward trend in world forests—no obvious 'losses' at all, and certainly no 'near catastrophic' loss." He later co-authored an op-ed piece in the *New York Times* under the headline "Facts, Not Species, Are Periled." Again he went after Myers, asserting a "complete absence of evidence for the claim that the extinction of species is going up rapidly—or even going up at all." Simon's worst disservice to logic in that statement and others was the denial that *inferential* evidence of wholesale extinction counts for anything. Of inferential evidence there was an abundance—for example, from the Centinela Ridge in a cloud-forest zone of western Ecuador, where in 1978 the botanist Alwyn Gentry and a colleague found thirty-eight species of narrowly endemic plants, including several with mysteriously black leaves. Before Gentry could get back, Centinela Ridge had been completely deforested, the native plants replaced by cacao and other crops. As for inferential evidence generally, we might do well to remember what it contributes to our conviction that approximately 105,000 Japanese civilians died in the atomic bombing of Hiroshima. The city's population fell abruptly on August 6, 1945, but there was no one-by-one identification of 105,000 bodies.

Nowadays a few younger writers have taken Simon's line, pooh-poohing the concern over extinction. As for Simon himself, who died earlier this year, perhaps the truest sentence he left behind was, "We must also try to get more reliable information about the number of species that might be lost with various changes in the forests." No one could argue.

But it isn't easy to get such information. Field biologists tend to avoid investing their precious research time in doomed tracts of forest. Beyond that, our culture offers little institutional support for the study of narrowly endemic species in order to register their existence *before* their habitats are destroyed. Despite these obstacles, recent efforts to quantify rates of extinction have supplanted the old warnings. These new estimates use satellite imaging and improved on-the-ground data about deforestation, records of the many human-caused extinctions on islands, and a branch of ecological theory called island biogeography, which connects documented island cases with the mainland problem of forest fragmentation. These efforts differ in particulars, reflecting how much uncertainty is still involved, but their varied tones form a chorus of consensus. I'll mention three of the most credible.

W. V. Reid, of the World Resources Institute, in 1992 gathered numbers on the average annual deforestation in each of sixty-three tropical countries during the 1980s and from them charted three different scenarios (low, middle, high) of presumable forest loss by the year 2040. He chose a standard mathematical model of the relationship between decreasing habitat area and decreasing species diversity, made conservative assumptions about the crucial constant, and ran his various deforestation estimates through the model. Reid's calculations suggest that by the year 2040, between 17 and 35 percent of tropical forest species will be extinct or doomed to be. Either at the high or the low end of this range, it would amount to a bad loss, though not as bad as the K-T event. Then again, 2040 won't mark the end of human pressures on biological diversity or landscape.

Robert M. May, an ecologist at Oxford, co-authored a similar effort in 1995. May and his colleagues noted the five causal factors that account for most extinctions: habitat destruction, habitat fragmentation, overkill, invasive species, and secondary effects cascading through an ecosystem from other extinctions. Each of those five is more intricate than it sounds. For instance, habitat fragmentation dooms species by consigning them to small, island-like parcels of habitat surrounded by an ocean of human impact and by then subjecting them to the same jeopardies (small population size, acted upon by environmental fluctuation, catastrophe, inbreeding, bad luck, and cascading effects) that make island species especially vulnerable to extinction. May's team concluded that most extant bird and mammal species can expect average life spans of between 200 and 400 years. That's equivalent to saying that about a third of one percent will go extinct each year until some unimaginable end point is reached. "Much of the diversity we inherited," May and his coauthors wrote, "will be gone before humanity sorts itself out."

The most recent estimate comes from Stuart L. Pimm and Thomas M. Brooks, ecologists at the University of Tennessee. Using a combination of published data on bird species lost from forest fragments and field data they gathered themselves, Pimm and Brooks concluded that 50 percent of the world's forest-bird species will be doomed to extinction by deforestation occurring over the next half century. And birds won't be the sole victims. "How many species will be lost if current trends continue?" the two scientists asked. "Somewhere between one third and two thirds of all species—easily making this event as large as the previous five mass extinctions the planet has experienced."

Jablonski, who started down this line of thought in 1978, offers me a reminder about the conceptual machinery behind such estimates. "All mathematical models," he says cheerily, "are wrong. They are approximations. And the question is: Are they usefully wrong, or are they meaninglessly wrong?" Models projecting present and future species loss are useful, he suggests, if they help people realize that *Homo sapiens* is perturbing Earth's biosphere to a degree it hasn't often been perturbed before. In other words, that this is a drastic experiment in biological drawdown we're engaged in, not a continuation of routine.

Behind the projections of species loss lurk a number of crucial but hard-to-plot variables, among which two are especially weighty: continuing landscape conversion and the growth curve of human population.

Landscape conversion can mean many things: draining wetlands to build roads and airports, turning tallgrass prairies under the plow, fencing savanna and overgrazing it with domestic stock, cutting second-growth forest in Vermont and consigning the land to ski resorts or vacation suburbs, slash-and-burn clearing of Madagascar's rain forest to grow rice on wet hillsides, industrial logging in Borneo to meet Japanese plywood demands. The ecologist John Terborgh and a colleague, Carel P. van Schaik, have described a four-stage process of landscape conversion that they call the land-use cascade. The successive stages are: 1) *wildlands*, encompassing native floral and faunal communities altered little or not at all by human impact; 2) *extensively used areas*, such as natural grasslands lightly grazed, savanna kept open for prey animals by infrequent human-set fires, or forests sparsely worked by slash-and-burn farmers at low density; 3) *intensively used areas*, meaning crop fields, plantations, village commons, travel corridors, urban and industrial zones; and finally 4) *degraded land*, formerly useful but now abused beyond value to anybody. Madagascar, again, would be a good place to see all four stages, especially the terminal one. Along a thin road that leads inland from a town called Mahajanga, on the west coast, you can gaze out over a vista of degraded land—chalky red hills and gullies, bare of forest, burned too often by graziers wanting a short-term burst of pasturage, sparsely covered in dry grass and scrubby fan palms, eroded starkly, draining red mud into the Betsiboka River, supporting almost no human presence. Another showcase of degraded land—attributable to fuelwood gathering, overgrazing, population density, and decades of apartheid—is the Ciskei homeland in South Africa. Or you might look at overirrigated crop fields left ruinously salinized in the Central Valley of California.

Among all forms of landscape conversion, pushing tropical forest from the *wildlands* category to the *intensively used* category has the greatest impact on biological diversity. You can see it in western India, where a spectacular deciduous ecosystem known as the Gir forest (home to the last surviving population of the Asiatic lion, *Panthera leo persica*) is yielding along its ragged edges to new mango orchards, peanut fields, and lime quarries for cement. You can see it in the central Amazon, where big tracts of rain forest have been felled and burned, in a largely futile attempt (encouraged by misguided government incentives, now revoked) to pasture cattle on sun-hardened clay. According to the United Nations Food and Agriculture Organization, the rate of deforestation in tropical countries has increased (contrary to Julian Simon's claim) since the 1970s, when Myers made his estimates. During the 1980s, as the FAO reported in 1993, that rate reached 15.4 million hectares (a hectare being the metric equivalent of 2.5 acres) annually. South America was losing 6.2 million hectares a year. Southeast Asia was losing less in area but more proportionally: 1.6 percent of its forests yearly. In terms of cumulative loss, as reported by other observers, the Atlantic coastal forest of Brazil is at least 95 percent gone. The Philippines, once nearly covered with rain forest, has lost 92 percent. Costa Rica has continued to lose forest, despite that country's famous concern for its biological resources. The richest of old-growth lowland forests in West Africa, India, the Greater Antilles, Madagascar, and elsewhere have been reduced to less than a tenth of their original areas. By the middle of the next century, if those trends continue, tropical forest will exist virtually nowhere outside of protected areas—that is, national parks, wildlife refuges, and other official reserves.

How many protected areas will there be? The present worldwide total is about 9,800, encompassing 6.3 percent of the planet's land area. Will those parks and reserves retain their full biological diversity? No. Species with large territorial needs will be unable to maintain viable population levels within small reserves, and as those species die away their absence will affect others. The disappearance of big predators, for instance, can release limits on medium-size predators and scavengers, whose overabundance can drive still other species (such as ground-nesting birds) to extinction. This has already happened in some habitat fragments, such as Panama's Barro Colorado Island, and been well

documented in the literature of island biogeography. The lesson of fragmented habitats is Yeatsian: Things fall apart.

Human population growth will make a bad situation worse by putting
ever more pressure on all available land.

Population growth rates have declined in many countries within the
past several decades, it's true. But world population is still increasing, and
even if average fertility suddenly, magically, dropped to 2.0 children per
female, population would continue to increase (on the momentum of
birth rate exceeding death rate among a generally younger and healthier populace) for some time. The annual increase is now 80 million
people, with most of that increment coming in less-developed countries.
The latest long-range projections from the Population Division of the
United Nations, released earlier this year, are slightly down from previous long-term projections in 1992 but still point toward a problematic
future. According to the U.N.'s middle estimate (and most probable?
hard to know) among seven fertility scenarios, human population will
rise from the present 5.9 billion to 9.4 billion by the year 2050, then to
10.8 billion by 2150, before leveling off there at the end of the twenty-
second century. If it happens that way, about 9.7 billion people will
inhabit the countries included within Africa, Latin America, the
Caribbean, and Asia. The total population of those countries—most of
which are in the low latitudes, many of which are less developed, and
which together encompass a large portion of Earth's remaining tropical
forest—will be more than twice what it is today. Those 9.7 billion
people, crowded together in hot places, forming the ocean within which
tropical nature reserves are insularized, will constitute 90 percent of
humanity. Anyone interested in the future of biological diversity needs
to think about the pressures these people will face, and the pressures
they will exert in return.

We also need to remember that the impact of *Homo sapiens* on the
biosphere can't be measured simply in population figures. As the population expert Paul Harrison pointed out in his book *The Third Revolution*, that impact is a product of three variables: population size,
consumption level, and technology. Although population growth is

highest in less-developed countries, consumption levels are generally far higher in the developed world (for instance, the average American consumes about ten times as much energy as the average Chilean, and about a hundred times as much as the average Angolan), and also higher among the affluent minority in any country than among the rural poor. High consumption exacerbates the impact of a given population, whereas technological developments may either exacerbate it further (think of the automobile, the air conditioner, the chainsaw) or mitigate it (as when a technological innovation improves efficiency for an established function). All three variables play a role in every case, but a directional change in one form of human impact—upon air pollution from fossil-fuel burning, say, or fish harvest from the seas—can be mainly attributable to a change in one variable, with only minor influence from the other two. Sulfur-dioxide emissions in developed countries fell dramatically during the 1970s and '80s, due to technological improvements in papermaking and other industrial processes; those emissions would have fallen still farther if not for increased population (accounting for 25 percent of the upward vector) and increased consumption (accounting for 75 percent). Deforestation, in contrast, is a directional change that *has* been mostly attributable to population growth.

According to Harrison's calculations, population growth accounted for 79 percent of the deforestation in less-developed countries between 1973 and 1988. Some experts would argue with those calculations, no doubt, and insist on redirecting our concern toward the role that distant consumers, wood-products buyers among slow-growing but affluent populations of the developed nations, play in driving the destruction of Borneo's dipterocarp forests or the hardwoods of West Africa. Still, Harrison's figures point toward an undeniable reality: more total people will need more total land. By his estimate, the minimum land necessary for food growing and other human needs (such as water supply and waste dumping) amounts to one fifth of a hectare per person. Given the U.N.'s projected increase of 4.9 billion souls before the human population finally levels off, that comes to another billion hectares of human-claimed landscape, a billion hectares less forest—even without allowing for any further deforestation by the current human population, or for any further loss of agricultural land to degradation. A billion hectares—in other words, 10 million square kilometers—is, by a conservative estimate, well more than half the remaining forest area in Africa, Latin America, and Asia. This raises the vision of a very exigent human population pressing snugly around whatever patches of natural landscape remain.

Add to that vision the extra, incendiary aggravation of poverty. According to a recent World Bank estimate, about 30 percent of the total population of less-developed countries lives in poverty. Alan Durning, in his 1992 book *How Much Is Enough? The Consumer Society and the Fate of the Earth*, puts it in a broader perspective when he says that the world's human population is divided among three "ecological classes": the consumers, the middle-income, and the poor. His consumer class includes those 1.1 billion fortunate people whose annual income per family member is more than $7,500. At the other extreme, the world's poor also number about 1.1 billion people—all from households with less than $700 annually per member. "They are mostly rural Africans, Indians, and other South Asians," Durning writes. "They eat almost exclusively grains, root crops, beans, and other legumes, and they drink mostly unclean water. They live in huts and shanties, they travel by foot, and most of their possessions are constructed of stone, wood, and other substances available from the local environment." He calls them the "absolute poor." It's only reasonable to assume that another billion people will be added to that class, mostly in what are now the less-developed countries, before population growth stabilizes. How will those additional billion, deprived of education and other advantages, interact with the tropical landscape? Not likely by entering information-intensive jobs in the service sector of the new global economy. Julian Simon argued that human ingenuity—and by extension, human population itself—is "the ultimate resource" for solving Earth's problems, transcending Earth's limits, and turning scarcity into abundance. But if all the bright ideas generated by a human population of 5.9 billion haven't yet relieved the desperate needfulness of 1.1 billion absolute poor, why should we expect that human ingenuity will do any better for roughly 2 billion poor in the future?

Other writers besides Durning have warned about this deepening class rift. Tom Athanasiou, in *Divided Planet: The Ecology of Rich and Poor*, sees population growth only exacerbating the division, and notes that governments often promote destructive schemes of transmigration and rain-forest colonization as safety valves for the pressures of land hunger and discontent. A young Canadian policy analyst named Thomas F. Homer-Dixon, author of several calm-voiced but frightening articles on the linkage between what he terms "environmental scarcity" and global sociopolitical instability, reports that the amount of cropland available per person is falling in the less-developed countries because of population growth and because millions of hectares "are being lost each year to a combination of problems, including encroachment by cities, erosion, depletion of nutrients, acidification, compacting and salinization and waterlogging from overirrigation." In the cropland pinch and other forms of environmental scarcity, Homer-Dixon foresees potential for "a widening gap" of two sorts—between demands on the state and its ability to deliver, and more basically between rich and poor. In conversation with the journalist Robert D. Kaplan, as quoted in Kaplan's book *The Ends of the Earth*, Homer-Dixon said it more vividly: "Think of a stretch limo in the potholed streets of New York City, where homeless beggars live. Inside the limo are the air-conditioned post-industrial regions of North America, Europe, the emerging Pacific Rim, and a few other isolated places, with their trade summitry and computer information highways. Outside is the rest of mankind, going in a completely different direction."

That direction, necessarily, will be toward ever more desperate exploitation of landscape. When you think of Homer-Dixon's stretch limo on those potholed urban streets, don't assume there will be room inside for tropical forests. Even Noah's ark only managed to rescue paired animals, not large parcels of habitat. The jeopardy of the ecological fragments that we presently cherish as parks, refuges, and reserves is already severe, due to both internal and external forces: internal, because insularity itself leads to ecological unraveling; and external, because those areas are still under siege by needy and covetous people. Projected forward into a future of 10.8 billion humans, of which perhaps

2 billion are starving at the periphery of those areas, while another 2 billion are living in a fool's paradise maintained by unremitting exploitation of whatever resources remain, that jeopardy increases to the point of impossibility. In addition, any form of climate change in the mid-term future, whether caused by greenhouse gases or by a natural flip-flop of climatic forces, is liable to change habitat conditions within a given protected area beyond the tolerance range for many species. If such creatures can't migrate beyond the park or reserve boundaries in order to chase their habitat needs, they may be "protected" from guns and chainsaws within their little island, but they'll still die.

We shouldn't take comfort in assuming that at least Yellowstone National Park will still harbor grizzly bears in the year 2150, that at least Royal Chitwan in Nepal will still harbor tigers, that at least Serengeti in Tanzania and Gir in India will still harbor lions. Those predator populations, and other species down the cascade, are likely to disappear. "Wildness" will be a word applicable only to urban turmoil. Lions, tigers, and bears will exist in zoos, period. Nature won't come to an end, but it will look very different.

The most obvious differences will be those I've already mentioned: tropical forests and other terrestrial ecosystems will be drastically reduced in area, and the fragmented remnants will stand tiny and isolated. Because of those two factors, plus the cascading secondary effects, plus an additional dire factor I'll mention in a moment, much of Earth's biological diversity will be gone. How much? That's impossible to predict confidently, but the careful guesses of Robert May, Stuart Pimm, and other biologists suggest losses reaching half to two thirds of all species. In the oceans, deepwater fish and shellfish populations will be drastically depleted by overharvesting, if not to the point of extinction then at least enough to cause more cascading consequences. Coral reefs and other shallow-water ecosystems will be badly stressed, if not devastated, by erosion and chemical runoff from the land. The additional dire factor is invasive species, fifth of the five factors contributing to our current experiment in mass extinction.

That factor, even more than habitat destruction and fragmentation, is a symptom of modernity. Maybe you haven't heard much about invasive species, but in coming years you will. The ecologist Daniel Simberloff takes it so seriously that he recently committed himself to founding an institute on invasive biology at the University of Tennessee, and Interior Secretary Bruce Babbitt sounded the alarm last April in a speech to a weed-management symposium in Denver. The spectacle of a cabinet secretary denouncing an alien plant called purple loosestrife struck some observers as droll, but it wasn't as silly as it seemed. Forty years ago, the British ecologist Charles Elton warned prophetically in a little book titled *The Ecology of Invasions by Animals and Plants* that "we are living in a period of the world's history when the mingling of thousands of kinds of organisms from different parts of the world is setting up terrific dislocations in nature." Elton's word "dislocations" was nicely chosen to ring with a double meaning: species are being moved from one location to another, and as a result ecosystems are being thrown into disorder.

The problem dates back to when people began using ingenious new modes of conveyance (the horse, the camel, the canoe) to travel quickly across mountains, deserts, and oceans, bringing with them rats, lice, disease microbes, burrs, dogs, pigs, goats, cats, cows, and other forms of parasitic, commensal, or domesticated creature. One immediate result of those travels was a wave of island-bird extinctions, claiming more than a thousand species, that followed oceangoing canoes across the Pacific and elsewhere. Having evolved in insular ecosystems free of predators, many of those species were flightless, unequipped to defend themselves or their eggs against ravenous mammals. *Raphus cucullatus*, a giant cousin of the pigeon lineage, endemic to Mauritius in the Indian Ocean and better known as the dodo, was only the most easily caricatured representative of this much larger pattern. Dutch sailors killed and ate dodos during the seventeenth century, but probably what guaranteed the extinction of *Raphus cucullatus* is that the European ships put ashore rats, pigs, and *Macaca fascicularis*, an opportunistic species of Asian monkey. Although commonly known as the crab-eating macaque, *M. fascicularis* will eat almost anything. The monkeys are still pestilential on Mauritius, hungry and daring and always ready to grab what they can, including raw eggs. But the dodo hasn't been seen since 1662.

The European age of discovery and conquest was also the great age of biogeography—that is, the study of what creatures live where, a branch of biology practiced by attentive travelers such as Carolus Linnaeus, Alexander von Humboldt, Charles Darwin, and Alfred Russel Wallace. Darwin and Wallace even made biogeography the basis of their discovery that species, rather than being created and plopped onto Earth by divine magic, evolve in particular locales by the process of natural selection. Ironically, the same trend of far-flung human travel that gave biogeographers their data also began to muddle and nullify those data, by transplanting the most ready and roguish species to new places and thereby delivering misery unto death for many other species. Rats and cats went everywhere, causing havoc in what for millions of years had been sheltered, less competitive ecosystems. The Asiatic chestnut blight and the European starling came to America; the American muskrat and the Chinese mitten crab got to Europe. Sometimes these human-mediated transfers were unintentional, sometimes merely shortsighted. Nostalgic sportsmen in New Zealand imported British red deer; European brown trout and Coastal rainbows were planted in disregard of the native cutthroats of Rocky Mountain rivers. Prickly-pear cactus, rabbits, and cane toads were inadvisedly welcomed to Australia. Goats went wild in the Galapagos. The bacterium that causes bubonic plague journeyed from China to California by way of a flea, a rat, and a ship. The Atlantic sea lamprey found its own way up into Lake Erie, but only after the Welland Canal gave it a bypass around Niagara Falls. Unintentional or otherwise, all these transfers had unforeseen consequences, which in many cases included the extinction of less competitive, less opportunistic native species. The rosy wolfsnail, a small creature introduced onto Oahu for the purpose of controlling a larger and more obviously noxious species of snail, which was itself invasive, proved to be medicine worse than the disease; it became a fearsome predator upon native snails, of which twenty species are now gone. The Nile perch, a big predatory fish introduced into Lake

Victoria in 1962 because it promised good eating, seems to have exterminated at least eighty species of smaller cichlid fishes that were native to the lake's Mwanza Gulf.

The problem is vastly amplified by modern shipping and air transport, which are quick and capacious enough to allow many more kinds of organism to get themselves transplanted into zones of habitat they never could have reached on their own. The brown tree snake, having hitchhiked aboard military planes from the New Guinea region near the end of World War II, has eaten most of the native forest birds of Guam. Hanta virus, first identified in Korea, burbles quietly in the deer mice of Arizona. Ebola will next appear who knows where. Apart from the frightening epidemiological possibilities, agricultural damages are the most conspicuous form of impact. One study, by the congressional Office of Technology Assessment, reports that in the United States 4,500 nonnative species have established free-living populations, of which about 15 percent cause severe harm; looking at just 79 of those species, the OTA documented $97 billion in damages. The lost value in Hawaiian snail species or cichlid diversity is harder to measure. But another report, from the U.N. Environmental Program, declares that almost 20 percent of the world's endangered vertebrates suffer from pressures (competition, predation, habitat transformation) created by exotic interlopers. Michael Soulé, a biologist much respected for his work on landscape conversion and extinction, has said that invasive species may soon surpass habitat loss and fragmentation as the major cause of "ecological disintegration." Having exterminated Guam's avifauna, the brown tree snake has lately been spotted in Hawaii.

Is there a larger pattern to these invasions? What do fire ants, zebra mussels, Asian gypsy moths, tamarisk trees, maleleuca trees, kudzu, Mediterranean fruit flies, boll weevils, and water hyacinths have in common with crab-eating macaques or Nile perch? Answer: They're *weedy* species, in the sense that animals as well as plants can be weedy. What that implies is a constellation of characteristics: They reproduce quickly, disperse widely when given a chance, tolerate a fairly broad range of habitat conditions, take hold in strange places, succeed especially in disturbed ecosystems, and resist eradication once they're established. They are scrappers, generalists, opportunists. They tend to thrive in human-dominated terrain because in crucial ways they resemble *Homo sapiens*: aggressive, versatile, prolific, and ready to travel. The city pigeon, a cosmopolitan creature derived from wild ancestry as a Eurasian rock dove (*Columba livia*) by way of centuries of pigeon fanciers whose coop-bred birds occasionally went AWOL, is a weed. So are those species that, benefiting from human impacts upon landscape, have increased grossly in abundance or expanded their geographical scope without having to cross an ocean by plane or by boat—for instance, the coyote in New York, the raccoon in Montana, the white-tailed deer in northern Wisconsin or western Connecticut. The brown-headed cowbird, also weedy, has enlarged its range from the eastern United States into the agricultural Midwest at the expense of migratory songbirds. In gardening usage the word "weed" may be utterly subjective, indicating any plant you don't happen to like, but in ecological usage it has these firmer meanings. Biologists frequently talk of weedy species, meaning animals as well as plants.

Paleontologists, too, embrace the idea and even the term. Jablonski himself, in a 1991 paper published in *Science*, extrapolated from past mass extinctions to our current one and suggested that human activities are likely to take their heaviest toll on narrowly endemic species, while causing fewer extinctions among those species that are broadly adapted and broadly distributed. "In the face of ongoing habitat alteration and fragmentation," he wrote, "this implies a biota increasingly enriched in widespread, weedy species—rats, ragweed, and cockroaches—relative to the larger number of species that are more vulnerable and potentially more useful to humans as food, medicines, and genetic resources." Now, as we sit in his office, he repeats: "It's just a question of how much the world becomes enriched in these weedy species." Both in print and in talk he uses "enriched" somewhat caustically, knowing that the actual direction of the trend is toward impoverishment.

Regarding impoverishment, let's note another dark, interesting irony: that the two converse trends I've described—partitioning the world's landscape by habitat fragmentation, and unifying the world's landscape by global transport of weedy species—produce not converse results but one redoubled result, the further loss of biological diversity. Immersing myself in the literature of extinctions, and making dilettantish excursions across India, Madagascar, New Guinea, Indonesia, Brazil, Guam, Australia, New Zealand, Wyoming, the hills of Burbank, and other semi-wild places over the past decade, I've seen those redoubling trends everywhere, portending a near-term future in which Earth's landscape is threadbare, leached of diversity, heavy with humans, and "enriched" in weedy species. That's an ugly vision, but I find it vivid. Wildlife will consist of the pigeons and the coyotes and the white-tails, the black rats (*Rattus rattus*) and the brown rats (*Rattus norvegicus*) and a few other species of worldly rodent, the crab-eating macaques and the cockroaches (though, as with the rats, not *every* species—some are narrowly endemic, like the giant Madagascar hissing cockroach) and the mongooses, the house sparrows and the house geckos and the houseflies and the barn cats and the skinny brown feral dogs and a short list of additional species that play by our rules. Forests will be tiny insular patches existing on bare sufferance, much of their biological diversity (the big predators, the migratory birds, the shy creatures that can't tolerate edges, and many other species linked inextricably with those) long since decayed away. They'll essentially be tall woody gardens, not forests in the richer sense. Elsewhere the landscape will have its strips and swatches of green, but except on much-poisoned lawns and golf courses the foliage will be infested with cheatgrass and European buckthorn and spotted knapweed and Russian thistle and leafy spurge and salt meadow cordgrass and Bruce Babbitt's purple loosestrife. Having recently passed the great age of biogeography, we will have entered the age *after* biogeography, in that virtually everything will live virtually everywhere, though the list of species that constitute "everything" will be small. I see this world implicitly foretold in the U.N. population projections, the FAO reports on deforestation, the northward advance into Texas of Africanized honeybees, the rhesus monkeys that haunt the parapets of public buildings in New Delhi, and every fat gray squirrel on a bird feeder in England. Earth will be a different sort of place—soon, in just five or six human generations. My label for that place, that time, that apparently unavoidable prospect, is the Planet of Weeds. Its main consoling felicity, as far as I can imagine, is that there will be no shortage of crows.

Now we come to the question of human survival, a matter of some interest to many. We come to a certain fretful leap of logic that otherwise thoughtful observers seem willing, even eager, to make: that the ultimate consequence will be the extinction of us. By seizing such a huge share of Earth's landscape, by imposing so wantonly on its providence and presuming so recklessly on its forgivingness, by killing off so many species, they say, we will doom our own species to extinction. This is a commonplace among the environmentally exercised. My quibbles with the idea are that it seems ecologically improbable and too optimistic. But it bears examining, because it's frequently offered as the ultimate argument against proceeding as we are.

Jablonski also has his doubts. Do you see *Homo sapiens* as a likely survivor, I ask him, or as a casualty? "Oh, we've got to be one of the most bomb-proof species on the planet," he says. "We're geographically widespread, we have a pretty remarkable reproductive rate, we're incredibly good at co-opting and monopolizing resources. I think it would take really serious, concerted effort to wipe out the human species." The point he's making is one that has probably already dawned on you: *Homo sapiens* itself is the consummate weed. Why shouldn't we survive, then, on the Planet of Weeds? But there's a wide range of possible circumstances, Jablonski reminds me, between the extinction of our species and the continued growth of human population, consumption, and comfort. "I think we'll be one of the survivors," he says, "sort of picking through the rubble." Besides losing all the pharmaceutical and genetic resources that lay hidden within those extinguished species, and all the spiritual and aesthetic values they offered, he foresees unpredictable levels of loss in many physical and biochemical functions that ordinarily come as benefits from diverse, robust ecosystems—functions such as cleaning and recirculating air and water, mitigating droughts and floods, decomposing wastes, controlling erosion, creating new soil, pollinating crops, capturing and transporting nutrients, damping short-term temperature extremes and longer-term fluctuations of climate, restraining outbreaks of pestiferous species, and shielding Earth's surface from the full brunt of ultraviolet radiation. Strip away the ecosystems that perform those services, Jablonski says, and you can expect grievous detriment to the reality we inhabit. "A lot of things are going to happen that will make this a crummier place to live—a more stressful place to live, a more difficult place to live, a less resilient place to live—before the human species is at any risk at all." And maybe some of the new difficulties, he adds, will serve as incentive for major changes in the trajectory along which we pursue our aggregate self-interests. Maybe we'll pull back before our current episode matches the Triassic extinction or the K-T event. Maybe it will turn out to be no worse than the Eocene extinction, with a 35 percent loss of species.

"Are you hopeful?" I ask.

Given that hope is a duty from which paleontologists are exempt, I'm surprised when he answers, "Yes, I am."

I'm not. My own guess about the mid-term future, excused by no exemption, is that our Planet of Weeds will indeed be a crummier place, a lonelier and uglier place, and a particularly wretched place for the 2 billion people comprising Alan Durning's absolute poor. What will increase most dramatically as time proceeds, I suspect, won't be generalized misery or futuristic modes of consumption but the gulf between two global classes experiencing those extremes. Progressive failure of ecosystem functions? Yes, but human resourcefulness of the sort Julian Simon so admired will probably find stopgap technological remedies, to be available for a price. So the world's privileged class—that's your class and my class—will probably still manage to maintain themselves inside Homer-Dixon's stretch limo, drinking bottled water and breathing bottled air and eating reasonably healthy food that has become incredibly precious, while the potholes on the road outside grow ever deeper. Eventually the limo will look more like a lunar rover. Ragtag mobs of desperate souls will cling to its bumpers, like groupies on Elvis's final

Cadillac. The absolute poor will suffer their lack of ecological privilege in the form of lowered life expectancy, bad health, absence of education, corrosive want, and anger. Maybe in time they'll find ways to gather themselves in localized revolt against the affluent class. Not likely, though, as long as affluence buys guns. In any case, well before that they will have burned the last stick of Bornean dipterocarp for firewood and roasted the last lemur, the last grizzly bear, the last elephant left unprotected outside a zoo.

Jablonski has a hundred things to do before leaving for Alaska, so after two hours I clear out. The heat on the sidewalk is fierce, though not nearly as fierce as this summer's heat in New Delhi or Dallas, where people are dying. Since my flight doesn't leave until early evening, I cab downtown and take refuge in a nouveau-Cajun restaurant near the river. Over a beer and jambalaya, I glance again at Jablonski's 1991 *Science* paper, titled "Extinctions: A Paleontological Perspective." I also play back the tape of our conversation, pressing my ear against the little recorder to hear it over the lunch-crowd noise.

Among the last questions I asked Jablonski was, What will happen *after* this mass extinction, assuming it proceeds to a worst-case scenario? If we destroy half or two thirds of all living species, how long will it take for evolution to fill the planet back up? "I don't know the answer to that," he said. "I'd rather not bottom out and see what happens next." In the journal paper he had hazarded that, based on fossil evidence in rock laid down atop the K-T event and others, the time required for full recovery might be 5 or 10 million years. From a paleontological perspective, that's fast. "Biotic recoveries after mass extinctions are geologically rapid but immensely prolonged on human time scales," he wrote. There was also the proviso, cited from another expert, that recovery might not begin until *after* the extinction-causing circumstances have disappeared. But in this case, of course, the circumstances won't likely disappear until *we* do.

Still, evolution never rests. It's happening right now, in weed patches all over the planet. I'm not presuming to alert you to the end of the world, the end of evolution, or the end of nature. What I've tried to describe here is not an absolute end but a very deep dip, a repeat point within a long, violent cycle. Species die, species arise. The relative pace of those two processes is what matters. Even rats and cockroaches are capable—given the requisite conditions, namely, habitat diversity and time—of speciation. And speciation brings new diversity. So we might reasonably imagine an Earth upon which, 10 million years after the extinction (or, alternatively, the drastic transformation) of *Homo sapiens*, wondrous forests are again filled with wondrous beasts. That's the good news.

Harper's, October 1998

JANISSE RAY

Janisse Ray (b. 1962) grew up in a junkyard near Baxley, Georgia, the daughter of Christian fundamentalists. If that doesn't sound like the standard resumé for an environmental writer, never mind—she is one of the finest voices to emerge in recent years. Much of her work explores the longleaf pine country of the Southeast, one of the most depleted ecosystems on the continent. But probably more importantly, she engages a culture that has long been ignored by environmentalists: the working-class South. It was a great breakthrough when *Ecology of a Cracker Childhood* (1999) was chosen for the "All Georgia Reading the Same Book Project." The questions she asks, though, are universal—in many ways, the whole planet is now as comprehensively trashed as the piney woods of the American South. If we're all living in a junkyard, we need just this kind of writing to help us understand what beauty still remains, and what kind of repairs we must begin.

from **Ecology of a Cracker Childhood**

The Keystone

One July day after I was grown I stopped at the fruit stand by the railroad track in Baxley to buy tangerines.

"Are these grapes good?" I inquired of the fruit-stand owner, a beefy, red-faced man who planted greens and onions on the strip of curb.

"Good," he said. "In fact, I just fed some to my turtle, trying to get him to eat."

"Turtle? What kind?"

"Go look in that wagon yonder," he said.

Inside the red metal wagon with foot-high sides, used for hauling produce, was a huge gopher tortoise. I didn't recognize it immediately because it had been recently spray-painted gold and silver, gold on its carapace and silver on the finely notched head. It was drooling profusely from the nose and mouth, scrambling relentlessly from side to side in the four-foot wagon. An intense midday sun beat down on it.

It looked like a circus animal, painted like that. No telling how old it was—fifteen, twenty years old—and because it was an elder in terms of gopher tortoises its predicament seemed even more an abomination.

"Who painted it?" I asked the peddler.

"I did."

"When?" I asked.

"I just did it," he said. "I bought paint for my tennis shoes and decided to paint him too."

"How long have you had him?"

"Since yesterday."

"Where did you get him?"

"Right there." He pointed toward Main Street. "I saw a van stop in the middle of the street and put a package on that strip of ground beside the railroad track. I thought it might be a bomb or something, somebody trying to blow up the train, and with me right here, they'd blow me up too. So I went over to see what they put out and it was this turtle."

"It's a gopher tortoise," I said.

"Yeah. Gopher."

"Has he been eating?" I could tell it was a he because his plastron, or under shell, curved inward.

"Naw," he said.

"He's gonna die out in this sun. They go into their holes when it's this hot out."

"He don't have a burrow."

"You know, this is an endangered species, and you could get into a fair amount of trouble having one in your possession," I said. "I'll take him and go find a piece of land with burrows to put him on."

"No, I want to keep him awhile," he replied.

"You might have to pay a fine if the wildlife officer comes by."

"Wildlife officer? He won't do anything. He's a friend of mine," he said.

"He's a friend of mine too."

"I'm gonna let him go. But I want to show him a little first."

I wanted to take a picture of the spectacle, and I walked to the truck for the camera. It was out of film.

"I want a picture of it," I said. "I'll be right back."

When I got back from Winn-Dixie two blocks away, the gopher tortoise was still prowling across the hot trailer, drooling steadily. Gopher tortoises, I knew, are prone to a disease of the upper respiratory tract, which they spread among themselves by nose-to-nose contact and which is taking a severe toll on some populations. The disease appears to be worse where tortoises are concentrated. Perhaps this tortoise was already infected, or more aptly, the atoms of paint had affected his respiratory system and the toxins would kill him before the heat did, or before he starved. Either way, what was happening to him was cruel, even if he had been saved from the highway. I tried again to persuade the fruit seller to let me relocate him to the wild.

"No. I want to show him off for a day or two and then I'll let him go."

I drove to the first phone I could find and called my father, who was home. I told him about the tortoise. I said I was minutes away from calling the sheriff, the wildlife officer, or whomever else I could find who might be sympathetic. I'd call Washington if I had to.

"Hold off on that," he said. "I'll go see what I can do." The fruit seller was a friend of his, and at Daddy's urging he agreed to release the tortoise at 6 P.M., still some hours away. Daddy called me right back. Because I couldn't locate the wildlife officer, that was what happened. Daddy carried the circus tortoise to a forest he owns. He brought his shovel with him, dug the tortoise a burrow two feet long and deposited it in its new hole. There it crouched as long as Daddy watched, but the next day when he returned to check on it, it had not deepened its man-made hole, but had moved on to make a new life for itself.

Of plants and animals native to the longleaf pine barren, the gopher tortoise may be most crucial, in the same way the keystone, or upper central stone in an arch, is thought to be most important in holding the other stones in place. The tortoise is central in holding the ecosystem together.

An ancient tortoise of great tolerance, it lives in a burrow in sand-hills, flatwoods, and other upland habitat, sharing its hole with more than three hundred species of vertebrates and arthropods. Among these commensals (meaning organisms that live in close association, one benefited by the relationship and the other—in this case the tortoise—unaffected) are the eastern diamondback rattlesnake, gopher frog, opossum, rabbit, Florida mouse, skunk, armadillo, lizard, and gopher cricket. Three kinds of scarab beetles that are candidates for federal listing use tortoise burrows, as do tineid moths, whose larvae feed on the tortoise's fecal pellets as well as decaying plant material. Tortoise burrows provide refuges from cold, heat, dryness, and predators, and are especially important during periodic forest fires, when the tortoise and its houseguests escape to the hole in the ground to wait the inferno's passing. Even flushed quail run into them.

A gopher tortoise can live up to fifty years, although they take a long time to mature. Females reach adulthood at ten to fifteen years of age. At the northern end of the range, south Georgia, they may require as much as twenty-one years. Mature, they weigh about as many pounds as they are old, and the diameter of the shell maxes out at twelve or thirteen inches.

Gopher tortoises feed on low-growing, sun-loving plants like wiregrass, broadleaf grasses, and legumes. They eat prickly pear cactus, blackberries, pawpaw, saw palmetto berries, and other fruits in season. Besides unsnarled and open vegetation, gopher tortoises require open sunny spots for laying eggs and dry, sandy soil for digging, since the burrows can be up to forty feet in length and ten feet deep. The record burrow was forty-seven and a half feet long.

The life of a gopher tortoise revolves around its burrow, although it can occupy more than one. Males use an average of four to nine burrows, while females use only two to four.

Their homes, typically eight or ten feet below the surface of the ground, are long, straight, and unbranched. The burrow opening corresponds to the size of their shells—the burrow is as wide as the length of the shell so the tortoise can turn around at any point—and slopes gently downward, usually with a turn. It is too dark and narrow to see far inside the burrow. An apron of weedless sand, marked by the tracks of animals and the drag of tortoise plastron, hems the opening of most burrows.

Tortoises mate in spring after elaborate courtships that involve visits by head-bobbing males to female burrows. The female decides when she's interested. Several weeks after mating, female tortoises deposit three to fifteen eggs in the sand mounds in front of their burrows or some other nearby sand flat. Incubation depends on climate and varies from seventy to one hundred days up the length of the tortoise range. Usually the female lays one clutch per year, but often raccoons, foxes, armadillos, skunks, and fire ants raid the eggs, so that only one nest in ten years survives.

After hatching, young tortoises either join their mother in her burrow or dig their own small version nearby. Many are eaten by predators until they get too big to be swallowed, at which time their enemies are few—humans, dogs, raccoons.

Their ancestors were one of at least twenty-three species of land tortoises that originated in western North America some sixty million years ago. Along with scrub jays and burrowing owls, they were part of a savanna fauna that migrated to the Southeast. Of four species of land tortoises remaining in North America, gopher tortoises are unique in their occurrence east of the Mississippi River. Some people, because of the inhospitable climate, refer to gopher tortoise habitat as the "southeastern desert."

During winter, tortoises hibernate, although on warm afternoons they trudge to the surface to sun on the patios of their burrows. During warmer months they stay underground during the heat of the day, coming out at dawn and dusk to feed.

The gopher tortoise has been broadsided by the absence of regenerative burning in pine forests. Because it relies upon herbaceous plants for food, it is confounded by dense understory vegetation—gallberry, blackberry brambles, sumac, turkey oak—which take over in the absence of fire. Food for tortoises becomes scarce.

Because slash and loblolly pines cannot tolerate fire, not only do they collapse food supplies, but the dense canopies that accompany pine monocultures whittle down sunny spots female tortoises need for nesting. Fire is vital in maintaining native ecosystems—most commonly longleaf pine sandhills—where gopher tortoises live.

Until it became protected by Georgia in 1977 and by Florida in 1988, the tortoise was hunted openly for food. It was a reliable source of meat during the Depression, thus the reference "Hoover chicken." In 1989, the gopher tortoise was designated the state reptile of Georgia and has been listed as a threatened species by the state since 1992.

Logging, development, and conversion to agricultural lands also have spelled its doom by destroying and fragmenting natural landscapes. Tortoises have been called the most relocated reptile in America, since developers often covet lands they inhabit. Tortoises are killed crossing highways or buried alive by heavy machinery, although studies have found tortoises able to dig out of burrows collapsed by tractors even in soil with a high clay content.

A tortoise shares its humble dwelling with over three hundred species of fauna and is, increasingly, homeless. Many of these three hundred may be doomed along with the gopher tortoise if we continue to wipe out its domain.

Second Coming

Through the acres of wrecks she came
With a wrench in her hand,

Through dust where the blacksnake dies
Of boredom, and the beetle knows
The compost has no more life.
—James Dickey, "Cherrylog Road"

When my father bought a ten-acre lowland out U.S. 1 north on the outskirts of Baxley, Georgia, intending to use it as a junkyard, it had already been logged. So the unhitching of the first junker wasn't so much a travesty as it was a monument to my deepest regret.

Birding in the junkyard now, one finds nothing very unusual: cardinals, brown thrashers, red-winged blackbirds, crows. They eat the ripe elderberries and the mosquitoes that rise from the environs of foundered vehicles. Although I did not as a child know their name, Carolina wrens nest in the old cars, from which anoles and snakes come crawling. Field mice birth pink babies into shredded foam under back seats.

But where are the eastern bluebirds, winter chickadees, yellow-rumped warblers, white-eyed vireos? Where are tree swallows and savanna sparrows? Where is yellow colic root and swamp coreopsis? Where is bird's-foot violet and blue-eyed grass? Where are meadowlarks? River swamp frogs and sweet bay magnolias should be there, an alligator or two. What happened to the cougar and the red wolf?

Sometimes I dream of restoring the junkyard to the ecosystem it was when Hernando de Soto sauntered into Georgia, looking for wealth but unable to recognize it. Because it is a lowland, perhaps transitional to a bog, slash pine would have dominated. Slash pines still grow here and there, as well as other flora native to a wet pinewood: hatpins, sundews, gallberry. I dream about it the way my brother dreams of restoring the '58 Studebaker, a fender at a time.

Eighty to 95 percent of the metals of vehicles of that era are recyclable, but what do you do with the gas tanks? What about heavy metal accumulations in the soil, lead contamination, battery acid leaks, the veins of spilled oil and gasoline? The topsoil would have to be scraped away: where would it go? What about the rubber, plastic, and broken glass? Would we haul it all to the county dump?

It might take a lifetime, one spent undoing. It might require even my son's lifetime. And where would we find all the replacement parts for this piece of wasted earth? Yet, might they not come, slowly, very slowly?

A junkyard is a wilderness. Both are devotees of decay. The nature of both is random order, the odd occurrence and juxtaposition of miscellany, backed by a semblance of method. Walk through a junkyard and you'll see some of the schemes a wilderness takes—Fords in one section, Dodges in another, or older models farthest from the house—so a brief logic of ecology can be found.

In the same way, an ecosystem makes sense: the canebrakes, the cypress domes. Pine trees regenerate in an indeterminate fashion, randomly here and there where seeds have fallen, but also with some predictability. Sunlight and moisture must be sufficient for germination, as where a fallen tree has made a hole in the canopy, after a rain. This, too, is order.

Without fail in a junkyard you encounter the unexpected—a doll's head, bodyless; a bike with no handlebars; a cache of wheat pennies; thirty feet of copper pipe; a boxy '58 Edsel. Likewise, in the middle of Tate's Hell Swamp you might look unexpectedly into the brown eyes of a barred owl ten feet away or come upon a purple stretch of carnivorous bladderworts in bloom, their BB-sized bladders full of aquatic microorganisms.

In junkyard as in wilderness there is danger: shards of glass, leaning jacks, weak chains; or rattlesnakes, avalanches, polar bears. In one as in the other you expect the creativity of the random, how the twisted metal protrudes like limbs, the cars dumped at acute, right, and obtuse angles, how the driveways are creeks and rivers.

This from my brother Dell:

> There is a place in the old junkyard that, when I encounter it, turns magical. I become a future savage, half-naked, silently creeping through the dense canopy of trees and scrub. A feeling of dread increases with each step but curiosity draws me on. My footsteps falter but never completely stop. Suddenly I see mammoth beasts, eyes staring sightless forward. I see huge shining teeth in these monsters. As I move my hand gently among their flanks, I realize that I am in a graveyard speckled with dead prehistoric creatures. I am filled with awe. I can only speculate about their lives, imagine them roaring about and shudder at what they fed on. I know that this is hallowed ground and I remember that this place was spoken of in soft mutterings of the old ones, long

dead, around the fires at night. But hunger pangs drive me on, for beyond this place are the animals that clothe and feed me. As I grope the haft of the spear and prepare to leave, I wonder if the pangs are from hunger or from a sense of loss.

Pine lilies don't grow in the junkyard anymore, nor showy orchis, and I've never seen a Bachman's sparrow flitting amid the junk. I'd like to. I have a dream for my homeland. I dream we can bring back the long-leaf pine forests, along with the sandhills and the savannas, starting now and that we can bring back all the herbs and trees and wild animals, the ones not irretrievably lost, which deserve an existence apart from slavery to our own.

Ecology of a Cracker Childhood (1999)

It was Julia Butterfly Hill's actions, not her words, that first made her a hero. In December 1997, as part of an ongoing protest by the group Earth First! (itself originally inspired by Ed Abbey's writings), Hill (b. 1974) climbed into a platform on an almost 200-foot-tall redwood that she and her cohorts called Luna. The idea was that the lumber company, cutting at a rapacious rate to finance the interest on a junk-bond-funded merger, would be reluctant to topple a tree with a human being clinging to its branches. That turned out to be, just barely, true, though only after Hill had endured not only storms but helicopter attacks and attempts to cut off her supply of food (and the cellphone batteries that allowed her to keep talking to reporters). By the time she finally climbed down two years later, a deal had been struck with the company to protect Luna and the trees around it, and she'd become a celebrity, using her fame to found the Circle of Life Foundation. A year later, an unidentified but evidently bitter anti-environmentalist tried again to cut Luna down, but only managed to get halfway through the trunk with a chainsaw; when the damage was discovered, arborists improvised a series of braces that so far have kept it upright.

from **The Legacy of Luna**

The Storm

Despite Kalani's help on the emotional front, the siege was taking its toll. For starters, I was running out of battery power for communication, so we had to pull off a resupply. We tried in the middle of the night. The attempt totally failed. The security guards, who stayed on duty round the clock, kept the floodlights illuminated. There was a demonstration staged, I later found out, down on Highway 101, which I can see from the top of Luna. A group of people was trying to create a diversion so the resupply could get to me. I found out about this later when I used my new cell phone batteries to call Almond.

The guards had become very vigilant about stopping resupply efforts. "Nobody's going to get to you," they said when three people were caught. "You are not going to get resupplied. We are going to starve you out, so you might as well come down."

One of the three people, a seventy-something woman known as Grandma Rosemary, told them she was my grandmother and that she wanted to hike up the hill to tell me to come down. The security guards told me they couldn't let my grandmother hike up for fear she'd have a heart attack; I had to come down to see her. If only they had known! This amazing woman had hiked the hill three times and later climbed all the way up the tree!

"I don't know who's down there, but it's not my grandmother," I retorted.

Then I asked them to describe the other two people they had stopped. One of the descriptions fit Almond.

"Look, if you want me to come down, find out if one of the people you have is Doug Fir," the media name Almond was using at the time. "If he's there, bring him up here. If he tells me to come down, I'll come down."

I actually hoped in a way that they did have Almond and that he would ask me to come down. I was so sad thinking of losing Luna to these destructive, greedy men. But I just couldn't imagine facing another freezing cold, stormy night like the preceding one. The night before had been one of the scariest nights of my life.

In Luna, the wind is a constant. And wind does something to you, something that rain doesn't. It makes your thoughts go wild. You can't focus. You can't read or write or paint or think. You feel disconnected and ungrounded. The sound of tarps whipping in the wind drives you crazy. You just sit here with a glaze, while your mind gets pummeled.

It was January, and gale-force winds, along with rain, sleet, and hail, had set in. I grew up with storms. I knew they passed. These didn't. This, as I later found out, was El Niño, one of the worst winters in recorded history in northern California.

The storms had been growing in power every week, each day worse than the last. The night before, the storm had completely shredded my tarps. I sat wrapped up like a burrito in what remained of a single tarp, getting beaten with hail and freezing. Another picked up the platform and tossed it about like a matchstick. That scared me so badly, I gave myself into the craziness of it all and laughed hysterically, holding onto my rapidly slipping shreds of sanity. I prayed like I haven't prayed in a long, long time. I prayed to every power and to every God. I begged and pleaded for my life, the life of my friend next to me, and the life of the goddess in whose arms I was being held. I even said a prayer for the safety of the Pacific Lumber security men on the ground below us.

The storms were so loud and I was so cold so much of the time that I couldn't sleep. After six or seven of these sleepless nights, I started to break down. Suddenly, I couldn't stop crying. The intensity I had undergone over the preceding weeks had drained everything out of me. But without a decent night's rest, I was never able to recharge. I reached empty, and still I kept draining.

"I cannot survive any longer this way," I thought. "I cannot go one more night on no sleep, just hearing the howling of the wind and the sleet pelting me through the cracks. I can't do it anymore. I just can't."

But the storms would get even worse—a lot worse. It was in this weather that a group of Earth Firstlers and others tried to resupply me with food and batteries.

The guards held the line. "I'm not bringing any more of you Earth Firstlers up this hill!" screamed one of them. "It's trespassing! It's private property! Just get the hell off it!"

By this stage, nine or ten Pacific Lumber people had gathered at the base of the tree, including one of their top brass. Despite their numbers, I kept clinging to the notion that somehow a new supply run would get through. I stared down the hill through intermittent hailstorms all afternoon. Nothing. I began to cry out of sheer exhaustion.

Finally, I was forced to accept that the supply runs had failed. I was so broken by that point that if anybody I trusted from my side had told me to come down, I probably would have.

Late that same afternoon, I saw these little colored specks coming up the mountain. In my sleep-deprived state, I still assumed that the supply run had failed again.

Then my pager sounded, and I saw our prearranged signal indicating a resupply. We had set up a few different codes via pager so I would know when a resupply team was headed out, when it was nearing the tree, and when to drop the duffel bag we used to haul up equipment and supplies. The code told me they were near.

I had to create a distraction. Several days before the siege, the activists had sent up a banner that said "Earth Jobs First!" So I unfurled all thirty-five feet of it—*Whooom!*

"Heads up!" I yelled to the guards, afraid that the banner might break some branches. Meanwhile, the resupply group of twenty activists crept stealthily closer. To cover up any noises, like breaking twigs, I started singing the same song I'd sung to the guards, and the loggers before them, as loudly as I could.

> *Love in any language,*
> *Straight from the heart,*
> *Pulls us all together,*
> *Never apart.*

The security guards didn't think anything about it because I'd been singing that one song over and over the whole time. Suddenly Shakespeare walked up to them.

"Hey, guys, how's it going?" he asked casually.

Nineteen other people popped up from the surrounding greenery and yelled at the tops of their lungs, "Twenty-three!" That was how old I was at the time. It was also our code to drop the haul line. I had previously lowered it part of the way through the branches. When I heard the code, I dropped it the rest of the way down.

The security guards and the activists, the latter cracking jokes and running around in circles, all dashed to the rope. Many of the activists had stuff sacks in their hands, but only some of those had supplies in them. The security guards didn't know whom to tackle. All they could do was go for the rope. Before they got there, one of the activists managed to clip a bag onto the rope.

"Twenty-three!" they shouted again, my cue to pull the haul bag back up.

A guard grabbed for it, but the activist took a flying leap and hit the bag downhill. The hill Luna stands on drops so steeply that one side of the tree's base is twelve feet lower than the other. By hitting the haul bag down toward the ravine, it flew above the security guard's hands. That was all I needed. My first yank pulled it up well above them, and then I was able to haul it safely to the top.

That same maneuver worked once more. The second time the haul bag was in a security guard's hands, but he didn't have a grip on it yet, so an activist jumped through the air and hit it again, sending it flying. While I pulled it up into the tree, the activists posed for pictures with big grins on their faces and then took off back into the bushes before the security guards showed up again.

As I unpacked my fresh fruit, cell phone batteries, and propane with which to cook tea on my stove, I thought about those twenty people—some Earth Firstlers, others from all walks of life—who were willing and ready to be arrested that day, and all the people who staged the demonstration below in order to resupply me. The beauty of so much love gave me the burst of energy I so desperately needed. Suddenly I felt supported instead of all alone. I was recharged and ready to keep going.

The successful resupply turned many Earth Firstlers around as well. In their eyes, this was war! The siege had provided them with a chance to shake things up, to be in the face of the corporate structure, which they love to do. That's one of their ways to publicize an issue. Now they were rallied behind the Luna tree-sit.

After the resupply, Carl Anderson, Pacific Lumber's head of security, chewed the guards up one side and down the other.

"What is wrong with you guys?" he demanded, cussing them out.

"Man, they were outnumbered," I called down. "There was nothing they could do."

Of course, without *my* team, there would have been nothing I could have done. Together, we were the tools trying to keep this vehicle of a movement running. In a car race, somebody is at the steering wheel, and at the finish line that driver gets the trophy and the spotlight. But everybody knows that he had a top-of-the-line car and a top-of-the-line pit crew, that all the bolts were tightened to perfection, and that everything was lubricated just right. So the trophy is not just for that car's driver, it represents the whole effort of all the people who worked on the car. And so with this movement: a victory comes from the efforts of everyone, not just me. Our trophy will be to find permanent protection for all the old growth while we save Luna. And we will all share that prize.

The storms got so bad that the guards pulled out two days after the resupply. Every night, the wind ripped huge branches off trees and flung them to the ground, making it extremely dangerous for anyone on the forest floor. Plus, the guards knew that the activists would continue to outwit them unless they brought in a whole bunch of extra security, and the company didn't seem willing to do that. So finally, two days after the resupply, they left without a word.

I never saw Kalani again, though I spoke with him over the telephone a couple of times, finding out in the process that he had quit Pacific Lumber security. I think of him as an angel, because angels are the people who pop into our lives at a needed time and then disappear without a trace, having helped us through a critical point.

On day seventy-one of the tree-sit, a photographer hiked up to Luna with a group of people and asked if he could come up and take photos. I hesitated. But he knew how to climb, and the group had brought all this food up for me. Feeling obligated, I agreed. Eric Slomanson turned out to be an upbeat, funny man who quickly put me at ease. Over the next two days, he took pictures while we talked and clowned around.

"You know, dahling," he said, pretending to be an agent, "if you really want to do this right, you've got to stay until the hundred-day mark, because the world record is ninety days, and Americans love record breaking, anniversaries, and numbers. So not only will you break the world record, you'll have a nice round number of a hundred."

We both laughed, but he was serious about my staying up.

"Are you crazy? That's three weeks away!" I exclaimed. "It's just not possible. Look at me. I'm dying here!"

"Yes, it is! You've been up here this long. Three weeks is nothing to you."

"There's no way I can last another three weeks," I insisted. "There's just no way."

I was so tired, cold, and wet, the only thing I could think about was a hot shower and a bunch of bottles of wine in a row. My nerves were shot. Every noise I heard convinced me that the tree was under attack again. But the quiet also scared me, because then I didn't know what was going on.

I even found myself missing the security guards. I had gotten used to their generators, their lights, their dogs, their chaos, and their cussing. And then all that went away, leaving me to wonder what the next barrage would be. It had to be something. Surely, they couldn't just roll over; they would have to save face.

Losing my mind from a lack of sleep, food, positive results, and emotional support, I began to feel like my whole being was under attack. I was near the breaking point, unable to fend off the devastating impact of the elements. When I'd get wet, the chill would work itself into my very core. My shivers would wrack my body for hours, even after I had dried off and settled into my sleeping bag.

"I'm soaking wet, I'm cold, and I'm miserable," I confessed to myself.

The cold and damp aggravated all the physical ailments that still lingered from my wreck. My shoulder bothered me. So did my back and neck.

"Man, why am I even here?" I wondered.

Not long after the security guards left, I thought that a bit of music might calm me down—anything other than the incessant flapping of tarps in the wind. Because of the helicopters and the storms and the siege, I hadn't listened to my radio in weeks. So I pulled it out of the five-gallon storage bucket and started messing with it. Finally, I got it to work.

I put on the headphones and nestled down into my sleeping bag, ready to relax. Instead of tunes, however, I heard warnings about another storm watch and upcoming seventy-mile-an-hour winds.

"That's for down there," I thought with trepidation. "God only knows what it's going to be like up here."

The mere thought terrified me. I kept wondering if this was a sign that I should go down. I remembered my father preaching about a man who hears that a flood is coming. So he goes and prays to God.

"God, please protect me," he asks. "Keep me safe from this flood."

"Ask and you shall receive," God responds.

The floodwaters begin to rise. As they flow over the front stoop and enter the first floor of his home, some people come by, paddling a canoe.

"Hey, brother, would you like a ride to safe ground?" they ask.

"No, no, that's okay," says the man. "I prayed to God, and he said he's going to take care of me."

The floodwaters continue to rise, and the man has to move up into the second story of his house. More people come by, this time in a motorboat.

"Hey, we're here to save you!"

"Oh, no, that's okay," says the man. "God said he is going to protect me and take care of me."

The floodwaters continue to rise, and he's standing on the roof of his house, and some people fly by in a helicopter.

"We're here to save you! We're here to save you!" they shout, hovering over him.

"No, thank you, God said he's going to protect me," the man responds.

"Are you nuts? Look at you, man! Your house is under water. We're the only ones who can save you. Hop on!"

"No, no, really," says the man. "God will save me. God said he would save me, so I know God will."

"You're nuts," they say as they fly off.

Sure enough, the man drowns.

He stands before God in heaven. "God, your answer to my prayer was, 'Ask and you shall receive.' Why did you let me drown?" the man asks.

"I sent a canoe, a motorboat, and a helicopter to save you!" God retorts. "What more do you want?"

I didn't want to let Luna fall. But I didn't want to be stupid. I didn't want to miss my opportunities to make it out alive. I wondered whether the worsening storms had been my sign—and my help—from up above to get out of the tree.

"Maybe this radio broadcast is going to be the last helper that God is going to send my way," I thought. "Or maybe my fear is simply trying to put me under its power and manipulate me into going down to where it seems safer, where I don't risk falling a hundred eighty feet and smashing into the ground, with branches skewering me like somebody's barbecue."

I couldn't tell. The only thing I knew for sure was that I wished I hadn't heard that radio alert. I tried meditating. I tried praying. I still didn't know what to do. I didn't want to get blown over or get blown out of the tree. I wasn't ready to die yet. If it was my time, then it was my time. But I didn't need to bring my time upon myself before it was meant to be.

I tried to figure out what I was supposed to do. I didn't feel any need to play Superwoman, but I knew that I had given my word that I wasn't coming down until I had done everything I possibly could to protect this area. To come down because I was afraid of a storm would be to break my word, and I believe beyond a shadow of a doubt that we are only as good as our word. If our actions don't meet our words, our value as people is lessened. That's just the way I was raised.

Still, I was torn. My survival instinct was telling me to go down to the ground, that the Pacific Lumber people had all left, and that I could just climb back up in the morning and nobody would ever know. But that would mean breaking my word, and I just couldn't do it.

Before the storm ended, however, a promise would be the last thing on my mind. I would just be trying to stay alive—and not doing a very good job of it.

The moment the storm hit, I couldn't have climbed down if I had wanted to. To climb you have to be able to move, and my hands were frozen. Massive amounts of rain, sleet, and hail mixed together, and the winds blew so hard I might have been ripped off a branch.

The storm was every bit as strong as they said it would be. Actually, up here, it was even stronger. When a gust would come through, it would flip the platform up into the air, bucking me all over the place.

"Boy! Whoaaah! Ooh! Whoa!"

The gust rolled me all the way up to the hammock. Only the rope that cuts an angle underneath it prevented me from slipping through the gap in the platform.

"I'm really ready for this storm to chill out. I'm duly impressed," I decided. "I've bowed and cowered once again before the great almighty gods of wind and rain and storm. I've paid my respects—and my dues—and I'd appreciate it if they got the heck out of here."

My thoughts seemed to anger the storm spirits.

"Whoa! Whoa!" I cried, as the raging wind flung my platform, straining the ropes that attached it.

"This is getting really intense! Oh, my God! Oh, my God! Okay, never mind, I take it back. Whoaaah!"

The biggest gust threw me close to three feet. I grabbed onto the branch of Luna that comes through the middle of the platform, and I prayed.

"I want to be strong for you, Luna. I want to be strong for the forest. I don't want to die, because I want to help make a difference. I want to be strong for the movement, but I can't even be strong for myself."

It seemed like it took all my will to stay alive. I was trying to hold onto life so hard that my teeth were clenched, my jaws were clenched, my muscles were clenched, my fists were clenched, everything in my body was clenched completely and totally tight.

I knew I was going to die.

The wind howled. It sounded like wild banshees, *rrahhh*, while the tarps added to the crazy cacophony of noise, *flap, flap, flap, bap, bap, flap, bap!* Had I remained tensed for the sixteen hours that the storm raged, I would have snapped. Instead, I grabbed onto Luna, hugging the branch that comes up through the platform, and prayed to her.

"I don't know what's happening here. I don't want to go down, because I made a pact with you. But I can't be strong now. I'm frightened out of my mind, Luna, I'm losing it. I'm going crazy!"

Maybe I was, maybe I wasn't, but in that moment I heard the voice of Luna speak to me.

"Julia, think of the trees in the storm."

And as I started to picture the trees in the storm, the answer began to dawn on me.

"The trees in the storm don't try to stand up straight and tall and erect. They allow themselves to bend and be blown with the wind. They understand the power of letting go," continued the voice. "Those trees and those branches that try too hard to stand up strong and straight are the ones that break. Now is not the time for you to be strong, Julia, or you, too, will break. Learn the power of the trees. Let it flow. Let it go. That is the way you are going to make it through this storm. And that is the way to make it through the storms of life."

I suddenly understood. So as I was getting chunked all over by the wind, tossed left and right, I just let it go. I let my muscles go. I let my jaw unlock. I let the wind blow and the craziness flow. I bent and flailed with it, just like the trees, which flail in the wind. I howled. I laughed. I whooped and cried and screamed and raged. I hollered and I jibbered and I jabbered. Whatever came through me, I just let it go.

"When my time comes, I'm going to die grinning," I yelled.

Everything around me was being ripped apart. My sanity felt like it was slipping through my fingers like a runaway rope. And I gave in.

"Fine. Take it. Take my life. Take my sanity. Take it all."

Once the storm ended, I realized that by letting go of all attachments, including my attachment to self, people no longer had any power over me. They could take my life if they felt the need, but I was no longer going to live my life out of fear, the way too many people do, jolted by our disconnected society. I was going to live my life guided from the higher source, the Creation source.

I couldn't have realized any of this without having been broken emotionally and spiritually and mentally and physically. I had to be pummeled by humankind. I had to be pummeled by Mother Nature. I had to be broken until I saw no hope, until I went crazy, until I finally let go. Only then could I be rebuilt; only then could I be filled back up with who I am meant to be. Only then could I become my higher self.

That's the message of the butterfly. I had come through darkness and storms and had been transformed. I was living proof of the power of metamorphosis.

The Legacy of Luna (2000)

CALVIN DeWITT

At least since Lynn White Jr.'s 1969 essay (see pages 405–12), many environmentalists had decided that Christianity was an obstacle to their work—which, with the rise of the religious right in the 1980s, made that work all the more difficult. But there were some in the evangelical movement determined to heal that breach, none earlier or more effectively than Calvin DeWitt (b. 1935). A mild-mannered midwesterner with a Ph.D. in zoology, he helped in 1979 to found the Au Sable Institute in northern Michigan. The institute devotes itself to organizing field courses and conferences that teach ecology, always stressing the Christian notion of stewardship, the idea that, as written in Genesis, we are to "dress and keep" the fertile earth. Over time, its courses and conferences helped spread the message; in 1993, DeWitt was a co-founder of the Evangelical Environmental Network, which ran a campaign to preserve the Endangered Species Act when it came under right-wing congressional fire. Most of his work, though, has been patient and nonconfrontational, and it was rewarded in spring 2006 when many of the nation's leading evangelical scholars and pastors signed a statement demanding federal action on global warming. This passage is from a talk that DeWitt gave at a seminar in Ecuador organized by Heifer Project International, a charity with Christian roots that delivers animals, and the principles of careful husbandry, to villagers around the world. It is delivered in DeWitt's trademark calm style—but it's worth noting that he can be roused to anger too. "We've spiritualized the devil," he said recently. "But when Exxon is funding think tanks to basically confuse the lessons that we're getting from this great book of creation, that's devilish work. We find ourselves praying to God to protect us from the wiles of the devil, but we can't see him when he's staring us in the face."

from *Inspirations for Sustaining Life on Earth*

Greeting Friends in Their Andean Gardens

About fifteen years ago I received a telephone call from the U.S. State Department to ask the question, "Do you have a set of ethical principles which we can use in negotiating international treaties on biodiversity?" It was a curious question. Thinking that they might not really want what they had asked, I said, "Would you like some scientific principles?" "No," was the reply, "we have the science all down."

Somewhat surprised by this, I asked, "Well, won't you have to believe these ethics?" I found the question irrelevant. "We are negotiators; we just need ethical principles to do the job." And so I gave them three principles and these are the same ones I am presenting to you. They have been used in negotiating international treaties on biodiversity, and I present them to you—with their roots in the Hebrew religious texts—as basic ethical principles for agroecology and development.

They are: Earthkeeping, Fruitfulness, and Sabbath. Memorize these three terms right now so that you can use them as descriptors of these three principles: Earthkeeping, Fruitfulness, Sabbath. I will conclude the presentation of these principles by putting all three of them within the frame work of "Con-Service," a framework I will explain.

In presenting these principles as derived from the Hebrew scriptures I am proposing that they really are universal principles. They are principles that are so broadly held that they will appear within the matrices of practically every religion and every culture. And yet it is important to respect fully the Hebrew text from which we will be working, and to deal with them with respectful scholarly study and analysis, as we would with any religious text.

Earthkeeping Principle

Here I am selecting an ancient text over three thousand years old, and one whose message is that human beings must take care of the garden, must take care of creation, must keep the earth. This message is one that is widely accepted across cultures from around the world. We must keep the very system that sustains us and all of life, we must keep and care for the world in which we live, we must not destroy the system that sustains life on earth.

In ancient Hebrew culture this is expressed in a number of ways. One of these is "bal taschit" or "do not destroy." It is out of respect for the earth and for the Creator that this principle is given. We must work to keep the earth. This is the earthkeeping principle.

The text of Genesis 2:15 expects that human beings to *abad* the garden and *shamar* it. *Shamar* means "to keep," and to keep in a very certain kind of way. Looking at another Hebrew word that means "to keep" is helpful in understanding its meaning, the word *natsar*. *Natsar* means preservationist keeping, like injecting a specimen with alcohol or formaldehyde to keep it on a museum shelf, or fixing a pressed plant specimen to an herbarium sheet to keep it in a herbarium. *Shamar*, however, means something quite different, perhaps best realized in the blessing of Aaron, "The Lord bless you and *shamar* you" (Numbers 6:24). The people who are blessed by their pastor or rabbi with this widely used benediction expect God to keep them, not as pickles in a jar, but keep them in all of their dynamic integrity. *Shamar* in this blessing means something like "May God, the Creator, keep you: with every-thing working right inside of you, everything working right psycholog-ically, everything working right between you and all the people, and everything working right between you and the soil, and the air, and the land, and the rest of creation—everything in the biosphere." That is the richness of the word *shamar*. And it is this word that is used in this famous text of Genesis 2:15. People are expected to keep the earth in the sense of the *shamar* word. We must keep the earth, not as we would a pickled specimen or an animal in a cage or a plant in an herbarium or a seed bank. This of course does not mean we should not have muse-ums, seed banks, or zoos—much like it does not mean that Noah should not build an ark! In an emergency we just might need an ark, to tide us and the creatures over, but we must always work to keep things in their place, and to get them back into place when they have been dislodged. Keeping of the creatures means keeping them within their habitats, not forever on arks!

For Heifer Project International, the ark symbol used in publications and logos images for us the fact that arks are necessary when the habitat of people and other creatures has been destroyed, but is a temporary measure that anticipates, and works toward restored habitats, restored community, and a restored creation.

Earthkeeping is a principle that is not unique to Hebrew culture and Judeo-Christian religion. Culture after culture, religion after religion we find beliefs and practices that serve a similar end of not destroying and of restoring what has been degraded. In the Brazilian rainforests it is to do the bidding of the Bushy Mama who is implored for permission to cut a tree of the forest. In ancient Israel it was seeking to do the will of God, the Maker and owner of heaven and earth. In Christendom it might be to do what is right in creation as followers of the Son through whom God created all things, holds everything together, and reconciles and restores all things.[1]

The film we saw yesterday was produced by the Union of Concerned Scientists (UCS) titled "Keeping the Earth."[2] That title was very carefully chosen by the UCS because it not only convicts those of Jewish and Christian traditions but people across all cultures. We and people everywhere and all times must work to keep the earth.

Fruitfulness Principle

Most of you know the story of Noah and the Ark. And reflecting the significance of this story is the HPI periodical, *The Ark*. This story is an interesting one even when read in a cursory way. But it is even more interesting—and more relevant—if we thoughtfully unpack it. An important discovery we can make in this unpacking is the principle of Fruitfulness.

1. See the hymn of Colossians recorded in Colossians 1:15–20. For the interested reader, the contribution of this hymn can be evaluated in the context of the related texts of John 1:1–8, Philippians 2:5–11, Hebrews 1:1–4, and Revelation 5:9–14.

2. *Keeping the Earth.* (Videotape: 27 minutes.) Produced by Union of Concerned Scientists, Two Brattle Square, Cambridge, MA 02238-9105 USA. Phone: (617) 547-5552.

The setting of the story is a society that is living in disregard for integrity of Creation and human society. People were not doing what they should to sustain themselves, their community, and their environment. They are living in disregard of the laws and ordinances of their community and of creation. And the consequence of this is that the world as they know it has come to the brink of destruction. An impending major disaster now threatens life on earth.

But there is an exception to this disregard in the life and family of Noah. Remaining faithful in a degraded society, in obedience to the Creator of all things, Noah puts every effort and expense into preserving the lineage of every animal species. When the great flood drowns the life of the earth, he has preserved sufficient domestic and wild life onto the ark so that each of the kinds can reinhabit the earth after the great flood subsides.

For us here there is an important lesson of faithfulness. And in our time in earth's history this story, told in chapters 6 through 9 of Genesis, illustrates the great importance of preserving the lineages of the creatures in the face of extinction. Creation's fruitfulness—its capacity to produce fruit from which each lineage is sustained—deserves a great deal of attention by us. And acting upon sustaining creation's fruitfulness must be pursued even if it requires an immense effort and resources.

But let's get to the Hebrew scripture directly:

"Be fruitful and multiply, and fill the skies and fill the seas . . ." So goes the blessing that the Creator gives to the birds and the fish, recited in Genesis 1:22. If you were deeply immersed within the teaching and significance of this passage and its context in this first chapter of the book of Genesis, during your trip tomorrow high into the Andes or down their great slopes toward the sea, you would see the abundance of birds above and creatures all around as fruitfulness. The sky is filled with birds, the sea is filled with fish. Earth swarms with living creatures, blessed by their Creator with fruitfulness!

Now you can see how this relates to our time. As we see all this abundant and diverse life, we enjoy it all, and may even say, "Thank God for this!" But as we see the air made uninhabitable for birds or the sea uninhabitable for fish, we have good reason to counter the things and forces that destroy and to do the things that preserve, sustain, and restore.

What we can gain from the fruitfulness principle is that we may take from creation, we may take the fruit, but must not destroy the fruitfulness of earth's living creatures. Their home in creation must be sustained, their habitats saved, their lineages preserved. In another of the five books of Hebrew law, the book of Deuteronomy, we read that when you come across a mother bird on her nest, you may take the young, but not the mother. The idea here is that if you take both the young and the mother, then you don't have any way to produce more birds. It is an expression of the Fruitfulness principle that you know well from your work in sustaining a crop: "Don't eat the seed corn that you depend upon for perpetuating your crop the next year!"

Filling out the richness of the Fruitfulness principle is Ezekiel 34:18: "Is it not enough for you to feed in the good pasture, must you trample the rest your feet? Is it not enough for you to drink the clear waters, must you foul the rest with your feet?" We may eat of the fruits of creation—from the green pasture or the still water—but we must not ruin the very pastures and waters that provide the needs for the life of us and other creatures.

When we ascend the mountains tomorrow and see alpacas and vicuñas and llamas, we'll also very likely see people who understand stewardship of their animals and grazing lands in ways that do not destroy the very lands and water they depend upon. The principle given in Genesis and Ezekiel is widely understood.

Sabbath Principle

During the French Revolution, as I have been told, there was an attempt made to change the weekly calendar from a seven-day week to a ten-day week, with work for nine days and rest on the tenth. But the horses died! (So I am told.) Now the 20th-century Hebrew rabbi, Abraham Joshua Heschel, says that the 7-day week with the seventh as Sabbath is a pattern in creation—it is part of the way the world works. Now whether that can be scientifically established is not important for us here, but it is important to observe that the 7-day week has been established as the pattern worldwide for all people. We should reflect on this and learn from it!

Now, what is the biblical teaching? In Deuteronomy and Exodus it is, "You rest on the Sabbath." And the reason for this is that God rested after making the heaven and the earth. We rest not because we need it, not because it makes us more productive. We rest because God rests. Rest is not a sign of weakness; it is part of the design of the world.

Some of us are, or know others who are, "workaholics." What this means is that work goes on seven days a week, week after week. We say we're on a treadmill and things like that. And we know the consequences of this. It is eventual collapse. And the Hebrew scriptures tell us that not only do we need Sabbath rest, but the whole creation does.

Some years ago, I met a farmer in Alberta, Canada, who gave his land a rest every second year. As we walked together on his farm, I asked him, "Why every two years?" and he said, "Because this is what the scriptures tell me." "But don't you have the numbers wrong?" I asked. "No," he replied, "you remember Christ's teaching in the New Testament—'The Sabbath is made for the land, not the land for the Sabbath.'" Now that was not a literal translation of the text that says "The Sabbath is made for people, not people for the Sabbath." And then he went on to say that "I give my land rest every two years because that is what my land needs." He was applying the principle of Sabbath, giving the land whatever rest it needs. If you are legalistic, the Sabbath for the land is one year in seven, but if you are principled about it, it's giving the land the rest it needs whenever it needs it. And we as ecologists, agriculturalists, and scientists even know of some lands that need a perpetual Sabbath.

The teaching on the Sabbath for the Land is given in the book of Exodus, another of the five books of the law, chapter 23 verse 10, reinforced in still another of these five books, Leviticus 25 and 26. Leviticus warns, "If you fail to observe these Laws, then you will no longer be supported by the Land, and after you are off the Land, the Land will then enjoy its Sabbaths, the Sabbaths it did not have when you lived there." You and I have seen such lands—lands that have been over-grazed and over-farmed and now, eroded and salinized, they no longer support our agriculture. The land must be given its times of rest. This is the teaching of the Sabbath.

Earthkeeping, Fruitfulness, Sabbath—these are the three principles I have summarized. And now we can encapsulate these three, putting them all together within the principle of Con-Service.

Con-Service—an Overarching Principle

Conservation is a word well known to all of us, and we know well how we have come to use and apply this word to our work and our world. In gaining insight into this word, and into the practice of conservation, it is very helpful for us to explore the concept as it emerges from the book of Genesis. We already have found that the text of Genesis 2:15 expects that human beings to *abad* the garden and *shamar* it. And we noted that *shamar* means "to keep." But now we will look at the word *abad*, and through this, understand the encapsulating principle of Con-Service.

People are expected to keep the earth in the sense of the *shamar* word. But they also are expected to *abad* the garden. Now if you look at how *abad* is translated by us modern folk, you find it translated "cultivate," "till," "work," "keep," "tend." Some of those words are better translations than others. The meaning of this word can be grasped by seeing how this word is used elsewhere in these great writings, and specifically the book of Joshua: "Choose ye this day whom you will *abad*; as for me and my house, we will *abad* Jehovah." *Abad* means "serve."

But these days, when a translator comes to the word *abad*, they usually do not translate it as "serve"; they use a term from what they understand about serving a garden. Only in Young's Literal Translation has it been translated "serve."

One of my botanist friends has just retired as the Director of Kew Gardens, the Royal Botanical Gardens, in England. (Ghillean Prance, incidentally, has done much work in the Amazon basin on the ethnobotany of indigenous people.) I often have thought of what his reaction might be to my arriving at the front gate of Kew Gardens in London on my tractor, pulling an eight-blade plow and saying to him, "Iain, I have come to till your garden." Could you imagine his response? Kew Gardens is a place where a plow is out of place and where even the use of a shovel would be carefully supervised. In the refrigerated house for high-altitude plants you will find tiny little plants for which a toothpick might be the tool of choice, if any cultivation is needed at all. This is an illustration of why it is important for us to read *abad* as "serve" and not as "till."

How do you serve a garden? How do you serve Creation? How do you serve the Land? I suppose that this text is written in a way that will raise the question, "Doesn't the Scripture have this backwards?" "Isn't the garden there to serve us?" Yet, it expects people to serve the garden.

In the Hebrew rabbinical tradition, one will take a text like this and "turn it about, turn it about." If this is done with this text, one first may think, "the garden serves us, we don't serve it." And this should generate in your mind the idea of reciprocal service, back-and-forth service. Human service to the garden is returned by its service to us, and we return its service to us with service to the garden. The soil that serves us by supporting growing plants is the soil we also serve with our love and care. That is con-servation. "Con" is the Latin prefix that means "with." So the service here is reciprocal. Con-servation here does not mean to set it aside. Conservation means to serve and to be served, in a community relationship.

Today, the word we are using for con-service is "stewardship." We can therefore use the word stewardship, but, if we could somehow reinstate the rich meaning of "con-servation" there would be no reason not to call it con-servation. I use the word *stewardship* but often use "conserving" or "con-servancy" or con-service—with a hyphen. The biblical idea is rich; it is extremely beautiful.

Now if you take the word "manage," manage relates to "hands." As soon as you use *manage* you're thinking of "hands on" something. But this word does not show the community between people and the land. *Management* is one-directional in its meaning because it does not allow Creation to come back and put its hands on you. But, with your hands, you can serve the garden, and the Creation with its photosynthesis, soil building capacity and all the rest, can come back and serve you. *Stewardship* and *con-service* are words for extremely powerful concepts. They represent ideas that have been with us for more than 3,000 years. Unfortunately, the richness of Hebrew biblical teaching, of Christian teaching, and the teaching of many other traditions, have been swamped out by a very utilitarian worldview which says the Creation is just Resource. But the Creation is this glorious, wonderful thing of which we are allowed to be part and be stewards. Creation is pouring out praise all the time. And responding, we have joy in its praise and service.

A concluding note: I was in Bogor on the Island of Java some years ago where early one morning I walked to the market place, before it opened. Here at the center of Bogor is a great botanical garden, with iron bars all around it. There is a gate, of course, where you can enter; but here at the market there are only the iron bars that make an abrupt transition between the street and the lush diversity of green wonder. The people there were the farmers. They had come from their fields and their plots and gardens with their things to sell, their booths were set up facing the street. But the farmers were facing the opposite direction. Standing with their hands on the bars, nearly every one of them were gazing into the garden. Their wares were on beautiful display but there were no buyers yet. And of 50 there, 45 now were turned, looking into the garden.

Gardens and Creation, each with their integrity, are what are in accord with who we are and why we are here. Plants and Creation's vegetation is not just to eat, just to sell, or just to grow; our being on earth is not that we merely eat, or even that we eat well. We are here to take joy in the beauty of this world and to keep it beautiful. Our world must be beautiful! It must have geraniums and potatoes. It must have heifers and humming birds! Then we have a beautiful world.

2001

Americans have increasingly taken to eating organic food—it's the fastest growing section of the supermarket. Some of this trend has to do with taste and freshness, but more involves fears over the effect of chemicals on our bodies, fears that, if often vague, are nonetheless pervasive. Sandra Steingraber (b. 1959), who has a Ph.D. in biology from the University of Michigan, has done much to substantiate those worries, in part because of her personal history: at 20, she was diagnosed with bladder cancer. Much of Steingraber's career has been spent investigating the ways in which human disease is caused by exposure to toxic chemicals. In *Living Downstream* (1997) she lays out the evidence for cancer clusters across the country's contaminated Rust Belt; in *Having Faith* (2001), an account of the birth of her daughter, she delves deeply into new research about fetal toxicology.

from Having Faith

The View from the Top

Two years before I was born, the Soviet Union sent into space *Sputnik 1*, the world's first human-made satellite. It was quickly followed by *Sputnik 2*, which contained in its payload a live dog. *Sputnik 3* contained a live man. The United States rushed to replicate these feats—founding the National Aeronautics and Space Administration along the way—and thus the Cold War entered the Space Age. Five years later, the American biologist Rachel Carson published *Silent Spring*, a best-selling book that warned about the ecological consequences of human technology, particularly chemical pesticides. I had just turned three.

Even though I'm too young to remember the launching of either *Sputnik* or *Silent Spring*, both profoundly influenced my education. In my tiny public elementary school, science became the subject of first priority. Even art classes had planetary themes, as when we were all put to work drawing the Solar System to scale. Our reading and social studies books might be taped and worn, their inside front covers bearing the names of their many previous owners, but our science books were spine-cracking new. Their first chapters invariably focused on the structure of atoms and molecules, and their final chapters were always devoted to ecology. I don't believe we ever actually made it to the end of our science books before the end of the school year, so I was left to explore the back pages on my own, during the dull moments of a spelling drill or a rained-out recess.

What fascinated me most were the elegant black-and-white diagrams representing ecological food chains. One year, the arrows of energy flowed from sunlight to grass, from grass to cows, and from cows to milk. Another year, it was sunlight to diatoms, diatoms to crustaceans, crustaceans to smelt, smelt to mackerel, mackerel to tuna. In each of these diagrams, it was man, as a drinker of milk and an eater of tuna fish, who occupied the top slot. At some point—I don't remember when exactly—the idea of biomagnification was introduced. This was Rachel Carson's big point, of course—that long-lived toxic chemicals, such as chlorinated pesticides, do not remain diluted when they are broadcast out into the environment. Instead, they magnify—are concentrated—inexorably as they move up the food chain. Smelt to mackerel. Mackerel to tuna. Tuna to man.

It was not until I studied ecology in college, however, that the underlying cause of this phenomenon became clear to me. Biomagnification follows from two laws of physics that appear in the front chapters of most elementary science books: the idea that matter can neither be created nor destroyed, and the contrasting proposition that some amount of usable energy is always lost whenever it is transformed from one type to another. Taken together, these principles mean that fewer and fewer individuals can occupy each ascending link of the food chain because fewer and fewer calories (energy) are available to feed them. The total amount of a persistent pollutant (matter), however, doesn't change. Thus, as the rarer members of the higher links dine upon the commoners below them, poisons dispersed among the many are drawn up into the bodies of the few. This process of concentration can be described mathematically, and I spent a lot of hours working out such equations. As a general rule, persistent toxic chemicals concentrate by a factor of 10 to 100 with every link ascended.

By the time I was teaching premedical biology as a graduate student, food chains and other topics of ecology were once again relegated to the back of the book—and we almost never made it there by the end of the spring semester. My remaining connection to the concept of biomagnification was a yellowing poster displayed in a glass case outside the laboratory where I taught. It depicted the flow of DDT in a marine estuary, and at the top of poster all the arrows ended, once again, with man, who was shown as a muscular male silhouette. But then a passing comment during an ecology seminar made me look at that poster more closely. *"Man,"* a visiting professor intoned wryly, "is not at the top of the food chain. His breastfed infants are."

Of course! After the tuna sandwiches and glasses of cow's milk are all consumed, there still remains one more chance for the contaminants they carry to magnify, and that takes place inside the breasts of nursing mothers, where the calories gleaned from food are transferred into human milk. The human food chain depicted on the bulletin board was missing an entire trophic level—as was every other diagram I'd studied, from grade school to graduate school. The absent link was the last one, the top one, the one occupied by nursing babies.

Why was the final link in the chain left out?

As a nursing mother, I still wonder about this. Twenty years later I have yet to find a poster or textbook that places a picture of a suckling child at the pinnacle of a human food chain, one full link above adult men and women. The reason for this omission eludes me. Perhaps it reflects a larger cultural denial of breastfeeding. In any case, a failure to acknowledge the unique position of the breastfed infant within the ecological world prevents us from having an informed public conversation about a very real problem: the biomagnified presence of persistent toxic chemicals in breast milk.

When it comes to persistent organic pollutants (POPs), breast milk is the most contaminated of all human foods. It typically carries concentrations of organochlorine pollutants that are ten to twenty times higher than those in cow's milk. Indeed, prevailing levels of chemical contaminants in human milk often exceed legally allowable limits in commercial foodstuffs. One leading researcher concluded in 1996, "Breast milk, if regulated like infant formula, would commonly violate Food and Drug Administration action levels for poisonous or deleterious substances in food and could not be sold."

The hard fact of biomagnification means that breastfed babies have greater dietary exposures to toxic chemicals than their parents. On average, in industrialized countries, breastfed infants ingest each day fifty times more PCBs per pound of body weight than do their parents. The same is true for dioxins, a special class of chlorinated contaminants (discussed below in more detail). These exposures typically exceed the maximum recommended limits for adults, as determined by the World Health Organization. For example, breastfed infants in Great Britain receive seventeen times the so-called tolerable amount of PCBs and dioxins in their daily diets.

Breastfed babies also experience greater dietary exposures to certain toxic chemicals than their formula-fed counterparts. Infant formula carries significantly lower levels of persistent organic pollutants than breast milk. It is also less contaminated than whole milk from cows. All the fats in infant formula derive from plant oils such as sesame, corn, palm, and coconut, and these plants are further down on the food chain than either nursing mothers or milk-producing cows. Indeed, a 1998 study of eleven-month-olds in Germany found that organochlorine contaminants are ten to fifteen times higher in the bodies of nursed babies than of formula-fed babies. Another study found a twentyfold difference in organochlorine intake between breast- and bottle-fed infants.

The stubbornly long lives of persistent organic pollutants mean that these differences persist beyond infancy. In the Netherlands, researchers examined PCB levels among three-and-a-half-year-old Dutch children. Those who had been breastfed at least six weeks as infants had nearly four times more PCBs in their blood serum than children who had been bottle-fed. And the longer they breastfed, the higher their body burden. Other studies consistently show that the more mother's milk children consume, the higher the concentration of organochlorines in their tissues. Even at twenty-five years of age, men and women who were breastfed as infants have elevated levels of organochlorines. Dutch researchers estimate that between 12 and 14 percent of the body burden of organochlorine chemicals comes from breast milk.

None of these studies is in dispute. Indeed, their results have been corroborated by many other studies, some published years and years ago. The very first report of breast-milk contamination came in 1951, when DDT was discovered in the milk of black mothers living in Washington, D.C. The presence of PCBs in breast milk was first discovered in 1966, when, after finding traces of these chemicals in the tissues of a dead eagle, a Swedish researcher thought to test the milk of his own wife. By 1981, researchers had already identified 200 different chemical contaminants in the milk of U.S. mothers. Today, DDT (in the form of DDE, a metabolic breakdown product of DDT) still remains the most widespread contaminant in human milk around the world, and PCBs remain the most prevalent contaminant in the milk of mothers living in industrialized countries. In addition to DDT and PCBs, common contaminants of breast milk include flame retardants, fungicides, wood preservatives, termite poisons, mothproofing agents, toilet deodorizers, cable-insulating materials, dry-cleaning fluids, gasoline vapors, and the chemical by-products of garbage incineration.

My office shelves contain stacks and stacks of published reports documenting the presence of environmental chemicals in human milk. All together they would fill a couple of large suitcases. But seldom do nursing mothers hear about them. Not only are our breastfed children omitted from popular depictions of the human food chain, but we ourselves are excluded from discussions of breast-milk contamination. Some researchers, public health officials, and lactation advocates argue in their defense that publicizing the problem would only serve to frighten women away from breastfeeding. But keeping secrets is seldom a good public health strategy, for how will we solve a problem whose existence we don't acknowledge?

Here, in the back pages of my own book, I begin to cast about for a way to make visible the final ecological link of the human food chain. I am searching for words that will provoke courage instead of fear, conversation instead of silence. On the one hand we have the chemical adulteration of human milk. On the other is the bodily sacrament between mother and child. Can we speak of them both in the same breath? Can we look at one without turning away from the other?

When Faith is nine months old, we move from our crowded apartment at the top of Somerville's Prospect Hill to a log cabin tucked into a wooded hollow just outside Ithaca, New York. The move offers me affiliation to a research university and its libraries. It offers Jeff cheap studio space and a five-hour bus trip to Manhattan. It offers Faith room to crawl, a pursuit she has just begun to consider. But beyond all this reasonableness is a deeper yearning—to live closer to the source of things.

Even though I've happily lived in cities for most of my adult life, they remain for me a kind of confusing movie, a thrilling but complicated show with an excess of characters and subplots. By contrast, I can decipher most countrysides. With a little time, I can make sense out of the placement of drainage tiles, windbreaks, orchards, wood lots, and wellheads. I can read something into the architecture of trees and the direction of the prevailing wind. My intuition works better in the rural world. I enjoy coming upon a clearing in the woods and thinking, say, *perfect goldfinch habitat*, and then, a second later, glimpsing a bobbing flash of gold among the branches. Or sensing, half consciously, that this particular grove of firs would be a great place for deer to bed down—and then looking down and seeing bowls of flattened grass. Or wondering why there are no blackberries in a sunny spot near a tree fall—and then, suddenly, there are blackberries. I wish my daughter similar insights.

In the woods behind our rented cabin there are blackberries. And deer. And goldfinches. Our wellhead is by the maples. The drainage flows east toward the swamp, out of which rise the occasional heron and great-horned owl, and around which crowd beech and basswood. Cherries

and white pine prefer the higher ground nearer the house. You can estimate the age of a white pine by counting the number of its lateral
branches. Cherry bark looks like layers of potato chips. Young beeches
hang on to their leaves all winter. Honeybees are notably fond of basswood flowers.

Faith's first word is "tree."

While nursing on a blanket in the backyard, she points at the sun-
splintered pines and leafy maples, mouthing "tree tree" into my breast.
Sometimes I take this as an invitation to issue a small lecture on the
wonders of photosynthesis—explaining how leaves spin sunlight, air,
and water into food for all to eat. Sometimes I just laugh.

Within a week of our move to the cabin, Faith attempts and then
masters the art of crawling. And thus begins the Era of Relentless Exploration. Our first act of housewarming is to install barriers, bars,
locks, and latches throughout the cabin. Jeff and I get down on the floor
and crawl, too. We peer at cabinets, stairwells, electrical outlets, toilet
bowls, and window sills from Faith's perspective, trying to anticipate
accidents, hoping to prevent and forestall harm. "Better safe than
sorry," we say with a sigh to each other, as we notice yet another potential hazard that needs attention.

The farther Faith voyages away from me under her own power, the
more interested she becomes in nursing when she returns. Nursing, in
turn, fuels her courage for more daring forays. She and I are no longer
one body, nor even two intertwined, symbiotic organisms. I have
become a harbor, a destination point, a launching pad, a rest stop along
the highway. Still, the milk threads connect us, one to the other, as
powerfully as gravity.

It is June 1999. Each morning I carry Faith out to the road to fetch
the newspaper from its crooked plastic box. A food crisis in Belgium is
making international headlines. Dioxin- and PCB-tainted eggs have
been pulled from supermarket shelves and sent to incinerators. No one
knows exactly how they became contaminated, but the problem has
been traced back to a batch of animal feed. According to the leading
theory, someone dumped used industrial oil into a recycling vat for
used frying oil sometime last winter. A fat-rendering company then

sold the contaminated oil to makers of animal feed, who mixed it with grain and sold it to farms throughout the country. By March, Belgian chicken farmers began noticing that eggs weren't hatching, chicks had nervous disorders, and hens were dying. Lab tests showed PCB contamination and dioxin levels that were 1,500 times the legal limit. But the government delayed taking action for six weeks, withholding information from the public and offering false reassurances.

Each day the newspaper brings announcements of new recalls. Chickens join eggs on the condemned list. Then hogs. Then veal, beef, milk, and cheese. Then milk chocolate, mayonnaise, cookies, egg noodles, aged hams, and anything made with butter. An investigation reveals that some of the tainted animal feed was distributed also in France and the Netherlands. The United States moves to ban imports of meat, eggs, and poultry products from all of Europe. By mid-June, the scandal brings down the Belgian government. But even these drastic measures are too little too late. Most of the contaminated food has already been eaten. Researchers call for those exposed as fetuses, infants, and young children to be followed for at least ten years, calculating that a single egg could contribute as much as 20 percent of the dioxin burden of a three-year-old. Immunological, neurological, and behavioral effects in infants and children are "to be expected but cannot be quantified."

While I am screwing on outlet covers, Faith circles me like a satellite. I think about all the eggs I ate during my pregnancy. I wonder about the imported cheese we bought last month. But mostly, I think about nursing mothers in Belgium.

Dioxin is a paradox. It has been called the most toxic chemical on earth, and yet there is no consensus on what a dioxin molecule is or what it does exactly inside the human body. It is an industrial substance, but it's never manufactured intentionally (except for use in laboratories), and it has no known purpose.

Dioxins can be defined two ways—in terms of chemical makeup or of biological reactivity. Chemically speaking, there are seventy-five dioxins. They're all built like bicycles, with two sturdy carbon wheels held together by a frame of oxygens and a varying number of chlorine flags flying out from the fenders.

But not all chemical dioxins are dioxins. And some chemicals that are not dioxins are dioxins. That's because there is another definition that is based on function rather than form. Biologically speaking, a dioxin is any foreign substance capable of combining with, and thereby activating, a molecule inside the body called the Ah (**a**ryl **h**ydrocarbon) receptor. By this definition, only seven of the seventy-five chemical dioxins qualify—but in addition, 12 of the 209 PCBs and 10 of the 135 chemicals known as furans qualify. (Furans look a lot like chemical dioxins but have one less atom of oxygen holding their carbon wheels together.) Thus, from a biological point of view, there are twenty-nine dioxins.

They are not all equally potent. Toxicity depends on how tightly they can bind to the Ah receptor. The most tenacious by far is a particular dioxin called TCDD. This is the one spoken of in hushed tones as the most poisonous molecule ever synthesized, the one generally meant when people speak of dioxin. Through its unwavering attraction for the Ah receptor, TCDD is capable of altering physiological processes inside the human body at levels so minute as to be nearly undetectable—at levels of parts per trillion. Just testing a single biological sample for the presence of this dioxin requires two days of work and a piece of expensive equipment called a high-resolution mass spectrometer. There are only a handful of laboratories in the United States capable of doing it.

The Ah receptor itself was only discovered in 1976, but it has apparently been around a very long time. This protein complex has been identified in monkeys, whales, ferrets, gerbils, ducks, alligators, newts, trout, and lampreys. The last common ancestor of both vertebrate and invertebrate animals—which lived more than 540 million years ago—clearly had a gene from which the present Ah receptor genes have descended.

What this receptor actually does is not known, but researchers have identified a few of its key activities. We know that certain cellular signals are propagated through it. And we know that it regulates several genes, including those that oversee the metabolism of harmful chemical substances. Thus, dioxin, through its liaison with the Ah receptor, disrupts our body's detoxification system.

Dioxin is capable of wreaking other kinds of havoc. Exposure in laboratory animals reduces fertility, exacerbates endometriosis, induces birth defects, damages the liver, alters the development of genitals, slows growth, affects thyroid functioning, triggers learning deficits, and decreases the responsiveness of immune cells. Less is known about its effects in humans because controlled experiments are not possible. But evidence is emerging that dioxin tampers with the human thyroid, depresses the immune system, causes birth defects, and interferes with glucose metabolism, thereby contributing to diabetes. Dioxin perturbs every hormone system investigated. Oh, and it also causes cancer. In 1997, the World Health Organization declared TCDD a proven human carcinogen.

Adding to dioxin's mysteries is the fact that no one knows exactly where it all comes from. About twice as much currently rains down from the atmosphere onto the earth than can be accounted for by its known sources on the earth. Waste incinerators, especially those that burn chlorinated plastics, are known to be a leading producer. Dioxin is also a by-product of manufacturing certain chemicals, such as pesticides. Some is also generated during metal smelting, especially from scrap operations that burn plastic coatings off old copper wire. Backyard trash burning is another likely source. Some researchers suspect the atmosphere itself is creating dioxin out of the evaporated vapors of common wood preservatives.

However it is made, dioxin reaches us when it falls from the sky. Blades of grass absorb it, are eaten by cows, and then by us. Oceanic algae absorb it, are eaten by crustaceans, are eaten by fish, and then by us. The crusty fronds of lichens absorb it, are eaten by caribou, and then by us.

And then we feed our babies.

Having Faith (2001)

BARBARA KINGSOLVER

Barbara Kingsolver (b. 1955) took her master's degree in ecology and evolutionary biology from the University of Arizona; she then evolved into one of America's most beloved novelists, her work regularly atop the bestseller list. Her fiction often has environmental themes—*Prodigal Summer* (2000), for instance, set in the hills of southern Appalachia, makes the wildness and the domesticity of people and coyotes come urgently alive. Most recently, she's joined the burgeoning movement toward local food, with *Animal, Vegetable, Miracle* (2007), her widely read chronicle of a year spent eating close to home.

Knowing Our Place

I have places where all my stories begin.

One is a log cabin in a deep, wooded hollow at the end of Walker Mountain. This stoic little log house leans noticeably uphill, just as half the tobacco barns do in this rural part of southern Appalachia, where even gravity seems to have fled for better work in the city. Our cabin was built of chestnut logs in the late 1930s, when the American chestnut blight ran roughshod through every forest from Maine to Alabama, felling mammoth trees more extravagantly than the crosscut saw. Those of us who'll never get to see the spreading crown of an American chestnut have come to understand this blight as one of the great natural tragedies in our continent's history. But the pragmatic homesteaders who lived in this hollow at that time simply looked up and saw a godsend. They harnessed their mule and dragged the fallen soldiers down off the mountain to build their home.

Now it's mine. Between May and August, my family and I happily settle our lives inside its knobby, listing walls. We pace the floorboards of its porch while rain pummels the tin roof and slides off the steeply pitched eaves in a limpid sheet. I love this rain; my soul hankers for it. Through a curtain of it I watch the tulip poplars grow. When it stops, I listen to the woodblock concerto of dripping leaves and the first indignant Carolina wrens reclaiming their damp territories. Then come the wood thrushes, heartbreakers, with their minor-keyed harmonies as resonant as poetry. A narrow beam of sun files between the steep mountains, and butterflies traverse this column of light, from top to bottom to top again, like fish in a tall aquarium. My daughters hazard the damp grass to go hunt box turtles and crayfish, or climb into the barn loft to inhale the scent of decades-old tobacco. That particular dusty sweetness, among all other odors that exist, invokes the most reliable nostalgia for my own childhood; I'm slightly envious and have half a mind to run after the girls with my own stick for poking into crawdad holes. But mostly I am glad to watch them claim my own best secrets for themselves.

On a given day I may walk the half mile down our hollow to the mailbox, hail our neighbors, and exchange a farmer's evaluation of the weather (*terrible*; it truly is always either too wet or too dry in these marginal tobacco bottoms). I'll hear news of a house mysteriously put up for sale, a dog on the loose, or a memorable yard sale. My neighbors use the diphthong-rich vowels of the hill accent that was my own first language. My great-grandfather grew up in the next valley over from this one, but I didn't even know that I had returned to my ancestral home when I first came to visit. After I met, fell in love with, and married the man who was working this land, and agreed to share his home as he also shares mine in a distant place, I learned that I have close relatives buried all through these hollows. Unaccustomed as I am to encountering others with my unusual surname, I was startled to hear neighbors in this valley say, "Why, used to be you couldn't hardly walk around here without stepping on a Kingsolver." Something I can never explain, or even fully understand, pulled me back here.

Now I am mostly known around these parts by whichever of my relatives the older people still remember (one of them, my grandfather's uncle, was a physician who, in the early 1900s, attended nearly every birth in this county requiring a doctor's presence). Or else I'm known as the gal married to that young fella that fixed up the old Smyth cabin. We are suspected of being hard up (the cabin is quite small and rustic for a family of four) or a little deranged; neither alternative prevents our being sociably and heartily welcomed. I am nowhere more at home than here, among spare economies and extravagant yard sales glinting with jewel-toned canning jars.

But even so, I love to keep to our hollow. Hard up or deranged I may be, but I know my place, and sometimes I go for days with no worldly exchanges beyond my walk to the mailbox and a regular evening visit on our favorite neighbor's porch swing. Otherwise I'm content to listen for the communiqués of pileated woodpeckers, who stay hidden deep in the woods but hammer elaborately back and forth on their hollow trees like the talking drummers of Africa. Sometimes I stand on the porch and just stare, transfixed, at a mountainside that offers up more shades of green than a dictionary has words. Or else I step out with a hand trowel to tend the few relics of Mrs. Smyth's garden that have survived her: a June apple, a straggling, etiolated choir of August lilies nearly shaded out by the encroaching woods, and one heroic wisteria that has climbed hundreds of feet into the trees. I try to imagine the life of this woman who grew corn on a steeper slope than most people would be willing to climb on foot, and who still, at day's end, needed to plant her August lilies.

I take walks in the woods, I hang out our laundry, I read stories to my younger child, I hike down the hollow to a sunnier spot where I look after the garden that feeds us. And most of all, I write. I work in a rocking chair on the porch, or at a small blue desk facing the window. I write a good deal by hand, on paper, which—I somehow can't ever forget—is made from the macerated hearts of fallen trees.

The rest of the year, from school's opening day in autumn till its joyful release in May, I work at a computer on a broad oak desk by a different window, where the view is very different but also remarkable. In this house, which my predecessors constructed not from trees (which are scarce in the desert Southwest) but of sunbaked mud (which is not), we nestle into what's called in this region a *bosque*—that is, a narrow riparian woodland stitched like a green ribbon through the pink and tan quilt of the Arizona desert. The dominant trees are mesquite and cottonwood, with their contrasting personalities: the former swarthy with a Napoleonic stature and confidence, the latter tall and apprehensive, trembling at the first rumor of wind. Along with Mexican elder, buttonwillow, and bamboo, the mesquites and cottonwoods grow densely along a creek, creating a shady green glen that is stretched long and thin. Picture the rich Nile valley crossing the Saharan sands, and you will understand the fecundity of this place. Picture the air hose connecting a diver's lips to the oxygen tank, and you will begin to grasp the urgency. A riparian woodland, if it remains unbroken, provides a corridor through which a horde of fierce or delicate creatures may prowl, flutter, swim, or hop from the mountains down through the desert and back again. Many that follow this path—willow flycatchers, Apache trout—can live nowhere else on earth. An ill-placed dam, well, ranch, or subdivision could permanently end the existence of their kind.

I tread lightly here, with my heart in my throat, like a kid who's stumbled onto the great forbidden presence (maybe sex, maybe an orchestra rehearsal) of a more mature world. If I breathe, they'll know I'm here. From the window of my study I bear witness to a small, tunnelish clearing in the woods, shaded by overarching mesquite boughs and carpeted with wildflowers. Looming over this intimate foreground are mountains whose purple crowns rise to an altitude of nine thousand feet above the Tucson basin. In midwinter they often wear snow on their heads. In fall and early spring, blue-gray storms draw up into their canyons, throwing parts of the strange topography into high relief. Nearer at hand, deer and jackrabbits and javelina halt briefly to browse my clearing, then amble on up the corridor of forest. On insomniac nights I huddle in the small glow of my desk lamp, sometimes pausing the clicking of my keys to listen for great horned owls out there in the dark, or the ghostly, spine-chilling rasp of a barn owl on the hunt. By day, vermilion flycatchers and western tanagers flash their reds and yellows in the top of my tall window, snagging my attention whenever they dance into the part of my eyesight where color vision begins. A roadrunner drops from a tree to the windowsill, dashes across the window's full length, drops to the ground, and moves on, every single day, running this course as smoothly as a toy train on a track. White-winged doves feed and fledge their broods outside just inches from my desk, oblivious to my labors, preoccupied with their own.

One day not long ago I had to pull myself out of my writerly trance, having become aware of a presence over my left shoulder. I turned my head slowly to meet the gaze of an adolescent bobcat at my window. Whether he meant to be the first to read the story on my computer screen or was lured in by his own reflection in the quirky afternoon light, I can't say. I can tell you, though, that I looked straight into bronze-colored bobcat eyes and held my breath, for longer than I knew I could. After two moments (his and mine) that were surely not equal— for a predator must often pass hours without an eyeblink, while a human can grow restless inside ten seconds—we broke eye contact. He turned and minced away languidly, tail end flicking, for all the world a *cat*. I presume that he returned to the routine conjectures and risks and re-membered scents that make up his bobcat-life, and I returned to mine, mostly. But some part of my brain drifted after him for the rest of the day, stalking the taste of dove, examining a predator's patience from the inside.

It's a grand distraction, this window of mine. "Beauty and grace are performed," writes Annie Dillard, "whether or not we will or sense them. The least we can do is try to be there." I agree, and tend to work where the light is good. This window is *the world* opening onto *me*. I find *I* don't look out so much as *it* pours in.

What I mean to say is, I have come to depend on these places where I live and work. I've grown accustomed to looking up from the page and letting my eyes relax on a landscape upon which no human artifact intrudes. No steel, pavement, or streetlights, no architecture lovely or otherwise, no works of public art or private enterprise—no hominid agenda. I consider myself lucky beyond words to be able to go to work every morning with something like a wilderness at my elbow. In the way of so-called worldly things, I can't seem to muster a desire for cellular phones or cable TV or to drive anything flashier than a dirt-colored sedan older than the combined ages of my children. My tastes are much more extreme: I want wood-thrush poetry. I want mountains.

It would not be quite right to say I *have* these things. The places where I write aren't actually mine. In some file drawer we do have mortgages and deeds, pieces of paper (made of dead trees—mostly pine, I should think), which satisfy me in the same way that the wren yammering his territorial song from my rain gutter has satisfied himself that all is right in *his* world. I have my ostensible claim, but the truth is, these places own *me*: They hold my history, my passions, and my capacity for honest work. I find I do my best thinking when I am looking out over a clean plank of planet earth. Evidently I need this starting point—the world as it appeared before people bent it to their myriad plans—from which to begin dreaming up my own myriad, imaginary hominid agendas.

And that is exactly what I do: I create imagined lives. I write about people, mostly, and the things they contrive to do for, against, or with one another. I write about the likes of liberty, equality, and world peace, on an extremely domestic scale. I don't necessarily write about wilderness in general or about these two places that I happen to love in particular. Several summers ago on the cabin porch, surrounded by summertime yard sales and tobacco auctions, I wrote about *Africa*, for heaven's sake. I wrote long and hard and well until I ended each day panting and exhilarated, like a marathon runner. I wrote about a faraway place that I once knew well, long ago, and I have visited more recently on research trips, and whose history and particulars I read about in books until I dreamed in the language of elephants. I didn't need to *be* in Africa as I wrote that book; I needed only to be someplace where I could think straight, remember, and properly invent. I needed the blessed emptiness of mind that comes from birdsong and dripping trees. I needed to sleep at night in a square box made of chestnut trees who died of natural causes.

It is widely rumored, and also true, that I wrote my first novel in a closet. Before I get all rapturous and carried away here, I had better admit to that. The house was tiny, I was up late at night typing while another person slept, and there just wasn't any other place for me to go but that closet. The circumstances were extreme. And if I have to—if the Furies should take my freedom or my sight—I'll go back to writing in the dark. Fish gotta swim, birds gotta fly, writers will go to stupefying lengths to get the infernal roar of words out of their skulls and onto paper. Probably I've already tempted fate by announcing that I need to look upon wilderness in order to write. (I can hear those Furies sharpening their knives now, clucking, *Which shall it be, dearie? Penury or cataracts?*) Let me back up and say that I am breathless with gratitude for the collisions of choice and luck that have resulted in my being able to work under the full-on gaze of mountains and animate beauty. It's a privilege to live any part of one's life in proximity to nature. It is a privilege, apparently, even to know that nature is out there at all. In the summer of 1996 human habitation on earth made a subtle, uncelebrated passage from being mostly rural to being mostly urban. More than half of all humans now live in cities. The natural habitat of our species, then, officially, is steel, pavement, streetlights, architecture, and enterprise—the hominid agenda.

With all due respect for the wondrous ways people have invented to amuse themselves and one another on paved surfaces, I find that this exodus from the land makes me unspeakably sad. I think of the children who will never know, intuitively, that a flower is a plant's way of making love, or what *silence* sounds like, or that trees breathe out what we breathe in. I think of the astonished neighbor children who huddled around my husband in his tiny backyard garden, in the city where he lived years ago, clapping their hands to their mouths in pure dismay at seeing him pull *carrots* from the *ground*. (Ever the thoughtful teacher, he explained about fruits and roots and asked, "What other foods do you think might grow in the ground?" They knit their brows, conferred, and offered brightly, "Spaghetti?") I wonder what it will mean for people to forget that food, like rain, is not a product but a process. I wonder how they will imagine the infinite when they have never seen how the stars fill a dark night sky. I wonder how I can explain why a wood-thrush song makes my chest hurt to a populace for whom wood is a construction material and thrush is a tongue disease.

What we lose in our great human exodus from the land is a rooted sense, as deep and intangible as religious faith, of why we need to hold on to the wild and beautiful places that once surrounded us. We seem to succumb so easily to the prevailing human tendency to pave such places over, build subdivisions upon them, and name them The Willows, or Peregrine's Roost, or Elk Meadows, after whatever it was that got killed there. Apparently it's hard for us humans to doubt, even for a minute, that this program of plunking down our edifices at regular intervals over the entire landmass of planet earth is overall a good idea. To attempt to slow or change the program is a tall order.

Barry Lopez writes that if we hope to succeed in the endeavor of protecting natures other than our own, "it will require that we reimagine our lives. . . . It will require of many of us a humanity we've not yet mustered, and a grace we were not aware we desired until we had tasted it."

And yet no endeavor could be more crucial at this moment. Protecting the land that once provided us with our genesis may turn out to be the only real story there is for us. The land *still* provides our genesis, however we might like to forget that our food comes from dank, muddy earth, that the oxygen in our lungs was recently inside a leaf, and that every newspaper or book we may pick up (including this one, ultimately, though recycled) is made from the hearts of trees that died for the sake of our imagined lives. What you hold in your hands right now, beneath these words, is consecrated air and time and sunlight and, first of all, a place. Whether we are leaving it or coming into it, it's *here* that matters, it is place. Whether we understand where we are or don't, that is the story: To be *here* or not to be. Storytelling is as old as our need to remember where the water is, where the best food grows, where we find our courage for the hunt. It's as persistent as our desire to teach our children how to live in this place that we have known longer than they have. Our greatest and smallest explanations for ourselves grow from place, as surely as carrots grow in the dirt. I'm presuming to tell you something that I could not prove rationally but instead feel as a religious faith. I can't believe otherwise.

A world is looking over my shoulder as I write these words; my censors are bobcats and mountains. I have a place from which to tell my stories. So do you, I expect. We sing the song of our home because we are animals, and an animal is no better or wiser or safer than its habitat and its food chain. Among the greatest of all gifts is to know our place.

Oh, how can I say this: People *need* wild places. Whether or not we think we do, we *do*. We need to be able to taste grace and know once again that we desire it. We need to experience a landscape that is timeless, whose agenda moves at the pace of speciation and glaciers. To be surrounded by a singing, mating, howling commotion of other species, all of which love their lives as much as we do ours, and none of which could possibly care less about our economic status or our running day calendar. Wildness puts us in our place. It reminds us that our plans are small and somewhat absurd. It reminds us why, in those cases in which our plans might influence many future generations, we ought to choose carefully. Looking out on a clean plank of planet earth, we can get shaken right down to the bone by the bronze-eyed possibility of lives that are not our own.

Small Wonder (2002)

MICHAEL POLLAN

Some of the best writing in the country right now can be found in a handful of slick magazines—the *Atlantic*, *The New Yorker*, *Harper's*, *The New York Times Magazine*. That's the world that Michael Pollan (b. 1955) came from, but in recent years, while still very much a reporter, he has grown steadily more pointed in his critique of the state of American agriculture and the economy and politics that built it. His most recent book, *The Omnivore's Dilemma* (2006), demonstrates that industrial agriculture has sickened both people and the landscape, moving the country away from diverse and sturdy farming tradition toward a few crops (principally corn) that are more feedstock than food. He avoids the sentimental (his first book, the powerful 1991 *Second Nature*, is an able attack on the idea that there's something peculiarly righteous about wildness), but with each passing year he becomes more of an environmental activist, most recently suggesting that the federal farm bill should be considered a food bill and used as a vehicle to transform the rural landscape and the dinner table. His writing never descends to polemic, nor strays to abstract generalization—it's often wry and always detailed and alive.

from **The Omnivore's Dilemma**

Traveling from the ranch to the feedyard, as 534 and I both did (in separate vehicles) the first week of January, feels a lot like going from the country to the big city. A feedlot is very much a premodern city, however, teeming and filthy and stinking, with open sewers, unpaved roads, and choking air rendered visible by dust.

The urbanization of the world's livestock being a fairly recent historical development, it makes a certain sense that cow towns like Poky Feeders would recall human cities centuries ago, in the days before

948

modern sanitation. As in fourteenth-century London, say, the workings of the metropolitan digestion remain vividly on display, the foodstuffs coming in, the streams of waste going out. The crowding into tight quarters of recent arrivals from all over, together with the lack of sanitation, has always been a recipe for disease. The only reason contemporary animal cities aren't as plague-ridden or pestilential as their medieval human counterparts is a single historical anomaly: the modern antibiotic.

I spent the better part of a day at Poky Feeders, walking the streets, cattle watching, looking up my steer, and touring local landmarks like the towering feed mill. In any city it's easy to lose track of nature—of the transactions between various species and the land on which everything ultimately depends. Back on the ranch the underlying ecological relationship could not have been more legible: It is a local food chain built upon grass and the ruminants that can digest grass, and it draws its energy from the sun. But what about here?

As the long shadow of the mill suggests, the feedlot is a city built upon America's mountain of surplus corn—or rather, corn plus the various pharmaceuticals a ruminant must have if it is to tolerate corn. Yet, having started out from George Naylor's farm, I understood that the corn on which this place runs is implicated in a whole other set of ecological relationships powered by a very different source of energy—the fossil fuel it takes to grow all that corn. So if the modern CAFO is a city built upon commodity corn, it is a city afloat on an invisible sea of petroleum. How this peculiar state of affairs came to seem sensible is a question I spent my day at Poky trying to answer.

It was only natural that I start my tour at the feed mill, the feedlot's thundering hub, where three meals a day for thirty-seven thousand animals are designed and mixed by computer. A million pounds of feed pass through the mill each day. Every hour of every day a tractor trailer pulls up to the loading dock to deliver another fifty tons of corn. The driver opens a valve in the belly of the truck and a golden stream of grain—one thin rivulet of the great corn river coursing out of the Middle West—begins to flow, dropping down a chute into the bowels of the mill. Around to the other side of the building, tanker trucks back up to silo-shaped tanks into which they pump thousands of gallons of liquefied fat and protein supplements. In a shed attached to the mill sit vats of liquid vitamins and synthetic estrogen beside pallets stacked with fifty-pound sacks of antibiotics—Rumensin and Tylosin. Along with alfalfa hay and silage (for roughage), all these ingredients will be automatically blended and then piped into the parade of dump trucks that three times a day fan out from here to keep Poky's eight and a half miles of trough filled.

The feed mill's pulsing din is the sound of two giant steel rollers turning against one another twelve hours a day, crushing steamed corn kernels into warm and fragrant flakes. (Flaking the corn makes it easier for cattle to digest it.) This was the only feed ingredient I sampled, and it wasn't half bad; not as crisp as a Kellogg's flake, but with a cornier flavor. I passed on the other ingredients: the liquefied fat (which on today's menu is beef tallow, trucked in from one of the nearby slaughterhouses), and the protein supplement, a sticky brown goop consisting of molasses and urea. The urea is a form of synthetic nitrogen made from natural gas, similar to the fertilizer spread on George Naylor's fields.

Before being put on this highly concentrated diet, new arrivals to the feedyard are treated to a few days of fresh long-stemmed hay. (They don't eat on the long ride and can lose up to one hundred pounds, so their rumens need to be carefully restarted.) Over the next several weeks they'll gradually step up to a daily ration of thirty-two pounds of feed, three-quarters of which is corn—nearly a half bushel a day.

What got corn onto the menu at this and almost every other American feedlot is price, of course, but also USDA policy, which for decades has sought to help move the mountain of surplus corn by passing as much of it as possible through the digestive tracks of food animals, who can convert it into protein.

We've come to think of "corn-fed" as some kind of old-fashioned virtue, which it may well be when you're referring to Midwestern children, but feeding large quantities of corn to cows for the greater part of their lives is a practice neither particularly old or virtuous. Its chief advantage is that cows fed corn, a compact source of caloric energy, get fat quickly; their flesh also marbles well, giving it a taste and texture American consumers have come to like. Yet this corn-fed meat is demonstrably less healthy for us, since it contains more saturated fat and less omega-3 fatty acids than the meat of animals fed grass. A growing body of research suggests that many of the health problems associated with eating beef are really problems with corn-fed beef. (Modern-day hunter-gatherers who subsist on wild meat don't have our rates of heart disease.) In the same way ruminants are ill adapted to eating corn, humans in turn may be poorly adapted to eating ruminants that eat corn.

Yet the USDA's grading system has been designed to reward marbling (a more appealing term than "intramuscular fat," which is what it is) and thus the feeding of corn to cattle. Indeed, corn has become so deeply engrained in the whole system of producing beef in America that whenever I raised any questions about it among ranchers or feedlot operators or animal scientists, people look at me as if I'd just arrived from another planet. (Or perhaps from Argentina, where excellent steaks are produced on nothing but grass.)

The economic logic behind corn is unassailable, and on a factory farm there is no other kind. Calories are calories, and corn is the cheapest, most convenient source of calories on the market. Of course, it was the same industrial logic—protein is protein—that made feeding rendered cow parts back to cows seem like a sensible thing to do, until scientists figured out that this practice was spreading bovine spongiform encephalopathy (BSE), more commonly known as mad cow disease. Rendered bovine meat and bonemeal represented the cheapest, most convenient way of satisfying a cow's protein requirement (never mind these animals were herbivores by evolution) and so appeared on the daily menus of Poky and most other feedyards until the FDA banned the practice in 1997.

We now understand that while at a reductive, molecular level protein may indeed be protein, at an ecological or species level, this isn't quite true. As cannibal tribes have discovered, eating the flesh of one's own species carries special risks of infection. Kuru, a disease bearing a striking resemblance to BSE, spread among New Guinea tribesmen who ritually ate the brains of their dead kin. Some evolutionary biologists believe that evolution selected against cannibalism as a way to avoid such infections; animals' aversion to their own feces, and the carcasses of their species, may represent a similar strategy. Through natural selection animals have developed a set of hygiene rules, functioning much like taboos. One of the most troubling things about factory farms is how cavalierly they flout these evolutionary rules, forcing animals to overcome deeply engrained aversions. We make them trade their instincts for antibiotics.

Though the industrial logic that made feeding cattle to cattle seem like a good idea has been thrown into doubt by mad cow disease, I was surprised to learn it hadn't been discarded. The Food and Drug Administration (FDA) ban on feeding ruminant protein to ruminants makes an exception for blood products and fat; my steer will probably dine on beef tallow recycled from the very slaughterhouse he's heading to in June. ("Fat is fat," the feedlot manager shrugged, when I raised an eyebrow.) Though Poky doesn't do it, the rules still permit feedlots to feed nonruminant animal protein to ruminants. Feather meal and chicken litter (that is, bedding, feces, and discarded bits of feed) are accepted cattle feeds, as are chicken, fish, and pig meal. Some public health experts worry that since the bovine meat and bonemeal that cows used to eat is now being fed to chickens, pigs, and fish, infectious prions could find their way back into cattle when they're fed the protein of the animals that have been eating them.

Before mad cow disease remarkably few people in the cattle business, let alone the general public, comprehended the strange new semicircular food chain that industrial agriculture had devised for the beef animal—and so, in turn, for the beef eater. When I mentioned to Rich Blair how surprised I'd been to learn cattle were eating cattle, he said, "To tell you the truth, it was kind of a shock to me, too."

Compared to all the other things we feed cattle these days, corn seems positively wholesome. And yet it too violates the biological or evolutionary logic of bovine digestion. During my day at Poky I spent a few hours with Dr. Mel Metzin, the staff veterinarian, learning more than any beef eater really should know about the gastrointestinal life of the modern cow. Dr. Mel, as he's known at Poky, oversees a team of eight cowboys who spend their days riding the yard's dusty streets, spotting sick animals and bringing them into Poky's three "hospitals" for treatment. Most of the health problems that afflict feedlot cattle can be traced either directly or indirectly to their diet. "They're made to eat forage," Dr. Metzin explained, "and we're making them eat grain."

"It's not that they can't adjust," he continues, "and now we're breeding cattle to do well in a feedyard." One way to look at the breeding work going on at ranches like the Blairs' is that the contemporary beef cow is being selected for the ability to eat large quantities of corn and efficiently convert it to protein without getting too sick. (These, after all, are precisely the genes prized in 534's father, Gar Precision 1680.) The species is evolving, in other words, to help absorb the excess biomass coming off America's cornfields. But the cow's not there quite yet, and a great many feedlot cattle—virtually all of them to one degree or another, according to several animal scientists I talked to—are simply sick.

Bloat is perhaps the most serious thing that can go wrong with a ruminant on corn. The fermentation in the rumen produces copious amounts of gas, which is normally expelled by belching during rumination. But when the diet contains too much starch and too little roughage, rumination all but stops, and a layer of foamy slime forms in the rumen that can trap the gas. The rumen inflates like a balloon until it presses against the animal's lungs. Unless action is taken promptly to relieve the pressure (usually by forcing a hose down the animal's esophagus), the animal suffocates.

A concentrated diet of corn can also give a cow acidosis. Unlike our own highly acid stomachs, the normal pH of a rumen is neutral. Corn renders it acidic, causing a kind of bovine heartburn that in some cases can kill the animal, but usually just makes him sick. Acidotic animals go off their feed, pant and salivate excessively, paw and scratch their bellies, and eat dirt. The condition can lead to diarrhea, ulcers, bloat, rumenitis, liver disease, and a general weakening of the immune system that leaves the animal vulnerable to the full panoply of feedlot diseases—pneumonia, coccidiosis, enterotoxemia, feedlot polio. Much like modern humans, modern cattle are susceptible to a set of relatively new diseases of civilization—assuming, that is, we're willing to put the modern feedlot under the rubric of civilization.

Cattle rarely live on feedlot diets for more than 150 days, which might be about as much as their systems can tolerate. "I don't know how long you could feed them this ration before you'd see problems," Dr. Metzin said; another vet told me the diet would eventually "blow out their livers" and kill them. Over time the acids eat away at the rumen wall, allowing bacteria to enter the animal's bloodstream. These microbes wind up in the liver, where they form abscesses and impair the liver's function. Between 15 percent and 30 percent of feedlot cows are found at slaughter to have abscessed livers; Dr. Mel told me that in some pens the figure runs as high as 70 percent.

What keeps a feedlot animal healthy—or healthy enough—are antibiotics. Rumensin buffers acidity in the rumen, helping to prevent bloat and acidosis, and Tylosin, a form of erythromycin, lowers the incidence of liver infection. Most of the antibiotics sold in America today end up in animal feed, a practice that, it is now generally acknowledged (except in agriculture), is leading directly to the evolution of new antibiotic-resistant superbugs. In the debate over the use of antibiotics in agriculture, a distinction is usually made between their clinical and nonclinical uses. Public health advocates don't object to treating sick animals with antibiotics; they just don't want to see the drugs lose their effectiveness because factory farms are feeding them to healthy animals to promote growth. But the use of antibiotics in feedlot cattle confounds this distinction. Here the drugs are plainly being used to treat sick animals, yet the animals probably wouldn't be sick if not for the diet of grain we feed them.

I asked Dr. Mel what would happens if drugs like Rumensin and Tylosin were banned from cattle feed, as some public health experts advocate. "We'd have a high death rate [it's currently about 3 percent, matching the industry average] and poorer performing cattle. We just couldn't feed them as hard." The whole system would have to change—and slow down.

"Hell, if you gave them lots of grass and space, I wouldn't have a job."

My first impression of pen 63, where my steer is spending his last five months, was, *Not a bad little piece of real estate, all considered.* The pen is far enough from the feed mill to be fairly quiet and it has a water view of what I thought was a pond or reservoir until I noticed the brown scum. The body of water is what is known, in the geography of CAFOs, as a manure lagoon. I asked the feedlot manager why they didn't just spray the liquefied manure on neighboring farms. The farmers don't want it, he explained. The nitrogen and phosphorus levels are so high that spraying the crops would kill them. He didn't say that feedlot wastes also contain heavy metals and hormone residues, persistent chemicals that end up in waterways downstream, where scientists have found fish and amphibians exhibiting abnormal sex characteristics. CAFOs like Poky transform what at the proper scale would be a precious source of fertility—cow manure—into toxic waste.

The pen 534 lives in is surprisingly spacious, about the size of a hockey rink, with a concrete feed bunk along the road, and a fresh water trough out back. I climbed over the railing and joined the ninety steers, which, en masse, retreated a few lumbering steps, and then stopped to see what I would do.

I had on the same carrot-colored sweater I'd worn to the ranch in South Dakota, hoping to elicit some glint of recognition from my steer. I couldn't find him at first; all the faces staring at me were either completely black or bore an unfamiliar pattern of white marks. And then I spotted him—the three white blazes—way off in the back. As I gingerly stepped toward him the quietly shuffling mass of black cowhide between us parted, and there stood 534 and I, staring dumbly at one another. Glint of recognition? None, none whatsoever. I told myself not to take it personally; 534 and his pen mates have been bred for their marbling, after all, not their ability to form attachments.

I noticed that 534's eyes looked a little bloodshot. Dr. Metzin had told me that some animals are irritated by feedlot dust. The problem is especially serious in the summer months, when the animals kick up clouds of the stuff and workers have to spray the pens with water to keep it down. I had to remind myself that this is not ordinary dirt dust, inasmuch as the dirt in a feedyard is not ordinary dirt; no, this is fecal dust. But apart from the air quality, how did feedlot life seem to be agreeing with 534? I don't know enough about the emotional life of a steer to say with confidence that 534 was miserable, bored, or indifferent, but I would not say he looked happy.

He's clearly eating well, though. My steer had put on a couple hundred pounds since we'd last met, and he looked it: thicker across the shoulder and round as a barrel through the middle. He carried himself more like a steer now than a calf, even though his first birthday was still two months away. Dr. Metzin complimented me on his size and conformation. "That's a handsome-looking beef you got there." (Shucks.)

If I stared at my steer hard enough, I could imagine the white lines of the butcher's chart dissecting his black hide: rump roast, flank steak, standing rib, tenderloin, brisket. One way of looking at 534—the feedlot way, the industrial way—was as a most impressive machine for turning number 2 field corn into cuts of beef. Every day between now and his slaughter in six months, 534 will convert thirty-two pounds of feed into four pounds of gain—new muscle, fat, and bone. This at least is how 534 appears in the computer program I'd seen at the mill: the ratio of feed to gain that determines his efficiency. (Compared to other food animals, cattle are terribly inefficient: The ratio of feed to flesh in chicken, the most efficient animal by this measure, is two pounds of corn to one of meat, which is why chicken costs less than beef.) Poky Feeders is indeed a factory, transforming—as fast as bovinely possible—cheap raw materials into a less cheap finished product, through the mechanism of bovine metabolism.

Yet metaphors of the factory and the machine obscure as much as they reveal about the creature standing before me. He has, of course, another, quite different identity—as an animal, I mean, connected as all animals must be to certain other animals and plants and microbes, as well as to the earth and the sun. He's a link in a food chain, a thread in a far-reaching web of ecological relationships. Looked at from this perspective, everything going on in this cattle pen appears quite different, and not nearly as far removed from our world as this manure-encrusted patch of ground here in Nowhere, Kansas, might suggest.

For one thing, the health of these animals is inextricably linked to our own by that web of relationships. The unnaturally rich diet of corn that undermines a steer's health fattens his flesh in a way that undermines the health of the humans who will eat it. The antibiotics these animals consume with their corn at this very moment are selecting, in their gut and wherever else in the environment they end up, for new strains of resistant bacteria that will someday infect us and withstand the drugs we depend on to treat that infection. We inhabit the same microbial ecosystem as the animals we eat, and whatever happens in it also happens to us.

Then there's the deep pile of manure on which I stand, in which 534 sleeps. We don't know much about the hormones in it—where they will end up, or what they might do once they get there—but we do know something about the bacteria, which can find their way from the manure on the ground to his hide and from there into our hamburgers. The speed at which these animals will be slaughtered and processed— four hundred an hour at the plant where 534 will go—means that sooner or later some of the manure caked on these hides gets into the meat we eat. One of the bacteria that almost certainly resides in the manure I'm standing in is particularly lethal to humans. *Escherichia coli* 0157:H7 is a relatively new strain of the common intestinal bacteria (no one had seen it before 1980) that thrives in feedlot cattle, 40 percent of which carry it in their gut. Ingesting as few as ten of these microbes can cause a fatal infection; they produce a toxin that destroys human kidneys.

Most of the microbes that reside in the gut of a cow and find their way into our food get killed off by the strong acids in our stomachs, since they evolved to live in the neutral pH environment of the rumen. But the rumen of a corn-fed feedlot steer is nearly as acidic as our own, and in this new, man-made environment new acid-resistant strains of *E. coli*, of which 0157:H7 is one, have evolved—yet another creature recruited by nature to absorb the excess biomass coming off the Farm Belt. The problem with these bugs is that they can shake off the acid bath in our stomachs—and then go on to kill us. By acidifying the rumen with corn we've broken down one of our food chain's most important barriers to infection. Yet another solution turned into a problem.

We've recently discovered that this process of acidification can be reversed, and that doing so can greatly diminish the threat from *E. coli* 0157:H7. Jim Russell, a USDA microbiologist on the faculty at Cornell, has found that switching a cow's diet from corn to grass or hay for a few days prior to slaughter reduces the population of *E. coli* 0157:H7 in the animal's gut by as much as 80 percent. But such a solution (*Grass?!*) is considered wildly impractical by the cattle industry and (therefore) by the USDA. Their preferred solution for dealing with bacterial contamination is irradiation—essentially, to try to sterilize the manure getting into the meat.

So much comes back to corn, this cheap feed that turns out in so many ways to be not cheap at all. While I stood in pen 63 a dump truck pulled up alongside the feed bunk and released a golden stream of feed. The black mass of cowhide moved toward the trough for lunch. The $1.60 a day I'm paying for three meals a day here is a bargain only by the narrowest of calculations. It doesn't take into account, for example, the cost to the public health of antibiotic resistance or food poisoning by *E. coli* 0157:H7. It doesn't take into account the cost to taxpayers of the farm subsidies that keep Poky's raw materials cheap. And it certainly doesn't take into account all the many environmental costs incurred by cheap corn.

I stood alongside 534 as he lowered his big head into the stream of fresh grain. How absurd, I thought, the two of us standing hock-deep in manure in this godforsaken place, overlooking a manure lagoon in the middle of nowhere somewhere in Kansas. Godforsaken perhaps, and yet not apart, I realized, as I thought of the other places connected to this place by the river of commodity corn. Follow the corn from this bunk back to the fields where it grows and I'd find myself back in the middle of that 125,000-mile-square monoculture, under a steady rain of pesticide and fertilizer. Keep going, and I could follow the nitrogen runoff from that fertilizer all the way down the Mississippi into the Gulf of Mexico, adding its poison to an eight-thousand-square-mile zone so starved of oxygen nothing but algae can live in it. And then go farther still, follow the fertilizer (and the diesel fuel and the petrochemical pesticides) needed to grow the corn all the way to the oil fields of the Persian Gulf.

I don't have a sufficiently vivid imagination to look at my steer and see a barrel of oil, but petroleum is one of the most important ingredients in the production of modern meat, and the Persian Gulf is surely a link in the food chain that passes through this (or any) feedlot. Steer 534 started his life part of a food chain that derived all of its energy from the sun, which nourished the grasses that nourished him and his mother. When 534 moved from ranch to feedlot, from grass to corn, he joined an industrial food chain powered by fossil fuel—and therefore defended by the U.S. military, another never-counted cost of cheap food. (One-fifth of America's petroleum consumption goes to producing and transporting our food.) After I got home from Kansas, I asked an economist who specializes in agriculture and energy if it might be possible to calculate precisely how much petroleum it will take to grow my steer to slaughter weight. Assuming 534 continues to eat twenty-five pounds of corn a day and reaches a weight of twelve hundred pounds, he will have consumed in his lifetime the equivalent of thirty-five gallons of oil—nearly a barrel.

So this is what commodity corn can do to a cow: industrialize the miracle of nature that is a ruminant, taking this sunlight- and prairie grass-powered organism and turning it into the last thing we need: another fossil fuel machine. This one, however, is able to suffer.

Standing there in the pen alongside my steer, I couldn't imagine ever wanting to eat the flesh of one of these protein machines. Hungry was the last thing I felt. Yet I'm sure that after enough time goes by, and the stink of this place is gone from my nostrils, I will eat feedlot beef again. Eating industrial meat takes an almost heroic act of not knowing or, now, forgetting. But I left Poky determined to follow this meat to a meal on a table somewhere, to see this food chain at least that far. I was curious to know what feedlot beef would taste like now, if I could taste the corn or even, since taste is as much a matter of what's in the head as it is about molecules dancing on the tongue, some hint of the petroleum. "You are what you eat" is a truism hard to argue with, and yet it is, as a visit to a feedlot suggests, incomplete, for you are what what you eat eats, too. And what we are, or have become, is not just meat but number 2 corn and oil.

The Omnivore's Dilemma (2006)

PAUL HAWKEN

Paul Hawken (b. 1946) has been at the center of the environmental movement in recent decades. A one-time entrepreneur (his Smith & Hawken catalogue company has outfitted many a well-heeled gardener), he has focused much of his thinking on the relations between ecology and business: President Clinton called his *Natural Capitalism* (1999), co-written with Amory and L. Hunter Lovins, one of the "five most important books in the world today." The chapter that follows comes from his most recent book, *Blessed Unrest* (2007), which chronicles the rise of what Hawken thinks is something very new: a loosely organized, worldwide movement of people intent on preserving and restoring their communities and battling corporate globalization. Published at a moment when some had begun to despair in the face of the seeming inevitability of global climate change, it came as a shot in the arm to a resurgent environmental movement—and a strong reminder that that movement only made sense coupled with the fight for the needs of the world's overwhelming poor majority.

from **Blessed Unrest**

I recently received three annual reports from movement organizations in the same week: the Audubon Society, Friends of the Earth, and the India Resource Center. The centennial Audubon annual report was a graphic masterpiece, printed in soft sepia tones on recycled paper. Inside were photographs from the Centennial Gala, featuring the Rockefellers and other black-tie attendees. At the back of the report was the list of the society's 44 vice presidents; 34 directors; 127 state offices, centers, and sanctuaries; and 492 chapters in fifty states, from the Arctic Audubon Society in Alaska to the Florida Keys Audubon Society, 3,457 miles away. One can only imagine how many flyways, species, sinkholes, inlets, forests, lakes, riparian corridors, and marine estuaries Audubon is able to keep an eye on, supported as it is by 254 corporations and 528 foundations, and more than half a million members.

The Friends of the Earth report was issued on a CD, to save paper, and listed sister organizations in seventy countries, which involved over a million activists. Its assets (U.S. only) are a half percent of those of the Audubon Society. In fact, Friends of the Earth has fewer staff in the United States than Audubon has directors, yet in the prior year it managed to stop snowmobiles in Rocky Mountain National Park, pressure JP Morgan to adopt environmental standards in lending, block logging in the Green Mountain National Forest, help obtain a ban on jet skis to protect manatees in the Florida Keys, help push through new rules in the International Maritime Organization on ship emissions, block the planting of biopharmaceutical rice in Missouri, lobby against Newmont Mining's plans in Peru, win a clean-air lawsuit against the EPA in the federal court of appeals, run advertisements in the *New York Times* against Ford Motor Company to improve its fleet's fuel economy, urge the World Bank to increase its funding of renewable energy projects, and more.

The third report I received was from the one-person India Resource Center, and it was e-mailed. IRC's total budget is equivalent to the salary of one staff person at Audubon. It is part of a larger network of NGOs taking on the world's biggest beverage company, Coca-Cola, over concerns about water pollution, toxicity, product safety, and worker rights. The movement against Coke is emblematic of how the smallest organizations confront large institutions. A coalition of tiny organizations comprising farmers, indigenous people, students, and Dalits (formerly untouchables) is using sit-ins, protests, Web sites, and phone cards to create a formidable international grassroots campaign against Coca-Cola that is singeing its global reputation and costing it tens of millions of dollars.[1]

The original protest began in Plachimada, Kerala, instigated by an Adavasi (indigenous) widow named Mylamma, who had farmed land

---

1. Steve Stecklow, "Virtual Battle: How a Global Web of Activists Gives Coke Problems in India," *The Wall Street Journal*, June 7, 2005, A1.

adjacent to a new Coca-Cola bottling plant all her life. Two years after the factory went into production in March 2000, the water table dropped from 150 to 500 feet, drying up the farmers' wells, and the water that Mylamma and the villagers were able to obtain was polluted and undrinkable. In 2003 the district medical officer declared the water hazardous to human health. Mylamma believed that Coca-Cola's pumping of groundwater was responsible for the water situation and led a series of protests that culminated in the local village council's canceling the company's license to operate. Coca-Cola sued, claiming the local council had no jurisdiction, but was turned down by the High Court, which ruled that the company had to obtain its water in some other manner because groundwater belonged to all of the community, and that it could draw no more groundwater from its thirty-four-acre site than could a farmer using it for agriculture.[2]

In 2003 the Center for Science and the Environment (CSE), a nonprofit institute in New Delhi, published analyses of popular soft drinks (including Coke and Pepsi) showing that they contained levels of pesticides, including DDT, lindane, and malathion, eleven to seventy times higher than those established by E.U. drinking water standards.[3] (CSE's analysis of American Coke and Pepsi showed zero pesticide residues.) The Indian parliament banned Coke and Pepsi from its cafeterias, and ten thousand schools and colleges on the subcontinent became Coke/Pepsi-Free Zones. The U.S. companies fought back. Allegedly, Secretary of State Colin Powell intervened at the highest levels. Lawyers swept in from the United States to lobby Indian officials. A massive ad campaign was mounted featuring Aamir Khan, one of the most popular film stars in India, assuring his countrymen that Coke was safe. In 2006 the tests were repeated, and Pepsi and Coke again contained the highest pesticide residues of all soft drinks analyzed.[4] Adding to the controversy, Coca-Cola had been distributing wastes

2. C. Surendranath, "Coca-Cola: Continuing Battle in Kerala," India Resource Center, July 10, 2003, http://www.indiaresource.org/campaigns/coke/

3. Stecklow, "Virtual Battle," A1.

4. "The Street Fight," *Down to Earth: Science and Environment Online*, Aug. 15, 2006, Center for Science and the Environment, New Delhi.

from its bottling plants containing lead, chromium, and cadmium to local farmers for use as fertilizer.

The India Coca-Cola protest movement runs on very little money, whereas Coca-Cola has a market capitalization exceeding $100 billion. The protests have spread to soft-drink plants throughout India and all the way to college and university campuses in South America, the United States, and Europe, spawning an organization called the Student Coalition to Cut Contracts with Cola-Cola. Michigan, Swarthmore, Bard, and other colleges have banned the sale of Coca-Cola products because of the company's environmental practices and violations of human rights. Despite such annoyances, the company's worst enemy has proven to be itself, not global activists. Responding to questions from a *Wall Street Journal* reporter, the company's spokesperson was caught dissembling, if not lying, about analyses of the heavy metal content of processed sludge distributed to farmers.[5] There is a perverse naivete in Coca-Cola's response, the credulity that comes with having read its own press releases for so long, that prohibits it from recognizing the obvious: the company is harming the environment and people. Coke sees no contradiction in promoting sixty-four-ounce plastic bottles of Coke containing more than a half-pound of sugar to American teenagers who drink sixty gallons of soft drinks every year, despite the rapid increase of obesity and diabetes in the United States, or in having Olympic athletes promote the product. Coke's so-called natural products, such as Fruitopia, contain 5 percent juice and even more sugar than a Classic Coke. Coke may not notice the 44 billion soft drink cans tossed into landfills and apparently looked in the opposite direction when offering farmers cadmium-tainted wastes from its bottling plant. It has no problem with its India Web site asserting, "Sugar does not cause heart disease, cancer, diabetes or obesity," a statement of farcical disregard for nutrition and medical science. The problems it faces are pathologies of intent and power.

The Coca-Cola conflict concerns the rights of a community versus the rights of a corporation, and in that respect is emblematic of NGO campaigns throughout the world. Coca-Cola has appealed to the Indian

5. Stecklow, "Virtual Battle," A1.

Supreme Court, hoping to overturn the High Court ruling, and in so doing it is pursuing a strategy universally employed by corporations: resorting to higher realms of governance if local bodies impede corporate goals. In 2005 Monsanto, one of the two largest companies in the world selling genetically modified seeds, pressured fourteen state legislatures to pass laws that would prohibit local restrictions on genetically engineered crops after they lost county elections that called for their ban. In 2005 factory farm and food lobbyists, including Coca-Cola, Pepsi, and Unilever, began to push legislation through the U.S. Congress that would overturn more than seventy-six different state laws regulating labels, toxins, and other issues of food safety. The federal government has always been able to set minimum safety standards, but under the National Food Uniformity Act of 2005, the logic is reversed. This legislation—which could also be called the Faster Food Bill—would prevent a state from setting different standards from the FDA's, and has passed the House at the time of this writing. Under California state law, for example, fish containing dangerous levels of mercury must be so labeled, a vital health issue with respect to food choices for pregnant women and their unborn children. Under the new federal law, such labeling would be forbidden. New legislation being passed and proposed increases the rights of business at the expense of consumers, much as WTO rulings can override national standards, as discussed earlier.

Karl Marx had one goal: to change the world. He was dismissive of those who spent their lives in an ongoing effort to interpret the world because he had the luxury of believing there was only one correct interpretation. Such a narrow view is common to ideologies, and it is why many diverse groups are arising in opposition to this sort of rigid thinking. Ideologies exclude openness, diversity, resiliency, and multiplicity, the very qualities that nourish life in any system, be it ecosystem, immune system, or social system.[6] Hundreds of thousands of

6. Philip Ball, *Critical Mass, How One Thing Leads to Another* (New York: Farrar, Straus and Giroux, 2004), pp. 459–60.

small groups are trying to ignite an array of ideas in the world, fanning them like embers. Ideas are living things; they can be changed and adapted, and can grow. Ideas do not belong to anyone, and require no approval. This may sound ethereal but it is in fact the essence of praxis, the application of grassroots democracy in a violent and exploitative age.

Some would argue that it is counterproductive to conflate all the different organizations and types of organizations into a single movement, that it is self-evident that such divergent aims cannot create an effective, unified body. It's true that pluralism, the de facto tactic of a million small organizations, functions best in a society that cultivates diversity, dialogue, and collaboration; in a you-are-either-with-us-or-against-us society, small, single-issue organizations are effectively marginalized. In the United States, the environmental and social justice movements emerged in what was a pluralistic society. Because that is increasingly not the case, the stratagems and goals of the movement may be inadequate to the increasing centralization of power. Volunteer organizations that focus on the health of a stream or riparian corridor are still needed, but their work may be futile if the larger issue of climate change is not addressed. Addressing climate change is futile, in turn, if political corruption is not eliminated. The corrupting influence of large corporations cannot be addressed unless campaign finance is addressed. Similarly, vaccinating the children of the developing world, an extraordinarily helpful act that has cascading benefits, including population reduction (families have fewer children if they are confident their children will survive), could be undermined by shifts in climate that could cause mass starvation.

Can myriad organizations work together to challenge deeper systemic issues? Do organizations step back and see where there is overlap? Do they cooperate sufficiently? Do they try to create synergies, maximize funding, encourage efficiencies, and sublimate their identities to a larger whole? Not as much as is possible, and is necessary. The fact that the movement is made up of pieces does not mean it can only work piecemeal. The Garfield Foundation, a small New York group, spent a year working with twelve nonprofit organizations and eight foundations in the Midwest to create and implement a plan whereby clean energy would rapidly increase as a proportion of overall consumption. They determined four leverage points, all of which were being addressed in some ways by a number of the groups, but not with the systematic approach that would produce results: retiring old coal-fired generating plants that produced the greatest pollution, stopping the licensing of new ones, increasing the production of renewable energy, and raising energy efficiency in the region. Then they went to work and spent months in meetings, with the group eventually growing to include thirty NGOs. From that collective came a unifying vision, ReAmp, with an agenda that was accessible to citizens, government, and business: to create a vibrant Midwest clean energy economy that would increase jobs, investment, and prosperity while addressing climate change, culminating in an 80 percent reduction of greenhouse gases by 2030.

If anything can offer us hope for the future it will be an assembly of humanity that is representative but not centralized, because no single ideology can ever heal the wounds of this world. History demonstrates all too eloquently that no ideology has ever amounted to more than a palliative for any dire condition. The immune system is the most complex system in the body, just as the body is the most complex organism on earth, and the most complicated assembly of organisms is human civilization.

The movement, for its part, is the most complex coalition of human organizations the world has ever seen. The incongruity of anarchists, billionaire funders, street clowns, scientists, youthful activists, indigenous and native people, diplomats, computer geeks, writers, strategists, peasants, and students all working toward common goals is a testament to human impulses that are unstoppable and eternal. The founder of Earth First, Dave Foreman, and the chair of the New York Council of the Alaska Conservation Foundation, David Rockefeller Jr., want the same things for Alaska: no drilling in the Arctic National Wildlife Refuge, moratoriums on indiscriminate game hunting, wildlife corridors for migratory species, permanent protection for the roadless areas of the Tongass and Chugach old-growth forests, elimination of all clear-cutting in the national forests, challenges to all timber sales and concessions by the Department of the Interior, and banishment of destructive bottom trawling in the fisheries.

The list goes on. The two Davids do not know each other. They do not have to hoist a pint or exchange e-mails to work together, because their goals are the same, however different their politics, backgrounds, wealth, and education. This is the promise of the movement: that the margins link up, that we discover through our actions and shared concerns that we are a global family.

The ability to respond to the endless injustices and hurts endured by the earth and its people requires concerted action and hinges in part on understanding both our function and potential as individuals and where we fit into a larger whole. Antigens dot the surface of our body's cells like lapel pins that proudly proclaim, "It's me, don't hurt me, I am you." Viruses and invasive diseases have their own antigens that warn the body that a "not me" has arrived. Millions of different kinds of antigens tag the different microorganisms and cells that find their way into the body, especially detrimental ones. With almost perfect symmetry, millions of different antibodies, proteins that can lock on to antigens as neatly as a key to a hasp, neutralize these invaders while simultaneously signaling for help. This is the beginning of the immune response, the ability of the body to maintain the self, to be a human rather than a petri dish for opportunistic microorganisms. The hundreds of thousands of organizations that make up the movement are social antibodies attaching themselves to pathologies of power. Many will fail, for at present it is often a highly imperfect, and sometimes clumsy movement. It can flail, overreach, and founder; it has much to learn about how to work together, but it is what the earth is producing to protect itself.

For much of medical history, the immune system and brain were considered two completely separate entities. Over the past two decades, science has mapped the many interactions between the two, demonstrating that each affects the other, right down to what we are thinking. Gerald Callahan, associate professor of immunology at Colorado State University, has upped the ante, stating what may be obvious from an evolutionary view: *the brain is part of the immune system.*[7] The immune

7. Gerald N. Callahan, *Faith, Madness, and Spontaneous Human Combustion: What Immunology Can Teach Us About Self-Perception* (New York: St. Martin's, 2002), p. 63.

system predates the brain by a good billion years. While the immune system responds to microscopic threats, the brain defends against risk that is too big for our natural immunity to handle. "The mind is for bears, coral snakes, sharks, snapping turtles, wife beaters, and Buicks," explains Callahan. The immune system addresses organisms that have been around for billions of years; the brain confronts relatively newer dangers.

The massive growth of citizen-based organizations responds to threats that are new, immense, and, in some cases, game-ending. These groups defend against corrupt politics and climate change, corporate predation and the death of oceans, governmental indifference and pandemic poverty, industrial forestry and farming, and depletion of soil and water. Five hundred years of ecological mayhem and social tyranny is a relatively short time for humanity to have learned to understand its self-created patterns of systematic pillage. What has changed recently, and has offered evidence that hope may be a rational act despite the onslaught of countervailing data, is the use of connectivity. Individuals are associating, hooking up, and identifying with one another. From that meeting and experience they are forming units, inventing again and again pieces of a larger organism, enjoining associations and volunteers and committees and groups, and assembling these into a mosaic of activity as if they were solving a jigsaw puzzle without ever having seen the picture on its box. The insanity of human destructiveness may be matched by an older grace and intelligence that is fastening us together in ways we have never before seen or imagined.

There is fierceness at work here. There is no other explanation for the raw courage and heart displayed over and again in the people who march, speak, create, resist, and build. It is the fierceness of knowing we are human and intend to survive. To witness the worldwide breakdown of civility into camps, ideologies, and wars, to watch the accelerating breakdown of our environmental systems, is harrowing and dispiriting.

But immune systems do fail; this movement most certainly could fail as well. What can help preserve it is the gift of self-perception, the gift of seeing who we truly are. We will either come together as one, globalized people, or we will disappear as a civilization. To come together we must know our place in a biological and cultural sense, and reclaim our role as engaged agents of our continued existence. Our minds were made to defend ourselves, born of an immune system that brought us to this stage in our development and evolution. We are surfeited with metaphors of war, such that when we hear the word *defense*, we think *attack*, but the defense of the world can truly be accomplished only by cooperation and compassion. Science now knows that while still in diapers, virtually all children exhibit altruistic behavior. Concern for the well-being of others is bred in the bone, endemic and hardwired. We became human by working together and helping one another. According to immunologist Gerald Callahan, faith and love are literally buried in our genes and lymphocytes, and what it takes to arrest our descent into chaos is one person after another remembering who and where they really are.

Blessed Unrest (2007)

The conversation that Thoreau began continues unabated. Here, Rebecca Solnit (b. 1961) reflects on the ways that environmentalism has often gone astray by concentrating only on part of his message. Solnit is a good example of the re-integration—her sharp essays, most recently collected in *Storming the Gates of Paradise* (2007), combine a love for the American West with a devotion to justice that takes her from the street battles in Seattle during the WTO protests to the barrios of the border towns. Her work appears in places that would seem familiar to Thoreau (this comes from *Orion* magazine, the most prominent forum for environmental writing in the country) and those that have arisen only in this century (she's a prominent voice at tomdispatch.org, a popular website). But her message—that environmentalism is about who we are and how we're going to live—comes full circle from that Concord cabin. With luck, Solnit and the other recent voices in this collection will provide as sturdy a foundation for future thinking.

The Thoreau Problem

Thoreau was emphatic about the huckleberries. In one of his two most famous pieces of writing, "Civil Disobedience," he concluded his account of a night in Concord's jail with, "I was put in jail as I was going to the shoemaker's to get a shoe which was mended. When I was let out the next morning, I proceeded to finish my errand, and having put on my mended shoe, joined a huckleberry party." He told the same story again in *Walden*, this time saying that he "returned to the woods in season to get my dinner of huckleberries on Fair-Haven Hill." That he told it twice suggests that he considered the conjunction of prisons and berry parties, of the landscape of incarceration and of pastoral pleasure, significant. But why?

The famous night in jail took place about halfway through his stay on Emerson's woodlot at Walden Pond. His two-year stint in the small cabin he built himself is often portrayed as a monastic retreat from the world of human affairs into the world of nature, though he went back to town to eat and talk with friends and family and to pick up money doing odd jobs that didn't fit into *Walden*'s narrative. He went to jail not only because he felt passionately enough about national affairs— slavery and the war on Mexico—to refuse to pay his tax, but also because the town jailer ran into him while he was getting his shoe mended.

Says the introduction to my paperback edition of *Walden* and "Civil Disobedience": "As much as Thoreau wanted to disentangle himself from other people's problems so he could get on with his own life, he sometimes found that the issue of black slavery spoiled his country walks. His social conscience impinged on his consciousness, even though he believed that his duty was not to eradicate social evils but to live his life independently." To believe this is to believe that the woods were far from Concord jail not merely by foot but by thought. To believe that conscience is an imposition upon consciousness is to regard engagement as a hijacker rather than a rudder, interference with one's true purpose rather than perhaps at least part of that purpose.

Thoreau did not believe so or wish that it were so, and he contradicted this isolationist statement explicitly in "Civil Disobedience" (completed, unlike *Walden*, shortly after those years in the woods), but many who have charge of his reputation do. These scholars and critics permit no conversation, let alone any unity, between Thoreau the rebel, intransigent muse to Gandhi and Martin Luther King, and that other Thoreau who wrote about autumnal tints, ice, light, color, grasses, woodchucks, and other natural histories, essays easily and often defanged and diced up into inspiring extracts. But for Thoreau, any subject was a good enough starting point to travel any distance, toward any destination.

This compartmentalizing of Thoreau is a microcosm of a larger partition in American thought, a fence built in the belief that places in the imagination can be contained. Those who deny that nature and culture, landscape and politics, the city and the country are inextricably inter-fused have undermined the connections for all of us (so few have been able to find Thoreau's short, direct route between them since). This makes politics dreary and landscape trivial, a vacation site. It banishes certain thoughts, including the thought that much of what the environ-mental movement dubbed wilderness was or is indigenous homeland—a very social and political space indeed, then and now—and especially the thought that Thoreau in jail must have contemplated the following day's huckleberry party, and Thoreau among the huckleberries must have ruminated on his stay in jail.

If "black slavery spoiled his country walks," it spoiled the slaves' country walks even more. Thus the unresisting walk to jail. "Eastward, I go only by force: but westward I go free," Thoreau wrote. His thoughts on the matter might be summed up this way: You head for the hills to enjoy the best of what the world is at this moment; you head for confrontation, for resistance, for picket lines to protect it, to liberate it. Thus it is that the road to paradise often runs through prison, thus it is that Thoreau went to jail to enjoy a better country, and thus it is that one of his greatest stu-dents, Martin Luther King Jr., found himself in jail and eventually in the way of a bullet on what got called the long road to freedom, whose goal he spoke of as the mountaintop.

Conventional environmental writing has often maintained a strict silence on or even an animosity toward the city, despite its importance as a lower-impact place for the majority to live, its intricate relations to the rural, and the direct routes between the two. Imagining the woods or any untrammeled landscape as an unsocial place, an outside, also depends on erasing those who dwelt and sometimes still dwell there, the original Americans—and one more thing that can be said in favor of Thoreau is that he spent a lot of time imaginatively repopulating with Indians the woods around Concord, and even prepared quantities of notes for a never-attempted history of Native America.

Not that those woods were unsocial even after the aboriginal popu-lation was driven out. "Visitors" was one of the chapters of *Walden*, and in it he describes meeting in the woods and guiding farther on the road to freedom runaway slaves. Rather than ruining his country walks, some slaves joined him on them, or perhaps he joined them in the act of becoming free. Some of those he guided were on the Underground Railroad, in which his mother and sisters in Concord were deeply involved, and a few months after that famous night in jail Thoreau hosted a meeting of Concord's most important abolitionist group, the Concord Female Anti-Slavery Society, at his Walden Pond hut. What kind of a forest was this, with slaves, rebels, and the ghosts of the original inhabitants all moving through the trees?

If he went to jail to demonstrate his commitment to the freedom of others, he went to the berries to exercise his own recovered freedom, the liberty to do whatever he wished, and the evidence in all his writing is that he very often wished to pick berries. There's a widespread belief, among both activists and those who cluck disapprovingly over insufficiently austere activists, that idealists should not enjoy any pleasure denied to others, that beauty, sensuality, delight all ought to be stalled behind some dam that only the imagined revolution will break. This schism creates, as the alternative to a life of selfless devotion, a life of flight from engagement, which seems to be one way those years at Walden Pond are sometimes portrayed. But change is not always by revolution, the deprived don't generally wish that the rest of us would join them in deprivation, and a passion for justice and pleasure in small things are not incompatible. That's part of what the short jaunt from jail to hill says.

Perhaps prison is anything that severs and alienates, paradise is the reclaimed commons with the fences thrown down, and so any step toward connection and communion is a step toward paradise, even if the route detours through jail. Thoreau was demonstrating on that one day in Concord in June of 1847 both what dedication to freedom was and what enjoyment of freedom might look like—free association, free roaming, the picking of the fruits of the Earth for free, free choice of commitments. That is the direct route to paradise, the one road worth traveling.

c. 15,000–10,000 BCE   *Homo sapiens* arrives in North America, having crossed a land bridge between Siberia and Alaska. (In the absence of definitive archaeological, genetic, or other evidence, theories about the early history of human settlement in the Western Hemisphere continue to be revised; alternate models have proposed ocean voyages by Pacific or Atlantic routes, much earlier dates of initial settlement, and multiple waves of migration.)

c. 10,000 BCE   The woolly mammoth (*Mammuthus primigenius*) becomes extinct over most of its range, which includes parts of the present United States. Climate change, human hunting, disease, or a combination of factors have been blamed for the species' demise. Most of North America's endemic Pleistocene megafauna—including horses, llamas, sloths, the mastodon, and big cats—disappear around the same time.

c. 2830 BCE   A Great Basin bristlecone pine (*Pinus longaeva*) germinates in the White Mountains of California. Now named "Methuselah," it is the world's oldest known surviving non-clonal organism.

c. 850–1150 CE   The Anasazi, or ancient Puebloans, build the irrigation systems, multistory "great houses," and astronomical sites of Chaco Canyon in present-day New Mexico. Around 1300 the canyon is abandoned, possibly as the result of climate change.

c. 1050–c. 1400   A Mississippian Indian city now known as Cahokia, near present-day St. Louis, Missouri, attains a population estimated at between 8,000 and 40,000, making it the largest settlement in pre-Columbian North America. The city is abandoned before 1400; disease, political disorder, and local environmental collapse caused by deforestation and over-hunting are among several hypotheses proposed to account for its demise.

1492   In October, an expedition led by Christopher Columbus arrives in the Bahamas, beginning a new phase in European exploration and inaugurating a major ecological event, the "Columbian Exchange" of species between the Old World and the New. The Native American population in the Western Hemisphere at the time of Columbus's voyages has been estimated at anywhere from about 8 million to over 100 million.

Native Americans significantly modify the lands they inhabit, clearing and burning forests for agriculture, cultivating fields, and hunting. In subsequent years, millions of Native Americans die from diseases introduced by Europeans or are killed.

1620   William Bradford, arriving at Cape Cod in the *Mayflower*, sees what he later describes as "a hideous and desolate wilderness, full of wild beasts and wild men."

1670   The Hudson's Bay Company is established by royal charter from Charles II and joins an already flourishing trade in furs between North America and Europe.

1681   In his "Concessions to the Province of Pennsylvania," William Penn stipulates that "in clearing the ground, care be taken to leave one acre of trees for every five acres cleared, especially to preserve oak and mulberries, for silk and shipping."

1739   Benjamin Franklin's *Pennsylvania Gazette* reports on a dispute over Philadelphia's tanneries, from which "many offensive and unwholesome Smells do arise . . . to the great Annoyance of the Neighbourhood." The Assembly accepts a proposal from the tanners to regulate their own trade; the *Gazette* argues that public rights ought to take precedence, and that tan-yards ought to be prohibited, as they are in other "well-regulated Towns and Cities."

1781   Thomas Jefferson compiles his *Notes on the State of Virginia*, detailing the natural and demographic features of the state for a French correspondent.

1785   Congress passes an ordinance for the disposal of western lands that authorizes the survey of newly acquired lands and their division into regular townships and sections. Sections of each township are set aside "for the maintenance of public schools" and for veterans' benefits. Boundaries established by the ordinance are often still visible and in use today.

1790   The first U.S. census reports a population of almost 4 million.

1800   U.S. population exceeds 5 million.

1802   Congress authorizes the creation of an Army Corps of Engineers.

1803   The United States buys the Louisiana Territory from France, doubling the nation's size; at a total price of just over $23 million, the final cost is about 4 cents an acre.

1804   On May 14 Meriwether Lewis and William Clark depart St. Louis with 30 soldiers, Lewis's slave York, and a Newfoundland dog. Their task is to explore the Louisiana Purchase and the territory between it and the Pacific at the behest of President Jefferson, who hopes they will find a way to reach the Pacific Ocean by boat. On the upper Missouri, they are joined by a Shoshone woman, Sacagawea. The Corps of Discovery arrives at the Pacific Ocean at the mouth of the Columbia River in 1805 and returns to St. Louis in 1806, producing extensive records and journals of the land and life encountered.

1808   John Jacob Astor founds the American Fur Company, which comes to dominate the U.S. fur trade.

1810   U.S. population grows to over 7 million.

1820   U.S. population grows to more than 9 million.

1824   With the passage of the General Survey Act and other legislation, the Army Corps of Engineers takes on increasing responsibility for public works, including road and canal surveys and river improvements.

1825   The Erie Canal, begun in 1798, is completed in October, linking the Hudson River with Lake Erie over a course of more than 350 miles; it enables transportation of immigrants, goods, and grain.

1827   John James Audubon begins publication of his *Birds of America*, completing the first edition in 1838.

1830   U.S. population reaches almost 13 million.

1834   Cyrus McCormick of Virginia patents a grain reaper that cuts and holds stalks for binding, significantly increasing farm productivity; along with his brothers, he later founds McCormick Harvesting Machine Company, one of the nation's largest manufacturers of agricultural equipment.

1840   U.S. population exceeds 17 million. In Paris, Alexis de Tocqueville publishes the second volume of his *Democracy in America*. "Europe is much concerned with the American wilderness," he writes, "but Americans themselves hardly give it a thought. The wonders of inanimate nature leave them cold, and it is hardly an exaggeration to say that they do not see the admirable forests that surround them until the trees fall to their axes. Another spectacle fills their eyes. The American people see themselves tramping through wilds, draining swamps, diverting rivers, populating solitudes, and taming nature."

1845   On July 4, Henry David Thoreau moves into a small house he had built for himself on the shore of Walden Pond in Concord, Massachusetts, on land owned by Ralph Waldo Emerson. He will spend two years, two months, and two days there, keeping careful notes of all his observations, and publish *Walden, or Life in the Woods* in 1854. Also in July, journalist John L. O'Sullivan coins the phrase "manifest destiny," and urges U.S. annexation of new territories "for the free development of our yearly multiplying millions."

1846   Anglo-American periodicals use the phrase "acid rain" to translate a report from Nismes, Belgium, describing the phenomenon for the first time. The U.S. whaling fleet reaches its peak size of more than 700 vessels.

1849   The U.S. Department of the Interior is established alongside the existing executive departments of State, Treasury, and War. The Swamp Land Act is passed, giving Louisiana authority to build levees and drains for flood and mosquito control; it is soon extended to a dozen other states.

1850   U.S. population exceeds 23 million. The town of Lowell, Massachusetts, about 25 miles from Walden Pond, is home to ten large spinning mill complexes, employing more than 10,000 workers. With a population of 33,000, Lowell is the leading factory town in the United States.

1857   In October, New York City's Board of Commissioners of the Central Park announces a design competition for a great park. They select the naturalistic "Greensward" plan, by Frederick Law Olmsted and Calvert Vaux.

1859   On August 30, the first oil is pumped from a well in Titusville, Pennsylvania. Titusville is later hailed as "the birthplace of the petroleum industry"; refined as kerosene, its products begin to replace whale oil as a preferred fuel for lighting and are adopted for many other purposes.

1860   U.S. population exceeds 31 million.

1861   Carleton E. Watkins takes the first of his widely reproduced photographs of Yosemite.

1862   In May, President Lincoln signs the Homestead Act, which grants 160 acres of undeveloped western land to citizens who build a small house on their quarter-section and farm it for at least five years. Subsequent amendments offer 640 acres in areas where the original allotment will not sustain a homestead; by 1900, settlers file claims for more than 80 million acres.

1864   *Man and Nature*, by George Perkins Marsh, is published. Marsh, a lawyer and former member of Congress, had been sent on diplomatic assignments to Greece and Italy, where he observed the arid land that had resulted from the heedless logging of forests. In June, President Lincoln signs a bill protecting Yosemite Valley and the nearby Mariposa Grove of giant sequoias as a public reserve, the Yosemite Grant, to remain inviolate forever; it is the first federal withdrawal of public lands for conservation purposes and effectively the first national park, though responsibility for the reserve is yielded to the state of California.

1866   Ernst Haeckel, a German biologist inspired by Charles Darwin's *Origin of Species* (1859), coins the term "oecologie."

1867   The United States buys Alaska from Russia—about 600,000 square miles for $7.2 million, or about 2 cents an acre.

1869   On May 10, the completion of the first transcontinental railroad is celebrated with the driving of a golden spike at Promontory Summit, Utah. On May 24, Major John Wesley Powell begins the first of two descents of the Green and Colorado rivers, leading a party of nine from what is now Green River, Wyoming, to Grand Wash Cliffs at the terminus of the Grand Canyon, where he arrives in late August.

1870   U.S. population approaches 39 million. In Cleveland, John D. Rockefeller incorporates Standard Oil, which soon dominates the fledgling oil industry. Congress passes "An Act to prevent the Extermination of Fur-bearing Animals in Alaska," regulating the seal hunt and leasing hunting rights.

1871   John Burroughs publishes *Wake-Robin*, his first collection of nature essays. Congress, noting that "the most valuable food fishes of the coast and the lakes of the United States are rapidly diminishing in number, to public injury," authorizes the President to appoint a Commissioner of Fish and Fisheries. Ferdinand Hayden of the U.S. Geological Survey of the Territories travels with photographer William Henry Jackson and artist Thomas Moran through Yellowstone.

1872   In March, Congress authorizes the creation of Yellowstone National Park in the Wyoming and Montana territories; in the absence of state governments it remains under federal management. The Union Pacific Railroad, envisioning a tourist attraction, had lobbied strenuously for the new park, which includes geysers and mud pots, elk and bison, Yellowstone Lake, and a magnificent waterfall. The state of Nebraska deems April 10 a "Tree-Planting Day"; it is the prototype of subsequent Arbor Day celebrations. In May, Congress passes the General Mining Act. It allows the staking of claims on federal land and, if the claim proves out, the patenting of land for $2.50 or $5 an acre, depending on whether the ore is in a seam or a placer deposit in a stream. The law prompts a land rush that will result in hundreds of thousands of acres passing from public to private ownership.

1876   John Ericsson, designer of the Civil War ironclad *Monitor*, publishes *Solar Investigations*, detailing his development of a solar-powered engine, the "sun-motor." "I had to abandon my various schemes," he later writes, "not being able to compete with the vast energy stored up in lumps of coal. But the time will come when such lumps will be scarce as diamonds."

1877   In June, *Forest and Stream* notes: "The City of New York is greatly indebted to the American Acclimatization Society for the setting at liberty [of] a large number of common starlings (*Sturnus vulgaris*) in the Central Park." In the wake of this and subsequent introductions, the European starling becomes an abundant and widespread invasive species, with a detrimental effect on native bird populations.

1878   In April, John Wesley Powell submits his *Report on the Lands of the Arid Region of the United States* to Secretary of the Interior Carl Schurz in which he predicts that "all the waters of all the arid lands will eventually be taken from their natural channels" for irrigation. He proposes a system of water law that would favor small landholders and prevent domination of the region by absentee corporate interests, but his vision for the West will largely be ignored. In October, Thomas Edison files the first of several patent applications leading to the development of practical electric lighting. Alexander Starbuck, in his *History of the American Whale Fishery*, writes: "Whaling as a business has declined; 1st, from the scarcity and shyness of the whales, requiring longer and more expensive voyages; 2d, extravagance in fitting out and refitting; 3d, the character of the men engaged; 4th, the introduction of coal-oils."

1879   The California Electric Light Company in San Francisco sets up the nation's first central electric utility station. Congress passes the Timber and Stone Act, offering federal land considered "unfit for farming" to small holders at $2.50 an acre; fraud enables large companies to buy much of the more valuable land.

1880   U.S. population exceeds 49 million.

1881   Chicago and Cincinnati pass the country's first air pollution ordinances.

1884   In January, the U.S. Circuit Court in San Francisco rules that hydraulic gold mining, which fills riverbeds with immense volumes of silt and gravel, flooding out farmers in California's Central Valley, is "a public and private nuisance," and issues an injunction against the practice.

1885   Coal becomes the principal source of energy in the U.S., surpassing wood, as demand from railroads and the steel industry increases. The Adirondack Forest Preserve, including some 6 million acres of public and private land, is created by act of the New York State Legislature; in 1894, the state's constitution decrees that these lands, now known as the Adirondack Park, "shall be forever kept as wild."

1886   The National Audubon Society is founded by naturalist and writer George Bird Grinnell. Its mission is to bring public attention to the killing of birds for their meat, eggs, and feathers; the fledgling organization collapses after 39,000 people join in its first year. (In 1896 Harriet Hemenway of Boston founds the Massachusetts Audubon Society, and in 1902, several state Audubon societies affiliate to become the new National Audubon Society.)

1887   The Boone and Crockett Club is formed by Theodore Roosevelt and George Bird Grinnell. Its purpose is to promote "manly sport with the rifle" and to defend the integrity of Yellowstone Park.

1889   In *The Extermination of the American Bison*, William T. Hornaday reports that only 1,091 bison (*Bison bison*) remain alive in North America—635 of them in the wild—out of an 1870 population estimated at over 5 million and pre-18th century numbers of at least 25 million. Albert Pope introduces the "safety" bicycle featuring same-size wheels, ball-bearings, and pneumatic tires; by 1896 four million Americans own "safeties."

1890   U.S. population approaches 63 million. In September, Congress authorizes the creation of Sequoia National Park, south of Yosemite. In October, after intense lobbying by John Muir and others, the Yosemite Reserve of 1864 is expanded and made into Yosemite National Park. The new park records 4,500 visitors in its first year (over 3.2 million will come in 2006); the state of California retains management authority over Yosemite Valley and the Mariposa Grove until 1906, when it cedes them back to the federal government after an intense legislative struggle.

1891   Congress passes the General Land Revision Act in March. (President Benjamin Harrison sets aside 13 million acres in the public domain as forest reserves by 1893; in 2007 there are approximately 190 million acres of national forests.)

1892   In February, in the wake of escalating tensions between Great Britain and the U.S. over pelagic seal hunting in the Bering Sea and dramatic declines in seal populations, a treaty is signed agreeing to resolve the dispute by arbitration. Great Britain argues that its ships have the right "to come and go upon the high sea without let or hindrance, and to take therefrom at will," while the U.S. claims the right to preserve its seal populations—"half human in their intelligence, valuable to mankind, almost the last of their species"—from unsustainable pelagic hunting. The arbitrators rule in Britain's favor, ordering large damages be paid for three vessels seized in 1886–87, while also ordering a one-year moratorium on pelagic hunting, imposing seasonal limits, and prohibiting the use of explosives, firearms, and nets. These measures fail to stem the seals' ongoing decline. Scottish-born naturalist and writer John Muir, the painter William Keith, several businessmen, bankers, and lawyers from San Francisco, and professors from Stanford and the University of California at Berkeley form the Sierra Club in May to defend Yosemite National Park against efforts to shrink its boundaries and to "explore, enjoy, and render accessible the mountain regions of the Pacific Coast."

1893   Historian Frederick Jackson Turner publishes "The Significance of the Frontier in American History," an essay arguing that "the forces dominating American character" had been shaped by the "return to primitive conditions" experienced during the westward expansion of European settlement in the U.S. According to Turner, the 1890 census announced the effective end of the frontier.

1899   Congress enacts the Rivers and Harbors Act, often referred to as the first federal environmental law. It bans the construction of bridges, dams, dikes, and other structures in or over navigable waters without congressional approval and forbids the unauthorized disposal of dredged or fill material in such waters as well. Gifford Pinchot, the first American to be formally trained in the new European science of forestry, is named head of the Division of Forestry with the responsibility to oversee the forest reserves. Pinchot and John Muir espouse opposing philosophies of natural-resource management; Muir campaigns for the preservation of large tracts of wilderness while Pinchot promotes the sustainable "wise use" of resources for the long-term public benefit of people ("each year cut no more than is grown").

1900   U.S. population exceeds 76 million. The Lacey Act becomes the first federal law protecting game, prohibiting the interstate shipment of illegally taken wildlife and importation of invasive non-native species. Enforcement of the act becomes the responsibility of the Biological Survey within the Department of Agriculture.

1902   Congress establishes the United States Reclamation Service (later renamed the Bureau of Reclamation) in July; the agency will eventually complete over 600 dams and reservoirs in western states, becoming the largest U.S. water wholesaler and the second-largest hydroelectric provider. The bison population of Yellowstone National Park—the last remaining wild herd in the U.S.—is counted at 23.

1903   The first Federal Bird Reservation is established by President Theodore Roosevelt on Pelican Island, Florida, and placed under the jurisdiction of the Biological Survey. (Pelican Island and other early federal wildlife reservations are re-designated as national wildlife refuges in 1942. Though the primary purpose of the refuges is to provide protected habitat for many species of wildlife, the managers of some of the refuges allow hunting, oil and gas drilling, logging, and practice bombing by the military.)

1904   An Asian bark fungus (*Cryphonectria parasitica*) is reported in American chestnut trees (*Castanea dentata*) in the Bronx Zoo; by 1950, the chestnut—an important part of Appalachian forest ecosystems from Maine to Florida—is largely wiped out.

1905   The Forest Service is established within the Department of

Agriculture to manage U.S. forest reserves (referred to as "National Forests" beginning in 1907), with Gifford Pinchot as its first chief. The agency manages federal forests and grasslands in the interests of wildlife habitat, watershed protection, recreation, and timber production.

1906   The Antiquities Act, which authorizes the President to set aside federal lands as national monuments or historic sites without congressional action, becomes law in June. Many areas, including the Grand Canyon, Grand Teton, Bryce Canyon, and Death Valley, are first protected under the Antiquities Act and later are made national parks by acts of Congress. (The act is challenged repeatedly in court as an unconstitutional infringement on congressional power, but the Supreme Court will uphold the law. Congress emends the act in 1950 to restrict its use in Wyoming, and in 1980 to limit it in Alaska.) The Department of Agriculture conducts its first inventory of "swamp and overflowed lands" in the U.S. to identify areas that can be reclaimed for farming and other uses.

1908   Grand Canyon National Monument is created by President Theodore Roosevelt, who says from the canyon's south rim: "Leave it as it is. The ages have been at work on it and man can only mar it." Roosevelt convenes the first Governors' Conference on Conservation, inspiring many state-level conservation measures, and creates a National Conservation Commission, chaired by Gifford Pinchot, to conduct an inventory of America's natural resources, which they present to Congress in 1909. The National Bison Range is established in Montana.

1910   U.S. population exceeds 92 million. Gifford Pinchot, dismissed from his government post by President Taft, serves as president of the recently founded National Conservation Association and publishes *The Fight for Conservation.*

1911   The output of the "modern" whaling industry—dominated by Norwegian factory vessels hunting in Antarctic waters—surpasses the peak levels attained by the American whaling fleet in the 1840s and 1850s. In July, the North Pacific Fur Seal Treaty joins Great Britain, Japan, Russia, and the U.S. in an agreement to ban pelagic sealing for 15 years and land sealing for five years. Russia and the U.S., together home to the principal seal rookeries, agree to share hunting revenues with the pelagic sealing nations. Seal populations—having fallen to around 300,000 from an estimated 3–4 million before commercial hunting—begin a dramatic recovery.

1913   After a decade-long dispute, Congress and President Wilson authorize the building of the O'Shaughnessy Dam at Hetch Hetchy Valley in Yosemite National Park despite vigorous opposition by John Muir and the Sierra Club

1914   Assembly-line production of the Ford Model-T automobile increases dramatically and Ford becomes the world's largest industrial enterprise. On September 1, the last surviving passenger pigeon (*Ectopistes migratorius*), named Martha, dies in the Cincinnati Zoo. Until the 19th century, passenger pigeons were among the most numerous birds in North America; they became extinct because of widespread hunting for food and the destruction of their forest habitat.

1916   The National Park Service is created to manage the growing number of federal parks. Housed in the Department of the Interior, its first director is Stephen Mather, a member of the Sierra Club who had favored the construction of the dam in Hetch Hetchy and feuded with John Muir.

1917   Mount McKinley National Park is established in the Alaska Territory.

1918   Save-the-Redwoods League is founded in California and raises money to buy surviving stands of old-growth *Sequoia sempervirens*, eventually deeding most of them to the state of California to become state parks. Congress passes the Migratory Bird Treaty Act, ratifying an earlier treaty protecting birds that migrate between the U.S. and Canada; subsequent agreements with Mexico (1936), Japan (1972), and the Soviet Union (1976) expand the list of protected bird species, now numbering over 800.

1919   Grand Canyon National Park is created, incorporating much of the national monument designated in 1908.

1920   U.S. population exceeds 106 million. The Mineral Leasing Act becomes law; it regulates the extraction of coal, oil, and natural gas on federal lands not covered by the General Mining Act of 1872.

1922   California's last known surviving grizzly bear (*Ursus arctos horribilis*) is shot and killed. The grizzly is the state's official mammal and appears on the state flag.

1924   In June, at the urging of Aldo Leopold, the Forest Service protects a section of the Gila National Forest as the Gila Wilderness; it is the first officially designated "wilderness" area in the U.S.

1930   U.S. population exceeds 123 million.

1931   In April, construction begins on the massive Boulder Canyon Project (later known as Hoover Dam) on the Colorado River. In the wake of a widening drought, the plains of the Midwest and the South experience several "black blizzards," harbingers of what will become known as the Dust Bowl. Dutch elm disease, already responsible for widespread "elm death" in northern Europe, is reported in trees in Cleveland and Cincinnati. Though attempts are made at containment, the disease begins to spread throughout North America, devastating both forest and urban plantings.

1933   In March, the administration of Franklin D. Roosevelt creates the Civilian Conservation Corps as part of its New Deal program. By 1942, when the Corps is disbanded, over 3 million people have been employed in a variety of projects: building park trails and logging roads, planting trees, and working to prevent soil erosion and forest fires. In May, President Roosevelt signs a bill establishing the Tennessee Valley Authority. The Soil Erosion Service is established in September. In December, the Supreme Court rules in favor of New Jersey in an ocean dumping case against New York City, preventing the city from disposing of "offensive or injurious matter" off the New Jersey coast. Construction begins on the Grand Coulee Dam on the Columbia River.

1934   In March, Congress passes the Migratory Bird Hunting Stamp Act, which requires bird hunters to buy a license stamp. Revenues from the program—over $670 million cumulatively by 2003—are used to preserve wetlands, and cartoonist J. N. "Ding" Darling, who conceived it, designs the first stamp. Beginning in the spring, vast dust storms bury the high plains of Oklahoma, Texas, New Mexico, Colorado, and Kansas under millions of tons of wind-blown soil and darken skies in Chicago and New York City. Severe wind erosion caused by drought and over-farming continues for years. An estimated 2.5 million people emigrate from the affected areas over the next half-decade.

1935   On April 14—"Black Sunday"—another massive dust storm rises from the plains; an Associated Press reporter traveling through Oklahoma coins the phrase "Dust Bowl." Within two weeks, Congress establishes the Soil Conservation Service (moving the Soil Erosion Service into the Department of Agriculture), and by December over 30,000 workers are assigned to erosion control projects. Ornithologists from Cornell University make film and sound recordings of the endangered ivory-billed wood-pecker (*Campephilus principalis*) in the Singer Tract, a remnant of old-growth forest in Louisiana; by 1944, after extensive logging in the Tract, only one bird is known to survive in the U.S. In May, President Roosevelt establishes the Rural Electrification Administration to bring electric power to rural communities (almost 90 percent of which are not connected to util-ities). In June, Congress passes the Taylor Grazing Act, which regulates grazing on federal lands in an attempt to prevent their deterioration. The General Wildlife Federation is created to protect habitat for birds and other species (in 1936 its name is changed to the National Wildlife Federation). The Wilderness Society is created by Robert Marshall, Benton MacKaye, Aldo Leopold, Bernard Frank, and Harvey Broome, with Robert Sterling Yard as its first president; its goal is to give permanent protection to wilderness throughout the country.

1936   Hoover Dam is completed in March. Lake Mead, behind the dam, is the largest man-made lake in the U.S.

1939   The Bureau of Fisheries and the Biological Survey are com-bined to become the Fish and Wildlife Service, under the jurisdiction of the Department of the Interior. The agency administers the national wildlife refuges and eventually the 1973 Endangered Species Act.

1940   U.S. population exceeds 132 million.

1942   In December, a group led by Nobel laureate Enrico Fermi achieves the first self-sustaining nuclear chain reaction in a laboratory under the University of Chicago football stadium.

1945   In July, the U.S. conducts a nuclear weapons test—the first of more than 1,000—near Alamogordo, New Mexico. In August, the U.S. drops atomic bombs on Hiroshima and Nagasaki, killing at least 115,000 people and prompting Japanese surrender in World War II. American farmers begin widespread use of the pesticide DDT.

1946   The Bureau of Land Management is created within the Interior Department by merging the Grazing Service and the General Land Office. The BLM oversees federal land not under the jurisdiction of the National Park Service, the Forest Service, the Fish and Wildlife Service, or the mili-tary. Much of it is rangeland, and the agency, which tends to favor resource extraction, is called "the Bureau of Livestock and Mining" by its critics. The Ecologists Union is founded, determined to take "direct action" to save threatened areas; it is later renamed The Nature Conservancy and in 1955 begins acquiring land for conservation. In August, President Truman signs the Atomic Energy Act, establishing the Atomic Energy Commission under civilian control and regulating the dissemination of information about nuclear power and nuclear weapons. The International Convention for the Regulation of Whaling, signed in Washington, D.C., in December, establishes the International Whaling Commission to oversee the conservation of declining whale fisheries.

1947   The Los Angeles Air Pollution Control District—the nation's first such agency—is established in October to confront the city's increasing smog problems. It regulates industrial air pollution and later bans residential incinerators. In December, President Truman dedicates the Everglades National Park, preserving what remains—about one-quarter—of the vast wetland that once covered the lower third of the Florida peninsula, much of the rest having been drained for agriculture and later housing development by the U.S. Army Corps of Engineers. Water diversion, polluted runoff from sugar-cane fields and cattle ranches, and ongoing development continue to damage the park's ecosystems.

1948   A weather inversion traps gases emitted by smelters operated by U.S. Steel at Donora, Pennsylvania, killing 21 people and sickening 6,000, one-third of the town's population. The National Park Service reports over a million visitors to Yellowstone National Park.

1949   Aldo Leopold's *A Sand County Almanac* is published.

1950   U.S. population approaches 152 million.

1951   Oil passes coal as the principal energy source in the U.S.

1952   David Brower is hired as the first executive director of the Sierra Club. Brower has been active in club affairs as editor of the *Sierra Club Bulletin* and a leader of hiking and climbing expeditions. He leads a campaign to block a plan to build two hydroelectric dams inside Dinosaur National Monument in northeast Utah. The campaign, which involves publication of a campaign book and newspaper advertising, succeeds when plans for the dams are dropped in 1955 as part of a deal in which the Sierra Club agrees not to oppose a dam at Glen Canyon. (Brower will later bitterly regret the compromise.)

1953   In December, President Dwight Eisenhower delivers his "Atoms for Peace" speech at the United Nations General Assembly, proposing international nuclear cooperation.

1954   In April, researchers at Bell Laboratories announce development of a silicon-based solar battery. *The New York Times* argues that the invention "may mark the beginning of a new era, leading eventually to the realization of one of mankind's most cherished dreams—the harnessing of the almost limitless energy of the sun." In August, President Eisenhower signs the Atomic Energy Act of 1954, easing restrictions on the international exchange of nuclear technology and enabling the commercial development of nuclear power.

1955   Under pressure from the timber industry, the Forest Service increases the "allowable cut" in federal forests to 8.6 billion board feet, up from 5.6 billion in 1949. The first commercial whale-watching cruises are offered from a San Diego municipal pier; thousands gather on the California coast to watch migrating gray whales (*Eschrichtius robustus*).

1957   In July, the Sodium Reactor Experiment, a nuclear facility at the Santa Susana Field Laboratory, near Los Angeles, begins supplying power to the local grid. In December, the Shippingport Reactor in Pennsylvania comes on line; it is the first large-scale commercial reactor in the U.S.

1960   U.S. population exceeds 179 million. *This Is the American Earth*—the first in the Sierra Club's "Exhibit Format" series of large, illustrated conservation books—is published in May. Based on an exhibit put together by Ansel Adams and Nancy Newhall for the Smithsonian Institution, with photographs by Adams and others and a text by Newhall, it is the subject of enthusiastic reviews and editorials across the country; Supreme Court Justice William O. Douglas calls it "one of the great statements in the history of conservation."

1962   *Silent Spring* is published. The author is Rachel Carson, a zoologist and marine biologist previously known for her best-selling books on marine and coastal wildlife. First published in *The New Yorker*, the book warns of the devastation that pesticides, particularly DDT, and other chemicals are wreaking on birds and other creatures. Carson is criticized by the chemical industry, parts of the food industry, and some academic scientists, but the book is a best seller and has an immense impact worldwide.

1963   Congress passes the Clean Air Act in July (significantly expanding it in 1970, 1977, and 1990), and ratifies the Limited Nuclear Test Ban Treaty in September, ending American, British, and Soviet testing of nuclear weapons in the atmosphere, underwater, and in space. (Although this treaty has only limited impact on the nuclear arms race, and other nations continue atmospheric tests for some years, it ends atmospheric testing of nuclear weapons by the U.S.)

1964   The Wilderness Act is passed and signed by President Lyndon Johnson eight years after it was first introduced. The law sets aside 9.1 million acres of national forest land to be preserved in perpetuity from any and all development, "where man is a visitor but does not remain." Congress will add national forest lands and lands managed by the National Park Service and the Bureau of Land Management to the system, which will grow to 100 million acres.

1965   The Department of the Interior announces in February that traces of DDT have been found in the tissue of Antarctic seals and penguins. In July, the Scenic Hudson Preservation Conference—an alliance of local residents and national environmental groups—files a lawsuit before the Federal Power Commission seeking to challenge permits sought by Consolidated Edison for a hydroelectric plant at Storm King Mountain on the Hudson River in New York. The commission argues that the organizations have no material interest in the matter and therefore lack legal standing to bring the case, but the U.S. Court of Appeals for the Second Circuit rules in December that "aesthetic, conservational, or recreational" interests can suffice to establish standing, a precedent that permits increased environmental litigation.

1966   In June, the Sierra Club publishes ads in several newspapers opposing Bureau of Reclamation efforts to build two hydroelectric dams inside the Grand Canyon. One ad is headlined "Should We Also Flood the Sistine Chapel So Tourists Can Get Closer to the Ceiling?" Immediately following publication, the IRS announces that it is reviewing the tax deductible status of contributions to the club. The club challenges the agency in court and loses, suffering a drop in major contributions but a large increase in membership. David Brower observes that "people may not know whether or not they like the Sierra Club, but they know what they think about the IRS." In October, the Enrico Fermi Nuclear Reactor near Detroit, Michigan, suffers a partial core meltdown. Though no radiation escapes, officials are forced to consider a large-scale evacuation.

1967   The Environmental Defense Fund is founded by attorneys and scientists in New York who begin litigation to ban the pesticide DDT. The U.S. Fish and Wildlife Service publishes its first list of endangered species.

1968   The discovery of an oil field beneath the North Slope of Alaska and the Beaufort Sea, larger than any previously known in the U.S., is announced in March, and within the year plans begin for the construction of a Trans-Alaska pipeline. *The Population Bomb*, by Stanford biologist Paul R. Ehrlich, becomes a best seller following its publication in May; it predicts widespread famine in the wake of global overpopulation. In September, Congress declines to fund the proposed construction of two dams inside the Grand Canyon. In October, President Johnson signs legislation creating the North Cascades National Park, Redwood National Park, and the Wild and Scenic Rivers System, protecting waterways with "outstandingly remarkable" features.

1969   An oil rig in the Santa Barbara Channel operated by Union Oil Company blows out, spilling 3 million gallons of crude oil into the ocean and creating a slick that eventually covers 800 square miles, fouling beaches and killing an estimated 10,000 birds. David Brower is forced to resign as executive director of the Sierra Club after an internal power struggle; he founds Friends of the Earth in the United States. (A year later, Les Amis de la Terre is founded in France. Friends of the Earth International eventually includes groups in about 70 nations.)

1970   U.S. population exceeds 203 million. U.S. domestic oil production, having risen sharply and consistently for many decades, peaks at about 9.5 million barrels per day. The National Environmental Policy Act (NEPA), introduced by Washington senator Henry "Scoop" Jackson, becomes law on January 1. It requires federal agencies to analyze the environmental impact of major federal projects, inform the public of pending projects and allow comments to be registered, and establishes the Council on Environmental Quality, a White House agency charged with coordinating environmental policy. In March, Alaska Native and environmental groups including the Environmental Defense Fund, Friends of the Earth, and The Wilderness Society file lawsuits to block construction of the Trans-Alaska pipeline, alleging failure to hire Native contractors and failure to study environmental impacts. The first Earth Day is celebrated on April 22. Conceived by Wisconsin senator Gaylord Nelson, it attracts an estimated 20 million participants nationwide. In June, the Ford Foundation awards $100,000 in seed money to the Natural Resources Defense Council, founded by a group of young lawyers. A major extension of the 1963 Clean Air Act becomes law, despite opposition from the automobile industry, establishing national ambient air quality standards and regulating tailpipe emissions and hazardous pollutants. In December, President Nixon establishes the Environmental Protection Agency by executive order.

1971   In January, two tankers operated by Standard Oil of California collide in dense fog under the Golden Gate Bridge, spilling 800,000 gallons of oil into San Francisco Bay and causing widespread damage and public outrage. In March, faced with citizen protests over exhaust and noise pollution, Congress votes to end funding for a supersonic passenger plane. In July, Oregon enacts the nation's first statewide container deposit law, the Oregon Bottle Bill. Similar laws are eventually passed in ten other states. In September, the *Phyllis Cormack*, rechristened *Greenpeace*, sails from Vancouver with a crew of U.S. and Canadian activists to protest an underground nuclear test in the Aleutian Islands; the group later attempts to disrupt French nuclear testing and Soviet whaling in the Pacific. (In 1979, Greenpeace International unites loosely affiliated Greenpeace groups that have been started throughout the world.) The Alaska Native Land Claim Settlement Act becomes law in December, transferring 44 million acres and nearly a billion dollars, half of which is to come from new oil revenues, to Native Alaskans. The law extinguishes Native claims for most of the state, sets up regional Native corporations to administer land grants, and removes a political obstacle impeding construction of the Trans-Alaska pipeline. Sierra Club Legal Defense Fund (later renamed Earthjustice) is created to provide legal services to the Sierra Club and other environmental organizations.

1972   In April, the Supreme Court issues its decision in *Sierra Club* v. *Morton* in a dispute over a large ski resort the Walt Disney Corporation plans to build in Mineral King valley in the Sierra Nevada. Though the Sierra Club loses its case, the litigation affirms the principle that conservation groups can take their grievances to the federal courts. (The ski resort is never built.) In June, Stockholm hosts the United Nations Conference on the Human Environment. More than a thousand journalists from across the world attend the gathering, along with thousands of activists. Whaling by Japan and other nations and the use of the toxic defoliant Agent Orange by the U.S. military are among the most hotly debated issues. During the last days of the conference, the EPA bans the use of DDT in the U.S. In September, at a conference in Bucharest, Norwegian philosopher Arne Naess presents the concept of "deep ecology" and calls for a holistic, egalitarian, and global approach to environmental problems. In October, Congress passes new environmental laws: the Marine Protection, Research and Sanctuaries Act (also known as the Ocean Dumping Act), which gives the EPA regulatory power over waste disposal in U.S. territorial waters; the Marine Mammal Protection Act; and the Federal Water Pollution Control Act (also known as the Clean Water Act).

1973   CITES, the Convention on International Trade in Endangered Species of Wild Fauna and Flora, is finalized in March. In May, the Izaak Walton League sues the Forest Service, claiming the agency's preferred logging method—clear cutting, which strips large expanses of forest bare of all trees—is illegal. A federal judge agrees and halts the practice nationwide, prompting legislative efforts to permit its return. In July, Vice President Spiro Agnew breaks a tie in the Senate, enabling passage of an amendment that declares the Trans-Alaska pipeline in compliance with the National Environmental Policy Act. In October, the Organization of Petroleum Exporting Countries suspends shipments of crude oil to nations that supported Israel during the Yom Kippur War, triggering long lines at filling stations, rationing, and a sharp spike in gasoline prices. In the wake of the embargo, the U.S. introduces the 55-mph national speed limit (in effect until 1995), an extended daylight saving time (until 1976), a Strategic Petroleum Reserve, Corporate Average Fuel Economy standards, and a cabinet-level Department of Energy. In November, President Nixon signs the Trans-Alaska Pipeline Authorization Act. The EPA announces regulations requiring a gradual phase-out of leaded gasoline. The Endangered Species Act becomes law in December. It sets up a system for listing rare species as "threatened" or "endangered," for designating "critical habitat," and for ensuring that actions undertaken or permitted by the federal government not "jeopardize" the species or hinder its chances of recovering. Construction begins on the Watts Bar Nuclear Generating Station near Spring City, Tennessee, the last commercial nuclear power plant in the U.S. to come on line (as of 2007). A group of 54 produce growers forms California Certified Organic Farmers, which promotes and sets standards for organic agriculture.

1974   President Gerald Ford signs the Safe Drinking Water Act in December.

1975   The Eastern Wilderness Act is signed into law in January after a campaign lasting several years. It protects 207,000 acres of wilderness in 13 states, mostly recovering forests that have been acquired by the federal government after extensive logging. Construction of the Trans-Alaska pipeline resumes in March.

1976   The National Forest Management Act becomes law, superseding the Organic Act of 1897 and allowing clear cutting to resume. The Federal Land Policy and Management Act is passed. It guides management of lands controlled by the Bureau of Land Management and allows Congress to consider creating wilderness areas on BLM lands; it also ends land claims under the 1862 Homestead Act, except in Alaska where the last Homestead Act claimant receives land in 1988. *Foreign Affairs* publishes an essay by Amory Lovins entitled "Energy Strategy, The Road Not Taken?" It describes a "hard path" relying on fossil fuels and nuclear fission, and a "soft path" that depends on conservation and renewable energy sources such as wind and solar power.

1977   In April, over 2,000 Clamshell Alliance protestors occupy the construction site of a nuclear reactor at Seabrook, New Hampshire; 1,414 are arrested and detained. (Only one of the two reactors planned for the site ultimately comes on line, and the owner of the Seabrook Station is bankrupted by the project.) In July, the Trans-Alaska pipeline delivers its first oil to the Valdez terminal on Prince William Sound.

1978   The Smithsonian Institution lists close to 10 percent of 22,000 plant species native to the continental U.S. as threatened or endangered, largely because of habitat loss. President Jimmy Carter declares an emergency at Love Canal, a neighborhood in Niagara Falls, New York, contaminated for years by toxic waste by Hooker Chemical Company. All residents are evacuated, and the federal government buys their abandoned property; a leader of the local protest group, Lois Gibbs, later moves to Washington, D.C., and starts the Citizens Clearinghouse for Hazardous Waste. The EPA bans the use of chlorofluorocarbon propellants in aerosol cans. In June, the Supreme Court upholds the Endangered Species Act in a case involving the snail darter (*Percina tanasi*), a tiny fish threatened by the Tellico Dam on the Little Tennessee River in eastern Tennessee. (Congress later exempts "economically important" federal projects from the provision of the ESA; a federal court finds the Tellico Dam not economically important; Congress votes to exempt the Tellico Dam from the ESA and the dam is built. Remnant populations of the snail darter are discovered elsewhere, and its status is lowered from "endangered" to "threatened.")

1979   In March, the Three Mile Island nuclear power plant near Harrisburg, Pennsylvania, suffers a partial meltdown, prompting evacuation of the surrounding area. The accident delivers a major setback to the American nuclear industry. In April, the EPA bans production of polychlorinated biphenyls, a notably toxic class of persistent organic pollutants. Facing a sharp spike in oil prices precipitated by the Iranian Revolution and a broader "crisis of confidence," President Carter addresses the nation in July, urging conservation. He lowers federal thermostats and installs solar panels on the White House roof. (President Reagan later has the panels removed.) Inspired by Edward Abbey's novel *The Monkey Wrench Gang* (1975), Earth First! is founded by four young men who feel that the mainstream environmental movement has become too willing to compromise. Its motto: "No Compromise in Defense of Mother Earth."

1980   U.S. population approaches 227 million. In June, the Supreme Court decides *Diamond* v. *Chakrabarty*, ruling that a genetically modified organism may be patented; Anand Chakrabarty, a General Electric engineer, had developed a transgenic bacterium to help clean up oil spills. In December, President Carter signs the Alaska National Interest Lands Conservation Act, protecting 104 million acres in parks, refuges, and wilderness areas; it expands Mount McKinley National Park, renamed Denali National Park, and the Arctic National Wildlife Refuge. Also in December, Congress passes the Comprehensive Environmental Response, Compensation and Liability Act, commonly known as the Superfund Act, in the wake of the Love Canal disaster; it identifies hazardous waste sites, determines parties responsible for cleanup, and provides funds for federal remediation where the original polluters are bankrupt or unidentifiable.

1981   James G. Watt becomes Secretary of the Interior after leading the Mountain States Legal Foundation, which represents the interests of miners, ranchers, timber companies, and other extractive industries. His nomination is opposed by a majority of environmental organizations; a petition calling for his ouster is signed by more than a million people. He resigns in 1983.

1982   The International Whaling Commission, meeting in Brighton, England, approves a moratorium on commercial whaling to take effect in 1985, the result of an intense campaign carried out by activists throughout the world. Japan and Norway defy the ban and continue whaling. Dr. Benjamin Chavis of the NAACP coins the term "environmental racism" in discussing the proposed placement of a PCB landfill in Warren County, North Carolina. Congress passes the Nuclear Waste Policy Act, seeking a 10,000-year disposal site for radioactive materials stored at a host of temporary locations. Under the Act, Nevada's Yucca Mountain is selected for development as a nuclear waste repository in 1987; the Department of Energy currently projects an opening date of 2017.

1983   In February, the EPA agrees to buy out and evacuate the residents of Times Beach, Missouri, following the revelation late in 1982 that dioxin contamination in the soil dramatically exceeded safe levels. (A contractor hired to spray oil on the town's roads, to suppress dust, had used toxic industrial waste.) Times Beach becomes a Superfund site, and is soon disincorporated and demolished. Plans to log a stand of old-growth trees in the Siskiyou National Forest in Oregon spark a protest, in April, by members of Earth First!, who block timber company bulldozers for months. The Forest Service later cancels the timber sale, and the area is incorporated into the South Kalmiopsis Roadless Area.

1984   In June, César Chávez of the United Farm Workers calls for a renewed boycott against the California table-grape industry to protest worker exposure to pesticides; he later goes on a 36-day hunger strike to draw attention to the issue. In December, an accident at a Union Carbide pesticide factory in Bhopal, India, releases methyl isocyanate and other toxic gases into the city, killing an estimated 7,000 people within a few days and ultimately causing an estimated 15,000 more deaths. Union Carbide, a U.S.-based multinational, denies responsibility; its CEO, later arrested on manslaughter charges, leaves India on bail and is not extradited.

1985   In the May issue of *Nature*, British scientists report a hole in the ozone layer over Antarctica; their finding suggests ozone depletion is occurring more rapidly than previously expected. The Department of Agriculture begins its "Swampbuster" program, denying federal subsidies to farmers who drain wetlands; the program is later expanded to offer incentives for wetlands restoration.

1986   Harvesting of trees from the national forests reaches 5 billion board feet, up from 900 million in 1946. (Only 10 percent of America's old-growth forests remain.) The USDA, the EPA, and the FDA establish the Coordinated Framework for Regulation of Biotechnology to regulate newly developed transgenic organisms.

1987   The Montreal Protocol on Substances that Deplete the Ozone Layer is adopted by more than 100 countries. It calls for a reduction in the emission of ozone-depleting chemicals by 2000, but is amended in 1990 and 1992 to call for a complete phase-out of the use of chlorofluorocarbons, halons, and carbon tetrachloride by 2000 and methyl chloroform by 2005.

1988   The Intergovernmental Panel on Climate Change is established to investigate whether carbon dioxide and other gases are causing a warming of the global atmosphere and, if so, whether human activity is a major contributor. After many years of warnings from the scientific community, NASA climatologist James Hansen declares that "global warming is here." The federal government, asserting damage to the Everglades National Park and the Loxahatchee National Wildlife Refuge, sues the state of Florida for failing to enforce environmental laws.

1989   In March, the oil tanker *Exxon Valdez* runs aground in Alaska's Prince William Sound, spilling an estimated 11 million gallons of North Slope crude. The spill covers over 6,000 square miles of ocean and over 800 miles of shoreline, killing hundreds of thousands of marine animals and causing long-term environmental degradation. Alar, a controversial agricultural chemical used mainly on apples, is withdrawn by its manufacturer in June following a *60 Minutes* report based on a study by the Natural Resources Defense Council; the EPA later bans the product. In October, international trade in elephant ivory is banned.

1990   U.S. population approaches 249 million. The northern spotted owl (*Strix occidentalis caurina*), dependent on the old-growth forests of Washington, Oregon, and California for its habitat, is listed as a threatened subspecies under the Endangered Species Act in June, following litigation brought by environmental groups. (The listing provokes considerable controversy, and becomes an issue in the 1992 presidential campaign.) Sulfur dioxide emissions from U.S. coal plants reach 28 million tons, almost double the emissions before World War II. In August, in the wake of the *Exxon Valdez* disaster, Congress passes the Oil Pollution Act.

The National Wetlands Inventory reports that, since the 1780s, the U.S. has lost over half of its wetlands.

1991   The first National People of Color Environmental Leadership Summit is held in Washington, D.C., attracting more than a thousand participants. In a negotiated settlement following a 1988 federal lawsuit, plans begin for restoring water flows in the Florida Everglades and regulating the use of agricultural chemicals in the surrounding region.

1992   Canada, Mexico, and the U.S. sign the North America Free Trade Agreement, easing trade restrictions among the three countries. The proposed treaty causes a rift within the environmental movement, with some organizations in support and others claiming that it could undermine environmental laws and labor protections in the U.S. The United Nations holds an Earth Summit in Rio de Janeiro on the 20th anniversary of the 1972 Stockholm conference; major treaties concerning climate and biodiversity are adopted.

1993   Water contaminated with cryptosporidium, a protozoan parasite, sickens more than 400,000 and kills more than 100 people in the Milwaukee area beginning in March. Blame is leveled at one of the city's water-treatment facilities, leading the EPA to tighten water-quality regulations. In April, President Bill Clinton hosts a "Forest Summit" in Portland, Oregon, to try to solve the timber conflict in the Northwest. Several Cabinet members attend, along with loggers, environmentalists, scientists, and others. As a result of the summit, a new Northwest Forest Plan aims to balance preservation with production of a sustainable supply of wood and pulp. The EPA establishes a 25-member National Environmental Justice Advisory Council in late September, bringing representatives of community, industry, governmental, tribal, activist, and academic groups together to discuss issues of environmental justice.

1994   President Clinton issues an executive order in February directing all federal agencies to conduct their activities in a way that will promote environmental justice. In May, the FDA allows the sale of the rot-resistant Flavr Savr™ tomato, the first genetically modified whole food intended for public consumption; after a variety of production problems, it is withdrawn from the market within a few years. Genetically modified canola, corn, and soybeans are subsequently approved by the FDA and begin to be widely adopted by U.S. farmers. In June, Exxon Mobil is ordered to pay $5 billion in damages in the wake of the *Exxon*

Valdez disaster; the company immediately appeals. (In 2007, the Supreme Court agrees to review the case.)

1995   In January, the National Park Service begins a controversial plan to reintroduce the gray wolf (*Canis lupus*) into Yellowstone National Park and central Idaho, which were part of its natural range until the 1920s. Fourteen wild gray wolves from Canada are released in the park. (In 2007, approximately 370 wolves live in Yellowstone, although both gray and red wolves remain endangered in most states.) The EPA identifies 126 types of ecosystems that are threatened or critically endangered. Approximately 5 million people live on farms in the U.S., down from over 31 million in 1920.

1997   In May, prompted in part by concerns over environmental justice, the Nuclear Regulatory Commission seeks "further study" before it will license a planned uranium-enrichment facility at Homer, Louisiana; the request effectively blocks the facility. In August, the National Cancer Institute reports on radiation exposures from Cold War atmospheric nuclear testing in Nevada; an estimated 120,000 excess thyroid cancers (above the statistical norm) and 6,000 deaths may have been caused by these tests. The Kyoto Protocol on greenhouse gases is agreed to in December and signed by the U.S., though President Clinton declines to submit it to the Senate in the wake of the Byrd-Hagel resolution, passed by a vote of 95–0, which opposes key provisions of the agreement. (President George W. Bush later withdraws the U.S. from the protocol.) Also in December, Julia Butterfly Hill takes up residence in an ancient redwood in the Headwaters forest in northern California. She names the tree Luna and pledges to save it from being logged. It will be two years before her feet touch the ground. She spends her days giving interviews to journalists from all over the world. Luna is spared, though vandalized after Hill leaves.

1999   In November, tens of thousands of loosely affiliated anti-globalization protestors—including a variety of environmental, labor, religious, student, and anarchist groups—stage demonstrations in Seattle and disrupt the third ministerial meeting of the World Trade Organization.

2000   The population of the U.S. exceeds 281 million. Three-fourths of Americans now live in and around cities, up from 20 percent at the time of the Civil War and 5 percent in 1790. (Between 1820 and 2000, the per capita income in the U.S. has doubled every 42 years, and since 1880 U.S.

industrial production has exceeded that of any other nation.) In August, Toyota introduces a hybrid gasoline-electric model, the Prius, which becomes a best seller among hybrid vehicles. The Census Bureau reports on the commutes of U.S. workers: 76 percent drive to work alone, 12 percent carpool, 4.7 percent use public transportation, 3.3 percent work at home, 2.9 percent walk, and 1.2 percent ride a bicycle or motorcycle.

2001   In a controversial November *Nature* article, University of California–Berkeley ecologist Ignacio Chapela presents evidence that genetically modified corn has contaminated wild varieties in the Mexican state of Oaxaca. The average fuel efficiency of U.S. cars and light trucks falls to 23.9 mpg, from a 1987–88 high of 25.9 mpg; over 3.5 million sport-utility vehicles are sold, up from just over 700,000 in 1990.

2002   The USDA creates the National Organic Program, regulating organic food production.

2003   The GloFish®, a genetically modified zebra fish (*Zebra danio*), is made available for sale in pet stores after the Food and Drug Administration offers no objection; it is the first transgenic organism sold as a pet.

2004   The National Wetlands Inventory reports that, since 1998, the U.S. has seen a small net gain in wetlands acreage: restoration programs and land set-asides have balanced ongoing losses from development.

2005   Hurricane Katrina, which devastates New Orleans and the Gulf Coast in August, heightens anxieties about global warming, a possible intensifier of the region's weather patterns. In December, on the initiative of New York governor George Pataki, the governors of seven northeastern states sign a memorandum agreeing to a mandatory cap-and-trade program to limit carbon dioxide emissions, the Regional Greenhouse Gas Initiative.

2006   *An Inconvenient Truth*, a documentary about global warming featuring former Vice President Al Gore, heightens concern over greenhouse gas emissions; it later wins an Academy Award for best documentary feature. In June, President George W. Bush protects the Northwestern Hawaiian Islands Marine National Monument (also known as the Papahānaumokuākea Marine National Monument) under the Antiquities Act, creating an ocean reserve of approximately 140,000 square miles. The state of California passes the Global Warming Solutions Act, mandating a reduction in greenhouse gases to 1990 levels by the year 2020. The estimated population of the U.S. passes 300 million in mid-October. In December, scientists describe widespread losses to commercial honey-bee colonies in the eastern U.S.; later named "Colony Collapse Disorder," the phenomenon is reported elsewhere and becomes a subject of ongoing research and concern.

2007   In January, the federal Fish and Wildlife Service proposes the addition of the polar bear (*Ursus maritimus*) to its list of threatened and endangered species as Arctic warming reduces the bear's summer habitat. After years of protection and recovery, the bald eagle (*Haliaeetus leucocephalus*) is removed from the list later in the year. In March, the Organization of American States receives a delegation of Inuit people from Alaska, Canada, and Russia who argue that the United States' failure to limit greenhouse gas emissions is destroying their way of life. In April, in a 5–4 decision in *Massachusetts* v. *Environmental Protection Agency*, the Supreme Court rules that the 1990 Clean Air Act gives the EPA regulatory authority over automobile greenhouse gas emissions, an authority the EPA had avoided claiming. In June, General Electric and Hitachi announce plans to build two new nuclear power plants in Matagorda County, Texas, scheduled to open in 2014; in August, the board of the Tennessee Valley Authority decides to complete Watts Bar 2, a nuclear reactor mothballed in 1988 and now expected to begin commercial generation in 2013. (Just over 100 commercial nuclear reactors are in operation in the U.S., providing around 20 percent of the nation's electricity, but no new plants have been ordered since 1978, and several have been decommissioned early.) In September, satellite imagery reveals that the Northwest Passage between the Atlantic and Pacific is free of ice and fully navigable. In October, Al Gore and the United Nations Intergovernmental Panel on Climate Change are named as winners of the Nobel Peace Prize. China is reported to have overtaken the U.S. as the world's leading emitter of greenhouse gases from fossil fuel consumption, though Americans are responsible for over six times as much greenhouse gas per capita.

NOTE ON THE ILLUSTRATIONS

1. Asher B. Durand, *Kindred Spirits* (1849).
    Courtesy Crystal Bridges Museum of American Art, Bentonville,
    Arkansas.

2. George Catlin, *Buffalo Hunt, Approaching in a Ravine* (1845).
    Handcolored lithograph from *Catlin's North American Indian Portfolio:
    Hunting Scenes and Amusements of the Rocky Mountains of
    America* (New York: James Ackerman), plate 11.
    Courtesy Rare Books Division, The New York Public Library, Astor,
    Lenox, and Tilden Foundations.

3. Henry D. Thoreau, manuscript survey of Walden Pond (1846).
    Courtesy Concord Free Public Library (Thoreau survey collection 133a).

4. Title page of Susan Fenimore Cooper's *Rural Hours* (1851).
    Lithographer: Endicott & Co., New York. Colorist unknown.
    Courtesy of the Department of Special Collections (Cairns Collection),
    Memorial Library, University of Wisconsin–Madison.
    Reprinted by permission.

5. Title page of Henry D. Thoreau's *Walden* (1854).
    Engraving: Baker & Andrew, after a sketch by Sophia Thoreau.
    Courtesy Concord Free Public Library.

6. Lydia Huntley Sigourney (1859).
    Photographer: Mathew B. Brady Studio.
    Courtesy of the Library of Congress.

7. George Perkins Marsh (c. 1861).
    Photographer: Mathew B. Brady Studio.
    Courtesy of the Library of Congress.

8. James Wallace Black, *Artists' Falls, North Conway* (1854).
    Courtesy of The Metropolitan Museum of Art, Robert O. Dougan
    Collection, Gift of Warner Communications, Inc., 1981
    (1981.1229.3). Image copyright © The Metropolitan Museum
    of Art.

9. Carleton Watkins, *Trees and Cabin with Yosemite Falls in Background*
    (1861).
    Courtesy of the Library of Congress.

10. Carleton Watkins, *The Three Graces, 272 Feet* (c. 1865–66).

Courtesy of The Metropolitan Museum of Art, Gift of Carole and Irwin
Lainoff, Ruth P. Lasser and Joseph R. Lasser, Mr. and Mrs. John T.
Marvin, Martin E. and Joan Messinger, Richard L. Yett and Sheri
and Paul Siegel, 1986 (1986.1189.69). Image copyright © The
Metropolitan Museum of Art.

11. William Henry Jackson, *Elk with Velvet on its Antlers, Yellowstone
National Park* (1871).
Courtesy of the Library of Congress.

12. Charles Leander Weed, *Yosemite Valley from Mariposa Trail* (1865).
Mammoth albumen print from wet collodion negative, 39.70 x 71.70 cm.
Copyright © The Cleveland Museum of Art, John L. Severance
Fund, 2002.43.
Reprinted by permission.

13. B. F. Upton, *On the Drive, Pineries of Minnesota* (c. 1867–75).
Half stereocard, from series *Upton's Minnesota and Northwestern
Views*. Photographer unknown.
Courtesy of the Library of Congress.

14. Buffalo skulls at Michigan Carbon Works, a Detroit charcoal and
fertilizer factory (c.1880).
Photographer unknown.
Courtesy Burton Historical Collection, Detroit Public Library.

15. Currier & Ives, *The Falls of Niagara* (*From the Canada Side*) (c. 1868).
Engraving: Parsons & Atwater, after a painting by B. Hess.
Courtesy of the Library of Congress.

16. William Henry Jackson, *Old Faithful* (1870).
Courtesy of The J. Paul Getty Museum, Los Angeles (85.XM.5.38).

17. Albert Bierstadt, *Hetch Hetchy Canyon* (1875).
Courtesy Mount Holyoke College Art Museum, South Hadley,
Massachusetts. Gift of Mrs. A. L. Williston and Mrs. E. H. Sawyer,
1876.

18. Harry Fenn (S.V. Hunt, engraver), *The Catskills: Sunrise from South
Mountain*
From William Cullen Bryant, ed., *Picturesque America* (New York:
D. Appleton, 1873).
Courtesy of the Library of Congress.

19. Timothy H. O'Sullivan, *Ancient Ruins in the Cañon de Chelle, N.M.*
(1873).
From *Photographs, Geographical Explorations and Surveys West of the*

100th Meridian (Washington, D.C.: United States Army Corps of
Engineers, 1874).
Courtesy of the Library of Congress.

20. *St. Peter's Dome on the C. S. & C. C. Short Line, Colo.* (1901)
Postcard, Detroit Photographic Co.
Courtesy of the Photography Collection, Miriam and Ira D. Wallach
Division of Art, Prints, and Photographs. The New York Public
Library, Astor, Lenox and Tilden Foundations.

21. *"A Bare Faced Steal"* (1905).
Postcard, Detroit Photographic Co.
Photography Collection, Miriam and Ira D. Wallach Division of Art,
Prints, and Photographs, The New York Public Library, Astor,
Lenox and Tilden Foundations.

22. Darius Kinsey, *On the Spring Boards and in the Undercut, Washington
Bolt Cutter and His Daughters* (1905).
Courtesy of the Library of Congress.

23. Darius Kinsey, *Logging in the Cascade Mountains, near Seattle*
(c. 1906).
Courtesy of The Library of Congress.

24. Theodore Roosevelt and John Muir at Glacier Point, Yosemite (1903).
Half stereocard, Underwood & Underwood.
Courtesy of the Library of Congress.

25. John Burroughs and John Muir at the Grand Canyon (1909).
Photographer: Karl Moon.
Courtesy Holt Atherton Special Collections, University of the Pacific
(John Muir Papers MSS 048).

26. John Muir with a Sierra Club group on the trail to Hetch Hetchy,
California (1909).
Photographer: George R. King.
Courtesy Holt Atherton Special Collections, University of the Pacific
(John Muir Papers MSS 048).

27. Herbert W. Gleason, *Northwest Cove of Walden, Ice Breaking Up
(Train in Distance)* (1920).
Courtesy Concord Free Public Library.

28. Herbert W. Gleason, *Walden in Winter (Arching Limb)* (1917).
Lantern slide, hand-colored by Lulu Rounds Gleason.
Courtesy Concord Free Public Library.

29. Alma Lavenson, *Zion Canyon* (*The Light Beyond*) (1927).
    Galerie Zur Stockeregg.
    Courtesy of Stockeregg Gallery, Zurich, Switzerland.

30. Gifford Pinchot at Partlow Lake in New York's Adirondack Park (c. 1892).
    H. S. Graves, photographer.
    Courtesy of the Photography Collection, Miriam and Ira D. Wallach Division of Art, Prints, and Photographs. The New York Public Library, Astor, Lenox and Tilden Foundations.

31. Mary Austin (c. 1920).
    Photographer unknown.
    Courtesy University of California–Berkeley.

32. Gene Stratton-Porter in California (c. 1920).
    Photographer: Edward S. Curtis.
    Gene Stratton-Porter State Historic Sites, Indiana State Museum.
    Courtesy of the Indiana State Museum and Historic Sites.

33. Arthur Rothstein, *Dust Clouds over Texas Panhandle* (1936).
    Courtesy of the Library of Congress.

34. Aldo Leopold examining red pines near his Sauk County, Wisconsin, shack (1946).
    Photographer: Robert McCabe.
    Aldo Leopold papers, University of Wisconsin–Madison; Aldo Leopold Foundation.
    Courtesy of the Aldo Leopold Foundation Archives.

35. Leopold's shack, Sauk County, Wisconsin (c. 1936).
    Photographer unknown.
    Aldo Leopold papers, University of Wisconsin–Madison; Aldo Leopold Foundation.
    Courtesy of the Aldo Leopold Foundation Archives.

36. Sigurd Olson stocking Minnesota's Crooked Lake with smallmouth bass fingerlings (August 1940)
    Photographer: Leland J. Prater.
    Copyright © CORBIS.

37. Ansel Adams, *Mount McKinley and Wonder Lake, Denali National Park, Alaska* (1947; revised print 1978).
    Copyright © The Ansel Adams Publishing Rights Trust / CORBIS.

38. Ansel Adams, *El Capitan, Yosemite National Park, California* (1952).
    Copyright © The Ansel Adams Publishing Rights Trust / CORBIS.

39.   Donora, Pennsylvania, on November 3, 1948. A day earlier, funeral
        services were held for victims of the Donora smog—a cloud of
        toxic gases that also sickened thousands of residents.
      Photographer unknown.
      Copyright © Bettmann / CORBIS.

40.   An insecticidal fogging machine in its first public test sprays DDT at
        Jones Beach, New York, July 8, 1945.
      Photographer unknown.
      Copyright © Bettmann / CORBIS.

41.   Cleveland firemen battle a blaze on the polluted Cuyahoga River,
        November 3, 1952.
      Photographer unknown.
      Copyright © Bettmann / CORBIS.

42.   Eliot Porter, *Pool in a Brook, Brook Pond, New Hampshire, October 4,
        1953.*
      Courtesy Amon Carter Museum.
      Copyright © 1990 Amon Carter Museum, Fort Worth, Texas, Bequest of
        the artist.

43.   Eliot Porter, *Arch and Box Elder Tree, Davis Gulch, Escalante River,
        Lake Powell, Utah, May 12, 1965.*
      Courtesy Amon Carter Museum.
      Copyright © 1990 Amon Carter Museum, Fort Worth, Texas, Bequest of
        the artist.

44.   Charles Pratt, *Woman and Flowering Tree, Hoboken, New Jersey*
        (c. 1963).
      Courtesy Robert Mann Gallery / Center for Creative Photography,
        University of Arizona.
      Copyright © The Estate of Charles Pratt.

45.   Philip Hyde, *South Rim in Winter, Grand Canyon, Arizona* (1964).
      Courtesy of the University of California Santa Cruz Special Collections,
        Philip Hyde Archive.
      Reprinted by permission.

46.   Rachel Carson, author of the newly published *Silent Spring*
        (September 1, 1962).
      Photographer: Alfred Eisenstaedt.
      Courtesy Time & Life Pictures / Getty Images.

47.   Hugh Barnes, David Brower, and Eliot Porter (*l. to r.*) examining proofs
        for *"In Wildness Is the Preservation of the World"*—the first of the

Sierra Club's "Exhibit Format" books—at Barnes Press in New York (c. 1962).

Photographer: Patricia Caulfield.

Grateful acknowledgment is made to the Colby Memorial Library of the Sierra Club for use of its historical archives.

Reprinted by permission of the photographer.

48. Stanley Mouse / Mouse Studios, poster for 10th Biennial Sierra Club Wilderness Conference (1967).

Colby Memorial Library, Sierra Club.

Grateful acknowledgment is made to the Colby Memorial Library of the Sierra Club for use of its historical archives.

49. Robert Rauschenberg, Earth Day poster (1970).

Copyright © Robert Rauschenberg / Licensed by VAGA, New York, New York.

50. Earth Day in New York City (April 22, 1970).

Photographer unknown.

Copyright © Bettmann / CORBIS.

51. Gary Snyder (1969).

Photographer: Philip Harrington.

Reprinted by permission of the Photographer.

52. Earth Day (April 22, 1970).

Photographer unknown.

Courtesy Hulton Archive / Getty Images.

53. N. Scott Momaday (c. 1969).

Photographer unknown.

Copyright © Bettmann / CORBIS.

54. A dead bird, covered in oil, in the wake of an oil spill off the coast of Santa Barbara (February 15, 1969).

Photographer: Vernon Merritt III.

Courtesy Time & Life Pictures / Getty Images.

55. The "Blue Marble" (December 7, 1972).

Photographer: *Apollo 17* crew, astronaut photograph AS17-148-22727.

Courtesy NASA Johnson Space Center Gateway to Astronaut Photography of Earth.

56. Robert Adams, *Newly Occupied Tract Houses, Colorado Springs* (1968).

Copyright © Robert Adams. Courtesy of the Yale University Art Gallery and Fraenkel Gallery, San Francisco.

57. Stephen Shore, *Second Street East and South Main Street, Kalispell, Montana, August 22, 1974*.
    Copyright © Stephen Shore, Courtesy of 303 Gallery, New York.

58. Vint Lawrence, *The William O. Douglas Wilderness Area* (1974).
    Offset lithograph. Reprinted by permission.

59. Edward Abbey in the Aztec Peak lookout tower, where he worked as a fire spotter (Tonto National Forest, Arizona, c. 1979).
    Photographer: Buddy Mays.
    Copyright © Buddy Mays / CORBIS.

60. Scott and Helen Nearing at home in Harborside, Maine (1975).
    Photographer unknown.
    Copyright © Bettmann / CORBIS.

61. Earth Day organizer Denis Hayes (1970).
    Photographer: John Olson.
    Courtesy Time & Life Pictures / Getty Images.

62. Marjory Stoneman Douglas, canoeing with a Miccosukee Indian at the Miccosukee Cultural Center in the Everglades (1983).
    Photographer unknown.
    Reprinted by permission of The State Archives of Florida.

63. Lois Gibbs at Love Canal (1978).
    Photographer: Katie Schneider.
    Copyright © 1978 by Katie Schneider. Reprinted by permission.

64. Timothy O'Sullivan, *Green River Buttes, Green River, Wyoming (1872)*.
    Courtesy United States Geological Survey.

65. Mark Klett & Gordon Bushaw for the Rephotographic Survey Project, *Castle Rock, Green River, Wyoming* (1979).
    Copyright © 1979 The Rephotographic Survey Project.

66. Emmet Gowin, *Aeration Pond, Toxic Water Treatment Facility, Pine Bluff, Arkansas* (1989).
    Copyright © Emmet and Edith Gowin. Courtesy Pace / MacGill Gallery, New York.

67. John Pfahl, *Trojan Nuclear Plant, Columbia River, Oregon, October 1982*.
    From the series "Power Places."
    Courtesy of the artist and Janet Borden, Inc.

68. Julia Butterfly Hill the branches of Luna (April 1, 1998).
    Photographer: Andrew Lichtenstein.
    Copyright © Andrew Lichtenstein / CORBIS SYGMA.

69. George Schaller, wildlife biologist, with a snow leopard kitten (c. 2000).
    Photographer unknown.
    Courtesy Wildlife Conservation Society, Bronx Zoo.

70. David Quammen in India's Gir Forest National Park, tracking
    endangered Asiatic lions (1997).
    Photographer: Michael Llewellyn.
    Copyright © 1997 Michael Llewellyn. All rights reserved.

71. E. O. Wilson with a model ant (September 18, 2002).
    Photographer: Rick Friedman.
    Copyright © Rick Friedman / CORBIS.

72. Robert Dawson, *Polluted New River, Calexico, California* (1989).
    From the "Farewell, Promised Land" project.
    Copyright © 1989 by Robert Dawson. Reprinted by permission.

73. Kim Stringfellow, *Pumping Out Flood Water, Salton Sea Beach,
    California (2004).*
    From *Greetings from the Salton Sea: Folly and Intervention in the
    Southern California Landscape, 1905–2005* (Santa Fe: Center for
    American Places, 2005).
    Copyright © 2004 by Kim Stringfellow. Reprinted by permission.

74. Richard Misrach, *Hazardous Waste Containment Site, Dow Chemical
    Corporation* (1998).
    Copyright © Richard Misrach. Courtesy Fraenkel Gallery, San
    Francisco; Pace MacGill Gallery, New York; and Marc Selwyn
    Gallery, Los Angeles.

75. Robert Glenn Ketchum, *The Chainsaws of Summer* (Tongass
    Rainforest, Alaska, 1992).
    Reprinted by permission of the artist.

76. Subhankar Banerjee, *Caribou Migration I* (from the series *Oil and the
    Caribou,* 2002).
    Photograph by Subhankar Banerjee / www.subhankarbanerjee.org.
    Reprinted with permission of the photographer.

77. Subhankar Banerjee, *Polar Bear on Bernard Harbor* (from the series *Oil
    and the Caribou,* 2001).
    Photograph by Subhankar Banerjee / www.subhankarbanerjee.org.
    Reprinted with permission of the photographer.

78. Christopher LaMarca, from *Forest Defenders* series (2005).
    Courtesy Christopher LaMarca / Redux.

79. Anti-pollution protestors from Greenaction for Health & Environmental
    Justice and the local community block the entrance to a power
    plant in San Francisco's Hunters Point neighborhood (December 9,
    2004).
    Photographer unknown.
    Courtesy of Greenaction for Health & Environmental Justice.

80. Chris Jordan, *Sawdust, Tacoma* (2004).
    From the series "Intolerable Beauty: Portraits of American Mass
    Consumption."
    Copyright © 2004 by Chris Jordan. Reprinted by permission.

81. Edward Burtynsky, *Oxford Tire Pile #1, Westley, California* (1999).
    Image Courtesy Edward Burtynsky and Charles Cowles Gallery,
    New York.

82. Mitch Epstein, *Amos Coal Power Plant, Raymond, West Virginia* (2004).
    From the "American Power" project.
    Copyright © Black River Productions, Ltd. / Mitch Epstein. Courtesy
    Sikkema Jenkins & Co., New York. Used with permission. All
    rights reserved.

SOURCES & ACKNOWLEDGMENTS

Edward Abbey, "Polemic: Industrial Tourism and the National Parks": *Desert Solitaire: A Season in the Wilderness* (New York: McGraw-Hill, 1968), pp. 39–59. Copyright © 1968 by Edward Abbey, renewed © 1996 by Clarke Abbey. Reprinted by permission of Don Congdon Associates, Inc.

David Abram, from "The Ecology of Magic": *The Spell of the Sensuous* (New York: Pantheon Books, 1996), pp. 3–21. Copyright © 1996 by David Abram. Used by permission of Pantheon Books, a division of Random House, Inc.

Carl Anthony and Renée Soule, "A Multicultural Approach to Ecopsychology": *The Humanistic Psychologist* 26.1–3 (1998): 155–61. Copyright © Carl Anthony and Renée Soule. Reprinted by permission.

Mary Austin, "The Scavengers": *The Land of Little Rain* (Boston: Houghton Mifflin, 1903), pp. 47–60.

Russell Baker, "The Great Paver": *The New York Times*, February 7, 1963, p. 5. Copyright © 1963 by The New York Times. All rights reserved. Used by permission and protected by the Copyright Laws of the United States. The printing, copying, redistribution, or retransmission of the Material without express written permission is prohibited.

P. T. Barnum, from *The Humbugs of the World: The Humbugs of the World: An Account of Humbugs, Delusions, Impositions, Quackeries, Deceits and Deceivers Generally, in All Ages* (New York: Carleton, 1866), pp. 27–29.

Rick Bass, from *The Ninemile Wolves: The Ninemile Wolves* (Livingston, Montana: Clark City Press, 1992), pp. 3–14. Copyright © 1992 by Rick Bass. Reprinted by permission of the author.

Wendell Berry, "Manifesto: The Mad Farmer Liberation Front": *The Country of Marriage* (New York: Harcourt Brace Jovanovich, 1973), pp. 16–17. Copyright © 1985 by Wendell Berry. Reprinted by permission of North Point Press, a division of Farrar, Straus and Giroux, LLC. "Preserving Wildness": *Home Economics* (New York: North Point Press, 1987), pp. 137–51. Copyright © 1987 by Wendell Berry. Reprinted by permission of North Point Press, a division of Farrar, Straus and Giroux, LLC. "The Making of a Marginal Farm": *Recollected Essays, 1965–1980* (San Francisco: North Point Press, 1981), pp. 329–40. Copyright © 1982 by Wendell Berry. Reprinted by arrangement with Counterpoint LLC.

Henry Beston, "Orion Rises on the Dunes": *The Outermost House* (Garden City: Doubleday, Doran, 1928), pp. 214–18. Copyright © 1928, 1949 by Henry Beston, copyright renewed © 1956 by Henry Beston, copyright renewed © 1977 by Elizabeth C. Beston. Reprinted by permission of Kate Beston Barnes.

Kenneth E. Boulding, from "The Economics of the Coming Spaceship Earth": *Environmental Quality in a Growing Economy* (Baltimore: Johns Hopkins Press, 1966), pp. 3–14. Copyright © 1966. Reprinted by permission of REF Press / Resources for the Future.

David R. Brower, "The Third Planet: Operating Instructions": *The New York Times Magazine*, March 16, 1975, p. 111. Copyright © 2000 by David Brower and Steve Chapple. Reprinted by permission of Sierra Club Books.

Robert D. Bullard, from *Dumping in Dixie*: *Dumping in Dixie* (Boulder: Westview Press, 1990), pp. 1–5, 55–59. Copyright © 1990, 1994, 2000 by Westview Press, A Member of the Perseus Books Group. Reprinted by permission.

John Burroughs, "The Art of Seeing Things"; "The Grist of the Gods": *Leaf and Tendril* (Boston: Houghton Mifflin, 1908), pp. 1–23; 199–213. "Nature Near Home": *Field and Study* (Boston: Houghton Mifflin, 1919), pp. 213–17.

Rachel Carson, from *Silent Spring*: *Silent Spring* (Cambridge: Houghton Mifflin, 1962), pp. 1–3, 103–26. Copyright © 1962 by Rachel L. Carson, renewed ©1990 by Roger Christie. Reprinted by permission of Houghton Mifflin Company. All rights reserved.

George Catlin, from *Letters and Notes on the Manners, Customs, and Condition of the North American Indians*: *Letters and Notes on the Manners, Customs, and Condition of the North American Indians* (London: George Catlin, 1841), pp. 258–64.

César Chávez, "Wrath of Grapes Boycott Speech": *The Words of César Chávez,* eds. Richard J. Jensen & John C. Hammerback (College Station, Texas: Texas A & M University Press, 2002), pp. 132–35. Copyright © 2002 by Richard J. Jensen and John C. Hammerback. Reprinted by permission of Texas A&M University Press. Speech originally delivered 1986; typescript in the United Farm Workers Papers, Wayne State University.

Susan Fenimore Cooper, from *Rural Hours*: *Rural Hours* (New York: G. P. Putnam, 1850), pp. 105–10, 187–94.

William Cronon, "Seasons of Want and Plenty": *Changes in the Land: Indians, Colonists, and the Ecology of New England* (New York: Hill and Wang, 1983), pp. 34–53. Copyright © 1983 by William Cronon. Reprinted by permission of Hill and Wang, a division of Farrar, Straus and Giroux, LLC.

R. Crumb, "A Short History of America": *CoEvolution Quarterly* 23 (Fall 1979): 21–24. Copyright © R. Crumb. Reprinted with permission of the author.

J. N. "Ding" Darling, "What a few more seasons will do to the ducks": *New York Herald*, September 17, 1930. The editorial cartoons of J. N. "Ding" Darling [CD-ROM]: The Cowles collection, Drake University 1912–1962 (Key Biscayne, Florida: J. N. "Ding" Darling Foundation, ©1999). Reproduced courtesy of the "Ding" Darling Wildlife Society.

Calvin DeWitt, from "Inspirations for Sustaining Life on Earth: Greeting Friends in Their Andean Gardens": "Inspirations for Sustaining Life on

Earth," Seminar Paper, Agroecology Roundtable, Heifer Project International, "Sustaining Life on Earth" meeting, Ecuador, 2001. Copyright © 2001 by Calvin DeWitt. Reprinted by permission.

Philip K. Dick, from *Do Androids Dream of Electric Sheep?*: *Philip K. Dick: Four Novels of the 1960s*, Jonathan Lethem, ed. (New York: The Library of America, 2007), pp. 462–64. Copyright © 1962, 1964, 1968, 1969 by Philip K. Dick, renewed 1990, 1992, 1996, 1997 by Laura Coelho, Christopher Dick, and Isa Dick. Reprinted by permission of the Philip K. Dick Testamentary Trust.

Annie Dillard, "Fecundity": *Pilgrim at Tinker Creek* (New York: Harper's Magazine Press, 1974), pp. 159–81. Copyright © 1974 by Annie Dillard. Reprinted by permission of HarperCollins Publishers.

Marjory Stoneman Douglas, from *The Everglades: River of Grass*: *The Everglades: River of Grass* (New York: Rinehart & Co., 1947), pp. 9–14. Copyright © 1947 by Marjory Stoneman Douglas. Reprinted with permission of the Marjory Stoneman Douglas Papers, Otto G. Richter Library, University of Miami, Florida.

William O. Douglas, from *My Wilderness: The Pacific West*: *My Wilderness: The Pacific West* (New York: Doubleday, 1960), pp. 152–60. Copyright © 1960 by William O. Douglas. Reprinted by permission of Cathleen Douglas Stone. Dissent in *Sierra Club* v. *Morton*: *Sierra Club* v. *Morton*, 405 U.S. 727 (1972).

Theodore Dreiser, "A Certain Oil Refinery": *The Color of a Great City* (New York: Boni & Liveright, 1923), pp. 200–06. First published as "The Standard Oil Works at Bayonne," *New York Call,* March 16, 1919.

Alan Durning, "The Dubious Rewards of Consumption": *How Much Is Enough?: The Consumer Society and the Future of the Earth* (New York: W. W. Norton, 1992), pp. 37–48. Copyright © 1992 by Woldwatch Institute. Used by permission of W. W. Norton & Company, Inc.

Paul R. Ehrlich, from *The Population Bomb*: *The Population Bomb* (New York: Ballantine Books, 1968), pp. 15–20. Copyright © 1968, 1971 by Paul R. Ehrlich. Used by permission of Ballantine Books, a division of Random House, Inc.

Loren Eiseley, "How Flowers Changed the World": *The Immense Journey* (New York: Random House, 1957), pp. 61–77. Copyright © 1946, 1950, 1951, 1953, 1955, 1956, 1957 by Loren Eiseley. Used by permission of Random House, Inc.

Colin Fletcher, "A Sample Day in the Kitchen": *The Complete Walker* (New York: Knopf, 1968), pp. 124–32. Copyright © 1968 by Colin Fletcher. Used by permission of Alfred A. Knopf, a division of Random House, Inc. A footnote to Fletcher's chapter title notes "[t]here are several similarities, here, to an account in *The Man Who Walked Through Time* (pages 19–24) of how I prepared an evening meal."

Friends of the Earth, from *The Stockholm Conference: Only One Earth* (London: Earth Island Limited, 1972), pp. 17–22. Copyright © 1972 by Friends of the Earth. Reprinted by permission.

R. Buckminster Fuller, "Spaceship Earth": *Operating Manual for Spaceship Earth* (Carbondale: Southern Illinois University Press, 1969), pp. 49–56. Copyright © 1963, 1971 Buckminster Fuller and The Estate of R. Buckminster Fuller. All rights reserved. Reprinted by permission.

Marvin Gaye, "Mercy Mercy Me (The Ecology)": *What's Going On* (Tamla TS 310, 1971, LP vinyl recording). Words and Music by Marvin Gaye © 1971 (Renewed 1999) JoBette Music Co., Inc. All Rights Controlled and Administered by EMI APRIL MUSIC INC. All Rights Reserved. International Copyright Secured. Used by permission.

Lois Marie Gibbs, from *Love Canal: My Story*: *Love Canal: My Story* (Albany: State University of New York Press, 1982), pp. 8–24. Copyright © 1982 by Lois Marie Gibbs. Used by permission of Grove/Atlantic, Inc.

Al Gore, "Speech at the Kyoto Climate Change Conference": "Remarks As Prepared for Delivery for Vice President Al Gore, Kyoto Climate Change Conference, December 8, 1997," National Archives Internet cache, accessed Sept. 20, 2007: *clinton3.nara.gov/WH/EOP/OVP/speeches/kyotofin.html*.

Woody Guthrie, "This Land Is Your Land": *Ten of Woody Guthrie's Songs. Book One* (Brooklyn: W. Guthrie, 1945), p. 7.

Garrett Hardin, from "The Tragedy of the Commons": *Science*, December 13, 1968, pp. 1243–48. Reprinted with permission from American Association for the Advancement of Science.

Paul Hawken, from *Blessed Unrest*: *Blessed Unrest: How the Largest Movement in the World Came into Being and Why No One Saw It Coming* (New York: Viking, 2007), pp. 158–65. Copyright © 2007 by Paul Hawken. Used by permission of Viking Penguin, a division of Penguin Group (USA), Inc.

Denis Hayes, "The Beginning": *Earth Day—The Beginning: A Guide for Survival*, ed. National Staff of Environmental Action (New York: Arno Press & The New York Times, 1970), pp. xv–xvii. Copyright © 1970 by Arno Press, Inc. Reprinted by permission.

Caroline Henderson, "Letter from the Dust Bowl": "Letters from the Dust Bowl," *The Atlantic*, May, 1936, pp. 540–43. Reprinted by permission of the University of Oklahoma Press.

Julia Butterfly Hill, from *The Legacy of Luna*: *The Legacy of Luna* (New York: HarperCollins, 2000), pp. 99–115. Copyright © 2000 by Julia Hill. Reprinted by permission of HarperCollins Publishers.

Linda Hogan, "Dwellings": *Dwellings: A Spiritual History of the Living World* (New York. W.W. Norton, 1995), pp. 117–24. Copyright © 1995 by Linda Hogan. Used by permission of W. W. Norton & Company, Inc.

William T. Hornaday, "The Bird Tragedy on Laysan Island": *Our Vanishing Wild Life* (New York: New York Zoological Society, 1913), pp. 137–42.

Jane Jacobs, from *The Death and Life of Great American Cities*: *The Death and Life of Great American Cities* (New York: Random House, 1961), pp. 443–48. Copyright © 1961, 1989 by Jane Jacobs. Used by permission of Random House, Inc.

Wes Jackson, "Outside the Solar Village: One Utopian Farm": *New Roots for Agriculture* (Washington, D.C.: Friends of the Earth, 1980), pp. 137–49. Copyright © 1980 by Wes Jackson, all rights reserved. Reprinted by permission.

Robinson Jeffers, "The Answer"; "Carmel Point": *The Selected Poetry of Robinson Jeffers,* Tim Hunt, ed. (Stanford: Stanford University Press, 2001), pp. 594, 676. "The Answer" originally published 1935; "Carmel Point" originally published 1953. "The Answer": Copyright © 1938, renewed 1966 by Garth Jeffers and Donnan Jeffers. All rights reserved. Used with permission of Stanford University Press, www.sup.org. "Carmel Point": Copyright © 1954 by Robinson Jeffers. Used by permission of Random House, Inc.

Lyndon B. Johnson, "Remarks at the Signing of the Highway Beautification Act of 1965": *Public Papers of the Presidents of the United States: Lyndon B. Johnson* (Washington, D.C., Government Printing Office, 1966), Book 2 (1965), pp. 1072–74.

Barbara Kingsolver, "Knowing Our Place": *Small Wonder* (New York: HarperCollins, 2002), pp. 31–40. Copyright © 2002 by Barbara Kingsolver. Reprinted by permission of HarperCollins Publishers. An early version of this essay appeared as the Introduction to *Off the Beaten Path: Stories of Place,* Joseph Barbato and Lisa Weinerman Horak, eds. (New York: North Point Press, 1998).

Joseph Lelyveld, "Millions Join Earth Day Observances Across the Nation": *The New York Times,* April 23, 1970, pp. 1, 30. Copyright © 1970 The New York Times. All rights reserved. Used by permission and protected by the Copyright Laws of the United States. The printing, copying, redistribution, or retransmission of the Material without express written permission is prohibited. The original text of this article in the *Times* includes a line of garbled copy. "Before he left Albany he / signed by Gov. William T. Ca- / pollution activities" has been rewritten in the present volume as "Before he left Albany he signed a bill organizing anti-pollution activities."

Aldo Leopold, from *A Sand County Almanac*: *A Sand County Almanac* (New York: Oxford University Press, 1949), pp. 95–101, 104–08, 129–33, 201–14, 223–26. Copyright © 1949 by Oxford University Press. Reprinted by permission of Oxford University Press, Inc.

Barry Lopez, "A Presentation of Whales": *Crossing Open Ground* (New York: Charles Scribner's Sons, 1988), pp. 117–46. Copyright © 1978, 1979, 1980, 1981, 1982, 1983, 1984, 1985, 1986, 1988 by Barry Lopez. Reprinted with permission of Sll/Sterling Lord Literistic, Inc.

Amory B. Lovins, from "Energy Strategy: The Road Not Taken?": *Foreign Affairs,* 55.1 (October, 1976), pp. 77–80, 91–95. Reprinted by permission of *Foreign Affairs* (55.1). Copyright © 1976 by the Council on Foreign Relations, Inc.

Benton MacKaye, "The Indigenous and the Metropolitan": *The New Exploration: A Philosophy of Regional Planning* (New York: Harcourt, Brace, 1928), pp. 56–74. Copyright © by Benton MacKaye. Reprinted by permission of John Barnes.

Don Marquis, "what the ants are saying": *The Lives and Times of Archy and Mehitabel* (Garden City, New York: Doubleday Doran, 1935), pp. 475–77. Copyright © 1927 by Doubleday, a division of Random House, Inc. Used by permission of Doubleday, a division of Random House, Inc.

George Perkins Marsh, from *Man and Nature: Man and Nature; or, Physical Geography as Modified by Human Action* (New York: Charles Scribner, 1864), pp. 35–44, 328–29.

Robert Marshall, from "Wintertrip into New Country": *Arctic Wilderness* (Berkeley: University of California Press, 1956), pp. 61–69. Copyright © 1956 by the Regents of the University of California. Reprinted by permission of the University of California Press. Written c. 1931 and published posthumously.

Bill McKibben, from *The End of Nature: The End of Nature* (New York: Random House, 1989), pp. 47–49, 86–91. Copyright © 1989, 2006 by William McKibben. Used by permission of Random House, Inc.

John McPhee, from *Encounters with the Archdruid: Encounters with the Archdruid* (New York: Farrar, Straus & Giroux, 1971), pp. 196–204. Copyright © 1971 by John McPhee. Reprinted by permission of Farrar, Straus and Giroux, LLC.

Ellen Meloy, "The Flora and Fauna of Las Vegas": *Raven's Exile: A Season on the Green River* (New York: Henry Holt, 1994), pp. 179–97. Copyright © 1994 by The Estate of Ellen Meloy. Reprinted by permission of Sll/Sterling Lord Literistic, Inc.

W. S. Merwin, "Place": *The Rain in the Trees* (New York: Alfred A. Knopf, 1988), p. 64. Copyright © 1988 by W. S. Merwin. Used by permission of Alfred A. Knopf, a division of Random House, Inc.

Stephanie Mills, "Mills College Valedictory Address": Typescript press release, June 1, 1969, Mills College (Oakland, California). Reprinted with permission of Stephanie Mills.

Joni Mitchell, "Big Yellow Taxi": *Ladies of the Canyon* (Reprise RS 6376, 1970, LP vinyl recording). Words and music by Joni Mitchell © 1970 (Renewed) Crazy Crow Music. All rights administered by Sony/ATV Music Publishing, 8 Music Square West, Nashville, TN 37203. All Rights Reserved. Used by permission of Alfred Publishing Co., Inc.

N. Scott Momaday, "A First American Views His Land": *National Geographic*, July 1976, pp. 13–18. Copyright © N. Scott Momaday. Reprinted by permission.

J. Sterling Morton, "About Trees": *Arbor Day Leaves*, N.H. Egleston, ed. (New York: American Book Company, 1893), pp. 3–5.

John Muir, from *A Thousand-Mile Walk to the Gulf: A Thousand-Mile Walk to the Gulf* (Boston: Houghton Mifflin, 1916), pp. 96–99, 136–42. "A Wind-Storm in the Forests"; from *My First Summer in the Sierra*; "Hetch Hetchy Valley": *John Muir: Nature Writings*, William Cronon, ed. (New York: The Library of America, 1997), pp. 465–73; 227–234; 810–17. "A Wind-Storm in the Forests" first published 1894. *My First Summer in the Sierras* first published 1911. "Hetch Hetchy Valley" first published 1912

W.H.H. Murray, from *Adventures in the Wilderness: Adventures in the Wilderness* (Boston, De Wolfe, Fiske, 1869), pp. 9–13, 32–28.

Helen and Scott Nearing, from *Living the Good Life: Living the Good Life* (Harborside, Maine: Social Science Institute, 1954), pp. 29–35. Copyright © 1954 and renewed 1982 by Helen Nearing. Used by permission of Schocken Books, a division of Random House, Inc.

Richard Nelson, from *Heart and Blood: Living with Deer in America: Heart and Blood: Living with Deer in America* (New York: Alfred A. Knopf, 1997), pp. 342–52. Copyright © 1997 by Richard Nelson. Reprinted by permission of Susan Bergholz Literary Services, New York, NY and Lamy, NM. All rights reserved.

Mary Oliver, "The Summer Day": *House of Light* (Boston: Beacon Press, 1990), p. 60. Copyright © 1990 by Mary Oliver. Reprinted by permission of Beacon Press, Boston.

Frederick Law Olmsted, from "A Review of Recent Changes, and Changes Which Have Been Projected, in the Plans of the Central Park": *Frederick Law Olmsted, Landscape Architect, 1822–1903*, vol. 2 (New York: G.P. Putnam's Sons, 1928), pp. 248–52. First published in 1872, in the 2nd Annual Report of the New York Department of Public Parks.

Sigurd F. Olson, "Northern Lights": *The Singing Wilderness* (New York: Alfred A. Knopf, 1956), pp. 183–87. Copyright © 1956 by Sigurd F. Olson. Copyright renewed 1984 by Elizabeth D. Olson and Alfred A. Knopf, Inc. Used by permission of Alfred A. Knopf, a division of Random House, Inc.

Donald Culross Peattie, "Birds That Are New Yorkers": *The New York Times Magazine,* February 16, 1936, pp. 11, 15. Copyright © 1936 by Donald C. Peattie. Reprinted with permission of the Peattie Literary Estate.

Gifford Pinchot, "Prosperity": *The Fight for Conservation* (New York: Doubleday, Page, 1910), pp. 3–20.

Michael Pollan, from *The Omnivore's Dilemma: The Omnivore's Dilemma* (New York: Penguin, 2006), pp. 72–84. Copyright © 2006 by Michael Pollan. Used by permission of The Penguin Press, a division of Penguin Group (USA) Inc.

Eliot Porter, "The Living Canyon": *The Place No One Knew: Glen Canyon on the Colorado* (San Francisco: Sierra Club, 1963), pp. 13–18. Copyright © 1963 by the Sierra Club and © 1988 by Eliot Porter. Reprinted by permission of Russell & Volkening as agents for the author.

David Quammen, "Planet of Weeds": *Harper's,* October 1998, pp. 57–69. Copyright © 1998 by David Quammen. Reproduced by permission of David Quammen.

Janisse Ray, from *Ecology of a Cracker Childhood*: *Ecology of a Cracker Childhood* (Minneapolis: Milkweed Editions, 1999), pp. 167–73, 267–70. Copyright © 1999 by Janisse Ray. Reprinted with permission from Milkweed Editions. (www.milkweed.org).

Theodore Roosevelt, To Frank Chapman; To John Burroughs: *Theodore Roosevelt: Letters and Speeches,* Louis Auchincloss, ed. (New York: The Library of America, 2004), pp. 167, 344. Copyright © 1951 by the President and Fellows of Harvard College. Reprinted by permission of the publisher. "Speech At Grand Canyon, Arizona, May 6, 1903": *Presidential Addresses and State Papers: February 19, 1902 to May 13, 1903* (New York: Review of Reviews, 1910), pp. 369–72.

Berton Roueché, "The Fog": *The New Yorker,* September 30, 1950, pp. 33–51. Copyright © 1950 by Berton Roueché. Reprinted with permission.

Scott Russell Sanders, "After the Flood": *Staying Put: Making a Home in a Restless World* (Boston: Beacon Press, 1993), pp. 3–15. Copyright © 1993 by Scott Russell Sanders. Copyright © 1993 by Scott Russell Sanders. Reprinted by permission of Beacon Press, Boston.

Nathaniel Southgate Shaler, from *Man and the Earth*: *Man and the Earth* (New York: Fox, Duffield, 1905), pp. 1–7.

George B. Schaller, from *The Last Panda*: *The Last Panda* (Chicago: University of Chicago Press, 1993), pp. 1–2. Copyright © 1993 by George Schaller. Reprinted by permission of the publisher.

Jonathan Schell, from *The Fate of the Earth*: *The Fate of the Earth* (New York: Alfred A. Knopf, 1982), pp. 114–23. Copyright © 1982 by Jonathan Schell. Originally published in *The Fate of the Earth*. Reprinted by permission of the author.

Lydia Huntley Sigourney, "Fallen Forests": *Scenes in My Native Land* (Boston: James Munroe, 1845), pp. 117–19.

Leslie Marmon Silko, from *Ceremony*: *Ceremony* (New York: Viking Press, 1977), pp. 184–92. Copyright © 1977 by Leslie Marmon Silko. Used by permission of Viking Penguin, a division of Penguin Group (USA) Inc.

Gary Snyder, "Smokey the Bear Sutra": Broadside ([San Francisco]: [Gary Snyder], 1969). "Covers the Ground": *Mountains and Rivers without End* (Washington, D.C.: Counterpoint, 1996), pp. 65–66. Copyright © 1996 by Gary Snyder. Reprinted by arrangement with his publisher.

Rebecca Solnit, "The Thoreau Problem": *Orion*, May/June 2007. Copyright © 2007 by Rebecca Solnit. Reprinted by permission of the author.

Sandra Steingraber, from *Having Faith*: *Having Faith: An Ecologist's Journey to Motherhood* (Cambridge, Massachusetts: Perseus, 2001), pp. 249–57. Copyright © 2001 by Sandra Steingraber. Reprinted by permission.

John Steinbeck, from *The Grapes of Wrath*: *The Grapes of Wrath and Other Writings, 1936–1941,* Robert DeMott & Elaine A. Steinbeck, eds. (New York: The Library of America, 1985), pp. 211–14. Copyright © 1939, renewed 1967 by John Steinbeck. Used by permission of Viking Penguin, a division of Penguin Group (USA) Inc. First published 1939.

Gene Stratton-Porter, "The Last Passenger Pigeon": *Tales You Won't Believe* (Garden City, New York: Grosset & Dunlap, 1925), pp. 211–30. Copyright © 1925 by Gene Stratton-Porter, Inc. All rights reserved. Copyright © 1923, 1924, 1925 by International Magazine Company. Reprinted by permission of James L. Meehan and Monica Meehan Berg.

from *Table Rock Album*: *Table Rock Album and Sketches of the Falls and Scenery Adjacent,* Thomas Barnett, ed. (Buffalo: Jewett, Thomas & Co., 1850), pp. 16–17.

Edwin Way Teale, "The Longest Day": *North with the Spring* (New York: Dodd, Mead, 1951), pp. 334–37. Used with permission of the University of Connecticut Libraries.

Lewis Thomas, "The World's Biggest Membrane": *The Lives of a Cell* (New York: Viking, 1974), pp. 145–48. Copyright © 1971, 1972, 1973 by The Massachusetts Medical Society, from *The Lives of a Cell* by Lewis Thomas. Used by permission of Viking Penguin, a division of Peguin Group (USA) Inc.

Henry David Thoreau, from *Journals*: *The Writings of Henry D. Thoreau: Journal (Volume 1, 1837–1844),* John C. Broderick, gen. ed. (Princeton: Princeton University Press, 1981), pp. 5, 34–35, 42; *Journal (Volume 2, 1842–1848),* John C. Broderick, gen. ed. (Princeton: Princeton University Press, 1984), pp. 380–81; *Journal (Volume 4, 1851–1852),* Robert Sattlemeyer, gen. ed. (Princeton: Princeton University Press, 1992), pp. 75–76, 227–31. Copyright © 1981 Princeton University Press. Reprinted by permission of Princeton University Press. From *Walden; or, Life in the Woods*: *A Week on the Concord and Merrimack Rivers; Walden; The Maine Woods; Cape Cod,* Robert F. Sayre, ed. (New York: The Library of America, 1985), pp. 354–65, 394–401, 579–80. From "Huckleberries": *Collected Essays and Poems,* Elizabeth Hall Witherell, ed. (New York: The Library of America, 2001), pp. 491–501. Berg Collection of English and American Literature. The New York Public Library. Astor, Lenox and Tilden Foundations. Reprinted by permission

Jack Turner, "The Song of the White Pelican": *The Abstract Wild* (Tucson: University of Arizona Press, 1996), pp. 69–80. Copyright © 1996 by John C. Turner. Reprinted by permission of the University of Arizona Press.

Alice Walker, "Everything Is a Human Being": *Living by the Word* (New York: Harcourt Brace, 1989), pp. 139–52. Copyright ©1984 by Alice Walker, reprinted by permission of Harcourt, Inc. First published as "When A Tree Falls: Alice Walker on the Future of the Planet," *Ms.,* January, 1984. A note in brackets at the beginning of the text in *Living by the Word* reads: "This was written to celebrate the birth of Martin Luther King, Jr., and delivered as a keynote address at the University of California, Davis, January 15, 1983."

Walt Whitman, from *Leaves of Grass*: *Walt Whitman: Poetry and Prose,* Justin Kaplan, ed. (New York: The Library of America, 1982), pp. 495–97, 351–55. "This Compost" first published in 1856; "Song of the Redwood-Tree" in 1874.

E. B. White, "Sootfall and Fallout": "Letter from the East," *The New Yorker,* November 3, 1956, pp. 198–207. Reprinted by permission; Copyright © E. B. White. Originally published in *The New Yorker.* All rights reserved. Retitled "Sootfall and Fallout" in *Essays of E. B. White* (1977).

Lynn White Jr., from "The Historical Roots of Our Ecologic Crisis": *Science* 155 (March 10, 1967): 1205–07. Reprinted with permission from American Association for the Advancement of Science.

Terry Tempest Williams, from *Refuge: An Unnatural History of Family and Place*: *Refuge: An Unnatural History of Family and Place* (New York: Pantheon, 1991), pp. 5–19, 281–90. Copyright © 1991 by Terry Tempest Williams. Used by permission of Pantheon Books, a division of Random House, Inc.

Edward O. Wilson, "Bernhardsdorp": *Biophilia* (Cambridge: Harvard University Press, 1984), pp. 3–22. Copyright © 1984 by the President and Fellows of Harvard College. Reprinted by permission of the publisher.

Howard Zahniser, from "The Wilderness Act of 1964": P.L. 88–577, *United States Statutes at Large* 78 Stat., pp. 890–91.

Designed by Fearn Cutler de Vicq, *American Earth* is set in 9.5 point Monotype Century Old Style, modeled on the font created in 1900 by Morris Fuller Benton, following the typeface originally created in 1894 for *Century Magazine*. The font used for display type is Helvetica Neue 83 Extended. Composition was by Dedicated Business Services, New Market, Iowa.

This printing uses Utopia Book Matte, an acid-free, high-opacity paper that meets the requirements for permanence of the American National Standards Institute yet includes post-consumer (recycled) waste content. The plates are printed on Utopia Two Xtra Green, an acid-free coated paper that contains over 30% post-consumer waste and is processed chlorine free. The endsheets are Speckletone Kraft, also acid-free and made of at least 30% post-consumer waste.

The printing and Smyth-sewn binding are by Edwards Brothers Malloy, Ann Arbor, Michigan. In 2014, virtually all of the ink used by Malloy was soy-, vegetable-, or water-based and approximately 90% of the paper came from sources certified by either the Sustainable Forestry Initiative (SFI) or the Forest Stewardship Council (FSC).

THE LIBRARY OF AMERICA SERIES

The Library of America fosters appreciation and pride in America's literary heritage by publishing, and keeping permanently in print, authoritative editions of America's best and most significant writing. An independent nonprofit organization, it was founded in 1979 with seed funding from the National Endowment for the Humanities and the Ford Foundation.

To subscribe to the series or to order individual copies, please visit www.loa.org or call (800) 964-5778.